Langenscheidt

Japanese – English
English – Japanese
Dictionary

Edited by the
Langenscheidt Editorial Staff

Compiled by LEXUS
with
秋山真有子 (Mayuko Akiyama)
八幡尚子 (Takako Y Hyland)
Anthony P Newell

General editor: Peter Terrell

*This edition published by Barnes & Noble, Inc.
by arrangement with Langenscheidt Publishers Inc.*

ISBN: 0-7607-7556-7

Printed in Germany

MP 9 8 7 6 5 4 3 2 1

Preface

Here is a new dictionary of English and Japanese, a tool with some 40,000 references for those who work with the English and Japanese languages at beginner's or intermediate level.

Focusing on modern usage, the dictionary offers coverage of everyday language, including vocabulary from areas such as computers and business.

The Japanese in this dictionary is written both in Japanese characters and in a romanized pronunciation system – a modified version of the standard Hepburn.

The two sides of this dictionary, the English-Japanese and the Japanese-English, are quite different in structure and purpose. The English-Japanese is designed for productive usage, for self-expression in Japanese. The Japanese-English, which can also be accessed through the Jōyō Kanji index, is a decoding dictionary, a dictionary to enable the native speaker of English to understand Japanese.

Clarity of presentation has been a major objective. The editors of this book have set out to provide the means to enable you, the user of the dictionary, to get straight to the translation that fits a particular context of use. Is the *mouse* you need for your computer, for example, the same in Japanese as the *mouse* you don't want in the house? Is *flimsy* referring to furniture the same in Japanese as *flimsy* referring to an excuse? The English-Japanese dictionary is rich in sense distinctions like this – and in translation options tied to specific, identified senses.

Grammatical or function words are treated in some detail, on both the English-Japanese and the Japanese-English sides. And a large number of idiomatic phrases are given to show how the two languages correspond in context.

All in all, this is a book full of information, which will, we hope, become a valuable part of your language toolkit.

Contents

How to use the dictionary

To get the most out of your dictionary you should understand how and where to find the information you need. Whether you are yourself writing a text in Japanese or wanting to understand a text written in Japanese, the following pages should help.

1. How and where do I find a word?

1.1 English headwords. The English word list is arranged in alphabetical order.

Sometimes you might want to look up terms made up of two separate words, for example **antivirus program**, or hyphenated words, for example **absent-minded**. These words are treated as though they were a single word and their alphabetical ordering reflects this. Compound words like **bookseller**, **bookstall**, **bookstore** are also listed in alphabetical order.

The only exception to this strict alphabetical ordering is made for English phrasal verbs - words like ♦**go off**, ♦**go out**, ♦**go up**. These are positioned directly after their main verb (in this case go), rather than being scattered around in alphabetical positions.

1.2 Japanese headwords. The Japanese word list is arranged in English alphabetical order by being sorted on the romanization system or romaji. So if you know how a word is pronounced, or how it is written in romaji, you can look it up straightforwardly.

If, however, you are decoding a Japanese character, and have no idea how it is pronounced or written in romaji, then you can make use of one of the three indexes of Japanese characters. These indexes are on pages 11-32.

1.3 Running heads

If you are looking for an English or a Japanese word you can use the **running heads** printed in bold in the top corner of each page. The running head on the left tells you the *first* headword on the left-hand page and the one on the right tells you the *last* headword on the right-hand page.

2. Swung dashes

2.1 A swung dash (~) replaces the entire headword when the headword is repeated within an entry:

sly zurui ずるい; ***on the ~*** kossori to こっそりと

Here ***on the ~*** means ***on the sly***.

2.2 When a headword changes form in an entry, for example if it is put in the past tense or in the plural, then the past tense or plural ending is added to the swung dash - but only if the rest of the word doesn't change:

fluster *v/t* menkurawaseru めんくらわせる; ***get ~ed*** urotaeru うろたえる

But:

horrify: ***I was horrified*** zotto shimashita ぞっとしました

2.3 Headwords made up of two, or sometimes three, words are replaced by a single swung dash:

♦**hold on** *v/i* (*wait*) matsu 待つ; TELEC kiranaide matsu 切らないで待つ; ***now ~ a minute!*** chotto matte ちょっと待って

♦**come in on**:~ ***a deal*** keiyaku ni sanka suru 契約に参加する

3. What do the different typefaces mean?

3.1 All Japanese and English headwords and the Arabic numerals differentiating English parts of speech appear in **bold**:

alcoholic 1 *n* arukōru-chūdoku-kanja アルコール中毒患者 **2** *adj* arukōru-iri (no) アルコール入り(の)

3.2 *italics* are used for :

a) abbreviated grammatical labels: *adj, adv, v/i, v/t* etc

b) all the indicating words which are the signposts pointing to the correct translation for your needs

c) explanations

mailbox (*in street*) posuto ポスト; (*of house*) yūbin'uke 郵便受け; COMPUT mērubokkusu メールボックス

Thai 1 *adj* Tai (no) タイ(の) **2** *n* (*person*) Tai-jin タイ人; (*language*) Tai-go タイ語

serve 1 *n* (*in tennis*) sābu サーブ **2** *v/t food, meal* dasu 出す; *customer in shop* ... no yō o ukagau ...の用をうかがう; *one's country, the people* ... ni tsukaeru ...に仕える

脚 **ashi** leg (*of table etc*)

あたし **atashi** I (*used mainly by women*)

な **na** (*forms adjectives*): 憶病(な) ***okubyô*** (***na***) cowardly

3.3 All phrases (examples and idioms) are given in ***secondary bold italics***:

損失 **sonshitsu** loss; 損失を出す ***sonshitsu o dasu*** make a loss

linguist (*professional*) gengo-gakusha 言語学者; ***she's a good ~*** kanojo wa gaikokugo ga jōzu da 彼女は外国語が上手だ

3.4 The normal typeface is used for the translations.

3.5 If a translation is given in italics, and not in the normal typeface, this means that the translation is more of an *explanation* in the other language and that an explanation has to be given because there is no real equivalent:

banker's card *chekku kādo, kogitte o tsukau toki ni hitsuyō na kādo* チェックカード、小切手を使うときに必要なカード

単身赴任 **tanshinfunin** *living away from one's family after a job transfer*

4. What do the various symbols and abbreviations tell you?

4.1 A solid black lozenge is used to identify a phrasal verb:

♦**auction off** ... o kyōbai ni kakete shobun suru ...を競売にかけて処分する

4.2 A white lozenge is used to divide up longer entries into more easily digested chunks of related bits of text:

a, an ◊ (*no translation*): ***a cat*** neko 猫; ***an apple*** ringo りんご ◊ (*with countword*): ***a pencil and an eraser*** enpitsu ippon to keshigomu ikko 鉛筆一本と消しゴム一個; ***five men and a woman*** go-nin no otoko to hitori no onna 五人の男と一人の女 ◊ (*per*): ***$50 a ride*** ikkai gojū doru 一回五十ドル; ***once a week*** isshūkan ni ikkai 一週間に一回

It is also used, in the Japanese-English dictionary, to split different translations when the part of speech of each translation is different:

いらいらする **iraira suru** frustrating; nerve-racking ◊ get worked up

海抜 **kaibatsu** altitude; elevation ◊ above sea level

4.3 The abbreviation F tells you that the word or phrase is used colloquially rather than in formal contexts. The abbreviation V warns you that a word or phrase is vulgar or taboo. Be careful how you use these words. The abbreviation H means that the word is used to make yourself humble before the person you are speaking to.

4.4 A colon before an English or Japanese word or phrase means that usage is restricted to this specific example (at least as far as this dictionary's choice of vocabulary is concerned):

accord: ***of one's own ~*** jihatsuteki ni 自発的に

次第 **shidai**: あなた次第です ***anata shidai desu*** it's up to you

4.5 The letters X and Y are used to indicate insertion points for other words if you are building a complete sentence in Japanese, for example:

get away 1 *v/i* (*leave*) tachisaru 立ち去る **2** *v/t*: ***get X away from Y*** Y kara X o toriageru YからXを取り上げる

shoestring: ***do X on a ~*** shōgaku-shikin de X suru 小額資金でXする

Suspension points (...) are used in a similar way:

below 1 *prep* ... no shita ni ...の下に; (*in amount, rate, level*) ... ika ni ...以下に

5. Does the dictionary deal with grammar too?

5.1 All English headwords are given a part of speech label, unless, in normal modern English, the headword is only used as one part of speech and so no confusion or ambiguity is possible. In these cases no part of speech label is needed.

abolish haishi suru 廃止する

lastly saigo ni 最後に

But:

glory *n* eikō 栄光 (*n* given because 'glory' could be a verb)

own[1] *v/t* shoyū suru 所有する (*v/t* given because 'own' is also an adjective)

5.2 Japanese headwords are not given part of speech labels. Where their English translations can be of more than one part of speech, then these are separated by a white lozenge. For example:

異なる**kotonaru** differ ◊ dissimilar

前**mae** front ◊ before; ago

5.3 Where a Japanese word has a grammatical function, this is illustrated:

な **-na** ◊ (*forms negative imperative*): 忘れるな ***wasureru-na*** don't forget ◊ (*for emphasis*): きれいだな ***kirei da na*** it's beautiful, isn't it!

か **ka** ◊ (*question particle*) いいですか ***ii desu ka*** is it OK? ◊: ...か...か ***... ka ... ka*** either ... or...

5.4 Object particles

Object particles such as 'no' and 'ni' are included with translations of transitive verbs in the English-Japanese half of the dictionary. If an object particle is not given, then you can assume that the correct particle to use is 'o'.

win 2 *v/t* ... ni katsu …に勝つ; *lottery, money, prize* ateru 当てる

In phrasal verbs the object particle is always given.

♦**live on 1** *v/t rice, bread* ... o tabete ikiru ...を食べて生きる

6. (no) and (na):

Where the Japanese translation of an adjective is given with (no) or (na) the general rule is that the 'no' or 'na' is only used if the adjective is placed before its noun:

quiet shizuka (na) 静か(な)

a quiet room shizuka na heya 静かな部屋

the room was quiet heya wa shizuka deshita 部屋は静かでした

flowery *pattern* hanamoyō (no) 花模様(の)

flowery dress hanamoyō no doresu 花模様のドレス

the dress is flowery doresu wa hanamoyō desu ドレスは花模様です

7. Verbs of activity and verbs of being

The translation of some basic prepositions (or postpositions in Japanese) depends on the type of verb used with the preposition. Verbs of activity are verbs like: work, run, eat, verbs of being are verbs like: live, be.

I used to work in Tokyo watashi wa Tōkyō de hataraite imashita 私は東京で働いていました

does he still live in Tokyo? kare wa mada Tōkyō ni sunde imasu ka 彼はまだ東京に住んでいますか

The pronunciation of Japanese

All Japanese characters in this dictionary are accompanied by a romanized script known as romaji. Not all romaji letters are pronounced as you would normally expect on the basis of English. The following is a guide to the pronunciation of romaji.

Vowels

There are only five vowel sounds in Japanese:

a	as in f*a*ther	o	as in p*o*rt (but shorter)
e	as in g*e*t or b*e*d	u	as in p*u*t
i	as in h*ea*t (but shorter)		

Remember that there are no silent letters. So when 'e', for example, comes at the end of a word it must be pronounced: 'are' is ah-reh' (not as in 'are' in English).

A bar, or macron, over a vowel means that it has twice the length of a vowel without a bar. Distinguish carefully between obasan (aunt) and obāsan (grandmother) or koji (orphan) and kōji (construction).

When two vowels are adjacent they should not be made into a single sound (as in English), but each should be pronounced separately:

ai	like Thai	ie	pronounced ee-eh
ae	pronounced ah-eh	oh	pronounced o-oo
ee	pronounced eh-eh	ue	pronounced oo-eh
ei	like the ay of pay		

Consonants

g	as in go or girl	s	always as in ma*ss* (never z)
j	as in *j*ar	y	as in *y*et

Note that 'y' is never a long 'i' sound. For example, the Kyū of Kyūshū is like the 'cu' of cute and never like the 'ki' of kite.

The letter 'r' sounds more like an 'l'.

Double consonants are an important feature of Japanese. Each part of a double consonant should be pronounced separately: anna is pronounced an-na; kippu is kip-pu; gakkō is gak-kō.

An apostrophe is used to indicate a slight pause when speaking.

Stress

To all intents and purposes there is no stress in Japanese. So give the same value to all syllables: say Yo-ko-ha-ma not Yo-ko-HA-ma.

Abbreviations

adj	adjective
adv	adverb
ANAT	anatomy
BIO	biology
BOT	botany
Br	British English
CHEM	chemistry
COM	commerce, business
COMPUT	computers, IT term
conj	conjunction
EDU	education
ELEC	electricity, electronics
F	familiar, colloquial
fig	figurative
FIN	financial
fml	formal usage
GRAM	grammar
H	humble, showing humility to the listener
interj	interjection
LAW	law
MATH	mathematics
MED	medicine
MIL	military
MOT	motoring
MUS	music
n	noun
NAUT	nautical
neg	negative
pej	pejorative
PHOT	photography
PHYS	physics
POL	politics
prep	preposition
pron	pronoun
PSYCH	psychology
RAD	radio
RAIL	railroad
REL	religion
s.o.	someone
SP	sports
sth	something
TECH	technology
TELEC	telecommunications
THEA	theatre
TV	television
V	vulgar
v/i	intransitive verb
v/t	transitive verb
→	see
®	registered trademark

Jōyō Kanji

Although Japanese uses more kanji than those listed here, this table, known as the Jōyō Kanji List, is the full listing of the 1,945 characters that the Japanese government recommends as a guideline for the Japanese press and for the general writing of Japanese by both native and non-native speakers.

1 stroke

一 ichi, itsu, hito(tsu)
乙 otsu

2 strokes

七 shichi, nana(tsu)
丁 tei, chō
九 kyū, ku, kokono(tsu)
二 ni, futa(tsu)
人 jin, nin, hito
入 nyū, i(ru), hai(ru)
八 hachi, ya(tsu), yat(tsu)
刀 tō, katana
力 ryoku, riki, chikara
十 jū, jit(tsu), tō,
又 mata
了 ryō

3 strokes

下 ka, ge, shita, shimo, moto, sa(geru), sa(garu), kuda(ru), kuda(su), kuda(saru), o(rosu), o(riru)
才 sai
三 san, mi(tsu),mit(tsu)
上 jō, shō, ue, uwa, kami, a(garu), a(geru), nobo(ru), nobo(seru), nobo(su)
丈 jō, take
万 man, ban
与 yo, ata(eru)
丸 gan, maru(i)
及 kyū, oyo(bu),
千 sen, chi
亡 bō, mō, na(i)
凡 bon, han
刃 jin, ha
勺 shaku
久 kyū, ku, hisa(shii)
口 kō, ku, kuchi
土 do, to, tsuchi
士 shi
夕 seki, yū
大 dai, tai, ō(kii), ō(ini)
女 jo, nyo, onna, me
子 shi, su, ko
寸 sun
小 shō, chii(sai), ko, o
山 san, yama
川 sen, kawa
工 kō, ku
己 ko, ki, onore
干 kan, ho(su), hi(ru)
弓 kyū, yumi

4 strokes

不 fu, bu
中 chū, naka
丹 tan
午 go
升 shō, masu
屯 ton
乏 bō, tobo(shii)
五 go, itsu(tsu)
互 go, taga(i)
井 sei, shō, i
介 kai
今 kon, kin, ima
化 ka, ke, ba(keru)
仁 jin, ni
仏 butsu, hotoke
元 gen, gan, moto
公 kō, ōyake
分 bun, fun, bu,

wa(keru), wa(karu)
六 roku, mu(tsu), mut(tsu)
円 en, maru(i)
内 nai, dai, uchi
冗 jō
凶 kyō
切 setsu, sai, ki(ru)
刈 ka(ru)
匁 monme
区 ku
匹 hitsu, hiki
反 han, hon, tan, so(ru)
厄 yaku
双 sō, futa
友 yū, tomo
予 yo
太 tai, ta, futo(i), futo(ru)
天 ten, ame, ama
夫 fu, fū, otto
孔 kō
少 shō, suku(nai)
尺 shaku, seki
幻 gen, maboroshi
引 in, hi(ku), hi(keru)
弔 chō, tomura(u)
心 shin, kokoro
戸 ko, to
手 shu, te, ta
支 shi, sasa(eru)
文 bun, mon, fumi
斗 to
斤 kin
方 hō, kata
日 nichi, jitsu, hi, ka
月 getsu, gatsu, tsuki
木 moku, boku, ki, ko
欠 ketsu, ka(keru), ka(ku)
止 shi, to(maru)
比 hi, kura(beru)
毛 mō, ke
氏 shi, uji
水 sui, mizu
火 ka, ko, hi, ho
父 fu, chichi
片 hen, kata
牛 gyū, ushi
犬 ken, inu
王 ō, kimi

5 strokes

以 i
北 hoku, kita
矛 mu, hoko
玉 gyoku, tama
巧 kō, taku(mi)
包 hō, tsutsu(mu)
丘 kyū, oka
凸 totsu
凹 ō
且 ka(tsu)
必 hitsu, kanara(zu)
斥 seki
矢 shi, ya
左 sa, hidari
丙 hei
出 shutsu, sui, de(ru), da(su)
民 min, tami
半 han, naka(ba)
収 shū, osa(maru)
本 hon, moto
末 matsu, batsu, sue
未 mi
失 shitsu, ushina(u)
生 sei, shō, i(kiru), i(kasu), i(keru), u(mareru), u(mu), o(u), ha(eru), ha(yasu), ki, nama
弁 ben
甘 kan, ama(i)
央 ō
甲 kō, kan
由 yū, yu, yui, yoshi
母 bo, haha
世 se, sei, yo
史 shi
申 shin, mō(su)
冊 satsu, saku
仙 sen
仕 shi, ji, tsuka(eru)
代 dai, tai, ka(waru), yo, shiro
他 ta
付 fu, tsu(ku)
令 rei
刊 kan
召 shō, me(su)
加 ka, kuwa(eru)
功 kō, ku
幼 yō, osana(i)
皮 hi, kawa

写 sha, utsu(su)
市 shi, ichi
玄 gen
古 ko, furu(i)
平 hei, hyō, tai(ra), hira
外 gai, ge, soto, hoka, hazu(su)
占 sen, shi(meru), urana(u)
正 sei, shō, tada(shii), masa
圧 atsu
用 yō, mochi(iru)
冬 tō, fuyu
処 sho
汁 jū, shiru
去 kyo, ko, sa(ru)
払 futsu, hara(u)
打 da, u(tsu)
兄 kei, kyō, ani
号 gō
台 dai, tai
可 ka
句 ku
司 shi
右 u, yū, migi
好 kō, kono(mu) , su(ku)
奴 do
布 fu, nuno
犯 han, oka(su)
穴 ketsu, ana
広 kō, hiro(i)
庁 chō
尼 ni, ama
囚 shū
四 shi, yon, yo(tsu), yot(tsu)
札 satsu, fuda
巨 kyo
旧 kyū
白 haku, byaku, shiro(i), shira
示 ji, shi, shime(su)
永 ei, naga(i)
氷 hyō, kōri, hi
礼 rei, rai
主 shu, su, omo, nushi
石 seki, shaku, koku, ishi
立 ritsu, ryū, ta(tsu)
目 moku, boku, me, ma
田 den, ta
皿 sara

6 strokes

多 ta, ō(i)
死 shi,shi(nu)
気 ki, ke
両 ryō
朱 shu
年 nen, toshi
西 sei, sai, nishi
衣 i, koromo
吏 ri
毎 mai
再 sai, sa, futata(bi)
曲 kyoku, ma(garu)
伏 fuku, fu(seru)
休 kyū, yasu(mu)
件 ken
伐 batsu
仲 chū, naka
任 nin, maka(seru)
仰 gyō, kō, ao(gu), ō(se)
伝 den, tsuta(eru)
仮 ka, ke, kari
全 zen, matta(ku)
企 ki, kuwada(teru)
合 gō, ga', ka', a(u)
会 kai, e, a(u)
肉 niku
次 ji, shi, tsugi, tsu(gu)
壮 sō
兆 chō, kiza(shi)
羽 u, ha, hane
印 in, shirushi
州 shū, su
刑 kei
列 retsu
交 kō, maji(waru), maji(eru), ma(jiru), ma(zaru), ma(zeru), ka(u), ka(wasu)
充 jū, a(teru)
妄 mō, bō
考 kō, kanga(eru)
老 rō, o(iru), fu(keru)
缶 kan
色 shiki, shoku, iro
争 sō, araso(u)
危 ki, abuna(i), aya(ui),

aya(bumu)
羊 yō, hitsuji
灰 kai, hai
辺 hen, ata(ri), be
込 ko(mu), ko(meru)
巡 jun, megu(ru)
迅 jin
同 dō, ona(ji)
匠 shō
式 shiki
弐 ni
池 chi, ike
汚 o, kitana(i) , kega(su), kega(rawashii), yogo(su)
汗 kan, ase
江 kō, e
忙 bō, isoga(shii)
各 kaku, onoono
地 chi, ji
寺 ji, tera
至 shi, ita(ru)
先 sen, saki
存 son, zon
在 zai, a(ru)
扱 atsuka(u)
吐 to, ha(ku)
叫 kyō, sake(bu)
吸 kyū, su(u)
舌 zetsu, shita
向 kō, mu(ku)
后 kō
名 mei, myō, na
如 nyo, jo
妃 hi
帆 han, ho
行 kō, gyō, an, i(ku), yu(ku), okona(u)

芋 imo
芝 shiba
共 kyō, tomo
安 an, yasu(i)
守 shu, su, mamo(ru), mori
宇 u
字 ji, aza
宅 taku
光 kō, hika(ru), hikari
当 tō, a(taru)
劣 retsu, oto(ru)
吉 kichi, kitsu
尽 jin, tsu(kiru)
回 kai, e, mawa(ru)
因 in, yo(ru)
団 dan, ton
朴 boku
机 ki, tsukue
朽 kyū, ku(chiru)
肌 hada
有 yū, u, a(ru)
早 sō, sa', haya(i)
旨 shi, mune
百 hyaku
旬 shun
灯 tō, hi
成 sei, jō, na(ru)
自 ji, shi, mizuka(ra)
血 ketsu, chi
糸 shi, ito
米 bei, mai, kome
舟 shū, fune, funa
虫 chū, mushi
耳 ji, mimi
竹 chiku, take

7 strokes

良 ryō, yo(i)
身 shin, mi
来 rai, ku(ru), kita(ru), kita(su)
束 soku, taba
里 ri, sato
我 ga, ware, wa
更 kō, sara(ni), fu(keru)
亜 a
寿 ju, kotobuki
位 i, kurai
伸 shin, no(basu)
伴 han, ban, tomona(u)
体 tai, tei, karada
伯 haku
佐 sa
作 saku, sa, tsuku(ru)
似 ji, ni(ru)
但 tada(shi)
低 tei, hiku(i)
住 jū, su(mu)
何 ka, nani, nan
伺 shi, ukaga(u)
余 yo, ama(ru)
含 gan, fuku(mu)
状 jō
冷 rei, tsume(tai), hi(eru), hi(yasu), sa(meru), sa(masu)
求 kyū, moto(meru)
防 bō, fuse(gu)
邦 hō

即 soku
卵 ran, tamago
却 kyaku
判 han, ban
別 betsu, waka(reru)
助 jo, tasu(keru), suke
励 rei, hage(masu)
努 do, tsuto(meru)
忘 bō, wasu(reru)
対 tai, tsui
克 koku
角 kaku, kado, tsuno
弟 dai, tei, de, otōto
谷 koku, tani
兵 hei, hyō
呉 go
医 i
沖 chū, oki
決 ketsu, ki(maru)
沈 chin, shizu(mu)
没 botsu
汽 ki
沢 taku, sawa
坊 bō, bo'
坑 kō
坂 han, saka
均 kin
走 sō, hashi(ru)
赤 seki, shaku, aka(i)
扶 fu
把 ha
折 setsu, o(ru)
抜 batsu, nu(ku)
抄 shō
抑 yoku, osa(eru)
批 hi
抗 kō
技 gi, waza
投 tō, na(geru)
択 taku
快 kai, kokoroyo(i)
吹 sui, fu(ku)
吟 gin
呈 tei
告 koku, tsu(geru)
否 hi, ina
乱 ran, mida(reru)
豆 tō, zu, mame
君 kun, kimi
妨 bō, samata(geru)
妊 nin
妙 myō
妥 da
希 ki
狂 kyō, kuru(u)
役 yaku, eki
形 kei, gyō, kata, katachi
芳 hō, kanba(shii)
花 ka, hana
芸 gei
孝 kō
究 kyū, kiwa(meru)
完 kan
肖 shō
労 rō
岐 ki
志 shi, kokorozashi, kokoroza(su)
壱 ichi
売 bai, u(ru)
声 sei, shō, koe, kowa
床 shō, yuka, toko
応 ō
序 jo
近 kin, chika(i)
迎 gei, muka(eru)
返 hen, kae(su)
廷 tei
尿 nyō
尾 bi, o
局 kyoku
困 kon, koma(ru)
囲 i, kako(mu)
図 zu, to, haka(ru)
杉 sugi
材 zai
村 son, mura
条 jō
肝 kan, kimo
児 ji, ni
災 sai, wazawa(i)
社 sha, yashiro
改 kai, arata(meru)
攻 kō, se(meru)
忍 nin, shino(bu)
忌 ki, i(mawashii)
戻 rei, modo(ru)
戒 kai, imashi(meru)
辛 shin, kara(i)
見 ken, mi(ru)
臣 jin, shin
利 ri, ki(ku)
私 shi, watakushi
秀 shū, hii(deru)
初 sho, haji(me), hatsu, ui, so(meru)
町 chō, machi
男 dan, nan, otoko

系 kei
言 gen, gon, i(u), koto
貝 kai
車 sha, kuruma
足 soku, ashi, ta(riru), ta(ru), ta(su)
麦 baku, mugi

8 strokes

非 hi
長 chō, naga(i)
表 hyō, omote, arawa(su)
画 ga, kaku
果 ka, ha(tasu)
東 tō, higashi
垂 sui, ta(reru)
奉 hō, tatematsu(ru)
毒 doku
事 ji, zu, koto
乳 nyū, chichi, chi
承 shō, uketamawa(ru)
依 i, e
使 shi, tsuka(u)
価 ka, atai
例 rei, tato(eru)
佳 ka
侍 ji, samurai
供 kyō, ku, tomo, sona(eru)
併 hei, awa(seru)
侮 bu, anado(ru)
舎 sha
念 nen
命 mei, myō, inochi
阻 so, haba(mu)
附 fu
邪 ja
邸 tei
制 sei
刺 shi, sa(su)
到 tō
刻 koku, kiza(mu)
刷 satsu, su(ru)
券 ken
劾 gai
効 kō, ki(ku)
叔 shuku
受 ju, u(keru)
夜 ya, yo, yoru
卒 sotsu
京 kei, kyō
享 kyō
育 iku, soda(tsu)
斉 sei
盲 mō
版 han
協 kyō
直 choku, jiki, tada(chini), nao(su)
奔 hon
卓 taku
免 men, manuka(reru)
並 hei, nara(bu), nami
典 ten
延 en, no(biru)
周 shū, mawa(ri)
殴 ō, nagu(ru)
泣 kyū, na(ku)
沸 futsu, wa(ku)
油 yu, abura
波 ha, nami
泌 hitsu, hi
泳 ei, oyo(gu)
泊 haku, to(maru)
注 chū, soso(gu)
泡 hō, awa
法 hō, ha', ho'
況 kyō
沿 en, so(u)
沼 shō, numa
治 chi, ji, osa(meru), nao(ru)
泥 dei, doro
河 ka, kawa
坪 tsubo
幸 ou, saiwa(i), sachi, shiawa(se)
拓 taku
拝 hai, oga(mu)
押 ō, o(su)
抽 chū
抹 matsu
拙 setsu
披 hi
拍 haku, hyō
抱 hō, da(ku), ida(ku), kaka(eru)
抵 tei
担 tan, katsu(gu), nina(u)
拐 kai
招 shō, mane(ku)
拡 kaku
拠 kyo, ko
拘 kō
拒 kyo, koba(mu)
性 sei, shō
怖 fu, kowa(i)
怪 kai, aya(shii)
味 mi, aji(wau)

呼 ko, yo(bu)
知 chi, shi(ru)
奇 ki
姓 sei, shō
妹 mai, imōto
姉 shi, ane
始 shi, haji(maru)
妻 sai, tsuma
学 gaku, mana(bu)
弦 gen, tsuru
彼 hi, kare, kano
征 sei
径 kei
往 ō
参 san, mai(ru)
苗 byō, nae, nawa
英 ei
茂 mo, shige(ru)
芽 ga, me
若 jaku, nyaku, waka(i), mo(shikuwa)
茎 kei, kuki
苦 ku, kuru(shii), niga(i), niga(ru)
昔 seki, shaku, mukashi
宗 sō, shū
宝 hō, takara
実 jitsu, mi, mino(ru)
宙 chū
官 kan
宜 gi
定 tei, jō, sada(maru)
突 totsu, tsu(ku)
空 kū, a(ku) , sora, kara
尚 shō
歩 ho, fu, bu, aru(ku), ayu(mu)
武 bu, mu
岬 misaki
岩 gan, iwa
岸 gan, kishi
岳 gaku, take
府 fu
底 tei, soko
店 ten, mise
届 todo(ku), todo(keru)
屈 kutsu
居 kyo, i(ru)
国 koku, kuni
固 ko, kata(i)
林 rin, hayashi
枚 mai
杯 hai, sakazuki
析 seki
松 shō, matsu
枝 shi, eda
枠 waku
板 han, ban, ita
枢 sū
肪 bō
肥 hi, ko(eru), koe
服 fuku
肢 shi
青 sei, shō,ao(i)
肯 kō
明 mei, myō, a(kasu), a(ku), a(keru), a(kari), aka(rui), aka(ramu), aki(raka)
昇 shō, nobo(ru)
易 eki, i, yasa(shii)
昆 kon
的 teki, mato
者 sha, mono
炊 sui, ta(ku)
炉 ro
炎 en, honō
祉 shi
祈 ki, ino(ru)
牧 boku, maki
物 butsu, motsu, mono
放 hō, hana(su)
欧 ō
忠 chū
肩 ken, kata
房 bō, fusa
所 sho, tokoro
具 gu
和 wa, o, yawa(ragu), nago(mu), nago(yaka)
委 i
季 ki
取 shu, to(ru)
金 kin, kon, kane, kana
雨 u, ame, ama
門 mon, kado

9 strokes

食 shoku, jiki, ta(beru), ku(u), ku(rau)
飛 hi, to(bu)
発 hatsu, hotsu
衷 chū
甚 jin,

hanaha(dashii)
巻 kan, ma(ku), maki
専 sen, moppa(ra)
奏 sō, kana(deru)
重 jū, chō, omo(i), kasa(naru), e
乗 jō, no(ru)
信 shin
促 soku, unaga(su)
便 ben, bin, tayo(ri)
係 kei, kaka(ru), kakari
俊 shun
保 ho, tamo(tsu)
侵 shin, oka(su)
俗 zoku
侯 kō
限 gen, kagi(ru)
郎 rō
郊 kō
卸 oroshi, oro(su)
削 saku, kezu(ru)
契 kei, chigi(ru)
勅 choku
勇 yū, isa(mu)
叙 jo
軍 gun
冠 kan, kanmuri
帝 tei
変 hen, ka(waru)
哀 ai, awa(remu)
亭 tei
南 nan, na, minami
貞 tei, sada
虐 gyaku, shiita(geru)
負 fu, ma(keru), o(u)
急 kyū, iso(gu)
首 shu, kubi
前 zen, mae
美 bi, utsuku(shii)
盆 bon
厘 rin
厚 kō, atsu(i)
迷 mei, mayo(u)
退 tai, shirizo(ku)
追 tsui, o(u)
逃 tō, ni(geru), ni(gasu), noga(su), noga(reru)
逆 gyaku, saka(rau)
送 sō, oku(ru)
迭 tetsu
述 jutsu, no(beru)
迫 haku, sema(ru)
建 ken, kon, ta(teru)
耐 tai, ta(eru)
風 fū, fu, kaze, kaza
段 dan
津 tsu, shin
浅 sen, asa(i)
洗 sen, ara(u)
洪 kō
活 katsu
浄 jō
洋 yō
海 kai, umi
派 ha
洞 dō, hora
城 jō, shiro
垣 kaki, kai
型 kei, kata
封 fū, hō
赴 fu, omomu(ku)
挟 kyō, hasa(mu)
拷 gō
挑 chō, ido(mu)
持 ji, mo(tsu)
括 katsu
拾 shū, jū, hiro(u)
指 shi, sa(su), yubi
咲 sa(ku)
品 hin, shina
姻 in
姿 shi, sugata
要 yō, i(ru)
帥 sui
独 doku, hito(ri)
狭 kyō, sema(i), seba(maru)
狩 shu, ka(ru)
弧 ko
律 ritsu, richi
待 tai, ma(tsu)
後 kō, go, oku(reru), ato, nochi, ushi(ro)
革 kaku, kawa
荘 sō
草 sō, kusa
荒 kō, a(reru), ara(i)
茶 cha, sa
宣 sen
客 kyaku, kaku
室 shitsu, muro
窃 setsu
栄 ei, saka(eru), ha(eru)
単 tan
孤 ko
県 ken
峡 kyō
峠 tōge

炭 tan, sumi
幽 yū
度 do, to, taku, tabi
庭 tei, niwa
屋 oku, ya
面 men, omo, omote, tsura
相 sō, shō, ai
柄 hei, e, gara
柱 chū, hashira
柳 ryū, yanagi
枯 ko, ka(reru)
査 sa
某 bō
柔 jū, nyū, yawa(rakai)
染 sen, so(maru), shi(miru)
架 ka, ka(keru)
胞 hō
胆 tan
肺 hai
胎 tai
背 hai, somu(ku), se, sei
映 ei, utsu(ru), utsu(su), ha(eru)
昨 saku
昭 shō
冒 bō, oka(su)
星 sei, shō, hoshi
是 ze
春 shun, haru
皆 kai, mina
泉 sen, izumi
昼 chū, hiru
畑 hatake, hata
点 ten
為 i
神 shin, jin, kami, kan, kō
祖 so
祝 shuku, shū, iwa(u)
珍 chin, mezura(shii)
皇 kō, ō
牲 sei
施 shi, se, hodoko(su)
政 sei, shō, matsurigoto
恨 kon, ura(mu)
恒 kō
悔 bu, anado(ru)
故 ko, yue
怒 do, oko(ru), ika(ru)
怠 tai, namake(ru), okota(ru)
威 i
研 ken, to(gu)
砂 sa, sha, suna
砕 saku, kuda(ku)
音 on, in, oto, ne
臭 shū, kusa(i)
看 kan
省 shō, sei, habu(ku), kaeri(miru)
盾 jun, tate
秋 shū, aki
秒 byō
科 ka
香 kō, kyō, kao(ru), ka,
胃 i
思 shi, omo(u)
界 kai
卑 hi, iya(shii)
疫 eki, yaku
級 kyū
糾 kyū
紀 ki
紅 kō, ku, beni, kurenai
約 yaku
計 kei, haka(ru)
訂 tei
則 soku
軌 ki

10 strokes

既 ki, sude(ni)
殊 shu, koto
射 sha, i(ru)
残 zan, noko(ru)
耗 mō, kō
耕 kō, tagaya(su)
倒 tō, tao(reru)
倣 hō, nara(u)
俳 hai
候 kō, sōrō
修 shū, shu, osa(maru)
倍 bai
俸 hō
俵 hyō, tawara
借 shaku, ka(riru)
倹 ken
倫 rin
値 chi, ne, atai
個 ko
倉 sō, kura
准 jun
凍 tō, kō(ru), kogo(eru)
将 shō
陣 jin

陛 hei
降 kō, fu(ru), o(riru), o(rosu)
院 in
除 jo, ji, nozo(ku)
陥 kan, ochii(ru), otoshii(reru)
郡 gun
剖 bō
剣 ken, tsurugi
剤 zai
剛 gō
帰 ki, kae(ru)
脅 kyō, obiya(kasu), odo(su), odo(kasu)
桑 sō, kuwa
衰 sui, otoro(eru)
恋 ren, ko(u), koi(shii)
高 kō, taka(i)
畜 chiku
真 shin, ma
索 saku
勉 ben
兼 ken, ka(neru)
差 sa, sa(su)
益 eki, yaku
翁 ō
原 gen, hara
辱 joku, hazukashi(meru)
連 ren, tsura(naru), tsu(reru)
速 soku, haya(i), haya(meru), sumi(yaka)
逓 tei
逐 chiku
逝 sei, yu(ku), i(ku)
透 tō, su(ku)
造 zō, tsuku(ru)
途 to
通 tsū, tsu, tō(ru), tō(su), kayo(u)
匿 toku
酒 shu, sake, saka
浦 ho, ura
浪 rō
浜 hin, hama
流 ryū, ru, naga(reru)
消 shō, ke(su), ki(eru)
浸 shin, hita(ru)
浴 yoku, a(biru)
涙 rui, namida
浮 fu, u(ku)
埋 mai, u(maru)
起 ki, o(kiru), o(koru)
挿 sō, sa(su)
捕 ho, to(ru), tora(eru), tsuka(maru)
捜 sō, saga(su)
振 shin, fu(ru)
唆 sa, sosonoka(su)
員 in
唇 shin, kuchibiru
哲 tetsu
娘 musume
娯 go
娠 shin
姫 hime
孫 son, mago
帯 tai, o(biru)
師 shi
弱 jaku, yowa(i)
徒 to
徐 jo
従 jū, shō, shitaga(u)
華 ka, ke, hana
荷 ni, ka
恭 kyō, uyauya(shii)
家 ka, ke, ie, ya
宰 sai
宴 en
害 gai
宮 kyū, gū, ku, miya
案 an
宵 yoi, shō
容 yō
挙 kyō, a(garu)
党 tō
峰 hō, mine
島 tō, shima
庫 ko, ku
座 za, suwa(ru)
唐 tō, kara
席 seki
展 ten
桟 san
株 kabu
根 kon, ne
桃 tō, momo
桜 ō, sakura
格 kō, kaku
核 kaku
校 kō
栓 sen
梅 bai, ume
殺 satsu, sai, setsu, koro(su)
朕 chin
脂 shi, abura

脈 myaku
胸 kyō, mune, muna
胴 dō
朗 rō, hoga(raka)
骨 kotsu, hone
能 nō
時 ji, toki
書 sho, ka(ku)
殉 jun
烈 retsu
祥 shō
珠 shu
班 han
特 toku
泰 tai
旅 ryo, tabi
致 chi, ita(su)
敏 bin
悟 go, sato(ru)
悩 nō, naya(mu)
悦 etsu
恵 kei, e, megu(mu)
息 soku, iki
恐 kyō, oso(reru), osoro(shii)
恩 on
扇 sen, ōgi
栽 sai
破 ha, yabu(ru)
砲 hō
竜 ryū, tatsu
眠 min, nemu(ru)
秩 chitsu
秘 hi, hi(meri)
租 so
称 shō
被 hi, kōmu(ru)
票 hyō
畔 han
留 ryū, ru, to(maru)
畝 se, une
鬼 ki, oni
疲 hi, tsuka(reru)
病 byō, hei, ya(mu), yamai
症 shō
疾 shitsu
紡 bō, tsumu(gu)
純 jun
紙 shi, kami
納 nō, na', na, nan, tō, osa(maru)
紛 fun, magi(reru)
紋 mon
素 so, moto
料 ryō
粋 sui
粉 fun, ko, kona
航 kō
般 han
蚊 ka
蚕 san, kaiko
恥 chi, ha(jiru), haji
笑 shō, wara(u), e(mu)
託 taku
討 tō, u(tsu)
記 ki, shiru(su)
訓 kun
財 zai, sai
貢 kō, ku, mitsu(gu)
軒 ken, noki
配 hai, kuba(ru)
酌 shaku, ku(mu)
針 shin, hari
飢 ki, u(eru)
隻 seki
夏 ka, ge, natsu
馬 ba, uma, ma

11 strokes

野 ya, no
粛 shuku
偶 gū
偽 gi, itsuwa(ru), nise
側 soku, gawa
停 tei
偵 tei
偏 hen, katayo(ru)
斜 sha, nana(me)
陳 chin
陪 bai
陸 riku
陵 ryō, misasagi
隆 ryū
陰 in, kage(ru)
険 ken, kewa(shii)
陶 tō
郵 yū
都 to, tsu, miyako
郷 gō, kyō
部 bu
郭 kaku
剰 jō
副 fuku
動 dō, ugo(ku)
勘 kan
率 ritsu, sotsu, hiki(iru)
斎 sai
商 shō, akina(u)
虚 kyo, ko
貧 hin, bin, mazu(shii)
瓶 bin

進	shin, susu(mu)
逮	tai
逸	itsu
週	shū
淑	shuku
渇	katsu, kawa(ku)
混	kon, ma(zaru)
淡	tan, awa(i)
渓	kei
清	sei, shō, kiyo(i)
渋	jū, shibu(i)
渉	shō
深	shin, fuka(i)
添	ten, so(u)
液	eki
済	sai, su(mu)
涼	ryō, suzu(shii)
涯	gai
域	iki
培	bai, tsuchika(u)
堀	hori
基	ki, moto, motoi
執	shitsu, shū, to(ru)
推	sui, o(su)
掛	ka(karu), kakari
排	hai
接	setsu, tsu(gu)
控	kō, hika(eru)
掲	kei, kaka(geru)
採	sai, to(ru)
授	ju, sazu(keru)
探	tan, sagu(ru), saga(su)
措	so
描	byō, ega(ku)
掃	sō, ha(ku)
捨	sha, su(teru)
掘	kutsu, ho(ru)
据	su(eru)
惨	san, zan, miji(me)
情	jō, sei, nasa(ke)
惜	seki, o(shimu)
悼	tō, ita(mu)
唯	yui, i
喝	katsu
唱	shō, tona(eru)
啓	kei
婚	kon
婦	fu
婆	ba
帳	chō
猫	byō, neko
猛	mō
猟	ryō
張	chō, ha(ru)
強	kyō, gō, tsuyo(i), tsuyo(maru), shi(iru)
術	jutsu
得	toku, e(ru), u(ru)
彩	sai, irodo(ru)
彫	chō, ho(ru)
尉	i
菓	ka
著	cho, arawa(su), ichijiru(shii)
黄	ō, kō, ki, ko
菜	sai, na
菊	kiku
菌	kin
寂	seki, jaku, sabi(shii)
宿	shuku, yado(ru)
密	mitsu
窓	sō, mado
寄	ki, yo(ru)
窒	chitsu
袋	tai, fukuro
巣	sō, su
蛍	kei, hotaru
常	jō, tsune, toko
堂	dō
崎	saki
崩	hō, kuzu(reru)
崇	sū
殻	kaku, kara
康	kō
庸	yō
麻	ma, asa
庶	sho
械	kai
豚	ton, buta
脚	kyaku, kya, ashi
脳	nō
脱	datsu, nu(gu)
曹	sō
習	shū, nara(u)
乾	kan, kawa(ku)
黒	koku, kuro(i)
視	shi
理	ri
球	kyū, tama
現	gen, arawa(reru)
望	bō, mō, nozo(mu)
旋	sen
族	zoku
救	kyū, suku(u)
教	kyō, oshi(eru), oso(waru)
赦	sha
務	mu, tsuto(meru)
欲	yoku, ho(shii),

hos(suru)
悪 aku, o, waru(i)
患 kan, wazura(u)
悠 yū
章 shō
産 san, u(mu), ubu
翌 yoku
眼 gan, gen, manako
眺 chō, naga(me)
規 ki
祭 sai, matsu(ru)
移 i, utsu(ru)
略 ryaku
累 rui
異 i, koto(naru)
盛 sei, jō, mo(ru), saka(ru), saka(n)
盗 tō, nusu(mu)
細 sai, hoso(i), hoso(ru), koma(kai)
紳 shin
紺 kon
組 so, ku(mu), kumi
終 shū, o(waru)
紹 shō
経 kei, kyō, he(ru)
粒 ryū, tsubu
粗 so, ara(i)
粘 nen, neba(ru)
釈 shaku
断 dan, ta(tsu), kotowa(ru)
舶 haku
船 sen, fune, funa
蛇 ja, da, hebi
第 dai
笛 teki, fue
符 fu
訪 hō, otozu(reru), tazu(neru)
許 kyo, yuru(su)
訟 shō
設 setsu, mō(keru)
訳 yaku, wake
敗 hai, yabu(reru)
販 han
貫 kan, tsuranu(ku)
責 seki, se(meru)
貨 ka
軟 nan, yawara(kai)
転 ten, koro(bu)
酔 sui, yo(u)
釣 chō, tsu(ru)
雪 setsu, yuki
問 mon, to(u), ton
閉 hei, to(jiru), to(zasu), shi(meru), shi(maru)
頂 chō, itadak(ku), itadaki
魚 gyo, uo, sakana
鳥 chō, tori

12 strokes

健 ken, suko(yaka)
備 bi, sona(eru)
偉 i, era(i)
傍 bō, katawa(ra)
傘 san, kasa
隅 gū, sumi
陽 yō
階 kai
隊 tai
割 katsu, wa(ru), wa(reru), wari, sa(ku)
創 sō, tsuku(ru)
勤 kin, gon, tsuto(meru)
蛮 ban
博 haku, baku
象 zō, shō
着 chaku, jaku, tsu(ku), tsu(keru), ki(ru), ki(seru)
善 zen, yo(i)
尊 son, tōto(i), tōto(bu), tatto(i), tatto(bu)
普 fu
遇 gū
達 tatsu
運 un, hako(bu)
遂 sui, to(geru)
道 dō, tō, michi
遍 hen
遅 chi, oso(i), oku(reru)
過 ka, ayama(tsu), su(giru), su(gosu)
遊 yū, yu, aso(bu)
測 soku, haka(ru)
湖 ko, mizūmi
港 kō, minato
湾 wan
温 on, atata(kai)
湿 shitsu, shime(ru)

湯 tō, yu
満 man, mi(chiru)
滋 ji
渡 to, wata(ru)
渦 ka, uzu
減 gen, he(ru)
堪 kan, ta(eru)
場 jō, ba
堤 tei, tsutsumi
塔 tō
塚 tsuka
塀 hei
堅 ken, kata(i)
堕 da
報 hō, muku(iru)
超 chō, ko(eru)
喪 sō, mo
揚 yō, a(geru)
提 tei, sa(geru)
援 en
揺 yō, yu(reru)
搭 tō
揮 ki
換 kan, ka(waru)
握 aku, nigi(ru)
喫 kitsu
喚 kan
就 shū, ju, tsu(ku)
登 tō, to, nobo(ru)
短 tan, mijika(i)
尋 jin, tazu(neru)
媒 bai
婿 sei, muko
帽 bō
幅 fuku, haba
猶 yū
弾 dan, hi(ku), hazu(mu), tama
御 go, gyo, on
街 gai, kai, machi
復 fuku
循 jun
裂 retsu, sa(ku)
装 sō, shō, yosō(u)
裁 sai, saba(ku), ta(tsu)
落 raku, o(chiru)
葬 sō, hōmu(ru)
葉 yō, ha
募 bo, tsuno(ru)
寒 kan, samu(i)
富 fu, fū, to(mu), tomi
営 ei, itona(mu)
覚 kaku, obo(eru), sa(masu)
掌 shō
喜 ki, yoroko(bu)
廃 hai, suta(reru)
廊 rō
属 zoku
圏 ken
棟 tō, mune, muna
棚 tana
極 kyoku, goku, kiwa(meru)
棋 ki
棒 bō
棺 kan
検 ken
植 shoku, u(eru)
森 shin, mori
脹 chō
勝 shō, ka(tsu), masa(ru)
腕 wan, ude
期 ki, go
朝 chō, asa
暁 gyō, akatsuki
晴 sei, ha(reru)
晩 ban
暑 sho, atsu(i)
晶 shō
景 kei
量 ryō, haka(ru)
最 sai, motto(mo)
替 tai, ka(waru)
焼 shō, ya(ku)
無 mu, bu, na(i)
煮 sha, ni(ru)
然 zen, nen
琴 kin, koto
散 san, chi(ru)
敬 kei, uyama(u)
敢 kan
欺 gi, azamu(ku)
款 kan
惰 da
慌 kō, awa(teru)
愉 yu
惑 waku, mado(u)
悲 hi, kana(shimu)
雇 ko, yato(u)
扉 hi, tobira
越 etsu, ko(su)
幾 ki, iku
硬 kō, kata(i)
硫 ryū
硝 shō
童 dō, warabe
殖 shoku, fu(eru)
程 tei, hodo
税 zei
補 ho, ogina(u)
裕 yū
塁 rui
畳 jō, tata(mu), tatami
番 ban
買 bai, ka(u)

衆 shū, shu
疎 so, uto(i)
痢 ri
痛 tsū, ita(mu)
痘 tō
結 ketsu, musu(bu), yu(u), yu(waeru)
絡 raku
給 kyū
絵 kai, e
絞 kō, shibo(ru), shi(meru), shi(maru)
統 tō, su(beru)
絶 zetsu, ta(eru)
紫 shi, murasaki
粧 shō
奥 ō, oku
歯 shi, ha
筆 hitsu, fude
策 saku
筋 kin, suji
等 tō, hito(shii)
答 tō, kota(eru)
筒 tō, tsutsu
訴 so, utta(eru)
評 hyō
証 shō
詐 sa
診 shin, mi(ru)
詔 shō, mikotonori
詠 ei, yo(mu)
詞 shi
貯 cho
費 hi, tsui(yasu)
貴 ki, tatto(i), tatto(bu), tōto(i), tōto(bu)
貿 bō
貸 tai, ka(su)
賀 ga
軸 jiku
軽 kei, karu(i), karo(yaka)
距 kyo
酢 saku, su
鈍 don, nibu(i)
飲 in, no(mu)
飯 han, meshi
雄 yū, osu, o
集 shū, tsudo(u), atsu(maru)
焦 sho, ko(geru), ase(ru)
雲 un, kumo
雰 fun
閑 kan
間 kan, ken, ma, aida
開 kai, a(keru), a(ku), hira(ku), hira(keru)
項 kō
順 jun

13 strokes

業 gyō, gō, waza
働 dō, hatara(ku)
傾 kei, katamu(ku)
傑 ketsu
僧 sō
傷 shō, ita(mu), kizu
債 sai
催 sai, moyō(su)
随 zui
隔 kaku, heda(teru)
勧 kan, susu(meru)
勢 sei, ikio(i)
裏 ri, ura
棄 ki
準 jun
艇 tei
虞 osore
虜 ryo
慈 ji, itsuku(shimu)
義 gi
農 nō
滑 katsu, sube(ru), name(raka)
滝 taki
溝 kō, mizo
滞 tai, todokō(ru)
溶 yō, to(keru)
漢 kan
漠 baku
源 gen, minamoto
滅 metsu, horo(biru)
塊 kai, katamari
塩 en, shio
塑 so
塗 to, nu(ru)
搬 han
携 kei, tazusa(eru)
摂 setsu, to(ru)
搾 saku, shibo(ru)
損 son, soko(nau)
嘆 tan, nage(ku)
嗣 shi
群 gun, mu(reru), mura
豊 hō, yuta(ka)
嫁 ka, totsu(gu),

yome
嫌 ken, gen, kira(u), iya
猿 en, saru
微 bi
夢 yume, mu
愛 ai
蓄 chiku, takuwa(eru)
蒸 jō, mu(su)
墓 bo, haka
幕 baku, maku
靴 ka, kutsu
寝 shin, ne(ru)
寛 kan
誉 yo, homa(re)
奨 shō
鼓 ko, tsuzumi
廉 ren
殿 den, ten, tono, dono
園 en, sono
楼 rō
楽 raku, gaku, tano(shii)
腰 yō, koshi
腹 fuku, hara
腸 chō
暇 ka, hima
暗 an, kura(i)
暖 dan, atata(kai)
幹 kan, miki
煩 han, bon, wazura(washii)
煙 en, kemu(ru), kemuri
照 shō, te(ru)
献 ken, kon
福 fuku
禅 zen
禍 ka
聖 sei
解 kai, ge, to(ku)
数 sū, su, kazo(eru), kazu
慨 gai
慎 shin, tsutsushi(mu)
愚 gu, oro(ka)
愁 shū, ure(eru)
想 sō, so
感 kan, kan(jiru)
戦 sen, tataka(u), ikusa
歳 sai, sei
碁 go
意 i
新 shin, atara(shii), ara(ta), nii
辞 ji, ya(meru)
睡 sui
督 toku
禁 kin
稚 chi
裸 ra, hadaka
褐 katsu
署 sho
罪 zai, tsumi
置 chi, o(ku)
盟 mei
痴 chi
絹 ken, kinu
続 zoku, tsuzu(ku)
継 kei, tsu(gu)
触 shoku, sawa(ru), fu(reru)
節 setsu, sechi, fushi
誠 sei, makoto
詩 shi
詰 kitsu, tsu(maru)
話 wa, hana(su), hanashi
誇 ko, hoko(ru)
該 gai
詳 shō, kuwa(shii)
試 shi, tame(su), kokoro(miru)
賄 wai, makana(u)
賊 zoku
賃 chin
資 shi
較 kaku
載 sai, no(seru)
践 sen
跳 chō, ha(neru), to(bu)
路 ro, ji
跡 seki, ato
酪 raku
酬 shū
鉢 hachi, hatsu
鉄 tetsu
鈴 rei, rin, suzu
鉛 en, namari
鉱 kō
飽 hō, a(kiru)
飾 shoku, kaza(ru)
飼 shi, ka(u)
雅 ga
雷 rai, kaminari
電 den
零 rei
頒 han
預 yo, azu(keru)
頑 gan

14 strokes

僕 boku
僚 ryō
像 zō
豪 gō
疑 gi, utaga(u)
暦 reki, koyomi
歴 reki
遭 sō, a(u)
適 teki
遮 sha, saegi(ru)
際 sai, kiwa
障 shō, sawa(ru)
隠 in, kaku(su)
遣 ken, tsuka(u)
遠 en, on, tō(i)
違 i, chiga(i)
漁 ryō
漸 zen
漂 hyō, tadayo(u)
漆 shitsu, urushi
漫 man
漬 tsu(karu)
演 en
滴 teki, shitata(ru), shizuku
漏 rō, mo(ru)
境 kyō, kei, sakai
増 zō, ma(su), fu(eru), fu(yasu)
塾 juku
墨 boku, sumi
摘 teki, tsu(mu)
鳴 mei, na(ru)
嫡 chaku
獄 goku
徴 chō
徳 toku
彰 shō
髪 hatsu, kami
慕 bo, shita(u)
暮 bo, ku(reru)
寡 ka
察 satsu
寧 nei
腐 fu, kusa(ru)
層 sō
概 gai
構 kō, kama(u)
模 mo, bo
様 yō, sama
膜 maku
静 sei, jō, shizu(maru), shizu(ka)
旗 ki, hata
歌 ka, uta(u)
憎 zō, niku(mu)
慢 man
慣 kan, na(reru)
態 tai
碑 hi
磁 ji
端 tan, hashi, ha, hata
種 shu, tane
稲 tō, ine, ina
穀 koku
複 fuku
魂 kon, tamashii
鼻 bi, hana
罰 batsu, bachi
維 i
練 ren, ne(ru)
緒 sho, cho, o
綿 men, wata
緑 ryoku, roku, midori
総 so
綱 kō, tsuna
網 mō, ami
精 sei, shō
製 sei
算 san
管 kan, kuda
箇 ka
誤 go, ayama(ru)
誘 yū, saso(u)
語 go, kata(ru)
誌 shi
読 doku, toku, tō, yo(mu)
認 min, mito(meru)
説 setsu, zei, to(ku)
誓 sei, chika(u)
踊 yō, odo(ru)
酷 koku
酸 san, su(i)
酵 kō
銭 sen, zeni
銀 gin
銘 mei
銑 sen
銃 jū
銅 dō
雌 shi, mesu, me
雑 zatsu, zō
奪 datsu, uba(u)
需 ju
聞 bun, mon, ki(ku)
閥 batsu
閣 kaku
関 kan, seki
領 ryō, rei
駄 da
駅 eki
駆 ku, ka(keru)

15 strokes

舞 bu, ma(u), mai
儀 gi
億 oku
劇 geki
褒 hō, ho(meru)
膚 fu
慮 ryō, omonbaka(ru)
養 yō, yashina(u)
遷 sen
選 sen, era(bu)
遺 i, yui
遵 jun
潮 chō, shio
潜 sen, mogu(ru), hiso(mu)
潟 kata
潔 ketsu, isagiyo(i)
澄 chō, su(mu)
潤 jun, uruo(u)
墜 tsui
墳 fun
舗 ho
撲 boku
撤 tetsu
撮 satsu, to(ru)
噴 fun, fu(ku)
嘱 shoku
器 ki, utsuwa
幣 hei
衝 shō, tsu(ku)
徹 tetsu
影 ei, kage
蔵 zō, kura
審 shin
寮 ryō
賓 hin
窮 kyū, kiwa(maru)
窯 yō, kama
導 dō, michibi(ku)
賞 shō
撃 geki, u(tsu)
摩 ma
慶 kei
憂 yū, ure(eru), u(i)
履 ri, ha(ku)
槽 sō
標 hyō
横 ō, yoko
権 ken, gon
暴 bō, baku, aba(ku)
暫 zan, shibara(ku)
熟 juku, u(reru)
勲 kun
熱 netsu, atsu(i)
黙 moku, dama(ru)
敷 shi(ku), fu
敵 teki, kataki
弊 hei
歓 kan
慰 i, nagusa(meru)
戯 gi, ge, tawamu(reru)
確 kaku, tashi(ka)
穂 sui, ho
稼 ka, kase(gu)
稿 kō
魅 mi
罷 hi
監 kan
盤 ban
縄 jō, nawa
線 sen
緩 kan, yuru(i)
縁 en, fuchi
締 tei, shi(maru)
編 hen, a(mu)
緊 kin
趣 shu, omomuki
範 han
箱 hako
課 ka
諸 sho
謁 etsu
談 dan
請 sei, shin, ko(u), u(keru)
諾 daku
論 ron
調 chō, shira(beru), totono(u), totono(eru)
誕 tan
賠 bai
賜 shi, tamawa(ru)
賦 fu
賛 san
質 shitsu, shichi, chi
輪 rin, wa
輩 hai
輝 ki, kagaya(ku)
踏 to, fu(mu)
鋳 chū, i(ru)
鋭 ei, surudo(i)
餓 ga
霊 rei, ryō, tama
震 shin, furu(eru)
閲 etsu
駐 chū

16 strokes

儒 ju
凝 gyō, ko(ru)
興 kyō, kō, oko(ru)
激 geki, hage(shii)
濃 nō, ko(i)
濁 daku, nigo(ru)
壊 kai, kowa(su)
壌 jō
壇 dan, tan
墾 kon
壁 heki, kabe
操 sō, ayatsu(ru), misao
擁 yō
撼 kan
嬢 jō
獲 kaku, e(ru)
衡 kō
衛 ei
薪 shin, takigi
薄 haku, usu(i)
薬 yaku, kusuri
薫 kun, kao(ru)
薦 sen, susu(meru)
憲 ken
磨 ma, miga(ku)
機 ki, hata
樹 ju
橋 kyō, hashi
膨 bō, fuku(ramu)
曇 don, kumo(ru)
燃 nen, mo(eru)
獣 jū, kemono
整 sei, totono(eru)
憤 fun, ikidō(ru)
憶 oku
懐 kai, natsuka(shimu), natsu(ku), futokoro
隣 rin, tona(ru), tonari
避 hi, sa(keru)
還 kan, kae(ru)
憩 kei, iko(u)
親 shin, shita(shii), oya
穏 on, oda(yaka)
積 seki, tsu(mu)
奮 fun, furu(u)
縦 jū, tate
縛 baku, shiba(ru)
緯 i
縫 hō, nu(u)
繁 han
糖 tō
融 yū
篤 toku
築 chiku, kizu(ku)
諮 shi, haka(ru)
謀 bō, mu, haka(ru)
謡 yō, uta(u), utai
諭 yu, sato(su)
賢 ken, kashiko(i)
輸 yu
錘 sui
錬 ren
錯 saku
錠 jō
録 roku
鋼 kō, hagane
館 kan
隷 rei
頼 rai, tano(mu), tayo(ru)
頭 tō, zu, to, atama, kashira

17 strokes

優 yū, yasa(shii), sugu(reru)
償 shō, tsuguna(u)
翼 yoku, tsubasa
濯 taku
擬 gi
擦 satsu, su(ru)
嚇 kaku
矯 kyō, ta(meru)
厳 gen, gon, kibi(shii), ogoso(ka)
謄 tō
燥 sō
環 kan
犠 gi
懇 kon, nengo(ro)
礁 shō
覧 ran
爵 shaku
療 ryō
繊 sen
績 seki
縮 shuku, chiji(mu)
齢 rei
聴 chō, ki(ku)
謝 sha, ayama(ru)
講 kō
謹 kin, tsutsushi(mu)
謙 ken
購 kō
轄 katsu
醜 shū, miniku(i)
鍛 tan, kita(eru)
霜 sō, shimo
頻 hin
鮮 sen, aza(yaka)

18 strokes

濫 ran
藩 han
繭 ken, mayu
曜 yō
覆 fuku, ō(u), kutsugae(su)
懲 chō, ko(riru)
礎 so, ishizue
瞬 shun, matata(ku)
臨 rin, nozo(mu)
観 kan
穫 kaku
襟 kin, eri
癖 heki, kuse
癒 yu
繕 zen, tsukuro(u)
織 shoku, shiki, o(ru)
糧 ryō, rō, kate
翻 hon, hirugae(ru)
職 shoku
簡 kan
贈 zō, sō, oku(ru)
鎖 sa, kusari
鎮 chin, shizu(meru)
難 nan, muzuka(shii), kata(i)
闘 tō, tataka(u)
類 rui
顔 gan, kao
顕 ken
額 gaku, hitai
題 dai
騎 ki
験 ken, gen
騒 sō, sawa(gu)

19 strokes

瀬 se
藻 sō, mo
麗 rei, uruwa(shii)
臓 zō
覇 ha
爆 baku
璽 ji
羅 ra
繰 ku(ru)
簿 bo
譜 fu
識 shiki
警 kei
韻 in
鏡 kyō, kagami
離 ri, hana(reru)
霧 mu, kiri
髄 zui
願 gan, nega(u)
鯨 gei, kujira
鶏 kei, niwatori

20 strokes

懸 ken, ke, ka(karu)
欄 ran
騰 tō
競 kyō, kei, kiso(u), se(ru)
籍 seki
譲 jō, yuzu(ru)
護 go
議 gi
醸 jō, kamo(su)
鐘 shō, kane
響 kyō, hibi(ku)

21 strokes

魔 ma
艦 kan
躍 yaku, odo(ru)
露 ro, rō, tsuyu
顧 ko, kaeri(miru)

22 strokes

襲 shū, oso(u)
驚 kyō, odoro(ku)

23 strokes

鑑 kan

Hiragana and Katakana Table

In addition to the *kanji*, or Chinese characters, Japanese uses two sets of characters known as *hiragana* and *katakana*. Unlike *kanji*, each *hiragana* or *katakana* character has a single reading and represents a sound rather than a meaning. Loan words are usually written in *katakana*.

ひらがな **hiragana**	カタカナ **katakana**	ローマ字 **rōmaji**
あ	ア	a
い	イ	i
う	ウ	u
え	エ	e
お	オ	o
か	カ	ka
き	キ	ki
く	ク	ku
け	ケ	ke
こ	コ	ko
さ	サ	sa
し	シ	shi
す	ス	su
せ	セ	se
そ	ソ	so
た	タ	ta
ち	チ	chi
つ	ツ	tsu
て	テ	te
と	ト	to
な	ナ	na
に	ニ	ni
ぬ	ヌ	nu
ね	ネ	ne
の	ノ	no
は	ハ	ha/wa
ひ	ヒ	hi
ふ	フ	fu
へ	ヘ	he/e
ほ	ホ	ho
ま	マ	ma
み	ミ	mi
む	ム	mu
め	メ	me
も	モ	mo
や	ヤ	ya
ゆ	ユ	yu
よ	ヨ	yo
ら	ラ	ra
り	リ	ri
る	ル	ru
れ	レ	re
ろ	ロ	ro
わ	ワ	wa
	ウィ	wi
	ウェ	we
	ウォ	wo
を	ヲ	o
ん	ン	n
	アー	ā
	イー	ī
	ウー	ū
	エー	ē

ひらがな hiragana	カタカナ katakana	ローマ字 rōmaji
おお/おう	オー	ō
が	ガ	ga
ぎ	ギ	gi
ぐ	グ	gu
げ	ゲ	ge
ご	ゴ	go
ざ	ザ	za
じ	ジ	ji
ず	ズ	zu
ぜ	ゼ	ze
ぞ	ゾ	zo
だ	ダ	da
ぢ	ヂ	ji
づ	ヅ	zu
で	デ	de
ど	ド	do
ば	バ	ba
び	ビ	bi
ぶ	ブ	bu
べ	ベ	be
ぼ	ボ	bo
ぱ	パ	pa
ぴ	ピ	pi
ぷ	プ	pu
ぺ	ペ	pe
ぽ	ポ	po
きゃ	キャ	kya
きゅ	キュ	kyu
きょ	キョ	kyo
しゃ	シャ	sha
しゅ	シュ	shu
しぇ	シェ	she
しょ	ショ	sho

ひらがな hiragana	カタカナ katakana	ローマ字 rōmaji
ちゃ	チャ	cha
ちゅ	チュ	chu
ちぇ	チェ	che
ちょ	チョ	cho
にゃ	ニャ	nya
にゅ	ニュ	nyu
にょ	ニョ	nyo
ひゃ	ヒャ	hya
ひゅ	ヒュ	hyu
ひょ	ヒョ	hyo
みゃ	ミャ	mya
みゅ	ミュ	myu
みょ	ミョ	myo
りゃ	リャ	rya
りゅ	リュ	ryu
りょ	リョ	ryo
ぎゃ	ギャ	gya
ぎゅ	ギュ	gyu
ぎょ	ギョ	gyo
じゃ	ジャ	ja
じゅ	ジュ	ju
じぇ	ジェ	je
じょ	ジョ	jo
びゃ	ビャ	bya
びゅ	ビュ	byu
びょ	ビョ	byo
ぴゃ	ピャ	pya
ぴゅ	ピュ	pyu
ぴょ	ピョ	pyo

A

あーあ **āa** oh God!; ah!; aha!; oh!
暴く **abaku** disclose; expose; show up
あばら屋 **abaraya** hovel
暴れまわる **abaremawaru** rampage
暴れる **abareru** become violent; act violently
浴びる **abiru** take *shower*
浴びせる **abiseru** throw *water*; shower (*with questions*)
あぶ **abu** horsefly
危ない **abunai** dangerous
脂 **abura** grease; fat
油 **abura** oil; 油をさす ***abura o sasu*** oil
油絵 **aburae** oil painting
脂っこい **aburakkoi** fatty; greasy
脂身 **aburami** fat
脂っぽい **aburappoi** greasy; oily
アーチ **āchi** arch
あちこち **achikochi** here and there; あちこち旅行する ***achikochi ryokô suru*** travel around
あちら **achira** over there
アダプター **adaputā** adapter
アダルトチルドレン **adaruto-chirudoren** screwed-up adult (*brought up in a dysfunctional family*); weirdo
アドバイス **adobaisu** advice
アドレス帳 **adoresuchō** address book
あえぐ **aegu** gasp; pant
亜鉛 **aen** zinc
アフガニスタン **Afuganisutan** Afghanistan
アフガニスタン(の) **Afuganisutan (no)** Afghan
あふれる **afureru** overflow
アフリカ **Afurika** Africa
アフリカ(の) **Afurika (no)** African
アフターサービス **afutā sābisu** after sales service
あがる **agaru** get nervous
上がる **agaru** go up, increase, rise; be up
揚がる **agaru** fly (*of flag*)
上がってくる **agatte kuru** come up
あげる **ageru** give; let out *groan, yell*
上げる **ageru** increase, raise; hold up *hand*; turn up *volume*
揚げる **ageru** deep-fry, fry; hoist
上げ相場 **agesōba** bull market
あご **ago** chin; jaw
あぐらをかく **agura o kaku** sit cross-legged
あひる **ahiru** duck
愛 **ai** love
愛着 **aichaku** love
間 **aida** through, during ◊ interval
アイデア **aidea** idea
アイドル **aidoru** idol
相いれない **aiirenai** incompatible
愛人 **aijin** lover; mistress
愛情 **aijō** affection; love; 愛情の深い ***aijô no fukai*** loving
合い鍵 **aikagi** duplicate key
相変わらず **aikawarazu** the same as ever
合気道 **aikidō** aikido
あいこだ **aiko da** be quits with
愛国者 **aikoku-sha** patriot
愛国心 **aikoku-shin** patriotism
愛国的(な) **aikokuteki (na)** patriotic
アイコン **aikon** icon
愛くるしい **aikurushii** adorable
IQ **ai-kyū** IQ
合間 **aima** interlude
あいまい(な) **aimai (na)** ambiguous; vague
あいにく **ainiku** unfortunately
アイヌ **Ainu** *ethnic group based in Hokkaido*
アイライナー **airainā** eyeliner
アイロン **airon** iron; アイロンをかける ***airon o kakeru*** iron
アイロン台 **airon-dai** ironing board

アイロンがけ **airon-gake** ironing
アイルランド **Airurando** Ireland
アイルランド(の) **Airurando** (no) Irish
あいさつ **aisatsu** greeting
あいさつする **aisatsu suru** greet; salute
アイシャドウ **aishadō** eye shadow
ICU **ai-shī-yū** intensive care (unit)
相性 **aishō** chemistry *fig*; affinity
愛称 **aishō** pet name; shortened form
愛想のいい **aisō no ii** amiable
愛想の悪い **aisō no warui** unfriendly
愛すべき **aisubeki** darling; lovable
アイスホッケー **aisuhokkē** (ice) hockey
アイスコーヒー **aisukōhī** iced coffee
アイスクリーム **aisukurīmu** ice cream
愛する **ai suru** love
(アイス)スケートリンク **(aisu)sukēto-rinku** ice rink
アイスティー **aisutī** iced tea
開いた **aita** open
相手 **aite** companion; opponent
空いている **aite iru** free; vacant
あいつ **aitsu** so-and-so; that guy
相次いで **aitsuide** successively
合図 **aizu** signal
合図する **aizu suru** signal
味 **aji** taste; savor
アジア **Ajia** Asia
アジア人 **Ajia-jin** Asian
アジア(の) **Ajia** (no) Asian
味気ない **ajikenai** bland
味見する **ajimi suru** taste
あじさい **ajisai** hydrangea
味付けする **ajitsuke suru** flavor
味わう **ajiwau** taste; savor
あか **aka** grime
赤 **aka** red
赤ちゃん **akachan** baby
赤い **akai** red; rosy
赤字 **akaji** deficit; 赤字である ***akaji de aru*** be in the red
赤味 **akami** glow; tinge of red
赤身(の) **akami** (no) lean *meat*
赤ん坊 **akanbō** baby
あからさま(な) **akarasama** (na) frank; open; stark *reminder, contrast etc*; obvious
明り **akari** light
明るい **akarui** bright; light; cheerful; rosy *future*
明るく **akaruku** brightly
明るくする **akaruku suru** brighten up; lighten
明るさ **akaru-sa** brightness
赤線地区 **akasen-chiku** red light district
赤信号 **akashingō** red light
明かす **akasu** unveil
明けましておめでとうございます **akemashite omedetō gozaimasu** Happy New Year!
開ける **akeru** open; undo; unwrap; make *hole*
空ける **akeru** vacate; empty
明ける **akeru** 梅雨が明ける ***tsuyu ga aketa*** the rainy season is over; 夜が明ける ***yo ga akeru*** dawn is breaking
秋 **aki** fall
空き **aki** opening
空き部屋 **akibeya** unoccupied room
明らか(な) **akiraka** (na) apparent, obvious, evident; visible *difference*
明らかにする **akiraka ni suru** specify; identify; manifest; disclose, reveal ◊ revealing; 明らかにされていない ***akiraka ni sarete inai*** untold
あきらめ **akirame** resignation
あきらめる **akirameru** give up; despair of
あきらめた **akirameta** resigned
あきれる **akireru** be shocked; be astonished
あきれた **akireta** outrageous; horrifying
飽きる **akiru** tire of
悪化させる **akka saseru** aggravate
悪化する **akka suru** degenerate; deteriorate, worsen
あこがれ **akogare** yearning
あこがれの的 **akogare no mato** heart throb
あこがれる **akogareru** worship; admire; yearn for
空く **aku** be empty
開く **aku** open

悪 aku evil
アクアラング akuarangu air tank, aqualung
あくび akubi yawn
あくびする akubi suru yawn
悪意 akui malice; spite; 悪意のある ***akui no aru*** malicious, malevolent
飽くことのない aku koto no nai insatiable
悪魔 akuma devil; demon; fiend
あくまで守る aku made mamoru stick up for
悪名の高い akumei no takai infamous, notorious
悪夢 akumu nightmare
悪人 akunin villain
アクロバット akurobatto acrobat; acrobatics
悪性(の) akusei (no) malignant; virulent
アクセル akuseru accelerator, gas pedal
アクセサリー akusesarī accessory
アクセスコード akusesu kōdo access code
アクション akushon action
握手 akushu handshake; 握手をする ***akushu o suru*** shake hands with
悪臭 akushū stench, stink
悪態 akutai verbal abuse, cursing; swear word; 悪態をつく ***akutai o tsuku*** swear
悪党 akutō crook; rogue
悪徳 akutoku vice
悪用 akuyō misuse
悪用する akuyō suru misuse
あま ama bitch
尼 ama nun
アマチュア amachua amateur
雨垂れ amadare raindrop
甘える amaeru act like a spoilt child; …に甘える ***... ni amaeru*** depend on the good will of
甘い amai sweet; indulgent; permissive; luscious
あま皮 amakawa cuticle
甘口(の) amakuchi (no) mild
甘くする amaku suru sweeten
あまり amari not so much; あまり…でない ***amari ... de nai*** not overly, not very
余る amaru be left over
余った amatta to spare
余っている amatte iru be left over
雨宿りの場所 amayadori no basho cover; shelter (from the rain)
甘やかされた amayaka sareta spoilt
甘やかし amayakashi indulgence
甘やかす amayakasu pamper; spoil
甘酒 amazake sweet sake
甘酸っぱい amazuppai sweet and sour
あめ ame candy
雨 ame rain; 雨が降る ***ame ga furu*** rain
雨模様 amemoyō rainy
アメリカ Amerika America
アメリカ合衆国 Amerika-gasshūkoku USA, United States of America
アメリカ合衆国(の) Amerika-gasshūkoku (no) American
アメリカ人 Amerika-jin American
アメリカ国防総省 Amerika-kokubō-sōshō the Pentagon
アメリカンフットボール Amerikan-futtobōru football
アメリカンフットボール競技場 Amerikan-futtobōru-kyōgijō gridiron
網 ami net
編み出す amidasu formulate
編み物 amimono knitting
編み物する amimono suru knit
アーモンド āmondo almond
編む amu knit; plait; weave
穴 ana hole; pit; puncture; leak; 穴のある ***ana no aru*** leaky
アナボリックステロイド anaborikku-suteroido anabolic steroid
あなご anago eel
アナログ式(の) anarogu-shiki (no) analog
あなた anata you (*singular polite form*); darling, honey
あなたの anata no your (*singular polite*)
あなたたち anatatachi you (*plural polite*)
あなたたちの anatatachi no your (*plural polite*)

アナウンサー **anaunsā** announcer
アナウンス **anaunsu** announcement
アンダーシャツ **andāshatsu** undershirt
安ど **ando** relief
姉 **ane** big sister
案外 **angai** unexpectedly
暗号 **angō** code
兄 **ani** big brother
アニメ **anime** cartoon
アニメ映画 **anime-eiga** animation
暗示 **anji** hint ; 暗示にかける ***anji ni kakeru*** influence by suggestion
アンケート **ankēto** questionnaire
暗記 **anki** memorizing
暗記している **anki shite iru** know by heart
暗記する **anki suru** memorize
あんこ **anko** sweet bean paste
あんこう **ankō** monkfish
暗黒 **ankoku** blackness
暗黒街 **ankokugai** underworld
暗黒(の) **ankoku (no)** black *fig*
アンコール **ankōru** encore
あんま **anma** massage
あんまり **anmari** not a lot, not really
暗黙(の) **anmoku (no)** implicit; tacit
あんな **anna** such a; that sort of
案内 **annai** information; guidance
案内係 **annaigakari** usher; attendant; guide
案内標識 **annai-hyōshiki** signpost
案内人 **annai-nin** guide
案内する **annai suru** guide; lead
案の定 **an no jō** sure enough
あの **ano** that; those
あのう **anō** well
あのね **anone** well; hey!
アノラック **anorakku** parka
あの世 **ano yo** the afterlife
あのよう(な) **ano yō (na)** such
アンプ **anpu** amplifier
安楽いす **anraku-isu** easy chair
安楽死 **anraku-shi** euthanasia
暗殺 **ansatsu** assassination
暗殺者 **ansatsu-sha** assassin
暗殺する **ansatsu suru** assassinate
安静 **ansei** rest cure
安心 **anshin** peace of mind
安心させる **anshin saseru** reassure ◊ reassuring
安心する **anshin suru** feel relieved
暗礁 **anshō** reef
暗証番号 **anshō-bangō** PIN, personal identification number
暗唱する **anshō suru** recite
安定 **antei** stability
安定させる **antei saseru** stabilize; steady
安定した **antei shita** firm; secure; stable; steady
安定する **antei suru** stabilize
アンテナ **antena** antenna
暗算 **anzan** mental arithmetic
安全 **anzen** safety
安全地帯 **anzen-chitai** (traffic) island
安全第一(の) **anzen-daiichi (no)** safety first
安全でない **anzen de nai** insecure
安全(な) **anzen (na)** safe; invulnerable
安全ピン **anzen-pin** safety pin
安全性 **anzensei** safety
安全対策 **anzen-taisaku** safeguard
あんず **anzu** apricot
青 **ao** blue
あおぐ **aogu** fan oneself
青い **aoi** blue
青写真 **aojashin** blueprint
青白い **aojiroi** pale, white; pasty; sickly; ghastly
青二才 **aonisai** greenhorn
あおりたてる **aoritateru** incite; inflame
あおる **aoru** whip up
アオサギ **aosagi** heron
青信号 **aoshingō** green light
青ざめる **aozameru** go pale
青ざめた **aozameta** wan
アパート **apāto** apartment; apartment block
アピール **apīru** appeal
アポストロフィー **aposutorofī** apostrophe
アップルパイ **appurupai** apple pie
アプローチ **apurōchi** approach
アラビア語 **Arabia-go** Arabic
アラビア(の) **Arabia (no)** Arabic
アラビア数字 **Arabia-sūji** Arabic numeral

アラブ(の) **Arabu** (**no**) Arab
荒い **arai** rough
粗い **arai** coarse
洗い流す **arainagasu** flush away
あらかじめ **arakajime** in advance
あらかじめ備えさせる **arakajime sonae saseru** forearm
あらまし **aramashi** outline
あら探しをする **arasagashi o suru** find fault with
あられ **arare** hail
あらし **arashi** storm
争い **arasoi** conflict; contest; struggle, fight; …を争っている ***... o arasotte iru*** be in contention for …; …と争っている ***... to arasotte iru*** be at odds with
争う **arasou** struggle; dispute; contest
荒す **arasu** damage; ruin
洗う **arau** clean; wash
あらわにする **arawa ni suru** reveal
現れる **arawareru** appear, show up
表れる **arawareru** manifest itself
表す **arawasu** embody; register *emotion*; show *interest, emotion*
あらゆる **arayuru** all kinds of
あれ **are** that one; that
荒れ地 **arechi** wasteland; wilderness
荒れ果てた **arehateta** dilapidated; godforsaken *place, town*
あれから **are kara** after that
あれこれ **are kore** this and that
荒れ狂う **arekuruu** rage
荒れ模様(の) **aremoyō** (**no**) stormy; inclement
荒れる **areru** get stormy; get worked up; get violent
アレルギー **arerugī** allergy; …にアレルギーがある ***... ni arerugī ga aru*** be allergic to …
荒れた **areta** rough; wild
あり **ari** ant
アリバイ **aribai** alibi
ありえる **arieru** probable
ありふれた **arifureta** common; everyday; trite; nondescript
ありがたい **arigatai** grateful
ありがたく思う **arigataku omou** appreciate
ありがとう **arigatō** thank you, thanks
アリゲーター **arigētā** alligator
あります **arimasu** there is; there are
ありそうもない **arisō mo nai** unlikely
ありそう(な) **arisō** (**na**) likely
ある **aru** be; be located, lie (*of place, building, object*); measure ◊ certain, particular; …がある ***... ga aru*** have...; there is / are; ある日 ***aru hi*** one day; ある意味で ***aru imi de wa*** in a sense; ある程度は ***aru teido wa*** to a certain extent
アルバイト **arubaito** part-time job; part-time work
アルバム **arubamu** album
アルファベット **arufabetto** alphabet
アルファベット順(の) **arufabetto-jun** (**no**) alphabetical
歩いて **aruite** on foot
歩いていく **aruite iku** walk
あるいは **arui wa** or; perhaps
歩き **aruki** walking
アルコール **arukōru** alcohol
アルコール中毒患者 **arukōru-chūdoku-kanja** alcoholic
歩く **aruku** pace; tread; walk
アルミニウム **aruminiumu** aluminum
アルゼンチン **Aruzenchin** Argentina
アルゼンチン(の) **Aruzenchin** (**no**) Argentinian
麻 **asa** hemp; linen
朝 **asa** morning
朝ごはん **asagohan** breakfast
浅黒い **asaguroi** swarthy
浅薄(な) **asahaka** (**na**) shallow *person*; unwise
朝日 **asahi** morning sun; rising sun
浅い **asai** shallow; superficial
朝飯 **asameshi** breakfast (*not a polite word*); 朝飯前です ***asameshi-mae desu*** be a piece of cake
朝寝坊 **asanebō** late riser
あさり **asari** short-neck clam
浅瀬 **asase** ford
あさって **asatte** the day after tomorrow
汗 **ase** sweat; 汗をかく ***ase o kaku*** sweat
あせる **aseru** get impatient; fade

汗ばんだ **asebanda** sweaty
汗びっしょりになる **asebisshori ni naru** covered in sweat
あせた **aseta** faded
あし **ashi** reed
足 **ashi** foot; paw; leg
脚 **ashi** leg (*of table etc*)
足跡 **ashiato** footprint
足場 **ashiba** scaffold(ing)
足留めされる **ashidome sareru** be stranded; be forced to stay in *hotel*
足取り **ashidori** way of walking, gait; tracks
足掛り **ashigakari** foothold; stepping stone
足ひれ **ashihire** flipper
足首 **ashikubi** ankle
足元に気をつけて **ashimoto ni ki o tsukete** mind the step!
足の裏 **ashi no ura** sole
足音 **ashioto** footstep; tread
アシスタント **ashisutanto** assistant
明日 **ashita** tomorrow
あそび **asobi** play TECH
遊び **asobi** game; play; pleasure
遊び回る **asobimawaru** play around
遊び人 **asobi-nin** playboy
遊び友達**asobitomodachi** playmate
遊ぶ **asobu** play; enjoy oneself
あそこ **asoko** over there ◊ that place
阿蘇山 **Aso-san** Mt Aso
あっさり **assari** simply; plainly; ***assari shita tabemono*** plain food
圧縮する **asshuku suru** compress
明日 **asu** tomorrow
アース **āsu** ground ELEC
アスパラガス **asuparagasu** asparagus
アスピリン **asupirin** aspirin
与える **ataeru** give; award; provide; spare
値する **atai suru** deserve ◊ worthy
頭 **atama** head
頭でっかち(の) **atamadekkachi (no)** top heavy
頭がいい **atama ga ii** smart; brainy; academic
頭が悪い **atama ga warui** dense; unintelligent
頭金 **atamakin** down payment
新しい **atarashii** fresh, new
新しくする **atarashiku suru** freshen
新しさ **atarashi-sa** freshness
あたり前 **atarimae** natural; reasonable
あたる **ataru** take it out on
当たる **ataru** strike; be right; win
あたし **atashi** I (*used mainly by women*)
温かい, 暖かい **atatakai** cordial; hot; warm
温かく, 暖かく **atatakaku** warmly
温かみ, 暖かみ **atatakami** warmth
温かさ, 暖かさ **atataka-sa** warmth
温まる, 暖まる **atatamaru** warm up
温める, 暖める **atatameru** warm up, heat up
当たった **atatta** winning
宛て **-ate** addressed to
宛て名 **atena** address
当てにならない **ate ni naranai** unreliable
当てにする **ate ni suru** bank on, count on
当てる **ateru** win
充てる **ateru** devote; set aside
あてずっぽう **atezuppō** guesswork
跡 **ato** mark; trace; trail
後味 **atoaji** aftertaste
後で **ato de** afterward; later, later on
後へ引かない **ato e hikanai** stand one's ground
あと片付け **atokatazuke** clearing away
後回しにする **atomawashi ni suru** put on the back burner
後戻り(の) **atomodori (no)** retrograde
後に **ato ni** after; behind
アトラクション **atorakushon** attraction
アトリエ **atorie** studio
後始末 **atoshimatsu** ordering
後ずさりする **atozusari suru** back away
熱々(の) **atsuatsu (no)** piping hot
厚切り (の) **atsugiri (no)** thickly-sliced

厚着する **atsugi suru** bundle up
厚い **atsui** heavy; thick
暑い **atsui** hot *weather, day*
熱い **atsui** hot *object, food, water*
扱い **atsukai** handling; treatment
扱いにくくなる **atsukainikuku naru** play up; be difficult to handle
扱いやすい **atsukaiyasui** manageable
厚かましい **atsukamashii** impudent
熱かん **atsukan** hot sake
扱う **atsukau** handle; treat; trade
集まり **atsumari** gathering; reunion
集まる **atsumaru** assemble; collect; congregate; rally around
集める **atsumeru** collect, gather; pick up *information*; raise *money*
圧力 **atsuryoku** pressure; 圧力をかける ***atsuryoku o kakeru*** pressure
圧力団体 **atsuryoku-dantai** lobby
厚さ **atsu-sa** thickness
暑さ **atsu-sa** heat (*weather*)
熱さ **atsu-sa** heat (*water*)
あっという間に **atto iu ma ni** in a flash
圧倒する **attō suru** overwhelm; …に圧倒される ***... ni attô sareru*** be overawed by
圧倒的(な) **attōteki (na)** overpowering; predominant; 圧倒的な勝利 ***attôteki na shôri*** landslide victory
あう **au** meet with *sth unfavorable*; get involved in; suit
合う **au** fit; go; match
会う **au** meet
アウトである **auto de aru** be out SP
アウトプット **autoputto** output
泡 **awa** bubble; froth; head (*on beer*); foam; lather
あわび **awabi** abalone
泡立て器 **awadateki** mixer; whisk
泡立てる **awadateru** whip; whisk
泡立つ **awadatsu** effervescent
淡い **awai** pale; faint
合わない **awanai** clash
阿波踊り **awa-odori** *festival dance in Tokushima*
哀れみ **awaremi** pity
哀れ(な) **aware (na)** miserable; pitiful; unfortunate; pathetic
合わせる **awaseru** join; set *alarm clock, broken limb*; チャンネルをあわせる ***channeru o awaseru*** tune in
あわただしい **awatadashii** hurried
あわただしさ **awatadashi-sa** scramble
あわてる **awateru** be flustered; panic
あわてている **awatete iru** be in a hurry
誤り(の) **ayamari (no)** false
謝る **ayamaru** apologize
誤る **ayamaru** make a mistake
誤った **ayamatta** misguided; mistaken
あやめ **ayame** iris
怪しげ(な) **ayashige (na)** sinister
怪しい **ayashii** shaky; fishy, suspicious
あやす **ayasu** rock; dandle; caress
操り人形 **ayatsuri-ningyō** puppet
操る **ayatsuru** manipulate
危うくする **ayauku suru** compromise; endanger
あゆ **ayu** sweetfish
あざ **aza** bruise; birthmark
あざけり **azakeri** derision; mockery; ridicule; taunt
あざける **azakeru** ridicule
あざらし **azarashi** seal
あざ笑う **azawarau** scoff; sneer
鮮やか(な) **azayaka (na)** vivid
鮮やかさ **azayaka-sa** brilliance
預ける **azukeru** leave

B

ば -**ba** if; when; whenever; 雨が降れば ***ame ga fureba ...*** if it rains ...; その音楽を聞けば ***sono ongaku o kikeba ...*** whenever I hear that music ...
場 **ba** scene; place
バー **bā** (cross)bar (*in high jump*); saloon (bar)
ばばシャツ **babashatsu** long-sleeved thermal undershirt
バーベキュー **bābekyū** barbecue
バーボン **bābon** bourbon
バブル経済 **baburu-keizai** bubble economy
ばち **bachi** drumstick
罰 **bachi** punishment
場違い(の) **bachigai (no)** unsuitable
バッジ **badji** badge; button
バドミントン **badominton** badminton
バーゲン **bāgen** sale (*at reduced prices*)
倍 **bai** double
場合 **bāi** occasion; case; situation
バイバイ **baibai** bye-bye
売買 **baibai** buying and selling
梅毒 **baidoku** syphilis
ばい菌 **baikin** bug, germ
バイク便 **baiku-bin** motorcycle courier
バインダー **baindā** binder
倍(の) **bai (no)** double
バイオリン **baiorin** violin
バイオリン奏者 **baiorin-sōsha** violinist
バイオテクノロジー **baiotekunorojī** biotechnology
バイパス **baipasu** bypass
バイリンガル(の) **bairingaru (no)** bilingual
バイセクシャル **baisekusharu** bisexual
陪審 **baishin** jury
陪審員 **baishin'in** juror
賠償 **baishō** recompense
売春 **baishun** prostitution
売春婦 **baishunfu** prostitute
売春宿 **baishun'yado** brothel
買収 **baishū** purchase; bribe
買収する **baishū suru** bribe; buy, take over COM
バイスプレジデント **baisu-purejidento** vice president
媒体 **baitai** medium; vehicle
売店 **baiten** booth
バイト **baito** byte; part-time job; part-time work
バイヤー **baiyā** buyer
ばか... **baka...** very; too; ridiculously
ばか **baka** idiot; fool, imbecile; jerk
ばかばかしいほど **bakabakashii-hodo** ridiculously
ばかばかしさ **bakabakashi-sa** absurdity
ばかげた **bakageta** absurd, ridiculous
ばか(な) **baka (na)** idiotic, silly, stupid
ばかにする **baka ni suru** deride; mock; 人をばかにした ***hito o baka ni shita*** contemptuous
ばからしい **bakarashii** ridiculous; silly
ばかり -**bakari** approximately; only; just; just because; 五人ばかり ***gonin-bakari*** approximately five people; 大人ばかり ***otona-bakari*** adults only; 着いたばかりだ ***tsuita-bakari da*** I've just arrived
ばかさわぎする **bakasawagi suru** go (out) on a spree; fool around
ばか笑い **bakawarai** guffaw
ばか笑いする **bakawarai suru** guffaw
馬券屋 **baken'ya** bookmaker
化ける **bakeru** disguise oneself as

バケツ **baketsu** bucket
罰金 **bakkin** fine, penalty
バック **bakku** back; backhand; reverse MOT
バックアップ **bakku-appu** backup, support
バックミラー **bakkumirā** mirror; rear-view mirror
バックパッカー **bakku-pakkā** backpacker
バックパック **bakku-pakku** backpack
バックル **bakkuru** buckle
バックさせる **bakku saseru** back, reverse
バックスペース(キー) **bakkusupēsu (kī)** backspace (key)
バックする **bakku suru** back, back up, reverse
バーコード **bākōdo** bar code
ばくち **bakuchi** gambling
ばくち打ち **bakuchiuchi** gambler
ばく大(な) **bakudai (na)** great; huge; vast; enormous; infinite
爆弾 **bakudan** bomb
爆弾騒ぎ **bakudan-sawagi** bomb scare
幕府 **bakufu** *government under the shogunate*
爆撃 **bakugeki** bomb attack
爆撃機 **bakugekiki** bomber
爆撃する **bakugeki suru** bomb
爆破する **bakuha suru** blast; blow up, bomb
爆発 **bakuhatsu** blast, explosion; outburst
爆発物 **bakuhatsu-butsu** shell
爆発させる **bakuhatsu saseru** detonate, explode
爆発する **bakuhatsu suru** detonate, blow up; explode, go off
暴露 **bakuro** exposure; revelation
暴露する **bakuro suru** expose, uncover
爆薬 **bakuyaku** explosive
漠然と **bakuzen to** indefinitely; vaguely
漠然とした **bakuzen to shita** indefinable; indeterminate
バン **ban** van
晩 **ban** evening
番 **ban** move; turn
バナナ **banana** banana
バンド **bando** band; vocal group; strap
バンドエイド **bando-eido** Band-Aid®
ばね **bane** spring
番号 **bangō** number
番号間違い **bangō-machigai** wrong number
晩ごはん **bangohan** evening meal
番組 **bangumi** program
バニラ **banira** vanilla
万事 **banji** everything
万能 **bannō** versatility
万能(の) **bannō (no)** all-purpose; all-round
バンパー **banpā** bumper
伴奏 **bansō** accompaniment; backing; 伴奏をする ***bansô o suru*** accompany
ばんそうこう **bansōkō** adhesive plaster, sticking plaster
万歳 **banzai** hurray!, hurrah!
番付 **banzuke** sumo rankings
抜本的(な) **bapponteki (na)** drastic
ばら **bara** rose
ばらばらに **barabara ni** out of sequence
ばらばらになる **barabara ni naru** come apart; disintegrate; be scattered
ばらばらにする **barabara ni suru** take to pieces
ばらばら(の) **barabara (no)** sporadic; in pieces
バラエティーショー **baraetī-shō** vaudeville
ばら色(の) **barairo (no)** rosy
ばらまく **baramaku** scatter
バランス **baransu** balance; coordination
バランスのとれた **baransu no toreta** balanced
バランスの悪い **baransu no warui** unbalanced
ばらす **barasu** take to pieces; reveal *secret*; kill
バレーボール **barēbōru** volleyball
バレエ **baree** ballet

バレエダンサー **baree dansā** ballet dancer
バレリーナ **barerīna** ballerina
ばれる **bareru** be out (*of secret*)
バリカン **barikan** hair clippers
バリケード **barikēdo** barricade
馬力 **bariki** horsepower; 馬力のある ***bariki no aru*** powerful
バロメーター **baromētā** barometer
バルブ **barubu** valve
場所 **basho** locality; place; location; site; spot; room, space
抜歯 **basshi** tooth extraction
抜糸をする **basshi o suru** take the stitches out
抜粋 **bassui** excerpt, extract
罰する **bassuru** discipline; punish
バス **basu** bass; bus
バスケット **basuketto** basket
バスケットボール **basukettobōru** basketball
バスマット **basu-matto** bath mat
バス(の) **basu (no)** bass
バスローブ **basu-rōbu** bathrobe
バスターミナル **basu-tāminaru** bus station; bus terminal
バスタオル **basu-taoru** bath towel
バス停 **basutei** bus stop
バスト **basuto** bust
バター **batā** butter
ばたんと閉まる **batan to shimaru** bang, slam
ばたんと閉める **batan to shimeru** bang, slam
バーテン **bāten** bartender
罰 **batsu** penalty; punishment
抜群 **batsugun** outstanding, excellent
ばつ(印) **batsu(jirushi)** cross
ばった **batta** grasshopper
バッター **battā** batter
バッテリー **batterī** battery
バット **batto** bat
バウンド **baundo** bound
バウンドさせる **baundo saseru** bounce
バウンドする **baundo suru** bounce
ベアリング **bearingu** bearing
ベビーベッド **bebī-beddo** crib
ベビーいす **bebī-isu** highchair
ベビーシッター **bebīshittā** baby-sitter; ベビーシッターをする ***bebîshittâ o suru*** baby-sit
ベッド **beddo** bed
ベッドカバー **beddokabā** bedspread
ベッドメーキングする **beddo-mēkingu suru** make the bed
べき **-beki** should, ought to; 驚くべき ***odoroku-beki*** surprising
別館 **bekkan** annex
別居 **bekkyo** separation
別居中(の) **bekkyochū (no)** estranged
別居した **bekkyo shita** separated
別居している **bekkyo shite iru** live apart
別居する **bekkyo suru** separate
ベーコン **bēkon** bacon
弁 **-ben** dialect
弁 **ben** speech; valve
便 **ben** convenience; feces
ベンチャー事業 **benchā-jigyō** venture
ベンチ **benchi** bench
弁護 **bengo** defense
弁護人 **bengo-nin** defense lawyer
弁護士 **bengo-shi** lawyer, attorney; counsel
弁護する **bengo suru** defend
ベニヤ板 **beniya-ita** plywood
便所 **benjo** toilet
弁解 **benkai** excuse
弁解がましい **benkai-gamashii** defensive
便器 **benki** lavatory
勉強 **benkyō** study
勉強家(の) **benkyōka (no)** hard-working
勉強させる **benkyō saseru** work
勉強する **benkyō suru** study; do *subject at school*; work
便秘 **benpi** constipation
便秘している **benpi shite iru** constipated
便利 **benri** convenience
便利(な) **benri (na)** convenient, handy
弁償 **benshō** recompense
弁償する **benshō suru** reimburse
弁当 **bentō** packed lunch; lunch box
ベランダ **beranda** balcony; porch; veranda

ベル **beru** bell
ベール **bēru** veil
ベルベット **berubetto** velvet
ベルギー **Berugī** Belgium
ベルギー(の) **Berugī** (**no**) Belgian
ベルト **beruto** belt
ベルトコンベヤー **beruto-konbeyā** conveyor belt
ベース **bēsu** bass
ベスト **besuto** vest; the best
ベストをつくす **besuto o tsukusu** do one's best
ベストセラー **besuto-serā** best-seller
ベテラン **beteran** veteran
ベテラン(の) **beteran** (**no**) veteran
べとべとした **betobeto shita** soggy; sticky; tacky
べとべとする **betobeto suru** gooey
ベトナム **Betonamu** Vietnam
ベトナム(の) **Betonamu** (**no**) Vietnamese
別 **betsu** difference; distinction
別々に **betsubetsu ni** independently of; separately
別(の) **betsu** (**no**) another; different; separate
備蓄 **bichiku** reserve; stockpile
備蓄する **bichiku suru** stockpile
ビデオ **bideo** video
ビデオカメラ **bideo-kamera** video camera
ビデオテープ **bideo-tēpu** video cassette
美人 **bijin** beautiful woman
ビジネスクラス **bijinesu-kurasu** business class
美人(の) **bijin** (**no**) beautiful
美術館 **bijutsukan** art gallery; gallery, museum
ビーカー **bīkā** beaker
ビキニ **bikini** bikini
びっくり仰天させる **bikkuri-gyōten saseru** shock
びっくりさせられる **bikkuri saserareru** be shocked by
びっくりさせる **bikkuri saseru** shock, astonish; scare ◊ shocking; stunning
びっくりする **bikkuri suru** shock, amaze
びくびくしている **bikubiku shite iru** jumpy
微妙(な) **bimyō** (**na**) delicate; subtle
びん **bin** bottle; jar
便 **bin** flight
貧乏 **binbō** poverty
ビニール袋 **binīru-bukuro** plastic bag
便乗する **binjō suru** get a ride; jump on the bandwagon
敏感(な) **binkan** (**na**) reponsive; sensitive
敏感さ **binkan-sa** sensitivity
便名 **binmei** flight number
便せん **binsen** notepaper; writing paper
ビラ **bira** bill, poster; handout
ビリヤード **biriyādo** billiards; snooker
ビール **bīru** beer
ビル **biru** building
ビルディング **birudingu** building
ビルマ **Biruma** Burma
ビルマ(の) **Biruma** (**no**) Burmese
微笑 **bishō** smile
微小(の) **bishō** (**no**) microscopic
びしょぬれになる **bishonure ni naru** be wet through
ビスケット **bisuketto** biscuit
ビタミン **bitamin** vitamin
ビタミン剤 **bitamin-zai** vitamin pill
美的(な) **biteki** (**na**) esthetic
ビート **bīto** beat
美徳 **bitoku** virtue
ビット **bitto** bit
琵琶湖 **Biwako** Lake Biwa
美容院 **biyōin** beauty parlor
美容(の) **biyō** (**no**) cosmetic
美容整形 **biyō-seikei** cosmetic surgery
美容師 **biyōshi** beautician; hairdresser
ビザ **biza** visa
微罪 **bizai** misdemeanor
棒 **bō** bar; pole; rod
防備なし(の) **bōbi nashi** (**no**) unprotected
ボブ **bobu** bob
墓地 **bochi** cemetery, graveyard
膨張 **bōchō** expansion

膨張する **bōchō suru** expand
膨大(な) **bōdai** (**na**) vast
防弾(の) **bōdan** (**no**) bullet-proof
ボディーチェック **bodīchekku** body search; …のボディーチェックをする ***… no bodīchekku o suru*** frisk
ボディーガード **bodīgādo** bodyguard
ボディーランゲージ **bodīrangēji** body language
ボディースーツ **bodīsūtsu** bodice; body (suit)
暴動 **bōdō** disorder; disturbances; riot; 暴動を起こす ***bôdô o okosu*** riot
防衛 **bōei** defense
防衛庁 **Bōeichō** Japan Defense Agency
防衛予算 **bōei-yosan** defense budget
貿易 **bōeki** trade
貿易収支 **bōeki-shūshi** balance of trade
望遠鏡 **bōenkyō** telescope
望遠レンズ **bōen-renzu** telephoto lens
防腐処理を施す **bōfu-shori o hodokosu** preserve; embalm
暴風雨 **bōfūu** hurricane; rainstorm
妨害 **bōgai** interference; disruption
妨害する **bōgai suru** disrupt; jam
墓碑銘 **bohimei** epitaph
ボーイ **bōi** bellhop
ボーイフレンド **bōifurendo** boyfriend
ボイコット **boikotto** boycott
ボイコットする **boikotto suru** boycott
母音 **boin** vowel
ボイラー **boirā** boiler; furnace
ボーイソプラノ **bōi-sopurano** treble
ボーイスカウト **bōi-sukauto** (boy)scout
傍受する **bōju suru** intercept
傍観する **bōkan suru** look on; stand by
ボーカル **bōkaru** vocalist
ぼかす **bokasu** blur; obscure
冒険 **bōken** adventure
簿記 **boki** bookkeeping
簿記係 **boki-gakari** bookkeeper
募金 **bokin** collection; fundraising
勃起 **bokki** erection
暴行 **bōkō** assault; beating
膀胱 **bōkō** bladder
母国 **bokoku** native country
母国語 **bokokugo** mother tongue
暴行する **bōkō suru** assault
牧場経営者 **bokujō-keiei-sha** rancher
撲滅 **bokumetsu** elimination
暴君 **bōkun** despot, tyrant
暴君(の) **bōkun** (**no**) tyrannical
ぼく **boku** I (*used mostly by males*)
ボクサー **bokusā** boxer
牧師 **bokushi** clergyman; minister
ボクシング **bokushingu** boxing
牧草地 **bokusōchi** meadow
忘却 **bōkyaku** oblivion
亡命 **bōmei** exile
亡命者 **bōmei-sha** exile
亡命する **bōmei suru** go into exile
盆 **bon** tray
ボーナス **bōnasu** bonus
凡人 **bonjin** ordinary person; mediocrity
ボンネット **bonnetto** hood
盆踊り **bon'odori** festival dance
盆栽 **bonsai** bonsai
ぼんやりした **bon'yari shita** absent-minded; blank, vacant; dim; hazy; misty; dazed
母乳 **bonyū** milk (*woman's*)
防音(の) **bōon** (**no**) soundproof
ぼっ発 **boppatsu** outbreak
ぼっ発する **boppatsu suru** flare up
暴落する **bōraku suru** crash; slump
ボランティア **borantia** volunteer
ボランティア(の) **borantia** (**no**) voluntary
ボレー **borē** volley
ボーリング **bōringu** bowling; ボーリングをする ***bôringu o suru*** bowl
ボーリング場 **bōringu-jō** bowling alley
ぼろ **boro** rag
ぼろぼろになる **boroboro ni naru** perish (*of material*)
ぼろぼろになった **boroboro ni natta** worn-out
ぼろぼろ(の) **boroboro** (**no**) ragged
ぼろ負け **boromake** massacre (*in*

game)
ぼろ負けする **boromake suru** be massacred, get a licking
ボール **bōru** ball; football; bowl (*for cooking, salad*)
ボール紙 **bōrugami** cardboard
ボールペン **bōrupen** ballpoint pen
ボルト **boruto** bolt; volt
暴力 **bōryoku** brute force; violence
暴力団員 **bōryokudan'in** mobster
暴力的(な) **bōryokuteki (na)** violent
ボリューム **boryūmu** volume
防災訓練 **bōsai-kunren** emergency drill
母性 **bosei** maternity
母性的(な) **boseiteki (na)** maternal, motherly
紡績工場 **bōseki-kōjō** mill
帽子 **bōshi** cap; hat
防止 **bōshi** prevention
母子家庭 **boshi katei** single parent family (*mother only*)
防止する **bōshi suru** prevent
募集 **boshū** recruitment
募集人員 **boshū-jin'in** intake
募集活動 **boshū-katsudō** recruitment drive
募集する **boshū suru** recruit
防臭剤 **bōshūzai** deodorant
没収する **bosshū suru** confiscate
防水(の) **bōsui (no)** showerproof; waterproof
防水シート **bōsui-shīto** tarpaulin
棒高跳び **bōtakatobi** polevault
ぼたん **botan** peony
ボタン **botan** button
ボート **bōto** rowboat; boat
冒頭 **bōtō** opening
冒とく **bōtoku** blasphemy; impudence; violation
冒とくする **bōtoku suru** blaspheme
没落 **botsuraku** downfall
ぼーっとさせる **bōtto saseru** stupefy
没頭する **bottō suru** be absorbed in; be devoted to; 仕事に没頭する ***shigoto ni bottô suru*** bury oneself in work
ぼやけた **boyaketa** fuzzy; hazy
ぼう然とした **bōzen to shita** dazed
ぼう然として **bōzen to shite** in a daze
坊主 **bōzu** Buddhist monk
部 **bu** department, division; part, section
歩合 **buai** commission; percentage
無愛想(な) **buaisō (na)** inhospitable; surly; unsociable
部分 **bubun** bit; part; component; piece
部分的(な) **bubunteki (na)** incomplete, partial
部分的に **bubunteki ni** partially, partly
ぶちまける **buchimakeru** pour out; disclose
部長 **buchō** head
仏陀 **Budda** Buddha
ぶどう **budō** grape
ぶどう園 **budōen** vineyard
ぶどうの木 **budō no ki** vine
部外者 **bugai-sha** outsider
舞楽 **bugaku** court dance
部品 **buhin** part; unit
ブイ **bui** buoy
ブーイング **būingu** booing
無事である **buji de aru** be safe
無事(な) **buji (na)** safe
無事に **buji ni** safely
侮辱 **bujoku** humiliation; insult, slight; snub
侮辱する **bujoku suru** insult; snub
武術 **bujutsu** martial arts
部下 **buka** subordinate
不格好(な) **bukakkō (na)** misshapen; crude
不格好にする **bukakkō ni suru** deform
武器 **buki** weapon; arms
無気味(な), 不気味(な) **bukimi (na)** ghostly; eerie; uncanny
ぶきっちょ **bukitcho** clumsy person
不器用 **bukiyō** clumsiness
不器用(な) **bukiyō (na)** clumsy
物価 **bukka** commodity prices
ぶっきらぼう(な) **bukkirabō (na)** abrupt; blunt; curt; gruff
ぶっきらぼうに **bukkirabō ni** bluntly
仏教 **Bukkyō** Buddhism
仏教(の) **Bukkyō (no)** Buddhist
仏教徒 **Bukkyōto** Buddhist

部門 **bumon** sector
ブーム **būmu** boom; craze; ブーム(の) ***bûmu*** **(no)** all the rage
文 **bun** sentence
分 **bun** portion
ぶな **buna** beech
分べん **bunben** labor (*in pregnancy*)
分べん室 **bunben-shitsu** labor ward
文房具 **bunbōgu** stationery
文房具店 **bunbōgu-ten** stationery store
分断された **bundan sareta** segmented
文学 **bungaku** literature
文学修士 **bungaku-shūshi** MA, Master of Arts (*person*)
文学修士号 **bungaku-shūshigō** MA, Master of Arts (*degree*)
分譲マンション **bunjō-manshon** condo
文化 **bunka** culture
文化の日 **Bunka no hi** Culture Day
分解する **bunkai suru** break up (*into component parts*); cannibalize; dismantle
文化的(な) **bunkateki (na)** cultural
分割 **bunkatsu** division; partition
分割払い **bunkatsu-barai** paying by installments
分割できない **bunkatsu dekinai** indivisible
分割する **bunkatsu suru** divide; partition
文系の学位 **bunkei no gakui** arts degree
文献目録 **bunken-mokuroku** bibliography
分岐する **bunki suru** branch off, diverge
分岐点 **bunkiten** fork
文庫本 **bunkobon** pocket-sized book
文明 **bunmei** civilization
文脈 **bunmyaku** context
分配 **bunpai** distribution; split, division
分配する **bunpai suru** distribute
分泌 **bunpitsu** secretion (*activity*)
分泌物 **bunpitsu-butsu** secretion (*product*)
分泌する **bunpitsu suru** secrete
文法 **bunpō** grammar
文法(の) **bunpō (no)** grammatical
文楽 **bunraku** *traditional Japanese puppet play*
分裂 **bunretsu** division; fission; split; disagreement
分裂させる **bunretsu saseru** divide; split
分裂する **bunretsu suru** split; disagree
分離 **bunri** separation
分離できない **bunri dekinai** inseparable
分離する **bunri suru** separate; isolate
分類 **bunrui** classification
分類する **bunrui suru** break down; classify, sort
分量 **bunryō** amount
分析 **bunseki** analysis
分析する **bunseki suru** analyze
分子 **bunshi** molecule
分子(の) **bunshi (no)** molecular
文書 **bunsho** document
文章 **bunshō** writing; composition
分数 **bunsū** fraction
文体 **buntai** style of writing
分担 **buntan** my / his / her etc share
分担する **buntan suru** share
文通 **buntsū** correspondence
文通相手 **buntsū-aite** correspondent
文通する **buntsū suru** correspond
分野 **bun'ya** area, field, sphere
物品 **buppin** article, item
ぶらぶらする **burabura suru** lounge around; mess around; take a stroll; wander around
ブラインド **buraindo** blind; shade
ブラジャー **burajā** brassiere
ブラジル **Burajiru** Brazil
ブラジル人 **Burajiru-jin** Brazilian
ブラジル(の) **Burajiru (no)** Brazilian
ブラックボックス **burakku-bokkusu** black box
ブラック(の) **burakku (no)** black *coffee*
ブラックリスト **burakku-risuto** blacklist

ブラックユーモア **burakku yūmoa** black mood, black humor
ブランチ **buranchi** brunch
ブランデー **burandē** brandy
ブランド **burando** brand
ブランド志向 **burando-shikō** brand loyalty
ブランコ **buranko** swing; trapeze
ぶら下がる **burasagaru** dangle
ぶら下げる **burasageru** dangle
ブラシ **burashi** brush; scrubbing brush; ブラシをかける ***burashi o kakeru*** brush
ブラスバンド **burasu-bando** brass band
ぶらつく **buratsuku** wander; stroll
ブラウニー **braunī** brownie
ブラウス **burausu** blouse
ブラウザー **burauzā** browser
無礼 **burei** rudeness
無礼(な) **burei (na)** rude
ブレーカー **burēkā** circuit breaker
ブレーキ **burēki** brake; ブレーキをかける ***burêki o kakeru*** brake
ブレンド **burendo** blend
ブレンドする **burendo suru** blend
ブレスレット **buresuretto** bracelet
ブレザー **burezā** blazer
ぶり **buri** yellowtail
ブリーチ **burīchi** bleach
ブリーダー **burīdā** breeder
ブリーフ **burīfu** briefs
ブリーフケース **burīfukēsu** briefcase
ブローチ **burōchi** brooch; pin
ブロードライ **burō-dorai** blow-dry
ブロッコリ **burokkori** broccoli
ブロック **burokku** block
ブロークン(な) **burōkun (na)** broken
ブロンズ **buronzu** bronze
ぶる **-buru**: いい子ぶる ***ii ko-buru*** pretend to be behaving well; 学者ぶる ***gakusha-buru*** pose as a scholar; 上品ぶる人 ***jôhin-buru hito*** person who puts on airs; prude
ブルドーザー **burudōzā** bulldozer
部類 **burui** category, class
ブルース **burūsu** blues
不作法 **busahō** misbehavior; bad manners; 不作法にふるまう ***busahô ni furumau*** misbehave
不作法(な) **busahō (na)** ill-mannered
物色する **busshoku suru** browse; hunt for
部署 **busho** post; place of duty
不精ひげ, 無精ひげ **bushōhige** bristles, stubble
無精ひげ(の) **bushōhige (no)** unshaven
無精(な) **bushō (na)** lazy
部首 **bushu** radical (*in Chinese character*)
武装解除 **busō-kaijo** disarmament
武装解除する **busō-kaijo suru** disarm
不足 **-busoku** shortage of; 水不足 ***mizu-busoku*** shortage of water; 睡眠不足 ***suimin-busoku*** lack of sleep
武装させる **busō saseru** arm
武装した **busō shita** armed
武装していない **busō shite inai** unarmed
物質 **busshitsu** material, substance; matter
物質主義 **busshitsu-shugi** materialism
物質主義者 **busshitsu-shugisha** materialist
物質主義的(な) **busshitsu-shugiteki (na)** materialistic
物質的(な) **busshitsuteki (na)** material
豚 **buta** hog; pig
豚皮 **buta-gawa** pigskin
豚小屋 **buta-goya** (pig)sty, pigpen *also fig*
舞台 **butai** scene; stage THEA
部隊 **butai** unit; corps
舞台げいこ **butai-geiko** dress rehearsal
舞台装置 **butai-sōchi** stage scenery
舞台裏で **butaiura de** behind the scenes
ブータン **Būtan** Bhutan
豚肉 **butaniku** pork
ブータン(の) **Būtan (no)** Bhutanese
豚野郎 **butayarō** pig
ブティック **butikku** boutique
ぶつ **butsu** beat; smack

ブーツ **būtsu** boot
ぶつぶつができる **butsubutsu ga dekiru** break out in a rash; blister
ぶつぶつ言う **butsubutsu iu** mumble; grumble
物々交換 **butsubutsu-kōkan** barter
物々交換する **butsubutsu-kōkan suru** barter
仏壇 **butsudan** Buddhist altar
ぶつかる **butsukaru** bump into; knock, hit
ぶつける **butsukeru** bang; bump
物理学 **butsuri-gaku** physics
物理学者 **butsuri-gakusha** physicist
物理療法 **butsuri-ryōhō** physiotherapy
物理療法士 **butsuri-ryōhōshi** physiotherapist
仏塔 **buttō** pagoda
ぶよ **buyo** gnat
ブザー **buzā** buzzer; doorbell; ブザーを鳴らす ***buzâ o narasu*** buzz
びょう **byō** tack
秒 **byō** second (*of time*)
屏風 **byōbu** screen
平等 **byōdō** equality
平等(な) **byōdo (na)** even
平等に **byōdō ni** equally
平等(の) **byōdō (no)** equal
平等主義(の) **byōdō-shugi (no)** egalitarian
病院 **byōin** hospital; infirmary
病弱(な) **byōjaku (na)** sickly
病気 **byōki** illness, disease; infirmity; sickness
病気になる **byōki ni naru** fall ill, be taken ill; sicken
病気(の) **byōki (no)** ailing; ill; sick
病人 **byōnin** invalid
病歴 **byōreki** case history, medical history
病理学 **byōrigaku** pathology
病理学者 **byōrigaku-sha** pathologist
描写 **byōsha** description; portrait; portrayal
描写 する **byōsha suru** describe
秒針 **byōshin** second hand
病室 **byōshitsu** sickroom
病的(な) **byōteki (na)** compulsive; morbid; pathological
病棟 **byōtō** ward
秒読み **byōyomi** countdown

C

茶 **cha** tea
茶番劇 **chabangeki** farce
ちゃち(な) **chachi (na)** flimsy; cheap
チャイム **chaimu** chime
茶色 **chairo** brown
茶色(の) **chairo (no)** brown
チャイルドシート **chairudo-shīto** car seat
着 **-chaku** order of arrival; マラソンで二着になった ***marason de nichaku ni natta*** I came second in the marathon ◊ *countword for clothes*
着々と **chakuchaku to** steadily
着服する **chakufuku suru** pocket, embezzle
着実(な) **chakujitsu (na)** steady, reliable
着陸 **chakuriku** landing, touchdown
着陸させる **chakuriku saseru** land
着陸装置 **chakuriku-sōchi** landing gear, undercarriage
着陸する **chakuriku suru** land, touch down
着席する **chakuseki suru** take a seat
着色する **chakushoku suru** stain;

color
着色剤 **chakushokuzai** coloring agent; stain
着水する **chakusui suru** splash down
ちゃん **-chan** *affectionate suffix added to names*
チャンネル **channeru** channel; station
チャンピオン **chanpion** champion
チャンス **chansu** chance; …にチャンスを与える ***... ni chansu o ataeru*** give a break
ちゃんと **chanto** straight; clearly; properly
ちゃんとした **chanto shita** proper
ちゃりんこ **charinko** bicycle
チャリティー **charitī** charity
チャーター便 **chātā-bin** charter flight
チャーターする **chātā suru** charter
茶わん **chawan** bowl
ちえっ **che'** blast, damn
チェック **chekku** check
チェックアウトする **chekku-auto suru** check out; チェックアウトの時間 ***chekkuauto no jikan*** checkout time
チェックイン(カウンター) **chekku-in (kauntā)** check-in (counter)
チェックインする **chekku-in suru** check in; チェックインの時間 ***chekku-in no jikan*** check-in time
チェック(の) **chekku (no)** check, checked, checkered
チェックリスト **chekku-risuto** checklist
チェコ共和国 **Cheko-kyōwakoku** the Czech Republic
チェコ(の) **Cheko (no)** Czech
チェーン **chēn** chain; snow chain
チェーンストア **chēn-sutoa** chain store
チェロ **chero** cello
血 **chi** blood
治安 **chian** law and order; 治安のいい ***chian no ii*** safe ; 治安の悪い ***chian no warui*** dangerous; rough
チアリーダー **chiarīdā** cheerleader
血走った **chibashitta** bloodshot
チベット **Chibetto** Tibet
チベット(の) **Chibetto (no)** Tibetan
乳房 **chibusa** breast; tit, boob
父 **chichi** father
乳 **chichi** milk; boob, tit
父方(の) **chichikata (no)** paternal
父親 **chichioya** father
父親(の) **chichioya (no)** paternal
父親のよう(な) **chichioya no yō (na)** fatherly
血だらけ(の) **chidarake (no)** bloody, covered in blood
知恵 **chie** wisdom; 知恵を絞る ***chie o shiboru*** rack one's brains
知恵遅れ(の) **chieokure (no)** backward, retarded
チフス **chifusu** typhus
違い **chigai** contrast; difference
違いない **-chigai nai** surely; 彼らはもう着いたに違いない ***karera wa mô tsuita ni chigainai*** they must have arrived by now
違いのわかる **chigai no wakaru** discerning; discriminating
違う **chigau** different
違う風に **chigau fū ni** differently, otherwise
ちぎる **chigiru** tear into small pieces
地平線 **chiheisen** horizon
地方 **chihō** district; region
地方分権にする **chihō-bunken ni suru** decentralize
地方自治体 **chihō-jichitai** local government
地方自治体(の) **chihō-jichitai (no)** municipal
地方検事 **chihō-kenji** DA, district attorney
地方(の) **chihō (no)** provincial; rural; regional
地位 **chii** level; position; rank; status
地域 **chiiki** area; neighborhood; terrain
小さい **chiisai** small, little; petty; low
小さくする **chiisaku suru** reduce; turn down
小さ(な) **chiisa (na)** small, little; petty; low
知事 **chiji** governor
縮こまる **chijikomaru** cower
縮み上がる **chijimiagaru** cower
縮む **chijimu** shrink

知人 **chijin** acquaintance
縮れた **chijireta** frizzy; curly
地上 **chijō** above ground
地上管制室 **chijō-kanseishitsu** ground control
地上整備員 **chijō-seibiin** ground crew, ground staff
地下 **chika** basement
地下貯蔵室 **chika-chozōshitsu** underground vaults (*for wine*)
地下で **chika de** underground
地下道 **chikadō** underpass
地階 **chikai** basement
近い **chikai** near; …に近い ***… ni chikai*** border on
誓い **chikai** vow
知覚 **chikaku** perception
近くに **chikaku ni** around; close by, near
知覚する **chikaku suru** perceive
近道 **chikamichi** short cut
地下(の) **chika** (**no**) underground
ちかん **chikan** groper
ちかんする **chikan suru** molest; feel up
力 **chikara** strength; force; power; might
力こぶ **chikarakobu** biceps
力ずく(の) **chikarazuku** (**no**) forcible
力強い **chikarazuyoi** strong; powerful; forceful
地下鉄 **chikatetsu** subway
誓う **chikau** pledge; swear; vow
近寄る **chikayoru** approach; …に近寄らない ***… ni chikayoranai*** keep away from …
近づける **chikazukeru** have access to
近づきにくい **chikazukinikui** unapproachable
近づく **chikazuku** draw near, draw on, approach; 近づかない ***chikazukanai*** keep away
遅刻する **chikoku suru** arrive late
遅刻した **chikoku shita** late
地区 **chiku** district; precinct; quarter
乳首 **chikubi** nipple; teat
チクチクする **chikuchiku suru** prickly; tickle
チクる **chikuru** inform on, snitch on
蓄積 **chikuseki** build-up, accumulation
蓄積する **chikuseki suru** accumulate
畜生 **chikushō** damn it!
地球 **chikyū** the earth; globe
地球儀 **chikyūgi** globe (*model*)
地球(の) **chikyū** (**no**) global; 地球の温暖化 ***chikyû no ondanka*** global warming
血まみれ(の) **chimamire** (**no**) bloodstained
致命傷を受けた **chimeishō o uketa** fatally injured
致命的(な) **chimeiteki** (**na**) deadly, fatal; mortal
チーム **chīmu** side; team
チームワーク **chīmuwāku** teamwork
鎮圧 **chin'atsu** suppression
鎮圧する **chin'atsu suru** suppress; put down
沈没 **chinbotsu** sinking
沈殿物 **chindenbutsu** sediment
賃金 **chingin** wages
賃金労働者 **chingin-rōdō-sha** wage earner
陳述 **chinjutsu** statement (*to police*)
沈下 **chinka** settlement; subsidence
沈下する **chinka suru** subside
珍味 **chinmi** delicacy
沈黙 **chinmoku** hush, silence
知能 **chinō** intelligence
血の気 **chi no ke** blood; 血の気を失う ***chi no ke o ushinau*** turn pale
知能(の) **chinō** (**no**) mental
知能指数 **chinō-shisū** IQ
チンパンジー **chinpanjī** chimpanzee
チンピラ **chinpira** hood, hoodlum
陳列している **chinretsu shite iru** be on display
陳列する **chinretsu suru** display; lay out
鎮静剤 **chinseizai** sedative
賃借契約 **chinshaku-keiyaku** lease
賃借する **chinshaku suru** lease
賃貸契約 **chintai-keiyaku** lease
賃貸契約書 **chintai-keiyakusho** rental agreement
賃貸料 **chintai-ryō** rental; rent
賃貸する **chintai suru** lease; rent

out
チップ **chippu** chip (*in gambling*); tip (*money*)
ちらちら光る **chirachira hikaru** shimmer
ちらちらする **chirachira suru** flicker
散らかった **chirakatta** untidy
散らかっている **chirakatte iru** be a mess
散らかす **chirakasu** scatter; make a mess
ちらりとひと目見る **chirari to hitome miru** catch a glimpse of
ちらし **chirashi** circular; leaflet
散らす **chirasu** disperse
ちらつく **chiratsuku** flicker; fall lightly (*of rain, snow*)
ちらっと見る **chiratto miru** glance at, give a quick look
ちり **chiri** litter; dust
地理 **chiri** geography (*of area*)
地理学 **chirigaku** geography (*subject*)
ちり紙 **chirigami** tissue paper
ちりぢりになる **chirijiri ni naru** be scattered
地理的(な) **chiriteki** (**na**) geographical
ちりとり **chiritori** dustpan
散る **chiru** scatter; disperse
治療 **chiryō** treatment
治療不可能(な) **chiryō-fukanō** (**na**) incurable
治療法 **chiryōhō** cure, remedy
治療法(の) **chiryōhō** (**no**) therapeutic
治療可能(な) **chiryō-kanō** (**na**) curable
治療過程 **chiryō-katei** course of treatment
治療する **chiryō suru** cure; treat
知性 **chisei** intellect, mind; mentality
治世 **chisei** reign
知識 **chishiki** familiarity; knowledge
知識人 **chishiki-jin** intellectual
知識のある **chishiki no aru** knowledgeable
致死(の) **chishi** (**no**) lethal
致死量 **chishiryō** overdose
地質 **chishitsu** geology (*of area*)
地質学 **chishitsugaku** geology (*subject*)
地質学(の) **chishitsugaku** (**no**) geological
地質学者 **chishitsugaku-sha** geologist
窒素 **chisso** nitrogen
窒息 **chissoku** suffocation
窒息させる **chissoku saseru** choke; smother; suffocate
窒息する **chissoku suru** suffocate
血筋 **chisuji** bloodline; lineage
地帯 **chitai** zone
知的(な) **chiteki** (**na**) intellectual, cerebral
膣 **chitsu** vagina
秩序 **chitsujo** order
散っていく **chitte iku** disperse
ちやほやする **chiyahoya suru** make a fuss of; pamper
地図 **chizu** map
チーズ **chīzu** cheese
地図帳 **chizuchō** atlas
チーズケーキ **chīzukēki** cheesecake
著 **-cho** written by
ちょう **chō** butterfly
腸 **chō** bowels; gut, intestine
長 **chō** head; 店長 ***tenchô*** store manager; 部長 ***buchô*** department chief
超 … **chō…** extremely
兆 **chō** trillion
町**chō** administrative division of city; area; block
庁**chō** government agency
跳馬 **chōba** vault
帳簿 **chōbo** accounts book
腸チフス **chō-chifusu** typhoid (fever)
貯蓄 **chochiku** saving
貯蓄する **chochiku suru** save up
ちょうど **chōdo** exactly, just; on the dot; now, immediately; just about; ちょうどその本 ***chôdo sono hon*** the very book
ちょうだい **chōdai** please
重複 **chōfuku** repetition
重複する **chōfuku suru** repeat; overlap
調合物 **chōgōbutsu** concoction

長波 **chōha** long wave
挑発 **chōhatsu** provocation
挑発的(な) **chōhatsuteki (na)** provocative
徴兵 **chōhei** draft, conscription
徴兵忌避者 **chōhei-kihisha** draft dodger
徴兵する **chōhei suru** draft
長編映画 **chōhen-eiga** feature movie
長方形 **chōhōkei** rectangle
長方形(の) **chōhōkei (no)** oblong, rectangular
超人的(な) **chōjinteki (na)** superhuman
帳尻が合う **chōjiri ga au** balance
長女 **chōjo** first daughter
頂上 **chōjō** summit; tip; crest
著述業 **chojutsugyō** writing
超過 **chōka** excess
懲戒(の) **chōkai (no)** disciplinary
聴覚 **chōkaku** hearing
朝刊 **chōkan** morning paper
超過料金 **chōka-ryōkin** excess fare
超過する **chōka suru** overrun
帳消しにする **chōkeshi ni suru** write off
貯金 **chokin** savings
貯金箱 **chokinbako** piggybank
長期(の) **chōki (no)** long-range; long-term
貯金する **chokin suru** save, put away
ちょっかい **chokkai**: …にちょっかいを出す ***... ni chokkai o dasu*** interfere with, mess with
直角 **chokkaku** right-angle
直感 **chokkan** intuition
直径 **chokkei** diameter
直行便 **chokkō-bin** nonstop flight
直行で **chokkō de** nonstop
直行(の) **chokkō (no)** direct, nonstop
直行列車 **chokkō-ressha** through train
徴候, 兆候 **chōkō** indication, sign
ちょこ **choko** sake cup
彫刻 **chōkoku** sculpture
彫刻家 **chōkoku-ka** sculptor
彫刻する **chōkoku suru** carve
チョコレート **chokorēto** chocolate
チョコレートケーキ **chokorēto-kēki** chocolate cake
超高層ビル **chōkōsō-biru** skyscraper
聴講する **chōkō suru** audit
チョーク **chōku** chalk
直面する **chokumen suru** confront; encounter
直立した **chokuritsu shita** erect; upright
直流 **chokuryū** direct current
直線 **chokusen** straight line
直接(の) **chokusetsu (no)** direct; firsthand; immediate *family*
直通バス **chokutsū-basu** through bus
直通(の) **chokutsū (no)** direct
長距離(の) **chōkyori (no)** long-distance; long-range
長距離通話料 **chōkyori-tsūwaryō** long-distance phone toll
調教師 **chōkyō-shi** trainer
超満員(の) **chōman'in (no)** overcrowded
著名(な) **chomei (na)** eminent
調味料 **chōmiryō** flavoring; seasoning
聴問会 **chōmonkai** hearing LAW
弔問客 **chōmonkyaku** mourner
蝶結び **chōmusubi** bow (*in hair etc*)
長男 **chōnan** eldest son
蝶ネクタイ **chōnekutai** bow tie
ちょんまげ **chonmage** topknot
超能力(の) **chōnōryoku (no)** psychic
超能力者 **chōnōryoku-sha** psychic (*person*)
超音波 **chōonpa** ultrasound
超音速(の) **chōonsoku (no)** supersonic
調理師 **chōrishi** cook, chef
調理室 **chōrishitsu** galley
調律する **chōritsu suru** tune
鳥類保護区 **chōrui-hogoku** bird sanctuary
調査 **chōsa** examination; investigation; inquest; probe; search; survey
著作権 **chosaku-ken** copyright
調査する **chōsa suru** examine; probe; check out, investigate

調整 **chōsei** coordination; adjustment
調整する **chōsei suru** coordinate; set, adjust; tune up
朝鮮 **Chōsen** Korea
挑戦 **chōsen** challenge
朝鮮語 **Chōsen-go** Korean
朝鮮人 **Chōsen-jin** Korean
朝鮮民主主義人民共和国 **Chōsen-minshu-shugi-jinmin-kyōwakoku** Democratic People's Republic of Korea, North Korea
朝鮮(の) **Chōsen (no)** Korean
挑戦者 **chōsen-sha** challenger; contender
挑戦する **chōsen suru** challenge; attempt
調節 **chōsetsu** regulation; adjustment
調節できる **chōsetsu dekiru** adjustable
調節する **chōsetsu suru** adjust; readjust; regulate
著者 **chosha** author
調子 **chōshi** pitch; tone MUS; 調子が合っている ***chôshi ga atte iru*** be in tune; 調子がはずれている ***chôshi ga hazurete iru*** be out of tune; 調子が悪くなる ***chôshi ga waruku naru*** play up; 調子がよい ***chôshi ga yoi*** fit; 調子を合わせる ***chôshi o awaseru*** tune up; 調子を悪くする ***chôshi o waruku suru*** trouble; 調子はどうですか ***chôshi wa dô desu ka*** how are you?, how are things?
聴診器 **chōshinki** stethoscope
聴診する **chōshin suru** sound *chest*
超自然(の) **chōshizen (no)** supernatural
超自然的(な) **chōshizenteki (na)** transcendental
長所 **chōsho** merit; strong point
調書 **chōsho** record; report; 調書をとる ***chôsho o toru*** put on record; book (*for speeding*)
朝食 **chōshoku** breakfast
聴衆 **chōshū** audience
徴収する **chōshū suru** levy
貯水池 **chosuichi** reservoir
超大国 **chōtaikoku** superpower
調停 **chōtei** arbitration, mediation
調停人 **chōtei-nin** troubleshooter
調停者 **chōteisha** mediator
調停する **chōtei suru** arbitrate, mediate
頂点 **chōten** culmination; high point; summit *fig*
ちょうつがい **chōtsugai** hinge
ちょっと **chotto** a little ◊ excuse me!, hello! (*to get attention*); 五十ちょっと ***gojû chotto*** 50 odd; ちょっと違いますね ***chotto chigai masu ne*** not exactly; ちょっといいですか ***chotto ii desu ka*** do you have a minute?; ちょっと聞いてもいいですか ***chotto kiite mo ii desu ka*** can I ask you something?; ちょっと待ちなさい ***chotto machinasai*** just you wait!; ちょっと待って下さい ***chotto matte kudasai*** just a second, please; ちょっと見てもいいですか ***chotto mite mo ii desu ka*** can I have a quick look?; ちょっと立ち寄る ***chotto tachiyoru*** drop in for a while
調和 **chōwa** harmony; unity; reconciliation
調和させる **chōwa saseru** harmonize; reconcile
調和しない **chōwa shinai** incongruous
調和した **chōwa shita** harmonious
調和して **chōwa shite** in keeping with
調和する **chōwa suru** match
跳躍 **chōyaku** leap; spring
調剤室 **chōzaishitsu** dispensary
貯蔵品 **chozōhin** stock, supplies (*food*)
貯蔵室 **chozō-shitsu** stockroom
貯蔵する **chozō suru** stock; store up
注 **chū** note, annotation
中 **-chū** during; within; throughout; 午前中 ***gozenchû*** in the morning
チューブ **chūbu** tube; inner tube
中部 **Chūbu** *central region of Honshu*
中断する **chūdan suru** interrupt, stop; put aside; pause
中道派 **chūdōha** center POL

中毒 **chūdoku** poisoning; addiction; 中毒になっている ***chûdoku ni natte iru*** be addicted to
中毒者 **chūdoku-sha** addict
中元 **chūgen** midsummer gift
中国 **Chūgoku** China; western region of Honshu
中国語 **Chūgoku-go** Chinese
中国語(の) **Chūgoku-go** (**no**) Chinese
中国人 **Chūgoku-jin** Chinese
中国系の **Chūgokukei no** of Chinese descent
中国(の) **Chūgoku** (**no**) Chinese
中位(の) **chūgurai** (**no**) medium, average
注意 **chūi** attention, heed; mind; …に注意を払う ***… ni chûi o harau*** heed *advice*; take notice of
注意深い **chūi-bukai** careful, cautious; observant; watchful
注意深く **chūibukaku** carefully, attentively
チューインガム **chūingamu** (chewing) gum
注意する **chūi suru** beware of; look out for; take note of
忠実(な) **chūjitsu** (**na**) loyal; staunch
仲介者 **chūkai-sha** go-between; intermediary
仲介する **chūkai suru** mediate
中華人民共和国 **Chūkajinmin-kyōwakoku** People's Republic of China
中間管理職 **chūkan-kanrishoku** middle management
中間(の) **chūkan** (**no**) halfway; neutral (*color*)
中華料理 **Chūka-ryōri** Chinese cuisine
中継放送 **chūkei-hōsō** outside broadcast
中継する **chūkei suru** relay
中近東 **Chūkintō** Middle East
中古で **chūko de** secondhand
忠告 **chūkoku** advice
忠告する **chūkoku suru** advise
中古(の) **chūko** (**no**) secondhand, used
中級(の) **chūkyū** (**no**) intermediate
注目 **chūmoku** publicity ; 注目の的になる ***chûmoku no mato ni naru*** be the focus of attention
注目に値する **chūmoku ni atai suru** notable
注目する **chūmoku suru** pay attention
注文 **chūmon** order
注文する **chūmon suru** order
チューナー **chūnā** tuner
中年(の) **chūnen** (**no**) middle-aged
中二階 **chūnikai** mezzanine (floor)
注入 **chūnyū** injection; transfusion
注入する **chūnyū suru** inject
中央 **chūō** center
中央分離帯 **chūō-bunritai** median strip
中央処理装置 **chūō-shori-sōchi** CPU, central processing unit
チューリップ **chūrippu** tulip
中立 **chūritsu** neutrality
中立(の) **chūritsu** (**no**) neutral, nonaligned
中流階級 **chūryū-kaikyū** the middle class(es)
中流階級(の) **chūryū-kaikyū** (**no**) middle class
仲裁 **chūsai** arbitration
仲裁する **chūsai suru** arbitrate; intercede
忠誠 **chūsei** devotion; 会社への忠誠心 ***kaisha e no chûseishin*** sense of corporate loyalty
中世 **Chūsei** the Middle Ages
中西部 **Chūseibu** Midwest
注射 **chūsha** injection, shot
駐車 **chūsha** parking
注射針 **chūshabari** hypodermic needle
駐車違反 **chūsha-ihan** parking violation
駐車違反の切符 **chūsha-ihan no kippu** parking ticket
駐車場 **chūshajō** car port; parking lot; parking garage
注射器 **chūshaki** syringe
駐車禁止 **chūsha-kinshi** no parking
注射する **chūsha suru** inject
駐車する **chūsha suru** park

中心 **chūshin** center; core; focus; heart
中止 **chūshi** stoppage
中止になる **chūshi ni naru** be off, be canceled
中心(の) **chūshin (no)** central; …に中心を置く ***… ni chûshin o oku*** center on
中心的(な) **chūshinteki (na)** central
中止する **chūshi suru** abandon; abort
中傷 **chūshō** slur, smear
抽象派(の) **chūshōha (no)** abstract
中小企業 **chūshō-kigyō** small and medium-sized enterprises
昼食 **chūshoku** lunch
昼食時 **chūshokudoki** lunch hour, lunchtime
中傷する **chūshō suru** libel; slander; smear; blacken
抽象的(な) **chūshōteki (na)** abstract
チューター **chūtā** tutor
中東 **Chūtō** the Middle East
中等教育 **chūtō-kyōiku** secondary education
中途に **chūto ni** midway
駐屯している **chūton shite iru** be stationed at
中途退学者 **chūto-taigaku-sha** dropout
中途退学する **chūto-taigaku suru** drop out
中和する **chūwa suru** counteract; neutralize
中絶 **chūzetsu** interruption; abortion
中絶する **chūzetsu suru** interrupt; abort

D

だ **da** be → ***desu***
打撲症 **dabokushō** bruise
だぶだぶ(の) **dabudabu (no)** baggy
ダブル **daburu** double
ダブルベッド **daburu-beddo** double bed
ダブル(の) **daburu (no)** double; double-breasted
ダブルルーム **daburu-rūmu** double room
ダブルス **daburusu** doubles
だ液 **daeki** saliva
だ円 **daen** ellipse
だ円形(の) **daenkei (no)** oval
だが **daga** but
打楽器 **dagakki** percussion instrument; percussion section
駄菓子屋 **dagashi-ya** confectioner; confectionery
打撃 **dageki** blow; hit; …に打撃を与える ***… ni dageki o ataeru*** deal a blow to; 打撃を受ける ***dageki o ukeru*** receive a blow; suffer damage
台 **dai** pedestal; stand
題 **dai** title
代 **-dai** generation; 六十代の人 ***rokujû dai no hito*** someone in their sixties
大 **dai** large, big; 大都市 ***daitoshi*** big city
第… **dai…** (*ordinal prefix*): 第一 ***daiichi*** first; 第二 ***daini*** second; 第三 ***daisan*** third
ダイバー **daibā** diver, frogman
大便 **daiben** feces; shit; 大便をする ***daiben o suru*** defecate; shit
代弁する **daiben suru** speak for
ダイビング **daibingu** dive (*underwater*)
大部分 **daibubun** bulk
大仏 **daibutsu** great Buddha
台地 **daichi** terrace; plateau

台帳 **daichō** ledger
台所 **daidokoro** kitchen; kitchenette
台所用品 **daidokoro-yōhin** kitchen utensil
ダイエット **daietto** diet
ダイエットする **daietto suru** diet, slim
大学 **daigaku** college; university
大学院(の) **daigakuin** (**no**) postgraduate
大学院生 **daigakuinsei** postgraduate (*person*)
大学(の) **daigaku** (**no**) university
大学生 **daigakusei** college student
代議士 **daigishi** Member of the Diet
大虐殺 **daigyakusatsu** carnage; massacre; holocaust
大ヒット **dai hitto** smash hit
代表 **daihyō** delegate; representative; representation
代表団 **daihyō-dan** delegation; deputation
代表する **daihyō suru** represent
大臣 **daijin** minister; secretary POL
大事(な) **daiji** (**na**) important
大事にする **daiji ni suru** value; prize; treat as important
大臣(の) **daijin** (**no**) ministerial
大丈夫 **daijōbu**: 大丈夫ですか **daijōbu desu ka** are you ok?
大丈夫(な) **daijōbu** (**na**) OK; safe
大韓民国 **Daikan-minkoku** the Republic of Korea, South Korea
大規模(な) **daikibo** (**na**) large-scale
代金**daikin** charge; price; bill
代金引き換え払い **daikin-hikikaebarai** COD, collect on delivery
大嫌い(な) **daikirai** (**na**) hateful; ゴキブリは大嫌いです ***gokiburi wa daikirai desu*** I hate cockroaches
大混乱 **daikonran** chaos; havoc
大工 **daiku** carpenter
代名詞 **daimeishi** pronoun
大名 **daimyō** feudal lord
ダイナマイト **dainamaito** dynamite
台無しにする **dainashi ni suru** mess up, ruin
大人気 **daininki** sensation; phenomenon
ダイレクトメール **dairekuto-mēru** junk mail
代理 **dairi** representative; substitute
代理母 **dairibo** surrogate mother
代理人 **dairi-nin** agent; proxy; deputy
代理(の) **dairi** (**no**) acting; 代理をする ***dairi o suru*** represent; stand in for
大理石 **dairiseki** marble
代理店 **dairiten** agency
大流行 **dairyūkō** craze
大災害 **daisaigai** catastrophe
第三世界 **Daisan-sekai** Third World
大聖堂 **daiseidō** cathedral
大成功 **daiseikō** coup *fig*; hit, success
大失敗 **daishippai** fiasco; mistake
大好き(な) **daisuki** (**na**) favorite; …が大好きだ ***…ga daisuki da*** have a soft spot for; adore; チョコレートは大好きです ***chokorêto wa daisuki desu*** I love chocolate
だいたい **daitai** more or less; roughl, approximately
大胆不敵(な) **daitanfuteki** (**na**) fearless
大胆(な) **daitan** (**na**) adventurous; bold; flamboyant
大胆さ **daitan-sa** audacity
大多数 **daitasū** majority
大邸宅 **daiteitaku** mansion
大統領 **daitōryō** president
大統領(の) **daitōryō** (**no**) presidential
大都市 **daitoshi** metropolis
大都市(の) **daitoshi** (**no**) metropolitan
ダイヤ**daiya** schedule (*for bus, train*); diamond
ダイヤモンド **daiyamondo** diamond
ダイヤル **daiyaru** dial
ダイヤルする **daiyaru suru** dial
代用品 **daiyōhin** replacement; substitute
代用する **daiyō suru** substitute
題材 **daizai** subject matter; topic
大豆 **daizu** soy bean
だじゃれ **dajare** pun

打開する **dakai suru** thrash out, resolve
だから **dakara** because; since; that's why, so; あなたがそれを嫌いだから ***anata ga sore o kirai dakara*** since you don't like it
…だけ **… dake** only; solely
だけど **dakedo** but
…だけれども **… da keredomo** although; however
抱き合う **dakiau** embrace
抱き締める **dakishimeru** clasp; cuddle; hug
抱き締めたくなる **dakishimetaku naru** cuddly
奪還する **dakkan suru** recapture
脱穀する **dakkoku suru** thresh
脱きゅうさせる **dakkyū saseru** dislocate
抱く **daku** embrace
妥協 **dakyō** compromise
妥協しない **dakyō shinai** uncompromising
妥協する **dakyō suru** compromise
黙らせる **damaraseru** silence, gag
黙る **damaru** shut up, pipe down
だまされる **damasareru** fall for
だまされやすい **damasare-yasui** credulous; gullible
だます **damasu** deceive; trick; rip off, cheat
黙っている **damatte iru** keep quiet about; keep … in the dark
だまし取る **damashitoru** swindle, cheat
ダメージ **damēji** damage
だめになる **dame ni naru** screwed up ◊ come unstuck
だめになって **dame ni natte** in ruins; spoilt
だめにする **dame ni suru** ruin, screw up
ダム **damu** dam
段 **dan** step; stair; rung
弾圧 **dan'atsu** repression
弾圧的(な) **dan'atsuteki (na)** repressive
暖房 **danbō** heating
段ボール紙 **danbōru-gami** corrugated cardboard
団地 **danchi** *apartment provided by local authorities*
だんだん **dandan** gradually; …にだんだんと向かう ***… ni dandan to mukau*** lead up to; だんだん激しくなる ***dandan hageshiku naru*** escalate; get more violent; だんだんと聞こえなくなる ***dandan to kikoenaku naru*** die away
断言 **dangen** declaration; assertion
断言する **dangen suru** declare
だんご **dango** dumpling
断食 **danjiki** fast (*not eating*)
男女 **danjo** men and women; the two sexes
男女同権主義(の) **danjo-dōkenshugi (no)** feminist
男女共学(の) **danjo-kyōgaku (no)** co-educational
段階 **dankai** stage; phase; point
段階的(な) **dankaiteki (na)** progressive
段階的に **dankaiteki ni** gradually, progressively; 段階的に導入する ***dankaiteki ni dônyû suru*** phase in; 段階的に廃止する ***dankaitekini haishi suru*** phase out
団結心 **danketsushin** team spirit
団結する **danketsu suru** unite
断固とした **danko to shita** determined; firm; strong-minded
断熱 **dannetsu** insulation
断熱する **dannetsu suru** insulate
断熱材 **dannetsuzai** insulation (*material*)
断片 **danpen** shred; fragment; piece
断片的(な) **danpenteki (na)** fragmentary
段落 **danraku** paragraph
暖炉 **danro** fireplace
弾力性 **danryokusei** elasticity
弾力性のある **danryokusei no aru** elastic; springy
段差 **dansa** bump; ramp (*in road*)
ダンサー **dansā** dancer
男性 **dansei** male
男性(の) **dansei (no)** male; masculine
男性的(な) **danseiteki (na)** masculine
男性用トイレ **dansei-yō toire** men's room, gents

男子生徒 **danshi-seito** schoolboy
男娼 **danshō** male prostitute
男尊女卑 **danson-johi** male domination
ダンス **dansu** dance; dancing
団体 **dantai** group
団体交渉 **dantai-kōshō** collective bargaining
断定する **dantei suru** conclude
弾薬 **dan'yaku** ammunition
だらだら長引く **daradara nagabiku** drag (*of day*); drag on (*of meeting*)
堕落させる **daraku saseru** corrupt
堕落した **daraku shita** tainted
堕落する **daraku suru** degenerate
だらしない **darashinai** untidy; loose *morals*; undisciplined
誰 **dare** who
誰でも **dare de mo** whoever; 彼女を知っている人誰でもと話した ***kanojo o shitte iru hito dare demo to hanashita*** I've spoken to everyone who knew her
誰か **dareka** anybody; somebody
誰も **dare mo** nobody; anybody; 誰も知らない ***dare mo shiranai*** nobody knows
誰(の) **dare** (**no**) whose
だれる **dareru** stagnate; lose enthusiasm
誰それ **daresore** so-and-so
だろう **-darō** will probably ◊ suppose
だるま **daruma** Dharma doll
ダサい **dasai** dowdy; provincial; awkward
駄作 **dasaku** trash; poor work
打算的(な) **dasanteki** (**na**) calculating, sly
惰性 **dasei de** out of habit
惰性で走る **dasei de hashiru** freewheel
出し物 **dashimono** act; turn (*in vaudeville*)
出し抜けに **dashinuke ni** abruptly
出し抜く **dashinuku** outwit
出し惜しみする **dashioshimi suru** grudge, be unwilling to give
出しっぱなしにする **dashippanashi ni suru** leave lying around; leave running
脱線 **dassen** digression
脱線する **dassen suru** be derailed
脱脂綿 **dasshimen** absorbent cotton
ダッシュボード **dasshubōdo** dash(board)
脱出する **dasshutsu suru** escape, break out; eject
脱走 **dassō** escape; desertion
脱走する **dassō suru** escape; desert; bolt
脱水機 **dassui-ki** spin-dryer
脱水症状 **dassui-shōjō** dehydration; 脱水症状を起こした ***dassui-shôjô o okoshita*** dehydrated
脱水する **dassui suru** spin-dry
ダース **dāsu** dozen
出す **dasu** issue *warning*; publish, bring out; put *question*; give; serve *dish*; hold out; take out; submit; send; show; stick out; break out (*of fever*); gather *speed*; open
ダストシュート **dasuto-shūto** chute
妥当でない **datō de nai** invalid; inappropriate
妥当(な) **datō** (**na**) reasonable; valid; appropriate
妥当性 **datōsei** validity
打倒する **datō suru** overturn, bring down *government*
脱毛剤 **datsumōzai** hair remover
脱落する **datsuraku suru** drop out
脱税 **datsuzei** tax evasion
脱退する **dattai suru** break away, secede
ダウ平均 **Dau-heikin** Dow Jones Average
ダウン **daun** down
ダウンロードする **daunrōdo suru** download
…で **… de** ◊ in; at; on; 家で ***ie de*** at home; …で休暇を過ごす ***...de kyûka o sugosu*** go to … on vacation; 一時間で着く ***ichijikan de tsuku*** I'll be there in an hour ◊ by; with; 自転車で ***jitensha de*** by bicycle; 鉛筆で ***enpitsu de*** with a pencil ◊ owing to; 病気で ***byôki de*** owing to illness
…である **… de aru** be

出会い **deai** encounter, meeting
出会う **deau** meet *person*; encounter *difficulty etc*
デビットカード **debitto-kādo** debit card
でぶ **debu** fatty, fatso
デビュー **debyū** début
出口 **deguchi** exit, way out
出入口 **deiriguchi** doorway
デジタル **dejitaru** digital
デジタルディバイド **dejitaru-dibaido** digital divide
デジタル式(の) **dejitaru-shiki (no)** digital
出かける **dekakeru** go out
デカンター **dekantā** decanter
出来 **deki** result
出来上がり **dekiagari** completion
出来上がる **dekiagaru** be finished
出来上がっている **dekiagatte iru** tight, smashed
出来合い(の) **dekiai (no)** ready-made
出来栄え **dekibae** workmanship; result
出来事 **dekigoto** event; occurrence
できもの **dekimono** spot; boil
出来のいい **deki no ii** good *result, quality*
出来の悪い **deki no warui** poor *result, quality*
できれば **dekireba** if possible; hopefully; preferably; できれば手伝います ***dekireba tetsudai masu*** I would help if I could
できる **dekiru** be able to; be ready; be finished; be capable of
できるだけ **dekiru dake** as … as possible; できるだけ早く ***dekiru dake hayaku*** as soon as possible; …をできるだけ活用する ***... o dekiru dake katsuyô suru*** make the most of; できるだけよい ***dekirudake yoi*** the best possible
でき死させる **dekishi saseru** drown
デッキ **dekki** deck
デッキチェア **dekkichea** deckchair
でこぼこ(な) **dekoboko (na)** irregular; uneven; bumpy; lumpy
出くわす **dekuwasu** run across, meet; run into *person, problem*; come across
出前 **demae** home delivery
デモ **demo** demonstration, demo; デモをする ***demo o suru*** demonstrate POL
でも **demo** ◊ but; though; でも私は行かない ***demo watashi wa ikanai*** but I am not going ◊: 誰でも ***dare demo*** anyone; どこでも ***doko demo*** anywhere ◊ even: 雨でも ***ame demo*** even if it rains ◊ or something; コーヒーでもいかがですか ***kôhî demo ikaga desu ka*** would you like to have coffee or something?
デモ行進 **demo-kōshin** march, demo
デモ行進する **demo-kōshin suru** march
でもね、**demo ne,** mind you,
デモンストレーション **demonsutorēshon** demonstration (*of equipment*)
デモテープ **demo-tēpu** demo (tape)
出迎える **demukaeru** meet
…でない **... de nai** not; un-; 本気でない ***honki de nai*** not serious; 安全でない ***anzen de nai*** unsafe; insecure
電圧 **den'atsu** voltage
電池 **denchi** battery
伝道師 **dendōshi** evangelist
伝導する **dendō suru** conduct ELEC
電源 **dengen** switch; power supply
電撃 **dengeki** shock ELEC
伝言 **dengon** message
デニム(の) **denimu (no)** denim
デニッシュ **Denisshu** Danish (pastry)
電化製品 **denka-seihin** appliance
伝記 **denki** biography
電気 **denki** electricity
電気技師 **denki-gishi** electrician
電気配線 **denki-haisen** wiring
電気いす **denki-isu** the (electric) chair
電気かみそり **denki-kamisori** shaver
電気(の) **denki (no)** electric; electrical

電気通信 **denki-tsūshin** telecommunications
電極 **denkyoku** electrode
電球 **denkyū** (light) bulb
デンマーク **Denmāku** Denmark
デンマーク(の) **Denmāku** (**no**) Danish
電熱器 **dennetsuki** hotplate
電報 **denpō** telegram, wire
でんぷん質 **denpunshitsu** carbohydrate; starch
電力 **denryoku** power
電流 **denryū** current
電線 **densen** power line; wire; run (*in pantyhose*)
伝染 **densen** transmission; infection
伝染性(の) **densensei** (**no**) contagious, catching
伝説 **densetsu** legend
電車 **densha** train
電子 **denshi** electron
電子データ処理 **denshi-dēta-shori** EDP, electronic data processing
電子工学 **denshi-kōgaku** electronics
電子工学(の) **denshi-kōgaku** (**no**) electronic
電子メール **denshi-mēru** e-mail
電信柱 **denshinbashira** telegraph pole
電子レンジ **denshi-renji** microwave (oven)
電卓 **dentaku** calculator; pocket calculator
伝達 **dentatsu** transmission; communication
伝統 **dentō** tradition
伝統的(な) **dentōteki** (**na**) traditional, conventional
電話 **denwa** (phone)call; (tele)phone; 電話をかける ***denwa o kakeru*** dial *number*; 電話を切る ***denwa o kiru*** cut off; 電話をかけ直す ***denwa o kakenaosu*** call back
電話番号 **denwa-bangō** (tele)phone number
電話帳 **denwachō** telephone directory, phone book
電話機 **denwaki** (tele)phone
電話交換室 **denwa-kōkanshitsu** telephone exchange
電話に出る **denwa ni deru** answer the telephone
電話線 **denwasen** line TELEC
電話セールス **denwa-sērusu** telesales
電話する **denwa suru** dial *number*; (tele)phone, call
デオドラント **deodoranto** deodorant
デオキシリボ核酸 **deokishiribo-kakusan** DNA, deoxyribonucleic acid
デパート **depāto** department store
デリカテッセン **derikatessen** delicatessen
デリケート(な) **derikēto** (**na**) delicate
デリケートさ **derikēto-sa** delicacy
出る **deru** come out (*of sun, results, product*); get out; be given; infuse; leave; make it (*to party, meeting etc*); run (*of faucet*); be issued; stick out; break out; show; attend; graduate
弟子 **deshi** disciple; pupil; apprentice
デシベル **deshiberu** decibel
でしょう **deshō** *polite form of* ***darô***
です **desu** *polite form of* ***da*** be; 学生です ***gakusei desu*** he's a student; どこです ***doko desu*** where is it?; 雨です ***ame desu*** it's raining; チャーリーです ***Chârî desu*** it's Charlie here
デスクトップパブリッシング **desukutoppu-paburisshingu** DTP, desktop publishing
ですが **desu ga** but
ですから **desu kara** so; therefore; because
データ **dēta** data
データベース **dēta-bēsu** database
データ保護 **dēta-hogo** data protection
データ管理 **dēta-kanri** data storage; data management
デタント **detanto** détente
でたらめ(な) **detarame** (**na**) haphazard; nonsensical
でたらめを言う **detarame o iu** bullshit
データ処理 **dēta-shori** data

processing
データ収集 **dēta-shūshū** data capture
でっちあげる **detchiageru** concoct; 帳簿をでっちあげる ***chôbo o detchi ageru*** fiddle the accounts
出て行く **dete iku** go out (*of person*); leave; clear out; move out; walk out; 出て行け ***dete ike*** (get) out!
出ている **dete iru** be out (*of sun*)
出てくる **dete kuru** leave; come out (*on date*)
では **dewa** well then; right
デート **dēto** date (*romantic*)
デザイン **dezain** design
デザイナー **dezainā** designer
デザインする **dezain suru** design
デザート **dezāto** dessert
DNA **dī-enu-ē** DNA
ディフェンス **difensu** defense
DJ **dī-jē** disc jockey
ディナー **dinā** dinner
ディーラー **dīrā** dealer
ディスコ **disuko** disco
ディスク **disuku** disk
ディスクドライブ **disuku-doraibu** disk drive
ディスクジョッキー **disuku-jokkī** disc jockey
ディスプレー **disupurē** display
ディーゼル **dīzeru** diesel
度 **do** degree; …に度が過ぎる ***… ni do ga sugiru*** go overboard for
どう **dō** how; what; どうですか ***dô desu ka*** how is it?; どうしますか ***dô shimasu ka*** what are you going to do?; 彼なんてどうでもいい ***kare nante dô demo ii*** to hell with him; どうでもよい ***dô de mo yoi*** it doesn't make any difference; …はどうですか ***… wa dô desu ka*** how about …?; どうしたの ***dô shita no*** what's the matter (with you)?, what's wrong?
銅 **dō** copper
胴 **dō** trunk (*of body*)
同 … **dō…** same; 同時代 ***dôjidai*** (**no**) contemporary
ドア **doa** door
土木技師 **doboku-gishi** civil engineer
動物 **dōbutsu** animal
動物園 **dōbutsuen** zoo
動物学 **dōbutsugaku** zoology
動物学(の) **dōbutsugaku** (**no**) zoological
同着 **dōchaku** dead heat
土着(の) **dochaku** (**no**) native
どちら **dochira** which
どちらでも **dochira demo** either; whichever
どちらか(の) **dochira ka no** either
どちらも **dochira mo** both
どちら(の) **dochira** (**no**) which
同調する **dōchō suru** sympathize
土台 **dodai** foundations
堂々とした **dōdō to shita** dignified; majestic; regal
同封する **dōfū suru** enclose
動議 **dōgi** motion (*at conference*)
どぎまぎさせる **dogimagi saseru** disconcert; embarrass
どぎまぎした **dogimagi shita** disconcerted; embarrassed
どぎまぎする **dogimagi suru** be disconcerted; feel embarrassed
道具 **dōgu** tool, device, implement
同輩 **dōhai** peer, equal
土俵 **dohyō** sumo ring
同意 **dōi** agreement, consent
同意語 **dōigo** synonym
同意する **dōi suru** concur, agree, consent
どういたしまして **dō itashimashite** don't mention it, you're welcome
ドイツ **Doitsu** Germany
ドイツ語 **Doitsu-go** German
ドイツ人 **Doitsu-jin** German
ドイツ(の) **Doitsu** (**no**) German
同時に **dōji ni** at the same time, together; simultaneously
同情 **dōjō** compassion; sympathy
同情する **dōjō suru** commiserate, sympathize
同情的(な) **dōjōteki** (**na**) sympathetic
どうか **dō ka** ◊ please; どうか手伝ってください ***dô ka tetsudatte kudasai*** please help ◊ whether (or not); 買うかどうか ***kau ka dô ka*** whether to buy or not; どうかと思う ***dô ka to omou*** I wonder

同化する **dōka suru** assimilate
同感する **dōkan suru** feel the same, agree
同形異義語**dōkei-igigo** homograph
どける **dokeru** remove
動機 **dōki** motivation; motive
動悸 **dōki** palpitations
どきどきする **dokidoki suru** flutter; pound (*of heart*)
ドック **dokku** dock
どこ **doko** where
瞳孔 **dōkō** pupil (*of eye*)
どこでも **doko demo** anywhere; everywhere
どこか **dokoka** somewhere
どこかで **dokoka de** anywhere
どこかに **dokoka ni** anywhere; somewhere
同国人 **dōkoku-jin** (fellow) countryman
どこも **doko mo** everywhere; anywhere
どこに **doko ni** where
どこにも **doko ni mo** anywhere; nowhere
どころか **dokoro ka** as well as; on the contrary
どことなく**dokotonaku** somehow
毒 **doku** poison; venom; …に毒を盛る ***… ni doku o moru*** poison
独房 **dokubō** solitary cell
独自(の) **dokuji** (**no**) original; unique
毒きのこ **doku kinoko** toadstool
独立 **dokuritsu** independence
独立記念日**Dokuritsu-kinenbi** Independence Day
独立(の) **dokuritsu** (**no**) independent
独立した **dokuritsu shita** sovereign
独立して **dokuritsu shite** independently
独力で **dokuryoku de** single-handedly
独力(の) **dokuryoku** (**no**) single-handed
独裁政治 **dokusai-seiji** dictatorship, tyranny
独裁者 **dokusai-sha** dictator
独裁的(な) **dokusaiteki** (**na**) dictatorial
独占する **dokusen suru** monopolize
独占的(な) **dokusenteki** (**na**) exclusive
独占欲の強い **dokusen'yoku no tsuyoi** possessive
読者 **dokusha** reader
独身(の) **dokushin** (**no**) single
読唇する **dokushin suru** lipread
読書 **dokusho** reading
読書する **dokusho suru** read
独奏 **dokusō** solo
独創性 **dokusōsei** originality; creativity
独特(な) **dokutoku** (**na**) distinctive
独特(の) **dokutoku** (**no**) unique
ドキュメンタリー **dokyumentarī** documentary
同級生 **dōkyūsei** classmate; peer
同盟 **dōmei** alliance
どうも **dōmo** ◊ thank you ◊ very much ◊ I suspect that; どうもありがとう ***dômo arigatô*** thanks very much
どう猛(な) **dōmō** (**na**) ferocious; vicious
どもる **domoru** stammer, stutter
ドーム **dōmu** dome
動脈 **dōmyaku** artery
どなる **donaru** bawl, bellow; shout
どうなる **dō naru**: どうなるかわかりませんね ***dô naru ka wakarimasen ne*** you never know; 彼女はどうなった **kanojo wa dō natta** what's become of her?
ドーナッツ **dōnattsu** donut
丼もの **donburimono** *bowl of rice with topping of meat, egg, fish etc*
どんちゃん騒ぎ **donchansawagi** drinking session
どんぐり **donguri** acorn
どうにか **dōnika** somehow; どうにか暮していく ***dônika kurashite iku*** manage to survive; どうにか…する ***dônika … suru*** contrive
鈍感 **donkan** insensitivity
鈍感(な) **donkan** (**na**) insensitive
どんな **donna** what?; what kind of?; 彼女はどんな人ですか ***kanojo wa***

donna hito desu ka what is she like?; どんな…でも ***donna ... demo*** whatever kind; どんな事情があっても ***donna jijô ga atte mo*** under no circumstances
どの **dono** which; any; どの辺り ***dono atari*** where abouts?; あなたがどのスタイルを選ぶにしても ***anata ga dono sutairu o erabu ni shite mo*** whichever style you choose; どのくらい ***dono kurai*** how much?; how many?; how far? how soon?
殿 **-dono** *polite title suffix used in formal letters after addressee's name*
どん欲 **don'yoku** greed
どん欲(な) **don'yoku (na)** acquisitive; greedy; voracious
どんよりした **don'yori shita** glazed; dull; lackluster
導入 **dōnyū** introduction
導入する **dōnyū suru** bring in
どん底に落ちる **donzoko ni ochiru** reach rock bottom
ドラゴン **doragon** dragon
ドライバー **doraibā** driver, motorist; screwdriver
ドライブ **doraibu** ride (*in vehicle*); run (*in car*); drive (*also* COMPUT)
ドライブインシアター **doraibuin-shiatā** drive-in
ドライクリーニングする **dorai-kurīningu suru** dryclean
ドライクリーニング屋 **dorai-kurīningu-ya** dry cleaner's
ドラマ **dorama** drama; play
ドラマー **doramā** drummer
ドラマチック(な) **doramachikku (na)** dramatic
ドラム **doramu** drum
動乱 **dōran** upheaval; disturbance
どれ **dore** which
どれでも **dore demo** whichever; どれでもいいから取りなさい ***dore demo ii kara torinasai*** take one, it doesn't matter which
どれほど **dore hodo** how much; どれほど大きくても / 金持ちでも ***dore hodo ôkikute mo / kanemochi demo*** however big / rich he / she is
奴隷 **dorei** slave
どれくらい **dore kurai** how; どれくらいかかりますか ***dore kurai kakarimasu ka*** how long does it take?; どれくらい前ですか ***dore kurai mae desu ka*** how long ago?
ドレッシング **doresshingu** (salad) dressing
ドレス **doresu** frock
ドレスアップする **doresuappu suru** dress up
ドリブルする **doriburu suru** dribble SP
ドリル **doriru** drill (*tool*)
泥 **doro** earth; muck; mud; …に泥を塗る ***...ni doro o nuru*** bring dishonor on
道路 **dōro** road
泥棒 **dorobō** thief
道路地図 **dōro-chizu** road map
泥だらけ(の) **doro darake (no)** muddy
道路標識 **dōro-hyōshiki** roadsign
道路工事 **dōro-kōji** road repairs
ドル **doru** dollar, buck
同僚 **dōryō** associate, colleague; peer
努力 **doryoku** effort; exertion; endeavor
動力 **dōryoku** power
努力する **doryoku suru** endeavor; exert oneself
同量(の) **dōryō (no)** equivalent
動作 **dōsa** movement
洞察 **dōsatsu** insight
洞察力 **dōsatsuryoku** insight, perception
どうせ **dōse** anyhow; at best
同棲 **dōsei** cohabitation
同性愛(の) **dōseiai (no)** homosexual
同性愛者 **dōseiai-sha** homosexual
同棲する **dōsei suru** cohabit
土砂降り(の) **doshaburi (no)** torrential
同志 **dōshi** comrade
動詞 **dōshi** verb
どうして **dōshite** how come?; what for?; why?; どうしていいか分からなくなる ***dôshite ii ka wakaranakunaru*** be at one's wits' end; どうしていやなの ***dôshite iya***

na no why not?
どうしても **dōshite mo** by any means
同室する **dōshitsu suru** double up
どうしようもない **dō shiyō mo nai** hopeless
同窓会 **dōsōkai** reunion
どっしりした **dosshiri shita** massive
同数(の) **dōsū** (**no**) equivalent
どっち **dotchi** which one?; どっちでもいいです ***dotchi demo ii desu*** I don't mind
どっちつかずの場合 **dotchitsukazu no bāi** borderline case
土手 **dote** bank (*of river*)
童貞 **dōtei** virgin; virginity (*male*)
同点 **dōten** tie (*in sports*); 二対二の同点 ***ni-tai-ni no dôten*** two all
同点にする **dōten ni suru** even the score
同点(の) **dōten** (**no**) level, tied
動転した **dōten shita** shattered, shocked
同等である **dōtō de aru** match; be equal; be on a par with
道徳 **dōtoku** ethics; morals; morality
道徳的(な) **dōtokuteki** (**na**) ethical; moral
同等(の) **dōtō** (**no**) equivalent
同等の人 **dōtō no hito** equal
ドット **dotto** dot
どうやって **dō yatte** how
動揺 **dōyō** agitation; upheaval; unrest
童謡 **dōyō** nursery rhyme
同様 **dōyō** same; similar; …と同様に ***… to dôyô ni*** in the same way as; as well as
土曜日 **doyōbi** Saturday
動揺させる **dōyō saseru** disturbing ◊ ruffle
動揺した **dōyō shita** agitated
動揺する **dōyō suru** be shaken; get ruffled
同然である **dōzen de aru** verge on; be equal to
どうぞ **dōzo** please; come in!; go ahead!; どうぞ試してみてください ***dôzo tameshite mite kudasai*** you're welcome to try some
銅像 **dōzō** bronze

E

柄 **e** handle; shaft
絵 **e** painting; picture; 絵をかく ***e o kaku*** draw; paint
へ **e** to; for; on; in
ええ **ē** yes; no; ええ、わかっています ***ê wakatte imasu*** yes, I know; ええ、どうぞ ***ê, dôzo*** please do
エーッ **ē'** (*expression of surprise, doubt or hesitation*) eh?; uh?; well, well!
エアコン **eakon** air conditioner; air conditioning
エアロビクス **earobikusu** aerobics
エアターミナル **eatāminaru** air terminal
えび **ebi** shrimp; prawn
枝 **eda** branch
エディター **editā** editor
江戸時代 **Edo-jidai** Edo period
絵筆 **efude** paintbrush
描く **egaku** depict, portray
笑顔 **egao** smiling face
エゴ **ego** ego
絵はがき **ehagaki** (picture) postcard
絵本 **ehon** picture book
英文学 **Eibungaku** English literature
HIV陽性(の) **eichi-ai-bui-yōsei** (**no**) HIV-positive
永遠 **eien** eternity
永遠(の) **eien** (**no**) eternal,

everlasting
映画 **eiga** movie, picture
映画界 **eigakai** cinema
映画館 **eigakan** movie theater
映画監督 **eiga-kantoku** movie director
英語 **Eigo** English; 英語で ***Eigo de*** in English
営業 **eigyō** selling
営業部 **eigyō-bu** sales (department)
営業中(の) **eigyōchū** (**no**) open for business
営業時間 **eigyō-jikan** business hours, office hours
営業課長 **eigyō-kachō** sales manager
営業する **eigyō suru** operate
栄光 **eikō** glory
栄光ある **eikō aru** glorious
英国 **Eikoku** GB, (Great) Britain; UK
英国人 **Eikoku-jin** the British; Briton
英国(の) **Eikoku** (**no**) British
影響 **eikyō** effect; impact; influence; repercussions; 影響を及ぼす ***eikyô o oyobosu*** affect; influence; 影響を受けやすい ***eikyô o ukeyasui*** susceptible; …に影響されない ***… ni eikyô sarenai*** impervious to
影響力 **eikyōryoku** clout, influence, pull; leverage
影響力のある **eikyōryoku no aru** influential
永久に **eikyū ni** forever; permanently
永久的(な) **eikyūteki** (**na**) permanent; perpetual
衛生 **eisei** hygiene
衛星 **eisei** satellite
衛生局 **eiseikyoku** sanitation department
衛生設備 **eisei-setsubi** sanitary facilities
衛生的(な) **eiseiteki** (**na**) hygienic, sanitary
衛星テレビ **eisei-terebi** satellite TV
映写機 **eishaki** projector
映写する **eisha suru** screen
英和辞典 **Eiwa jiten** English-Japanese dictionary
栄養 **eiyō** nourishment; nutrition
栄養分 **eiyōbun** goodness
栄養不足(の) **eiyōbusoku** (**no**) underfed
栄養のある **eiyō no aru** nourishing, nutritious
栄養失調**eiyō-shitchō** malnutrition
英雄 **eiyū** hero
英雄的(な) **eiyūteki** (**na**) heroic
永続させる **eizoku saseru** perpetuate
永続する **eizoku suru** enduring
エイズ **eizu** Aids
エジプト**Ejiputo** Egypt
エジプト(の) **Ejiputo** (**no**) Egyptian
絵かき **ekaki** painter
駅 **eki** (railroad) station; stop; depot
駅弁 **ekiben** lunch box
疫病 **ekibyō** plague
液晶表示 **ekishō-hyōji** LCD, liquid crystal display
エキスパート**ekisupāto** expert
液体 **ekitai** liquid
液体(の) **ekitai** (**no**) liquid
エキゾチック(な) **ekizochikku** (**na**) exotic
エックス線 **ekkususen** X-ray
eコマース **e komāsu** e-commerce
エコノミークラス **ekonomī-kurasu** economy class
えくぼ **ekubo** dimple
エメラルド **emerarudo** emerald
エメラルド色 **emerarudo-iro** emerald
獲物 **emono** prey
エムサイズ **em-saizu** medium
円 **en** circle; yen
縁 **en** karma, fate
エナメル **enameru** enamel
円盤 **enban** discus; disk
えん尾服 **enbifuku** tail coat
延長 **enchō** extension
延長コード **enchō-kōdo** extension cable
延長する **enchō suru** extend; roll over; prolong
円柱 **enchū** column

演台 **endai** dais
円高 **endaka** appreciation of the yen
演壇 **endan** platform; rostrum; pulpit
縁談 **endan** marriage proposal
えんどう豆 **endōmame** pea
えんえんと **en'en to** on and on, endlessly
エネルギー **enerugī** energy
沿岸警備隊 **engan-keibitai** coastguard
沿岸(の) **engan (no)** coastal
園芸 **engei** gardening; horticulture
園芸家 **engei-ka** gardener
演劇 **engeki** drama
演劇(の) **engeki (no)** dramatic; theatrical
演技 **engi** acting; performance; portrayal
縁起 **engi** sign; omen; 縁起をかつぐ ***engi o katsugu*** be superstitious
縁起のいい **engi no ii** lucky
縁起の悪い **engi no warui** unlucky
援護 **engo** backup; protection
援軍 **engun** reinforcements
エンジン **enjin** engine, motor
エンジニア **enjinia** engineer
演じる **enjiru** interpret, play *role*
援助 **enjo** aid, assistance; input
炎上している **enjō shite iru** be ablaze
援助する **enjo suru** aid, stake
宴会 **enkai** dinner party; banquet
円形(の) **enkei (no)** circular
延期 **enki** postponement; reprieve
延期する **enki suru** postpone, put off
えん曲語法 **enkyoku-gohō** euphemism
円満(な) **enman (na)** amiable; peaceful; harmonious
絵の具 **enogu** paint
鉛筆 **enpitsu** pencil
鉛筆削り **enpitsu-kezuri** pencil sharpener
遠慮 **enryo** reserve; personal restraint
遠征試合 **ensei-jiai** away match
遠視(の) **enshi (no)** far-sighted, long-sighted
炎症 **enshō** inflammation
円周 **enshū** circumference
演出 **enshutsu** direction
演出家 **enshutsu-ka** director
演出する **enshutsu suru** direct
塩素 **enso** chlorine
演奏 **ensō** performance; rendering
遠足 **ensoku** excursion, outing
演奏者 **ensō-sha** musician; player
演奏する **ensō suru** interpret; perform; play MUS
円すい形 **ensuikei** cone
エンストする **ensuto suru** stall (*of vehicle*)
エンターテイナー **entāteinā** entertainer
円筒形(の) **entōkei (no)** cylindrical
煙突 **entotsu** chimney
円安 **en'yasu** depreciation of the yen
遠洋航海(の) **en'yō-kōkai (no)** seagoing
演説をする **enzetsu o suru** make a speech
演説者 **enzetsu-sha** speaker, orator
演説する **enzetsu suru** speak; speak to
演ずる **enzuru** perform
エピローグ **epirōgu** epilog
えら **era** gills
選ばれた **erabareta** selected
選び出す **erabidasu** select, pick on
選ぶ **erabu** choose, pick, plump for; single out
偉い **erai** eminent; great
エラーメッセージ **erā-messēji** error message
偉そうに **erasō ni** self-importantly; …に偉そうに指図する ***... ni erasô ni sashizu suru*** boss around
エレベーター **erebētā** elevator
エレガント(な) **ereganto (na)** elegant; dressy
エレクトロン **erekutoron** electron
襟 **eri** collar
エリート **erīto** elite
エリート(の) **erīto (no)** elite
エロティック(な) **erotikku (na)** erotic
エロティシズム **erotishizumu** eroticism

得る **eru** earn; gain; obtain, get
えさ **esa** bait; えさをやる ***esa o yaru*** feed
エッセイ **essei** essay
エース **ēsu** ace
エスカレーター **esukarētā** escalator
エッチ(な) **etchi (na)** naughty; warped; perverted
エッチング **etchingu** etching
えーっと… **ētto …** well …

F

ファイバーグラス **faibā-gurasu** fiberglass
ファインダー **faindā** viewfinder
ファイル **fairu** file; folder
ファイルマネジャー **fairu-manejā** file manager
ファイルする **fairu suru** file
ファックス **fakkusu** fax; …をファックスする ***… o fakkusu suru*** send by fax
ファン **fan** fan; enthusiast; follower; supporter; 映画ファン ***eiga-fan*** moviegoer
ファンベルト **fanberuto** fan belt
ファシスト **fashisuto** fascist
ファシズム **fashizumu** fascism
ファッション **fasshon** fashion
ファッションデザイナー **fasshon-dezainā** fashion designer
ファッションモデル **fasshon-moderu** model
ファスナー **fasunā** fastener; zipper; ファスナーを下げる ***fasunâ o sageru*** unzip
ファーストフード **fāsuto fūdo** fast food
ファーストクラス **fāsuto kurasu** firstclass
ファウル **fauru** foul
フェミニスト **feminisuto** feminist
フェミニスト(の) **feminisuto (no)** feminist
フェミニズム **feminizumu** feminism
フェンダー **fendā** fender
フェンス **fensu** fence
フェラチオ **ferachio** fellatio; blow job
フェリー **ferī** ferry
フェルト **feruto** felt
フェルトペン **ferutopen** felt tip
フィギュアスケート **figyua-sukēto** figure skating
フィンランド **Finrando** Finland
フィンランド(の) **Finrando (no)** Finnish
フィリピン(の) **Firipin(no)** Philippine
フィリピン諸島 **Firipin-shotō** the Philippines
フィールド種目 **fīrudo-shumoku** field events
フィルム **firumu** film; …にフィルムを入れる ***… ni firumu o ireru*** load
フィルター **firutā** filter; filter tip
フィート **fīto** foot
フィットネスクラブ **fittonesu kurabu** fitness center
フォアハンド **foahando** forehand
フォーク **fōku** fork
フォークダンス **fōku-dansu** folk dance
フォークミュージック **fōku-myūjikku** folk music
フォークソング **fōku-songu** folk song
フォーマットする **fōmatto suru** format
フォーメーション **fōmēshon** formation
フォント **fonto** font
フォローする **forō suru** follow up
フォルダ **foruda** folder
フォワード **fowādo** forward
不… **fu …** non…; un…
封 **fū** seal

不安 **fuan** insecurity; misgiving; unrest
不安(な) **fuan** (**na**) perturbing
不安にさせる **fuan ni saseru** disturb; upset; perturb
不安定 **fuantei** instability
不安定(な) **fuantei** (**na**) erratic; unstable; wobbly; precarious; uncertain; uneasy
不安定に **fuantei ni** precariously
不払い **fubarai** nonpayment
不便(な) **fuben** (**na**) inconvenient
不便さ **fuben-sa** inconvenience
不備(な) **fubi** (**na**) unsatisfactory; defective
吹雪 **fubuki** blizzard, snowstorm
不文律 **fubunritsu** unwritten law
不平等 **fubyōdō** inequality
不平等(な) **fubyōdō** (**na**) unequal
縁 **fuchi** frame; brink; edge
縁取る **fuchidoru** edge
不調 **fuchō** malfunction; failure
不注意(な) **fuchūi** (**na**) careless; slack; inattentive
札 **fuda** tag
普段着 **fudangi** casual wear
普段着(の) **fudangi** (**no**) casual
普段(の) **fudan** (**no**) informal
不断(の) **fudan** (**no**) tireless; perpetual
筆 **fude** writing brush
フード **fūdo** hood (*on head*)
不動産 **fudōsan** real estate
不動産屋 **fudōsan-ya** real estate agent
不道徳 **fudōtoku** immorality
不道徳(な) **fudōtoku** (**na**) immoral
笛 **fue** whistle
増える **fueru** increase; multiply
夫婦 **fūfu** married couple
不服従 **fufukujū** disobedience
夫婦(の) **fūfu no** marital
風変わり(な) **fūgawari** (**na**) eccentric
不合理(な) **fugōri** (**na**) illogical; irrational
ふぐ **fugu** blowfish; puffer
不具 **fugu** physically handicapped person
腐敗 **fuhai** decay, rot
腐敗した **fuhai shita** corrupt
腐敗する **fuhai suru** decompose
不平 **fuhei** grievance, beef; fuss; 不平をいう ***fuhei o iu*** complain, beef
普遍的(な) **fuhenteki** (**na**) universal
不必要(な) **fuhitsuyō** (**na**) unnecessary
不法(な) **fuhō** (**na**) illicit
不法侵入者 **fuhō-shinnyū-sha** trespasser
不法侵入している **fuhō-shinnyū shite iru** trespass on
不法侵入する **fuhō-shinnyū suru** trespass
不評(の) **fuhyō** (**no**) unpopular
不意に **fui ni** just like that; unexpectedly
ふいにする **fui ni suru** blow; miss an opportunity
不一致 **fuitchi** clash
不意打ち **fuiuchi** surprise attack; …に不意打ちをくらわせる ***… ni fuiuchi o kurawaseru*** catch unawares
藤 **fuji** wisteria
不時着 **fujichaku** crash landing; forced landing
藤色 **fujiiro** lilac
不死身 **fujimi** immortal
婦人科 **fujinka** gynecologist
婦人警官 **fujin-keikan** policewoman
富士山 **Fuji-san** Mt Fuji
不実 **fujitsu** deception; faithlessness
不自由(な) **fujiyū** (**na**) physically handicapped; inconvenient
不十分(な) **fujūbun** (**na**) inadequate; scarce; inconclusive
不純(な) **fujun** (**na**) impure
負荷 **fuka** load ELEC; …に負荷をかけすぎる ***… ni fuka o kakesugiru*** overload
深い **fukai** deep; profound
不快(な) **fukai** (**na**) offensive
不可解(な) **fukakai** (**na**) baffling; enigmatic
ふ化器 **fukaki** incubator
深く **fukaku** profoundly
不確実 **fukakujitsu** uncertainty
深くなる **fukaku naru** deepen
深くする **fukaku suru** deepen

深まる **fukamaru** deepen
不可能 **fukanō** impossibility
不可能(な) **fukanō** (**na**) impossible
不感症(の) **fukanshō** (**no**) frigid
不完全(な) **fukanzen** (**na**) imperfect; incomplete; patchy
不活発(な) **fukappatsu** (**na**) inactive
深さ **fuka-sa** depth
ふかす **fukasu** rev up; puff at *cigarette*
ふけ **fuke** dandruff
父兄 **fukei** parents (*of schoolchildren*)
風景画 **fūkeiga** landscape painting
不景気 **fukeiki** slump
不景気になる **fukeiki ni naru** slacken off
不敬(な) **fukei** (**na**) irreverent
不経済(な) **fukeizai** (**na**) uneconomic; wasteful
不健康(な) **fukenkō** (**na**) unhealthy *person*
不健全(な) **fukenzen** (**na**) unhealthy *atmosphere, economy*
ふける **fukeru** immerse oneself in; indulge in
不潔(な) **fuketsu** (**na**) filthy; foul; squalid
不潔さ **fuketsu-sa** squalor
吹きだまり **fukidamari** snowdrift
吹きだまる **fukidamaru** drift
噴き出す **fukidasu** spurt out; burst out laughing
不機嫌である **fukigen de aru** be in a temper
吹替えする **fukikae suru** dub
噴きかける **fukikakeru** squirt *water*
吹き消す **fukikesu** blow out, extinguish
吹き込む **fukikomu** indoctrinate
ふきん **fukin** cloth; tea towel
付近 **fukin** neighborhood
不謹慎(な) **fukinshin** (**na**) indiscreet
不謹慎な行動 **fukinshin na kōdō** indiscretion
封切り **fūkiri** première, film release
不規則(な) **fukisoku** (**na**) erratic; irregular
不規則に **fukisoku ni** unevenly
吹き倒す **fukitaosu** blow over
吹き飛ばす **fukitobasu** blow away; blow off
吹き飛ぶ **fukitobu** be blown away
不吉(な) **fukitsu** (**na**) ominous
吹っかける **fukkakeru** rip off
復活 **fukkatsu** revival
復活祭 **Fukkatsusai** Easter
復活させる **fukkatsu saseru** revive; bring back, reintroduce
復活する **fukkatsu suru** revive
復帰させる **fukki saseru** reinstate
復帰する **fukki suru** return
フック **fukku** hook; peg
ふっくらする **fukkura suru** fill out, put on weight
不幸 **fukō** unhappiness
不幸(な) **fukō** (**na**) unfortunate, unlucky; unhappy
不公正 **fukōsei** injustice
ふく **fuku** mop up; wipe
吹く **fuku** blow
服 **fuku** clothes; 服を着る ***fuku o kiru*** dress; 服を着せる ***fuku o kiseru*** dress; 服を脱ぐ ***fuku o nugu*** get undressed, undress
福 **fuku** good fortune
副… **fuku…** vice-; deputy; 副大統領 ***fuku-daitôryô*** vice-president; 副リーダー ***fuku-rîdâ*** deputy leader
副木 **fukuboku** splint
腹部 **fukubu** abdomen; belly
腹部(の) **fukubu** (**no**) abdominal
複合(の) **fukugō** (**no**) multiple
副業 **fukugyō** sideline
服従 **fukujū** obedience
含める **fukumeru** include
含めて **fukumete** including, inclusive, inclusive of
含む **fukumu** embrace, take in; include
ふくらはぎ **fukurahagi** calf (*of leg*)
膨らます **fukuramasu** inflate, blow up
膨らますことができる **fukuramasu koto ga dekiru** inflatable
膨らみ **fukurami** bulge
膨れ上がった **fukureagatta** bloated
膨れる **fukureru** bulge; pout
膨れた **fukureta** swollen
複利 **fukuri** compound interest

袋 **fukuro** bag; pack
ふくろう **fukurō** owl
袋小路 **fukurokōji** impasse; dead end
袋に入れる **fukuro ni ireru** pack
副産物 **fukusanbutsu** by-product; spin-off
副作用 **fukusayō** side effect
複製 **fukusei** copy; replica; reproduction
複製する **fukusei suru** copy, duplicate; reproduce
副社長 **fuku-shachō** vice president
副詞 **fukushi** adverb
福祉 **fukushi** welfare
副支配人 **fukushihai-nin** assistant manager
福祉事業 **fukushi-jigyō** welfare work
福祉国家 **fukushi-kokka** welfare state
副署する **fukusho suru** countersign
復習 **fukushū** review (*of lessons*)
復しゅう **fukushū** revenge, vengeance; …に復しゅうする ***... ni fukushû suru*** take one's revenge
復しゅう心に燃えた **fukushūshin ni moeta** vindictive
復習する **fukushū suru** review; revise
服装 **fukusō** dress, clothing
副操縦士 **fuku-sōjūshi** copilot
複数形 **fukusūkei** plural
複数(の) **fukusū (no)** multiple; plural
副店長 **fukutenchō** assistant manager
腹痛 **fukutsū** stomach ache; colic
腹話術師 **fukuwajutsu-shi** ventriloquist
服用法 **fukuyō-hō** directions MED
複雑(な) **fukuzatsu (na)** complex; intricate; mixed *feelings*
不況 **fukyō** depression (*economic*)
不協和音 **fukyō-waon** discord
不満 **fuman** discontent; dissatisfaction
不満(な) **fuman (na)** unhappy; dissatisfied; discontented
不満(の) **fuman (no)** disgruntled
不満足(な) **fumanzoku (na)** unsatisfactory
不明 **fumai** unclear
不明りょう(な) **fumeiryō (na)** indistinct; unclear; vague
不名誉 **fumeiyo** dishonor, disgrace
不名誉(な) **fumeiyo (na)** dishonorable, disgraceful
不滅 **fumetsu** immortality
不滅(の) **fumetsu (no)** immortal
風味 **fūmi** flavor
踏み入れる **fumiireru** step into; set foot in
踏切 **fumikiri** grade crossing
不眠 **fumin** insomnia
踏みつける **fumitsukeru** trample (on)
不毛 **fumō** infertility
不毛(な) **fumō (na)** barren
不毛(の) **fumō (no)** infertile
ふもと **fumoto** bottom
踏む **fumu** tread on
不向き(な) **fumuki (na)** unfit
ふん **fun** dung
分 **fun** minute; 十五分 ***jûgo fun*** 15 minutes
船便 **funabin** shipping; 船便で送る ***funabin de okuru*** ship
船旅 **funatabi** cruise; voyage
船酔い(の) **funayoi (no)** seasick
船酔いする **funayoi suru** get seasick
分別のある **funbetsu no aru** reasonable
船 **fune** boat; ship; vessel
船(の) **fune (no)** nautical
不燃性(の) **funensei (no)** fireproof, non(in)flammable
憤慨 **fungai** indignation
雰囲気 **fun'iki** atmosphere; mood; tone
不妊 **funin** infertility
不妊(の) **funin (no)** infertile; sterile
噴火 **funka** eruption
噴火口 **funkakō** crater
噴火する **funka suru** erupt
粉砕する **funsai suru** pulverize
紛失 **funshitsu** loss
噴出 **funshutsu** eruption
噴出口 **funshutsu-kō** nozzle
紛争 **funsō** dispute; trouble
紛争地帯 **funsō-chitai** hot spot

噴水 **funsui** fountain
ふぬけ **funuke** sissy; coward
フラッドライト **furaddo-raito** floodlight
ふらふら(の) **furafura (no)** shaky
ふらふらした **furafura shita** unsteady
フライにする **furai ni suru** deep-fry
フライパン **furaipan** frying pan; pan
フライトレコーダー **furaito-rekōdā** flight recorder
フランス **Furansu** France
フランス語 **Furansu-go** French
フランス人 **Furansu-jin** the French
フランス(の) **Furansu (no)** French
フラッシュ **furasshu** flash(light)
フラッシュバック **furasshu-bakku** flashback
フレアー **fureā** flare
フレックスタイム **furekkusutaimu** flexitime
フレーム **furēmu** frame, rim (*of eyeglasses*)
フレームワーク **furēmuwāku** framework
フレンチフライ **furenchi-furai** (French) fries
触れる **fureru** touch
不利 **furi** disadvantage
フリー **furī** freelancer
フリーダイアル **furī-daiaru** toll-free
振り出しに戻る **furidashi ni modoru** go back to the drawing board; we're back to square one
フーリガン **fūrigan** hooligan
ふりがな **furigana** *small kana written beside kanji as a pronunciation aid*
振り返る **furikaeru** turn around
ふりかける **furikakeru** sprinkle
フリーキック **furī-kikku** free kick
振り回す **furimawasu** brandish; thrash around
不倫 **furin** adultery
不利(な) **furi (na)** disadvantageous
不利にする **furi ni suru** penalize
フリー(の) **furī (no)** freelance
ふりをする **furi o suru** pretend; act; playact
振り落とす **furiotosu** throw off; shake off
フリル **furiru** frill
振り袖 **furisode** long-sleeved kimono
振り付け **furitsuke** choreography
振り付け師 **furitsukeshi** choreographer
風呂 **furo** bath; 風呂に入る ***furo ni hairu*** take a bath, bathe
フロア **furoa** floor
フロアランプ **furoarampu** floor lamp
フローチャート **furōchāto** flowchart
浮浪児 **furōji** street urchin
付録 **furoku** appendix
フロンガス **furongasu** CFC, chlorofluorocarbon
フロント **furonto** reception desk; reception; room clerk
フロント係 **furonto-gakari** desk clerk; receptionist
フロントガラス **furonto-garasu** windshield
風呂おけ **furooke** tub
フロッピーディスク **furoppī-disuku** floppy (disk)
浮浪者 **furō-sha** tramp, bum, hobo
降る **furu** fall (*of rain, snow*)
振る **furu** shake; wag; waggle; wave; swing; jilt
振るう **furū** wield
震える **furueru** shudder; quiver; shake (*of voice, hand*); tremble; shiver ◊ wobbly
ふるい **furui** sieve; ふるいにかける ***furui ni kakeru*** sift
古い **furui** old; old-fashioned
奮い立たせる **furuitataseru** summon up
ふるい分ける **furui wakeru** sift through
古くなった **furuku natta** stale
古くさい **furukusai** antiquated; old-fashioned; stale; stuffy *person*
ふるまい **furumai** behavior; conduct; goings-on
ふるまう **furumau** behave; conduct oneself; treat (*to food and drink*)
フルート **furūto** flute
フルーツ **furūtsu** fruit
不良 **furyō** juvenile delinquent
房 **fusa** lock (*of hair*); tassel
封鎖 **fūsa** blockade

ふさふさした髪 **fusafusa shita kami** bushy hair
ふさぎ込む **fusagikomu** mope; feel gloomy
ふさぐ **fusagu** obstruct, block
夫妻 **fusai** husband and wife; 山田夫妻 ***Yamada fusai*** Mr and Mrs Yamada
負債者 **fusai-sha** debtor
不採用 **fusaiyō** rejection
不採用にする **fusaiyō ni suru** reject
不賛成 **fusansei** disapproval
封鎖する **fūsa suru** blockade; seal off
ふさわしい **fusawashii** fit (*morally*); fitting, appropriate
防ぐ **fusegu** prevent; save
不正 **fusei** wrong; injustice
不誠実 **fuseijitsu** insincerity; unfaithfulness; …に対して不誠実である ***… ni taishite fuseijitsu de aru*** be unfaithful to
不誠実(な) **fuseijitsu (na)** unfaithful; insincere; dishonest
不正確(な) **fuseikaku (na)** incorrect
不正(な) **fusei (na)** crooked; fraudulent; unjust
不正資金 **fusei-shikin** slush fund
不正操作する **fuseisōsa suru** rig
風船 **fūsen** balloon
風船ガム **fūsengamu** bubble gum
風車 **fūsha** windmill
不死 **fushi** immortality
風刺 **fūshi** satire
不幸せ(な) **fushiawase (na)** unhappy
ふしだら(な) **fushidara (na)** dissolute; sloppy
不思議(な) **fushigi (na)** mysterious
不思議なことに **fushigi na koto ni** mysteriously
不思議にも **fushigi ni mo** strangely enough
父子家庭 **fushi katei** single parent family (*father only*)
節くれだった **fushikuredatta** gnarled
風刺漫画 **fūshi-manga** caricature
節目 **fushime** turning point
不信感 **fushinkan** distrust, mistrust
不審(な) **fushin (na)** questionable
不死(の) **fushi (no)** immortal
不親切(な) **fushinsetsu (na)** unfriendly; unkind
風刺的(な) **fūshiteki (na)** satirical
不自然(な) **fushizen (na)** unnatural
不正直 **fushōjiki** dishonesty
不正直(な) **fushōjiki (na)** deceitful; dishonest
腐食 **fushoku** corrosion; decay
腐食させる **fushoku saseru** corrode
腐食する **fushoku suru** corrode; erode
負傷者 **fushō-sha** the injured
負傷する **fushō suru** injure
不足 **fusoku** deficiency; shortage; shortfall; …が不足している ***… ga fusoku shite iru*** be deficient in …; 不足する ***fusoku suru*** be in short supply
不相応(な) **fusōō (na)** undeserved; disproportionate; out of keeping
風水 **fūsui** feng shui
ふすま **fusuma** sliding screen
ふた **futa** cap; flap; lid; top
双子 **futago** twin
二けた(の) **futaketa no** double
二股(の) **futamata (no)** forked
負担 **futan** burden; strain; 負担をかける ***futan o kakeru*** strain
負担する **futan suru** bear (*costs*)
二人 **futari** two people
二人組 **futarigumi** couple; pair
再び **futatabi** again; 再び現れる ***futatabi arawareru*** reappear
不貞 **futei** infidelity
不定冠詞 **futei-kanshi** indefinite article
不定(の) **futei (no)** indefinite
不定詞 **futeishi** infinitive
不適切(な) **futekisetsu (na)** improper
不適当(な) **futekitō (na)** inadequate; inappropriate; unsuitable
ふと **futo** suddenly; …をふと思いつく ***… o futo omoitsuku*** hit on
ふ頭 **futō** wharf
封筒 **fūtō** envelope
不凍液 **futōeki** antifreeze

太い **futoi** thick *rope*; deep *voice*; shameless
太字 **futoji** bold *letters*
不登校 **futōkō** refusal to attend school
不透明(な) **futōmei** (**na**) opaque
ふとん **futon** futon
不当(な) **futō** (**na**) undeserved; unfair
不当に **futō ni** unduly; unjustly
太りすぎ(の) **futorisugi** (**no**) overweight
太る **futoru** put on weight
太った **futotta** fat; stout
普通株式 **futsū-kabushiki** equities
二日前 **futsuka-mae** two days ago
二日酔い **futsukayoi** hangover
二日酔い(の) **futsukayoi** (**no**) hung-over
普通(の) **futsū** (**no**) normal; ordinary; usual
不つり合い(な) **futsuriai** (**na**) disproportionate
普通は **futsū wa** mostly; usually
普通預金口座 **futsū-yokin-kōza** savings account
普通郵便 **futsū-yūbin** surface mail
沸騰させる **futtō saseru** boil
沸騰する **futtō suru** boil
不運 **fuun** bad luck
不運(な) **fuun** (**na**) ill-fated
不和 **fuwa** breach; discord; friction
ふわふわした **fuwafuwa shita** fluffy; spongy
不渡り手形 **fuwatari-tegata** bounced check
増やす **fuyasu** boost; increase
扶養家族 **fuyō-kazoku** dependent
不用(の) **fuyō** (**no**) waste
扶養料 **fuyōryō** maintenance (*of family*)
扶養する **fuyō suru** maintain, provide for
冬 **fuyu** winter
不愉快(な) **fuyukai** (**na**) distasteful; unpleasant; repulsive
冬らしい **fuyurashii** wintry
不在 **fuzai** absence
不在(の) **fuzai** (**no**) absent
ふざける **fuzakeru** fool around
ふざけて **fuzakete** jokingly
風俗 **fūzoku** manners; customs
風俗犯罪取り締まり班 **fūzokuhanzai-torishimarihan** vice squad
付属(の) **fuzoku** (**no**) affiliated
付属装置 **fuzoku-sōchi** add-on
ふぞろい(の) **fuzoroi** (**no**) irregular; uneven
付随的(な) **fuzuiteki** (**na**) incidental

G

が **ga** but ◊ (*subject particle*): 私がやった ***watashi ga yatta*** I did it
蛾 **ga** moth
画板 ***gaban*** drawing board
画びょう **gabyō** thumbtack
がちょう **gachō** goose
ガードマン **gādoman** guard
ガード下 **gādo shita** underpass
雅楽 **gagaku** court music
害 **gai** harm
外部 **gaibu** exterior
外部(の) **gaibu** (**no**) exterior, external
害虫 **gaichū** pest; vermin
害虫駆除 **gaichū-kujo** pest control
ガイド **gaido** guide
ガイドブック **gaido-bukku** guide(book)
外人 **gaijin** foreigner *pej*
害獣 **gaijū** pest; vermin
外貨 **gaika** foreign currency
外観 **gaikan** façade

外見 **gaiken** appearance; exterior (*of person*)
外交 **gaikō** diplomacy
外交儀礼 **gaikō-girei** protocol
外交官 **gaikōkan** diplomat
外交官(の) **gaikōkan (no)** diplomatic
外交官特権 **gaikōkan-tokken** diplomatic immunity
外国 **gaikoku** foreign country
外国で **gaikoku de** abroad
外国へ **gaikoku e** abroad
外国語 **gaikoku-go** foreign language
外国人 **gaikoku-jin** foreigner; alien
外国為替 **gaikoku-kawase** foreign exchange
外国(の) **gaikoku (no)** foreign; alien
外国通貨 **gaikoku-tsūka** foreign currency
外交(の) **gaikō (no)** diplomatic
外交政策 **gaikō-seisaku** foreign policy
外向的(な) **gaikōteki (na)** outgoing, extrovert
外向的な人 **gaikōteki na hito** extrovert
がい骨 **gaikotsu** skeleton
街区 **gaiku** block
外務 **gaimu** foreign affairs
外務大臣 **Gaimu-daijin** (Japanese) Secretary of State
外務省 **Gaimu-shō** (Japanese) State Department
概念 **gainen** concept
外来語 **gairaigo** loanword
概算で **gaisan de** approximately
概説 **gaisetsu** survey; outline
概して **gaishite** as a rule; typically
外食する **gaishoku suru** eat out
外出中である **gaishutsuchū de aru** be out
街灯 **gaitō** lamppost; streetlight
該当する **gaitō suru** satisfy *requirements*; apply
概要 **gaiyō** gloss (*general explanation*); profile, description
画家 **gaka** artist; painter
がけ **gake** cliff
がき **gaki** kid; brat; urchin
学科 **gakka** department
学会 **gakkai** academic association; academic conference
がっかりした **gakkari shita** disappointed; disheartened; downcast
楽器 **gakki** (musical) instrument
学期 **gakki** semester
学校 **gakkō** school; academy; 学校に行く ***gakkô ni iku*** go to school
がっくりさせる **gakkuri saseru** depress, get down
学級崩壊 **gakkyū-hōkai** classroom disruption
額 **gaku** amount, sum; frame
学 **gaku** learning; knowledge; study; 言語学 ***gengo-gaku*** linguistics; 地理学 ***chiri-gaku*** geography
学部 **gakubu** department; faculty
学部長 **gakubuchō** dean
学長 **gakuchō** college president
楽団 **gakudan** band; orchestra
楽譜 **gakufu** score MUS
学費 **gakuhi** tuition fees
学位 **gakui** degree; 学位を取る ***gakui o toru*** get one's degree
額面 **gakumen** denomination; face value; …を額面通りに受け取る ***... o gakumen dôri ni uketoru*** take at face value
学問 **gakumon** scholarship
学問的(な) **gakumonteki (na)** academic
学年 **gakunen** academic year; grade; class (*in school*)
学歴 **gakureki** educational background
学生 **gakusei** student
学生時代 **gakusei-jidai** school days
学生かばん **gakusei-kaban** schoolbag, satchel
学生寮 **gakuseiryō** college dorm; hostel
学者 **gakusha** academic; scholar
楽章 **gakushō** movement MUS
学習 **gakushū** learning
学習曲線 **gakushū-kyokusen** learning curve
学習者 **gakushū-sha** learner
学習する **gakushū suru** study
楽屋 **gakuya** dressing room

楽屋口**gakuya-guchi** stage door
学友**gakuyū** school pal
我慢できない**gaman dekinai** unbearable ◊ I won't tolerate it
我慢できる**gaman dekiru** tolerable
我慢する**gaman suru** bear; tolerate; stand for; endure; resist
我慢強い**gamanzuyoi** patient
我慢強く**gamanzuyoku** patiently
画面**gamen** screen
画面に出る**gamen ni deru** be on (the) screen
がん**gan** cancer
がんばる**ganbaru** persevere
がんばって**ganbatte** good luck!
願望**ganbō** longing
がにまた(の)**ganimata (no)** bandy-legged
元日**Ganjitsu** New Year's Day
頑丈(な)**ganjō (na)** strong; solid; robust; heavy-duty
眼科医**gankai** ophthalmologist
頑健(な)**ganken (na)** rugged, robust
頑固**ganko** obstinacy
頑固(な)**ganko (na)** stubborn; headstrong; confirmed, inveterate *bachelor*
眼球**gankyū** eyeball
眼精疲労**gansei-hirō** eye strain
岩石**ganseki** rock
元旦**Gantan** New Year's Day
合併**gappei** merger
合併症**gappeishō** complications MED
合併する**gappei suru** combine; merge; amalgamate
がら**gara** character; build; pattern; がらが悪い ***gara ga warui*** vulgar; ill-mannered; がらの大きい ***gara no ôkii*** well-built; 派手ながら ***hade na gara*** a loud pattern
がらがら**garagara** rattle; …にがらがら音を立てさせる ***… ni garagara oto o tatesaseru*** rattle
がらがらへび **garagarahebi** rattlesnake
がらくた**garakuta** garbage; junk; odds and ends; trash
がらくた市**garakuta-ichi** rummage sale
がらんとした**garan to shita** bare, empty
ガラス**garasu** glass
ガレージ**garēji** garage
がれき**gareki** rubble
がり**-gari** sensitive to; 怖がり ***kowagari*** timid person
がり勉**gariben** plodder
画廊**garō** art gallery
ガロン**garon** gallon
がる**-garu** be sensitive to; 寒がる ***samugaru*** be sensitive to the cold
ガールフレンド **gārufurendo** girlfriend
ガールスカウト**gārusukauto** girl scout
ガソリン**gasorin** gas, gasoline
ガソリンスタンド**gasorin-sutando** gas station, filling station
がっしりした**gasshiri shita** hefty; stocky; sturdy
合唱団**gasshōdan** chorus
合唱する**gasshō suru** sing in unison
合宿する**gasshuku suru** go to training camp
ガス**gasu** wind, flatulence
ガーター**gātā** garter
がたがた(の)**gatagata (no)** ramshackle; shaky
がたがた動く**gatagata ugoku** jerky
合致する**gatchi suru** check with, tally with
ガッツ**gattsu** guts
ガウン**gaun** gown
側**gawa** side
ガーゼ**gāze** gauze
下**ge** low grade
解毒剤**gedokuzai** antidote
下品(な)**gehin (na)** vulgar; indelicate
芸術**geijutsu** art
芸術家**geijutsuka** artist
芸術作品**geijutsu-sakuhin** work of art
芸術的(な)**geijutsuteki (na)** artistic; cultural
芸能人**geinō-jin** show business people
芸能界**geinōkai** show business
芸者**geisha** geisha

外科 **geka** surgery; 外科手術を受ける ***geka-shujutsu o ukeru*** undergo surgery
外科医 **gekai** surgeon
外科的(な) **gekateki** (**na**) surgical
劇 **geki** play, drama
激怒 **gekido** fury, rage
激怒させる **gekido saseru** incense, infuriate
激怒した **gekido shita** furious, livid
激怒する **gekido suru** fly into a rage, go wild
激減する **gekigen suru** decimate
劇場 **gekijō** theater
激化 **gekika** escalation, intensification
激流 **gekiryū** torrent
劇作家 **geki-sakka** dramatist, playwright
撃退する **gekitai suru** repel
劇的(な) **gekiteki** (**na**) dramatic; spectacular
激痛 **gekitsū** acute pain; twinge
月刊(の) **gekkan** (**no**) monthly
月刊誌 **gekkanshi** monthly (magazine)
月桂樹 **gekkeiju** laurel
月給 **gekkyū** monthly salary
ゲーム **gēmu** game
ゲームセンター **gēmu-sentā** arcade
弦 **gen** string (*on instrument*)
現場 **genba** scene
原爆 **genbaku** atom bomb
現地時間 **genchi-jikan** local time
現代(の) **gendai** (**no**) modern, contemporary, present-day
現代的(な) **gendaiteki** (**na**) modern *way of thinking*
限度 **gendo** limit; …に限度を置く ***… ni gendo o oku*** draw the line at
現役(の) **gen'eki** (**no**) active; 現役で合格する ***gen'eki de gôkaku suru*** pass straight from high school *college entrance exam*
弦楽器 **gengakki** stringed instrument
言語 **gengo** language
元号 **gengō** era name
言語学者 **gengogaku-sha** linguist
言語(の) **gengo** (**no**) linguistic
言語療法士 **gengo-ryōhōshi** speech therapist
言語障害 **gengo-shōgai** speech impediment, speech defect
原因 **gen'in** cause
源氏物語 **Genji-monogatari** The Tale of Genji
現実主義 **genjitsu-shugi** realism
現実主義者 **genjitsu-shugi-sha** realist
現実的(な) **genjitsuteki** (**na**) realistic; practical; hardheaded
原住民 **genjūmin** native
厳重に **genjū ni** strictly
原価 **genka** cost price
限界 **genkai** limit, threshold; limitation; frontier *fig*
厳格(な) **genkaku** (**na**) austere; puritanical; straightlaced
厳格さ **genkaku-sa** rigor
玄関 **genkan** entrance; doorway; front door; hall
原型 **genkei** prototype
減刑する **genkei suru** commute *sentence*
元気 **genki** vigor; vitality; 元気である ***genki de aru*** be well; be full of life; 元気がない ***genki ga nai*** be feeling low; 元気 -元気です ***genki - genki desu*** how are you? – fine; 元気を出す ***genki o dasu*** cheer up
現金 **genkin** cash
元気(な) **genki** (**na**) frisky
現金自動支払機 **genkin-jidō-shiharaiki** ATM
現金化する **genkinka suru** cash *check*
現金割引 **genkin-waribiki** cash discount
元気づける **genkizukeru** cheer up, perk up; refresh
原稿 **genkō** copy (*written material*); manuscript
現行犯で **genkōhan de** in the very act; 現行犯で捕まえる ***genkôhan de tsukamaeru*** catch red-handed
原告 **genkoku** claimant, plaintiff
現行(の) **genkō** (**no**) going, current
言及 **genkyū** reference
言及しない **genkyū shinai** stay silent
幻滅 **genmetsu** disillusionment

幻滅させる genmetsu saseru disillusion
幻滅する genmetsu suru disenchanted with
厳密(な) genmitsu (na) strict; rigorous; meticulous
現なま gennama dough; cash
原理 genri principle
原料 genryō raw materials
減産 gensan slowdown; decrease in output
原産(の) gensan (no) native
原子 genshi atom
原子物理学 genshi-butsurigaku nuclear physics
原子(の) genshi (no) atomic
原始(の) genshi (no) primitive
原子炉 genshiro nuclear reactor
原子力 genshiryoku atomic energy, nuclear energy,
原子力爆弾 genshiryoku-bakudan atom bomb
原子力発電所 genshiryoku-hatsudensho nuclear power station
原子力(の) genshiryoku (no) nuclear
原始的(な) genshiteki (na) primitive
減少 genshō decrease; reduction; decline
現象 genshō phenomenon
減少させる genshō saseru decrease
減少する genshō suru decrease; diminish; slide
厳粛(な) genshuku (na) solemn
元素 genso element CHEM
幻想 gensō illusion; fantasy
原則 gensoku general principle
減速する gensoku suru throttle back
原則的には gensokuteki ni wa in principle
限定された gentei sareta qualified, limited
限定する gentei suru qualify, limit, restrict
原油 gen'yu crude (oil)
現在 genzai right now ◊ the present
現在形 genzaikei present GRAM
現在(の) genzai (no) present, current; existing
現像 genzō development (*of film*)
現存(の) genzon (no) in existence
現像する genzō suru develop *film*
げっぷ geppu belch, burp; げっぷをする ***geppu o suru*** belch, burp
げっぷさせる geppu saseru burp *baby*
下落 geraku fall, decline
下落する geraku suru fall, decline
ゲレンデ gerende ski run
下劣(な) geretsu (na) vile
下痢 geri diarrhea
ゲリラ兵 gerira-hei guerrilla
下船する gesen suru disembark
下宿人 geshuku-nin boarder, lodger
下宿する geshuku suru board with
げっ歯類 gesshirui rodent
月食 gesshoku eclipse (of the moon)
下水 gesui sewage
下水道 gesuidō sewer
下水処理場 gesui-shorijō sewage plant
下駄 geta thonged clogs
ゲート gēto gate
月曜日 getsuyōbi Monday
下剤 gezai laxative
下山 gezan descent
下山する gezan suru descend
ギア gia gear
議案 gian bill POL
議長 gichō chair; chairperson; chairman; …の議長を務める ***… no gichô o tsutomeru*** chair; preside at
議題 gidai agenda
ギフト gifuto gift
ギガバイト gigabaito gigabyte
議員 giin councilor; member of the Diet
議事録 gijiroku minutes (*of meeting*)
技術 gijutsu skill; craft; expertise; technique
議会 gikai Congress; assembly, council; parliament
議会(の) gikai (no) Congressional; parliamentary

ぎこちない **gikochinai** awkward; stiff
疑問 **gimon** doubt; skepticism; qualm; 疑問がある ***gimon ga aru*** be in doubt; 疑問のある ***gimon no aru*** debatable
疑問符 **gimonfu** question mark
疑問詞 **gimonshi** interrogative GRAM
義務 **gimu** duty, responsibility; obligation; liability
義務教育 **gimu-kyōiku** compulsory education
義務(の) **gimu (no)** obligatory
義務づける **gimuzukeru** bind LAW
銀 **gin** silver
銀行 **ginkō** bank FIN
銀行振替為替 **ginkō-furikae-kawase** giro
銀行家 **ginkōka** banker
銀行口座 **ginkō-kōza** bank account
銀めっき(の) **gin mekki (no)** silver-plated
ぎんなん **ginnan** gingko nut
銀(の) **gin (no)** silver
銀髪(の) **ginpatsu (no)** gray-haired; silver-haired
ギプス **gipusu** plaster cast
ぎらぎら光る **giragira hikaru** glare
義理 **giri**: …に義理がある ***… ni giri ga aru*** be under an obligation to
義理と人情 **giri to ninjō** duty and human feelings
義理(の) **giri (no)** in-law; 義理の姉 ***giri no ane*** sister-in-law
ギリシア **Girishia** Greece
ギリシア(の) **Girishia (no)** Greek
議論 **giron** argument, reasoning; discussion
議論する **giron suru** argue
議論好き(な) **gironzuki (na)** argumentative
犠牲 **gisei** cost *fig*; sacrifice; 犠牲にする ***gisei ni suru*** sacrifice *fig*; victimize; 犠牲をはらう ***gisei o harau*** make sacrifices
犠牲者 **gisei-sha** martyr *fig*; victim
犠牲者の数 **gisei-sha no kazu** toll (*deaths*)
議席 **giseki** seat POL
技師 **gishi** engineer
儀式 **gishiki** ceremony; ritual
儀式(の) **gishiki (no)** ceremonial
儀式的(な) **gishikiteki (na)** ritual
偽証 **gishō** perjury
偽証する **gishō suru** perjure oneself
ぎっしり詰まって **gisshiri tsumatte** chock-full
ギター **gitā** guitar
ギタリスト **gitarisuto** guitarist
ぎざぎざ(の) **gizagiza (no)** jagged
偽善 **gizen** hypocrisy
偽善者 **gizen-sha** hypocrite
偽善的(な) **gizenteki (na)** hypocritical
偽造 **gizō** forgery
偽造文書 **gizō-bunsho** forgery
偽造(の) **gizō (no)** counterfeit
偽造者 **gizō-sha** forger
偽造する **gizō suru** counterfeit, forge
五 **go** five
語 **go** word
碁 **go** game of Go
後 **-go** after; in; 三日後 ***mikkago*** after three days; in three days
御 …, ご … **go …** (*honorific prefix*): ご家族 ***gokazoku*** your family; ご案内致します ***goannai itashimasu*** I'll show you the way
合弁事業 **gōben-jigyō** joint venture
語尾 **gobi** ending GRAM
五分五分に **gobugobu ni** fifty-fifty
ごちゃごちゃ **gochagocha** muddle
ごちゃごちゃにする **gochagocha ni suru** muddle up
ごちゃ混ぜにする **gochamaze ni suru** mix up
ごちそう **gochisō** feast, spread
ごちそうさまでした **gochisōsama deshita** that was delicious
護衛 **goei** escort; guard
護衛する **goei suru** escort; guard
語学 **gogaku** language
五月 **gogatsu** May
午後 **gogo** afternoon; 午後に ***gogo ni*** in the afternoon; 午後(の) ***gogo (no)*** pm
ゴーグル **gōguru** goggles
ご飯 **gohan** rice (*cooked*)

ご飯茶碗**gohan-jawan** rice bowl
合法化する**gōhōka suru** legalize
合法的(な)**gōhōteki (na)** legal; legitimate
語い**goi** vocabulary
合意**gōi** consensus, agreement; understanding
強引(な)**gōin (na)** assertive; pushy
合意する**gōi suru** agree
強情(な)**gōjō (na)** pigheaded
五十**gojū** fifty
誤解**gokai** misunderstanding; misconception; misinterpretation; …の誤解を招く***… no gokai o maneku*** mislead; 誤解をしている ***gokai o shite iru*** be under a misapprehension; be mistaken
誤解する**gokai suru** misinterpret, misread; misunderstand
合格点**gōkakuten** pass mark
合格する**gōkaku suru** pass *exam*
語幹**gokan** root, stem (*of word*)
強かん**gōkan** rape
豪華(な)**gōka (na)** luxurious; de luxe; plush
互換性**gokansei** compatibility
互換性のある**gokansei no aru** compatible
互換性のない**gokansei no nai** incompatible
強かん者**gōkan-sha** rapist
強かんする**gōkan suru** rape
合計**gōkei** sum, total
合計(の)**gōkei (no)** total
合計する**gōkei suru** add; add up
ごきぶり**gokiburi** cockroach
合金**gōkin** alloy
…ごっこをして遊ぶ**… gokko o shite asobu** play
後光**gokō** halo
ごく**goku** extremely
極悪(の)**gokuaku (no)** wicked
ごくごく飲む**gokugoku nomu** gulp down
ご苦労さま**gokurōsama** well done!; thanks for your help
極小型(の)**gokushōgata (no)** midget; miniature
ごくわずか(の)**goku wazuka (no)** least
ごまかし**gomakashi** deception; whitewash
ごまかす**gomakasu** fiddle *accounts, results*; stall (*for time*)
ごう慢**gōman** arrogance
ごう慢(な)**gōman (na)** arrogant, superior *pej*
ごまをする**goma o suru** suck up to
ごめんなさい**gomen nasai** I beg your pardon?, pardon me?; I'm sorry
ごみ**gomi** garbage; litter
ごみ入れ**gomiire** ash can
ごみの山**gomi no yama** scrap heap
ごみ捨て場**gomi-suteba** refuse dump
拷問**gōmon** torture; 拷問にかける ***gômon ni kakeru*** torture
ゴム**gomu** rubber
ゴムボート**gomu-bōto** dinghy
ゴムひも**gomuhimo** piece of elastic
ごう音**gōon** roar
娯楽**goraku** recreation, entertainment
娯楽施設**goraku-shisetsu** amusements
合理化**gōrika** rationalization
合理化された**gōrika sareta** streamlined
合理化する**gōrika suru** rationalize; streamline
ゴリラ**gorira** gorilla
合理性**gōrisei** rationality
合理的(な)**gorīteki (na)** rational
…頃**…goro** around
ごろごろとのどを鳴らす**gorogoroto nodo o narasu** purr
ゴロゴロ鳴る**gorogoro naru** rumble
ごろつき**gorotsuki** ruffian
ゴール**gōru** finish, finishing line; goal
ゴールデンアワー**gōruden-awā** prime time
ゴールデンウィーク**gōruden-wīku** Golden Week (*string of national holidays between April 29 and May 5*)
ゴルファー**gorufā** golfer
ゴルフ**gorufu** golf
ゴルフコース**gorufu-kōsu** golf course

ゴルフクラブ **gorufu-kurabu** golf club
ゴールキーパー **gōru-kīpā** goalkeeper
ゴールポスト **gōru-posuto** goalpost
合流する **gōryū suru** join; link up
誤算 **gosan** miscalculation
合成(の) **gōsei (no)** synthetic
ごしごし洗う **goshigoshi arau** scour; scrub
誤審 **goshin** miscarriage of justice
誤植 **goshoku** misprint
強盗 **gōtō** robber; mugger; robbery; mugging; raid; 強盗に入る ***gôtô ni hairu*** raid
ごとに **-goto ni** every, each
ごと(の) **-goto (no)** every; each
強盗する **gōtō suru** burglarize; raid
豪雨 **gōu** deluge; monsoon
誤用 **goyō** misuse
誤用する **goyō suru** misuse
ございます **gozaimasu** *polite form of* ***aru, desu***
午前 **gozen** a.m.
午前0時 **gozen reiji** midnight
具合 **guai** condition; 体の具合 ***karada no guai*** health; 具合の悪い ***guai no warui*** ill
ぐち **guchi** complaint; beef; ぐちを言う ***guchi o iu*** complain; beef
郡 **gun** county
軍 **gun** army; troops
軍備縮小 **gunbi-shukushō** disarmament; arms reduction
軍備縮小する**gunbi-shukushō suru** disarm; cut down on armaments
軍事演習 **gunji-enshū** exercise MIL
軍事教練 **gunji-kyōren** drill MIL
軍人 **gunjin** serviceman; soldier
軍事(の) **gunji (no)** military
軍事施設 **gunji-shisetsu** military installation
軍艦 **gunkan** warship
軍法会議 **gunpō-kaigi** court martial
群衆 **gunshū** crowd; mob; throng
軍隊 **guntai** armed forces; the military; troops
軍隊(の) **guntai (no)** military
軍用機 **gunyōki** warplane
グラビア雑紙 **gurabia-zasshi** glossy (magazine)
グラフ **gurafu** graph
ぐらぐらした **guragura shita** unsteady
ぐらぐらする **guragura suru** wobble
ぐらい **gurai** around; これぐらい大きい/高い ***koregurai ôkii / takai*** this big / high
グライダー **guraidā** glider
グラマー(な) **guramā (na)** busty
グラム **guramu** gram
グランドピアノ **gurando-piano** grand piano
グラニュー糖 **guranyū-tō** granulated sugar
グラス **gurasu** tumbler
グレードアップする **gurēdo appu suru** upgrade
グレープフルーツ**gurēpufurūtsu** grapefruit
グリニッジ標準時 **gurinidji-hyōjun ji** GMT, Greenwich Mean Time
グリーン車 **gurīn-sha** first class (*on bullet train*)
グリップ **gurippu** grip SP
グリル **guriru** grill
グローバルスタンダード**gurōbaru-sutandādo** global standard
グローブ **gurōbu** glove
ぐるぐる巻く **guruguru maku** coil (up)
グルメ **gurume** gourmet, food freak
グループ **gurūpu** bunch; group; in-group
ぐるっと **gurutto** all around
ぐっすり **gussuri** soundly
ぐっすり眠らせる **gussuri nemuraseru** knock out
偶数(の) **gūsū (no)** even
具体化させる **gutaika saseru** crystallize
具体化する **gutaika suru** crystallize
具体的(な) **gutaiteki (na)** concrete
偶然 **gūzen** coincidence; 偶然見つける ***gûzen mitsukeru*** stumble across
偶然に **gūzen ni** by accident, by chance
偶然(の) **gūzen (no)** accidental
偶像 **gūzō** icon; idol

ぐずぐずする **guzuguzu suru** dawdle; delay
ギャグ **gyagu** gag, joke
逆 **gyaku** opposite, converse
逆風 **gyakufū** headwind
逆効果(の) **gyakukōka (no)** counterproductive
逆に **gyaku ni** conversely
逆にする **gyaku ni suru** invert, reverse
逆(の) **gyaku (no)** opposite; reverse
虐殺 **gyakusatsu** slaughter; bloodshed
虐殺する **gyakusatsu suru** massacre; slaughter
逆説 **gyakusetsu** paradox
逆説的(な) **gyakusetsuteki (na)** paradoxical
虐待 **gyakutai** abuse, maltreatment
虐待する **gyakutai suru** abuse, maltreat, illtreat
ギャンブル **gyanburu** gamble; gambling
ギャング **gyangu** gangster, mobster
行 **gyō** line (*of text*)
行儀 **gyōgi** manners; behavior; 行儀良くする ***gyôgi yoku suru*** behave (oneself)
行儀のいい **gyōgi no ii** well-behaved
行儀の悪い **gyōgi no warui** naughty
行事 **gyōji** festivities; function, reception; occasion, event
魚介類 **gyokairui** seafood
漁獲 **gyokaku** haul, catch
凝結する **gyōketsu suru** condense
凝固する **gyōko suru** coagulate; congeal; curdle
行列 **gyōretsu** procession
行政 **gyōsei** administration
行政(の) **gyōsei (no)** administrative
業績 **gyōseki** achievement
漁船 **gyosen** fishing boat
凝視 **gyōshi** stare
仰天 **gyōten** amazement
仰天させる **gyōten saseru** amaze
仰天する **gyōten suru** be amazed
ぎゅうぎゅう詰めである **gyūgyūzume de aru** be crowded, be jammed
ぎゅうぎゅう詰め(の) **gyūgyūzume (no)** jam-packed
牛肉 **gyūniku** beef
牛乳 **gyūnyū** milk
ぎゅっと **gyutto** firmly; tightly; ぎゅっと絞る ***gyutto shiboru*** squeeze

H

刃 **ha** blade
歯 **ha** tooth; cog; 歯をくいしばる ***ha o kuishibaru*** clench one's teeth; 歯(の) ***ha*** (***no***) dental
葉 **ha** leaf; foliage
幅 **haba** breadth; range; 幅十メートル ***haba jû mêtoru*** 10m across; 幅を広げる ***haba o hirogeru*** let out
把握する **haaku suru** comprehend; grasp
羽ばたく **habataku** flap
幅跳び **habatobi** broadjump, long jump
派閥 **habatsu** in-group
ハブ **habu** hub
ハーブ **hābu** herb
省く **habuku** leave out
歯ブラシ **ha-burashi** toothbrush
はち **hachi** wasp
鉢 **hachi** bowl
八 **hachi** eight
八月 **hachigatsu** August
はちまき **hachimaki** headband
はちみつ **hachimitsu** honey
はちの巣 **hachi no su** hive; honeycomb

波長**hachō** wavelength; 波長が合う ***hachô ga au*** be on the same wavelength; 波長を変える ***hachô o kaeru*** scramble
ハ長調**hachōchō** C major
は虫類**hachūrui** reptile
肌**hada** skin
裸で**hadaka de** in the nude
裸にする**hadaka ni suru** strip
裸(の)**hadaka (no)** naked, nude, bare
肌の色**hada no iro** coloring
裸足(の)**hadashi (no)** barefoot
肌寒い**hadazamui** chilly
派手(な)**hade (na)** loud, flamboyant; ostentatious, showy
ハードディスク**hādo disuku** hard disk
ハードカバー**hādo kabā** hardback
ハードル**hādoru** hurdle; hurdles
ハードウェア**hādowea** hardware
ハエ**hae** fly
生える**haeru** grow
ハーフタイム**hāfu-taimu** half time
葉書**hagaki** postcard
はがれる**hagareru** come unstuck; peel off
はがす**hagasu** rub off; strip, remove; take up *carpet etc*
はげ**hage** baldness
励まし**hagemashi** encouragement
励ます**hagemasu** encourage, urge on
励ますよう(な)**hagemasu yō (na)** encouraging
励みになる**hagemi ni naru** encouraging
はげ落ちる**hageochiru** flake off; peel
激しい**hageshii** stormy *relationship*; violent *emotion, storm*; acute *pain*; fiery; heavy *rain*; intense; strenuous
激しく**hageshiku** severely; violently
激しくなる**hageshiku naru** intensify
激しさ**hageshi-sa** intensity; violence
はげた**hageta** bald; bare
はげたか**hagetaka** vulture; condor
はげてきている**hagete kite iru** receding
歯ぐき**haguki** gum (*in mouth*)
はぐらかす**hagurakasu** evade, dodge
はぐれる**hagureru** stray
はぐれた**hagureta** stray
歯車**haguruma** cogwheel
母**haha** mother; 母の日 ***Haha no hi*** Mother's Day
母方(の)**hahakata (no)** maternal
母親**hahaoya** mother
破片**hahen** fragment; splinter
はい**hai** yes; no (*see* ***yes*** *p670*); uh-huh (*I'm listening*); はい、ここにあります ***hai, koko ni arimasu*** here it is
灰**hai** ash; ashes
胚**hai** embryo
肺**hai** lung
敗北**haiboku** defeat, whipping
ハイボール**haibōru** whiskey and soda
ハイブリッド**haiburiddo** hybrid
配置**haichi** arrangement
配置する**haichi suru** arrange; position; post; station
肺炎**haien** pneumonia
配布**haifu** distribution
ハイフン**haifun** hyphen
肺がん**haigan** lung cancer
配偶者**haigū-sha** partner; spouse
ハイヒール**haihīru** stilettos
灰色(の)**haiiro (no)** gray
ハイジャック**haijakku** hijack
ハイジャックする**haijakku suru** hijack
ハイジャンプ**haijanpu** high jump
ハイカー**haikā** hiker; rambler
配管**haikan** plumbing
配管工**haikankō** plumber
廃刊にする**haikan ni suru** be discontinued; fold
背景**haikei** background; context; scenes THEA; …の背景を考えて ***... no haikei o kangaete*** looking at ... in context
拝啓**haikei** Dear Sir
肺結核**haikekkaku** pulmonary tuberculosis
拝見する**haiken suru** H see
敗血症**haiketsushō** blood

poisoning
廃棄**haiki** disposal
廃棄物**haikibutsu** waste; waste product
排気ガス**haiki-gasu** exhaust fumes
排気管**haikikan** exhaust (pipe)
ハイキング**haikingu** hike; ramble; rambling; walking
ハイキングする**haikingu suru** walk; ramble
排気量**haikiryō** capacity
俳句**haiku** haiku
配給する**haikyū suru** ration; distribute
排尿する**hainyō suru** urinate
ハイパーテキスト**haipātekisuto** hypertext
ハイライト**hairaito** highlight
排卵誘発剤**hairan-yūhatsuzai** fertility drug
はいる**hairu** percolate
入る**hairu** enter, come in; fit, slot in; 入ることができる ***hairu koto ga dekiru*** be able to enter; have access to
配線盤**haisenban** circuit board
歯医者**haisha** dentist
敗者**haisha** loser
廃止する**haishi suru** abolish, ax; discontinue; dismantle
配色**haishoku** color scheme
排出**haishutsu** emission
排水**haisui** drainage
排水管**haisuikan** drain, drainpipe; drainage
排水口**haisuikō** overflow (pipe)
排水溝**haisuikō** storm drain
排水する**haisui suru** drain
歯痛**haita** toothache
敗退**haitai** elimination; defeat
敗退する**haitai suru** be eliminated, be out (*from competition*)
配達**haitatsu** delivery
配達状**haitatsu-jō** delivery note
配達する**haitatsu suru** deliver
ハイテク**haiteku** hi-tech
ハイテク(の)**haiteku (no)** hi-tech
配当金**haitōkin** dividend
配役する**haiyaku suru** cast
俳優**haiyū** actor, player
灰皿**haizara** ashtray
配属**haizoku** posting
配属する**haizoku suru** post; assign
恥**haji** disgrace; shame; embarrassment; humiliation; 恥をかかせる ***haji o kakaseru*** embarrass; humiliate
はじく**hajiku** flip, flick
初まり**hajimari** beginning, start; onset; dawn
始まる**hajimaru** begin, start
初め**hajime** beginning; outset; 十月の初め ***jûgatsu no hajime*** early October
はじめまして**hajimemashite** how do you do?, pleased to meet you
初め(の) **hajime (no)** initial
始める**hajimeru** begin, start; mount *campaign*; take up *new job*
初めて**hajimete** for the first time
初めは**hajime wa** at first, initially
恥さらし**hajisarashi** a disgrace
恥知らず(の)**hajishirazu (no)** shameless
墓**haka** grave; tomb
破壊**hakai** destruction; ruin
破壊できない**hakai dekinai** indestructible
破壊行動**hakai-kōdō** vandalism
破壊工作**hakai-kōsaku** sabotage
破壊される**hakai sareru** be ruined
墓石**hakaishi** gravestone; tombstone
破壊する**hakai suru** destroy; knock out *power lines etc*; sabotage; vandalize
破壊的(な)**hakaiteki (na)** destructive; subversive
はかま**hakama** *traditional pants, like culottes*
はかり**hakari** scales
はかりしれない **hakari-shirenai** incalculable, inestimable; inscrutable; untold
測る**hakaru** measure
計る**hakaru** take *temperature*
量る**hakaru** weigh
図る**hakaru** plan; plot
博士号**hakase-gō** doctorate, PhD
はけ**hake** paintbrush
はけ口**hakeguchi** outlet
派遣**haken** temp

派遣で働く **haken de hataraku** temp
派遣する **haken suru** send in; dispatch
吐き出す **hakidasu** exhale; spit out; give vent to
吐き気 **hakike** sickness, vomiting; nausea
吐き気がする **hakike ga suru** feel nauseous
はきもの **hakimono** footwear
破棄する **haki suru** break off *engagement*; tear up *agreement*
掃き寄せる **hakiyoseru** sweep up
ハッカー **hakkā** hacker
発覚 **hakkaku** disclosure
発覚する **hakkaku suru** be out (*of scandal etc*); be discovered
発汗 **hakkan** perspiration
発見 **hakken** detection; discovery; strike (*of oil*)
発見者 **hakken-sha** discoverer
発見する **hakken suru** discover; unearth; strike *oil*
白血病 **hakketsubyō** leukemia
はっきり **hakkiri** clearly; …にはっきり言う ***… ni hakkiri iu*** give … a piece of one's mind; はっきり物を言う ***hakkiri mono o iu*** vocal; はっきりは言えませんが ***hakkiri wa iemasen ga*** I couldn't say for sure
はっきりさせる **hakkiri saseru** clarify
はっきりしない **hakkiri shinai** dull; inarticulate; uncertain; vague ◊ be a bit hazy
はっきりした **hakkiri shita** clear; decided, definite; distinct; vivid
はっきりする **hakkiri suru** become clear
はっきりと **hakkiri to** clearly, distinctly; explicitly
発揮する **hakki suru** exhibit; display; show
発酵 **hakkō** fermentation
発行 **hakkō** issue
発行部数 **hakkō-busū** circulation
発行物 **hakkōbutsu** issue
発光ダイオード **hakkō-daiōdo** LED, light-emitting diode
発行者 **hakkō-sha** publisher
発効する **hakkō suru** come into effect
発酵する **hakkō suru** ferment
発行する **hakkō suru** issue
発光する **hakkō suru** emit light
発掘 **hakkutsu** excavation
発掘する **hakkutsu suru** excavate; uncover; unearth
発狂した **hakkyō shita** demented, deranged
箱 **hako** box; carton; crate; pack
運ぶ **hakobu** carry; convey
はく **haku** wear; put on *footwear, pants*
吐く **haku** blow; vomit, throw up; 息を吐く ***iki o haku*** breathe; breathe out
掃く **haku** sweep
泊 **-haku** overnight stay; 二泊する ***ni-haku suru*** stay for two nights
白亜 ***hakua*** chalk
博物学者 **hakubutsugaku-sha** naturalist
博物館 **hakubutsukan** museum
白鳥 **hakuchō** swan
白昼 **hakuchū** broad daylight
白昼夢 **hakuchūmu** daydream
迫害 **hakugai** persecution
迫害する **hakugai suru** persecute
白人 **hakujin** white (person)
白人(の) **hakujin (no)** white
白状する **hakujō suru** confess, own up
博識(の) **hakushiki (no)** well-read
白紙(の) **hakushi (no)** blank
拍手 **hakushu** applause
拍手する **hakushu suru** applaud, clap
破局 **hakyoku** bust-up, catastrophe
浜辺 **hamabe** beach
はまぐり **hamaguri** clam
葉巻き **hamaki** cigar
ハマる **hamaru** get caught out; be crazy about
はまった **hamatta** be trapped
はめ込む **hamekomu** slot in
はめる **hameru** wear *gloves, rings*
破滅 **hametsu** doom; devastation
歯みがき粉 **ha-migakiko** toothpaste
ハミングする **hamingu suru** hum
ハーモニー **hāmonī** harmony

ハーモニカ **hāmonika** mouthorgan
ハム **hamu** ham
ハムスター **hamusutā** hamster
班 **han** crew
版 **han** edition
判 **han** stamp; seal
半 **-han** half; 十時半 ***jûji han*** half (past) ten
藩 **han** clan
反… **han…** anti; 反政府団体 ***hanseifu-dantai*** anti-government group
花 **hana** bloom; blossom; flower
鼻 **hana** nose; snout; trunk; 鼻をかむ ***hana o kamu*** blow one's nose
鼻柱 **hanabashira** bridge (*of nose*)
花火 **hanabi** fireworks
花びら **hanabira** petal
鼻血 **hanaji** nosebleed; 鼻血が出る ***hanaji ga deru*** have a nosebleed
鼻くそ**hanakuso** snot; 鼻くそをほじる ***hanakuso o hojiru*** pick one' s nose
花見 **hanami** blossom viewing
鼻水 **hanamizu** mucus; 鼻水が垂れる ***hanamizu ga tareru*** run (*of nose*)
花模様(の) **hanamoyō** (**no**) flowery
花婿 **hanamuko** bridegroom
鼻にかかった **hana ni kakatta** nasal
鼻の穴 **hana no ana** nostril
離れられない **hanarerarenai** inseparable
離れる **hanareru** break away; leave
離れた **hanareta** remote
離れて **hanarete** apart (*in distance*); off (*in distance*)
離れている **hanarete iru** stay away
話 **hanashi** story; あなたに話があります ***anata ni hanashi ga arimasu*** I need to talk to you
話し合い **hanashiai** discussion
話し合う **hanashiau** talk; talk over, discuss
話中(の) **hanashichū** (**no**) busy TELEC; 話中である ***hanashichû* de aru** be on the telephone
話しかける **hanashikakeru** speak to; address
話し方 **hanashikata** speech; way of speaking
話し言葉 **hanashi-kotoba** vernacular
話好き(な) **hanashizuki** (**na**) communicative
話好き(の) **hanashizuki** (**no**) chatty
離す **hanasu** separate; disengage
放す **hanasu** release; let go; let off
話す **hanasu** speak; talk; relate; tell; …に話す ***…ni hanasu*** have a word with
花束 **hanataba** bouquet, bunch of flowers
鼻歌を歌う **hanauta o utau** hum
花輪 **hanawa** garland; wreath
花屋 **hana-ya** florist
華やか(な) **hanayaka** (**na**) gorgeous; flowery; brilliant
花嫁 **hanayome** bride
花盛り(の) **hanazakari** (**no**) in full bloom
鼻詰まり **hanazumari** congestion
ハンバーガー **hanbāgā** hamburger
販売 **hanbai** sale; 販売されている ***hanbai sarete iru*** be on sale
販売業者 **hanbai-gyō-sha** dealer
販売会議 **hanbai-kaigi** sales meeting
販売促進 **hanbai-sokushin** promotion
販売する **hanbai suru** sell; distribute
販売店 **hanbaiten** outlet
半分 **hanbun** half
半分にする **hanbun ni suru** halve
半分(の) **hanbun** (**no**) half
判断 **handan** judgment; 判断の尺度 ***handan no shakudo*** yardstick; 判断を誤る ***handan o ayamaru*** misjudge
判断する **handan suru** judge
ハンディ **handi** handicap
反動 **handō** backlash
ハンドバッグ **handobaggu** bag; pocketbook, purse
ハンドブック**handobukku** handbook
ハンドル **handoru** handlebars; (steering) wheel
半導体 **handōtai** semiconductor

反動的(な)**handōteki (na)** reactionary
羽**hane** wing; feather; propeller
羽根**hane** feather; shuttlecock
跳ね上る**haneagaru** buck (*of horse*)
羽ぶとん**hanebuton** eiderdown
繁栄**han'ei** prosperity
繁栄した**han'ei shita** prosperous
繁栄する**han'ei suru** flourish, prosper
はね返る**hanekaeru** rebound
跳ねかける**hanekakeru** splash; splatter
ハネムーン**hanemūn** honeymoon
半円**han'en** semicircle
半円(の)**han'en (no)** semicircular
はねる**haneru** bound; knock down, knock over
はねつける**hanetsukeru** scorn; shoot down *suggestion*
ハンガー**hangā** clothes hanger, coathanger
版画**hanga** engraving; woodblock print
半額(の)**hangaku (no)** half-price
ハンガリー**Hangarī** Hungary
ハンガリー(の)**Hangarī (no)** Hungarian
反撃**hangeki** counter-attack
反撃する**hangeki suru** counter, counter-attack, retaliate
反逆**hangyaku** revolt
反逆者**hangyaku-sha** rebel; traitor
反逆する**hangyaku suru** revolt
反逆罪**hangyakuzai** treason
範囲**han'i** area; scope; spectrum; sphere; …の範囲内で ***…no han'inai de*** within
はにかんだ**hanikanda** coy; shy
判事**hanji** judge
繁盛している**hanjō shite iru** prospering; flourishing
ハンカチ**hankachi** handkerchief
繁華街**hankagai** busy shopping district
繁華街(の)**hankagai (no)** downtown
反感**hankan** antipathy; 反感を買う ***hankan o kau*** alienate
半径**hankei** radius
半券**hanken** stub
判決**hanketsu** judgment; 判決を下す ***hanketsu o kudasu*** pass sentence; Xに有罪/無罪判決を下す ***X ni yûzai/muzai hanketsu o kudasu*** find X innocent/guilty
はんこ**hanko** signature seal
反抗**hankō** defiance; rebellion
反抗する**hankō suru** rebel
反抗的(な)**hankōteki (na)** defiant; rebellious; disobedient; insubordinate
半狂乱(の)**hankyōran (no)** frantic
反響する**hankyō suru** echo
半球**hankyū** hemisphere
ハンマー**hanmā** hammer; sledgehammer
ハンモック**hanmokku** hammock
反目**hanmoku** antagonism
犯人**hannin** culprit
反応**hannō** reaction; response
反応する**hannō suru** react
歯(の)**ha (no)** dental
反乱**hanran** mutiny, rebellion; 反乱を起こす ***hanran o okosu*** rebel, mutiny
反乱軍**hanran-gun** rebel troops
はんらんさせる**hanran saseru** flood
はんらんする**hanran suru** overflow
判例**hanrei** precedent; case LAW
販路**hanro** market; outlet
反論する**hanron suru** contradict; dispute
ハンサム(な)**hansamu (na)** handsome
反省する**hansei suru** reflect on; be sorry
帆船**hansen** sailing ship
反射**hansha** reflection
反社会的(な)**hanshakaiteki (na)** antisocial
反射能力**hansha-nōryoku** reflex
反射する**hansha suru** reflect
反射的(な)**hanshateki (na)** involuntary
反射運動**hansha-undō** reflex reaction
反して**hanshite** contrary to
繁殖**hanshoku** breeding; reproduction
繁殖(の)**hanshoku (no)**

reproductive
繁殖させる **hanshoku saseru** breed
繁殖する **hanshoku suru** breed; reproduce; multiply
反証する **hanshō suru** disprove
半そで(の) **hansode (no)** short-sleeved
反則する **hansoku suru** foul SP
半数(の) **hansū (no)** half
反する **hansuru** oppose
ハンター **hantā** hunter
反対 **hantai** dissent; opposition
反対である **hantai de aru** be opposed to; be disapprove of
反対尋問を行う **hantai-jinmon o okonau** cross-examine
反対(の) **hantai (no)** contrary; opposite
反体制になる **hantaisei ni naru** become anti-establishment; go underground
反対する **hantai suru** object; oppose; protest
半島 **hantō** peninsula
犯罪 **hanzai** crime, offense
犯罪(の) **hanzai (no)** criminal
犯罪者 **hanzai-sha** criminal, offender
半ズボン **han-zubon** shorts
はおり **haori** half-length Japanese coat
葉っぱ **happa** leaf
発破をかける **happa o kakeru** urge on; give a pep talk
発砲される **happō sareru** go off (*of gun*)
発泡ワイン **happō-wain** sparkling wine
発表 **happyō** announcement
発表する **happyō suru** announce; bring out; air
ハープ **hāpu** harp
腹 **hara** belly; gut; insides; 腹を立てる ***hara o tateru*** lose one's temper; resent; …に対して腹を立てている ***... ni taishite hara o tatete iru*** be angry with
腹ごしらえする **haragoshirae suru** grab a quick bite
腹黒い **haraguroi** scheming; wicked
払い込む **haraikomu** pay in
払い戻し **haraimodoshi** rebate; refund
払い戻す **haraimodosu** refund, reimburse; repay
払いのける **harainokeru** brush; brush off
波乱に富んだ **haran ni tonda** eventful
腹ペコ(の) **harapeko (no)** ravenous
払う **harau** pay, fork out; 注意を払う ***chûi o harau*** pay attention
腫れ **hare** swelling
腫れぼったい **harebottai** puffy
晴れ(の) **hare (no)** fine *day*
晴れる **hareru** brighten up; clear; lift; swell (*of wound, limb*)
晴れた **hareta** bright; clear; sunny; swollen
破裂 **haretsu** burst; rupture
破裂させる **haretsu saseru** burst; bust, break
破裂した **haretsu shita** burst
破裂する **haretsu suru** burst; rupture
晴やかさ **hareyaka-sa** brightness
はり **hari** beam; rafter
針 **hari** hand (*of clock*); needle; spike; spine (*on hedgehog*)
張り **hari** strain, tension
ハリ治療 **harichiryō** acupuncture
張り出す **haridasu** jut out
はり紙 **harigami** notice
針金 **harigane** wire
ハリケーン **harikēn** hurricane
張り切る **harikiru** be enthusiastic; be in high spirits
はりねずみ **harinezumi** hedgehog
はり付ける **haritsukeru** stick (up); paste
張り付く **haritsuku** stick to, follow
張り詰めた **haritsumeta** tense; anxious
はる **haru** post; affix; stick up
張る **haru** stretch; spread; tense up; pitch *tent*
春 **haru** spring
春一番 **haruichiban** first south wind of spring
はるかに **haruka ni** far, much
挟まれている **hasamarete iru** lie between; be caught between

はさみ **hasami** scissors; shears
挟み込む **hasamikomu** tuck; tuck in
挟む **hasamu** sandwich, squeeze
破産 **hasan** bankruptcy
破産させる **hasan saseru** bankrupt, ruin
破産した **hasan shita** bankrupt, insolvent
破産する **hasan suru** go bankrupt, go bust, go under; be ruined (*financially*)
派生(の) **hasei** (**no**) derivative
はし **hashi** chopsticks
橋 **hashi** bridge
端 **hashi** edge; end
はしご **hashigo** ladder
はしか **hashika** measles
はしけ **hashike** barge NAUT
はし置き **hashioki** chopstick rest
柱 **hashira** pillar; post
走り書き **hashirigaki** scribble
走る **hashiru** run
はした金 **hashitagane** chickenfeed, peanuts
橋渡し **hashiwatashi** mediation; buffer *fig*
破傷風 **hashōfū** tetanus
破損 **hason** break; breakage
発生 **hassei** creation; eruption (*of violence*)
発生する **hassei suru** erupt; flare up
発車 **hassha** departure
発射 **hassha** launch; shot
発射する **hassha suru** launch; blast off; fire, shoot
発しん **hasshin** rash
発信音 **hasshin'on** dial tone
発送 **hassō** shipping, sending
発送する **hassō suru** dispatch, send off
発する **hassuru** give off; utter; issue
ハッスル **hassuru** hustle
はす **hasu** lotus
ハスキー(な) **hasukī** (**na**) husky
旗 **hata** flag; colors MIL
はたち, 二十歳 **hatachi** twenty (years old)
畑 **hatake** field
はためく **hatameku** flap; flutter
破たん **hatan** breakup, failure
働かせる **hatarakaseru** exercise *caution, restraint*; (make) work
働き者(の) **hatarakimono** (**no**) hard-working
働きすぎる **hataraki-sugiru** overwork
働く **hataraku** function; work
果たす **hatasu** fulfill
ハッチ **hatchi** hatch
ハッチバック車 **hatchibakku-sha** hatchback
果てしない **hateshinai** never-ending, unending
はと **hato** dove; pigeon
ハート **hāto** hearts
波止場 **hatoba** jetty; wharf
はと派 **hatoha** dove *fig*
初(の) **hatsu** (**no**) first
発 **-hatsu** departure; 大阪発 ***Ōsakahatsu*** departure from Osaka
発売 **hatsubai** launch, release (*of product*)
発売する **hatsubai suru** launch, release *new product*
発病 **hatsubyō** onset
発病させる **hatsubyō saseru** develop
発電機 **hatsudenki** dynamo; generator
発電所 **hatsudensho** power station
発電する **hatsuden suru** generate electricity
発煙筒 **hatsuentō** flare
発がん性物質 **hatsugansei-busshitsu** carcinogen
発がん性(の) **hatsugansei** (**no**) carcinogenic
発芽する **hatsuga suru** sprout
発言 **hatsugen** remark; contribution (*to debate*)
発言する **hatsugen suru** contribute
はつかだいこん **hatsuka-daikon** radish
発明 **hatsumei** invention
発明者 **hatsumei-sha** inventor
発明する **hatsumei suru** invent
初耳 **hatsumimi**: 初耳だ ***hatsumimi da*** it's the first time I've heard that

初詣 **hatsumōde** *first visit to a shrine in New Year*
発音 **hatsuon** pronunciation
発音する **hatsuon suru** pronounce
はったり **hattari** bluff; はったりをきかせる ***hattari o kikaseru*** bluff
発達 **hattatsu** development; growth
発達する **hattatsu suru** develop; grow
発展 **hatten** growth; development; evolution
発展させる **hatten saseru** develop
発展する **hatten suru** grow; grow up; develop; evolve
発展途上国 **hatten-tojōkoku** developing country
はう **hau** crawl; wriggle
ハウスボート **hausubōto** houseboat
早い **hayai** early
速い **hayai** fast, quick, swift, speedy
早死に **hayajini** untimely death
早く **hayaku** early ◊ be quick!
速く **hayaku** fast
早まった **hayamatta** premature
早め(の) **hayame** (**no**) early
早める **hayameru** precipitate; hasten
早送り **hayaokuri** fast forward
早送りする **hayaokuri suru** fast forward
はやり(の) **hayari** (**no**) trendy, in
はやる **hayaru** become popular; become fashionable; flourish
速さ **haya-sa** speed, rapidity
早過ぎた **hayasugita** premature
はず **-hazu** should; ought; be supposed to
恥ずべき **hazubeki** disgraceful; shameful
恥ずかしがり(の) **hazukashigari** (**no**) shy
恥ずかしい **hazukashii** ashamed; embarrassing; …を恥ずかしく思う ***… o hazukashiku omou*** be ashamed of
辱める **hazukashimeru** disgrace; shame
恥ずかしそう(な) **hazukashisō** (**na**) sheepish
弾ませる **hazumaseru** bounce
弾み **hazumi** bound
はずみ **hazumi** impetus
弾む **hazumu** bounce
はずれ **hazure** fringe, edge; miss; outskirts
はずす **hazusu** undo, unfasten; ボタンをはずす ***botan o hazusu*** unbutton
屁 **he** fart; 屁をこぐ ***he o kogu*** fart
ヘアブラシ **heaburashi** hairbrush
ヘアダイ **headai** rinse
ヘアドライヤー **headoraiyā** hairdrier, hairdryer
ヘアカット **heakatto** haircut
ヘアピン **heapin** barrette; hairpin
ヘアピンカーブ **heapin-kābu** hairpin curve
ヘアスプレー **heasupurē** lacquer
ヘアスタイル **heasutairu** hairstyle
へび **hebi** snake
ヘビー級(の) **hebī-kyū** (**no**) heavyweight
ヘビースモーカー **hebī-sumōkā** heavy smoker
隔たり **hedatari** gap, distance
ヘッドハンター **heddo-hantā** headhunter
ヘッドホン **heddo-hon** headphones
ヘッドライト **heddo-raito** headlamp, headlight
ヘディング **hedingu** header (*in soccer*)
ヘディングする **hedingu suru** head *ball*
平凡 **heibon** mediocrity; triviality
平凡(な) **heibon** (**na**) average; mediocre; indifferent; conventional; humdrum
平地 **heichi** plain
兵役 **heieki** military service
平服 **heifuku** clothes for everyday wear
併合する **heigō suru** annex; merge
平方 **heihō** square MATH; 平方マイル ***heihô mairu*** square mile
平日 **heijitsu** weekday
陛下 **Heika** Your Majesty
閉館時間 **heikan-jikan** closing time
兵器 **heiki** armaments
平均 **heikin** average
平気(な) **heiki** (**na**) OK; unconcerned

平均寿命 **heikin-jumyō** life expectancy
平均して **heikin shite** on average
平均的(な) **heikinteki** (**na**) average
平行(の) **heikō** (**no**) parallel
平衡を保つ **heikō o tamotsu** maintain a balance
閉口させる **heikō saseru** stump, perplex
平行線 **heikōsen** parallel lines
平面図 **heimenzu** ground plan
平熱 **heinetsu** normal temperature
平穏(な) **heion** (**na**) quiet, peaceful
閉鎖 **heisa** closure
閉鎖される **heisa sareru** be closed down
閉鎖された **heisa sareta** disused
閉鎖する **heisa suru** close down, shut down
平成時代 **Heisei-jidai** Heisei era (*1989-*)
平静 **heisei** calm; 平静を保つ ***heisei o tamotsu*** keep one's temper
閉所恐怖症 **heisho-kyōfushō** claustrophobia
閉店 **heiten** closure
閉店時間 **heiten-jikan** closing time
閉店する **heiten suru** close
平和 **heiwa** peace
平和部隊 **Heiwa-butai** Peace Corps
平和主義 **heiwa-shugi** pacifism
平和主義者 **heiwa-shugi-sha** pacifist
平和的(な) **heiwateki** (**na**) peaceful
平然と **heizen to** calmly; coolly; in cold blood
平然とした **heizen to shita** nonchalant; unflappable
壁画 **hekiga** mural
へこませる **hekomaseru** dent
へこみ **hekomi** dent
へま **hema** blunder; へまをする ***hema o suru*** blunder; goof, trip up
偏 **hen** radical of a Chinese character
変圧器 **hen'atsuki** transformer
変動 **hendō** fluctuation; upheaval
変動する **hendō suru** fluctuate; float FIN
返事 **henji** answer, reply; 返事をする ***henji o suru*** answer
変人 **henjin** crank; freak; eccentric
変化 **henka** change; shift; variation; variety
変換 **henkan** conversion
変化に富んだ **henka ni tonda** checkered; varied
変換する **henkan suru** export COMPUT; convert COMPUT
変化する **henka suru** vary; change; transform
変形 **henkei** transformation
変形させる **henkei saseru** transform
偏見 **henken** bias; prejudice; myth *fig*; …に偏見を抱かせる ***... ni henken o idakaseru*** prejudice
偏見に基づいた **henken ni motozuita** bias(s)ed
偏見のある **henken no aru** prejudiced
変更 **henkō** alteration, change; revision
変更できない **henkō dekinai** irrevocable
変更する **henkō suru** change
返却 **henkyaku** return
返却する **henkyaku suru** return
編曲 **henkyoku** arrangement
編曲する **henkyoku suru** arrange
偏狭(な) **henkyō** (**na**) intolerant; narrow-minded
変(な) **hen** (**na**) odd, strange, weird
変な風に **hen na fū ni** funnily, oddly
へんぴ(な) **henpi** (**na**) out-of-the-way; remote
返済 **hensai** repayment
返済する **hensai suru** wipe out
変色させる **henshoku saseru** discolor
編集長 **henshūchō** editor-in-chief (*of magazine*)
編集局長 **henshū-kyokuchō** editor (*of newspaper*)
編集(の) **henshū** (**no**) editorial
編集者 **henshū-sha** editor (*of book*)
編集する **henshū suru** compile; edit
変装 **hensō** disguise; …に変装する ***... ni hensô suru*** disguise oneself as

変速機 **hensokuki** transmission MOT
変速レバー **hensoku-rebā** gear lever, gear shift
返送する **hensō suru** send back
変数 **hensū** variable MATH
変態 **hentai** pervert
変態(の) **hentai (no)** kinky
扁桃腺 **hentōsen** tonsils
扁桃腺炎 **hentōsen-en** tonsillitis
変造する **henzō suru** falsify; forge
偏頭痛 **henzutsū** migraine
減らす **herasu** reduce, cut down (on); run down; work off *flab*
へり **heri** border; hem; fringe
ヘリコプター **herikoputā** helicopter
ヘロイン **heroin** heroin
減る **heru** decline, drop off; shrink
ヘルメット **herumetto** helmet, crash helmet
ヘルニア **herunia** hernia
ヘルパー **herupā** helper
ヘルペス **herupesu** herpes
ヘルプ画面 **herupu-gamen** help screen
へそ **heso** navel
へそ曲り **hesomagari** contrary; sullen
へその緒 **heso no o** umbilical cord
下手(な) **heta (na)** incompetent; poor; lame *excuse*
下手に **heta ni** badly, poorly
へとへとになる **hetoheto ni naru** worn-out
へとへと(の) **hetoheto (no)** grueling; run-down
へつらう **hetsurau** butter up; flatter
部屋 **heya** room; apartment
部屋ばき **heyabaki** slippers
日 **hi** day
火 **hi** fire; 火がつく ***hi ga tsuku*** catch fire; light up *cigarette*; Xに火をつける ***X ni hi o tsukeru*** set X on fire
比 **hi** ratio; equal
費 **-hi** expenses
非… **hi…** non-; un-; im-
干上がる **hiagaru** parch; dry up
火花 **hibana** spark
非番である **hiban de aru** be off duty
ひばり **hibari** skylark
ひび **hibi** crack; ひびが入る ***hibi ga hairu*** crack
響き **hibiki** ring (*of voice*)
響く **hibiku** reverberate
ひび割れた **hibiwareta** cracked
ひぼう文書 **hibō-bunsho** libel
非暴力 **hi-bōryoku** nonviolence
非暴力(の) **hi-bōryoku (no)** nonviolent
ひだ飾り **hidakazari** ruffle (*on dress*)
左 **hidari** left
左側 **hidarigawa** left
左側(の) **hidarigawa (no)** left-hand
左利き(の) **hidarikiki (no)** left-handed
左(の) **hidari (no)** left
左手(の) **hidarite (no)** left-hand
ひどい **hidoi** bad, awful; acute *embarrassment*; gross *exaggeration*; heavy *cold*; murderous *look*; total *disaster* ◊ it's a disgrace
日時計 **hidokei** sundial
ひどく **hidoku** badly; bitterly *cold*; dreadfully *expensive, sorry, pretty*; seriously; violently *object*
冷え **hie** chill
非衛生的(な) **hieiseiteki (na)** unsanitary, unhygienic
冷える **hieru** freeze
皮膚 **hifu** skin
日帰り旅行 **higaeri-ryokō** daytrip
被害 **higai** damage; loss; 被害を受ける ***higai o ukeru*** be damaged
被害者 **higai-sha** victim
彼岸 **higan** the Equinoctial Week
日傘 **higasa** sunshade
東 **higashi** east
東から(の) **higashi kara (no)** east, easterly
東(の) **higashi (no)** east, eastern
東シナ海 **Higashi-shinakai** East China Sea
ひげ **hige** beard; whiskers; ひげをそる ***hige o soru*** have a shave
悲劇 **higeki** tragedy
悲劇(の) **higeki (no)** tragic
非現実的(な) **higenjitsuteki (na)** impractical; unrealistic; unreal
ひげそり **higesori** shaver; razor

非合法(の) **higōhō (no)** illegal
日ごとに **higoto ni** day by day
ひぐま **higuma** brown bear
批判 **hihan** criticism
批判する **hihan suru** criticize
批判的(な) **hihanteki (na)** critical; unfavorable
批評 **hihyō** review, write-up
批評する **hihyō suru** review
ひいき **hiiki** favor; partiality
ひいき目 **hiikime** bias
ひいき目に見て **hiikime ni mite** bias(s)ed
ひいきにする **hiiki ni suru** patronize
ひじ **hiji** elbow
ひじ掛け **hijikake** armrest
ひじ掛け椅子 **hijikakeisu** armchair
非常口 **hijōguchi** emergency exit, fire escape
非常階段 **hijō-kaidan** fire escape
非常勤(の) **hijōkin (no)** part-time
非情(な) **hijō (na)** heartless
非常に **hijō ni** very; highly; greatly; much; unusually
非常識(な) **hijōshiki (na)** thoughtless; lacking common sense
控え目(な) **hikaeme (no)** modest; reserved; unobtrusive; unpretentious
日陰 **hikage** out of the sun, in the shade
日陰(の) **hikage (no)** shady
比較 **hikaku** comparison
非核地帯 **hikakuchitai** nuclear-free zone
比較できる **hikaku dekiru** comparable
比較する **hikaku suru** compare
比較的 **hikakuteki** comparative ◊ comparatively, relatively
悲観論 **hikanron** pessimism
悲観論者 **hikanron-sha** pessimist
悲観的(な) **hikanteki (na)** pessimistic
ひかれる **hikareru** have an affinity for; be fascinated by; be attracted to
光 **hikari** light; 光を注ぐ ***hikari o sosogu*** shed light on
光り輝く **hikari-kagayaku** brilliant
光る **hikaru** gleam; glint; shine
光った **hikatta** shiny
非建設的(な) **hikensetsuteki (na)** destructive
秘訣 **hiketsu** formula; secret; key
ひき **hiki** *countword for animals, fish etc*
引き上げ ***hikiage*** rise, hike
引き上げる **hikiageru** raise *wages*; withdraw *army*
引き合う **hikiau** pay off; be profitable
引き出し **hikidashi** drawer; withdrawal
引き出す **hikidasu** draw, withdraw, take out
引き戸 **hikido** sliding door
ひきがえる **hikigaeru** toad
引き金 **hikigane** trigger; 引き金になる ***hikigane ni naru*** trigger; set off
引き離す **hikihanasu** separate, pull apart; pull away
率いる **hikiiru** head, lead
引き換えに **hikikae ni** in exchange
引き返す **hikikaesu** turn back, double back; retrace
引き込まれる **hikikomareru** compelling
引き逃げ事故 **hikinige-jiko** hit-and-run accident
ひき肉 **hikiniku** ground meat
引き伸ばし **hikinobashi** enlargement, blow-up (*of photo*)
引き伸ばす **hikinobasu** enlarge, blow up *photo*; pad *speech*; spin out
引き抜く **hikinuku** extract; pull; pull up
引き起こす **hikiokosu** cause; create; generate; provoke; rouse; stir up
引き落し **hikiotoshi** debit
引き落しされる **hikiotoshi sareru** be debited
引き下がる **hikisagaru** retreat; back off; climb down
引き下げる **hikisageru** lower; reduce
引き裂く **hikisaku** tear *paper, cloth*
引き締まった **hikishimatta** firm; lean; trim
引き潮 **hikishio** ebb tide
引き止める **hikitomeru** detain, keep; stall

引き継ぐ **hikitsugu** take over
引き付ける **hikitsukeru** attract
引き続いて **hikitsuzuite** in the wake of, following
引き受ける **hikiukeru** undertake
引き分け **hikiwake** draw, tie
引き分ける **hikiwakeru** draw
引き渡し **hikiwatashi** extradition; surrender
引き渡し条約 **hikiwatashi-jōyaku** extradition treaty
引き渡す **hikiwatasu** extradite; hand over (*to authorities*); surrender
引き寄せる **hikiyoseru** draw, attract; draw up *chair*
引き算 **hikizan** subtraction
引きずり出す **hikizuridasu** drag out
引きずる **hikizuru** drag; 足を引きずって歩く ***ashi o hikizutte aruku*** shuffle
引っかける **hikkakeru** hitch; suspend; catch; throw on *clothes*; splash *water*; deceive; pick up *man, woman*
引っかき傷 **hikkakikizu** scratch
引っかく **hikkaku** scratch
ひっきりなしに **hikkirinashi ni** perpetually
引っ込める **hikkomeru** retract; draw back
引込み思案(の) **hikkomijian (no)** retiring; conservative
引っ込んでいる **hikkonde iru** make oneself scarce
引っ越す **hikkosu** move out, move house
ひっくり返る **hikkurikaeru** overturn; capsize
ひっくり返す **hikkurikaesu** capsize; knock over; overturn; reverse *decision*
飛行 **hikō** flight; navigation
非行 **hikō** delinquency
飛行時間 **hikō-jikan** flight time
飛行場 **hikōjō** airfield; landing field, landing strip
被後見人 **hikōken-nin** ward (*child*)
飛行機 **hikōki** airplane; 飛行機で ***hikôki de*** by air
飛行機雲 **hikōki-gumo** vapor trail
被告 **hikoku** defendant
被告弁護人 **hikoku-bengo-nin** defense lawyer
被告側証人 **hikokugawa-shō-nin** defense witness
被告人 **hikoku-nin** the accused; defendant
非行に走った **hikō ni hashitta** delinquent
非公式には **hikōshiki ni wa** unofficially; 非公式に言う ***hikôshiki ni iu*** say off the record
非公式(の) **hikōshiki (no)** informal
非行少年 **hikō-shōnen** juvenile delinquent
飛行する **hikō suru** navigate
ひく **hiku** run down, knock down; grind *coffee, meat*; saw *wood*
引く **hiku** attract, draw; go down (*of swelling*); subtract
弾く **hiku** play MUS
低い **hikui** deep; low
低くする **hikuku suru** lower; muffle
低さ **hiku-sa** depth
非居住者 **hi-kyojūsha** nonresident
卑きょう(な) **hikyō (na)** unfair; cowardly
非協力的(な) **hikyōryokuteki (na)** uncooperative
暇 **hima** leisure
ひ孫 **himago** great-grandchild
肥満 **himan** obesity
暇(な) **hima (na)** idle
悲鳴 **himei** scream; shriek; yelp; 悲鳴をあげる ***himei o ageru*** scream; shriek; yelp
秘密 **himitsu** secret, confidence
秘密(の) **himitsu (no)** secret; confidential; clandestine; hidden
ひも **himo** band; cord; string
ひな祭り **Hina-matsuri** Doll Festival
非難 **hinan** accusation; blame; attack; reproach; condemnation
避難 **hinan** shelter; refuge
ひな人形 **hinaningyō** *set of ornamental dolls*
避難させる **hinan saseru** evacuate
非難すべき **hinansubeki** reprehensible

避難する **hinan suru** shelter, take refuge; evacuate
非難する **hinan suru** attack; accuse; condemn; rebuke
日なた **hinata** sunshine; sunny place
日なたぼっこする **hinatabokko suru** bask in the sun
頻度 **hindo** frequency
ひねくれた **hinekureta** warped, twisted
皮肉 **hiniku** cynicism; sarcasm; irony
皮肉(な) **hiniku (na)** cynical; ironic(al); dry
皮肉屋 **hiniku-ya** cynic
避妊 **hinin** birth control, contraception
避妊具 **hinin-gu** contraceptive device
否認する **hinin suru** disclaim; deny
避妊薬 **hinin-yaku** contraceptive
貧弱(な) **hinjaku (na)** lamentable
貧血である **hinketsu de aru** be anemic
貧困 **hinkon** poverty
品目 **hinmoku** item
日の出 **hinode** sunrise
日の丸 **hinomaru** Japanese national flag, Rising Sun
非能率的(な) **hinōritsuteki (na)** inefficient
頻繁(な) **hinpan (na)** frequent
品詞 **hinshi** part of speech
品質 **hinshitsu** quality
品質管理 **hinshitsu-kanri** quality control
品種 **hinshu** breed; type; category
ヒント **hinto** hint
ひいおばあさん **hīobāsan** great-grandmother
ひいおじいさん **hīojīsan** great-grandfather
引っ張りだこである **hipparidako de aru** in demand, very popular
引っ張る **hipparu** pull, draw; yank; tow
引っぱたく **hippataku** whack; smack
ひらがな **hiragana** *the rounded Japanese syllabary*
避雷針 **hiraishin** lightning conductor
開いた **hiraita** open
開く **hiraku** open; unfold; throw *party*
ひらめ **hirame** plaice; sole
ひらめき **hirameki** brainstorm
ひらめく **hirameku** have a flash of inspiration
平泳ぎ **hiraoyogi** breaststroke
平手打ち **hirateuchi** smack; slap
ひれ **hire** fin
比例した **hirei shita** proportional
ヒレ肉 **hireniku** fillet
ヒレステーキ **hire sutēki** fillet steak
卑劣(な) **hiretsu (na)** contemptible; rotten; shabby
ひりひり痛む **hirihiri itamu** sting; smart
ひりひりする **hirihiri suru** sting; smart
疲労 **hirō** fatigue
ヒーロー **hīrō** hero
広場 **hiroba** square
広々とした **hirobiro to shita** open; roomy, spacious
披露宴 **hirōen** wedding reception
広がり **hirogari** expanse; spread; stretch
広がる **hirogaru** dilate; extend; unfold; stretch ◊ pervasive
広がった **hirogatta** widespread
広げる **hirogeru** broaden; enlarge; expand; unfold; unroll; spread, lay
広い **hiroi** broad, wide; great
ヒロイン **hiroin** heroine
拾い読み **hiroiyomi**: 本を拾い読みする ***hon o hiroiyomi suru*** browse through a book
広く **hiroku** widely
広くなる **hiroku naru** broaden, widen
広くする **hiroku suru** widen
広まる **hiromaru** become widespread; pervade
広める **hiromeru** spread
広さ **hiro-sa** breadth, width
拾う **hirou** pick up
昼 **hiru** midday; daytime
ヒール **hīru** heel
昼ごはん **hirugohan** lunch
昼間 **hiruma** day
昼休み **hiruyasumi** lunch break
被災地 **hisaichi** disaster area

悲惨(な) **hisan (na)** disastrous
悲惨さ **hisan-sa** misery
ひさし **hisashi** eaves
ひさしぶり **hisashiburi** a long time; ひさしぶりです ***hisashiburi desu*** long time no see
非生産的(な) **hiseisanteki (na)** unproductive
ひし形 **hishi-gata** diamond (*shape*); lozenge
秘書 **hisho** secretary
秘書(の) **hisho (no)** secretarial
ひそか(な) **hisoka (na)** furtive, stealthy; covert
ひそかに **hisoka ni** secretly; ひそかに…する ***hisoka ni … suru*** do … in secret
筆跡 **hisseki** handwriting
必死で **hisshi de** like mad
必死に **hisshi ni** madly
必死(の) **hisshi (no)** desperate
必修(の) **hisshū (no)** compulsory
必須(の) **hissu (no)** mandatory; imperative
ひすい **hisui** jade
ヒステリー **hisuterī** hysteria
ヒーター **hītā** heater
額 **hitai** forehead, brow
ひたむき(な) **hitamuki (na)** single-minded
悲嘆 **hitan** lament; 悲嘆にくれている ***hitan ni kurete iru*** be prostrate with grief
浸す **hitasu** steep; dip
ヒッチハイクする **hitchi-haiku suru** hitch, hitchhike
否定 **hitei** denial
否定できない **hitei dekinai** undeniable
否定(の) **hitei (no)** negative
否定する **hitei suru** contradict; deny, repudiate
人 **hito** man; person; character; creature
一… **hito…** (*prefix*) one; a; 一きれ ***hitokire*** a slice; 一口 ***hitokuchi*** a bite; a gulp; 一組 ***hitokumi*** a deck, a pack (*of cards*); a block (*of shares*)
人々 **hitobito** people, folk
ひとで **hitode** starfish
人手 **hitode** hand, worker
人手不足(の) **hitode-busoku (no)** short-staffed, understaffed
ひとでなし **hitodenashi** beast (*person*); brute; monster
人柄 **hitogara** character; personality
人込み **hitogomi** crowd, crush
人殺し **hitogoroshi** killer; murderer
人質 **hitojichi** hostage; 人質にとられる ***hitojichi ni torareru*** be taken hostage
一言 **hitokoto** a (brief) word
人前で **hitomae de** in public
ひとまとめにする **hitomatome ni suru** bundle up
ひと目 **hitome** a glimpse
ヒト免疫不全ウィルス **hito-men'eki-fuzen-uirusu** human immunodeficiency virus, HIV
人並みはずれた **hitonami-hazureta** uncanny
人なつこい **hitonatsukoi** friendly
人(の) **hito (no)** human
ひとり **hitori** one person; ひとり息子/娘 ***hitori-musuko / musume*** only son / daughter
ひとりで **hitori de** alone; by oneself, on one's own
独り言 **hitorigoto** talking to oneself
ひとりっこ **hitorikko** only child
一人(の) **hitori (no)** one (*person*)
ひとりよがり(の) **hitoriyogari (no)** self-righteous; smug
ひとさじ **hitosaji** a spoonful; a portion; a drop
人さし指 **hitosashiyubi** index finger, forefinger
一騒ぎ **hitosawagi** a fuss
等しい **hitoshii** equal
等しく **hitoshiku** equally
一坪 **hitotsubo** *area measure of 3.6 square yards*
一つ **hitotsu** one
ひとつまみ **hitotsumami** a pinch
一つにする **hitotsu ni suru** unite
一つ(の) **hitotsu (no)** one (*thing*); single, sole
一山 **hitoyama** a pile; a heap
人里離れた **hitozato hanareta** secluded

ひつぎ **hitsugi** casket, coffin
羊 **hitsuji** sheep
羊の肉 **hitsuji no niku** mutton
必需品 **hitsujuhin** commodity; necessity
悲痛(な) **hitsū (na)** heartbreaking; poignant
必要 **hitsuyō** necessity; need
必要経費 **hitsuyō-keihi** expense account
必要(な) **hitsuyō (na)** necessary, required; obligatory
必要とする **hitsuyō to suru** require, necessitate
必然的に **hitsuzenteki ni** inevitably; necessarily
ひったくる **hittakuru** snatch, grab
匹敵する **hitteki suru** be comparable; be similar ◊ equal, rival
匹敵するもの **hitteki suru mono** equal
ヒット **hitto** hit
ヒットチャート **hitto-chāto** charts MUS
ヒット作 **hittosaku** blockbuster
引っつける **hittsukeru** tape; stick
引っつく **hittsuku** stick; stick to
悲運 **hiun** misfortune; doom
冷や **hiya** cold sake
冷やかす **hiyakasu** tease; make fun of
日焼け **hiyake** sunburn; suntan, tan
日焼け止め **hiyake-dome** sunblock
日焼けする **hiyake suru** get a suntan
飛躍的発展 **hiyakuteki-hatten** breakthrough
冷やす **hiyasu** chill *wine*
費用 **hiyō** cost, expense
日よけ **hiyoke** awning; sunshade
ひよこ **hiyoko** chick
肥沃(な) **hiyoku (na)** fertile, rich
比喩的(な) **hiyuteki (na)** figurative, metaphorical
膝 **hiza** knee, lap
日差し**hizashi** sunlight
ひざ掛け **hizakake** (travel) rug
膝小僧 **hizakozō** kneecap
ひざまずく**hizamazuku** kneel down
日付 **hizuke** date; 日付を入れる ***hizuke o ireru*** date *check etc*
帆 **ho** sail
ほお **hō** cheek
法 **hō** act, law
方 **hō** direction; side; …の方へ ***… no hô e*** to; toward; やめておいた方がいい ***yamete oita hô ga ii*** I'd really better not; …のほうを好む ***… no hô o konomu*** prefer
法案 **hōan** bill POL
ホバークラフト **hobākurafuto** hovercraft
ほお紅 **hōbeni** blusher
ほうび **hōbi** reward
保母 **hobo** nursery school teacher
ほお骨 **hōbone** cheekbone
放置 **hōchi** neglect
補聴器 **hochōki** hearing aid
程 **hodo** around; 一週間程 ***isshûkan hodo*** around a week; 早ければ早い程いい ***hayakereba hayai hodo ii*** the sooner the better
歩道 **hodō** sidewalk; walk
報道 **hōdō** journalism; coverage (*by media*); report; publication
ほどほどに **hodohodo ni** in moderation
報道陣 **hōdōjin** the press
報道記事 **hōdō-kiji** news report
ほどく **hodoku** disentangle; undo; unfold; untie
歩道橋 **hodōkyō** footbridge
報道する **hōdō suru** report
ほどよい **hodoyoi** moderate
放映されている **hōei sarete iru** be on (*of TV program*)
ほえる **hoeru** bark; bellow; roar
報復 **hōfuku** reprisal; retaliation
報復する **hōfuku suru** take reprisals; retaliate
豊富(な) **hōfu (na)** abundant; plentiful; rich
豊富にする **hōfu ni suru** enrich
豊富さ **hōfu-sa** abundance; plenty
邦画 **hōga** Japanese movie
法外(な) **hōgai (na)** exorbitant, prohibitive
方角 **hōgaku** direction; compass point

法学 **hōgaku** law (*as subject*)
捕鯨 **hogei** whaling
砲撃 **hōgeki** shellfire
砲撃される **hōgeki sareru** come under shellfire
砲撃する **hōgeki suru** shell
方言 **hōgen** dialect
保護 **hogo** conservation; protection
縫合 **hōgō** stitches; seam; suture
保護観察官 **hogo-kansatsukan** probation officer
保護区域 **hogo-kuiki** sanctuary
保護する **hogo suru** protect; safeguard; shield
縫合する **hōgō suru** stitch up
ほぐす **hogusu** relax; unravel
方法 **hōhō** manner, way; means; method; system
ほほ笑み **hohoemi** smile
ほほ笑む **hohoemu** smile
包囲 **hōi** siege
方位磁針 **hōi-jishin** compass
保育 **hoiku** nursing
保育園 **hoikuen** nursery (school)
ホイル **hoiru** tinfoil, foil
保持者 **hoji-sha** holder
補助教材 **hojo-kyōzai** teaching aid
補助(の) **hojo (no)** auxiliary
補助的(な) **hojoteki (na)** subsidiary; subordinate
補充する **hojū suru** refill; supplement
他, ほか **hoka** etc
放火 **hōka** arson
放課後 **hōkago** after school; 放課後に残す ***hôkago ni nokosu*** keep in (*at school*)
崩壊 **hōkai** fall, collapse (*of government*)
崩壊した **hōkai shita** broken *home*
崩壊する **hōkai suru** crumble; disintegrate; fall
捕獲 **hokaku** capture
保管 **hokan** storage
他に **hoka ni** apart from, besides; as well as, in addition to; 他にだれがそこにいましたか ***hoka ni dare ga soko ni imashita ka*** who else was there?; 他にだれも…ない ***hoka ni dare mo i nai*** there's no one else here; ほかに何か ***hoka ni nani ka*** anything else?
他(の) **hoka (no)** other; 他の人 ***hoka no hito*** the other; 他の人たち ***hoka no hitotachi*** (other) people; 他の物 ***hoka no mono*** another; the other; 他の場所では ***hoka no basho de wa*** elsewhere; 他の人たちは皆行く ***hoka no hitotachi wa mina iku*** everyone else is going
保管されている **hokan sarete iru** be in storage
保管する **hokan suru** keep safe; look after
包括的(な) **hōkatsuteki (na)** comprehensive
保険 **hoken** insurance; 保険に入っている ***hoken ni haitte iru*** be insured; 保険をかける ***hoken o kakeru*** insure
保険会社 **hoken-gaisha** insurance company
保険料 **hokenryō** insurance premium; 保険料運賃込み価格 ***hokenryô-unchin-komkakaku*** CIF, cost insurance freight
保険証 **hokenshō** health insurance identity card
保険証券 **hoken-shōken** (insurance) policy
保険証書 **hoken-shōsho** (insurance) policy
補欠 **hoketsu** reserve, substitute
ほうき **hōki** broom
保菌者 **hokin-sha** carrier (*of disease*)
放棄する **hōki suru** renounce
北海道 **Hokkaidō** Hokkaido
ホッケー **hokkē** (ice) hockey
ホック **hokku** hook; snap fastener
北極 **Hokkyoku** North Pole
北極(の) **hokkyoku (no)** polar
方向 **hōkō** direction
歩行器 **hokōki** walker
報告 **hōkoku** account; submission
報告書 **hōkoku-sho** report
報告する **hōkoku suru** report
ほこり **hokori** dust ; ほこりを払う ***hokori o harau*** dust
誇り **hokori** pride; 誇りに思う ***hokori***

ni omou be proud of; 誇りにする ***hokori ni suru*** pride oneself on
ほこりっぽい **hokorippoi** dusty
歩行者 **hokō-sha** pedestrian
方向転換 **hōkō-tenkan** turn
方向転換する **hōkō-tenkan suru** turn; turn around
方向づける **hōkōzukeru** shape
北米 **Hokubei** North America
ほくろ **hokuro** mole (*on skin*)
北西 **hokusei** northwest
北東 **hokutō** northeast
補強する **hokyō suru** reinforce
ほめ言葉 **homekotoba** compliment
方面 **hōmen** direction; district; line (of business)
ほめる **homeru** compliment
ホモ **homo** homosexual, gay; fag
訪問 **hōmon** visit
ホモ(の) **homo (no)** homosexual, gay
訪問者 **hōmon-sha** caller
訪問する **hōmon suru** visit
ホーム **hōmu** home; home base; (railroad) platform
ホームムービー **hōmu-mūbī** home movie
ホームラン **hōmu ran** home run
ホームレス **hōmuresu** the homeless, streetpeople
ホームレス(の) **hōmuresu (no)** homeless
ホームシックになる **homushikku ni naru** be homesick
法務省 **Hōmushō** Japanese Ministry of Justice
本 **hon** book
本 **-hon** *countword for long thin things*
本… **hon…** real, genuine
本部 **honbu** headquarters
本文 **honbun** text
本題 **hondai** the main issue; 本題に入る ***hondai ni hairu*** get to the point
本棚 **hondana** bookcase
本土 **hondo** mainland
本堂 **hondō** *main building of a temple*
骨 **hone** bone; 骨の折れる ***hone no oreru*** painstaking
骨組 **honegumi** frame; framework
本格的(な) **honkakuteki (na)** real; authentic
本気でない **honki de nai** playful; not serious
本気になる **honki ni naru** knuckle down
香港 **Honkon** Hong Kong
本拠地 **honkyochi** base, center; 本拠地にする ***honkyochi ni suru*** be based in
本物 **honmono** the real thing
本物(の) **honmono (no)** authentic; original; real
本音と建て前 **honne to tatemae** what you really think and the face you put on
本人 **honnin** the person in question
ほんの **hon no** mere; 彼はほんの六歳です ***kare wa hon no rokusai desu*** he' s only 6
本能 **honnō** instinct
本能的に **honnōteki ni** instinctively
ほのお **honō** flame
ほのか(な) **honoka (na)** vague; faint
ほのめかす **honomekasu** imply, insinuate
本来 **honrai** originally; from the beginning; fundamentally
本籍地 **honsekichi** official address (*for registration purposes*)
本社 **honsha** head office
本質 **honshitsu** nature; essence
本質的に **honshitsuteki ni** essentially
本州 **Honshū** Honshu
本当に **hontō ni** absolutely, completely; actually; really, truly; indeed; very much
本当(の) **hontō (no)** real; true
本屋 **hon-ya** bookseller; bookstore
翻訳 **hon'yaku** translation
翻訳者 **hon'yaku-sha** translator
翻訳する **hon'yaku suru** translate; 英語に翻訳する ***Eigo ni hon'yaku suru*** translate into English
ほ乳びん **honyūbin** bottle
ほ乳動物 **honyū-dōbutsu** mammal
北方領土 **Hoppō-ryōdo** Northern Territories

ホップ **hoppu** hop
ほら **hora** hey; ほら、やってごらんなさい ***hora, yatte goran nasai*** go on, do it!; ほらを吹く ***hora o fuku*** brag; tell a tall story
洞穴 **hora-ana** cave
ほら話 **horabanashi** yarn, tall story
ホラー映画 **horā-eiga** horror movie
ほうれん草 **hōrensō** spinach
掘り出し物 **horidashimono** catch; lucky find; bargain
ほうり出す **hōridasu** fling out, throw out
掘り起こす **horiokosu** dig up, dredge up
法律 **hōritsu** law; statute; legislation
法律違反 **hōritsu-ihan** violation of the law
法律(の) **hōritsu (no)** legal
ほうろう **hōrō** enamel
滅びる **horobiru** be ruined; die out; become extinct
ホログラム **horoguramu** hologram
放浪する **hōrō suru** wander around
掘る **horu** dig; excavate; drill
彫る **horu** engrave
ホール **hōru** hall
ホルモン **horumon** hormone
捕虜 **horyo** captive; prisoner of war
保留する **horyū suru** reserve; withhold
補佐官 **hosakan** assistant, aide
宝石 **hōseki** gem; jewel; (precious) stone
宝石類 **hōseki-rui** jewelry
宝石商 **hōseki-shō** jeweler
保釈 **hoshaku** bail; 保釈中で ***hoshakuchû de*** on bail
保釈金 **hoshakukin** bail (*money*)
保釈させる **hoshaku saseru** bail out
放射能 **hōshanō** radiation, radioactivity
放射性(の) **hōshasei (no)** radioactive
放射線療法 **hōshasen-ryōhō** radiotherapy
放射する **hōsha suru** radiate
星 **hoshi** star
欲しい **hoshii** want; would like to; wish, hope
干しぶどう **hoshibudō** currant; raisin
星印 **hoshijirushi** asterisk
干し草 **hoshikusa** hay
方針 **hōshin** course of action; policy
星占い **hoshiuranai** astrology; horoscope
星占い師 **hoshiuranai-shi** astrologer
保証 **hoshō** guarantee; warranty; assurance; security (*in job*)
保障 **hoshō** guarantee
補償 **hoshō** compensation
補償額 **hoshō-gaku** (insurance) cover
保証期間 **hoshō-kikan** guarantee period
補償金 **hoshō-kin** compensation
捕食動物 **hoshoku-dōbutsu** predator
保証人 **hoshō-nin** guarantor; witness; sponsor; 保証人となる ***hoshô-nin to naru*** sponsor; 保証人としてサインする ***hoshô-nin toshite sain suru*** witness
保証する **hoshō suru** guarantee; answer for, vouch for
補償する **hoshō suru** compensate
報酬 **hōshū** compensation; remuneration
保守的(な) **hoshuteki (na)** conservative, conventional
放送 **hōsō** broadcast; broadcasting
包装 **hōsō** packaging
細い **hosoi** fine; thin
補足料金 **hosoku-ryōkin** supplementary fee
包装紙 **hōsōshi** wrapping paper
舗装する **hosō suru** pave
放送する **hōsō suru** broadcast
包装する **hōsō suru** package
発作 **hossa** bout; fit; seizure
発足する **hossoku suru** inaugurate
ほっそりした **hossori shita** slender, slim
干す **hosu** dry
ホース **hōsu** hose
ホスピス **hosupisu** hospice
ホステス **hosutesu** hostess
包帯 **hōtai** bandage; dressing; 包帯をする ***hôtai o suru*** bandage

ほたる **hotaru** firefly
ホッチキス **hotchikisu®** stapler
法廷 **hōtei** court; courtroom; law court
方程式 **hōteishiki** equation
ほてる **hoteru** glow; feel warm
ホテル **hoteru** hotel
放とう **hōtō** debauchery
仏 **Hotoke** Buddha
仏 **hotoke** the deceased
ほとんど **hotondo** almost; nearly, all but ◊ most; ほとんど…ない ***hotondo...nai*** scarcely; ほとんど…しない ***hotondo... shinai*** little; ほとんど…と同じ ***hotondo ... to onaji*** in comparison with, next to; ほとんど残っていない ***hotondo nokotte inai*** there are very few of them left
ほととぎす **hototogisu** Japanese cuckoo
ほったらかしにされた **hottarakashi ni sareta** neglected
ほったらかしにする **hottarakashi ni suru** neglect
ほったらかし(の) **hottarakashi (no)** unattended
ホットドッグ **hotto-doggu** hot dog
ホットケーキ **hotto-kēki** pancake
ほっとした **hotto shita** that's a relief
ホワイトハウス **Howaito-hausu** White House
ホワイトカラー **howaito-karā** white-collar worker
抱擁 **hōyō** cuddle; embrace
保存 **hozon** preservation
保存する **hozon suru** preserve; save COMPUT; store COMPUT; cure *meat, fish*
保存剤 **hozonzai** preservative
百科辞典 **hyakka-jiten** encyclopedia
百 **hyaku** hundred; 百番目(の) ***hyakubanme (no)*** hundredth
百万 **hyakuman** million
百万長者 **hyakuman-chōja** millionaire
百周年 **hyakushūnen** centenary, centennial
百日ぜき **hykunichizeki** whooping cough
ひょう **hyō** hail; leopard
表 **hyō** table (*of figures*)
票 **hyō** vote
評判 **hyōban** reputation; standing
評判の良い **hyōban no yoi** reputable
表題 **hyōdai** heading, title
氷河 **hyōga** glacier
表現 **hyōgen** expression; show, display
表現力 **hyōgenryoku** expressive power
表現する **hyōgen suru** express; phrase; represent
標本 **hyōhon** specimen MED
表示 **hyōji** sign
表情 **hyōjō** expression
表情に富む **hyōjō ni tomu** expressive
表情の豊か(な) **hyōjō no yutaka (na)** expressive
標準 **hyōjun** standard; 標準以下である ***hyôjun ika de aru*** not be up to standard
標準語 **hyōjungo** standard Japanese / English etc; standard language
標準以下(の) **hyōjun-ika (no)** substandard
評価 **hyōka** valuation; evaluation
評価する **hyōka suru** assess, evaluate; consider
票決 **hyōketsu** vote
標高 **hyōkō** altitude
表明する **hyōmei suru** voice *opinions*
表面 **hyōmen** surface
表面(の) **hyōmen (no)** cosmetic *changes, reasons*
表面上は **hyōmenjō wa** on the surface, superficially
表面的(な) **hyōmenteki (na)** outward; superficial
評論 **hyōron** criticism; review
評論家 **hyōronka** critic, reviewer
漂流する **hyōryū suru** drift
表紙 **hyōshi** (front) cover
標識 **hyōshiki** sign
氷点 **hyōten** freezing point
氷山 **hyōzan** iceberg
ヒューズ **hyūzu** fuse; ヒューズが飛んだ ***hyûzu ga tonda*** the fuse blew

I

胃 **i** stomach
位 **-i** rank; position; 第4位 ***daiyon'i*** fourth
医 **-i** doctor; 外科医 ***gekai*** surgeon
いばる **ibaru** brag; be arrogant
居場所 **ibasho** whereabouts
いびき **ibiki** snoring; いびきをかく ***ibiki o kaku*** snore
いぼ **ibo** wart
異母兄弟 **ibo-kyōdai** stepbrother
異母姉妹 **ibo-shimai** stepsister
イブニングドレス **ibuningu-doresu** evening dress
いぶす **ibusu** smoke *bacon*
遺物 **ibutsu** relic
一 **ichi** one; 一か八かやってみる ***ichi ka bachi ka yatte miru*** take a chance
位置 **ichi** position
市場 **ichiba** market; marketplace
一番 **ichiban** the best, the top
一番に **ichiban ni** first
一番(の) **ichiban (no)** foremost
一番好き(な) **ichiban suki (na)** favorite
一番少ない **ichiban sukunai** least
一番遠く(の) **ichiban tōku (no)** furthest
一番年上(の) **ichiban toshiue (no)** eldest
一番上(の) **ichiban ue (no)** topmost
一べつ **ichibetsu** glance
一部 **ichibu** part; fraction; segment; patch
一部分は **ichibubun wa** part, partly
一部始終 **ichibu-shijū** all the details; the whole story
一団 **ichidan** batch; convoy; corps; group
一度 **ichido** once
一度に **ichido ni** all at once
一月 **ichigatsu** January
いちご **ichigo** strawberry
一合 **ichigō** *measure of 0.38 pints*
一群 **ichigun** a cluster
一員 **ichiin** member
いちじく **ichijiku** fig
一陣の風 **ichijin no kaze** blast; gust
一時(の) **ichiji (no)** temporary
著しい **ichijirushii** marked; conspicuous; remarkable
著しく **ichijirushiku** eminently
一時停止標識 **ichijiteishi-hyōshiki** stop sign
一時停止する **ichiji-teishi suru** pause
一時的(な) **ichijiteki (na)** momentary
一畳 **ichijō** *area measure of a tatami mat*
一枚 **ichimai** a copy (*of record, CD*); an exposure; 紙切れ一枚 ***kami ichimai*** a piece of paper
一面 **ichimen** front page; 一面のニュース ***ichimen no nyûsu*** front page news
一面の **ichimen no** a blanket of
一味 **ichimi** gang
一文なし(の) **ichimon-nashi (no)** broke, penniless
一年間(の) **ichinenkan (no)** annual, yearly
一日 **ichinichi** one day
一人前 **ichinin-mae** a portion
一応 **ichiō** for the time being; roughly
一卵性双生児 **ichiransei-sōseiji** identical twins
一連(の) **ichiren (no)** stream of; string of; sequence
一律に **ichiritsu ni** across the board; evenly
一流(の) **ichiryū (no)** first-class, first-rate; classic, definitive
位置している **ichi shite iru** be situated

一話 **ichiwa** one episode, one installment
一族 **ichizoku** clan
いちょう **ichō** gingko
偉大(な) **idai (na)** great
遺伝 **iden** inheritance
遺伝性(の) **idensei (no)** hereditary
遺伝子 **idenshi** gene
遺伝子学 **idenshi-gaku** genetics
遺伝子学者 **idenshi-gakusha** geneticist
遺伝子工学 **idenshi-kōgaku** genetic engineering
遺伝子(の) **idenshi (no)** genetic
イデオロギー **ideologī** ideology
緯度 **ido** latitude
井戸 **ido** well
移動 **idō** migration; transfer
移動させる **idō saseru** move; transfer
移動する **idō suru** move; transfer; relocate; migrate
家 **ie** house
家出する **iede suru** run away from home
家柄 **iegara** pedigree; lineage
家元 **iemoto** *principal of a school of one of the Japanese arts*
イエローページ **ierōpēji** yellow pages
イエス **Iesu** Jesus
イエスキリスト **Iesu Kirisuto** Jesus Christ
イエスマン **iesuman** yesman
衣服 **ifuku** garment
以外 **igai** except; 八月以外なら ***hachigatsu igai nara*** except (for) August
意外 **igai** surprising; unexpected
医学 **igaku** medicine
医学博士 **igaku-hakushi** MD, Doctor of Medicine
医学(の) **igaku (no)** medical
鋳型 **igata** cast, mold
異議 **igi** objection
意義 **igi** significance
意義のある **igi no aru** meaningful
異議を唱える **igi o tonaeru** challenge; raise an objection
イギリス **Igirisu** Britain
イギリス人 **Igirisu-jin** British; Briton
イギリスポンド **Igirisu-pondo** pound sterling
以後 **igo** after; since; from now on
囲碁 **igo** the game of Go
居心地 **igokochi**: 居心地のいい ***igokochi no ii*** friendly; comfortable; 居心地の悪い ***igokochi no warui*** uncomfortable
偉業 **igyō** exploits; great undertaking
違反 **ihan** breach, violation
違反(の) **ihan (no)** illegal
違反する **ihan suru** violate, contravene
違法(の) **ihō (no)** illegal
違法行為 **ihō-kōi** misconduct
いい **ii** good; いいですね ***ii desu ne*** good idea!; いいですよ ***ii desu yo*** you're on; no problem; …といい仲になる ***… to ii naka ni naru*** have a good time with (*sexually*)
言い表せない **iiarawasenai** indescribable; inexpressible
言い表す **iiarawasu** describe; express
言い分 **iibun**: 言い分がある ***iibun ga aru*** have one's say
いいえ **iie** no; yes (*see* **no** *p504*)
言い張る **iiharu** insist
言いかえる **iikaeru** paraphrase
言い返す **iikaesu** retort
いい加減(な) **iikagen (na)** perfunctory; slack; いいかげんにしなさい ***iikagen ni shinasai*** that' s enough, calm down!; いいかげんにしてよ ***iikagen ni shite yo*** do me a favor!
言い方 **iikata** phrase
いい子ぶりっこ **iikoburikko** goody-goody
言い回し **iimawashi** expression; wording
委員 **iin** committee member
委員長 **iinchō** chairperson
委員会 **iinkai** board; committee; commission
言い逃れする **iinogare suru** stonewall
言い伝え **iitsutae** tradition
言い訳 **iiwake** excuse
言いようのない **iiyō no nai**

indescribable
言い寄る **iiyoru** proposition; make advances
維持 **iji** maintenance
意地 **iji** nature; pride; 意地の悪い ***iji no warui*** mean; nasty
維持管理 **iji-kanri** upkeep
いじくる **ijikuru** meddle; toy with
いじめ **ijime** bullying
いじめっ子 **ijimekko** bully
いじめる **ijimeru** bully; pick on; tease
いじる **ijiru** fumble; interfere with; tinker with; twiddle
維持する **iji suru** hold, maintain; preserve
意地悪(な) **ijiwaru** (**na**) bitchy; spiteful; wicked
異常 **ijō** freak
以上 **ijō** not less than; plus; それはいやなんです, 以上 ***sore wa iya nan desu, ijô*** I don't want to, period!; …以上(で) ***… ijô*** (***de***) above; これ以上言う必要がありますか ***kore ijô iu hitsuyô ga arimasu ka*** need I say more?
異常(な) **ijō** (**na**) abnormal; freak
異常に **ijō ni** extraordinarily; remarkably
移住 **ijū** emigration; immigration
移住者 **ijū-sha** emigrant; immigrant
移住する **ijū suru** emigrate; immigrate; migrate
いか **ika** squid
以下 **ika** below; not more than ◊ the following; 以下次号 ***ika-jigô*** to be continued
…以下に **… ika ni** below
以下の事 **ika no koto** the following
いかだ **ikada** raft
いかが **ikaga** how; how about; クッキーはいかがですか ***kukkî wa ikaga desu ka*** would you like some cookies?
いかがわしい **ikagawashii** disreputable; indecent; shady; unsavory; juicy *news*
いかに **ika ni** how
いかにも **ika ni mo** really; indeed; very
いかれている **ikarete iru** be mentally unbalanced
いかり **ikari** anchor; いかりを下ろす ***ikari o orosu*** anchor
怒り **ikari** anger; displeasure
怒り出す **ikaridasu** erupt
怒り狂う **ikarikuruu** rage
いかさま **ikasama** cheat; deception; con; いかさまをする ***ikasama o suru*** cheat
生かす **ikasu** keep alive; make the best use of
池 **ike** pond
生け花 **ikebana** flower arrangement
生け垣 **ikegaki** hedge
胃けいれん **ikeiren** stomach cramps
いけません **ikemasen** not permitted; forbidden; bad ◊ must; must not
意見 **iken** opinion, (point of) view; observation; judgment; verdict; 意見が合わない ***iken ga awanai*** differ; disagree; disagree with
いけにえ **ikenie** sacrifice
生ける **ikeru** arrange *flowers*
息 **iki** breath; 息が切れる ***iki ga kireru*** be out of breath; 息が詰まる ***iki ga tsumaru*** choke; 息を切らした ***iki o kirashita*** breathless; 息をこらす ***iki o korasu*** hold one's breath; 息をのむ ***iki o nomu*** gasp; 息をする ***iki o suru*** breathe; 息を吸う ***iki o suu*** breathe
行き **iki**: …行きである ***… iki de aru*** be going to; be bound for
遺棄 **iki** abandonment; desertion
行き止まり **ikidomari** cul-de-sac; dead end
憤り **ikidōri** indignation; outrage
息切れする **ikigire suru** pant
息苦しい **ikigurushii** stifling, suffocating
生き生きした **ikiiki shita** lively
生き返る **ikikaeru** be resurrected; be revived
生き物 **ikimono** being; creature
いき(な) **iki** (**na**) stylish
生き延びる **ikinobiru** survive
生き残る **ikinokoru** survive
勢い **ikioi** momentum; power; energy
勢いのある **ikioi no aru** vigorous

生きる **ikiru** live
生きている **ikite iru** be alive ◊ living
生き写しである **ikiutsushi de aru** be the (spitting) image
生き写し(の) **ikiutsushi (no)** lifelike
行き詰まり **ikizumari** blind alley; deadlock
一ヶ月(の) **ikkagetsu (no)** monthly
一回 **ikkai** once; one episode; first inning; one round
一階 **ikkai** first floor
一回分 **ikkaibun** one dose
一貫性 **ikkansei** consistency
一貫した **ikkan shita** consistent
一括払い **ikkatsubarai** lump sum
一括契約 **ikkatsu-keiyaku** package deal
一見 **ikken** a look
一斤 **ikkin** a loaf
一気に **ikki ni** in one go; at a stretch
いっこうに **ikkōni**: いっこうに平気だ ***ikkô ni heiki da*** I couldn't care less
一曲 **ikkyoku** piece of music
一級(の) **ikkyū (no)** choice, top quality
…以降 **… ikō** from … onward
eコマース **ī-komāsu** e-commerce
遺骨 **ikotsu** ashes
行く **iku** come; go; visit; cover *distance*
意気地のない **ikuji no nai** spineless, cowardly
幾人か **ikuninka** a few people
幾人か(の) **ikuninka (no)** a few; several
いくら **ikura** how much?
いくらか **ikuraka** some
いくらか(の) **ikuraka (no)** some, a number of
いくつ **ikutsu** how many; how old
いくつか **ikutsuka** a few; several
いくつか(の) **ikutsuka (no)** a few; some; several
異教徒 **ikyōto** heathen
今 **ima** now; right now
居間 **ima** living room, lounge
今風(の) **imafū (no)** fashionable
今頃 **imagoro** about this time; by now
いまいましい **imaimashii** damn, cursed
今から **ima kara** from now on
今までで **ima made de** ever
今までに **ima made ni** ever; till now
今にも…しそうである **ima ni mo …shisō de aru** be on the verge of
今のところ **ima no tokoro** at present, at the moment, currently; for the time being
います **imasu** *polite form of* ***iru***
今すぐ **ima sugu** straight away
イメージ **imēji** image
Eメール **īmēru** email
意味 **imi** meaning; point, purpose; implication
意味ありげ(な) **imiarige (na)** meaningful
移民 **imin** immigrant
意味する **imi suru** mean, imply; signify
イミテーション **imitēshon** imitation
芋 **imo** sweet potato
妹 **imōto** (younger) sister
医務室 **imushitsu** dispensary; medical office
韻 **in** rhyme; …と韻を踏む ***… to in o fumu*** rhyme with
稲光 **inabikari** lightning
いなご **inago** locust
いない **inai** there is / are not
…以内で **…inai de** within
田舎 **inaka** countryside; country; the sticks
田舎者 **inakamono** hick, hillbilly
田舎(の) **inaka (no)** rural
いななく **inanaku** neigh
稲荷神社 **inari-jinja** *shrine for the celebration of the harvest*
陰謀 **inbō** plot; conspiracy; intrigue
インチ **inchi** inch
いんちき(の) **inchiki (no)** bogus
インデックス **indekkusu** index
インディアン **Indian** American Indian, Native American
インド **Indo** India
インドア(の) **indoa (no)** indoor
インドネシア **Indoneshia** Indonesia
インドネシア(の) **Indoneshia (no)** Indonesian
インド(の) **Indo (no)** Indian
インドシナ **Indoshina** Indochina
稲 **ine** rice plant

居眠り **inemuri** snooze
居眠りする **inemuri suru** snooze; have a snooze; nod off
インフレ **infure** inflation; インフレを引き起こす ***infure o hikiokosu*** inflationary
インフレ(の) **infure (no)** inflationary
インフルエンザ **infuruenza** influenza
隠語 **ingo** slang
イングランド **Ingurando** England
イングランド人 **Ingurando-jin** English person; the English
イングランド(の) **Ingurando (no)** English
委任 **inin** delegation; proxy
委任権 **ininken** power of attorney
イニシャル **inisharu** initial
イニシアチブ **inishiachibu** initiative
印鑑 **inkan** signature seal
陰険(な) **inken (na)** insidious; sneaky
陰気(な) **inki (na)** dingy; dreary; dismal, sad
インコース **inkōsu** inside lane SP
インク **inku** ink
陰毛 **inmō** pubic hair
命 **inochi** life
命にかかわる **inochi ni kakawaru** life-threatening
命取り **inochitori** killer
居残る **inokoru** stay behind; work overtime
祈り **inori** praying, prayer
祈る **inoru** pray
いのしし **inoshishi** wild boar
インポ **inpo** impotence
インポ(の) **inpo (no)** impotent
インプット **inputto** input
引力 **inryoku** gravity
飲料水 **inryōsui** drinking water
飲料用(の) **inryōyō (no)** drinkable
インサイダー取り引き **insaidā-torihiki** insider trading
印刷物 **insatsubutsu** printed matter
印刷業者 **insatsu-gyōsha** printer
印刷機 **insatsuki** printing press
印刷する **insatsu suru** print; run off
いん石 **inseki** meteorite
印象 **inshō** impression
印章 **inshō** seal, stamp
印象的(な) **inshōteki (na)** impressive; memorable
飲酒 **inshu** drinking
インシュリン **inshurin** insulin
飲酒運転 **inshu-unten** drunk driving
インスピレーション **insupirēshon** inspiration
インスタントコーヒー **insutanto-kōhī** instant coffee
インスタント食品 **insutanto-shokuhin** convenience food
インストラクター **insutorakutā** instructor
インストール **insutōru** installation
インストールする **insutōru suru** install
インタビュー **intabyū** interview
インタビューア **intabyūa** interviewer
インタビューする **intabyū suru** interview
インターチェンジ **intāchenji** exit; interchange
インターホン **intāhon** intercom
インターネット **intānetto** Internet
インテリ **interi** intellectual, egghead
インテリア **interia** décor; decoration
インテリアデザイナー **interia-dezainā** interior decorator; interior designer
犬 **inu** dog
犬小屋 **inugoya** kennel
引用 **in'yō** quotation, quote
引用符 **in'yōfu** quotation marks
引用する **inyō suru** quote
印税 **inzei** royalty
硫黄 **iō** sulfur
…一杯 **… ippai** a drink of … ; お茶一杯 ***ocha ippai*** a cup of tea
いっぱいになる **ippai ni naru** fill up
いっぱい(の) **ippai (no)** full, full up
一泊 **ippaku** night
一泊(の) **ippaku (no)** overnight
一般化 **ippanka** generalization
一般化する **ippanka suru** generalize
一般に **ippan ni** in general
一般(の) **ippan (no)** civilian; popular

一般的(な) **ippanteki (na)** general; prevailing
一般的に **ippanteki ni** generally
一片 **ippen** piece; fragment; flake
一匹おおかみ **ippikiōkami** loner
一品 **ippin** course; dish
逸品 **ippin** gem; superb specimen
一歩 **ippo** pace; step
一方では…で、もう一方では…だ **ippō dewa … de, mō ippō dewa … da** on the one hand …, on the other hand
一本 **ippon** length (*of cloth, wood*); strand
一方的(な) **ippōteki (na)** one-sided; unilateral
一方通行 **ippō-tsūkō** one-way street
いらだち **iradachi** annoyance, irritation
いらだたせる **iradataseru** vex
依頼 **irai** commission; request
以来 **irai** since; あなたが去って以来 ***anata ga satte irai*** since you left
依頼人 **irai-nin** client
いらいらさせる **iraira saseru** annoy, irritate, bug
いらいらして **iraira shite** impatiently
いらいらする **iraira suru** frustrating; nerve-racking ◊ get worked up
依頼する **irai suru** commission; request
イラク **Iraku** Iraq
イラク(の) **Iraku (no)** Iraqi
いらくさ **irakusa** nettle
イラン **Iran** Iran
イラン(の) **Iran (no)** Iranian
いらっしゃいませ **irasshaimase** welcome
いらっしゃる **irassharu** (*polite*) be; come; go
イラスト **irasuto** illustration
イラストレーター **irasutorētā** illustrator
入れ歯 **ireba** dentures, false teeth
入れ物 **iremono** container; holder; tub
入れる **ireru** make, brew; turn on *faucet, heater*; pour; engage *clutch, gear*; include; insert
いれずみ **irezumi** tattoo
入り江 **irie** cove; inlet; estuary
入り口 **iriguchi** entrance, way in; gateway
色 **iro** color; hue
色合い **iroai** shade; tint
色々(な) **iroiro (na)** varied; various
色気 **iroke** sex appeal
いる **iru** be; be present; live; have; …がいる ***… ga iru*** there is / are; 彼女は子供が二人いる ***kanojo wa kogomo ga futari iru*** she has two children
要る **iru** need; require
炒る **iru** roast; toast
鋳る **iru** cast *metal*; mint *coins*
射る **iru** shoot, fire *arrow*
衣類 **irui** clothing
いるか **iruka** dolphin
イルミネーションで飾る **iruminēshon de kazaru** illuminate
医療 **iryō** medical treatment, medical care
衣料品 **iryōhin** clothing
医療過誤 **iryō-kago** malpractice
威力 **iryoku** power
医療(の) **iryō (no)** medical
いさかい **isakai** fight; quarrel
遺産 **isan** heritage; inheritance; legacy
異性 **isei** opposite sex
異性愛者 **isei-aisha** heterosexual
遺跡 **iseki** ruins
医者 **isha** doctor
石 **ishi** stone; rock
意志 **ishi** will, willpower; 意志が弱い ***ishi ga yowai*** weak-willed
意思 **ishi** intention; wish; mind
医師 **ishi** doctor
意識 **ishiki** awareness; consciousness; 意識を失う / 取り戻す ***ishiki o ushinau / torimodosu*** lose / regain consciousness
意識不明(の) **ishiki-fumei (no)** unconscious
意識もうろう **ishiki-mōrō** stupor
意識のある **ishiki no aru** conscious
石切り場 **ishikiriba** quarry
意識的(な) **ishikiteki (na)** conscious, deliberate

意志の強い **ishi no tsuyoi** strong-willed
意思疎通 **ishi-sotsū** communication; mutual understanding
遺失物取扱所 **ishitsubutsu-toriatsukaijo** lost-and-found (office)
衣装 **ishō** costume; clothes
移植 **ishoku** graft; transplant
移植する **ishoku suru** transplant
急がせる **isogaseru** rush *person*
忙しい **isogashii** busy; full; eventful
急がす **isogasu** hustle
急ぐ **isogu** hurry (up); rush; speed; 急いで ***isoide*** hurry up!; don't be long!
急いでいる **isoide iru** be in a rush
一切込み(の) **issaikomi (no)** inclusive
一酸化炭素 **issanka-tanso** carbon monoxide
一冊 **issatsu** a copy
一斉 **issei** volley
一節 **issetsu** passage; stanza
一式 **isshiki** set (*of tools, books etc*)
一生 **isshō** life; lifetime
一升 **isshō** *liquid measure of 3.8 pints*
一生涯 **isshōgai** all his / her / my life
一緒に **issho ni** together; along (with); with; …と一緒に暮らす ***… to issho ni kurasu*** live with
一生(の) **isshō (no)** lifelong
一周 **isshū** circuit, lap
一週間 **isshūkan** one week
一掃する **issō suru** clean up; sweep away
いす **isu** chair
イスラエル **Isuraeru** Israel
イスラエル(の) **Isuraeru (no)** Israeli
イスラム教 **Isuramu-kyō** Islam
イスラム教(の) **Isuramu-kyō (no)** Islamic
イースト **īsuto** yeast
板 **ita** board; plank
板ばさみになる **itabasami ni naru** be in a dilemma, be torn between two alternatives
いただけますか **-itadakemasu ka** could you…?
いただきます **itadakimasu** *words spoken before eating*
痛い **itai** painful, sore; tender
遺体 **itai** remains
板前 **itamae** chef
痛ましい **itamashii** miserable; poignant
傷める **itameru** hurt; injure; strain; bruise
炒める **itameru** (stir-)fry
痛めつける **itametsukeru** torment; treat harshly
痛み **itami** pain; prick; ache; tenderness; 痛みがある ***itami ga aru*** be in pain
痛み止め **itamidome** painkiller
痛む **itamu** hurt; ache
傷む **itamu** bruise
イタリア **Itaria** Italy
イタリア語 **Itaria-go** Italian
イタリア人 **Itaria-jin** Italian
イタリア(の) **Itaria (no)** Italian
いたるところに **itaru tokoro ni** everywhere
いたします **itashimasu** H do
いたわる **itawaru** be kind to
いたずら **itazura** practical joke; prank; mischief; hoax; いたずらをする ***itazura o suru*** play a prank; molest
いたずらっ子 **itazurakko** rascal, monkey
いたずら(な) **itazura (na)** mischievous
一致 **itchi** correspondence, match; agreement
一致した **itchi shita** concerted ◊ in unison
一致して **itchi shite** in line with …
一致する **itchi suru** correspond, match; agree
意図 **ito** intention; aim
糸 **ito** thread, yarn; 糸を通す ***ito o tôsu*** thread
いとこ **itoko** cousin
糸巻き **itomaki** spool
意図的(な) **itoteki (na)** intentional
いつ **itsu** when
逸脱 **itsudatsu** departure; deviation

いつでも **itsu demo** whenever; いつでも協力します ***itsu demo kyôryoku shimasu*** I am at your disposal
いつか **itsuka** sometime; one day; once; ever; before
いつかは **itsuka wa** sooner or later
慈しみ **itsukushimi** fondness; affection
いつまでも **itsu made mo** for ever; persistently
いつも **itsumo** always, invariably
いつも(の) **itsumo (no)** usual; customary; habitual; いつもの手順で ***itsumo no tejun de*** as a matter of routine; いつものように ***itsumo no yô ni*** as usual; as is his / her / my custom
いつのまにか **itsu no ma ni ka** before you know it; unnoticed
一体… **ittai …** … on earth; 一体誰が ***ittai dare ga*** who on earth?; whoever?; 一体どこに… ***ittai doko ni*** where on earth?; wherever?
いったん…すれば **ittan … sureba** once
行ったり来たり **ittari kitari** to and fro
一定(の) **ittei (no)** uniform; fixed; definite
いってきます **itte kimasu** see you; I'm off now
いってらっしゃい **itterasshai** good luck!; have a nice day
一等 **ittō** first class
言う **iu** say; describe; …は言うまでもなく ***… wa iu made mo naku*** to say nothing of
岩 **iwa** rock
岩だらけ(の) **iwadarake (no)** rocky
祝い **iwai** celebration; congratulations
いわし **iwashi** sardine
祝う **iwau** celebrate
岩山 **iwayama** crag
いわゆる **iwayuru** so-called
いやがらせ **iyagarase** harassment; …にいやがらせをする ***… ni iyagarase o suru*** harass
イヤホン **iyahon** earphones
いやいやながら **iyaiya-nagara** reluctantly
違約条項 **iyaku-jōkō** penalty clause
嫌み **iyami** unpleasantness; sarcasm; bad taste
嫌み(な) **iyami (na)** sarcastic; in bad taste
嫌(な) **iya (na)** unpleasant; disagreeable; dismal; nasty; disgusting; hideous
嫌なやつ **iya na yatsu** a pain in the neck; prick (*person*); swine
嫌になる **iya ni naru** turn off (*sexually*)
いやらしい **iyarashii** unpleasant; disgusting; indecent
イヤリング **iyaringu** earring
癒し **iyashi** healing; soothing; stress-relieving
卑しい **iyashii** humble; vulgar; despicable
卑しめる **iyashimeru** degrade
意欲 **iyoku** will; aspiration; desire
意欲的(な) **iyokuteki (na)** enthusiastic
居酒屋 **izakaya** bar
いざこざ **izakoza** misunderstanding; quarrel
以前 **izen** before; 私は以前彼が好きだった ***watashi wa izen kare ga suki datta*** I used to like him
以前(の) **izen (no)** former, past
以前は **izen wa** formerly
イーゼル **īzeru** easel
遺族 **izoku** the bereaved
依存 **izon** dependence, dependency; reliance
依存心の強い **izonshin no tsuyoi** clingy
依存する **izon suru** depend on, rely on
泉 **izumi** spring (*of water*)
いずれ **izure** some day; some other time; いずれの場合においても ***izure no bâi ni oite mo*** in any case; いずれも ***izure mo*** all; each one; any

J

じゃあ **jā** well; then; in that case; じゃあ、また ***jâ, mata*** see you later!
邪悪(な) **jaaku (na)** evil
じゃがいも **jagaimo** potato
蛇口 **jaguchi** faucet
ジャージー **jājī** jersey
ジャケット **jaketto** jacket
ジャッキ **jakki** jack MOT
ジャック **jakku** jack (*in cards*)
ジャクージ **jakūji** whirlpool, jacuzzi®
弱者 **jakusha** underdog
弱点 **jakuten** weakness
邪魔 **jama** disruption; interruption; hindrance; intrusion; 邪魔になる ***jama ni naru*** be in the way; 邪魔をする ***jama o suru*** interrupt; disrupt; distract; thwart
ジャム **jamu** jam, conserve; jelly
ジャーナリスト **jānarisuto** journalist
ジャーナリズム **jānarizumu** journalism
ジャングル **janguru** jungle
じゃんけん **janken** *game of stone, paper, scissors*
ジャンパー **janpā** jumper SP
ジャンプ **janpu** jump
砂利 **jari** gravel; grit; shingle
ジャズ **jazu** jazz
ジェイアール **jei-āru** Japan Railways, JR
ジェル **jeru** gel
ジェットエンジン **jetto-enjin** jet engine
ジェット機 **jetto-ki** jet
ジェットコースター **jetto-kōsutā** roller coaster
字 **ji** written character; letter
時 **-ji** o'clock
ぢ **ji** piles MED
耳鼻科 **jibika** ear and nose department; otorhinology
自分 **jibun** oneself
自分で **jibun de** personally, in person; by oneself
自治権 **jichiken** autonomy
時代 **jidai** age, era, epoch
時代劇 **jidaigeki** historical drama
時代後れで **jidaiokure de** out of date
時代後れ(の) **jidaiokure (no)** dated; outdated; out-of-date
自動振替 **jidō-furikae** banker's order
自動販売機 **jidōhanbaiki** slot machine, vending machine
自動化する **jidōka suru** automate
自動(の) **jidō (no)** automatic
自動車 **jidōsha** auto, automobile
自動車教習 **jidōsha-kyōshū** driving lesson
自動車教習所 **jidōsha-kyōshūjo** driving school
自動詞 **jidōshi** intransitive verb
自動的(な) **jidōteki (na)** automatic
自営業(の) **jieigyō (no)** self-employed
自衛隊 **jieitai** Japan Self-Defense Forces
ジーエヌピー **jī-enu-pī** GNP, gross national product
時限爆弾 **jigen bakudan** time bomb
地獄 **jigoku** hell
ジグソー(パズル) **jigusō(pazuru)** jigsaw (puzzle)
ジグザグ **jiguzagu** zigzag; ジグザグに進む ***jiguzagu ni susumu*** zigzag
事業 **jigyō** business enterprise; concern
自白 **jihaku** confession
自白する **jihaku suru** admit, confess
自発的(な) **jihatsuteki (na)** voluntary; spontaneous
自発的に **jihatsuteki ni** of one's own accord
自閉症(の) **jiheishō (no)** autistic
慈悲 **jihi** mercy

慈悲深い **jihibukai** benevolent; charitable; merciful
時事問題 **jiji-mondai** current affairs, current events
事実 **jijitsu** reality; fact
事実上(の) **jijitsujō** (**no**) virtual
事情 **jijō** circumstances; situation; matter
二乗 **jijō** square MATH
自叙伝 **jijoden** autobiography
事情通(の) **jijōtsū** (**no**) streetwise
自覚 **jikaku** consciousness; awareness
時間 **jikan** time; hour; 時間どおり ***jikan dôri*** on time; 時間を合わせる ***jikan o awaseru*** synchronize
時間切れである **jikangire de aru** time is up
時間給で **jikankyū de** at an hourly rate of
時間のずれ **jikan no zure** time-lag
時間を守る **jikan o mamoru** prompt
時間割 **jikan-wari** schedule
自家製(の) **jikasei** (**no**) homemade
自活している **jikatsu shite iru** independent
自活する **jikatsu suru** support oneself
事件 **jiken** case (*for police*); incident
時期 **jiki** season; time
磁器 **jiki** porcelain
磁器(の) **jiki** (**no**) porcelain
実感 **jikkan** realization
実感する **jikkan suru** realize
実験 **jikken** experiment
実験台 **jikkendai** guinea pig
実験する **jikken suru** experiment
実験的(な) **jikkenteki** (**na**) experimental
実行 **jikkō** execution
実行する **jikkō suru** carry out; execute, put into effect; set things in motion
じっくり **jikkuri** properly; じっくり考える ***jikkuri kangaeru*** ponder; contemplate
実況放送 **jikkyō-hōsō** live broadcast
実況(の) **jikkyō** (**no**) live
事故 **jiko** accident; mishap
自己 **jiko** self
自己防衛 **jiko-bōei** self-defense
自己中心(の) **jiko-chūshin** (**no**) self-centered
自己中心的(な) **jiko-chūshinteki** (**na**) egocentric
自己不信 **jiko-fushin** self-doubt
自己規制 **jiko-kisei** self-discipline
時刻 **jikoku** time; hour
時刻表 **jikoku-hyō** schedule, timetable
自己満足 **jiko-manzoku** complacency
自己満足(の) **jiko-manzoku** (**no**) self-satisfied
自己満足した **jiko-manzoku shita** complacent
自己紹介 **jikoshōkai** self-introduction
自己主張する **jiko-shuchō suru** assert oneself
軸 **jiku** axle; shaft; axis
持久力 **jikyūryoku** endurance; stamina
字幕 **jimaku** subtitles; 字幕をつける ***jimaku o tsukeru*** subtitle
自慢 **jiman** boast; pride
自慢する **jiman suru** boast, talk big
自明(の) **jimei** (**no**) self-evident
じめじめした **jimejime shita** swampy; damp
地面 **jimen** ground
地道な人 **jimichi na hito** steady worker
地味(な) **jimi** (**na**) conservative, modest
地元で **jimoto de** locally
地元(の) **jimoto** (**no**) local
ジム **jimu** gym
事務 **jimu** business; office work
事務員 **jimuin** clerk
事務室 **jimushitsu** office
事務所 **jimusho** firm; office
事務的(な) **jimuteki** (**na**) matter-of-fact; businesslike; mechanical
ジン **jin** gin
人 **-jin** person; アメリカ人 ***Amerika-jin*** American; 日本人 ***Nihon-jin*** Japanese
人文科学 **jinbun-kagaku** the arts

陣地**jinchi** position
人道的(な)**jindōteki (na)** humanitarian
人員**jin'in** manpower; staff; personnel
辞任**jinin** resignation
辞任する**jinin suru** resign, step down
自認する**jinin suru** acknowledge
人為的(な)**jin'iteki (na)** human; man-made
神社**jinja** shrine
人事**jinji** personnel affairs
人事部**jinjibu** human resources, personnel (*department*)
人事部長**jinji-buchō** personnel manager
人格**jinkaku** personality
人口**jinkō** population
人工知能**jinkō-chinō** artificial intelligence
人工衛星**jinkō-eisei** satellite
人工保育器**jinkō-hoikuki** incubator
人工呼吸装置**jinkōkokyū-sōchi** respirator
人口密度**jinkō-mitsudo** population density
人工(の)**jinkō (no)** artificial, man-made
ジンクス**jinkusu** jinx
人命**jinmei** human life
人命救助用(の)**jinmei-kyūjoyō (no)** life-saving
尋問**jinmon** interrogation
尋問者**jinmon-sha** interrogator
尋問する**jinmon suru** question; interrogate
人類**jinrui** humanity; mankind; human race
人生**jinsei** human life
人生観**jinseikan** outlook on life; philosophy of life
人種**jinshu** race
人種平等**jinshu-byōdō** racial equality
人種(の)**jinshu (no)** racial
人種差別**jinshu-sabetsu** racism
迅速(な)**jinsoku (na)** prompt; rapid
じん帯**jintai** ligament
人体**jintai** human body
地主**jinushi** land owner
人材スカウト係**jinzai-sukauto-gakari** headhunter
腎臓**jinzō** kidney
ジーンズ**jīnzu** jeans, denims
ジーパン**jīpan** jeans
ジープ**jīpu** jeep
ジプシー**jipushī** gypsy, gipsy
地雷**jirai** landmine
地雷原**jiraigen** minefield
じらした**jirashita** tantalizing
ジレンマ**jirenma** dilemma
じりじりと進む**jirijiri to susumu** edge forward
自立した**jiritsu shita** emancipated; self-reliant
時差ぼけ**jisa-boke** jetlag
自殺**jisatsu** suicide
自殺する**jisatsu suru** commit suicide, kill oneself
自制**jisei** self control
時制**jisei** tense GRAM
自制する**jisei suru** contain oneself, control oneself
磁石**jishaku** magnet
磁石(の)**jishaku (no)** magnetic
自信**jishin** confidence; self-confidence; 自信がある***jishin ga aru*** be confident
地震**jishin** earthquake
自信がない**jishin ga nai** insecure
自信のある**jishin no aru** confident; self-confident
辞書**jisho** dictionary
地所**jisho** estate; plot (*land*)
自首する**jishu suru** surrender; 警察へ自首する***keisatsu e jishu suru*** give oneself up to the police
自主的(な)**jishuteki (na)** independent
時速…マイル**jisoku ... mairu** mph, miles per hour
自尊心**jisonshin** ego; pride; self-respect
自尊心の強い**jisonshin no tsuyoi** proud
実際には**jissai ni wa** in practice
実際(の)**jissai (no)** actual
実際的(な)**jissaiteki (na)** businesslike; practical

実際は **jissai wa** in fact, as a matter of fact
実績 **jisseki** achievement; accomplishment
実践 **jissen** practice
実践的(な) **jissenteki (na)** hands-on
実施される **jisshi sareru** come into force
実施されて **jisshi sarete** effective
実施する **jisshi suru** enforce; put into effect
実質的(な) **jisshitsuteki (na)** substantive
実質的には **jisshitsuteki ni** practically; essentially; virtually
地滑り **jisuberi** landslide
自炊**jisui** self-catering
辞退する **jitai suru** refuse
自宅 **jitaku** home
実地(の) **jitchi (no)** practical
時点 **jiten** point in time
辞典 **jiten** dictionary
自転車 **jitensha** bicycle, cycle, bike
実物 **jitsubutsu** the real thing; 実物に会う ***jitsubutsu ni au*** meet/see a person in the flesh
実物大(の) **jitsubutsudai (no)** lifesized
実現 **jitsugen** fulfillment; realization
実現する **jitsugen suru** realize; come true
実業家 **jitsugyōka** businessman; industrialist
実は **jitsu wa** actually
実力 **jitsuryoku** capability; competence; ability
実用性 **jitsuyōsei** usefulness, utility
実用主義 **jitsuyō-shugi** pragmatism
実用的(な) **jitsuyōteki (na)** practical; pragmatic
じっと **jitto** quietly; intently; without moving
じっと見る **jitto miru** peer at; scrutinize
じっと見つめる **jitto mitsumeru** stare at; gaze at
じっとりした **jittori shita** clammy; damp
じっとしている **jitto shite iru** stand still
自由 **jiyū** freedom; scope; liberty; latitude
自由経済 **jiyū-keizai** free market economy
自由民主党 **Jiyū-minshu-tō** LDP, Liberal Democratic Party
自由(な) **jiyū (na)** free; liberated; open
自由にする **jiyū ni suru** liberate
自由の女神像 **Jiyū no Megamizō** Statue of Liberty
自由主義(の) **jiyū-shugi (no)** liberal
自在ドア **jizai-doa** swing-door
慈善 **jizen** charity
慈善団体 **jizen-dantai** charitable organization
慈善事業 **jizen-jigyō** philanthropy
慈善家 **jizen-ka** philanthropist; do-gooder
事前(の) **jizen (no)** prior
地蔵 **jizō** *guardian deity of children and travelers*
持続 **jizoku** persistence
持続する **jizoku suru** maintain; endure; hold out
上 **jō** best; top
情 **jō** emotion; feelings; affection
状 **-jō** letter; card; 招待状 ***shôtaijô*** invitation
乗馬 **jōba** ride; riding; 乗馬をする ***jôba o suru*** ride
序文 **jobun** introduction; preface
丈夫(な) **jōbu (na)** hardy; sturdy; indestructible
上部(の) **jōbu (no)** upper
情緒不安定(な) **jōcho-fuantei (na)** emotionally unstable; emotionally disturbed
助長する **jochō suru** encourage, foster
冗談 **jōdan** joke, crack; witticism; 冗談を言う ***jôdan o iu*** joke; jest; kid; quip; 冗談じゃない ***jôdan ja nai*** you've got to be joking!
上映される **jōei sareru** show, be screened
上映する **jōei suru** perform *play*; enact; show *movie*
上演する **jōen suru** put on, perform

除外 **jogai** omission
除外する **jogai suru** eliminate; exclude; omit; drop
助言 **jogen** advice; hint, pointer
ジョギング **jogingu** jog; jogging, running
ジョギングシューズ **jogingu-shūzu** jogger
ジョギングする **jogingu suru** go for a run
蒸発させる **jōhatsu saseru** vaporize
蒸発する **jōhatsu suru** evaporate
城壁 **jōheki** rampart; castle wall
上品(な) **jōhin** (**na**) distinguished; dignified; stylish
譲歩 **jōho** concession; information; intelligence (*news*)
情報 **jōhō** information
情報部 **jōhōbu** intelligence service
情報源 **jōhōgen** source of information
情報科学 **jōhō-kagaku** information science
情報工学 **jōhō-kōgaku** information technology, IT
情報処理 **jōhō-shori** data processing
譲歩する **jōho suru** back down; concede
情報提供者 **jōhō-teikyō-sha** informant
除氷する **johyō suru** de-ice; defrost
女医 **joi** woman doctor
上院 **Jōin** Senate; Upper House
上院議員 **jōin-giin** senator
上位(の) **jōi** (**no**) senior
ジョイントベンチャー **jointo-benchā** joint venture
情事 **jōji** (love) affair
徐々(の) **jojo** (**no**) gradual
情状酌量 **jōjō-shakuryō** mitigating circumstances
ジョーカー **jōkā** joker
助監督 **jokantoku** assistant director
浄化する **jōka suru** purify
条件 **jōken** condition, term, requirement; proviso
条件付き(の) **jōkentsuki** (**no**) conditional; provisional
条件付け **jōkenzuke** conditioning
蒸気 **jōki** vapor; steam
上機嫌(の) **jōkigen** (**no**) good-humored
常勤で **jōkin de** full-time
常勤(の) **jōkin** (**no**) full-time
上記(の) **jōki** (**no**) above-mentioned
ジョッキー **jokkī** jockey
条項 **jōkō** article (*section*); clause (*in agreement*); provision
除光液 **jokōeki** nail polish remover
乗客 **jōkyaku** passenger; occupant (*of vehicle*)
除去 **jokyo** removal, elimination
状況 **jōkyō** conditions, circumstances; matter
情況 **jōkyō** scene
助教授 **jokyōju** associate professor
序曲 **jokyoku** overture
上級(の) **jōkyū** (**no**) advanced
錠前屋 **jōmae-ya** locksmith
常務 **jōmu** managing director
乗務員 **jōmuin** crew; crew member
静脈 **jōmyaku** vein
静脈内(の) **jōmyakunai** (**no**) intravenous
静脈瘤 **jōmyakuryū** varicose vein
情熱 **jōnetsu** passion
情熱的(な) **jōnetsuteki** (**na**) intense; passionate
女王 **joō** queen
女王ばち **joō-bachi** queen bee
常連 **jōren** regular (customer)
上陸する **jōriku suru** go ashore
じょうろ **jōro** watering can
常緑樹 **jōryokuju** evergreen
助力する **joryoku suru** assist
上流階級 **jōryū-kaikyū** upper classes
上流階級(の) **jōryū-kaikyū** (**no**) upper class
上流に **jōryū ni** upstream
上流(の) **jōryū** (**no**) upper-class
上流社会 **jōryū-shakai** high society
蒸留酒 **jōryūshu** distilled spirits
如才ない **josainai** tactful; shrewd
如才なさ **josainasa** diplomacy
助産婦 **josanpu** midwife
女性 **josei** woman; female
情勢 **jōsei** situation; state of affairs

女性実業家 **josei-jitsugyōka** businesswoman
女性形 **joseikei** feminine GRAM
助成金 **joseikin** subsidy
女性(の) **josei (no)** female
女性らしい **josei-rashii** feminine
女性用トイレ **joseiyō toire** ladies' room
乗船している **jōsen shite iru** be aboard
乗船する **jōsen suru** embark, go aboard
除雪機 **josetsuki** snowplow
乗車している **jōsha shite iru** be aboard
乗車する **jōsha suru** go aboard
上司 **jōshi** boss; superior
常識 **jōshiki** (common) sense
常識のある **jōshiki no aru** sensible; well-balanced
常識的に **jōshikiteki ni** reasonably
女子 **joshi** girl; woman
女子大 **joshi-dai** women's college
女子生徒 **joshi-seito** schoolgirl
上昇 **jōshō** rise
上昇させる **jōshō saseru** boost
上昇する **jōshō suru** climb; look up, improve
助手 **joshu** assistant
助手席 **joshuseki** passenger seat
常習的(な) **jōshūteki (na)** habitual
助走 **josō** run-up SP
上訴 **jōso** appeal
上訴する **jōso suru** appeal
除草剤 **josōzai** weedkiller
除隊 **jotai** discharge MIL
状態 **jōtai** circumstances; condition, state
上達 **jōtatsu** improvement
上達させる **jōtatsu saseru** improve
上達する **jōtatsu suru** improve; progress
譲渡できる **jōto dekiru** transferable
上等(の) **jōtō (no)** excellent; very good
除夜のかね **joya no kane** *temple bells on New Year's Eve*
条約 **jōyaku** treaty
常用漢字 **Jōyō kanji** *Chinese characters in common use*
情欲 **jōyoku** passion; lust
女優 **joyū** actress
錠剤 **jōzai** tablet
醸造業者 **jōzō-gyōsha** brewer
醸造所 **jōzōjo** brewery
醸造する **jōzō suru** brew
上手である **jōzu de aru** be good at
上手(な) **jōzu (na)** good, skillful
銃 **jū** gun
十 **jū** ten
中 **-jū** throughout; 年中 ***nenjû*** throughout the year, all year round
重圧 **jūatsu** heavy pressure
十分, 充分 **jūbun** enough
十分(な) **jūbun (na)** adequate; enough; ample; plentiful
十分に **jūbun ni** enough; sufficiently; fully
十代 **jūdai** adolescence
重大(な) **jūdai (na)** important; drastic; grave; serious
十代(の) **jūdai (no)** adolescent
充電する **jūden suru** charge; recharge
柔道 **jūdō** judo
樹液 **jueki** sap
十月 **jūgatsu** October
銃撃 **jūgeki** gunfire
授業 **jugyō** class, lesson
従業員 **jūgyōin** employee
獣医 **jūi** veterinary surgeon, vet
十一月 **jūichigatsu** November
十字架 **jūjika** cross REL
充実感 **jūjitsu-kan** fulfillment
充実した **jūjitsu shita** fulfilling
従順(な) **jūjun (na)** docile; submissive
受刑者 **jukei-sha** convict; inmate
受験 **juken** taking an exam
受験者 **juken-sha** candidate; entrant (*for exam*)
熟考 **jukkō** consideration, reflection, thought
熟考する **jukkō suru** deliberate; ponder; pore over
重婚 **jūkon** bigamy
受講手続 **jukō-tetsuzuki** course registration; lecture enrollment
塾 **juku** crammer
ジュークボックス **jūku-bokkusu** jukebox

熟読する **jukudoku suru** pore over
熟練 **jukuren** proficiency
熟練工 **jukuren-kō** skilled worker
熟練(の) **jukuren (no)** skilled
熟練した **jukuren shita** accomplished; expert; experienced; proficient
熟する **juku suru** ripen
熟達 **jukutatsu** mastery
儒教 **Jukyō** Confucianism
住民 **jūmin** inhabitant; people
住民投票 **jūmin-tōhyō** referendum
寿命 **jumyō** life
順 **jun** order, sequence
柔軟(な) **jūnan (na)** flexible; supple; pliable
柔軟仕上げ剤 **jūnan-shiagezai** conditioner
順番に **junban ni** in sequence
準備 **junbi** organization; preparation(s) ; …の準備で ***… no junbi de*** in preparation for; 準備ができた ***junbi ga dekita*** ready; …の準備をする ***… no junbi o suru*** get … ready
準備中で **junbichū de** in the pipeline
準備金 **junbikin** reserves FIN
準備する **junbi suru** arrange; prepare; set up; lay on; get oneself ready; set the table
順調(な) **junchō (na)** smooth, trouble-free
順位 **jun'i** place, position (*in race, competition*)
十二月 **jūnigatsu** December
十二支 **jūnishi** *the twelve Chinese year signs*
順序 **junjo** order; sequence
準々決勝 **junjun-kesshō** quarter-final
巡回 **junkai** patrol; round (*of mailman, doctor*)
巡回中である **junkaichū de aru** be on patrol
巡回する **junkai suru** patrol
循環 **junkan** circulation
循環する **junkan suru** circulate
潤滑油 **junkatsuyu** lubricant
準決勝 **junkesshō** semifinal
純潔 **junketsu** purity
純潔(な) **junketsu (na)** pure
純血(の) **junketsu (no)** pedigree
殉教者 **junkyōsha** martyr
順応する **junnō suru** conform to; adapt to
巡礼 **junrei** pilgrimage
巡礼者 **junrei-sha** pilgrim
純利益 **junrieki** net profit
巡査 **junsa** patrolman
巡査部長 **junsa-buchō** police sergeant
潤色する **junshoku suru** embellish
純粋(な) **junsui (na)** pure
純粋(の) **junsui (no)** solid
純粋さ **junsui-sa** purity
十億 **jū-oku** billion
重量挙げ **jūryōage** weightlifting
重力 **jūryoku** gravity
受領書 **juryō-sho** receipt
受領通知 **juryō-tsūchi** acknowledgment of receipt
銃声 **jūsei** sound of gunfire
受精する **jusei suru** be fertilized
樹脂 **jushi** resin
受信機 **jushinki** receiver TV, RAD
住所 **jūsho** address
重傷 **jūshō** serious injury
受賞者 **jushō-sha** prizewinner
受賞した **jushō shita** prizewinning
ジュース **jūsu** juice; deuce
受胎 **jutai** conception
渋滞 **jūtai** congestion
重体で **jūtai de** critically ill
重体(な) **jūtai (na)** critical
渋滞した **jūtai shita** congested
渋滞している **jūtai shite iru** be jammed
住宅 **jūtaku** housing; residence
住宅地 **jūtakuchi** residential district
住宅ローン **jūtaku-rōn** mortgage
受託者 **jutaku-sha** trustee
じゅうたん **jūtan** carpet; rug
重点 **jūten** emphasis, stress
充てん **jūten** filling; plugging
充当する **jūtō suru** commit; allot; appropriate
受話器 **juwaki** receiver TELEC; 受話器をはずして ***juwaki o hazushite*** off the hook
重役 **jūyaku** executive

重役会議 **jūyaku-kaigi** board meeting
受容 **juyō** acceptance
需要 **juyō** demand COM
重要である **jūyō de aru** count, matter; be important
重要でない **jūyō de nai** insignificant; unimportant
重要(な) **jūyō (na)** important; vital; prominent; significant
重要性 **jūyōsei** importance
授与する **juyo suru** confer, award
重罪 **jūzai** felony
じゅず **juzu** prayer beads; rosary

K

か **ka** ◊ (*question particle*): いいですか ***ii desu ka*** is it OK? ◊: …か…か ***… ka … ka*** either … or…
日 **-ka** (*countword for days*); 二日 ***futsu-ka*** two days; the second (*of the month*)
下 **-ka** below; under; 支配下 ***shihai-ka*** under the control of
化 **-ka** transform into; make into; 自由化 ***jiyû-ka*** liberalization
科 **-ka** department; 日本語科 ***Nihongo-ka*** Department of Japanese
家 **-ka** person; profession; 音楽家 ***ongaku-ka*** musician; 小説家 ***shôsetsu-ka*** novelist
課 **ka** section; department; lesson; 第一課 ***dai-ikka*** Lesson 1
蚊 **ka** mosquito
かば **kaba** hippopotamus
カバー **kabā** cover; jacket (*of book*)
かばん **kaban** bag
カバーレター **kabā-retā** covering letter
かばう **kabau** protect; defend; cover up
かばやき **kabayaki** broiled eels
壁 **kabe** wall
壁紙 **kabegami** wallpaper
かび **kabi** mold
かび臭い **kabikusai** musty
花瓶 **kabin** vase
かびのはえた **kabi no haeta** moldy
過敏症 **kabinshō** hypersensitive
かぼちゃ **kabocha** pumpkin
かぶ **kabu** turnip
株 **kabu** share FIN
カーブ **kābu** bend; curve; twist
歌舞伎 **Kabuki** Kabuki
株主 **kabunushi** stockholder, shareholder
かぶる **kaburu** wear *hat*
株式 **kabushiki** stock
株式会社 **kabushiki-gaisha** incorporated ◊ limited company
株式公開買付 **kabushiki-kōkai-kaitsuke** takeover bid
株式市場 **kabushiki-shijō** stockmarket; securities market
かぶと **kabuto** helmet
かぶと虫 **kabutomushi** beetle
価値 **kachi** merit; value; valuation; 価値がある ***kachi ga aru*** be good value; be worth; 価値が下がる ***kachi ga sagaru*** depreciate; 価値がない ***kachi ga nai*** worthless
勝ち **kachi** win; victory
かちあう **kachiau** clash; coincide
カチカチなる **kachikachi naru** tick
家畜 **kachiku** domestic animal
勝ち目のない人 **kachime no nai hito** outsider (*in race etc*); underdog
かちんと鳴る **kachin to naru** clink; click
課長 **kachō** section chief
課題 **kadai** assignment
過大評価された **kadai-hyōka sareta** overrated
過大に評価する **kadai ni hyōka**

suru overestimate
花壇 **kadan** (flower)bed
カーディガン **kādigan** cardigan
角 **kado** corner
カード **kādo** card
…かどうか **…ka dō ka** whether
門松 **kadomatsu** *New Year's pine decoration*
過度に **kado ni** overly
可動性 **kadōsei** mobility
替え玉 **kaedama** double; stand-in
かえで **kaede** maple; sycamore
帰り **kaeri** return journey
帰りの便 **kaeri no bin** return flight
かえる **kaeru** frog ◊ hatch out (*of eggs*)
変える **kaeru** change; shift
代える, 替える **kaeru** replace; convert
帰る **kaeru** return
返す **kaesu** return, give back; put back; take back; pay back
カフェイン **kafein** caffeine
カフェテラス **kafeterasu** sidewalk café
カフェテリア **kafeteria** cafeteria
花粉 **kafun** pollen
花粉症 **kafunshō** hay fever
カフス **kafusu** cuff
カフスボタン **kafusubotan** cuff link
化学 **kagaku** chemistry
科学 **kagaku** science
科学技術 **kagaku-gijutsu** technology
科学技術恐怖症 **kagaku-gijutsu-kyōfushō** technophobia
科学技術(の) **kagaku-gijutsu** (**no**) technological
化学兵器戦争 **kagaku-heiki-sensō** chemical warfare
化学肥料 **kagaku-hiryō** fertilizer
化学(の) **kagaku** (**no**) chemical
化学療法 **kagaku-ryōhō** chemotherapy
化学者 **kagaku-sha** chemist
科学者 **kagaku-sha** scientist
科学的(な) **kagakuteki** (**na**) scientific
化学薬品 **kagaku-yakuhin** chemicals
かがめる **kagameru** bend; bow
鏡 **kagami** mirror
かがむ **kagamu** bend; stoop; crouch
輝き **kagayaki** glow
輝く **kagayaku** glow; shine; sparkle; twinkle
輝くよう(な) **kagayaku yō** (**na**) radiant
陰 **kage** shadow; 陰で ***kage de*** behind the scenes; 陰で糸を引く ***kage de ito o hiku*** mastermind
影 **kage** shadow; silhouette
過激派 **kagekiha** extremist
過激(な) **kageki** (**na**) extreme; radical
加減 **kagen** adjustment; extent; physical condition
加減する **kagen suru** adjust; moderate
鍵 **kagi** key; lock; 鍵を開ける ***kagi o akeru*** unlock; 鍵をかける ***kagi o kakeru*** lock
鍵穴 **kagiana** keyhole
かぎ回る **kagimawaru** nose around
限られた **kagirareta** restricted
限りのない **kagiri no nai** boundless
限り **kagiri**: …である限りは ***… de aru kagiri wa*** so long as; 今度限り ***kondo kagiri*** just this once
限る **kagiru** confine
かぎつける **kagitsukeru** detect; get wind of
かご **kago** basket; cage
化合物 **kagōbutsu** compound CHEM
化合する **kagō suru** combine
かぐ **kagu** smell; sniff
家具 **kagu** furniture
家具一式 **kagu-isshiki** suite
加虐的(な) **kagyakuteki** (**na**) sadistic
下半身麻痺の人 **kahanshin-mahi no hito** paraplegic
過半数を占める **kahansū o shimeru** be in the majority
かい **kai** paddle
会 **kai** association
階 **kai** floor, story
回 **kai** round (*of drinks*); time, occasion
貝 **kai** seashell; shellfish

海抜 **kaibatsu** altitude; elevation ◊ above sea level
解剖学 **kaibō-gaku** anatomy
怪物 **kaibutsu** monster
会長 **kaichō** president; chairman
懐中電灯 **kaichū-dentō** flashlight
買いだめする **kaidame suru** stock up on
階段 **kaidan** stairs; staircase
会談 **kaidan** consultation; discussion
解読する **kaidoku suru** decipher; decode
回復 **kaifuku** recovery; restoration; revival
回復期 **kaifuku-ki** convalescence
回復させる **kaifuku saseru** revive
回復する **kaifuku suru** recover; recuperate; pull through; survive
絵画 **kaiga** painting
海外で **kaigai de** overseas
海外に **kaigai ni** overseas
海外(の) **kaigai (no)** overseas
海岸 **kaigan** coast
海岸通り **kaigandōri** seafront
海岸線 **kaigansen** coastline
貝殻 **kaigara** shell
戒厳令 **kaigenrei** martial law
会議 **kaigi** conference; congress; meeting
会議場 **kaigijō** convention center
会議室 **kaigishitsu** board room; conference room
懐疑的 **kaigiteki** skeptical
介護 **kaigo** care; nursing (*of the elderly*)
会合 **kaigō** meeting; assembly
海軍 **kaigun** navy
海軍基地 **kaigun-kichi** naval base
海軍大尉 **kaigun-taii** lieutenant
開業医 **kaigyōi** doctor in private practice
開業する **kaigyō suru** set up, establish
開発 **kaihatsu** development
開発業者 **kaihatsu-gyōsha** developer
開発する **kaihatsu suru** develop
回避 **kaihi** evasion
会費 **kaihi** membership fee
回避する **kaihi suru** evade; shirk; deflect
回避的(な) **kaihiteki (na)** evasive
解放 **kaihō** emancipation; release
解放する **kaihō suru** free
開票 **kaihyō** counting (*of votes*)
会員 **kaiin** member
会員資格 **kaiin-shikaku** membership
会員証 **kaiinshō** pass
会場 **kaijō** venue
開会式 **kaikaishiki** opening ceremony
開会する **kaikai suru** begin a session; open a meeting
改革 **kaikaku** reform
改革する **kaikaku suru** reform
快感 **kaikan** pleasant feeling; kick
階下に **kaika ni** downstairs
階下(の) **kaika (no)** downstairs
快活 **kaikatsu** vivacity
快活(な) **kaikatsu (na)** irrepressible; sunny *disposition*
会計 **kaikei** accounts
会計係 **kaikei-gakari** accountant; cashier; treasurer
会計上(の) **kaikei-jō (no)** fiscal
会計課 **kaikeika** accounts department
会計監査 **kaikei-kansa** audit
会計監査官 **kaikei-kansakan** auditor
会計年度 **kaikei-nendo** financial year, fiscal year
会計士 **kaikeishi** accountant
会見 **kaiken** meeting; interview; 会見する ***kaiken suru*** meet with
解決 **kaiketsu** answer; resolution; 解決できない ***kaiketsu dekinai*** insoluble
解決法 **kaiketsu-hō** fix; way out
解決する **kaiketsu suru** resolve; settle; work out
回帰線 **kaikisen** the tropics
解雇 **kaiko** dismissal
回顧 **kaiko** retrospective
蚕 **kaiko** silkworm
回顧録 **kaikoroku** memoirs
解雇される **kaiko sareru** be laid off
解雇する **kaiko suru** dismiss; lay off; fire
海峡 **kaikyō** strait; channel

階級 **kaikyū** social class; rank
階級社会 **kaikyū-shakai** class society
階級闘争 **kaikyū-tōsō** class warfare
解明する **kaimei suru** unravel
買い物 **kaimono** purchase; shopping; 買い物に行く ***kaimono ni iku*** go shopping; 買い物をする ***kaimono o suru*** shop
買い物客 **kaimono-kyaku** shopper
下院 **Kain** House of Representatives; Lower House
飼い慣らされた **kainarasareta** tame
飼い慣らす **kainarasu** domesticate
下院議員 **Kain-giin** Congressman; representative
下位(の) **kai** (**no**) inferior
飼い主 **kainushi** owner; keeper (*of pet*)
介入 **kainyū** intervention
介入する **kainyū suru** intervene
かいらい政権 **kairai-seiken** puppet government
回覧する **kairan suru** circulate
海里 **kairi** nautical mile
回路 **kairo** circuit
カイロプラクター **kairopurakutā** chiropractor
改良 **kairyō** improvement; reform
海流 **kairyū** current (*in sea*)
開催地 **kaisaichi** venue
開催する **kaisai suru** hold; open
解散する **kaisan suru** dismiss; dissolve; break up
改札係 **kaisatsugakari** ticket collector
改札口 **kaisatsuguchi** ticket barrier
快晴 **kaisei** fine weather
改正 **kaisei** reform; revision
改正する **kaisei suru** reform; revise
懐石料理 **kaiseki-ryōri** Japanese-style haute cuisine
回戦 **kaisen** round (*in tournament*)
回線 **kaisen** telephone line
会戦 **kaisen** battle, encounter
開戦 **kaisen** outbreak of war
解説 **kaisetsu** comment
解説者 **kaisetsu-sha** commentator
会社 **kaisha** business, company, firm
解釈 **kaishaku** interpretation
解釈する **kaishaku suru** interpret
開始 **kaishi** initiation
買い占める **kaishimeru** buy up
開始する **kaishi suru** commence; initiate; open; inaugurate
会衆 **kaishū** congregation REL
回収 **kaishū** recovery; recall
改宗させる **kaishū saseru** convert REL
改修する **kaishū suru** repair; renovate
回収する **kaishū suru** repossess; retrieve
階層 **kaisō** layer
海草 **kaisō** seaweed
快速 **kaisoku** fast train
改装する **kaisō suru** redecorate
回数 **kaisū** frequency
回数券 **kaisūken** multi-journey ticket
開拓する **kaitaku suru** cultivate; develop; open up
買い手 **kaite** buyer, purchaser
快適(な) **kaiteki** (**na**) pleasant
快適さ **kaiteki-sa** comfort
回転 **kaiten** revolution, turn; rotation; spin
回転盤 **kaitenban** turntable
回転ドア **kaiten-doa** revolving door
回転させる **kaiten saseru** spin; turn
回転する **kaiten suru** revolve; rotate; spin
開店する **kaiten suru** open (for business); establish
解答 **kaitō** answer; response; solution
買い取る **kaitoru** buy out
解答する **kaitō suru** answer; respond; solve
解凍する **kaitō suru** defrost, thaw; 圧縮ファイルを解凍する ***asshuku fairu o kaitô suru*** unzip
会話 **kaiwa** conversation; talk
会話集 **kaiwa-shū** phrasebook
会話(の) **kaiwa** (**no**) conversational
かいよう **kaiyō** ulcer
海洋(の) **kaiyō** (**no**) seafaring
改善 **kaizen** improvement
改善する **kaizen suru** improve
改造 **kaizō** conversion; modification; renovation

解像力 **kaizō-ryoku** resolution
改造する **kaizō suru** adapt, modify; renovate
海図 **kaizu** (nautical) chart
かじ **kaji** rudder
火事 **kaji** blaze, fire
家事 **kaji** housekeeping; housework
かじかんだ **kajikanda** numb
かじき **kajiki** swordfish
カジノ **kajino** casino
かじる **kajiru** chew; gnaw; nibble
箇条書にする **kajōgaki ni suru** itemize
過剰(の) **kajō (no)** excess; excessive
カジュアル(な) **kajuaru (na)** casual
カジュアルウェア **kajuaru-wea** casual wear
果樹園 **kajuen** orchard
抱える **kakaeru** embrace; hold; employ
掲げる **kakageru** put up; hoist; hold up; publish
価格 **kakaku** value
係り **kakari** person in charge; subsection of an office
係り長 **kakarichō** assistant manager
かかる **kakaru** cost; take *time*; catch
掛かる **kakaru** hang
かかと **kakato** heel
かかっていない **kakatte inai** be off (*of brake*)
かかっている **kakatte iru** be on (*of brake*); span
かかわらず **kakawarazu**: …にかかわらず ***… ni kakawarazu*** whatever; regardless of
かかわり合い **kakawariai** involvement; …とかかわり合いになる ***… to kakawariai ni naru*** get mixed up with
かかわる **kakawaru** engage in; get involved with
賭け **kake** bet
駆け足 **kakeashi** run
掛け布団 **kakebuton** quilt, duvet
かけがえのない **kakegae no nai** indispensable; invaluable; irreplaceable
掛け金 **kakegane** latch
掛け声 **kakegoe** chant; 掛け声を掛ける ***kakegoe o kakeru*** chant
賭け事 **kakegoto** gamble; gambling; 賭け事をする ***kakegoto o suru*** bet
家計 **kakei** budget
家系 **kakei** descent; lineage
掛け軸 **kakejiku** hanging scroll
賭け金 **kakekin** stake
駆け落ちする **kakeochi suru** elope
かけら **kakera** bit; piece; fragment
かける **kakeru** put on *glasses, necklace*; build; cover; sprinkle; impose *tax*; switch on; tie up
賭ける **kakeru** bet, stake; back
掛ける **kakeru** hang; multiply; sit down
欠ける **kakeru** lack; wane
欠けている **kakete iru** be lacking; be devoid of
可決する **kaketsu suru** pass, carry *proposal*
掛け算 **kakezan** multiplication
かき **kaki** oyster
柿 **kaki** persimmon
夏期 **kaki** summer; summer semester
かき氷 **kakigōri** *crushed ice with syrup*
かき込む **kakikomu** tuck away; shovel in
かき混ぜる **kakimazeru** stir; toss
書き直す **kakinaosu** rewrite
かき鳴らす **kakinarasu** strum
下記に **kaki ni** below
下記参照 **kaki-sanshō** see below
書き手 **kakite** writer
書留めで送る **kakitome de okuru** send a letter registered
書き留める **kakitomeru** write down, note down
書留書簡 **kakitome-shokan** registered letter
書き取り **kakitori** dictation
書き初め **kakizome** New Year calligraphy
活気 **kakki** activity; vitality; dynamism; …に活気を与える ***… ni kakki o ataeru*** enliven
活気のある **kakki no aru** lively; exuberant
活気のない **kakki no nai** dead *place*; sleepy *town*; slack *period*

画期的(な) **kakkiteki** (**na**) epoch-making
活気づける **kakkizukeru** stimulate; inspire; give life to
活気づく **kakkizuku** become lively; boom
かっこ **kakko** bracket
格好 **kakkō** form; appearance
格好いい **kakkō ii** stylish; attractive
確固たる **kakko taru** solid, firm; determined
確固とした **kakko to shita** pronounced, definite; unswerving
格好悪い **kakkō warui** unattractive, ugly
過去 **kako** past
下降 **kakō** downturn
河口 **kakō** mouth (*of river*)
過去分詞 **kako-bunshi** past participle
花こう岩 **kakōgan** granite
囲い **kakoi** enclosure; compound; pen; fold; corral
囲い込む **kakoikomu** fence in
過去形 **kakokei** past tense
囲む **kakomu** enclose; surround; 囲まれている ***kakomarete iru*** be surrounded by
加工していない **kakō shite inai** raw
加工する **kakō suru** process
かく **kaku** scratch
欠く **kaku** be lacking; neglect; chip; crack
描く **kaku** paint; draw
書く **kaku** write, put down (in writing)
核 **kaku** core; nucleus
各 **kaku** each; every
格上げする **kakuage suru** upgrade; promote
核分裂 **kakubunretsu** nuclear fission
拡張 **kakuchō** enlargement; expansion
拡張する **kakuchō suru** expand; extend
拡大 **kakudai** enlargement; expansion; escalation
拡大鏡 **kakudaikyō** magnifying glass
拡大する **kakudai suru** expand; enlarge; magnify
角度 **kakudo** angle
角刈り **kakugari** crew cut
覚悟 **kakugo** readiness
核廃棄物 **kaku-haikibutsu** nuclear waste
核兵器 **kaku-heiki** nuclear weapon
確保する **kakuho suru** secure, obtain
確実(な) **kakujitsu** (**na**) definite; sure; safe; hard *facts, evidence*
確実に **kakujitsu ni** reliably
確実にする **kakujitsu ni suru** ensure
確実性 **kakujitsusei** certainty; safety (*of prediction*)
かくまう **kakumau** harbor, shelter
革命 **kakumei** revolution; 革命を起こす ***kakumei o okosu*** revolutionize
革命家 **kakumei-ka** revolutionary
革命(の) **kakumei** (**no**) revolutionary
革命的(な) **kakumeiteki** (**na**) revolutionary
確認 **kakunin** confirmation, verification
確認する **kakunin suru** check; confirm; recognize
核(の) **kaku** (**no**) nuclear
架空(の) **kakū** (**no**) fictitious, imaginary
格納庫 **kakunōko** hangar
隠れ家 **kakurega** retreat
かくれんぼ **kakurenbo** hide-and-seek
隠れる **kakureru** hide; go into hiding
隠れている **kakurete iru** be in hiding
隔離 **kakuri** seclusion; quarantine
隔離病棟 **kakuri-byōtō** isolation ward
確率 **kakuritsu** probability
確立する **kakuritsu suru** establish
隠された **kakusareta** hidden
覚せい剤 **kakuseizai** stimulant
かくしゃくとした **kakushaku to shita** sprightly
隠しきれない **kakushikirenai** telltale

確信 **kakushin** assurance; certainty; belief
核心 **kakushin** core, heart (*of problem*)
革新 **kakushin** innovation
確信のある **kakushin no aru** assured
確信させる **kakushin saseru** convince
革新者 **kakushin-sha** innovator
確信している **kakushin shite iru** be certain
革新的(な) **kakushinteki (na)** innovative
隠す **kakusu** hide; cover; disguise; mask; withhold
確定申告書 **kakutei-shinkokusho** tax return
確定する **kakutei suru** determine, establish
カクテル **kakuteru** cocktail
獲得する **kakutoku suru** capture; land *job*; poll *votes*
格闘する **kakutō suru** fight; wrestle
獲得する **kakutoku suru** win; obtain
格付けする **kakuzuke suru** rank; grade
窯 **kama** kiln
かま **kama** sickle
かまう **kamau** mind, object to; かまうものか ***kamau mono ka*** I don't care!
かまわずに **kamawazu ni** regardless
かめ **kame** tortoise; turtle; tub
カメラ **kamera** camera
カメラマン **kameraman** photographer; cameraman
神 **kami** God, Lord; deity; god
紙 **kami** paper
髪 **kami** hair
かみ合わせる **kamiawaseru** engage, mesh
紙挟み **kamibasami** clipboard
紙袋 **kamibukuro** paper bag
神棚 **kamidana** Shinto altar
髪型 **kamigata** hairdo
神風 **kamikaze** kamikaze
紙コップ **kamikoppu** paper cup
紙くず **kamikuzu** wastepaper
雷 **kaminari** bolt (*of lightning*); thunder
神(の) **kami (no)** divine
紙(の) **kami (no)** paper
髪の毛 **kami no ke** hair
仮眠する **kamin suru** grab some sleep
神様 **kamisama** god; ace; champion
かみそり **kamisori** razor
紙テープ **kami-tēpu** streamer
かみつきそう(な) **kamitsukisō (na)** snappy
かみつく **kamitsuku** bite; snap
紙やすり **kami-yasuri** sandpaper
かも **kamo** duck; sucker (*person*)
科目 **kamoku** subject
かもめ **kamome** (sea)gull
…かもしれない **… kamo shirenai** may, might; 彼は決心したかもしれない ***kare wa kesshin shita kamo shirenai*** he may have decided
貨物 **kamotsu** freight
貨物機 **kamotsu-ki** freighter, cargo plane
貨物列車 **kamotsu-ressha** freight train
貨物船 **kamotsu-sen** freighter
貨物室 **kamotsushitsu** hold
貨物輸送 **kamotsu-yusō** shipment
かむ **kamu** bite; chew
カムバックする **kamubakku suru** make a comeback
カムフラージュ **kamufurāju** camouflage
カムフラージュする **kamufurāju suru** camouflage
缶 **kan** can
勘 **kan** feeling; intuition; 勘が鈍る ***kan ga niburu*** be losing one's grip
間 **-kan** for; during; between; 一時間 ***ichiji-kan*** for an hour; 東京-シカゴ間 ***Tôkyô-Shikago-kan*** between Tokyo and Chicago
巻 **-kan** *countword for books, volumes*
かな **kana** (*question particle*): 雨かな ***ame kana*** is it raining?
仮名 **kana** Japanese syllabary
金網 **kanaami** wire netting
カナダ **Kanada** Canada
カナダ人 **Kanada-jin** Canadian

カナダ(の) **Kanada (no)** Canadian
かなえる **kanaeru** grant
家内 **kanai** wife
金切り声 **kanakirigoe** screech; squeal; 金切り声をあげる ***kanakirigoe o ageru*** screech; squeal
金物類 **kanamonorui** hardware
必ず **kanarazu** without fail
必ずしも **kanarazushimo** not necessarily
かなり **kanari** considerably; rather; fairly, quite; quite a lot
カナリア **kanaria** canary
かなり(の) **kanari (no)** considerable, substantial; significant; a good deal of ◊ quite a few; a number of
かなりたくさん(の) **kanari takusan (no)** a good many
悲しげ(な) **kanashige (na)** mournful
悲しい **kanashii** sad; disconsolate
悲しませる **kanashimaseru** upset
悲しみ **kanashimi** sadness; sorrow; grief; 悲しみに沈んだ ***kanashimi ni shizunda*** mournful
悲しむ **kanashimu** grieve; feel sad
悲しそう(な) **kanashisō (na)** sad; plaintive
かなう **kanau** come true; be fulfilled; measure up to; be consistent with; 法にかなう ***hô ni kanau*** follow the rules
かなづち **kanazuchi** hammer; non-swimmer
干ばつ **kanbatsu** drought
勘弁 **kanben** forgiveness
カンボジア **Kanbojia** Cambodia
カンボジア(の) **Kanbojia (no)** Cambodian
かん木 **kanboku** shrub
陥没 **kanbotsu** cave-in; subsidence
幹部 **kanbu** executive
看病する **kanbyō suru** nurse; look after
干潮 **kanchō** low tide
館長 **kanchō** curator
寛大(な) **kandai (na)** generous; lenient
かん高い **kandakai** high-pitched; strident
感動させる **kandō saseru** move, touch (*emotionally*)
勘当する **kandō suru** disown; disinherit
感動する **kandō suru** be impressed
感動的(な) **kandōteki (na)** emotional; moving; stirring
金 **kane** money
鐘 **kane** bell
金貸し **kanekashi** moneylender; moneylending
金持ち **kanemochi** the rich
金持ち(の) **kanemochi (no)** rich; well-heeled
肝炎 **kan'en** hepatitis
金のかかる **kane no kakaru** expensive
金の無駄 **kane no muda** waste of money
可燃性(の) **kanensei (no)** (in)flammable, combustible
兼ねる **kaneru** combine; serve several functions
カーネーション **kānēshon** carnation
加熱する **kanetsu suru** heat up
金づる **kanezuru** financial supporter; meal ticket
考え **kangae** idea, notion; thought; mind; plan; intention
考え出す **kangaedasu** dream up, think up; come up with
考え方 **kangaekata** mentality, mindset; viewpoint
考え込む **kangaekomu** brood
考え込んだ **kangaekonda** thoughtful
考え直す **kangaenaosu** reconsider
考えられない **kangaerarenai** inconceivable, unthinkable
考えられる **kangaerareru** conceivable
考える **kangaeru** think; assume; figure
かんがい **kangai** irrigation
かんがいする **kangai suru** irrigate
管楽器 **kangakki** wind instrument
歓迎 **kangei** welcome, reception
歓迎する **kangei suru** welcome
感激する **kangeki suru** be touched; be moved
看護 **kango** nursing; care

看護婦 **kangofu** nurse
看護士 **kangoshi** male nurse
かに **kani** crab
カーニバル **kānibaru** carnival
果肉 **kaniku** flesh; pulp (*of fruit*)
患者 **kanja** patient
漢字 **kanji** Chinese character
感じ **kanji** sense
肝心(の) **kanjin** (**no**) essential
感じのいい **kanji no ii** agreeable; pleasant; pleasing
感じられる **kanjirareru** feel
感じる **kanjiru** feel; sense
勘定 **kanjō** bill; check; counting; 勘定を払う ***kanjô o harau*** pay
感情 **kanjō** emotion; feeling
冠状動脈血栓 **kanjō-dōmyaku-kessen** coronary
勘定書き **kanjōgaki** check (*in restaurant etc*)
感情的(な) **kanjōteki** (**na**) emotional
感覚 **kankaku** feeling; sensation; sense
間隔 **kankaku** interval
感覚のない **kankaku no nai** numb
かんかんになっている **kankan ni natte iru** be fuming
関係 **kankei** connection; relationship; dealings; involvement; …と関係がある ***... to kankei ga aru*** be connected with; be mixed up in
関係のない **kankei no nai** unrelated
関係者以外立ち入り禁止 **kankeisha-igai-tachiiri-kinshi** private
関係している **kankei shite iru** be associated with
関係する **kankei suru** be concerned; be involved
簡潔(な) **kanketsu** (**na**) concise, succinct
歓喜 **kanki** jubilation
換気 **kanki** ventilation
換気孔 **kankikō** ventilation shaft
監禁 **kankin** confinement
換金性 **kankinsei** liquidity
缶切り **kankiri** can opener
換気装置 **kanki-sōchi** ventilator
換気する **kanki suru** ventilate; air
観光 **kankō** sightseeing
観光案内所 **kankō annaisho** tourist (information) office
観光事業 **kankō jigyō** tourism
韓国 **Kankoku** Korea
韓国語 **Kankoku-go** Korean
韓国人 **Kankoku-jin** Korean
韓国(の) **Kankoku** (**no**) Korean
観光客 **kankō-kyaku** tourist; visitor; sightseer
観客 **kankyaku** audience; spectator
観客席 **kankyakuseki** auditorium
環境 **kankyō** environment; setting; surroundings; 環境にやさしい ***kankyôniyasashii*** environmentally friendly
環境庁 **Kankyōchō** Environment Agency
環境保護 **kankyō-hogo** environmental protection
環境保護(の) **kankyō-hogo** (**no**) ecological, green
環境保護論者 **kankyō-hogo-ronsha** environmentalist
環境(の) **kankyō** (**no**) environmental
環境汚染 **kankyō-osen** environmental pollution
緩慢(な) **kanman** (**na**) sluggish
甘味料 **kanmiryō** sweetener
かんな **kanna** plane (*tool*)
カンニングをする **kanningu o suru** cheat
観音 **kannon** goddess of mercy
官能的(な) **kannōteki** (**na**) sensual; voluptuous; sultry
かんぬき **kannuki** bolt; bar
神主 **kannushi** Shinto priest
彼女 **kanojo** she ◊ girlfriend
彼女(の) **kanojo** (**no**) her
可能(な) **kanō** (**na**) feasible; possible
可能性 **kanōsei** chance; possibility; potential; liability
化膿する **kanō suru** fester
乾杯 **kanpai** toast ◊ cheers!, your health!
完敗する **kanpai suru** be wiped out, be totally beaten
乾杯する **kanpai suru** toast
完ぺき **kanpeki** perfection

完ぺき(な) **kanpeki** (**na**) perfect; flawless
完ぺき主義者 **kanpeki-shugi-sha** perfectionist
漢方薬 **kanpōyaku** Chinese herbal medicine
慣例 **kanrei** institution
関連 **kanren** link; relevance
関連させる **kanren saseru** link
関連する **kanren suru** relevant
関連づける **kanrenzukeru** connect; implicate
管理 **kanri** administration; control
管理人 **kanri-nin** caretaker; superintendent
管理(の) **kanri** (**no**) administrative
管理する **kanri suru** look after; control; manage
管理者 **kanri-sha** administrator
管理職 **kanrishoku** administration; management
簡略 **kanryaku** informality; simplicity
官僚 **kanryō** bureaucracy; bureaucrat
完了形 **kanryōkei** perfect GRAM
官僚主義 **kanryō-shugi** bureaucracy, red tape
完了する **kanryō suru** accomplish
官僚的(な) **kanryōteki** (**na**) bureaucratic
関西 **Kansai** *area around Osaka, Kyoto and Hyogo*
閑散期(の) **kansanki** (**no**) offpeak
監査する **kansa suru** audit
観察 **kansatsu** observation
観察地点 **kansatsu-chiten** viewpoint (*place*)
観察者 **kansatsu-sha** observer
観察する **kansatsu suru** observe; study
観察点 **kansatsuten** vantage point
歓声 **kansei** cheer; cheering; 歓声を上げる ***kansei o ageru*** cheer
完成 **kansei** completion
完成する **kansei suru** complete; perfect
艦船 **kansen** fleet
感染 **kansen** infection
幹線道路 **kansen-dōro** highway; main road
感染した **kansen shita** septic
感染する **kansen suru** become infected; go septic ◊ infectious
関節 **kansetsu** joint ANAT
関節炎 **kansetsuen** arthritis
間接経費 **kansetsu-keihi** overhead FIN
間接的(な) **kansetsuteki** (**na**) indirect
間接的に **kansetsuteki ni** indirectly
感謝 **kansha** gratitude; appreciation; thanks
かんしゃく **kanshaku** tantrum
感謝している **kansha shite iru** thankful
感謝する **kansha suru** grateful ◊ thank; be grateful to
冠詞 **kanshi** article GRAM
感心 **kanshin** admiration
関心 **kanshin** concern; 関心がある ***kanshin ga aru*** care about; 関心のない ***kanshin no nai*** unconcerned
関心事 **kanshinji** a matter of concern
感心する **kanshin suru** admire
監視されている **kanshi sarete iru** come under scrutiny
監視する **kanshi suru** monitor; observe
関して **kan shite**: …に関して ***… ni kan shite*** in connection with, with reference to, as regards
鑑賞 **kanshō** appreciation
干渉 **kanshō** interference; intervention
感傷 **kanshō** sentiment, sentimentality
感触 **kanshoku** touch
干渉する **kanshō suru** interfere, meddle; intervene
感傷的(な) **kanshōteki** (**na**) sentimental; sloppy
看守 **kanshu** guard
慣習 **kanshū** convention; custom
感想 **kansō** thoughts; impressions; feedback
乾燥機 **kansō-ki** dryer, drier
観測所 **kansokujo** observatory
観測する **kansoku suru** observe; survey

簡素(な) **kanso (na)** plain; austere
乾燥した **kansō shita** arid; dried; seasoned
感嘆符 **kantanfu** exclamation point
簡単(な) **kantan (na)** easy, simple
簡単にする **kantan ni suru** simplify
簡単さ **kantan-sa** simplicity
感嘆させる **kantan saseru** dazzle
観点 **kanten** point of view
関東 **Kantō** *central eastern district of Tokyo, Kanagawa*
監督 **kantoku** direction; director; supervisor
監督する **kantoku suru** direct; oversee; supervise
かんと鳴る **kan to naru** clang
カントリー **kantorī** country and western
貫通する **kantsū suru** penetrate; pierce
カヌー **kanū** canoe
緩和 **kanwa** relief; easing
慣用 **kan'yō** usage
寛容 **kan'yō** tolerance
慣用句 **kan'yōku** idiom
寛容(な) **kan'yō (na)** tolerant
慣用的(な) **kan'yōteki (na)** idiomatic
加入する **kanyū suru** join; take out *insurance*
換算 **kanzan** conversion
換算表 **kanzan-hyō** conversion table
換算する **kanzan suru** convert
関税 **kanzei** tariff
完全(な) **kanzen (na)** complete; full; perfect
肝臓 **kanzō** liver (*in body*)
缶詰にする **kanzume ni suru** can
缶詰(の) **kanzume (no)** canned
顔 **kao** face; 顔に泥を塗る ***kao ni doro o nuru*** bring shame on; 顔を赤くする ***kao o akaku suru*** go red in the face; 顔を出す ***kao o dasu*** put in an appearance; 顔をしかめる ***kao o shikameru*** frown; scowl; 顔を背ける ***kao o somukeru*** turn away, look away; 顔をつぶす ***kao o tsubusu*** make lose face; 顔をつぶされる ***kao o tsubusareru*** lose face
顔立ち **kaodachi** features
顔色 **kaoiro** color; complexion; 顔色が悪い ***kaoiro ga warui*** look pale; have a bad complexion
香り **kaori** scent; perfume; aroma; bouquet
カーペット **kāpetto** carpet
かっぱ **kappa** water imp
活発(な) **kappatsu (na)** vigorous; vivacious; brisk
カップ **kappu** cup
カップル **kappuru** couple
カプセル **kapuseru** capsule
から **kara** from; after; off; because; so; 十八世紀から ***jûhasseiki kara*** from the 18th century; 十人から十五人まで ***jû-nin kara jûgo-nin made*** from 10 to 15 people; 五時から ***goji kara*** after five o'clock; 雨が降っているから ***ame ga futte iru kara*** because it's raining
殻 **kara** husk; shell
カラー **karā** color; collar
カーラー **kārā** roller
体 **karada** body; 体に合わない ***karada ni awanai*** disagree with (*of food*)
辛い **karai** hot, spicy
からかう **karakau** make fun of; play a joke on
辛口(の) **karakuchi (no)** dry *wine*
絡まる **karamaru** become entangled in
絡ませる **karamaseru** wind
絡み付く **karamitsuku** wind (*of ivy etc*)
空になる **kara ni naru** empty
空にする **kara ni suru** empty
空(の) **kara (no)** blank
カラオケ **karaoke** karaoke
空っぽ **karappo** emptiness
空っぽ(の) **karappo (no)** empty, hollow
カラー写真 **karā-shashin** color photograph
からし **karashi** (Japanese) mustard
からす **karasu** crow
枯らす **karasu** kill *plant*; parch *crops*
空手 **karate** karate
空手チョップ **karate choppu** karate chop

カラーテレビ **karā-terebi** color TV
カラット **karatto** carat
彼 **kare** he; him ◊ boyfriend
かれい **karei** plaice; flounder
華麗に **karei ni** gorgeously; magnificently
カレンダー **karendā** calendar
彼の **kare no** his
彼ら **karera** they; them
彼らの **karera no** their ◊ theirs
枯れる **kareru** wither
枯れ山水 **karesanzui** rock garden with raked gravel
彼氏 **kareshi** boyfriend
狩り **kari** hunt
借り **kari** debt
カリフラワー **karifurawā** cauliflower
刈り込み **karikomi** trim
刈り込む **karikomu** clip; crop
借り越す **karikosu** overdraw
カリキュラム **karikyuramu** curriculum
借りる **kariru** borrow; rent
仮出所 **karishussho** parole
カリスマ **karisuma** charisma
借りている **karite iru** on loan ◊ owe
過労 **karō** overwork
かろうじて **karōjite** barely; narrowly; only just
カロリー **karorī** calorie
過労死 **karōshi** death from overwork
狩る **karu** hunt
刈る **karu** mow
カール **kāru** curl
カルチャーショック **karuchā-shokku** culture shock
軽い **karui** frivolous; minor; light; idle *threat*
軽くなる **karuku naru** ease up
軽くする **karuku suru** lighten
軽さ **karu-sa** lightness
カルシウム **karushiumu** calcium
カールする **kāru suru** curl
カルテル **karuteru** cartel
カルテット **karutetto** quartet
かさ **kasa** lampshade
傘 **kasa** umbrella
かさばった **kasabatta** bulky
かさぶた **kasabuta** scab
火災 **kasai** fire
火災報知機 **kasai-hōchiki** fire alarm
かさかさと鳴る **kasakasa to naru** rustle
重なる **kasanaru** overlap
重ねる **kasaneru** pile up; repeat
稼ぎ手 **kasegite** breadwinner
稼ぐ **kasegu** earn, make
家政婦 **kaseifu** housekeeper
化石 **kaseki** fossil
下線を引く **kasen o hiku** underline
仮説 **kasetsu** hypothesis
仮説上(の) **kasetsujō (no)** hypothetical
カセット **kasetto** cassette
カセットテープ **kasetto-tēpu** tape
貨車 **kasha** freight car
かし **kashi** oak
華氏 **kashi** Fahrenheit
歌詞 **kashi** lyrics
菓子 **kashi** cake; candy
貸し倒れ金 **kashidaorekin** bad debt
貸し家あり **kashiie ari** house for rent
賢い **kashikoi** wise
かしこまりました **kashikomarimashita** (*acknowledging order, request etc*) yes, sir; sure; thank you (*said by sales clerk*)
カシミヤ(の) **kashimiya (no)** cashmere
かしら **kashira** I wonder; I hope
頭文字 **kashira-moji** initial
貸付金 **kashitsukekin** loan
加湿器 **kashitsuki** humidifier
柏餅 **kashiwamochi** *rice cake wrapped in an oak leaf with sweetbean paste*
過小評価する **kashō-hyōka suru** undervalue
歌手 **kashu** singer
火葬 **kasō** cremation; 火葬にする ***kasô ni suru*** cremate
仮装 **kasō** fancy dress
火葬場 **kasō-ba** crematorium
仮想現実 **kasō-genjitsu** virtual reality
加速 **kasoku** acceleration
加速する **kasoku suru** accelerate

カーソル **kāsoru** cursor
仮装する **kasō suru** dress up
滑車 **kassha** pulley
滑走路 **kassōro** runway
かす **kasu** dregs; scum
課す **kasu** impose
貸す **kasu** loan; rent (out)
かすか(な) **kasuka** (**na**) dim; faint; vague
かすかな光 **kasuka na hikari** glimmer
かすめる **kasumeru** graze; skim past; steal
かすみ **kasumi** haze
かすむ **kasumu** glaze over; mist over
かすんだ **kasunda** misty
かすり傷 **kasurikizu** graze
かする **kasuru** brush; brush against
カスタードクリーム **kasutādo-kurīmu** custard
カースト **kāsuto** caste
方 **kata** person (*polite*)
方 **-kata** how to…; 書き方 ***kakikata*** how to write
…方 **… kata** care of, c/o
過多 **kata** excess
型 **kata** version; kind; 型にはまらない ***kata ni hamaranai*** unconventional; 型にはまる ***kata ni hamaru*** be in a rut; 型にはまった ***kata ni hamatta*** conventional; set *views, ideas*
潟 **kata** lagoon
肩 **kata** shoulder; 肩をすくめる ***kata o sukumeru*** shrug (one's shoulders)
形 **katachi** figure; form; shape
形になる **katachi ni naru** form
形作る **katachizukuru** form
かたどる **katadoru** model on; imitate
肩書き **katagaki** title
型紙 **katagami** pattern
方々 **katagata** people (*polite*)
肩口 **kataguchi** socket
肩ひも **katahimo** strap
片方 **katahō** one side; one of a pair
硬い, 固い, 堅い **katai** rigid; solid; stiff; tough; tight *drawer, screw*; serious *company*
かたかな **katakana** *the angular Japanese syllabary*
堅くなる **kataku naru** harden; stiffen up
かたくり粉 **katakuriko** cornstarch
堅苦しい **katakurushii** uptight; stiff (*in manner*); stilted
堅く絞める **kataku shimeru** tighten
家宅捜索令状 **katakusōsaku-reijō** search warrant
固まり **katamari** block; chunk; clot
固まる **katamaru** harden; solidify; set
片道切符 **katamichi-kippu** one-way ticket
傾ける **katamukeru** lean
傾き **katamuki** slope
傾く **katamuku** lean; slant; tilt
刀 **katana** samurai sword
片親(の) **kataoya** (**no**) single parent
カタログ **katarogu** catalog; literature
語る **kataru** relate; talk
固さ, 硬さ, 堅さ **kata-sa** hardness; rigidity
片手 **katate** one hand
片手なべ **katate-nabe** saucepan
かたつむり **katatsumuri** snail
偏らない **katayoranai** impartial; fair; varied
偏った, 片寄った **katayotta** biased; unfair
固ゆで(の) **katayude** (**no**) hard-boiled
片付ける **katazukeru** clear away; tidy up
仮定 **katei** assumption
家庭 **katei** home
過程 **katei** process
家庭教師 **katei-kyōshi** (private) tutor
家庭(の) **katei** (**no**) domestic
仮定する **katei suru** assume
家庭的(な) **kateiteki** (**na**) homeloving, homely
カーテン **kāten** drapes, curtains
カート **kāto** baggage cart
過渡期(の) **katoki** (**no**) transitional
カートリッジ **kātoridji** cartridge
カトリック(の) **katorikku** (**no**) Roman Catholic

カトリック信者**katorikku-shinja** Roman Catholic
勝つ **katsu** win; prevail; …に勝つ ***… ni katsu*** win a victory over …
活動 **katsudō** activity
活動家 **katsudōka** activist
活動的(な) **katsudōteki** (**na**) active; dynamic
担ぐ**katsugu** shoulder; carry; play tricks on
活字 **katsuji** type (*printing*)
活字体 **katsujitai** block letters
かつお **katsuo** bonito
かつら **katsura** wig
活力 **katsuryoku** dynamism; spirit
かつて **katsute** once; long ago
活躍する **katsuyaku suru** be active
活用する **katsuyō suru** use, employ; conjugate
飼っている **katte iru** have, keep *pet*
勝手気ままにさせる **katte kimama ni saseru** run wild
勝手(な) **katte** (**na**) arbitrary; 勝手にしなさい ***katte ni shinasai*** please yourself!
カット **katto** cut
かっとなる **katto naru** lose one's cool; blow up
カットする **katto suru** cut
買う **kau** buy
飼う **kau** keep *pet*; raise
カウボーイ **kaubōi** cowboy
カウチポテト **kauchi-poteto** couch potato
カウンセラー **kaunserā** counselor
カウンセリング **kaunseringu** counseling
カウンター **kauntā** bar, counter
カウント **kaunto** count
皮 **kawa** crust; peel; leather; hide (*of animal*); 皮をはぐ ***kawa o hagu*** skin; 皮をむく ***kawa o muku*** peel; 皮をなめす ***kawa o namesu*** tan *leather*
川, 河 **kawa** river
革 **kawa** leather
川床 **kawadoko** riverbed
川岸 **kawagishi** riverside
かわいがる **kawaigaru** fondle
かわいい **kawaii** cute; sweet
かわいらしい **kawairashii** endearing; pretty
かわいそう(な) **kawaisō** (**na**) pitiful; poor
乾いた **kawaita** dry
皮ジャン **kawajan** bomber jacket
乾かす **kawakasu** dry
乾く **kawaku** drain; dry
皮(の) **kawa** (**no**) leather
かわら **kawara** roof tile
代わり **kawari** substitute; exchange; fill in
代わりに **kawari ni** instead (of)
代わり(の) **kawari** (**no**) alternate; alternative
変わりやすい **kawariyasui** unsettled; changeable
変わる **kawaru** swing (*of opinion*); change; break (*of boy's voice*)
代わる **kawaru** replace
為替相場 **kawase-sōba** exchange rate
かわす **kawasu** evade; ward off; duck
変わった **kawatta** unusual
かわうそ **kawauso** otter
蚊帳 **kaya** mosquito net
火薬 **kayaku** gunpowder
火曜日 **kayōbi** Tuesday
通う **kayou** attend *school*; commute; frequent *place*
かゆい **kayui** itchy
かゆみ **kayumi** itch
火山 **kazan** volcano
火山灰 **kazanbai** ash
飾り **kazari** decoration; ornament; trimming
飾り(の) **kazari** (**no**) decorative; ornamental
飾る **kazaru** decorate; garnish; trim
風 **kaze** wind; 風の強い ***kaze no tsuyoi*** windy
風邪 **kaze** cold; 風邪を引く ***kaze o hiku*** catch (a) cold
課税 **kazei** taxation
課税する **kazei suru** tax
風通しのよい **kazetōshi no yoi** airy
数えきれない **kazoekirenai** countless
数える **kazoeru** count
家族 **kazoku** family; household

家族計画 **kazoku-keikaku** family planning
数 **kazu** count; number; 数に入る ***kazu ni hairu*** count; qualify; 数に入れる ***kazu ni ireru*** count
毛 **ke** hair (*single*); bristles
気 **ke** touch; sign; indication
家 **-ke** family
毛穴 **keana** pore
けばだった **kebadatta** fuzzy
けばけばしい **kebakebashii** flashy; garish, gaudy
毛深い **kebukai** hairy
ケーブルカー **kēburu-kā** cable car; funicular
ケーブルテレビ **kēburu-terebi** cable television, cable (TV)
ケチャップ **kechappu** ketchup
けち **kechi** miser; けちをつける ***kechi o tsukeru*** find fault with
けちけちした **kechikechi shita** niggardly
けち(な) **kechi (na)** mean; miserly; tight-fisted
けちる **kechiru** be stingy with
けだもの **kedamono** brute
怪我 **kega** injury; 怪我をさせる ***kega o saseru*** injure; 怪我をする ***kega o suru*** injure
怪我をした **kega o shita** injured
汚す **kegasu** ruin; violate; tarnish
毛皮 **kegawa** fur; coat (*of animal*)
刑 **kei** punishment; sentence
敬愛する **keiai suru** revere
競馬 **keiba** the races
競馬場 **keiba-jō** racecourse
刑罰 **keibatsu** punishment
軽べつ **keibetsu** contempt; scorn
軽べつした **keibetsu shita** scornful
軽べつする **keibetsu suru** despise; pour scorn on
軽べつ的(な) **keibetsuteki (na)** derogatory, pejorative
警備 **keibi** security guard
警備部門 **keibi-bumon** security
警備員 **keibiin** security guard
警備する **keibi suru** guard
警備隊 **keibitai** guard
警棒 **keibō** nightstick
経度 **keido** longitude
経営 **keiei** administration; management
経営学 **keieigaku** business studies; management studies
経営学大学院 **keieigaku-daigakuin** business school
経営学修士 **keieigaku-shūshi** MBA, master in business administration
経営陣 **keieijin** management team
経営コンサルタント **keiei-konsarutanto** management consultant
経営(の) **keiei (no)** managerial; administrative
経営者 **keiei-sha** manager; administrator
経営者側 **keieisha-gawa** management
経営する **keiei suru** manage; run; administer
軽減する **keigen suru** alleviate
敬語 **keigo** honorific language
敬具 **keigu** (Kind) regards; Yours truly
経費 **keihi** expenses
景品 **keihin** free gift; giveaway
警報 **keihō** alarm; alert; 暴風警報 ***bôfû-keihô*** storm warning; 警報を発する ***keihô o hassuru*** raise the alarm
敬意 **keii** respect; deference; 敬意を払う ***keii o harau*** show respect to
刑事 **keiji** detective
掲示 **keiji** notice
掲示版 **keijiban** bulletin board
軽自動車 **kei-jidōsha** compact MOT
経過 **keika** passage
警戒警報 **keikai-keihō** security alert
軽快(な) **keikai (na)** nimble; springy
警戒している **keikai shite iru** be on the alert
計画 **keikaku** project; plan, scheme
計画性のない **keikakusei no nai** disorganized
計画する **keikaku suru** plan; propose; stage *demonstration*
計画的(な) **keikakuteki (na)** premeditated
警官 **keikan** policeman

経過する **keika suru** elapse
経験 **keiken** experience
敬けん(な) **keiken (na)** devout; pious
経験のない **keiken no nai** inexperienced
経験する **keiken suru** experience; undergo
経験豊か(な) **keiken yutaka (na)** experienced; seasoned
計器 **keiki** gauge
景気 **keiki** economic conditions; the market; 景気沈滞している ***keiki-chintai shite iru*** be sluggish (*of business*); be in the doldrums
景気後退 **keiki-kōtai** recession
けいこ **keiko** practice
傾向 **keikō** tendency, inclination; trend
警告 **keikoku** caution; warning
渓谷 **keikoku** ravine
警告する **keikoku suru** warn
蛍光(の) **keikō (no)** fluorescent
蛍光ペン **keikō-pen** marker, highlighter
啓もうする **keimō suru** enlighten
刑務所 **keimu-sho** jail, prison; 刑務所に入れる ***keimusho ni ireru*** imprison, lock up
敬礼 **keirei** salute
経歴 **keireki** career history; background
けいれん **keiren** cramp; spasm; convulsion; twitch
けいれんする **keiren suru** twitch; have a fit; get cramp
経理部 **keiribu** accounts (department)
敬老の日 **Keirō no hi** Respect-for-the-Aged Day
計略 **keiryaku** trick; plot
計算 **keisan** calculation; count
計算まちがい **keisan machigai** miscalculation
計算する **keisan suru** calculate; count; figure out
警察 **keisatsu** police
警察庁 **Keisatsuchō** National Police Agency
警察官 **keisatsukan** officer
警察国家 **keisatsu-kokka** police state
警察署 **keisatsu-sho** police station
警察署長 **keisatsu-shochō** police chief; marshal
形成外科 **keisei-geka** plastic surgery
形成外科医 **keisei-gekai** plastic surgeon
形成する **keisei suru** mold, shape
形跡 **keiseki** signs; traces; evidence
傾斜 **keisha** slant
警視庁 **Keishichō** Metropolitan Police Department
形式 **keishiki** formality
敬称 **keishō** polite form of address; honorific
軽食 **keishoku** refreshments; snack
軽食堂 **keishokudō** snack bar; truck stop
軽率(な) **keisotsu (na)** hasty, rash; indiscreet; thoughtless
携帯電話 **keitai-denwa** cell phone, mobile phone *Br*
携帯用(の) **keitaiyō (no)** portable
携帯用テレビ **keitaiyō terebi** portable (TV)
毛糸 **keito** wool; yarn
系統 **keitō** system
系統的に **keitōteki ni** systematically
契約 **keiyaku** agreement; contract
契約不履行 **keiyaku-furikō** breach of contract
契約上(の) **keiyakujō (no)** contractual
契約書 **keiyakusho** contract
形容詞 **keiyōshi** adjective
経由で **keiyu de** via, by way of
経済 **keizai** economy
経済学 **keizai-gaku** economics
経済学者 **keizai-gakusha** economist
経済状態 **keizaī-jōtai** economic circumstances
経済企画庁 **Keizai-kikakuchō** Economic Planning Agency of Japan
経済緊縮 **keizai-kinshuku** austerity
経済的(な) **keizaiteki (na)** economical
ケーキ **kēki** cake

結果 **kekka** effect; result; …の結果 ***… no kekka*** result from; …の結果である ***… no kekka de aru*** be due to
結核 **kekkaku** tuberculosis
血管 **kekkan** blood vessel
欠陥 **kekkan** defect
欠陥のある **kekkan no aru** defective, faulty
欠勤 **kekkin** absence
欠勤(の) **kekkin** (**no**) absent
結婚 **kekkon** marriage; matrimony
結構(な) **kekkō** (**na**) decent; good; sufficient; enough; adequate; 結構です ***kekkô desu*** no, thank you
結婚記念日 **kekkon-kinenbi** wedding anniversary
結婚式 **kekkon-shiki** marriage, wedding
結婚した **kekkon shita** married
結婚する **kekkon suru** get married; marry
結婚指輪 **kekkon-yubiwa** wedding ring
決行する **kekkō suru** carry out
結局 **kekkyoku** after all; ultimately
血球 **kekkyū** corpuscle
獣 **kemono** beast
煙い **kemui** smoky
煙に巻く **kemu ni maku** mystify
煙 **kemuri** fumes; smoke
毛虫 **kemushi** caterpillar
圏 **ken** sphere; circle; bloc
腱 **ken** tendon
県 **ken** prefecture
券 **ken** ticket
軒 **-ken** *countword for houses*
件 **ken** matter, affair
剣 **ken** sword
けなした **kenashita** disparaging
けなす **kenasu** criticize; get at; put down
顕微鏡 **kenbikyō** microscope
見物 **kenbutsu** sightseeing
見物人 **kenbutsu-nin** sightseer; visitor; onlooker
建築 **kenchiku** architecture
建築現場 **kenchiku-genba** construction site
建築業者 **kenchiku-gyōsha** builder
建築家 **kenchiku-ka** architect
剣道 **kendō** kendo
検閲 **ken'etsu** censorship
検閲する **ken'etsu suru** censor
見学する **kengaku suru** visit; tour
権限 **kengen** authority; mandate; power
権威 **ken'i** authority
献辞 **kenji** dedication (*in book*)
検事 **kenji** public prosecutor
堅実(な) **kenjitsu** (**na**) sound; sensible
けんか **kenka** argument; quarrel; fight
けんかっぱやい **kenkappayai** quarrelsome
けんかする **kenka suru** argue; fall out; quarrel; fight; brawl
献血 **kenketsu** blood donation
献金 **kenkin** contribution; donation
健康 **kenkō** fitness; health
健康保険 **kenkō-hoken** health insurance
肩甲骨 **kenkōkotsu** shoulder blade
建国記念日 **Kenkoku-kinenbi** National Foundation Day
健康(な) **kenkō** (**na**) healthy
健康に悪い **kenkō ni warui** unhealthy
健康に良い **kenkō ni yoi** wholesome
健康診断 **kenkō-shindan** medical, checkup
健康診断書 **kenkō-shindansho** medical certificate
健康食品 **kenkō-shokuhin** health food
健康的(な) **kenkōteki** (**na**) healthy
謙虚 **kenkyo** modesty
検挙 **kenkyo** arrest
謙虚(な) **kenkyo** (**na**) modest
検挙する **kenkyo suru** arrest; round up
研究 **kenkyū** research; study
研究所 **kenkyū-jo** laboratory, lab
研究開発 **kenkyū-kaihatsu** R&D, research and development
研究休暇 **kenkyū-kyūka** sabbatical
研究者 **kenkyū-sha** researcher
研究室 **kenkyū-shitsu** laboratory, lab (*room*)

賢明(な) **kenmei** (**na**) judicious; wise
賢明さ **kenmei-sa** wisdom
検問所 **kenmonjo** checkpoint
嫌悪 **ken'o** hatred; disgust; revulsion
憲法 **kenpō** constitution POL
憲法記念日 **kenpō-kinenbi** Constitution Day
憲法(の) **kenpō** (**no**) constitutional
権利 **kenri** claim; right; 権利を与える ***kenri o ataeru*** entitle
権力 **kenryoku** power
検査 **kensa** inspection; check; examination
検査係 **kensa-gakari** inspector
検索する **kensaku suru** retrieve
検査する **kensa suru** examine; inspect
検札係 **kensatsu-gakari** inspector (*on bus etc*)
検察側 **kensatsugawa** prosecution
検察官 **kensatsukan** public prosecutor
建設 **kensetsu** building, construction; 建設中で ***kensetsu-chû de*** under construction
建設現場 **kensetsu-genba** building site
建設業 **kensetsugyō** building trade
建設業界 **kensetsu-gyōkai** construction industry
建設する **kensetsu suru** construct
建設的(な) **kensetsuteki** (**na**) constructive
検死 **kenshi** autopsy, postmortem
検死官 **kenshi-kan** coroner
検診 **kenshin** checkup
献身 **kenshin** dedication; devotion
献身的(な) **kenshinteki** (**na**) devoted
研修 **kenshū** training
研修会 **kenshū-kai** refresher course
研修コース **kenshū kōsu** training course
研修生 **kenshūsei** trainee
研修する **kenshū suru** train
検出器 **kenshutsu-ki** detector
謙そん **kenson** humility; modesty
検討 **kentō** examination; investigation; exploration
見当 **kentō** speculation; aim; direction; 見当もつかない ***kentô mo tsukanai*** I haven't a clue
見当違いで **kentō-chigai de** beside the point
見当はずれ(な) **kentōhazure** (**na**) misplaced
検討する **kentō suru** explore *possibility*; discuss; take stock
倹約 **ken'yaku** thrift
健全(な) **kenzen** (**na**) healthy; robust; wholesome
建造物 **kenzōbutsu** construction
潔白 **keppaku** innocence
けれど(も) **keredo**(**mo**) but; however; though
ける **keru** kick; kick around
けさ **kesa** this morning
消しゴム **keshi-gomu** eraser
消印 **keshiin** postmark
景色 **keshiki** landscape; scenery; sights; view
化身 **keshin** embodiment; incarnation
化粧 **keshō** make-up; 化粧をする ***keshô o suru*** make up, put on make-up
化粧品 **keshōhin** cosmetics
化粧ポーチ **keshō-pōchi** vanity case
化粧室 **keshōshitsu** powder room
決済 **kessai** settlement
傑作 **kessaku** masterpiece
決算 **kessan** settlement; financial results
欠席 **kesseki** absence
欠席(の) **kesseki** (**no**) absent
欠席する **kesseki suru** miss
血栓症 **kessenshō** thrombosis
決心 **kesshin** resolution
決心する **kesshin suru** decide, make up one's mind
決して…ない **kesshite… nai** never
血色の良い **kesshoku no yoi** ruddy
決勝戦 **kesshōsen** final
決勝点 **kesshōten** winning post
傑出した **kesshutsu shita** outstanding
結束 **kessoku** unity; solidarity

消す **kesu** switch off; put out; erase; delete; extinguish; drown *sound*
ケース **kēsu** holder; case; housing
けた **keta** figure; digit; beam; girder
ケータイ **kētai** cell phone
決着 **ketchaku** conclusion; settlement; 決着をつける ***ketchaku o tsukeru*** settle
けつ **ketsu** V ass
血圧 **ketsuatsu** blood pressure
欠乏 **ketsubō** lack
血液型 **ketsuekigata** blood group
血液銀行 **ketsueki-ginkō** blood bank
血液検査 **ketsueki-kensa** blood test
血縁関係(の) **ketsuen-kankei (no)** related by birth
決議 **ketsugi** resolution
結合する **ketsugō suru** unite
決意 **ketsui** determination
欠員 **ketsuin** opening
結膜炎 **ketsumakuen** conjunctivitis
結末 **ketsumatsu** conclusion
けつの穴 **ketsu no ana** V asshole
欠落 **ketsuraku** omission; lack
決裂 **ketsuretsu** breakdown; rupture
結露 **ketsuro** condensation
結論 **ketsuron** conclusion; decision; 結論に達しない ***ketsuron ni tasshinai*** inconclusive; 結論を下す ***ketsuron o kudasu*** conclude
血流 **ketsuryū** bloodstream
決定 **kettei** decision; ruling
決定戦 **ketteisen** decider
決定者 **kettei-sha** decision-maker
決定する **kettei suru** decide; shape *future*
決定的(な) **ketteiteki (na)** conclusive; decisive; definitive; fatal *error*
欠点 **ketten** drawback; flaw, shortcoming
欠点のない **ketten no nai** faultless; immaculate
血統 **kettō** pedigree; blood line
険しい **kewashii** rugged; steep
毛染め **kezome** dye; tint
削る **kezuru** whittle; shave; sharpen
木 **ki** tree
気 **ki** mood; feeling; will; mind; 気が重い ***ki ga omoi*** feel down; mind; 気が変わった ***ki ga kawatta*** have changed one's mind; 気を失う ***ki o ushinau*** lose consciousness ; 気が強い ***ki ga tsuyoi*** strong-willed; … 気がする … ***ki ga suru*** have a feeling that; 気をつけて ***ki o tsukete*** take care; 気がいい ***ki ga ii*** good-natured; 気を静めなさい ***ki o shizumenasai*** calm down; …気がない ***… ki ga nai*** don't want to …; → *also* **ki ga …, ki ni …, ki no …, ki o …**
キー **kī** key COMPUT, MUS
気圧 **kiatsu** air pressure
気圧計 **kiatsukei** barometer
きば **kiba** fang; tusk
基盤 **kiban** base; foundation
気晴らし **kibarashi** amusement; distraction
きびきびした **kibikibi shita** brisk; energetic
機敏(な) **kibin (na)** agile
厳しい **kibishii** strict; severe; rigorous; grim; bitter *weather*; inhospitable *climate*; rigid *principles*; tight *security*
厳しく **kibishiku** severely; strictly
厳しくする **kibishiku suru** tighten
厳しさ **kibishi-sa** difficulty; severity
規模 **kibo** scale, size
希望 **kibō** hope; wish; 希望を持つ ***kibô o motsu*** hope
キーボード **kībōdo** keyboard
希望的観測 **kibōteki-kansoku** wishful thinking
気分 **kibun** frame of mind; 行きたい気分です ***ikitai kibun desu*** I feel like going
気分がいい **kibun ga ii** feel well
気分がさわやかになる **kibun ga sawayaka ni naru** feel refreshed
気分がすぐれない **kibun ga sugurenai** poorly
気分が悪い **kibun ga warui** unwell
気分転換に **kibun-tenkan ni** for a change
基地 **kichi** base MIL
気違い **kichigai** insane; lunatic
気違いじみた **kichigaijimita** insane

きちんと **kichin to** properly; conscientiously; tight *shut*
きちんとした **kichin to shita** neat, tidy; きちんとした服装をする ***kichin to shita fukusô o suru*** dress up
きちんとする **kichin to suru** tidy oneself up
機長 **kichō** captain (*of aircraft*)
基調演説 **kichō-enzetsu** keynote speech
貴重品 **kichōhin** valuables
きちょうめんな **kichōmen na** methodical; scrupulous
貴重(な) **kichō (na)** precious, valuable
気立てのよい **kidate no yoi** good-natured
軌道 **kidō** orbit; …を軌道に乗せる ***… o kidô ni noseru*** send into orbit
機動部隊 **kidō-butai** task force
気取らない **kidoranai** unassuming
気取る **kidoru** put on airs
起動させる **kidō saseru** boot up
起動する **kidō suru** boot up; log on
気取った **kidotta** pretentious
消える **kieru** disappear; go away; go out (*of light*); fade
寄付 **kifu** contribution; donation
寄付者 **kifu-sha** contributor
寄付する **kifu suru** contribute; donate
飢餓 **kiga** starvation
気が合う **ki ga au** compatible
着替え **kigae** change of clothes
着替える **kigaeru** change *clothes*
気がかりである **kigakari de aru** be on tenterhooks
気が変わる **ki ga kawaru** change one's mind
気が狂う **ki ga kuruu** go mad; be out of one's mind
気が狂った **ki ga kurutta** crazy
気軽(な) **kigaru (na)** cheerful; lighthearted
気が進まない **ki ga susumanai** disinclined; reluctant
気が立つ **ki ga tatsu** get worked up
気がついている **ki ga tsuite iru** be conscious; be aware of, be conscious of
気がつかない **ki ga tsukanai** be unaware of, be unconscious of
気がつく **ki ga tsuku** regain consciousness, come to; become aware of; notice; observe
喜劇 **kigeki** comedy
喜劇(の) **kigeki (no)** comic
機嫌 **kigen** humor; mood; temper; 機嫌がよい/悪い ***kigen ga yoi/warui*** be in a good/bad mood
起源 **kigen** origin
期限 **kigen** deadline; time limit; 期限が切れる ***kigen ga kireru*** be up, have expired
期限切れ **kigengire** expiry
期限切れで **kigengire de** out of date
記号 **kigō** symbol
器具 **kigu** instrument; gadget; appliance; apparatus
企業 **kigyō** enterprise; company
企業秘密 **kigyō-himitsu** trade secret
企業家 **kigyō-ka** entrepreneur
企業家(の) **kigyō-ka (no)** entrepreneurial
企業(の) **kigyō (no)** corporate
規範 **kihan** norm; model
気品 **kihin** elegance; grace; dignity
基本 **kihon** basis; foundation
基本的(な) **kihonteki (na)** basic; fundamental; underlying
キーホルダー **kī-horudā** key-ring
黄色 **kiiro** yellow; 黄色で ***kiiro de*** at amber MOT
黄色(の) **kiiro (no)** yellow
きじ **kiji** pheasant
記事 **kiji** article; item; story
生地 **kiji** dough; fabric, material
期日 **kijitsu** deadline; 期日が来ている ***kijitsu ga kite iru*** be due
基準 **kijun** standard; benchmark; criterion
基準利率 **kijun-riritsu** base rate
幾何学 **kikagaku** geometry
幾何学的(な) **kikagakuteki (na)** geometric(al)
機会 **kikai** chance, opportunity
機械 **kikai** machine; mechanism
機械化する **kikaika suru** mechanize
機械工 **kikaikō** mechanic

機械(の) **kikai (no)** mechanical
機械類 **kikairui** machinery
機械的(な) **kikaiteki (na)** mechanical
規格 **kikaku** standard
企画 **kikaku** plan; project
規格化する **kikakuka suru** standardize
期間 **kikan** duration; period; term
機関 **kikan** institution
器官 **kikan** organ ANAT
帰還 **kikan** return
季刊(の) **kikan (no)** quarterly
機関銃 **kikanjū** machine gun
機関士 **kikanshi** engineer NAUT, RAIL
気管支炎 **kikanshi-en** bronchitis
帰化する **kika suru** become naturalized
着飾る **kikazaru** dress up
奇形 **kikei** deformity
棄権 **kiken** abstention
危険 **kiken** risk; danger; hazard; 危険にさらされている ***kiken ni sarasarete iru*** be at stake; 危険にさらす ***kiken ni sarasu*** endanger; jeopardize; risk; 危険を冒す ***kiken o okasu*** take a risk; risk
危険人物 **kiken-jinbutsu** security risk
危険(な) **kiken (na)** dangerous; risky
棄権する **kiken suru** abstain
危機 **kiki** crisis
聞き出す **kikidasu** extract *information*; worm out of
聞き返す **kikikaesu** ask back; ask again
聞き間違える **kikimachigaeru** mishear
効き目 **kikime** effect; 効き目がある ***kikime ga aru*** effective; potent ◊ tell, have an effect
ききん **kikin** famine
基金 **kikin** foundation; fund
聞き覚えがある **kikioboe ga aru** that sounds familiar
危機的(な) **kikiteki (na)** critical
聞き取る **kikitoru** catch
きっかけ **kikkake** cue; hint; opportunity
きっかりに **kikkari ni** promptly, on the dot
キック **kikku** kick
キックオフ **kikku-ofu** kickoff
気候 **kikō** climate
寄稿 **kikō** contribution
聞こえない **kikoenai** inaudible
聞こえる **kikoeru** hear; sound; seem ◊ audible
帰国 **kikoku** return to one's own country
着込む **kikomu** wrap up warmly
寄稿する **kikō suru** contribute
菊 **kiku** chrysanthemum
聞く **kiku** listen; ask; listen to
効く **kiku** work, take effect
気配り **kikubari** consideration; care
気球 **kikyū** balloon
気前がいい **kimae ga ii** generous
気前のよさ **kimae no yosa** generosity
気まぐれ **kimagure** whim
気まぐれ(な) **kimagure (na)** inconsistent; fickle; quirky; volatile
決まり **kimari** rule
決まり文句 **kimarimonku** cliché
きまりの悪い **kimari no warui** embarrassed
決まった **kimatta** fixed
決まっていない **kimatte inai** undecided
気まずい **kimazui** awkward; embarrassing; 気まずい思いをさせる ***kimazui omoi o saseru*** embarrass
決める **kimeru** arrange; decide
黄身 **kimi** yolk
君 **kimi** you (*familiar*)
気味 **kimi** feeling; a touch of ; 気味の悪い ***kimi no warui*** eerie; 風邪気味だ ***kazegimi da*** I have a slight cold
君が代 **Kimigayo** Kimigayo (*Japanese national anthem*)
君(の) **kimi (no)** your (*familiar*)
君達 **kimitachi** you (*plural familiar*)
君達(の) **kimitachi (no)** your (*plural familiar*)
機密 **kimitsu** secret
機密(の) **kimitsu (no)** classified
気持ち **kimochi** feeling

気持ちのいい **kimochi no ii** delightful; pleasant
気持ちの悪い **kimochi no warui** disgusting; lousy
気持ちよく **kimochi yoku** nicely
キモい **kimoi** lousy, crap
着物 **kimono** kimono
気難しい **kimuzukashii** demanding; morose
奇妙なことに **kimyō na koto ni** strangely enough
金 **kin** gold
機内(の) **kinai** (**no**) inflight
勤勉(な) **kinben** (**na**) industrious; painstaking
緊張 **kinchō** tension
緊張緩和 **kinchō-kanwa** détente
緊張した **kinchō shita** tense
緊張して **kinchō shite** keyed-up
緊張する **kinchō suru** tense up
近代化する **kindaika suru** modernize
近代的(な) **kindaiteki** (**na**) modern
禁断症状 **kindan-shōjō** withdrawal symptoms
禁煙 **kin'en** smoking forbidden, no smoking
記念 **kinen** commemoration; memento
記念日 **kinenbi** anniversary
記念碑 **kinenhi** memorial; monument
記念品 **kinenhin** memento
記念(の) **kinen** (**no**) memorial
記念する **kinen suru** commemorate; 記念して ***kinen shite*** in memory of
金額 **kingaku** sum, amount
近眼(の) **kingan** (**no**) shortsighted
キング **kingu** king (*in cards*)
キングサイズ(の) **kingu-saizu** (**no**) king-size(d)
金魚 **kingyo** gold fish
気に入る **ki ni iru** take a liking to; appeal to
気にかかる **ki ni kakaru** bother; worry
気にかける **ki ni kakeru** care
気になる **ki ni naru** worry
キニーネ **kinīne** quinine
金色(の) **kin'iro** (**no**) golden
気にさわる **ki ni sawaru** obnoxious; offensive
気にする **ki ni suru** mind
均一料金 **kin'itsu-ryōkin** flat rate
禁じられた **kinjirareta** forbidden
禁じる **kinjiru** forbid; prohibit
近所 **kinjo** vicinity
金欠(の) **kinketsu** (**no**) broke
近畿 **Kinki** *western district of Osaka, Kyoto and Hyogo etc*
金庫 **kinko** safe
近郊 **kinkō** environs; suburbs
均衡 **kinkō** equilibrium; balance
禁固刑 **kinkokei** imprisonment
金婚式 **kinkonshiki** golden wedding anniversary
金庫室 **kinkoshitsu** vaults
緊急着陸**kinkyū-chakuriku** emergency landing
緊急脱出装置**kinkyū-dasshutsu-sōchi** escape chute
緊急事態 **kinkyū-jitai** emergency; state of emergency
緊急(な) **kinkyū** (**na**) urgent
金めっき **kinmekki** gilt
勤務日 **kinmubi** workday
勤務中である **kinmuchū de aru** be on duty
勤務時間 **kinmu-jikan** office hours
勤務時間中 **kinmu-jikanchū** during work hours
筋肉 **kinniku** muscle
金(の) **kin** (**no**) gold
機能 **kinō** faculty; function
昨日 **kinō** yesterday
気の合う **ki no au** congenial
気の小さい **ki no chiisai** nervous
気の毒に思う **ki no doku ni omou** pity; take pity on
気のきいた **ki no kiita** clever
きのこ **kinoko** mushroom
気の狂った **ki no kurutta** mad, loony, nutty, crackbrained
気の狂っている **ki no kurutte iru** mental
気の短い **ki no mijikai** impatient
気の抜けた **ki no nuketa** flat *beer*
気乗りのしない **kinori no shinai** half-hearted; lukewarm
気の強い **ki no tsuyoi** strong-willed; tough

緊迫 **kinpaku** tension
金髪(の) **kinpatsu** (**no**) fair *hair*
きんぽうげ **kinpōge** buttercup
勤労感謝の日 **Kinrō-kansha no hi** Labor Thanksgiving Day
禁止 **kinshi** ban, prohibition
近視眼的(な) **kinshiganteki** (**na**) shortsighted, myopic
近視(の) **kinshi** (**no**) near-sighted, myopic
近親相かん **kinshin-sōkan** incest
禁止する **kinshi suru** ban, prohibit
禁酒 **kinshu** abstinence from alcohol
きんたま **kintama** V balls, nuts
均等に **kintō ni** evenly; equally
絹 **kinu** silk
絹(の) **kinu** (**no**) silk
金曜日 **kin'yōbi** Friday
金融(の) **kin'yū** (**no**) monetary
金融市場 **kin'yū-shijō** money market
記入する **kinyū suru** complete; enter; fill out
金細工師 **kinzaikushi** goldsmith
金属 **kinzoku** metal
金属(の) **kinzoku** (**no**) metal, metallic
金属的(な) **kinzokuteki** (**na**) metallic
禁ずる **kinzuru** forbid
記憶 **kioku** memory
記憶力 **kiokuryoku** memory
記憶容量 **kioku-yōryō** storage capacity COMPUT
気温 **kion** temperature
気を落ち着ける **ki o ochitsukeru** compose oneself; calm oneself
気を静める **ki o shizumeru** pull oneself together
気をそらす **ki o sorasu** create a diversion
キオスク **kiosuku** kiosk
気を使う **ki o tsukau** worry about; 気を使わないで下さい ***ki o tsukawanaide kudasai*** you needn't have bothered
気をつける **ki o tsukeru** take care, watch out; make sure
気を失う **ki o ushinau** faint, pass out
きっぱりした **kippari shita** decisive
きっぱりと **kippari to** point-blank
切符 **kippu** ticket
切符売場 **kippu-uriba** ticket office; box office
嫌い **kirai** hate; dislike
きらきら光る **kirakira hikaru** glisten; twinkle
気楽(な) **kiraku** (**na**) easygoing; lighthearted
きらめき **kirameki** blaze; glint
きらめく **kirameku** glint; twinkle
嫌う **kirau** dislike
嫌われている **kirawarete iru** be in the doghouse
切れ **-kire** *countword for slices of bread, meat, cakes etc*
切れ端 **kirehashi** shred; scrap
きれい(な) **kirei** (**na**) nice, pretty, lovely; clean
きれいにする **kirei ni suru** clean; clean out
切れ目 **kireme** nick, cut
切れる **kireru** run out; be cut off; be sharp; expire
キレる **kireru** snap, lose control
切れた **kireta** flat; off (*of switch*); 電話が切れた ***denwa ga kireta*** I was disconnected
切れている **kirete iru** worn out; be out (*of light*)
亀裂 **kiretsu** rift; crack
きり **kiri** paulownia
霧 **kiri** fog; mist; 霧のかかった ***kiri no kakatta*** misty
切り上げる **kiriageru** revalue; round up *figure*; cut short
切り出す **kiridasu** broach; begin to talk about; quarry
切り離す **kiri hanasu** isolate
切り開く **kirihiraku** slit, cut open
切り株 **kirikabu** stump
切り替える **kirikaeru** switch; change; transfer
切り傷 **kirikizu** cut; slash
切り口 **kirikuchi** cut, slit
きりん **kirin** giraffe
切り抜ける **kirinukeru** negotiate; wriggle out of
切り抜き **kirinuki** clipping, cutting
切り抜く **kirinuku** cut out
切り落とす **kiriotosu** lop off; shave

off
切り下げ **kirisage** devaluation; reduction
切り下げる **kirisageru** devalue; reduce
霧雨 **kirisame** drizzle
切りそろえる **kirisoroeru** trim
キリスト **Kirisuto** Christ
キリスト教 **Kirisuto-kyō** Christianity
キリスト教(の) **Kirisuto-kyō (no)** Christian
キリスト教徒 **Kirisuto-kyōto** Christian
切り倒す **kiritaosu** chop down, cut down
切り立った **kiritatta** sheer
切り取る **kiritoru** cut off
規律 **kiritsu** discipline, order
起立 **kiritsu** stand up; all stand!
切り詰める **kiritsumeru** cut back; trim, prune
規律正しい **kiritsutadashii** orderly
切り分ける **kiriwakeru** carve
キロバイト **kirobaito** kilobyte
キログラム **kiroguramu** kilogram
記録 **kiroku** chronicle; record(s); log; reading (*from meter etc*)
記録文書 **kiroku-bunsho** transcript
記録係 **kiroku-gakari** scorer
記録保持者 **kiroku-hojisha** record holder
記録する **kiroku suru** record; document; keep score
記録破り(の) **kirokuyaburi (no)** record-breaking
キロメーター **kiromētā** kilometer
切る **kiru** cut; disconnect; switch off; hang up; shuffle *cards*; write *check*
着る **kiru** wear; put on
気力 **kiryoku** spirit; mental energy
器量の悪い **kiryō no warui** homely, ugly
気さく(な) **kisaku (na)** approachable, friendly
規制 **kisei** controls; regulation
寄生虫 **kiseichū** parasite
既製服(の) **kiseifuku (no)** ready-to-wear
既製(の) **kisei (no)** off the peg, ready-made
規制する **kisei suru** control, regulate
奇跡 **kiseki** miracle
奇跡的(な) **kisekiteki (na)** miraculous
着せる **kiseru** dress; help … dress
季節 **kisetsu** season
記者 **kisha** journalist, reporter; correspondent
記者会見 **kisha-kaiken** press conference
岸 **kishi** shore
きしむ **kishimu** creak; squeak
気質 **kishitsu** disposition, temperament
気性 **kishō** nature; temperament
気象学 **kishōgaku** meteorology
気象学者 **kishōgaku-sha** meteorologist
気象(の) **kishō (no)** meteorological
騎手 **kishu** rider; jockey
基礎 **kiso** basis, foundation; rudiments
起訴 **kiso** prosecution LAW
基礎知識 **kiso-chishiki** working knowledge
基礎準備 **kiso-junbi** groundwork
規則 **kisoku** regulation, rule
規則的(な) **kisokuteki (na)** even, regular
起訴する **kiso suru** charge, prosecute
基礎的(な) **kisoteki (na)** basic, fundamental, rudimentary
喫茶店 **kissaten** coffee shop
キス **kisu** kiss; キスをする ***kisu o suru*** kiss
奇数(の) **kisū (no)** odd *number*
北 **kita** north
北アメリカ **Kita-Amerika** North America
北アメリカ人 **Kita-Amerika-jin** North American
北アメリカ(の) **Kita-Amerika (no)** North American
北ベトナム **Kita-Betonamu** North Vietnam
北ベトナム(の) **Kita-Betonamu (no)** North Vietnamese
北朝鮮 **Kita-Chōsen** North Korea
北朝鮮人 **Kita-Chōsen-jin** North Korean

北朝鮮(の) **Kita-Chōsen (no)** North Korean
鍛える **kitaeru** exercise; train
期待 **kitai** expectation(s)
機体 **kitai** fuselage
気体 **kitai** gas
期待はずれ **kitaihazure** disappointment
期待はずれ(な) **kitaihazure (na)** disappointing
期待する **kitai suru** expect
帰宅する **kitaku suru** return home
汚い **kitanai** dirty, grubby; sordid
北(の) **kita (no)** north; northerly; northern
キッチン **kitchin** kitchen; kitchenette
きっちり **kitchiri** tightly; punctually; exactly
既定値(の) **kiteichi (no)** default COMPUT
起点 **kiten** starting point
気転, 機転 **kiten** tact; 気転のきかない ***kiten no kikanai*** tactless; 機転のきく ***kiten no kiku*** quickwitted
喫煙 **kitsuen** smoking
喫煙家 **kitsuen-ka** smoker
喫煙車 **kitsuen-sha** smoking car
きつい **kitsui** demanding; punishing; tight
きつね **kitsune** fox
切手 **kitte** stamp
きっと **kitto** no doubt, surely
きっと…する **kitto … suru** be bound to do
際立って **kiwadatte** striking, conspicuous
きわどい **kiwadoi** narrow; risky; きわどい差で ***kiwadoi sa de*** by a narrow margin
きわめて **kiwamete** extremely
器用(な) **kiyō (na)** deft; ingenious
器用さ **kiyō-sa** dexterity; ingenuity
刻む **kizamu** cut; carve; chop
兆し **kizashi** hint; symptom
気絶させる **kizetsu saseru** stun
気絶する **kizetsu suru** faint
寄贈 **kizō** donation
寄贈者 **kizō-sha** donor
寄贈する **kizō suru** donate
傷 **kizu** damage; wound; blemish; flaw; blot; 傷を負わせる ***kizu o owaseru*** wound; 傷を付ける ***kizu o tsukeru*** damage
傷跡 **kizuato** scar; 傷跡を残す ***kizuato o nokosu*** leave a scar
傷口 **kizuguchi** sore; wound
気づいていない **kizuite inai** unsuspecting
気づいている **kizuite iru** be conscious of
気づかって **kizukatte** concerned, caring
気付 **kizuke** c/o, care of
築き上げる **kizukiageru** build up
気づく **kizuku** become aware of
気詰まり **kizumari**: 彼と居ると気詰まりである ***kare to iru to kizumari de aru*** I feel uncomfortable with him
きずな **kizuna** bond
傷ついた **kizutsuita** injured
傷ついていない **kizutsuite inai** undamaged; uninjured
傷つける **kizutsukeru** wound; hurt; bruise
傷つきやすい **kizutsukiyasui** vulnerable
傷つく **kizutsuku** get hurt; be injured
子 **ko** child; 男の子 ***otoko no ko*** boy
故 **ko** the late; deceased
個 **ko** *countword for small objects*
香 **kō** incense
考案者 **kōan-sha** designer; inventor
考案する **kōan suru** devise
高圧ガス **kōatsu-gasu** propellant
高圧的(な) **kōatsuteki (na)** strongarm; high-pressure; authoritative
こう配 **kōbai** gradient, slope
購買意欲 **kōbai-iyoku** consumer confidence
購買契約 **kōbai-keiyaku** subscription
交番 **kōban** police box
こびる **kobiru** flatter; flirt
小人 **kobito** dwarf
こぼれる **koboreru** spill
こぼす **kobosu** spill, slop
こぶ **kobu** bump; hump

後部 **kōbu** back, rear
子分 **kobun** protégé; follower; henchman
後部(の) **kōbu** (**no**) rear
こぶし **kobushi** fist; こぶしで殴る ***kobushi de naguru*** punch; こぶしを握り締める ***kobushi o nigirishimeru*** clench one's fist
子豚 **kobuta** piglet
好物 **kōbutsu** favorite (food)
鉱物 **kōbutsu** mineral
紅茶茶碗 **kōcha-jawan** teacup
こう着状態 **kōchaku-jōtai** stalemate; deadlock
コーチ **kōchi** coach
こちら **kochira** this (*polite*) ◊ this way ◊ this one; this person; こちらへどうぞ ***kochira e dôzo*** please come this way
拘置する **kōchi suru** detain
校長 **kōchō** principal EDU
好調(な) **kōchō** (**na**) in good condition; good
誇張する **kochō suru** exaggerate; magnify
広大(な) **kōdai** (**na**) vast
古代(の) **kodai** (**no**) ancient
誇大宣伝 **kodai-senden** hype
こだま **kodama** echo
こだわらない **kodawaranai** easy-going
こだわる **kodawaru** be obsessive; dwell on
鼓動 **kodō** beat; heartbeat; throb (*of heart*)
コード **kōdo** cable, cord
高度 **kōdo** altitude; height
行動 **kōdō** behavior; action; 行動を起こす ***kôdô o okosu*** take action
小道具 **kodōgu** stage props
孤独 **kodoku** loneliness; solitude
孤独(な) **kodoku** (**na**) lonely; solitary
子供 **kodomo** child, kid; offspring
子供の日 **Kodomo no hi** Children's Day
子供だまし **kodomodamashi** childish nonsense
子供じみた **kodomojimita** childish
高度(な) **kōdo** (**na**) sophisticated
コードレス電話 **kōdoresu-denwa** cordless phone
鼓動する **kodō suru** beat; throb; pulsate
行動する **kōdō suru** behave; act
コーデュロイ **kōdyuroi** corduroy
声 **koe** voice; 声を出して ***koe o dashite*** aloud
小枝 **koeda** twig
光栄(な) **kōei** (**na**) privileged
公園 **kōen** park
後援 **kōen** patronage, sponsorship
公演 **kōen** performance
声(の) **koe** (**no**) vocal
後援者 **kōen-sha** backer; patron
後援する **kōen suru** patronize
公演する **kōen suru** perform
越える **koeru** exceed, surpass
越えて **koete** beyond
校閲者 **kōetsu-sha** editor
校閲する **kōetsu suru** edit
坑夫 **kōfu** miner
交付金 **kōfukin** subsidy
幸福 **kōfuku** bliss; well-being
降伏 **kōfuku** submission, surrender
降伏する **kōfuku suru** surrender
古墳 **kofun** burial mound
興奮 **kōfun** excitement, buzz
古風(な) **kofū** (**na**) quaint
興奮させる **kōfun saseru** excite; stimulate; turn on (*sexually*)
興奮した **kōfun shita** excited; wild *applause*; heated *discussion*; horny (*sexually*)
興奮している **kōfun shite iru** be in a flap
興奮する **kōfun suru** get excited
交付する **kōfu suru** grant
郊外 **kōgai** outskirts; suburbs
口がい **kōgai** palate
公害 **kōgai** environmental pollution
戸外で **kogai de** in the open air
郊外(の) **kōgai** (**no**) suburban
子会社 **kogaisha** subsidiary
工学 **kōgaku** engineering
高額(の) **kōgaku** (**no**) expensive
こう丸 **kōgan** testicle
小柄(の) **kogara** (**no**) undersized
焦がす **kogasu** burn; scorch; singe
小型化する **kogataka suru** downsize

小型(の) **kogata (no)** miniature, pocket; compact
小型トラック **kogata-torakku** pick-up (truck)
攻撃 **kōgeki** aggression; attack, offensive
攻撃する **kōgeki suru** attack, lay into
攻撃的(な) **kōgekiteki (na)** aggressive
高原 **kōgen** plateau
公言する **kōgen suru** profess
焦げる **kogeru** burn
焦げた **kogeta** charred
抗議 **kōgi** outcry; protest
講義 **kōgi** lecture; talk; 講義をする ***kôgi o suru*** lecture, give a lecture
こぎれい(な) **kogirei (na)** tidy; neat
こぎれいにする **kogirei ni suru** smarten up
抗議者 **kōgi-sha** protester
抗議集会 **kōgi-shūkai** protest
抗議する **kōgi suru** protest
小切手 **kogitte** check FIN
皇后 **kōgō** empress
凍えた **kogoeta** frozen
交互に **kōgo ni** alternately; mutually
口語(の) **kōgo (no)** colloquial
小言を言う **kogoto o iu** nag
こぐ **kogu** paddle; row
工業 **kōgyō** industry
鉱業 **kōgyō** mining
工業団地 **kōgyō-danchi** industrial park
工業化する **kōgyōka suru** industrialize
工業(の) **kōgyō (no)** industrial
後輩 **kōhai** junior
荒廃して **kōhai shite** in ruins
後半 **kōhan** second half
小春日和 **koharu-biyori** Indian summer
公平(な) **kōhei (na)** fair; sporting; impartial, unbias(s)ed
公平さ **kōhei-sa** fairness
コーヒー **kōhī** coffee
コーヒーブレイク **kōhī-bureiku** coffee break
コーヒーメーカー **kōhī-mēkā** coffee maker
コーヒーポット **kōhī-potto** coffee pot
子羊 **kohitsuji** lamb
公報 **kōhō** bulletin; official report
広報活動 **kōhō-katsudō** PR, public relations
候補者 **kōho-sha** candidate; contender
候補する **kōho suru** be a candidate; run for office
公表 **kōhyō** disclosure, publication
好評 **kōhyō** rave review
公表されていない **kōhyō sarete inai** unofficial
公表する **kōhyō suru** publicize; release *information*; post *profits*
こい **koi** koi, carp
恋 **koi** romantic love; 恋に落ちる ***koi ni ochiru*** fall in love
濃い **koi** thick; strong; dense; dark
行為 **kōi** act, deed; action
好意 **kōi** willingness; goodwill
恋人 **koibito** boyfriend; girlfriend; partner
故意でない **koi de nai** unintentional
コイン **koin** coin; token
故意に **koi ni** knowingly; intentionally
故意(の) **koi (no)** deliberate, intentional
こいのぼり **koinobori** carp banners
コインランドリー **koin-randorī** laundromat
子犬 **koinu** puppy, pup
小石 **koishi** pebble
恋しがる **koishigaru** pine for
恋しい **koishii** dear; cherished; beloved ◊ miss
恋している **koi shite iru** be in love
更衣室 **kōishitsu** changing room
好意的(な) **kōiteki (na)** favorable; sympathetic; high *opinion*
孤児 **koji** orphan
工事 **kōji** construction
こじ開ける **kojiakeru** force open
こじき **kojiki** beggar
故人 **kojin** the deceased
個人 **kojin** individual
個人秘書 **kojin-hisho** personal assistant

個人(の) **kojin** (**no**) individual; personal
個人主義者**kojin-shugisha** individualist
個人的(な) **kojinteki** (**na**) intimate; personal; private
口実 **kōjitsu** pretext; excuse
控除 **kōjo** deduction
工場 **kōjō** factory, plant
甲状腺 **kōjōsen** thyroid (gland)
口述する **kōjutsu suru** dictate
硬貨 **kōka** coin
降下 **kōka** descent
効果 **kōka** effect
高架道路 **kōka-dōro** overpass
航海 **kōkai** crossing; sailing
後悔 **kōkai** regret; penitence; 激しい後悔 ***hageshii kôkai*** remorse
公会堂 **kōkaidō** auditorium; public hall
航海術 **kōkaijutsu** navigation
コカイン **kokain** cocaine, coke
航海(の) **kōkai** (**no**) nautical
公開(の) **kōkai** (**no**) public
航海士 **kōkaishi** mate; navigator
後悔している **kōkai shite iru** penitent
航海する **kōkai suru** cruise
公開する **kōkai suru** exhibit; release
後悔する **kōkai suru** regret; repent
コカコーラ **koka-kōra** Coke®
甲殻類 **kōkakurui** crustaceans
降格する **kōkaku suru** downgrade; demote
高官 **kōkan** dignitary
交換 **kōkan** exchange
高価(な) **kōka** (**na**) expensive, dear; valuable
交換できる **kōkan dekiru** interchangeable; exchangeable
高架(の) **kōka** (**no**) overhead, elevated
効果のない **kōka no nai** ineffective
交換留学 **kōkan-ryūgaku** (academic) exchange
交換する **kōkan suru** trade, swap, exchange
効果的(な) **kōkateki** (**na**) effective; forcible
こけ **koke** moss
口径 **kōkei** caliber
光景 **kōkei** image; sight
後継者 **kōkei-sha** replacement; successor
貢献 **kōken** contribution
後見人 **kōken-nin** guardian
貢献する **kōken suru** contribute
こけし **kokeshi** kokeshi doll
高潔 **kōketsu** integrity
高血圧 **kōketsuatsu** high blood pressure; hypertension
高潔(な) **kōketsu** (**na**) virtuous, high-minded
後期 **kōki** second semester; second half; 20世紀後期 ***nijusseiki-kôki*** the late 20th century
高気圧 **kōkiatsu** high pressure
拘禁 **kōkin** detention
高貴(な) **kōki** (**na**) noble
拘禁する **kōkin suru** confine; detain; intern
こきおろす **kokiorosu** disparage; criticize
高貴さ **kōki-sa** nobility
好奇心 **kōkishin** curiosity; 好奇心の強い ***kôkishin no tsuyoi*** curious
国家 **kokka** nation, state
国歌 **kokka** national anthem
国会 **Kokkai** the Diet; Congress; national assembly
国会議員 **Kokkai-giin** member of Congress
国家(の) **kokka** (**no**) national
こっけい(な) **kokkei** (**na**) comical
国旗 **kokki** national flag
コック **kokku** cook
コックピット **kokkupitto** cockpit
国境 **kokkyō** border, frontier
ここ **koko** here; ここだけの話 ***koko dake no hanashi*** between you and me
航行 **kōkō** navigation
高校 **kōkō** high school, high
ココア **kokoa** cocoa
心地悪い **kokochiwarui** uncomfortable
心地よい **kokochiyoi** pleasing
考古学 **kōkogaku** archeology
考古学者 **kōkogaku-sha** archeologist

故国 **kokoku** home, native country
広告 **kōkoku** advertisement, advertising; 広告を出す ***kôkoku o dasu*** advertise
公告 **kōkoku** notice
広告代理店 **kōkoku-dairiten** advertising agency
広告業界 **kōkoku-gyōkai** advertising
広告主 **kōkokunushi** advertiser
ココナッツ **kokonattsu** coconut
ここに **koko ni** in here; here
個々(の) **koko (no)** individual
心 **kokoro** mind; 心に抱く ***kokoro ni idaku*** harbor; cherish
心当たりがある **kokoroatari ga aru** happen to know of; 心当たりがありますか ***kokoroatari ga arimasu ka*** any idea …?
心細い **kokorobosoi** downhearted
心がける **kokorogakeru** bear in mind
心から **kokoro kara** dearly; sincerely; warmly
心から(の) **kokoro kara (no)** heartfelt; whole-hearted; warm
試み **kokoromi** try, attempt
試みる **kokoromiru** try, attempt
心無い **kokoronai** thoughtless; heartless
心に浮かぶ **kokoro ni ukabu** strike
心の温かい **kokoro no atatakai** warm-hearted
心の広い **kokoro no hiroi** broadminded, open-minded, liberal
心のこもった **kokoro no komotta** loving
心の中で **kokoro no naka de** inwardly, mentally
心の狭い **kokoro no semai** narrow-minded, petty
心の安らぎ **kokoro no yasuragi** peace of mind
心をかき乱す **kokoro o kakimidasu** stir up
心を奪う **kokoro o ubau** enthrall
快く **kokoroyoku** gladly
志 **kokorozashi** ambition; aspiration; wish
志ざす **kokorozasu** aspire to; aim to
心遣い **kokorozukai** thoughtfulness
心付け **kokorozuke** gratuity
心強い **kokorozuyoi** encouraging; reassuring
高校生 **kōkōsei** high school student
航行する **kōkō suru** navigate
航空 **kōkū** aviation
黒板 **kokuban** blackboard
航空便で **kōkūbin de** by air, by airmail
航空母艦 **kōkū-bokan** aircraft carrier
国防省長官 **Kokubōshō-chōkan** Defense Secretary
国防総省 **Kokubō-sōshō** Department of Defense
国土 **kokudo** country; land
国道 **kokudō** national route
克服できない **kokufuku dekinai** insurmountable
克服する **kokufuku suru** overcome; master
航空会社 **kōkū-gaisha** airline
国外退去命令 **kokugai-taikyo-meirei** deportation order
航空学(の) **kōkūgaku (no)** aeronautical
国語 **kokugo** national language; Japanese
告白 **kokuhaku** admission, confession
告白する **kokuhaku suru** confess
告発 **kokuhatsu** accusation
告発する **kokuhatsu suru** accuse
酷評する **kokuhyō suru** criticize severely; hit out at
刻印 **kokuin** stamp; imprint
黒人 **kokujin** black (*person*)
航空管制 **kōkū-kansei** air-traffic control
航空管制塔 **kōkū-kanseitō** control tower
航空機 **kōkūki** aircraft
国民 **kokumin** subject; fellow citizen; the public
国民の休日 **Kokumin no kyūjitsu** 4th of May holiday
国民総生産 **kokumin-sōseisan**

GNP, gross national product
穀物 **kokumotsu** cereal, grain
国務長官 **Kokumu-chōkan** Secretary of State
国務省 **Kokumushō** State Department
国内(の) **kokunai** (**no**) domestic, internal
国内線 **kokunai-sen** domestic flight
国内総生産 **kokunai-sōseisan** GDP, gross domestic product
国王 **kokuō** king
国連 **Kokuren** UN
国立公園 **kokuritsu-kōen** national park
コクる **kokuru**: …にコクった ***… ni kokutta*** he / she said he / she loved
国債 **kokusai** national debt
国際 **kokusai** international
国際電話 **kokusai-denwa** international call
国際競技会 **kokusai-kyōgikai** international competition
国際連合 **Kokusai-rengō** United Nations
国際収支 **kokusai-shūshi** balance of payments
国際的(な) **kokusaiteki** (**na**) international, cosmopolitan
国際通貨基金 **Kokusai-tsūka-kikin** IMF, International Monetary Fund
国籍 **kokuseki** nationality
航空写真 **kōkū-shashin** aerial photograph
酷使 **kokushi** abuse
航空書簡 **kōkū-shokan** air letter
告訴されている **kokuso sarete iru** be accused of
告訴する **kokuso suru** accuse; sue
航空宇宙産業 **kōkū-uchū-sangyō** aerospace industry
国有化する **kokuyūka suru** nationalize
国税庁 **Kokuzeichō** Internal Revenue (Service); National Tax Administration
航空図 **kōkūzu** chart
顧客 **kokyaku** client, patron
故郷 **kokyō** home; home town
皇居 **Kōkyo** Imperial Palace
公共事業 **kōkyō-jigyō** public utilities
交響曲 **kōkyōkyoku** symphony
公共(の) **kōkyō** (**no**) public
呼吸 **kokyū** respiration, breathing
高級官僚 **kōkyū-kanryō** mandarin; high-ranking official
高級(な) **kōkyū** (**na**) exclusive; high-class; high-quality
こま **koma** counter, piece, man
細かい **komakai** detailed; finicky; fine *distinction*
鼓膜 **komaku** eardrum
コマ漫画 **koma-manga** (comic) strip
小間物 **komamono** notions
こま結び **komamusubi** square knot; reef knot
高慢ちき(な) **kōmanchiki** (**na**) conceited; stuck-up
高慢(な) **kōman** (**na**) haughty
困らせる **komaraseru** puzzle; put on the spot
困る **komaru** be in trouble; be badly off
コマーシャル **komāsharu** commercial, ad
コマーシャルソング **komāsharu-songu** (advertising) jingle
困った **komatta** troubled; vexed
困っている **komatte iru** be in a fix
米 **kome** rice (*uncooked*)
コメディアン **komedian** comedian
こめかみ **komekami** temple ANAT
コメント **komento** comment
込み合った **komiatta** packed, crowded
小道 **komichi** lane; path, track
小見出し **komidashi** subheading
込み入った **komiitta** involved, complex
項目 **kōmoku** item
顧問 **komon** adviser, consultant
顧問料 **komon-ryō** fee, retainer
こうもり **kōmori** bat
子守歌 **komoriuta** lullaby
込む **komu** be crowded
小麦 **komugi** wheat
小麦粉 **komugiko** flour
公務員 **kōmuin** civil servant, official

こうむる **kōmuru** incur, suffer; receive
鉱脈 **kōmyaku** deposit; vein (*of ore*)
巧妙(な) **kōmyō (na)** ingenious; subtle
コミュニケーション **komyunikēshon** communication
コミュニティー **komyunitī** community
コーン **kōn** cone
粉 **kona** powder
粉々になる **konagona ni naru** smash; …を粉々にする ***… o konagona ni suru*** smash to pieces
粉々に割れる **konagona ni wareru** shatter
粉々に割る **konagona ni waru** shatter
構内 **kōnai** campus; yard
コーナーキック **kōnā kikku** corner kick, corner
粉ミルク **konamiruku** formula
コンバイン **konbain** combine harvester
今晩 **konban** this evening, tonight;
こんばんは **konbanwa** good evening
コンビニエンスストア **konbiniensu-sutoa** convenience store
こん棒 **konbō** club; stick
こんぶ **konbu** kelp
昆虫 **konchū** insect
込んだ **konda** crowded
込んでいる **konde iru** busy
コンデンスミルク **kondensu-miruku** condensed milk
今度 **kondo** this time; next time
コンドミニアム **kondominiamu** condo(minium)
コンドーム **kondōmu** condom
今度(の) **kondo (no)** forthcoming
混同する **kondō suru** confuse, muddle
子猫 **koneko** kitten
光年 **kōnen** light year
更年期 **kōnenki** menopause
こねる **koneru** knead
コーンフレーク **kōnfurēku** cereal
婚外(の) **kongai (no)** extramarital
懇願する **kongan suru** plead with
根源 **kongen** root
今月 **kongetsu** this month
混合 **kongō** mixture
公認会計士 **kōnin-kaikeishi** certified public accountant
公認されていない **kōnin sarete inai** unofficial
後任者 **kōnin-sha** successor
紺色 **kon'iro** navy blue
根気 **konki** perseverance
根気強さ **konkizuyo-sa** patience; persistence
コンクリート **konkurīto** concrete
根拠 **konkyo** ground, reason; cause; basis (*of argument*)
根拠のない **konkyo no nai** groundless, unfounded
コンマ **konma** comma
こんな **konna** this kind of; such
困難 **konnan** hardship
こんなに **konna ni** so; to this extent; こんなにたくさん ***konna ni takusan*** so many
困難(な) **konnan (na)** painful
こんにちは **konnichiwa** good afternoon; hello, hi; how are you?
この **kono** this; the
このあいだ **kono aida** the other day; that time
このごろは **kono goro wa** nowadays
この辺に **kono hen ni** around here
この前 (の) **kono mae (no)** the last; the one before this
好ましい **konomashii** agreeable; pleasant
好ましくない **konomashiku nai** undesirable; unsavory
好み **konomi** choice, preference, inclination; taste
木の実 **konomi** nut
好む **konomu** like; be fond of
このよう(な) **kono yō (na)** such
この世の **kono yo no** earthly
コンパクトディスク **konpakuto-disuku** CD, compact disc
コンパス **konpasu** compasses
根本 **konpon** foundation; base
根本的(な) **konponteki (na)** radical; basic
コンプレックス **konpurekkusu** complex

コンピューター **konpyūtā** computer
コンピューターゲーム **konpyūtā-gēmu** computer game
混乱 **konran** confusion, muddle; disruption
混乱させる **konran saseru** confuse, muddle; muddle up
混乱した **konran shita** confused, disoriented
混乱している **konran shite iru** be mixed up
コンサルタント **konsarutanto** consultant
コンサルタント業 **konsarutanto-gyō** consultancy
コンサート **konsāto** concert
コンサートマスター **konsāto-masutā** concertmaster
コンセント **konsento** outlet
今週 **konshū** this week
コンタクトレンズ **kontakuto-renzu** contact lens
コンテナ **kontena** container
コンテスト **kontesuto** competition, contest
コントラバス **kontorabasu** double-bass
コントラスト **kontorasuto** contrast
コントロール **kontorōru** control
コントロールパネル **kontorōru-paneru** control panel
コントロールする **kontorōru suru** control
困惑させる **konwaku saseru** baffle
困惑する **konwaku suru** be baffled
コニャック **konyakku** cognac
婚約 **kon'yaku** engagement
婚約者 **kon'yaku-sha** fiancé; fiancée
婚約している **kon'yaku shite iru** engaged
婚約する **kon'yaku suru** get engaged
婚約指輪 **kon'yaku-yubiwa** engagement ring
購入 **kōnyū** purchase; purchasing
購入品 **kōnyūhin** purchase
購入する **kōnyū suru** purchase
混雑する **konzatsu suru** be crowded
婚前(の) **konzen** (**no**) premarital
根絶する **konzetsu suru** eradicate, stamp out
コピー **kopī** photocopy; copy
コピー犯罪 **kopī-hanzai** copycat crime
コピー機 **kopī-ki** photocopier, copier
コピーライター **kopī-raitā** copy-writer
コピーする **kopī suru** photocopy; copy
こっぴどく **koppidoku** soundly; severely
コップ **koppu** glass
甲羅 **kōra** shell
こらえる **koraeru** bear; persevere; repress
こらこら **korakora** now, now!
行楽地 **kōrakuchi** resort
行楽客 **kōrakukyaku** vacationer
コラム **koramu** column
コラムニスト **koramunisuto** columnist
凍らせる **kōraseru** freeze
コーラス **kōrasu** chorus
これ **kore** this; this one; これだけです ***kore dake desu*** that's all, thanks; これでおしまい ***kore de oshimai*** that's it!
高齢者 **kōrei-sha** senior citizen
これから **kore kara** from now on
コレクション **korekushon** collection; selection, assortment
コレクトコール **korekuto-kōru** collect call
これまでで **kore made de** yet
これら **korera** these
これらの **korera no** these
コレステロール **koresuterōru** cholesterol
氷 **kōri** ice; ice cube
凝り固まった **korikatamatta** entrenched; fanatical
こりる **koriru** learn one's lesson
孤立 **koritsu** isolation
公立学校 **kōritsu-gakkō** public school
公立(の) **kōritsu** (**no**) public
孤立させる **koritsu saseru** isolate, cut off
孤立した **koritsu shita** isolated

効率的(な) **kōritsuteki** (na) efficient
頃 **koro** time ◊ when; 子供の頃 ***kodomo no koro*** when I was a child
転ぶ **korobu** fall over
転がる **korogaru** roll
転がす **korogasu** roll over
こおろぎ **kōrogi** cricket
ころころ変わる **korokoro kawaru** changeable ◊ change a lot
ころころ転がる **korokoro korogaru** roll over and over
コロン **koron** colon
殺し屋 **koroshi-ya** hired killer; hitman
殺す **korosu** kill; slay
こる **koru** become stiff; be absorbed in
凍る **kōru** freeze, freeze over
コルク **koruku** cork
コールスロー **kōrusurō** coleslaw
凍るよう(な) **kōru yō** (na) freezing
攻略する **kōryaku suru** capture; conquer
考慮 **kōryo** consideration; 考慮に入れる ***kôryo ni ireru*** make allowances
綱領 **kōryō** summary; outline; platform
考慮する **kōryo suru** consider; think about
荒涼とした **kōryō to shita** desolate, stark
交流 **kōryū** alternating current
拘留されている **kōryū sarete iru** be in custody
拘留する **kōryū suru** detain, hold
濃さ **ko-sa** depth (*of color*); shade; thickness
こう彩 **kōsai** iris (*of eye*)
交際する **kōsai suru** associate with; go out with
耕作 **kōsaku** cultivation
小作人 **kosaku-nin** farmworker
耕作する **kōsaku suru** cultivate
降参する **kōsan suru** give in, surrender
交差する **kōsa suru** cross, intersect
交差点 **kōsaten** intersection; junction
個性 **kosei** individuality; personality
構成 **kōsei** composition; formation; organization; structure
後世 **kōsei** posterity
抗生物質 **kōsei-busshitsu** antibiotic
公正(な) **kōsei** (na) unbias(s)ed, just
高性能(の) **kōseinō** (no) high performance; high-powered
構成されている **kōsei sarete iru** be comprised of, be made up of
厚生省 **Kōseishō** Ministry of Health and Welfare
構成する **kōsei suru** compose, comprise, constitute; structure, plan
校正する **kōsei suru** proofread
校正刷り **kōseizuri** proof (*of book*)
鉱石 **kōseki** ore
航跡 **kōseki** wake (*of ship*)
戸籍係 **koseki-gakari** registrar
戸籍登記所 **koseki-tōkisho** registrar's office
交戦 **kōsen** engagement MIL
光線 **kōsen** ray
好戦的(な) **kōsenteki** (na) belligerent
後者 **kōsha** the latter
校舎 **kōsha** school building
腰 **koshi** hip; waist
孔子 **Kōshi** Confucius
公使 **kōshi** envoy; minister
格子 **kōshi** grate, grating, grid
講師 **kōshi** lecturer
腰掛ける **koshikakeru** sit; perch
こし器 **koshiki** strainer
公式 **kōshiki** formula
公式訪問 **kōshiki-hōmon** official visit; state visit
公式(の) **kōshiki** (no) formal; official; ceremonial
行進 **kōshin** march
更新 **kōshin** renewal; update
香辛料 **kōshinryō** spice; 香辛料の利いた ***kôshinryô no kiita*** spicy
行進する **kōshin suru** march; parade
更新する **kōshin suru** renew, roll over; update

行使する **kōshi suru** use; exercise *right*
こうして **kōshite** thus
個室 **koshitsu** private room
固執する **koshitsu suru** persist, keep on; cling to
こしょう **koshō** pepper
故障 **koshō** breakdown
呼称 **koshō** form of address
交渉 **kōshō** negotiation
故障中で **koshōchū de** out of order
故障のない **koshō no nai** trouble-free
故障する **koshō suru** break down
交渉する **kōshō suru** negotiate
絞首台 **kōshudai** gallows
公衆電話 **kōshū-denwa** pay phone
公衆電話ボックス **kōshū-denwa-bokkusu** (tele)phone booth
絞首刑にする **kōshukei ni suru** hang
こそ **-koso** (*intensifier*): これこそぼくが見たものだ ***kore-koso boku ga mita mono da*** this is the very one that I saw
高僧 **kōsō** high priest
構想 **kōsō** idea; blueprint; plan
高層ビル **kōsō-biru** high rise
こそ泥 **kosodoro** thief; pilferer
高速道路 **kōsoku-dōro** expressway, freeway
高速ギヤ **kōsoku-giya** high (gear)
拘束力のある **kōsokuryoku no aru** binding
拘束する **kōsoku suru** tie down
酵素洗剤 **kōso-senzai** biological detergent
骨折 **kossetsu** break, fracture
骨折した **kossetsu shita** broken
骨折する **kossetsu suru** break, fracture
こっそり **kossori** stealthily; secretly
こっそりと **kossori to** on the sly
こす **kosu** filter, strain
越す **kosu** exceed
コース **kōsu** track; course
香水 **kōsui** perfume, scent
降水量 **kōsuiryō** rainfall
こする **kosuru** rub; scrape
コスト **kosuto** cost
答え **kotae** answer, response
こたえる **kotaeru** affect; respond; 暑さが彼の身にこたえる ***atsusa ga kare no mi ni kotaeru*** the heat is telling on him; 期待にこたえる ***kitai ni kotaeru*** live up to expectations
答える **kotaeru** respond; answer固体 **kotai** solid
抗体 **kōtai** antibody
後退 **kōtai** retreat; regression; setback
交替 **kōtai** alternation; shift; 交替で…をする ***kôtai de … o suru*** take turns in doing; do … in rotation
交替する, 交代する **kōtai suru** alternate; change places; take over
光沢 **kōtaku** luster
こたつ **kotatsu** heated table with quilt cover
こっち **kotchi** this; this one
こて **kote** curling tongs
皇帝 **kōtei** emperor
行程 **kōtei** journey; stage (*of journey*)
公定歩合 **kōtei-buai** bank rate
固定概念 **koteigainen** stereotype
皇帝(の) **kōtei (no)** imperial
固定された **kotei sareta** secure; fixed
固定した **kotei shita** fixed
固定する **kotei suru** secure, fix
肯定する **kōtei suru** answer in the affirmative
公的(な) **kōteki (na)** official
古典 **koten** classic
好転 **kōten** upturn; improvement
こてんぱんにやっつける **kotenpan ni yattsukeru** massacre
好転させる **kōten saseru** turn around; change for the better
鋼鉄 **kōtetsu** steel
鋼鉄製(の) **kōtetsusei (no)** steel
事, こと **koto** business; matter, affair, thing
琴 **koto** *Japanese string instrument*
コート **kōto** court SP
こう頭 **kōtō** larynx
言葉 **kotoba** language; phrase; word
言葉につまる **kotoba ni tsumaru** be lost for words

言葉の壁 **kotoba no kabe** language barrier
言葉を選ぶ **kotoba o erabu** choose one's words
言葉遣い **kotobazukai** wording; language
…ことができる… **koto ga dekiru** can, be able to
高等(な) **kōtō (na)** advanced; high-level
異なる **kotonaru** differ ◊ dissimilar
口頭(の) **kōtō (no)** oral
今年 **kotoshi** this year
断る **kotowaru** refuse, turn down
ことわざ **kotowaza** proverb, saying
こつ **kotsu** knack, trick
交通 **kōtsū** traffic
骨盤 **kotsuban** pelvis
好都合 **kōtsugō** convenience
交通標識 **kōtsū-hyōshiki** traffic sign
交通違反 **kōtsū-ihan** traffic violation
交通事故 **kōtsū-jiko** traffic accident
交通渋滞 **kōtsū-jūtai** traffic congestion; (traffic) jam; gridlock
交通機関 **kōtsū-kikan** means of transportation
こつこつ **kotsukotsu**: こつこつやる ***kotsukotsu yaru*** plug away, persevere
凝った **kotta** elaborate; ornate; fussy
凍った **kōtta** frozen
こってりした **kotteri shita** thick; heavy; rich
骨とう品 **kottō-hin** antique
コットン **kotton** cotton
骨とう屋 **kottō-ya** antique dealer
幸運, 好運 **kōun** good luck; lucky break; fortune; 幸運を祈る ***kôun o inoru*** keep one's fingers crossed; wish … well
幸運(な) **kōun (na)** fortunate; happy
幸運(の) **kōun (no)** lucky
小売業者 **kouri-gyōsha** retailer
小売価格 **kouri-kakaku** retail price
小売値で **kourine de** retail
小売りされる **kouri sareru** retail
子牛 **koushi** calf
子牛肉 **koushiniku** veal
こわばる **kowabaru** stiffen; 顔がこわばる ***kao ga kowabaru*** wince
こわばった **kowabatta** stiff
怖がらせる **kowagaraseru** frighten, scare
怖がる **kowagaru** be afraid; be frightened of; dread
怖い **kowai** scary
壊れない **kowarenai** unbreakable; indestructible
壊れる **kowareru** break, come apart
壊れた **kowareta** broken
壊れやすい **kowareyasui** breakable, fragile
壊す **kowasu** break; ruin
小屋 **koya** hut, shed
荒野 **kōya** the wilds; wilderness
肥やし **koyashi** manure
雇用 **koyō** employment
こよみ **koyomi** calendar
雇用者 **koyō-sha** employer
小指 **koyubi** little finger; little toe
口座 **kōza** account
講座 **kōza** course
小細工 **kozaiku** gimmick; cheap trick
鉱山 **kōzan** mine
小銭 **kozeni** change, small change
公然(の) **kōzen (no)** public
公然と **kōzen to** publicly
構造 **kōzō** mechanism; structure
構造工学 **kōzō-kōgaku** structural engineering
構造的(な) **kōzōteki (na)** structural
洪水 **kōzui** flood; flooding
小遣い **kozukai** allowance
小突く **kozuku** poke; nudge; jog
小包 **kozutsumi** package, parcel
句 **ku** phrase
区 **ku** ward (*of city*); district; zone
配る **kubaru** deal; distribute, give out
区別 **kubetsu** distinction; 区別をする ***kubetsu o suru*** differentiate between, distinguish between; mark out, single out
首 **kubi** neck; 首を切る ***kubi o kiru*** decapitate; fire
首になる **kubi ni naru** be fired
首にする **kubi ni suru** fire

くぼみ **kubomi** dip; recess
くぼんだ **kubonda** hollow
口 **kuchi** mouth; 口が軽い ***kuchi ga karui*** be talkative; 口がうまい ***kuchi ga umai*** have a smooth tongue; 口が悪い ***kuchi ga warui*** have a sharp tongue; 口をはさむ ***kuchi o hasamu*** interrupt, break in
くちばし **kuchibashi** beak
口紅 **kuchibeni** lipstick
唇 **kuchibiru** lip
口笛 **kuchibue** whistle; 口笛をふく ***kuchibue o fuku*** whistle
口げんか **kuchigenka** row
口げんかする **kuchigenka suru** have words
口汚い **kuchigitanai** abusive
口答えする **kuchigotae suru** answer back
口ひげ **kuchihige** mustache
口(の) **kuchi (no)** oral
口のきけない **kuchi no kikenai** dumb, mute
口先だけ **kuchisaki dake** lip service
口うるさい **kuchiurusai** nagging
口調 **kuchō** tone of voice
空調 **kūchō** air-conditioning
空中で **kūchū de** in midair
空中(の) **kūchū (no)** aerial
管 **kuda** tube
砕ける **kudakeru** splinter; be smashed
くだけた **kudaketa** chatty; informal; plain; easy
果物 **kudamono** fruit
くだらない **kudaranai** trashy; trifling
下りになる **kudari ni naru** descend
下り坂(の) **kudarizaka (no)** downhill
下さい **kudasai** please; ドアを締めて下さい ***doa o shimete kudasai*** would you close the door, please?
下さる **kudasaru** give (*polite*); be kind enough to do
下す **kudasu** bring in; hand down; lower
クーデター **kūdetā** coup
くどい **kudoi** persistent; repetitive; tedious
口説く **kudoku** make advances; seduce
空腹 **kūfuku** hunger
九月 **kugatsu** September
くぎ **kugi** nail; spike
空軍 **kūgun** air force
空軍基地 **kūgun-kichi** airbase
空白 **kūhaku** vacuum
くい **kui** stake, post
食いぶち **kuibuchi** keep; ***kuibuchi o kasegu*** earn one's keep
食い違う **kuichigau** clash
区域 **kuiki** area; sector
食い込む **kuikomu** eat into; encroach on
食い物にする **kuimono ni suru** prey on
食い止める **kuitomeru** keep in check, hold in check
食いつく **kuitsuku** bite
クイズ **kuizu** quiz
クイズ番組 **kuizu-bangumi** quiz program
くじゃく **kujaku** peacock
くじ **kuji** raffle
くじ引き **kujibiki** draw
鯨 **kujira** whale
苦情 **kujō** complaint; 苦情を言う ***kujô o iu*** complain
駆除する **kujo suru** exterminate
茎 **kuki** stalk; stem
空気 **kūki** air
クッキー **kukkī** cookie
屈強(な) **kukkyō (na)** brawny
空港 **kūkō** airport
苦境 **kukyō** plight, predicament
空虚 **kūkyo** void, emptiness
くま **kuma** bear
くま手 **kumade** rake
組 **kumi** class; team
組合 **kumiai** association
組み合わせ **kumiawase** combination
組み合わせる **kumiawaseru** combine
組曲 **kumikyoku** suite MUS
組み立て **kumitate** assembly
組み立てる **kumitateru** assemble, put together
くも **kumo** spider
雲 **kumo** cloud

苦もん **kumon** agony
クモの巣 **kumo no su** cobweb, spiderweb
くもりガラス **kumori-garasu** opaque glass
曇り **kumori** cloudy weather
曇り(の) **kumori** (**no**) dull
曇る **kumoru** cloud over; mist up
曇った **kumotta** cloudy; overcast
組む **kumu** unite; pair; assemble; fold *arms*; cross *legs*
君 **-kun** Mr; Ms (*to address younger people*)
宮内庁 **Kunaichō** Imperial Household Agency
くねくねした **kunekune shita** wavy; zigzag
くねくねする **kunekune suru** wriggle
くねらす **kunerasu** wiggle
くねる **kuneru** crooked; wind round; twist
国 **kuni** country, nation; 国の内外で ***kuni no naigai de*** at home and abroad
くんくんかぐ **kunkun kagu** sniff
くんくん泣く **kunkun naku** whine
苦悩 **kunō** anguish; distress
苦悩した **kunō shita** martyred
訓練する **kunren suru** drill; train; groom
君臨する **kunrin suru** reign
勲章 **kunshō** medal; decoration
クーポン **kūpon** voucher, coupon
くら **kura** saddle
倉 **kura** storehouse
比べものにならない **kurabemono ni naranai** there's no comparison
比べる **kuraberu** compare
クラブ **kurabu** club, society
暗がり **kuragari** dark; gloom
くらげ **kurage** jellyfish
くらい **-kurai** around, approximately ◊ like ◊ at least
位 **kurai** rank; grade; throne
暗い **kurai** dark; somber; dismal
暗い色(の) **kurai iro** (**no**) dark
クライマックス **kuraimakkusu** climax, high point
クラッカー **kurakkā** cracker
暗くなる **kuraku naru** darken, dim
くらくらする **kurakura suru** feel dizzy; be in a whirl
クラクション **kurakushon** horn MOT
クラリネット **kurarinetto** clarinet
暮し **kurashi** living
クラシック(な) **kurashikku** (**na**) classical
暮しに困らない **kurashi ni komaranai** be comfortable
クラッシュ **kurasshu** crash COMPUT
クラッシュする **kurasshu suru** crash COMPUT
クラス **kurasu** class
暮らす **kurasu** live
クラスメート **kurasumēto** classmate
クラッチ **kuratchi** clutch MOT
暗やみ **kurayami** darkness
クレジット **kurejitto** credit
クレジットカード **kurejitto-kādo** credit card, charge card
クレーン **kurēn** crane
くれる **kureru** give
暮れる **kureru** get dark; come to an end; be absorbed in
クレヨン **kureyon** crayon
くり **kuri** chestnut
クリアランスセール **kuriaransu-sēru** clearance sale
繰り返し **kurikaeshi** chorus, refrain; repetition
繰り返し(の) **kurikaeshi** (**no**) repetitive
繰り返している **kurikaeshite iru** duplicate
繰り返して言う **kurikaeshite iu** repeat
繰り返す **kurikaesu** repeat; echo
クリック **kurikku** click COMPUT; …をクリックする ***… o kurikku suru*** click on
クリーム **kurīmu** cream
クリームチーズ **kurīmu-chīzu** cream cheese
クリーム色 **kurīmu-iro** cream
クリームソーダ **kurīmu sōda** soda
クリーニングする **kurīningu suru** clean
クリーニング店 **kurīningu-ten** laundry
クリップ **kurippu** clip; paperclip
クリスマス **Kurisumasu** Christmas;

Christmas Day
クリスタルガラス **kurisutaru-garasu** crystal
黒 **kuro** black
苦労 **kurō** effort, struggle, trouble; toil
黒い **kuroi** black
黒字で **kuroji de** in the black, in credit
黒子 **kuroko** puppeteer in Bunraku
クロコダイル **kurokodairu** crocodile
クローク **kurōku** checkroom, cloakroom
黒幕 **kuromaku** mastermind
クロム **kuromu** chrome, chromium
黒帯 **kuro-obi** black belt
黒っぽい **kuroppoi** dark
クロール **kurōru** crawl
クロスカントリー(スキー) **kurosu-kantorī (sukī)** cross-country (skiing)
苦労する **kurō suru** struggle ◊ you'll / he'll etc have a job
クロスワードパズル **kurosuwādo-pazuru** crossword (puzzle)
クローズアップ **kurōzu-appu** close-up
クローズアップする **kurōzu-appu suru** close up, move closer; zoom in
来る **kuru** come; fall (*of night*)
くるくる回る **kurukuru mawaru** whirl
くるくる回す **kurukuru mawasu** twirl
車 **kuruma** vehicle; car
車いす **kurumaisu** wheelchair
車回し **kuruma-mawashi** driveway
くるみ **kurumi** walnut
くるみ割り **kurumiwari** nutcrackers
くるむ **kurumu** wrap; tuck in (*in bed*)
苦しい **kurushii** agonizing
苦しめる **kurushimeru** distress
苦しみ **kurushimi** suffering; torment
苦しむ **kurushimu** suffer
狂った **kurutta** unbalanced
クルーズ **kurūzu** cruise
草 **kusa** grass
くさび **kusabi** wedge
くさい **kusai** smelly
鎖 **kusari** chain; lead, leash
腐る **kusaru** decay, rot, go bad
腐った **kusatta** rotten, bad, tainted; rancid; sick *society*
癖 **kuse** habit; peculiarity
くせに **kuse ni** although; in spite of
癖になる **kuse ni naru** be addictive
くしゃくしゃにする **kushakusha ni suru** rumple
くしゃみ **kushami** sneeze; くしゃみをする ***kushami o suru*** sneeze
くし **kushi** comb
苦心した **kushin shita** labored
くそ **kuso** V fuck!; shit!
空想 **kūsō** fantasy; 空想にふける ***kûsô ni fukeru*** daydream
くそったれ **kusottare** V asshole
クッション **kusshon** cushion
くすぶる **kusuburu** smolder
くすぐる **kusuguru** tickle
くすぐったがり(の) **kusuguttagari (no)** ticklish
くすぐったい **kusuguttai** ticklish
くすくす笑い **kusukusu warai** chuckle, giggle
くすくす笑う **kusukusu warau** chuckle, giggle, titter
薬 **kusuri** drug, medicine
薬指 **kusuri-yubi** ring finger
くたばっちまえ **kutabatchimae** V fuck off!
くたびれる **kutabireru** get tired; become worn out
くたくた(の) **kutakuta (no)** exhausted; worn out
苦闘 **kutō** struggle
苦闘する **kutō suru** struggle
句読点 **kutōten** punctuation marks
句読点の打ち方 **kutōten no uchikata** use of punctuation
靴 **kutsu** shoe
苦痛 **kutsū** distress; pain; agony
靴べら **kutsu-bera** shoehorn
覆す **kutsugaesu** demolish
靴ひも **kutsu-himo** shoelace
屈辱 **kutsujoku** humiliation
屈辱的(な) **kutsujokuteki (na)** degrading, humiliating
靴直し **kutsunaoshi** heel bar
くつろぐ **kutsurogu** relax, unwind; make oneself at home

くつろいだ **kutsuroida** free and easy
靴下 **kutsushita** sock
靴屋 **kutsu-ya** shoestore
靴墨 **kutsuzumi** shoe polish
くっついている **kuttsuite iru** stick together
くっつける **kuttsukeru** knit together
くっつく **kuttsuku** adhere
桑 **kuwa** mulberry
加える **kuwaeru** add; ...に加えて ***... ni kuwaete*** in addition to
くわがたむし **kuwagatamushi** stag beetle
詳しい **kuwashii** detailed; knowledgeable ◊ be well versed in
詳しく **kuwashiku** at length
加わらない **kuwawaranai** keep out
加わる **kuwawaru** join; be a party to
悔やむ **kuyamu** regret
悔しい **kuyashii** regrettable
くよくよ悩む **kuyokuyo nayamu** fret
空輸する **kūyu suru** fly, send by air
くず **kuzu** crumb; scrap; trash, garbage
くず入れ **kuzuire** trashcan
くずかご **kuzukago** waste basket
崩れ落ちる **kuzureochiru** topple
崩れる **kuzureru** collapse, give way; crumble
崩す **kuzusu** change *money*; destroy; crumble
キャベツ **kyabetsu** cabbage
キャビア **kyabia** caviar
キャディー **kyadī** caddie
キャド-キャム **kyado-kyamu** CAD-CAM
客観的(な) **kyakkanteki (na)** objective
却下する **kyakka suru** throw out, reject
客 **kyaku** customer; diner (*person*); guest, visitor
脚注 **kyakuchū** footnote
脚本 **kyakuhon** script
脚本家 **kyakuhon-ka** scriptwriter
客間 **kyakuma** guestroom
客船 **kyakusen** cruise liner
客車 **kyakusha** coach
客室 **kyakushitsu** cabin; compartment
客室係 **kyakushitsu-gakari** cabin crew; maid
脚色 **kyakushoku** dramatization, adaptation
脚色する **kyakushoku suru** dramatize, adapt
キャンバス **kyanbasu** canvas
キャンデー **kyandē** candy; toffee
キャンパス **kyanpasu** campus
キャンピングカー **kyanpingu-kā** camper, motor home
キャンプ **kyanpu** camp; camping
キャンプ場 **kyanpu-jō** camp ground, campsite
キャンプする **kyanpu suru** camp
キャンセル待ち(の) **kyanseru machi (no)** on standby
キャピタルゲイン税 **kyapitarugein-zei** capital gains tax
キャップ **kyappu** cap
キャプテン **kyaputen** captain
キャラバン **kyaraban** trailer
キャリア **kyaria** career
きゃしゃ(な) **kyasha (na)** petite; slight
キャスター **kyasutā** broadcaster; newscaster; caster (*on chair*)
脚立 **kyatatsu** stepladder
キャッチャー **kyatchā** catcher
今日 **kyō** today
競売 **kyōbai** auction; 競売にかける ***kyôbai ni kakeru*** auction
狂暴になる **kyōbō ni naru** go berserk
共謀する **kyōbō suru** conspire
強調 **kyōchō** accent, emphasis, stress
共著者 **kyōcho-sha** co-author
強調する **kyōchō suru** accentuate, stress
強打 **kyōda** bang, whack, sock
鏡台 **kyōdai** dressing table
巨大(な) **kyodai (na)** enormous, huge
兄弟(の) **kyōdai (no)** fraternal
兄弟姉妹 **kyōdai-shimai** brothers and sisters
強打する **kyōda suru** smash; punch, sock
共同ビル **kyōdō-biru** complex

共同経営事業 **kyōdō-keiei-jigyō** partnership
共同経営者 **kyōdō-keiei-sha** partner; partnership
共同研究する **kyōdō-kenkyū suru** collaborate
協同組合(の) **kyōdō-kumiai (no)** cooperative
共同(の) **kyōdō (no)** collective, joint
虚栄心 **kyoeishin** vanity
恐怖 **kyōfu** fright, terror; horror; 恐怖にかられた ***kyôfu ni karareta*** be terrified
強風 **kyōfū** gale
恐怖症 **kyōfushō** phobia
狂言 **kyōgen** Noh comedy
協議 **kyōgi** consultation; conference
教義 **kyōgi** dogma; doctrine
競技 **kyōgi** athletics competition; 競技に出る ***kyôgi ni deru*** race
競技場 **kyōgijō** stadium, arena; field
競技会 **kyōgikai** meet
協議する **kyōgi suru** confer, discuss
競合できる **kyōgō dekiru** competitive
脅迫 **kyōhaku** threat
強迫観念 **kyōhaku-kannen** compulsion, obsession
強迫されて **kyōhaku sarete** under duress
脅迫する **kyōhaku suru** threaten
共犯者 **kyōhan-sha** accomplice, accessory
拒否 **kyohi** refusal; denial
拒否権 **kyohiken** veto; …に拒否権を行使する ***… ni kyohiken o kôshi suru*** veto
拒否する **kyohi suru** deny, refuse
脅威 **kyōi** menace, threat
教育 **kyōiku** education
教育実習生 **kyōiku-jisshūsei** student teacher
教育(の) **kyōiku (no)** educational
教育のある **kyōiku no aru** educated
教育する **kyōiku suru** educate; train
教育的(な) **kyōikuteki (na)** educational
教員研修 **kyōin-kenshū** teacher training
虚弱 **kyojaku** weakling
巨人 **kyojin** giant
狂人 **kyōjin** maniac
狂女 **kyōjo** madwoman
教条主義的(な) **kyōjō-shugiteki (na)** dogmatic
教授 **kyōju** professor
居住可能(な) **kyojū-kanō (na)** inhabitable
居住者 **kyojū-sha** resident
居住する **kyojū suru** reside
許可 **kyoka** permission; authority; clearance; 許可を得る ***kyoka o eru*** get permission; 許可を与える ***kyoka o ataeru*** clear; authorize
協会 **kyōkai** association, organization, society
境界 **kyōkai** boundary, limit
教会 **kyōkai** church
共感 **kyōkan** sympathy; empathy; …に共感する ***… ni kyôkan suru*** sympathize with; empathize with
許可証 **kyokashō** permit
教科書 **kyōkasho** textbook
許可する **kyoka suru** allow; permit
強化する **kyōka suru** strengthen; reinforce
恐喝者 **kyōkatsu-sha** blackmailer
狂犬病 **kyōkenbyō** rabies
狂気 **kyōki** insanity, madness
狂気(の) **kyōki (no)** insane
狂喜する **kyōki suru** go wild with joy
強硬派 **kyōkōha** hardliner
強固(な) **kyōko (na)** strong; stubborn
局 **kyoku** bureau
極 **kyoku** pole (*of the earth*)
曲 **kyoku** musical composition
極地(の) **kyokuchi (no)** polar
極度の疲労 **kyokudo no hirō** exhaustion
教訓 **kyōkun** moral (*of story*)
曲線 **kyokusen** curve
局所麻酔 **kyokusho-masui** local anesthetic
極端 **kyokutan** extreme
極端(な) **kyokutan (na)** drastic, extreme
極東 **Kyokutō** Far East
極右 **kyokuu** extreme right
供給 **kyōkyū** provision, supply

供給する **kyōkyū suru** furnish, supply, provide
興味 **kyōmi** interest; …に興味がある ***… ni kyômi ga aru*** be interested in; 興味を持つ ***kyômi o motsu*** take up; have an interest in
去年 **kyonen** last year
狂乱した **kyōran shita** raving mad
強烈(な) **kyōretsu (na)** forceful; overpowering
距離 **kyori** distance
協力 **kyōryoku** collaboration; cooperation; interaction
強力(な) **kyōryoku (na)** strong, powerful
協力者 **kyōryoku-sha** collaborator
協力する **kyōryoku suru** collaborate; cooperate
協力的(な) **kyōryokuteki (na)** cooperative
狭量(な) **kyōryō (na)** narrow-minded
恐竜 **kyōryū** dinosaur
恐妻家 **kyōsai-ka** henpecked husband
共産主義**Kyōsan-shugi** Communism
共産主義者 **Kyōsan-shugisha** Communist
共産党 **Kyōsan-tō** Japanese Communist Party
虚勢 **kyosei** bravado
強勢 **kyōsei** stress, emphasis
矯正器 **kyōseiki** brace (*on teeth*)
強制送還**kyōsei-sōkan** deportation
強制送還する**kyōsei-sōkan suru** deport
去勢する **kyosei suru** castrate, neuter
強制する **kyōsei suru** force, compel
強制的(な) **kyōseiteki (na)** compulsory; forced
教師 **kyōshi** teacher; 教師をする ***kyôshi o suru*** teach
狭心症 **kyōshinshō** angina
教室 **kyōshitsu** classroom
教職 **kyōshoku** teaching
拒食症 **kyoshokushō** anorexia
郷愁 **kyōshū** nostalgia
競争 **kyōsō** competition; race; 競争の激しい ***kyôsô no hageshii*** competitive
競走 **kyōsō** race; running
競争相手 **kyōsō-aite** competition, competitor(s)
競走馬 **kyōsō-ba** racehorse
競争社会 **kyōsō-shakai** rat race
競争する **kyōsō suru** compete; race
競走する **kyōsō suru** race
強壮剤 **kyōsōzai** tonic
協定 **kyōtei** pact; 協定を結ぶ ***kyôtei o musubu*** reach agreement on
拠点 **kyoten** stronghold; base
京都 **Kyōto** Kyoto
共通に **kyōtsū ni** in common
共通(の) **kyōtsū (no)** common, mutual, shared
共和国 **kyōwakoku** republic
共和党員 **Kyōwatōin** Republican
共和党(の) **Kyōwatō (no)** Republican
教養のある **kyōyō no aru** cultivated, cultured
教養のない人 **kyōyō no nai hito** philistine
許容量 **kyoyōryō** limit
共用する **kyōyō suru** share
許容する **kyoyō suru** allow; permit
共有(の) **kyōyū (no)** communal
拒絶 **kyozetsu** rebuff; rejection; refusal
拒絶される **kyozetsu sareru** get the brushoff
拒絶する **kyozetsu suru** reject
共存 **kyōzon** coexistence
共存する **kyōzon suru** coexist
キュー **kyū** cue
九 **kyū** nine
球 **kyū** sphere
旧 **kyū** old; former
宮殿 **kyūden** palace
休業 **kyūgyō** closure, shutdown
吸引 **kyūin** suction
求人 **kyūjin** employment opportunity
求人広告 **kyūjin-kōkoku** want ad
休日 **kyūjitsu** holiday
救助 **kyūjo** rescue
救助員 **kyūjoin** lifeguard
急上昇 **kyūjōshō** jump, sudden rise

急上昇する **kyūjōshō suru** soar, rocket
救助する **kyūjo suru** rescue
救助隊 **kyūjo-tai** rescue party
九十 **kyūjū** ninety
休暇 **kyūka** vacation; leave; day off
休会 **kyūkai** recess, adjournment
休会する **kyūkai suru** adjourn
休火山 **kyūkazan** dormant volcano
休憩 **kyūkei** rest; break
休憩時間 **kyūkei-jikan** intermission, interval
休憩する **kyūkei suru** take a break
急行 **kyūkō** fast train
急行バス **kyūkō-basu** express bus
急降下 **kyūkōka** dive
急降下する **kyūkōka suru** dive; take a dive
球根 **kyūkon** bulb
急行(の) **kyūkō (no)** express
急行列車 **kyūkō-ressha** express train
窮屈(な) **kyūkutsu (na)** narrow; tight; formal; ill at ease
究極(の) **kyūkyoku (no)** ultimate
救急箱 **kyūkyū-bako** first-aid box, first-aid kit
救急車 **kyūkyūsha** ambulance
救急処置 **kyūkyū-shochi** first aid
救命ベルト **kyūmei-beruto** life belt
救命ボート **kyūmei-bōto** dinghy; lifeboat
救命胴衣 **kyūmei-dōi** life vest
救命具 **kyūmeigu** life preserver
休眠中(の) **kyūminchū (no)** dormant
急(な) **kyū (na)** urgent; sudden
急に **kyū ni** suddenly
吸入器 **kyūnyūki** inhaler
急落 **kyūraku** plunge
急落する **kyūraku suru** plummet, plunge
きゅうり **kyūri** cucumber
給料 **kyūryō** pay, salary, wage; payroll (*money*); pay check
給料日 **kyūryōbi** payday
給料体系 **kyūryō-taikei** salary scale
急流 **kyūryū** rapids
救済する **kyūsai suru** rescue, bail out
旧姓 **kyūsei** maiden name ◊ née
休戦 **kyūsen** truce
急進派 **kyūshin-ha** radical
急進的(な) **kyūshinteki (na)** radical
休職 **kyūshoku** leave of absence
給食 **kyūshoku** school meals
求職 **kyūshoku** job hunting
九州 **Kyūshū** Kyushu
吸収性(の) **kyūshūsei (no)** absorbent
吸収する **kyūshū suru** absorb, soak up
急襲する **kyūshū suru** pounce
救出する **kyūshutsu suru** extricate, free
休息 **kyūsoku** respite
急速に **kyūsoku ni** rapidly
吸水しやすい **kyūsui shiyasui** porous
休廷する **kyūtei suru** adjourn
急用 **kyūyō** urgent business
給油ポンプ **kyūyu-ponpu** gas pump
急増 **kyūzō** surge, sudden increase

M

間 **ma** interval; pause; 間をあける ***ma o akeru*** pause
まあ **mā** well!; oh!
まあじ **maaji** horse mackerel
真新しい **maatarashii** brand-new
まばたきする **mabataki suru** blink
幻 **maboroshi** vision REL
まぶしい **mabushii** blinding; dazzling
まぶた **mabuta** eyelid

町 **machi** town
待合室 **machiaishitsu** waiting room
待ち合わせ **machiawase** rendezvous
待ち合わせる **machiawaseru** arrange to meet; rendezvous
待ち針 **machibari** pin
待ちぼうけを食わす **machibōke o kuwasu** break an appointment; stand up
待ち伏せ **machibuse** ambush
待ち伏せする **machibuse suru** ambush; lurk
待ち遠しい **machidōshii** long for; look forward to
間違える **machigaeru** mistake, confuse
間違えて **machigaete** by mistake
間違え様のない **machigae-yō no nai** unmistakable
間違い **machigai** error, mistake, slip
間違った **machigatta** false, wrong
間違っている **machigatte iru** be in the wrong; be wrong
間違う **machigau** make a mistake, go wrong
待ち時間 **machi-jikan** wait; waiting
マチネ **machine** matinée
待ち受ける **machiukeru** wait for; expect
まだ **mada** still, as yet; まだです ***mada desu*** it's not ready; まだ一時です ***mada ichiji desu*** it's only one o'clock
…まで **... made** until; …までどれくらいですか ***... made dore kurai desu ka*** how far is it to …?
…までに ***... made ni*** by; 月曜日までに ***getsuyôbi made ni*** by Monday
窓 **mado** window
窓ガラス **mado-garasu** glazing; pane; windowpane
窓口 **madoguchi** teller; wicket
前 **mae** front ◊ before; ago
前払い **maebarai** advance payment, cash in advance
前払いする **maebarai suru** pay in advance
前触れ **maebure** foretaste
前書き **maegaki** foreword
前髪 **maegami** fringe
前借り **maegari** receive in advance
前金 **maekin** (money paid in) advance
前もって **maemotte** in advance; beforehand
前向き(な) **maemuki** (**na**) positive; facing the front; …に前向きである ***... ni maemuki de aru*** be receptive to
前に **mae ni** before, previously; forward; in front
前(の) **mae** (**no**) front; previous, old; preceding
前売り **maeuri** advance booking
マフィア **mafia** the Mafia
マフィン **mafin** muffin
マフラー **mafurā** muffler MOT; scarf
真冬 **mafuyu** midwinter
曲り角 **magarikado** corner; turn
曲がりくねる **magarikuneru** twist
曲がりくねった **magarikunetta** twisting, winding
マーガリン **māgarin** margarine
曲がる **magaru** bend, curve; turn; wind; round
曲がった **magatta** crooked
曲げる **mageru** bend; compromise
紛らわしい **magirawashii** confusing; misleading
孫 **mago** grandchild
孫息子 **mago-musuko** grandson
孫娘 **mago-musume** granddaughter
まごつく **magotsuku** be confused
マグカップ **magukappu** mug
まぐれ(の) **magure** (**no**) lucky
まぐろ **maguro** tuna
麻ひ **mahi** paralysis
麻ひさせる **mahi saseru** cripple; paralyze
魔法 **mahō** magic; magic spell
魔法瓶 **mahōbin** thermos flask, vacuum flask
魔法(の) **mahō** (**no**) magical
まい **-mai** (*negative suffix*) not; 言うまい ***iumai*** I won't say
枚 **-mai** *countword for flat items*
毎... **mai...** every; 毎分 ***maifun*** every minute; per minute; 毎度 ***maido*** every time; always

舞い上がる **maiagaru** soar
迷子 **maigo** lost child
マイコン **maikon** microcomputer
マイク **maiku** microphone, mike
マイクロバス **maikurobasu** minibus
マイクロチップ **maikurochippu** (micro)chip
マイクロフィルム **maikurofirumu** microfilm
マイナス **mainasu** minus
マイナス(の) **mainasu (no)** negative
毎日 **mainichi** every day
毎日(の) **mainichi (no)** daily
舞い下りる **maioriru** fly down; swoop
マイル **mairu** mile
参る **mairu** be defeated; surrender; be exhausted; be in love; visit *temple, grave*; H go; H come
毎週 **maishū** weekly
埋葬 **maisō** burial
埋葬する **maisō suru** bury
毎年 **maitoshi** yearly
毎月 **maitsuki** monthly
麻雀 **mājan** mah-jong
間仕切り **majikiri** partition wall
まじめ(な) **majime (na)** earnest, serious; straight; conservative
混じる **majiru** be mixed
魔女 **majo** witch
任せる **makaseru** entrust; delegate
負かす **makasu** beat, defeat
負け **make** defeat
負け惜しみ **make-oshimi** sour grapes
負ける **makeru** lose
負けている **makete iru** be behind SP
マーケティング **māketingu** marketing
まき **maki** firewood
巻 **maki** reel; roll
巻き上げる **makiageru** hoist
巻き毛(の) **makige (no)** curly
巻尺 **makijaku** tape measure
巻き戻す **makimodosu** rewind
巻き物 **makimono** scroll
巻き付ける **makitsukeru** wind
巻き添え **makizoe** involvement
真っ赤(な) **makka (na)** crimson; 真っ赤なうそ ***makka na uso*** a downright lie
末期(の) **makki (no)** terminal; 末期の病気 ***makki no byôki*** terminally ill
真っ暗(な) **makkura (na)** pitch dark
真っ黒(な) **makkuro (na)** jet-black
誠に **makoto ni** really; truly; 誠にありがとうございます ***makoto ni arigatô gozaimasu*** thank you very much indeed
まく **maku** scatter; sow
幕 **maku** act; curtain THEA; screen
膜 **maku** membrane
巻く **maku** coil; curl; wrap
幕あい **makuai** intermission; interlude
枕 **makura** pillow
枕カバー **makura-kabā** pillowcase, pillowslip
マクロ **makuro** macro
まくる **makuru** roll up; tuck up
まま **mama** like that; as is: そのままにして***sono mama ni shite*** leave it as it is
ママ **mama** mom
まあまあ **māmā** so-so
まま父 **mama-chichi** stepfather
まま母 **mama-haha** stepmother
まま息子 **mama-musuko** stepson
まま娘 **mama-musume** stepdaughter
まあまあ(の) **māmā (no)** moderate; ok, passable
マーマレード **māmarēdo** marmalade
まめ **mame** blister; corn
豆 **mame** bean
豆まき **mamemaki** bean scattering (*at the Setsubun festival*)
真水 **mamizu** freshwater
まもなく **mamonaku** before long; presently, soon
守られている **mamorarete iru** sheltered
守る **mamoru** uphold; protect; defend, stand up for; meet, keep to *deadline*
まむし **mamushi** pit viper
万 **man** ten thousand
学ぶ **manabu** learn; study
真夏 **manatsu** midsummer

万引き **manbiki** shoplifter; shoplifting
満潮 **manchō** high tide, high water
まね **mane** imitation, impersonation
マネージャー **manējā** manager
招き猫 **maneki-neko** beckoning cat (*small figure seen in shops and restaurants to invite customers in*)
マネキン人形 **manekin-ningyō** mannequin, dummy
招く **maneku** invite; beckon; incur
まねる **maneru** copy, imitate
まねし **maneshi** copycat
まねする **mane suru** copy; imitate
漫画 **manga** comic; cartoon
満月 **mangetsu** full moon
マニア **mania** fan; enthusiast; fanatic
間に合う **ma ni au** be suitable; be enough; be in time; catch
間に合わせ(の) **ma ni awase (no)** makeshift
間に合わせる **ma ni awaseru** make do with
万一の事 **man'ichi no koto** contingency
マニキュア **manikyua** manicure; (nail) varnish, (nail) polish
満員 **man'in** full
満場一致(の) **manjō-itchi (no)** unanimous
満期 **manki** maturity; 満期になる ***manki ni naru*** mature
真ん中 **mannaka** middle; …の真ん中に ***… no mannaka ni*** in the middle of
万年筆 **mannenhitsu** (fountain) pen
間の取り方 **ma no torikata** timing
満杯(の) **manpai (no)** full
満腹(の) **manpuku (no)** full (up)
慢性(の) **mansei (no)** chronic
マンション **manshon** apartment; apartment block; condominium
満州 **Manshū** Manchuria
免れる **manugareru** escape from; be relieved of; be excepted from; absolve
まぬけ **manuke** dope, moron
マニュアル **manyuaru** manual
漫才 **manzai** comic duo, comic double act
満足 **manzoku** contentment, satisfaction
満足で **manzoku de** content
満足感 **manzoku-kan** gratification; feeling of satisfaction
満足(な) **manzoku (na)** satisfactory; adequate
満足させる **manzoku saseru** gratify; indulge; satisfy
満足した **manzoku shita** full; satisfied
満足する **manzoku suru** be satisfied
マラソン **marason** marathon
まれ(な) **mare (na)** rare
マレーシア **Marēshia** Malaysia
マレーシア人 **Marēshia-jin** Malay
マレーシア(の) **Marēshia (no)** Malaysian
マリファナ **marifana** joint; marijuana, pot
マリーナ **marīna** marina
マリネ **marine** marinade
丸 **maru** circle; 丸で囲む ***maru de kakomu*** encircle; 丸一日 ***maru ichinichi*** an entire day ◊ (*suffix for names of ships*)
マルチメディア **maruchi-media** multimedia
まるで **marude** completely, entirely; まるで…であるかのように ***marude … de aru ka no yô ni*** as if
丸裸で **maruhadaka de** stark naked
丸い **marui** round
丸首セーター **marukubi sētā** crew neck
丸くなる **maruku naru** curl
円くなる **maruku naru** mellow
丸くする **maruku suru** round off
マルクス主義 **Marukusu-shugi** Marxism
マルクス主義者 **Marukusu-shugi-sha** Marxist
丸める **marumeru** roll up; screw up *paper etc*
丸ぽちゃ(の) **marupocha (no)** chubby
丸太 **maruta** log
丸太小屋 **maruta-goya** log cabin

魔力 **maryoku** magic power
まさぐる **masaguru** grope; feel around
まさか **masaka** surely not!; come on! (*in disbelief*)
まさか…ない **masaka … nai** never
まさに **masa ni** exactly
勝る **masaru** outdo; surpass; predominate
摩擦 **masatsu** friction
マシュマロ **mashumaro** marshmallow
マッサージ **massāji** massage
マッサージ師 **massāji-shi** masseur; masseuse
真っ盛り **massakari** height (*of season*); heyday
真っ逆さまに **massakasama ni** head over heels, headlong
真っ青(の) **massao (no)** pale, pallid
抹殺 **massatsu** elimination, murder
抹殺する **massatsu suru** eliminate, kill
真っ白(な) **masshiro (na)** pure white
マッシュポテト **masshupoteto** mashed potatoes
マッシュルーム **masshurūmu** mushroom
真っすぐ **massugu** straight
真っすぐ(な) **massugu (na)** straight
真っすぐにする **massugu ni suru** straighten
真っ直ぐ(の) **massugu (no)** straight; erect
ます **masu** square (*in board game*); trout; box seat (*for sumo*)
ます **-masu** (*polite verbal suffix*): 私が行きます ***watashi ga ikimasu*** I'm going
増す **masu** increase; build up; mount; enhance *taste*
麻酔 **masui** anesthetic
麻酔医 **masuii** anesthetist
マスカラ **masukara** mascara
マスコミ **masukomi** the media
マスコミ業界**masukomi-gyōkai** journalism; mass media
マスコット **masukotto** mascot
マスク **masuku** mask
ますます **masumasu** increasingly, more and more; ますます長い時間 ***masumasu nagai jikan*** more and more time
ますます良い **masumasu yoi** all the better
マスメディア **masumedia** mass media
マスターベーションをする **masutābēshon o suru** masturbate
マスタード **masutādo** mustard
マスターキー **masutā-kī** master key; skeleton key
マスト **masuto** mast
また **mata** again; also; またね ***mata ne*** see you!
又貸しする **matagashi suru** sublet
マタニティーウェア **matanitī-wea** maternity dress
または **mata wa** or
抹茶 **matcha** powdered green tea
マッチ **matchi** match
マッチ箱 **matchibako** matchbox
的 **mato** target; butt (*of joke*); 的にする ***mato ni suru*** target
まとまりのない **matomari no nai** disjointed, rambling
まとまる **matomaru** be settled; be concluded; have coherence
まとめ **matome** round-up
まとめる **matomeru** settle; conclude; form; collect; arrange
まとも(な) **matomo (na)** decent; straight
まともにする **matomo ni suru** straighten out
まとわりつく **matowari tsuku** cling
松 **matsu** pine
待つ **matsu** wait, hold on
松葉杖 **matsubazue** crutch
まつげ **matsuge** (eye)lash
松かさ **matsukasa** pinecone
祭り **matsuri** festival
まったく **mattaku** altogether, completely; decidedly; honestly!; まったく構いません ***mattaku kamaimasen*** not at all!
まったく(の) **mattaku (no)** absolute, total; downright
まったく同じよう(な) **mattaku onaji yō (na)** identical

待っている **matte iru** expectant ◊ watch for
マット **matto** mat; doormat
まっとう(な) **mattō (na)** decent
マットレス **mattoresu** mattress
マウンド **maundo** mound
マウンテンバイク **mauntenbaiku** mountain bike
マウス **mausu** mouse COMPUT
マウスパッド **mausupaddo** mouse mat
マウスピース **mausupīsu** mouthpiece
マウスウォッシュ **mausu-wosshu** mouthwash
回り **mawari** circumference; rotation; spread ◊ via
回り道 **mawarimichi** detour ◊ indirect
回りに **mawari ni** around
回る **mawaru** turn; spin; rotate; swivel
まわし **mawashi** belt
回す **mawasu** pass around; pass on
回っている **mawatte iru** be spinning
麻薬 **mayaku** drug; narcotic; dope; 麻薬をやっている ***mayaku o yatte iru*** be on drugs
麻薬常用者 **mayaku-jōyō-sha** drug addict
麻薬密売 **mayaku-mitsubai** drug trafficking
麻薬密売人 **mayaku-mitsubai-nin** (drug) dealer, pusher
麻薬捜査官 **mayaku-sōsakan** narcotics agent
麻薬取り引き **mayaku-torihiki** (drug) dealing
真夜中 **mayonaka** midnight
マヨネーズ **mayonēzu** mayonnaise
迷う **mayou** stray, wander; lose one's way; 道に迷った ***michi ni mayotta*** I'm lost
まゆ **mayu** eyebrow
混ざる, 交ざる **mazaru** mingle
混ぜ合わせる **mazeawaseru** combine
混ぜる **mazeru** mix, blend in
マゾヒスト **mazohisuto** masochist
マゾヒズム **mazohizumu** masochism
まず **mazu** first of all; まず第一に ***mazu daiichi ni*** in the first place; まず最初に ***mazu saisho ni*** firstly, first of all
まずい **mazui** tasteless; unfortunate *choice of words*
貧しい **mazushii** poor; deprived; needy
貧しくなった **mazushiku natta** impoverished
目 **me** eye; 目が回る ***me ga mawaru*** heady; dizzy; 目をくらませる ***me o kuramaseru*** blind, dazzle; 目をくらます ***me o kuramasu*** blinding; 目をそらす ***me o sorasu*** look away; 目を奪う ***me o ubau*** mesmerize
芽 **me** germ; sprout
目新しい **meatarashii** novel; fresh
目新しさ **meatarashi-sa** novelty
めちゃくちゃ(な) **mechakucha (na)** disorganized
めちゃくちゃに **mechakucha ni** absurdly; めちゃくちゃに壊す ***mechakucha ni kowasu*** smash
めちゃめちゃにする **mechamecha ni suru** mangle
目立ちたがり屋 **medachitagariya** exhibitionist
目玉焼き **medamayaki** fried egg
メダリスト **medarisuto** medalist
メダル **medaru** medal
目立たない **medatanai** discreet; inconspicuous; unobtrusive
目立つ **medatsu** conspicuous; imposing; predominant ◊ stand out, stick out
目立って **medatsu** striking
目立った **medatta** noticeable
メドレー **medorē** medley
メガバイト **megabaito** megabyte
女神 **megami** goddess
目がない **me ga nai** have a weakness for
眼鏡 **megane** (eye)glasses
眼鏡屋 **megane-ya** optician
目が覚める **me ga sameru** wake (up)
目が覚めて **me ga samete** awake
恵まれない **megumarenai** underprivileged
恵まれている **megumarete iru** be blessed with

目薬 **megusuri** (eye)drops
めい **mei** niece
銘 **mei** inscription
名 **mei** excellent; renowned; 名ピアニスト ***mei-pianisuto*** a renowned pianist ◊ (*countword for people*): 三名 ***san-mei*** three people
名案 **meian** brainwave
名簿 **meibo** directory; list, roll
命中する **meichū suru** hit; strike
めい福を祈る **meifuku o inoru** pay one's last respects (to)
銘柄 **meigara** brand
銘柄名 **meigara-mei** brand name
明白(な) **meihaku (na)** clear, plain explicit; glaring; pronounced *accent*
明治維新 **Meiji-ishin** Meiji Restoration
明治時代 **Meiji-jidai** Meiji period
名人 **meijin** virtuoso
命じる **meijiru** give orders; order
明確(な) **meikaku (na)** definite; precise
明確さ **meikaku-sa** precision
名門 **meimon** dynasty; distinguished family
名門(の) **meimon (no)** prestigious; renowned
命令 **meirei** command, order
命令形 **meireikei** imperative GRAM
命令する **meirei suru** command
迷路 **meiro** maze
明朗(な) **meirō (na)** bright; cheerful; hearty
明りょうさ **meiryō-sa** clarity
名作 **meisaku** masterpiece
名声 **meisei** fame, renown; prestige
明せきさ **meiseki-sa** clarity
名刺 **meishi** (business) card
名詞 **meishi** noun
迷信 **meishin** superstition
迷信深い **meishin-bukai** superstitious
名所 **meisho** famous place
めい想 **meisō** meditation
めい想する **meisō suru** meditate
迷惑 **meiwaku** inconvenience; 迷惑をかける ***meiwaku o kakeru*** trouble; bother; impose oneself on; 人に迷惑をかける ***hito ni meiwaku o kakeru*** make a nuisance of oneself
迷惑(な) **meiwaku (na)** disruptive
名誉 **meiyo** credit; honor; privilege
名誉棄損 **meiyo-kison** defamation; libel; 名誉棄損にあたる ***meiyo-kison ni ataru*** defamatory
目隠し **mekakushi** blindfold
メキシコ **Mekishiko** Mexico
メキシコ人 **Mekishiko-jin** Mexican
メキシコ(の) **Mekishiko (no)** Mexican
メークアップをする **mēkuappu o suru** make up
めくる **mekuru** turn over, turn
めまい **memai** giddiness; vertigo
めまいがする **memai ga suru** feel dizzy, feel giddy
メモ **memo** memo; note
メモ帳 **memochō** notepad
目盛り **memori** scale; divisions on a scale
メモリー **memorī** memory COMPUT
メモする **memo suru** jot down
めん **men** noodles
面 **men** mask; face; aspect; 面と向かって ***men to mukatte*** face to face
綿 **men** cotton
メンバー **menbā** member
めん棒 **menbō**; rolling pin
綿棒 **menbō** absorbent cotton swab
面目 **menboku** reputation; face; …の面目をつぶす ***… no menboku o tsubusu*** embarrass, make lose face; 面目を失う ***menboku o ushinau*** lose face
面目を失って **menboku o ushinatte** in disgrace
面倒 **mendō** bother, nuisance, trouble
面倒くさい **mendō-kusai** annoying, tiresome
面倒(な) **mendō (na)** laborious; troublesome; 面倒なことになる ***mendô na koto ni naru*** get into trouble
めんどり **mendori** hen
免疫 **men'eki** immunity
免疫のある **men'eki no aru** immune

目に見えない **me ni mienai** invisible
目に見える **me ni mieru** visible
目にみえて **me ni miete** visibly
免除 **menjo** exemption; immunity
免除される **menjo sareru** be exempt from
免除された **menjo sareta** exempt; immune
免除する **menjo suru** exempt; excuse; exonerate
面会 **menkai** interview; meeting
面会時間 **menkai-jikan** visiting hours
めんくらわせる **menkurawaseru** fluster
免許 **menkyo** license
免許証 **menkyoshō** license; certificate
綿密(な) **menmitsu (na)** detailed; scrupulous
綿(の) **men (no)** cotton
目の不自由(な) **me no fujiyū (na)** blind; visually impaired
面積 **menseki** area
面接 **mensetsu** interview
面接者 **mensetsu-sha** interviewer
面接する **mensetsu suru** interview
面している **menshite iru** facing, looking on to
メンテナンス **mentenansu** maintenance
メニュー **menyū** menu
免税品 **menzei-hin** duty-free
免税(の) **menzei (no)** duty-free, tax-free
メリーゴーラウンド **merī-gōraundo** carousel, merry-go-round
メロディー **merodī** melody, tune
メロン **meron** melon
メールボックス **mērubokkusu** mailbox COMPUT
メル友 **merutomo** e-mail pen pal
めし **meshi** rice; food; meal (*familiar*)
召し上がる **meshiagaru** (*polite*) eat; drink
メッセージ **messēji** message
メス **mesu** scalpel
雌 **mesu** female
メーター **mētā** meter
メートル **mētoru** meter
メートル法(の) **mētoruhō (no)** metric
めったに…ない **metta ni … nai** rarely, seldom
目上ぶった **meuebutta** patronizing
目上の人 **meue no hito** superior
目覚まし時計 **mezamashi-dokei** alarm clock
めざす **mezasu** aim at
目ざわり **mezawari** eyesore
めずらしい **mezurashii** rare, uncommon
めずらしく **mezurashiku** unusually
実 **mi** fruit; nut; ear
身 **mi** body; person; meat; 身の毛のよだつ ***mi no ke no yodatsu*** hair-raising; 身を引く ***mi o hiku*** stand down, withdraw; 身をかがめる ***mi o kagameru*** get down
未 … **mi…** not yet; 未解決 (の) ***mikaiketsu (no)*** unsolved
見上げる **miageru** look up
見合い **miai** arranged marriage meeting
未亡人 **mibōjin** widow
身分 **mibun** status
身分証明書 **mibun-shōmeisho** identity card, (identity) papers
身ぶり **miburi** gesture; 身ぶりで話す ***miburi de hanasu*** gesticulate; 身ぶりでまねる ***miburi de maneru*** mime
身震い **miburui** shudder
道 **michi** road; way; means; path, trail
道案内する **michiannai suru** guide; show the way
導く **michibiku** guide; steer
未知(の) **michi (no)** unknown
道のり **michinori** distance; journey; drive
満ちる **michiru** come in ◊ incoming
満ち潮 **michishio** flood tide; incoming tide
みだら **midara** sensuality
乱れる **midareru** be disordered; be chaotic; be corrupt
乱れた **midareta** disheveled; tousled

見出し **midashi** header; headline
身だしなみ **midashinami** personal hygiene; 身だしなみのよい ***midashinami no yoi*** well-groomed
乱す **midasu** disrupt; ruffle
ミディアム **midiamu** medium
緑の日 **Midori no hi** Green Day
緑色(の) **midori-iro (no)** green
見えなくする **mienaku suru** blot out
見える **mieru** show, show up; look; see
見え透いた **miesuita** transparent
磨く **migaku** clean; polish
身代わり **migawari** scapegoat
右 **migi** right
右側に **migigawa ni** on the right-hand side
右側(の) **migigawa (no)** right-hand
右ハンドル(の) **migi-handoru (no)** right-hand drive
右利き(の) **migikiki (no)** right-handed
右に **migi ni** right; on the right
右(の) **migi (no)** right, right-hand
右腕 **migiude** right-hand man
身ごもっている **migomotte iru** be pregnant
見事(な) **migoto (na)** splendid, wonderful
見事に **migoto ni** beautifully, marvellously
見苦しい **migurushii** unsightly; disgraceful
未払い(の) **miharai (no)** unpaid, outstanding
見晴らし **miharashi** view
見張り **mihari** lookout; sentry; 見張りをする ***mihari o suru*** keep watch; 見張っている ***mihatte iru*** keep an eye on
見本 **mihon** pattern; sample, specimen
見本市 **mihon'ichi** trade fair
短い **mijikai** brief, short
短くする **mijikaku suru** abbreviate; shorten; take up *dress etc*
身近(な) **mijika (na)** familiar; closely related
みじめ(な) **mijime (na)** dismal; miserable
みじん切りにする **mijingiri ni suru** shred
未熟児 **mijukuji** premature baby
未熟(な) **mijuku (na)** immature; unskilled
未開地 **mikaichi** wilderness
未解決(の) **mikaiketsu (no)** unsolved
未開の地 **mikai no chi** bush
見かけ **mikake** look, appearance
見かけ倒し(の) **mikake-daoshi (no)** shoddy
見かける **mikakeru** see; catch sight of
味覚 **mikaku** palate; taste (*sense*)
みかん **mikan** mandarin orange; tangerine
未完成(の) **mikansei (no)** incomplete, unfinished
味方 **mikata** ally; 味方をする ***mikata o suru*** take sides; be behind; side with
見方 **mikata** slant; viewpoint
三日月 **mikazuki** crescent moon
未決定(の) **mikettei (no)** pending; undecided
幹 **miki** stem; trunk
ミキサー **mikisā** blender
密告者 **mikkoku-sha** informer
密告する **mikkoku suru** turn in, inform on
密航者 **mikkō-sha** stowaway
密航する **mikkō suru** stow away
ミックスした **mikkusu shita** mixed
みこ (巫女) **miko** shrine maiden
見込み **mikomi** likelihood, probability; prospect
見込みなし **mikominashi** no-hoper
見込みのある **mikomi no aru** prospective
見込みのない **mikomi no nai** improbable
見込む **mikomu** allow for; expect; anticipate
未婚(の) **mikon (no)** unmarried
みこし **mikoshi** ceremonial palanquin
見くびる **mikubiru** underestimate, underrate
見下す **mikudasu** look down on
見舞い **mimai** visit (*to sick person*)

...未満で **... miman de** under, less than
見回る **mimawaru** patrol
耳 **mimi** ear; 耳が聞こえない ***mimi ga kikoenai*** deaf; 耳が遠い ***mimi ga tôi*** hard of hearing; 耳に心地よい ***mimi ni kokochi yoi*** pleasant-sounding; musical; 耳にする ***mimi ni suru*** overhear; 耳をそば立てる ***mimi o sobadateru*** strain the ears; prick up one's ears; 耳を立てる ***mimi o tateru*** prick up its ears
耳あか **mimiaka** wax
耳寄りの情報 **mimiyori no jōhō** tip, piece of advice
耳障り(な) **mimizawari (na)** grating; unmusical
身もだえする **mimodae suru** writhe, squirm
身元 **mimoto** identity; background
身元保証人 **mimoto-hoshō-nin** referee (*for job*)
身元確認 **mimoto-kakunin** identification
皆 **mina** all
南 **minami** south
南から(の) **minami kara (no)** southerly
源 **minamoto** source
見直す **minaosu** overhaul
見習い **minarai** apprentice
見習い看護婦 **minarai-kangofu** student nurse
見習う **minarau** learn by observation
身なり **minari** appearance; clothes
身なりの良い **minari no yoi** well-dressed
皆さん **mina-san** everyone, folks; ladies and gentlemen
みなす **minasu** consider
港 **minato** harbor, port
港町 **minatomachi** seaport
峰 **mine** mountain, peak
ミネラルウォーター **mineraru-wōtā** mineral water
民芸品 **mingeihin** folkcraft
醜い **minikui** ugly, hideous
身にしみる **mi ni shimiru** piercing
ミニスカート **minisukāto** miniskirt
身につける **mi ni tsukeru** put on; wear; carry; acquire
身につけている **mi ni tsukete iru** have on
民間放送 **minkan-hōsō** independent television
民間人 **minkan-jin** civilian
民間企業 **minkan-kigyō** private sector
民間(の) **minkan (no)** independent; private *industry*; civil (*not military*)
ミンク **minku** mink
皆 **minna** everyone; ねえ、みんな ***nê, minna*** hey, you guys
見逃す **minogasu** overlook
実りある **minori aru** fruitful
実りのない **minori no nai** unproductive
実る **minoru** bear fruit
身代金 **minoshirokin** ransom
民宿 **minshuku** Japanese B&B
民主主義 **minshu-shugi** democracy
民主主義国家 **minshu-shugi-kokka** democracy
民主主義者 **minshu-shugisha** democrat
民主的(な) **minshuteki (na)** democratic
ミント **minto** mint
民謡 **min'yō** folk music
民族 **minzoku** people
民族(の) **minzoku (no)** ethnic
民族集団 **minzoku-shūdan** ethnic group
民族主義 **minzoku-shugi** nationalism
見覚え **mioboe** recollection; recognition
見送る **miokuru** see off; give a send-off; pass up; miss
見下ろす **miorosu** overlook
見落とし **miotoshi** oversight
見落とす **miotosu** miss, overlook
身を寄せ合う **mi o yoseau** huddle together
密閉(の) **mippei (no)** airtight; sealed
密閉する **mippei suru** seal
未来 **mirai** future
未来形 **miraikei** future tense
ミリグラム **miriguramu** milligram
ミリメーター **mirimētā** millimeter

見る **miru** look; watch; see; view; look at; …と見る ***... to miru*** characterize as
みる **-miru** try to; 説得してみる ***settoku shite miru*** try to persuade
ミルク **miruku** milk
魅力 **miryoku** attraction; appeal
魅力的(な) **miryokuteki (na)** attractive; appealing; fascinating
魅了する **miryō suru** attract; enchant; fascinate
ミサイル **misairu** missile
岬 **misaki** cape
店 **mise** store, shop; place (*bar, restaurant*)
見せびらかす **misebirakasu** parade, show off
未成年(の) **miseinen (no)** underage
未成年者 **miseinen-sha** juvenile, minor
見せかけ **misekake** act, pretense; make-believe; 全部見せかけだけである ***zenbu misekake dake de aru*** it's all done for show
見せかけ(の) **misekake (no)** mock
魅せられた **miserareta** spellbound
見せる **miseru** demonstrate; show; display; exhibit
ミシン **mishin** sewing machine
見知らぬ人 **mishiranu hito** stranger
見知っている **mishitte iru** know by sight
未使用(の) **mishiyō (no)** unused
みそ **miso** soybean paste
みそ汁 **miso shiru** miso soup
密生した **missei shita** dense; thick
密接して **missetsu shite** close together
密集した **misshū shita** crowded; dense
密集する **misshū suru** cluster; crowd; mass
ミス **misu** mistake; unmarried woman
みすぼらしい **misuborashii** scruffy; seedy
未遂 **misui** failed attempt
見捨てない **misutenai** stick by
ミステリー **misuterī** mystery
見捨てる **misuteru** abandon; walk out on; leave; jettison
みたい **-mitai**: 夢みたい ***yume-mitai*** like a dream; 金持ちみたい ***kanemochi-mitai*** wealthy-looking; ***baka-mitai*** idiotic
満たす **mitasu** fill; fulfill; meet; satisfy
見たところ **mita tokoro** apparently; on the face of it
未定 **mitei** undecided
ミートボール **mītobōru** meatball
認められない **mitomerarenai** unacceptable
認められる **mitomerareru** acceptable; discernible
認める **mitomeru** accept; admit; acknowledge; attach *importance*; award *damages*; discern; vindicate
見通し **mitōshi** outlook, prospects; 見通しの利かない ***mitôshi no kikanai*** blind *corner*
ミツバチ **mitsubachi** bee
密売する **mitsubai suru** push *drugs*
密度 **mitsudo** density
三つ子 **mitsugo** triplets
見つかる **mitsukaru** be found
見つけ出す **mitsukedasu** discover; track down
見つける **mitsukeru** find; observe; gaze; catch sight of; spot, notice; work out *solution*
見つめる **mitsumeru** stare at; gaze at
見積もり **mitsumori** quotation, quote; estimate; projection
見積もる **mitsumoru** calculate; estimate; cost
密林地帯 **mitsurin-chitai** jungle
密漁する **mitsuryō suru** poach (*for fish etc*)
密輸 **mitsuyu** smuggling
密輸業者 **mitsuyu-gyōsha** smuggler
密輸する **mitsuyu suru** smuggle
ミット **mitto** mitt
みっともない **mittomonai** disreputable; shameful

身動きする **miugoki suru** stir
見失う **miushinau** lose sight of
見分けがつく **miwake ga tsuku** recognizable
見分けのつかない **miwake no tsukanai** indistinguishable
見分ける **miwakeru** identify, distinguish; make out, see
魅惑する **miwaku suru** fascinate; charm
魅惑的(な) **miwakuteki (na)** ravishing; seductive; tempting
見渡す **miwatasu** scan; survey
みやげ **miyage** souvenir
溝 **mizo** ditch; drain (*under street*); gutter; gulf; groove
みぞれ **mizore** sleet
水 **mizu** water; 水をやる ***mizu o yaru*** water; 水を跳ねる ***mizu o haneru*** splash; 水を通さない ***mizu o tôsanai*** watertight
水辺(の) **mizube (no)** waterside
水浸し(の) **mizubitashi (no)** soggy
水ぼうそう **mizubōsō** chicken pox
水ぶくれ **mizubukure** blister
水着 **mizugi** swimsuit
水気を切る **mizuke o kiru** strain
湖 **mizūmi** lake
みずみずしい **mizumizushii** juicy
水っぽい **mizuppoi** runny, watery
水差し **mizusashi** carafe; pitcher
水玉 **mizutama** dewdrop; polka dot
水玉(の) **mizutama (no)** spotted
水たまり **mizutamari** puddle
水割り **mizuwari** whiskey and water
…も **… mo** also, as well; …も…も ***… mo … mo*** both…and…; …も…もない ***… mo … mo nai*** neither … nor …
喪 **mo** mourning
もう **mō** already; still; more ◊ another; もう彼はきましたか - まだです ***mô kare wa kimashita ka – mada desu*** is he here yet? - not yet; 彼はもうここでは働いていません ***kare wa mô koko de wa hataraite imasen*** he no longer works here; もう一度 ***mô ichido*** again, once more; もう少し ***mô sukoshi*** a little bit more; もう一つ ***mô hitotsu*** another (one); もう、我慢できない ***mô gaman dekinai*** that's the last straw!; もう限界だ ***mô genkai da*** that's the limit!
モバイル **mobairu** cell phone; palmtop; organizer; PDA
もち **mochi** rice cake
持ち上がる **mochiagaru** arise, crop up; be raised
持ち上げる **mochiageru** elevate; lift, raise
持ち歩く **mochiaruku** carry
持ち場 **mochiba** post (*of soldier*)
持ち出す **mochidasu** bring up *subject*; run away with
持ち運ぶ **mochihakobu** carry
持ちこたえる **mochikotaeru** endure; hold out
持ち物 **mochimono** belongings, things
持ち逃げする **mochinige suru** make off with
持ち主 **mochinushi** owner
もちろん **mochiron** of course, certainly; surely
持ちよる **mochiyoru** pool *resources*
盲腸 **mōchō** appendix
盲腸炎 **mōchōen** appendicitis
喪中である **mochū de aru** be in mourning
もだえる **modaeru** squirm, writhe
モデム **modemu** modem
モデル **moderu** model
モード **mōdo** mode
盲導犬 **mōdōken** seeing-eye dog
戻る **modoru** return; go back; come back; resume
戻す **modosu** return, put back
戻ってくる **modotte kuru** come back
燃え上がる **moeagaru** flare up
燃える **moeru** burn
燃え立つ **moetatsu** blaze ◊ fiery
燃えている **moete iru** alight ◊ be on fire
毛布 **mōfu** blanket
喪服 **mofuku** mourning (clothes)
もがく **mogaku** struggle; wriggle
模擬(の) **mogi (no)** mock
もぎ取る **mogitoru** wrench; break off; pull off; snatch

もぐ **mogu** pick, pluck
模範 **mohan** model; example
模範的(な) **mohanteki (na)** exemplary
猛威 **mōi** ferocity; fury
もじゃもじゃ(の) **mojamoja (no)** bushy; shaggy, unkempt
文字 **moji** character (*in writing*); letter; script, writing
文字盤 **moji-ban** dial
文字どおり(の) **mojidōri (no)** literal
もじもじする **mojimoji suru** squirm; fidget
盲人 **mōjin** the blind
もうかる **mōkaru** pay, be profitable
模型 **mokei** miniature; model; mock-up
模型(の) **mokei (no)** model
もうけになる **mōke ni naru** profitable
設ける **mōkeru** institute, set up
木管楽器 **mokkan-gakki** woodwind (instrument)
目撃者 **mokugeki-sha** (eye)witness
目撃する **mokugeki suru** witness
目標 **mokuhyō** goal, target; landmark
目標期日 **mokuhyō- kijitsu** target date
目次 **mokuji** table of contents
木目 **mokume** grain
目録 **mokuroku** inventory, list
木製(の) **mokusei (no)** wooden
目的 **mokuteki** aim, purpose, objective
目的地 **mokutekichi** destination
目的語 **mokutekigo** object GRAM
木曜日 **mokuyōbi** Thursday
木材 **mokuzai** wood
木造(の) **mokuzō (no)** made of wood; wooden
…もまた **…mo mata** too; …もまた…ない ***… mo mata …nai*** nor
木綿 **momen** cotton
もめる **momeru** have a dispute; be at odds
もみじ **momiji** Japanese maple
もみ消し **momikeshi** coverup
もみ消す **momikesu** cover up, hush up
もみの木 **momi no ki** fir
もも **momo** thigh
桃 **momo** peach
盲目(の) **mōmoku (no)** blind
もむ **momu** massage; rub
門 **mon** gate
文部省 **Monbushō** Ministry of Education, Science, Sports and Culture
もん着 **monchaku** trouble; dispute; もん着を起こす ***monchaku o okosu*** cause trouble; make a fuss
問題 **mondai** matter, affair; problem; 問題の ***mondai no*** in question; 問題を生む ***mondai o umu*** pose a problem
問題解決 **mondai- kaiketsu** troubleshooting
門限 **mongen** curfew
モンゴル **Mongoru** Mongolia
モンゴル (の) **Mongoru (no)** Mongolian
モーニングコール **mōningu-kōru** wake-up call
モニター **monitā** display; visual display unit
文句 **monku** phrase; complaint; 文句を言う ***monku o iu*** complain; make a fuss
文句無し(の) **monku nashi (no)** entirely satisfactory; undisputed
文盲(の) **monmō (no)** illiterate
物, もの **mono** object, thing; stuff
者 **mono** person
ものだ **-monoda** used to
物語 **monogatari** narrative; story, tale
物乞いする **monogoi suru** beg
ものまね **monomane** impression; …のものまねをする ***… no monomane o suru*** impersonate; mimic
もの珍しそうに **monomezurashisō ni** curiously, inquisitively
もの覚えがいい **mono-oboe ga ii** have a good memory
もの覚えが悪い **mono-oboe ga warui** have a poor memory
物置 **mono-oki** storeroom; shed
もの思いにふける **mono-omoi ni fukeru** muse

もの思いに沈んだ**mono-omoi ni shizunda** pensive
もの惜しみしない**mono-oshimi shinai** lavish
物音を立てる**mono-oto o tateru** make a noise
モノローグ **monorōgu** monolog(ue)
物差し, ものさし **monosashi** rule, ruler; gauge
ものしり顔(の) **monoshiri gao (no)** knowing
もの静か(な) **mono-shizuka (na)** quiet
ものすごい **monosugoi** terrific, awesome
もの笑いの種になる**monowarai no tane ni naru** become a laughing stock
もの好き(な) **monozuki (na)** curious; inquisitive
もっぱら**moppara** entirely
モップ **moppu** mop
モラルハザード**moraru-hazādo** decline in moral standards
漏らす **morasu** divulge
もらう **morau** receive
もらう **-morau** (*causative*): 洗ってもらった ***aratte moratta*** I had it washed; ちょっと手伝ってもらえますか ***chotto tetsudatte moraemasu ka*** can you help me?
漏れ **more** escape, leak
漏れる **moreru** escape, leak out
猛烈(な) **mōretsu (na)** fierce; intense; impetuous
猛烈に **mōretsu ni** fiercely; with a vengeance
森 **mori** forest
盛り上がり **moriagari** upsurge; climax; hump
もろい **moroi** brittle; frail; fragile
もうろく **mōroku** senility
もうろくした **mōroku shita** senile
もうろうとした **mōrō to shita** hazy; dim
漏る **moru** leak
モルヒネ **moruhine** morphine
モルモット **morumotto** guinea pig
モルタル **morutaru** mortar
もし **moshi** if; もし必要なら ***moshi hitsuyô nara*** if need be; もし…の場合に備えて ***moshi ... no bâi ni sonaete*** in case ...
申し分ないほど **mōshibun nai hodo** perfectly, impeccably
申し分のない **mōshibun no nai** impeccable; irreproachable
申し出 **mōshide** approach, offer; proposal
申し入れをする **mōshiire o suru** make overtures to
もしかしたら **moshikashitara** maybe
申し込み **mōshikomi** application
申込用紙 **mōshikomi-yōshi** application form
申し込む **mōshikomu** apply for; challenge
もしもし **moshimoshi** hello TELEC
申し立て **mōshitate** allegation; statement; testimony
申す **mōsu** H say; …と申しますが ***... to môshimasu ga*** this is TELEC
もうすぐ **mōsugu** soon, directly
モスクワ **Mosukuwa** Moscow
モーター **mōtā** motor
モーターボート **mōtābōto** motorboat, speedboat
毛沢東 **Mō Takutō** Mao Zedong
もたらす **motarasu** bring; produce, bring about; yield
もたれる **motareru** recline on; lean on
持たせる **motaseru** give; stretch; make last
もたつく **motatsuku** fumble; dawdle
盲点 **mōten** blind spot
もてなす **motenasu** entertain
もてる **moteru** be popular
モーテル **mōteru** motel
もと, 基, 元 **moto** origin; cause; 元に戻す ***moto ni modosu*** reinstate; replace, put back; 基にする ***moto ni suru*** be based on
元… **moto ...** ex-
求める **motomeru** seek; ask for
もともと **motomoto** naturally; originally
もと(の) **moto (no)** original, first
基づかせる **motozukaseru** base
基づく **motozuku** rest on ...
もつ **motsu** hold out (*of supplies*); keep (*of food, milk*); last

持つ**motsu** have; hold
もつれ**motsure** tangle
もつれる**motsureru** get tangled up
もったいぶった**mottaibutta** pompous
もったいない**mottainai** wasteful
持って行く**motte iku** take away; bring along
持っている**motte iru** possess, have; hang on to; keep
持ってくる**motte kuru** bring; take along
もっと**motto** more; もっと大きな ***motto ôki na*** bigger
モットー**mottō** motto
最も**mottomo** most; 最も上手(な) ***mottomo jôzu (na)*** best
もっとも(な)**mottomo (na)** justifiable; reasonable
もっともらしい**mottomorashii** plausible
燃やす**moyasu** burn
模様**moyō** motif; design; pattern
模様替え**moyōgae** reorganization
模様替えする**moyōgae suru** reorganize *room*; remodel
模様入り(の)**moyō-iri (no)** patterned
催し**moyōshi** meeting; event
モザイク**mozaiku** mosaic
模造品**mozōhin** imitation
無…**mu…** non-; un-
無防備(な)**mubōbi (na)** defenseless, helpless
無茶(な)**mucha (na)** reckless
無知**muchi** ignorance
むち**muchi** whip
無知(な)**muchi (na)** ignorant
無秩序**muchitsujo** anarchy; chaos
無秩序(の)**muchitsujo (no)** chaotic
むち打ち**muchiuchi** hiding; whipping
むち打つ**muchiutsu** flog; whip
夢中である**muchū de aru** be hooked on; be engrossed in
無駄**muda** useless; unnecessary
無駄足**mudaashi** wildgoose chase
無駄話をする**mudabanashi o suru** prattle
無駄である**muda de aru** it's no use
無駄(な)**muda (na)** feeble; futile; vain; 彼等の努力は無駄だった ***karera no doryoku wa muda datta*** their efforts were in vain
無断で**mudan de** without permission
無駄にする**muda ni suru** undo; waste; spoil
無駄使いする**mudazukai suru** waste
無鉛(の)**muen (no)** lead-free, unleaded
無害(な)**mugai (na)** harmless
無学(な)**mugaku (na)** uneducated
無限**mugen** infinity
無限(の)**mugen (no)** infinite
麦**mugi** barley; wheat
麦わら**mugiwara** straw
無言で**mugon de** in silence
無言(の)**mugon (no)** mute
むごたらしい**mugotarashii** bloody; cruel; tragic
無法(の)**muhō (no)** lawless
無表情(な)**muhyōjō (na)** impassive
無一文(の)**muichimon (no)** penniless
無意味(な)**muimi (na)** meaningless, empty; pointless, senseless
無意識に**muishiki ni** mechanically; unintentionally
無意識(の)**muishiki (no)** unconscious
むいていない**muite inai** incompetent
無邪気**mujaki** innocence
無邪気(な)**mujaki (na)** innocent
無慈悲(な)**mujihi (na)** merciless
無人(の)**mujin (no)** uninhabited; unmanned
無地(の)**muji (no)** plain
無尽蔵(の)**mujinzō (no)** inexhaustible
無条件(の)**mujōken (no)** unconditional
矛盾**mujun** contradiction; discrepancy
矛盾した**mujun shita** contradictory; inconsistent
矛盾する**mujun suru** conflict; …と矛盾する ***... to mujun suru*** be at odds with

迎えに行く **mukae ni iku** collect, pick up
迎えに来る**mukae ni kuru** come for
向かい風 **mukaikaze** headwind
むかむかさせる **mukamuka saseru** nauseate
無関係(な) **mukankei (na)** irrelevant
無関心 **mukanshin** indifference
無関心(な) **mukanshin (na)** indifferent
昔 **mukashi** ancient times; the old days
昔から(の) **mukashi kara (no)** old
昔々 **mukashimukashi** once upon a time
むかつかせる **mukatsukaseru** disgust; repel; sicken ◊ revolting
ムカつく **mukatsuku** be mad, be pissed
むかつくよう(な) **mukatsuku yō (na)** nauseating
向かう **mukau** head for, make for
向けである **muke de aru** be meant for
むける **mukeru** peel
向ける **mukeru** direct; point; steer; …に向けたものである ***… ni muketa mono de aru*** be meant for
無血(の) **muketsu (no)** bloodless
向き **muki** direction; 向きを変える ***muki o kaeru*** turn around; 向きを変えて立ち去る ***muki o kaete tachisaru*** turn away
無機物(の) **mukibutsu (no)** inorganic
むき出しにする **mukidashi ni suru** expose
無期限(の) **mukigen (no)** open-ended; indefinite
無記名投票 **mukimei-tōhyō** secret ballot
無気力(な) **mukiryoku (na)** apathetic; lethargic
無傷(の) **mukizu (no)** intact; unscathed
婿 **muko** bridegroom
無効で **mukō de** null and void
向こう側に **mukōgawa ni** across, over
向こう側(の) **mukōgawa (no)** opposite
むこうみず(な) **mukōmizu (na)** foolhardy
無効(な) **mukō (na)** invalid
向こうに **mukō ni** beyond
無効にする **mukō ni suru** annul; invalidate; revoke; overule
向うずね **mukōzune** shin
むく **muku** peel; scrape; shell
向く **muku** face
無口(な) **mukuchi (na)** reticent
むくどり **mukudori** starling
むくんだ **mukunda** swollen, puffy
無許可(の) **mukyoka (no)** unauthorized
無給(の) **mukyū (no)** unpaid
無名(の) **mumei (no)** obscure
むなしい **munashii** empty ◊ in vain
むなしさ **munashi-sa** emptiness; vanity (*of hopes*)
胸 **mune** chest; bosom; breast ; 胸に秘める ***mune ni himeru*** cherish; 胸をうつ ***mune o utsu*** touching
胸やけ **muneyake** heartburn
無認可(の) **muninka (no)** unauthorized
無能 **munō** incompetence
無能(な) **munō (na)** incapable; incompetent
無農薬(の) **munōyaku (no)** organic
村 **mura** village
群がる **muragaru** mob; cluster; swarm
むら気(な) **muraki (na)** capricious; erratic
むらのある **mura no aru** inconsistent; patchy
紫色(の) **murasakiiro (no)** violet; purple
群れ **mure** clump; crop; flock; herd; swarm
無理 **muri** impossible; unreasonable
無理強い(の) **murijii (no)** forced
無理に **muri ni** by force
無理に抑える **muri ni osaeru** bottle up
無理やり **muriyari** forcibly; 無理やり聞き出す ***muriyari kikidasu*** extract; drag out of; Xを無理やりYに引きずり込む ***X o muriyari Y ni hikizurikomu*** drag X into Y

ムール貝 **mūru-gai** mussel
無類(の) **murui** (**no**) incomparable
無料 **muryō** free of charge
無料で **muryō de** for free
無力(な) **muryoku** (**na**) helpless; powerless
無料(の) **muryō** (**no**) complimentary, free
無差別(な) **musabetsu** (**na**) indiscriminate
無差別(の) **musabetsu** (**no**) indiscriminate; wholesale
むさぼる **musaboru** devour
無作為抽出 **musakui-chūshutsu** random sample
無作為(の) **musakui** (**no**) random
無生物(の) **museibutsu** (**no**) inanimate
無制限(の) **museigen** (**no**) unlimited
無声(の) **musei** (**no**) silent
無責任(な) **musekinin** (**na**) irresponsible
無せきつい動物 **musekitsui-dōbutsu** invertebrate
無線 **musen** radio
無線電話 **musen-denwa** radio telephone
無線タクシー **musen-takushī** radio taxi
虫 **mushi** bug; worm
無視 **mushi** disregard
蒸し暑い **mushiatsui** humid, muggy, sultry
虫歯 **mushiba** bad tooth; cavity; 虫歯になる ***mushiba ni naru*** decay, rot
蒸し器 **mushiki** steamer
虫眼鏡 **mushi-megane** magnifying glass
無神経(な) **mushinkei** (**na**) insensitive
無神論者 **mushinron-sha** atheist
むしろ **mushiro** rather
虫刺され **mushisasare** bite; sting
無視する **mushi suru** ignore; dismiss; brush off, discount
虫よけ **mushiyoke** (insect) repellent
夢想家 **musō-ka** dreamer
蒸す **musu** steam
結び目 **musubime** knot
結び付ける **musubitsukeru** bind; knit together; XとYを結び付ける ***X to Y o musubitsukeru*** relate X to Y
結ぶ **musubu** form; tie up, do up; knot
息子 **musuko** son
息子さん **musuko-san** son
娘 **musume** daughter
娘さん **musume-san** daughter
無敵(の) **muteki** (**no**) invincible; unbeaten
むとんちゃく(な) **mutonchaku** (**na**) nonchalant; casual
無痛(の) **mutsū** (**no**) painless
むっとした **mutto shita** annoyed; stuffy, airless
むっとしている **mutto shite iru** be in a huff
むっとする **mutto suru** be annoyed
むっつりした **muttsuri shita** glum; sullen
無欲(の) **muyoku** (**no**) selfless
夢遊病者 **muyūbyō- sha** sleepwalker
無罪 **muzai** innocence; 無罪にする ***muzai ni suru*** acquit; exonerate; 無罪を主張する ***muzai o shuchô suru*** plead not guilty
無罪(の) **muzai** (**no**) innocent
無造作(な) **muzōsa** (**na**) offhand ◊ easily
難しい **muzukashii** difficult, hard
難しさ **muzukashi-sa** difficulty
脈拍 **myakuhaku** pulse
脈打つ **myakuutsu** pulsate
ミャンマー **Myanmā** Burma, Myanmar
ミャンマー (の) **Myanmā** (**no**) Burmese, Myanmar
妙案 **myōan** inspiration
名字 **myōji** family name, surname
妙(な) **myō** (**na**) peculiar
妙に **myō ni** curiously
ミュージカル **myūjikaru** musical
ミュージシャン **myūjishan** musician

N

な -na ◊ (*forms negative imperative*): 忘れるな ***wasureru-na*** don't forget ◊ (*for emphasis*): きれいだな ***kirei da na*** it's beautiful, isn't it!
な na (*forms adjectives*): 憶病(な) ***okubyô*** (**na**) cowardly
名 **na** name; renown
名ばかり(の) **nabakari** (**no**) so-called
なべ **nabe** pot
ナビゲーター **nabigētā** navigator
名高い **nadakai** prestigious
なだめる **nadameru** soothe; pacify
なだれ **nadare** avalanche
なでる **naderu** caress, stroke
なでつける **nadetsukeru** smooth
など **nado** et cetera, and so on
苗 **nae** seedling
苗床 **naedoko** nursery
名札 **nafuda** nametag
長引いた **nagabiita** protracted
長引かせる **nagabikaseru** drag out
長靴 **nagagutsu** boots
長い **nagai** lengthy, long
長い間 **nagai aida** a long while
長生きする **nagaiki suru** live for a long time
長い目で見れば **nagai me de mireba** in the long term
長いす **nagaisu** couch
長く **nagaku** long
眺め **nagame** view
眺める **nagameru** look at; gaze at
長持ちする **nagamochi suru** last ◊ resilient
長年にわたる **naganen ni wataru** long-standing
ながら **-nagara** (*linking two actions*) while; though; 歩きながら食べる ***arukinagara taberu*** eat while walking
流れ **nagare** current; flow; timescale
流れ星 **nagare-boshi** shooting star
流れ者 **nagare-mono** drifter
流れる **nagareru** break (*of news*); flow (*of current, traffic*); run (*of river, paint*); flush
流れ作業 **nagare-sagyō** assembly line
長さ **naga-sa** length
流し **nagashi** sink
長袖(の) **nagasode** (**no**) long-sleeved
流す **nagasu** flush; flush away; shed
長続きする **nagatsuzuki suru** durable ◊ endure, last
長屋 **nagaya** row houses
投げかける **nagekakeru** cast; throw; hurl
嘆かわしい **nagekawashii** deplorable; lamentable; sad
嘆き悲しむ **nagekikanashimu** mourn
嘆く **nageku** deplore; lament
投げる **nageru** throw, pitch; toss; throw up
投げつける **nagetsukeru** hurl; pelt
なごませる **nagomaseru** disarming; calming
名残 **nagori** remains; traces; 名残を惜しむ ***nagori o oshimu*** be reluctant to leave
なごやか(な) **nagoyaka** (**na**) peaceful; gentle
なぐり書き **nagurigaki** scrawl, scribble
なぐり書きする **nagurigaki suru** scrawl
殴る **naguru** thump; knock around
慰め **nagusame** consolation, comfort
慰める **nagusameru** console, comfort
慰めようのない **nagusameyō no nai** inconsolable
ない **-nai** (*negative suffix*) not; 私は行かない ***watashi wa ikanai*** I won't go

無い, ない**nai** there is/are not; do not have
内部**naibu** inside
内部情報**naibu-jōhō** inside information
内部(の)**naibu (no)** interior, internal
内縁の妻**naien no tsuma** common-law wife
ナイフ**naifu** knife
内服薬**naifukuyaku** medicine for internal use
内報する**naihō suru** tip off
内耳**naiji** inner ear
内科医**naikai** physician
内閣**naikaku** cabinet POL
内閣総理大臣**naikaku-sōridaijin** Japanese Prime Minister
内向的(な)**naikōteki (na)** introverted
内面(の)**naimen (no)** inner
内密で**naimitsu de** secretly
内密(の)**naimitsu (no)** undercover
内務省**Naimushō** Department of the Interior
内陸(の)**nairiku (no)** inland; interior (*of country*)
ナイロン**nairon** nylon
内政不干渉**naisei-fukanshō** noninterference, nonintervention (*in the affairs of other nations*)
内戦**naisen** civil war
内線**naisen** extension TELEC
内心(の)**naishin (no)** inward, innermost
内緒(の)**naisho (no)** secret
内装**naisō** décor, decoration
内装業者**naisō-gyōsha** interior decorator
内装する**naisō suru** decorate
ナイトクラブ**naitokurabu** nightclub
ナイトスポット**naitosupotto** nightspot
内容**naiyō** content
内臓**naizō** internal organs
内蔵(の)**naizō (no)** built-in
なじみのない**najimi no nai** alien, unfamiliar
なじむ**najimu** become familiar with
なじる**najiru** taunt; rebuke; blame
中**naka** inside
仲**naka** relationship; relations
半ば**nakaba** half; middle
中だるみする**naka-darumi suru** sag
中で**naka de** inside
仲買人**nakagai-nin** middle man
中ごろに**nakagoro ni** in the middle of
中から**naka kara** from within
仲間**nakama** circle, group, set; company; crony; comrade
仲間意識**nakama-ishiki** comradeship
中身, 中味**nakami** contents; filling; …の中身をあける ***... no nakami o akeru*** empty
なかなか**nakanaka** very; quite; rather; なかなか消えない ***nakanaka kienai*** linger; なかなか立ち去らない ***nakanaka tachisaranai*** linger
仲直りをする**nakanaori o suru** make up, be reconciled
仲直りさせる**nakanaori saseru** reconcile, patch up
中に**naka ni** in; inside; 中に入る ***naka ni hairu*** go in
中庭**nakaniwa** courtyard, quadrangle; patio
中(の)**naka (no)** inside
仲のよい**naka no yoi** harmonious; on good terms
なければならない **-nakereba naranai** must ; 勉強しなければならない ***benkyô shinakereba naranai*** I have to study
泣き声**nakigoe** wail; 泣き声をあげる ***nakigoe o ageru*** give a wail
泣き言を言う**nakigoto o iu** whine
泣きじゃくる**nakijakuru** sob
泣き崩れる**nakikuzureru** break down
泣き叫ぶ**nakisakebu** bawl; wail
仲人**nakōdo** go-between
泣く**naku** cry, have a cry
なくなる**nakunaru** run out; go (*of pain etc*)
亡くなる**nakunaru** pass away
なくす**nakusu** abolish, do away with; eliminate; lose

なくてはならない **-nakute wa naranai** must; 行かなくてはならない ***ikanakute wa naranai*** I must leave
ナマあし **namaashi** *not wearing socks or pantyhose*
生ビール **nama-bīru** draft (beer)
名前 **namae** name; given name
生臭い **namagusai** smelly; smelling of fish
生意気 **namaiki** impertinence
生意気(な) **namaiki (na)** impertinent, fresh; saucy
生意気になる **namaiki ni naru** get smart with
怠け者 **namakemono** layabout
怠け者(の) **namakemono (no)** idle
怠ける **namakeru** idle away; laze around
怠けている **namakete iru** lazy
生(の) **nama (no)** live *broadcast*; raw
なまぬるい **namanurui** tepid
なまり **namari** accent
鉛 **namari** lead
生焼け(の) **namayake (no)** underdone
なまず **namazu** catfish
なめくじ **namekuji** slug
なめらか(な) **nameraka (na)** smooth
なめらかにする **nameraka ni suru** smooth down
なめらかさ **nameraka-sa** fluency
なめる **nameru** lick
波 **nami** wave (*in sea*)
涙 **namida** tear; 涙が出る ***namida ga deru*** run, water; be wet (*of eyes*); 涙にくれる ***namida ni kureru*** be in tears
涙でいっぱい(の) **namida de ippai (no)** tearful
並はずれた **namihazureta** uncommon; extraordinary
波に揺れる **nami ni yureru** bob
並(の) **nami (no)** average; satisfactory
七 **nana** seven
斜めになる **naname ni naru** slope
斜め(の) **naname (no)** diagonal; slanting
ナンバー **nanbā** number; license (plate) number
ナンバープレート **nanbāpurēto** license plate
南米 **Nanbei** South America
南米人 **Nanbei-jin** South American
南米(の) **Nanbei (no)** South American
南部 **nanbu** south
南部(の) **nanbu (no)** southern
難題 **nandai** difficult problem; challenge
何だか **nandaka** somehow; kind of, sort of
何でも **nan demo** whatever; 私は何でもかまいません ***watashi wa nan demo kamaimasen*** it's all the same to me; 私は何でも食べられます ***watashi wa nan demo taberaremasu*** I could eat anything
難読症 **nandokushō** dyslexia
難読症患者 **nandokushō-kanja** dyslexic
何度も **nando mo** many times
何 **nani** what; 何があったの ***nani ga atta no*** what has happened?
何気ない **nanigenai** casual; unconcerned
何か **nani ka** anything; something; 何かあった ***nani ka atta*** what's up?
何も **nani mo** nothing; anything; 何も不自由していない ***nani mo fujiyû shite inai*** want for nothing; 何も残っていません ***nani mo nokotte imasen*** there isn't/aren't any left
何よりも **nani yori mo** most of all
何よりもまず **nani yori mo mazu** above all
軟弱(な) **nanjaku (na)** weak; soft; effeminate
何時 **nanji** what time?; what time is it?
何時間でも **nanjikan demo** for hours on end
何十もの… **nanjū mono …** dozens of
何回も **nankai mo** time and again
軟化する **nanka suru** soften

南京錠 **nankinjō** padlock
軟こう **nankō** ointment
南極 **Nankyoku** Antarctic, South Pole
南極(の) **Nankyoku (no)** polar
難民 **nanmin** refugee
難問 **nanmon** difficult problem; puzzle
難なく **nannaku** without difficulty
何年も **nannen mo** for years
何(の) **nan (no)** what; 何のために ***nanno tame ni*** what for?
…なので **… na node** as; …なので私も来れます ***…na node watashi mo koremasu*** so I can come too
菜の花 **nanohana** rape blossom
名乗り出る **nanorideru** come forward; give oneself up; claim
難破 **nanpa** shipwreck
難破させる **nanpa saseru** wreck
難破船 **nanpasen** wreck
難破する **nanpa suru** be shipwrecked
南西 **nansei** southwest
南西部(の) **nanseibu (no)** southwestern
ナンセンス **nansensu** nonsense
何て **nante** what; 何て言った ***nante itta*** what (did you say)?; 何てきれいな娘だろう ***nante kirei na ko darô*** what a beautiful girl!; 何ておかしいんだろう ***nante okashiin darô*** how funny!
南東 **nantō** southeast
南東部(の) **nantōbu (no)** southeastern
何と **nan to** what; 彼女が何と言おうとも ***kanojo ga nan to iô tomo*** no matter what she says
何とか **nantoka** somehow; 何とかパスする ***nantoka pasu suru*** scrape through; 何とか生活する ***nantoka seikatsu suru*** scrape a living; どう－何とかやっているよ ***dô – nantoka yatte iru yo*** how are you? – surviving
何とかして **nantoka shite** somehow
何とかする **nantoka suru** stretch *rules*
何とかという **nantoka to iu** thingumajig
何となく **nantonaku** vaguely; somehow
南東(の) **nantō (no)** southeast
直る **naoru** be repaired
治る **naoru** heal; be cured; feel better
直す **naosu** correct; put right
治す **naosu** heal
ナプキン **napukin** napkin
なら **nara** Japanese oak
… なら **… nara** if; provided that
並べ直す **narabenaosu** rearrange
並べる **naraberu** lay, set out
並ぶ **narabu** line up; form a line; stand in line
習い始める **narai hajimeru** take up, begin to learn
ならない **-naranai** should not ; 行ってはならない ***itte wa naranai*** you should not go
並んで **narande** side by side
慣らす **narasu** condition; familiarize
鳴らす **narasu** beep; honk; ring
習う **narau** learn
なれなれしい **narenareshii** familiar
慣れる **nareru** get accustomed to, get used to
ナレーション **narēshon** narration
ナレーター **narētā** narrator
成り上がり **nariagari** upstart
鳴り響く **narihibiku** go off; ring out; reverberate
なりすます **narisumasu** impersonate
成り立っている **naritatte iru** be composed of
なる **naru** go, become *sad, green, quiet etc*; result in; work out to; constitute; follow
鳴る **naru** sound; crash; ring; toll
なるべく **narubeku** as … as possible
なるほど **naruhodo** I see, indeed
情け深い **nasakebukai** compassionate; philanthropic
情けない **nasakenai** pitiful; disappointing; shameful
なさる **nasaru** *polite form of* **suru**
なし **nashi** pear
なしで **nashi de** without
なす **nasu** eggplant

夏**natsu** summer
懐かしい**natsukashii** nostalgic ◊ miss
ナット**natto** nut
納豆**nattō** fermented soybeans
納得する**nattoku suru** understand
縄**nawa** rope; cord
縄跳びする**nawatobi suru** skip
納屋**naya** barn
悩ませる**nayamaseru** perplex; trouble, worry
悩ます**nayamasu** annoy; bother; plague
悩み**nayami** distress; worry
悩む**nayamu** bother; get worried
なぜ**naze** why
なぜか**nazeka** somehow
なぞ**nazo** enigma, mystery
なぞめいた**nazomeita** enigmatic, mysterious
なぞなぞ**nazonazo** riddle (*game*)
名づける**nazukeru** name
ね**-ne** (*for emphasis*): きれいだね ***kirei da ne*** it's beautiful, isn't it!
根**ne** root
値**ne** price
ねえ**nē** hey
値上がりする**neagari suru** go up in price; appreciate FIN
値上げする**neage suru** mark up
ねばねばした**nebaneba shita** sticky
粘り強い**nebarizuyoi** dogged; persistent
粘る**nebaru** persist; be sticky
値引きする**nebiki suru** mark down, discount
寝坊する**nebō suru** sleep late
寝袋**nebukuro** sleeping bag
値段**nedan** price
ねだる**nedaru** pester for
値札**nefuda** price tag
寝返りをうつ**negaeri o utsu** roll over (in bed); toss about (in bed)
願い**negai** desire
願う**negau** request; desire; ask for; hope
ねぎ**negi** leek; spring onion
値切る**negiru** bargain; haggle
音色**neiro** tone
ネイティブスピーカー**neitibu-supīkā** native speaker
ねじ**neji** screw; ねじを巻く ***neji o maku*** wind up
ねじれ**nejire** twist
ねじれる**nejireru** be twisted
ねじる**nejiru** contort; twist
寝かせる**nekaseru** lay, put down
ネックレス**nekkuresu** necklace; beads
ネック**nekku** bottleneck; neckline
熱狂**nekkyō** mania
熱狂的(な)**nekkyōteki (na)** enthusiastic; ecstatic; fanatical
猫**neko** cat
寝転ぶ**nekorobu** lie down
根こそぎにする**nekosogi ni suru** root out
ネクタイ**nekutai** necktie
寝巻き**nemaki** nightshirt
眠い**nemui** drowsy, sleepy
眠れる**nemureru** sleep well; have a good night
眠れない**nemurenai** have a restless night ◊ sleepless
眠り込む**nemurikomu** drop off
眠る**nemuru** fall asleep; sleep
年**nen** (*countword for years, grades*) year; grade; 三年 **san-nen** three years; third grade
粘着テープ**nenchaku-tēpu** adhesive tape
年長(の)**nenchō (no)** senior
年代順(の)**nendaijun (no)** chronological
粘土**nendo** clay
年度**nendo** (academic) year; fiscal year
ねーねー**nēnē** hey
年賀状**nengajō** New Year's card
年号**nengō** era name
根に持って**ne ni motte** bitter
念入り(な)**nen'iri (na)** careful; elaborate
年次総会**nenji-sōkai** annual general meeting
年中**nenjū** throughout the year
年中無休**nenjū-mukyū** open all year
年間**nenkan**: 十年間 ***jû-nenkan*** ten years; 年間を通じて ***nenkan o tsûjite*** throughout the year; 昭和

年間 ***Shôwa-nenkan ni*** in the Hirohito years
年金 **nenkin** pension
年末 **nenmatsu** year end
年配(の) **nenpai** (**no**) elderly
年齢 **nenrei** age
年利 **nenri** APR, annual percentage rate
燃料 **nenryō** fuel
年生 **-nensei** -grade student; 二年生 ***ni nensei*** second grade student, sophomore
燃焼 **nenshō** combustion
ねんざ **nenza** sprain, wrench
ねんざする **nenza suru** sprain, wrench; twist one's ankle
ネオン灯 **neon-tō** neon light
ネパール **Nepāru** Nepal
ネパール (の) **Nepāru** (**no**) Nepalese
熱波 **neppa** heatwave
ねらい **nerai** aim; message
ねらう **nerau** aim
寝る **neru** go to bed; go to sleep; go to bed with
練る **neru** knead; polish up
寝る時間 **nerujikan** bedtime
値下がりする **nesagari suru** go down in price
値下げ **nesage** reduction (in price)
値下げした **nesage shita** reduced (in price)
寝そべる **nesoberu** lie; sprawl
熱射病 **nesshabyō** heatstroke
熱心(な) **nesshin** (**na**) enthusiastic; eager
熱心さ **nesshin-sa** eagerness
寝過ごす **nesugosu** oversleep
寝たきり(の) **netakiri** (**no**) bedridden
ねたみ **netami** envy
ねたむ **netamu** be jealous; envy; grudge
熱中している **netchū shite iru** be mad about, be crazy about ◊ enthusiastic
熱中する **netchū suru** be enthusiastic about; go in for
熱 **netsu** temperature, fever; heat; 熱がある ***netsu ga aru*** have a temperature; 熱をあげる ***netsu o ageru*** have a crush on
熱意 **netsui** enthusiasm, zest
熱意のない **netsui no nai** lukewarm
熱情 **netsujō** zeal; passion
根付け **netsuke** netsuke (*small carved toggle*)
熱っぽい **netsuppoi** feverish
熱烈(な) **netsuretsu** (**na**) ardent; impassioned; effusive; glowing
熱帯地方 **nettai-chihō** tropics
熱帯(の) **nettai** (**no**) tropical
熱帯雨林 **nettai-urin** tropical rain forest
ネット **netto** basket; net
ネットサーフィンをする **netto-sāfin o suru** surf the Net
ネットワーク **nettowāku** network
値打ち **neuchi** value; worth; merit
値打ちのある **neuchi no aru** valuable
値打ちのない **neuchi no nai** worthless; poor quality; bad
寝酒 **nezake** nightcap
ねずみ **nezumi** mouse; rat
…に… **ni** at; in; to; by; on; for ◊ and ◊ (*forms adverbs*): 段階的に ***dankaiteki ni*** gradually
二 **ni** two; 二、三人 ***ni, san-nin*** two or three people; 二、三の ***ni, san no*** two or three; a couple of
ニアミス **niamisu** near miss
似合う **niau** flattering ◊ suit
二倍 **nibai** double, twice as much
二倍になる **nibai ni naru** double
鈍い **nibui** blunt; dull; stupid
二分 **nibun** dichotomy
日米安全保障条約 **Nichibei-anzen-hoshō-jōyaku** Japan-US Security Treaty
日没 **nichibotsu** sunset
日時 **nichiji** date (and time)
日常(の) **nichijō** (**no**) everyday; routine
日露戦争 **Nichiro-sensō** Russo-Japanese War
日曜日 **nichiyōbi** Sunday
日曜大工 **nichiyō-daiku** DIY, do-it-yourself
荷台 **nidai** roofrack; pallet
二段ベッド **nidan-beddo** bunk beds
煮える **nieru** boil; be boiled

苦い **nigai** bitter
逃がす **nigasu** set free; let go; lose
苦手である **nigate de aru** be bad at
二月 **nigatsu** February
逃げ出す **nigedasu** run off
逃げる **nigeru** escape, break away; flee; run away
握り **nigiri** grip
にぎわう **nigiwau** be crowded; be active
にぎやか(な) **nigiyaka (na)** busy; lively
にぎやかにする **nigiyaka ni suru** jazz up
濁る **nigoru** not be clear (*of water etc*); become muddy
荷車 **niguruma** cart
日本 **Nihon** Japan
日本晴れ **Nihon-bare** very fine day without a cloud in the sky
日本舞踊 **Nihon-buyō** Japanese dance
日本髪 **Nihon-gami** traditional Japanese hairstyle
日本銀行 **Nihon-ginkō** The Bank of Japan
日本語 **Nihon-go** Japanese
日本人 **Nihon-jin** Japanese
日本海 **Nihon-kai** Sea of Japan
日本国憲法 **Nihon-koku-kenpō** Constitution of Japan
日本(の) **Nihon (no)** Japanese
日本列島 **Nihon-rettō** the Japanese Islands
日本製 **Nihon-sei** made in Japan
日本庭園 **Nihon-teien** Japanese garden
虹 **niji** rainbow
にじませる **nijimaseru** spread
にじみ出る **nijimideru** spread; ooze
にじむ **nijimu** run (*of color*); spread
二次的(な) **nijiteki (na)** secondary
二十 **nijū** twenty
二重あご **nijū-ago** double chin
二重ガラス **nijū-garasu** double glazing
二重人格 **nijū-jinkaku** split personality
二重にする **nijū ni suru** double
二重(の) **nijū (no)** double; dual
二重唱 **nijūshō** duo (*singing*)
二重奏 **nijūsō** duo (*instrumental*)
24時間営業 **nijūyojikan-eigyō** open 24 hours
二回 **nikai** twice
二階 **nikai** second story; upper floor
にきび **nikibi** spot; pimple
日刊紙 **nikkan-shi** daily
日記 **nikki** diary, journal
日光 **nikkō** sunshine
にっこり笑う **nikkori warau** grin
日光浴する **nikkōyoku suru** sunbathe
ニックネーム **nikkunēmu** nickname
肉 **niku** flesh; meat; 肉が付く ***niku ga tsuku*** fill out; put on weight
肉眼では **nikugan de wa** to the naked eye
にくい **-nikui** difficult to…; 食べにくい ***tabe-nikui*** difficult to eat
憎い **nikui** detestable
憎む **nikumu** hate
憎しみ **nikushimi** hate, hatred
肉親 **nikushin** blood relation, blood relative
肉体 **nikutai** body; flesh
肉体関係 **nikutai-kankei** intimacy; relationship
肉体労働者 **nikutai-rōdō-sha** blue-collar worker; laborer
肉体的(な) **nikutaiteki (na)** physical
肉屋 **niku-ya** butcher
二枚舌を使う **nimaijita o tsukau** doublecross
…にも…にも… **… ni mo … ni mo** neither … nor …
にもかかわらず **ni mo kakawarazu** *fml* despite
荷物 **nimotsu** luggage; baggage; cargo
荷物受け取り所 **nimotsu-uketorijo** baggage reclaim
人 **-nin** (*countword for people*): 十人 ***jû-nin*** ten people
人間 **ningen** human (being); man, humanity
人間味のある **ningenmi no aru** humane
人間味のない **ningenmi no nai** impersonal; inhumane
人間らしい **ningenrashii** human

人間性 **ningensei** humanity
人形 **ningyō** doll
任意(の) **nin'i (no)** optional
にんじん **ninjin** carrot
人情 **ninjō** → ***giri***
認可 **ninka** permission; sanction; 認可を受ける ***ninka o ukeru*** be licensed
認可する **ninka suru** authorize, sanction; license
人気 **ninki** popularity
任期 **ninki** term of office; stint; 大統領の任期 ***daitôryô no ninki*** presidency
人気がある **ninki ga aru** be popular ◊ popular
人気のない **ninki no nai** unpopular
にんまりする **ninmari suru** gloat
任命 **ninmei** appointment, nomination
任命する **ninmei suru** appoint, nominate; assign; delegate
任務 **ninmu** assignment; mission; mandate
にんにく **ninniku** garlic
妊婦 **ninpu** expectant mother
認識 **ninshiki** awareness; perception; recognition
認識票 **ninshiki-hyō** dog tag
認識する **ninshiki suru** recognize; perceive; acknowledge
妊娠 **ninshin** pregnancy
妊娠中絶 **ninshin-chūzetsu** abortion; 妊娠中絶をする ***ninshin-chûzetsu o suru*** have an abortion
妊娠している **ninshin shite iru** pregnant ◊ be pregnant
妊娠する **ninshin suru** conceive
人称代名詞 **ninshō-daimeishi** personal pronoun
人相 **ninsō** features; looks
忍耐 **nintai** endurance; patience
認定された **nintei sareta** qualified
人数 **ninzū** number of people
におい **nioi** smell; においがする ***nioi ga suru*** smell; においをかぐ ***nioi o kagu*** smell, sniff
におう **niou** smell, odor; reek, stink
日本 **Nippon** Japan
日本語 **Nippon-go** Japanese
日本人 **Nippon-jin** Japanese
日本(の) **Nippon (no)** Japanese
にらむ **niramu** glare at; stare at
煮る **niru** boil; cook
似る **niru** resemble
二流(の) **niryū (no)** second-rate
偽物 **nisemono** fake
偽(の) **nise (no)** fake, phony
西 **nishi** west
西側(の) **Nishigawa (no)** Western
西側諸国 **Nishigawa-shokoku** the West
にしん **nishin** herring
二進法(の) **nishinhō (no)** binary
日射病 **nisshabyō** sunstroke
日誌 **nisshi** log(book)
日清戦争 **Nisshin-sensō** Sino-Japanese War (*1894-95*)
日食 **nisshoku** eclipse
日数 **nissū** number of days
ニス **nisu** varnish
日中 **nitchū** by day
日中戦争 **Nitchū-sensō** Chinese-Japanese War (*1937-45*)
似ている **nite iru** be alike; be close; resemble
二等 **nitō** second class
日程 **nittei** daily schedule
ニットウェア **nitto-wea** knitwear
庭 **niwa** garden
…には **…niwa** concerning; about
にわか雨 **niwaka-ame** scattered showers
にわとり **niwatori** chicken
にやにや笑い **niyaniya-warai** smirk
にやにや笑う **niyaniya warau** smirk
荷造りをする **nizukuri o suru** pack
…の **…no** of; from; with; at; on ◊ (*forms adjectives*): 文法(の) ***bunpô (no)*** grammatical
能 **Nō** No play
脳 **nō** brain
延ばす **nobasu** defer, delay
伸ばす **nobasu** lengthen; spread; stretch; smooth out
延べ **nobe** total; 延べ時間 ***nobe jikan*** the total number of hours
述べる **noberu** extend *thanks, congratulations*; state
伸びをする **nobi o suru** stretch
延びる **nobiru** be postponed
伸びる **nobiru** grow; stretch

上る**noboru** mount, go up
登る**noboru** climb; be up (*of sun*)
昇る**noboru** rise, come up
のぼせる**noboseru** feel hot; be crazy about
ノブ **nobu** handle; knob
…ので **...node** because; as; since
のど **nodo** throat; gullet; のどがからからである ***nodo ga karakara de aru*** be parched; のどを鳴らす ***nodo o narasu*** gurgle; purr
のどあめ **nodo-ame** throat lozenges
のどか(な) **nodoka (na)** calm; peaceful
のどが渇いて **nodo ga kawaite** thirsty; dehydrated
逃れる **nogareru** elude; escape
逃す **nogasu** miss out on; set free
脳外科医 **nōgekai** brain surgeon
農業 **nōgyō** agriculture
農業(の) **nōgyō (no)** agricultural
野原 **nohara** field
ノウハウ **nōhau** expertise, knowhow
ノイローゼ **noirōze** nervous breakdown
農場 **nōjō** farm
農場主 **nōjōshu** farmer
野宿する **nojuku suru** sleep rough
農家 **nōka** farmhouse
ノック **nokku** knock
ノックアウト **nokku-auto** knockout
ノックアウトする **nokku-auto suru** knock out
ノックする **nokku suru** knock
のこぎり **nokogiri** saw
ノーコメント **nō komento** no comment
残らず **nokorazu** completely; without exception
残り **nokori** remainder, rest; remnant
残り物 **nokorimono** left-overs
残る **nokoru** remain, be left
残す **nokosu** leave, bequeath
能面 **Nōmen** No mask
のめり込む **nomerikomu** be into, get enthusiastic about
のみ **nomi** chisel; flea
のみ **-nomi** *fml* only
飲み干す **nomihosu** drink up; lap up
飲み込む **nomikomu** swallow; engulf
飲物 **nomimono** drink
農民 **nōmin** peasant
飲みに行く **nomi ni iku** go for a drink
のみ屋 **nomi-ya** bookmaker, bookie
飲む **nomu** drink; consume
飲んべえ **nonbē** heavy drinker
のんびりした **nonbiri shita** carefree; laidback; lazy *day*
飲んだくれ **nondakure** drunk; drunkard
ノンフィクション **non-fikushon** nonfiction
のに **-noni** although; if only; in order to; 熱いのに ***atsui noni*** although it's hot; 勉強しておけばよかったのに ***benkyô shite okeba yokatta noni*** if only I'd studied
のんき(な) **nonki (na)** happy-go-lucky
ののしり **nonoshiri** abuse
ののしる **nonoshiru** abuse; call names; curse; swear at
納入日 **nōnyūbi** delivery date
納入業者 **nōnyū-gyōsha** supplier
野良犬 **nora-inu** stray
のらくら暮らす **norakura kurasu** laze around; loaf around
野良猫 **nora-neko** stray (*cat*)
のれん **noren** *short cloth curtain at the entrance to a restaurant or store*
のり **nori** paste (*adhesive*); sheet of seaweed
乗り出す **noridasu** set out; embark on
乗り物酔い **norimonoyoi** travelsick
乗り換え **norikae** transfer
乗り換える **norikaeru** change
乗り切る **norikiru** get over; overcome; weather
乗り越える **norikoeru** surmount; get over *fence, disappointment etc*
乗組員 **norikumiin** crew
乗り物 **norimono** vehicle
乗り遅れる **noriokureru** miss *bus, train etc*
乗捨てる **norisuteru** abandon *ship*; drop off *one-way rental car*

乗り手 **norite** rider
能率的に **nōritsuteki ni** efficiently
のろい **noroi** slow; sluggish; dull-witted ◊ curse
のろのろ進む **noronoro susumu** crawl; drag (*of time*)
のろのろと **noronoro to** at a crawl
のろう **norou** curse
乗る **noru** board, get on; get in (*to car*), catch, get; mount; ride
載る **noru** be on top of; be printed
ノルマ **noruma** norm
能力 **nōryoku** ability; capacity; competence
乗せる **noseru** carry; pick up (*in car*)
載せる **noseru** load; put; place; print
乗せて行く **nosete iku** drive; take; give a ride to
脳しんとう **nōshintō** concussion
濃縮された **nōshuku sareta** concentrated
濃淡 **nōtan** light and shade; tone
ノート **nōto** notebook
ノートブック **nōto-bukku** notebook (computer)
乗っ取り **nottori** hijack
乗っ取り犯 **nottorihan** hijacker
乗っ取る **nottoru** hijack; take over *company*
…のうち **... no uchi** between; among; within ; 十人のうち一人 ***jû-nin no uchi hitori*** one in ten
納税者 **nōzei-sha** tax payer
除いて **nozoite** except for, aside from
のぞき穴 **nozokiana** peephole
のぞき見する **nozokimi suru** peek, peep
除く **nozoku** exclude
望ましい **nozomashii** advisable; desirable
望み **nozomi** hope; prospect; wish
望む **nozomu** wish; hope
ノズル **nozuru** nozzle
ヌード **nūdo** nude (*painting*)
ヌード雑誌 **nūdo-zasshi** girlie magazine
ヌガー **nugā** nougat
脱ぐ **nugu** remove, take off *clothes*; undo *shirt*
ぬぐう **nuguu** mop; wipe
ぬいぐるみ **nuigurumi** stuffed toy, cuddly toy
縫い目 **nuime** seam; stitching
縫い物 **nuimono** sewing; needlework
縫いつける **nuitsukeru** sew on
抜け穴 **nukeana** loophole
抜け出す **nukedasu** slip out; sneak away
抜け目のない **nukeme no nai** shrewd, smart
抜ける **nukeru** fall out; come off; escape; be missing
抜き取り検査 **nukitori-kensa** spot check
抜き打ち検査をする **nukiuchi kensa o suru** carry out spot checks
抜く **nuku** extract, take out *tooth*; pull out; draw *gun, knife*; drain; pluck
沼地 **numachi** marsh; swamp
布 **nuno** cloth, fabric
ぬらす **nurasu** soak
ぬれた **nureta** wet
塗りたくる **nuritakuru** daub
塗る **nuru** spread; paint
ぬるい **nurui** lukewarm
ぬるぬるした物 **nurunuru shita mono** slimy; slippery
盗み **nusumi** theft
盗み聞きする **nusumigiki suru** eavesdrop; listen in
盗み見する **nusumimi suru** sneak a glance at
盗む **nusumu** steal
縫う **nuu** sew; stitch
にゃあ **nyā** miaow
尿 **nyō** urine
入学願書 **nyūgaku-gansho** application form
入学させる **nyūgaku saseru** admit (*to school*)
入学式 **nyūgaku-shiki** admission ceremony
入学する **nyūgaku suru** enroll; matriculate; enter *school, college*
入学手続 **nyūgaku-tetsuzuki** registration; 入学手続きをする ***nyûgaku-tetsuzukiosuru*** register

乳がん **nyūgan** breast cancer
入院患者 **nyūin-kanja** inmate; in-patient
入院させる **nyūin saseru** admit (*to hospital*); keep in the hospital
入院する **nyūin suru** go into *hospital*
ニュージーランド **Nyū-Jīrando** New Zealand
ニュージーランド人 **Nyū-Jīrando-jin** New Zealander
入場 **nyūjō** admission, entry
入場券 **nyūjōken** pass; platform ticket
入場無料 **nyūjō-muryō** admission free
入場料 **nyūjōryō** entrance fee
入場させる **nyūjō saseru** admit (*to a place*)
入会させる **nyūkai saseru** admit (*to organization*)
入館者 **nyūkan-sha** visitor (*to museum etc*)
入金 **nyūkin** credit (*payment received*)
入国 **nyūkoku** entry (*to country*)
入国ビザ **nyūkoku-biza** entry visa
入国管理局 **Nyūkoku-kanrikyoku** Immigration
入国審査 **nyūkoku-shinsa** passport control
入力 **nyūryoku** input
入力する **nyūryoku suru** enter, input, key (in) COMPUT
入札 **nyūsatsu** bid; tender COM
乳製品 **nyū-seihin** dairy products
入社式 **nyūsha-shiki** induction ceremony
入社する **nyūsha suru** join a company
入賞する **nyūshō suru** win a prize
ニュース **nyūsu** news
ニュースキャスター **nyūsu-kyasutā** anchor man
ニュース速報 **nyūsu-sokuhō** news flash
ニュートラル **nyūtoraru** neutral (*gear*)
ニューヨーク **Nyū-Yōku** New York
入浴する **nyūyoku suru** take a bath

O

お **o** (*honorific*): お友達 ***o-tomodachi*** your friend; また明日お電話いたします ***mata ashita o-denwa itashimasu*** I'll call you again tomorrow
を **o** (*direct object particle*): 映画を見に行く ***eiga o mi ni iku*** go to see a movie
尾 **o** tail
王 **ō** king
オアシス **oashisu** oasis
おば **oba** aunt
オーバー **ōbā** overcoat
おばあちゃん **obāchan** grandma, granny
大ばか **ōbaka** lunatic
お化けの出そう(な) **obake no desō (na)** spooky
オーバーオール **ōbāōru** dungarees
おばさん **obasan** aunt
おばあさん **obāsan** grandmother; granny
欧米 **ōbei** the West; Europe and the US
お弁当 **obentō** lunch box
おび **obi** cloth belt (*kimono sash*)
おびえさせる **obiesaseru** terrorize
おびえる **obieru** be frightened
おびき寄せる **obikiyoseru** lure
脅かす **obiyakasu** threaten, menace
応募 **ōbo** application
覚えがある **oboe ga aru** recognize
覚え書き **oboegaki** reminder

覚える **oboeru** remember; memorize; feel; pick up *language, skill*
覚えやすい **oboeyasui** catchy
お盆 **Obon** O-bon (*Buddhist festival in August*)
横暴(な) **ōbō** (**na**) domineering; high-handed
おぼれる **oboreru** drown; be drowned
お坊さん **obōsan** Buddhist priest
応募者 **ōbo-sha** applicant
応募する **ōbo suru** apply for
オーブン **ōbun** oven
オーブン皿 **ōbun-zara** oven tray
お茶 **ocha** Japanese tea
落ち **ochi** punch line
落ち込む **ochikomu** sink, fall; have the blues
落ちる **ochiru** come out, go (*of stain*); fail *exam*; fall down; drop; land (*of ball*); slacken off (*of pace*)
落ち着いた **ochitsuita** calm, composed; balanced
落ち着かない **ochitsukanai** feel ill at ease ◊ restless; unsettled; uncomfortable
落ち着かせる **ochitsukaseru** cool down
落ち着き **ochitsuki** balance, composure, poise
落ち着く **ochitsuku** calm; cool (down); wind down; settle (down); feel at ease
王朝 **ōchō** dynasty
お中元 **o-chūgen** mid-year gift
殴打 **ōda** blow; thrashing
お大事に **odaiji ni** bless you (*when s.o. sneezes*); take care (*said to s.o. who is ill*)
オーダーメイド(の) **ōdāmēdo** (**no**) made-to-measure
黄だん **ōdan** jaundice
横断できない **ōdan dekinai** impassable
横断歩道 **ōdan-hodō** crosswalk
横断幕 **ōdanmaku** banner
横断する **ōdan suru** go across
穏やか(な) **odayaka** (**na**) calm; mild; peaceable; serene
穏やかさ **odayaka-sa** mildness
おでき **odeki** boil; skin eruption
オーディオ(の) **ōdio** (**no**) audio
オーディション **ōdishon** audition; screen test; オーディションを受ける ***ôdishon o ukeru*** audition
オードブル **ōdoburu** hors d'oeuvre
脅かす **odokasu** threaten; scare
踊り **odori** dance
大通り **ōdōri** main street; avenue
踊り場 **odoriba** landing (*top of staircase*)
驚かす **odorokasu** astonish, surprise; startle
驚き **odoroki** astonishment; surprise; wonder; fright; alarm
驚く **odoroku** be astonished
驚くべき **odoroku beki** amazing, surprising
驚くほど **odoroku hodo** suprisingly
驚くほど(の) **odoroku hodo** (**no**) astonishing, phenomenal
踊る **odoru** dance
脅し **odoshi** intimidation; menace
脅しつける **odoshitsukeru** browbeat
脅す **odosu** intimidate; menace
応援する **ōen suru** support
終える **oeru** cease; end, finish; round off; conclude
OL **ōeru** *female clerical employee*
オフィス **ofisu** office
オフィスビル **ofisubiru** office block
オフホワイト(の) **ofuhowaito** (**no**) off-white
往復 **ōfuku** round trip ◊ there and back
往復切符 **ōfuku-kippu** round trip ticket
往復する **ōfuku suru** shuttle
オフライン式(の) **ofurain-shiki** (**no**) off-line
オフサイド(の) **ofusaido** (**no**) offside SP
オフシーズン **ofushīzun** low season
大がかり(な) **ōgakari** (**na**) ambitious; large scale
おがくず **ogakuzu** sawdust
拝む **ogamu** pray; worship
オーガニック **ōganikku** organic

大型(の) **ōgata (no)** large-sized
小川 **ogawa** stream, creek
オーガズム **ōgazumu** orgasm
お元気で **ogenki de** all the best!
(お)元気ですか **(o) genki desu ka** how are you?
大げさ **ōgesa** exaggeration
大げさ(な) **ōgesa (na)** melodramatic; ornate
補い合う **oginaiau** complementary
補う **oginau** compensate for; supplement; complement
大声 **ōgoe** shout; 大声を出す ***ôgoe o dasu*** cry out; 大声で呼ぶ ***ôgoe de yobu*** call out
おごる **ogoru** buy a drink / meal for, treat; 一杯おごらせてください ***ippai ogorasete kudasai*** can I buy you a drink?
大幅に **ōhaba ni** greatly; drastically
お払い箱にする **oharaibako ni suru** dismiss; sack; pension off
おはよう(ございます) **ohayō (gozaimasu)** good morning
横柄(な) **ōhei (na)** insolent; arrogant
尾ひれをつける **ohire o tsukeru** embroider
大広間 **ōhiroma** hall
お昼 **ohiru** lunch
お冷や **ohiya** iced water
オホーツク海 **Ohōtsuku-kai** Sea of Okhotsk
おい **oi** nephew ◊ hey!
覆い **ōi** coating, layer; hood (*over cooker*)
多い **ōi** much; many; frequent
追い出す **oidasu** throw out, kick out
追い払う **oiharau** repel; chase away, see off; send away
追いかける **oikakeru** chase
覆い隠す **ōikakusu** hide; screen
追い風 **oikaze** tail wind
王位継承 **ōi-keishō** succession (*to the throne*)
追い込む **oikomu** drive into *situation, corner*; condemn
追い越し車線 **oikoshi-shasen** fast lane
追い越す **oikosu** pass, overtake
大いに **ōi ni** very much
オイル **oiru** oil
お医者さん **oishasan** doctor
おいしい **oishii** good; nice; delicious
おいしそう(な) **oishisō (na)** appetizing; tempting; gorgeous *smell*
大急ぎ **ōisogi** hurry, rush; …を大急ぎで病院に連れていった ***… o ôisogi de byôin ni tsurete itta*** rush … to the hospital
おいて **oite**: この点において ***kono ten ni oite*** in this respect
置いてある **oite aru** stand; be placed
置いて行く **oite iku** deliver, drop off; leave behind
追いつく **oitsuku** catch up; overtake
追い詰める **oitsumeru** corner
お祝い **oiwai** celebration; お祝いの言葉 ***oiwai no kotoba*** congratulations
おじ **oji** uncle
王子 **ōji** prince
おじぎ **ojigi** bow (*greeting*); おじぎをする ***ojigi o suru*** bow
おじいちゃん **ojiichan** granddad, grandpa
おじいさん **ojiisan** grandfather; grandpa
おじけづく **ojikezuku** lose courage; get frightened
応じる **ōjiru** respond, react; live up to, come up to
おじさん **ojisan** uncle
王女 **ōjo** princess
お嬢さん **ojōsan** daughter; ma'am
お上手(の) **ojōzu (no)** flattering
丘 **oka** hill; mound
おかえりなさい **okaerinasai** welcome home
おかげで **okage de** thanks to
横隔膜 **ōkakumaku** diaphragm
お構いなく **okamainaku** with no regard for
おおかみ **ōkami** wolf
お金 **okane** money
お金持ち(の) **okanemochi (no)** loaded, rich
お勘定 **o-kanjō** check, bill; お勘定

お願い ***o-kanjô o-negai*** the check, please
オカルト **okaruto** occult
お母さん **okāsan** mother
お菓子 **okashi** confectionery
おかしい **okashii** humorous; odd; suspicious
おかし(な) **okashi (na)** funny, strange
おかしなことに **okashi na koto ni** funnily enough
冒す **okasu** brave *danger*; affect
犯す **okasu** commit
侵す **okasu** invade; infringe
おかわり **okawari** 紅茶のおかわりは ***kôcha no okawari wa*** some more tea?
おかず **okazu** side dishes
おけ **oke** bucket
オーケー **ōkē** ok
オーケストラ **ōkesutora** orchestra
置き場 **okiba** storage space; yard
大きい **ōkii** big; loud
置き換え **okikae** substitution
大きくする **ōkiku suru** enlarge
お決まり(の) **okimari (no)** routine
大き(な) **ōki (na)** great, big; large; 大きなお世話だ ***ôkina osewa da*** that's none of your business
起き直る **okinaoru** sit up (in bed)
沖縄 **Okinawa** Okinawa
お気に入り **oki ni iri** favorite
置きに **oki ni** every other ; 一日置きに ***ichi-nichi oki ni*** every other day
起きる **okiru** get up (*in morning*); be up (*out of bed*)
大きさ **ōki-sa** size, magnitude
起きている **okite iru** sit up, stay up (*at night*)
置き忘れる **okiwasureru** leave (behind); mislay
おこがましい **okogamashii** impertinent; presumptuous
王国 **ōkoku** kingdom
行い **okonai** conduct; deed
行う **okonau** perform; carry out; transact
行われる **okonawareru** take place
お好み焼き **okonomiyaki** Japanese savory pancake
怒らせる **okoraseru** anger; displease; offend, insult; provoke
怒り出す **okoridasu** flare up
怒りっぽい **okorippoi** bad-tempered, cranky; irritable
起こりうる **okoriuru** potential
怒る **okoru** get angry
起こる **okoru** happen, occur; break out (*of fight*); get up (*of wind*); arise
起こす **okosu** wake, rouse
…お断り **...okotowari** please do not …
怒った **okotta** angry; exasperated; annoyed
怒っている **okotte iru** cross, angry; resentful
奥 **oku** back (*of room, drawer*)
億 **oku** hundred million
置く **oku** deposit, place, put, set
オーク **ōku** oak (tree)
奥歯 **okuba** molar
憶病 **okubyō** cowardice
憶病者 **okubyō-mono** coward
憶病(な) **okubyō (na)** cowardly; timid
屋外(の) **okugai (no)** outdoor, open-air
屋内(の) **okunai (no)** indoor
多く(の) **ōku (no)** much; many
大蔵大臣 **Ōkura-daijin** Minister of Finance
遅らせる **okuraseru** hold up, make late; set back, delay; slow down
大蔵省 **Ōkura-shō** Treasury Department; Japanese Ministry of Finance
遅れ **okure** delay, hold up
遅れる **okureru** be delayed; lag behind; lose (*of clock*)
遅れた **okureta** backward; late; overdue
遅れている **okurete iru** be slow (*of clock*); be behind
送り出す **okuridasu** see out, see to the door
送りがな **okurigana** *syllabary letters added to Chinese characters to show inflection*
贈り物 **okurimono** gift
贈る **okuru** present, give

送る **okuru** send, ship; transmit; see off (*at airport etc*); take back *person*
奥さん **okusan** wife; ma'am
オークション **ōkushon** auction
憶測 **okusoku** speculation, guess
憶測する **okusoku suru** speculate, guess
お悔やみ **okuyami** condolences
奥行き **okuyuki** depth
奥行きの深い **okuyuki no fukai** deep
オーク材 **ōku-zai** oak
お経 **okyō** Buddhist sutra
応急(の) **ōkyū (no)** emergency
応急処置 **ōkyū-shochi** first aid; emergency treatment
お前 **omae** you (*familiar*)
お孫さん **omago-san** grandchild; grandson; granddaughter
お参りする **omairi suru** visit a shrine
おまけ **omake** bonus, extra; free gift
おまけに **omake ni** on top of that
お守り **omamori** lucky charm
おまる **omaru** potty; bedpan
大また **ōmata** stride; 大またで歩く ***ômata de aruku*** stride
お待たせしました **omatase shimashita** sorry to keep you waiting
お祭り **omatsuri** festival
お巡りさん **omawari-san** cop
おめでとう **omedetō** best wishes; congratulations on …; well done; …におめでとうと言う ***... ni omedetô to iu*** congratulate
汚名 **omei** stigma, shame
お目にかかる **ome ni kakaru** (*polite*) see *person*
大目に見る **ōme ni miru** make allowances
お見合い **omiai** meeting to discuss an arranged marriage
おみくじ **omikuji** *written oracle received at shrine*
大みそか **Ōmisoka** New Year's Eve
おもちゃ **omocha** toy
重い **omoi** heavy; serious; tough
思い上った **omoiagatta** conceited
思い違い **omoichigai** misunderstanding
思い出させる **omoidasaseru** bring back; be reminiscent of
思い出す **omoidasu** remember, recollect; remind
思い出 **omoide** memory, recollection
思い出話をする **omoidebanashi o suru** reminisce
思い通りにする **omoidōri ni suru** have one's (own) way
思いがけない **omoigakenai** unexpected, unforeseen
思い切り **omoikiri** with all one's might; as hard/fast as you can; 思い切り遊ぶ ***omoikiri asobu*** have a great time
思い切って…する **omoikitte … suru** dare; venture; 思い切ってやってみる ***omoikitte yatte miru*** take the plunge
思い込む **omoikomu** have the impression that; be convinced that
思い過ごしです **omoisugoshi desu** it's all in your imagination
思いとどまらせる **omoi-todomaraseru** dissuade, put off
思いつき **omoitsuki** plan; idea
思いつく **omoitsuku** hit on a plan
思いやり **omoiyari** consideration; empathy
思いやりのある **omoiyari no aru** caring; considerate; understanding; unselfish
思いやりのない **omoiyari no nai** inconsiderate
思いやる **omoiyaru** consider
大文字 **ōmoji** capital letter
大もうけする **ōmōke suru** make a killing, clean up
主(な) **omo (na)** chief, main
重荷 **omoni** burden, millstone
主に **omo ni** mainly, mostly
大物 **ōmono** tycoon
重さ **omo-sa** weight; 重さが…である ***omo-sa ga ... de aru*** weigh; 重さを量る ***omo-sa o hakaru*** weigh
おもしろがる **omoshirogaru** be amused at

おもしろ半分で **omoshiro hanbun de** (just) for kicks; for fun
おもしろい **omoshiroi** entertaining; amusing; hilarious; interesting
おもしろく **omoshiroku** funnily
重たい **omotai** heavy
表 **omote** front
表向き **omotemuki** front, cover
表向きは **omotemuki wa** officially
おもてなし **omotenashi** hospitality
思う **omou** think; expect; feel; reckon; ...と思う ***... to omou*** regard as; ...と思われる ***... to omowareru*** it appears that; ...と思われている ***... to omowarete iru*** it is considered to be
思う存分 **omouzonbun** to one's heart's content
思わず **omowazu** involuntarily, in spite of oneself; 思わず笑ってしまう ***omowazu waratte shimau*** I couldn't help laughing
おうむ **ōmu** parrot
大麦 **ōmugi** barley
オムレツ **omuretsu** omelet
おむすび **omusubi** rice ball
おむつ **omutsu** diaper
恩 **on** debt of gratitude; indebtedness
オーナー **ōnā** owner
同じ **onaji** the same; ...と同じだけ ***... to onaji dake*** as much as
同じくらいに **onaji kurai ni** as; ...と同じくらい高い/かわいい ***... to onaji kurai takai / kawaii*** as high / pretty as
おなか **onaka** tummy; belly; おなかが一杯になる ***onaka ga ippai ni naru*** be full up; おなかがペコペコである ***onaka ga pekopeko de aru*** I'm starving; おなかがすいた ***onaka ga suita*** I'm hungry; おなか一杯食べる ***onaka-ippai taberu*** eat one's fill; おなかをこわしている ***onaka o kowashite iru*** have an upset stomach
おなか痛 **onakaita** stomach-ache
おんぶ **onbu** piggyback
御中 **onchū** *fml* to; Messrs
温度 **ondo** temperature
温度計 **ondokei** thermometer
おんどり **ondori** cock, cockerel
尾根 **one** ridge
お願い **onegai** favor; request
お願いします **onegai shimasu** please
お願いする **onegai suru** request
恩返しする **ongaeshi suru** repay
お姉さん **onēsan** elder sister
音楽 **ongaku** music
音楽家 **ongakuka** musician
音楽(の) **ongaku (no)** musical
音楽的でない **ongakuteki de nai** unmusical
音楽的(な) **ongakuteki (na)** melodious
音楽好き(な) **ongakuzuki (na)** musical
鬼 **oni** devil
鬼ばば **onibaba** dragon; nag
おにぎり **onigiri** rice ball
大人数 **ōninzū** large number of people
お兄さん **onīsan** elder brother
恩人 **onjin** benefactor
音階 **onkai** scale MUS
音感のよい **onkan no yoi** musical
穏健派 **onkenha** moderate
穏健(な) **onken (na)** moderate
恩着せがましい **onkisegamashii** condescending
音響効果 **onkyō-kōka** acoustics
女 **onna** woman; female; chick
女形 **onnagata** *female impersonator in Kabuki*
女の子 **onna no ko** girl
女らしい **onna-rashii** feminine
女主人 **onna-shujin** landlady; mistress (*of servant*)
女たらし **onnatarashi** womanizer, wolf
女友達 **onna-tomodachi** girlfriend (*of girl*)
おの **ono** ax; chopper (*tool*)
音符 **onpu** note MUS
オンライン(の) **onrain (no)** on-line
オンラインサービス **onrain-sābisu** on-line service
温泉 **onsen** hot spring
音節 **onsetsu** syllable
恩赦 **onsha** amnesty; pardon

恩知らず **onshirazu** ingratitude
恩知らず(の) **onshirazu (no)** ungrateful
温室 **onshitsu** conservatory; greenhouse
温室効果 **onshitsu-kōka** greenhouse effect
温床 **onshō** breeding ground
オンス **onsu** ounce
温水 **onsui** heated water
温帯 **ontai** temperate zone
音訳する **on'yaku suru** transliterate
オンザロック **on-za-rokku** on the rocks ◊ whiskey and water
おおやまねこ **ōyamaneko** lynx
オペラ **opera** opera
オペラグラス **operagurasu** opera glasses
オペレーター **operētā** operator TELEC
オペレーティングシステム **operētingu-shisutemu** operating system
オープンチケット **ōpun-chiketto** open ticket
オープンカー **ōpun-kā** convertible
オープンプランオフィス **ōpun-puran-ofisu** open plan office
オプション **opushon** optional extras
往来 **ōrai** traffic
オランダ **Oranda** Holland
オランダ語 **Oranda-go** Dutch
オーラルセックス **ōraru-sekkusu** oral sex
おれ **ore** (*familiar, used by men*) I
お礼 **orei** bow; thanks; remuneration
オレンジ **orenji** orange
オレンジ色 **orenji-iro** orange
折れる **oreru** break
おり **ori** cage; occasion
オリーブオイル **orību-oiru** olive oil
折り紙 **origami** origami
オリジナル **orijinaru** original *painting etc*
折り返し **orikaeshi** cuff (*of pants*)
折り返し(で) **orikaeshi (de)** by return (*of mail*); …に折り返し電話する ***… ni orikaeshi denwa suru*** call back
折返し運転 **orikaeshi-unten** shuttle service
折り返す **orikaesu** turn back *edges, sheets*; turn up *collar*
折り込み広告 **orikomi kōkoku** insert
折り目 **orime** crease (*in pants*); fold
織物 **orimono** textile; tissue
折りの悪い **ori no warui** untimely
オリンピック **Orinpikku** Olympics
降りる, 下りる **oriru** descend; climb down; go down; come down; disembark; get off
折りたたみ式ベッド **oritatami-shiki-beddo** folding bed
折りたたみ式(の) **oritatami-shiki (no)** folding
折りたたむ **oritatamu** fold (up)
往路 **ōro** outward journey
愚か(な) **oroka (na)** stupid; mindless
愚かさ **oroka-sa** stupidity; folly
卸で **oroshi de** wholesale
おろし金 **oroshigane** grater
卸(の) **oroshi (no)** wholesale
下ろす **orosu** let down *hair, blinds*
降ろす **orosu** drop (off) (*from car*); lower
折る **oru** break; break off
織る **oru** weave
オール **ōru** oar
オルガン **orugan** organ MUS
横領 **ōryō** misappropriation
横領する **ōryō suru** misappropriate
抑えきれない **osaekirenai** irrepressible
抑える **osaeru** check, restrain; keep back; keep down *costs etc*; repress; bring under control
押さえつける **osaetsukeru** pin, hold down
おさげ髪 **osagegami** braid; plait; pigtail
大さじ **ōsaji** tablespoon
大阪 **Ōsaka** Osaka
収まる **osamaru** subside, blow over, quieten down
納まる **osamaru** fit, go in
治める **osameru** govern
納める **osameru** settle *debts*
お産 **osan** confinement MED

幼い **osanai** very young; infantile
大騒ぎ **ōsawagi** scene (*argument*); uproar; 大騒ぎをする ***ôsawagi o suru*** make a scene
大騒ぎ(の) **ōsawagi (no)** wild
オセアニア **Oseania** Oceania
おせち料理 **osechi-ryōri** *traditional New Year food*
お歳暮 **o-seibo** year-end gift
おう盛(な) **ōsei (na)** hearty; active
お世辞 **oseji** flattery; お世辞のうまい ***oseji no umai*** smooth; お世辞を言う ***oseji o iu*** flatter
おせっかいな人 **osekkai na hito** busybody
お説教をする **osekkyō o suru** preach
汚染 **osen** pollution; contamination
汚染物質 **osen-busshitsu** pollutant
汚染する **osen suru** pollute; infect
応接室 **ōsetsushitsu** drawing room; room for visitors
おしゃべり **oshaberi** gossip; chat; banter; chatterbox
おしゃべり(な) **oshaberi (na)** talkative
おしゃべりする **oshaberi suru** chat
おしゃぶり **oshaburi** pacifier
おしゃれ(な) **oshare (na)** stylish
押し上げる **oshiageru** push off *lid*; push up *prices*
押しボタン **oshi-botan** button, push-button
おしどり **oshidori** mandarin duck
教える **oshieru** educate; teach, instruct
惜しい **oshii** regrettable; unfortunate ◊ be precious
押し入れ **oshiire** storage space
押し入る **oshiiru** jam, squeeze
押しかける **oshikakeru** gatecrash
おしっこをする **oshikko o suru** pee
押し込み強盗 **oshikomi-gōtō** burglary, break-in; housebreaking
押し込む **oshikomu** jam, ram; squeeze in
おしまい **oshimai** conclusion, end
おしめ **oshime** diaper
惜しむ **oshimu** regret; be ungenerous; begrudge
押しのける **oshinokeru** elbow out of the way
おしろい **oshiroi** face powder; …におしろいを塗る ***… ni oshiroi o nuru*** powder
押し進む **oshisusumu** push along
押し倒す **oshitaosu** overpower
押しつぶす **oshitsubusu** crush
押しつける **oshitsukeru** coerce; force
押し売り **oshiuri** high-pressure selling
押し売り(の) **oshiuri (no)** high-pressure *salesman*
押し寄せる **oshiyoseru** close in
汚職 **oshoku** corruption; bribery
押収 **ōshū** seizure
押収する **ōshū suru** seize
遅い **osoi** late (*in day*); tardy; slow
襲いかかる **osoikakaru** attack; pounce on; go for
大掃除 **ōsōji** spring-cleaning
遅くなった **osoku natta** belated; 遅くなってきた ***osoku natte kita*** it's getting late; 遅くなります ***osoku narimasu*** I won't be back until late
お粗末(な) **osomatsu (na)** flimsy; poor; crude
お供え **osonae** offering
おそらく **osoraku** possibly, perhaps; おそらく…しない ***osoraku … shinai*** hardly; not likely
恐れ **osore** fear
恐れいります **osore irimasu** (*polite*) thank you
恐れる **osoreru** fear
おそろい(の) **osoroi (no)** matching
恐ろしい **osoroshii** terrifying; frightening
襲う **osou** attack; break (*of storm*)
おっしゃる **ossharu** (*polite*) say; tell
雄 **osu** male (*animal*)
押す **osu** press; push, shove
雄猫 **osuneko** tomcat
オーストラレーシア **Ōsutorarēshia** Australasia
オーストラリア **Ōsutoraria** Australia
オーストラリア人 **Ōsutoraria-jin** Australian

オーストラリア(の) **Ōsutoraria (no)** Australian
オーストリア **Ōsutoria** Austria
オーストリア (の) **Ōsutoria (no)** Austrian
おたふくかぜ **otafukukaze** mumps
お互いに **otagai ni** one another, each other
応対に出る **ōtai ni deru** answer the door
応対する **ōtai suru** deal with customers
おたま **otama** ladle
おたまじゃくし **otamajakushi** tadpole
お誕生日おめでとう **otanjōbi omedetō** happy birthday!
王手 **ōte** checkmate
お手洗 **otearai** rest room, washroom
お手柄 **otegara** great feat
おてんば **otenba** tomboy
お手伝い **otetsudai** maid
音 **oto** noise, sound
おう吐 **ōto** vomiting
オートバイ **ōtobai** motorbike, motorcycle
おとぎ話 **otogi-banashi** fairy tale
男 **otoko** man
男の子 **otoko no ko** boy
男っぽい **otokoppoi** macho
男っぽさ **otokoppo-sa** machismo
男らしい **otokorashii** manly; virile
男らしさ **otokorashi-sa** masculinity; virility
男やもめ **otokoyamome** widower
お得意さん **otokuisan** good customer
お徳用 **otokuyō** economy size
オートマチック **ōtomachikku** automatic
オートメーション **ōtomēshon** automation
大人 **otona** adult, grown-up
おとなしい **otonashii** meek, mild
おとなしく **otonashiku** meekly
おとり **otori** decoy, diversion
衰える **otoroeru** weaken; ebb away
劣る **otoru** be inferior
お父さん **otōsan** father; dad
落し穴 **otoshiana** catch, pitfall
落し物 **otoshimono** lost and found
お年寄り **otoshiyori** old person
落とす **otosu** drop; droop (*of shoulders*); slacken; shed *leaves*
弟 **otōto** younger brother
おととい **ototoi** the day before yesterday
弟さん **otōtosan** younger brother
おととし **ototoshi** year before last
劣った **ototta** inferior
訪れる **otozureru** visit; arrive
おつまみ **otsumami** nibbles; snacks
お釣り **otsuri** change
追っ手 **otte** those in pursuit; 追って通知する ***otte tsûchi suru*** until further notice
夫 **otto** husband
追う **ou** chase; pursue; follow
負う **ou** bear *responsibility, debt*; carry on one's back
覆う **ōu** coat, cover; cover up; envelop
大売り出し **ōuridashi** clearance sale
雄牛 **oushi** bull; ox
おわび **owabi** apology
おわん **owan** bowl
大笑い **ōwarai** hysterics
大笑いする **ōwarai suru** howl, roar with laughter
終わらせる **owaraseru** terminate; finish off; put an end to
終わり **owari** end; ending
終わりである **owari de aru** be over, be finished
終わりのない **owari no nai** endless
終わる **owaru** finish; end; be through (*of couple*); result in
親 **oya** parent; dealer (*in card games*)
おや、まあ **oya, mā** oh dear!, good heavens!
親会社 **oyagaisha** holding company; parent company
公(の) **ōyake (no)** public
親子 **oyako** parent and child; family
親(の) **oya (no)** parental
親知らず **oyashirazu** wisdom tooth
おやすみ(なさい) **oyasumi (nasai)** good night

親指 **oyayubi** thumb
及び **oyobi** and; as well as
及ぼす **oyobosu** influence; affect; exert
及ぶ **oyobu** reach; extend to
泳ぎ**oyogi** swimming; 泳ぎに行く ***oyogi ni iku*** go swimming, go for a swim
泳ぐ **oyogu** swim
大喜び **ōyorokobi** delight
大喜び(の) **ōyorokobi** (**no**) elated; overjoyed; jubilant
大喜びする **ōyorokobi suru** exult
およそ **oyoso** around, approximately
おおよそ(の) **ōyoso** (**no**) approximate
王座 **ōza** throne
大酒 **ōzake** heavy drinking; bender
大ざっぱ(な) **ōzappa** (**na**) broad, general; sketchy; 大ざっぱに言って ***ôzappa ni itte*** broadly speaking
大皿 **ōzara** platter
大勢 **ōzei crowd**
大関 **ōzeki** sumo champion
王族 **ōzoku** royalty
オゾン **ozon** ozone
オゾン層 **ozon-sō** ozone layer
応ずる **ōzuru** comply

P

パー **pā** par (*in golf*)
パブ **pabu** pub
パチンコ **pachinko** Japanese pinball
ぱちぱちと音を立てる**pachipachi to oto o tateru** crackle
パッド **paddo** pad
パイ **pai** flan; pie
パイ生地 **pai-kiji** pastry
パイナップル **painappuru** pineapple
パイプ **paipu** pipe
パイロット**pairotto** pilot
パジャマ **pajama** pajamas
パーキングメーター **pākingu-mētā** parking meter
パキスタン **Pakisutan** Pakistan
パック **pakku** carton; pack; packet
パック旅行 **pakku-ryokō** package tour
パーコレーター**pākorētā** percolator
パーマ **pāma** perm; パーマをかける ***pâma o kakeru*** perm
パン **pan** bread
パンチ **panchi** punch
パンダ **panda** panda
パネル **paneru** panel
パンフレット**panfuretto** brochure; booklet; pamphlet
パニック **panikku** panic, scare; パニック状態になる ***panikku-jôtai ni naru*** panic
パンジー **panjī** pansy (*flower*)
パン粉 **panko** breadcrumbs
パンク **panku** blow-out (*of tire*)
パンクした **panku shita** flat
パンクする **panku suru** blow (*of tire*)
パンくず **pankuzu** breadcrumbs
パノラマ **panorama** panorama
パンティー **pantī** panties
パンティーストッキング**pantī-sutokkingu** pantyhose
パンツ **pantsu** underpants
パン屋 **pan-ya** baker; bakery
パパ **papa** dad
パラボラアンテナ **parabora-antena** satellite dish
パラサイトシングル**parasaito-shinguru** *person who lives with his/her parents for a long time*
パラシュート **parashūto** parachute; パラシュートで降りる ***parashûto de oriru*** parachute

パラソル **parasoru** parasol
パレード **parēdo** parade
パレードする **parēdo suru** parade
ぱりっとした **paritto shita** crisp *shirt, bank bills*
パルプ **parupu** pulp (*for papermaking*)
パーセント **pāsento** percent
パセリ **paseri** parsley
パソコン **pasokon** PC, personal computer
パス **pasu** pass SP
パスポート **pasupōto** passport
パスする **pasu suru** pass SP
パステル **pasuteru** pastel (*color*)
パステル調(の) **pasuteru-chō (no)** pastel
パスワード **pasuwādo** password
パターン **patān** pattern
パッチワーク **patchiwāku** patchwork
パーティー **pātī** party
パート **pāto** part MUS; part-time job
パトカー **patokā** patrol car
パートナー **pātonā** partner (*in particular activity*)
パトロール **patorōru** patrol
パートタイム(の) **pātotaimu (no)** part-time
パワーシャベル **pawā-shaberu** excavator
パワーステアリング **pawā-sutearingu** power(-assisted) steering
パワーユニット **pawā-yunitto** power unit
パズル **pazuru** puzzle
ペア **pea** pair
ぺちゃくちゃしゃべる **pechakucha shaberu** yap; chatter
ペチコート **pechikōto** underskirt
ペダル **pedaru** pedal; ペダルを踏む ***pedaru o fumu*** pedal
ページ **pēji** page
北京語 **Pekingo** Mandarin Chinese
ぺこぺこする **pekopeko suru** fawn (on); kowtow (to)
ペン **pen** pen
ペナント **penanto** pennant
ペナルティー **penarutī** penalty SP; ペナルティーを科す ***penarutī o kasu*** penalize
ペナルティーエリア **penarutī-eria** penalty area
ペンチ **penchi** pliers
ペンダント **pendanto** pendant
ペンフレンド **pen-furendo** pen friend
ペニシリン **penishirin** penicillin
ペンキ **penki** paint; ペンキを塗る ***penki o nuru*** paint
ペンキ塗り **penki-nuri** painting (*decorating*)
ペンキ塗りたて **penki-nuritate** wet paint
ペンキ屋 **penki-ya** painter (*decorator*)
ペンネーム **pen-nēmu** pseudonym, pen name
ペーパーバック **pēpābakku** paperback
ペパーミント **pepāminto** peppermint
ぺらぺら(の) **perapera (no)** fluent; talkative
ペッサリー **pessarī** diaphragm (*contraceptive*)
ペース **pēsu** pace, speed
ペースメーカー **pēsumēkā** pacemaker
ペストリー **pesutorī** pastry
ぺてん師 **peten-shi** swindler; impostor
ペッティングする **pettingu suru** pet (*of couple*)
ペット **petto** pet, domestic animal
ペットホテル **petto-hoteru** pet hotel
ピアニスト **pianisuto** pianist
ピアノ **piano** piano
ピーアール **pīāru** public relations
ピアスをする **piasu o suru** pierce
ピエロ **piero** clown
ぴかぴか(の) **pikapika (no)** sparkling; flashing
ぴかぴか光る **pikapika hikaru** glitter; flash
ピーク **pīku** peak, high point
ピーク時 **pīku-ji** peak hours
ピクニック **pikunikku** picnic
ぴくぴく動く **pikupiku ugoku**

twitch; move jerkily
ピクルス **pikurusu** pickles
ピーマン **pīman** pepper
ピン **pin** pin; ピンで留める ***pin de tomeru*** pin; attach
ピーナッツ **pīnattsu** ground nut, peanut
ピーナッツバター **pīnattsu-batā** peanut butter
ピンチ **pinchi** pinch; fix; difficulty
ピンク色 **pinku-iro** pink
ピンポン **pinpon** ping-pong ◊ *used to indicate a correct answer*
ピンセット **pinsetto** forceps; tweezers
ピンストライプ **pinsutoraipu** pinstripe
ピント **pinto** focus; ピントが合っている/ずれている ***pinto ga atte iru / zurete iru*** be in / out of focus; …にピントを合わせる ***… ni pinto o awaseru*** focus on
ぴんと張った **pin to hatta** taut; tense
ぴりぴりした **piripiri shita** uptight, nervous, jittery
ぴりぴりする **piripiri suru** sting; smart
ぴりっとした **piritto shita** savory; sharp *taste*
ピル **piru** the pill; ピルを飲んでいる ***piru o nonde iru*** be on the pill
ぴしゃりとたたく **pishari to tataku** slap
ピシャッと打つ **pishatto utsu** slap; smack
ピストン **pisuton** piston
ピストル **pisutoru** pistol
ピッチャー **pitchā** pitcher
ぴったり **pittari**: ぴったり合った ***pittari atta*** snug, tight-fitting; ぴったりだ ***pittari da*** it's a good fit; 体にぴったり(の) ***karada ni pittari (no)*** skin-tight
ピザ **piza** pizza
ポーチ **pōchi** pouch; porch
ぽい **-poi**: 子供っぽい ***kodomoppoi*** childish
ポーカー **pōkā** poker
ポケット **poketto** pocket
ポケットベル **poketto-beru** pager
ぽきんと折れる **pokin to oreru** snap, break
ぽきんと折る **pokin to oru** snap, break
ポン引き **ponbiki** pimp
ポニー **ponī** pony
ポニーテール **ponītēru** ponytail
ポンプ **ponpu** pump
ぽんという音 **pon to iu oto** pop
ぽんと抜く **pon to nuku** pop
ポピー **popī** poppy
ポップコーン **poppukōn** popcorn
ポップス **poppusu** pop; pop song
ポップス(の) **poppusu (no)** pop
ポーランド **Pōrando** Poland
ポリエチレン **poriechiren** polyethylene
ポリ塩化ビニール **pori-enka-binīru** PVC
ポリエステル **poriesuteru** polyester
ポリスチレン **porisuchiren** polystyrene
ポロシャツ **poroshatsu** polo shirt
ポルノ **poruno** pornography, porn
ポルトガル **Porutogaru** Portugal
ポルトガル語 **Porutogaru-go** Portuguese (*language*)
ポスター **posutā** poster
ポスト **posuto** mailbox
ぽっちゃりした **potchari shita** plump
ポテトチップス **poteto-chippusu** potato chip
ポテトフライ **poteto-furai** fried potatoes
ポット **potto** pot
ポーズをとる **pōzu o toru** pose
プードル **pūdoru** poodle
プンプンにおう **punpun niou** have a strong smell
プンプン怒る **punpun okoru** be furious
プラチナ **purachina** platinum
プラチナ製(の) **purachina-sei (no)** platinum
プラグ **puragu** plug ELEC
プライバシー **puraibashī** privacy
プライド **puraido** pride
プラカード **purakādo** placard
プラム **puramu** plum

プランテーション **purantēshon** plantation
プラス **purasu** plus (sign)
プラス(の) **purasu** (**no**) positive ELEC
プラスチック **purasuchikku** plastic
プラスチック製(の) **purasuchikku-sei** (**no**) plastic, made of plastic
プラトニック(な) **puratonikku** (**na**) platonic
プラットホーム **purattohōmu** platform
プレー **purē** play SP
プレハブ(の) **purehabu** (**no**) prefabricated
プレイボーイ **purei-bōi** flirt (*male*)
プレイガール **purei-gāru** flirt (*female*)
プレッシャー **puresshā** pressure; プレッシャーを感じる ***puresshâ o kanjiru*** be under pressure
プレーする **purē suru** play
プレゼン **purezen** presentation
プレゼント **purezento** present
プリンター **purintā** printer
プリント **purinto** print, photograph; handout (*for class*); hard copy
プリントアウト **purinto-auto** printout
プリントアウトする **purinto-auto suru** print out
ぷりぷりする **puripuri suru** be in a huff
プリーツ **purītsu** pleat
プロ **puro** professional, pro; プロに転向する ***puro ni tenkô suru*** turn professional
プロバイダー **purobaidā** service provider
プロデューサー **purodyūsā** film-maker; producer
プログラマー **puroguramā** programmer
プログラム **puroguramu** program
プロモーション **puromōshon** promotion
プロ並み(の) **puro-nami** (**no**) professional
プロンプト **puronputo** prompt COMPUT
プロパガンダ **puropaganda** propaganda
プロポーズ **puropōzu** proposal
プロポーズする **puropōzu suru** propose
プロテスタント **Purotesutanto** Protestant
プール **pūru** (swimming) pool; pool (*game*)
プルーン **purūn** prune
プルタブ **puru-tabu** ring-pull
ぴょんと飛ぶ **pyon to tobu** hop

R

らば **raba** mule
ラベンダー **rabendā** lavender
ラベル **raberu** label; ラベルをはる ***raberu o haru*** label
ラブ **rabu** love
ラブレター **raburetā** love letter
ラード **rādo** lard
ラフ **rafu** rough
ラガービール **ragābīru** lager
ライバル **raibaru** competition; rival
ライダー **raidā** motorcyclist
ライフル **raifuru** rifle
来月 **raigetsu** next month
来客 **raikyaku** guest; visitor
ライム **raimu** lime
ライン **rain** line
来年 **rainen** next year
来日する **ranichi suru** visit Japan
ラインズマン **rainzuman** linesman
ライオン **raion** lion
ライラック **rairakku** lilac (*flower*)

来週 **raishū** next week
ライス **raisu** rice (*cooked*)
ライター **raitā** lighter
ライトアップする **raitoappu suru** light, light up, illuminate
ライト級 **raito-kyū** lightweight
ライトウイング **raito-uingu** right wing SP
雷雨 **raiu** thunderstorm
ラジエーター **rajiētā** radiator
ラジオ **rajio** radio
ラジオ放送局 **rajio-hōsōkyoku** radio station
ラケット **raketto** bat; racket
楽観論 **rakkanron** optimism
楽観論者 **rakkanron-sha** optimist
楽観的(な) **rakkanteki (na)** optimistic
楽観要因 **rakkan-yōin** feelgood factor
落下傘兵 **rakkasanhei** paratrooper
ラック **rakku** rack
楽 **raku**: 楽である ***raku de aru*** be comfortable; 楽をする ***raku o suru*** live comfortably; take the easy course
落第する **rakudai suru** fail an exam (*and not be able to move up a grade*)
落書き **rakugaki** graffiti
落書きする **rakugaki suru** scribble
落語 **rakugo** comic story-telling
落後者 **rakugo-sha** dropout; loser
楽に走る **raku ni hashiru** cruise
楽々とした **rakuraku to shita** effortless
落成する **rakusei suru** be completed; inaugurate
落選する **rakusen suru** be defeated
楽勝 **rakushō** walkover
落胆した **rakutan shita** dejected, downhearted
ラーメン **rāmen** Chinese noodles
ラム **ramu** lamb; RAM
ラム酒 **ramu-shu** rum
らん **ran** orchid
欄 **ran** box (*on form*); column (*of text*)
乱暴 **ranbō** violence; hooliganism
乱暴(な) **ranbō (na)** rough, violent; rowdy; destructive
ランチ **ranchi** lunch; launch (*boat*)
ランチョンマット **ranchonmatto** place mat
ランドリー **randorī** laundry
ランジェリー **ranjerī** lingerie
乱気流 **rankiryū** turbulence
ランプ **ranpu** lamp; ramp
卵子 **ranshi** ovum, egg
卵巣 **ransō** ovary
乱闘 **rantō** scuffle
乱用 **ran'yō** abuse
乱用する **ran'yō suru** abuse
乱雑 **ranzatsu** disorder
乱雑(な) **ranzatsu (na)** disorderly
ラオス **Raosu** Laos
ラオス (の) **Raosu (no)** Laotian
ラップ **rappu** clingfilm; shrink-wrapping; lap (*in athletics*); rap MUS
ラップで包む **rappu de tsutsumu** shrink-wrap
ラップトップ **rapputoppu** laptop
られる **-rareru** ◊ (*polite*): 学長は来られますか ***gakuchô wa koraremasu ka*** will the college president come? ◊ (*ability*): 信じられない ***shinjirarenai*** I can't believe it ◊ (*passive*): 部屋は白く塗られていた ***heya wa shiroku nurarete ita*** the room had been painted white ◊ (*intuition*): 何か起こったと感じられた ***nani ka okotta to kanjirareta*** I felt that something must have happened
ラリー **rarī** rally
ら旋階段 **rasen kaidan** spiral staircase
ら旋形 **rasenkei** spiral
らしい **-rashii** apparently ◊ it appears that ◊ typical of; あなたらしい ***anatarashii*** that's typical of you!
ラッシュアワー **rasshu-awā** rush hour
ラストスパートをかける **rasuto-supāto o kakeru** put on a final spurt
ラテンアメリカ **Raten-Amerika** Latin America

ラテンアメリカ人 **Raten-Amerika-jin** Latin American, Hispanic
ラテンアメリカ(の) **Raten-Amerika-(no)** Latin American, Hispanic
ラウンド **raundo** round (*in boxing*)
ラズベリー **razuberī** raspberry
レア **rea** rare
レバー **rebā** lever; liver (*food*)
レベル **reberu** level, amount
レビュー **rebyū** revue
レーダー **rēdā** radar
レフトウイング **refuto-uingu** left wing SP
例 **rei** case, example
礼 **rei** etiquette; thanks; reward; fee; bow
零 **rei** zero
霊 **rei** spirit (*of dead person*)
霊安室 **reianshitsu** mortuary
レイアウトする **reiauto suru** lay out
霊媒師 **reibaishi** medium
冷房 **reibō** air conditioning
例外 **reigai** exception
例外的(な) **reigaiteki (na)** exceptional, special
礼儀 **reigi** courtesy; decency; social niceties
礼儀知らず(の) **reigishirazu (no)** ignorant; impolite
礼儀正しい **reigi-tadashii** polite, civil; respectful; well-mannered
礼儀正しさ **reigitadashi-sa** politeness
礼拝 **reihai** worship
礼拝堂 **reihaidō** chapel
令状 **reijō** warrant
零下 **reika** below zero
霊感 **reikan** inspiration; …から霊感を得る ***… kara reikan o eru*** be inspired by
冷血(の) **reiketsu (no)** cold-blooded
礼金 **reikin** key money (*deposit on apartment*)
冷酷 **reikoku** ruthlessness
冷酷(な) **reikoku (na)** ruthless; cold-blooded; unfeeling; remorseless
冷酷に **reikoku ni** in cold blood
冷却期間 **reikyaku-kikan** cooling-off period; break
冷却する **reikyaku suru** cool; refrigerate
霊きゅう車 **reikyū-sha** hearse
例年(の) **reinen (no)** annual
レインコート **reinkōto** raincoat
冷静(な) **reisei (na)** cool; level-headed; objective; philosophical
冷静さ **reisei-sa** detachment, objectivity
冷笑 **reishō** sneer
冷淡(な) **reitan (na)** cool, icy *welcome*; callous
冷淡に **reitan ni** coolly; indifferently
霊的(な) **reiteki (na)** spiritual
冷凍庫 **reitōko** freezer, deep freeze; freezing compartment
冷凍(の) **reitō (no)** frozen
冷凍室 **reitō-shitsu** icebox
冷凍食品 **reitō-shokuhin** (deep-) frozen food
冷凍する **reitō suru** freeze
冷蔵庫 **reizōko** refrigerator, fridge
冷蔵する **reizō suru** refrigerate
レジ **reji** checkout, cash desk
レジデント(の) **rejidento (no)** resident
レジ係 **reji-gakari** cashier
レジスター **rejisutā** cash register
歴史 **rekishi** history
歴史上(の) **rekishijō (no)** historical
歴史家 **rekishi-ka** historian
レッカー車 **rekkā-sha** wrecker, tow truck
列挙する **rekkyo suru** recite, enumerate
レコード **rekōdo** record MUS
レコードプレイヤー **rekōdo-pureiyā** record player
レモン **remon** lemon
レモネード **remonēdo** lemonade
レモンティー **remon-tī** lemon tea
恋愛 **ren'ai** love; romance
恋愛映画 **ren'ai-eiga** romance (*movie*)
恋愛関係 **ren'ai-kankei** love affair
恋愛小説 **ren'ai-shōsetsu** romance (*novel*)
恋愛する **ren'ai suru** fall in love
れんが **renga** brick
連合 **rengō** confederation; union

連合王国 **Rengō-ōkoku** United Kingdom
レンジ **renji** stove; burner
連日 **renjitsu** day after day
連盟 **renmei** league
練乳 **rennyū** condensed milk
連発 **renpatsu** torrent
連邦 **renpō** federation
連邦(の) **renpō (no)** federal
連絡 **renraku** contact; liaison; から連絡がある ***kara renraku ga aru*** hear from; 連絡が途絶える ***renraku ga todaeru*** lose touch with
連絡道路 **renraku-dōro** access road
連絡先 **renraku-saki** contact number; contact address
連絡している **renraku shite iru** keep in touch with
連絡する **renraku suru** contact; communicate
連絡役を務める **renrakuyaku o tsutomeru** liaise with
連立内閣 **renritsu-naikaku** coalition cabinet
連鎖反応 **rensa-hannō** chain reaction
連載される **rensai sareru** be serialized
練習 **renshū** practice; training; 練習不足である ***renshû-busoku de aru*** be out of practice; be out of training
練習帳 **renshūchō** exercise book
練習計画 **renshū-keikaku** training scheme
練習問題 **renshū-mondai** exercise EDU
練習する **renshū suru** practice
レンタカー **renta-kā** rental car
レントゲン **rentogen** X-ray; レントゲン写真を取る ***rentogen-shashin o toru*** X-ray
連続 **renzoku** sequence, series, succession
連続ホームコメディー **renzoku hōmu-komedī** sitcom
連続公演 **renzoku-kōen** run (*of play*)
連続公演する **renzoku-kōen suru** run (*of play*)
連続メロドラマ **renzoku merodorama** soap (opera)
連続(の) **renzoku (no)** consecutive
連続殺人犯 **renzoku-satsujinhan** serial killer
連続性 **renzokusei** continuity
連続して **renzoku shite** in succession
連続する **renzoku suru** continue
レンズ **renzu** aperture; lens
レオタード **reotādo** leotard
レポート **repōto** report; paper
レプリカ **repurika** replica
れる **-reru** → ***rareru***
レール **rēru** rail
レーサー **rēsā** racing driver
列車 **ressha** train
レシーバー **reshībā** receiver
レーシングカー **rēshingu-kā** racing car
レシピ **reshipi** recipe
レシート **reshīto** receipt
レッスン **ressun** lesson
レース **rēsu** lace; race
レスラー **resurā** wrestler
レスリング **resuringu** wrestling
レストラン **resutoran** restaurant
レタス **retasu** lettuce
レート **rēto** rate
列 **retsu** column; row; tier; line; 列に並ぶ ***retsu ni narabu*** stand in line
劣等感 **rettōkan** inferiority complex
レーザー **rēzā** laser
レーザー光線 **rēzā-kōsen** laser beam
レーザープリンター **rēzā-purintā** laser printer
レズビアン **rezubian** lesbian
リアルタイム **riarutaimu** real time
リバイバル **ribaibaru** revival
リベート **ribēto** kickback
リビア **Ribia** Libya
リビングルーム **ribingu-rūmu** living room, sitting room
リボン **ribon** ribbon
リボルバー **riborubā** revolver
リーダー **rīdā** chief; leader
リーダーシップ **rīdā-shippu** leadership
リード **rīdo** lead (*in race*); リードして

rîdo shite in the lead, in front
リードする **rīdo suru** lead *race*
利益 **rieki** benefit; profit; yield; 利益を上げる ***rieki o ageru*** realize a profit; yield a profit FIN; 利益を得る ***rieki o eru*** benefit; profit
利益のない **rieki no nai** unprofitable
リフレーション **rifureishon** reflation
リーグ **rīgu** league
利幅 **rihaba** mark-up; profit margin
リハーサル **rihāsaru** rehearsal; リハーサルをする ***rihâsaru o suru*** rehearse
理科 **rika** science; science department
理解 **rikai** understanding, comprehension
理解できない **rikai dekinai** incomprehensible ◊ be puzzled
理解できる **rikai dekiru** intelligible
理解し合う **rikai shiau** communicate
理解する **rikai suru** understand; assimilate; take on board
立候補 **rikkōho** candidacy
リコーダー **rikōdā** recorder MUS
離婚 **rikon** divorce
利口(な) **rikō** (**na**) intelligent, clever, bright
離婚した **rikon shita** divorced
離婚する **rikon suru** divorce, get divorced
離婚手当 **rikon-teate** alimony
利口さ **rikō-sa** intelligence
利己主義 **riko-shugi** self-interest
陸 **riku** land
リクエスト **rikuesuto** request
陸軍 **rikugun** army
陸上で **rikujō de** on land
陸上競技場 **rikujō-kyōgijō** athletics stadium
陸路で **rikuro de** by land, overland
理屈 **rikutsu** reason; argument; pretext
リキュール **rikyūru** liqueur
リモートアクセス **rimōto-akusesu** remote access
リモートコントロール **rimōto-kontorōru** remote control
リム **rimu** rim
リムジン **rimujin** limo, limousine
リネン **rinen** linen
りんご **ringo** apple
リング **ringu** ring
林業 **ringyō** forestry
臨時(の) **rinji** (**no**) temporary; extraordinary
臨時職員 **rinji-shokuin** temp
輪郭 **rinkaku** contour; outline
臨機応変(の) **rinki-ōhen** (**no**) resourceful
リンク **rinku** rink
輪ね **rinne** reincarnation
リンパ腺 **rinpasen** lymph gland
倫理学 **rinri-gaku** ethics
リンリンと鳴る音 **rinrin to naru oto** tinkle; jingle
倫理的(な) **rinriteki** (**na**) ethical
隣接(の) **rinsetsu** (**no**) adjacent
隣接した **rinsetsu shita** neighboring
隣接する **rinsetsu suru** border on
臨床(の) **rinshō** (**no**) clinical
リンス **rinsu** conditioner
輪タク **rintaku** pedicab
立派(な) **rippa** (**na**) honorable; noble; admirable; respectable
立法府 **rippōfu** legislature
立法権のある **rippōken no aru** legislative
立法(の) **rippō** (**no**) legislative
立方体 **rippōtai** cube
リレー **rirē** relay (race)
履歴書 **rirekisho** résumé
離陸 **ririku** takeoff
離陸する **ririku suru** rise; take off (*of airplane*)
リリースする **rirīsu suru** bring out *video, CD*
利率 **riritsu** interest rate
理論 **riron** theory
理論的(な) **rironteki** (**na**) theoretical
理論的には **rironteki ni wa** in theory
リール **rīru** reel, spool
リサイクル **risaikuru** recycling
リサイタル **risaitaru** recital
理性 **risei** mind, sanity; reason

理性的(な) **riseiteki** (**na**) rational
利子 **rishi** interest; rate of interest
理想 **risō** role model
理想の高い **risō no takai** idealistic
理想的(な) **risōteki** (**na**) ideal, model
立証 **risshō** demonstration, proof
立食 **risshoku** buffet
立証する **risshō suru** demonstrate, prove
りす **risu** squirrel
リスト **risuto** list
リターン **ritān** return
利他的(な) **ritateki** (**na**) altruistic
立地条件 **ritchi-jōken** location; neighborhood
利点 **riten** advantage, plus
率 **ritsu** rate
立案者 **ritsuan-sha** draftsman; planner
立案する **ritsuan suru** form a plan
立体影像 **rittaieizō** hologram
立体交差 **rittai-kōsa** (overhead) interchange
立体的 **rittaiteki** three-dimensional
リットル **rittoru** liter
利用できる **riyō dekiru** have access to ◊ available
利用する **riyō suru** utilize; use *pej*: *person*; exploit *resources*; take advantage of *opportunity*
理由 **riyū** reason; 理由もなく ***riyû mo naku*** for nothing, for no reason
利ざや **rizaya** (profit) margin
リゾート **rizōto** resort
リズム **rizumu** rhythm; throb; リズムを打つ ***rizumu o utsu*** throb
ろうあ(の) **rōa** (**no**) deaf-and-dumb
ろば **roba** donkey
ろうばい **rōbai** consternation
ろうばい売り **rōbai uri** panic selling
ロビー **robī** lobby; lounge (*in hotel, airport*)
ロボット **robotto** robot
ロブスター **robusutā** lobster
労働 **rōdō** labor
労働ビザ **rōdō-biza** work permit
労働組合 **rōdō-kumiai** labor union
朗読する **rōdoku suru** read out; recite
労働力 **rōdōryoku** workforce
労働者 **rōdō-sha** worker; laborer
労働者階級 **rōdōsha-kaikyū** working class
労働争議 **rōdō-sōgi** industrial dispute
漏えい **rōei** leak; disclosure
ローファー **rōfā** loafer (*shoe*)
ロゴ **rogo** logo
浪費 **rōhi** waste
浪費家 **rōhi-ka** spendthrift
浪費する **rōhi suru** waste; squander
路地 **roji** alley, lane
老人 **rōjin** elderly person
老人ホーム **rōjin-hōmu** nursing home
廊下 **rōka** corridor
路肩 **rokata** verge
ロケ中で **roke-chū de** on location
ロケット **roketto** locket; rocket
ロッカー **rokkā** locker
ろっ骨 **rokkotsu** rib
ロック **rokku** rock MUS
ロックンロール **rokkun-rōru** rock'n'roll
ロックスター **rokku-stā** rock star
六 **roku** six
録画 **rokuga** video recording
録画する **rokuga suru** video
六月 **rokugatsu** June
録音 **rokuon** recording
録音する **rokuon suru** tape
録音スタジオ **rokuon-sutajio** recording studio
ロム **ROM** ROM, read only memory
ローマ法王 **Rōma-hōō** Pope
ローマ字 **rōmaji** Roman script, romaji
ロマンチック(な) **romanchikku** (**na**) romantic
路面電車 **romen-densha** streetcar
論 **ron** theory
ローン **rōn** bank loan
論文 **ronbun** paper (*academic*); thesis
老年 **rōnen** old age
老年医学 **rōnen-igaku** geriatric
ロングドレス **rongu-doresu** gown
ロング(の) **rongu** (**no**) full-length
浪人 **rōnin** *student who will resit*

college entrance examinations
論じる **ronjiru** discuss; maintain, assert; argue
論破 **ronpa** refutation; demolition
論理 **ronri** logic
論理的(な) **ronriteki (na)** logical
論争 **ronsō** conflict, dispute; controversy
ロープ **rōpu** rope
ローラーブレード **rōrā-burēdo** roller blade
ローラースケート **rōrā-sukēto** roller skate
老齢身障者医療保険制度 **rōrei-shinshōsha-iryō-hoken-seido** Medicare
老練(な) **rōren (na)** experienced; veteran
ロールパン **rōru-pan** bread roll
労力 **rōryoku** labor; workforce
ロシア **Roshia** Russia
ロシア語 **Roshia-go** Russian (*language*)
ロシア人 **Roshia-jin** Russian (*person*)
ローション **rōshon** lotion
露出不足(の) **roshutsu-busoku (no)** underexposed
露出狂 **roshutsukyō** exhibitionist
露出する **roshutsu suru** expose
ろうそく **rōsoku** candle
ろうそく立て **rōsokutate** candlestick
ロースト **rōsuto** roast
ローストビーフ **rōsuto-bīfu** roast beef
ロータリー **rōtarī** traffic circle
露天風呂 **rotenburo** open-air hot spa
ルビー **rubī** ruby
類似 **ruiji** analogy; similarity
類人猿 **ruijin'en** ape
類似した **ruiji shita** similar
類似点 **ruijiten** resemblance, likeness; parallel
ルームサービス **rūmu-sābisu** room service
ルール **rūru** rule
留守番電話 **rusuban-denwa** answerphone; voicemail
留守番する **rusuban suru** look after the house / apartment
留守である **rusu de aru** be out; be away
ルート **rūto** route
ルーツ **rūtsu** roots
るつぼ **rutsubo** melting pot
略 **ryaku** abbreviation; …の略である ***... no ryaku de aru*** stand for
略奪者 **ryakudatsu-sha** looter
略奪する **ryakudatsu suru** loot
略する **ryaku suru** abbreviate
量 **ryō** amount, quantity; volume
寮 **ryō** dormitory
漁 **ryō** fishing
猟 **ryō** hunting
両開き(の) **ryōbiraki (no)** double *doors*
領土 **ryōdo** territory
領土(の) **ryōdo (no)** territorial
両替する **ryōgae suru** exchange
両側 **ryōgawa** both sides
両端 **ryōtan** both ends
両方(の) **ryōhō (no)** both; 両方とも ***ryôhô tomo*** both of them
領域 **ryōiki** preserve; domain
領事 **ryōji** consul
領事館 **ryōji-kan** consulate
領海 **ryōkai** territorial waters
了解する **ryōkai suru** agree; understand
旅館 **ryokan** Japanese-style inn
旅券 **ryoken** passport
料金 **ryōkin** fee; charge; rate
料金表 **ryōkinhyō** price list; tariff
料金所 **ryōkin-jo** toll booth
旅行 **ryokō** journey; trip; travels
旅行代理店 **ryokō-dairiten** tour operator
旅行会社 **ryokō-gaisha** tour operator
旅行保険 **ryokō-hoken** travel insurance
旅行かばん **ryokō-kaban** suitcase
旅行者 **ryokō-sha** traveler
旅行者用小切手 **ryokōshayō-kogitte** traveler's check
旅行する **ryokō suru** travel; tour
領空 **ryōkū** airspace
緑茶 **ryokucha** green tea
両極化する **ryōkyokuka suru** polarize

料理 **ryōri** cooking (*food*); dish (*part of meal*)
料理(の) **ryōri** (**no**) cookery; culinary
料理する **ryōri suru** cook
両立する **ryōritsu suru** be compatible
量産する **ryōsan suru** mass produce
寮生 **ryōsei** *student who lives on campus*
良性(の) **ryōsei** (**no**) benign
漁師 **ryōshi** fisherman
猟師 **ryōshi** hunter
良心 **ryōshin** conscience; 良心のとがめ ***ryôshin no togame*** scruples
両親 **ryōshin** parents
良心的(な) **ryōshinteki** (**na**) conscientious
領収書 **ryōshū-sho** receipt
両手 **ryōte** both hands
料亭 **ryōtei** quality restaurant
療養所 **ryōyō-jo** sanitarium
竜 **ryū** dragon
留置場 **ryūchijō** police cell; lockup
流ちょうに **ryūchō ni** fluently
流動体 **ryūdōtai** fluid
留学する **ryūgaku suru** study abroad
留学生 **ryūgakusei** overseas student
流儀 **ryūgi** fashion; style
流感 **ryūkan** flu
流血 **ryūketsu** bloodshed
リュックサック **ryukku-sakku** rucksack
流行 **ryūkō** epidemic; fashion, style
流行(の) **ryūkō** (**no**) fashionable
流行遅れである **ryūkō-okure de aru** be out (of fashion)
流行遅れになる **ryūkō-okure ni naru** go out of style
流行する **ryūkō suru** be in fashion; break out (*of disease*)
竜骨 **ryūkotsu** keel
琉球 **Ryūkyū** *historical name for Okinawa*
リューマチ **ryūmachi** rheumatism
留年する **ryūnen suru** repeat a year
流星 **ryūsei** meteor
流星のよう(な) **ryūsei no yō** (**na**) meteoric
流線形(の) **ryūsenkei** (**no**) streamlined
粒子 **ryūshi** particle
流出する **ryūshutsu suru** drain away, drain off
流通 **ryūtsū** distribution
流通業者 **ryūtsū-gyōsha** distributor
流産 **ryūzan** miscarriage

S

さ **-sa** (*familiar emphatic particle used mostly by men*): もう、いいさ ***mô iisa*** that's enough
差 **sa** difference; gap; remainder; 2、3分の差で ***ni, sanpun no sa de*** by a couple of minutes
さあ **sā** well; right; come on!
さば **saba** mackerel
サーバー **sābā** scoop; server (*in tennis*), COMPUT; サーバーにデータを送る ***sâbâ ni dêta o okuru*** upload
さばけた **sabaketa** down-to-earth; wordly-wise
砂漠 **sabaku** desert
差別 **sabetsu** discrimination; segregation
差別する **sabetsu suru** discriminate
さび **sabi** rust
さびない **sabinai** rust-proof
さびれた **sabireta** bleak; deserted
さびれている **sabirete iru** run-down

さびる **sabiru** rust
寂しい **sabishii** lonely; …がいなくなって寂しい ***… ga inaku natte sabishii*** miss
サービス **sābisu** service
サービスエリア **sābisu-eria** service area
サービス(の) **sābisu** (**no**) complimentary
サービス料 **sābisu-ryō** service charge
サービス産業 **sābisu-sangyō** service industry, service sector
さびた **sabita** rusty
さび取り剤 **sabitorizai** rust remover
さぼる **saboru** skip *class*; 学校をさぼる ***gakkô o saboru*** play hooky
サボタージュ **sabotāju** go-slow
さぼてん **saboten** cactus
サーブ **sābu** serve (*in tennis*)
サーブする **sābu suru** serve (*in tennis*)
サーチ **sāchi** search COMPUT
サーチライト **sāchiraito** searchlight
定まらない **sadamaranai** variable
定める **sadameru** set, arrange
サディスト **sadisuto** sadist
サディズム **sadizumu** sadism
茶道 **sadō** tea ceremony
作動していない **sadō shite inai** be down (*not working*)
作動する **sadō suru** go, work; run; start to operate
…さえ **… sae** even
さえぎる **saegiru** obstruct; block
さえない **saenai** drab; plain
さえずる **saezuru** twitter; warble (*of birds*)
サーファー **sāfā** (wind)surfer
サファイア **safaia** sapphire
サーフィン **sāfin** surfing
サーフボード **sāfu-bōdo** sailboard; surfboard
差額 **sagaku** balance, remainder
砂岩 **sagan** sandstone
下がる **sagaru** drop, come down (*in price etc*)
捜し出す **sagashidasu** trace; dig out, root out
探し回る, 捜しまわる **sagashimawaru** poke around; scour, search
探す, 捜す **sagasu** search for, hunt for, seek
下がっている **sagatte iru** be down (*of price, rate*); stand back, keep back
下げる **sageru** reduce, lower; keep down *voice, noise*; bow *head*
下げ相場 **sagesōba** bear market
さぎ **sagi** heron
詐欺 **sagi** fraud; racket (*criminal*), scam; rip-off
詐欺師 **sagishi** fraud, trickster
探り出す **saguridasu** dig up *information*
さぐる **saguru** spy on; grope for, feel for
作業 **sagyō** work; operation
作業場 **sagyōba** workshop
作業台 **sagyōdai** (work)bench
左派 **saha** left POL
さい **sai** rhinoceros
際 **sai** occasion
才 **sai** ability; gift; years old
歳 **-sai** years old
最愛(の) **saiai** (**no**) beloved
最悪(の) **saiaku** (**no**) worst; 最悪の場合には ***saiaku no bâi ni wa*** if the worst comes to worst; 最悪の事態 ***saiaku no jitai*** the worst
栽培する **saibai suru** cultivate; grow *flowers, vegetables*
裁判 **saiban** trial, court case; judgment
裁判官 **saibankan** judge; 裁判にかけられて ***saiban ni kakerarete*** on trial
裁判所 **saiban-sho** courthouse
裁判所命令 **saibansho-meirei** court order
裁判する **saiban suru** try LAW
サイバースペース **saibāsupēsu** cyberspace
細胞 **saibō** cell BIO
再分割する **saibunkatsu suru** subdivide
再調整する **saichōsei suru** rearrange, reschedule
最中 **saichū** middle
再注文 **saichūmon** repeat order

最大限 saidaigen maximum; 最大限に利用する ***saidaigen ni riyô suru*** make the best of
最大にする saidai ni suru maximize
最大(の) saidai (no) maximum; utmost
祭壇 saidan altar
サイドブレーキ saidoburēki parking brake
サイドライン saidorain sideline
サイドライト saidoraito sidelight
財布 saifu pocketbook, wallet
災害 saigai disaster
再現する saigen suru reconstruct *crime*; reproduce *atmosphere*
さい疑心 saigishin paranoia
最期 saigo last moments; death
最後に saigo ni in conclusion, finally, lastly
最後(の) saigo (no) final, last; latest; 最後は…になる ***saigo wa ... ni naru*** end up (*doing something*)
最後通ちょう saigotsūchō ultimatum
再軍備する saigunbi suru rearm
再発 saihatsu relapse
再発する saihatsu suru have a relapse; recur
再編成 saihensei reorganization; shake-up
再編成する saihensei suru reorganize
裁縫 saihō sewing
再放送 saihōsō repeat
細字部分 saiji-bubun small print
再上演する saijōen suru revive *play etc*
最上階 saijōkai top *floor*
最上(の) saijō (no) best
最重要(の) saijūyō (no) of prime importance
再開 saikai renewal
再開発する saikaihatsu suru redevelop
再会させる saikai saseru reunite
再開する saikai suru renew *discussions*; reopen *business*
債券 saiken bond FIN
債権者 saiken-sha creditor
再建する saiken suru reconstruct *city*
再検討 saikentō review
再検討する saikentō suru review
細菌 saikin bacteria
最近 saikin recently, lately, of late
細菌戦争 saikin-sensō germ warfare
最高 saikō top *speed, note*
最後尾(の) saikōbi (no) rearmost
最高幹部 saikō-kanbu top *management, official*
最高機密(の) saikō-kimitsu (no) top secret
最高記録 saikō-kiroku high (*in statistics*); record SP
最高(の) saikō (no) best; maximum; supreme; utmost; top
再婚する saikon suru remarry
さいころ saikoro dice
最高裁判所 Saikō-saibansho Supreme Court
最高責任者 Saikō-sekininsha CEO, Chief Executive Officer
最高司令官 saikō-shireikan commander-in-chief, supreme commander
サイクリング saikuringu cycling
サイクル saikuru cycle
採掘 saikutsu extraction (*of coal, oil*)
採掘する saikutsu suru mine; extract
催眠状態 saimin-jōtai hypnosis
催眠術をかける saiminjutsu o kakeru hypnotize
催眠療法 saimin-ryōhō hypnotherapy
サイン sain autograph
最年長者 sainenchō-sha eldest
才能 sainō aptitude; talent, flair; 才能がある ***sainô ga aru*** talented; gifted ◊ be gifted
さいの目に切る sai no me ni kiru dice, cut
歳入 sainyū revenue
サイレン sairen siren
再利用できる sairiyō dekiru reusable
再利用する sairiyō suru recycle, reuse
催涙ガス sairui-gasu tear gas
再三(の) saisan (no) repeated

再生 **saisei** playback, replay; reproduction
再生する **saisei suru** play; rerun *tape*
さい銭 **saisen** money offering REL
最先端 **saisentan** frontier
最先端(の) **saisentan (no)** leading-edge
妻子 **saishi** family; wife and children
再試合 **saishiai** replay
最新版 **saishinban** update; latest edition
最新技術(の) **saishin-gijutsu (no)** state-of-the-art
最新(の) **saishin (no)** latest; up-to-date
細心(の) **saishin (no)** meticulous
最新流行(の) **saishin-ryūkō (no)** up-to-date
最新式(の) **saishinshiki (no)** up-to-date
最初は **saisho wa** at first; originally
最小限(の) **saishōgen (no)** minimal
菜食主義(の) **saishoku-shugi (no)** vegetarian
菜食主義者 **saishoku-shugisha** vegetarian
最初に **saisho ni** first, beforehand
最小にする **saishō ni suru** minimize
最初のうちは **saisho no uchi wa** to begin with, at first
最終 **saishū** end
最終決定する **saishū-kettei suru** finalize
最終(の) **saishū (no)** final, last
最終的(な) **saishūteki (na)** eventual
最終的には **saishūteki ni wa** at the last count
催促状 **saisokujō** reminder (*for payment*)
催促する **saisoku suru** remind; urge
咲いた **saita** open *flower*
再逮捕する **saitaiho suru** recapture
最低 **saitei** a minimum of
最低賃金 **saitei-chingin** minimum wage
最低記録 **saitei-kiroku** low (*in statistics*)
最低にする **saitei ni suru** minimize
最低(の) **saitei (no)** lousy; minimum
咲いている **saite iru** be out, be open (*of flower*)
最適条件 **saiteki-jōken** optimum
最適(な) **saiteki (na)** optimum
再点検する **saitenken suru** doublecheck
採点する **saiten suru** correct, mark
再統合する **saitōgō suru** reunite
再統一 **saitōitsu** reunification
幸いにも **saiwai ni mo** luckily, happily
採用 **saiyō** adoption (*of plan*)
採用する **saiyō suru** adopt *plan*
最善を尽くす **saizen o tsukusu** do one's best, do one's utmost
最前列 **saizenretsu** front row
サイズ **saizu** format; size
さじ **saji** spoon
坂 **saka** slope; hill
酒場 **sakaba** bar
栄える **sakaeru** thrive
境 **sakai** border; boundary
魚 **sakana** fish
魚屋 **sakana-ya** fishmonger
盛ん(な) **sakan (na)** flourishing
さかのぼる **sakanoboru** date back, go back ◊ retroactive
逆らう **sakarau** contradict; disobey
盛りにある **sakari ni aru** be in one's prime
盛りを過ぎる **sakari o sugiru** go to seed; go down in the world
逆さまに **sakasama ni** upside down
逆さま(の) **sakasama (no)** topsy-turvy
サーカス **sākasu** circus
酒屋 **sakaya** liquor store
酒 **sake** alcohol; liquor; rice wine; 酒を飲む ***sake o nomu*** drink *alcohol*; 酒を絶つ ***sake o tatsu*** stop drinking
さけ **sake** salmon
叫び声 **sakebigoe** cry, call; yell; shouting
叫ぶ **sakebu** cry, call; yell; exclaim
裂け目 **sakeme** rip, tear; split (*in fabric, wood*); 裂け目をいれる ***sakeme o ireru*** crack, decipher *code*
酒飲み **sakenomi** drinker

避けられない **sakerarenai** inevitable, unavoidable
避ける **sakeru** avoid; avert; evade; shun
裂ける **sakeru** split, tear
先 **saki** point, tip; 先へ進む ***saki e susumu*** continue, push on; 先を考える ***saki o kangaeru*** think ahead
先駆け **sakigake** pioneer
先物取引 **sakimono-torihiki** futures FIN
先(の) **saki** (**no**) former; recent; future
サーキット **sākitto** circuit
作家 **sakka** writer
サッカー **sakkā** soccer, football
錯覚 **sakkaku** delusion, illusion
サッカリン **sakkarin** saccharin
さっき **sakki** a little while ago; some time ago
殺菌した **sakkin shita** sterile
殺菌する **sakkin suru** sterilize
作曲 **sakkyoku** composition MUS
作曲家 **sakkyoku-ka** composer
作曲する **sakkyoku suru** compose MUS
鎖国 **sakoku** national seclusion
鎖骨 **sakotsu** collarbone
さく **saku** barrier; fence; railings
策 **saku** plan; scheme; policy
咲く **saku** open (*of flower*) ; 花が咲く ***hana ga saku*** bloom, flower
裂く **saku** rip; split
作文 **sakubun** composition, essay
削減 **sakugen** cut, cutback
削減する **sakugen suru** ax; reduce, cut back
作品 **sakuhin** work (*of art, literature*)
索引 **sakuin** index (*of book*)
昨日 **sakujitsu** yesterday
削除 **sakujo** deletion
削除する **sakujo suru** delete
昨年 **sakunen** last year
桜 **sakura** cherry blossom
さくらんぼ **sakuranbo** cherry (*fruit*)
策略 **sakuryaku** maneuver; trap, set-up; 策略に富む ***sakuryaku ni tomu*** tactical
作成する **sakusei suru** prepare, draw up *document*
作戦 **sakusen** maneuver; tactics
作者 **sakusha** author
作詞家 **sakushi-ka** lyricist, songwriter
搾取 **sakushu** exploitation
搾取する **sakushu suru** exploit
サクソフォーン **sakusofōn** saxophone
昨夜 **sakuya** last night
砂丘 **sakyū** sand dune
…様 **… sama** Mr/Mrs/Ms (*in addresses*)
冷ます **samasu** cool down
覚ます **samasu** wake up
妨げる **samatageru** hinder, hamper; prevent; obstruct
さまよう **samayou** roam; drift (*of person*)
様々(な) **samazama** (**na**) diverse, varied; various, several
さめ **same** shark
冷める **sameru** cool, cool down; die down (*of excitement*)
覚める **sameru** wake up; sober up
サミット **samitto** summit
さもないと **samonai to** otherwise, or else
サーモスタット **sāmostatto** thermostat
寒い **samui** cold; fresh *weather*
寒気 **samuke** chill (*illness*); 寒気がする ***samuke ga suru*** chilly ◊ I'm chilly
侍 **samurai** samurai
寒さ **samu-sa** cold; freshness
酸 **san** acid
…さん **… san** Mr; Mrs; Ms; 賢さん ***Ken-san*** Ken
…山 **… san** Mount
三 **san** three
三倍になる **sanbai ni naru** treble
賛美歌 **sanbika** hymn
散文 **sanbun** prose
産地 **sanchi** home
散弾銃 **sandanjū** shotgun
サンダル **sandaru** sandal
サンドイッチ **sandoitchi** sandwich
産婦人科 **sanfujinka** obstetrics and gynecology
三月 **sangatsu** March
参議院 **sangiin** House of Councilors

さんご **sango** coral
サングラス **sangurasu** sunglasses, dark glasses
産業 **sangyō** industry
産業廃棄物 **sangyō-haikibutsu** industrial waste
三乗(の) **sanjō (no)** cubic
三重奏 **sanjūsō** trio MUS
参加 **sanka** participation
酸化物 **sankabutsu** oxide
産科病棟 **sanka-byōtō** maternity ward
産科医 **sankai** obstetrician
三角形 **sankakkei** triangle
三角巾 **sankakukin** sling (*for arm*)
三角(の) **sankaku (no)** triangular
参加させる **sanka saseru** involve, bring in
参加者 **sanka-sha** participant; competitor
参加する **sanka suru** participate; compete, take part
参考 **sankō** reference
参考図書 **sankōtosho** reference book
三脚 **sankyaku** tripod
産休 **sankyū** maternity leave
さんま **sanma** saury
山脈 **sanmyaku** range (*of mountains*)
参入 **sannyū** penetration (*of market*)
参入する **sannyū suru** penetrate
散髪する **sanpatsu suru** have a haircut
賛否両論 **sanpi-ryōron** the pros and cons
散歩 **sanpo** stroll
山腹 **sanpuku** hillside, slope
サンプル **sanpuru** sample
三輪車 **sanrinsha** tricycle
三流(の) **sanryū (no)** third-rate
山菜 **sansai** edible wild plant
賛成 **sansei** approval, blessing
賛成している **sansei shite iru** agreeable, in agreement
賛成する **sansei suru** agree, assent; approve; go along; hold with
酸性雨 **sanseiu** acid rain
参照する **sanshō suru** refer to, consult *dictionary etc*
酸素 **sanso** oxygen
算数 **sansū** arithmetic
サンタクロース **santakurōsu** Santa Claus
さっぱりした **sappari shita** refreshing
さっぱりする **sappari suru** freshen up
皿 **sara** dish; plate
サラブレッド **sarabureddo** thoroughbred
サラダ **sarada** salad
再来年 **sarainen** the year after next
再来週 **saraishū** the week after next
さらに **sara ni** in addition, moreover; even more, still more; さらに大きく/よく ***sara ni ôkiku / yoku*** even bigger / better
サラリーマン **sararīman** salaried office worker, salaryman
さらさらと鳴る **sarasara to naru** rustle
さらされる **sarasareru** bear the brunt of; be exposed; 風雨にさらされた ***fûu ni sarasareta*** weather-beaten
さらす **sarasu** subject; expose
さらう **sarau** dredge; drag *canal, river*; kidnap
される **sareru** ◊ (*polite form of* **suru**): 教授が講演される ***kyôju ga kôen sareru*** the professor will also give us a lecture ◊ (*passive of* **suru**): 連載される ***rensai sareru*** be serialized
さりげない **sarigenai** throw-away, casual *remark*
サーロイン **sāroin** sirloin
去る **saru** go (*of people*); leave
猿 **saru** monkey
猿ぐつわ **sarugutsuwa** gag; 猿ぐつわをかませる ***sarugutsuwa o kamaseru*** gag
支える **sasaeru** bear *weight*; support; prop up; keep in place
捧げる **sasageru** dedicate, devote; donate
ささい(な) **sasai (na)** trivial; little
ささいなこと **sasai na koto** detail, trifle, irrelevancy

ささやか(な) **sasayaka (na)** modest *house*
ささやき **sasayaki** whisper
ささやく **sasayaku** whisper
…させられる **… saserareru** be made to
…させる **… saseru** let, allow; make; 彼の思うようにさせる ***kare no omou yô ni saseru*** leave himself to his own resources; 意識を回復させる ***ishiki o kaifuku saseru*** bring around
差し上げる **sashiageru** (*polite*) give; present; offer
差し当たり **sashiatari** for the moment
差出人 **sashidashi-nin** sender
差し出す **sashidasu** hold out, put out *hand*
挿絵 **sashie** illustration, picture
差し引く **sashihiku**: YからXを差し引く ***Y kara X o sashihiku*** deduct X from Y
差し込む **sashikomu** insert
さしみ **sashimi** sashimi
差し迫った **sashisematta** impending, imminent; dire
差し迫っている **sashisematte iru** be pending, be about to happen
指し示す **sashishimesu** point out, indicate
指図 **sashizu** directions; instructions
査証 **sashō** visa
誘う **sasou** entice; invite
サッシ **sasshi** sash (*in window*)
早速 **sassoku** immediately; at once
察する **sassuru** guess; infer; imagine
刺す **sasu** bite; sting; prick, jab; stab; ナイフで刺す ***naifu de sasu*** knife, stab
指す **sasu** point; point to
さすがに **sasuga ni** as expected
サスペンダー **sasupendā** suspenders
サスペンション **sasupenshon** suspension (*of vehicle*)
サスペンス **sasupensu** suspense
刺すよう(な) **sasu yō (na)** piercing
殺虫剤 **satchūzai** insecticide; pesticide
さて **sate** right; now; well
査定 **satei** evaluation, assessment
査定する **satei suru** assess, evaluate
サテン **saten** satin
砂糖 **satō** sugar
里帰り **satogaeri** homecoming
里子 **satogo** foster child
砂糖きび **satō kibi** sugar cane
里親 **satooya** foster parents
悟り **satori** enlightenment
悟る **satoru** be enlightened; realize
冊 **satsu** *countword for books*
札 **satsu** paper money; bill
撮影現場 **satsuei-genba** (film) set
撮影所 **satsuei-sho** (film) studio
撮影する **satsuei suru** film; shoot *movie*
殺害する **satsugai suru** murder
札入れ **satsuire** billfold
殺人 **satsujin** homicide, murder, killing
殺人犯 **satsujin-han** killer, murderer
殺人鬼 **satsujinki** butcher, murderer
殺人捜査課 **satsujin-sōsa-ka** homicide (*department*)
さつま芋 **satsuma-imo** sweet potato
さっと **satto** suddenly; quickly
殺到 **sattō** stampede; rush; deluge
殺到する **sattō suru** flood
サウジアラビア **Sauji-Arabia** Saudi Arabia
サウジアラビア(の) **Sauji-Arabia (no)** Saudi Arabian
サウナ **sauna** sauna
サウンドトラック **saundotrakku** soundtrack
騒がしい **sawagashii** noisy; boisterous
騒ぎ **sawagi** commotion, hullabaloo; noise; trouble; 騒ぎを起こす ***sawagi o okosu*** make a fuss; cause a stir
騒ぎ立てる **sawagitateru** carry on, make a fuss
さわら **sawara** Spanish mackerel
触る **sawaru** touch; feel
障る **sawaru** grate; jar on

さわやか(な) **sawayaka (na)** fresh, cool; invigorating *climate*; crisp *weather*
さわやかさ **sawayaka-sa** freshness (*of weather*)
さや **saya** husk; pod; sheath (*for knife*)
左翼 **sayoku** left-wing
さようなら **sayōnara** goodbye
左右する **sayū suru** affect; influence; decide
さざえ **sazae** top shell
さざ波 **sazanami** ripple
さぞ **sazo** how; surely
授かる **sazukaru** be given; be blessed with; be taught
授ける **sazukeru** give; award; teach
背 **se** back; spine (*of book*); height; 背が高い ***se ga takai*** tall; 背の低い ***se no hikui*** short; …に背を向ける ***… ni se o mukeru*** turn one's back on
背広 **sebiro** suit (*for men*)
背骨 **sebone** spine; spinal column,
セーブ **sēbu** save SP
セーブする **sēbu suru** save SP
世代 **sedai** generation; 世代の断絶 ***sedai no danzetsu*** generation gap
セダン **sedan** sedan
セーフティーコーン **sēfutī-kōn** (traffic) cone
せがむ **segamu** press for *reform, payment*
せい **sei** fault; あなた/私のせいです ***anata/watashi no sei desu*** it's your/my fault; せいにする ***sei ni suru*** blame
性 **sei** gender
姓 **sei** family name
性別 **seibetsu** sex, gender
整備された **seibi sareta** roadworthy; tuned up; serviced
整備する **seibi suru** provide; equip
西部 **seibu** west (*of a country*)
西部劇 **seibugeki** western (*movie*)
生物 **seibutsu** organism
生物学 **seibutsugaku** biology
性病 **seibyō** venereal disease
成長 **seichō** growth
成長できる **seichō dekiru** viable (*able to survive*)
成長する **seichō suru** grow up
静電気 **seidenki** static (electricity)
制度 **seido** system
青銅 **seidō** bronze (*metal*)
精鋭(の) **seiei (no)** elite
精液 **seieki** semen; sperm
声援する **seien suru** cheer, cheer on
政府 **seifu** government
征服 **seifuku** conquest
制服 **seifuku** uniform
征服者 **seifuku-sha** conqueror
征服する **seifuku suru** conquer
製粉工場 **seifun-kōjō** mill (*for grain*)
請願書 **seigansho** petition
制限 **seigen** limit, restriction
制限速度 **seigen-sokudo** speed limit
制限する **seigen suru** limit, restrict
正義 **seigi** justice
正義感の強い **seigikan no tsuyoi** moral
制御盤 **seigyoban** control panel
正反対(の) **seihantai (no)** inverse; opposite; diametrically opposed
製品 **seihin** product
正方形 **seihōkei** square (*shape*)
製本 **seihon** binding (*of book*)
声域 **seiiki** range (*of voice*)
聖域 **seiiki** sanctuary
誠意のない **seii no nai** insincere
静寂 **seijaku** silence; tranquility
政治 **seiji** politics
政治部記者 **seijibu-kisha** political correspondent
政治犯 **seijihan** political detainee
政治家 **seijika** politician
成人の日 **Seijin no hi** Adult's Day
成人映画 **seijin-eiga** adult film
成人教育 **seijin-kyōiku** adult education
政治(の) **seiji (no)** political
政治体制 **seiji-taisei** political system; regime
政治的(な) **seijiteki (na)** political
誠実 **seijitsu** fidelity; sincerity
誠実(な) **seijitsu (na)** truthful; sincere; faithful
正常 **seijō** normality
正常化する **seijōka suru** normalize

relationship
星条旗 **Seijōki** Stars and Stripes
正常に **seijō ni** normally
成熟 **seijuku** maturity; ripeness
成熟期 **seijukuki** maturity, adulthood
成熟する **seijuku suru** mature (*of person*)
正解 **seikai** correct answer
性格 **seikaku** character, nature; 性格の不一致 ***seikaku no fuitchi*** incompatibility (*of people*); 性格の悪い ***seikaku no warui*** ill-natured; 性格のいい ***seikaku no ii*** good-natured
正確である **seikaku de aru** be right (*of clock*)
正確(な) **seikaku (na)** accurate; exact, precise
正確さ **seikaku-sa** accuracy; precision
聖歌隊 **seikatai** choir
生活 **seikatsu** life; livelihood
生活費 **seikatsu-hi** cost of living; housekeeping (money); keep
生活保護を受けている **seikatsu-hogo o ukete iru** be on welfare
生活協同組合 **seikatsu-kyōdō-kumiai** cooperative (*store*)
生活習慣病 **seikatsu-shūkanbyō** lifestyle disease
生活水準 **seikatsu-suijun** standard of living
生活様式 **seikatsu-yōshiki** way of life
生計 **seikei** livelihood; 生計を立てる ***seikei o tateru*** earn one's living
整形外科(の) **seikei-geka (no)** orthopedic
整形手術 **seikei-shujutsu** plastic surgery
政権 **seiken** political power; government, administration; 政権を握った ***seiken o nigitta*** in power
清潔(な) **seiketsu (na)** clean; spotless
生気 **seiki** animation, liveliness; 生気のない ***seiki no nai*** lifeless
世紀 **seiki** century
性器 **seiki** genitals
正規(の) **seiki (no)** regular; formal; full-time *student*
成功 **seikō** success
性交 **seikō** (sexual) intercourse
性交感染病 **seikō-kansen-byō** sexually transmitted disease
成功した **seikō shita** prosperous, successful
成功する **seikō suru** succeed
請求 **seikyū** claim (*for damages, insurance*)
請求書 **seikyūsho** bill; invoice; 請求書を送る ***seikyûsho o okuru*** bill; invoice
請求する **seikyū suru** charge *sum of money*; claim
声明 **seimei** statement, announcement
生命 **seimei** life; existence
姓名 **seimei** full name
青年 **seinen** youth; young person
生年月日 **seinengappi** date of birth
成年期 **seinenki** manhood, maturity
性能 **seinō** performance (*of machine*)
性能が悪い **seinō ga warui** perform badly
性能がよい **seinō ga yoi** perform well
生来(の) **seirai (no)** innate
聖霊 **Seirei** Holy Spirit
西暦 **Seireki** Western calendar; AD
整列する **seiretsu suru** line up
生理 **seiri** menstruation; period; 生理がある ***seiri ga aru*** menstruate
セーリングする **sēringu suru** sail
整理する **seiri suru** order, sort out; arrange
成立する **seiritsu suru** come into existence; be established
生理用ナプキン **seiriyō napukin** (sanitary) napkin
清涼飲料水 **seiryō-inryōsui** soft drink
精力 **seiryoku** energy (*of person*); strength (*of organization*); 精力を傾けた ***seiryoku o katamuketa*** energetic *measures*; 精力を使い果たす ***seiryoku o tsukaihatasu*** burn oneself out
勢力 **seiryoku** power; influence

精力的(な) **seiryokuteki (na)** energetic; spirited
制裁 **seisai** punishment; penalty
政策 **seisaku** policy
製作 **seisaku** production (*of movie etc*)
製作費 **seisakuhi** production costs
製作する **seisaku suru** produce *movie etc*
清算 **seisan** settlement *of debts*; liquidation
生産 **seisan** production
生産物 **seisanbutsu** product
生産高 **seisandaka** output
生産力 **seisanryoku** capacity (*of factory*); 生産力の高い ***seisanryoku no takai*** productive
生産性 **seisansei** productivity
生産者 **seisan-sha** producer
清算する **seisan suru** go into liquidation; settle, pay *bill*
生産する **seisan suru** produce
生産的(な) **seisanteki (na)** productive
精製所 **seisei-jo** refinery
生成する **seisei suru** generate
精製する **seisei suru** refine
成績 **seiseki** grade; result; performance
正社員 **seishain** permanent employee
正社員(の) **seishain (no)** full-time
生死 **seishi** life and death
精子 **seishi** sperm
精子銀行 **seishi-ginkō** sperm bank
正式(の) **seishiki (no)** formal
精神 **seishin** soul, spirit; 精神が錯乱した ***seishin ga sakuran shita*** delirious
精神安定剤 **seishin-anteizai** tranquilizer
精神分裂症 **seishin-bunretsushō** schizophrenia
精神分析 **seishin-bunseki** psychoanalysis
精神分析医 **seishin-bunsekii** psychoanalyst
精神分析をする **seishin-bunseki o suru** psychoanalyse
精神病 **seishin-byō** mental illness
精神病院 **seishin-byōin** (mental) asylum, mental hospital
精神医学 **seishin-igaku** psychiatry
精神異常者 **seishin-ijōsha** psychopath
精神科医 **seishinkai** psychiatrist
精神科(の) **seishinka (no)** psychiatric
精神力 **seishinryoku** willpower
精神的虐待 **seishinteki-gyakutai** mental cruelty
精神的(な) **seishinteki (na)** mental
制止する **seishi suru** stop; restrain
静止する **seishi suru** stand still; freeze *video*
性質 **seishitsu** nature (*of person*)
聖書 **seisho** Bible, the (Holy) Scriptures
清書 **seisho** clean copy
生殖力 **seishokuryoku** fertility
聖職者 **seishoku-sha** clergy
青少年 **seishōnen** youth, young people
青春 **seishun** adolescence
正装 **seisō** formal clothes
生息地 **seisokuchi** habitat; home
整体 **seitai** manipulation (*of bones*)
声帯 **seitai** vocal cords
整体治療する **seitai-chiryō suru** manipulate *bones*
生態学 **seitaigaku** ecology
生態系 **seitaikei** ecosystem
整体師 **seitaishi** chiropractor
生誕地 **seitanchi** birthplace
制定する **seitei suru** enact; 法律を制定する ***hôritsu o seitei suru*** legislate
性的いやがらせ **seiteki iyagarase** sexual harassment
性的(な) **seiteki (na)** sexual
性的能力 **seiteki-nōryoku** virility (*sexual*)
性的倒錯 **seiteki-tōsaku** (sexual) perversion
性的欲求不満 **seiteki-yokkyūfuman** sexual frustration
晴天 **seiten** good weather
青天のへきれき **seiten no hekireki** like a bolt from the blue
生徒 **seito** pupil; student; schoolchild
政党 **seitō** political party

正当化する **seitōka suru** justify; rationalize
正当(な) **seitō (na)** just, right; lawful; rightful
正当に **seitō ni** duly, properly
整とんされた **seiton sareta** neat, tidy
整とんする **seiton suru** arrange, put in order
精通している **seitsū shite iru** knowledgeable ◊ be conversant
制約 **seiyaku** constraint, restriction
製薬(の) **seiyaku (no)** pharmaceutical
西洋 **Seiyō** the West
西洋人 **Seiyō-jin** Westerner
西洋化 **seiyōka** westernized
西洋なし **seiyōnashi** pear
星座 **seiza** signs of the zodiac
正座 **seiza** *formal Japanese sitting position, kneeling, with legs tucked under*
せいぜい **seizei** at (the) most
整然とした **seizen to shita** in order, shipshape
製造 **seizō** manufacture
製造番号 **seizō bangō** serial number
製造中止にする **seizō-chūshi ni suru** discontinue *product*
製造業 **seizōgyō** manufacturing (*industry*)
製造業者 **seizō-gyōsha** manufacturer
生存 **seizon** survival; existence
生存者 **seizon-sha** survivor
生存する **seizon suru** exist; live on, continue living
製造する **seizō suru** manufacture
製図法 **seizuhō** graphics
製図工 **seizukō** draftsman
セージ **sēji** sage (*herb*)
世界 **sekai** world
世界経済 **sekai-keizai** global economy
世界市場 **sekai-shijō** global market
世界大戦 **sekaitaisen** world war
世界的(な) **sekaiteki (na)** worldwide
セカンド **sekando** second (gear)
せかす **sekasu** hurry; press, urge
世間話 **sekenbanashi** small talk
世間知らず(な) **sekenshirazu (na)** naive
せき **seki** family register; cough; barrier; dam; せきをする ***seki o suru*** cough
席 **seki** seat, place; 席に着く ***seki ni tsuku*** sit down; take one's seat
隻 **seki** *countword for boats*
籍 **seki** family register
せき払い **seki-barai** cough
赤道 **sekidō** equator
せき止め薬 **sekidome-yaku** cough medicine, cough syrup
赤外線(の) **sekigaisen (no)** infra-red
赤十字 **Sekijūji** Red Cross
赤面 **sekimen** blush
赤面する **sekimen suru** blush
責任 **sekinin** fault; accountability; liability; guilt; blame; 責任がある ***sekinin ga aru*** be responsible, be to blame; 責任を取る ***sekinin o toru*** accept responsibility
責任感 **sekininkan** sense of responsibility; commitment (*in professional relationship*)
責任(の) **sekinin (no)** responsible; guilty
責任のある **sekinin no aru** be liable
責任の重い **sekinin no omoi** responsible *job*
責任者である **sekinin-sha de aru** be in charge
責任転嫁をする **sekinin-tenka o suru** pass the buck
セキセイインコ **sekiseiinko** budgerigar
石炭 **sekitan** coal
せきたてる **sekitateru** hurry up; push, pressure
関取 **sekitori** ranking sumo wrestler
せきつい **sekitsui** spine; vertebra
せきつい動物 **sekitsui-dōbutsu** vertebrate
石油 **sekiyu** oil; petroleum
石油会社 **sekiyu-gaisha** oil company
石油化学(の) **sekiyu-kagaku (no)** petrochemical

石油タンカー **sekiyu-tankā** oil tanker
切開 **sekkai** incision
石灰 **sekkai** lime (*substance*)
設計 **sekkei** design
設計ミス **sekkei-misu** design fault
設計者 **sekkei-sha** designer
設計する **sekkei suru** design, plan
石けん **sekken** soap
接近 **sekkin** approach; access
セックス **sekkusu** sex; セックスをする ***sekkusu o suru*** make love (to), have sex (with); sleep with
セックスライフ **sekkusu-raifu** lovelife
セックスする **sekkusu suru** make love (to), have sex (with)
説教 **sekkyō** sermon; lecture, criticism; 説教をする ***sekkyô o suru*** preach
積極的(な) **sekkyokuteki (na)** positive, optimistic
施行 **sekō** execution (*of work*, *law*)
施行する **sekō suru** execute *work*, *law*
セクハラ **sekuhara** sexual harrassment
セクシー(な) **sekushī (na)** sexy
セキュリティーチェック **sekyuritī-chekku** security check
狭い **semai** narrow; small; cramped
狭苦しい **semakurushii** poky, cramped
迫る **semaru** approach; draw near; compel
迫っている **sematte iru** brew (*of trouble*)
セメント **semento** cement
責める **semeru** blame; persecute
せめて **semete** at least
せみ **semi** cicada
セミナー **seminā** seminar
千 **sen** thousand
線 **sen** line; 線を引く ***sen o hiku*** draw a line; mark out, set apart
栓 **sen** plug, stopper; 栓をする ***sen o suru*** plug
背中 **senaka** back (*of person*)
専売 **senbai** monopoly
旋盤 **senban** lathe
選抜 **senbatsu** selection (*that/those chosen*)
選抜方法 **senbatsu-hōhō** selection process
せんべい **senbei** rice cracker
戦没者追悼記念日 **Senbotusha-tsuitōkinenbi** Memorial Day
センチメートル **senchimētoru** centimeter
船長 **senchō** captain, skipper
宣伝 **senden** publicity; endorsement
宣伝文句 **senden-monku** blurb (*on book*)
宣伝する **senden suru** publicize; promote
扇動者 **sendō-sha** agitator
扇動する **sendō suru** incite (*to riot*)
洗顔料 **senganryō** facial cleanser
宣言 **sengen** declaration (*of independence etc*)
宣言する **sengen suru** declare; proclaim; pronounce
先月 **sengetsu** last month
戦後(の) **sengo (no)** postwar
繊維 **sen'i** fiber, roughage
繊維光学 **sen'i-kōgaku** fiber optics
船員 **sen'in** seaman
戦時 **senji** wartime
先日 **senjitsu** the other day, recently
戦場 **senjō** battlefield, battleground
旋回する **senkai suru** circle (*of plane, bird*)
先見の明 **senken no mei** foresight
せん光 **senkō** flash
線香 **senkō** incense
専攻 **senkō** major (*academic*); specialty
宣告 **senkoku** sentence LAW
専攻する **senkō suru** specialize in *subject*; major in
先駆者 **senku-sha** forerunner; pioneer
先駆的(な) **senkuteki (na)** pioneering
占拠 **senkyo** occupation; capture
選挙 **senkyo** election
選挙人 **senkyo-nin** elector
選挙制度 **senkyo-seido** electoral system
選挙する **senkyo suru** elect

選挙運動 **senkyo-undō** election campaign; 選挙運動をする ***senkyo-undô o suru*** campaign, canvass
洗面台 **senmendai** (wash)basin
洗面所 **senmenjo** bathroom
洗面器 **senmenki** washbowl; basin
洗面用具 **senmen yōgu** toiletries
専門 **senmon** specialty
専門医 **senmon-i** specialist MED
専門家 **senmonka** specialist
専門家(の) **senmonka** (**no**) professional
専門にする **senmon ni suru** specialize in
専門職の人 **senmonshoku no hito** professional
専門的(な) **senmonteki** (**na**) technical
専門用語 **senmon-yōgo** terminology, jargon
専務取締役 **senmu-torishimariyaku** managing director
専念する **sennen suru** concentrate; focus
せん熱 **sennetsu** glandular fever
洗脳 **sennō** brainwashing
洗脳する **sennō suru** brainwash
栓抜き **sennuki** bottle-opener; corkscrew
先入観 **sennyūkan** preconceived idea
先輩 **senpai** *one's senior at school or work*
船舶 **senpaku** shipping, sea traffic
戦犯 **senpan** war criminal
扇風機 **senpūki** fan (*electric*)
洗礼 **senrei** baptism
先例 **senrei** precedent
洗礼する **senrei suru** christen
洗練された **senren sareta** sophisticated; refined
洗練する **senren suru** civilize; refine
戦利品 **senrihin** spoils of war; booty; loot
線路 **senro** track; rail
戦略 **senryaku** strategy
戦略的(な) **senryakuteki** (**na**) strategic
染料 **senryō** dye
占領 **senryō** occupation (*of country*)
戦力 **senryoku** military capability
占領する **senryō suru** occupy *country*
繊細(な) **sensai** (**na**) delicate
繊細さ **sensai-sa** delicacy
せん索する **sensaku suru** pry; poke one's nose into
せん索好き(な) **sensakuzuki** (**na**) nosy
先生 **sensei** (school)teacher; doctor (*form of address*)
宣誓 **sensei** oath LAW
占星術 **senseijutsu** astrology
宣誓供述書 **senseikyōjutsusho** deposition
宣誓就任する **sensei-shūnin suru** swear in *witnesses*
宣誓する **sensei suru** swear (*on oath*)
センセーション **sensēshon** sensation (*event*)
センセーショナル(な) **sensēshonaru** (**na**) sensational
洗車 **sensha** car wash
戦車 **sensha** tank MIL
戦士 **senshi** warrior
戦死 **senshi** death in action
先史時代(の) **senshi-jidai** (**no**) prehistoric
線審 **senshin** linesman, touch judge
先進(の) **senshin** (**no**) advanced
船首 **senshu** bow (*of ship*)
船主 **senshu** shipowner
選手 **senshu** player; contender; 飛び込みの選手 ***tobikomi no senshu*** diver
先週 **senshū** last week
選手権 **senshuken** championship (*title*)
選手権大会 **senshuken-taikai** championship (*event*)
選出する **senshutsu suru** select; elect
戦争 **sensō** war; warfare
戦争の放棄 **sensō no hōki** renunciation of war
戦争中である **sensōchū de aru** be at war
センス **sensu** good sense; taste
扇子 **sensu** fan (*handheld*)

潜水艦 **sensuikan** submarine
潜水する **sensui suru** submerge
センター **sentā** center (*building*)
船体 **sentai** hull (*of ship*)
選択 **sentaku** choice, option; selection; 選択の余地がなかった ***sentaku no yochi ga nakatta*** I had no choice
洗濯できる **sentaku dekiru** washable
洗濯機 **sentakuki** washing machine
洗濯物 **sentaku-mono** laundry, washing
選択(の) **sentaku** (**no**) elective; optional
選択肢 **sentakushi** alternative
洗濯室 **sentakushitsu** laundry (*place*)
洗濯する **sentaku suru** do the laundry; do the washing
先端 **sentan** tip (*of cigarette*); top (*of mountain, tree*)
せん定ばさみ **senteibasami** pruning shears
せん定する **sentei suru** prune
先天性(の) **sentensei** (**no**) congenital
セント **sento** cent
せん塔 **sentō** spire, steeple
先頭 **sentō** head; leader; 先頭に立つ ***sentô ni tatsu*** take the lead
戦闘 **sentō** combat
銭湯 **sentō** public bath
戦闘機 **sentōki** fighter (*airplane*)
先頭(の) **sentō** (**no**) leading
セントラルヒーティング **sentoraru-hītingu** central heating
洗剤 **senzai** detergent; dishwashing liquid
潜在意識 **senzai-ishiki** the subconscious (mind)
潜在的(な) **senzaiteki** (**na**) insidious *effect*; potential *customer*
戦前(の) **senzen** (**no**) prewar
先祖 **senzo** forefathers
背負う **seou** carry on one's back; be burdened with
背泳ぎ **seoyogi** backstroke
セラピー **serapī** therapy
セラピスト **serapisuto** therapist
せりふ **serifu** speech (*in play*); …にせりふをつける ***... ni serifu o tsukeru*** prompt
セーリング **sēringu** sailing
セロハン **serohan** cellophane
世論 **seron** public opinion
世論調査 **seron-chōsa** poll, survey
世論調査員 **seron-chōsain** pollster
セロリ **serori** celery
せる **seru** compete
セール **sēru** sale (*at reduced price*)
セルフサービス(の) **serufu-sābisu** (**no**) self-service
セールスマン **sērusuman** salesman, (sales) rep
セールスポイント **sērusu-pointo** selling point
節制のない **sessei no nai** immoderate
せっせと働く **sesse to hataraku** work hard; beaver away
摂氏 **sesshi** centigrade
摂氏零度 **sesshi-reido** freezing
接触 **sesshoku** contact
接触する **sesshoku suru** touch
セッション **sesshon** session
節操のない **sessō no nai** unprincipled
接する **sessuru** touch; contact; serve; receive; border on
セーター **sētā** sweater
接着する **setchaku suru** glue; bond (*of glue*)
接着テープ **setchaku-tēpu** sticky tape
接着剤 **setchakuzai** adhesive, glue
設置する **setchi suru** set up
瀬戸際 **setogiwa** brink
瀬戸物 **setomono** ceramics
節 **setsu** clause; verse
設備 **setsubi** facilities, amenities; equipment
設備完備(の) **setsubi-kanbi** (**no**) self-contained
切望 **setsubō** longing
切望する **setsubō suru** long, yearn; be anxious for
節分 **setsubun** last day of winter
切断する **setsudan suru** amputate; sever; mutilate
節度 **setsudo** moderation, restraint

接合する **setsugō suru** cement; fuse; link
切除 **setsujo** removal MED
切除する **setsujo suru** remove MED
雪辱を果たす **setsujoku o hatasu** get even; get revenge
説明 **setsumei** explanation; account; illustration
説明文 **setsumeibun** caption
説明できない **setsumei dekinai** unaccountable; inexplicable
説明する **setsumei suru** explain, set out; illustrate (*with examples*)
設立 **setsuritsu** foundation, setting up
設立する **setsuritsu suru** establish, set up
節約 **setsuyaku** saving, economy
節約して **setsuyaku shite** economically, thriftily
節約する **setsuyaku suru** save; conserve; economize
接続 **setsuzoku** connection
接続便 **setsuzoku-bin** connecting flight
接続詞 **setsuzoku-shi** conjunction GRAM
接続する **setsuzoku suru** connect
設定 **settei** setting
設定する **settei suru** set *movie, novel etc*; establish; create
セット **setto** scenery; set (*in tennis*)
窃盗 **settō** theft; larceny
接頭辞 **sēttōji** prefix
説得 **settoku** persuasion
説得力のある **settokuryoku no aru** be convincing ◊ persuasive; compelling; forceful
説得する **settoku suru** persuade; reason with
セットメニュー **setto-menyū** set menu
セットする **setto suru** do *hair*; 髪をセットしてもらう ***kami o setto shite morau*** have one's hair done
窃盗罪 **settōzai** larceny
世話 **sewa** care (*of baby, pet etc*); 世話をする ***sewa o suru*** attend to; take care of; look after; 世話をやく ***sewa o yaku*** meddle; interfere
せわしなく動き回る **sewashinaku ugokimawaru** bustle around
世話やき(の) **sewayaki (no)** interfering; over-protective
世俗(の) **sezoku (no)** common; secular
世俗的(な) **sezokuteki (na)** worldly
しゃべる **shaberu** talk; chat
シャベル **shaberu** shovel
シャボン玉 **shabondama** (soap) bubble
しゃぶしゃぶ **shabushabu** *fondue-style dish with beef*
社長 **shachō** head, president (*of company*)
遮断する **shadan suru** block out *light*; cut off; insulate
車道 **shadō** roadway
しゃがむ **shagamu** squat
しゃがれ声 **shagaregoe** husky voice; croak; しゃがれ声を出す ***shagaregoe o dasu*** croak
しゃがれ声(の) **shagaregoe (no)** hoarse; husky
社員 **shain** staff; employee
写実的(な) **shajitsuteki (na)** graphic, vivid
社会 **shakai** community; society
社会復帰させる **shakai-fukki saseru** rehabilitate
社会福祉事業 **shakaifukushi-jigyō** social work
社会学 **shakai-gaku** sociology
社会(の) **shakai (no)** social; 社会のくず ***shakai no kuzu*** the dregs of society
社会主義 **shakai-shugi** socialism
社会主義(の) **shakai-shugi (no)** socialist
社会主義者 **shakai-shugi-sha** socialist
社会党 **Shakaitō** Social Democratic Party
しゃきしゃきした **shakishaki shita** crisp *lettuce, apple*
借金 **shakkin** debt; 借金をしている ***shakkin o shite iru*** be in debt, be in the red; …に借金をしている ***... ni shakkin o shite iru*** owe
しゃっくり **shakkuri** hiccup
しゃっくりする **shakkuri suru** have

the hiccups
車庫 **shako** garage
社交(の) **shakō (no)** social
社交的(な) **shakōteki (na)** sociable
借地人 **shakuchi-nin** tenant
赤銅色 **shakudōshoku** tan (*color*)
尺八 **shakuhachi** bamboo flute
釈放 **shakuhō** release
釈放する **shakuhō suru** release
釈明 **shakumei** defense, justification
釈明する **shakumei suru** defend, justify
しゃくし定規(な) **shakushi-jōgi (na)** pedantic
借用証書 **shakuyō-shōsho** IOU
斜面 **shamen** slope
赦免する **shamen suru** pardon; absolve
三味線 **shamisen** Japanese banjo
シャム双生児 **Shamu-sōseiji** Siamese twins
車内 **shanai** *inside of a train car*
社内(の) **shanai (no)** in-house
シャンデリア **shanderia** chandelier
シャンパン **shanpan** champagne
シャンプー **shanpū** shampoo
シャンプーする **shanpū suru** shampoo
しゃれ **share** joke; pun
しゃれた **shareta** classy; stylish, elegant
車両 **sharyō** car (*of train*)
車両立ち入り禁止区域 **sharyō-tachiiri-kinshi-kuiki** pedestrian precinct
射殺する **shasatsu suru** gun down
写生する **shasei suru** sketch
車線 **shasen** lane MOT
斜線 **shasen** oblique
社説 **shasetsu** editorial
写真 **shashin** photo(graph); 写真をとる ***shashin o toru*** photograph
写真撮影 **shashin-satsuei** photography
写真うつりのよい **shashin'utsuri no yoi** photogenic
車掌 **shashō** ticket inspector; conductor
射手 **shashu** marksman; archer
車体 **shatai** bodywork
射程距離 **shatei-kyori** range (*of gun*)
シャトル **shatoru** shuttlecock
シャトルバス **shatoru-basu** shuttlebus
シャツ **shatsu** shirt
シャッター **shattā** shutter
シャワー **shawā** shower; シャワーを浴びる ***shawâ o abiru*** take a shower, shower
シャワーカーテン **shawā-kāten** shower curtain
シャワーキャップ **shawā-kyappu** shower cap
社用車 **shayō-sha** company car
謝罪 **shazai** apology
シェフ **shefu** chef
シェイク **sheiku** milk shake
し **-shi** and; and besides that ; りんごも好きだし、みかんも好きだ ***ringo mo suiki da shi, mikan mo suki da*** I like both apples and tangerines
死 **shi** death; loss
四 **shi** four
詩 **shi** poem; poetry, verse
市 **shi** city
氏 **shi** *polite form of* ***san***; Mr; Ms
仕上がり **shiagari** finish (*of product*)
仕上げをする **shiage o suru** polish up *work*
試合 **shiai** competition; match; game (*in tennis*); 試合をする ***shiai o suru*** play
シーアイエー(中央情報局) **Shī-ai-ē (Chūō-jōhō-kyoku)** CIA, Central Intelligence Agency
試合開始 **shiai-kaishi** kickoff
指圧 **shiatsu** shiatsu (*massage*)
幸せ **shiawase** happiness; welfare
幸せ(な) **shiawase (na)** happy; …を幸せにする ***… o shiawase ni suru*** make happy
芝生 **shibafu** lawn; grass
芝居 **shibai** play; drama
芝刈り機 **shibakariki** lawn mower
しばらく **shibaraku** for a while, for a time
縛り付ける **shibaritsukeru** tie down (*with rope*)
縛る **shibaru** bind, tie up

しばしば **shibashiba** frequently
しびれる **shibireru** go numb; have pins and needles
しびれた **shibireta** numb
志望 **shibō** wish; hope
脂肪 **shibō** fat
死亡 **shibō** death
死亡事故 **shibō-jiko** fatality
死亡記事 **shibō-kiji** obituary
死亡率 **shibō-ritsu** mortality, death rate
絞る **shiboru** press *grapes, olives*; wring out
死亡者数 **shibō-sha-sū** death toll
志望する **shibō suru** wish; hope
死亡する **shibō suru** die
渋い **shibui** sour; astringent; sullen; austere; tasteful
しぶき **shibuki** spray; splash
四分音符 **shibu-onpu** quarternote
渋る **shiburu** hesitate; falter
試着する **shichaku suru** try on *clothes*
七福神 **Shichi-fukujin** the Seven Deities of Good Luck
七月 **shichigatsu** July
七五三 **Shichigosan** Shichi-Go-San (*festival for children aged 3, 5 and 7*)
七面鳥 **shichimenchō** turkey
質に入れる **shichi ni ireru** pawn
質屋 **shichi-ya** pawnbroker; pawnshop
市長 **shichō** mayor
視聴覚(の) **shichōkaku (no)** audiovisual
視聴者 **shichō-sha** audience; viewer
シチュー **shichū** stew
支柱 **shichū** support
シダ **shida** fern
次第 **shidai**: あなた次第です ***anata shidai desu*** it's up to you
次第に **shidai ni** by degrees, gradually
仕出し業者 **shidashi-gyōsha** caterer
仕出しをする **shidashi o suru** cater for
CD **shī-dī** CD, compact disc
指導 **shidō** guidance; tuition
私道 **shidō** private road
シード **shīdo** seed (*in tennis*)
指導権争い **shidōken-arasoi** leadership contest
指導者 **shidō-sha** mentor; advisor; coach
指導する **shidō suru** coach, teach
始動する **shidō suru** start
指導的地位 **shidōteki-chii** leadership
支援 **shien** support, backing
支援者 **shien-sha** sympathizer
支援する **shien suru** support, back up
シーフード **shīfūdo** seafood
私服 **shifuku de** plain clothes
至福感 **shifukukan** euphoria
私腹をこやす **shifuku o koyasu** line one's own pockets
シフトキー **shifuto kī** shift key
…しがちである **... shigachi de aru** be liable to, be prone to
市外 **shigai** suburbs; area beyond city limits
市外局番 **shigai-kyokuban** area code
紫外線(の) **shigaisen (no)** ultraviolet
しがみつく **shigamitsuku** cling to (*of child*)
志願者 **shigan-sha** volunteer
四月 **shigatsu** April
刺激 **shigeki** incentive; stimulation; irritation MED
刺激する **shigeki suru** arouse (*sexually*); goad; stimulate; irritate MED
刺激的(な) **shigekiteki (na)** pungent; stimulating; electric *fig*
茂み **shigemi** bush
資源 **shigen** resource; stock, reserves
茂る **shigeru** grow thickly; be luxuriant
死後(の) **shigo (no)** posthumous
仕事 **shigoto** work; job, task; business affair
仕事中である **shigotochū de aru** be at work
仕事中毒 **shigoto-chūdoku** workaholic
支配 **shihai** control; domination;

reign; sway, influence
支配人 **shihai-nin** manager (*of restaurant, hotel etc*)
支配者 **shihai-sha** ruler (*of state*)
支配する **shihai suru** rule; reign; control; dominate
支配的(な) **shihaiteki (na)** dominant
四半期(の) **shihanki (no)** quarterly
支払い **shiharai** payment (*of bill*); 支払いをする ***shiharai o suru*** pay
支払う **shiharau** meet *payment*; pay
支払うべき **shiharaubeki** payable
支払われるべき **shiharawarerubeki** due, owed
始発 **shihatsu** the first train
紙幣 **shihei** bank bill
司法権 **shihōken** jurisdiction
資本 **shihon** capital (*money*)
資本家 **shihon-ka** capitalist
司法(の) **shihō (no)** judicial
資本主義 **shihon-shugi** capitalism
資本主義(の) **shihon-shugi (no)** capitalist
資本主義者 **shihon-shugi-sha** capitalist, believer in capitalism
指標 **shihyō** index; indicator; guidelines
子音 **shiin** consonant
仕入れる **shiireru** purchase; buy in
虐げる **shiitageru** tyrannize; oppress
指示 **shiji** directions, instructions
詩人 **shijin** poet
支持者 **shiji-sha** follower, supporter
支持する **shiji suru** bear out, confirm; support; stand by
指示する **shiji suru** instruct
市場 **shijō** market; market place
市場調査 **shijō-chōsa** market research
市場経済 **shijō-keizai** market economy
市場シェア **shijō-shea** market share
しか **shika** deer
しか **-shika** only, just
仕返しをする **shikaeshi o suru** take revenge; get even with, pay back
視界 **shikai** visual field; visibility
市会議員 **shikai-giin** councilman
司会をする **shikai o suru** front *TV program*
司会者 **shikai-sha** host (*of TV program*); master of ceremonies
仕掛け **shikake** device; mechanism
仕掛ける **shikakeru** begin; set *trap*
四角形 **shikakkei** quadrangle
資格 **shikaku** certificate; qualification; 資格を与える ***shikaku o ataeru*** qualify; 資格を得る ***shikaku o eru*** qualify (*in competition*); 資格を取る ***shikaku o toru*** qualify (*get degree etc*)
死角 **shikaku** blind spot
資格のある **shikaku no aru** eligible
資格のない **shikaku no nai** ineligible; unqualified
視覚障害 **shikaku-shōgai** visual deficiency
視覚的(な) **shikakuteki (na)** visual
しかめる **shikameru** contort; screw up *eyes*
しかめっ面 **shikamettsura** frown; scowl; grimace
しかも **shikamo** besides; in addition; and also
士官 **shikan** officer
歯冠 **shikan** crown (*on tooth*)
しか肉 **shikaniku** venison
歯科(の) **shika (no)** dental
しかりとばす **shikaritobasu** bawl out, chew out
しかる **shikaru** scold
しかし **shikashi** at the same time, however, but
仕方 **shikata** method; way
しかたがない **shikata ga nai**: 待っていてもしかたがない ***matte itemo shikata ga nai*** it's no use waiting; 寂しくてしかたがない ***sabishikute shikata ga nai*** I cannot help feeling sad; …をしかたがないと受け入れる ***... o shikata ga nai to ukeireru*** reconcile oneself to
死刑 **shikei** capital punishment; death penalty; 電気いすで死刑になる ***denki-isu de shikei ni naru*** go to the chair
死刑執行人 **shikei-shikkō-nin** executioner
死刑執行猶予 **shikeishikkō-yūyo** reprieve from the death penalty

試験 **shiken** examination; paper; 試験に合格する ***shiken ni gôkaku suru*** pass an exam; 試験に受かる/落ちる ***shiken ni ukaru / ochiru*** pass / fail an exam; 試験を受ける ***shiken o ukeru*** take an exam
試験官 **shiken-kan** examiner
試験管 **shikenkan** test tube
試験管ベビー **shikenkan-bebī** test tube baby
試験採用期間 **shiken-saiyō-kikan** probation period
試験する **shiken suru** examine
式 **shiki** ceremony; style
士気 **shiki** morale, spirits
指揮 **shiki** conducting; command
四季 **shiki** the four seasons
敷布団 **shikibuton** bottom futon
敷地 **shikichi** location; premises
指揮台 **shikidai** podium
式服 **shikifuku** ceremonial robe
敷居 **shikii** threshold
色覚異常(の) **shikikaku-ijō (no)** color-blind
敷物 **shikimono** carpet; rug
資金 **shikin** fund; 資金を出す ***shikin o dasu*** fund, finance
至近距離で **shikin-kyori de** at point-blank range
仕切り **shikiri** partition; compartment
しきりに **shikiri ni** eagerly
仕切り屋 **shikiri-ya** control freak
仕切る **shikiru** partition off
色彩 **shikisai** color; 色彩に富んだ ***shikisai ni tonda*** colorful
指揮者 **shiki-sha** conductor MUS
指揮する **shiki suru** conduct MUS
式典 **shikiten** ceremony
失格する **shikkaku suru** be disqualified; be eliminated
しっかり **shikkari** tight; しっかり焼けた ***shikkari yaketa*** well-done *meat*
しっかりした **shikkari shita** solid; stalwart; steady
湿気 **shikke** humidity
漆器 **shikki** lacquerware
失効となる **shikkō to naru** expire
執行猶予 **shikkō-yūyo** probation
しっくい **shikkui** plaster
失脚 **shikkyaku** downfall
失脚する **shikkyaku suru** fall from power
歯こう **shikō** plaque (*on teeth*)
四国 **Shikoku** Shikoku
しこり **shikori** lump, swelling
敷く **shiku** lay *cable, carpet*
しくじる **shikujiru** botch, bungle ◊ put one's foot in it
仕組み **shikumi** structure; device; mechanism
しくしく泣く **shikushiku naku** weep
死去 **shikyo** demise
至急 **shikyū** urgently; immediately
子宮 **shikyū** uterus, womb
子宮摘出手術 **shikyū-tekishutsu-shujutsu** hysterectomy
支給する **shikyū suru** supply; issue *supplies*
しま **shima** stripe
島 **shima** island
姉妹 **shimai** sisters
しまい込む **shimaikomu** put away
姉妹都市 **shimai-toshi** twin town
しま模様(の) **shimamoyō (no)** striped
閉まる **shimaru** close, shut
します **shimasu** (*polite present tense of* ***suru***): 私がします ***watashi ga shimasu*** I'll do it
始末する **shimatsu suru** dispose of; put away *animal*
閉まった **shimatta** closed
しまった **shimatta** damn!
閉まっている **shimatte iru** be on (*of lid, top*)
しまっておく **shimatte oku** keep (*in specific place*)
しまう **shimau** store, stow; put away (*in closet etc*)
しまうま **shimauma** zebra
締め出す **shimedasu** bar; exclude; lock out (*of house*)
締め金 **shimegane** clamp
氏名 **shimei** full name
指名する **shimei suru** designate, nominate
指名手配中(の) **shimei-tehai chū (no)** wanted (*by police*)
締め切り **shimekiri** deadline; time limit

締め切る **shimekiru** close; keep shut; refuse to accept because a deadline has passed
絞め殺す **shimekorosu** strangle
締めくくる **shimekukuru** finish, wind up
湿っぽい **shimeppoi** damp
湿らせる **shimeraseru** dampen, moisten
湿り気 **shimerike** moisture
湿る **shimeru** get damp
占める **shimeru** account for, constitute; occupy, take up
閉める **shimeru** close; shut; wind up *car window*
締める **shimeru** fasten *seat belt*; tighten *screw*; tie *necktie*
示す **shimesu** show; indicate, point to; mark; reveal
湿った **shimetta** damp, moist
染み **shimi** stain, mark; blot; smear; 染みがつく ***shimi ga tsuku*** mark (*of fabric*)
染み込む **shimikomu** sink in
市民 **shimin** citizen; fellow citizen; the people
市民権 **shiminken** citizenship; civil rights
市民(の) **shimin (no)** civic; civil
染み抜き **shiminuki** stain remover
しみる **shimiru** penetrate; pierce; sting
霜 **shimo** frost; 霜の降りた ***shimo no orita*** frosty
指紋 **shimon** fingerprint
霜取りをする **shimotori o suru** defrost
しもやけ **shimoyake** frostbite; chilblain
シミュレートする **shimyurēto suru** simulate
しん **shin** core (*of fruit*) ; しんをくり抜く ***shin o kurinuku*** core
新… **shin…** new
竹刀 **shinai** bamboo sword
市内 **shinai** area within city limits
市内通話 **shinai-tsūwa** local call
シナモン **shinamon** cinnamon
品物 **shinamono** article; thing; goods
シナリオ **shinario** scenario
しなやか(な) **shinayaka (na)** supple; flexible
シンボルマーク **shinboru-māku** emblem
辛抱する **shinbō suru** be patient; endure
新聞 **shinbun** (news)paper
新聞雑誌 **shinbun-zasshi** the press
新聞雑誌販売店 **shinbun-zasshi-hanbaiten** newsagent
新陳代謝 **shinchin-taisha** metabolism
身長 **shinchō** height
慎重(な) **shinchō (na)** cautious, prudent
慎重に **shinchō ni** carefully; gingerly
慎重さ **shinchō-sa** discretion; prudence
真ちゅう **shinchū** brass
死んだ **shinda** dead; lifeless
寝台 **shindai** berth, bunk; couchette
寝台車 **shindai-sha** sleeping car
診断 **shindan** diagnosis
診断する **shindan suru** diagnose
神殿 **shinden** *main building of a shrine*
震度 **shindo** magnitude (*of quake*)
進度 **shindo** progress
震動 **shindō** tremor
振動 **shindō** vibration; oscillation; swing
震動する **shindō suru** quake; tremble
振動する **shindō suru** vibrate
深えん **shin'en** abyss; depths
深遠(な) **shin'en (na)** profound, deep
心不全 **shinfuzen** heart failure
侵害 **shingai** infringement; violation
侵害する **shingai suru** violate; encroach on; trespass on
神学 **shingaku** theology
シンガポール **Shingapōru** Singapore
シンガポール (の) **Shingapōru (no)** Singaporean
震源地 **shingenchi** epicenter
新月 **shingetsu** new moon
審議会 **shingikai** council

信号 **shingō** traffic light; signal
信号無視 **shingō-mushi** jaywalking
寝具 **shingu** bedclothes; bedding
シングル盤 **shinguru-ban** single MUS
シングルマザー **shinguru-mazā** single mother
シングル(の) **shinguru (no)** single-breasted
シングルス **shingurusu** singles (*in tennis*)
新方針 **shin-hōshin** new direction; new departure
死に物狂い **shinimonogurui** desperation
シニヨン **shiniyon** chignon; bun (*hairstyle*)
信者 **shinja** believer
信じがたい **shinjigatai** farfetched
信心深い **shinjinbukai** pious, religious
新人類 **shinjinrui** *pej* younger generation
信じられない **shinjirarenai** incredible; unbelievable
信じる **shinjiru** believe
真実 **shinjitsu** truth
信条 **shinjō** creed (*beliefs*)
真珠 **shinju** pearl
心中 **shinjū** double suicide
真珠湾 **Shinjuwan** Pearl Harbor
進化 **shinka** evolution
新幹線 **shinkansen** bullet train
進化論 **shinka-ron** evolution
進化する **shinka suru** evolve
神経 **shinkei** nerve; 神経が参っている ***shinkei ga maitte iru*** be a nervous wreck; 神経にさわる ***shinkei ni sawaru*** jar, grate
神経過敏 **shinkei-kabin** hypersensitivity
神経過敏(の) **shinkei-kabin (no)** neurotic; hypersensitive
神経科医 **shinkeikai** neurologist
神経(の) **shinkei (no)** nervous
神経質(な) **shinkeishitsu (na)** nervous; high-strung; sensitive
神経症 **shinkeishō** neurosis
真剣(な) **shinken (na)** serious; intense; solemn
しん気楼 **shinkirō** mirage
信仰 **shinkō** faith, belief
進行中である **shinkōchū de aru** be under way
深刻(な) **shinkoku (na)** deep *trouble*; somber; serious
深刻さ **shinkoku-sa** severity
申告する **shinkoku suru** declare (*at customs*)
深呼吸をする **shinkokyū o suru** take a deep breath
新婚カップル **shinkon-kappuru** newlyweds
信仰する **shinkō suru** believe in
進行する **shinkō suru** proceed, progress
真空 **shinkū** vacuum
真紅色(の) **shinkuiro (no)** scarlet
真空パック(の) **shinkū-pakku (no)** vacuum-packed
新境地 **shin-kyōchi** new departure
進級する **shinkyū suru** move up (*in school*)
新芽 **shinme** shoot
新年 **Shinnen** New Year
新任(の) **shinnin (no)** incoming
侵入 **shinnyū** penetration
進入禁止 **shinnyū-kinshi** no entry
新入生 **shinnyūsei** freshman
侵入者 **shinnyū-sha** intruder
新入社員 **shinnyū-shain** newcomer, recruit (*to company*)
侵入する **shinnyū suru** break in (*of burglar*); encroach on
市(の) **shi (no)** civic; municipal
忍び寄る **shinobiyoru** creep; sneak
しのぐ **shinogu** eclipse, outdo; overtake
死の灰 **shi no hai** fallout
しのんで **shinonde** in memory of
心配 **shinpai** anxiety, concern, worry
心配(な) **shinpai (na)** disturbed, concerned; worrying
心配させる **shinpai saseru** alarm; worry, concern
心配して **shinpai shite** anxious
心配している **shinpai shite iru** be worried ◊ apprehensive; concerned
心配そう(な) **shinpaisō (na)** worried
心配する **shinpai suru** worry
審判 **shinpan** referee; umpire; judge

審判する **shinpan suru** judge
新兵 **shinpei** recruit
神秘的(な) **shinpiteki (na)** mystical; occult; enigmatic
進歩 **shinpo** advance, progress
進歩させる **shinpo saseru** advance
信奉者 **shinpō-sha** believer
進歩する **shinpo suru** make progress, advance, come on
進歩的(な) **shinpoteki (na)** progressive
新婦 **shinpu** bride
信ぴょう性 **shinpyōsei** reliability; credibility
信頼 **shinrai** belief; faith; confidence, trust
信頼できない **shinrai dekinai** unreliable
信頼できる **shinrai dekiru** authoritative; credible; reliable; responsible
信頼性 **shinraisei** reliability
信頼する **shinrai suru** trust; rely on
辛らつ(な) **shinratsu (na)** cutting; hurtful; pointed *remark, question*
真理 **shinri** truth
心理 **shinri** state of mind
心理学 **shinrigaku** psychology
心理学者 **shinri-gakusha** psychologist
心理学的(な) **shinrigakuteki (na)** psychological
森林 **shinrin** woods; forest
森林警備隊員 **shinrin-keibi-taiin** forest ranger
心理的(な) **shinriteki (na)** psychological
針路 **shinro** course (*of ship, plane*)
新郎 **shinrō** groom
侵略 **shinryaku** invasion
侵略する **shinryaku suru** invade; overrun
診療 **shinryō** medical treatment
診療所 **shinryōjo** clinic
審査する **shinsa suru** screen, vet; process *application*
診察 **shinsatsu** examination (*of patient*)
診察料 **shinsatsu-ryō** medical fee
診察する **shinsatsu suru** examine *patient*
申請 **shinsei** application
神聖(な) **shinsei (na)** holy, sacred
神聖さ **shinsei-sa** sanctity
申請書 **shinseisho** application form
申請する **shinsei suru** apply for; put in for
親せき **shinseki** relation, relative
新鮮(な) **shinsen (na)** fresh
新鮮さ **shinsen-sa** freshness
親切 **shinsetsu** kindness
親切(な) **shinsetsu (na)** genial; obliging; kind
紳士 **shinshi** gentleman
紳士的(な) **shinshiteki (na)** gallant
寝室 **shinshitsu** bedroom
侵食 **shinshoku** encroachment; erosion
侵食する **shinshoku suru** encroach on; erode
伸縮性のある **shinshukusei no aru** elastic; flexible
進出する **shinshutsu suru** advance
進水 **shinsui** launch
浸水した **shinsui shita** waterlogged
進水する **shinsui suru** launch
身体障害 **shintai-shōgai** physical disability, physical handicap; 身体障害のある ***shintai-shôgai no aru*** be disabled
身体障害者 **shintai-shōgai-sha** the disabled
身体的(な) **shintaiteki (na)** physical; bodily
信託 **shintaku** trust FIN
進展 **shinten** breakthrough; development
親展 **shinten** private, confidential
新展開 **shin-tenkai** new departure, new development
進展させる **shinten saseru** develop, improve on
神道 **Shintō** Shinto
死ぬ **shinu** die
神話 **shinwa** myth; mythology
神話学 **shinwagaku** mythology
深夜料金 **shin'ya-ryōkin** late-night fare
信用できない **shin'yō dekinai** untrustworthy
信用できる **shinyō dekiru** trustworthy; credible; reliable

針葉樹 **shinyōju** conifer
信用された **shin'yō sareta** trusted
信用性 **shinyōsei** credibility
信用しない **shinyō shinai** distrust, mistrust
信用照会状 **shinyō-shōkaijō** letter of credit
信用する **shinyō suru** trust; rely on
親友 **shin'yū** close friend
親善 **shinzen** friendship
新参者 **shinzanmono** newcomer
心臓 **shinzō** heart; heart attack
心臓発作 **shinzō-hossa** heart attack
心臓移植 **shinzo-ishoku** heart transplant
心臓(の) **shinzō** (**no**) cardiac, coronary
塩 **shio** salt
潮 **shio** tide; 潮が満ちる/引く ***shio ga michiru*** / ***hiku*** the tide is in / out
塩味(の) **shioaji** (**no**) savory; salty
塩辛い **shiokarai** salty
しおれる **shioreru** wilt, droop; be depressed
失敗 **shippai** failure, flop; 失敗に終わる ***shippai ni owaru*** break down (*of talks*)
失敗した **shippai shita** unsuccessful
失敗する **shippai suru** fail; flunk; misfire (*of scheme*)
しっぺ返し **shippegaeshi** retort; tit for tat
尻尾 **shippo** tail
湿布 **shippu** compress
調べ **shirabe** investigation; enquiry
調べる **shiraberu** check; find out; study, examine; look at; look up
しらふ(の) **shirafu** (**no**) sober
白髪(の) **shiraga** (**no**) gray-haired
しらかば **shirakaba** silver birch
しらみ **shirami** louse
知らない **shiranai** strange, unknown; unfamiliar
知られていない **shirarete inai** unheard of, unknown
知らせ **shirase** word, news
知らせる **shiraseru** break *news*; keep posted
試練 **shiren** trial; ordeal
しり **shiri** bottom, buttocks, butt; しりに敷かれた ***shiri ni shikareta*** henpecked
知り合い **shiriai** acquaintance
知り合いである **shiriai de aru** be acquainted with; know
知り合いになる **shiriai ni naru** get to know
知り合う **shiriau** know; get to know
しりごみさせる **shirigomi saseru** daunt
しりごみする **shirigomi suru** flinch
シリコン **shirikon** silicon
シリコンチップ **shirikon chippu** silicon chip
シリンダー **shirindā** cylinder
知りたがり(の) **shiritagari** (**no**) inquisitive
私立(の) **shiritsu** (**no**) private
市立(の) **shiritsu** (**no**) municipal
私立探偵 **shiritsu-tantei** private detective
退ける **shirizokeru** dismiss; reject; repel
白 **shiro** white
城 **shiro** castle
白い **shiroi** white; fair *complexion*
しろかび **shirokabi** mildew
白くま **shirokuma** polar bear
白黒(の) **shirokuro** (**no**) black and white
しろめ **shirome** pewter
白身 **shiromi** (egg) white
素人 **shirōto** amateur; layman
素人(の) **shirōto** (**no**) unprofessional; amateurish
汁 **shiru** soup; juice; sap
知る **shiru** know
白ワイン **shiro wain** white wine
印 **shirushi** mark, sign; brand; checkmark; 印を付ける ***shirushi o tsukeru*** check, check off
資料 **shiryō** data, material
飼料 **shiryō** fodder
視力 **shiryoku** eyesight, vision
資料請求券 **shiryō-seikyū-ken** coupon
支流 **shiryū** tributary
示唆 **shisa** suggestion, implication
資産 **shisan** asset; equity
示唆する **shisa suru** suggest, imply

視察 **shisatsu** inspection
視察する **shisatsu suru** inspect
姿勢 **shisei** position, stance; posture
私生児 **shiseiji** bastard, illegitimate child
視線 **shisen** gaze
施設 **shisetsu** establishment; institute
使節団 **shisetsudan** mission
支社 **shisha** branch office
死者 **shisha** dead person; the deceased
四捨五入 **shisha-gonyū** *rounding off to the nearest whole number*
試写会 **shishakai** preview
指針 **shishin** pointer, indication
司書 **shisho** librarian
私書箱 **shishobako** PO Box
死傷者 **shishō-sha** casualty
ししゅう **shishū** embroidery; needlework
思春期 **shishunki** puberty
支出 **shishutsu** expenditure
しそ **shiso** perilla (*plant*)
思想 **shisō** idea; thought
子孫 **shison** descendant; …の子孫である ***... no shison de aru*** be descended from…
湿疹 **shisshin** eczema
失神させる **shisshin saseru** knock unconscious
失そう **shissō** disappearance
質素(な) **shisso (na)** humble; thrifty; plain; simple
質素さ **shisso-sa** modesty, simplicity
失そうする **shissō suru** disappear
システム **shisutemu** system COMPUT
システムアナリスト **shisutemu-anarisuto** systems analyst
システムキッチン **shisutemu-kitchin** fitted kitchen
下 **shita** bottom (*of pile*); lower part; 下で ***shita de*** under; 下に ***shita ni*** below; down; 下(の) ***shita (no)*** junior, subordinate
舌 **shita** tongue
下取り **shitadori** part exchange
下取りする **shitadori suru** trade in; take in part exchange
下書き **shitagaki** (rough) draft
したがって **shitagatte** accordingly; therefore; thus; …にしたがって ***... ni shitagatte*** in accordance with
従う **shitagau** abide by; comply with; follow; obey
下着 **shitagi** underwear
死体 **shitai** corpse, cadaver
支度 **shitaku** preparations; arrangements
下町 **shitamachi** downtown
下向き(の) **shitamuki (no)** downward
舌なめずりする **shitanamezuri suru** lick one's lips
親しい **shitashii** close; intimate; …と親しい ***... to shitashii*** be friendly with
親しくなる **shitashiku naru** make friends with; get involved with
親しくしている **shitashiku shite iru** be close to
親しさ **shitashi-sa** intimacy; familiarity
舌足らず **shitatarazu** lisp
したたる **shitataru** drip
下手投げ(の) **shitate nage (no)** underarm
仕立て(の) **shitate (no)** tailor-made
仕立てる **shitateru** tailor; sew; train; prepare
慕っている **shitatte iru** be attached to
慕う **shitau** adore
下請け会社 **shitauke-gaisha** subcontractor
下請けさせる **shitauke saseru** subcontract
舌触り **shitazawari** texture (*of food*)
指定する **shitei suru** designate; specify
指定図書 **shitei-tosho** set book; set reading
私的(な) **shiteki (na)** personal, private
詩的(な) **shiteki (na)** poetic
指摘する **shiteki suru** point out; bring to the attention of
支店 **shiten** branch (*of bank, company*)
私鉄 **shitetsu** private railroad
シートベルト **shīto-beruto** seat belt

しとしと **shitoshito**: 雨がしとしと降っている ***ame ga shitoshito futte iru*** it's spitting with rain
質 **shitsu** quality (*of goods etc*)
シーツ **shītsu** sheet
失望 **shitsubō** disappointment; dismay; frustration
湿度 **shitsudo** humidity
失業 **shitsugyō** unemployment
失業中(の) **shitsugyōchū (no)** idle
失業者 **shitsugyō-sha** the unemployed
失業した **shitsugyō shita** unemployed
失業している **shitsugyō shite iru** be out of work
しつけ **shitsuke** upbringing; training
しつける **shitsukeru** discipline; train
しつこい **shitsukoi** insistent; nagging *pain*; strident *demands*; heavy *food*
失明させる **shitsumei saseru** blind
質問 **shitsumon** question, query
質問する **shitsumon suru** ask a question; query; question
室内(の) **shitsunai (no)** interior (*of house*)
室内装飾 **shitsunai-sōshoku** interior design
室温 **shitsuon** room temperature
失礼 **shitsurei** disrespect; 失礼ですが ***shitsurei desu ga*** excuse me (*interrupting s.o.*); 失礼します ***shitsurei shimasu*** excuse me
失礼(な) **shitsurei (na)** disrespectful; offensive
知ったかぶり屋 **shittakaburi-ya** wise guy
知っている **shitte iru** know
しっと **shitto** jealousy
しっと深い **shittobukai** jealous
しわ **shiwa** crease, wrinkle; しわがよる ***shiwa ga yoru*** shrivel; wrinkle, crease; しわにする ***shiwa ni suru*** crumple, crease; しわを寄せる ***shiwa o yoseru*** wrinkle
視野 **shiya** field of vision; 視野の狭い ***shiya no semai*** narrow-minded
市役所 **shiyakusho** city hall, town hall
しよう **shiyō** let's; 仕事をしよう ***shigoto o shiyô*** let's do business; ...しようと努力する ***...shiyô to doryoku suru*** try to; resolve to
仕様 **shiyō** means; method; specifications
使用 **shiyō** use
使用できる **shiyō dekiru** usable
使用法 **shiyō-hō** directions (for use)
使用可能(な) **shiyō-kanō (na)** live *ammunition*
試用期間 **shiyō-kikan** trial period (*for employee*); 試用期間中で ***shiyôkikan chû de*** on probation (*in job*)
使用説明 **shiyō-setsumei** instruction; operating instructions
使用者 **shiyō-sha** user
私有(の) **shiyū (no)** private
死産した **shizan shita** be stillborn
自然 **shizen** nature
自然保護区域 **shizen-hogo-kuiki** nature reserve
自然保護論者 **shizen-hogo-ronsha** conservationist
自然科学 **shizen-kagaku** natural science
自然科学者 **shizen-kagakusha** natural scientist
自然に **shizen ni** naturally
自然(の) **shizen (no)** natural
静か(な) **shizuka (na)** peaceful; quiet; subdued; still *water, trees*; smooth *ride*
静かに **shizuka ni** quiet!, silence! ◊ softly
静かにさせる **shizuka ni saseru** quieten down
静けさ **shizuke-sa** calm; peace
滴 **shizuku** drip; drop
静まる **shizumaru** die down (*of storm*); drop (*of wind*); settle down; calm down
沈める **shizumeru** sink *ship*
沈む **shizumu** sink, go under
シーズン **shīzun** season (*for tourism etc*)
シーズンオフ **shīzun'ofu** off-season
ショー **shō** cabaret; show
賞 **shō** award, prize
章 **shō** chapter; section
省 **shō** department, ministry,

商売 **shōbai** business; 商売をする ***shôbai o suru*** do business; deal
処罰する **shobatsu suru** penalize, punish
小便 **shōben** urine; 小便をする ***shôben o suru*** urinate
消防車 **shōbō-sha** fire truck
消防士 **shōbō-shi** firefighter
消防署 **shōbō-sho** fire department
勝負 **shōbu** match; game; victory or defeat, result; ここが勝負勝負だ ***koko ga shôbu da*** this is the crucial moment
処分 **shobun** disposal; punishment
処分する **shobun suru** dispose of; punish
承知する **shōchi suru** consent; understand; be aware of
所長 **shochō** director; warden
象徴 **shōchō** symbol
象徴する **shōchō suru** symbolize
象徴的(な) **shōchōteki (na)** symbolic
承諾 **shōdaku** acceptance; compliance
承諾する **shōdaku suru** accept
商談をまとめる **shōdan o matomeru** clinch a deal
書道 **shodō** calligraphy
衝動 **shōdō** impulse, urge
衝動買い **shōdōgai** impulse buy; 衝動買いをする ***shôdôgai o suru*** go on a shopping spree
消毒綿 **shōdokumen** swab
消毒(の) **shōdoku (no)** antiseptic
消毒する **shōdoku suru** disinfect
消毒剤 **shōdokuzai** antiseptic; disinfectant
衝動的(な) **shōdōteki (na)** impulsive
衝動的に **shōdōteki ni** on the spur of the moment
省エネ(の) **shō-ene (no)** energy-saving
しょうが **shōga** ginger
障害 **shōgai** barrier; obstacle; hindrance; disorder MED
渉外 **shōgai** public relations; customer relations
生涯 **shōgai** lifetime
障害物 **shōgaibutsu** obstacle, obstruction; blockage
障害物走 **shōgaibutsu-sō** steeplechase
小学校 **shōgakkō** elementary school
小学校教師 **shōgakkō-kyōshi** elementary teacher
奨学金 **shōgakukin** grant; scholarship
小学生 **shōgakusei** elementary school student
しょうがない **shō ga nai** it can't be helped
正月 **shōgatsu** New Year season
衝撃 **shōgeki** impact (*of new manager etc*); knock, blow
衝撃的(な) **shōgekiteki (na)** devastating; traumatic; shocking
証言する **shōgen suru** testify, give evidence
将棋 **shōgi** Japanese chess
正午 **shōgo** midday, noon
将軍 **shōgun** general MIL
商業 **shōgyō** commerce
商業化する **shōgyōka suru** commercialize
商業(の) **shōgyō (no)** commercial
商業的(な) **shōgyōteki (na)** commercial
消費 **shōhi** consumption
商品 **shōhin** goods, merchandise; stock
賞品 **shōhin** prize
商品化 **shōhinka** merchandising
商品券 **shōhinken** gift token, gift voucher
消費量 **shōhi-ryō** consumption
消費者 **shōhi-sha** consumer
消費社会 **shōhi-shakai** consumer society
消費する **shōhi suru** consume, use
消費財 **shōhi-zai** consumer goods
初歩(の) **shoho (no)** elementary, rudimentary
処方せん **shohōsen** prescription
処方する **shohō suru** prescribe
初歩的(な) **shohoteki (na)** rudimentary
所持 **shoji** possession (*of gun, drugs*)
障子 **shōji** sliding paper door
正直 **shōjiki** honesty

正直(な) **shōjiki (na)** honest, straight; upright
正直に **shōjiki ni** honestly; 正直に言うと ***shôjiki ni iu to*** to be brutally frank; to be honest with you
所持規制薬物**shojikisei-yakubutsu** controlled substance
精進料理 **shōjin-ryōri** vegetarian Japanese cuisine
所持する **shoji suru** possess *gun, drugs*
処女 **shojo** virgin (*female*); virginity (*female*)
少女 **shōjo** girl
症状 **shōjō** symptom; 症状がある ***shôjô ga aru*** be symptomatic of
賞状 **shōjō** certificate of merit
処女航海 **shojo-kōkai** maiden voyage
消化 **shōka** digestion
消化不良 **shōka-furyō** indigestion
紹介 **shōkai** introduction (*to person*); presentation (*of product*)
照会番号 **shōkai-bangō** reference number
紹介する **shōkai suru** introduce
消火器 **shōka-ki** fire extinguisher
昇格する **shōkaku suru** move up (*in league*)
召喚状 **shōkan-jō** subpoena
召喚する **shōkan suru** subpoena
償還する **shōkan suru** repay; redeem *debt*
消火栓 **shōkasen** hydrant
消化する **shōka suru** digest
処刑 **shokei** execution (*of criminal*)
処刑する **shokei suru** execute *criminal*
証券 **shōken** bonds; securities; stocks
証券ブローカー**shōken-burōkā** broker
証券市場 **shōken-shijō** stock market; 証券市場の暴落 ***shôken-shijô no bôraku*** stockmarket crash
証券取引所**shōken-torihiki-sho** stock exchange
初期 **shoki** infancy (*of state, institution*)
正気 **shōki** sanity
初期化する **shokika suru** format
賞金 **shōkin** reward; winnings; 賞金を与える ***shôkin o ataeru*** reward
初期(の) **shoki (no)** early; initial
正気(の) **shōki (no)** sane, lucid
触角 **shokkaku** antenna, feeler
食券 **shokken** voucher (*for food*)
食器 **shokki** tableware
食器棚 **shokkidana** dresser; sideboard
ショッキング(な) **shokkingu (na)** shocking
ショック **shokku** shock; ショックを与える ***shokku o ataeru*** stun, shock; electrify *fig*
ショック状態にある **shokku jōtai ni aru** be in shock
証拠 **shōko** evidence, proof; testament (*to s.o.*)
証拠物件 **shōko-bukken** evidence
商工会議所**Shōkō-kaigisho** Chamber of Commerce
しょう紅熱 **shōkōnetsu** scarlet fever
職 **shoku** job, post; office, position; 職探しをしている ***shokusagashi o shite iru*** be job hunting
触媒 **shokubai** catalyst
植物 **shokubutsu** plant
植物学 **shokubutsugaku** botany
植物(の) **shokubutsu (no)** botanical
食中毒 **shoku-chūdoku** food poisoning
食堂 **shokudō** canteen; diner; dining room
食堂車 **shokudōsha** dining car, restaurant car
職業 **shokugyō** employment; business; profession
職業(の) **shokugyō (no)** vocational
職業倫理に反する**shokugyōrinri ni hansuru** unprofessional
職業紹介所**shokugyō-shōkaijo** employment agency
触発する **shokuhatsu suru** touch off; trigger; provoke
食費 **shokuhi** spending on food
食品 **shokuhin** food products
職員 **shokuin** personnel, staff
職員室 **shokuin-shitsu** staffroom
食事 **shokuji** meal; 食事を出す

shokuji o dasu serve food, give out food; 食事をする ***shokuji o suru*** dine
食事時間 **shokuji-jikan** mealtime; sitting (*for meal*)
食事療法 **shokuji-ryōhō** diet (*for health reasons*)
植民地 **shokuminchi** colony
植民地化する **shokuminchika suru** colonize
職務 **shokumu** duty, responsibility
職務内容 **shokumu-naiyō** job description
職人 **shokunin** tradesman, workman; craftsman
食料 **shokuryō** food
食料雑貨屋 **shokuryō-zakka-ya** grocer
食生活 **shokuseikatsu** diet (*regular food*)
触手 **shokushu** feeler; antenna; tentacle
食卓 **shokutaku** dining table
食欲 **shokuyoku** appetite
食前酒 **shokuzenshu** appetizer, apéritif
焼却炉 **shōkyakuro** incinerator
消極的(な) **shōkyokuteki (na)** passive; negative
初級 **shokyū** beginner's course; elementary level
昇給 **shōkyū** raise, rise (*in salary*)
署名 **shomei** signature
照明 **shōmei** lighting
証明 **shōmei** verification; identification; proof
証明書 **shōmeisho** certificate
署名する **shomei suru** sign
証明する **shōmei suru** certify; prove
正面 **shōmen** front (*of building, book*)
書面で **shomen de** in writing
正面入り口 **shōmen-iriguchi** front entrance
正面観覧席 **shōmen-kanranseki** grandstand
正面(の) **shōmen (no)** head-on
消滅 **shōmetsu** disappearance
賞味期限の日付け **shōmikigen no hizuke** best before date
庶民 **shomin** the people, the masses
正味(の) **shōmi (no)** net *weight, amount*
消耗する **shōmō suru** consume; exhaust
少年 **shōnen** boy
少年非行 **shōnen-hikō** delinquency
少年(の) **shōnen (no)** juvenile
少年のよう(な) **shōnen no yō(na)** boyish
初日 **shonichi** première
小児科 **shōnika** pediatrics
小児科医 **shōnikai** pediatrician
小児まひ **shōni-mahi** polio
承認 **shōnin** acknowledg(e)ment; recognition (*of state, s.o.'s achievements*); approval
証人 **shōnin** witness
商人 **shōnin** merchant; shopkeeper
証人席 **shōnin-seki** witness stand
承認する **shōnin suru** approve; grant *request*; recognize
しょう乳洞 **shōnyūdō** limestone cave
消音装置 **shōon-sōchi** silencer
ショッピングセンター **shoppingu-sentā** shopping mall, plaza
将来 **shōrai** future
症例 **shōrei** case MED
奨励 **shōrei** encouragement
奨励する **shōrei suru** encourage
勝利 **shōri** win, victory; triumph; 勝利を得た ***shôri o eta*** victorious
勝利者 **shōri-sha** victor
処理する **shori suru** handle, take care of; process *data*; treat *materials*
小論文 **shōronbun** essay
ショール **shōru** shawl
書類 **shorui** documentation, papers
ショールーム **shōrūmu** showroom
省略 **shōryaku** omission
省略形 **shōryakukei** abbreviation
省略する **shōryaku suru** omit; abbreviate
少量 **shōryō** dash, drop
書斎 **shosai** den; study
詳細 **shōsai** detail
詳細に **shōsai ni** in minute detail, minutely
称賛 **shōsan** applause, praise; 称賛に値する ***shôsan ni atai suru*** creditable; praiseworthy

称賛する **shōsan suru** applaud, praise
小冊子 **shōsasshi** booklet
小説 **shōsetsu** fiction; novel
小説家 **shōsetsu-ka** novelist
勝者 **shō-sha** winner
商社 **shōsha** trading company
昇進 **shōshin** promotion
昇進させる **shōshin saseru** promote *employee*
初心者 **shoshin-sha** beginner, novice
正真正銘(の) **shōshin-shōmei (no)** genuine
昇進する **shōshin suru** be promoted
証書 **shōsho** (title) deed; certificate
少々 **shōshō** a bit; a little; mildly
招集する **shōshū suru** call, summon, convene
召集する **shōshū suru** summon, call out
消息通 **shōsokutsū** insider
小数 **shōsū** decimal; minority ◊ few, not many
少数派である **shōsūha de aru** be in the minority
少数民族 **shōsū-minzoku** ethnic minority
少数(の) **shōsū (no)** few, not many
小数点 **shōsūten** decimal point
招待 **shōtai** invitation
正体 **shōtai** true character; 正体を現わす ***shôtai o arawasu*** give oneself away
招待状 **shōtaijō** invitation (*card*)
招待する **shōtai suru** invite, ask
焦点 **shōten** focus; …の焦点を絞る ***… no shôten o shiboru*** focus on
商店 **shōten** store
商店主 **shōten-shu** storekeeper; merchant
ショート **shōto** short circuit
所得 **shotoku** earnings; 所得から控除される ***shotoku kara kôjo sareru*** tax deductible
所得税 **shotokuzei** income tax
衝突 **shōtotsu** crash, collision
衝突させる **shōtotsu saseru** crash, collide
衝突する **shōtotsu suru** collide; run into
ショーツ **shōtsu** briefs
ショット **shotto** photograph, shot
小宇宙 **shōuchū** microcosm
昭和時代 **Shōwa-jidai** Showa period (*1926-1989*)
昭和天皇 **Shōwa-tennō** Emperor Hirohito
ショーウィンドウ **shō-windō** store window
賞与 **shōyo** bonus; reward
所有 **shoyū** possession, ownership
しょうゆ **shōyu** soy sauce
所有物 **shoyūbutsu** possession; possessions, property
所有地 **shoyūchi** land (*property*)
所有格(の) **shoyūkaku (no)** possessive GRAM
所有権 **shoyū-ken** ownership
所有者 **shoyū-sha** holder, owner
所有する **shoyū suru** own, possess
肖像画 **shōzōga** portrait
所属する **shozoku suru** belong to
種 **shu** species
州 **shū** province, state
週 **shū** week
守備 **shubi** defense; fielding SP
首謀者 **shubō-sha** ringleader
秋分 **shūbun** autumnal equinox
秋分の日 **Shūbun no hi** Day of the Autumnal Equinox
執着 **shūchaku** attachment; persistence; obsession
執着する **shūchaku suru** be attached; stick
主張 **shuchō** case, argument; cause; claim; assertion
しゅう長 **shūchō** chief; headman
主張する **shuchō suru** claim, maintain; argue that; protest
集中治療室 **shūchū-chiryōshitsu** intensive care (unit)
集中コース **shūchū-kōsu** crash course
集中講座 **shūchū-kōza** intensive course
集中力 **shūchūryoku** concentration
集中する **shūchū suru** concentrate
集中的(な) **shūchūteki (na)** intensive

主題 **shudai** subject, topic
手段 **shudan** avenue *fig*; vehicle *fig*; expedient
集団 **shūdan** group
集団療法 **shūdan-ryōhō** group therapy
終電 **shūden** last train of the day
修道院 **shūdōin** abbey; monastery
修道女 **shūdōjo** nun
主導権 **shudōken** initiative
修道士 **shūdōshi** monk
収益 **shūeki** proceeds; profits
収益性 **shūekisei** profitability
主演させる **shuen saseru** star
主演する **shuen suru** star
主夫 **shufu** house-husband
主婦 **shufu** housewife
修復 **shūfuku** restoration (*of building*)
修復できない **shūfuku dekinai** irreparable
修復する **shūfuku suru** restore
手芸 **shugei** handicraft
襲撃 **shūgeki** assault, attack; raid
襲撃する **shūgeki suru** assault, attack; raid
主義 **shugi** doctrine; principle; 主義として ***shugi to shite*** on principle
衆議院 **Shūgiin** House of Representatives
集合 **shūgō** gathering; assembly; set MATH
主語 **shugo** subject GRAM
就業時間 **shūgyō-jikan** work day
宗派 **shūha** cult, sect; denomination
周波数 **shūhasū** frequency, wavelength
周辺 **shūhen** periphery
周辺機器 **shūhen-kiki** peripheral
首位 **shui** first place; leader
周囲 **shūi** perimeter
周囲(の) **shūi (no)** surrounding
習字 **shūji** calligraphy
主人 **shujin** landlord; master
囚人 **shūjin** prisoner
手術 **shujutsu** operation MED; 手術をする ***shujutsu o suru*** operate on; 手術を受ける ***shujutsu o ukeru*** have an operation
手術室 **shujutsushitsu** operating room
手術する **shujutsu suru** operate MED
集会 **shūkai** rally POL
臭覚 **shūkaku** sense of smell
収穫 **shūkaku** crop; harvest; yield; catch (*of fish*)
収穫する **shūkaku suru** reap
習慣 **shūkan** habit; routine; practice, custom
週間 **shūkan** week
週刊 **shūkan** weekly *magazine*
主観的(な) **shukanteki (na)** subjective
主権 **shuken** sovereignty, independence
集結地点 **shūketsu-chiten** rendezvous MIL
周期 **shūki** cycle (*series of events*)
周期的(な) **shūkiteki (na)** periodic
集金 **shūkin** collecting money; bill collection
出血 **shukketsu** hemorrhage
出血している **shukketsu shite iru** bleeding
出血する **shukketsu suru** bleed
出勤する **shukkin suru** go off to work
出国審査 **shukkoku-shinsa** passport control (*for departure*)
出港する **shukkō suru** sail, depart
宿題 **shukudai** homework
祝福 **shukufuku** blessing
祝福する **shukufuku suru** bless
宿泊客 **shukuhaku-kyaku** guest; visitor; resident
宿泊させる **shukuhaku saseru** accommodate
宿泊設備 **shukuhaku-setsubi** accommodations
宿泊する **shukuhaku suru** stay
祝日 **shukujitsu** holiday (*one day*)
縮小 **shukushō** decrease
縮小する **shukushō suru** decrease; wind down (*of business*)
宿敵 **shukuteki** old enemy; mortal enemy
縮図 **shukuzu** scale (*of map*); scale drawing
宗教 **shūkyō** religion
宗教(の) **shūkyō (no)** religious
週末 **shūmatsu** weekend

趣味 **shumi** hobby; pastime, pursuit
趣味のよい **shumi no yoi** tasteful; esthetic
種目 **shumoku** event SP
春分 **shunbun** vernal equinox
春分の日 **Shunbun no hi** Day of the Vernal Equinox
周年 **-shūnen** anniversary
執念深い **shūnen-bukai** relentless; persistent
就任式(の) **shūninshiki (no)** inaugural
就任する **shūnin suru** be inaugurated; be appointed
瞬間 **shunkan** instant, moment
春期 **shunki** springtime
州(の) **shū (no)** state
収納箱 **shūnōbako** chest
首脳会議 **shunō-kaigi** summit
シュノーケル **shunōkeru** snorkel
収入 **shūnyū** income, revenue
出版 **shuppan** publication (*of book, report*); publishing
出版物 **shuppanbutsu** publication (*book, newspaper*)
出版されている **shuppan sarete iru** be published, be out
出版社 **shuppan-sha** publisher, publishing company
出版する **shuppan suru** publish, bring out
出発 **shuppatsu** departure
出発便 **shuppatsubin** outgoing flight
出発地点**shuppatsu-chiten** starting point
出発時刻**shuppatsu-jikoku** departure time
出発ラウンジ**shuppatsu-raunji** departure lounge
出発する **shuppatsu suru** leave
出品物 **shuppinbutsu** exhibit; entry, item submitted
シュレッダー **shureddā** shredder; シュレッダーにかける ***shureddâ ni kakeru*** shred
修理工 **shūrikō** mechanic
修理工場 **shūri-kōjō** body shop; garage (*for repairs*)
修理する **shūri suru** repair, mend; fix; recondition
種類 **shurui** brand, make; sort, variety; form (*of government, address*)
狩猟 **shuryō** hunting
終了 **shūryō** termination
終了する **shūryō suru** log off; shut down COMPUT; complete
修了する **shūryō suru** complete
手りゅう弾 **shuryūdan** grenade
主催者 **shusai-sha** organizer; promoter
主催する **shusai suru** sponsor; host
修正 **shūsei** amendment; revision
修正液 **shūseieki** white-out, correcting fluid
修正する **shūsei suru** amend; revise *text, figures*; touch up *photo*
臭跡 **shūseki** scent (*of animal*)
集積回路 **shūseki-kairo** integrated circuit
収支 **shūshi** income and expenditure; 収支を合わせる ***shûshi o awaseru*** balance the books
終止符 **shūshifu** full stop
修士号 **shūshigō** master's (degree)
首相 **shushō** prime minister, premier
主食 **shushoku** staple diet
就職する **shūshoku suru** find work; get a job
収集家 **shūshūka** collector
収縮する **shūshuku suru** contract, shrink
収集した **shūshū shita** collected *works*
収集する **shūshū suru** collect (*as hobby*)
しゅうしゅうという音を立てる**shūshū to iu oto o tateru** hiss; sizzle
出産 **shussan** birth, labor; childbirth; delivery (*of baby*)
出産前(の) **shussanmae (no)** antenatal, prenatal
出生証明書**shussei-shōmeisho** birth certificate
出席 **shusseki** attendance
出席者 **shusseki-sha** those attending; turnout (*of people*)
出席している **shusseki shite iru** be present

出席する **shusseki suru** attend
出世する **shusse suru** be promoted
出身である **shusshin de aru** originate from, come from
出資者 **shusshi-sha** investor; financier
出生率 **shusshōritsu** birthrate
出所する **shussho suru** get out (*from prison*); be released
首都 **shuto** capital
シュート **shūto** chute
取得する **shutoku suru** acquire
習得する **shūtoku suru** master *skill, language*
しゅうとめ **shūtome** mother-in-law
主として **shu to shite** chiefly, largely
出馬する **shutsuba suru** run (*in election*); 大統領選に出馬する ***daitôryô-sen ni shutsuba suru*** run for President
出演 **shutsuen** appearance (*in movie etc*)
出演者 **shutsuen-sha** cast
出演する **shutsuen suru** appear (*in movie etc*)
出願 **shutsugan** application
出願する **shutsugan suru** apply for
出現 **shutsugen** birth, appearance
出現させる **shutsugen saseru** materialize
出場させる **shutsujō saseru** enter (*in race*)
出場者 **shutsujō-sha** contestant
出場する **shutsujō suru** enter (*in competition*); play, take part SP
出力 **shutsuryoku** output
出張 **shutchō** business trip
出張旅費 **shutchō-ryohi** travel expenses
出廷 **shuttei** appearance (*in court*)
出廷する **shuttei suru** appear (*in court*)
出頭命令 **shuttō-meirei** summons (*to court*)
出頭する **shuttō suru** report (*to police*); present oneself
手話 **shuwa** sign language
手腕 **shuwan** prowess
しゅよう **shuyō** growth MED; tumor
主要(な) **shuyō** (**na**) main; major, primary
収容力 **shūyōryoku** capacity
収容する **shūyō suru** accommodate; take in; intern
取材する **shuzai suru** collect *news*; gather *material*; cover (*of journalist*)
種族 **shuzoku** tribe
そう **sō** so; yes; in that way ◊ seeming; うれしそうな顔 ***ureshi-sô na kao*** a happy-looking face; そうですね ***sô desu ne*** that's right, isn't it?; そうではないだろう ***sô dewa nai darô*** I guess not; そう希望します / そう思います ***sô kibô shimasu / omoimasu*** I hope / think so
層 **sō** layer; tier
粗悪さ **soaku-sa** inferiority
そば **soba** buckwheat noodles
相場 **sōba** market; market price
そばかす **sobakasu** freckles
そばに **soba ni** beside; by
送別会 **sōbetsukai** farewell party
装備 **sōbi** gear, equipment
そびえる **sobieru** tower over; soar over; dominate
そびえ立つ **sobietatsu** lofty
ソビエト連邦 **Sobieto-renpō** Soviet Union
装備されている **sōbi sarete iru** be supplied with
祖母 **sobo** grandmother
素朴(な) **soboku** (**na**) simple, unsophisticated
装置 **sōchi** device
そうだ **sō da** that's right; I hear that …; looks like; そうだとは思いません ***sô da to wa omoimasen*** I don't think so; そうだとよいと思う ***sô da to yoi to omou*** I hope so; みんなうまくいきそうだ ***minna umaku ikisô da*** it looks like everything is going to be fine
ソーダ **sōda** soda (water)
壮大(な) **sōdai** (**na**) grand, magnificent
壮大さ **sōdai-sa** magnificence
相談 **sōdan** session
相談料 **sōdan-ryō** fee
相談する **sōdan suru** consult
相談役 **sōdan'yaku** adviser

そうだろう **sō darō** I guess so
育てる **sodateru** raise, bring up *child*
育つ **sodatsu** develop, grow; thrive
そで **sode** sleeve
そでなし(の) **sodenashi** (**no**) sleeveless
騒動 **sōdō** tumult; 騒動を起こす ***sôdô o okosu*** make a scene
疎遠になる **soen ni naru** drift apart
ソファ **sofa** sofa
ソファベッド **sofa-beddo** sofa-bed
祖父 **sofu** grandfather
祖父母 **sofubo** grandparents
ソフト **sofuto** software
双眼鏡 **sōgankyō** binoculars
狙撃班 **sogekihan** hit squad
狙撃兵 **sogekihei** sniper
草原 **sōgen** prairie
争議 **sōgi** dispute (*industrial*)
葬儀場 **sōgijō** funeral home
葬儀屋 **sōgiya** mortician
相互依存した **sōgo-izon shita** interdependent
相互(の) **sōgo** (**no**) mutual, reciprocal
相互作用 **sōgo-sayō** interaction; reciprocal action
総合的(な) **sōgōteki** (**na**) comprehensive
操業短縮する **sōgyō-tanshuku suru** be on short time; reduce operations
双方で **sōhō de** bilateral
相違 **sōi** disparity; 意見の相違 ***iken no sôi*** difference; disagreement; dissension
そういう **sō iu** such a ◊ so; そういうつもりはなかった ***sô iu tsumori wa nakatta*** that's not what I intended
掃除 **sōji** cleaning
掃除夫 **sōjifu** cleaner (*male*)
掃除婦 **sōjifu** cleaner (*female*); cleaning woman
掃除機 **sōjiki** vacuum cleaner; 掃除機をかける ***sôjiki o kakeru*** vacuum
掃除する **sōji suru** clean, clean up
早熟(な) **sōjuku** (**na**) precocious
操縦室 **sōjū-shitsu** flight deck
操縦装置 **sōjū-sōchi** controls
操縦する **sōjū suru** fly *airplane*
総会 **sōkai** general meeting; plenary session
送還する **sōkan suru** repatriate
総計…になる **sōkei … ni naru** amount to…
ソケット **soketto** socket, outlet
送金 **sōkin** transfer (*of money*)
速記 **sokki** shorthand
即金で払う **sokkin de harau** cash down
そっくりである **sokkuri de aru** be the spitting image of
即興で演じる **sokkyō de enjiru** improvise
そこ **soko** over there; down there
底 **soko** base, bottom; bed (*of sea, river*); 底をつく ***soko o tsuku*** bottom out (*of recession etc*)
倉庫 **sōko** storehouse; warehouse; storeroom
そこで **soko de** there; then; accordingly
走行距離 **sōkō-kyori** mileage
損なう **sokonau** deface; harm; spoil
底値(の) **sokone** (**no**) rock-bottom
そこに **soko ni** down there; there
装甲車 **sōkōsha** armored vehicle
足 **-soku** *countword for footwear*
束縛 **sokubaku** restriction; tie
速度 **sokudo** rate; velocity; 速度を増す ***sokudo o masu*** gain speed
速度計 **sokudo-kei** speedometer
即時(の) **sokuji** (**no**) instant, instantaneous
即時再生ビデオ **sokuji-saisei-bideo** action replay
側面 **sokumen** side; flank MIL
測量 **sokuryō** survey (*of building*)
測量技師 **sokuryō-gishi** surveyor
測量する **sokuryō suru** survey *building*
側線 **sokusen** sidetrack
促進 **sokushin** promotion
促進する **sokushin suru** encourage; promote; facilitate; further
速達 **sokutatsu** express delivery
測定 **sokutei** measurement
測定する **sokutei suru** gauge
即座に **sokuza ni** instantly; promptly

染まる **somaru** dye; be dyed; be tainted
粗末(な) **somatsu** (**na**) cheap; poor; shabby; low *quality*
染める **someru** dye
そもそも **somosomo** in the first place
背く **somuku** go against; defy; offend
損 **son** loss; 損をする ***son o suru*** lose out; be out of pocket
備える **sonaeru** provide; be equipped with
供える **sonaeru** offer (*at an altar*)
備え付けられている **sonaetsukerarete iru** be fixed
備え付ける **sonaetsukeru** equip; install; provide
遭難信号 **sōnan-shingō** distress signal
遭難する **sōnan suru** meet with disaster
尊重する **sonchō suru** respect; value
尊大(な) **sondai** (**na**) dictatorial; haughty; arrogant
損益分岐点 **son'eki-bunkiten** break-even point
損害 **songai** damage; 損害を与える ***songai o ataeru*** damage
損害賠償 **songai-baishō** damages
損害賠償保険 **songaibaishō-hoken** third-party insurance
尊敬 **sonkei** deference; respect
尊敬する **sonkei suru** respect
そんな **sonna** such a, so; そんなばかなことはない ***sonna baka na koto wa nai*** that's not acceptable; そんなこと知ったことじゃない ***sonna koto shitta koto ja nai*** I don't give a damn!; そんなにかかるのですか ***sonna ni kakaru no desu ka*** as much as that?; そんなにたくさん ***sonna ni takusan*** so much
その **sono** that; those; the
その間に **sono aida ni** meanwhile
その後 **sono ato** subsequently
その後(の) **sono ato** (**no**) subsequent; succeeding
その場で **sono ba de** on the spot, immediately
その場しのぎ(の) **sono ba shinogi** (**no**) temporary; stopgap
その辺 **sono hen** somewhere near
その代わりに **sono kawari ni** instead; alternatively
その結果 **sono kekka** consequently; so, for that reason
そのくらい **sono kurai** thereabouts
そのまま **sono mama**: そのまま真っすぐ行く ***sono mama massugu iku*** carry straight on; そのままお待ちください ***sono mama omachi kudasai*** please hold the line; そのまま立っていて ***sono mama tatte ite*** stand still!
その当時 **sono tōji** then, at that time
その当時は **sono tōji wa** in those days
そのとおり **sono tōri** exactly!; that's it!; that's right
そのうち **sono uchi** sometime
そのうちに **sono uchi ni** in due course; eventually
そのうえ **sono ue** besides
そのよう(な) **sono yō** (**na**) such
損失 **sonshitsu** loss; 損失を出す ***sonshitsu o dasu*** make a loss
挿入 **sōnyū** insertion, inserting
存在 **sonzai** existence; presence
存在しない **sonzai shinai** nonexistent
存在する **sonzai suru** exist
騒音 **sōon** din, racket
ソプラノ **sopurano** soprano
空 **sora** sky
そらす **sorasu** avert; distract; divert
それ **sore** that; that one
それで **sore de** so, and then; in order that ◊ so what?; それでいい－ちょっと違う ***sore de ii - chotto chigau*** is that right? - not quite; それで十分だ ***sore de jûbun da*** that will do!
それでも **soredemo** still, ◊ yet; nevertheless
それでもなお **sore demo nao** nonetheless
それどころか **sore dokoro ka** on the contrary
それ程 **sore hodo** so; that

それ以上(の) **sore ijō** (**no**) further, additional
それ以来 **sore irai** ever since; since
それじゃ **sore ja** well; so
それから **sore kara** then, after that; since then
それまで **sore made** until then
それなら **sore nara** in that case, then
それに加えて **sore ni kuwaete** plus, in addition to that
それにもかかわらず **sore ni mo kakawarazu** nevertheless
それに応じて **sore ni ōjite** accordingly
それら **sorera** they; those
それらの **sorera no** their; those ◊ theirs
それる **soreru** stray, wander; swerve
それとも **sore tomo** or
それぞれ **sorezore** each; respectively
それぞれ(の) **sorezore** (**no**) each ◊ respective
そり **sori** sled(ge), sleigh, toboggan
総理大臣 **sōri-daijin** prime minister, premier
そりおとす **soriotosu** shave off
ソリスト **sorisuto** soloist
創立者 **sōritsu-sha** founder
創立する **sōritsu suru** found; start, establish
そろばん **soroban** abacus
そろえる **soroeru** put in order; arrange; make uniform
そろそろ **sorosoro** soon; slowly
そろう **sorou** be complete; be equal; gather
そる **soru** shave
総領事 **sōryōji** consul general
ソリューション **soryūshon** solution, fix
操作 **sōsa** operation; handling
捜査 **sōsa** investigation
捜査方針 **sōsa-hōshin** line of inquiry
創作 **sōsaku** creation
捜索 **sōsaku** hunt
創作者 **sōsaku-sha** creator
創作する **sōsaku suru** create
捜索する **sōsaku suru** search; hunt
捜索隊 **sōsaku-tai** search party
操作する **sōsa suru** manipulate; operate
ソーセージ **sōsēji** sausage
祖先 **sosen** ancestor
総選挙 **sōsenkyo** general election
総選挙日 **sōsenkyobi** election day
創設者 **sōsetsu-sha** creator
走者 **sōsha** runner
ソーシャルワーカー **sōsharu-wākā** social worker, welfare worker
組織 **soshiki** outfit, organization; system; set-up, structure; tissue ANAT
葬式 **sōshiki** funeral
組織する **soshiki suru** organize; put together
組織的(な) **soshikiteki** (**na**) methodical, systematic
装身具 **sōshingu** accessories; trinkets
送信機 **sōshinki** transmitter
送信する **sōshin suru** transmit; beam
阻止する **soshi suru** check, stop; deter
そして **soshite** and (then)
素質 **soshitsu** nature; character; predisposition
訴訟 **soshō** lawsuit
装飾する **sōshoku suru** decorate; embellish
そう祖父 **sōsofu** great-grandfather
そう祖母 **sōsobo** great-grandmother
注ぎ口 **sosogiguchi** spout
注ぐ **sosogu** pour; devote oneself to
そそのかす **sosonokasu** instigate; egg on
そそる **sosoru** excite; incite; arouse
ソース **sōsu** sauce
そうすると **sō suru to** in that case; if so; then
相対的(な) **sōtaiteki** (**na**) relative
そっち **sotchi** over there ◊ you (*informal*)
率直(な) **sotchoku** (**na**) candid; open; direct; outspoken
率直さ **sotchoku-sa** candor
外 **soto** outside; 外を見る ***soto o miru*** look out
外側 **sotogawa** outside

外側(の) **sotogawa (no)** outer; outside
相当(な) **sōtō (na)** substantial; suitable
外に **soto ni** outdoors, outside; 外に出す ***soto ni dasu*** let out (*of room, building*); 外に出ている ***soto ni dete iru*** be out, be outside
ソートする **sōto suru** sort COMPUT
相当する **sōtō suru** correspond to; be equivalent to
卒業 **sotsugyō** graduation
卒業生 **sotsugyō-sei** graduate
卒業式 **sotsugyō-shiki** graduation ceremony
卒業証書 **sotsugyō-shōsho** diploma
卒業する **sotsugyō suru** graduate; leave *school*
そつのない **sotsu no nai** diplomatic, tactful
そった **sotta** shaven
そっと **sotto** quietly; softly; stealthily
沿う **sou** run along; follow; go along
添う **sou** meet; answer; accompany
そわそわする **sowasowa suru** fidget
そよ風 **soyokaze** breeze
総菜屋 **sōzai-ya** delicatessen
粗雑(な) **sozatsu (na)** crude
想像 **sōzō** imagination; 想像がつく ***sôzô ga tsuku*** I can just imagine it
創造 **sōzō** creation
想像できない **sōzō dekinai** unimaginable
想像できる **sōzō dekiru** imaginable
相続人 **sōzoku-nin** heir; heiress
相続する **sōzoku suru** inherit
想像力 **sōzōryoku** imagination; 想像力の豊か(な) ***sôzôryoku no yutaka (na)*** imaginative
騒々しい **sōzōshii** boisterous; rowdy; tumultuous
想像する **sōzō suru** imagine; visualize
創造する **sōzō suru** create
巣 **su** nest; 巣をつくる ***su o tsukuru*** spin (*of spider*)
酢 **su** vinegar
巣箱 **subako** nesting box; hive
素晴らしい **subarashii** amazing, wonderful, brilliant, great
素晴らしく **subarashiku** beautifully
素早い **subayai** nimble
素早く **subayaku** quickly, speedily
滑らない **suberanai** nonslip
滑らせる **suberaseru** slide
滑り台 **suberidai** slide
滑る **suberu** glide; slip
すべて(の) **subete (no)** all; every
スチュワーデス **suchuwādesu** flight attendant; stewardess
スチュワード **suchuwādo** steward
すだれ **sudare** bamboo blind
すでに **sude ni** already
末 **sue** end; trifle; tip; future
スエード **suēdo** suede
末っ子 **suekko** youngest child
据え付ける **suetsukeru** install; set up
スエットスーツ **suetto-sūtsu** jogging suit
数学 **sūgaku** math
数学者 **sūgaku-sha** mathematician
数学的(な) **sūgakuteki (na)** mathematical
すがすがしい **sugasugashii** refreshing
姿 **sugata** image; 姿を表す ***sugata o arawasu*** surface
すっごく **suggoku** really; extremely; way
杉 **sugi** Japanese cedar
過ぎる **sugiru** pass by; slip away (*of time*); expire; go too far
…すぎる **…sugiru** too; ごはんが多すぎる ***gohan ga ô-sugiru*** there is too much rice
過ぎ去る **sugisaru** speed by
すごい **sugoi** super, terrific; unbelievable
すごく **sugoku** very; extremely
過ごす **sugosu** spend, pass the time
すぐ **sugu** right away; directly; すぐ近くに ***sugu chikaku ni*** nearby; すぐそば ***sugu soba*** right next door; close; すぐそこです ***sugu soko desu*** it's around the corner; it's just down the road
すぐに **sugu ni** immediately; soon; right now

優れる **sugureru** shine; excel
優れた **sugureta** excellent
すぐさま **sugusama** immediately
崇拝 **sūhai** worship
崇拝者 **sūhai-sha** worshiper; admirer
崇拝する **sūhai suru** idolize; worship
水分 **suibun** moisture; water
垂直(の) **suichoku (no)** perpendicular; vertical
水中翼船 **suichū-yokusen** hydrofoil
水田 **suiden** ricefield
水道 **suidō** water supply
水道管 **suidōkan** water pipe
水道水 **suidōsui** running water
水泳 **suiei** swimming; swim
吸い殻 **suigara** butt, stub
水源地 **suigenchi** source
水銀 **suigin** mercury, quicksilver
水兵 **suihei** sailor
水平(の) **suihei (no)** horizontal
水平線 **suiheisen** horizon
水位 **suii** water level
衰弱した **suijaku shita** emaciated; worn out
衰弱する **suijaku suru** become weak; be worn out
炊事 **suiji** cooking
水蒸気 **suijōki** steam
水上スキー **suijō-sukī** waterskiing
水準 **suijun** level; standard
スイカ **suika** water melon
吸い込む **suikomu** inhale, breathe in
水面 **suimen** surface
睡眠 **suimin** sleep
睡眠薬 **suimin'yaku** sleeping pill
推理 **suiri** inference; speculation
推理小説 **suiri-shōsetsu** detective novel
水路 **suiro** waterway
推論 **suiron** deduction
推論する **suiron suru** deduce
水力 **suiryoku** water power
水力発電(の) **suiryoku-hatsuden (no)** hydroelectric
水彩絵の具 **suisai-enogu** watercolor (*paint*)
水彩画 **suisaiga** watercolor (*painting*)
すい星 **suisei** comet
水性白色塗料 **suisei-hakushoku-toryō** whitewash
推薦 **suisen** endorsement; recommendation; nomination
水仙 **suisen** daffodil
推薦状 **suisenjō** reference, testimonial
推薦する **suisen suru** endorse; recommend
推進力 **suishin-ryoku** driving force
推進する **suishin suru** propel
水晶 **suishō** crystal; quartz
水素 **suiso** hydrogen
水素爆弾 **suiso-bakudan** hydrogen bomb
吹奏楽団 **suisō-gakudan** brass band
推測 **suisoku** conjecture; guess
推測する **suisoku suru** gather; guess
スイス **Suisu** Switzerland
スイス(の) **Suisu (no)** Swiss
スイッチ **suitchi** switch
推定 **suitei** estimate; inference; presumption
推定する **suitei suru** presume; assume
吸い取り紙 **suitorishi** blotter; blotting paper
吸い取る **suitoru** absorb
スイートルーム **suīto-rūmu** suite (*of rooms*)
水曜日 **suiyōbi** Wednesday
水族館 **suizokukan** aquarium
筋 **suji** action; plot; gristle; tendon; 筋の通った ***suji no tôtta*** coherent
数字 **sūji** digit, figure, number; numeral
筋張った **sujibatta** wiry
筋違い **sujichigai** crick in the neck
筋書き **sujigaki** scenario
数字に強い **sūji ni tsuyoi** numerate
スカーフ **sukāfu** headscarf
スカイライン **sukairain** skyline
数か国語を話せる **sūkakokugo o hanaseru** multilingual *person*
好かれる **sukareru** likeable
スカッシュ **sukasshu** squash
スカート **sukāto** skirt

すけすけ(の) **sukesuke (no)** see-through
スケーター **sukētā** skater
スケッチ **suketchi** drawing; sketch
スケッチブック **suketchi bukku** sketchbook
スケート **sukēto** skate; skating
スケートボード **sukēto-bōdo** skateboard
すき **suki** plow; spade
スキー **sukī** ski; skiing
好きである **suki de aru** like ◊ be enthusiastic about; be into
すき間 **sukima** chink; gap; slit
すきま風 **sukimakaze** draft; すきま風の入る ***sukimakaze no hairu*** drafty
すき間のない **sukima no nai** solid
スキムミルク **sukimu miruku** skimmed milk
スキンダイビング **sukin daibingu** skin diving
好きになる **suki ni naru** like, take to
スキップ **sukippu** skip
スキップする **sukippu suru** skip
スキーリフト **sukī-rifuto** chair lift, ski lift
透き通る **sukitōru** be transparent
スキーヤー **sukīyā** skier
すきやき **sukiyaki** sukiyaki
すっからかんになる **sukkarakan ni naru** go broke, go bankrupt
すっかり **sukkari** right, completely; head over heels *fall in love*; in full; すっかり目が覚めている ***sukkari me ga samete iru*** be wide awake; すっかりなくなる ***sukkari nakunaru*** be all gone; すっかり大人になった ***sukkari otona ni natta*** full-grown
すっきりする **sukkiri suru** feel refreshed; be satisfied
スコア **sukoa** score MUS, SP
崇高(な) **sūkō (na)** lofty; sublime
スコップ **sukoppu** scoop; spade
少し **sukoshi** a little, a bit; scrap; touch ◊ rather, somewhat; slightly ◊ some; 少しだけ ***sukoshi dake*** just a bit; not a lot
少しも…ない **sukoshi mo …nai** not at all; not in the least; 少しも残っていない ***sukoshi mo nokotte inai*** there is none left
少し(の) **sukoshi (no)** a little; a bit (of)
少しの間 **sukoshi no aida** briefly
少しずつ **sukoshi zutsu** bit by bit, little by little
スコッチウイスキー **sukotchi-uisukī** Scotch (whiskey)
スコットランド **Sukottorando** Scotland
すく **suku** become less full; be hungry; be transparent; plow
救い **sukui** rescue; relief; help
すくい上げる **sukuiageru** scoop up
救い出す **sukuidasu** salvage
救いがたい **sukuigatai** incorrigible
少ない **sukunai** few
少なくとも **sukunaku tomo** at least
スクープ **sukūpu** scoop (*story*)
スクランブルエッグ **sukuranburu eggu** scrambled eggs
スクラップブック **sukurappu-bukku** scrapbook
スクリーン **sukurīn** monitor; screen
スクリーンセーバー **sukurīn-seibā** screen saver
スクロールする **sukurōru suru** scroll up/down
スクリュー **sukuryū** propeller
スクーター **sukūtā** motorscooter; scooter
すくう **sukuu** scoop
救う **sukuu** redeem; save, rescue
スキャン **sukyan** scan; scanner; スキャンをかける ***sukyan o kakeru*** scan
スキャナー **sukyanā** scanner; スキャナーで読み込む ***sukyanâ de yomikomu*** scan in
スキャンダル **sukyandaru** scandal
スキューバダイビング **sukyūba-daibingu** scuba diving
住まい **sumai** house; residence
すまない **sumanai** inexcusable; sorry; すまないと思う ***sumanai to omou*** regret
すませる **sumaseru** settle
すまし汁 **sumashijiru** clear soup
スマッシュ **sumasshu** smash
済ます **sumasu** finish
スマートカード **sumāto-kādo** smart

card
スマート(な) **sumāto (na)** stylish; slim
住める **sumeru** habitable
炭 **sumi** charcoal
隅 **sumi** corner; nook
墨 **sumi** Chinese ink
炭火焼き(の) **sumibiyaki (no)** charbroiled
墨絵 **sumie** ink painting
すみません **sumimasen** excuse me; (I'm) sorry!; thank you; ちょっとすみません ***chotto sumimasen*** excuse me; すみませんが、塩をとっていただけますか ***sumimasen ga, shio o totte itadakemasu ka*** will you pass the salt please
住みにくい **suminikui** inhospitable
すみれ **sumire** violet (*plant*)
相撲 **sumō** sumo
相撲取り **sumō-tori** sumo wrestler
スモッグ **sumoggu** smog
住む **sumu** live, reside; live in
澄む **sumu** be clear
済む **sumu** be finished; manage without
砂 **suna** grit; sand
砂場 **sunaba** sandpit
砂袋 **suna-bukuro** sandbag
素直(な) **sunao (na)** docile; obedient
スナップ写真 **sunappu shashin** snap(shot)
すなわち **sunawachi** namely
澄んだ **sunda** clear; pure
すね **sune** shin
すねる **suneru** sulk
すねた **suneta** sulky; sullen
スニーカー **sunīkā** sneakers
寸法 **sunpō** dimension, measurement
寸法直し **sunpō-naoshi** alteration
寸前 **sunzen** immediately before; 寸前である ***sunzen de aru*** be on the verge of
スロットル **surottoru** throttle
スパゲティ **supageti** spaghetti
スパイ **supai** secret agent, spy; スパイをする ***supai o suru*** spy
スパイ防止活動 **supai-bōshi-katsudō** counterespionage
スパイ行為 **supai-kōi** espionage
スパイク **supaiku** spike (*on shoe*)
スーパーマーケット **sūpāmāketto** supermarket
スパナ **supana** wrench (*tool*)
スパート **supāto** spurt
スペアミント **supeaminto** spearmint
スペアリブ **supearibu** spare ribs
スペアタイヤ **supea-taiya** spare tire; spare wheel
スペード **supēdo** spades (*in card game*)
スペイン **Supein** Spain
スペイン語 **Supein-go** Spanish
スペイン人 **Supein-jin** Spaniard
スペイン(の) **Supein (no)** Spanish
スペクタクル **supekutakuru** spectacle
スペリング **superingu** spelling
スペルチェッカー **superu-chekkā** spellchecker
スペルチェック **superu-chekku** spellcheck
スペースバー **supēsu-bā** space bar
スペースシャトル **supēsu-shatoru** space shuttle
スピーチ **supīchi** speech
スピード **supīdo** speed; …のスピードを上げる ***... no supîdo o ageru*** accelerate; スピードを出す ***supîdo o dasu*** speed up, put one's foot down; スピードを落とす ***supîdo o otosu*** slow down
スピード違反 **supīdo-ihan** speeding
スピーカー **supīkā** speaker; loudspeaker
スポーク **supōku** spoke
スポークスマン **supōkusuman** spokesperson
スポンジ **suponji** sponge
スポンサー **suponsā** sponsor; スポンサーになる ***suponsâ ni naru*** sponsor
スポーティー(な) **supōtī (na)** sporty
スポーツ **supōtsu** sport
スポーツカー **supōtsu-kā** sportscar
スポーツクラブ **supōtsu-kurabu** health club
スポーツマン **supōtsu-man** sportsman

スポーツ(の) **supōtsu (no)** athletic; sporting
スポーツニュース **supōtsu-nyūsu** sports news
スポーツ欄 **supōtsu-ran** sports page
スポーツウーマン **supōtsu-ūman** sportswoman
スポットライト **supottoraito** spotlight
酸っぱい **suppai** sour (*not sweet*)
酸っぱくなった **suppaku natta** sour (*not fresh*)
素っぴん(の) **suppin (no)** unmade-up
スープ **sūpu** soup, broth
スプーン **supūn** spoon
スプレー **supurē** atomizer; spray
スプレッドシート **supureddoshīto** spreadsheet
スプレー缶 **supurē-kan** aerosol
スプリンクラー **supurinkurā** sprinkler
スープ皿 **sūpu-zara** soup bowl
すら **-sura** even
スライド **suraido** slide PHOT
スラックス **surakkusu** slacks
スラム街 **suramugai** slum
スラング **surangu** slang
スラッシュ **surasshu** slash
すらすら言う **surasura iu** rattle off
すれば **sureba**: ...とすれば ***...to sureba*** supposing that
すれ違う **surechigau** brush past; pass each other
すり **suri** pickpocket
すりガラス **suri-garasu** frosted glass
擦り減らす **suriherasu** wear away; wear out
擦り減る **suriheru** wear away; wear out
擦り切れる **surikireru** wear (*of carpet, fabric*)
擦り切れた **surikireta** threadbare
擦り傷 **surikizu** abrasion
擦りむく **surimuku** chafe; graze
すりおろす **suriorosu** grate
スリッパ **surippa** slipper
スリップ **surippu** skid; slip
スリップする **surippu suru** skid
スリラー **surirā** thriller
スリル **suriru** thrill
スリーサイズ **surī-saizu** vital statistics
スリット **suritto** slit
スローガン **surōgan** slogan
スローイン **surō-in** throw-in
スローモーションで **surō-mōshon de** in slow motion
スロープ **surōpu** ramp
スロットマシン **surotto-mashin** slot machine
スロットル **surottoru** throttle
する **suru** ◊ do; have *meal, walk, wash*; play *game*; lift; render *service*; wear *make-up*; choose; decide on; cost; ...すること ***... suru koto*** to (*with verbs*); ...することができない ***... suru koto ga deki nai*** be incapable of doing ... ◊ (*forms verbs*): 大量生産する ***tairyô-seisan suru*** mass produce
擦る **suru** rub; grind; chafe
刷る **suru** print
...する間 **... suru aida** while
鋭い **surudoi** acute, sharp; incisive *mind*; penetrating *analysis*; perceptive
鋭くする **surudoku suru** sharpen
鋭さ **surudo-sa** edge (*in voice*)
すると **suruto** and then; just then
すし **sushi** sushi
すそ **suso** hem; bottom edge; foot (*of mountain*)
すす **susu** soot
すすぐ **susugu** rinse
すすき **susuki** Japanese pampas grass
勧められない **susumerarenai** inadvisable
進める **susumeru** advance; go ahead with
勧める **susumeru** advise; offer
薦める **susumeru** recommend
進む **susumu** progress, come along; flow (*of work*); proceed
進んで **susunde** readily, willingly
進んでいる **susunde iru** be fast (*of clock*)
すすり泣き **susurinaki** sob
すする **susuru** sip; slurp; はなをすする ***hana o susuru*** sniff

スター **sutā** star
スタイリスト **sutairisuto** stylist
スタイル **sutairu** figure (*of person*); style; スタイルのいい ***sutairu no ii*** shapely
スタジアム **sutajiamu** stadium
スタジオ **sutajio** television studio
スタミナ **sutamina** energy; stamina
スタンド **sutando** stand; stall; the bleachers; lamp
スタンプ **sutanpu** stamp; スタンプを押す ***sutanpu o osu*** postmark
スタント **sutanto** stunt
スタントマン **sutantoman** stuntman
すたれる **sutareru** decline; be abolished; die out
すたれた **sutareta** obsolete
スターター **sutātā** starter
ステアリング **sutearingu** steering
ステイタスシンボル **suteitasu-shinboru** status symbol
素敵(な) **suteki (na)** cute; gorgeous; swell
ステーキ **sutēki** steak
ステッカー **sutekkā** sticker
ステッキ **sutekki** walking stick
ステンドグラス **sutendo-gurasu** stained-glass
ステンレス **sutenresu** stainless steel
ステレオ **sutereo** stereo
ステレオタイプ **sutereotaipu** stereotype
ステロイド **suteroido** steroids
捨てる **suteru** abandon; discard; throw out
スト **suto** strike, industrial action
ストーブ **sutōbu** stove
ストーカー **sutōkā** stalker
ストッキング **sutokkingu** stocking
ストップする **sutoppu suru** stop
ストップウォッチ **sutoppu-wotchi** stopwatch
ストライキ **sutoraiki** strike, industrial action; ストライキに入る ***sutoraiki ni hairu*** go on strike; ストライキをする ***sutoraiki o suru*** strike
ストライク **sutoraiku** strike (*in baseball*)
ストライキ中である **sutoraikichū de aru** be on strike
ストラップ **sutorappu** strap
ストレス **sutoresu** stress; ストレスがたまっている ***sutoresu ga tamatte iru*** stressed out; ストレスのある ***sutoresu no aru*** be under stress ◊ stressful
ストレート(の) **sutorēto (no)** black *tea*; neat, straight-up *whiskey etc*
ストリッパー **sutorippā** stripper
ストリップ小屋 **sutorippu-goya** strip club
ストリップショー **sutorippu-shō** strip show; striptease
ストロー **sutorō** straw
スーツ **sūtsu** suit
スーツケース **sūtsukēsu** suitcase
スツール **sutsūru** stool
吸う **suu** inhale; suck; smoke
座り心地のよい **suwarigokochi no yoi** comfortable
座る **suwaru** sit, sit down
スウェーデン **Suwēden** Sweden
スウェーデン(の) **Suwēden (no)** Swedish
スウェットスーツ **suwetto-sūtsu** tracksuit
すやすや眠る **suyasuya nemuru** sleep peacefully; be fast asleep
すず **suzu** tin
鈴 **suzu** bell
酢漬けにする **suzuke ni suru** pickle
すずき **suzuki** sea bass
すずめ **suzume** sparrow; すずめの涙 ***suzume no namida*** pittance
すずめばち **suzumebachi** hornet
鈴虫 **suzumushi** cricket (*insect*)
すずらん **suzuran** lily of the valley
涼しい **suzushii** cool
涼しくなる **suzushiku naru** cool down

T

田 ta paddy field; rice field
他 ta other
束 taba bundle; wad; tuft
タバコ tabako cigarette; tobacco; タバコを吸う ***tabako o suu*** smoke; have a smoke
束ねる tabaneru bundle; tie up
食べ物 tabemono food
食べられない taberarenai uneatable; inedible
食べられる taberareru eatable; edible
食べる taberu eat
旅 tabi journey
足袋 tabi *traditional split-toed Japanese socks*
タービン tābin turbine
度々 tabitabi often; repeatedly; 度々起こる ***tabitabi okoru*** recurrent
タブ tabu tab (*in text*)
たぶん tabun maybe, perhaps; probably; presumably
タブー(の) tabū (no) taboo
タブロイド taburoido tabloid
立ち上がる tachiagaru get up, rise, stand up; set up
立場 tachiba position
たちどころに tachidokoro ni at once; there and then; like magic
立ち止まる tachidomaru stop
立入禁止 tachiiri-kinshi no admittance; no trespassing; keep out
たちまち tachimachi instantly; at once
立ち見席 tachimiseki standing room
立ち向かう tachimukau stand up to; confront
立ち直る tachinaoru recover; make a comeback
立ち退かせる tachinokaseru evict
立ち去る tachisaru leave, go away; get away
立ち寄る tachiyoru call, come by; stop over
ただ tada just, only
ただで tada de for nothing, for free
ただいま tadaima I'm home
ただし tadashi however; but
正しい tadashii correct, right ◊ be right; be in the right
正しく tadashiku right, correctly
正す tadasu rectify; correct
漂う tadayou drift
たどり着く tadoritsuku arrive at; struggle along to
耐えがたい taegatai excruciating, unbearable
絶え間ない taema nai continual, perpetual
絶え間なく taema naku incessantly; nonstop
耐えられない taerarenai intolerable, unbearable
耐えられる taerareru bearable
耐える taeru withstand
耐え忍ぶ taeshinobu endure
絶えず taezu continuously
タフガイ tafu gai tough guy
互いに tagai ni mutually; (with) each other
多額(の) tagaku (no) a lot of; a large sum of
たがる -tagaru want; 知りたがる ***shiri-tagaru*** want to know
耕す tagayasu plow, till
タグボート tagubōto tug
タイ Tai Thailand
たい tai sea bream
たい -tai want; 行きたい ***ikitai*** want to go
対 tai versus; 三対一 ***san tai ichi*** three to one
体罰 taibatsu corporal punishment
大病 taibyō severe illness

体調 **taichō** condition (*of health*)
怠惰 **taida** indolence
怠惰(な) **taida** (**na**) indolent
対談する **taidan suru** talk; converse
態度 **taido** attitude, manner
台風 **taifū** typhoon
たいがい **taigai** mostly; generally
退学処分 **taigaku-shobun** expulsion
体現する **taigen suru** embody
タイ語 **Tai-go** Thai (*language*)
待遇 **taigū** service; treatment
退廃的(な) **taihaiteki** (**na**) decadent
太平洋 **Taiheiyō** Pacific (Ocean)
太平洋横断(の) **Taiheiyō-ōdan** (**no**) transpacific
太平洋戦争 **Taiheiyō-sensō** Pacific War
大変 **taihen** most, very
大変(な) **taihen** (**na**) difficult; terrible; tough; enormous
待避所 **taihijo** pull-in (*at roadside*)
対比する **taihi suru** contrast
逮捕 **taiho** arrest; capture
大砲 **taihō** artillery
逮捕されている **taiho sarete iru** be under arrest
逮捕する **taiho suru** arrest; pick up
体育 **taiiku** gymnastics
体育の日 **Taiiku no hi** Sports Day
体育館 **taiikukan** gymnasium, gym
退院 **taiin** discharge
退院させる **taiin saseru** discharge
退位する **taii suru** abdicate
胎児 **taiji** embryo; fetus; unborn baby
タイ人 **Tai-jin** Thai
退治する **taiji suru** exterminate; subdue; conquer
退場 **taijō** exit
退場させる **taijō saseru** expel from the game
体重 **taijū** weight
体重計 **taijūkei** scales
大会 **taikai** convention
体格 **taikaku** build, physique
耐火性(の) **taikasei** (**no**) fireproof
体系 **taikei** system
体系的 **taikeiteki** systematic
体験 **taiken** experience
対決 **taiketsu** confrontation, showdown
大気 **taiki** atmosphere
大気圏 **taikiken** atmosphere
大金 **taikin** a large sum of money
大気汚染 **taiki-osen** air pollution, atmospheric pollution
待機する **taiki suru** stand by, be ready
太鼓 **taiko** drum
太鼓腹 **taikobara** paunch
太鼓橋 **taikobashi** arched bridge
対抗する **taikō suru** counter; oppose
退屈(な) **taikutsu** (**na**) boring; dull
退屈させる **taikutsu saseru** bore
退屈する **taikutsu suru** be bored
退却 **taikyaku** retreat
退却する **taikyaku suru** retreat
耐久性 **taikyūsei** endurance; 耐久性のある ***taikyûsei no aru*** durable
大麻 **taima** hemp; cannabis
タイマー **taimā** timer, time switch
怠慢 **taiman** neglect; negligence
たいまつ **taimatsu** torch
タイミング **taimingu** timing; タイミングがいい ***taimingu ga ii*** timely; well-timed
タイムアウト **taimu-auto** time out SP
タイムレコーダー **taimu-rekōdā** time clock
耐熱(の) **tainetsu** (**no**) resistant to heat
タイ(の) **Tai** (**no**) Thai
滞納金 **tainōkin** arrears
滞納している **tainō shite iru** be in arrears
体温 **taion** (body) temperature
体温計 **taionkei** clinical thermometer
対応する **taiō suru** correspond (to); cope (with)
タイピスト **taipisuto** typist
タイプ **taipu** type; sort; タイプを打つ ***taipu o utsu*** type
タイプライター **taipu-raitā** typewriter
タイプする **taipu suru** type
平らげる **tairageru** eat up; put away; subjugate
平ら(な) **taira** (**na**) even, level; flat
平らにする **taira ni suru** flatten
大陸 **tairiku** continent

大陸(の) **tairiku** (**no**) continental
対立 **tairitsu** conflict, clash; rift
対立する **tairitsu suru** confront
タイル **tairu** tile
大量 **tairyō** mass; 大量に ***tairyô ni*** in bulk
体力 **tairyoku** strength; stamina
大量生産 **tairyō-seisan** mass production
大量生産する **tairyō-seisan suru** mass produce
大作 **taisaku** epic
対策 **taisaku** measures; steps
体制 **taisei** system; structure; Establishment
体勢 **taisei** footing, balance
大勢 **taisei** general situation; current trend
大西洋(の) **Taiseiyō** (**no**) Atlantic
大西洋横断(の) **Taiseiyō-ōdan** (**no**) transatlantic
体積 **taiseki** volume
対戦する **taisen suru** meet SP
大切(な) **taisetsu** (**na**) important; valuable
大切にする **taisetsu ni suru** cherish, prize, treasure
貸借対照表 **taishaku-taishōhyō** balance sheet
退社する **taisha suru** leave work; resign; retire
大使 **taishi** ambassador
大使館 **taishikan** embassy
たいした **taishita** great; important ; たいしたことではない ***taishita koto de wa nai*** it doesn't matter; nothing much
対して **taishite** against; concerning
体質 **taishitsu** constitution (*of person*)
対称 **taishō** symmetry
対象 **taishō** target; object
対照 **taishō** contrast; comparison
大正時代 **Taishō-jidai** Taisho period
退職 **taishoku** retirement; departure
大食 **taishoku** gluttony
大食家 **taishokuka** glutton
退職金 **taishokukin** golden handshake
退職した **taishoku shita** retired
退職する **taishoku suru** retire
対処する **taisho suru** cope with; deal with; tackle
対称的(な) **taishōteki** (**na**) symmetrical; regular
対照的(な) **taishōteki** (**na**) contrasting
対照的に **taishōteki ni** as opposed to; in contrast to
体臭 **taishū** BO, body odor
大衆 **taishū** the masses; 大衆向けに ***taishûmuke ni*** downmarket
体操 **taisō** gymnastics
体操選手 **taisō-senshu** gymnast
たいてい **taitei** most of the time
たいてい(の) **taitei** (**no**) most
対等(の) **taitō** (**no**) equal
タイトル **taitoru** title
対話 **taiwa** dialog
台湾 **Taiwan** Taiwan
台湾語 **Taiwan-go** Taiwanese (*dialect*)
台湾人 **Taiwan-jin** Taiwanese
タイヤ **taiya** tire
太陽 **taiyō** sun
太陽電池板 **taiyō-denchiban** solar panel
太陽エネルギー **taiyō-enerugī** solar energy
耐用年数 **taiyō nensū** life (*of a building*)
滞在 **taizai** stay
滞在する **taizai suru** stay
たか **taka** hawk
たか派 **takaha** hawk *fig*
高い **takai** high; tall; expensive; prominent
多角経営 **takaku-keiei** diversification
多角経営する **takaku-keiei suru** diversify
高まり **takamari** upsurge; build-up; rise
高める **takameru** boost, enhance
宝 **takara** treasure
宝くじ **takara-kuji** lottery
たかり **takari** scrounger, sponger; blackmailer
たかる **takaru** bum, cadge; sponge off; extort; swarm; be infested with
高さ **takasa** height

竹 **take** bamboo
丈 **take** height; size; stature
竹の子 **takenoko** bamboo shoot
竹馬 **takeuma** stilts
滝 **taki** waterfall
たき火 **takibi** bonfire
タキシード **takishīdo** tuxedo
タックル **takkuru** tackle SP
タックルする **takkuru suru** tackle
卓球 **takkyū** table tennis
宅急便 **takkyūbin®** express home delivery service
たこ **tako** kite; octopus; callus
多国籍企業 **takokuseki-kigyō** multinational (company)
多国籍(の) **takokuseki (no)** multinational
たく **taku** burn; heat
宅 **taku** home; house
炊く **taku** boil; cook
たくましい **takumashii** strong; robust
巧み(な) **takumi (na)** professional, workmanlike
巧みに **takumi ni** professionally; 巧みに操る ***takumi ni ayatsuru*** maneuver
たくらみ **takurami** scheme, plot
たくらむ **takuramu** engineer; plot, scheme
たくさん **takusan** a lot, lots; much
たくさん(の) **takusan (no)** many, much; big
タクシー **takushī** cab, taxi
タクシードライバー **takushī-doraibā** cab driver
タクシー乗り場 **takushī-noriba** cab rank, cab stand
タクシー運転手 **takushī-untenshu** cab driver, taxi driver
蓄え **takuwae** hoard; store
蓄える **takuwaeru** hoard
玉 **tama** ball; bead; jewel
球 **tama** ball
弾 **tama** bullet
卵 **tamago** egg
卵焼き **tamagoyaki** Japanese omelet
たまねぎ **tamanegi** onion
たまに **tama ni** occasionally
たまには **tama ni wa** for a change
たま(の) **tama (no)** infrequent, occasional
たまらない **tamaranai** unendurable
たまらない **-tamaranai** be desperate; 飲みたくてたまらない ***nomitakute tamaranai*** be desperate for a drink
たまり **tamari** puddle; pool
たまり場 **tamariba** meeting place; haunt; joint
たまる **tamaru** accumulate, mount up; pile up
貯まる **tamaru** be saved up
魂 **tamashii** soul REL
たまたま **tamatama** accidentally; by chance
玉突き場 **tamatsukijō** pool hall
玉突き衝突 **tamatsuki-shōtotsu** pile-up
ため息 **tameiki** sigh; ため息をつく ***tameiki o tsuku*** sigh
ため(に) **tame (ni)** due to; owing to; because of; in favor of; for the sake of
ためになる **tame ni naru** rewarding; worthwhile
ためらい **tamerai** hesitation
ためらいがち(な) **tameraigachi (na)** tentative
ためらう **tamerau** hesitate; hold back
ためる **tameru** accumulate, collect; straighten; remedy
貯める **tameru** save; put by
試してみる **tameshite miru** try out; experiment with
試す **tamesu** test; try
ターミナル **tāminaru** terminal; terminus
保つ **tamotsu** keep, retain
棚 **tana** ledge; shelf; shelves; rack; cabinet
七夕 **Tanabata** Star Festival
棚ぼた **tanabota** windfall; godsend
棚卸し **tanaoroshi** stocktaking
田んぼ **tanbo** paddy field
探知 **tanchi** detection
探知器 **tanchi-ki** detector
探知する **tanchi suru** detect
短調 **tanchō** minor; ニ短調 ***ni tanchô*** D minor
単調 **tanchō** monotony

単調(な) **tanchō** (**na**) flat; monotonous; uneventful
単独(の) **tandoku** (**no**) isolated; solo
種 **tane** pip, seed; cause; trick; topic; quality
種馬 **taneuma** stallion; stud
嘆願 **tangan** plea; appeal
嘆願する **tangan suru** plead for; implore
単語 **tango** word
タンゴ **tango** tango
谷 **tani** valley
単位 **tan'i** unit
他人 **tanin** outsider, stranger
単一(の) **tan'itsu** (**no**) single
誕生 **tanjō** birth
誕生日 **tanjōbi** birthday
単純(な) **tanjun** (**na**) menial; simple; straightforward
単価 **tanka** unit cost
担架 **tanka** stretcher
短歌 **tanka** tanka (*31-syllable Japanese poem*)
タンカー **tankā** tanker
短剣 **tanken** dagger
探検 **tanken** expedition; exploration
探検家 **tankenka** explorer
探検する **tanken suru** explore
探検隊 **tankentai** expedition
短気 **tanki** impatience
短期間(の) **tankikan** (**no**) short-term
短気(な) **tanki** (**na**) short-tempered, testy
炭鉱 **tankō** coal mine
炭坑 **tankō** pit, coal mine
タンク **tanku** cistern; tank
タンクローリー **tanku-rōrī** tanker (*truck*)
短距離競走 **tankyori-kyōsō** sprint
短距離選手 **tankyori-senshu** sprinter
端末 **tanmatsu** terminal
単に **tan ni** purely, simply, merely
胆のう **tannō** gall bladder
頼み **tanomi** request; Xの頼みを聞く ***X no tanomi o kiku*** do X a favor
頼む **tanomu** ask; request; beg
楽しい **tanoshii** pleasant; enjoyable; delightful
楽しませる **tanoshimaseru** amuse, entertain
楽しみ **tanoshimi** amusement; entertainment; fun; enjoyment, pleasure; 楽しみにする ***tanoshimi ni suru*** anticipate; look forward to
楽しむ **tanoshimu** enjoy, relish; have a good time
楽しそうに **tanoshisō ni** happily
短波 **tanpa** high-frequency; short wave
たんぱく質 **tanpakushitsu** protein
短編小説 **tanpen-shōsetsu** short story
担保 **tanpo** security; mortgage
タンポン **tanpon** tampon
たんぽぽ **tanpopo** dandelion
炭酸入り(の) **tansan'iri** (**no**) carbonated
胆石 **tanseki** gallstone
端子 **tanshi** terminal ELEC
単身赴任 **tanshinfunin** *living away from one's family after a job transfer*
短所 **tansho** shortcoming; fault
短縮する **tanshuku suru** condense, make shorter; curtail
たんす **tansu** bureau, chest of drawers
単数 **tansū** singular GRAM
淡水 **tansui** freshwater
炭水化物 **tansuika-butsu** carbohydrate
単刀直入(な) **tantō-chokunyū** (**na**) point-blank
担当する **tantō suru** be in charge of
たぬき **tanuki** raccoon dog
倒れる **taoreru** collapse; tumble; fall down; fall over
タオル **taoru** towel
倒す **taosu** bring down; knock down; overthrow, topple
タペストリー **tapesutorī** tapestry
タップダンス **tappu-dansu** tap dance
たっぷり(の) **tappuri** (**no**) abundant; hearty; lavish
たっぷりした **tappuri shita** substantial
たら **tara** cod
たら **-tara** if; when; how about; まじめに勉強したら ***majime ni benkyô***

shitara if you study hard; 駅に着いたら電話してください ***eki ni tsuitara denwa shite kudasai*** call me when you get to the station; 映画を見に行ったらどう ***eiga o mi ni ittara dô*** how about going to see a movie?
たらふく食う **tarafuku kuu** gorge oneself
タラップ **tarappu** airbridge; landing steps; gangway
垂らす **tarasu** drop; let fall; suspend
垂れる **tareru** dribble; droop
垂れている **tarete iru** floppy
たり **-tari** (*for example actions*): 彼は本を読んだりなど決してしない ***kare wa hon o yondari nado kesshite shinai*** he never does things like reading books ◊ (*for successive actions*): 食べたり飲んだりする ***tabetari nondari suru*** eating and drinking; 雨が降ったりやんだりしている ***ame ga futtari yandari shite iru*** it's raining on and off
足りない **tarinai** be short of, be low on
足りる **tariru** be enough; suffice
たる **taru** barrel
タール **tāru** tar
たるみ **tarumi** flab
たるむ **tarumu** sag
たるんだ **tarunda** flabby; loose, slack
タルト **taruto** tart
多量(の) **taryō** (**no**) a large quantity of
多才 **tasai** versatility
多才(の) **tasai** (**no**) versatile
多作(な) **tasaku** (**na**) prolific
確かめる **tashikameru** make certain
確か(な) **tashika** (**na**) certain; sure; 確かな筋から聞いたところによると ***tashika na suji kara kiita tokoro ni yoru to*** I am reliably informed that
確かに **tashika ni** certainly, definitely; sure; by far
足し算 **tashizan** addition MATH
足し算する **tashizan suru** add
たそがれ **tasogare** dusk, twilight
達成 **tassei** achievement
達成する **tassei suru** accomplish, achieve
達する **tassuru** arrive at, reach; meet
足す **tasu** add; 2足す2は4だ ***ni tasu ni wa yon da*** 2 plus 2 is 4
多数 **tasū** many
助かる **tasukaru** be saved; be helpful; survive
助け **tasuke** favor; help
助ける **tasukeru** help
多数(の) **tasū** (**no**) numerous; many
多胎(の) **tatai** (**no**) of a multiple birth
戦い **tatakai** battle; fight
闘い **tatakai** battle, fight
戦う **tatakau** fight
闘う **tatakau** battle, fight, combat; contend with
たたき上げの人 **tatakiage no hito** self-made man
たたき出す **tatakidasu** throw out; evict; flush out
たたく **tataku** beat, hit; hammer; swat
畳 **tatami** tatami mat
たたむ **tatamu** fold up; close *umbrella*; wind up *company*
タッチ **tatchi** touch SP
タッチダウン **tatchi-daun** touchdown
タッチダウンする **tatchi-daun suru** touch down
縦 **tate** length; height
盾 **tate** shield
たてがみ **tategami** mane
縦書き **tategaki** writing in vertical lines
建具屋 **tategu-ya** joiner
建て替える **tatekaeru** rebuild; remodel
立てかける **tatekakeru** lean against
建て前 **tatemae** → ***honne***
建物 **tatemono** building
縦向き **tatemuki** vertical; portrait *print*
建て直す **tatenaosu** rebuild
立て直す **tatenaosu** rebuild, reconstruct
建てる **tateru** build, erect, put up
立てる **tateru** raise; stand
たとえ **tatoe** example; simile; metaphor
例えば **tatoeba** for example
たとえ…でも **tatoe ... de mo** even

if; even as; たとえそうでも ***tatoe sô de mo*** even so
タートル **tātoru** turtleneck (sweater)
たつ **tatsu** pass, go by; get on (*of time*)
立つ **tatsu** stand
発つ **tatsu** leave
絶つ **tatsu** sever; discontinue
建つ **tatsu** be up, be built
達人 **tatsujin** master
竜巻 **tatsumaki** tornado
たった **tatta** only
立っている **tatte iru** stand, be
建っている **tatte iru** stand, be situated (*of building*)
田植え **taue** rice-planting
たわごと **tawagoto** nonsense, garbage
たわみ **tawami** sag; bend
たやすい **tayasui** easy
便り **tayori** news
頼りになる **tayori ni naru** dependable
頼りにする **tayori ni suru** rely on
頼る **tayoru** rely on
多様性 **tayōsei** diversity
頼っている **tayotte iru** dependent
たゆまぬ **tayumanu** steady; untiring
手綱 **tazuna** rein
尋ねる **tazuneru** ask, check with
訪ねる **tazuneru** visit (with), come around
て **-te** and; 安くて汚い ***yasukute kitanai*** cheap and dirty ◊ -ing; 雨が降っています ***ame ga futte imasu*** it's raining ◊ since; 雨が降って行けなかった ***ame ga futte ikenakatta*** since it was raining, I couldn't go ◊ (*as imperative*): 早く起きて ***hayaku okite*** quick, wake up! ◊ (*as a participle in combination with other verbs*): 送ってもらう ***okutte morau*** have … sent; 試してみる ***tameshite miru*** try out
手 **te** hand; move (*in board game*); 手が空いている ***te ga aite iru*** available; 手に入りやすい ***te ni hairiyasui*** accessible; 手に入れられる ***te ni irerareru*** available, obtainable; 手に入れる ***te ni ireru*** get; pick up, buy; 手に負えない ***te ni oenai*** disorderly, unruly; uncontrollable; 手の届かないところ ***te no todokanai tokoro*** out of reach; 手の届くところ ***te no todoku tokoro*** within reach; 手をあげろ ***te o agero*** hands up!; 手を出す ***te o dasu*** dabble in; mess with; 手を振る ***te o furu*** wave; 手を引く ***te o hiku*** back out, pull out; 手を伸ばす ***te o nobasu*** reach out; 手をつなぐ ***te o tsunagu*** hold
手足 **teashi** limbs
手当たり次第に **teatari shidai ni** at random
手当たり次第(の) **teatari shidai (no)** random
手当 **teate** allowance; medical treatment; 手当をする ***teate o suru*** dress; treat
手放す **tebanasu** part with
手早く **tebayaku** lightly; quickly
手引き **tebiki** guidebook
手袋 **tebukuro** glove
手振り **teburi** gesture
テーブル **tēburu** table
テーブルクロス **tēburu-kurosu** tablecloth
テーブルスプーン **tēburu-supūn** tablespoon
手違い **techigai** mix-up; mistake
手帳 **techō** small notebook; diary
手取り給料 **tedori-kyūryō** take-home pay
テフロン加工(の) **tefuron-kakō (no)** nonstick
手がかり **tegakari** clue; purchase, grip
手書き(の) **tegaki (no)** handwritten
手紙 **tegami** letter; correspondence
手柄 **tegara** credit
手軽(な) **tegaru (na)** handy; light; easy
手際 **tegiwa** skill; 手際がいい ***tegiwa ga ii*** skillful; 手際が悪い ***tegiwa ga warui*** awkward; clumsy
手ごろ(な) **tegoro (na)** handy; convenient; reasonably priced
手配 **tehai** arrangements
手配する **tehai suru** fix, fix up; arrange for
手本 **tehon** model; example

提案 **teian** proposal, suggestion, proposition
提案する **teian suru** propose, suggest
堤防 **teibō** dike (*wall*); embankment
停電 **teiden** power outage, blackout
程度 **teido** degree, extent, measure
定義 **teigi** definition
定義する **teigi suru** define
停泊場所 **teihaku-basho** berth
定員 **teiin** capacity (*of elevator, vehicle*)
提示 **teiji** presentation
定住所 **teijūsho** permanent address
定住する **teijū suru** settle down
低下 **teika** decline, drop, fall
定価 **teika** list price
定冠詞 **teikanshi** definite article
低カロリー(の) **tei-karorī** (**no**) low-calorie
低下させる **teika saseru** decrease
低下する **teika suru** decline, decrease, fall
提携する **teikei suru** link up TV
定期 **teiki** commuter pass
低気圧 **teikiatsu** depression, low (*in weather*)
低気圧域 **teikiatsu-iki** low-pressure area
定期便 **teikibin** scheduled flight
定期券 **teikiken** season ticket, pass (*for transport*)
定期購読者 **teiki-kōdokusha** subscriber
定期購読する **teiki-kōdoku suru** subscribe to
定期船 **teikisen** liner
提起する **teiki suru** raise *question*
定期的(な) **teikiteki** (**na**) regular
定期的に **teikiteki ni** periodically
抵抗 **teikō** resistance
帝国 **teikoku** empire
定刻 **teikoku** scheduled time
定刻どおり **teikoku dōri** on schedule
抵抗力 **teikō-ryoku** resistance
抵抗する **teikō suru** resist
テイクアウト **teikuauto** take-away
提供 **teikyō** offer; donation MED
提供者 **teikyō-sha** donor MED
提供する **teikyō suru** contribute; put up *money*; offer *services*; present TV, RAD donate MED
定休日 **teikyūbi** closing day
ていねい語 **teinei-go** polite word
ていねい(な) **teinei** (**na**) polite
ていねいに **teinei ni** politely
定年 **teinen** retirement age
帝王切開 **teiō-sekkai** Cesarean
手入れをする **teire o suru** take care of
手入れされた **teire sareta** trim
手入れされて **teire sarete** in good trim
手入れする **teire suru** swoop on; make a raid
停留所 **teiryū-jo** depot; bus stop
体裁 **teisai** appearance; format
偵察 **teisatsu** reconnaissance
訂正 **teisei** correction
訂正する **teisei suru** correct
停戦 **teisen** cease-fire
停車禁止 **teisha-kinshi** no stopping
停車する **teisha suru** stop; call at
停止 **teishi** cessation; halt
低脂肪(の) **teishibō** (**no**) low-fat
低姿勢(な) **teishisei** (**na**) low profile
停止信号 **teishi-shingō** stoplight
停止している **teishi shite iru** be at a standstill
停止する **teishi suru** come to a halt
定職 **teishoku** permanent job
停職 **teishoku** suspension (*from duty*)
定食 **teishoku** set menu
停職処分にする **teishoku-shobun ni suru** suspend (*from office, duties*)
提出する **teishutsu suru** advance *theory*; submit; put in
停滞した **teitai shita** stagnant
停滞している **teitai shite iru** be backed up
抵当 **teitō** pledge, security
手近に **tejika ni** close at hand
手品 **tejina** conjuring tricks, magic; magic trick
手品師 **tejina-shi** conjurer, magician
手錠 **tejō** handcuffs
手順 **tejun** process; procedure
敵 **teki** adversary, enemy

的中する **tekichū suru** hit the bull's-eye
適度(な) **tekido** (**na**) modest
適度に **tekido ni** within limits; moderately
適度(の) **tekido** (**no**) moderate
適合性 **tekigōsei** compatibility
適合している **tekigō shite iru** be compatible
適合する **tekigō suru** conform; fit; suit
敵意 **tekii** animosity, hostility, ill will; 敵意のある ***tekii no aru*** hostile
的確(な) **tekikaku** (**na**) precise; accurate
適応させる **tekiō saseru** adjust; accommodate
適応性 **tekiōsei** compatibility; 適応性のある ***tekiôsei no aru*** adaptable
適応する **tekiō suru** adapt
適性 **tekisei** aptitude
適切(な) **tekisetsu** (**na**) appropriate, apt; neat *solution*; right, fair
適している **tekishite iru** be suited for, be cut out for
適所 **tekisho** niche; the right place
適する **teki suru** be suitable
テキスト **tekisuto** text; textbook
敵対行為 **tekitai-kōi** hostilities
適当(な) **tekitō** (**na**) proper, right, suitable
適用できない **tekiyō dekinai** inapplicable
適用できる **tekiyō dekiru** applicable
適用させる **tekiyō sareru** apply; apply to
適用する **tekiyō suru** apply
撤回する **tekkai suru** retract, withdraw
鉄筋コンクリート **tekkin-konkurīto** reinforced concrete
てこ **teko** lever; てこの作用 ***teko no sayô*** leverage
手首 **tekubi** wrist
手間 **tema** time; trouble
テーマ **tēma** theme
手前 **temae** this side; front
手招きする **temaneki suru** beckon
テーマ音楽 **tēma-ongaku** signature tune
テーマソング **tēma-songu** theme song
ても **-te mo** even if; whether; however; 雪が降っても ***yuki ga futte mo*** even if it snows; 高くても ***takakute mo*** however expensive it is
...てもいい **...temo ii** can; タクシーで行ってもいい ***takushii de itte mo ii*** can we go by taxi?
点 **ten** dot; point
天 **ten** heaven; sky
手直し **tenaoshi** correction; touching up
店長 **tenchō** manager
天国 **tengoku** heaven, paradise
手荷物 **tenimotsu** (hand) luggage, baggage
手荷物預かり所 **tenimotsu-azukarijo** (baggage) checkroom
店員 **ten'in** sales clerk
テニス **tenisu** tennis
テニスコート **tenisu-kōto** tennis court
テニスプレイヤー **tenisu-pureiyā** tennis player
点字 **tenji** braille
展示 **tenji** display
展示中 **tenjichū** on show, on display
展示品 **tenjihin** exhibit
展示してある **tenji shite aru** be on display
展示する **tenji suru** exhibit, display, show
天井 **tenjō** ceiling
添乗員 **tenjōin** courier, tour conductor
天井桟敷 **tenjō-sajiki** gallery THEA
添加物 **tenkabutsu** additive
展開する **tenkai suru** unfold, develop
てんかん **tenkan** epilepsy
転換 **tenkan** shift, switch; convert
てんかん患者 **tenkan-kanja** epileptic
点火装置 **tenka-sōchi** ignition
点火する **tenka suru** ignite
典型 **tenkei** model; pattern; type; cross-section
典型である **tenkei de aru** representative

典型的(な) **tenkeiteki (na)** typical, representative; vintage, classic
点検修理 **tenken-shūri** service (*for car*)
点検修理する **tenken-shūri suru** service *car*
点検する **tenken suru** check, look over
天気 **tenki** weather
転勤する **tenkin suru** be transferred
天気予報 **tenki-yohō** weather forecast
点呼 **tenko** roll call
転向させる **tenkō saseru** convert
転向者 **tenkō-sha** convert
転校する **tenkō suru** change schools
天窓 **tenmado** skylight
点滅 **tenmetsu** blip
点滅する **tenmetsu suru** blink; flash on and off
天文学 **tenmongaku** astronomy
天文学者 **tenmongaku-sha** astronomer
天文学的(な) **tenmongakuteki (na)** astronomical
天然 **tennen** nature
天然ガス **tennen-gasu** natural gas
天然痘 **tennentō** smallpox
天皇 **tennō** emperor
天皇誕生日**Tennō-tanjōbi** Emperor's Birthday
手のひら **tenohira** palm (*of hand*)
テノール **tenōru** tenor
テンポ **tenpo** tempo
転覆させる **tenpuku saseru** turn over, put upside down
転覆する **tenpuku suru** overturn; capsize
てんぷら **tenpura** tempura (*deep-fried food*)
転落 **tenraku** fall
転落する **tenraku suru** fall
展覧会 **tenrankai** exhibition
天才 **tensai** genius, prodigy
天災 **tensai** natural disaster
点線 **tensen** dotted line
天使 **tenshi** angel
転職 **tenshoku** career change
天職 **tenshoku** vocation, calling
店主 **tenshu** shopkeeper
転送する **tensō suru** forward
点数 **tensū** mark, point; 点数かせぎをする ***tensûkasegi o suru*** earn Brownie points
点滴 **tenteki** drip MED
テント **tento** marquee; tent
転倒 **tentō** fall
店頭 **tentō** storefront
てんとうむし **tentōmushi** ladybug
転倒する **tentō suru** fall
手ぬるい **tenurui** lax; permissive
点在している **tenzai shite iru** be scattered
点在する **tenzai suru** be dotted about
手遅れ(の) **teokure (no)** too late
手おの **teono** hatchet
手押し車**teoshi-guruma** wheelbarrow; pushcart
鉄板 **teppan** iron plate; hot plate
鉄砲 **teppō** gun
テープデッキ **tēpu-dekki** tape deck
テープレコーダー **tēpu-rekōdā** tape recorder
寺 **tera** temple
テラコッタ **terakotta** terracotta
照らす **terasu** shine
テラス **terasu** terrace, patio
テラスハウス **terasu-hausu** row house
テレビ **terebi** television set, TV
テレビ番組 **terebi-bangumi** TV program
テレビ電話**terebi-denwa** videophone
テレビゲーム **terebi-gēmu** video game
テレビ放送 **terebi-hōsō** television
テレビ会議 **terebi-kaigi** video conference
テレホンカード**terehon-kādo** phonecard
テレパシー **terepashī** telepathy
テロ **tero** terrorism
テロリスト **terorisuto** terrorist
テロ組織 **tero-soshiki** terrorist organization
照る **teru** shine
手探りする **tesaguri suru** fumble around, grope
手作業(の) **tesagyō (no)** manual
手先 **tesaki** fingers; agent; pawn *fig*

手製(の) **tesei (no)** handmade
手仕事 **teshigoto** handiwork
手数 **tesū** trouble; inconvenience
手すり **tesuri** handrail; banister
手数料 **tesūryō** commission; handling fee
テスト **tesuto** test, trial
テスト期間 **tesuto-kikan** trial period
鉄 **tetsu** iron
鉄棒 **tetsubō** bar (*gymnastics*)
手伝い **tetsudai** helper
手伝う **tetsudau** help
鉄道 **tetsudō** railroad
鉄道線路 **tetsudō-senro** track
哲学 **tetsugaku** philosophy
哲学者 **tetsugaku-sha** philosopher
哲学的(な) **tetsugakuteki (na)** philosophical
手付け金 **tetsukekin** deposit
鉄製品 **tetsuseihin** ironworks
徹夜する **tetsuya suru** stay up all night
手続き **tetsuzuki** procedure
撤退 **tettai** withdrawal
撤退させる **tettai saseru** pull out, withdraw
撤退する **tettai suru** pull out, withdraw
徹底している **tettei shite iru** be thorough
徹底する **tettei suru** be thorough
徹底的(な) **tetteiteki (na)** thorough; exhaustive
徹底的に **tetteiteki ni** thoroughly; downright; systematically
鉄塔 **tettō** steel tower; mast
…てはいけない **…te wa ikenai** must not
手分けする **tewake suru** divide
手渡す **tewatasu** hand on; hand over, pass
手触り **tezawari** texture; touch
手詰まり **tezumari** stalemate; deadlock
ティー **tī** tee
ティーバッグ **tībaggu** teabag
ティーンエイジャー **tīn'eijā** teenager
ティーポット **tīpotto** teapot
ティールーム **tīrūmu** tearoom
ティーセット **tīsetto** tea service, tea set
ティーシャツ **tī-shatsu** T-shirt
ティースプーン **tīspūn** teaspoon
ティッシュペーパー **tisshu-pēpā** tissue paper
…と … **to** and; パンとバター ***pan to batâ*** bread and butter ◊ with; 友達と映画を見に行った ***tomodachi to eiga o mi ni itta*** I went with a friend to see a movie ◊ if; 入試に合格しないと ***nyûshi ni gôkaku shinai to*** if you don't pass your entrance exams ◊ whenever; 雨が降ると ***ame ga furu to*** whenever it rains ◊ : 彼と同じ大学を卒業した ***kare to onaji daigaku o sotsugyô shita*** I graduated from the same university as him; 何といいましたか ***nan to iimashita ka*** what did you say?
戸 **to** door
都 **to** metropolis; capital; city
塔 **tō** pagoda; tower
党 **tō** political party
頭 **-tō** *countword for large animals*
答案 **tōan** answer sheet
当番 **tōban** duty; person on duty
当番表 **tōbanhyō** duty rota
飛ばす **tobasu** skip; blow *fuse*
飛び上がる **tobiagaru** spring
飛び散る **tobichiru** splash; scatter
飛び出す **tobidasu** rush out; jump out; jut out
飛び道具 **tobidōgu** missile; projectile
飛び跳ねる **tobihaneru** bounce
飛び石 **tobiishi** stepping stone
飛び板 **tobiita** springboard
飛びかかる **tobikakaru** jump, attack; tackle
とびきり(の) **tobikiri (no)** exceptional; out of this world
跳び越える **tobikoeru** jump, leap
飛び込み **tobikomi** dive; plunge; high diving
飛び込み台 **tobikomi-dai** diving board
飛び込む, 跳び込む **tobikomu** dive; plunge; leap
飛び回る **tobimawaru** jump around; fly around
飛びのく **tobinoku** jump back; jump

aside
飛び乗る **tobinoru** jump into *car*
飛び下りる **tobioriru** jump down; jump out; jump off
扉 **tobira** (double) door
飛びつく **tobitsuku** jump at
逃亡 **tōbō** flight, escape
遠吠えする **tōboe suru** howl
逃亡者 **tōbō-sha** fugitive
乏しい **toboshii** scarce; meager
とぼとぼ歩く **tobotobo aruku** plod, trudge
飛ぶ **tobu** blow (*of fuse*); fly; fly in
跳ぶ **tobu** jump, leap
東部 **tōbu** east
等分する **tōbun suru** divide into equal parts
到着 **tōchaku** arrival, appearance
到着ロビー **tōchaku-robī** arrivals
到着する **tōchaku suru** arrive
到着予定時刻 **tōchaku-yotei-jikoku** ETA, estimated time of arrival
父ちゃん **tōchan** pop, dad
土地 **tochi** land, property; 土地の人 ***tochi no hito*** local
統治 **tōchi** rule
土地開発業者 **tochi-kaihatsu-gyōsha** property developer
統治する **tōchi suru** rule; administer
盗聴器 **tōchōki** bug (*device*); 盗聴器を仕掛ける ***tôchôki o shikakeru*** bug
盗聴する **tōchō suru** listen in; tap
途中 **tochū** midway; on the way
途中下車 **tochū-gesha** stopover
灯台 **tōdai** lighthouse
戸棚 **todana** closet; cupboard
都道府県 **todōfuken** prefectures
届出 **todokede** report; notification; registration
届け出る **todokederu** notify; register
届ける **todokeru** deliver, pass on
滞りなく **todokōri naku** duly; without a hitch
届く **todoku** reach, come to (*of hair, dress, water*); be through (*of news etc*)
とどまる **todomaru** remain, stay put
頭取 **tōdori** bank president
とどろき **todoroki** boom; roll (*of thunder*)
とどろく **todoroku** boom
とうふ **tōfu** tofu, bean curd
塗布する **tofu suru** apply *ointment*
とがめる **togameru** find fault; blame
とうがらし **tōgarashi** chili (pepper)
とがる **togaru** taper; be pointed
とげ **toge** prickle; spine; thorn; splinter
峠 **tōge** pass (*in mountains*)
とげだらけ(の) **togedarake (no)** prickly
陶芸 **tōgei** ceramics; pottery
遂げる **togeru** achieve; accomplish
討議 **tōgi** debate
途切れなく **togirenaku** uninterrupted
途切れ途切れ(の) **togiretogire no** fitful
投獄 **tōgoku** imprisonment
統語論 **tōgoron** syntax
研ぐ **togu** sharpen; wash *rice*
戸口 **toguchi** doorstep
徒歩 **toho** walk
東北 **Tōhoku** *northern region of Honshu*
途方もない **tohō mo nai** absurd; preposterous; fantastic
途方に暮れる **tohō ni kureru** be at a loss
徒歩旅行 **toho-ryokō** walking tour, hike
投票 **tōhyō** polls; vote; voting
投票箱 **tōhyō-bako** ballot box
投票所 **tōhyō-jo** polling booth, voting booth
投票者 **tōhyō-sha** voter
投票数 **tōhyō-sū** vote, votes cast
投票用紙記入所 **tōhyō-yōshi-kinyūjo** voting booth
投票する **tōhyō suru** go to the polls, vote
とい **toi** gutter (*on roof*)
遠い **tōi** distant, remote
問い合わせ **toiawase** inquiry
問い合わせる **toiawaseru** inquire; apply to
トイレ **toire** bathroom, toilet; トイレに行く ***toire ni iku*** go to the toilet
トイレットペーパー **toiretto-pēpā**

toilet paper
問いただす **toitadasu** question; grill
統一 **tōitsu** unification
統一する **tōitsu suru** unify
…といって **... to itte** just because
当時 **tōji** at that time; then
冬至 **tōji** winter solstice
陶磁器 **tōjiki** ceramics; china; crockery
閉じ込める **tojikomeru** confine; lock in; block in
戸締り **tojimari** locking up
閉じる **tojiru** close
閉じた **tojita** closed
当日 **tōjitsu** (on) that day; the scheduled day
登場 **tōjō** entrance
登場人物 **tōjō-jinbutsu** character
搭乗券 **tōjōken** boarding card, boarding pass
搭乗している **tōjō shite iru** be aboard
搭乗する **tōjō suru** go aboard
登場する **tōjō suru** appear; enter THEA
…とか **... toka** and so on; something like; 山田とかいう人 ***Yamada toka iu hito*** somebody called Yamada or something like that
とかげ **tokage** lizard
都会 **tokai** city
投かんする **tōkan suru** mail
とかす **tokasu** comb
溶かす **tokasu** dissolve; melt; melt down
時計 **tokei** clock
統計 **tōkei** statistics (*figures*)
統計学 **tōkei-gaku** statistics (*science*)
時計仕掛け **tokeijikake** clockwork
統計上 **tōkeijō** statistically
時計回り **tokeimawari** clockwise
時計屋 **tokei-ya** watchmaker
溶け込ませる **tokekomaseru** integrate
溶け込む **tokekomu** merge; blend in; fit in
溶けない **tokenai** insoluble
溶ける **tokeru** dissolve; melt, thaw ◊ soluble
凍結路面 **tōketsu-romen** black ice
凍結する **tōketsu suru** freeze
時 **toki** when; 子供/学生の時 ***kodomo / gakusei no toki*** as a child / student; 道をわたっている時に ***michi o watatte iru toki ni*** when crossing the road
陶器 **tōki** earthenware, china; pottery
投機 **tōki** venture; speculation
冬季 **tōki** winter; the winter season
登記 **tōki** registration
時々 **tokidoki** now and again, sometimes
解き放す **tokihanasu** release; set free
投機家 **tōki-ka** speculator
時には **toki ni wa** sometimes
投棄する **tōki suru** dump, throw away
投機する **tōki suru** speculate
特権 **tokken** privilege; 特権のある ***tokken no aru*** privileged
取っ組み合う **tokkumiau** grapple with
とっくに **tokku ni** long ago; long since; already
とっくり **tokkuri** sake flask
特許 **tokkyo** patent
特急 **tokkyū** express train
床 **toko** floor; bed; 床についている ***toko ni tsuite iru*** be confined to one's bed
陶工 **tōkō** potter
床の間 **tokonoma** alcove
所, ところ **tokoro** place; area; point; space; house ◊ about to; on the point of; have only just; ちょうど寝たところ ***chôdo neta tokoro*** when I had just gone to bed
ところで **tokoro de** incidentally, by the way
所々 **tokoro dokoro** here and there
ところが **tokoro ga** but; while; however
床屋 **tokoya** barber
得 **toku** advantage; profit; benefit; 得をする ***toku o suru*** profit; gain an advantage
解く **toku** answer; solve
特売 **tokubai** sale (*reduced prices*)
特別(な) **tokubetsu (na)** special
特別に **tokubetsu ni** specially;

particularly
特別(の) **tokubetsu** (**no**) particular, special
特別対策本部**tokubetsu-taisaku-honbu** task force
特徴 **tokuchō** character, personality; special feature
特徴づける**tokuchōzukeru** characterize
特大(の) **tokudai** (**no**) king-size(d); outsize
特派員 **tokuhain** correspondent, reporter
得意(な) **tokui** (**na**) skillful; …が得意である ***… ga tokui de aru*** be good at…
得意先 **tokuisaki** customer; client
特異点 **tokuiten** idiosyncrasy
匿名(の) **tokumei** (**no**) anonymous
特に **toku ni** especially, particularly; exceptionally
遠くに **tōku ni** in the distance ◊ far
トークショー **tōku-shō** talk show
特色 **tokushoku** characteristic, trait; specialty
特集記事 **tokushū-kiji** feature article
特殊(な) **tokushu** (**na**) special; particular; unique
特定(の) **tokutei** (**no**) particular, specific
得点 **tokuten** goal; score
特典 **tokuten** privilege; advantage
得点者 **tokuten-sha** scorer
得点する **tokuten suru** score
特有(の) **tokuyū** (**no**) characteristic
東京 **Tōkyō** Tokyo
当局 **tōkyoku** the authorities
等級 **tōkyū** grade, quality; 等級をつける ***tôkyû o tsukeru*** grade
投球する **tōkyū suru** pitch
とまどい **tomadoi** perplexity, puzzlement
とまどった **tomadotta** perplexed
止り木 **tomarigi** perch
止まる **tomaru** stop; bring to a standstill; perch
泊まる **tomaru** stay the night; ホテルに泊まる ***hoteru ni tomaru*** stay in a hotel
留まる **tomaru** fasten
トマト **tomato** tomato
トマトケチャップ **tomato-kechappu** tomato ketchup
止まっている **tomatte iru** be off (*of machine*) ◊ stationary
遠回りする **tōmawari suru** make a detour; go the long way around
遠回し(な) **tōmawashi** (**na**) coy; indirect
遠回しに言う **tōmawashi ni iu** beat around the bush
留め金 **tomegane** catch
留め具 **tomegu** clasp, fastener
透明度 **tōmeido** transparency
透明(の) **tōmei** (**no**) transparent
当面(の) **tōmen** (**no**) in hand
止める **tomeru** disconnect; turn off; stop; stall; halt; break up
泊める **tomeru** put up, take in *person*
留める **tomeru** do up; staple
富 **tomi** wealth
冬眠する **tōmin suru** hibernate
糖蜜 **tōmitsu** molasses; syrup
とも **-tomo** both; all ◊ wherever;両方とも ***ryôhô tomo*** both of them どこへ行こうとも ***doko e ikô tomo*** wherever you go; 少なくとも ***sukunaku tomo*** at least; 遅くとも ***osoku tomo*** at the latest
友 **tomo** friend
共働き **tomo-bataraki** dual-income family
友達 **tomodachi** friend, buddy, pal; 友達ができる ***tomodachi ga dekiru*** make a friend; 友達になる ***tomodachi ni naru*** make friends
伴う **tomonau** take along; be accompanied; involve; entail
とうもろこし **tōmorokoshi** corn; sweetcorn
富む **tomu** be wealthy; abound in
トン **ton** ton
トナー **tonā** toner
唱える **tonaeru** recite; chant; advocate
トーナメント **tōnamento** tournament
東南アジア **Tōnan Ajia** Southeast Asia
盗難報知機 **tōnan-hōchiki** burglar alarm
隣 **tonari** house next door; neighbor

隣り合わせ(の) **tonariawase (no)** adjoining
隣に **tonari ni** next-door; …の隣に ***… no tonari ni*** next to
隣(の) **tonari (no)** next; next-door; 隣の人 ***tonari no hito*** neighbor
とんぼ **tonbo** dragonfly
とんぼ返り **tonbogaeri** somersault
とんぼ返りする **tonbogaeri suru** somersault
とんだ **tonda** unexpected; terrible; serious
飛んで行く **tonde iku** fly, rush; fly off (*of hat etc*)
飛んで帰る **tonde kaeru** fly back
とんでもない **tondemonai** absolutely not!; of course not; my pleasure! ◊ unreasonable; scandalous, shocking; 彼はとんでもない ***kare wa tondemonai*** he's unbelievable
とんでもなく **tondemonaku** dreadfully
とにかく **tonikaku** anyhow; in any case, at all events
とんかち **tonkachi** hammer
とんま **tonma** clown, fool
トンネル **tonneru** tunnel
とんとんたたく **tonton tataku** rap
問屋 **ton'ya** wholesaler
糖尿病 **tōnyōbyō** diabetes
糖尿病患者 **tōnyōbyō-kanja** diabetic
糖尿病(の) **tōnyōbyō (no)** diabetic
投入 **tōnyū** injection (*of capital*), investment
投入口 **tōnyūguchi** slot
投入する **tōnyū suru** inject, invest
突破する **toppa suru** break through; smash through
突飛(な) **toppi (na)** wild; erratic
トッピング **toppingu** topping
トップ **toppu** leader; top
突風 **toppū** gusty wind
トップギア **toppu-gia** top (gear)
トップレベル(の) **toppureberu (no)** high-level
トップレス(の) **toppuresu (no)** topless
とら **tora** tiger
トラベラーズチェック **toraberāzu-chekku** traveler's check
トラブル **toraburu** problem
トラブルメーカー **toraburu-mēkā** troublemaker
捕らえる **toraeru** capture, portray; seize
トラック **torakku** racetrack; rig, truck
トラクター **torakutā** tractor
トランク **toranku** trunk
トランクス **torankusu** swimsuit
トランペット **toranpetto** trumpet
トランポリン **toranporin** trampoline
トランプ **toranpu** playing card
トランシーバー **toranshībā** walkie-talkie
トランジスター **toranjistā** transistor
とらわれの身 **toraware no mi** prisoner; captive
トレイ **torei** tray
トレーナー **torēnā** sweatshirt; trainer
トレーニング **torēningu** workout
トレーニングする **torēningu suru** work out
トレーラー **torērā** semi; trailer
取れる **toreru** come away; come off; be obtained; be interpreted
採れる **toreru** be extracted; be picked
鳥 **tori** bird
通り **tōri** street
通り **-tōri** as; 先生のいう通りにしなさい ***sensei no iu tôri ni shinasai*** do as your teacher tells you
とりあえず **toriaezu** for the time being
取り上げる **toriageru** pick up; take away; bring up
取り扱い **toriatsukai** treatment
取り扱い注意 **toriatsukai-chūi** (handle) with care
取扱説明 **toriatsukai-setsumei** instructions for use
取扱説明書 **toriatsukai-setsumeisho** instruction manual
取り扱う **toriatsukau** handle, deal with
取り違える **torichigaeru** mix up
取り散らかした **torichirakashita** messy
取り散らかす **torichirakasu** mess up
取り出す **toridasu** eject; extract,

take out; produce, bring out
とりで **toride** fort
取柄 **torie** merit; redeeming feature
鳥肌 **torihada** gooseflesh
取り計らう **torihakarau** arrange; see about, look into
取り払う **toriharau** remove, clear away
取りはずせる **torihazuseru** detachable
取りはずす **torihazusu** detach; disconnect
取り引き **torihiki** bargain, deal; transaction
取り引きする **torihiki suru** trade; deal with
鳥居 **torii** *gateway to Shinto shrine*
取り入れる **toriireru** incorporate; introduce
取り入る **toriiru** ingratiate oneself with
取替部品 **torikae-buhin** replacement part
取り替える **torikaeru** change; exchange; switch
取り返しのつかない **torikaeshi no tsukanai** irretrievable
取り返す **torikaesu** get back; retrieve
取りかかる **torikakaru** go ahead; launch; start
取り囲む **torikakomu** encircle
取り交わす **torikawasu** exchange
取り消し **torikeshi** cancelation; withdrawal
取り消す **torikesu** cancel; withdraw
取り決める **torikimeru** arrange; settle; negotiate
とりこになる **toriko ni naru** be captivated
取り壊し **torikowashi** demolition
取り壊す **torikowasu** demolish, pull down
取り組み方 **torikumi kata** approach
取り組む **torikumu** tackle *problem*; grapple with, wrestle with
通り道 **tōrimichi** route
取り巻く **torimaku** surround
取り乱した **torimidashita** distraught; confused
取り戻す **torimodosu** recover, get back; regain; recapture; 遅れを取り戻す ***okure o torimodosu*** catch up on
取りにいく **tori ni iku** collect, pick up
鳥肉 **toriniku** chicken (*food*); poultry (*meat*)
取りにくる **tori ni kuru** come for, collect
取り除く **torinozoku** clear; remove; weed out; take away
通り抜けられない **tōrinukerarenai** impassable
通り抜ける **tōrinukeru** get by, pass; pass through
取り下げる **torisageru** drop
取り去る **torisaru** take away; remove
取り締まり **torishimari** management; discipline; crackdown
取締役 **torishimariyaku** director
取り締まる **torishimaru** clamp down on
取り調べ **torishirabe** investigation
取り調べる **torishiraberu** investigate
通り過ぎる **tōrisugiru** go by, pass (by)
とりとめのない **toritome no nai** rambling; incoherent *speech*
取り次ぐ **toritsugu** act as an agent; pass on; convey
取りつかれたよう(な) **toritsukareta yō (na)** obsessive
取りつかれている **toritsukarete iru** be obsessed by / with
取り付け **toritsuke** installation; fittings
取り付ける **toritsukeru** attach; fix; install
取り止める **toriyameru** call off, cancel
とろ火 **torobi** low flame
トローチ **torōchi** lozenge
トロフィー **torofī** cup, trophy
登録 **tōroku** enrolment, registration
登録簿 **tōrokubo** register
登録商標 **tōroku-shōhyō** registered trademark
登録する **tōroku suru** enroll, register
討論 **tōron** debate, discussion
トロンボーン **toronbōn** trombone
討論する **tōron suru** debate

トロール船 **torōru-sen** trawler
とろとろ歩く **torotoro aruku** trudge
とる **toru** have *meal*
取る **toru** remove; seize; take *math, French etc*; take off (*discount*); take on *job*; occupy *time*; steal; subscribe to; record
捕る **toru** catch *fish*
撮る **toru** take *photograph, photocopy*
通る **tōru** penetrate
トルコ **Toruko** Turkey
トルコ(の) **Toruko (no)** Turkish
取るに足らない **toru ni taranai** unimportant; insignificant; negligible; petty
塗料 **toryō** paint
倒産 **tōsan** bankruptcy; crash
倒産させる **tōsan saseru** bankrupt
倒産した **tōsan shita** bankrupt
倒産する **tōsan suru** go bankrupt
と殺 **tosatsu** slaughter
と殺する **tosatsu suru** slaughter
当選者 **tōsen-sha** winner
当選する **tōsen suru** win
年 **toshi** year; age; 年をとる ***toshi o toru*** age, get on; 年をとった ***toshi o totta*** old
都市 **toshi** city
投資 **tōshi** investment, stake
闘士 **tōshi** fighter; activist; militant
都市化 **toshika** urbanization
都心部 **toshinbu** inner city
都市(の) **toshi (no)** urban
投資者 **tōshi-sha** investor
年下(の) **toshishita (no)** junior
投資する **tōshi suru** invest
…として **... to shite** as; by way of, in the form; …として機能する ***... to shite kinô suru*** function as; …として務める ***... to shite tsutomeru*** act as
通して **tōshite** through the medium of; 通して読む ***tôshite yomu*** go through, read through
年上 **toshiue** elder
年寄り **toshiyori** elderly person
図書 **tosho** books
投書 **tōsho** letter to the editor; contribution
凍傷 **tōshō** frostbite
図書館 **toshokan** library
党首 **tōshu** leadership
とそ **toso** New Year spiced sake
塗装 **tosō** paintwork
逃走 **tōsō** escape; flight; getaway
逃走車 **tōsō-sha** getaway car
闘争的(な) **tōsōteki (na)** militant
とっさに **tossa ni** at once; instantly
突進する **tosshin suru** dart, dash; surge forward
通す **tōsu** run through *details*; send in; thread
トースト **tōsuto** toast
…とたん **... totan** just when, the moment that; as soon as
到達する **tōtatsu suru** arrive at, reach
とうてい **tōtei** absolutely, utterly
とても **totemo** very; much; really
とうとう **tōtō** at last; after all
整える **totonoeru** organize, prepare; make *bed*; typeset
整う **totonou** be prepared; be completed
突撃する **totsugeki suru** charge, attack
突然 **totsuzen** all at once, suddenly
突然(の) **totsuzen (no)** abrupt, sudden
とって **totte** …にとって ***... ni totte*** to; for; 私にとって非常に不便だった ***watashi ni totte hijô ni fuben datta*** it was very inconvenient for me
取っ手 **totte** handle, knob
取って食う **totte kuu** prey on
取ってくる **totte kuru** get, fetch
とっても **tottemo** very; much; really
取っておく **totte oku** keep; set aside *money*; save; reserve
当惑 **tōwaku** discomfort, embarrassment
当惑させる **tōwaku saseru** perplex; embarrass; bewilder; dismay
投薬量 **tōyaku-ryō** dosage
東洋 **Tōyō** East, Orient
東洋人 **Tōyō-jin** Oriental
東洋(の) **Tōyō (no)** Eastern, Oriental
投与する **tōyo suru** administer, give *medication*

灯油 **tōyu** kerosene
東西 **Tōzai** East and West
当座借越 **tōza-karikoshi** overdraft
遠ざかる **tōzakaru** go away; get faint; drift apart
遠ざける **tōzakeru** shun; keep at a distance; abstain from
登山 **tozan** climb; mountaineering
登山家 **tozanka** mountaineer
登山者 **tozan-sha** climber
登山する **tozan suru** climb
当座預金口座 **tōza-yokin-kōza** checking account
当然 **tōzen** justly, rightly; naturally, of course; 当然だ ***tôzen da*** no wonder
当然(の) **tōzen (no)** due, proper; natural, obvious; 当然のこととして ***tôzen no koto to shite*** as a matter of course
盗賊 **tōzoku** bandit
つ **tsu** *countword for small objects*
通 **tsū** connoisseur
つば **tsuba** saliva; brim (*of hat*); guard (*on sword*); つばを吐く ***tsuba o haku*** spit
つばき **tsubaki** camellia
つばめ **tsubame** swallow (*bird*)
翼 **tsubasa** wing
つぼ **tsubo** urn
坪 **tsubo** *unit of area, 3. 6 square yards*
つぼみ **tsubomi** bud
粒 **tsubu** grain; speck ◊ *countword for small round objects and grain*
つぶれる **tsubureru** be crushed; go bankrupt; fold
つぶれそう(な) **tsuburesō(na)** tumbledown
つぶれた **tsubureta** broken
つぶす **tsubusu** kill *time*; smash; crush; thwart
つぶやき **tsubuyaki** murmur; muttering
つぶやく **tsubuyaku** murmur, mutter
土 **tsuchi** earth, soil
通知票 **tsūchi-hyō** report card
通知する **tsūchi suru** inform, notify
通帳 **tsūchō** bank book
つえ **tsue** cane; walking stick
つがい **tsugai** pair
つがいになる **tsugai ni naru** mate
告げ口する **tsugeguchi suru** snitch; inform on
告げ口屋 **tsugeguchi-ya** snitch, telltale
つぎ **tsugi** patch
接ぎ木 **tsugiki** graft BOT
つぎ込む **tsugikomu** invest, sink *funds*; put in
継ぎ目 **tsugime** join; joint
次に **tsugi ni** next
次(の) **tsugi (no)** next, following; 次の方どうぞ ***tsugi no kata dôzo*** next, please; 次のとおり ***tsugi no tôri*** as follows; 次の次 ***tsugi no tsugi*** the next but one
都合 **tsugō** circumstances; convenience; 都合のいい ***tsugô no ii*** suitable, convenient; 都合の悪い ***tsugô no warui*** inconvenient; あなた/私の都合の良い時に ***anata / watashi no tsugô no yoi toki ni*** at your / my convenience
つぐ **tsugu** join; piece together; pour, pour out
継ぐ **tsugu** inherit; succeed to
償う **tsugunau** compensate; make amends
通報する **tsūhō suru** report
つい **tsui** just; only; by accident; in spite of oneself; つい笑ってしまった ***tsui waratte shimatta*** I couldn't help laughing; ついさっき ***tsui sakki*** just now, a few moments ago
対 **tsui** pair
ついでに **tsuide ni** while I'm / you're etc about it
追放 **tsuihō** expulsion
追放された **tsuihō sareta** outcast
追放する **tsuihō suru** eject, expel, oust; exile
追加 **tsuika** addition
つい間板ヘルニア **tsuikanban herunia** slipped disc
追加(の) **tsuika (no)** additional
追加料金 **tsuika-ryōkin** surcharge
追加する **tsuika suru** add
追求 **tsuikyū** pursuit, search
追求する **tsuikyū suru** pursue
ツインベッド **tsuin-beddo** twin beds

ついに **tsui ni** in the end, eventually; at last; ついに…となる ***tsui ni ... to naru*** culminate in
墜落 **tsuiraku** crash
墜落する **tsuiraku suru** crash
ついさっき **tsui sakki** a few moments ago
追跡 **tsuiseki** chase, pursuit; 犯人追跡 ***hannin-tsuiseki*** manhunt
追跡者 **tsuiseki-sha** pursuer
追伸 **tsuishin** PS, postscript
追体験する **tsuitaiken suru** relive
ついたて **tsuitate** partition, screen
ついて **tsuite** per; about; concerning; …について聞く ***... ni tsuite kiku*** hear about; …についてよく知っている ***... ni tsuite yoku shitte iru*** have a good knowledge of; …については ***... ni tsuite wa*** as for
ついて行けない **tsuite ikenai** be out of one's depth
ついて行く **tsuite iku** follow; accompany; keep up with
ついている **tsuite iru** be lucky; be on (*of light, TV etc*); hold
ついてくる **tsuite kuru** keep up
ついて回る **tsuite mawaru** dog
追悼(の) **tsuitō (no)** memorial
費やす **tsuiyasu** spend
通じない **tsūjinai** dead *phone*
通じる **tsūjiru** lead to; reach by phone; communicate; …に通じる ***... ni tsûjiru*** give onto
つじつまが合う **tsujitsuma ga au** add up, make sense; be consistent
つじつまの合わない **tsujitsuma no awanai** incoherent; inconsistent
通常(の) **tsūjō (no)** regular, normal
通貨 **tsūka** currency; money
使えない **tsukaenai** useless
使える **tsukaeru** run (*of software*); be usable
仕える **tsukaeru** serve
使い **tsukai** errand
使い古し(の) **tsukaifurushi (no)** battered
使い古した **tsukaifurushita** well-worn; worn-out; dog-eared
使い古す **tsukaifurusu** wear
使い果たす **tsukaihatasu** exhaust, use up
使い込み **tsukaikomi** embezzlement
使い込む **tsukaikomu** embezzle
使いこなす **tsukaikonasu** master
使い道の多い **tsukaimichi no ōi** versatile
使い慣れる **tsukainareru** get used to
使いにくい **tsukainikui** unfriendly, not easy to use
使いすぎる **tsukaisugiru** overwork
使い捨て(の) **tsukaisute (no)** disposable
使い尽くす **tsukaitsukusu** eat up, use up
使いやすい **tsukaiyasui** user-friendly, easy to use
捕まえにくい **tsukamaenikui** elusive
捕まえる **tsukamaeru** capture, catch
捕まらないで **tsukamaranaide** at large
つかむ **tsukamu** grab; seize; catch hold of
通貨(の) **tsūka (no)** monetary
つかの間(の) **tsuka no ma (no)** fleeting; short-lived
通関手続 **tsūkan-tetsuzuki** customs formalities
疲れ果てた **tsukarehateta** weary
疲れ切った **tsukarekitta** exhausted
疲れる **tsukareru** wearing, tiring ◊ tire
疲れさせる **tsukare saseru** wear out, tire
疲れた **tsukareta** tired
通過する **tsūka suru** pass through
使う **tsukau** use; spend; take *credit cards*; run *car*
つけ **tsuke** charge account; credit
付け合わせ **tsukeawase** relish, sauce; side dish
つけ込む **tsukekomu** cash in on; take advantage of
付け加える **tsukekuwaeru** add, say; add on
漬物 **tsukemono** pickled vegetables
付け値 **tsukene** bid
つけっぱなしにする **tsukeppanashi ni suru** leave on *computer etc*
つける **tsukeru** immerse; dunk

cookie; soak; mop up *liquid* ; strike *match*; switch on, turn on *light etc*
着ける **tsukeru** put on; wear
付ける **tsukeru** fit, attach; build up
月 **tsuki** month; moon
月(の) **tsuki (no)** lunar; 月の光 ***tsuki no hikari*** moonlight
つき **tsuki** …につき ***… ni tsuki*** per
付き合い **tsukiai** companionship, company ◊ *afterwork socializing with people from work*; …と付き合いを続ける ***… to tsukiai o tsuzukeru*** keep up with
突き当たり **tsukiatari** bottom (*of street*)
付き合う **tsukiau** date, go out with; mix, socialize; keep … company
突き出す **tsukidasu** poke
突き出る **tsukideru** project, stick out
突き出た **tsukideta** prominent *chin*
月日 **tsukihi** time; days; years
通気孔 **tsūkikō** vent
つきまとう **tsukimatou** stalk *person*; lurk (*of doubt*); haunt
通勤ラッシュ **tsūkin-rasshu** commuter traffic
通勤列車 **tsūkin-ressha** commuter train
通勤者 **tsūkin-sha** commuter
通勤する **tsūkin suru** commute
尽きる **tsukiru** be used up
突き刺す **tsukisasu** plunge
突き刺すよう(な) **tsukisasu yō (na)** penetrating
付き添い **tsukisoi** nurse; orderly
付き添う **tsukisou** accompany; attend
突き飛ばす **tsukitobasu** push away
つきとめる **tsukitomeru** isolate, pinpoint; ascertain
月夜 **tsukiyo** moonlit night
つっかえさせる **tsukkaesaseru** jam
突っ込む **tsukkomu** plunge; poke, stick; shove in
通行権 **tsūkō-ken** right of way
通告 **tsūkoku** notice; …に通告する ***… ni tsûkoku suru*** give … his / her notice
通行人 **tsūkō-nin** passer-by
通行料 **tsūkō-ryō** toll
通行証 **tsūkōshō** pass, permit
つく **tsuku** increase; tell *lie*; leave for; pound; strike *bell*
付く **tsuku** be joined to; stick; be smeared; accompany; cost; be in luck
突く **tsuku** jab, prod; thrust
着く **tsuku** arrive; come; reach, come to; get
机 **tsukue** desk
作り上げる **tsukuriageru** make out *list*
作り話 **tsukuribanashi** lie, story
作り出す **tsukuridasu** make; produce; devise
作り付け(の) **tsukuritsuke (no)** built-in
繕い **tsukuroi** darning, mending
繕う **tsukurou** darn, mend
作る **tsukuru** create; make; fix *lunch*; form *past tense etc*
造る **tsukuru** build; manufacture; construct
尽くす **tsukusu** use up; exhaust
妻 **tsuma** wife
つまみ **tsumami** pinch (*of salt*); knob; snacks; 塩ひとつまみ ***shio hito-tsumami*** a pinch of salt
つまらない **tsumaranai** uninteresting; unsuccessful; tame *joke*
つまらなさ **tsumaranasa** boredom
詰まらせる **tsumaraseru** clog up; 彼はのどに骨を詰まらせた ***kare wa nodo ni hone o tsumaraseta*** he choked on a bone
つまり **tsumari** that is to say
詰まり **tsumari** blockage
つまる **tsumaru** be at a loss for words
詰まる **tsumaru** clog up, stop up; be packed; shrink; run short
つま先 **tsumasaki** toe (*of shoe*); つま先立ちで ***tsumasakidachi de*** on tippy-toe
つましい **tsumashii** economical, thrifty
つまようじ **tsumayōji** toothpick
つまずく **tsumazuku** stumble, trip
つめ **tsume** claw; fingernail
詰め合わせ **tsumeawase** assortment

つめ切り **tsume-kiri** nail clippers; nail scissors
詰め込まれる **tsumekomareru** be squeezed in
詰め込む **tsumekomu** cram
詰めもの **tsumemono** padding; stuffing
詰める **tsumeru** move up, squeeze up; pack; take in *clothes*
冷たい **tsumetai** cold; cool *drink*; frosty *welcome*
つめやすり **tsume-yasuri** nail file
罪 **tsumi** sin, crime; 罪を犯す ***tsumi o okasu*** sin
積み上げる **tsumiageru** heap up, pile up
罪深い **tsumibukai** sinful
積み重ね **tsumikasane** heap
積み重ねる **tsumikasaneru** stack
積み込み渡し **tsumikomi-watashi** FOB, free on board
積み荷 **tsumini** cargo, load
つもり **tsumori** intention; ...のつもりはまったくない ***... no tsumori wa mattaku nai*** I have no intention of; つもりである ***tsumori de aru*** mean, intend
摘む **tsumu** pick
積む **tsumu** load
つむぐ **tsumugu** spin *wool, cotton*
つむじ風 **tsumujikaze** whirlwind
つむじ曲り(の) **tsumujimagari** (**no**) perverse
綱 **tsuna** cable
ツナ **tsuna** tuna
つながり **tsunagari** link
つながる **tsunagaru** link up
つなげる **tsunageru** connect; link
つなぎ合わせる **tsunagiawaseru** piece together
つなぐ **tsunagu** connect, join; moor, tie up *boat*; tether *horse*; tie *hands*
津波 **tsunami** tidal wave, tsunami
常に **tsune ni** always
つねる **tsuneru** pinch
角 **tsuno** horn; 角で突く ***tsuno de tsuku*** butt
ツーピース **tsūpīsu** two-piece
面 **tsura** mug (*face*)
つらい **tsurai** upsetting, painful; trying, annoying
貫く **tsuranuku** pierce, penetrate
つらら **tsurara** icicle
連れ **tsure** companion
通例 **tsūrei** usually; as a rule ◊ standard
連れて行く **tsurete iku** take, accompany
連れてかえる **tsurete kaeru** fetch *person*
連れてくる **tsurete kuru** bring *person*
痛烈(な) **tsūretsu** (**na**) scathing
釣り **tsuri** fishing; change; 釣りをする ***tsuri o suru*** fish
つり上がった **tsuriagatta** slanting *eyes*
釣り合い **tsuriai** balance; proportions, dimensions; 釣り合いのとれた ***tsuriai no toreta*** balanced, fair; 釣り合いを取る ***tsuriai o toru*** balance
釣り合っていない **tsuriatte inai** unevenly matched
釣り合わせる **tsuriawaseru** counterbalance
釣り針 **tsuribari** hook
つり橋 **tsuribashi** suspension bridge
釣り道具 **tsuri-dōgu** fishing tackle
釣り糸 **tsuri-ito** fishing line
釣ざお **tsuri-zao** fishing rod
通路 **tsūro** aisle; passage, passageway; 通路側の席 ***tsûrogawa no seki*** aisle seat
つる **tsuru** crane (*bird*)
釣る **tsuru** catch *fish with rod*
つるす **tsurusu** suspend, hang
通信衛星 **tsūshin-eisei** communications satellite
通信販売カタログ **tsūshin-hanbai-katarogu** mail-order catalog
通信社 **tsūshinsha** news agency
通信手段 **tsūshin-shudan** communications
通信する **tsūshin suru** correspond; communicate
通商産業省 **Tsūshō-Sangyōshō** Ministry of International Trade and Industry
つた **tsuta** creeper; ivy
伝える **tsutaeru** communicate, convey, pass on, relay; hand down
伝わる **tsutawaru** carry (*of sound*);

come across; be communicated
つて **tsute** connection, contact; つてがある ***tsute ga aru*** be well connected
勤まる **tsutomaru** be fit for; be equal to
勤める **tsutomeru** serve; be employed
務める **tsutomeru** make efforts; work (*for a company*); 議長を務める ***gichô o tsutomeru*** act as chairperson
勤め先 **tsutomesaki** place of employment
筒 **tsutsu** cylinder
つつく **tsutsuku** peck, bite; poke; incite; criticize
つつましい **tsutsumashii** humble, modest; frugal
包み **tsutsumi** bundle; wrapper
包む **tsutsumu** envelop, wrap
慎み **tsutsushimi** modesty; self-control
慎む **tsutsushimu** refrain from; be discreet
つや **tsuya** gloss, shine
つや出し **tsuyadashi** polishing
つや消し(の) **tsuyakeshi** (**no**) matt; frosted
通訳 **tsūyaku** interpretation; interpreter
通訳する **tsūyaku suru** interpret
強火でいためる **tsuyobi de itameru** stir-fry
強い **tsuyoi** strong; forceful *argument*; vigorous *denial*; profound *shock, effect*
強く **tsuyoku** strongly
強くなる **tsuyoku naru** intensify; strengthen
強くする **tsuyoku suru** strengthen; turn up
強める **tsuyomeru** heighten, intensify
強み **tsuyomi** advantage; strength
強さ **tsuyo-sa** strength
つゆ **tsuyu** soup; sauce
梅雨 **tsuyu** rainy season
露 **tsuyu** dew
続ける **tsuzukeru** carry on, continue
続き **tsuzuki** continuation, sequel
続く **tsuzuku** continue; persist, last; to be continued
つづり **tsuzuri** spelling
つづる **tsuzuru** spell

U

乳母車 **ubaguruma** baby carriage, buggy
奪う **ubau** rob; deprive; fascinate
家 **uchi** house; home; family ◊ I (*familiar*); 家に帰る ***uchi ni kaeru*** come home
内 **uchi** inside; indoors; in-group; ◊ between; 両者の内で ***ryôsha no uchi de*** between the two of them
打ち上げ **uchiage** blast-off, lift-off
打ち上げられる **uchiagerareru** lift off (*of rocket*)
打ち明ける **uchiakeru** confide
打ち合わせ **uchiawase** prior arrangement; briefing
打ち合わせる **uchiawaseru** make a prior arrangement
内側 **uchigawa** inside
内側(の) **uchigawa** (**no**) inner; inside
内側車線 **uchigawa-shasen** inside lane
打ち掛け **uchikake** *traditional Japanese wedding dress*
打ち勝つ **uchikatsu** conquer; overcome
内気 **uchiki** shyness
内気(な) **uchiki** (**na**) shy

打ち消す **uchikesu** deny; contradict
打ち込む **uchikomu** drive in, hammer in
打ち切る **uchikiru** break off; discontinue
撃ち殺す **uchikorosu** shoot (*and kill*)
打ち壊す **uchikowasu** break down *door*
打ち砕く **uchikudaku** dash *hopes*
打ち負かす **uchimakasu** defeat, whip, thrash
内に **uchi ni** in ◊ while
家の **uchi no** (*familiar*) my
打ちのめされる **uchinomesareru** go to pieces
打ちのめす **uchinomesu** devastate; beat up
撃ち落とす **uchiotosu** shoot down, bring down
内ポケット **uchi-poketto** inside pocket
打ち解ける **uchitokeru** open up (*of person*)
うちわ **uchiwa** fan (*round, made of paper*)
内輪 **uchiwa** family circle; inner circle
内訳 **uchiwake** breakdown; details
打ち寄せる波 **uchiyoseru nami** surf; breakers
有頂天 **uchōten** ecstasy, rapture; 有頂天になった ***uchôten ni natta*** entranced
有頂天(の) **uchōten (no)** ecstatic
宇宙 **uchū** universe
宇宙服 **uchū-fuku** spacesuit
宇宙飛行士 **uchū-hikōshi** astronaut
宇宙人 **uchū-jin** alien
宇宙旅行 **uchū-ryokō** voyage (in space); space travel
宇宙船 **uchū-sen** space module, spacecraft
宇宙ステーション **uchū-sutēshon** space station
うだるよう(な) **udaru yō (na)** sweltering
腕 **ude** arm
腕時計 **udedokei** wrist watch
腕組みをする **udegumi o suru** fold one's arms
腕前 **udemae** ability; skill
腕立て伏せ **udetatefuse** push-up
うどん **udon** noodles
上 **ue** top; upper part; brow (*of hill*); 兄は僕より三歳上です ***ani wa boku yori sansai ue desu*** my elder brother is three years older than me; 上に ***ue ni*** on; on top of; upstairs; 山の上を飛ぶ ***yama no ue o tobu*** fly over the mountains; ピアニストである上に ***pianisuto de are ue ni*** as well as being a pianist
飢え **ue** hunger
ウエーブのかかった **uēbu no kakatta** wavy
ウエディングドレス **uedingu-doresu** wedding dress
ウエディングケーキ **uedingu-kēki** wedding cake
上側 **uegawa** top part
ウエハース **uehāsu** wafer
ウエイター **ueitā** waiter; ウエイターをする ***ueitâ o suru*** wait table
ウエイトレス **ueitoresu** waitress
飢え死にする **uejini suru** starve to death
植木 **ueki** garden plant; potted plant
植木鉢 **uekibachi** flowerpot; pot
植え込み **uekomi** shrubbery
上向きに **uemuki ni** upward
上に **ue ni** above ◊ up
植える **ueru** plant
飢える **ueru** starve
ウエスト **uesuto** waist; waistline
ウエストポーチ **uesuto pōchi** fanny pack
うがいをする **ugai o suru** gargle
動いていない **ugoite inai** idle *machinery*
動かない **ugokanai** be out of action ◊ motionless
動かなくなる **ugokanaku naru** jam, stick; seize up
動かす **ugokasu** move, shift; work *machine*; drive TECH
動き **ugoki** activity; movement; move; motion
動き回る **ugokimawaru** get around, be mobile; move around
動く **ugoku** move, budge, shift;

operate, work (*of machine*) ◊ moving (*which can move*)
うぐいす **uguisu** bush warbler
右派 **uha** right wing
ウイークデー **uīkudē** weekday
ウイークエンド **uīkuendo** weekend
ウィンドサーフィン **uindosāfin** windsurfing, sailboarding
ウインドーショッピングをする **uindō-shoppingu o suru** go window-shopping
ウイング **uingu** wing SP
ウインカー **uinkā** indicator MOT; ウインカーを出す ***uinkâ o dasu*** indicate
ウインク **uinku** wink
ウインクする **uinku suru** wink
ウイルス **uirusu** virus
ウイルス(の) **uirusu (no)** viral
ウイスキー **uisukī** whiskey
うじゃうじゃしている **ujauja shite iru** crawl with, swarm with
うじ **uji** maggot
うじ虫 **ujimushi** grub (*of insect*)
浮かべる **ukaberu** set afloat; sail; picture, imagine
浮かぶ **ukabu** float
うかがう **ukagau** H call on; visit; ask; hear
う回路 **ukairo** detour, diversion
う回させる **ukai saseru** divert, reroute
う回する **ukai suru** bypass
浮かんで **ukande** afloat
受かる **ukaru** pass *exam*
受け入れ **ukeire** acceptance
受け入れる **ukeireru** accept; take on board
受身 **ukemi** passive GRAM
受け持ち(の) **ukemochi (no)** in charge; having responsibility
受け持つ **ukemotsu** take charge
受ける **ukeru** take *exam, degree*; undergo *surgery*; take up, accept
受取人 **uketori-nin** addressee; recipient; payee
受け取る **uketoru** accept, take; get, receive; perceive, view
受け継ぐ **uketsugu** inherit; succeed to; take over
受付 **uketsuke** reception, reception desk
受付係 **uketsuke-gakari** receptionist
受け付けない **uketsukenai** reject
受け付ける **uketsukeru** accept
受け皿 **ukezara** saucer
雨季, 雨期 **uki** monsoon season
浮き彫り **ukibori** relief (*in art*)
浮き沈み **ukishizumi** ups and downs
浮き浮きした **ukiuki shita** cheerful; excited; buoyant; exhilarating
浮世絵 **ukiyoe** wood block print
うっかり **ukkari** carelessly; うっかり言う ***ukkari iu*** blurt out; let slip
浮く **uku** float
馬 **uma** horse
うまい **umai** delicious; skillful; clever; good; lucrative
うまく **umaku** cleverly; nicely; successfully; うまくいかない ***umaku ikanai*** go wrong, fail; うまくいく ***umaku iku*** do well; turn out well; うまくなる ***umaku naru*** get better; うまくやる ***umaku yaru*** do well (*of person*); うまくやっていく ***umaku yatte iku*** get on; be friendly with
ウーマンリブ **ūman ribu** women's lib
生まれ故郷(の) **umarekokyō (no)** native
生まれる **umareru** be born; originate
生まれたて(の) **umaretate (no)** newborn
生まれつき(の) **umaretsuki (no)** inborn
梅 **ume** (Japanese) plum
埋め合せ **umeawase** compensation
埋め合わせる **umeawaseru** compensate for
梅干し **umeboshi** pickled plum
うめき **umeki** groan; moan
うめき声 **umekigoe** groan
うめく **umeku** groan, moan
埋める **umeru** bridge *gap*; bury; fill in *hole*
埋め立て **umetate** (land) reclamation
埋め立てる **umetateru** reclaim *land*
うみ **umi** pus
海 **umi** sea; ocean
海辺 **umibe** seaside
生み出す **umidasu** generate, create

海(の) **umi** (**no**) marine; maritime
海の日 **Umi no hi** Sea Day
羽毛 **umō** down; feather
有無 **umu** presence; existence
うむ **umu** fester
生む **umu** yield; bring in *interest, income*
産む **umu** bear *children*; lay *eggs*; give birth to
うん **un** yes; OK; that's right
運 **un** chance, luck; 運のいい ***un no ii*** lucky; 運の悪い事に ***un no warui koto ni*** unluckily
うなぎ **unagi** eel
うなじ **unaji** nape of the neck
うなり声 **unarigoe** bellow; growl
うなる **unaru** growl; wail; whirr
うなずき **unazuki** nod
うなずく **unazuku** nod; agree
運賃 **unchin** fare
運賃込み価格 **unchin-komi kakaku** cost and freight
運動 **undō** campaign, drive; crusade; movement; exercise; 運動を起こす ***undô o okosu*** campaign
運動不足(の) **undōbusoku** (**no**) unfit
運動場 **undōjō** playing field
運動家 **undō-ka** campaigner
運動(の) **undō** (**no**) athletic
運動させる **undō saseru** exercise
運動する **undō suru** exercise, take exercise
運営 **un'ei** management; operation
運営する **un'ei suru** manage; operate; run
うねり **uneri** swell (*of sea*)
運河 **unga** canal
うに **uni** sea urchin
うんこ **unko** shit
運行 **unkō** running (*of trains etc*); movement (*of planets*)
運行する **unkō suru** run, operate (*of trains etc*); move (*of planet*)
運命 **unmei** destiny, fate
うのみにする **unomi ni suru** lap up; swallow
運搬する **unpan suru** transport; convey
運送 **unsō** haulage
運送会社 **unsō-gaisha** haulage company, haulier
運送業 **unsō-gyō** haulage
運送業者 **unsō-gyōsha** forwarding agent; movers
運送料 **unsō-ryō** freight
運転 **unten** driving; navigation
運転台 **untendai** driver's cab
運転免許試験 **unten-menkyo-shiken** driving test
運転免許証 **unten-menkyoshō** driver's license
運転者 **unten-sha** operator
運転士 **unten-shi** engineer RAIL
運転手 **unten-shu** driver; chauffeur
運転する **unten suru** drive; steer
うんと **unto** a great deal; severely
うぬぼれ **unubore** conceit; pride, arrogance
うぬぼれた **unuboreta** conceited; big-headed
うぬぼれている **unuborete iru** vain
うぬぼれや **unubore-ya** show-off
運よく **un'yoku** luckily
運輸業者 **un'yu-gyōsha** carrier
運輸省 **Un'yushō** Department of Transportation
うんざりした **unzari shita** bored; fed up
うんざりする **unzari suru** be fed up with
魚 **uo** fish
うっぷんを晴らす **uppun o harasu** work off *bad mood*; vent *anger*
裏 **ura** back; bottom; reverse; 裏をかく ***ura o kaku*** foil, outwit
裏返しに **uragaeshi ni** inside out
裏切り **uragiri** disloyalty; betrayal; treachery
裏切り者(の) **uragirimono** (**no**) disloyal
裏切る **uragiru** betray; 期待を裏切る ***kitai o uragiru*** let down
裏口 **uraguchi** backdoor
裏地 **uraji** lining; backing
裏階段 **urakaidan** backstairs
裏目に出る **urame ni deru** backfire
恨み **urami** feud; rancor; grudge; resentment; 恨みを晴らす ***urami o harasu*** have a score to settle with; 恨みを持っている ***urami o motte iru*** bear a grudge

恨む **uramu** bear a grudge
裏道 **uramichi** back road
占い師 **uranaishi** fortune teller
ウラニウム **uraniumu** uranium
裏庭 **uraniwa** backyard, yard
裏表 **uraomote** both sides; 裏表のある ***uraomote no aru*** two-faced
うらやましげ(な) **urayamashige (na)** envious
うらやましい **urayamashii** enviable ◊ envy; be jealous of
裏付け **urazuke** confirmation; backing, support
裏付ける **urazukeru** back up; corroborate; confirm; reinforce
売れる **ureru** sell; be in demand
熟れる **ureru** ripen; be ripe
うれしい **ureshii** glad
熟れた **ureta** ripe
売れていない **urete inai** unsuccessful
売り上げ **uriage** takings; turnover
売上高 **uriagedaka** sales figures
売り場 **uriba** department (*of store*)
売り出す **uridasu** offer for sale
売り切れ **urikire** sold out
売り込み **urikomi** sales patter
売り崩し **urikuzushi** raid FIN
売り物(の) **urimono (no)** for sale
売りに出す **uri ni dasu** put up for sale
うり類 **uriruі** squash (*vegetable*)
売り手 **urite** seller, vendor
売り渡し証 **uriwatashishō** bill of sale
うろこ **uroko** scale (*on fish*)
うろたえる **urotaeru** be in a flap; get flustered
うろつく **urotsuku** loiter; prowl
うろうろする **urouro suru** mill around; hang around
売る **uru** sell
ウール **ūru** wool
うるう年 **urūdoshi** leap year
ウール(の) **ūru (no)** woolen
うるさい **urusai** noisy; loud; persistent; annoying; fussy
漆 **urushi** lacquer
うさぎ **usagi** rabbit
牛 **ushi** cow; bull; cattle
失う **ushinau** lose; forfeit
失われた **ushinawareta** lost
後ろ **ushiro** back (*of car, bus*)
後ろへ **ushiro e** backward
後ろ前 **ushiromae** back to front
うしろめたい **ushirometai** have a guilty conscience
うしろめたさ **ushirometa-sa** guilt feelings
後ろに **ushiro ni** backward; behind; 後ろに下がる ***ushiro ni sagaru*** draw back, back off
後ろ(の) **ushiro (no)** back, rear
うそ **uso** lie; うそをつく ***uso o tsuku*** lie
うそ(の) **uso (no)** false, untrue; phony
うそつき **usotsuki** liar
うっ積した **usseki shita** pent-up
薄茶色 **usuchairo** buff; light brown
薄汚ない **usugitanai** dingy
薄暗い **usugurai** dim; obscure
薄い **usui** thin; light; weak; flimsy; 薄いピンク色 ***usui pinku-iro*** pale pink
薄く**usuku** thinly
薄める **usumeru** dilute
うすのろ(の) **usunoro (no)** dumb, stupid
薄っぺらい **usupperai** superficial; thin; flimsy
薄れる **usureru** abate; wane
歌 **uta** song
疑い **utagai** doubt; suspicion; reservation; 疑いのある ***utagai no aru*** suspected; 疑いをもっている ***utagai o motte iru*** be doubtful (*of person*)
疑い深い **utagaibukai** skeptical; suspicious
疑いもなく **utagai mo naku** unquestionably
疑いない **utagai nai** doubtless
疑いなく **utagai naku** distinctly, decidedly
疑う **utagau** question, doubt; suspect
疑う余地なく **utagau yochi naku** undoubtedly
疑わない **utagawanai** unquestioning
疑わしげ(な) **utagawashige (na)** questioning

疑わしげに **utagawashige ni** doubtfully
疑わしい **utagawashii** doubtful, dubious; questionable
うたた寝 **utatane** doze; nap; うたた寝をする ***utatane o suru*** doze; have a nap
歌う **utau** sing
うとうとする **utouto suru** doze off
打つ **utsu** hit; thrash; bat; bounce; strike (*of clock*)
撃つ **utsu** shoot
うつ病 **utsubyō** depression MED
美しい **utsukushii** beautiful
美しさ **utsukushi-sa** beauty
うつむく **utsumuku** hang one's head; look down
移り変わり **utsurikawari** change; transition
うつりやすい **utsuri-yasui** contagious
うつろ(な) **utsuro (na)** hollow; empty; vacant
うつる **utsuru** be infectious
移る **utsuru** move; transfer; change
映る **utsuru** be reflected; be shown (*on a screen*); suit
うつす **utsusu** transfer; transmit; pass on; 病気をうつす ***byôki o utsusu*** infect
映す **utsusu** project; reflect; mirror
写す **utsusu** take a photo; copy; trace; draw
訴え **uttae** lawsuit; complaint
訴える **uttaeru** complain of; bring an action against
うってつけ(の) **uttetsuke (no)** perfect, ideal
うっとりさせる **uttori saseru** charm
うっとりする **uttori suru** go into a trance
うっとりするよう(な) **uttori suru yō (na)** enchanting
うっとうしい **uttōshii** gloomy; oppressive
うわべだけ(の) **uwabe dake (no)** glib; hollow
上着 **uwagi** coat, jacket; top
うわ言を言う **uwagoto o iu** be delirious MED; rave
浮気(な) **uwaki (na)** unfaithful
浮気をする **uwaki o suru** fool around; have an affair
うわの空(の) **uwa no sora (no)** preoccupied; distracted
うわさ **uwasa** rumor
うわさ話 **uwasabanashi** gossip; うわさ話をする ***uwasabanashi o suru*** gossip
うわさで **uwasa de** by hearsay
上役 **uwayaku** superior; senior official
敬う **uyamau** respect; honor
うやうやしい **uyauyashii** reverent
右翼 **uyoku** right wing; right-winger
渦 **uzu** whirlpool; eddy; curl (*of smoke*)
うずく **uzuku** hurt; ache; smart; throb
渦巻 **uzumaki** whirlpool
渦巻く **uzumaku** whirl
うずら **uzura** quail

W

わ **wa** bundle; sheaf ◊ (*familiar softening or emphasizing particle used mostly by women*): 私が一緒に行くわ ***watashi ga issho ni ikuwa*** I'll come with you
は **wa** (*subject particle*): 私はアメリカ人です ***watashi wa Amerika-jin desu*** I'm American
和 **wa** peace; harmony; sum
和… **wa…** Japanese(-style)
羽 **-wa** *countword for birds and rabbits*

輪 **wa** hoop, loop; link (*in chain*); ring, circle
わーっ **wā'** wow!
わび **wabi** apology
わびる **wabiru** apologize
わび寂び **wabisabi** *restrained quiet beauty of stark simplicity*
わびしい **wabishii** lonely; miserable
わだち **wadachi** rut (*in road*)
話題 **wadai** topic; subject
話題(の) **wadai (no)** in question ◊ topical
ワッフル **waffuru** waffle
和服 **wafuku** Japanese clothes (*traditional*)
和風(の) **wafū (no)** Japanese-style
我が **waga** my; our
わがまま(な) **wagamama (na)** selfish; willful
和菓子 **wagashi** Japanese candy and cakes
輪ゴム **wagomu** rubber band
ワゴン車 **wagon-sha** station wagon
ワイン **wain** wine
ワインリスト **wainrisuto** wine list
ワイパー **waipā** windshield wiper
わいろ **wairo** bribe; kickback
わいせつ(な) **waisetsu (na)** obscene, lewd; dirty, smutty
ワイシャツ **waishatsu** shirt
和歌 **waka** waka (*31-syllable poem*)
分かち合う **wakachiau** share
若鶏 **wakadori** chicken; broiler
若い **wakai** young
和解 **wakai** reconciliation
和解できない **wakai dekinai** irreconcilable
わかめ **wakame** seaweed
若者 **wakamono** youngster
わからない **wakaranai** not understand; not know
わからせる **wakaraseru** get through
別れ **wakare** farewell, parting
別れる **wakareru** break up, split up; leave; finish with
わかりにくい **wakarinikui** obscure, hard to understand
わかりやすい **wakariyasui** clear, lucid; illuminating
わかる **wakaru** understand; tell *the difference*; わかりません ***wakarimasen*** I don't know; わかりました ***wakarimashita*** I see
沸かす **wakasu** boil; heat; excite
若々しい **wakawakashii** youthful
訳, わけ **wake** reason; cause; meaning; sense; どういうわけで ***dô iu wake de*** why?; そういうわけで ***sô iu wake de*** that's the reason why; そういうわけなら ***sô iu wake nara*** if that's the case; 心配しないわけにはいかない ***shinpai shinai wake ni wa ikanai*** I can't help worrying; わけのわからない ***wake no wakaranai*** puzzling
分け前 **wakemae** share, slice
分け目 **wakeme** part (*in hair*)
分ける **wakeru** divide, share; part, separate
わき **waki** side; わきへ入る ***waki e hairu*** turn off (*of car, driver*)
わき腹 **wakibara** flank; わき腹が痛む ***wakibara ga itamu*** have a stitch
わき道 **wakimichi** side street; わき道へそれる ***wakimichi e soreru*** digress
わき見する **wakimi suru** look away
わきに **waki ni** aside
わきの下 **waki no shita** armpit
ワックス **wakkusu** wax
沸く **waku** boil; be heated; be enthusiastic
枠 **waku** frame
ワクチン **wakuchin** vaccine
惑星 **wakusei** planet
ワークショップ **wāku-shoppu** workshop
ワークステーション **wāku-sutēshon** work station
わくわくさせる **wakuwaku saseru** thrilling
わくわくする **wakuwaku suru** exciting ◊ be thrilled
わめき声 **wamekigoe** shout; yell; roar
わめく **wameku** shout; howl; roar; rave
湾 **wan** bay; gulf
わな **wana** setup, trap; わなにかける ***wana ni kakeru*** frame, set up; trap
わに **wani** crocodile

ワンマン(な) **wanman (na)** dictatorial; one-man
ワンピース **wanpīsu** dress
ワンルームマンション **wanrūmu-manshon** studio apartment
わんわん **wanwan** doggie, bow-wow
和音 **waon** chord
ワープ **wāpu** timewarp
ワープロ **wāpuro** word processor
わら **wara** straw
笑い **warai** laugh; laughter
笑い声 **waraigoe** laughter
笑い事じゃない **waraigoto ja nai** it's no joke
笑いもの **waraimono** mockery, travesty; 笑いものになる ***waraimono ni naru*** make a fool of oneself
笑う **warau** laugh
笑わせる **warawaseru** amuse
割れ目 **wareme** crevice; split
我を忘れる **ware o wasureru** be beside oneself
割れる **wareru** break; break up; split
割れた **wareta** broken
我々 **wareware** we
割 **wari** rate; ratio; 10%; 二割 ***niwari*** 20%; 割に合わない ***wari ni awanai*** thankless; 割の合う ***wari no au*** remunerative
割合 **wariai** percentage; proportion; part
割り当て **wariate** quota
割り当てる **wariateru** allocate, allot, assign
割りばし **waribashi** disposable chopsticks
割引 **waribiki** discount
割引券 **waribiki-ken** coupon
割り引く **waribiku** discount
割り勘にする **warikan ni suru** go Dutch
割り切れる **warikireru** divisible
割り込む **warikomu** interrupt; cut in
割増料金 **warimashi-ryōkin** surcharge
わりに **wari ni** rather; somewhat
割り算 **warizan** division MATH
割る **waru** divide MATH; break; crack; split; chop
悪ふざけ **warufuzake** practical joke
悪賢い **warugashikoi** devious, cunning
悪賢さ **warugashiko-sa** cunning
悪気 **warugi** ill will; malice
悪口 **waruguchi** slander
悪い **warui** bad; evil
悪く **waruku** badly
悪くない **waruku nai** it's not bad ◊ fair, not bad
悪くなる **waruku naru** deteriorate, go downhill
ワルツ **warutsu** waltz
わさび **wasabi** Japanese horse radish
わし **washi** eagle
和紙 **washi** Japanese paper
ワシントン **Washinton** Washington
和室 **washitsu** Japanese room
和食 **washoku** Japanese cuisine
忘れ物 **wasuremono** something left behind; lost and found
わすれなぐさ **wasurenagusa** forget-me-not
忘れっぽい **wasureppoi** forgetful
忘れられない **wasurerarenai** memorable, unforgettable
忘れられる **wasurerareru** be forgotten, fall into oblivion
忘れられた **wasurerareta** neglected
忘れる **wasureru** forget; get over *lover etc*
綿 **wata** cotton
綿あめ **wata-ame** cotton candy
私 **watakushi** I (*polite*)
渡る **wataru** cross, go across
私 **watashi** I; me
私の **watashi no** my ◊ mine
私達 **watashitachi** we; us
私達の **watashitachi no** our ◊ ours
渡す **watasu** give in, hand in
ワット **watto** watt
わっと泣き出す **watto nakidasu** burst into tears
わざと **wazato** deliberately, intentionally, on purpose
わざとらしい **wazatorashii** artificial; theatrical
わざわざ **wazawaza** expressly
わずか(な) **wazuka (na)** slender, slight; meager; miserly
わずかに **wazuka ni** remotely;

slightly
わずらわしい **wazurawashii** annoying
わずらわしさ **wazurawashi-sa** annoyance
ウェブページ **webu-pēji** web page
ウェブサイト **webu-saito** web site
ウェールズ **Wēruzu** Wales
ウォッカ **wokka** vodka
ウォークマン **wōkuman** personal stereo, Walkman®
ウォームアップする **wōmu-appu suru** warm up
ウォール街 **Wōru-gai** Wall Street

Y

や **ya** (*particle linking nouns used as examples*) and; or; 肉や魚を食べない ***niku ya sakana o tabenai*** I don't eat things like meat or fish
矢 **ya** arrow
やばい **yabai** dangerous; terrible
野蛮人 **yaban-jin** savage
野蛮(な) **yaban (na)** savage
やぶ医者 **yabuisha** quack
破れる **yabureru** be ripped; be broken; break down
敗れる **yabureru** lose; be defeated
破る **yaburu** break; tear up ◊ outrage
破ることのできない **yaburu koto no dekinai** unbreakable
家賃 **yachin** rent, rental
宿 **yado** inn; hotel
ヤード **yādo** yard (*measurement*)
宿屋 **yadoya** inn
野外(の) **yagai (no)** outdoor
やがて **yagate** before long; soon
やぎ **yagi** goat
やはり **yahari** after all; as expected; also
やじ **yaji** jeering
やじる **yajiru** boo; heckle
矢印 **yajirushi** arrow
やじ馬 **yajiuma** curious bystander; rubber-neck
やかましい **yakamashii** noisy; particular; strict
やかん **yakan** kettle
夜間 **yakan** night time
夜間フライト **yakan-furaito** night flight
夜間外出禁止令 **yakan-gaishutsu-kinshirei** curfew
夜間学校 **yakan-gakkō** night school
夜間勤務 **yakan-kinmu** night shift
やけど **yakedo** burn
やけどさせる **yakedo saseru** scald
やけどする **yakedo suru** get burned
焼け焦げ **yakekoge** burn
焼ける **yakeru** burn; roast (*of food*)
焼き網 **yakiami** grill; broiler (*on stove*)
焼き増し **yakimashi** additional print of a photo
やきもち **yakimochi** toasted rice cake; jealousy; やきもちをやく ***yakimochi o yaku*** be jealous
焼き肉 **yakiniku** grilled meat
夜勤する **yakin suru** work nights
焼きすぎる **yaki-sugiru** overdo *meat etc*
焼きすぎた **yaki-sugita** overdone *meat etc*
やきとり **yakitori** *grilled chicken and vegetables on a skewer*
焼き尽くす **yakitsukusu** burn down
やっかい者 **yakkai mono** menace, pest
やっかい(な) **yakkai (na)** troublesome; awkward; messy
薬局 **yakkyoku** drugstore; pharmacy
焼く **yaku** burn; get a tan; bake; fry; grill; roast; toast; broil

約 **yaku** in the region of, roughly
訳 **yaku** translation
役 **yaku** part (*in play, movie*); 役を割り当てる ***yaku o wariateru*** cast
薬品 **yakuhin** medicine; chemical
役員会 **yakuinkai** board (of directors)
役目 **yakume** role; duty
役人 **yakunin** public servant; bureaucrat
役に立たない **yaku ni tatanai** useless
役に立つ **yaku ni tatsu** be worthwhile; be helpful; pay; benefit ◊ helpful
役者 **yakusha** actor
役者になる **yakusha ni naru** go on the stage
役所 **yakusho** government office
役職 **yakushoku** managerial position
約束 **yakusoku** appointment, date; meeting; promise, pledge; 約束を守る ***yakusoku o mamoru*** keep a promise
約束する **yakusoku suru** promise; commit oneself
訳す **yakusu** translate
役立たず **yakutatazu** good-for-nothing
役立たず(の) **yakutatazu (no)** useless, worthless
役得 **yakutoku** perk (*of job*)
役割 **yakuwari** function, role
薬用(の) **yakuyō (no)** medicated; medicinal
やくざ **yakuza** yakuza, gangster
薬剤師 **yakuzaishi** druggist, pharmacist
野球 **yakyū** baseball; ball game; 野球のバット ***yakyû no batto*** baseball bat; 野球のボール ***yakyû no bôru*** baseball (*ball*)
野球帽 **yakyū-bō** baseball cap
野球場 **yakyū-jō** ballpark
野球選手 **yakyū-senshu** baseball player
山 **yama** hill; mountain; pile, mound, stack; guess; 山が当たった ***yama ga atatta*** my guess was right!; 山の多い ***yama no ôi*** mountainous
やまあらし **yama-arashi** porcupine
山歩き **yamaaruki** hike
山ほどの **yamahodo no** a pile of
山のよう(な) **yama no yō (na)** mammoth, enormous
やましい **yamashii** remorseful; やましいところのない ***yamashii tokoro no nai*** clear *conscience*
やますそ **yamasuso** foothills
山分けする **yamawake suru** divide equally
やめる **yameru** drop, give up, abandon; stop
辞める **yameru** resign; quit
やめさせる **yamesaseru** stop, put a stop to
やみ **yami** darkness
やみ経済 **yamikeizai** black economy
やみ市場 **yamishijō** black market
病みつき(の) **yamitsuki (no)** compulsive
やむ **yamu** stop, let up; subside
やむを得ない **yamuoenai** unavoidable
やむを得ず **yamuoezu** unwillingly, reluctantly
柳 **yanagi** willow tree
屋根 **yane** roof
屋根裏 **yaneura** loft
屋根裏部屋 **yaneura-beya** attic, garret
ヤンキー **Yankī** Yank
八百長する **yaochō suru** fix *boxing match etc*
八百屋 **yaoya** greengrocer
やっぱり **yappari** after all; as expected; also
やれやれ **yareyare** thank God!
やり合う **yariau** compete; argue; haggle
やりがいのある **yarigai no aru** worthwhile
やり返す **yarikaesu** hit back
やり方 **yarikata** method; way
やりくりする **yarikuri suru** manage (*financially*); stretch *income*
やり直す **yarinaosu** brush up; go over
やりすぎ **yari-sugi** overdose;

excess; やりすぎだ ***yari-sugi da*** you went too far
やりすぎる **yari-sugiru** overdo, exaggerate; be over the top
やりたがる **yaritagaru** be enthusiastic to do
やり遂げる **yaritogeru** accomplish; pull off *deal etc*
やりとり **yaritori** give and take; exchange (*of letters*)
やる **yaru** play; do; give; V fuck
やる気 **yaruki** drive, energy; やる気がわいて ***yaruki ga waite*** in a burst of energy; やる気にさせる ***yaruki ni saseru*** motivate; やる気をなくす ***yaruki o nakusu*** become demoralized
野菜 **yasai** vegetable
やさしい **yasashii** easy
優しい **yasashii** loving, affectionate, tender; gentle; soft, kind, lenient; gracious
やさしさ **yasashi-sa** ease
優しさ **yasashi-sa** tenderness
野生動物 **yasei-dōbutsu** wildlife
野生(の) **yasei** (**no**) wild
やせこけた **yasekoketa** gaunt; haggard; sunken
やせ衰える **yaseotoroeru** waste away
やせっぽち(の) **yaseppochi** (**no**) puny
やせる **yaseru** get thin; lose weight
やせた **yaseta** lanky; skinny
やし **yashi** palm (tree)
野心 **yashin** ambition *pej*
養う **yashinau** support, provide for, keep
野心的(な) **yashinteki** (**na**) ambitious
安い **yasui** cheap, inexpensive; downmarket; low *salary, price*; weak *currency*
やすい **-yasui** easy to; 使いやすい ***tsukai-yasui*** easy to use, user-friendly
休まず **yasumazu** without a letup
休み **yasumi** break, rest; vacation; 休みである ***yasumi de aru*** be off
休み時間 **yasumi-jikan** recess (*at school*)
休みなく **yasumi naku** without respite
休みなしで **yasumi nashi de** without a break
休む **yasumu** rest
安物 **yasumono** cheap item
安っぽい **yasuppoi** cheap, tacky; sleazy
やすり **yasuri** file; やすりをかける ***yasuri o kakeru*** sand; file
安売り(の) **yasuuri** (**no**) cut-price
安売りされている **yasuuri sarete iru** be on sale (*at reduced prices*)
やすやすと **yasuyasu to** with ease
屋台 **yatai** street stall
やたら(に) **yatara** (**ni**) at random; indiscriminately; recklessly; extremely; やたら忙しい ***yatara isogashii*** hectic; やたらかわいがる ***yatara kawaigaru*** dote on
野党 **yatō** opposition POL
雇う **yatou** employ, hire, take on
雇われている **yatowarete iru** be on the payroll
やつ **yatsu** fellow, guy
やつれた **yatsureta** careworn, haggard
やっていく **yatte iku** get along, progress
やって来る **yatte kuru** come along, turn up
やってみる **yatte miru** have a try at; やってみよう ***yatte miyô*** let's risk it
やっと **yatto** finally; barely
やっとこ **yattoko** pincers
やっつける **yattsukeru** defeat; finish; criticize
和らげる **yawarageru** deaden; cushion, soften; defuse; ease, relieve; soothe
和らぐ **yawaragu** soften; ease off, moderate
柔らかい **yawarakai** muted, subdued; soft; tender
柔らかくなる **yawarakaku naru** soften
柔らか(な) **yawaraka na** soft; tender; mellow
柔らかさ **yawaraka-sa** tenderness
やや **yaya** rather; somewhat
ややこしい **yayakoshii** tricky

よ **yo** (*exclamatory particle*): 行こうよ ***ikô yo*** come on, let's go!; 何をしてるんだよ ***nani o shiterun da yo*** what the hell are you doing?
夜 **yo** night
世 **yo** world; 世が世なら***yo ga yo nara*** if times hadn't changed
よう **-yō** let's; 食べよう ***tabeyô*** let's eat
用 **yō** business; use; service
洋… **yō…** Western(-style)
夜明け **yoake** dawn, daybreak
夜遊び **yoasobi** nightlife
曜日 **yōbi** day of the week
呼び出し **yobidashi** call; summon
呼び出す **yobidasu** page (*with pager*); ask for
呼び入れる **yobiireru** call in, summon
呼びかける **yobikakeru** call out; call out to
予備校 **yobikō** prep school
呼び戻す **yobimodosu** call back, recall
呼び物 **yobimono** special attraction, draw
予備(の) **yobi** (**no**) auxiliary; spare
呼び起こす **yobiokosu** arouse; evoke, conjure up; inspire
予備選挙 **yobi-senkyo** primary POL
呼び捨て **yobisute** *using a person's name without courtesy titles*
予備的(な) **yobiteki** (**na**) preliminary
予防 **yobō** prevention
容ぼう **yōbō** looks; features
要望 **yōbō** request; requirement
予防注射する **yobō-chūsha suru** vaccinate
予防(の) **yobō** (**no**) preventive
予防接種 **yobō-sesshu** inoculation, vaccination
予防接種する **yobō-sesshu suru** inoculate
予防する **yobō suru** prevent
呼ぶ **yobu** call, shout; summon
養分 **yōbun** nutrient
余分(な) **yobun** (**na**) extra; spare; redundant; 余分に五個あります ***yobun ni goko arimasu*** there are 5 to spare
余分(の) **yobun** (**no**) extra
余地 **yochi** room, scope
予知 **yochi** prediction; prognosis
幼稚園 **yōchien** kindergarten
よちよち歩く **yochiyochi aruku** waddle; toddle
幼虫 **yōchū** larva
ようだ **yō da** → ***yô na***
容態 **yōdai** condition MED
余談 **yodan** padding (*in speech etc*)
よだれ **yodare** dribble; よだれが出ている ***yodare ga dete iru*** my mouth is watering; よだれを垂らす ***yodare o tarasu*** dribble; slobber
よだれ掛け **yodarekake** bib
よだれの出そう(な) **yodare no desō** (**na**) mouthwatering
よどんだ **yodonda** stagnant; stale
夜更かしする **yofukashi suru** stay up late
溶液 **yōeki** solution, mixture
洋服ダンス **yōfuku-dansu** wardrobe
洋服一式 **yōfuku-isshiki** wardrobe (*clothes*)
洋服掛け **yōfuku-kake** hanger; hook
洋服屋 **yōfuku-ya** tailor
洋風(の) **yōfū** (**no**) Western
洋画 **yōga** Western movie
溶岩流 **yōganryū** lava flow
洋菓子 **yōgashi** cake; pastries
予言 **yogen** prediction, prophecy
予言する **yogen suru** foretell, predict; prophesy
容疑 **yōgi** suspicion; charge LAW; 容疑を晴らす ***yôgi o harasu*** clear, acquit
容疑者 **yōgi-sha** suspect
用語 **yōgo** language; term
擁護 **yōgo** defense; protection
汚れ **yogore** dirt, filth
汚れる **yogoreru** stain
擁護者 **yōgo-sha** champion (*of cause*)
養護施設 **yōgo-shisetsu** orphanage
用語集 **yōgoshū** glossary; vocabulary
汚す **yogosu** dirty, soil, stain; smudge

擁護する **yōgo suru** defend, champion *cause*
夜ごとに **yogoto ni** nightly
用具 **yōgu** equipment; materials; utensil
ヨーグルト **yōguruto** yoghurt
余白 **yohaku** blank, space; margin
よう兵 **yōhei** mercenary (*soldier*)
予報 **yohō** weather forecast
余程 **yohodo** very much; almost
予報する **yohō suru** forecast
よい, 良い, 善い **yoi** good; nice
酔い **yoi** drunkenness; 酔いが覚める ***yoi ga sameru*** sober up; 酔いがすぐ回る ***yoi ga sugu mawaru*** heady *drink*
用意 **yōi** preparations
養育権 **yōikuken** custody
要因 **yōin** main cause; primary factor
容易(な) **yōi** (**na**) simple; easy
容易に **yōi ni** easily, with ease
容易さ **yōi-sa** ease
用意する **yōi suru** prepare; arrange
幼児 **yōji** infant
用事 **yōji** engagement; business
用心 **yōjin** caution; precaution
要人 **yōjin** very important person, VIP
用心棒 **yōjinbō** bodyguard; bouncer
用心深い **yōjin-bukai** cautious; alert; wary
用心のため(の) **yōjin no tame** (**no**) precautionary
用心する **yōjin suru** be careful; be wary of; guard against
よじれ **yojire** kink; twist
よじれる **yojireru** be twisted
余剰 **yojō** surplus
余剰(の) **yojō** (**no**) surplus
余暇 **yoka** leisure time; spare time
溶解した **yōkai shita** molten
予感 **yokan** foreboding, premonition; hunch
よかれと思ってする **yokare to omotte suru** mean well
余計(な) **yokei** (**na**) unnecessary; superfluous
用件 **yōken** business
よければ **yokereba** if you like
よける **yokeru** avoid; shun; dodge
予期 **yoki** expectation; anticipation
容器 **yōki** container
預金 **yokin** deposit
陽気(な) **yōki** (**na**) cheerful; lively
預金する **yokin suru** deposit; …銀行に預金する ***… ginkô ni yokin suru*** bank with
預金残高 **yokin-zandaka** bank balance
予期する **yoki suru** expect; anticipate
欲求不満 **yokkyū-fuman** frustration
欲求不満にさせる **yokkyū-fuman ni saseru** frustrate
欲求不満(の) **yokkyū-fuman** (**no**) frustrated
横 **yoko** side; width
横笛 **yokobue** flute
横書き **yokogaki** write horizontally
横顔 **yokogao** profile (*of face*)
横切る **yokogiru** cross; go across
横切って **yokogitte** through, across
横浜 **Yokohama** Yokohama
予告 **yokoku** warning
予告編 **yokokuhen** preview (*of movie*)
横道にそれる **yokomichi ni soreru** get sidetracked; wander (*of attention*)
横向きに **yokomuki ni** sideways
横になる **yoko ni naru** lie; lie down
溶鉱炉 **yōkōro** blast furnace
横綱 **yokozuna** grand champion
よく **yoku** often; well
欲 **yoku** appetite; greed
翌朝 **yokuasa** the following morning
抑圧する **yokuatsu suru** repress, stifle; oppress
欲張り **yokubari** greedy person
欲張る **yokubaru** be greedy
欲望 **yokubō** desire, lust
翌日 **yokujitsu** the following day
良くない **yoku nai** poor; unfavorable; wrong
良くなる **yoku naru** improve, pick up; look up
翌年 **yokunen** the following year
抑制 **yokusei** control; restraint; suppression

抑制されない **yokusei sarenai** unrestrained
抑制されている **yokusei sarete iru** inhibited
抑制した **yokusei shita** muted
抑制する **yokusei suru** curb; inhibit
抑止力 **yokushiryoku** deterrent
浴室 **yokushitsu** bathroom
翌週 **yokushū** the following week
浴槽 **yokusō** bathtub
欲得ずくの **yokutokuzuku no** selfish; mercenary *attitude*
抑揚 **yokuyō** intonation; inflection
要求 **yōkyū** demand, call; requirement; 要求を満たす ***yôkyû o mitasu*** cater for
要求者 **yōkyū-sha** claimant
要求する **yōkyū suru** demand; insist on
嫁 **yome** daughter-in-law
読める **yomeru** readable
読み **yomi** reading (*of a character*)
読み違える **yomichigaeru** misread
よみがえる **yomigaeru** come back to life; revive
読み書きができる **yomikaki ga dekiru** be literate
読み方 **yomikata** reading; pronunciation
読み物 **yomimono** reading matter
読みにくい **yominikui** difficult to read; illegible
読み取る **yomitoru** read *diskette*
読みやすい **yomiyasui** easy to read; legible
よもぎ **yomogi** mugwort
読む **yomu** read
四 **yon** four
よう(な) **yō** (**na**): …のよう(な) ***… no yô*** (***na***) like; such as; …のようである ***… no yô de aru*** be like, look like; seem like; 彼は来ないようだ ***kare wa konai yô da*** it looks like he's not coming
夜中 **yonaka** middle of the night; small hours
幼年時代 **yōnen-jidai** infancy
…ように **… yō ni** as, like; …のように ***… no yô ni*** as though; …のように見える ***… no yô ni mieru*** appear; seem
容認できる **yōnin dekiru** acceptable
容認する **yōnin suru** accept; allow; condone
四十 **yonjū** forty
世の中 **yo no naka** the world; society
酔っ払い **yopparai** drunk
酔っ払い(の) **yopparai** (**no**) drunken
酔っ払った **yopparatta** drunk
酔っ払う **yopparau** get drunk
よれば **yoreba** according to
よれよれ(の) **yoreyore** (**no**) shabby; worn-out
より **yori** from; than; 五月一日より ***gogatsu tsuitachi yori*** effective as from May 1; …より金がある ***… yori kane ga aru*** be better off than; …より前に ***… yori mae ni*** prior to; YよりXのほうが好きである ***Y yori X no hô ga suki de aru*** prefer X to Y
より好みする **yorigonomi suru** pick and choose
寄りかかる **yorikakaru** lean against; rely on
寄り目(の) **yorime** (**no**) cross-eyed
寄り道する **yorimichi suru** stop over; drop in
寄り添う **yorisou** snuggle up to
より優れた **yori sugureta** superior, better
より分ける **yoriwakeru** classify; sort out
よろいかぶと **yoroikabuto** armor
養老院 **yōrōin** rest home
喜ばす **yorokobasu** please
喜び **yorokobi** pleasure; joy
喜んだ **yorokonda** pleased
喜んで **yorokonde** gladly, willingly
喜んでいる **yorokonde iru** be delighted
よろめく **yoromeku** lurch, stagger; wobble; totter
ヨーロッパ **Yōroppa** Europe
ヨーロッパ人 **Yōroppa-jin** European
ヨーロッパ(の) **Yōroppa** (**no**) European
よろしい **yoroshii** good; OK
よろしく **yoroshiku** please do; はじめましてどうぞよろしくお願いします

hajimemashite, dôzo yoroshiku onegai shimasu hello, how do you do?; 彼女によろしく ***kanojo ni yoroshiku*** give her my love; give her my best wishes
よろよろする **yoroyoro suru** stagger; totter
よる **yoru** according to ◊ be based on; be relative to
夜 **yoru** night
夜中 **yorujū** the whole night ◊ in the night
要領 **yōryō** main point; knack; 要領がいい ***yôryô ga ii*** shrewd; clever; 要領が悪い ***yôryô ga warui*** awkward; clumsy
容量 **yōryō** volume, quantity
要さい **yōsai** fortress
予算 **yosan** budget; 予算がある ***yosan ga aru*** be on a budget; 予算にいれる ***yosan ni ireru*** budget for; 予算を立てる ***yosan o tateru*** budget
寄せ集め **yoseatsume** mixture; jumble; medley
寄せ集める **yoseatsumeru** gather up; put together
よう精(妖精) **yōsei** fairy
要請 **yōsei** request
陽性(の) **yōsei (no)** positive *medical test*
養成する **yōsei suru** train; educate
容積 **yōseki** cubic capacity, volume
溶接工 **yōsetsu-kō** welder
溶接する **yōsetsu suru** weld
容赦ない **yōsha nai** remorseless, unrelenting; cut-throat
養子 **yōshi** adopted child; 養子にする ***yôshi ni suru*** adopt
用紙 **yōshi** form (*document*)
善し悪し **yoshiashi** good and bad
様式 **yōshiki** mode, form; style, method
洋室 **yōshitsu** Western-style room
洋書 **yōsho** book written in a Western language
洋食 **yōshoku** Western cuisine
養殖 **yōshoku** cultivation; breeding
予習する **yoshū suru** prepare one's lessons
よそ **yoso** another place; another person; out-group
予想 **yosō** anticipation, expectation; forecast; 予想のつく ***yosô no tsuku*** predictable
ヨウ素 **yōso** iodine
要素 **yōso** element; factor; ingredient
予想できない **yosō dekinai** unpredictable
予測できる **yosoku dekiru** foreseeable
予想する **yosō suru** anticipate, expect; envisage
よそよそしい **yosoyososhii** cold; distant
様子 **yōsu** appearance; aspect; state of affairs; 様子を聞く ***yôsu o kiku*** ask after
用水路 **yōsuiro** irrigation canal
要する **yō suru** need; cost; entail
要するに **yō suru ni** in short; in a nutshell
世捨て人 **yosutebito** hermit
よたよた歩く **yotayota aruku** hobble; totter; waddle
予定 **yotei** arrangement, plan; 予定で一杯になる ***yotei de ippai ni naru*** be booked up; 予定がある ***yotei ga aru*** have on, have planned
予定である **yotei de aru** intend to; plan on
予定どおりである **yotei dōri de aru** be on schedule
予定されている **yotei sarete iru** be on, be scheduled
予定説 **yoteisetsu** predestination
予定する **yotei suru** intend; plan
要点 **yōten** main point; gist
与党 **yotō** ruling party
用途 **yōto** use; application
腰痛 **yōtsū** lumbago
四つ足(の) **yotsuashi (no)** quadruped
四つ子 **yotsugo** quadruplets
四つ角 **yotsukado** intersection
酔った **yotta** intoxicated
よって **yotte**: …によって ***… ni yotte*** with; by; by means of; according to; depending on
ヨット **yotto** yacht, sailboat

ヨットマン **yottoman** yachtsman, sailor
酔う **you** get drunk; get sick; 飛行機に酔う ***hikôki ni you*** get airsick
弱い **yowai** delicate *health*; floppy, weak; light
弱い者いじめ **yowaimono-ijime** bullying
弱気(な) **yowaki** (**na**) timid; weak-minded
弱気になる **yowaki ni naru** weaken
弱くなる **yowaku naru** weaken
弱くする **yowaku suru** weaken; turn down *heating*
弱まる **yowamaru** die down
弱める **yowameru** undermine
弱虫 **yowamushi** chicken, wimp; weakling
弱らせる **yowaraseru** sap
弱る **yowaru** weaken; flag, tire
弱さ **yowa-sa** weakness; frailty
酔わせる **yowaseru** make drunk
弱った **yowatta** impaired; infirm
弱っている **yowatte iru** be weak
弱々しい **yowayowashii** feeble
予約 **yoyaku** reservation; advance booking; appointment; 予約で一杯になる ***yoyaku de ippai ni naru*** be booked up
ようやく **yōyaku** finally; just, barely
要約 **yōyaku** summary, précis, résumé
予約帳 **yoyakuchō** appointments diary
予約係 **yoyaku-gakari** booking clerk
予約(の) **yoyaku** (**no**) reserved
予約する **yoyaku suru** book, reserve
要約する **yōyaku suru** summarize, sum up; compress *information*; abridge
余裕 **yoyū** leeway; margin; 余裕を持つ ***yoyû o motsu*** allow for; calculate for; 余裕がない ***yoyû ga nai*** have none to spare; not be able to afford to
湯 **yu** hot water
優 **yū** grade A; excellent
油圧式(の) **yuatsushiki** (**no**) hydraulic
ゆうべ **yūbe** last night
雄弁 **yūben** eloquence
雄弁家 **yūben-ka** speaker, orator
雄弁(な) **yūben** (**na**) eloquent
指 **yubi** finger
郵便 **yūbin** mail
優美(な) **yūbi** (**na**) dainty; exquisite; graceful
郵便番号 **yūbin-bangō** zip code
郵便振替為替 **yūbin-furikae-kawase** giro
指人形 **yubiningyō** finger puppet
郵便為替 **yūbin-kawase** money order
郵便局 **yūbinkyoku** post office
郵便(の) **yūbin** (**no**) postal
郵便受け **yūbin'uke** mailbox
指貫 **yubinuki** thimble
郵便屋さん **yūbin'ya-san** mailman
優美さ **yūbi-sa** grace
指先 **yubisaki** fingertip
指さす **yubisasu** point at
指輪 **yubiwa** ring
有望(な) **yūbō** (**na**) hopeful; promising
夕立 **yūdachi** evening shower
雄大(な) **yūdai** (**na**) grand; epic
雄大さ **yūdai-sa** grandeur
油断する **yudan suru** be careless; be off guard
ユダヤ人 **Yudaya-jin** Jew
ユダヤ(の) **Yudaya** (**no**) Jewish
ゆでる **yuderu** boil; poach
ゆで卵 **yude-tamago** boiled egg
湯豆腐 **yudōfu** hot bean curd
有毒(な) **yūdoku** (**na**) poisonous, toxic
有益(な) **yūeki** (**na**) informative, instructive; beneficial; salutary
遊園地 **yūenchi** amusement park, funfair
裕福(な) **yūfuku** (**na**) wealthy, well-off
有害(な) **yūgai** (**na**) detrimental, harmful
ゆがめる **yugameru** distort, warp
ゆがむ **yugamu** buckle; warp
優雅(な) **yūga** (**na**) elegant; gracious
優雅さ **yūga-sa** elegance, style
夕方 **yūgata** evening

湯気 **yuge** steam
融合 **yūgō** fusion
夕暮れ **yūgure** twilight
夕飯 **yūhan** dinner; evening meal
夕日 **yūhi** setting sun
遊歩道 **yūhodō** promenade; boardwalk
遺言 **yuigon** will LAW; 遺言で譲る ***yuigon de yuzuru*** bequeath
唯一(の) **yuiitsu (no)** exclusive, sole; only
友人 **yūjin** friend
友情 **yūjō** friendship
優柔不断 **yūjū-fudan** indecisiveness
優柔不断(の) **yūjū-fudan (no)** indecisive; wishy-washy
床 **yuka** floor (*of room*)
誘拐 **yūkai** kidnapping
誘拐犯 **yūkai-han** kidnapper
愉快(な) **yukai (na)** pleasant
誘拐する **yūkai suru** abduct; kidnap, snatch
床板 **yukaita** floorboard
夕刊 **yūkan** evening paper
勇敢(な) **yūkan (na)** brave, valiant; intrepid
勇敢さ **yūkan-sa** bravery
有価証券 **yūka-shōken** securities
浴衣 **yukata** summer kimono
有権者 **yūken-sha** elector, voter; electorate
輸血 **yuketsu** blood transfusion
雪 **yuki** snow; 雪が降る ***yuki ga furu*** snow
行き **yuki** going to; bound for; …行きの列車 ***…yuki no ressha*** a train for
勇気 **yūki** courage; nerve; 勇気のある ***yûki no aru*** courageous
雪玉 **yukidama** snowball
雪だるま **yukidaruma** snowman
有機肥料 **yūki-hiryō** organic fertilizer
勇気を出す **yūki o dasu** pluck up courage
ゆっくり **yukkuri** slowly; at leisure; ゆっくり歩く ***yukkuri aruku*** stroll; ゆっくり考える ***yukkuri kangaeru*** reflect, think; sleep on
ゆっくりした **yukkuri shita** easy
有効期限 **yūkō-kigen** expiry date; 有効期限が切れる ***yûkô-kigen ga kireru*** expire
有効(な) **yūkō (na)** valid
有効にする **yūkō ni suru** validate
有効性 **yūkōsei** validity
友好的(な) **yūkōteki (na)** friendly
行方不明である **yukue-fumei de aru** be missing
行方不明(の) **yukue-fumei (no)** missing
油膜 **yumaku** oil slick
夢 **yume** dream, ambition; 夢が実現する ***yume ga jitsugen suru*** a dream come true; 夢を見る ***yume o miru*** have a dream
有名人 **yūmei-jin** celebrity, personality
有名(な) **yūmei (na)** famous, well-known
有名になる **yūmei ni naru** make a name for oneself
夢見る **yumemiru** daydream
夢見るよう(な) **yumemiru yō (na)** dreamy
夢にも思わない **yume ni mo omowanai** undreamt-of
夢のよう(な) **yume no yō (na)** dream *house etc*
夢うつつ **yumeutsutsu** trance; *state between sleep and wakefulness*
弓 **yumi** bow MUS
ユーモア **yūmoa** humor, wit; ユーモアのある ***yûmoa no aru*** be witty; ユーモアのセンス ***yûmoa no sensu*** sense of humor
ユーモラス(な) **yūmorasu (na)** humorous
ユニフォーム **yunifōmu** uniform
ユニーク(な) **yunīku (na)** unique
ユニット **yunitto** module, unit
ユニット式(の) **yunitto-shiki (no)** modular
ゆのみ **yunomi** Japanese tea cup
有能(な) **yūnō (na)** able, skillful; capable
輸入 **yunyū** import
輸入業者 **yunyū-gyōsha** importer
輸入する **yunyū suru** import
揺らぐ **yuragu** waver; flicker; swing; shake

由来する **yurai suru** be derived from
揺れ **yure** shake; motion; swing; tremor
幽霊 **yūrei** ghost
揺れる **yureru** sway; rock; shake, shudder, quake; quiver; swing; wag (*of tail*)
揺れ動く **yure ugoku** rock
ゆり **yuri** lily
揺りいす **yuriisu** rocking chair
揺りかご **yurikago** cradle
有利(な) **yūri (na)** advantageous
揺り動かす **yuri ugokasu** rock
ユーロ **yūro** euro FIN
揺るがす **yurugasu** shake; shock; undermine
緩い **yurui** loose, slack; runny
緩く **yuruku** loosely
緩める **yurumeru** ease off; loosen; relax; slacken
許されない **yurusarenai** inexcusable
許される **yurusareru** permissible; 許されていない ***yurusarete inai*** it's not allowed
許せない **yurusenai** unforgivable
許し **yurushi** forgiveness
許しがたい **yurushigatai** outrageous
許す **yurusu** allow, permit; excuse, forgive, pardon
有料 **yūryō** charge; fee; toll
有料道路 **yūryō-dōro** toll road
優良株 **yūryō-kabu** blue chip; gilts
有料高速道路 **yūryō-kōsoku-dōro** turnpike
有力(な) **yūryoku (na)** important; leading; powerful; strong
優良(な) **yūryō (na)** high-grade
揺さぶる **yusaburu** shake; jolt; sway
油井 **yusei** oil well
優勢 **yūsei** dominance; supremacy
優勢(な) **yūsei (na)** superior; dominant
優性(の) **yūsei (no)** dominant
優先事項 **yūsen-jikō** priority
優先権 **yūsen-ken** right of way
優先(の) **yūsen (no)** preferential
優先される **yūsen sareru** give priority to; take precedence
優先する **yūsen suru** have priority
融資する **yūshi suru** finance
有刺鉄線 **yūshi-tessen** barbed wire
夕食 **yūshoku** dinner, supper
有色人種(の) **yūshoku-jinshu (no)** non-white; colored
優勝する **yūshō suru** win; be victorious
優秀(な) **yūshū (na)** brilliant, distinguished
輸出 **yushutsu** export
輸出業者 **yushutsu-gyōsha** exporter
輸出品 **yushutsuhin** export (*product*)
輸出禁止 **yushutsu-kinshi** export ban; embargo
輸出する **yushutsu suru** export
輸送 **yusō** transport
輸送貨物 **yusō-kamotsu** consignment
輸送機関 **yusō-kikan** (means of) transportation
郵送料 **yūsōryō** postage
郵送先名簿 **yūsōsaki-meibo** mailing list
郵送する **yūsō suru** mail; transport
ゆすぐ **yusugu** rinse
ユースホステル **yūsu-hosuteru** youth hostel
ゆすり **yusuri** blackmail, extortion
ゆする **yusuru** blackmail; extort; shake
豊か(な) **yutaka (na)** affluent; lavish; rich
豊かにする **yutaka ni suru** enrich
Uターン **yū-tān** U-turn
ゆとり **yutori** room; space; clearance
優等生 **yūtōsei** honor student
ゆったりした **yuttari shita** leisurely; loose, roomy *clothes*
憂うつ **yūutsu** gloom, melancholy
憂うつである **yūutsu de aru** be down, be depressed
憂うつ(な) **yūutsu (na)** depressed; dismal, gloomy; depressing
誘惑 **yūwaku** lure; seduction; temptation; 誘惑に負ける ***yûwaku ni makeru*** succumb to temptation
誘惑する **yūwaku suru** seduce; tempt

ゆうゆうと **yūyū to** calmly; in a relaxed way; easily
有罪 **yūzai** guilt LAW
有罪判決 **yūzai-hanketsu** conviction LAW; 有罪判決を下す ***yûzai-hanketsu o kudasu*** convict
有罪にする **yūzai ni suru** incriminate
有罪(の) **yūzai (no)** guilty LAW
ゆず **yuzu** yuzu (*small citrus fruit*)
融通の利かない **yūzū no kikanai** inflexible, rigid
融通の利く **yūzū no kiku** adaptable, flexible
譲る **yuzuru** yield, give way; transfer; sell

Z

ザブンという音 **zabun to iu oto** splash (*noise*)
ざぶとん **zabuton** (floor) cushion
座談会 **zadankai** meeting; round-table discussion
罪悪感 **zaiakukan** feelings of guilt
財閥 **zaibatsu** financial conglomerate
財団 **zaidan** foundation (*organization*)
在学する **zaigaku suru** be in school; attend school
財宝 **zaihō** treasure
在住 **zaijū** residence, stay
在庫 **zaiko** stock; 在庫がある/ない ***zaiko ga aru / nai*** be in / out of stock
在庫品 **zaikohin** supplies
材木 **zaimoku** lumber, timber
罪人 **zainin** sinner
材料 **zairyō** ingredient
在留許可 **zairyū-kyoka** residence permit
財産 **zaisan** assets; estate; wealth; means (*financial*)
財政 **zaisei** finance
財政上(の) **zaiseijō (no)** financial
在籍する **zaiseki suru** be enrolled; be registered
在席する **zaiseki suru** be in one's own seat; be at one's desk
在宅勤務する **zaitaku-kinmu suru** work from home
在宅する **zaitaku suru** be at home
雑貨 **zakka** sundries
座骨神経痛 **zakotsu-shinkeitsū** sciatica
ざくざく音を立てる **zakuzaku oto o tateru** crunch
残高 **zandaka** balance (*of bank account*)
残がい **zangai** debris, wreckage; wreck
ざんげする **zange suru** confess
ざんごう **zangō** trench
残虐行為 **zangyaku-kōi** atrocity
残業 **zangyō** overtime
残酷 **zankoku** cruelty
残酷(な) **zankoku (na)** cruel; savage, vicious
残酷に **zankoku ni** brutally
残念 **zannen** hard luck!; what a pity!; what a shame!
残念(な) **zannen (na)** regrettable; sorry
残念ながら **zannen-nagara** regrettably, unfortunately; 残念ながらそう思います ***zannen-nagara sô omoimasu*** I'm afraid so
残念なことに **zannen na koto ni** sadly, regrettably
残念に思う **zannen ni omou** feel bad about
残忍(な) **zannin (na)** brutal, savage
残忍さ **zannin-sa** brutality
残留物 **zanryūbutsu** residue
雑費 **zappi** incidental expenses
ざらざらした **zarazara shita** rough; gritty; sandy
ざりがに **zarigani** crayfish

ざるをえない **-zaru o enai** cannot help but; have to
座席 **zaseki** seat
ざ折させる **zasetsu saseru** defeat; frustrate *plans*
ざ折する **zasetsu suru** fall through
座礁する **zashō suru** strand
雑誌 **zasshi** magazine; journal, periodical
雑誌売り場 **zasshi uriba** bookstall
雑種 **zasshu** hybrid; mongrel
雑草 **zassō** weed
雑談 **zatsudan** chat
雑(な) **zatsu (na)** careless; scrappy
雑音 **zatsuon** noise, interference
雑用 **zatsuyō** chores
雑然とした **zatsuzen to shita** jumbled; confused
雑多(な) **zatta (na)** miscellaneous; unsorted
ざっと **zatto** briefly; ざっと目を通す ***zatto me o tôsu*** skim through, scan
雑踏 **zattō** hustle and bustle
座薬 **zayaku** suppository
座右の銘 **zayū no mei** motto
座禅 **zazen** Zen meditation
ぜ **ze** (*familiar exclamatory particle used mostly by men*): やろうぜ ***yarô ze*** let's do it!
ぜひ **zehi** by all means; ぜひどうぞ ***zehi dôzo*** by all means, of course
税 **zei** duty (*on goods*)
税関 **zeikan** customs
税関審査 **zeikan-shinsa** customs inspection
税金 **zeikin** tax; taxation; 税金を払う ***zeikin o harau*** pay a tax
税金を加えて **zeikin o kuwaete** plus tax
税引き後 **zeibikigo** after tax
税込み **zeikomi** including tax
税務査察官 **zeimu-sasatsukan** tax inspector
税務署 **zeimusho** tax office
税抜き(の) **zeinuki (no)** net *price*
ぜいたく **zeitaku** extravagance; luxury
ぜいたく(な) **zeitaku (na)** luxurious
ゼイゼイ言う **zeizei iu** wheeze
絶好(の) **zekkō (no)** ideal; perfect
絶交する **zekkō suru** drop; sever relations
絶叫する **zekkyō suru** scream; shout; exclaim
禅 **Zen** Zen
善 **zen** virtue; good
全 … **zen...** (*prefix*) all, the whole; 全国 ***zenkoku*** the whole country
前… **zen...** (*prefix*) former; previous; ex-
善悪 **zen'aku** good and evil
全部 **zenbu** all; everything ◊ fully; 全部払う ***zenbu harau*** pay in full; 全部飲む ***zenbu nomu*** drink up
前部 **zenbu** front
全部で **zenbu de** altogether, in all
全部(の) **zenbu (no)** complete; overall
前置詞 **zenchishi** preposition
前代未聞(の) **zendaimimon (no)** unheard-of
前衛的(な) **zen'eiteki (na)** avant-garde; futuristic
前夫 **zenfu** ex (*former husband*)
前言を撤回する **zengen o tekkai suru** backpedal *fig*
前後 **zengo** around; about; before and after; back and forth
前半 **zenhan** first half
善意 **zen'i** goodwill
全員 **zen'in** everybody; all the members
善意(の) **zen'i (no)** well-meaning
前日 **zenjitsu** the previous day
前科 **zenka** criminal record
全会一致である **zenkai itchi de aru** be unanimous on
全快する **zenkai suru** recover completely
前景 **zenkei** foreground
前期 **zenki** first semester
全国 **zenkoku** entire country
全国的(な) **zenkokuteki (na)** nationwide
全面的(な) **zenmenteki (na)** sweeping
全面的に **zenmenteki ni** overall; entirely
全滅させる **zenmetsu saseru** wipe out, destroy, kill
全滅する **zenmetsu suru** be

completely destroyed
前任者 **zennin-sha** predecessor (*in job*)
全般的(な) **zenpanteki (na)** overall; general
前方へ **zenpō e** onward
前例のない **zenrei no nai** unprecedented
全輪駆動 **zenrin-kudō** all-wheel drive
前輪駆動 **zenrin-kudō** front-wheel drive
前略 **zenryaku** hi there (*at start of informal letters*)
全力 **zenryoku** with all one's might; 全力で走る ***zenryoku de hashiru*** they pelted along the road
全力疾走 **zenryoku-shissō** sprint, race
前菜 **zensai** appetizer; starter
前妻 **zensai** ex (*former wife*)
全世界 **zensekai** entire world
全世界的(な) **zensekaiteki (na)** global, worldwide
前線 **zensen** weather front
前者 **zensha** the former
全身 **zenshin** the whole body; all over
全身(の) **zenshin (no)** full-length
前進する **zenshin suru** advance
全焼する **zenshō suru** burn down
禅宗 **Zenshū** Zen Buddhism
ぜんそく **zensoku** asthma
全速力で **zensokuryoku de** at full speed; flat out *work, run, drive*
全体 **zentai** whole; 町全体 ***machi-zentai*** the whole town
全体(の) **zentai (no)** entire, whole
全体主義(の) **zentai-shugi (no)** totalitarian
全体的(な) **zentaiteki (na)** general, widespread; global
全体として **zentai to shite** on the whole
前提 **zentei** premise; presupposition; prerequisite
前提条件 **zentei-jōken** precondition
前途有望(な) **zento-yūbō (na)** promising
前夜 **zen'ya** eve
全然 **zenzen** 全然…ではない ***zenzen... de wa nai*** not at all; anything but; 全然かまいません ***zenzen kamaimasen*** it's no bother; 全然思い当たりませんか ***zenzen omoiatarimasen ka*** have you any idea at all?
絶版で **zeppan de** out of print
ゼリー **zerī** jelly
ゼロ **zero** zero; ゼロから始める ***zero kara hajimeru*** start from scratch
ゼロエミッション **zero-emisshon** zero emission
ゼロ成長 **zero-seichō** zero growth
絶頂 **zetchō** pinnacle
絶望 **zetsubō** despair
絶望して **zetsubō shite** in despair
絶望する **zetsubō suru** despair; despair of
絶望的(な) **zetsubōteki (na)** desperate, hopeless
絶縁 **zetsuen** breaking off relations; insulation ELEC
絶縁する **zetsuen suru** break off relations; insulate ELEC
絶縁体 **zetsuentai** insulation
絶縁テープ **zetsuen-tēpu** friction tape
絶滅 **zetsumetsu** extinction
絶滅した **zetsumetsu shita** extinct
絶滅する **zetsumetsu suru** die out; exterminate
絶対 **zettai** 彼は絶対休暇をとるべきだ ***kare wa zettai kyûka o toru beki da*** he badly needs a rest; 絶対に確実(な) ***zettai ni kakujitsu (na)*** infallible; 絶対に…ない ***zettai ni ...nai*** on no account
絶対的(な) **zettaiteki (na)** absolute *power*; implicit *trust*
ぞ **zo** (*exclamatory particle used by men*): 無理だぞ ***muri da zo*** it's impossible!
象 **zō** elephant
像 **zō** statue
増築 **zōchiku** extension (*to house*)
増大 **zōdai** increase
象眼細工 **zōgan-zaiku** inlay
象牙 **zōge** ivory
増減する **zōgen suru** fluctuate; go up and down

増加 **zōka** increase; growth
増加する **zōka suru** increase; grow
造形(の) **zōkei (no)** figurative; formative
ぞうきん **zōkin** duster; cloth, rag
俗物 **zokubutsu** person with vulgar taste; snob
俗物(の) **zokubutsu (no)** snobbish
俗語 **zokugo** slang; colloquial word
属性 **zokusei** attribute
属する **zoku suru** belong
続々 **zokuzoku** successively; one after another; 続々出てくる ***zokuzoku dete kuru*** stream, pour
ぞくぞくさせる **zokuzoku saseru** thrill
ぞくぞくする **zokuzoku suru** be excited; have the shivers
増強する **zōkyō suru** reinforce; build up
雑煮 **zōni** rice cake soup
存じる **zon jiru** H know; think
ぞんざい(な) **zonzai (na)** rude; coarse; cursory; slipshod
ぞうり **zōri** Japanese sandals
増量 **zōryō** increase
増刷 **zōsatsu** reprint
増刷する **zōsatsu suru** reprint
造船 **zōsen** shipbuilding
造船所 **zōsen-jo** dockyard, shipyard
増進 **zōshin** boost
蔵書 **zōsho** (personal) library
増収 **zōshū** rise in income
贈呈票 **zōteihyō** compliments slip
ぞっとさせる **zotto saseru** appall; give the creeps
図 **zu** diagram; drawing; graphic
ズボン **zubon** pants; ズボンのチャック **zubon no chakku** fly (*on pants*)
ずぶぬれになる **zubunure ni naru** get drenched
ずぶぬれにする **zubunure ni suru** drench
ずぶぬれ(の) **zubunure (no)** dripping (wet)
図太さ **zubuto-sa** audacity, impudence
頭がい骨 **zugaikotsu** skull
図表 **zuhyō** chart
ずいぶん **zuibun** really; very; a lot
随筆 **zuihitsu** essay
髄膜炎 **zuimakuen** meningitis
頭上(の) **zujō (no)** overhead
図面 **zumen** plan (*drawing*)
ズームレンズ **zūmu-renzu** zoom lens
ずんぐりした **zunguri shita** stocky; thickset
頭脳 **zunō** brains, intelligence
づらい **-zurai** difficult to; 聞きづらい ***kiki-zurai*** difficult to hear
ずらす **zurasu** shift; stagger *breaks etc*
ずれ **zure** difference; gap (*in the market*)
ずれる **zureru** be shifted; be postponed
ずる賢い **zurugashikoi** wily
ずるい **zurui** crafty, sly; shifty
ずるずる滑る **zuruzuru suberu** slither; be slippery
ずさん(な) **zusan (na)** sloppy, slipshod
ずたずたになって **zutazuta ni natte** in tatters, in shreds
ずつ **-zutsu** each; of each; at a time; ひとつずつ ***hitotsu-zutsu*** one of each; 少しずつ ***sukoshi-zutsu*** little by little
頭痛 **zutsū** headache
ずっと **zutto** all the time, all along; a whole lot; ずっと前に ***zutto mae ni*** long ago; ずっと遠くに ***zutto tôku ni*** far off
ずうずうしい **zūzūshii** shameless; nervy
ずうずうしさ **zūzūshi-sa** nerve, impudence

A

a, **an**◊ (*no translation*): ***a cat*** neko 猫; ***an apple*** ringo りんご ◊ (*with countword*): ***a pencil and an eraser*** enpitsu ippon to keshigomu ikko 鉛筆一本と消しゴム一個; ***five men and a woman*** go-nin no otoko to hitori no onna 五人の男と一人の女 ◊ (*per*): ***$50 a ride*** ikkai gojū doru 一回五十ドル; ***once a week*** isshūkan ni ikkai 一週間に一回

abacus soroban そろばん

abalone awabi あわび

abandon *object* suteru 捨てる; *person* misuteru 見捨てる; *car* norisuteru 乗捨てる; *plan* chūshi suru 中止する

abbreviate mijikaku suru 短くする

abbreviation shōryakukei 省略形

abdomen fukubu 腹部

abdominal fukubu (no) 腹部(の)

abduct yūkai suru 誘拐する

♦ **abide by** … ni shitagau …に従う

ability nōryoku 能力

ablaze ***be ~*** enjō shite iru 炎上している

able (*skillful*) yūnō (na) 有能(な); ***be ~ to*** … koto ga dekiru …ことができる; ***I wasn't ~ to see / hear*** watashi wa miru koto ga dekinakatta / kiku koto ga dekinakatta 私は見ることができなかった/聞くことができなかった

abnormal ijō (na) 異常(な)

aboard 1 *prep* … ni notte …に乗って **2** *adv*: ***be ~*** (*on ship*) jōsen shite iru 乗船している; (*on plane*) tōjō shite iru 搭乗している; (*on train*) jōsha shite iru 乗車している; ***go ~*** (*onto ship*) jōsen suru 乗船する; (*onto plane*) tōjō suru 搭乗する; (*onto train*) jōsha suru 乗車する

abolish haishi suru 廃止する

abort *v/t launch, program* chūshi suru 中止する

abortion ninshin-chūzetsu 妊娠中絶; ***have an ~*** ninshin-chūzetsu o suru 妊娠中絶をする

about 1 *prep* (*concerning*) … ni tsuite (no) …について(の); ***a book ~ France*** Furansu ni tsuite no hon フランスについての本; ***what's it ~?*** (*brook, movie*) nani ni tsuite desu ka 何についてですか **2** *adv* (*roughly: number*) … gurai …ぐらい; (*time*) …goro …頃; ***be ~ to …*** … tokoro desu …ところです; ***I was just ~ to leave*** watashi wa chōdo deru tokoro deshita 私はちょうど出るところでした

above 1 *prep* (*higher than*) … no ue (ni) …の上(に); (*more than*) … ijō (de) …以上(で); ***~ all*** nani yori mo mazu 何よりもまず **2** *adv* ue ni 上に; ***on the floor ~*** ikkai ue ni 一階上に

above-mentioned jōki (no) 上記(の)

abrasion surikizu 擦り傷

abrasive *person* hageshii 激しい

abridge yōyaku suru 要約する

abroad *live* gaikoku de 外国で; *go* gaikoku e 外国へ

abrupt *departure* totsuzen (no) 突然(の); *manner* bukkirabō (na) ぶっきらぼう(な)

abscess nōyō 膿瘍

absence (*of person*) fuzai 不在; (*from school*) kesseki 欠席; (*from work*) kekkin 欠勤; (*lack*) ketsuraku 欠落

absent *adj* fuzai (no) 不在(の); (*from school*) kesseki (no) 欠席(の); (*from work*) kekkin (no) 欠勤(の)

absent-minded bon'yari shita ぼんやりした

absolute *power* zettaiteki (na) 絶対的(な); *idiot* mattaku (no) まったく(の)

absolutely (*completely*) hontō ni 本当に; **~ *not!*** tondemonai とんでもない; ***do you agree? - ~*** sansei desu ka - mochiron 賛成ですか - もちろん
absolve manugareru 免れる
absorb kyūshū suru 吸収する; ***~ed in ...*** … ni muchū ni natte …に夢中になって
absorbent kyūshūsei (no) 吸収性(の)
absorbent cotton dasshimen 脱脂綿
abstain (*from voting*) kiken suru 棄権する
abstention (*in voting*) kiken 棄権
abstract *adj* chūshōteki (na) 抽象的(な); *art* chūshōha (no) 抽象派(の)
absurd bakageta ばかげた
absurdity bakabakashi-sa 馬鹿馬鹿しさ
abundance hōfu-sa 豊富さ
abundant hōfu (na) 豊富(な)
abuse[1] *n* (*insults*) nonoshiri ののしり; (*of child*) gyakutai 虐待; (*of thing*) kokushi 酷使; (*of drug*) ran'yō 乱用
abuse[2] *v/t* (*physically*) gyakutai suru 虐待する; (*verbally*) nonoshiru ののしる; (*take advantage of*) ran'yō suru 乱用する
abusive *language* kuchigitanai 口汚い; ***become ~*** akutai o tsukidasu 悪態をつきだす
abysmal (*very bad*) hidoi ひどい
abyss shin'en 深えん
academic 1 *n* gakusha 学者 **2** *adj* gakumonteki (na) 学問的(な); *person* atama no yoi 頭の良い; ***~ year*** gakunen 学年
academy gakkō 学校
accelerate 1 *v/i* kasoku suru 加速する **2** *v/t production* … no supīdo o ageru …のスピードを上げる
acceleration (*of car*) kasoku 加速
accelerator akuseru アクセル
accent (*when speaking*) namari なまり; (*emphasis*) kyōchō 強調
accentuate kyōchō suru 強調する
accept 1 *v/t offer, suggestion* ukeireru 受け入れる; *present* uketoru 受け取る; *behavior, conditions* mitomeru 認める **2** *v/i* shōdaku suru 承諾する; ***thank you, I'd be pleased to ~*** arigatō, yorokonde o-uke shimasu 有り難う、喜んでお受けします
acceptable konomashii 好ましい
acceptance (*of offer*) shōdaku 承諾; (*recognition*) juyō 受容
access 1 *n*: ***have ~ to*** *building* … ni hairu koto ga dekiru …に入ることができる; *computer* … o riyō dekiru …を利用できる; *child* … to no menkaiken ga aru …との面会権がある; *information* … ni chikazukeru …に近付ける **2** *v/t information* … ni chikazuku …に近付く; *files* … ni akusesu suru …にアクセスする
access code COMPUT akusesu kōdo アクセスコード
accessible ikiyasui 行きやすい; *information* te ni hairiyasui 手に入りやすい
accessory (*for wearing*) akusesarī アクセサリー; LAW kyōhan-sha 共犯者
access road renraku-dōro 連絡道路
access time COMPUT akusesu-taimu アクセスタイム
accident jiko 事故; ***by ~*** gūzen ni 偶然に
accidental gūzen (no) 偶然(の)
acclimate, acclimatize *v/t* … ni narasu …に慣らす
accommodate shukuhaku saseru 宿泊させる; *special requirements* tekiō saseru 適応させる
accommodations shukuhaku-setsubi 宿泊設備
accompaniment MUS bansō 伴奏
accompany … ni tsuite iku …について行く; MUS bansō o suru 伴奏をする
accomplice kyōhan-sha 共犯者
accomplish *task* kanryō suru 完了する
accomplished jukuren shita 熟練した

accord: ***of one's own ~*** jihatsuteki ni 自発的に
accordance: ***in ~ with*** … ni shitagatte …に従って
according: ***~ to*** … ni yoru to …によると
accordingly (*consequently*) shitagatte したがって; (*appropriately*) sore ni ōjite それに応じて
account *n* (*financial*) kōza 口座; (*report, description*) hōkoku 報告; ***give an ~ of*** … no setsumei o suru …の説明をする; ***on no ~*** zettai ni…nai 絶対に…ない; ***on ~ of*** … no tame (ni) …のため(に); ***take … into ~***, ***take ~ of …*** … o kōryo ni ireru …を考慮に入れる
♦**account for** (*explain*) … no setsumei o suru …の説明をする; (*make up, constitute*) shimeru 占める
accountability sekinin 責任
accountable: ***be held ~*** sekinin ga aru 責任がある
accountant kaikeishi 会計士
accounts kaikei 会計; (*department*) keiribu 経理部
accumulate 1 *v/t* tameru ためる **2** *v/i* tamaru たまる
accuracy seikaku-sa 正確さ
accurate seikaku (na) 正確(な)
accusation hinan 非難; (*public*) kokuhatsu 告発
accuse hinan suru 非難する; (*publicly*) kokuhatsu suru 告発する; ***he ~d me of lying*** kare wa watashi ga uso o tsuita to hinan shita 彼は私が嘘をついたと非難した; ***be ~d of …*** LAW … de kokuso sarete iru …で告訴されている; ***the ~d*** hikoku-nin 被告人
accustom: ***get ~ed to*** … ni nareru …に慣れる; ***be ~ed to*** … ni narete iru …に慣れている
ace (*in cards, tennis*) ēsu エース
ache 1 *n* itami 痛み **2** *v/i* itamu 痛む
achieve tassei suru 達成する
achievement (*of ambition*) tassei 達成; (*thing achieved*) gyōseki 業績
acid *n* san 酸
acid rain sanseiu 酸性雨
acid test *fig* genkaku na kijun 厳格な基準
acknowledge mitomeru 認める
acknowledg(e)ment shōnin 承認; (*letter*) juryō-tsūchi 受領通知
acorn donguri どんぐり
acoustics onkyō-kōka 音響効果
acquaint: ***be ~ed with*** … to shiriai de aru …と知り合いである
acquaintance (*person*) shiriai 知り合い
acquire *skill, knowledge* mi ni tsukeru 身に付ける; *property* shutoku suru 取得する
acquisitive don'yoku (na) どん欲(な)
acquit LAW muzai ni suru 無罪にする
acre ēkā エーカー
acrobat akurobatto アクロバット
acrobatics akurobatto アクロバット
across 1 *prep* (*on other side of*) … no mukōgawa ni …の向こう側に; (*to other side of*) … o ōdan shite …を横断して; ***~ the table from me*** tēburu o hasande shōmen ni テーブルをはさんで正面に; ***sail ~ the Atlantic*** Taiseiyō o ōdan suru 大西洋を横断する **2** *adv* (*to other side*) mukōgawa e 向こう側へ; ***10m ~*** haba jūmētoru 幅十メートル; ***walk / run ~*** aruite / hashtte wataru 歩いて/走って渡る
act 1 *v/i* THEA enjiru 演じる; (*pretend*) furi o suru ふりをする; ***~ as*** … to shite tsutomeru …として務める **2** *n* (*deed*) kōi 行為; (*of play*) maku 幕; (*in vaudeville*) dashimono 出し物; (*pretense*) misekake 見せかけ; (*law*) hō 法
acting 1 *n* engi 演技 **2** *adj* (*temporary*) dairi (no) 代理(の)
action kōi 行為; (*in movie*) jiken 事件; ***be out of ~*** ugokanai 動かない; ***take ~*** kōdō o okosu 行動を起こす; ***bring an ~ against*** LAW … o uttaeru …を訴える; ***full of ~*** *novel, movie* akushon no ōi アクションの多い

action replay TV sokuji-saisei-bideo 即時再生ビデオ

active katsudōteki (na) 活動的(な); *party member* gen'eki (no) 現役(の); GRAM nōdō (no) 能動(の)

activist POL katsudōka 活動家

activity (*doing things*) katsudō 活動; (*economic, mental etc*) ugoki 動き; (*on the streets etc*) kakki 活気; (*pastime, thing to do*) goraku 娯楽

actor haiyū 俳優

actress joyū 女優

actual jissai (no) 実際(の)

actually (*in fact, to tell the truth*) jitsu wa 実は; (*surprise*) hontō ni 本当に; ***~ I do know him*** (*stressing converse*) jitsu wa kare o shitte imasu 実は彼を知っています

acupuncture harichiryō ハリ治療

acute *pain* hageshii 激しい; *embarrassment* hidoi ひどい; *sense* surudoi 鋭い

ad kōkoku 広告

adapt 1 *v/t* (*for the stage, TV etc*) kyakushoku suru 脚色する; *machine* kaizō suru 改造する **2** *v/i* (*of person*) tekiō suru 適応する

adaptable *person, plant* tekiōsei no aru 適応性のある; *vehicle etc* yūzū no kiku 融通の利く

adaptation (*of play etc*) kyakushoku 脚色

adapter ELEC adaputā アダプター

add 1 *v/t* MATH gōkei suru 合計する; (*say*) tsukekuwaeru 付け加える; *comment, sugar etc* kuwaeru 加える **2** *v/i* MATH tashizan suru 足し算する

♦ **add on** *15% etc* … o tsukekuwaeru …を付け加える

♦ **add up 1** *v/t* … o gōkei suru …を合計する **2** *v/i fig* tsujitsuma ga au つじつまが合う

addict *n* chūdoku-sha 中毒者

addicted ***be ~ to*** … no chūdoku ni natte iru …の中毒になっている

addiction (*to drugs, TV etc*) chūdoku 中毒

addictive ***be ~*** (*of drugs*) shūkansei no aru 習慣性のある; (*of TV, chocolate etc*) kuse ni naru 癖になる

addition MATH tashizan 足し算; (*to list, company etc*) tsuika 追加; ***in ~*** sara ni さらに; ***in ~ to*** … ni kuwaete …に加えて

additional tsuika (no) 追加(の)

additive tenkabutsu 添加物

add-on fuzoku-sōchi 付属装置

address 1 *n* jūsho 住所; ***form of ~*** keishō 敬称 **2** *v/t letter* … ni atena o kaku …に宛名を書く; *audience* … ni enzetsu suru …に演説する; *person* … ni hanashikakeru …に話しかける

address book adoresuchō アドレス帳

addressee uketori-nin 受取人

adequate jūbun (na) 十分(な); (*satisfactory*) manzoku (na) 満足(な)

adhere kuttsuku くっつく

♦ **adhere to** *surface* … ni shikkari to kuttsuku …にしっかりとくっつく; *rules* mamoru 守る

adhesive setchakuzai 接着剤

adhesive plaster bansōkō ばんそうこう

adhesive tape nenchaku-tēpu 粘着テープ

adjacent rinsetsu (no) 隣接(の)

adjective keiyōshi 形容詞

adjoining tonariawase (no) 隣り合わせ(の)

adjourn *v/i* (*of court*) kyūtei suru 休廷する; (*of meeting*) kyūkai suru 休会する

adjust *v/t* chōsetsu suru 調節する; *behavior* tekiō saseru 適応させる

adjustable chōsetsu dekiru 調節できる

administer *medicine* tōyo suru 投与する; *company* keiei suru 経営する; *country* tōchi suru 統治する

administration kanri 管理; (*of company*) keiei 経営; (*of country*) gyōsei 行政; (*government*) seiken 政権

administrative keiei (no) 経営(の); *tasks* kanri (no) 管理(の); (*in government*) gyōsei (no) 行政(の)

administrator (*in company*) kanri-

sha 管理者; (*civil servant*) gyōseikan 行政官
admirable rippa (na) りっぱ(な)
admiral teitoku 提督
admiration kanshin 感心
admire kanshin suru 感心する
admirer sūhai-sha 崇拝者
admissible yōnin dekiru 容認できる
admission (*confession*) kokuhaku 告白; **~ *ceremony*** nyūgaku-shiki 入学式; **~ *free*** nyūjō-muryō 入場無料
admit (*to a place*) nyūjō saseru 入場させる; (*to school*) nyūgaku saseru 入学させる; (*to hospital*) nyūin saseru 入院させる; (*to organization*) nyūkai saseru 入会させる; (*confess*) jihaku suru 自白する; (*accept*) mitomeru 認める
admittance: *no* ~ tachiiri-kinshi 立入禁止
adolescence jūdai 十代
adolescent 1 *n* jūdai 十代 **2** *adj* jūdai (no) 十代(の)
adopt *child* yōshi ni suru 養子にする; *plan* saiyō suru 採用する
adoption (*of child*) yōshi-engumi 養子縁組み; (*of plan*) saiyō 採用
adorable aikurushii 愛くるしい
adore *person* shitau 慕う; *chocolate, movie, book etc* … ga daisuki de aru …が大好きである
adult 1 *n* otona 大人 **2** *adj* otona (no) 大人(の); **~ *movie*** seijin-eiga 成人映画
Adult's Day Seijin no hi 成人の日
adultery furin 不倫
advance 1 *n* (*on payment*) maekin 前金; (*on salary*) maegari 前借り; (*in science etc*) shinpo 進歩; MIL shingun 進軍; ***in* ~** maemotte 前もって; (*get money*) maekin de 前金で; ***make ~s*** (*progress*) shinpo suru 進歩する; (*sexually*) kudoku 口説く **2** *v/i* MIL zenshin suru 前進する; (*make progress*) shinpo suru 進歩する **3** *v/t theory* teishutsu suru 提出する; *money* maebarai suru 前払いする; *cause* susumeru 進める; *knowledge* shinpo saseru 進歩させる
advance booking yoyaku 予約
advanced *country* senshin (no) 先進(の); *level, learner* jōkyū (no) 上級(の)
advance payment maebarai 前払い
advantage riten 利点; (*of person*) tsuyomi 強み; ***it's to your* ~** sore ga anata no tame ni naru それがあなたのためになる; ***take ~ of*** *opportunity* … o riyō suru …を利用する
advantageous yūri (na) 有利(な)
adventure bōken 冒険
adventurous daitan (na) 大胆(な)
adverb fukushi 副詞
adversary teki 敵
advertise 1 *v/t* kōkoku suru 広告する **2** *v/i* kōkoku o dasu 広告を出す
advertisement kōkoku 広告
advertiser kōkokunushi 広告主
advertising kōkoku 広告; (*industry*) kōkoku-gyōkai 広告業界
advertising agency kōkoku-dairiten 広告代理店
advice chūkoku 忠告, adobaisu アドバイス; ***take X's* ~** X no chūkoku o kiku Xの忠告を聞く
advisable nozomashii 望ましい
advise *person* … ni chūkoku suru …に忠告する; *caution* susumeru 勧める; **~ *X to …*** X ni …suru yō susumeru Xに…するよう勧める
adviser sōdan'yaku 相談役; (*to company*) komon 顧問
aerial kūchū (no) 空中(の)
aerial photograph kōkū-shashin 航空写真
aerobics earobikusu エアロビクス
aerodynamic kūki-rikigaku o ōyō shita 空気力学を応用した
aeronautical kōkūgaku (no) 航空学(の)
aerosol supurē-kan スプレー缶
aerospace industry kōkū-uchū-sangyō 航空宇宙産業
affair (*matter*) koto こと; (*business*) shigoto 仕事; (*love*) jōji 情事; ***foreign ~s*** gaimu 外務; ***have an ~ with*** … to uwaki suru …と浮気する
affect MED okasu 冒す; (*influence, concern*) … ni eikyō o oyobosu …に

影響を及ぼす
affection aijō 愛情
affectionate yasashii 優しい
affinity ruijisei 類似性; ***have an ~ with / for*** ... ni hikareru ...にひかれる
affirmative: ***answer in the ~*** kōtei suru 肯定する
affluent yutaka (na) 豊か(な); ***~ society*** yutaka na shakai 豊かな社会
afford (*financially*) suru yoyū ga aru する余裕がある
Afghan 1 *adj* Afuganisutan (no) アフガニスタン(の) **2** *n* (*person*) Afuganisutan-jin アフガニスタン人
Afghanistan Afuganisutanアフガニスタン
afloat *boat* ukande 浮かんで
afraid: ***be ~*** kowagaru 怖がる; ***be ~ of*** *cats etc* ... o kowagaru ...を怖がる; *of upsetting him etc* ... o shinpai suru ...を心配する; ***I'm ~*** (*regretting*) zannen-nagara 残念ながら; ***I'm ~ so*** zannen-nagara sō omoimasu 残念ながらそう思います; ***I'm ~ not*** zannen-nagara sō de wa naiyō desu 残念ながらそうではないようです
Africa Afurika アフリカ
African 1 *adj* Afurika (no) アフリカ(の) **2** *n* Afurika-jin アフリカ人
after 1 *prep* (*in order*) ... no tsugi ni ...の次に; (*in position*) ... no ushiro ni ...の後ろに; (*in time*) ... no ato de ...の後で; (*with names of months, telling the time etc*) ... ikō ...以降; ***~ 2 o'clock / March*** niji sn-gatsu ikō 二時/三月以降; ***~ all*** kekkyoku 結局; ***~ that*** sorekara それから; ***it's ten ~ two*** niji juppun sugi desu 二時十分過ぎです **2** *adv* ato ni 後に; ***the day ~*** sono yokujitsu ni その翌日に; ***~ you*** dōzo osaki ni どうぞお先に
afternoon gogo 午後; ***in the ~*** gogo ni 午後に; ***this ~*** kyō no gogo 今日の午後; ***good ~*** konnichi wa こんにちは
after sales service afutā sābisu アフターサービス
aftershave afutā shēbu アフターシェーブ
aftertaste atoaji 後味
afterward ato de 後で
again mō ichido もう一度
against (*lean etc*: *~ person*) ... ni yorikakatte ...に寄り掛かって; (*~ thing*) ... ni tatekakete ...に立て掛けて; ***America ~ Brazil*** SP Amerika tai Burajiru アメリカ対ブラジル; ***I'm ~ the idea*** watashi wa sono kangae ni hantai desu 私はその考えに反対です; ***what do you have ~ her?*** anata wa kanojo no nani ga kirai nan desu ka あなたは彼女の何がきらいなんですか; ***~ the law*** hōritsu-ihan 法律違反
age 1 *n* nenrei 年齢; (*era*) jidai 時代; ***at the ~ of*** ...sai de ...歳で; ***under ~*** miseinen de 未成年で; ***she's five years of ~*** kanojo wa gosai desu 彼女は五歳です **2** *v/i* toshi o toru 年をとる
agency dairiten 代理店
agenda gidai 議題; ***on the ~*** gidai to natte 議題となって
agent dairi-nin 代理人
aggravate akka saseru 悪化させる
aggression kōgeki 攻撃
aggressive sekkyokuteki (na) 積極的(な); (*dynamic*) kōgekiteki (na) 攻撃的(な)
agile kibin (na) 機敏(な)
agitated dōyō shita 動揺した
agitation dōyō 動揺
agitator sendō-sha 扇動者
ago: ***2 days ~*** futsuka-mae 二日前; ***long ~*** zutto mae ni ずっと前に; ***how long ~?*** dore kurai mae desu ka どれくらい前ですか
agonizing kurushii 苦しい
agony kumon 苦もん
agree 1 *v/i* sansei suru 賛成する; (*of figures, accounts*) itchi suru 一致する; (*reach agreement*) gōi suru 合意する; ***I ~*** watashi wa sansei desu 私は賛成です; ***I don't ~*** watashi wa sansei dekimasen 私は賛成できません; ***~ with*** ... ni dōi suru ... に同意する; ***it doesn't ~ with me*** (*of food*) watashi no karada ni aimasen 私の体に合いま

せん **2** *v/t price, date* … ni gōi suru … に合意する; **~ *that something should be done*** nanika shinakereba naranai to iu koto ni gōi shita 何かしなければならないということに合意した

agreeable (*pleasant*) kanji no ii 感じのいい; (*in agreement*) sansei shite iru 賛成している

agreement (*consent*) dōi 同意; (*contract*) keiyaku 契約; ***reach ~ on*** … no kyōtei o musubu …の協定を結ぶ

agricultural nōgyō (no) 農業(の)

agriculture nōgyō 農業

ahead: ***be ~ of*** … ni katte iru …に勝っている; ***plan ~*** saki no keikaku o tateru 先の計画をたてる; ***think ~*** saki o kangaeru 先を考える

aid 1 *n* enjo 援助 **2** *v/t* enjo suru 援助する

Aids eizu エイズ

aikido aikidō 合気道

ailing byōki (no) 病気(の); *economy* fushin (no) 不振(の)

aim 1 *n* (*in shooting*) nerai ねらい; (*objective*) mokuteki 目的 **2** *v/i* (*in shooting*) nerau ねらう; **~ *to do …*** … suru tsumori de aru …するつもりである **3** *v/t*: ***be ~ed at*** (*of remark etc*) … ni muketa mono de aru …に向けたものである; (*of guns*) … o neratte iru …をねらっている

air 1 *n* kūki 空気; ***by ~*** *travel* hikōki de 飛行機で; *send mail* kōkūbin de 航空便で; ***in the open ~*** kogai de 戸外で; ***on the ~*** RAD, TV hōsō sarete 放送されて **2** *v/t room* kanki suru 換気する; *fig*: *views* happyō suru 発表する

airbase kūgun-kichi 空軍基地; **air-conditioned** eakon-tsuki (no) エアコン付き(の); **air-conditioning** kūchō 空調; **aircraft** kōkūki 航空機; **aircraft carrier** kōkū-bokan 航空母艦; **air cylinder** akuarangu アクアラング; **airfield** hikōjō 飛行場; **air force** kūgun 空軍; **air hostess** suchuwādesu スチュワーデス; **air letter** kōkū-shokan 航空書簡; **airline** kōkū-gaisha 航空会社; **airmail**: ***by ~*** kōkūbin de 航空便で; **airplane** hikōki 飛行機; **air pollution** taiki-osen 大気汚染; **airport** kūkō 空港; **airsick**: ***get ~*** hikōki ni you 飛行機に酔う; **airspace** ryōkū 領空; **air terminal** eatāminaru エアターミナル; **airtight** *container* mippei (no) 密閉(の); **air traffic** kōkū-kōtsūryō 航空交通量; **air-traffic control** kōkū-kansei 航空管制; **air-traffic controller** kōkū-kanseikan 航空管制官

airy *room* kazetōshi no yoi 風通しのよい; *attitude* kaikatsu (na) 快活(な)

aisle tsūro 通路

aisle seat tsūrogawa no seki 通路側の席

alarm 1 *n* keihō 警報; ***raise the ~*** keihō o hassuru 警報を発する **2** *v/t* shinpai saseru 心配させる

alarm clock mezamashi-dokei 目覚まし時計

album arubamu アルバム

alcohol arukōru アルコール; (*alcoholic drink*) sake 酒

alcoholic 1 *n* arukōru-chūdoku-kanja アルコール中毒患者 **2** *adj* arukōru-iri (no) アルコール入り(の)

alert 1 *n* (*signal*) keihō 警報; ***be on the ~*** keikai shite iru 警戒している **2** *v/t* … ni keihō o dasu …に警報を出す **3** *adj* yōjin-bukai 用心深い

alibi aribai アリバイ

alien 1 *n* gaikokujin 外国人; (*from space*) uchūjin 宇宙人 **2** *adj* gaikoku (no) 外国(の); (*strange*) najimi no nai なじみのない; ***be ~ to*** … no shō ni awanai …の性にあわない

alienate … no hankan o kau …の反感を買う

alight *adj* moete iru 燃えている

alike 1 *adj*: ***be ~*** nite iru 似ている **2** *adv*: ***old and young ~*** rōjin mo wakamono mo onajiyō ni 老人も若者も同じように

alimony rikon-teate 離婚手当

alive: ***be ~*** ikite iru 生きている
all 1 *adj* subete (no) すべて(の)
2 *pron* zenbu 全部, mina 皆; ***he ate ~ of it*** kare wa zenbu tabemashita 彼は全部食べました; ***~ of us / ~ of them*** watashitachi wa mina / karera wa mina 私達は皆/彼等は皆; ***that's ~, thanks*** kore dake desu これだけです; ***for ~ I care*** watashi no shitta koto ja nai 私の知ったことじゃない; ***for ~ I know*** tabun たぶん; ***~ at once*** totsuzen 突然; ***~ but…*** (*except*) … o nozoite …を除いて; ***~ the time*** zutto ずっと **3** *adv*: ***~ the better*** masumasu yoi ますます良い; ***~ but*** (*nearly*) hotondo ほとんど; ***they're not at ~ alike*** karera wa mattaku nite inai 彼らはまったく似ていない; ***not at ~!*** (*you're welcome*) zenzen kamaimasen 全然構いません; ***two ~*** (*in score*) ni-tai-ni no dōten 二対二の同点
allegation shuchō 主張; LAW mōshitate 申し立て
alleged … to sarete iru …とされている; ***an ~ murderer*** satsujinhan to sarete iru hito 殺人犯とされている人
allergic: ***be ~ to …*** … ni arerugī ga aru …にアレルギーがある
allergy arerugī アレルギー
alleviate keigen suru 軽減する
alley roji 路地
alliance dōmei 同盟
alligator arigētā アリゲーター
allocate wariateru 割り当てる
allot wariateru 割り当てる
allow yurusu 許す; (*of person in authority*) kyoka suru 許可する; (*calculate for*) yoyū o motsu 余裕を持つ; ***it's not ~ed*** yurusarete inai 許されていない; ***~ X to …*** X ni …sasete oku Xに…させておく
♦**allow for** … o mikomu …を見込む
allowance (*money*) teate 手当; (*to child*) kozukai 小遣い; ***make ~s*** (*for thing, weather etc*) kōryo ni ireru 考慮に入れる; (*for person*) ōme ni miru 大目に見る
alloy gōkin 合金
all-purpose bannō (no) 万能(の); **all-round** *athlete* bannō (no) 万能(の); *improvement* tahōmen ni wataru 多方面にわたる; **all-time**: ***be at an ~ low*** saitei-kiroku de aru 最低記録である
♦**allude to** … o honomekasu …をほのめかす
alluring miryokuteki (na) 魅力的(な)
all-wheel drive zenrin-kudō 全輪駆動
ally *n* mikata 味方
almond āmondo アーモンド
almost hotondo ほとんど◊ (*negative consequences*) ayauku あやうく; ***he was ~ killed*** kare wa ayauku korosareru tokoro datta 彼はあやうく殺されるところだった
alone hitori de ひとりで
along 1 *prep* (*moving forward*) tōtte 通って; (*situated beside*) … ni sotte …に沿って; ***walk ~ this path*** kono michi o zutto aruku この道をずっと歩く **2** *adv*: ***~ with*** … to issho ni … と一緒に; ***all ~*** (*all the time*) zutto ずっと
aloud koe o dashite 声を出して
alphabet arufabetto アルファベット
alphabetical arufabetto-jun (no) アルファベット順(の)
already sude ni すでに
alright: ***that's ~*** (*doesn't matter*) sore de kamaimasen それで構いません; (*when s.o. says thank you*) dōitashimashite どう致しまして; (*is quite good*) nakanaka ii desu なかなかいいです; ***I'm ~*** (*not hurt*) daijōbu 大丈夫; (*have got enough*) kekkō desu 結構です; ***~, that's enough!*** hai, kekkō desu はい、結構です; ***don't do it again – ~*** mata shinaide ne – wakarimashita またしないでね ーわかりました
also … mo …も
altar saidan 祭壇
alter *v/t* kaeru 変える
alteration henkō 変更; (*to clothes*) sunpō-naoshi 寸法直し
alternate 1 *v/i* kōtai suru 交替する; (*of mood*) korokoro kawaru ころこ

ろ変わる **2** *adj* hitotsu-oki (no) 一つ置き(の); *plan* kawari (no) 代わり(の)

alternating current kōryū 交流

alternative 1 *n* kawari no hōhō 代わりの方法; (*choice*) sentakushi 選択肢 **2** *adj* kawari (no) 代わり(の)

alternatively sono kawari ni その代わりに

although … keredomo …けれども; ***~ he hadn't paid for it*** kare wa sore o haratte inai keredomo 彼はそれを払っていないけれども

altitude (*of plane*) kōdo 高度; (*of mountain*) hyōkō 標高; (*of city*) kaibatsu 海抜

altogether (*completely*) mattaku まったく; (*in all*) zenbu de 全部で

altruistic ritateki (na) 利他的(な)

aluminum aruminiumu アルミニウム

always itsumo いつも

a.m. gozen 午前; ***10 ~*** gozen jūji午前十時

amalgamate *v/i* (*of companies*) gappei suru 合併する

amateur *n* shirōto 素人; SP amachua アマチュア

amaze gyōten saseru 仰天させる

amazement gyōten 仰天

amazing odoroku beki 驚くべき; (*very good*) subarashii 素晴らしい

ambassador taishi 大使

amber: ***at ~*** kiiro de 黄色で

ambiguous aimai (na) あいまい(な)

ambition yume 夢; *pej* yashin 野心

ambitious yashinteki (na) 野心的(な); *plan* ōgakari (na) 大がかり(な)

ambulance kyūkyūsha 救急車

ambush 1 *n* machibuse 待ち伏せ **2** *v/t* machibuse suru 待ち伏せする

amend shūsei suru 修正する

amendment shūsei 修正

amends: ***make ~*** tsugunau 償う

amenities setsubi 設備

America Amerika アメリカ

American 1 *adj* Amerika (no) アメリカ(の) **2** *n* Amerika-jin アメリカ人

amiable aisō no yoi 愛想のよい

amicable enman (na) 円満(な)

ammunition dan'yaku 弾薬; *fig* kōgeki-zairyō 攻撃材料

amnesty onsha 恩赦

among(st) … ni kakomarete …に囲まれて; (*in the set of*) … no naka ni …のなかに; ***this is just one ~ many*** kore wa tan ni takusan no naka no hitotsu desu これは単にたくさんの中のひとつです

amount ryō 量; (*of money*) gaku 額

♦**amount to** sōkei … ni naru 総計…になる; (*of work*) … ni hitoshii …に等しい

ample jūbun (na) 十分(な)

amplifier anpu アンプ

amplify *sound* kakudai suru 拡大する

amputate setsudan suru 切断する

amuse (*make laugh etc*) warawaseru 笑わせる; (*entertain*) tanoshimaseru 楽しませる

amusement (*merriment*) tanoshimi 楽しみ; (*entertainment*) kibarashi 気晴らし; ***~s*** (*games*) goraku-shisetsu 娯楽施設; ***to our great ~*** totemo omoshiroi koto ni とても面白いことに

amusement park yūenchi 遊園地

amusing omoshiroi おもしろい

anabolic steroid anaborikku-suteroido アナボリック・ステロイド

analog COMPUT anarogu-shiki (no) アナログ式(の)

analogy ruiji 類似

analysis bunseki 分析; PSYCH seishin-bunseki 精神分析

analyze bunseki suru 分析する; PSYCH … no seishin-bunseki o suru …の精神分析をする

anarchy muchitsujo 無秩序

anatomy kaibō-gaku 解剖学; (*body*) karada 体

ancestor sosen 祖先

anchor 1 *n* NAUT ikari いかり **2** *v/i* NAUT ikari o orosu いかりを下ろす

anchor man TV nyūsu-kyasutā ニュースキャスター

ancient *adj* kodai (no) 古代(の)

and ◊ (*joining nouns, adjectives for*

distinct properties) … to … と; ***cats ~ dogs*** inu to neko 犬と猫; ***yellow ~ green*** kiiro to midori 黄色と緑◊ (*with verbs*) …shi … し; ***he can play the violin ~ sing*** kare wa baiorin mo hikerushi uta mo utaeru 彼はバイオリンもひけるし歌も歌える◊ (*in order to, joining adjectives jointly describing*) …te … て; ***I ate too much ~ I have a stomach-ache*** tabesugite onaka ga itaku natta 食べ過ぎておなかが痛くなった; ***it is small ~ inexpensive*** chiisakute yasui 小さくて安い◊ (*and then*) soshite そして, …te … て; ***I want to go there ~ take some photos*** soko e itte shashin o toritai そこへ行って写真を撮りたい◊ (*doing two things at the same time*) …tari …tari; ***we drank ~ talked*** nondari hanashitari shita 飲んだり話したりした◊: ***he talked ~ talked*** kare wa hanashi tsuzuketa 彼は話し続けた; ***he ran faster ~ faster*** kare wa masumasu hayaku hashitta 彼はますます速く走った; ***~ so on*** nadonado 等々

anemia hinketsushō 貧血症

anemic: ***be ~*** MED hinketsu de aru 貧血である

anesthetic *n* masui 麻酔

anesthetist masuii 麻酔医

anger 1 *n* ikari 怒り **2** *v/t* okoraseru 怒らせる

angina kyōshinshō 狭心症

angle *n* kakudo 角度

angry okotta 怒った; ***be ~ with*** … ni taishite hara o tatete iru …に対して腹を立てている; ***get ~*** okoru 怒る

anguish kunō 苦悩

animal dōbutsu 動物

animated ikiiki shita 生き生きした

animated cartoon anime-eiga アニメ映画

animation seiki 生気; (*movie*) animēshon-seisaku アニメーション製作

animosity tekii 敵意

ankle ashikubi 足首

annex 1 *n* (*building*) bekkan 別館 **2** *v/t state* heigō suru 併合する

anniversary kinenbi 記念日; ***wedding ~*** kekkon-kinenbi 結婚記念日

announce happyō suru 発表する

announcement happyō 発表; (*at airport*) anaunsu アナウンス

announcer RAD, TV, anaunsā アナウンサー

annoy iraira saseru いらいらさせる; ***be ~ed*** mutto suru むっとする

annoyance (*anger*) iradachi いら立ち; (*nuisance*) wazurawashi-sa わずらわしさ

annoying wazurawashii わずらわしい; *person* urusai うるさい

annual *adj* (*once a year*) reinen (no) 例年(の); (*of a year*) ichinenkan (no) 一年間(の)

annul *marriage* mukō ni suru 無効にする

anonymous tokumei (no) 匿名(の)

anorak anorakku アノラック

anorexia kyoshokushō 拒食症

anorexic: ***be ~*** kyoshokushō de aru 拒食症である

another 1 *adj* (*different*) betsu (no) 別(の); (*additional: thing, way*) mō hitotsu (no) もう一つ(の); (*person*) mō hitori (no) もう一人(の) **2** *pron* (*different one*) hoka no mono 他のもの; (*additional one*) mō hitotsu もう一つ; (*person*) mō hitori もう一人; ***one ~*** otagai ni お互いに; ***they helped one ~*** karera wa otagai ni tasukeatta 彼等はお互いに助け合った

answer 1 *n* henji 返事; (*to problem*) kaiketsu 解決; (*to question*) kotae 答え **2** *v/t* … ni henji o suru …に返事をする; *question* toku 解く; ***~ the door*** ōtai ni deru 応対に出る; ***~ the telephone*** denwa ni deru 電話に出る

♦ **answer back 1** *v/t person* … ni kuchigotae suru …に口答えする **2** *v/i* kuchigotae suru 口答えする

♦ **answer for** … no sekinin o toru … の責任をとる

answerphone rusuban-denwa 留守番電話

ant ari あり

antagonism hanmoku 反目
Antarctic *n* Nankyoku 南極
antenatal shussan mae (no) 出産前(の)
antenna shokkaku 触角; (*for TV*) antena アンテナ
antibiotic *n* kōsei-busshitsu 抗生物質
antibody kōtai 抗体
anticipate yosō suru 予想する; (*look forward to*) tanoshimi ni suru 楽しみにする
anticipation yosō 予想
antidote gedokuzai 解毒剤
antifreeze futōeki 不凍液
antipathy hankan 反感
antiquated furukusai 古くさい
antique *n* kottō-hin 骨とう品
antique dealer kottō-ya 骨とう屋
antiseptic 1 *adj* shōdoku (no) 消毒(の) **2** *n* shōdokuzai 消毒剤
antisocial hanshakaiteki (na) 反社会的(な)
antivirus program uirusu-chekkā ウイルスチェッカー
anxiety shinpai 心配
anxious shinpai shite 心配して; (*eager*) setsubō shite 切望して; ***be ~ for …*** (*for news etc*) … o setsubō suru …を切望する
any 1 *adj* ◊ (*usually not translated*): ***are there ~ diskettes / glasses?*** furoppī / gurasu wa arimasu ka フロッピー/グラスはありますか; ***is there ~ bread?*** pan wa arimasu ka パンはありますか; ◊ (*with abstracts*) nanika 何か; ***is there ~ improvement?*** nanika kaizen saremashita ka 何か改善されましたか; ***there isn't ~ improvement*** nani mo kaizen sarete imasen 何も改善されていません ◊ (*emphatic*) ***have you ~ idea*** (***at all***)***?*** zenzen omoi-atarimasen ka 全然思い当たりませんか; ***take ~ one you like*** dore demo suki na mono o totte kudasai どれでも好きなものを取ってください **2** *pron*: ***do you have ~?*** motte imasu ka 持っていますか; ***there isn't / aren't ~ left*** nani mo nokotte imasen 何も残っていません; ***~ of them could be guilty*** karera no uchi dare ka ga yūzai kamo shiremasen 彼らのうち誰かが有罪かもしれません **3** *adv*: ***is that ~ better?*** sukoshi wa yoku narimashita ka 少しは良くなりましたか; ***is that ~ easier?*** sukoshi wa kantan ni nari mashita ka 少しは簡単になりましたか; ***I don't like it ~ more*** watashi wa sore ga mō suki de nakunarimashita わたしはそれがもう好きでなくなりました
anybody ◊ (*with questions, conditionals*) dareka 誰か; ***is ~ at home?*** dareka iru 誰かいる; ***if ~ thinks …*** moshi dareka ga… to kangaetara もし誰かが…と考えたら… ◊ (*with negatives*) dare mo 誰も; ***there wasn't ~ there*** soko ni wa dare mo inakatta そこには誰もいなかった ◊ (*in statements, emphatic*) dare demo 誰でも; ***~ who has …*** … o motte iru hito wa dare demo …を持っている人は誰でも; ***it could have been ~*** dare de atte mo okashiku nai 誰であってもおかしくない
anyhow (*regardless*) tonikaku とにかく; ***he did it ~*** (*carelessly*) kare wa ozanari ni yarimashita 彼はおざなりにやりました
anyone → ***anybody***
anything ◊ (*with questions, conditionals*) nanika 何か; ***~ else?*** hoka ni nanika ほかに何か ◊ (*with negatives*) nani mo 何も; ***I didn't hear ~*** watashi ni wa nani mo kikoenakatta 私には何も聞こえなかった; ◊ (*in statements, emphatic*) nan demo 何でも; ***I could eat ~*** watashi wa nan demo taberaremasu 私は何でも食べられます ◊: ***~ but*** zenzen… de wa nai 全然…ではない; ***~ but sad*** zenzen kanashiku nai 全然悲しくない
anyway → ***anyhow***
anywhere ◊ (*with questions, conditionals*) dokoka de どこかで; ***do you see him ~?*** dokoka de kare o mikake mashita ka どこかで彼を

見かけましたか; ***if you see one ~*** moshi dokoka de sore o mikaketara もしどこかでそれを見かけたら ◊ (*with negatives*) doko ni mo どこにも; ***I can't find it ~*** doko ni mo mitsukaranai どこにも見つからない ◊ (*in statements, emphatic*) doko demo どこでも; ***you can go ~ you like*** doko demo suki na tokoro ni ikeru どこでも好きなところにいける

apart (*in distance*) hanarete 離れて; ***keep the two sides ~*** ryōgawa o hanashite oku 両側を離しておく; ***live ~*** bekkyo shite iru 別居している; ***~ from*** (*excepting*) … wa betsu to shite …は別として; (*in addition to*) … no hoka ni …のほかに

apartment apāto アパート, manshon マンション

apartment block apāto アパート, manshon マンション

apathetic mukiryoku (na) 無気力(な)

ape *n* ruijin'en 類人猿

aperture PHOT renzu レンズ

apologize ayamaru 謝る

apology shazai 謝罪

apostrophe aposutorofī アポストロフィー

appall zotto saseru ぞっとさせる

appalling osoroshii 恐ろしい; *language* hidoi ひどい

apparatus kigu 器具

apparent (*clear*) akiraka (na) 明らか(な); (*seeming*) mitatokoro 見た所; ***become ~ that …*** … to iu koto ga akiraka ni naru …ということが明らかになる

apparently …rashii …らしい; ***~ they have all been sold*** sorera wa zenbu ureta rashii それらは全部売れたらしい

appeal 1 *n* (*charm*) miryoku 魅力; (*for funds etc*) apīru アピール; LAW jōso 上訴 **2** *v/i* LAW jōso suru 上訴する

♦ **appeal for** … o motomete uttaeru …を求めて訴える

♦ **appeal to** (*be attractive to*) … no ki ni iru …の気に入る

appear arawareru 現れる; (*in movie etc*) shutsuen suru 出演する; (*of new product*) tōjō suru 登場する; (*in court*) shuttei suru 出廷する; (*look, seem*) … no yōni mieru …のように見える; ***it ~s that …*** … to omowareru …と思われる

appearance (*arrival*) tōchaku 到着; (*look*) gaiken 外見; (*in movie etc*) shutsuen 出演; (*in court*) shuttei 出廷; ***put in an ~*** kao o dasu 顔を出す

appendicitis mōchōen 盲腸炎

appendix MED mōchō 盲腸; (*of book etc*) furoku 付録

appetite shokuyoku 食欲; *fig* yoku 欲

appetizer (*food*) zensai 前菜; (*drink*) shokuzenshu 食前酒

appetizing oishisō (na) おいしそう(な)

applaud 1 *v/i* hakushu suru 拍手する **2** *v/t* … ni hakushu o okuru …に拍手を送る; *fig* shōsan suru 称賛する

applause hakushu 拍手; (*praise*) shōsan 称賛

apple ringo りんご

apple pie appurupai アップルパイ

apple sauce ringo-sōsu りんごソース

appliance kigu 器具; (*household*) denka-seihin 電化製品

applicable tekiyō dekiru 適用できる

applicant ōbo-sha 応募者

application (*for job etc*) ōbo 応募; (*for passport, visa*) shinsei 申請; (*for university*) shutsugan 出願

application form mōshikomi-yōshi 申込用紙; (*for visa*) shinseisho 申請書; (*for university*) nyūgaku-gansho 入学願書

apply 1 *v/t* tekiyō suru 適用する; *ointment* tofu suru 塗布する **2** *v/i* (*of rule, law*) tekiyō sareru 適用される

♦ **apply for** *job* … ni ōbo suru …に応募する; *passport* … o shinsei suru …を申請する; *university* … ni shutsugan suru …に出願する

♦ **apply to** (*contact*) … ni toiawaseru …に問い合わせる; (*affect*) … ni tekiyō sareru …に適用される

appoint (*to position*) ninmei suru 任命する
appointment (*meeting*) yakusoku 約束; (*at hairdresser, dentist*) yoyaku 予約; (*to position*) ninmei 任命
appointments diary yoyakuchō 予約帳
appreciate 1 *v/t* (*value*) hyōka suru 評価する; (*be grateful for*) arigataku omou ありがたく思う; (*acknowledge*) rikai suru 理解する; ***thanks, I ~ it*** arigatō, kansha shite imasu ありがとう、感謝しています **2** *v/i* FIN neagari suru 値上がりする
appreciation (*of kindness etc*) kansha 感謝; (*of music etc*) kanshō 鑑賞; (*understanding*) rikai 理解
apprehensive shinpai shite iru 心配している
apprentice minarai 見習い
approach 1 *n* sekkin 接近; (*offer etc*) mōshide 申し出, apurōchi アプローチ; (*to problem*) torikumi kata 取り組み方 **2** *v/t* (*get near to*) … ni chikazuku …に近づく; (*contact*) … ni hanashi o mochikakeru …に話を持ちかける; *problem* … to torikumu …と取り組む
approachable *person* kisaku (na) 気さく(な)
appropriate *adj* tekisetsu (na) 適切(な)
approval sansei 賛成; (*of something official*) shōnin 承認
approve 1 *v/i* sansei suru 賛成する **2** *v/t* … ni sansei suru …に賛成する; *sth official* shōnin suru 承認する
♦**approve of** … o yoi to omou …を良いと思う
approximate *adj* ōyoso (no) おおよそ(の)
approximately ōyoso おおよそ
APR (= ***annual percentage rate***) nenri 年利
apricot anzu あんず
April shigatsu 四月
apt *pupil* rikō (na) 利口(な); *remark* tekisetsu (na) 適切(な); ***be ~ to …*** … suru keikō ga aru …する傾向がある
aptitude sainō 才能
aquarium suizokukan 水族館
aquatic suisei (no) 水生(の)
Arab 1 *adj* Arabu (no) アラブ(の) **2** *n* Arabu-jin アラブ人
Arabic 1 *adj* Arabia (no) アラビア(の); ***~ numerals*** Arabia-sūji アラビア数字 **2** *n* Arabia-go アラビア語
arable kōsaku ni tekishita 耕作に適した
arbitrary shiiteki (na) 恣意的(な); *remark* katte (na) 勝手(な); *attack* musabetsu (na) 無差別(な)
arbitrate *v/i* (*in public affair*) chōtei suru 調停する; (*in private*) chūsai suru 仲裁する
arbitration (*in public affair*) chōtei 調停; (*in private*) chūsai 仲裁
arcade (*with slot machines*) gēmu-sentā ゲームセンター
arch *n* āchi アーチ
archeologist kōko-gakusha 考古学者
archeology kōko-gaku 考古学
archer shashu 射手
architect kenchiku-ka 建築家
architecture kenchiku 建築
archives kōbunsho-hozonjo 公文書保存所
archway *āchi no kakatta iriguchi* アーチの架かった入り口
Arctic *n* Hokkyoku-chihō 北極地方
ardent netsuretsu (na) 熱烈(な)
area (*region*) chiiki 地域; (*part*) han'i 範囲; (*of activity*) bun'ya 分野; (*square metres etc*) menseki 面積
area code TELEC shigai-kyokuban 市外局番
arena SP kyōgijō 競技場
Argentina Aruzenchin アルゼンチン
Argentinian 1 *adj* Aruzenchin (no) アルゼンチン(の) **2** *n* Aruzenchin-jin アルゼンチン人
arguably osoraku おそらく
argue 1 *v/i* (*quarrel*) kenka suru けんかする; (*reason*) giron suru 議論する **2** *v/t*: ***~ that*** … to ronjiru …と論じる
argument (*quarrel*) kenka けんか;

(*reasoning*) giron 議論
argumentative gironzuki (na) 議論好き(な)
arid *land* kansō shita 乾燥した
arise (*of situation*) okoru おこる
arithmetic sansū 算数
arm[1] *n* ude 腕; (*of chair*) hijikake ひじ掛け
arm[2] *v/t* busō saseru 武装させる
armaments heiki 兵器
armchair hijikakeisu ひじ掛け椅子
armed busō shita 武装した
armed forces guntai 軍隊
armed robbery busō-gōtō 武装強盗
armor bōdan-chokki 防弾チョッキ; (*for Samurai*) yoroikabuto よろいかぶと
armored vehicle sōkōsha 装甲車
armpit waki no shita わきの下
arms (*weapons*) buki 武器
army rikugun 陸軍
aroma kaori 香り
around 1 *prep* (*in circle*) … no mawari ni …の回りに; (*roughly*) oyoso … およそ…; (*with expressions of time*) … goro …ごろ; ***it's ~ the corner*** kado o magatta tokoro desu 角を曲がったところです; ***Christmas is just ~ the corner*** kurisumasu wa mō sugu desu クリスマスはもうすぐです **2** *adv* (*in the area*) chikaku ni 近くに; (*encircling*) mawari ni 回りに; ***there are a lot of people ~*** atari ni wa takusan no hito ga iru 辺りにはたくさんの人がいる; ***he lives ~ here*** kare wa konohen ni sunde iru 彼はこの辺に住んでいる; ***walk ~*** burabura aruku ぶらぶら歩く; ***she has been ~*** (*has traveled, is experienced*) kanojo wa keiken ga hōfu de aru 彼女は経験が豊富である
arouse yobiokosu 呼び起こす; (*sexually*) shigeki suru 刺激する
arrange (*put in order*) seiton suru 整とんする; *furniture* haichi suru 配置する; *flowers* ikeru 生ける; *music* henkyoku suru 編曲する; *meeting, party* junbi suru 準備する; *time, place* kimeru 決める; ***I've ~d to meet her*** watashi wa kanojo ni au yakusoku o shimashita 私は彼女と会う約束をしました
♦ **arrange for** … o tehai suru …を手配する
arranged marriage omiai-kekkon お見合い結婚
arrangement (*plan*) yotei 予定; (*agreement*) yakusoku 約束; (*layout: of furniture etc*) haichi 配置; (*of flowers*) ikebana 生け花; (*of music*) henkyoku 編曲
arrears tainōkin 滞納金; ***be in ~*** tainō shite iru 滞納している
arrest 1 *n* taiho 逮捕; ***be under ~*** taiho sarete iru 逮捕されている **2** *v/t* taiho suru 逮捕する
arrival tōchaku 到着; ***~s*** (*at airport*) tōchaku-robī 到着ロビー
arrive tsuku 着く
♦ **arrive at** *place* … ni tōchaku suru …に到着する; *decision etc* … ni tassuru …に達する
arrogance gōman 傲慢
arrogant gōman (na) 傲慢(な)
arrow ya 矢; (*on sign*) yajirushi 矢印
arson hōka 放火
art geijutsu 芸術; ***the ~s*** jinbun-kagaku 人文科学; ***~s degree*** bunkei no gakui 文系の学位
artery MED dōmyaku 動脈
art gallery bijutsukan 美術館; (*private*) garō 画廊
arthritis kansetsuen 関節炎
article buppin 物品; (*in newspaper*) kiji 記事; (*section*) jōkō 条項; GRAM kanshi 冠詞
articulate *adj* hyōgen no meikaku (na) 表現の明確(な)
artificial jinkō (no) 人工(の); (*not sincere*) wazatorashii わざとらしい
artificial intelligence jinkō-chinō 人工知能
artillery taihō 大砲
artisan shokunin 職人
artist gaka 画家; (*artistic person*) geijutsuka 芸術家
artistic geijutsuteki (na) 芸術的(な)
as 1 *conj* (*at the same time as*) … (suru) toki ni …(する)ときに; ***he***

came in ~ I was going out kare wa watashi ga dekakeru toki ni kita 彼は私が出かけるときに来た◊ (*while*) ...(shi)nagara ...(し)ながら; ***she whistled ~ she worked*** kanojo wa shigoto o shinagara kuchibue o fuita 彼女は仕事をしながら口笛を吹いた◊ (*because*) ... no de ...ので; ***~ it is still raining*** mada ame ga futte iru no de まだ雨が降っているので◊ (*like*) ... yō ni ...ように; ***~ I do*** watashi ga suru yō ni 私がするように◊: ***~ if*** marude ... de aru ka no yō ni まるで...であるかのように; ***~ usual*** itsumo no yō ni いつものように; ***~ necessary*** hitsuyō na dake 必要なだけ **2** *adv* onaji kurai 同じくらい; ***~ high / pretty*** ... to onaji kurai takai / kawaii ...と同じくらい高い/かわいい; ***will it cost ~ much ~ that?*** sonna ni kakaru no desu ka そんなにかかるのですか **3** *prep* (*in capacity of*) ... to shite ... として; (*when*) ... no toki ni ...のときに; ***~ a child / student*** kodomo no / gakusei no toki 子供の/学生の時; ***work ~ a teacher / ~ a translator*** sensei to shite / hon'yaku-sha to shite hataraite iru 先生として/翻訳者として働いている; ***~ for*** ... ni tsuite wa ...については; ***~ Hamlet*** Hamuretto yaku de ハムレット役で

asap (= ***as soon as possible***) dekiru dake hayaku できるだけ早く

ash hai 灰; (*volcanic*) kazanbai 火山灰; ***~es*** (*after cremation*) ikotsu 遺骨

ashamed hazukashii 恥ずかしい; ***be ~ of*** ... o hazukashiku omou ...を恥ずかしく思う; ***you should be ~ of yourself*** haji o shirinasai 恥を知りなさい

ash can gomiire ごみ入れ

ashore riku de 陸で; ***go ~*** jōriku suru 上陸する

ashtray haizara 灰皿

Asia Ajia アジア

Asian 1 *adj* Ajia (no) アジア(の) **2** *n* Ajia-jin アジア人

aside waki ni わきに; ***~ from*** ... o nozoite ...を除いて

ask 1 *v/t* (*put question to*) kiku 聞く; (*inquire*) tazuneru 尋ねる; (*invite*) shōtai suru 招待する; *favor* tanomu 頼む; ***can I ~ you something?*** chotto kiite mo ii desu ka ちょっと聞いてもいいですか; ***~ a question*** shitsumon suru 質問する; ***~ X for ...*** X ni ... o tanomu Xに...を頼む; ***~ X to do Y*** X ni Y suru yō tanomu XにYするよう頼む; ***~ X about Y*** X ni Y ni tsuite kiku XにYについて聞く **2** *v/i* tazuneru 尋ねる

♦ **ask after** *person* ... no yōsu o kiku ...の様子を聞く

♦ **ask for** ... o motomeru ...を求める; *person* ... o yobidasu ...を呼び出す

♦ **ask out** ... o sasou ...を誘う

asking price iine 言い値

asleep: ***be*** (***fast***) ***~*** (gussuri) nemutte iru (ぐっすり) 眠っている; ***fall ~*** nemuru 眠る

asparagus asuparagasu アスパラガス

aspect (*angle*) men 面; (*appearance*) yōsu 様子

aspirin asupirin アスピリン

ass[1] (*idiot*) baka 馬鹿

ass[2] V ketsu けつ; (*sex*) sekkusu セックス

assassin ansatsu-sha 暗殺者

assassinate ansatsu suru 暗殺する

assassination ansatsu 暗殺

assault 1 *n* bōkō 暴行 **2** *v/t* ... ni bōkō suru ...に暴行する

assemble 1 *v/t parts* kumitateru 組み立てる **2** *v/i* (*of people*) atsumaru 集まる

assembly (*of parts*) kumitate 組み立て; POL gikai 議会

assembly line nagaresagyō 流れ作業

assembly plant kumitate-kōjō 組み立て工場

assent *v/i* sansei suru 賛成する

assert: ***~ oneself*** jiko-shuchō suru 自己主張する

assertive *person* gōin (na) 強引(な)

assess *situation* satei suru 査定する; *value* hyōka suru 評価する

asset FIN shisan 資産; *fig* zaisan 財産
asshole V ketsu no ana けつの穴; (*idiot*) kusottare くそったれ
assign *person* ninmei suru 任命する; *thing* wariateru 割り当てる
assignment (*task, study*) kadai 課題; (*job*) ninmu 任務; ***his ~ to this position*** kare no kono pozishon e no ninmei 彼のこのポジションへの任命
assimilate *v/t information* rikai suru 理解する; *person into group* … ni dōka suru …に同化する
assist joryoku suru 助力する
assistance enjo 援助
assistant joshu 助手, ashisutanto アシスタント; (*of minister etc*) hosakan 補佐官
assistant director (*in movies*) jokantoku 助監督
assistant manager ashisutanto-manējā アシスタントマネージャー; (*of hotel, restaurant*) fuku-shihainin 副支配人; (*of store*) fuku-tenchō 副店長
associate 1 *v/t*: ***~ X with Y*** X o Y to musubitsukete kangaeru XをYと結び付けて考える; ***be ~ed with*** (*organization*) … to kankei shite iru …と関係している **2** *v/i*: ***~ with*** … to kōsai suru …と交際する **3** *n* dōryō 同僚
associate professor jokyōju 助教授
association kyōkai 協会, kumiai 組合; ***in ~ with*** … to kyōdō shite …と共同して
assortment (*of food*) tsumeawase 詰め合わせ; (*of people*) iroiro na hito いろいろな人
assume (*suppose*) … to kangaeru …と考える; (*take for granted*) … to katei suru …と仮定する
assumption katei 仮定
assurance hoshō 保証; (*confidence*) kakushin 確信
assure (*reassure*) … ni hoshō suru …に保証する
assured (*confident*) kakushin no aru 確信のある
asterisk hoshi-jirushi 星印
asthma zensoku ぜんそく
astonish odorokasu 驚かす; ***be ~ed*** odoroku 驚く
astonishing odorokuhodo (no) 驚くほど(の)
astonishment odoroki 驚き
astrologer hoshiuranai-shi 星占い師
astrology senseijutsu 占星術
astronaut uchū-hikōshi 宇宙飛行士
astronomer tenmon-gakusha 天文学者
astronomical tenmongaku (no) 天文学(の); *price etc* tenmongakuteki (na) 天文学的(な)
astronomy tenmongaku 天文学
asylum (*mental*) seishin-byōin 精神病院; POL hinansho 避難所
at ◊ (*place*) (*with verbs of being*) … ni …に; (*with verbs of activity*) … de …で; ***it's still ~ the cleaner's*** sore wa mada drai-kurīningu-ya no tokoro ni aru それはまだドライクリーニング屋のところにある; ***we all met ~ Joe's*** Jō no tokoro de aou ジョーのところで会おう ◊: ***~ 10 dollars*** jū doru de 十ドルで; ◊: ***~ the age of 18*** jūhassai de 十八歳で ◊: ***~ 5 o'clock*** goji ni 五時に; ***~ 150 mph*** jisoku hyakugojū mairu de 時速百五十マイルで ◊: ***be good / bad ~*** … ga tokui / … ga nigate de aru …が得意/…が苦手である
atheist mushinron-ja 無神論者
athlete supōtsu-senshu スポーツ選手
athletic undō (no) 運動(の), supōtsu (no) スポーツ(の)
athletics undō-kyōgi 運動競技
Atlantic *n* Taiseiyō 大西洋
atlas chizuchō 地図帳
ATM (= ***automated teller machine***) genkin-jidō-shiharaiki 現金自動支払機, ATM (*always in romaji*)
atmosphere (*of earth*) taiki 大気; (*ambience*) fun'iki 雰囲気
atmospheric pollution taiki-osen 大気汚染
atom genshi 原子
atom bomb genshiryoku-bakudan 原子力爆弾
atomic genshi (no) 原子(の)
atomic energy genshiryoku 原子力

atomic waste kaku-haikibutsu 核廃棄物
atomizer supurē スプレー
atrocious hidoi ひどい
atrocity zangyaku-kōi 残虐行為
attach toritsukeru 取り付ける; ***be ~ed to*** (*fond of: thing*) … ni aichaku o motte iru …に愛着を持っている; (*person*) … o shitatte iru …を慕っている; ***don't ~ too much importance to what he says*** kare no iu koto o jyūyōshi shinai de 彼の言うことを重要視しないで
attack 1 *n* shūgeki 襲撃; MIL kōgeki 攻撃; (*verbal*) hinan 非難 **2** *v/t* osou 襲う; MIL kōgeki suru 攻撃する; (*verbally*) hinan suru 非難する
attempt 1 *n* kokoromi 試み **2** *v/t* kokoromiru 試みる
attend … ni shusseki suru …に出席する
♦**attend to** … o shori suru …を処理する; *customer* … no sewa o suru … の世話をする
attendance shusseki 出席
attendant (*in museum etc*) annaigakari 案内係
attention chūi 注意; ***bring to the ~ of …*** … o shiteki suru …を指摘する; ***your ~ please*** chotto okiki kudasai ちょっとお聞きください; ***pay ~*** chūi o harau 注意を払う
attentive *listener* nesshin (na) 熱心(な)
attic yaneura-beya 屋根裏部屋
attitude taido 態度
attn (= ***for the attention of***) … sama ate …様宛て
attorney bengoshi 弁護士; ***power of ~*** ininken 委任権
attract hikitsukeru 引き付ける; *attention* hiku 引く; ***be ~ed to*** … ni hikarete iru …にひかれている
attraction (*charm*) miryoku 魅力; (*asset: of city*) yobimono 呼び物, atorakushon アトラクション
attractive miryokuteki (na) 魅力的(な)
attribute[1] *v/t*: ***~ X to …*** X o … no sei ni suru Xを…のせいにする; *painting, poem* X o … no saku to kangaeru Xを…の作と考える
attribute[2] *n* zokusei 属性
auction 1 *n* kyōbai 競売, ōkushon オークション **2** *v/t* kyōbai ni kakeru 競売にかける
♦**auction off** … o kyōbai ni kakete shobun suru …を競売にかけて処分する
audacious daitan (na) 大胆(な)
audacity daitan-sa 大胆さ
audible kikoeru 聞こえる
audience (*of speaker*) chōshū 聴衆; (*in theater, at show*) kankyaku 観客; (*of TV program*) shichō-sha 視聴者
audio *adj* ōdio (no) オーディオ(の)
audiovisual shichōkaku (no) 視聴覚(の)
audit 1 *n* kaikei-kansa 会計監査 **2** *v/t* … no kaikei o kansa suru …の会計を監査する; *course* chōkō suru 聴講する
audition 1 *n* ōdishon オーディション **2** *v/i* ōdishon o ukeru オーディションを受ける
auditor kaikei-kansakan 会計監査官
auditorium (*of theater etc*) kankyakuseki 観客席; (*building*) kōkaidō 公会堂
August hachigatsu 八月
aunt (*own*) oba おば; (*s.o. else's*) obasan おばさん
austere *interior* kanso (na) 簡素(な); *person* genkaku (na) 厳格(な)
austerity (*economic*) keizai-kinshuku 経済緊縮
Australasia Ōsutorarēshia オーストラレーシア
Australia Ōsutoraria オーストラリア
Australian 1 *adj* Ōsutoraria (no) オーストラリア(の) **2** *n* Ōsutoraria-jin オーストラリア人
Austria Ōsutoria オーストリア
Austrian 1 *adj* Ōsutoria (no) オーストリア(の) **2** *n* Ōsutoria-jin オーストリア人
authentic honmono (no) 本物(の)
authenticity honmono de aru koto 本物であること

author sakusha 作者; (*of text*) chosha 著者
authoritative keni no aru 権威のある; *source* shinrai dekiru 信頼できる
authority (*of officials, ministers*) kengen 権限; (*of parent, teacher*) ken'i 権威; (*permission*) kyoka 許可; ***be an ~ on …*** … no ken'i de aru … の権威である; ***the authorities*** tōkyoku 当局
authorize ninka suru 認可する; ***be ~d to …*** … suru kengen o ataerarete iru …する権限を与えられている
autistic jiheishō (no) 自閉症(の)
auto *n* jidōsha 自動車
autobiography jijoden 自叙伝
autograph sain サイン
automate jidōka suru 自動化する
automatic 1 *adj* jidō (no) 自動(の); *gesture, response* jidōteki (na) 自動的(な) **2** *n* (*car, gun etc*) ōtomatikku オートマティック
automatically jidōteki ni 自動的に
automation ōtomēshon オートメーション
automobile jidōsha 自動車
automobile industry jidōsha-gyōkai 自動車業界
autonomy jichiken 自治権
autopilot jidō-sōjū-sōchi 自動操縦装置
autopsy kenshi 検死
Autumn Equinox Day Shūbun no hi 秋分の日
auxiliary *adj services etc* hojo (no) 補助(の); *generator etc* yobi (no) 予備(の)
available *service* riyō dekiru 利用できる; *book, information* te ni irerareru 手に入れられる; *person* te ga aite iru 手が空いている
avalanche nadare なだれ
avenue ōdōri 大通り; *fig* shudan 手段
average 1 *adj* heikinteki (na) 平均的(な); (*ordinary*) nami (no) 並(の); (*mediocre*) heibon (na) 平凡(な) **2** *n* heikin 平均; ***above / below ~*** heikin ijō / ika de 平均以上/以下で; ***on ~*** heikin shite 平均して **3** *v/t* heikin … to naru 平均…となる
♦ **average out** *v/t* heikin o … to mitsumoru 平均を…と見積もる
♦ **average out at** heikin suru to … ni naru 平均すると…になる
aversion: ***have an ~ to*** … ga daikirai de aru …が大嫌いである
avert *one's eyes* sorasu そらす; *crisis* sakeru 避ける
aviary tori yō no ori 鳥用のおり
aviation kōkū 航空
avid nesshin (na) 熱心(な)
avoid sakeru 避ける
awake *adj* me ga samete 目が覚めて; ***it's keeping me ~*** watashi o nemurasezu ni iru 私を眠らせずにいる
award 1 *n* (*prize*) shō 賞 **2** *v/t* ataeru 与える; *damages* mitomeru 認める
aware: ***be ~ of*** … ni ki ga tsuite iru … に気が付いている; ***become ~ of*** … ni ki ga tsuku …に気が付く
awareness ninshiki 認識; (*knowledge*) ishiki 意識
away: ***be ~*** (*traveling, sick etc*) rusu ni suru 留守にする; ***walk ~*** arukisaru 歩き去る; ***run ~*** hashirisaru 走り去る; ***look ~*** me o sorasu 目をそらす; ***it's 2 miles ~*** ni-mairu hanarete iru 二マイル離れている; ***Christmas is still six weeks ~*** Kurisumasu wa mada roku-shūkan mo saki da クリスマスはまだ六週間も先だ; ***take X ~ from Y*** Y kara X o torisaru YからXを取り去る
away game SP ensei-jiai 遠征試合
awesome F (*terrific*) monosugoi ものすごい
awful hidoi ひどい
awkward (*clumsy*) gikochinai ぎこちない; (*difficult*) yakkai (na) やっかい(な); (*embarrassing*) kimazui 気まずい; ***feel ~*** kimazui 気まずい
awning hiyoke 日よけ
ax 1 *n* ono おの **2** *v/t project etc* haishi suru 廃止する; *budget, job* sakugen suru 削減する
axle jiku 軸

B

BA (= ***Bachelor of Arts***) gakushi-gō 学士号
baby *n* akanbō 赤ん坊
baby carriage ubaguruma 乳母車; **baby-sit** bebīshittā o suru ベビーシッターをする; **baby-sitter** bebīshittā ベビーシッター
bachelor dokushin no otoko 独身の男
back 1 *n* (*of person*) senaka 背中; (*of car, bus*) ushiro 後ろ, kōbu 後部; (*of paper, clothes, house, book*) ura 裏; (*of drawer*) oku 奥; (*of chair*) se 背; SP bakku バック; ***in ~*** ura ni 裏に; ***in the ~ of the car*** kuruma no kōbu-zaseki ni 車の後部座席に; ***at the ~ of the bus*** basu no kōbu-zaseki ni バスの後部座席に; ***~ to front*** ushiromae 後ろ前; ***at the ~ of beyond*** henpi na tokoro へんぴなところ **2** *adj* ushiro (no) 後ろ(の); ***~ road*** uramichi 裏道 **3** *adv*: ***please move ~/ stand ~*** ushiro ni sagatte kudasai / sagattete kudasai 後ろに下がって下さい/下がってて下さい; ***two meters ~ from the edge*** hashi kara ni mētoru bakku shita 端から二メートルバックした; ***~ in 1935*** sen-kyūhyaku-sanjūgo nen ni modotte 千九百三十五年に戻って; ***give X ~ to Y*** Y ni X o kaesu YにXを返す; ***she'll be ~ tomorrow*** kanojo wa ashita modotte kuru deshō 彼女は明日戻ってくるでしょう; ***when are you coming ~?*** itsu modotte kimasu ka いつ戻ってきますか; ***I'm ~*** tadaima ただいま; ***take X ~ to the store*** (*because unsatisfactory*) X o mise ni henpin suru Xを店に返品する; ***they wrote ~/ phoned ~*** karera wa henji o kureta / orikaeshi denwa o kureta 彼らは返事をくれた/折り返し電話をくれた; ***he hit me ~*** kare wa watashi o nagurikaeshita 彼は私を殴り返した **4** *v/t* (*support*) shien suru 支援する; *car* bakku saseru バックさせる; *horse* … ni kakeru …に賭ける **5** *v/i* (*of driver*) bakku suru バックする
♦**back away** atozusari suru 後ずさりする
♦**back down** jōho suru 譲歩する
♦**back off** ushiro ni sagaru 後ろにさがる; (*from danger*) hikisagaru 引き下がる
♦**back onto** ushirogawa de … ni menshite iru 後ろ側で…に面している
♦**back out** (*of commitment*) te o hiku 手を引く
♦**back up 1** *v/t* (*support*) … o shien suru …を支援する; *claim, argument* urazukeru 裏付ける; *file* bakku-appu バックアップ; ***be backed up*** (*of traffic*) teitai shiteiru 停滞している **2** *v/i* (*in car*) bakku suru バックする
back burner: ***put … on the ~*** … o atomawashi ni suru …を後回しにする; **backdate** sakanobotte yūkō ni suru さかのぼって有効にする; **backdoor** uraguchi 裏口
backer kōen-sha 後援者
backfire *v/i fig* urame ni deru 裏目に出る; **background** haikei 背景; (*of person*) keireki 経歴; **backhand** *n* (*in tennis*) bakku バック
backing (*support*) shien 支援; MUS bansō 伴奏
backing group MUS bansō-gurūpu 伴奏グループ
backlash handō 反動; **backlog** tamatta shigoto たまった仕事; **backpack 1** *n* bakku-pakku バックパック **2** *v/i* bakku-pakku o seotte ryokō suru バックパックを背負っ

て旅行する; **backpacker** bakku-pakkā バックパッカー; **backpedal** *fig* zengen o tekkai suru 前言を撤回する; **backspace (key)** bakku-supēsu (kī) バックスペース(キー); **backstairs** urakaidan 裏階段; **backstroke** SP seoyogi 背泳ぎ

backup (*support*) bakku-appu バックアップ, engo 援護; COMPUT bakku-appu バックアップ; ***take a ~*** COMPUT bakku-appu shiteoku バックアップしておく

backup disk bakku-appu no furoppī バックアップのフロッピー

backward 1 *adj child* chieokure (no) 知恵遅れ(の); *society* okureta 遅れた; *glance* ushiro e (no) 後ろへ(の) **2** *adv* ushiro ni 後ろに

backyard *also fig* uraniwa 裏庭; ***the not in my ~ syndrome*** watashitachi ni wa kankei nai shōkōgun 私達には関係ない症候群

bacon bēkon ベーコン

bacteria saikin 細菌

bad warui 悪い; *weather, conditions, cold, etc* hidoi ひどい; *mistake, accident* ōki (na) 大き(な); (*rotten*) kusatta 腐った; ***it's not ~*** waruku nai 悪くない; ***that's really too ~*** hontō ni zannen desu 本当に残念です; ***feel ~ about*** … o zannen ni omou …を残念に思う; ***be ~ at*** nigate de aru 苦手である; ***Friday's ~, how about Thursday?*** kin'yōbi wa tsugō ga warui desu, mokuyōbi wa dō desu ka 金曜日は都合が悪いです、木曜日はどうですか

bad debt kashidaorekin 貸し倒れ金

bad language akutai 悪態

badge badji バッジ

badger *v/t* nayamasu 悩ます

badly waruku 悪く; *work* heta ni 下手に; *injured, damaged* hidoku ひどく; (*very much*) totemo とても; ***he ~ needs a haircut / rest*** kare wa zettai kami no ke o kiru beki da / kyūka o torubeki da 彼は絶対髪の毛をきるべきだ/休暇をとるべきだ; ***he is ~ off*** kare wa seikatsu ga kurushii 彼は生活が苦しい

badminton badominton バドミントン

baffle konwaku saseru 困惑させる; ***be ~d*** konwaku suru 困惑する

baffling fukakai (na) 不可解(な)

bag (*plastic, paper*) fukuro 袋; (*for school, traveling*) kaban かばん

baggage tenimotsu 手荷物

baggage car RAIL tenimotsu-sha 手荷物車; **baggage cart** kāto カート; **baggage check** tenimotsu-ichiji-azukarijo 手荷物一時預り所; **baggage reclaim** nimotsu-uketorijo 荷物受け取り所

baggy dabudabu (no) だぶだぶ(の)

bail *n* LAW hoshaku 保釈; (*money*) hoshakukin 保釈金; ***on ~*** hoshakuchū de 保釈中で

♦**bail out 1** *v/t* LAW … o hoshaku saseru …を保釈させる; *fig* … o kyūsai suru …を救済する **2** *v/i* (*from airplane*) parashūto de dasshutsu suru パラシュートで脱出する

bait *n* esa えさ

bake *v/t* yaku 焼く

baked potato beikuto-poteto ベイクト・ポテト

baker pan-ya パン屋

bakery pan-ya パン屋

balance 1 *n* tsuriai 釣り合い, baransu バランス; (*mental*) ochitsuki 落ち着き; (*remainder*) sagaku 差額; (*of bank account*) zandaka 残高 **2** *v/t* … no tsuriai o toru …の釣り合いを取る; ***~ the books*** shūshi o awaseru 収支を合わせる **3** *v/i* heikō o tamotsu 平衡を保つ; (*of accounts*) chōjiri ga au 帳尻が合う

balanced (*fair*) tsuriai no toreta 釣り合いのとれた; *diet* baransu no toreta バランスのとれた; *personality* ochitsuita 落ち着いた

balance of payments kokusai-shūshi 国際収支; **balance of trade** bōeki-shūshi 貿易収支; **balance sheet** taishaku-taishōhyō 貸借対照表

balcony (*of house*) beranda ベランダ; (*in theater*) nikai-sajiki 二階桟敷

bald hageta はげた; ***he's going ~*** kare wa hagete kita 彼ははげてきた
ball bōru ボール; ***on the ~*** *fig* yūnō na 有能な; ***play ~ with …*** *fig* … to kyōryoku suru …と協力する; ***the ~'s in his court*** *fig* kondo wa kare no ban da 今度は彼の番だ
ball bearing bōru-bearingu no tama ボール・ベアリングの球
ballerina barerīna バレリーナ
ballet baree バレエ
ballet dancer baree dansā バレエダンサー
ball game (*baseball*) yakyū 野球; ***that's a different ~*** sore wa zenzen betsu no hanashi desu それは全然別の話です
ballistic missile dandōdan 弾道弾
balloon (*child's*) fūsen 風船; (*for flight*) kikyū 気球
ballot 1 *n* mukimei-tōhyō 無記名投票 **2** *v/t* tōhyō de kimeru 投票で決める
ballot box tōhyōbako 投票箱
ballpark yakyūjō 野球場; ***in the right ~*** *fig* gaisan de 概算で
ballpark figure ōyoso no sūji おおよその数字
ballpoint (pen) bōrupen ボールペン
balls V kintama きんたま; (*courage*) yūki 勇気
bamboo take 竹
bamboo flute shakuhachi 尺八
bamboo shoots takenoko 竹の子
ban 1 *n* kinshi 禁止 **2** *v/t* kinshi suru 禁止する
banana banana バナナ
band gakudan 楽団; (*pop*) bando バンド; (*material*) himo ひも
bandage 1 *n* hōtai 包帯 **2** *v/t* hōtai o suru 包帯をする
Band-Aid® bando-eido バンドエイド
bandit tōzoku 盗賊
bandwagon: ***jump on the ~*** binjō suru 便乗する
bandy *legs* ganimata (no) がにまた(の)
bang 1 *n* (*noise*) batan to iu oto ばたんという音; (*blow*) kyōda 強打 **2** *v/t door* batan to shimeru ばたんと閉める; (*hit*) butsukeru ぶつける **3** *v/i* batan to shimaru ばたんと閉まる
banjo banjō バンジョー; ***Japanese ~*** shamisen 三味線
bank[1] (*of river*) dote 土手
bank[2] **1** *n* FIN ginkō 銀行; ***The Bank of Japan*** Nihon-ginkō 日本銀行 **2** *v/i*: ***~ with*** (*of individual*) ginkō ni yokin suru 銀行に預金する; ~ (*of company*) ginkō to torihiki suru 銀行と取り引きする **3** *v/t money* ginkō ni yokin suru 銀行に預金する
♦**bank on** … o ate ni suru …を当てにする; ***don't ~ it*** sore o ate ni shinaide それを当てにしないで
bank account ginkō-kōza 銀行口座; **bank balance** yokin-zandaka 預金残高; **bank bill** shihei 紙幣
banker ginkō-ka 銀行家
banker's card *chekku kādo, kogitte o tsukau toki ni hitsuyō na kādo* チェックカード、小切手を使うときに必要なカード
banker's order jidō-furikae 自動振替
bank loan rōn ローン; **bank manager** ginkō-shitenchō 銀行支店長; **bank rate** kōtei-buai 公定歩合; **bankroll** *v/t* … ni shikin o teikyō suru …に資金を提供する
bankrupt 1 *adj person* hasan shita 破産した; *company* tōsan shita 倒産した; ***go ~*** hasan suru 破産する; (*of company*) tōsan suru 倒産する **2** *v/t* hasan saseru 破産させる; *company* tōsan saseru 倒産させる
bankruptcy hasan 破産; (*of company*) tōsan 倒産
bank statement kōzashūshi-hōkokusho 口座収支報告書
banner ōdanmaku 横断幕
banns kekkon-yokoku 結婚予告
banquet enkai 宴会
banter *n* oshaberi おしゃべり
baptism senrei 洗礼
baptize … ni senrei o hodokosu … に洗礼を施す
bar[1] (*iron*) bō 棒; (*for drinks*) sakaba 酒場; (*counter*) kauntā カウ

ンター; ***a ~ of soap*** sekken ikko 石けん一個; ***a ~ of chocolate*** itachoko ichimai 板チョコ一枚; ***be behind ~s*** keimusho ni hairu 刑務所に入る

bar[2] *v/t* shimedasu 締め出す

bar[3] *prep* (*except*) … o nozoite …を除いて

barbecue 1 *n* bābekyū バーベキュー; (*equipment*) bābekyū-dai バーベキュー台 **2** *v/t* bābekyū ni suru バーベキューにする

barbed wire yūshi-tessen 有刺鉄線

barber tokoya 床屋

bar code bākōdo バーコード

bare *adj arms earth* hadaka (no) 裸(の); *room, shelf* garan to shita がらんとした; *mountainside* hageta はげた; *floor* jūtan no shiite inai じゅうたんの敷いていない

barefoot: ***be ~*** hadashi de aru 裸足である

bare-headed bōshi nashi de 帽子なしで

barely karōjite かろうじて

bargain 1 *n* (*deal*) torihiki 取り引き; (*good buy*) yasui kaimono 安い買物; ***it's a ~!*** (*deal*) sore de kimari それで決まり **2** *v/i* nebiki no kōshō o suru 値引きの交渉をする

♦**bargain for** (*expect*) … o yoki suru …を予期する

barge *n* NAUT hashike はしけ

bark[1] **1** *n* (*of dog*) hoeru koe ほえる声 **2** *v/i* hoeru ほえる

bark[2] (*of tree*) ki no kawa 木の皮

barley ōmugi 大麦

barn naya 納屋

barometer kiatsukei 気圧計; *fig* barométā バロメーター

barracks MIL heisha 兵舎

barrel taru たる

barren *land* fumō (na) 不毛(な)

barrette baretta バレッタ

barricade *n* barikēdo バリケード

barrier saku さく; (*cultural*) shōgai 障害; ***language ~*** kotoba no kabe 言葉の壁

bartender bāten バーテン

barter 1 *n* butsubutsu-kōkan 物々交換 **2** *v/t*: ***~ X for Y*** X o Y to butsubutsu-kōkan suru XをYと物々交換する

base 1 *n* (*bottom*) soko 底; (*center*) honkyochi 本拠地; MIL kichi 基地 **2** *v/t* motozukaseru 基づかせる; ***~ X on Y*** X wa Y o moto ni shite iru X はYを基にしている; ***be ~d in*** (*in city, country*) … o honkyochi ni suru …を本拠地にする

baseball (*ball*) yakyū no bōru 野球のボール; (*game*) yakyū 野球

baseball bat yakyū no batto 野球のバット; **baseball cap** yakyūbō 野球帽; **baseball player** yakyū-senshu 野球選手

basement (*of house*) chika 地下; (*of store*) chikai 地階

base rate FIN kijun-riritsu 基準利率

basic (*rudimentary*) kisoteki (na) 基礎的(な); (*fundamental*) kihonteki (na) 基本的(な)

basically kihonteki ni 基本的に

basics: ***the ~*** kisoteki na koto 基礎的なこと; ***get down to ~*** kihonteki na koto ni torikakaru 基本的なことに取り掛かる

basis kiso 基礎; (*of argument*) konkyo 根拠

bask hinatabokko suru ひなたぼっこする

basket kago かご, basuketto バスケット; (*in basketball*) netto ネット

basketball basukettobōru バスケットボール

bass 1 *n* (*part*) basu バス; (*singer*) basu-kashu バス歌手; (*instrument*) bēsu ベース **2** *adj* basu (no) バス(の)

bastard shiseiji 私生児; F kusoyarō くそ野郎; ***poor / stupid ~*** kawaisō na / baka na yatsu かわいそうな/ばかなやつ

bat[1] **1** *n* (*for baseball*) batto バット; (*for table tennis*) raketto ラケット **2** *v/i* (*in baseball*) utsu 打つ

bat[2]: ***he didn't ~ an eyelid*** sukoshi mo odorokanakatta 少しも驚かなかった

bat[3] (*animal*) kōmori こうもり

batch *n* (*of bread*) hitokama 一かま;

(*of goods*) hitoyama 一山; (*of students*) ichidan 一団

bath furo 風呂; ***have a ~, take a ~*** furo ni hairu 風呂に入る

bathe *v/i* (*have a bath*) furo ni hairu 風呂に入る

bath mat basu-matto バスマット; **bathrobe** basu-rōbu バスローブ; **bathroom** (*for bath*) yokushitsu 浴室; (*for washing hands*) senmenjo 洗面所; (*toilet*) toire トイレ; **bath towel** basu-taoru バスタオル; **bathtub** yokusō 浴槽

batter *n* tane たね; (*in baseball*) battā バッター

battery denchi 電池; MOT batterī バッテリー

battle 1 *n* tatakai 戦い; *fig* tatakai 闘い **2** *v/i fig* tatakau 闘う

battlefield, battleground senjō 戦場

bawdy waisetsu (na) わいせつ(な)

bawl (*shout*) donaru どなる; (*weep*) nakisakebu 泣き叫ぶ

♦ **bawl out** *v/t* F … o shikaritobasu … をしかりとばす

bay (*inlet*) wan 湾

bay window demado 出窓

be ◊ (*written form*) … de aru …である; (*plain form*) … da …だ; (*polite form*) … desu …です; ***it's me*** watashi desu 私です; ***I'm 15*** watashi wa jūgo sai da 私は十五歳だ; ***how much is / are …?*** … wa ikura desu ka …はいくらですか ◊ (*written and plain form*: *of humans, animals*) iru いる; (*polite form*) imasu います; (*written and plain form*: *of objects*) aru ある; (*polite form*) arimasu あります; ***was she there?*** kanojo wa soko ni imashita ka 彼女はそこにいましたか; ***there is / are*** (*of humans, animals*) … ga iru …がいる; (*polite form*) … ga imasu …がいます; (*of objects*) … ga aru …がある; (*polite form*) … ga arimasu …があります ◊ (*imperatives*) …te …て; ***~ careful*** ki o tsukete 気をつけて; ***don't ~ sad*** kanashi-garanaide 悲しがらないで ◊: ***has the mailman been?*** yūbin'ya-san wa mō kimashita ka 郵便屋さんはもう来ましたか; ***I've never been to Japan*** watashi wa Nihon ni itta koto ga arimasen 私は日本に行ったことがありません; ***I've been here for hours*** watashi wa koko ni nanjikan mo imasu 私はここに何時間もいます ◊ (*tags*) … ne …ね; ***that's right, isn't it?*** sō desu ne そうですね; ***she's Chinese, isn't she?*** kanojo wa Chūgoku-jin desu ne 彼女は中国人ですね ◊ (*auxiliary*): ***I am thinking*** watashi wa kangaete imasu 私は考えています; ***he was running*** kare wa hashitte imashita 彼は走っていました; ***you're ~ing silly*** anata wa baka na mane o shite imasu あなたはばかなまねをしています ◊ (*obligation*): ***you are to do what I tell you*** watashi no iu tōri ni shinasai 私の言う通りにしなさい; ***I was to tell you this*** watashi wa kore o iu koto ni natte imashita 私はこれを言うことになっていました; ***you were not to tell anyone*** anata wa dare ni mo iubeki de wa nakatta あなたは誰にもいうべきではなかった ◊ (*passive*): ***he was killed*** kare wa korosareta 彼は殺された; ***they have been sold*** sorera wa urete shimatta それらは売れてしまった

♦ **be in for** … ni kitto au …にきっとあう

beach hamabe 浜辺

beachwear bīchiwea ビーチウェア

beads nekkuresu ネックレス; (*rosary*) juzu じゅず

beak kuchibashi くちばし

beaker bīkā ビーカー

be-all: ***the ~ and end-all*** mottomo jūyō na koto 最も重要なこと

beam 1 *n* (*in ceiling etc*) hari はり **2** *v/i* (*smile*) egao 笑顔 **3** *v/t* (*transmit*) sōshin suru 送信する

bean mame 豆; ***be full of ~s*** genki ippai de aru 元気いっぱいである

bear[1] (*animal*) kuma くま

bear[2] **1** *v/t weight* sasaeru 支える; *costs* futan suru 負担する;

(*tolerate*) gaman suru 我慢する; *child* umu 産む **2** *v/i*: ***bring pressure to ~ on*** … ni atsuryoku o kakeru …に圧力をかける
♦**bear out** (*confirm*) … o shiji suru …を支持する
bearable taerareru 耐えられる
beard hige ひげ
bearing (*in machine*) bearingu ベアリング; ***that has no ~ on the case*** sore wa jiken to mattaku kankei ga nai それは事件とまったく関係がない
bear market FIN sagesōba 下げ相場
beast kemono 獣
beat 1 *n* (*of heart*) kodō 鼓動; (*of music*) bīto ビート **2** *v/i* (*of heart*) kodō suru 鼓動する; (*of rain*) utsu 打つ; ***~ about the bush*** tōmawashi ni iu 遠回しに言う **3** *v/t* (*in competition*) makasu 負かす; (*hit*) butsu ぶつ; (*pound*) tataku たたく; ***~ it!*** F deteke 出てけ; ***it ~s me*** F sore ni wa maitta それにはまいった
♦**beat up** … o uchinomesu …を打ちのめす
beaten: ***off the ~track*** henpi na tokoro へんぴなところ
beating (*physical*) bōkō 暴行
beat-up F tsukaifurushi (no) 使い古し(の)
beautician biyōshi 美容師
beautiful utsukushii 美しい; *meal, vacation, story, movie* subarashii 素晴らしい; ***thanks, that looks ~!*** arigatō, mattaku subarashii ありがとう、まったくすばらしい
beautifully *cooked, done* migoto ni 見事に; *simple* subarashiku 素晴らしく
beauty (*of woman, sunset*) utsukushi-sa 美しさ
beauty parlor biyōin 美容院
♦**beaver away** F sesse to hataraku せっせと働く
because … kara …から; ***we can't go there ~ it is too expensive*** sore wa takasugiru kara ikenai それは高すぎるから行けない; ***~ of*** … no tame ni …のために; (*referring to sth negative*) … no seide …のせいで
beckon *v/i* … ni temaneki suru …に手招きする
become … ni naru …になる; ***what's ~ of her?*** kanojo wa dō natta 彼女はどうなった
bed beddo ベッド; (*of flowers*) kadan 花壇; (*of sea, river*) soko 底; ***go to ~*** neru 寝る; ***he's still in ~*** kare wa mada nete iru 彼はまだ寝ている; ***go to ~ with*** … to neru …と寝る
bedclothes shingu 寝具
bedding shingu 寝具
bedridden netakiri (no) 寝たきり(の); **bedroom** shinshitsu 寝室; **bedspread** beddokabā ベッドカバー; **bedtime** nerujikan 寝る時間
bee mitsubachi ミツバチ
beech buna ぶな
beef 1 *n* gyūniku 牛肉; F (*complaint*) fuhei 不平 **2** *v/i* F (*complain*) fuhei o iu 不平をいう
♦**beef up** … o kyōka suru …を強化する
beefburger hanbāgā ハンバーガー
beehive mitsubachi no subako ミツバチの巣箱
beeline: ***make a ~ for*** … e massugu ni iku …へまっすぐに行く
beep 1 *n* bītto naru oto ビーッと鳴る音 **2** *v/i* bītto naru ビーッと鳴る **3** *v/t* (*on pager*) narasu 鳴らす
beeper pokettoberu ポケットベル
beer bīru ビール
beetle kabutomushi かぶと虫
before 1 *prep* (*time, space, order*) … no mae ni …の前に **2** *adv* mae ni 前に; ***I've seen this movie ~*** kono eiga maeni mita koto ga aru この映画前に見たことがある; ***I didn't know that ~*** ima made shiranakatta 今まで知らなかった; ***you should have told me ~*** motto hayaku itte kurereba yokatta no ni もっと早く言ってくれればよかったのに; ***the week / day ~*** isshūkan / ichinichi mae 一週間/一日前 **3** *conj* … (suru) mae ni … (する)前に

beforehand maemotte 前もって
beg 1 *v/i* monogoi suru 物ごいする **2** *v/t*: ***~ X to ...*** X ni ... o tanomu Xに...を頼む
beggar kojiki こじき
begin 1 *v/i* hajimaru 始まる; ***to ~ with*** (*at first*) saisho no uchi wa 最初のうちは; (*in the first place*) mazu saisho ni まず最初に **2** *v/t* hajimeru 始める
beginner shoshin-sha 初心者
beginner driver unten-renshū-sha 運転練習者
beginning hajime 初め; (*origin*) hajimari 初まり
behalf: ***on*** *or* ***in ~ of*** ... ni kawatte ...に代わって; ***on my / his ~*** watashi no / kare no kawari ni 私の/彼の代わりに
behave *v/i* furumau ふるまう; **~ (*oneself*)** gyōgi yoku suru 行儀良くする; **~ (*yourself*)!** gyōgi yoku shinasai 行儀良くしなさい
behavior kōdō 行動
behind 1 *prep* (*in position*) ... no ushiro ni ...の後ろに; (*in race, competition etc*) ... yori okurete ...より遅れて; ***be ~ ...*** (*responsible for*) ... no ura ni iru ...の裏にいる; (*support*) ... ni mikata suru ...に味方する **2** *adv* (*at the back*) ushiro ni 後ろに; *leave, stay* ato ni あとに; ***be ~ with*** ...ga okurete iru ...が遅れている
being (*existence*) sonzai 存在; (*creature*) ikimono 生き物
belated osokunatta 遅くなった
belch 1 *n* geppu げっぷ **2** *v/i* geppu o suru げっぷをする
Belgian 1 *adj* Berugī (no) ベルギー(の) **2** *n* Berugī-jin ベルギー人
Belgium Berugī ベルギー
belief shinrai 信頼; (*religious*) shinkō 信仰
believe shinjiru 信じる
♦**believe in** REL ... o shinkō suru ...を信仰する; *ghosts* ... no sonzai o shinjiru ...の存在を信じる; (*trust*) ... o shinrai suru ...を信頼する; (*have confidence in abilities of*) ... o yoi to omou ...を良いと思う
believer shinja 信者; *fig* shinpō-sha 信奉者
bell beru ベル
bellhop bōi ボーイ
belligerent *adj* kōsenteki (na) 好戦的(な)
bellow 1 *n* unarigoe うなり声; (*of bull*) hoegoe ほえ声 **2** *v/i* donaru どなる; (*of bull*) hoeru ほえる
belly (*of person*) hara 腹; (*fat stomach*) onaka おなか; (*of animal*) fukubu 腹部
bellyache *v/i* F guchi o iu ぐちを言う
belong *v/i*: ***where does this ~?*** kore wa doko no mono desu ka これはどこのものですか; ***I don't ~ here*** watashi wa koko ni wa awanai 私はここには合わない
♦**belong to** ... no mono de aru ...のものである; *club, organization* ... ni shozoku suru ...に所属する
belongings mochimono 持ち物
beloved *adj* saiai (no) 最愛(の)
below 1 *prep* ... no shita ni ...の下に; (*in amount, rate, level*) ... ika ni ...以下に **2** *adv* shita ni 下に; (*in text*) kaki ni 下記に; ***see ~*** kaki-sanshō 下記参照; ***10 degrees ~*** reika jūdo 零下十度
belt beruto ベルト; ***tighten one's ~*** *fig* taibō-seikatsu o suru 耐乏生活をする
bench benchi ベンチ; (*work~*) sagyōdai 作業台
benchmark kijun 基準
bend 1 *n* kābu カーブ **2** *v/t* mageru 曲げる **3** *v/i* magaru 曲がる; (*of person*) kagamu かがむ
♦**bend down** karada o kagameru 体をかがめる
bender F ōzake 大酒
beneath 1 *prep* ... no shita ni ...の下に; (*in status, value*) ... yori ototte ...より劣って **2** *adv* shita ni 下に
benefactor onjin 恩人
beneficial yūeki (na) 有益(な)
benefit 1 *n* rieki 利益 **2** *v/t* ... no yaku ni tatsu ...の役に立つ **3** *v/i* rieki o eru 利益を得る
benevolent jihibukai 慈悲深い

benign yasashii 優しい; MED ryōsei (no) 良性(の)
bequeath yuigon de yuzuru 遺言で譲る; *fig* nokosu 残す
bereaved 1 *adj* ato ni nokosareta あとに残された **2** *n*: ***the ~*** ato ni nokosareta hitobito あとに残された人々; (*family*) izoku 遺族
berry ichigo-rui いちご類
berserk: ***go ~*** kyōbō ni naru 狂暴になる
berth (*for sleeping*) shindai 寝台; (*for ship*) teihaku-basho 停泊場所; ***give … a wide ~*** … o keien suru …を敬遠する
beside … no soba ni …のそばに; ***be ~ oneself*** ware o wasureru 我を忘れる; ***that's ~ the point*** sore wa mato hazure de aru それは的はずれである
besides 1 *adv* sono ue そのうえ **2** *prep* (*apart from*) … no hoka ni …のほかに
best 1 *adj* mottomo yoi 最もよい **2** *adv* mottomo yoku 最もよく; ***it would be ~ if …*** …suru no ga ichiban da to omou …するのが一番だと思う; ***I like her ~*** kanojo ga ichiban suki da 彼女がいちばん好きだ **3** *n*: ***do one's ~*** saizen o tsukusu 最善を尽くす; ***the ~*** (*thing*) saikō no mono 最高のもの; (*person*) ichiban 一番; ***I did the ~ I could*** watashi wa jibun de dekiru saikō no koto o shimashita 私は自分でできる最高のことをしました; ***make the ~ of*** … o saidaigen ni riyō suru …を最大限に利用する; ***all the ~!*** ogenki de お元気で
best before date shōmikigen no hizuke 賞味期限の日付け; **best man** (*at wedding*) shinrō-tsukisoi-nin 新郎付添人; **best-seller** besuto-serā ベストセラー
bet 1 *n* kake 賭け **2** *v/i* (*gamble*) kakegoto o suru 賭け事をする; (*on horse etc*) kakeru 賭ける; ***you ~!*** mochiron もちろん **3** *v/t* (*reckon*) … to dangen suru …と断言する
betray uragiru 裏切る
betrayal uragiri 裏切り
better 1 *adj* motto yoi もっとよい; *actor, swimmer, driver etc* motto jōzu (na) もっと上手(な); ***get ~*** umaku naru うまくなる; (*in health*) kaifuku suru 回復する; ***he's ~*** (*in health*) kare wa daibu yoi 彼はだいぶよい **2** *adv* motto yoku もっとよく; *act, swim, drive etc* motto jōzu ni もっと上手に; ***you'd ~ ask permission*** kyoka o morau beki da 許可をもらうべきだ; ***I'd really ~ not*** yamete oita hō ga ii やめておいた方がいい; ***all the ~ for us*** watashitachi no tame ni wa sono hōga ii 私達のためにはその方がいい; ***I like her ~*** kanojo no hō ga suki da 彼女のほうが好きだ
better-off …yori kane ga aru …より金がある
between *prep* … no aida ni …の間に; ***~ you and me*** koko dake no hanashi da ga ここだけの話だが
beverage *fml* nomimono 飲み物
beware: ***~ of*** chūi suru 注意する
bewilder tōwaku saseru 当惑させる
beyond 1 *prep* … o koete …を越えて; ***it's ~ me*** (*don't understand*) watashi ni wa wakaranai 私にはわからない; (*can't do it*) watashi ni wa dekinai 私にはできない **2** *adv* mukō ni 向こうに
Bhutan Būtan ブータン
Bhutanese 1 *adj* Būtan (no) ブータン(の) **2** *n* (*person*) Būtan-jin ブータン人
bias *n* henken 偏見; (*favorable*) hiikime ひいき目
bias(s)ed henken ni motozuita 偏見に基づいた; (*favorably*) hiikime ni mite ひいき目に見て
bib (*for baby*) yodarekake よだれ掛け
Bible seisho 聖書
bibliography bunken-mokuroku 文献目録
biceps chikarakobu 力こぶ
bicker kenka suru けんかする
bicycle *n* jitensha 自転車, F charinko ちゃりんこ
bid 1 *n* (*at auction*) tsukene 付け値; (*attempt*) kokoromi 試み **2** *v/i* (*at*

auction) kyōbai ni sanka suru 競売に参加する
biennial *adj* ni-nen goto (no) 二年ごと(の)
big 1 *adj* ōkii 大きい; ~ ***brother*** ani 兄; ~ ***sister*** ane 姉; ~ ***name*** ichiryū 一流 **2** *adv*: ***talk*** ~ jiman suru 自慢する
bigamy jūkon 重婚
big-headed unuboreta うぬぼれた
bike 1 *n* jitensha 自転車 **2** *v/i* jitensha ni noru 自転車に乗る
bikini bikini ビキニ
bilingual bairingaru (no) バイリンガル(の)
bill 1 *n* (*money*) shihei 紙幣; (*for electricity etc*) seikyūsho 請求書; *Br* (*in restaurant*) o-kanjō お勘定; POL gian 議案; (*poster*) bira ビラ **2** *v/t* (*invoice*) … ni seikyūsho o okuru … に請求書を送る
billboard kōkokuban 広告板
billfold satsuire 札入れ
billiards biriyādo ビリヤード
billion jū-oku 十億
bill of exchange kawase tegata 為替手形
bill of sale uriwatashishō 売り渡し証
bin (*for storage*) chozōbako 貯蔵箱
binary nishinhō (no) 二進法(の)
bind *v/t* (*connect*) musubi-tsukeru 結び付ける; (*tie*) shibaru 縛る; (LAW: *oblige*) gimuzukeru 義務づける
binder (*for papers*) baindā バインダー
binding 1 *adj agreement, promise* kōsokuryoku no aru 拘束力のある **2** *n* (*of book*) seihon 製本
binoculars sōgankyō 双眼鏡
biodegradable mugai-busshitsu ni kangen dekiru 無害物質に還元できる
biography denki 伝記
biological seibutsugaku-jō (no) 生物学上(の)
biological detergent kōso-senzai 酵素洗剤
biological parents jitsu no ryōshin 実の両親
biology seibutsugaku 生物学
biotechnology baiotekunorojī バイオテクノロジー
birch: ***silver*** ~ shirakaba しらかば
bird tori 鳥
bird of prey mōkin 猛きん
bird sanctuary chōrui-hogoku 鳥類保護区
birth (*of child*) tanjō 誕生; (*labor*) shussan 出産; *fig* (*of country*) shutsugen 出現; ***give ~ to*** *child* … o umu …を産む; ***date of*** ~ seinengappi 生年月日
birth certificate shussei-shōmeisho 出生証明書; **birth control** hinin 避妊; **birthday** tanjōbi 誕生日; ***happy ~!*** otanjōbi omedetō お誕生日おめでとう; **birthplace** seitanchi 生誕地; **birthrate** shusshōritsu 出生率
biscuit bisuketto ビスケット
bisexual 1 *adj* baisekusharu (no) バイセクシャル(の) **2** *n* baisekusharu バイセクシャル
bishop (*catholic*) shikyō 司教; (*protestant*) shukyō 主教
bit *n* (*of a whole*) kakera かけら; (*part, section*) bubun 部分; (*in book, movie*) tokoro ところ; COMPUT bitto ビット; ***a*** ~ (*a little*) sukoshi 少し; ***a ~ of*** (*a little*) sukoshi (no) 少し(の); ***a ~ of news / advice*** chotto shita nyūsu / adobaisu ちょっとしたニュース/アドバイス; ~ ***by*** ~ sukoshi zutsu 少しずつ; ***I'll be there in a*** ~ watashi wa soko ni sukoshi shitara ikimasu 私はそこに少ししたら行きます
bitch 1 *n* (*dog*) mesuinu 雌犬; F (*woman*) ama あま **2** *v/i* F (*complain*) monku o iu 文句を言う
bitchy F ijiwaru (na) 意地悪(な)
bite 1 *n* kamikizu かみ傷; (*of mosquito, flea*) mushisasare 虫刺され; (*of food*) hitokuchi 一口; ***get a*** ~ (*of angler*) kuitsuki 食い付き; ***a ~*** (***to eat***) tabemono 食べ物 **2** *v/t* kamu かむ; (*of mosquito, flea*) sasu 刺す **3** *v/i* kamitsuku かみつく; (*of mosquito, flea*) sasu 刺す; (*of fish*) kuitsuku 食いつく
bitter *taste* nigai 苦い; *person* ne ni motte 根に持って; *weather* kibishii

厳しい; *argument* hageshii 激しい
bitterly *cold* hidoku ひどく
black 1 *adj* kuroi 黒い; *person* kokujin (no) 黒人(の); *coffee* burakku (no) ブラック(の); *tea* sutorēto (no) ストレート(の); *fig* ankoku (no) 暗黒(の) **2** *n* (*color*) kuro 黒; (*person*) kokujin 黒人; ***in the ~*** FIN kuroji de 黒字で
♦**black out** *v/i* ishiki o ushinau 意識を失う
black belt kuro-obi 黒帯; **blackberry** burakkuberī ブラックベリー; **blackbird** kurōtadori クロウタドリ; **blackboard** kokuban 黒板; **black box** burakku-bokkusu ブラックボックス; **black economy** yamikeizai やみ経済
blacken *name* chūshō suru 中傷する
black eye aoaza 青あざ; **black ice** tōketsu-romen 凍結路面; **blacklist 1** *n* burakkurisuto ブラックリスト **2** *v/t* burakkurisuto ni noseru ブラックリストに載せる; **blackmail 1** *n* yusuri ゆすり; ***emotional ~*** hito no yowami ni tsukekomu koto 人の弱味に付け込むこと **2** *v/t* yusuru ゆする; **blackmailer** kyōkatsu-sha 恐喝者; **black market** yamishijō やみ市場
blackness ankoku 暗黒
blackout ELEC teiden 停電; MED ishikisōshitsu 意識喪失
bladder bōkō 膀胱
blade (*of knife, sword*) ha 刃; (*of helicopter*) hane 羽根; ***a ~ of grass*** kusa ippon 草一本
blame 1 *n* hinan 非難; (*responsibility*) sekinin 責任 **2** *v/t* … no sei ni suru …のせいにする; ***~ X for Y*** Y o X no sei ni suru YをXのせいにする
bland ajikenai 味気ない
blank 1 *adj* (*not written on*) hakushi (no) 白紙(の); *tape* kara (no) から(の); *look* bon'yari shita ぼんやりした **2** *n* (*empty space*) yohaku 余白; ***my mind's a ~*** atama ga karappo de aru 頭が空っぽである
blank check kingaku no kaite inai kogitte 金額の書いていない小切手
blanket *n* mōfu 毛布; ***a ~ of*** *fig* ichimen (no)… 一面(の)…
blare *v/i* yakamashiku naru やかましく鳴る
♦**blare out 1** *v/i* yakamashiku naru やかましく鳴る **2** *v/t* … o yakamashiku narasu …をやかましく鳴らす
blaspheme bōtoku suru 冒とくする
blast 1 *n* (*explosion*) bakuhatsu 爆発; (*gust*) ichijin no kaze 一陣の風 **2** *v/t* bakuha suru 爆破する **3** *interj* che' ちぇっ
♦**blast off** (*of rocket*) hassha suru 発射する
blast furnace yōkōro 溶鉱炉
blast-off uchiage 打ち上げ
blatant zūzūshii ずうずうしい
blaze 1 *n* (*fire*) kaji 火事; ***a ~ of color*** kagayaku yō na iro 輝くような色 **2** *v/i* (*of fire*) moetatsu 燃え立つ
♦**blaze away** (*with gun*) tsuzukete happō suru 続けて発砲する
blazer burezā ブレザー
bleach 1 *n* burīchi ブリーチ **2** *v/t hair* burīchi suru ブリーチする
bleak *countryside* sabireta さびれた; *weather* samuzamu shita 寒々した; *future* kurai 暗い
bleary-eyed me ga shoboshobo shita 目がしょぼしょぼした
bleat *v/i* (*of sheep*) mē to naku めーと泣く
bleed 1 *v/i* shukketsu suru 出血する **2** *v/t fig* kane o shibori toru 金を搾り取る
bleeding *n* shukketsu 出血
bleep 1 *n* pī to iu oto ぴーという音 **2** *v/i* pī to naru ぴーと鳴る
bleeper pokettoberu ポケットベル
blemish 1 *n* kizu 傷 **2** *v/t reputation* … o sokonau …を損なう
blend 1 *n* burendo ブレンド **2** *v/t* burendo suru ブレンドする
♦**blend in 1** *v/i* tokekomu 溶け込む **2** *v/t* (*in cooking*) … o mazeru …を混ぜる
blender mikisā ミキサー
bless shukufuku suru 祝福する; (***God***) ***~ you!*** kamisama no

omegumi ga arimasuyō ni 神様のお恵みがありますように; **~ you** (*in response to sneeze*) odaiji ni お大事に; **be ~ed with** … ni megumarete iru …に恵まれている

blessing REL shukufuku 祝福; *fig* (*approval*) sansei 賛成

blind 1 *adj* mōmoku (no) 盲目(の); *corner* mitōshi no kikanai 見通しの利かない; **~ to** … ni ki ga tsukanai …に気がつかない **2** *n*: **the ~** mōjin 盲人 **3** *v/t* shitsumei saseru 失明させる; *fig* me o kuramaseru 目をくらませる

blind alley *also fig* ikizumari 行き詰まり; **blind date** buraindo-dēto ブラインド・デート; **blindfold 1** *n* mekakushi 目隠し **2** *v/t* … ni mekakushi o suru …に目隠しをする **3** *adv* mekakushi o shite 目隠しをして

blinding me o kuramasu 目をくらます

blind spot (*in road*) shikaku 死角; *fig* mōten 盲点

blink *v/i* (*of person*) mabataki suru まばたきする; (*of light*) chiratsuku ちらつく

blip (*on radar screen*) tenmetsu 点滅; *fig* tankiteki na mono 短期的なもの

bliss kōfuku 幸福

blister 1 *n* mizubukure 水ぶくれ **2** *v/i* mizubukure ni naru 水ぶくれになる; (*of paint*) butsubutsu ga dekiru ぶつぶつができる

blizzard fubuki 吹雪

bloated fukureagatta ふくれ上がった

blob (*of liquid*) hitotarashi ひとたらし

bloc POL ken 圏

block 1 *n* katamari かたまり; (*in town*) burokku ブロック, gaiku 街区; (*blockage*) shōgaibutsu 障害物 **2** *v/t* fusagu ふさぐ

♦**block in** (*with vehicle*) … o tojikomeru …を閉じ込める

♦**block out** *light* … o shadan suru …を遮断する

♦**block up** *v/t sink etc* … o sukkari fusagu …をすっかりふさぐ

blockade 1 *n* fūsa 封鎖 **2** *v/t* fūsa suru 封鎖する

blockage tsumari 詰まり

blockbuster hittosaku ヒット作

block letters katsujitai 活字体

blond *adj* kinpatsu (no) 金髪(の)

blonde *n* (*woman*) kinpatsu no josei 金髪の女性

blood chi 血; **in cold ~** reikoku ni 冷酷に

blood bank ketsueki-ginkō 血液銀行; **blood donor** kenketsu-sha 献血者; **blood group** ketsuekigata 血液型

bloodless *coup* muketsu (no) 無血(の)

blood poisoning haiketsushō 敗血症; **blood pressure** ketsuatsu 血圧; **blood relation**, **blood relative** nikushin 肉親; **blood sample** ketsueki-sanpuru 血液サンプル; **bloodshed** ryūketsu 流血; **bloodshot** chibashitta 血走った; **bloodstain** kekkon 血こん; **bloodstream** ketsuryū 血流; **blood test** ketsueki-kensa 血液検査; **blood transfusion** yuketsu 輸血; **blood vessel** kekkan 血管

bloody *hands etc* chidarake (no) 血だらけ(の); *battle* mugotarashii むごたらしい

bloody mary buradī-marī ブラディーマリー

bloom 1 *n* hana 花; **in full ~** hanazakari (no) 花盛り(の) **2** *v/i* hana ga saku 花が咲く; *fig* massakari de aru 真っ盛りである

blossom 1 *n* hana 花; **~ viewing** hanami 花見 **2** *v/i* hana o tsukeru 花をつける; *fig* kaikatsu ni naru 快活になる

blot 1 *n* shimi 染み; *fig* kizu 傷 **2** *v/t* (*dry*) suitotte kawakasu 吸い取って乾かす

♦**blot out** … o kesu …を消す; *view* … o mienaku suru …を見えなくする

blotch hasshin 発疹

blotchy shimi darake (no) 染みだらけ(の)

blouse burausu ブラウス

blow[1] *n* ōda 殴打; *fig* dageki 打撃

blow[2] **1** *v/t* (*of wind*) fukitobasu 吹き飛ばす; *smoke* haku 吐く; *whistle* fuku 吹く; F (*spend*) rōhi suru 浪費する; F *opportunity* fui ni suru ふいにする; ~ ***one's nose*** hana o kamu 鼻をかむ **2** *v/i* (*of wind*) fuku 吹く; (*of whistle*) naru 鳴る; (*of person*) haku 吐く; (*of fuse*) tobu 飛ぶ; (*of tire*) panku suru パンクする

♦**blow off 1** *v/t* … o fukitobasu …を吹き飛ばす **2** *v/i* fukitobu 吹き飛ぶ

♦**blow out 1** *v/t candle* … o fukikesu …を吹き消す **2** *v/i* (*of candle*) kaze de kieru 風で消える

♦**blow over 1** *v/t* … o fukitaosu …を吹き倒す **2** *v/i* fukitobasareru 吹き飛ばされる; (*of storm*) shizumaru 静まる; (*of argument*) osamaru 収まる

♦**blow up 1** *v/t* (*with explosives*) … o bakuha suru …を爆破する; *balloon* fukuramasu 膨らます; *photograph* hikinobasu 引き伸ばす **2** *v/i* bakuhatsu suru 爆発する; F (*get angry*) katto naru かっとなる

blow-dry *n* burō-dorai ブロードライ; **blow job** V ferachio フェラチオ; **blow-out** (*of tire*) panku パンク; F (*big meal*) gochisō ごちそう; **blow-up** (*of photo*) hikinobashi 引き伸ばし

blue 1 *adj* aoi 青い; *movie* poruno (no) ポルノ(の) **2** *n* ao 青

blueberry burūberī ブルーベリー; **blue chip** yūryō kabu 優良株; **blue-collar worker** nikutai-rōdō-sha 肉体労働者; **blueprint** aojashin 青写真; (*plan*) keikaku 計画

blues MUS burūsu ブルース; ***have the ~*** ochikomu 落ち込む

blues singer burūsu-kashu ブルース歌手

bluff 1 *n* (*deception*) hattari はったり **2** *v/i* hattari o kikaseru はったりをきかせる

blunder 1 *n* hema へま **2** *v/i* hema o suru へまをする

blunt *adj* nibui 鈍い; *person* bukkirabō (na) ぶっきらぼう(な)

bluntly *speak* bukkirabō ni ぶっきらぼうに

blur 1 *n* bon'yari shita mono ぼんやりしたもの **2** *v/t* bokasu ぼかす

blurb (*on book*) senden-monku 宣伝文句

♦**blurt out** … o dashinuke ni iidasu …を出し抜けに言い出す

blush 1 *n* sekimen 赤面 **2** *v/i* sekimen suru 赤面する

blusher (*cosmetic*) hōbeni ほお紅, chīku チーク

BO (= ***body odor***) taishū 体臭

board 1 *n* ita 板; (*for game*) bōdo ボード; (*for notices*) keijiban 掲示板; (*committee*) iinkai 委員会; ~ **(*of directors*)** yakuinkai 役員会; ***on ~*** (*plane*) hikōki ni notte 飛行機に乗って; (*train*) ressha ni notte 列車に乗って; (*boat*) fune ni notte 船に乗って; ***take on ~*** *comments etc* rikai suru 理解する; (*fully realize truth of*) ukeireru 受け入れる; ***across the ~*** ichiritsu ni 一律に **2** *v/t airplane etc* … ni noru …に乗る **3** *v/i* (*of passengers*) noru 乗る

♦**board up** … ni ita o haru …に板を張る

♦**board with** … ni geshuku suru …に下宿する

board and lodging makanai-tsuki geshuku 賄い付き下宿

boarder geshukunin 下宿人; EDU ryōsei 寮生

board game bōdo-gēmu ボードゲーム

boarding card tōjōken 搭乗券; **boarding house** geshukuya 下宿屋; **boarding pass** tōjōken 搭乗券; **boarding school** kishuku-gakkō 寄宿学校

board meeting jūyaku-kaigi 重役会議; **board room** kaigishitsu 会議室; **boardwalk** yūhodō 遊歩道

boast 1 *n* jiman 自慢 **2** *v/i* jiman suru 自慢する

boat fune 船; (*small, for leisure*) bōto ボート; ***go by ~*** fune de iku 船で行く

bob[1] (*haircut*) bobu ボブ

bob[2] *v/i* (*of boat etc*) nami ni yureru 波に揺れる

♦ **bob up** arawareru 現れる
bobsleigh, **bobsled** bobusurē ボブスレー
bodice bodīsūtsu ボディースーツ
bodily 1 *adj* shintaiteki (na) 身体的(な) **2** *adv eject* karada goto 体ごと
body karada 体; (*dead*) shitai 死体; **~ *of water*** koshō 湖沼; **~ (*suit*)** (*undergarment*) bodīsūtsu ボディースーツ
bodyguard bodīgādo ボディーガード; **body language** bodīrangēji ボディーランゲージ; **body odor** taishū 体臭; **body shop** MOT shūri-kōjō 修理工場; **bodywork** MOT shatai 車体
boggle: ***it ~s the mind!*** shinjirarenai 信じられない
bogus inchiki (no) いんちき(の)
boil[1] *n* (*swelling*) odeki おでき
boil[2] **1** *v/t liquid* futtō saseru 沸騰させる; *egg, vegetables* yuderu ゆでる **2** *v/i* futtō suru 沸騰する
♦ **boil down to** … to naru …となる
♦ **boil over** (*of milk etc*) … ga fukikoboreru …が吹きこぼれる
boiler boirā ボイラー
boisterous sōzōshii 騒々しい
bold 1 *adj* daitan (na) 大胆(な) **2** *n* (*print*) futoji 太字; ***in ~*** futojitai de 太字体で
bolster *v/t confidence* shiji suru 支持する
bolt 1 *n* boruto ボルト; (*on door*) kannuki かんぬき; (*of lightning*) kaminari 雷; ***like a ~ from the blue*** seiten no hekireki no yō ni 青天のへきれきのように **2** *adv*: ***~ upright*** massugu ni まっすぐに **3** *v/t* (*fix with bolts*) boruto de shimeru ボルトで締める; *door* … ni kannuki o kakeru …にかんぬきを掛ける **4** *v/i* (*run off*) hashiridasu 走り出す; (*of prisoner*) dassō suru 脱走する
bomb 1 *n* bakudan 爆弾 **2** *v/t* bakuha suru 爆破する; MIL bakugeki suru 爆撃する
bombard: ***~ with questions*** shitsumonzeme ni suru 質問ぜめにする
bomb attack bakugeki 爆撃
bomber (*airplane*) bakugekiki 爆撃機; (*terrorist*) bakugeki-hannin 爆撃犯人
bomber jacket kawajan 皮ジャン
bomb scare bakudan-sawagi 爆弾騒ぎ
bond 1 *n* (*tie*) kizuna きずな; FIN saiken 債券 **2** *v/i* (*of glue*) setchaku suru 接着する
bone 1 *n* hone 骨 **2** *v/t meat, fish* … no hone o nuku …の骨を抜く
bonfire takibi たき火
bonsai bonsai 盆栽
bonus (*money*) bōnasu ボーナス; (*something extra*) omake おまけ
boo 1 *n* būingu ブーイング **2** *v/t & v/i* yajiru やじる
book 1 *n* hon 本; **~ *of matches*** hagitori matchi はぎ取りマッチ **2** *v/t* (*reserve*) yoyaku suru 予約する; (*of policeman*) chōsho o toru 調書をとる **3** *v/i* (*reserve*) yoyaku suru 予約する
bookcase hondana 本棚
booked up: ***be ~*** (*of hotel, flight*) yoyaku de ippai ni naru 予約で一杯になる; (*of person*) yotei de ippai ni naru 予定で一杯になる
bookie F nomi-ya のみ屋
booking (*reservation*) yoyaku 予約
booking clerk yoyaku-gakari 予約係
bookkeeper boki-gakari 簿記係
bookkeeping boki 簿記
booklet shōsasshi 小冊子
bookmaker baken-ya 馬券屋
books (*accounts*) chōbo 帳簿; ***do the ~*** chōbo o tsukeru 帳簿をつける
bookseller hon-ya 本屋; **bookstall** zasshi uriba 雑誌売り場; **bookstore** hon-ya 本屋
boom[1] **1** *n* būmu ブーム **2** *v/i* (*of business*) kakkizuku 活気づく
boom[2] **1** *n* (*noise*) todoroki とどろき **2** *v/i* todoroku とどろく
boonies: ***out in the ~*** F henpi na tokoro へんぴなところ
boost 1 *n* (*to sales, confidence*) zōka 増加; (*to economy*) zōshin 増進 **2** *v/t production, sales* fuyasu 増やす; *prices* jōshō saseru 上昇させる;

morale takameru 高める
boot *n* būtsu ブーツ
♦**boot out** F … o oidasu …を追い出す
♦**boot up 1** *v/i* COMPUT kidō suru 起動する **2** *v/t* COMPUT … o kidō saseru …を起動させる
booth (*at market, fair*) baiten 売店; (*in restaurant*) shikiriseki 仕切り席
booze *n* F sake 酒
booze-up *Br* F donchansawagi どんちゃん騒ぎ
border 1 *n* (*between countries*) kokkyō 国境; (*edge*) heri へり **2** *v/t country, river* … to rinsetsu suru …と隣接する
♦**border on** *country* … to rinsetsu suru …と隣接する; (*be almost*) … ni chikai …に近い
borderline: ***a ~ case*** dotchitsukazu no bāi どっちつかずの場合
bore[1] *v/t hole* akeru あける
bore[2] **1** *n* (*person*) taikutsu na hito 退屈な人 **2** *v/t* taikutsu saseru 退屈させる; ***be ~d*** taikutsu suru 退屈する
bored unzari shita うんざりした
boredom tsumarana-sa つまらなさ
boring taikutsu (na) 退屈(な)
born: ***be ~*** umareru 生まれる; ***where were you ~?*** anata wa doko de umaremashita ka あなたはどこで生まれましたか; ***be a ~ …*** umarenagara no … de aru 生まれながらの…である
borrow kariru 借りる
bosom (*of woman*) mune 胸
boss jōshi 上司
♦**boss around** … ni erasō ni sashizu suru …に偉そうに指図する
bossy ibarichirasu いばり散らす
botanical shokubutsu (no) 植物(の)
botany shokubutsugaku 植物学
botch *v/t* shikujiru しくじる
both 1 *adj & pron* ryōhō (no) 両方(の); (*as subject of sentence*) … wa ryōhō tomo …は両方とも; ***I know ~ (of the) brothers*** ryōhō no kyōdai o shitte iru 両方の兄弟を知っている; ***~ (of the) brothers were there*** kyōdai wa ryōhō tomo soko ni ita 兄弟は両方ともそこにいた; ***~ of them*** (*things*) ryōhō tomo 両方とも; (*people*) futari tomo 二人とも **2** *adv*: ***~ my mother and I*** haha mo watashi mo 母も私も; ***he's ~ handsome and intelligent*** kare wa hansamu de shikamo kashikoi 彼はハンサムでしかも賢い; ***is it business or pleasure? - ~*** sore wa shigoto desu ka, asobi desu ka - ryōhō それは仕事ですか、遊びですかー両方
bother 1 *n* mendō 面倒; ***it's no ~*** zenzen kamaimasen 全然かまいません **2** *v/t* (*disturb*) … ni meiwaku o kakeru …に迷惑をかける; *person working* … no jama o suru …の邪魔をする; (*worry*) shinpai saseru 心配させる **3** *v/i* nayamu 悩む; ***don't ~!*** yamete やめて; ***you needn't have ~ed*** ki o tsukawanai de kudasai 気を使わないで下さい
bottle 1 *n* bin びん; (*for baby*) honyūbin ほ乳びん **2** *v/t* bin ni ireru びんに入れる
♦**bottle up** *feelings* … o muri ni osaeru …を無理に抑える
bottle bank akibin-kaishūbako 空きびん回収箱
bottled water botoru-iri mineraru-wōtā ボトル入りミネラルウォーター
bottleneck *n* (*in road*) kyū ni semaku natte iru michi 急に狭くなっている道; (*in production*) nekku ネック
bottle-opener sennuki 栓抜き
bottom 1 *adj* mottomo shita (no) 最も下(の) **2** *n* (*underside*) ura 裏; (*on the inside*) soko 底; (*of hill*) fumoto ふもと; (*of pile*) shita 下; (*of street*) tsukiatari 突き当たり; (*of garden*) ichiban oku いちばん奥; (*buttocks*) shiri 尻; ***at the ~ of the screen*** sukurīn no shita no bubun ni スクリーンの下の部分に
♦**bottom out** soko o tsuku 底をつく
bottom line (*outcome*) kekka 結果; (*the real issue*) hondai 本題
boulder ōkina maruishi 大きな丸石
bounce 1 *v/t ball* hazumaseru 弾ませ

る; SP baundo saseru バウンドさせる **2** *v/i* (*of ball*) hazumu 弾む; SP baundo suru バウンドする; (*on sofa etc*) tobihaneru 飛び跳ねる; (*of rain etc*) utsu 打つ; (*of check*) fuwatari de modoru 不渡りで戻る
bouncer yōjinbō 用心棒
bound[1]: ***be ~ to do …*** (*sure to*) kitto … suru きっと…する; (*obliged to*) … suru gimu ga aru …する義務がある
bound[2]: ***be ~ for*** (*of ship*) … iki de aru …行きである
bound[3] **1** *n* (*jump*) hazumi 弾み **2** *v/i* haneru はねる
boundary kyōkai 境界
boundless kagiri no nai 限りのない
bouquet hanataba 花束; (*of wine*) kaori 香り
bourbon bābon バーボン
bout MED hossa 発作; (*in boxing*) ichishiai 一試合
boutique butikku ブティック
bow[1] **1** *n* (*as greeting*) ojigi おじぎ **2** *v/i* ojigi o suru おじぎをする **3** *v/t head* sageru 下げる
bow[2] (*knot*) chōmusubi 蝶結び; MUS yumi 弓
bow[3] (*of ship*) senshu 船首
bowels chō 腸
bowl[1] (*container*) hachi 鉢; (*for rice*) chawan 茶わん; (*for Japanese soup*) owan おわん; (*for cooking, salad*) bōru ボール
bowl[2] *v/i* (*in bowling*) bōringu o suru ボーリングをする
♦**bowl over** *fig* … o bikkuri saseru …をびっくりさせる
bowling bōringu ボーリング
bowling alley bōringu-jō ボーリング場
bow tie chōnekutai 蝶ネクタイ
box[1] *n* (*container*) hako 箱; (*on form*) ran 欄
box[2] *v/i* bokushingu o suru ボクシングをする
boxer bokusā ボクサー
boxing bokushingu ボクシング
boxing match bokushingu no shiai ボクシングの試合
box office kippu-uriba 切符売り場
boy otoko no ko 男の子; (*son*) musuko 息子
boycott 1 *n* boikotto ボイコット **2** *v/t* boikotto suru ボイコットする
boyfriend bōifurendo ボーイフレンド, kareshi 彼氏
boyish shōnen no yō (na) 少年のよう(な)
boyscout bōisukauto ボーイスカウト
bra burajā ブラジャー
brace (*on teeth*) kyōseiki 矯正器
bracelet buresuretto ブレスレット
bracket (*for shelf*) udeki 腕木; (*in text*) kakko かっこ
brag *v/i* hora o fuku ほらを吹く
braid *n* (*in hair*) osagegami おさげ髪; (*trimming*) mōru モール
braille tenji 点字
brain *n* nō 脳
brainless F nōmiso no taranai 脳みその足らない
brains (*intelligence*) zunō 頭脳
brainstorm (*bright idea*) hirameki ひらめき; **brainstorming** burēnsutōmingu ブレーンストーミング; **brain surgeon** nōgekai 脳外科医; **brainwash** sennō suru 洗脳する; **brainwashing** sennō 洗脳; **brainwave** (*brilliant idea*) meian 名案
brainy F atama no ii 頭のいい
brake 1 *n* burēki ブレーキ **2** *v/i* burēki o kakeru ブレーキをかける
brake light burēki-ranpu ブレーキランプ
brake pedal burēki-pedaru ブレーキペダル
branch *n* (*of tree*) eda 枝; (*of bank, company*) shiten 支店
♦**branch off** (*of road*) bunki suru 分岐する
♦**branch out** jigyō o kakuchō suru 事業を拡張する
brand 1 *n* meigara 銘柄, burando ブランド **2** *v/t*: ***be ~ed a liar*** usotsuki no rakuin o osareru うそつきのらく印を押される
brand image burando-imēji ブランドイメージ
brandish furimawasu 振り回す

brand leader ichiban urete iru burando いちばん売れているブランド; **brand loyalty** burando-shikō ブランド志向; **brand name** meigara-mei 銘柄名, burando-mei ブランド名
brand-new maatarashii 真新しい
brandy burandē ブランデー
brass (*alloy*) shinchū 真ちゅう
brass band burasu-bando ブラスバンド
brassiere burajā ブラジャー
brat *pej* gaki がき
bravado kyosei 虚勢
brave *adj* yūkan (na) 勇敢(な)
bravery yūkan-sa 勇敢さ
brawl 1 *n* kenka けんか **2** *v/i* kenka suru けんかする
brawny kukkyō (na) 屈強(な)
Brazil Burajiru ブラジル
Brazilian 1 *adj* Burajiru (no) ブラジル(の) **2** *n* Burajiru-jin ブラジル人
breach (*violation*) ihan 違反; (*in party*) fuwa 不和
breach of contract LAW keiyaku-furikō 契約不履行
bread *n* pan パン
breadcrumbs (*for cooking*) panko パン粉; (*for bird*) pankuzu パンくず
breadth (*of road*) haba 幅; (*of knowledge*) hiro-sa 広さ
breadwinner kasegite 稼ぎ手
break 1 *n* hason 破損; (*in bone*) kossetsu 骨折; (*rest*) yasumi 休み; (*in relationship*) reikyaku-kikan 冷却期間; ***give … a ~*** (*opportunity*) … ni chansu o ataeru …にチャンスを与える; ***take a ~*** kyūkei suru 休憩する; ***without a ~*** *work, travel* yasumi nashi de 休みなしで **2** *v/t device, toy* kowasu 壊す; *stick* oru 折る; *arm, leg* kossetsu suru 骨折する; *china, glass, egg* waru 割る; *law, promise, record* yaburu 破る; *news* shiraseru 知らせる **3** *v/i* (*of device, toy*) kowareru 壊れる; (*of china, glass, egg*) wareru 割れる; (*of stick*) oreru 折れる; (*of news*) nagareru 流れる; (*of storm*) osou 襲う; (*of boy's voice*) kawaru 変わる
♦**break away** *v/i* (*escape*) nigeru 逃げる; (*from family, tradition*) hanareru 離れる; (*from organization*) dattai suru 脱退する
♦**break down 1** *v/i* (*of vehicle, machine*) koshō suru 故障する; (*of talks*) shippai ni owaru 失敗に終わる; (*in tears*) nakikuzureru 泣き崩れる; (*mentally*) seishinteki ni mairu 精神的に参る **2** *v/t door* uchikowasu 打ち壊す; *figures* bunrui suru 分類する
♦**break even** COM sontoku nashi ni owaru 損得なしに終わる
♦**break in** (*interrupt*) kuchi o hasamu 口をはさむ; (*of burglar*) shinnyū suru 侵入する
♦**break off 1** *v/t* … o mogitoru …をもぎ取る; *damage* … o oru …を折る; *engagement* … o haki suru …を破棄する; ***they've broken it off*** *engagement* karera wa kon'yaku haki ni natta 彼等は婚約破棄になった **2** *v/i* (*stop talking*) kyū ni hanashi o yameru 急に話をやめる
♦**break out** (*start up*) okoru 起こる; (*of disease*) ryūkō suru 流行する; (*of prisoners*) dasshutsu suru 脱出する; ***he broke out in a rash*** kare wa totsuzen hasshin ga deta 彼は突然発しんが出た
♦**break up 1** *v/t* (*into component parts*) … o bunkai suru …を分解する; *fight* … o tomeru …をとめる **2** *v/i* (*of ice*) wareru 割れる; (*of couple*) wakareru 別れる; (*of band, meeting*) kaisan suru 解散する
breakable kowareyasui 壊れやすい
breakage hason 破損
breakdown (*of vehicle, machine*) koshō 故障; (*of talks*) ketsuretsu 決裂; (*nervous ~*) noirōze ノイローゼ; (*of figures*) uchiwake 内訳
break-even point son'eki-bunkiten 損益分岐点
breakfast *n* chōshoku 朝食, asagohan 朝ごはん; ***have ~*** chōshoku o toru 朝食をとる
break-in oshikomi-gōtō 押し込み強盗
breakthrough (*in talks*) shinten 進展;

(*in science, technology*) hiyakuteki-hatten 飛躍的発展; (*personal achievement*) toppa 突破
breakup (*of marriage, partnership*) hatan 破たん
breast (*of woman*) mune 胸
breastfeed *v/t* bonyū de sodateru 母乳で育てる
breaststroke hiraoyogi 平泳ぎ
breath hitoiki ひと息; ***be out of ~*** iki ga kireru 息が切れる; ***take a deep ~*** shinkokyū o suru 深呼吸をする
Breathalyzer®, breath analyzer inshu-kenchiki 飲酒検知器
breathe 1 *v/i* iki o suru 息をする **2** *v/t* (*inhale*) suu 吸う; (*exhale*) haku 吐く
♦**breathe in 1** *v/i* iki o suikomu 息を吸い込む **2** *v/t* … o suikomu …を吸い込む
♦**breathe out** *v/i* iki o haku 息を吐く
breathing kokyū 呼吸
breathless iki o kirashita 息を切らした
breathlessness ikigurushi-sa 息苦しさ
breathtaking iki o nomu yō (na) 息を飲むよう(な)
breed 1 *n* hinshu 品種 **2** *v/t* hanshoku saseru 繁殖させる; *fig* hikiokosu 引き起こす **3** *v/i* (*of animals*) hanshoku suru 繁殖する
breeding (*of animals*) hanshoku 繁殖
breeding ground *fig* onshō 温床
breeze soyokaze そよ風
brew 1 *v/t beer* jōzō suru 醸造する; *tea* ireru 入れる **2** *v/i* (*of storm*) okorō to shite iru 起ころうとしている; (*of trouble*) sematte iru 迫っている
brewer jōzō-gyōsha 醸造業者
brewery jōzōjo 醸造所
bribe 1 *n* wairo わいろ **2** *v/t* baishū suru 買収する
bribery oshoku 汚職
brick renga れんが
bricklayer renga-shokunin れんが職人
bride hanayome 花嫁
bridegroom hanamuko 花婿
bridesmaid hanayome-tsukisoi-nin 花嫁付添人
bridge[1] **1** *n* hashi 橋; (*of nose*) hanabashira 鼻柱; (*of ship*) buridji ブリッジ **2** *v/t gap* umeru うめる
bridge[2] (*card game*) buridji ブリッジ
brief[1] *adj* mijikai 短い
brief[2] **1** *n* (*mission*) ninmu 任務 **2** *v/t*: ***~ X on Y*** X ni Y ni tsuite no jōhō o ataeru XにYについての情報を与える
briefcase burīfukēsu ブリーフケース
briefing uchiawase 打ち合せ
briefly sukoshi no aida 少しの間; (*in a few words*) kantan ni 簡単に; (*to sum up*) kantan ni ieba 簡単に言えば
briefs (*for women*) shōtsu ショーツ; (*for men*) burīfu ブリーフ
bright *color, smile, future* akarui 明るい; (*sunny*) hareta 晴れた; (*intelligent*) rikō (na) 利口(な)
brighten (*of face, person*) akaruku naru 明るくなる
♦**brighten up 1** *v/t* … o akaruku suru …を明るくする **2** *v/i* (*of weather*) hareru 晴れる
brightly akaruku 明るく
brightness (*of weather*) hareyaka-sa 晴やかさ; (*of smile*) akaru-sa 明るさ; (*intelligence*) rikō-sa 利口さ
brilliance (*of person*) meiseki-sa 明せきさ; (*of color*) azayaka-sa 鮮やかさ
brilliant *sunshine* hikarikagayaku 光り輝く; *idea, performance* subarashii 素晴らしい; (*very intelligent*) yūshū (na) 優秀(な)
brim (*of container, hat*) fuchi ふち
brimful afurenbakari (no) あふれんばかり(の)
bring *object* motte kuru 持ってくる; *person* tsurete kuru 連れてくる; *peace, happiness etc* motarasu もたらす; ***~ it here, will you*** koko e motte kite kudasai ne ここへ持ってきて下さいね; ***can I ~ a friend?*** tomodachi o tsuretekite iidesu ka 友達を連れてきていいですか

♦**bring about** … o motarasu …をもたらす
♦**bring around** (*from a faint*) … no ishiki o kaifuku saseru …の意識を回復させる; (*persuade*) … o settoku suru …を説得する
♦**bring back** (*return*) … o kaesu …を返す; (*re-introduce*) … o fukkatsu saseru …を復活させる; *memories* … o omoidasaseru …を思い出させる; ***the song brought back memories of my childhood*** sono uta o kiku to kodomo no koro o omoidasu その歌を聞くと子どものころを思い出す
♦**bring down** *fence, tree* … o taosu …を倒す; *government* … o datō suru …を打倒する; *bird, airplane* … o uchiotosu …を撃ち落とす; *inflation, price* … o sageru …を下げる
♦**bring in** *interest, income* … o umu …を生む; (*earn*) … no kane ga hairu …の金が入る; *legislation* … o dōnyū suru …を導入する; *verdict* … o kudasu …を下す; (*involve*) … o sanka saseru …を参加させる
♦**bring out** (*produce: book*) … o shuppan suru …を出版する; *video, CD* … o rirīsu suru …をリリースする; *new product* … o happyō suru …を発表する
♦**bring to** (*from a faint*) … no ishiki o kaifuku saseru …の意識を回復させる
bring up *child* … o sodateru …を育てる; *subject* … o mochidasu …を持ち出す; (*vomit*) … o haku …を吐く
brink fuchi ふち; *fig* setogiwa 瀬戸際
brisk *person, voice, walk* kibikibi shita きびきびした; *trade* kappatsu (na) 活発(な)
bristles (*on chin*) bushōhige 不精ひげ; (*of brush*) ke 毛
bristling: ***be ~ with*** … de ippai de aru …でいっぱいである
Britain Eikoku, 英国, Igirisu イギリス
British 1 *adj* Eikoku (no) 英国(の), Igirisu (no) イギリス(の) **2** *n* ***the ~*** Eikoku-jin 英国人, Igirisu-jin イギリス人
Briton Eikoku-jin 英国人, Igirisu-jin イギリス人
brittle *adj* moroi もろい
broach *subject* kiridasu 切り出す
broad 1 *adj* hiroi 広い; (*general*) ōzappa (na) 大ざっぱ(な); ***in ~ daylight*** hakuchū ni 白昼に **2** *n* F (*woman*) onna 女
broadcast 1 *n* hōsō 放送 **2** *v/t* hōsō suru 放送する
broadcaster kyasutā キャスター
broadcasting hōsō 放送
broaden 1 *v/i* hiroku naru 広くなる **2** *v/t* hirogeru 広げる
broadjump habatobi 幅跳び
broadly: ***~ speaking*** ōzappa ni itte 大ざっぱに言って
broadminded kokoro no hiroi 心の広い
broccoli burokkori ブロッコリ
brochure panfuretto パンフレット
broil *v/t* yakiami de yaku 焼き網で焼く
broiler *n* (*on stove*) yakiami 焼き網; (*chicken*) wakadori 若鶏
broke F (*temporarily*) kinketsu (no) 金欠(の); (*long term*) ichimon-nashi (no) 一文なし(の); ***go ~*** (*bankrupt*) sukkarakan ni naru すっからかんになる
broken *adj* kowareta 壊れた; *glass, window* wareta 割れた; *neck, arm* kossetsu shita 骨折した; *home* hōkai shita 崩壊した; *marriage* hatan shita 破綻した; *English* burōkun (na) ブロークン(な)
broken-hearted kanashimi ni kureta 悲しみにくれた
broker (*stock~*) shōken-burōkā 証券ブローカー; (*insurance ~*) hoken-dairinin 保険代理人
bronchitis kikanshi-en 気管支炎
bronze *n* seidō 青銅; (*medal*) buronzu ブロンズ
brooch burōchi ブローチ
brood *v/i* (*of person*) kangaekomu 考え込む
broom hōki ほうき

broth (*soup*) sūpu スープ; (*stock*) niku no dashijiru 肉のだし汁
brothel baishun'yado 売春宿
brother (*own, elder*) ani 兄; (*somebody else's, elder*) onīsan お兄さん; (*own, younger*) otōto 弟; (*somebody else's, younger*) otōtosan 弟さん; ***they're ~s*** karera wa kyōdai desu 彼らは兄弟です; ***~s and sisters*** kyōdai-shimai 兄弟姉妹
brother-in-law (*own, elder*) giri no ani 義理の兄; (*somebody else's, elder*) giri no onīsan 義理のお兄さん; (*own, younger*) giri no otōto 義理の弟; (*somebody else's, younger*) giri no otōtosan 義理の弟さん; ***they're brothers-in-law*** karera wa giri no kyōdai desu 彼らは義理の兄弟です
brotherly kyōdai no yō (na) 兄弟のよう(な)
browbeat odoshitsukeru 脅しつける
brow (*forehead*) hitai 額; (*of hill*) ue 上
brown 1 *n* chairo 茶色 **2** *adj* chairo (no) 茶色(の); (*tanned*) hi ni yaketa 日に焼けた **3** *v/t* (*in cooking*) chairoku itameru 茶色く炒める **4** *v/i* (*in cooking*) chairo ni irozuku 茶色に色づく
brownbag: ***~ it*** F bentō o jisan suru 弁当を持参する
Brownie Buraunī ブラウニー
Brownie points: ***earn ~*** tensūkasegi o suru 点数かせぎをする
brownie (*cake*) buraunī ブラウニー
brown-nose *v/t* F … ni pekopeko suru …にぺこぺこする
browse (*in store*) busshoku suru 物色する; ***~ through a book*** hon o hiroiyomi suru 本を拾い読みする
browser COMPUT burauzā ブラウザー
bruise 1 *n* dabokushō 打撲症 **2** *v/t* aza o tsukeru あざをつける; *fruit* itameru 傷める **3** *v/i* (*of person*) aza ni naru あざになる; (*of fruit*) itamu 傷む
bruising *adj fig* tsurai つらい
brunch buranchi ブランチ
brunette burunetto ブルネット
brunt: ***bear the ~ of …*** … ni sarasareru …にさらされる
brush 1 *n* burashi ブラシ; (*for hair*) hea-burashi ヘアブラシ; (*for paint*) fude 筆; (*for teeth*) ha-burashi 歯ブラシ; (*conflict*) isakai いさかい **2** *v/t* burashi o kakeru ブラシをかける; (*touch lightly*) kasuru かする; (*move away*) harainokeru 払いのける
♦**brush against** … o kasuru …をかする
♦**brush aside** … o mushi suru …を無視する
♦**brush off** … o harainokeru …を払いのける; *criticism* … o mushi suru …を無視する
♦**brush up** … o yarinaosu …をやり直す
brushoff F kyozetsu 拒絶; ***get the ~*** kyozetsu sareru 拒絶される
brusque bukkirabō (na) ぶっきらぼう(な)
Brussels sprouts mekyabetsu 芽キャベツ
brutal zannin (na) 残忍(な)
brutality zannin-sa 残忍さ
brutally zankoku ni 残酷に; ***be ~ frank*** shōjiki ni iu to 正直に言うと
brute kedamono けだもの
brute force chikara 力; (*dispelling crowd*) bōryoku 暴力
bubble *n* awa 泡; (*soap ~*) shabondama しゃぼん玉
bubble gum fūsengamu 風船ガム
buck[1] *n* F (*dollar*) doru ドル
buck[2] *v/i* (*of horse*) haneagaru 跳ね上る
buck[3]: ***pass the ~*** sekinin-tenka o suru 責任転嫁をする
bucket *n* baketsu バケツ
buckle[1] **1** *n* bakkuru バックル **2** *v/t belt* … o bakkuru de shimeru …をバックルで締める
buckle[2] *v/i* (*of metal*) yugamu ゆがむ
bud *n* BOT tsubomi つぼみ
Buddha Budda 仏陀; ***Great ~*** daibutsu 大仏
Buddhism Bukkyō 仏教

Buddhist 1 *n* Bukkyōto 仏教徒 **2** *adj* Bukkyō (no) 仏教(の); **~ *altar*** butsudan 仏壇; **~ *monk*** bōzu 坊主; **~ *sutra*** okyō お経

buddy F aibō 相棒; ***hey ~, move your car, will you?*** anta, kuruma dokete kurenai あんた車どけてくれない

budge 1 *v/t* ugokasu 動かす; (*make reconsider*) … no iken o kaeru …の意見を変える **2** *v/i* ugoku 動く; (*change one's mind*) iken o kaeru 意見を変える

budgerigar sekiseiinko セキセイインコ

budget 1 *n* yosan 予算; (*of a family*) kakei 家計; ***be on a ~*** yosan ga aru 予算がある **2** *v/i* yosan o tateru 予算を立てる

♦**budget for** … o yosan ni ireru …を予算にいれる

buff[1] *adj* (*color*) usuchairo 薄茶色

buff[2] *n*: ***a movie / jazz ~*** eiga / jazu-kyō 映画 / ジャズ狂

buffalo baffarō バッファロー

buffer RAIL kanshōki 緩衝器; COMPUT kanshōkioku-sōchi 緩衝記憶装置; *fig* hashiwatashi 橋渡し

buffet[1] *n* (*meal*) risshoku 立食

buffet[2] *v/t* (*of wind*) … ni uchitsukeru …に打ちつける

bug 1 *n* (*insect*) mushi 虫; (*virus*) baikin ばい菌; (*spying device*) tōchōki 盗聴器; COMPUT bagu バグ **2** *v/t room, telephone* … ni tōchōki o shikakeru …に盗聴器を仕掛ける; F (*annoy*) iraira saseru いらいらさせる

buggy (*for baby*) ubaguruma 乳母車

build 1 *n* (*of person*) taikaku 体格 **2** *v/t* tateru 建てる

♦**build up 1** *v/t strength* … o tsukeru …をつける; *relationship* … o kizukiageru …を築き上げる; *collection* … o fuyashite iku …を増やしていく **2** *v/i* masu 増す

builder kenchiku-gyōsha 建築業者

building kensetsu 建設; (*house, office block etc*) tatemono 建物, birudingu ビルディング

building site kensetsu-genba 建設現場

building trade kensetsugyō 建設業

build-up (*accumulation*) chikuseki 蓄積; (*publicity*) senden 宣伝

built-in tsukuritsuke (no) 作り付け(の); *flash* naizō (no) 内蔵(の)

built-up area jūtakugai 住宅街

bulb BOT kyūkon 球根; (*light ~*) denkyū 電球

bulge 1 *n* fukurami 膨らみ; (*bigger and noticeable*) deppari 出っ張り **2** *v/i* (*of pocket*) fukureru 膨れる; (*of wall, eyes*) depparu 出っ張る

bulk daibubun 大部分; ***in ~*** tairyō ni 大量に

bulky kasabatta かさばった

bull (*animal*) oushi 雄牛

bulldoze (*demolish*) burudōzā de sarachi ni suru ブルドーザーでさら地にする; ***~ X into Y*** *fig* X ni Y o gorioshi suru XにYをごり押しする

bulldozer burudōzā ブルドーザー

bullet tama 弾

bulletin kōhō 公報

bulletin board *also* COMPUT keijiban 掲示版

bullet-proof bōdan (no) 防弾(の)

bullet train (*in Japan*) shinkansen 新幹線

bull market FIN agesōba 上げ相場

bull's-eye mato no chūshin 的の中心; ***hit the ~*** tekichū suru 的中する

bullshit V **1** *n* tawagoto たわごと **2** *v/i* detarame o iu でたらめを言う

bully 1 *n* yowaimono-ijime suru hito 弱い者いじめする人; (*child*) ijimekko いじめっ子 **2** *v/t* ijimeru いじめる

bum 1 *n* F (*tramp*) furō-sha 浮浪者; (*worthless person*) yōnashi 用無し **2** *adj* (*useless*) yaku ni tatanai 役に立たない **3** *v/t cigarette etc* takaru たかる

♦**bum around** F (*travel*) burabura tabi o suru ぶらぶら旅をする; (*be lazy*) bōtto shite sugosu ぼーっとして過ごす

bumblebee maruhanabachi まるはなばち

bump 1 *n* (*swelling*) kobu こぶ; (*in road*) dansa 段差; ***get a ~ on the head*** atama o butsukeru 頭をぶつける **2** *v/t* butsukeru ぶつける

♦**bump into** *table* … ni butsukaru …にぶつかる; (*meet*) … ni hyokkori au …にひょっこり会う

♦**bump off** F … o korosu …を殺す

♦**bump up** F *prices* … o ageru …を上げる

bumper *n* MOT banpā バンパー

bumpy dekoboko (na) でこぼこ(な)

bun (*hairstyle*) shiniyon シニヨン; (*for eating*) marupan 丸パン

bunch (*of people*) gurūpu グループ; ***a ~ of flowers*** hanataba 花束; ***a ~ of grapes*** hitofusa no budō 一房のぶどう; ***thanks a ~*** (*ironic*) sore wa dōmo それはどうも

bundle (*of clothes*) tsutsumi 包み; (*of wood*) taba 束

♦**bundle up** *v/t* … o hitomatome ni suru …をひとまとめにする; (*dress warmly*) … o atsugi saseru …を厚着させる

bungle *v/t* shikujiru しくじる

bunk shindai 寝台

bunk beds nidan-beddo 二段ベッド

buoy *n* bui ブイ

buoyant ukiuki shita 浮き浮きした; *economy* kakki no aru 活気のある

burden 1 *n* omoni 重荷; *fig* futan 負担 **2** *v/t*: ***~ X with Y*** Y de X o nayamasu YでXを悩ます

bureau (*chest of drawers*) tansu たんす; (*government department*) kyoku 局; (*office*) ka 課

bureaucracy (*red tape*) kanryō-shugi 官僚主義; (*system*) kanryō 官僚

bureaucrat kanryō 官僚

bureaucratic kanryōteki (na) 官僚的(な)

burger hanbāgā ハンバーガー

burglar gōtō 強盗

burglar alarm tōnan-hōchiki 盗難報知機

burglarize gōtō suru 強盗する

burglary gōtō 強盗

burial maisō 埋葬

burly takumashii たくましい

Burma Biruma ビルマ, Myanmā ミャンマー

Burmese 1 *adj* Biruma (no) ビルマ(の), Myanmā (no) ミャンマー(の) **2** *n* (*person*) Biruma-jin ビルマ人, Myanmā-jin ミャンマー人

burn 1 *n* yakekoge 焼け焦げ; (*on finger etc*) yakedo やけど **2** *v/t* moyasu 燃やす; *toast, meat* kogasu 焦がす; *finger, tongue etc* yakedo suru やけどする; (*consume*) moyasu 燃やす **3** *v/i* moeru 燃える; (*of house*) yakeru 焼ける; (*of toast*) kogeru 焦げる; (*get sunburnt*) hi ni yakeru 日に焼ける

♦**burn down 1** *v/t* yakitsukusu 焼き尽くす **2** *v/i* zenshō suru 全焼する

♦**burn out** *v/t*: ***burn oneself out*** seiryoku o tsukaihatasu 精力を使い果たす; ***a burned-out car*** yaketa kuruma 焼けた車

burner (*on cooker*) konro コンロ

burp 1 *n* geppu げっぷ **2** *v/i* geppu suru げっぷする **3** *v/t baby* geppu saseru げっぷさせる

burst 1 *n* (*in water pipe*) haretsu 破裂; (*of gunfire*) rensha 連射; ***in a ~ of energy*** yaruki ga waite やる気がわいて **2** *adj tire* haretsu shita 破裂した **3** *v/t balloon* haretsu saseru 破裂させる **4** *v/i* (*of balloon, tire*) haretsu suru 破裂する; ***~ into a room*** heya ni tobikomu 部屋に飛び込む; ***~ into tears*** watto nakidasu わっと泣き出す; ***~ out laughing*** kyū ni waraidasu 急に笑い出す

bury *person* maisō suru 埋葬する; *animal* umeru 埋める; (*conceal*) umete kakusu 埋めて隠す; ***be buried under*** (*covered by*) … no shita ni umatte iru …の下に埋まっている; ***~ oneself in one's work*** shigoto ni bottō suru 仕事に没頭する

bus 1 *n* basu バス **2** *v/t* basu de idō saseru バスで移動させる

busboy shokudō-kyūji no joshu 食堂給仕の助手

bush (*plant*) shigemi 茂み; (*land*) mikai no chi 未開の地

bushed F (*tired*) kutakuta (no) くたくた(の)

bushy *beard* mojamoja (no) もじゃもじゃ(の)

business (*trade*) shōbai 商売; (*company*) kaisha 会社; (*work*) shigoto 仕事; (*sector*) shokugyō 職業; (*affair, matter*) koto 事; (*as subject of study*) keieigaku 経営学; ***on ~*** shigoto de 仕事で; ***that's none of your ~!, mind your own ~!*** ōkina osewa da 大きなお世話だ

business card meishi 名刺; **business class** bijinesu-kurasu ビジネスクラス; **business hours** eigyō-jikan 営業時間; **businesslike** jissaiteki (na) 実際的(な); **business lunch** bijinesu-ranchi ビジネスランチ; **businessman** jitsugyōka 実業家; **business meeting** kaigō 会合; **business school** keieigaku-daigakuin 経営学大学院; **business studies** keieigaku 経営学; **business suit** sūtsu スーツ, sebiro 背広; **business trip** shutchō 出張; **businesswoman** josei-jitsugyōka 女性実業家

bus station basu-tāminaru バスターミナル

bus stop basutei バス停

bust[1] *n* (*of woman*) basuto バスト

bust[2] F **1** *adj* (*broken*) tsubureta つぶれた; ***go ~*** hasan suru 破産する **2** *v/t* haretsu saseru 破裂させる

♦**bustle around** sewashinaku ugokimawaru せわしなく動き回る

bust-up F hakyoku 破局

busty guramā (na) グラマー(な)

busy 1 *adj* isogashii 忙しい; *street* nigiyaka (na) にぎやか(な); *shop, restaurant*: *making money*) hanjō shite iru 繁盛している; (*full of people*) konde iru 混んでいる; TELEC hanashichū (no) 話中(の); ***be ~ doing ...*** ... shite ite isogashii ...していて忙しい **2** *v/t*: ***~ oneself with*** ... de isogashii ...で忙しい

busybody osekkai na hito おせっかいな人

busy signal hanashichū no oto 話中の音

but 1 *conj* keredomo けれども; ***I tried, ~ I couldn't*** tameshite mita keredomo dekinakatta 試してみたけれどもできなかった; ***~ that's not fair!*** demo sore wa fukōhei da でもそれは不公平だ; ***it's not me ~ my father you want*** hitsuyō na no wa watashi de wa naku chichi desu 必要なのは私ではなく父です; ***~ then (again)*** shikashi しかし **2** *prep*: ***all ~ him*** kare o nozoite 彼をのぞいて; ***the last ~ one*** saigo kara nibanme 最後から二番目; ***the next ~ one*** tsugi no tsugi 次の次; ***~ for you*** kimi ga inakattara 君がいなかったら; ***nothing ~ the best*** saikō no mono dake 最高のものだけ; ***nothing ~ problems*** mondai bakari 問題ばかり

butcher *n* niku-ya 肉屋; (*murderer*) satsujinki 殺人鬼

butt 1 *n* (*of cigarette*) suigara 吸い殻; (*of joke*) mato 的; F (*buttocks*) shiri 尻 **2** *v/t* atama de tsuku 頭で突く; (*of goat, bull*) tsuno de tsuku 角で突く

♦**butt in** ... ni kuchi o hasamu ...に口をはさむ

butter 1 *n* batā バター **2** *v/t* ... ni batā o nuru ...にバターを塗る

♦**butter up** F ... ni hetsurau ...にへつらう

buttercup kinpōge きんぽうげ

butterfly (*insect*) chō ちょう

buttocks shiri 尻

button 1 *n* botan ボタン; (*on machine*) oshi-botan 押しボタン; (*badge*) badji バッジ **2** *v/t* botan o tomeru ボタンを留める

buttonhole 1 *n* (*in suit*) botanhōru ボタンホール **2** *v/t* hikitomete hanasu 引きとめて話す

buxom nikuzuki no yoi 肉づきのよい

buy 1 *n* kaimono 買い物 **2** *v/t* kau 買う; ***can I ~ you a drink?*** ippai ogorasete kudasai 一杯おごらせてください; ***$50 doesn't ~ much*** gojū doru de wa amari kaenai 50ドルではあまり買えない

♦**buy off** (*bribe*) ... o baishū suru ...

を買収する
♦**buy out** COM … o kaitoru …を買い取る
♦**buy up** … o kaishimeru …を買い占める
buyer kaite 買い手; (*for store*) shiiregakari 仕入れ係; (*for luxury goods*) baiyā バイヤー
buzz 1 *n* bunbun iu oto ぶんぶんいう音; F (*thrill*) kōfun 興奮 **2** *v/i* (*of insect*) bunbun iu ぶんぶんいう; (*with buzzer*) buzā o narasu ブザーを鳴らす **3** *v/t* (*with buzzer*) buzā de yobu ブザーで呼ぶ
♦**buzz off**: **~!** F dete ike 出て行け
buzzer buzā ブザー
by 1 *prep* ◊ (*agency*) … ni …に; ***she was knocked down ~ a bus*** kanojo wa basu ni hikareta 彼女はバスにひかれた; ***a painting ~ Picasso*** Pikaso no e ピカソの絵; ***a play ~ …*** … no kaita shibai …の書いた芝居 ◊ (*near, next to*) … no soba ni …のそばに; ***~ the window*** mado no soba ni 窓のそばに ◊ (*past*) soba o tōri sugite そばを通り過ぎて; ***we drove ~ the church*** ◊ (*mode of transport*) … de …で; ***~ bus / train*** basu / densha de バス/電車で ◊ (*no later than*) … made ni …までに; ***~ Friday*** kin'yōbi made ni 金曜日までに; ***~ 9 o'clock*** kuji made ni 九時までに; ***~ this time tomorrow*** ashita no kono jikan ni wa 明日のこの時間には ◊ (*during*): ***~ day / ~ night*** nitchū / yorujū 日中/夜中 ◊ (*according to*): ***~ my watch*** watashi no tokei de wa 私の時計では ◊ (*measuring*): ***~ the hour / ton*** jikan / ton tan'i de 時間/トン単位で; ***~ a couple of minutes*** ni, sanpun no sa de ２、３分の差で; ***2 ~ 4*** ni kakeru yon ２掛ける４ ◊: ***~ oneself*** hitori de ひとりで **2** *adv*: ***~ and ~*** yagate やがて
bye(-bye) baibai バイバイ
bygone: ***let ~s be ~s*** sugita koto wa mizu ni nagase 過ぎたことは水に流せ
bypass 1 *n* (*road*) baipasu バイパス; MED baipasu バイパス **2** *v/t* ukai suru う回する
by-product fukusanbutsu 副産物
bystander yaji umatachi やじ馬たち
byte baito バイト

C

cab (*taxi*) takushī タクシー; (*of truck*) untendai 運転台
cabaret furoā-shō フロアーショー
cabbage kyabetsu キャベツ
cab driver takushī-doraibā タクシードライバー
cabin (*of plane, ship*) kyakushitsu 客室
cabin crew kyakushitsu-gakari 客室係
cabinet todana 戸棚; POL naikaku 内閣
cable (*of electrical appliance, telephone*) kōdo コード; (*for securing*) tsuna 綱; **~ (*TV*)** kēburu-terebi ケーブルテレビ
cable car kēburu-kā ケーブルカー;
cable television kēburu-terebi ケーブルテレビ; **cab stand** takushī noriba タクシー乗り場
cactus saboten さぼてん
cadaver shitai 死体
CAD-CAM kyado-kyamu キャド-キャム
caddie 1 *n* (*in golf*) kyadī キャディー **2** *v/i*: ***~ for*** … no kyadī o suru …のキャディーをする
cadet shikan-gakkō-seito 士官学校

生徒

cadge: ~ ***X from Y*** Y ni X o takaru YにXをたかる

café kafe カフェ

cafeteria kafeteria カフェテリア

caffeine kafein カフェイン

cage (*for bird*) kago かご; (*for lion*) ori おり

cagey keikai shite iru 警戒している

cahoots: ***be in ~ with*** … to guru ni natte iru …とぐるになっている

cake 1 *n* kēki ケーキ; ***be a piece of ~*** *fig* asameshimae desu 朝飯前です **2** *v/i* katamaru 固まる

calcium karushiumu カルシウム

calculate (*work out*) mitsumoru 見積もる; (*in arithmetic*) keisan suru 計算する

calculating dasanteki (na) 打算的(な)

calculation keisan 計算

calculator dentaku 電卓

calendar karendā カレンダー

calf[1] (*young cow*) koushi 子牛

calf[2] (*of leg*) fukurahagi ふくらはぎ

caliber (*of gun*) kōkei 口径; ***a man of his ~*** sugoude no hito すご腕の人

call 1 *n* TELEC denwa 電話; (*shout*) koe 声; (*demand*) yōkyū 要求; ***there's a ~ for you*** anata ni denwa desu あなたに電話です **2** *v/t* (*on phone*) … ni denwa o suru …に電話をする; (*summon*) shōshū suru 招集する; (*shout*) yobu 呼ぶ; ***he ~ed me a liar*** kare wa watashi o usotsuki da to itta 彼は私をうそつきだと言った; ***what have they ~ed the baby?*** karera wa akanbō o nan to nazukemashita ka 彼らは赤ん坊を何と名付けましたか; ***but we ~ him Tom*** dakedo watashitachi wa kare o Tomu to yonde imasu だけど私たちは彼をトムと呼んでいます; ***~ … names*** … o nonoshiru …をののしる **3** *v/i* (*on phone*) denwa o kakeru 電話をかける; (*shout*) yobu 呼ぶ; (*visit*) tachiyoru 立ち寄る

♦**call at** (*stop at*) … ni chotto tachiyoru …にちょっと立ち寄る; (*of train*) … ni teisha suru …に停車する

♦**call back 1** *v/t* (*on phone*) … ni orikaeshi denwa suru …に折り返し電話する; (*summon*) … o yobimodosu …を呼び戻す **2** *v/i* (*on phone*) denwa o kakenaosu 電話をかけ直す; (*make another visit*) ato de mata tachiyoru あとでまた立ち寄る

♦**call for** (*collect*) … o tori ni tachiyoru …を取りに立ち寄る; (*demand*) … o yōkyū suru …を要求する; (*require*) … o hitsuyō to suru …を必要とする

♦**call in 1** *v/t* (*summon*) … o yobiireru …を呼び入れる **2** *v/i* (*phone*) denwa o ireru 電話を入れる

♦**call off** (*cancel*) … o toriyameru …を取り止める

♦**call on** (*urge*) … ni yōkyū suru …に要求する; (*visit*) … o hōmon suru …を訪問する

♦**call out** (*shout*) ōgoe de yobu 大声で呼ぶ; (*summon*) … o shōshū suru …を招集する

♦**call up** *v/t* (*on phone*) … ni denwa o kakeru …に電話をかける; COMPUT … o konpyūtā de yobidasu …をコンピューターで呼び出す

caller (*on phone*) denwa o kaketa hito 電話をかけた人; (*visitor*) hōmon-sha 訪問者

call girl baishunfu 売春婦

calligraphy shodō 書道

callous reitan (na) 冷淡(な)

calm 1 *adj sea* odayaka (na) 穏やか(な); *person* ochitsuita 落ち着いた **2** *n* (*of countryside*) shizuke-sa 静けさ; (*of person*) heisei 平静 **3** *v/t* shizumeru 静める

♦**calm down 1** *v/t* … o shizumeru …を静める **2** *v/i* (*of sea, wind*) shizuka ni naru 静かになる; (*of person*) ochitsuku 落ち着く

calorie karorī カロリー

Cambodia Kanbojia カンボジア

Cambodian 1 *adj* Kanbojia (no) カンボジア(の) **2** *n* (*person*) Kanbojia-jin カンボジア人

camcorder bideo-kamera ビデオカメラ

camellia tsubaki つばき
camera kamera カメラ
cameraman kameraman カメラマン
camouflage 1 *n* kamufurāju カムフラージュ **2** *v/t* kamufurāju suru カムフラージュする
camp 1 *n* kyanpu キャンプ **2** *v/i* kyanpu suru キャンプする
campaign 1 *n* undō 運動 **2** *v/i* undō o okosu 運動を起こす
campaigner undō-ka 運動家
camper (*person*) kyanpu o suru hito キャンプをする人; (*vehicle*) kyanpingu-kā キャンピングカー
camp ground kyanpu-jō キャンプ場
camping kyanpu キャンプ
campsite kyanpu-jō キャンプ場
campus kōnai 構内, kyanpasu キャンパス
can[1] ◊ (*ability*) … koto ga dekiru … ことができる; ***I ~ use a computer*** konpyūtā o tsukau koto ga dekiru コンピューターを使うことができる; ***~ you hear me?*** kikoemasu ka 聞こえますか; ***I ~'t see*** mienai 見えない; ***~ you speak French?*** Furansu-go ga hanasemasu ka フランス語が話せますか; ***I ~'t speak French*** Furansu-go ga hanasemasen フランス語が話せません; ***as fast as you ~*** dekiru dake hayaku できるだけ速く ◊ (*request*) … te mo ii desu ka … てもいいですか; ***~ he call me back?*** kare ni denwa o kakenaoshite morattemo ii desu ka 彼に電話をかけなおしてもらってもいいですか; ***~ you help me?*** tetsudatte morattemo ii desu ka 手伝ってもらってもいいですか; ***~ I have a beer / coffee?*** bīru / kōhī o itadaitemo ii desu ka ビール/コーヒーをいただいてもいいですか ◊ (*permission*) … te mo ii desu ka … てもいいですか; ***~ I borrow the car?*** kuruma o karite mo ii desu ka 車を借りてもいいですか ◊ (*prohibition*): ***~not*** … te wa ikenai … てはいけない; ***you ~not stay without a visa*** vizanashi de taizai shite wa ikenai ビザなしで滞在してはいけない ◊ (*offer*): ***~ I help you?*** nanika otetsudai shimashō ka 何かお手伝いしましょうか ◊ (*disbelief*): ***that ~'t be right*** sore wa machigatte iru ni chigainai それは間違っているに違いない
can[2] **1** *n* (*for drinks etc*) kan 缶 **2** *v/t* kanzume ni suru 缶詰にする
Canada Kanada カナダ
Canadian 1 *adj* Kanada (no) カナダ(の) **2** *n* Kanada-jin カナダ人
canal (*waterway*) unga 運河
canary kanaria カナリア
cancel torikesu 取り消す
cancellation torikeshi 取り消し
cancer gan がん
c & f (= ***cost and freight***) unchin-komi kakaku 運賃込み価格
c & i (= ***cost and insurance***) hokenryō-komi kakaku 保険料込み価格
candid sotchoku (na) 率直(な)
candidacy rikkōho 立候補
candidate (*for position*) kōho-sha 候補者; (*in exam*) juken-sha 受験者
candle rōsoku ろうそく
candlestick rōsokutate ろうそく立て
candor sotchoku-sa 率直さ
candy kyandī キャンディー
cannabis taima 大麻
canned *fruit, tomatoes* kanzume (no) 缶詰(の); (*recorded*) rokuon sareta 録音された
cannibalize bunkai suru 分解する
cannot → ***can***[1]
canoe kanū カヌー
can opener kankiri 缶切り
cant tatemae 建て前
can't → ***can***[1]
canteen (*in factory*) shokudō 食堂
canvas (*for painting*) kyanbasu キャンバス; (*material*) kyanbasu-ji キャンバス地
canvass 1 *v/t* (*seek opinion of*) … no iken o kiku … の意見を聴く **2** *v/i* POL senkyo-undō o suru 選挙運動をする
canyon kyōkoku 峡谷

cap (*hat*) bōshi 帽子; (*of bottle, jar*) futa ふた; (*of pen, lens ~*) kyappu キャップ
capability (*of person*) nōryoku 能力; (*of military*) senryoku 戦力
capable (*efficient*) yūnō (na) 有能(な); ***be ~ of*** … ga dekiru …ができる
capacity (*of container*) yōseki 容積; (*of building*) shūyōryoku 収容力; (*of elevator*) teiin 定員; (*of car engine*) haikiryō 排気量; (*of factory*) seisanryoku 生産力; (*ability*) nōryoku 能力; ***in my ~ as …*** … no shikaku de …の資格で
cape (*land*) misaki 岬
capital *n* (*of country*) shuto 首都; (*letter*) ōmoji 大文字; (*money*) shihon 資本
capital expenditure shihon-shishutsu 資本支出; **capital gains tax** kyapitarugein-zei キャピタルゲイン税; **capital growth** shihon-seichō 資本成長
capitalism shihon-shugi 資本主義
capitalist 1 *adj* shihon-shugi (no) 資本主義(の) **2** *n* shihon-shugisha 資本主義者; (*businessman*) shihon-ka 資本家
capital letter ōmoji 大文字
capital punishment shikei 死刑
capitulate kōfuku suru 降伏する
capsize 1 *v/i* hikkurikaesu ひっくり返る **2** *v/t* hikkurikaesu ひっくり返す
capsule (*of medicine*) kapuseru カプセル; (*space ~*) roketto no kapuseru ロケットのカプセル
captain *n* (*of ship*) senchō 船長; (*of aircraft*) kichō 機長; (*of team*) kyaputen キャプテン
caption *n* setsumeibun 説明文
captivate miryō suru 魅了する
captive horyo 捕虜
captivity toraware no mi とらわれの身
capture 1 *n* (*of city*) senkyo 占拠; (*of criminal*) taiho 逮捕; (*of animal*) hokaku 捕獲 **2** *v/t person, animal* tsukamaeru 捕まえる; *city, building* kōryaku suru 攻略する; *market share* kakutoku suru 獲得する; (*portray*) toraeru 捕らえる
car kuruma 車; (*of train*) sharyō 車両; ***by ~*** kuruma de 車で
carafe (*for wine*) karafu カラフ
carat karatto カラット
carbohydrate denpunshitsu でんぷん質, tansuika-butsu 炭水化物
carbonated tansan'iri (no) 炭酸入り(の)
carbon monoxide issanka-tanso 一酸化炭素
carbureter, **carburetor** kyaburetā キャブレター
carcinogen hatsugansei-busshitsu 発がん性物質
carcinogenic hatsugansei (no) 発がん性(の)
card (*to mark special occasion*) kādo カード; (*post~*) hagaki 葉書; (*business ~*) meishi 名刺; (*playing ~*) toranpu トランプ
cardboard bōrugami ボール紙
cardiac shinzō (no) 心臓(の)
cardiac arrest shinzō-teishi 心臓停止
cardigan kādigan カーディガン
card index kādoshiki-sakuin カード式索引
card key kādoshiki no kagi カード式のかぎ
care 1 *n* (*of baby, pet*) sewa 世話; (*of the elderly*) kaigo 介護; (*of sick person*) kango 看護; (*medical ~*) iryō 医療; (*worry*) nayami 悩み; ***~ of …*** … kata …方, … kizuke …気付; ***take ~*** (*be cautious*) ki o tsukeru 気をつける; ***take ~ (of yourself)!*** (*goodbye*) ki o tsukete 気をつけて; ***take ~ of*** *baby, dog* … no sewa o suru …の世話をする; *tools, house, garden* … no teire o suru …の手入れをする; (*deal with*) … o shori suru …を処理する; (***handle***) ***with ~!*** (*on label*) toriatsukai-chūi 取り扱い注意 **2** *v/i* ki ni kakeru 気にかける; ***I don't ~!*** kamau mono ka かまうものか; ***I couldn't ~ less*** zenzen ki ni shinai 全然気にしない
♦ **care about** … ni kanshin ga aru …

に関心がある
♦ **care for** (*look after*) … no sewa o suru …の世話をする; (*like, be fond of*) … ga suki de aru …が好きである; ***would you ~ …?*** … ga hoshii desu ka …が欲しいですか
career (*profession*) shokugyō 職業; (*path through life*) kyaria キャリア
carefree nonbiri shita のんびりした
careful (*cautious*) chūibukai 注意深い; (*thorough*) nen'iri (na) 念入り(な); (***be***) ***~!*** ki o tsukete 気をつけて
carefully (*with caution*) shinchō ni 慎重に; *worded etc* nen'iri ni 念入りに
careless fuchūi (na) 不注意(な); ***you are so ~!*** anata mo zuibun ukkari shite imasu ne あなたもずいぶんうっかりしていますね
caress **1** *n* naderu koto なでること **2** *v/t* naderu なでる
caretaker kanri-nin 管理人
careworn yatsureta やつれた
cargo tsumini 積み荷
caricature *n* fūshi-manga 風刺漫画
caring *adj* omoiyari no aru 思いやりのある
carnage daigyakusatsu 大虐殺
carnation kānēshon カーネーション
carnival idō-yūenchi 移動遊園地; (*festival*) kānibaru カーニバル
carol *n* kurisumasu-kyaroru クリスマスキャロル
carousel (*at airport*) enkei-beruto-konbeyā 円形ベルトコンベヤー; (*for slide projector*) enkei-suraido-torē 円形スライドトレー; (*merry-go-round*) merī-gōraundo メリーゴーラウンド
carpenter daiku 大工
carpet kāpetto カーペット
carpool **1** *n* ainori-hōshiki 相乗り方式 **2** *v/i* ainori suru 相乗りする
car port chūshajō 駐車場
carrier (*company*) un'yu-gyōsha 運輸業者; (*of disease*) hokin-sha 保菌者
carrot ninjin にんじん; ***~ and stick*** ame to muchi あめとムチ
carry **1** *v/t* (*of person: in hand*) mochihakobu 持ち運ぶ; (*from one place to another*) hakobu 運ぶ; (*have on one's person*) mochiaruku 持ち歩く; (*of pregnant woman*) migomotte iru 身ごもっている; *disease* kin o motte iru 菌を持っている; (*of ship, plane, bus etc*) noseru 乗せる; *proposal* kaketsu suru 可決する; ***get carried away*** muchū ni naru 夢中になる **2** *v/i* (*of sound*) tsutawaru 伝わる
♦ **carry on** **1** *v/i* (*continue*) tsuzukeru 続ける; (*make a fuss*) sawagitateru 騒ぎ立てる; (*have an affair*) uwaki suru 浮気する **2** *v/t* (*conduct*) … o tsuzukeru …を続ける
♦ **carry out** *survey etc* … o okonau …を行う; *orders etc* … o jikkō suru …を実行する
car seat (*for child*) chairudo-shīto チャイルドシート
cart niguruma 荷車
cartel karuteru カルテル
carton (*for storage, transport*) hako 箱; (*for milk, eggs, cigarettes etc*) pakku パック
cartoon (*in newspaper, magazine*) manga 漫画; (*on TV, movie*) anime アニメ
cartridge (*for gun*) kātoridji カートリッジ
carve *meat* kiriwakeru 切り分ける; *wood* chōkoku suru 彫刻する
carving (*figure*) horimono 彫り物
car wash sensha 洗車
case[1] (*container*) kēsu ケース; (*of Scotch, wine*) hitohako ひと箱; *Br* (*suitcase*) sūtsu-kēsu スーツケース
case[2] *n* (*instance*) rei 例; (*situation*) ba-ai 場合; (*argument*) shuchō 主張; (*for police etc*) jiken 事件; MED shōrei 症例; LAW hanrei 判例; ***in ~ …*** moshi … no ba-ai ni sonaete もし…の場合に備えて; ***in any ~*** tonikaku とにかく; ***in that ~*** sore nara それなら
case history MED byōreki 病歴
cash **1** *n* genkin 現金; ***~ down*** sokkin de harau 即金で払う; ***pay*** (***in***) ***~***

genkin de shiharau 現金で支払う; **~ *in advance*** maebarai de 前払いで **2** *v/t check* genkinka suru 現金化する

♦ **cash in on** … ni tsukekomu …につけ込む

cash cow kane no naru ki 金のなる木; **cash desk** reji レジ; **cash discount** genkin-waribiki 現金割引; **cash flow** kyasshu-furō キャッシュフロー

cashier *n* (*in store etc*) reji-gakari レジ係

cash machine genkin-jidō-shiharaiki 現金自動支払機, ATM (*always in romaji*)

cashmere *adj* kashimiya (no) カシミヤ(の)

cash register rejisutā レジスター

casino kajino カジノ

casket (*coffin*) hitsugi ひつぎ

cassette kasetto カセット

cassette player kasetto-pureiyā カセットプレイヤー

cassette recorder kasetto-rekōdā カセットレコーダー

cast 1 *n* (*of play*) shutsuen-sha 出演者; (*mold*) igata 鋳型 **2** *v/t doubt, suspicion* nagekakeru 投げかける; *metal* chūzō suru 鋳造する; *play* haiyaku suru 配役する; *actor* yaku o wariateru 役を割り当てる

♦ **cast off** *v/i* (*of ship*) nawa o toku 綱を解く

caste kāsuto カースト

caster (*on chair etc*) kyasutā キャスター

cast iron *n* chūtetsu 鋳鉄

cast-iron chūtetsu (no) 鋳鉄(の)

castle shiro 城

castor → ***caster***

castor oil himashiyu ひまし油

castrate kyosei suru 去勢する

casual (*chance*) nanigenai 何気ない; (*offhand*) mutonchaku (na) むとんちゃく(な); (*not formal*) kajuaru (na) カジュアル(な), fudangi (no) 普段着(の); (*not permanent*) rinji (no) 臨時(の)

casualty shishō-sha 死傷者

casual wear kajuaru-wea カジュアルウェア, fudangi 普段着

cat neko 猫

catalog *n* katarogu カタログ

catalyst *fig* shokubai 触媒

catalytic converter shokubai-konbātā 触媒コンバーター

catastrophe daisaigai 大災害

catch 1 *n* hokyū 捕球; (*of fish*) shūkaku 収穫; (*locking device*) tomegane 留め金; (*problem*) otoshiana 落し穴 **2** *v/t ball, escaped prisoner* tsukamaeru 捕まえる; (*get on: bus, train*) … ni noru …に乗る; (*not miss: bus, train*) … ni ma ni au …に間に合う; *fish with rod* tsuru 釣る; *fish with net* toru 捕る; (*in order to speak to*) tsukamaeru 捕まえる; (*hear*) kikitoru 聞き取る; *illness* … ni kakaru …にかかる; **~ (*a*) *cold*** kaze o hiku 風邪を引く; **~ *X's eye*** (*of person, object*) X no chūi o hiku Xの注意を引く; **~ *sight of*** … o miru …を見る; **~ *X doing Y*** X ga Y shite iru tokoro o mitsukeru XがYしているところを見つける

♦ **catch on** (*become popular*) ninki o haku suru 人気を博する; (*understand*) wakaru わかる

♦ **catch up** *v/i* oitsuku 追いつく

♦ **catch up on** … no okure o torimodosu …の遅れを取り戻す

catch-22 ***it's a ~ situation*** dōshiyōmonai jōkyō de aru どうしようもない状況である

catcher (*in baseball*) kyatchā キャッチャー

catching *disease* densensei (no) 伝染性(の); *fear, panic* utsuru 移る

catchy *tune* oboeyasui 覚えやすい

category burui 部類

♦ **cater for** (*meet the needs of*) … no yōkyū o mitasu …の要求を満たす; (*provide food for*) … no shidashi o suru …の仕出しをする

caterer shidashi-gyōsha 仕出し業者

caterpillar kemushi 毛虫

cathedral daiseidō 大聖堂

Catholic 1 *adj* Katorikku (no) カトリック(の) **2** *n* Katorikku-kyōto カトリック教徒

catsup kechappu ケチャップ
cattle ushi 牛
catty ijiwaru (na) 意地悪(な)
cauliflower karifurawā カリフラワー
cause 1 *n* gen'in 原因; (*grounds*) konkyo 根拠; (*aim of movement*) shuchō 主張 **2** *v/t* hikiokosu 引き起こす
caution 1 *n* (*carefulness*) yōjin 用心; **~ *is advised*** gochūi negaimasu 御注意願います **2** *v/t* (*warn*) keikoku suru 警告する
cautious shinchō (na) 慎重(な)
cave hora-ana 洞穴
♦ **cave in** (*of roof*) kanbotsu 陥没
caviar kyabia キャビア
cavity mushiba 虫歯
cc 1 *n* kopī-haifusaki コピー配布先 **2** *v/t* … no kopī o okuru …のコピーを送る
CD (= ***compact disc***) shī-dī ＣＤ
CD-ROM shīdī-romu ＣＤロム
CD-ROM drive shīdī-romu-doraibu ＣＤロムドライブ
cease 1 *v/i* owaru 終わる **2** *v/t* oeru 終える
cease-fire teisen 停戦
cedar: ***Japanese ~*** sugi 杉
ceiling tenjō 天井; (*limit*) saikō-gendo 最高限度
celebrate *v/t & v/t* iwau 祝う
celebrated yūmei (na) 有名(な); ***be ~ for*** … de yūmei de aru …で有名である
celebration oiwai お祝い
celebrity yūmei-jin 有名人
celery serori セロリ
cell (*for prisoner*) dokubō 独房; BIO saibō 細胞
cello chero チェロ
cellophane serohan セロハン
cell(ular) phone keitai-denwa 携帯電話
cement 1 *n* semento セメント **2** *v/t* setsugō suru 接合する; *friendship* katameru 固める
cemetery bochi 墓地
censor *v/t* ken'etsu suru 検閲する
censorship ken'etsu 検閲
cent sento セント
centennial *n* hyakushūnen 百周年
center 1 *n* (*middle*) chūshin 中心; (*building*) sentā センター; (*region*) chūshin 中心; POL chūdōha 中道派; ***in the ~ of*** … no chūshin de …の中心で **2** *v/t* chūshin ni oku 中心に置く
♦ **center on** … ni chūshin o oku …に中心を置く
centigrade sesshi 摂氏; ***10 degrees ~*** sesshi jū-do 摂氏十度
centimeter senchimētoru センチメートル
central chūshin (no) 中心(の); *location, apartment* chūshinbu de benri (na) 中心部で便利(な); (*main*) chūshinteki (na) 中心的(な); ***be ~ to*** kore ga … no chūshin to naru これが…の中心となる
central heating sentoraru-hītingu セントラル・ヒーティング
centralize chūō ni atsumeru 中央に集める
central locking MOT sentoraru-rokku セントラルロック
central processing unit → ***CPU***
century seiki 世紀
CEO (= ***Chief Executive Officer***) saikō-sekininsha 最高責任者
ceramic tōjiki (no) 陶磁器(の)
ceramics (*objects*) tōjiki 陶磁器; (*art*) tōgei 陶芸; (*Japanese ~*) setomono 瀬戸物
cereal (*grain*) kokumotsu 穀物; (*breakfast ~*) shiriaru シリアル
ceremonial 1 *adj* gishiki (no) 儀式(の) **2** *n* gishiki 儀式
ceremony (*event*) shikiten 式典; (*ritual*) gishiki 儀式
certain (*sure*) kakushin shite iru 確信している; (*particular*) aru ある; ***it's ~ that …*** … wa hobo kakujitsu da …はほぼ確実だ; ***a ~ Mr S.*** esu-shi toka iu hito S氏とかいう人; ***make ~*** tashikameru 確かめる; ***know / say for ~*** hakkiri shitte iru / iu はっきり知っている/言う
certainly (*definitely*) tashika ni 確かに; (*of course*) mochiron もちろん; ***~ not!*** tondemonai とんでもない

certainty (*confidence*) kakushin 確信; (*inevitability*) kakujitsusei 確実性; ***it's / he's a ~*** sore / kare wa kakujitsu da それ/彼は確実だ
certificate (*qualification*) shikaku 資格; (*official paper*) shōmeisho 証明書
certified public accountant kōnin-kaikeishi 公認会計士
certify shōmei suru 証明する
Cesarean *n* teiō-sekkai 帝王切開
cessation teishi 停止
CFC (= ***chlorofluorocarbon***) furongasu フロンガス
chafe *v/t* surimuku すりむく
chain 1 *n* kusari 鎖; (*for bicycle, of stores, hotels*) chēn チェーン **2** *v/t*: ***~ X to Y*** X o Y ni kusari de tsunagu XをYに鎖でつなぐ
chain reaction rensa-hannō 連鎖反応; **chain smoke** tsuzukezama ni tabako o suu 続けざまにたばこを吸う; **chain smoker** chēn-sumōkā チェーンスモーカー; **chain store** chēn-sutoa チェーンストア
chair 1 *n* isu いす; (*arm~*) hijikake-isu ひじ掛けいす; (*at university*) shunin-kyōju 主任教授; ***the ~*** (*electric ~*) denki-isu 電気いす; (*at meeting*) gichō 議長; ***take the ~*** gichō o tsutomeru 議長を務める **2** *v/t meeting* gichō o tsutomeru 議長を務める
chair lift sukī-rifuto スキーリフト; **chairman** gichō 議長; **chairperson** gichō 議長; **chairwoman** gichō 議長
chalk (*for writing*) chōku チョーク; (*in soil*) hakua 白亜
challenge 1 *n* (*difficulty*) nandai 難題; (*in race, competition*) chōsen 挑戦 **2** *v/t* (*defy*) yōkyū suru 要求する; (*to race, debate*) mōshikomu 申し込む; (*call into question*) igi o tonaeru 異議を唱える
challenger chōsen-sha 挑戦者
challenging yarigai no aru やりがいのある
chambermaid mēdo メード
Chamber of Commerce shōkō-kaigisho 商工会議所
chamois (leather) sēmu-gawa セーム皮
champagne shanpan シャンパン
champion 1 *n* SP chanpion チャンピオン; (*of cause*) yōgo-sha 擁護者 **2** *v/t cause* yōgo suru 擁護する
championship (*event*) senshuken-taikai 選手権大会; (*title*) senshuken 選手権
chance (*possibility*) kanōsei 可能性; (*opportunity*) kikai 機会; (*risk*) kiken 危険; (*luck*) un 運; ***by ~*** gūzen ni 偶然に; ***take a ~*** ichi ka bachi ka yatte miru 一か八かやってみる; ***I'm not taking any ~s*** kiken o okashitari shinai 危険を冒したりしない
Chancellor (*in Germany*) shushō 首相; ~ (***of the Exchequer***) (*in Britain*) ōkura-daijin 大蔵大臣
chandelier shanderia シャンデリア
change 1 *n* (*to plan, idea, script*) henkō 変更; (*in society, climate, condition*) henka 変化; (*small coins*) kozeni 小銭; (*from purchase*) otsuri お釣り; (*different situation etc*) kibun-tenkan 気分転換; ***for a ~*** tama ni wa たまには; ***a ~ of clothes*** kigae 着替え **2** *v/t* (*alter*) kaeru 変える; *bank bill* kuzusu くずす; (*replace*) torikaeru 取り替える; *trains, planes* norikaeru 乗り換える; *one's clothes* kigaeru 着替える **3** *v/i* kawaru 変わる; (*put on different clothes*) kigaeru 着替える; (*take different train / bus*) norikaeru 乗り換える
channel RAD, TV channeru チャンネル; (*waterway*) suiro 水路
chant 1 *n* kakegoe 掛け声 **2** *v/i* kakegoe o kakeru 掛け声を掛ける
chaos daikonran 大混乱
chaotic muchitsujo (no) 無秩序(の)
chapel reihaidō 礼拝堂
chapped hibi no kireta ひびの切れた
chapter (*of book*) shō 章; (*of organization*) chihō-shibu 地方支部
character (*nature*) seikaku 性格; (*person*) hito 人; (*in book, play*)

tōjō-jinbutsu 登場人物; (*personality*) tokuchō 特徴; (*in writing*) moji 文字; ***he's a real ~*** kare wa taishita jinbutsu da 彼はたいした人物だ; ***Chinese ~*** kanji 漢字

characteristic 1 *n* tokushoku 特色 **2** *adj* tokuyū (no) 特有(の)

characterize (*be typical of*) tokuchōzukeru 特徴づける; (*describe*) … to miru …と見る

charbroiled sumibiyaki (no) 炭火焼き(の)

charcoal (*for barbecue*) sumi 炭; (*for drawing*) mokutan 木炭

charge 1 *n* (*fee*) ryōkin 料金; LAW yōgi 容疑; ***free of ~*** muryō 無料; ***will that be cash or ~?*** genkin to kādo no dochira desu ka 現金とカードのどちらですか; ***be in ~*** sekinin-sha de aru 責任者である; ***take ~*** ukemotsu 受け持つ **2** *v/t sum of money* seikyū suru 請求する; (*put on account*) kādo de harau カードで払う; LAW kiso suru 起訴する; *battery* jūden suru 充電する **3** *v/i* (*attack*) totsugeki suru 突撃する

charge account tsuke つけ

charge card ka-do カード

charisma karisuma カリスマ

charitable *institution, donation* jizen-katsudō (no) 慈善活動(の); *person* jihibukai 慈悲深い

charity (*assistance*) charitī チャリティー, jizen 慈善; (*organization*) jizen-dantai 慈善団体

charm 1 *n* (*appealing quality*) miryoku 魅力; (*on bracelet etc*) omamori お守り **2** *v/t* (*delight*) uttori saseru うっとりさせる

charming miryokuteki (na) 魅力的(な)

charred kogeta 焦げた

chart (*diagram*) zuhyō 図表; NAUT kaizu 海図; (*for airplane*) kōkūzu 航空図; ***the ~s*** MUS hitto-chāto ヒットチャート

charter *v/t* chātā suru チャーターする

charter flight chātā-bin チャーター便

chase 1 *n* tsuiseki 追跡 **2** *v/t* oikakeru 追いかける

♦ **chase away** … o oiharau …を追い払う

chaser (*drink*) chēsā チェーサー

chassis (*of car*) shāshī シャーシー

chat 1 *n* oshaberi おしゃべり **2** *v/i* oshaberi suru おしゃべりする

chatter 1 *n* oshaberi おしゃべり **2** *v/i* pechakucha to shaberu ぺちゃくちゃとしゃべる; (*of teeth*) katakata naru かたかた鳴る

chatterbox oshaberi おしゃべり

chatty *person* hanashizuki (no) 話好き(の); *letter* kudaketa くだけた

chauffeur *n* untenshu 運転手

chauvinist (*male ~*) danson-johi no hito 男尊女卑の人

cheap *adj* (*inexpensive*) yasui 安い; (*nasty*) yasuppoi 安っぽい; (*mean*) kechi (na) けち(な)

cheat 1 *n* (*person*) ikasamashi いかさま師 **2** *v/t*: ***~ X out of Y*** X kara Y o damashitoru XからYをだまし取る **3** *v/i* (*in exam*) kanningu o suru カンニングをする; (*in cards etc*) ikasama o suru いかさまをする; ***~ on one's wife*** okusan ni kakurete uwaki o suru 奥さんにかくれて浮気をする

check[1] **1** *adj shirt* chekku (no) チェック(の) **2** *n* chekku チェック

check[2] *n* FIN kogitte 小切手; (*in restaurant etc*) kanjōgaki 勘定書き; ***~ please*** o-kanjō o-negai お勘定お願い

check[3] **1** *n* (*to verify sth*) kensa 検査; ***keep in ~, hold in ~*** … o kuitomeru …を食い止める; ***keep a ~ on*** … o kanri suru …を管理する **2** *v/t* (*verify*) kakunin suru 確認する; *machinery* tenken suru 点検する; (*restrain*) osaeru 抑える; (*stop*) soshi suru 阻止する; (*with a ~ mark*) shirushi o tsukeru 印を付ける; *coat, package etc* azukeru 預ける **3** *v/i* shiraberu 調べる; ***~ for*** … o shiraberu …を調べる

♦ **check in** (*at airport, hotel*) chekku-in suru チェックインする

♦**check off** shirushi o tsukeru 印を付ける
♦**check on** … o shiraberu …を調べる
♦**check out 1** *v/i* (*of hotel*) chekku-auto suru チェックアウトする **2** *v/t* (*look into*) … o chōsa suru …を調査する; *club, restaurant etc* … ni itte miru …に行ってみる
♦**check up on** … o shiraberu … を調べる
♦**check with** (*of person*) … ni tazuneru …に尋ねる; (*tally: of information*) gatchi suru 合致する
checkbook kogittechō 小切手帳
checked *material* chekku (no) チェック(の)
checkerboard chekkā-ban チェッカー盤
checkered *pattern* chekku (no) チェック(の); *career* haran ni tonda 波乱に富んだ
checkers chekkā チェッカー
check-in (counter) chekku-in (kauntā) チェックイン（カウンター）
checking account tōza-yokin-kōza 当座預金口座
check-in time chekku-in no jikan チェックインの時間; **checklist** chekku-risuto チェックリスト; **checkmark** chekku no shirushi チェックの印; **checkmate** *n* chekku-meito チェックメイト, ōte 王手; **checkout** reji レジ; **checkout time** (*from hotel*) chekku-auto no jikan チェックアウトの時間; **checkpoint** (*military, police*) kenmonjo 検問所; (*in race etc*) chekku-pointo チェックポイント; **checkroom** (*for coats*) kurōku クローク; (*for baggage*) tenimotsu-azukarisho 手荷物預かり所; **checkup** (*medical*) kenkō-shindan 健康診断; (*dental*) kenshin 検診
cheek hō ほお
cheekbone hōbone ほお骨
cheer 1 *n* kansei 歓声; **~s!** (*toast*) kanpai 乾杯 **2** *v/t* seien suru 声援する **3** *v/i* kansei o ageru 歓声を上げる
♦**cheer on** … o seien suru …を声援する
♦**cheer up 1** *v/i* genki o dasu 元気を出す; **~!** genki dashite 元気出して **2** *v/t* genki zukeru 元気づける
cheerful kigen no ii 機嫌のいい
cheering kansei 歓声
cheerleader chiarīdā チアリーダー
cheese chīzu チーズ
cheeseburger chīzubāgā チーズバーガー
cheesecake chīzukēki チーズケーキ
chef shefu シェフ; (*for Japanese cuisine*) itamae 板前
chemical 1 *adj* kagaku (no) 化学(の) **2** *n* kagaku-yakuhin 化学薬品
chemical warfare kagakuheiki-sensō 化学兵器戦争
chemist kagaku-sha 化学者
chemistry kagaku 化学; *fig* aishō 相性
chemotherapy kagaku-ryōhō 化学療法
cherish taisetsu ni suru 大切にする; *memory, hope* mune ni himeru 胸に秘める
cherry (*fruit*) sakuranbo さくらんぼ; (*tree*) sakura no ki 桜の木; **~ *blossom*** sakura 桜
chess chesu チェス
chessboard chesu-ban チェス盤
chest (*of person*) mune 胸; (*box*) shūnōbako 収納箱; ***get … off one's ~*** … o uchiakeru …を打ち明ける; **~ *of drawers*** tansu たんす
chestnut kuri くり; (*tree*) kuri no ki くりの木
chew *v/t* kamu かむ; (*of dog, rats*) kajiru かじる
♦**chew out** F … o shikaritobasu …をしかりとばす
chewing gum chūingamu チューインガム
chick hiyoko ひよこ; F (*girl*) onna 女
chicken 1 *n* niwatori にわとり; (*food*) toriniku とり肉; F (*coward*) yowamushi 弱虫 **2** *adj* F (*cowardly*) okubyō (na) おくびょう(な)
♦**chicken out** ojikezuite yameru おじけづいてやめる

chickenfeed F hashitagane はした金
chicken pox mizubōsō 水ぼうそう
chief 1 *n* (*head*) rīdā リーダー; (*of tribe*) shūchō しゅう長 **2** *adj* omo (na) 主(な)
chiefly shu to shite 主として
chilblain shimoyake しもやけ
child kodomo 子供; *pej* kodomojimita hito 子供じみた人
childbirth shussan 出産
childhood kodomo no koro 子供の頃
childish *pej* kodomojimita 子供じみた
childishness kodomoppo-sa 子供っぽさ
childless kodomo no inai 子供のいない
childlike kodomo no yō (na) 子供のよう(な)
Children's Day Kodomo no hi 子供の日
chill 1 *n* (*in air*) hie 冷え; (*illness*) samuke 寒気 **2** *v/t wine* hiyasu 冷やす
chilli (pepper) tōgarashi とうがらし
chilly *weather* hadazamui 肌寒い; *welcome* hiyayaka (na) 冷やか(な); ***I'm ~*** samuke ga suru 寒気がする
chime *v/i* chaimu チャイム
chimney entotsu 煙突
chimpanzee chinpanjī チンパンジー
chin ago あご
china tōjiki 陶磁器; (*material*) setomono 瀬戸物
China Chūgoku 中国
Chinese 1 *adj* Chūgoku (no) 中国(の); (*in Chinese*) Chūgoku-go (no) 中国語(の); ***~ character*** kanji 漢字 **2** *n* (*language*) Chūgoku-go 中国語; (*person*) Chūgoku-jin 中国人
chink (*gap*) sukima すきま; (*sound*) kachin to iu oto かちんという音
chip 1 *n* (*fragment*) kakera かけら; (*damage*) kaketa tokoro 欠けたところ; (*in gambling*) chippu チップ; COMPUT maikuro-chippu マイクロチップ; ***~s*** potetochippu ポテトチップ **2** *v/t* (*damage*) kaku 欠く
♦ **chip in** (*interrupt*) kuchi o hasamu 口をはさむ; (*with money*) sukoshi zutsu dashiau 少しずつ出し合う
chiropractor seitaishi 整体師, kairopurakutā カイロプラクター
chirp *v/i* chunchun naku ちゅんちゅん鳴く
chisel *n* nomi のみ
chivalrous kishidō-seishin no aru 騎士道精神のある
chives chaibu チャイブ
chlorine enso 塩素
chockfull gisshiri tsumatte ぎっしり詰まって
chocolate chokorēto チョコレート; ***hot ~*** hotto-chokorēto ホットチョコレート
chocolate cake chokorēto-kēki チョコレートケーキ
choice 1 *n* sentaku 選択; (*selection*) sentaku no haba 選択の幅; (*preference*) konomi 好み; ***I had no ~*** sentaku no yochi ga nakatta 選択の余地がなかった **2** *adj* (*top quality*) ikkyū (no) 一級(の)
choir gasshōdan 合唱団; REL seikatai 聖歌隊
choke 1 *n* MOT chōku チョーク **2** *v/i* iki ga tsumaru 息が詰まる; ***he ~d on a bone*** kare wa nodo ni hone o tsumaraseta 彼はのどに骨をつまらせた **3** *v/t* chissoku saseru 窒息させる
cholesterol koresuterōru コレステロール
choose *v/t & v/i* erabu 選ぶ
choosey F urusai うるさい
chop 1 *n* (*meat*) choppu チョップ **2** *v/t wood* waru 割る; *meat, vegetables* kiru 切る
♦ **chop down** *tree* … o kiritaosu …を切り倒す
chopper (*tool*) ono おの; F (*helicopter*) herikoputā ヘリコプター
chopsticks hashi はし; ***disposable ~*** waribashi わりばし; ***~ rest*** hashioki はし置き
chord MUS waon 和音
chore zatsuyō 雑用
choreographer furitsukeshi 振り付け師
choreography furitsuke 振り付け

chorus (*singers*) gasshōdan 合唱団, kōrasu コーラス; (*of song*) kurikaeshi 繰り返し
Christ Iesu Kirisuto イエスキリスト; ***~!*** chikushō 畜生
christen senrei suru 洗礼する
Christian 1 *n* Kirisuto-kyōto キリスト教徒 **2** *adj* Kirisuto-kyō (no) キリスト教(の)
Christianity kirisuto-kyō キリスト教
Christian name namae 名前
Christmas Kurisumasu クリスマス; ***at ~*** Kurisumasu no koro ni クリスマスの頃に; ***Merry ~!*** Merī-Kurisumasu メリークリスマス
Christmas card Kurisumasu-kādo クリスマスカード; **Christmas Day** Kurisumasu クリスマス; **Christmas Eve** Kurisumasu-ibu クリスマスイブ; **Christmas present** Kurisumasu-purezento クリスマスプレゼント; **Christmas tree** Kurisumasu-tsurī クリスマスツリー
chrome, chromium kuromu クロム
chronic mansei (no) 慢性(の)
chronological nendaijun (no) 年代順(の); ***in ~ order*** nendaijun ni 年代順に
chrysanthemum kiku 菊
chubby marupocha (no) 丸ぽちゃ(の)
chuck *v/t* F hōru ほうる
♦ **chuck out** *object* ... o suteru ...を捨てる; *person* ... o oidasu ...を追い出す
chuckle 1 *n* kusukusu warai くすくす笑い **2** *v/i* kusukusu warau くすくす笑う
chunk katamari かたまり
church kyōkai 教会
chute shūto シュート; (*for garbage*) dasuto-shūto ダストシュート
CIA (= ***Central Intelligence Agency***) shī-ai-ē シーアイエー(中央情報局)
cicada semi せみ
cider ringo-shu リンゴ酒
CIF (= ***cost insurance freight***) hokenryō unchin-komi kakaku 保険料運賃込み価格
cigar hamaki 葉巻き
cigarette tabako たばこ
cinema (*Br*: *building*) eigakan 映画館; (*as institution*) eigakai 映画界
cinnamon shinamon シナモン
circle 1 *n* en 円; (*group*) nakama 仲間 **2** *v/t* (*draw circle around*) maru de kakomu 丸で囲む **3** *v/i* (*of plane, bird*) senkai suru 旋回する
circuit kairo 回路; (*lap*) isshū 一周
circuit board haisenban 配線盤
circuit breaker burēkā ブレーカー
circular 1 *n* (*giving information*) chirashi ちらし **2** *adj* enkei (no) 円形(の)
circulate 1 *v/i* junkan suru 循環する **2** *v/t memo* kairan suru 回覧する
circulation BIO junkan 循環; (*of newspaper, magazine*) hakkō-busū 発行部数
circumference enshū 円周
circumstances jijō 事情; (*financial*) keizai-jōtai 経済状態; ***under no ~*** donna jijō ga atte mo どんな事情があっても; ***under the ~*** sō iu jijō na node そういう事情なので
circus sākasu サーカス
cistern tanku タンク
citizen shimin 市民
citizenship shiminken 市民権
city toshi 都市; ***~ center*** hankagai 繁華街; ***~ hall*** shiyakusho 市役所
civic *adj* shi (no) 市(の); *pride, responsibilities* shimin (no) 市民(の)
civil (*not military*) minkan (no) 民間(の); *disobedience, duties etc* shimin (no) 市民(の); (*polite*) reigi-tadashii 礼儀正しい
civil engineer doboku-gishi 土木技師
civilian 1 *n* minkan-jin 民間人 **2** *adj clothes* ippan (no) 一般(の)
civilization bunmei 文明
civilize *person* senren suru 洗練する
civil rights shiminken 市民権; **civil servant** kōmuin 公務員; **civil service** seifu-kanchō(gun igai) 政府官庁(軍以外); **civil war** naisen 内戦

claim 1 *n* (*request*) seikyū 請求; (*right*) kenri 権利; (*assertion*) shuchō 主張 **2** *v/t* (*ask for as a right*) seikyū suru 請求する; (*assert*) shuchō suru 主張する; *lost property* nanorideru 名乗り出る; ***they have ~ed responsibility for the attack*** karera wa shūgeki no hankō-seimei o dashita 彼らは襲撃の犯行声明を出した

claimant yōkyū-sha 要求者; LAW genkoku 原告

clam hamaguri はまぐり

♦ **clam up** F totsuzen kuchi o tsugumu 突然口をつぐむ

clammy jittori shita じっとりした

clamor (*noise*) sakebi 叫び; (*outcry*) koe 声

♦ **clamor for** … o yakamashiku yōkyū suru …をやかましく要求する

clamp 1 *n* (*fastener*) shimegane 締め金, kuranpu クランプ **2** *v/t* (*fasten*) shimegane de shimeru 締め金で締める

♦ **clamp down** genjū ni torishimaru 厳重に取り締まる

♦ **clamp down on** … o genjū ni torishimaru …を厳重に取り締まる

clan ichizoku 一族

clandestine himitsu (no) 秘密(の)

clang 1 *n* kān to iu oto カーンという音 **2** *v/i* kān to naru カーンと鳴る

clap 1 *v/i* hakushu suru 拍手する **2** *v/t* … ni hakushu suru …に拍手する

clarify hakkiri saseru はっきりさせる

clarinet kurarinetto クラリネット

clarity meiryō-sa 明りょうさ

clash 1 *n* shōtotsu 衝突; (*of personalities*) fuitchi 不一致 **2** *v/i* shōtotsu suru 衝突する; (*of opinions*) kuichigau 食い違う; (*of colors*) awanai 合わない; (*of events*) kachiau かちあう

clasp 1 *n* tomegu 留め具 **2** *v/t* (*in hand*) nigirishimeru 握りしめる; (*to self*) dakishimeru 抱き締める

class 1 *n* (*lesson*) jugyō 授業; (*group of people*) kurasu クラス; (*category*) burui 部類; (*social ~*) kaikyū 階級 **2** *v/t* minasu みなす

classic 1 *adj* (*typical*) tenkeiteki (na) 典型的(な); (*definitive*) ichiryū (no) 一流(の) **2** *n* meisaku 名作

classical *music, style* kurashikku (no) クラシック(の); *literature* koten (no) 古典(の)

classification bunrui 分類

classified *information* kimitsu (no) 機密(の)

classified ad(vertisement) kōmokubetsu-kōkoku 項目別広告

classify (*categorize*) bunrui suru 分類する

classmate dōkyūsei 同級生, kurasumēto クラスメート

classroom kyōshitsu 教室

class warfare kaikyū-tōsō 階級闘争

classy F shareta しゃれた

clatter 1 *n* katakata to iu oto かたかたという音 **2** *v/i* katakata oto o tateru かたかた音を立てる

clause (*in agreement*) jōkō 条項; GRAM setsu 節

claustrophobia heisho-kyōfushō 閉所恐怖症

claw 1 *n* tsume つめ **2** *v/t* (*scratch*) tsume de hikkaku つめでひっかく

clay nendo 粘土

clean 1 *adj* kirei (na) きれい(な) **2** *adv* F (*completely*) kanzen ni 完全に **3** *v/t* kirei ni suru きれいにする; *teeth, shoes* migaku 磨く; *house, room* sōji suru 掃除する; *car, hands, face* arau 洗う; *clothes* kurīningu suru クリーニングする; ***get one's jacket ~ed*** uwagi o kurīningu suru 上着をクリーニングする

♦ **clean out** *room, cupboard* kirei ni suru きれいにする; *fig* ichimon nashi ni suru 一文なしにする

clean up 1 *v/t* katazukeru 片付ける; *fig* issō suru 一掃する **2** *v/i* sōji suru 掃除する; (*wash*) arau 洗う; (*on stock market etc*) ōmōke suru 大もうけする

cleaner (*male*) sōjifu 掃除夫; (*female*) sōjifu 掃除婦; ***dry ~*** dorai-kurīningu-ya ドライクリー

ニング屋

cleaning woman sōjifu 掃除婦

cleanse *skin* kurenjingu suru クレンジングする

cleanser senganryō 洗顔料

clear 1 *adj voice,photograph,vision* hakkiri shita はっきりした; (*easy to understand*) wakariyasui わかりやすい; (*obvious*) akiraka (na) 明らか(な); *weather*, *sky* hareta 晴れた; *water*, *eyes* sunda 澄んだ; *skin* kenkō-sō (na) 健康そう(な); *conscience* yamashii tokoro no nai やましいところのない; ***I'm not ~ about it*** watashi ni wa yoku wakaranai 私にはよくわからない; ***I didn't make myself ~*** watashi wa hakkiri sasenakatta 私ははっきりさせなかった **2** *adv*: ***stand ~ of*** … kara hanarete tatsu …から離れて立つ; ***steer ~ of*** … o sakeru …を避ける **2** *v/t roads etc* torinozoku 取り除く; (*acquit*) yōgi o harasu 容疑を晴らす; (*authorize*) kyoka o ataeru 許可を与える; (*earn*) kasegu 稼ぐ; ***~ one's throat*** sekibarai o suru せき払いをする **3** *v/i* (*of sky*, *mist*) hareru 晴れる; (*of face*) akaruku naru 明るくなる

♦ **clear away** *v/t* … o katazukeru …を片付ける

♦ **clear off** *v/i* isoide tachisaru 急いで立ち去る

♦ **clear out 1** *v/t* (*cupboard*) … o kara ni suru …を空にする **2** *v/i* dete iku 出ていく

♦ **clear up 1** *v/i* katazuke o suru 片付けをする; (*of weather*) hareagaru 晴れ上がる; (*of illness*, *rash*) naoru 治る **2** *v/t* (*tidy*) katazukeru 片付ける; *mystery*, *problem* kaiketsu suru 解決する

clearance (*space*) yutori ゆとり; (*authorization*) kyoka 許可

clearance sale kurabarai-ōuridashi 蔵払い大売り出し, kuriaransu-sēru クリアランスセール

clearly (*with clarity*) hakkiri to はっきりと; (*evidently*) akiraka ni 明らかに

clemency kandai na shochi 寛大な処置

clench *teeth* ha o kuishibaru 歯をくいしばる; *fist* kobushi o nigirishimeru こぶしを握り締める

clergy seishoku-sha 聖職者

clergyman bokushi 牧師

clerk jimuin 事務員; (*in store*) ten'in 店員

clever *person*, *animal* rikō (na) 利口(な); *idea* umai うまい; *gadget*, *device* ki no kiita 気のきいた

click 1 *n* COMPUT kurikku クリック **2** *v/i* kachiri to oto ga suru かちりと音がする

♦ **click on** COMPUT … o kurikku suru …をクリックする

client (*of lawyer etc*) irainin 依頼人; (*customer*) kokyaku 顧客

cliff gake がけ

climate kikō 気候

climax *n* kuraimakkusu クライマックス

climb 1 *n* (*up mountain*) tozan 登山 **2** *v/t* … ni noboru …に登る **3** *v/i* noboru 登る; (*up mountain*) tozan suru 登山する; *fig* (*increase*) jōshō suru 上昇する

♦ **climb down** oriru 降りる; *fig* hikisagaru 引き下がる

climber (*person*) tozan-sha 登山者

clinch: ***~ a deal*** F shōdan o matomeru 商談をまとめる

cling (*of clothes*) matowari tsuku まとわりつく

♦ **cling to** (*of child*) … ni shigamitsuku …にしがみつく; *ideas*, *tradition* … ni koshitsu suru …に固執する

clingfilm rappu ラップ

clingy *child*, *boyfriend* izonshin no tsuyoi 依存心の強い

clinic shinryōjo 診療所

clinical rinshō (no) 臨床(の)

clink 1 *n* (*noise*) kachin to iu oto かちんという音 **2** *v/i* kachin to naru かちんと鳴る

clip[1] **1** *n* (*fastener*) kurippu クリップ **2** *v/t*: ***~ X to Y*** X o Y ni kurippu de tomeru XをYにクリップで止める

clip[2] **1** *n* (*extract*) kurippu クリップ

2 *v/t hair, hedge* karikomu 刈り込む
clipboard kamibasami 紙挟み
clippers (*for hair*) barikan バリカン; (*for nails*) tsume-kiri つめ切り; (*for gardening*) senteibasami せん定ばさみ
clipping (*from newspaper*) kirinuki 切り抜き
cloakroom kurōku クローク
clock tokei 時計
clock radio tokei-tsuki rajio 時計付きラジオ; **clockwise** tokeimawari 時計回り; **clockwork** tokeijikake 時計仕掛け; ***it went like ~*** todokōri naku itta 滞りなく行った
clog: ***thonged ~s*** geta 下駄
♦ **clog up 1** *v/i* tsumaru 詰まる **2** *v/t* … o tsumaraseru …を詰まらせる
close[1] **1** *adj family, friend* shitashii 親しい; *resemblance* nite iru 似ている **2** *adv* sugu soba すぐそば; ***~ at hand*** tejika ni 手近に; ***~ by*** chikaku ni 近くに; ***be ~ to*** (*emotionally*) … to shitashiku shite iru …と親しくしている
close[2] **1** *v/t* shimeru 閉める; (*permanently: business*) yameru やめる; *factory* heisa suru 閉鎖する **2** *v/i* (*of door, store*) shimaru 閉まる; (*of eyes*) tojiru 閉じる; (*of store: permanently*) heiten suru 閉店する
close down 1 *v/t* heisa suru 閉鎖する **2** *v/i* (*permanently*) heisa sareru 閉鎖される
♦ **close in** *v/i* oshiyoseru 押し寄せる
♦ **close up 1** *v/t building* … o shimeru …を閉める **2** *v/i* (*move closer*) kurōzu-appu suru クローズアップする
closed *store* shimatta 閉まった; *eyes* tojita 閉じた
closed-circuit television kurōzudo-sākitto-terebi クローズドサーキットテレビ
closely *listen, watch* chūibukaku 注意深く; *cooperate* missetsu shite 密接して
closet todana 戸棚
close-up kurōzu-appu クローズアップ
closing time (*of store*) heiten-jikan 閉店時間; (*of museum, library*) heikan-jikan 閉館時間
closure (*permanent*) heisa 閉鎖; (*of shop*) heiten 閉店
clot 1 *n* (*of blood*) katamari 固まり **2** *v/i* (*of blood*) katamaru 固まる
cloth (*fabric*) nuno 布; (*for kitchen*) fukin ふきん; (*for cleaning etc*) zōkin ぞうきん
clothes fuku 服; (***traditional***) ***Japanese ~*** wafuku 和服
clothes brush ifukuyō-burashi 衣服用ブラシ
clothes hanger hangā ハンガー
clothing irui 衣類
cloud *n* kumo 雲; ***a ~ of smoke / dust*** mōmō to shita kemuri / hokori もうもうとした煙/ほこり
♦ **cloud over** (*of sky*) kumoru 曇る
cloudburst doshaburi どしゃ降り
cloudy kumotta 曇った
clout *fig* (*influence*) eikyōryoku 影響力
clown (*in circus*) piero ピエロ; (*joker*) itazuramono いたずら者; *pej* tonma とんま
club *n* (*weapon*) konbō こん棒; (*golf iron*) gorufu-kurabu ゴルフクラブ; (*organization*) kurabu クラブ; ***~s*** (*in cards*) kurōbā クローバー
clue tegakari 手がかり; ***I haven't a ~*** kentō mo tsukanai 見当もつかない
clued-up seitsū shite iru 精通している
clump *n* (*of earth*) katamari かたまり; (*group*) mure 群れ
clumsiness bukiyō 不器用
clumsy *person* bukiyō (na) 不器用(な)
cluster 1 *n* (*of people*) ichidan 一団; (*of houses*) ichigun 一群 **2** *v/i* (*of people*) muragaru 群がる; (*of houses*) misshū suru 密集する
clutch 1 *n* MOT kuratchi クラッチ **2** *v/t* shikkari nigiru しっかり握る
♦ **clutch at** … o tsukamō to suru … をつかもうとする
Co. (= ***Company***) kaisha 会社
c/o (= ***care of***) kizuke 気付, kata 方
coach 1 *n* (*trainer*) kōchi コーチ **2** *v/t*

shidō suru 指導する
coagulate (*of blood*) gyōko suru 凝固する
coal sekitan 石炭
coalition renritsu 連立
coal-mine tankō 炭鉱
coarse kime no arai きめの粗い; *hair* katai 硬い; (*vulgar*) gehin (na) 下品(な)
coast *n* kaigan 海岸; ***at the ~*** kaigan de 海岸で
coastal engan (no) 沿岸(の)
coastguard engan-keibitai 沿岸警備隊; (*person*) engan-keibitaiin 沿岸警備隊員
coastline kaigansen 海岸線
coat 1 *n* uwagi 上着; (*over~*) ōbā オーバー; (*of animal*) kegawa 毛皮; (*of paint etc*) nuri 塗り **2** *v/t* (*cover*) ōu 覆う
coathanger hangā ハンガー
coating ōi 覆い
coax settoku suru 説得する
cobweb kumo no su クモの巣
cocaine kokain コカイン
cock *n* (*chicken*) ondori おんどり; (*any male bird*) osu 雄
cockeyed *idea etc* bakageta ばかげた
cockpit kokkupitto コックピット
cockroach gokiburi ごきぶり
cocktail kakuteru カクテル
cocoa kokoa ココア
coconut kokonattsu ココナッツ
coconut palm kokoyashi no ki ココヤシの木
COD (= ***collect on delivery***) chakubarai 着払い
cod tara たら
coddle *sick person* daiji ni suru 大事にする; *child* amayakasu 甘やかす
code *n* angō 暗号
co-educational danjo-kyōgaku (no) 男女共学(の)
coerce kyōsei suru 強制する
coexist kyōzon suru 共存する
coexistence kyōzon 共存
coffee kōhī コーヒー
coffee break kōhī-bureiku コーヒーブレイク; **coffee maker** kōhī-mēkā コーヒーメーカー; **coffee pot** kōhī-potto コーヒーポット; **coffee shop** kissaten 喫茶店; **coffee table** kōhī-tēburu コーヒーテーブル
coffin hitsugi ひつぎ
cog ha 歯
cognac konyakku コニャック
cogwheel haguruma 歯車
cohabit dōsei suru 同棲する
coherent suji no tōtta 筋の通った
coil 1 *n* (*of rope*) hitomaki ひと巻き **2** *v/t* maku 巻く
coin *n* kōka 硬貨
coincide dōji ni okoru 同時に起こる
coincidence gūzen 偶然
coke F (*cocaine*) kokain コカイン
Coke® koka-kōra コカコーラ
cold 1 *adj* tsumetai 冷たい; *weather, day, room* samui 寒い; ***I'm (feeling) ~*** samui desu 寒いです; ***it's ~*** samui desu 寒いです; ***in ~ blood*** heizen to 平然と; ***get ~ feet*** *fig* ojikezuku おじけづく **2** *n* samusa 寒さ; ***I have a ~*** kaze o hiite iru 風邪をひいている
cold-blooded reiketsu (no) 冷血(の); *fig* reikoku (na) 冷酷(な); **cold cuts** hamu-rui ハム類; **cold sore** kōshin-herupesu 口唇ヘルペス
coleslaw kōrusurō コールスロー
colic fukutsū 腹痛
collaborate kyōryoku suru 協力する; (*in research*) kyōdō-kenkyū suru 共同研究する; (*on book*) kyōdō de kaku 共同で書く
collaboration kyōryoku 協力
collaborator kyōryoku-sha 協力者; (*in writing book*) kyōcho-sha 共著者
collapse kuzureru 崩れる; (*of person*) taoreru 倒れる
collapsible oritatameru 折りたためる
collar eri 襟
collarbone sakotsu 鎖骨
colleague dōryō 同僚
collect 1 *v/t person* mukae ni iku 迎えにいく; *tickets, cleaning etc* tori ni iku 取りにいく; (*as hobby*) shūshū suru 収集する; (*gather*) atsumeru 集める **2** *v/i* (*gather together*) atsumaru

集まる **3** *adv*: ***call ~*** … ni korekuto-kōru o kakeru …にコレクトコールをかける

collect call korekuto-kōru コレクトコール

collected *works, poems etc* shūshū shita 収集した; *person* ochitsuita 落ち着いた

collection korekushon コレクション; (*in church*) bokin 募金

collective kyōdō (no) 共同(の)

collective bargaining dantai-kōshō 団体交渉

collector shūshūka 収集家

college daigaku 大学

collide shōtotsu suru 衝突する

collision shōtotsu 衝突

colloquial kōgo (no) 口語(の)

colon (*punctuation*) koron コロン; ANAT ketchō 結腸

colonel taisa 大佐

colonial *adj* shokuminchi (no) 植民地(の)

colonize *country* shokuminchika suru 植民地化する

colony shokuminchi 植民地

color 1 *n* iro 色; (*in cheeks*) kaoiro 顔色; ***in ~*** (*movie etc*) karā de カラーで; ***~s*** MIL hata 旗 **2** *v/t one's hair* iro o tsukeru 色をつける **3** *v/i* (*blush*) kao o akaku suru 顔を赤くする

color-blind shikikaku-ijō (no) 色覚異常(の)

colored *adj person* yūshoku-jinshu (no) 有色人種(の)

color fast iro-ochi shinai 色落ちしない

colorful shikisai ni tonda 色彩に富んだ

coloring hada no iro 肌の色

color photograph karā-shashin カラー写真; **color scheme** haishoku 配色; **color TV** karā-terebi カラーテレビ

colt osu no kouma 雄の子馬

column retsu 列; (*architectural*) enchū 円柱; (*of text*) ran 欄; (*newspaper feature*) koramu コラム

columnist koramunisuto コラムニスト

comb 1 *n* kushi くし **2** *v/t* tokasu とかす; *area* tetteiteki ni sagasu 徹底的に捜す

combat 1 *n* sentō 戦闘 **2** *v/t* … to tatakau …と闘う

combination kumiawase 組み合わせ; (*of safe*) kumiawase-bangō 組み合わせ番号

combine 1 *n* COM gappei suru 合併する **2** *v/t* kumiawaseru 組み合わせる; *ingredients* mazeawaseru 混ぜ合わせる **3** *v/i* (*of chemical elements*) kagō suru 化合する

combine harvester konbain コンバイン

combustible kanensei (no) 可燃性(の)

combustion nenshō 燃焼

come (*toward speaker*) kuru 来る; (*toward listener*) iku 行く; (*of train, bus*) tsuku 着く; ***you'll ~ to like it*** sore o suki ni naru to omoimasu それを好きになると思います; ***how ~?*** F dōshite どうして

♦ **come about** (*happen*) okoru 起こる

♦ **come across 1** *v/t* (*find*) … ni dekuwasu …に出くわす **2** *v/i* (*of idea, humor*) tsutawaru 伝わる; ***she comes across as …*** kanojo wa … to iu inshō o ataeru 彼女は…という印象を与える

♦ **come along** (*come too*) issho ni kuru いっしょに来る; (*turn up*) yatte kuru やって来る; (*progress*) susumu 進む

♦ **come apart** barabara ni naru ばらばらになる; (*break*) kowareru 壊れる

♦ **come around** (*to place*) tazuneru 訪ねる; (*regain consciousness*) ki ga tsuku 気がつく

♦ **come away** (*leave*) dete kuru 出て来る; (*of button etc*) toreru とれる

♦ **come back** modotte kuru 戻ってくる; ***it came back to me*** omoidashita 思い出した

♦ **come by 1** *v/i* tachiyoru 立ち寄る **2** *v/t* (*acquire*) … o te ni ireru …を手に入れる

♦ **come down** *v/i* oriru 降りる; (*in*

price, amount etc) sagaru 下がる; (*of rain, snow*) furu 降る; ***he came down the stairs*** kare wa kaidan o orita 彼は階段を降りた

♦**come for** (*collect: thing*) … o tori ni kuru …を取りにくる; *person* … o mukae ni kuru …を迎えにくる; (*attack*) … ni osoi kakaru …に襲いかかる

♦**come forward** nanorideru 名乗り出る

♦**come from** … shusshin de aru …出身である

♦**come in** hairu 入る; (*of train*) haittekuru 入ってくる; (*of tide*) michiru 満ちる; **~!** dōzo どうぞ

♦**come in for**: **~ *criticism*** hihan o ukeru 批判を受ける

♦**come in on**:**~ *a deal*** keiyaku ni sanka suru 契約に参加する

♦**come off** (*of handle etc*) toreru とれる

♦**come on** (*progress*) shinpo suru 進歩する; **~!** sā, hayaku さあ早く; (*in disbelief*) masaka まさか

♦**come out** (*of person*) dete kuru 出てくる; (*of sun, results, product*) deru 出る; (*of stain*) ochiru 落ちる

♦**come to 1** *v/t place* tsuku 着く; (*of hair, dress, water*) todoku 届く; ***that comes to $70*** nana-jū doru ni naru 70ドルになる **2** *v/i* (*regain consciousness*) ki ga tsuku 気がつく

♦**come up** agatte kuru 上がってくる; (*of sun*) noboru 昇る; ***something has ~*** nanika ga okotta 何かが起こった

♦**come up with** *new idea etc* … o kangaedasu …を考え出す

comeback: ***make a ~*** kamubakku suru カムバックする

comedian komedian コメディアン; *pej* tonma とんま

comedown kitaihazure 期待外れ

comedy kigeki 喜劇

comet suisei すい星

comeuppance: ***he'll get his ~*** sono uchi kare wa tōzen no mukui o ukeru darō そのうち彼は当然の報いを受けるだろう

comfort 1 *n* kaiteki-sa 快適さ; (*consolation*) nagusame 慰め **2** *v/t* nagusameru 慰める

comfortable *chair* suwarigokochi no yoi 座り心地のよい; *house, room* igokochi no yoi 居心地のよい; ***be ~*** (*of person*) raku de aru 楽である; (*financially*) kurashi ni komaranai 暮しに困らない

comic 1 *n* (*to read*) manga 漫画 **2** *adj* kigeki (no) 喜劇(の)

comical kokkei (na) こっけい(な)

comic book mangabon 漫画本

comics rensai-manga 連載漫画

comma konma コンマ

command 1 *n* meirei 命令 **2** *v/t* meirei suru 命令する

commander shireikan 司令官

commander-in-chief saikō-shireikan 最高司令官

commemorate kinen suru 記念する

commemoration: ***in ~ of*** … o kinen shite …を記念して

commence 1 *v/i* hajimaru 始まる **2** *v/t* kaishi suru 開始する

comment 1 *n* kaisetsu 解説, komento コメント; ***no ~!*** nōkomento ノーコメント **2** *v/i* iken o noberu 意見を述べる

commentary jikkyō-hōsō 実況放送

commentator kaisetsu-sha 解説者

commerce shōgyō 商業

commercial 1 *adj firm, bank, English, college* shōgyō (no) 商業(の); *success* shōgyōteki (na) 商業的(な) **2** *n* (*advert*) komāsharu コマーシャル

commercial break komāsharu コマーシャル

commercialize *v/t* shōgyōka suru 商業化する

commercial traveler sērusuman セールスマン

commiserate dōjō suru 同情する

commission 1 *n* (*payment*) buai 歩合; (*job*) irai 依頼; (*committee*) iinkai 委員会 **2** *v/t* (*for a job*) irai suru 依頼する

commit *crime* okasu 犯す; *money* jūtō suru 充当する; **~ *oneself*** yakusoku suru 約束する

commitment (*in professional*

relationship) sekininkan 責任感; (*in personal relationship*) kenshin 献身; (*responsibility*) sekinin 責任
committee iinkai 委員会
commodity shōhin 商品
common (*not rare*) arifureta ありふれた; (*shared*) kyōtsū (no) 共通(の); ***in ~*** kyōtsū ni 共通に; ***have something in ~ with*** … to nanika kyōtsūten ga aru …と何か共通点がある
common law wife naien no tsuma 内縁の妻; **commonplace** *adj* arifureta ありふれた; **common sense** jōshiki 常識
commotion sawagi 騒ぎ
communal kyōyū (no) 共有(の)
communicate 1 *v/i* (*have contact*) renraku o toru 連絡をとる; (*make self understood*) rikai shiau 理解し合う **2** *v/t* tsutaeru 伝える
communication komyunikēshon コミュニケーション, ishi-sotsū 意思疎通
communications tsūshin-shudan 通信手段
communications satellite tsūshin-eisei 通信衛星
communicative *person* hanashizuki (na) 話好き(な)
Communism kyōsan-shugi 共産主義
Communist 1 *adj* kyōsan-shugi (no) 共産主義(の) **2** *n* Kyōsan-shugi-sha 共産主義者
community shakai 社会, komyunitī コミュニティー
commute 1 *v/i* tsūkin suru 通勤する **2** *v/t* LAW genkei suru 減刑する
commuter tsūkin-sha 通勤者
commuter pass teikiken 定期券; **commuter traffic** tsūkin rasshu 通勤ラッシュ; **commuter train** tsūkin-ressha 通勤列車
compact 1 *adj* kogata (no) 小型(の) **2** *n* MOT kei-jidōsha 軽自動車
compact disc konpakuto-disuku コンパクトディスク
companion aite 相手
companionship tsukiai 付き合い
company COM kaisha 会社; (*companionship*) tsukiai 付き合い; (*guests*) raikyaku 来客; ***he's good ~*** kare wa omoshiroi nakama da 彼はおもしろい仲間だ; ***keep X ~*** X ni tsukiau Xにつきあう
company car shayō-sha 社用車
company law kaisha-hō 会社法
comparable (*which can be compared*) hikaku dekiru 比較できる; (*similar*) hitteki suru 匹敵する
comparative 1 *adj* (*relative*) hikakuteki 比較的; *study* hikaku (no) 比較(の); GRAM hikakukyū (no) 比較級(の) **2** *n* GRAM hikakukyū 比較級
comparatively hikakuteki 比較的
compare 1 *v/t* hikaku suru 比較する; ***~ X with Y*** X o Y to kuraberu XをYと比べる; ***~d with …*** … to kuraberu to …と比べると **2** *v/i* hitteki suru 匹敵する
comparison hikaku 比較; ***there's no ~*** kurabemono ni naranai 比べものにならない
compartment shikiri 仕切り
compass hōi-jishin 方位磁針; NAUT rashinban 羅針盤; (*for geometry*) konpasu コンパス
compassion dōjō 同情
compassionate nasakebukai 情け深い
compatibility (*of people*) tekiōsei 適応性; (*of software*) gokansei 互換性; (*of blood types*) tekigōsei 適合性
compatible *people* ki ga au 気が合う; *blood types*, *life styles* tekigō shite iru 適合している; COMPUT gokansei no aru 互換性のある; ***we're not ~*** watashitachi wa uma ga awanai 私達はうまが合わない
compel kyōsei suru 強制する
compelling *argument* settokuryoku no aru 説得力のある; *movie*, *book* hikikomareru 引き込まれる
compensate 1 *v/t* (*with money*) hoshō suru 補償する **2** *v/i*: ***~ for*** … o umeawaseru …を埋め合わせる
compensation (*money*) hoshō-kin 補償金; (*reward*) hōshū 報酬; (*comfort*) umeawase 埋め合わせ
compete kyōsō suru 競争する; (*take

part) sanka suru 参加する; **~ *for*** … o mezashite kyōsō suru …をめざして競争する
competence nōryoku 能力
competent *person* yūnō (na) 有能(な); *work* deki no ii できのいい; ***I'm not ~ to judge*** watashi wa handan suru shikaku ga nai 私は判断する資格がない
competition kyōsō 競争; SP shiai 試合; (*competitors*) kyōsō-aite 競争相手, raibaru ライバル; ***the government wants to encourage ~*** seifu wa kyōsō o shōrei shite iru 政府は競争を奨励している
competitive *person* kyōsōshin ga tsuyoi 競争心が強い; *price*, *offer* kyōgō dekiru 競合できる; *profession* kyōsō no hageshii 競争の激しい
competitor (*in contest*) sanka-sha 参加者; COM kyōsōaite 競争相手
compile henshū suru 編集する
complacency jiko-manzoku 自己満足
complacent jiko-manzoku shita 自己満足した
complain *v/i* fuhei o iu 不平を言う; (*to shop*, *manager*) kujō o iu 苦情を言う; **~ *of*** MED … o uttaeru …を訴える
complaint (*grumble*) monku 文句; (*of striker*) uttae 訴え; MED byōki 病気
complement *v/t* oginau 補う; ***they ~ each other*** karera wa tarinai tokoro o oginaiatte iru 彼等は足りない所をを補い合っている
complementary oginaiau 補い合う
complete 1 *adj* (*total*) kanzen (na) 完全(な); (*full*) zenbu (no) 全部(の); (*finished*) kansei shite 完成して **2** *v/t task*, *building etc* kansei suru 完成する; *course* shūryō suru 修了する; *form* kinyū suru 記入する
completely kanzen ni 完全に
completion kansei 完成
complex 1 *adj* fukuzatsu (na) 複雑(な) **2** *n* PSYCH konpurekkusu コンプレックス; (*of buildings*) kyōdō-biru 共同ビル
complexion (*facial*) kao no irotsuya 顔の色つや
compliance shōdaku 承諾
complicate fukuzatsu ni suru 複雑にする
complicated fukuzatsu (na) 複雑(な)
complication mondai 問題; **~s** MED gappeishō 合併症
compliment 1 *n* homekotoba ほめ言葉 **2** *v/t* homeru ほめる
complimentary shōsan o hyōshita 賞賛を表した; (*free*) muryō (no) 無料(の); (*in restaurant*, *hotel*) sābisu (no) サービス(の)
compliments slip zōteihyō 贈呈票
comply ōzuru 応ずる; **~ *with …*** … ni shitagau …に従う
component bubun 部分
compose *v/t* kōsei suru 構成する; MUS sakkyoku suru 作曲する; ***be ~d of*** … kara naritatte iru …から成り立っている; **~ *oneself*** ki o ochitsukeru 気を落ち着ける
composed ochitsuita 落ち着いた
composer MUS sakkyoku-ka 作曲家
composition (*make-up*) kōsei 構成; MUS sakkyoku 作曲; (*essay*) sakubun 作文
composure ochitsuki 落ち着き
compound *n* CHEM kagōbutsu 化合物
compound interest fukuri 複利
comprehend (*understand*) rikai suru 理解する
comprehension rikai 理解
comprehensive hōkatsuteki (na) 包括的(な); *account* sōgōteki (na) 総合的(な)
compress 1 *n* MED shippu 湿布 **2** *v/t air*, *gas* asshuku suru 圧縮する; *information* yōyaku suru 要約する
comprise kōsei suru 構成する; ***be ~d of*** … de kōsei sarete iru …で構成されている
compromise 1 *n* dakyō 妥協 **2** *v/i* dakyō suru 妥協する **3** *v/t principles* mageru 曲げる; (*jeopardize*) ayauku suru 危うくする; **~ *oneself*** taimen o kizutsukeru 体面を傷付ける
compulsion PSYCH kyōhaku-

kannen 強迫観念
compulsive *behavior* byōteki (na) 病的(な); *reading* yamitsuki (no) 病みつき(の)
compulsory kyōseiteki (na) 強制的(な); *subject* hisshū (no) 必修(の); **~ *education*** gimu-kyōiku 義務教育
computer konpyūtā コンピューター; ***have … on ~*** konpyūtā ni … ga nyūryoku shite aru コンピューターに…が入力してある
computer-controlled konpyūtā-seigyo (no) コンピューター制御(の)
computer game konpyūtā-gēmu コンピューターゲーム
computerize konpyūtā de shori suru コンピューターで処理する; *workplace* … ni konpyūtā o sonaeru …にコンピューターを備える
computer literate konpyūtā o tsukaeru hito コンピューターを使える人; **computer science** konpyūtā-kagaku コンピューター科学; **computer scientist** konpyūtā-kagaku-sha コンピューター科学者
computing (*use of computers*) konpyūtā-sōsa コンピューター操作; (*computers*) konpyūtā-riyō コンピューター利用
comrade nakama 仲間; POL dōshi 同志
comradeship nakama-ishiki 仲間意識
con 1 *n* F ikasama いかさま **2** *v/t* F damasu だます
conceal kakusu 隠す
concede (*admit*) mitomeru 認める
conceit unubore うぬぼれ
conceited omoiagatta 思い上った
conceivable kangaerareru 考えられる
conceive *v/i* (*of woman*) ninshin suru 妊娠する; **~ *of*** (*imagine*) … o sōzō suru …を想像する
concentrate 1 *v/i* shūchū suru 集中する; (*on task*) sennen suru 専念する **2** *v/t one's attention, energies* shūchū suru 集中する
concentrated *juice etc* nōshuku sareta 濃縮された
concentration shūchūryoku 集中力
concept gainen 概念
conception (*of child*) jutai 受胎
concern 1 *n* (*anxiety*) shinpai 心配; (*care*) kanshin 関心; (*business*) kanshinji 関心事; (*company*) jigyō 事業 **2** *v/t* (*involve*) … ni kankei ga aru …に関係がある; (*worry*) shinpai saseru 心配させる; **~ *oneself with*** … ni kanshin o motsu …に関心を持つ
concerned (*anxious*) shinpai shite iru 心配している; (*caring*) kizukatte 気づかって; (*involved*) kankei suru 関係する; ***as far as I'm ~*** watashi no mikata to shite wa 私の見方としては
concerning *prep* … ni kanshite …に関して
concert konsāto コンサート
concerted itchi shita 一致した
concertmaster konsāto-masutā コンサートマスター
concerto kyōsōkyoku 協奏曲
concession (*giving in*) jōho 譲歩
conciliatory kaijūteki (na) 懐柔的(な)
concise kanketsu (na) 簡潔(な)
conclude 1 *v/t* (*deduce*) ketsuron o kudasu 結論を下す; (*end*) oeru 終える **2** *v/i* owaru 終わる
conclusion (*deduction*) ketsuron 結論; (*end*) ketsumatsu 結末; ***in ~*** saigo ni 最後に
conclusive ketteiteki (na) 決定的(な)
concoct *meal, drink* mazeawasete tsukuru 混ぜ合わせて作る; *excuse, story* detchiageru でっちあげる
concoction (*food, drink*) chōgōbutsu 調合物
concrete[1] *adj* (*not abstract*) gutaiteki (na) 具体的(な)
concrete[2] *n* konkurīto コンクリート
concur *v/i* dōi suru 同意する
concussion nōshintō 脳しんとう
condemn *action* hinan suru 非難する; *building* futeki to nintei suru 不適と認定する; (*doom*) oikomu 追い込む

condemnation (*of action*) hinan 非難
condensation ketsuro 結露
condense 1 *v/t* (*make shorter*) tanshuku suru 短縮する **2** *v/i* (*of steam*) gyōketsu suru 凝結する
condensed milk kondensu-miruku コンデンスミルク, rennyū 練乳
condescend: ***he ~ed to speak to me*** kare wa onkisegamashiku hanashikakete kita 彼は恩着せがましく話しかけてきた
condescending (*patronizing*) onkisegamashii 恩きせがましい
condition 1 *n* (*state*) jōtai 状態; (*of health*) taichō 体調; MED yōdai 容態; (*requirement, term*) jōken 条件; ***~s*** (*circumstances*) jōkyō 状況; ***on ~ that ...*** ... to iu jōken de ...という条件で **2** *v/t* PSYCH narasu 慣らす
conditional 1 *adj acceptance* jōkentsuki (no) 条件付き(の) **2** *n* GRAM jōkenhō 条件法
conditioner (*for hair*) rinsu リンス; (*for fabric*) jūnan-shiagezai 柔軟仕上げ剤
conditioning PSYCH jōkenzuke 条件付け
condo kondominiamu コンドミニアム, bunjō-manshon 分譲マンション
condolences okuyami お悔やみ
condom kondōmu コンドーム
condominium → ***condo***
condone yōnin suru 容認する
conducive: ***~ to*** ... no tame ni naru ...のためになる
conduct 1 *n* (*behavior*) okonai 行い **2** *v/t* (*carry out*) okonau 行う; ELEC dendō suru 伝導する; MUS shiki suru 指揮する; ***~ oneself*** furumau ふるまう
conducted tour gaido-tsuki kengaku ガイド付き見学
conductor MUS shiki-sha 指揮者; (*on train*) shashō 車掌
cone ensuikei 円すい形; (*for ice cream*) kōn コーン; (*of pine tree*) matsukasa 松かさ; (*on highway*) sēfutī-kōn セーフティーコーン
confectioner dagashi-ya 駄菓子屋
confectioners' sugar aishingu-yō shugā アイシング用シュガー
confectionery (*candy*) okashi お菓子
confederation rengō 連合
confer 1 *v/t* (*bestow*) juyo suru 授与する **2** *v/i* (*discuss*) kyōgi suru 協議する
conference kaigi 会議
conference room kaigishitsu 会議室
confess 1 *v/t* hakujō suru 白状する; REL zange suru ざんげする; (*admit*) mitomeru 認める; (*to the police*) jihaku suru 自白する; ***I ~ I don't know*** zannen desu ga shirimasen 残念ですが知りません **2** *v/i* mitomeru 認める; (*to police*) jihaku suru 自白する; REL zange suru ざんげする; ***~ to a weakness for ...*** ... ni taisuru yowasa o mitomeru ...に対する弱さを認める
confession kokuhaku 告白; (*to police*) jihaku 自白; REL zange ざんげ
confessional REL zange-shitsu ざんげ室
confessor REL chōzai-shisai 聴罪司祭
confide 1 *v/t* uchiakeru 打ち明ける **2** *v/i*: ***~ in*** ... ni himitsu o uchiakeru ...に秘密を打ち明ける
confidence (*assurance*) jishin 自信; (*trust*) shinrai 信頼; (*secret*) himitsu 秘密; ***in ~*** himitsu de 秘密で
confident (*self-assured*) jishin no aru 自信のある; (*convinced*) kakushin shite 確信して
confidential himitsu (no) 秘密(の)
confine (*imprison*) tojikomeru 閉じ込める; (*restrict*) kagiru 限る; ***be ~d to one's bed*** toko ni tsuite iru 床についている
confined *space* semai 狭い
confinement (*imprisonment*) kankin 監禁; MED osan お産
confirm *v/t* kakunin suru 確認する; *theory, fears* urazukeru 裏付ける
confirmation kakunin 確認; (*of theory, fears*) urazuke 裏付け
confirmed (*inveterate*) ganko (na) 頑固(な)

confiscate bosshū suru 没収する
conflict 1 *n* (*disagreement*) ronsō 論争; (*clash*) tairitsu 対立; (*war*) arasoi 争い **2** *v/i* (*clash*) kachiau かちあう; (*of theories*) mujun suru 矛盾する
conform junnō suru 順応する; (*of product*) tekigō suru 適合する; ***~ to government standards*** seifu no kijun ni shitagau 政府の基準に従う
conformist *n* taisei ni tsuku hito 大勢につく人
confront … ni tachimukau …に立ち向かう
confrontation taiketsu 対決
Confucianism Jukyō 儒教
Confucius Kōshi 孔子
confuse (*muddle*) konran saseru 混乱させる; ***~ X with Y*** X to Y o kondō suru XとYを混同する
confused konran shita 混乱した
confusing magirawashii 紛らわしい
confusion konran 混乱
congeal gyōko suru 凝固する
congenial tanoshii 楽しい
congenital MED sentensei (no) 先天性(の)
congested *roads* jūtai shita 渋滞した
congestion (*on roads*) jūtai 渋滞; (*in lungs*) kikan-heisoku 気管閉塞; (*in nose*) hanazumari 鼻詰まり; ***traffic ~*** kōtsū-jūtai 交通渋滞
congratulate … ni omedetō to iu …におめでとうと言う
congratulations oiwai no kotoba お祝いの言葉; ***~ on …*** … omedetō …おめでとう
congregate atsumaru 集まる
congregation REL kaishū 会衆
congress (*conference*) kaigi 会議; ***Congress*** (*of US*) Gikai 議会
Congressional Gikai (no) 議会(の)
Congressman Kain-giin 下院議員
Congresswoman Kain-giin 下院議員
conifer shinyōju 針葉樹
conjecture *n* (*speculation*) suisoku 推測
conjugate *v/t* GRAM katsuyō suru 活用する
conjunction GRAM setsuzoku-shi 接続詞; ***in ~ with*** … to tomo ni …とともに
conjunctivitis ketsumakuen 結膜炎
♦ **conjure up** (*produce*) … o tachidokoro ni tsukuridasu …をたちどころに作り出す; (*evoke*) … o yobiokosu …を呼び起こす
conjurer, conjuror tejina-shi 手品師
conjuring tricks tejina 手品
con man F ikasama-shi いかさま師
connect (*join*), TELEC tsunagu つなぐ; (*link*) kanrenzukeru 関連づける; (*to power supply*) setsuzoku suru 接続する
connected: ***be well ~*** tsute ga aru つてがある; ***be ~ with …*** … to kankei ga aru …と関係がある
connecting flight setsuzoku-bin 接続便
connection (*in wiring*) setsuzoku 接続; (*link*) kankei 関係; (*when traveling*) setsuzoku 接続; (*personal contact*) tsute つて; ***in ~ with …*** … ni kanshite …に関して
connoisseur tsū 通
conquer seifuku suru 征服する; *fear etc* uchikatsu 打ち勝つ
conqueror seifuku-sha 征服者
conquest (*of territory*) seifuku 征服
conscience ryōshin 良心; ***a guilty ~*** yamashii kokoro やましい心; ***it has been on my ~*** ki ni kakatte ita 気にかかっていた
conscientious ryōshinteki (na) 良心的(な)
conscientious objector ryōshinteki-heieki-kyohi-sha 良心的兵役拒否者
conscious *adj* (*aware*) ki ga tsuite iru 気がついている; (*deliberate*) ishikiteki (na) 意識的(な); MED ishiki no aru 意識のある; ***be ~ of …*** … ni kizuite iru …に気付いている
consciousness (*awareness*) jikaku 自覚; MED ishiki 意識; ***lose / regain ~*** ishiki o ushinau / torimodosu 意識を失う/取り戻す
consecutive renzoku (no) 連続(の)
consensus gōi 合意
consent 1 *n* dōi 同意 **2** *v/i* dōi suru 同

意する
consequence (*result*) kekka 結果
consequently sono kekka その結果
conservation hogo 保護
conservationist *n* shizen-hogoron-sha 自然保護論者, kankyō-hozenron-sha 環境保全論者
conservative *adj* (*conventional*) hoshuteki (na) 保守的(な); *clothes* jimi (na) 地味(な); *estimate* hikaeme (no) 控え目(の)
conservatory (*for plants*) onshitsu 温室; MUS ongaku-gakkō 音楽学校
conserve 1 *n* (*jam*) jamu ジャム **2** *v/t energy*, *strength* setsuyaku suru 節約する
consider (*regard*) … to minasu …とみなす; (*show regard for*) omoiyaru 思いやる; (*think about*) yoku kangaeru よく考える; ***it is ~ed to be …*** … to omowarete iru …と思われている
considerable kanari (no) かなり(の)
considerably kanari かなり
considerate omoiyari no aru 思いやりのある
consideration (*thought*) jukkō 熟考; (*thoughtfulness*, *concern*) omoiyari 思いやり; (*factor*) kōryo subeki ten 考慮すべき点; ***take … into ~*** … o kōryo ni ireru …を考慮に入れる
consignment COM yusō-kamotsu 輸送貨物
♦**consist of** … kara naru …から成る
consistency (*texture*) kata-sa 固さ; (*unchangingness*) ikkansei 一貫性
consistent (*unchanging*) ikkan shita 一貫した
consolation nagusame 慰め
console *v/t* nagusameru 慰める
consonant *n* GRAM shiin 子音
consortium kyōkai 協会
conspicuous medatsu 目立つ
conspiracy inbō 陰謀
conspire kyōbō suru 共謀する
constant (*continuous*) taezu tsuzuku 絶えず続く
consternation rōbai ろうばい
constipated benpi shite iru 便秘している
constipation benpi 便秘
constituent *n* (*component*) kōsei-yōso 構成要素
constitute (*account for*) kōsei suru 構成する; (*represent*) … to naru …となる
constitution POL kenpō 憲法; (*of person*) taishitsu 体質
constitutional *adj* POL kenpō (no) 憲法(の)
Constitution Day Kenpō-kinenbi 憲法記念日
constraint seiyaku 制約
construct *v/t building etc* kensetsu suru 建設する
construction (*of building etc*) kensetsu 建設; (*building*) kenzōbutsu 建造物; (*trade*) kensetsu-gyō 建設業; ***under ~*** kensetsu-chū de 建設中で
construction industry kensetsu-gyōkai 建設業界; **construction site** kenchiku-genba 建築現場; **construction worker** kensetsu-rōdō-sha 建設労働者
constructive kensetsuteki (na) 建設的(な)
consul ryōji 領事
consulate ryōji-kan 領事館
consult … ni sōdan suru …に相談する
consultancy (*company*) konsarutanto-gyō コンサルタント業; (*advice*) adobaisu アドバイス
consultant komon 顧問, konsarutanto コンサルタント
consultation kyōgi 協議
consume (*eat*) taberu 食べる; (*drink*) nomu 飲む; (*use*) shōhi suru 消費する
consumer (*purchaser*) shōhi-sha 消費者
consumer confidence kōbai-iyoku 購買意欲; **consumer goods** shōhi-zai 消費財; **consumer society** shōhi-shakai 消費社会
consumption shōhi 消費; (*of energy*) shōhi-ryō 消費量; ***~ tax*** shōhi-zei 消費税
contact 1 *n* (*person*) tsute つて; (*communication*) renraku 連絡;

(*physical*) sesshoku 接触; ***keep in ~ with*** … to renraku o toru …と連絡をとる **2** *v/t* … ni renraku suru …に連絡する
contact lens kontakuto-renzu コンタクトレンズ
contact number renraku-saki 連絡先
contagious densensei (no) 伝染性(の); *fig* utsuri-yasui うつりやすい
contain *tears, laughter* osaeru 抑える; ***it ~ed my camera*** sono naka ni watashi no kamera ga haitte ita その中に私のカメラが入っていた; ***~ oneself*** jisei suru 自制する
container iremono 入れ物; COM kontena コンテナ
container ship kontena-sen コンテナ船
contaminate osen suru 汚染する
contamination osen 汚染
contemplate *v/t* (*look at*) jitto mitsumeru じっと見つめる; (*think about*) jikkuri kangaeru じっくり考える
contemporary 1 *adj* gendai (no) 現代(の) **2** *n* dōjidai no hito 同時代の人
contempt keibetsu 軽べつ; ***be beneath ~*** keibetsu ni mo atai shinai 軽べつにも値しない
contemptible hiretsu (na) 卑劣(な)
contemptuous hito o baka ni shita 人をばかにした
contend *~ for …* … o arasou …を争う; ***~ with …*** … to tatakau …と闘う
contender SP senshu 選手; (*in competition*) sanka-sha 参加者; (*against champion*) chōsen-sha 挑戦者; POL kōho-sha 候補者
content[1] *n* naiyō 内容
content[2] **1** *adj* manzoku de 満足で **2** *v/t*: ***~ oneself with*** … de manzoku suru …で満足する
contented manzokusō (na) 満足そう(な)
contention (*assertion*) shuchō 主張; ***be in ~ for …*** … o arasotte iru …を争っている
contentment manzoku 満足
contents nakami 中身
contest[1] (*competition*) kontesuto コンテスト; (*struggle, for power*) arasoi 争い
contest[2] *leadership etc* … o arasou …を争う; (*oppose*) … ni igi o tonaeru …に異議を唱える
contestant kyōsō-sha 競争者; (*in competition*) shutsujō-sha 出場者
context bunmyaku 文脈; ***look at X in ~*** X no haikei o kangaete Xの背景を考えて
continent *n* tairiku 大陸
continental tairiku (no) 大陸(の)
contingency man'ichi no koto 万一の事
continual taema nai 絶え間ない
continuation tsuzuki 続き
continue 1 *v/t* tsuzukeru 続ける; ***to be ~d*** tsuzuku 続く **2** *v/i* tsuzuku 続く
continuity renzokusei 連続性
continuous taema nai 絶え間ない
contort *face* shikameru しかめる; *body* nejiru ねじる
contour rinkaku 輪郭
contraception hinin 避妊
contraceptive *n* (*device*) hinin-gu 避妊具; (*pill*) hinin-yaku 避妊薬
contract[1] *n* keiyaku 契約
contract[2] **1** *v/i* (*shrink*) shūshuku suru 収縮する **2** *v/t illness* … ni kakaru …にかかる
contractor ukeoinin 請負人
contractual keiyakujō (no) 契約上(の)
contradict *statement* hitei suru 否定する; *colleague* hanron suru 反論する; *parent, teacher* sakarau 逆らう
contradiction mujun 矛盾
contradictory mujun shita 矛盾した
contraption F kikai 機械
contrary[1] **1** *adj* hantai (no) 反対(の); ***~ to …*** … ni hanshite …に反して **2** *n*: ***on the ~*** soredokoroka それどころか
contrary[2] (*perverse*) hesomagari へそ曲り
contrast 1 *n* chigai 違い, kontorasuto コントラスト **2** *v/t* taihi suru 対比する **3** *v/i* … to ichijirushiku chigau …と著しく違う

contrasting taishōteki (na) 対照的(な)
contravene … ni ihan suru …に違反する
contribute 1 *v/i* (*with money, material*) kifu suru 寄付する; (*with time*) kōken suru 貢献する; (*to magazine, paper*) kikō suru 寄稿する; (*to discussion*) hatsugen suru 発言する; (*help to cause*) ichiin to naru 一因となる **2** *v/t money* kifu suru 寄付する; *time, suggestion* teikyō suru 提供する
contribution (*money*) kifu 寄付; (*to political party, church*) kenkin 献金; (*of time, effort*) kōken 貢献; (*to debate*) hatsugen 発言; (*to magazine*) kikō 寄稿
contributor (*of money*) kifu-sha 寄付者; (*to magazine*) kikō-sha 寄稿者
contrive dōnika … suru どうにか…する
control 1 *n* (*of country, organization*) shihai 支配; (*domination*) kanri 管理; (*of emotion*) yokusei 抑制; (*in ball game*) kontorōru コントロール; ***be in ~ of …*** … o shihai shite iru …を支配している; ***bring … under ~*** … o osaeru …を抑える; ***get out of ~*** … o seishikirenaku naru …を制しきれなくなる; ***lose ~ of …*** … o seishikirenaku naru …を制しきれなくなる; ***lose ~ of oneself*** jibun no kanjō o osaekirenaku naru 自分の感情を抑えきれなくなる; ***the situation is under ~*** banji umaku itte iru 万事うまくいっている; ***circumstances beyond our ~*** jōkyō ga te ni oenai 状況が手に負えない; **~s** (*of aircraft, vehicle*) sōjū-sōchi 操縦装置; (*restrictions*) kisei 規制 **2** *v/t* (*govern*) shihai suru 支配する; *class* kontorōru suru コントロールする; (*restrict*) kisei suru 規制する; (*regulate*) kanri suru 管理する; ***~ oneself*** jisei suru 自制する
control center kontorōru-sentā コントロールセンター
control freak F shikiri-ya 仕切り屋
controlled substance shojikisei-yakubutsu 所持規制薬物
controlling interest FIN shihai-mochibun 支配持ち分
control panel kontorōru-paneru コントロールパネル, seigyoban 制御盤
control tower kōkū-kanseitō 航空管制塔
controversial ronsō no mato ni natte iru 論争の的になっている
controversy ronsō 論争
convalesce kaifuku suru 回復する
convalescence kaifuku-ki 回復期
convene *v/t* shōshū suru 招集する
convenience benri 便利; (*of arrangement, time*) kōtsugō 好都合; ***at your/my ~*** anata / watashi no tsugō no yoi toki ni あなた/私の都合の良い時に; ***all (modern) ~s*** (gendaiteki) setsubi-kanbi (現代的) 設備完備
convenience food insutanto-shokuhin インスタント食品
convenience store konbini コンビニ
convenient *location, device* benri (na) 便利(な); *time, arrangement* tsugō no yoi 都合のよい
convent joshi-shūdōin 女子修道院
convention (*tradition*) kanshū 慣習; (*conference*) taikai 大会
conventional *person, ideas* kata ni hamatta 型にはまった; *family* heibon (na) 平凡(な); *method* dentōteki (na) 伝統的(な)
convention center kaigijō 会議場
conventioneer taikai-sanka-sha 大会参加者
conversant: ***be ~ with …*** … ni seitsū shite iru …に精通している
conversation kaiwa 会話
conversational kaiwa (no) 会話(の)
converse *n* (*opposite*) gyaku 逆
conversely gyaku ni 逆に
conversion henkan 変換; (*of part of house etc*) kaizō 改造; (*of yards to meters etc*) kanzan 換算; REL kaishū 改宗
conversion table kanzan-hyō 換算表

convert 1 *n* tenkō-sha 転向者 **2** *v/t* kaeru 変える; *unit of measurement* kanzan suru 換算する; *person* tenkō saseru 転向させる; REL kaishū saseru 改宗させる
convertible *n* (*car*) ōpun-kā オープンカー
convey (*transmit*) tsutaeru 伝える; (*carry*) hakobu 運ぶ
conveyor belt beruto-konbeyā ベルトコンベヤー
convict 1 *n* jukei-sha 受刑者 **2** *v/t* LAW yūzai-hanketsu o kudasu 有罪判決を下す; **~ *X of Y*** Y ni tsuite X ni yūzai-hanketsu o kudasu YについてXに有罪判決を下す
conviction LAW yūzai-hanketsu 有罪判決; (*belief*) kakushin 確信
convince kakushin saseru 確信させる
convincing settokuryoku no aru 説得力のある
convivial yōki (na) 陽気(な)
convoy (*of ships*) sendan 船団; (*of vehicles*) ichidan 一団
convulsion MED keiren けいれん
cook 1 *n* kokku コック, ryōri-nin 料理人 **2** *v/t* ryōri suru 料理する; ***a ~ed meal*** atatakai shokuji 暖かい食事 **3** *v/i* ryōri suru 料理する
cookbook ryōri no hon 料理の本
cookery ryōri (no) 料理(の)
cookie kukkī クッキー
cooking (*food*) ryōri 料理
cool 1 *n* F: ***keep one's ~*** katto naranai かっとならない; ***lose one's ~*** katto naru かっとなる **2** *adj weather, breeze* suzushii 涼しい; *drink* tsumetai 冷たい; (*calm*) reisei (na) 冷静(な); (*unfriendly*) reitan (na) 冷淡(な); F (*great*) kakko ii かっこいい **3** *v/i* (*of food*) sameru さめる; (*of tempers*) ochitsuku 落ち着く; (*of interest*) sameru さめる **4** *v/t*: **~ *it!*** F ochitsuite 落ち着いて
♦**cool down 1** *v/i* sameru さめる; (*of weather*) suzushiku naru 涼しくなる; (*of tempers*) ochitsuku 落ち着く **2** *v/t food* samasu さます; *fig* ochitsukaseru 落ち着かせる
cooperate kyōryoku suru 協力する
cooperation kyōryoku 協力
cooperative 1 *n* COM seikatsu-kyōdō-kumiai 生活協同組合 **2** *adj* COM seikatsu-kyōdō-kumiai (no) 生活協同組合(の); (*helpful*) kyōryokuteki (na) 協力的(な)
coordinate *activities* chōsei suru 調整する
coordination (*of activities*) chōsei 調整; (*of body*) baransu バランス
cop F omawari-san お巡りさん
cope taiō suru 対応する; **~ *with ...*** … ni taiō suru …に対応する; ***how does she ~ when she has six kids?*** kodomo ga rokunin mo ite kanjo wa dō yatte iru no kashira 子供が六人もいて彼女はどうやっているのかしら
copier (*machine*) kopī-ki コピー機
copilot fuku-sōjūshi 副操縦士
copious takusan (no) たくさん(の)
copper *n* (*metal*) dō 銅
copy 1 *n* (*duplicate, imitation*) fukusei 複製; (*photo~*) kopī コピー; (*of book*) issatsu 一冊; (*of record, CD*) ichimai 一枚; (*written material*) genkō 原稿; ***make a ~ of a file*** COMPUT fairu o kopī suru ファイルをコピーする **2** *v/t* (*imitate*) maneru まねる; *painting* fukusei suru 複製する; (*on photocopier, computer*) kopī suru コピーする; (*from blackboard, another person's work*) utsusu 写す
copy cat F maneshi まねし; **copycat crime** kopī-hanzai コピー犯罪; **copyright** *n* chosaku-ken 著作権; **copy-writer** (*in advertising*) kopī-raitā コピーライター
coral (*on seabed*) sango さんご
cord (*string*) himo ひも; (*cable*) kōdo コード
cordial *adj* atatakai 温かい
cordless phone kōdoresu-denwa コードレス電話
cordon hijōsen 非常線
♦**cordon off** hijōsen o haru 非常線を張る
cords (*pants*) kōdyuroi no zubon コーデュロイのズボン
corduroy kōdyuroi コーデュロイ

core 1 *n* (*of fruit*) shin しん; (*of problem*) kakushin 核心; (*of organization, party*) chūshin 中心 **2** *adj issue, meaning* jūyō (na) 重要(な)
cork (*in bottle*) koruku-sen コルク栓; (*material*) koruku コルク
corkscrew sennuki 栓抜き
corn tōmorokoshi とうもろこし
corner 1 *n* (*of page, room*) sumi 隅; (*of table, street*) kado 角; (*bend: on road*) magarikado 曲り角; (*in soccer*) kōnā kikku コーナーキック; ***in the ~*** sumi ni 隅に; ***on the ~*** (*of street*) kado de / ni 角で/に **2** *v/t person* oitsumeru 追い詰める; ***~ the market*** shijō o shihai suru 市場を支配する **3** *v/i* (*of driver, car*) kado o magaru 角を曲がる
corner kick kōnā kikku コーナーキック
cornstarch katakuriko かたくり粉
corny F tsumaranai つまらない
coronary 1 *adj* shinzō (no) 心臓(の) **2** *n* kanjō-dōmyaku-kessen 冠状動脈血栓
coroner kenshi-kan 検死官
corporal *n* gochō 伍長
corporal punishment taibatsu 体罰
corporate COM kigyō (no) 企業(の); ***~ image*** kigyō no imēji 企業のイメージ; ***sense of ~ loyalty*** kaisha e no chūseishin 会社への忠誠心
corporation (*business*) kigyō 企業
corps ichidan 一団
corpse shitai 死体
corpulent himan(no) 肥満(の)
corpuscle kekkyū 血球
corral *n* kakoi 囲い
correct 1 *adj* tadashii 正しい **2** *v/t* naosu 直す; *homework* saiten suru 採点する; *proofs* teisei suru 訂正する
correction teisei 訂正
correspond (*match*) itchi suru 一致する; (*write letters*) buntsū suru 文通する; ***~ to ...*** ... ni sōtō suru ...に相当する; ***~ with ...*** ... to itchi suru ...と一致する
correspondence (*matching*) itchi 一致; (*letters*) tegami 手紙; (*exchange of letters*) buntsū 文通
correspondent *letter writer* buntsū-aite 文通相手; (*reporter: abroad*) tokuhain 特派員; (*reporter: domestic*) kisha 記者
corresponding (*equivalent*) taiō suru 対応する
corridor (*in building*) rōka 廊下
corroborate urazukeru 裏付ける
corrode 1 *v/t* fushoku saseru 腐食させる **2** *v/i* fushoku suru 腐食する
corrosion fushoku 腐食
corrugated cardboard danbōru-gami 段ボール紙
corrugated iron hajō-totan'ita 波状トタン板
corrupt 1 *adj* fuhai shita 腐敗した; COMPUT mojibake suru 文字化けする **2** *v/t* daraku saseru 堕落させる; (*bribe*) baishū suru 買収する
corruption oshoku 汚職
cosmetic *adj* biyō (no) 美容(の); *fig* hyōmen dake (no) 表面だけ(の)
cosmetics keshōhin 化粧品
cosmetic surgeon biyō-seikei-gekai 美容整形外科医
cosmetic surgery biyō-seikei 美容整形
cosmonaut uchū-hikōshi 宇宙飛行士
cosmopolitan *city* kokusaiteki (na) 国際的(な)
cost 1 *n* hiyō 費用; *fig* gisei 犠牲; ***~s*** COM kosuto コスト **2** *v/t* kakaru かかる; *time* yō suru 要する; FIN *proposal, project* mitsumoru 見積もる; ***how much does it ~?*** kore wa ikura desu ka これはいくらですか; ***it ~ me my health*** watashi no kenkō ga gisei ni natta 私の健康が犠牲になった
cost and freight COM unchinkomi no nedan de 運賃込みの値段で; **cost-conscious** kosuto ishiki o motte コスト意識を持って; **cost-effective** hiyō-kōka no takai 費用効果の高い; **cost, insurance and freight** COM hokenryō unchinkomi no nedan de 保険料 運賃込みの値段で
costly *mistake etc* takaku tsuku 高

くっつく
cost of living seikatsu-hi 生活費
cost price genka 原価
costume (*for actor*) ishō 衣装
costume jewelry mozō-hōsekirui 模造宝石類
cot (*folding*) oritatami-shiki beddo 折りたたみ式ベッド
cottage shōkaoku 小家屋
cottage cheese kotēji-chīzu コテージチーズ
cotton 1 *n* wata 綿, kotton コットン **2** *adj* men (no) 綿(の)
♦**cotton on** F wakaru わかる
♦**cotton on to** F … ga wakaru …がわかる
♦**cotton to** F … ga suki ni naru …が好きになる
cotton candy wataame 綿あめ
couch *n* nagaisu 長いす
couch potato kauchi-poteto カウチポテト
couchette shindai 寝台
cough 1 *n* seki せき; (*to get attention*) seki-barai せき払い **2** *v/i* seki o suru せきをする; (*to get attention*) seki-barai o suru せき払いをする
♦**cough up 1** *v/t blood etc* … o haku …を吐く; F *money* … o shibushibu dasu …をしぶしぶ出す **2** *v/i* F (*pay*) okane o shibushibu harau お金をしぶしぶ払う
cough medicine, cough syrup sekidome-yaku せき止め薬
could: **~ *I have my key?*** kagi o totte itadakemasu ka かぎを取って頂けますか; **~ *you help me?*** tetsudatte itadakemasu ka 手伝って頂けますか; ***this ~ be our bus*** kore ga watashitachi no basu kamo shiremasen これが私達のバスかもしれません; ***you ~ be right*** anata ga tadashii kamo shiremasen あなたが正しいかもしれません; ***I ~n't say for sure*** hakkiri wa iemasen ga はっきりは言えませんが; ***he ~ have got lost*** kare wa mayotte ita kamo shiremasen 彼は迷っていたかもしれません; ***you ~ have warned me!*** anata wa watashi ni keikoku dekita no ni あなたは私に警告できたのに
council (*assembly*) gikai 議会; (*advisory body*) shingikai 審議会
councilman shikai-giin 市会議員
councilor giin 議員
counsel 1 *n* (*advice*) jogen 助言; (*lawyer*) bengo-shi 弁護士 **2** *v/t course of action* susumeru 勧める; *person* … ni jogen o ataeru …に助言を与える
counseling kaunseringu カウンセリング
counselor (*adviser*) kaunserā カウンセラー; LAW bengo-nin 弁護人
count 1 *n* (*number arrived at*) kazu 数; (*action of ~ing*) kanjō 勘定; (*in baseball, boxing*) kaunto カウント; ***keep ~ of …*** … no kazu o oboete oku …の数を覚えておく; ***lose ~ of …*** … no kazu o wasureru …の数を忘れる; ***at the last ~*** saishūteki ni wa 最終的には **2** *v/i* (*to ten etc*) kazu o kazoeru 数を数える; (*calculate*) keisan suru 計算する; *be important* jūyō de aru 重要である; *qualify* kazu ni hairu 数に入る **3** *v/t* (*~ up*) kazoeru 数える; (*calculate*) keisan suru 計算する; (*include*) kazu ni ireru 数に入れる
♦**count on** … o ate ni suru …を当てにする
countdown byōyomi 秒読み
countenance *v/t* yōnin suru 容認する
counter[1] (*in shop, café*) kauntā カウンター; (*in game*) koma こま
counter[2] **1** *v/t* … ni taikō suru …に対抗する **2** *v/i* (*retaliate*) hangeki suru 反撃する
counter[3]: ***run ~ to …*** … ni han suru …に反する
counteract chūwa suru 中和する; **counter-attack 1** *n* hangeki 反撃 **2** *v/i* hangeki suru 反撃する; **counterbalance** tsuriawaseru 釣り合わせる; **counterclockwise** han-tokeimawari (no) 反時計回り(の); **counterespionage** supai-bōshi-katsudō スパイ防止活動; **counterfeit 1** *v/t* gizō suru 偽造す

る **2** *adj* gizō (no) 偽造(の);
counterpart (*person*) sōtō suru hito 相当する人;
counterproductive gyakukōka (no) 逆効果(の); **countersign** *v/t* … ni fukusho suru …に副署する
countless kazoekirenai 数えきれない
country kuni 国; (*as opposed to town*) inaka 田舎; ***in the ~*** inaka ni 田舎に
country and western MUS kantorī カントリー
countryman (*fellow ~*) dōkoku-jin 同国人
countryside inaka 田舎
county gun 郡
coup POL kūdetā クーデター; *fig* daiseikō 大成功
couple (*married*) fūfu 夫婦; (*romantically involved*) kappuru カップル; (*two people*) futarigumi 二人組; ***just a ~*** sukoshi dake 少しだけ; ***a ~ of*** ni, san no 二、三の; (*people*) ni, san-nin no 二、三人の
coupon (*form*) shiryō-seikyū-ken 資料請求券; (*voucher*) waribiki-ken 割引券
courage yūki 勇気
courageous yūki no aru 勇気のある
courier (*messenger*) kūrie クーリエ; (*with tourist party*) tenjōin 添乗員; ***motorcycle ~*** baiku-bin バイク便
course *n* (*series of lessons*) kōza 講座, kōsu コース; (*part of meal*) ippin 一品; (*of ship, plane*) shinro 針路; (*for sports event*) kōsu コース; ***of ~*** mochiron もちろん; ***of ~ not*** tondemonai とんでもない; ***~ of action*** hōshin 方針; ***~ of treatment*** chiryō-katei 治療過程; ***in the ~ of …*** … no aida ni …の間に; ***can I open the window? - of ~!*** mado o akete mo ii desu ka - ē dōzo 窓を開けてもいいですかええどうぞ
court *n* LAW hōtei 法廷; (*~house*) saiban-sho 裁判所; SP kōto コート; ***take … to ~*** … o kiso suru …を起訴する
court case saiban 裁判
court dance (*Japanese-style*) bugaku 舞楽
courteous reigi-tadashii 礼儀正しい
courtesy reigi 礼儀
courthouse saiban-sho 裁判所;
court martial 1 *n* gunpō-kaigi 軍法会議 **2** *v/t* gunpō-kaigi ni kakeru 軍法会議にかける; **court music** (*Japanese-style*) gagaku 雅楽; **court order** saibansho-meirei 裁判所命令; **courtroom** hōtei 法廷;
courtyard nakaniwa 中庭
cousin itoko いとこ
cove (*small bay*) irie 入り江
cover 1 *n* (*protective*) kabā カバー; (*of book, magazine*) hyōshi 表紙; (*for bed*) beddo-kabā ベッドカバー; (*shelter*) kakure-basho 隠れ場所; (*shelter from rain*) amayadori no basho 雨宿りの場所; (*insurance*) hoshō-gaku 補償額 **2** *v/t* ōu 覆う; (*hide*) kakusu 隠す; (*of insurance policy*) … ni hoken o kakeru …に保険をかける; *distance* iku 行く; (*of journalist*) shuzai suru 取材する
♦ **cover up 1** *v/t* … o ōu …を覆う; *fig* momikesu もみ消す **2** *v/i fig* kabau かばう; ***~ for*** (*for person*) … o kabau …をかばう
coverage (*by media*) hōdō 報道
covering letter dōfū no tegami 同封の手紙, kabā-retā カバーレター
covert hisoka (na) ひそか(な)
coverup (*of crime etc*) momikeshi もみ消し
cow *n* ushi 牛
coward okubyō-mono おくびょう者
cowardice okubyō おくびょう
cowardly okubyō (na) おくびょう(な)
cowboy kaubōi カウボーイ
cower chijikomaru ちぢこまる
coy (*evasive*) tōmawashi (na) 遠回し(な); (*flirtatiously*) hanikanda はにかんだ
cozy igokochi no yoi 居心地のよい
CPU (= ***central processing unit***) chūō-shori-sōchi 中央処理装置
crab *n* kani かに
crack 1 *n* hibi ひび; (*joke*) jōdan 冗談 **2** *v/t cup, glass* hibi o ireru ひびを

入れる; *nut* waru 割る; (*solve*) kaiketsu suru 解決する; *code* sakeme o ireru 裂け目をいれる; ***~ a joke*** jōdan o tobasu 冗談を飛ばす **3** *v/i* hibi ga hairu ひびが入る; ***get ~ing*** sassoku shigoto ni torikakaru 早速仕事に取りかかる

♦**crack down on** … o kibishiku torishimaru …を厳しく取り締まる

♦**crack up** *v/i* (*have breakdown*) noirōze ni naru ノイローゼになる; F (*laugh*) warau 笑う

crackdown torishimari 取り締まり

cracked *cup, glass* hibiwareta ひび割れた

cracker (*to eat*) kurakkā クラッカー

crackle *v/i* (*of fire*) pachipachi to oto o tateru ぱちぱちと音を立てる

cradle *n* (*of baby*) yurikago 揺りかご

craft[1] NAUT fune 船

craft[2] (*skill*) gijutsu 技術; (*trade*) shokugyō 職業

craftsman shokunin 職人

crafty zurui ずるい

crag (*rocky*) iwaba 岩場

cram *v/t* tsumekomu 詰め込む

cramped *apartment* semai 狭い

cramps ikeiren 胃けいれん

cranberry kuranberī クランベリー, kiichigo 木いちご

crane 1 *n* (*machine*) kurēn クレーン; (*bird*) tsuru つる **2** *v/t*: ***~ one's neck*** kubi o nobasu 首を伸ばす

crank *n* (*person*) henjin 変人

crankshaft kuranku-jiku クランク軸

cranky (*bad-tempered*) okorippoi 怒りっぽい

crap *n* kuso くそ; *fig* V (*nonsense*) tawagoto たわごと; (*poor quality item*) dekisokonai 出来そこない

crash 1 *n* (*noise*) gachan to iu oto がちゃんという音; (*accident*) shōtotsu 衝突; (*plane ~*) tsuiraku 墜落; COM tōsan 倒産; COMPUT kurasshu クラッシュ **2** *v/i* (*make noise*) monosugoi oto o tateru ものすごい音を立てる; (*of thunder*) naru 鳴る; (*of car*) shōtotsu suru 衝突する; (*of airplane*) tsuiraku suru 墜落する; (*of market*) bōraku suru 暴落する; COMPUT kurasshu suru クラッシュする; F (*sleep*) neru 寝る; ***the vase ~ed to the ground*** kabin ga jimen ni ochite oto o tatete wareta 花瓶が地面に落ちて音をたてて割れた **3** *v/t car* shōtotsu saseru 衝突させる

♦**crash out** F (*fall asleep*) neru 寝る

crash course shūchū-kōsu 集中コース; **crash diet** shūchū-daietto 集中ダイエット; **crash helmet** herumetto ヘルメット; **crash landing** fujichaku 不時着

crate (*packing case*) hako 箱

crater (*of volcano*) funkakō 噴火口

crave hidoku hoshigaru ひどく欲しがる

craving tsuyoi yokkyū 強い欲求

crawl 1 *n* (*in swimming*) kurōru クロール; ***at a ~*** (*very slowly*) noronoro to のろのろと **2** *v/i* (*on floor*) hau はう; (*move slowly*) noronoro susumu のろのろ進む

♦**crawl with** … de ujauja shite iru … でうじゃうじゃしている

crayon kureyon クレヨン

craze dairyūkō 大流行; ***the latest ~*** saishin-ryūkō 最新流行

crazy *adj* ki ga kurutta 気が狂った; ***be ~ about*** … ni netchū shite iru … に熱中している

creak 1 *n* kiikii iu oto きいきいいう音 **2** *v/i* kishimu きしむ

cream 1 *n* (*for skin, coffee, cake*) kurīmu クリーム; (*color*) kurīmu-iro クリーム色 **2** *adj* kurīmu-iro (no) クリーム色(の)

cream cheese kurīmu-chīzu クリームチーズ

creamer (*pitcher*) mirukuire ミルク入れ; (*for coffee*) kōhī-yō kurīmu コーヒー用クリーム

creamy (*with lots of cream*) kurīmu tappuri (no) クリームたっぷり(の)

crease 1 *n* (*accidental*) shiwa しわ; (*deliberate*) orime 折り目 **2** *v/t* (*accidentally*) shiwa o tsukeru しわをつける

create 1 *v/t* hikiokosu 引き起こす; *garden, jobs, opportunity* tsukuru 作る **2** *v/i* (*be creative*) sōzō suru 創

造する
creation hassei 発生; (*of employment, opportunity*) sōshutsu 創出; (*something created*) sōsaku 創作; ***Creation*** REL tenchi-sōzō 天地創造
creative sōzōsei ga aru 創造性がある
creator sōsaku-sha 創作者; (*author*) saku-sha 作者; (*founder*) sōsetsu-sha 創設者; ***the Creator*** REL sōzō-shu 創造主
creature (*animal*) ikimono 生き物; (*person*) hito 人
credibility (*of person*) shinrai dekiru koto 信頼できること; (*of story*) shin'yōsei 信用性
credible (*believable*) shin'yō dekiru 信用できる; *candidate etc* shinrai dekiru 信頼できる
credit 1 *n* FIN tsuke つけ; (*use of ~ cards*) kurejitto クレジット; (*honor*) meiyo 名誉; (*payment received*) nyūkin 入金; ***be in ~*** kuroji de aru 黒字である; ***get the ~ for …*** … ni kansuru shin'yō o eru …に関する信用を得る **2** *v/t* (*believe*) shinjiru 信じる; ***~ an amount to an account*** aru kingaku o kōza ni nyūkin suru ある金額を口座に入金する
creditable shōsan ni atai suru 称賛に値する
credit card kurejitto-kādo クレジットカード
credit limit (*of credit card*) kādo-shiyō-gendogaku カード使用限度額
creditor saiken-sha 債権者
creditworthy shinyōgashi dekiru 信用貸しできる
credulous damasare-yasui だまされやすい
creed shinjō 信条
creek (*stream*) ogawa 小川
creep 1 *n pej* kobiru yatsu こびるやつ **2** *v/i* shinobiyoru 忍び寄る
creeper BOT tsuru-shokubutsu つる植物
creeps: ***the house gives me the ~*** zotto suru yō na ie da ぞっとするような家だ
creepy zotto suru ぞっとする
cremate kasō ni suru 火葬にする
cremation kasō 火葬
crematorium kasō-ba 火葬場
crescent *n* (*shape*) mikazuki 三日月
crest (*of hill*) chōjō 頂上; (*of bird*) tosaka とさか
crestfallen gakkari shita がっかりした
crevice wareme 割れ目
crew *n* (*of ship, plane*) norikumiin 乗組員; (*of repairmen etc*) han 班; (*crowd, group*) nakama 仲間
crew cut kakugari 角刈り
crew neck marukubi sētā 丸首セーター
crib *n* (*for baby*) bebī-beddo ベビーベッド
crick: ***~ in the neck*** sujichigai 筋違い
cricket (*insect*) kōrogi こおろぎ
crime (*offense*) hanzai 犯罪; (*shameful act*) tsumi 罪
criminal 1 *n* hanzai-sha 犯罪者 **2** *adj* (*relating to crime*) hanzai (no) 犯罪(の); (LAW: *not civil*) keiji (no) 刑事(の); (*shameful*) keshikaran けしからん
crimson *adj* makka (na) 真っ赤(な)
cringe chijimiagaru 縮み上がる
cripple 1 *n* (*disabled person*) fugu 不具 **2** *v/t person* fugu ni suru 不具にする; *fig* mahi saseru 麻ひさせる
crisis kiki 危機
crisp *adj weather, air* sawayaka (na) さわやか(な); *lettuce, apple* shakishaki shita しゃきしゃきした; *bacon, toast* karitto shita かりっとした; *shirt* paritto shita ぱりっとした; *bank bill* te no kireru yō (na) 手の切れるよう(な)
criterion (*standard*) kijun 基準
critic hyōron-ka 評論家
critical (*making criticisms*) hihanteki (na) 批判的(な); (*serious*) kikiteki (na) 危機的(な); *moment etc* jūdai (na) 重大(な); MED jūtai (no) 重体(の)
critically *speak etc* hihanteki ni 批判的に; ***~ ill*** jūtai de 重体で

criticism hihan 批判
criticize *v/t* hihan suru 批判する
croak 1 *n* (*of frog*) gerogero to naku koe げろげろと鳴く声; (*of person*) shagaregoe しゃがれ声 **2** *v/i* (*of frog*) gerogero naku げろげろ鳴く; (*of person*) shagaregoe o dasu しゃがれ声を出す
crockery tōjiki 陶磁器
crocodile wani わに, kurokodairu クロコダイル
crony F nakama 仲間
crook *n* (*dishonest*) akutō 悪党
crooked (*not straight*) magatta 曲がった; (*dishonest: person*) fuseijitsu (na) 不誠実(な); *business* fusei (na) 不正(な)
crop 1 *n* shūkaku 収穫; *fig* mure 群れ **2** *v/t hair* karikomu 刈り込む; *photo* hashi o kiriotosu 端を切り落とす
♦ **crop up** mochiagaru 持ち上がる
cross 1 *adj* (*angry*) okotte iru 怒っている **2** *n* (*X*) batsu(jirushi) ばつ（印）; (*Christian symbol*) jūjika 十字架 **3** *v/t* (*go across*) wataru 渡る; **~ *oneself*** REL jūji o kiru 十字を切る; **~ *one's legs*** ashi o kumu 足を組む; ***keep one's fingers ~ed*** kōun o inoru 幸運を祈る; ***it never ~ed my mind*** sore wa omoitsukanakatta それは思いつかなかった **4** *v/i* (*go across*) wataru 渡る; (*of lines*) kōsa suru 交差する
♦ **cross off, cross out** … o kesu …を消す
crossbar (*of goal*) yokogi 横木; (*of bicycle*) ue-paipu 上パイプ; (*in high jump*) bā バー
cross-country (skiing) kurosu-kantorī (sukī) クロスカントリー（スキー）
crossed check senbiki-kogitte 線引き小切手
cross-examine LAW hantai-jinmon o okonau 反対尋問を行う
cross-eyed yorime (no) 寄り目の
crossing NAUT kōkai 航海
crossroads kōsaten 交差点; **cross-section** (*of people*) tenkei 典型;
crosswalk ōdan-hodō 横断歩道;
crossword (puzzle) kurosuwādo-pazuru クロスワードパズル
crouch *v/i* kagamu かがむ
crow *n* (*bird*) karasu からす; ***as the ~ flies*** massugu ni ikeba 真っ直ぐに行けば
crowd *n* gunshū 群衆; (*at sports event*) kankyaku 観客; (*in department store, bar etc*) hitogomi 人込み; ***I don't like ~s*** hitogomi ga kirai desu 人込みがきらいです
crowded konda 込んだ
crown 1 *n* (*on tooth*) shikan 歯冠, kuraun クラウン **2** *v/t tooth* … ni kuraun o kabuseru …にクラウンをかぶせる
crucial jūdai (na) 重大(な)
crude 1 *adj* (*vulgar*) gehin (na) 下品(な); (*unsophisticated*) sozatsu (na) 粗雑(な) **2** *n*: **~ (*oil*)** gen'yu 原油
cruel zankoku(na) 残酷(な)
cruelty gyakutai-kōi 虐待行為
cruise 1 *n* funatabi 船旅, kurūzu クルーズ **2** *v/i* (*in ship*) kōkai suru 航海する; (*of car*) raku ni hashiru 楽に走る; (*of plane*) junkō-sokudo de hikō suru 巡航速度で飛行する
cruise liner kyakusen 客船
cruising speed junkō-sokudo 巡航速度
crumb kuzu くず
crumble 1 *v/t* kuzusu 崩す **2** *v/i* (*of bread, stonework*) kuzureru 崩れる; *fig* (*of opposition etc*) hōkai suru 崩壊する
crumple 1 *v/t* (*crease*) shiwa ni suru しわにする **2** *v/i* (*collapse*) kuzureru 崩れる
crunch 1 *n* F: ***when it comes to the ~*** iza to iu toki ni wa いざというときには **2** *v/i* (*of snow, gravel*) zakuzaku oto o tateru ざくざく音を立てる
crusade *n fig* undō 運動
crush 1 *n* (*crowd*) hitogomi 人込み; ***have a ~ on*** … ni netsu o ageru …に熱をあげる **2** *v/t* oshitsubusu 押しつぶす; (*crease*) shiwakucha ni suru しわくちゃにする; ***they were***

~ed to death karera wa gekitotsushi shita 彼等は激突死した
crust (*on bread*) kawa 皮
crutch (*for injured person*) matsubazue 松葉杖
cry 1 *n* (*call*) sakebigoe 叫び声; ***have a ~*** naku 泣く **2** *v/t* (*call*) sakebu 叫ぶ **3** *v/i* (*weep*) naku 泣く
♦ **cry out 1** *v/t* ... o ōgoe de iu ...を大声で言う **2** *v/i* ōgoe o dasu 大声を出す
♦ **cry out for** (*need*) ... o ōi ni hitsuyō to suru ...を多いに必要とする
crystal (*mineral*) suishō 水晶; (*glass*) kurisutaru-garasu クリスタルガラス
crystallize 1 *v/t* gutaika saseru 具体化させる **2** *v/i* (*of thoughts etc*) gutaika suru 具体化する
cub ko 子
cube (*shape*) rippōtai 立方体
cubic sanjō (no) 三乗(の)
cubic capacity TECH yōseki 容積
cubicle (*changing room*) kōishitsu 更衣室
cucumber kyūri きゅうり
cuddle 1 *n* hōyō 抱擁 **2** *v/t* dakishimeru 抱き締める
cuddly *kitten etc* dakishimetaku naru 抱き締めたくなる; (*liking cuddles*) dakko saretagaru だっこされたがる
cue *n* (*for actor, pool*) kyū キュー; ***that's my ~ to leave*** sore ga kaeru kikkake to natta それが帰るきっかけとなった
cuff *n* (*of shirt*) kafusu カフス; (*of pants*) orikaeshi 折り返し; (*blow*) hirateuchi 平手打ち; ***off the ~*** tossa no kiten de とっさの機転で
cuff link kafusubotan カフスボタン
cuisine: ***Japanese ~*** washoku 和食; ***western ~*** yōshoku 洋食; ***Chinese ~*** chūka-ryōri 中華料理
cul-de-sac ikidomari 行き止まり
culinary ryōri (no) 料理(の)
culminate: ***~ in ...*** tsui ni ... to naru ついに...となる
culmination chōten 頂点
culprit hannin 犯人
cult (*sect*) shūha 宗派
cultivate *land* kōsaku suru 耕作する; *person* kankei o kizuku 関係を築く
cultivated *person* kyōyō no aru 教養のある
cultivation (*of land*) kōsaku 耕作
cultural (*of the arts*) geijutsuteki (na) 芸術的(な); (*of a country's identity*) bunkateki (na) 文化的(な)
culture *n* (*artistic*) geijutsu 芸術; (*of a country*) bunka 文化
Culture Day Bunka no hi 文化の日
cultured (*cultivated*) kyōyō no aru 教養のある
culture shock karuchā-shokku カルチャーショック
cumbersome yakkai (na) やっかい(な)
cunning 1 *n* warugashiko-sa 悪賢さ **2** *adj* warugashikoi 悪賢い
cup *n* kappu カップ; (*trophy*) torofī トロフィー; ***a ~ of tea*** ippai no ocha 一杯のお茶
cupboard todana 戸棚
curable chiryō-kanō (na) 治療可能(な)
curator (*of museum*) kanchō 館長
curb 1 *n* (*of street*) fuchiishi 縁石; (*on powers etc*) yokusei 抑制 **2** *v/t* yokusei suru 抑制する
curdle *v/i* (*of milk*) gyōko suru 凝固する
cure 1 *n* MED chiryōhō 治療法 **2** *v/t* MED chiryō suru 治療する; *meat, fish* hozon suru 保存する
curfew MIL yakan-gaishutsu-kinshirei 夜間外出禁止令; *fig* mongen 門限
curiosity (*inquisitiveness*) kōkishin 好奇心
curious (*inquisitive*) kōkishin no tsuyoi 好奇心の強い; (*strange*) kimyō (na) 奇妙(な)
curiously (*inquisitively*) monomezurashisō ni もの珍しそうに; (*strangely*) myō ni 妙に; ***~ enough*** kimyō ni mo 奇妙にも
curl 1 *n* (*in hair*) kāru カール; (*of smoke*) uzu 渦 **2** *v/t hair* kāru

saseru カールさせる; (*wind*) maku 巻く **3** *v/i* (*of hair*) kāru suru カールする; (*of leaf, paper etc*) maruku naru 丸くなる
♦ **curl up** maruku natte neru 丸くなって寝る
curly *hair* makige (no) 巻き毛(の); *tail* kāru shita カールした
currant hoshibudō 干しぶどう
currency (*money*) tsūka 通貨; ***foreign ~*** gaika 外貨
current 1 *n* (*in river*) nagare 流れ; (*in sea*) kairyū 海流; ELEC denryū 電流 **2** *adj* (*present*) genzai (no) 現在(の)
current affairs, current events jiji-mondai 時事問題
current affairs program jiji-mondai-bangumi 時事問題番組
currently ima no tokoro 今のところ
curriculum karikyuramu カリキュラム
curse 1 *n* (*spell*) noroi のろい; (*swearword*) akutai 悪態 **2** *v/t* norou のろう; (*swear at*) nonoshiru ののしる **3** *v/i* nonoshiru ののしる
cursor COMPUT kāsoru カーソル
cursory zonzai (na) ぞんざい(な)
curt bukkirabō (na) ぶっきらぼう(な)
curtail tanshuku suru 短縮する
curtain kāten カーテン; THEA maku 幕
curve 1 *n* kyokusen 曲線, kābu カーブ **2** *v/i* magaru 曲がる
cushion 1 *n* (*for couch etc*) kusshon クッション **2** *v/t blow, fall* yawarageru 和らげる
custard kasutādo-kurīmu カスタードクリーム
custody (*of children*) yōikuken 養育権; ***in ~*** LAW kōryū sarete 拘留されて
custom (*tradition*) kanshū 慣習; (*habit*) shūkan 習慣; COM hiiki ひいき; ***as was his ~*** itsumo no yō ni いつものように
customary itsumo (no) いつも(の); (*required by tradition*) kanshū (no) 慣習(の); ***it is ~ to …*** … suru no ga kanshū to natte iru …するのが慣習となっている
customer kyaku 客
customer relations shōgai 渉外
custom-made ōdāmeido (no) オーダーメイド(の)
customs zeikan 税関
customs clearance tsūkan-tetsuzuki 通関手続; **customs inspection** zeikan-shinsa 税関審査; **customs officer** zeikanri 税官吏
cut 1 *n* (*with knife, scissors*) kirikuchi 切り口; (*injury*) kirikizu 切り傷; (*of garment, hair*) katto カット; (*reduction*) katto カット, sakugen 削減; ***my hair needs a ~*** kami o katto shitai 髪をカットしたい **2** *v/t* kiru 切る; (*reduce*) katto suru カットする, sakugen suru 削減する; ***get one's hair ~*** kami o kitte morau 髪を切ってもらう
♦ **cut back 1** *v/i* (*in costs*) kiritsumeru 切り詰める **2** *v/t employees* … o sakugen suru …を削減する
♦ **cut down 1** *v/t tree* … o kiritaosu …を切り倒す **2** *v/i* (*in smoking etc*) herasu 減らす
♦ **cut down on** *smoking etc* … o herasu …を減らす
♦ **cut off** (*with knife, scissors etc*) kiritoru 切り取る; (*isolate*) koritsu saseru 孤立させる; TELEC denwa o kiru 電話を切る; ***we were ~*** kirete shimai mashita 切れてしまいました
♦ **cut out** (*with scissors*) … o kirinuku …を切り抜く; (*eliminate*) … o yameru …をやめる; ***cut that out!*** F yamenasai やめなさい; ***be ~ for*** … ni tekishite iru …に適している
♦ **cut up** *v/t meat etc* … o kiru …を切る
cutback sakugen 削減
cute (*pretty*) kawaii かわいい; (*sexually attractive*) suteki (na) 素敵(な); (*smart, clever*) nukeme no nai 抜け目のない
cuticle amakawa あま皮
cut-price yasuuri (no) 安売り(の)
cut-throat *competition* yōsha no nai

容赦のない

cutting 1 *n* (*from newspaper etc*) kirinuki 切り抜き **2** *adj remark* shinratsu (na) 辛らつ(な)

cyberspace saibāsupēsu サイバースペース

cycle 1 *n* (*bicycle*) jitensha 自転車; (*series of events*) shūki 周期 **2** *v/i*: **~ *to work*** jitensha de shigoto ni iku 自転車で仕事に行く

cycling saikuringu サイクリング

cyclist saikuringu suru hito サイクリングする人; (*in race*) jitensha no senshu 自転車の選手

cylinder (*container*) tsutsu 筒; (*in engine*) shirindā シリンダー

cylindrical entōkei (no) 円筒形(の)

cynic hiniku-ya 皮肉屋

cynical hiniku (na) 皮肉(な)

cynicism hiniku 皮肉

cyst nōshu のうしゅ

Czech 1 *adj* Cheko (no) チェコ(の); ***the ~ Republic*** Cheko-kyōwakoku チェコ共和国 **2** *n* (*person*) Cheko-jin チェコ人; (*language*) Cheko-go チェコ語

D

DA (= ***district attorney***) chihō-kenji 地方検事

dab 1 *n* (*small amount*) hitonuri ひと塗り **2** *v/t* (*remove*) tebayaku fuku 手早くふく; (*apply*) tebayaku nuru 手早く塗る

♦ **dabble in** … ni te o dasu …に手を出す

dad otōsan お父さん, papa パパ; (*when talking to outsiders about own father*) chichi 父

daffodil suisen 水仙

dagger tanken 短剣

daily 1 *n* (*paper*) nikkan-shi 日刊紙 **2** *adj* mainichi (no) 毎日(の)

dainty yūbi (na) 優美(な)

dairy products nyū-seihin 乳製品

dais endai 演台

dam 1 *n* (*for water*) damu ダム **2** *v/t river* … ni damu o tsukuru …にダムを造る

damage 1 *n* songai 損害; *fig* (*to reputation etc*) kizu 傷, damēji ダメージ **2** *v/t* songai o ataeru 損害を与える; *fig*: *reputation etc* kizu o tsukeru 傷を付ける

damages LAW songai-baishō 損害賠償

damaging songai o ataeru 損害を与える

dame F (*woman*) onna 女

damn 1 *interj* shimatta しまった **2** *n*: ***I don't give a ~!*** sonna koto shitta koto ja nai そんなこと知ったことじゃない **3** *adj* imaimashii いまいましい **4** *adv* hidoku ひどく **5** *v/t* (*condemn*) hinan suru 非難する; ***~ it!*** chikushō 畜生; ***I'm ~ed if …*** … da nante jōdan ja nai …だなんて冗談じゃない

damned → ***damn*** *adj*, *adv*

damp *building*, *room* shimeppoi 湿っぽい; *cloth* shimetta 湿った

dampen shimeraseru 湿らせる

dance 1 *n* dansu ダンス; (*social event*) dansu-pātī ダンスパーティー; ***Japanese ~*** Nihon-buyō 日本舞踊 **2** *v/i* odoru 踊る; ***would you like to ~?*** odorimasen ka 踊りませんか

dancer odoru hito 踊る人; (*performer*) dansā ダンサー

dancing dansu ダンス

dandelion tanpopo たんぽぽ

dandruff fuke ふけ

Dane Denmāku-jin デンマーク人

danger kiken 危険; ***out of ~*** (*of patient*) kiki o dasshite 危機を脱

して

dangerous kiken (na) 危険(な)

dangle 1 *v/t* burasageru ぶら下げる **2** *v/i* burasagaru ぶら下がる

Danish 1 *adj* Denmāku (no) デンマーク(の) **2** *n* (*language*) Denmāku-go デンマーク語

Danish (pastry) Denisshu デニッシュ

dare 1 *v/i* omoikitte … suru 思い切って…する; ***how ~ you!*** yoku mo mā よくもまあ **2** *v/t*: ***~ X to do Y*** X ni Y dekiru nara yatte miro to keshikakeru XにYできるならやってみろとけしかける

daring *adj* daitan (na) 大胆(な)

dark 1 *n* kuragari 暗がり; ***after ~*** kuraku natte kara 暗くなってから; ***keep … in the ~*** *fig* … ni damatte oku …に黙っておく **2** *adj room, night* kurai 暗い; *hair, eyes* kuroppoi 黒っぽい; *color* koi 濃い; *clothes* kurai iro (no) 暗い色(の); ***~ blue*** kon 紺; ***~ green*** fukamidori 深緑; ***a ~er blue*** koi ao 濃い青

darken (*of sky*) kuraku naru 暗くなる

dark glasses sangurasu サングラス

darkness kurayami 暗やみ

darling 1 *n* (*woman to man*) anata あなた; (*man to woman*) nē ねえ; ***he's a ~*** kare wa kawaii hito da 彼はかわいい人だ **2** *adj* aisubeki 愛すべき

darn[1] 1 *n* (*mend*) tsukuroi 繕い **2** *v/t* (*mend*) tsukurou 繕う

darn[2], darned → ***damn*** *adj, adv*

dart 1 *n* (*for throwing*) dātsu ダーツ **2** *v/i* tosshin suru 突進する

dash 1 *n* (*punctuation*) dasshu ダッシュ; (*small amount*) shōryō 少量; (MOT: *dashboard*) dasshubōdo ダッシュボード; ***a ~ of brandy*** shōryō no burandē 少量のブランデー; ***make a ~ for*** … ni tosshin suru …に突進する **2** *v/i* tosshin suru 突進する **3** *v/t hopes* uchikudaku 打ち砕く

♦**dash off 1** *v/i* isoide iku 急いで行く **2** *v/t* (*write quickly*) … o isoide kaku …を急いで書く

dashboard dasshubōdo ダッシュボード

data shiryō 資料, dēta データ

database dēta-bēsu データベース; **data capture** dēta-shūshū データ収集; **data processing** jōhō-shori 情報処理, dēta-shori データ処理; **data protection** dēta-hogo データ保護; **data storage** dēta-kanri データ管理

date[1] (*fruit*) natsumeyashi no mi なつめやしの実

date[2] 1 *n* hizuke 日付; (*romantic*) dēto デート; (*person*) dēto no aite デートの相手; ***what's the ~ today?*** kyō wa nannichi desu ka 今日は何日ですか; ***out of ~*** *clothes* jidaiokure de 時代後れで; *passport* kigengire de 期限切れで; ***up to ~*** saishinshiki de 最新式で **2** *v/t letter* hizuke o ireru 日付を入れる; (*go out with*) tsukiau つき合う; ***that ~s you*** toshi ga bareru 年がばれる

dated jidaiokure (no) 時代後れ(の)

daub *v/t* nuritakuru 塗りたくる

daughter (*own*) musume 娘; (*s.o. else's*) ojō-san お嬢さん, musume-san 娘さん

daughter-in-law giri no musume 義理の娘; (*s.o. else's*) giri no musume-san 義理の娘さん

daunt *v/t* shirigomi saseru しりごみさせる

dawdle *v/i* guzuguzu suru ぐずぐずする

dawn 1 *n* yoake 夜明け; *fig* (*of new age*) hajimari 始まり **2** *v/i*: ***it ~ed on me that …*** … da to wakatte kita …だとわかってきた

day hi 日; (*daytime*) hiruma 昼間; ***what ~ is it today?*** kyō wa nan'yōbi desu ka 今日は何曜日ですか; ***~ off*** kyūka 休暇; ***by ~*** nitchū ni 日中に; ***~ by ~*** higoto ni 日ごとに; ***the ~ after*** sono tsugi no hi その次の日; ***the ~ after tomorrow*** asatte あさって; ***the ~ before*** sono mae no hi その前の日; ***the ~ before yesterday*** ototoi おととい; ***~ in ~ out*** kuru hi mo kuru hi mo 来る日も来る日も; ***in those ~s*** sono tōji wa

その当時は; ***one ~*** (*in past*) aru hi ある日; (*in future*) itsuka いつか; ***the other ~*** (*recently*) senjitsu 先日; ***let's call it a ~!*** kyō wa kore de o-shimai ni shiyō 今日はこれでおしまいにしよう ◊ (*with count word*) nichi 日; ***a ~*** ichi nichi 一日; ***two ~s*** futsuka 二日; ***three ~s*** mikka 三日; ***four ~s*** yokka 四日; ***five ~s*** itsuka 五日; ***six ~s*** muika 六日; ***seven ~s*** nanoka 七日; ***eight ~s*** yōka 八日; ***nine ~s*** kokonoka 九日; ***ten ~s*** tōka 十日; ***twenty ~s*** hatsuka 二十日

daybreak yoake 夜明け; **daydream 1** *n* hakuchūmu 白昼夢 **2** *v/i* kūsō ni fukeru 空想にふける; **daylight** hi no hikari 日の光; **daytime**: ***in the ~*** hiruma ni 昼間に; **daytrip** higaeri-ryokō 日帰り旅行

daze: ***in a ~*** bōzen to shite ぼう然として

dazed (*by news*) bōzen to shita ぼう然とした; (*by a blow*) bon'yari shite ぼんやりして

dazzle *v/t* (*of light*) … no me o kuramaseru …の目をくらませる; *fig* kantan saseru 感嘆させる

dead 1 *adj person* shinda 死んだ; *plant* kareta 枯れた; *battery* kirete iru 切れている; *phone* tsūjinai 通じない; *flashlight*, *light bulb* tsukanai つかない; F *place* kakki no nai 活気のない **2** *adv* F (*very*) sugoku すごく; ***~ beat, ~ tired*** hetoheto ni tsukareta へとへとに疲れた; ***that's ~ right*** hontō ni tadashii 本当に正しい **3** *n*: ***the ~*** shinda hito 死んだ人; ***in the ~ of night*** mayonaka ni 真夜中に

deaden *pain, sound* yawarageru 和らげる

dead end (*street*) ikidomari 行きどまり; **dead-end job** shōraisei no nai shigoto 将来性のない仕事; **dead heat** dōchaku 同着; **deadline** saishū-kigen 最終期限; (*for submissions*) shimekiri 締め切り; **deadlock** *n* (*in talks*) ikizumari 行き詰まり

deadly *adj* (*fatal*) chimeiteki (na) 致命的(な); F (*boring*) hidoku tsumaranai ひどくつまらない

deaf mimi ga kikoenai 耳が聞こえない

deaf-and-dumb rōa (no) ろうあ(の)

deafen mimi o kikoenaku suru 耳を聞こえなくする

deafening mimi o tsunzaku yō (na) 耳をつんざくよう(な)

deafness mimi no kikoenai koto 耳の聞こえない事

deal 1 *n* torihiki 取り引き; ***it's a ~*** COM kore de kimari desu ne これで決まりですね; (*I agree*) notta のった; (*it's a promise*) yakusoku desu yo 約束ですよ; ***a good ~*** (*bargain*) toku na kaimono 得な買物; (*a lot*) kanari (no) かなり(の); ***a great ~ of*** (*lots*) takusan (no) たくさん(の) **2** *v/t cards* kubaru 配る; ***~ a blow to*** … ni dageki o ataeru …に打撃を与える

♦ **deal in** (*trade in*) … no baibai o suru …の売買をする

♦ **deal out** *cards* … o kubaru …を配る

♦ **deal with** (*handle*) … o atsukau …を扱う; (*do business with*) … to torihiki suru …と取り引きする

dealer (*merchant*) hanbai-gyō-sha 販売業者, dīrā ディーラー; (*drug ~*) mayaku-mitsubainin 麻薬密売人; (*at cards*) dīrā ディーラー, oya 親

dealing (*drug ~*) mayaku-torihiki 麻薬取り引き

dealings (*business*) kankei 関係

dean (*of college*) gakubuchō 学部長

dear *adj* shin'ai (na) 親愛(な); (*expensive*) kōka (na) 高価(な); ***Dear Sir*** haikei 拝啓; ***Dear Richard / Margaret*** richādo-san / māgaretto-san リチャードさん/マーガレットさん, *fml* richādo-sama / māgaretto-sama リチャード様/マーガレット様; **(*oh*) *~!, ~ me!*** oya, mā おや、まあ

dearly *love* kokoro kara 心から

death shi 死

death penalty shikei 死刑

death toll shibōsha-sū 死亡者数

debatable gimon no aru 疑問のある

debate 1 *n* tōgi 討議; POL tōron 討論

2 *v/t & v/i* tōron suru 討論する
debauchery hōtō 放とう
debit 1 *n* hikiotoshi 引き落し **2** *v/t account* hikiotoshi sareru 引き落しされる; *amount* karikata ni kinyū suru 借り方に記入する
debris zangai 残がい
debt shakkin 借金; ***be in ~*** shakkin shite iru 借金している
debtor fusai-sha 負債者
debug *room* tōchōki o torinozoku 盗聴器を取り除く; COMPUT konpyūtā no puroguramu o tenaoshi suru コンピューターのプログラムを手直しする
début *n* debyū デビュー
decade jū nenkan 十年間
decadent taihaiteki (na) 退廃的(な)
decaffeinated kafein o nuita カフェインを抜いた
decanter dekantā デカンター
decapitate kubi o kiru 首を切る
decay 1 *n* (*process*) fuhai 腐敗; (*decayed matter*) fushoku 腐食; (*in teeth*) mushiba 虫歯 **2** *v/i* kusaru 腐る; (*of teeth*) mushiba ni naru 虫歯になる
deceased: ***the ~*** kojin 故人
deceit damashi だまし
deceitful fushōjiki (na) 不正直(な)
deceive damasu だます
December jūnigatsu 十二月
decency reigi 礼儀; ***he had the ~ to …*** kare wa … suru reigi o wakimaeteita 彼は…する礼儀をわきまえていた
decent *person* mattō (na) まっとう(な); *salary*, *price* kekkō (na) 結構(な); *meal*, *sleep* matomo (na) まとも(な); (*adequately dressed*) chanto fuku o kite iru ちゃんと服を着ている
decentralize *administration* chihō-bunken ni suru 地方分権にする
deception gomakashi ごまかし; (*sexual*) fujitsu 不実
deceptive mikake to nakami no chigatta 見かけと中身の違った
deceptively: ***it looks ~ simple*** mikake wa shinpuru da ga 見かけはシンプルだが
decibel deshiberu デシベル
decide 1 *v/t* kimeru 決める, kettei suru 決定する; (*settle*) sayū suru 左右する; ***I haven't ~d what I'm going to do*** watashi wa nani o suru ka kimete inai 私は何をするか決めていない **2** *v/i* kimeru 決める; ***you ~*** kimete kudasai 決めて下さい
decided (*definite*) hakkiri shita はっきりした
decider (*game*) ketteisen 決定戦
decimal *n* shōsū 小数
decimal point shōsūten 小数点
decimate gekigen suru 激減する
decipher kaidoku suru 解読する
decision kettei 決定; ***it's your ~*** anata ga kimeru koto desu あなたが決めることです; ***it was your ~ to come here*** koko e kuru no wa anata ga kimeta koto desu ここへ来るのはあなたが決めたことです; ***come to a ~ on*** … ni kimeru …に決める; ***we need a ~*** kimenakereba narimasen 決めなければなりません
decision-maker kettei-sha 決定者
decisive kippari shita きっぱりした; (*crucial*) ketteiteki (na) 決定的(な)
deck (*of ship*) dekki デッキ; (*of cards*) hitokumi 一組
deckchair dekkichea デッキチェア
declaration (*statement*) dangen 断言; (*of independence*) sengen 宣言; (*of war*) fukoku 布告
declare (*state*) dangen suru 断言する; *independence* sengen suru 宣言する; *war* fukoku suru 布告する; (*at customs*) shinkoku suru 申告する
decline 1 *n* (*fall*) genshō 減少; (*in standards*, *health*) teika 低下 **2** *v/t invitation* kotowaru 断わる; ***~ to comment*** komento o sashihikaeru コメントをさしひかえる **3** *v/i* (*refuse*) kotowaru 断わる; (*decrease*) genshō suru 減少する; (*of health*) teika suru 低下する
declutch kuratchi o kiru クラッチを切る
decode kaidoku suru 解読する
decompose fuhai suru 腐敗する

décor naisō 内装, interia インテリア
decorate (*with paint, paper*) naisō suru 内装する; (*adorn*) kazaru 飾る; *soldier* … ni kunshō o sazukeru …に勲章を授ける
decoration (*paint, paper*) naisō 内装, interia インテリア; (*ornament*) kazari 飾り
decorative kazari (no) 飾り(の)
decorator (*interior ~*) naisō-gyōsha 内装業者
decoy *n* otori おとり; (*model duck*) dekoi デコイ
decrease 1 *n* (*in number*) genshō 減少; (*in size*) shukushō 縮小; (*in value, production, speed*) teika 低下 **2** *v/t number* genshō saseru 減少させる; *size* shukushō suru 縮小する; *value, speed, production* teika saseru 低下させる **3** *v/i* (*of number*) genshō suru 減少する; (*of size*) shukushō suru 縮小する; (*of value, speed, production*) teika suru 低下する
dedicate *book etc* sasageru 捧げる; **~ *oneself to …*** … ni sennen suru …に専念する
dedication (*in book*) kenji 献辞; (*to cause, work*) kenshin 献身
deduce suiron suru 推論する
deduct: **~ *X from Y*** Y kara X o sashihiku YからXを差し引く
deduction (*from salary*) kōjo 控除; (*conclusion*) suiron 推論
deed *n* (*act*) okonai 行い; LAW shōsho 証書
deep *hole, water* fukai 深い; *shelf* okuyuki no fukai 奥行きの深い; *trouble* shinkoku (na) 深刻(な); *voice* hikui 低い; *color* koi 濃い; *thinker* kangae no fukai 考えの深い
deepen 1 *v/t* fukaku suru 深くする **2** *v/i* fukaku naru 深くなる; (*of mystery*) fukamaru 深まる; (*of crisis*) masu 増す
deep freeze *n* reitōko 冷凍庫; **deep-frozen food** reitō-shokuhin 冷凍食品; **deep-fry** ageru 揚げる, furai ni suru フライにする
deer shika しか
deface sokonau 損なう
defamation meiyo-kison 名誉棄損
defamatory meiyo-kison ni ataru 名誉棄損にあたる
default *adj* COMPUT kiteichi (no) 既定値(の)
defeat 1 *n* haiboku 敗北 **2** *v/t* makasu 負かす; (*of task, problem*) zasetsu saseru ざ折させる
defeatist *adj attitude* haiboku-shugi (no) 敗北主義(の)
defect *n* kekkan 欠陥
defective kekkan no aru 欠陥のある
defend mamoru 守る; *cause* yōgo suru 擁護する; (*stand by*) kabau かばう; (*justify*) shakumei suru 釈明する; LAW bengo suru 弁護する
defendant hikoku 被告; (*in criminal case*) hikoku-nin 被告人
defense *n* bōei 防衛; SP difensu ディフェンス; LAW bengo 弁護; (*justification*) shakumei 釈明; (*of cause*) yōgo 擁護; ***come to X's ~*** X o tasukeru Xを助ける; (*verbally*) … o bengo suru …を弁護する
defense budget bōei-yosan 防衛予算
defense lawyer hikoku-bengonin 被告弁護人
defenseless mubōbi (na) 無防備(な)
defense player SP difensu no senshu ディフェンスの選手; **Defense Secretary** Kokubōshō-chōkan 国防省長官; **defense witness** hikokugawa-shōnin 被告側証人
defensive 1 *n*: ***on the ~*** mamori ni mawatte 守りに回って; ***go on the ~*** shusei ni tatsu 守勢に立つ **2** *adj weaponry* bōeiyō (no) 防衛用(の); *person* benkai-gamashii 弁解がましい
defer *v/t* nobasu 延ばす
deference sonkei 尊敬; keii 敬意
deferential keii o arawasu 敬意を表す
defiance hankō 反抗; ***in ~ of…*** … o mushi shite …を無視して
defiant hankōteki (na) 反抗的(な)
deficiency (*lack*) fusoku 不足

deficient: ***be ~ in ...*** … ga fusoku shite iru …が不足している
deficit akaji 赤字
define *word* teigi suru 定義する; *goal* akiraka ni suru 明らかにする
definite *date, time* hakkiri to kimatta はっきりと決まった; *answer, improvement* meikaku (na) 明確(な); (*certain*) kakujitsu (na) 確実(な); ***are you ~ about that?*** sore wa tashika desu ka それは確かですか; ***nothing ~ has been arranged*** nani mo hakkiri to kimatte inai 何もはっきりと決まっていない
definite article teikanshi 定冠詞
definitely tashika ni 確かに
definition (*of word*) teigi 定義; (*of objective*) setsumei 説明
definitive ketteiteki (na) 決定的(な)
deflect *ball, blow* kawasu かわす; *criticism* kaihi suru 回避する; (*from course of action*) mage-saseru 曲げさせる; ***be ~ed from*** … o kaeru …を変える
deform bukakkō ni suru 不格好にする
deformity kikei 奇形
defraud … kara damashitoru …からだまし取る
defrost *v/t food* kaitō suru 解凍する; *fridge* … no shimotori o suru …の霜取りをする
deft kiyō (na) 器用(な)
defuse *bomb* shinkan o torinozoku 信管を取り除く; *situation* yawarageru 和らげる
defy mushi suru 無視する
degenerate *v/i* (*of behavior*) daraku suru 堕落する; MED akka suru 悪化する; ***the discussion ~d into a fight*** giron kara kenka ni hatten shita 議論からけんかに発展した
degrade iyashimeru 卑しめる
degrading *position, work* kutsujokuteki (na) 屈辱的(な)
degree do 度; (*from university*) gakui 学位; (*amount*) teido 程度; ***by ~s*** shidai ni 次第に; ***get one's ~*** gakui o toru 学位を取る
dehydrated dassui-shōjō o okoshite 脱水症状を起こして
de-ice johyō suru 除氷する
de-icer johyō-supurē 除氷スプレー
deign: ***~ to ...*** …shite kudasatta …して下さった
deity kami 神
dejected rakutan shita 落胆した
delay 1 *n* okure 遅れ **2** *v/t* nobasu 延ばす; ***be ~ed*** okureru 遅れる **3** *v/i* guzuguzu suru ぐずぐずする
delegate 1 *n* daihyō 代表 **2** *v/t task* makaseru 任せる; *person* ninmei suru 任命する
delegation (*of task*) inin 委任; (*people*) daihyō-dan 代表団
delete sakujo suru 削除する; (*cross out*) kesu 消す
deletion (*act*) sakujo 削除; (*that deleted*) sakujo-bubun 削除部分
deli → ***delicatessen***
deliberate 1 *adj* koi (no) 故意(の) **2** *v/i* jukkō suru 熟考する
deliberately waza to わざと
delicacy (*of fabric*) sensai-sa 繊細さ; (*of problem*) bimyō-sa 微妙さ, derikēto-sa デリケートさ; (*of health*) yowa-sa 弱さ; (*tact*) kikubari 気配り; (*food*) chinmi 珍味
delicate *fabric* sensai (na) 繊細(な), derikēto (na) デリケート(な); *problem* bimyō (na) 微妙(な), derikēto (na) デリケート(な); *health* yowai 弱い
delicatessen derikatessen デリカテッセン, sōzai-ya 総菜屋
delicious oishii おいしい; ***that was ~*** oishikatta おいしかった; (*to hostess, waiter etc*) gochisōsama deshita ごちそうさまでした
delight *n* ōyorokobi 大喜び
delighted yorokonde iru 喜んでいる; ***be ~ to ...*** yorokonde… suru 喜んで…する
delightful tanoshii 楽しい
delimit han'i o sadameru 範囲を定める
delinquent *n* hikō ni hashitta 非行に走った
delirious MED uwagoto o iu うわ言をいう; (*ecstatic*) uchōten (no) 有

頂天(の)
deliver haitatsu suru 配達する; *message* todokeru 届ける; *baby* shussan o tasukeru 出産を助ける; ~ ***a speech*** enzetsu o suru 演説をする
delivery (*of goods, mail*) haitatsu 配達; (*of baby*) shussan 出産
delivery date nōnyūbi 納入日; **delivery note** haitatsu-jō 配達状; **delivery van** haitatsuyō-torakku 配達用トラック
delude damasu だます; ***you're deluding yourself*** anata wa jibun o damashite iru あなたは自分をだましている
deluge 1 *n* gōu 豪雨; *fig* sattō 殺到 **2** *v/t fig* sattō saseru 殺到させる
delusion sakkaku 錯覚
de luxe gōka (na) 豪華(な)
demand 1 *n* yōkyū 要求; COM juyō 需要; ***in*** ~ hipparidako de aru 引っ張りだこである **2** *v/t* yōkyū suru 要求する; (*require*) hitsuyō to suru 必要とする
demanding *job* kitsui きつい; *person* kimuzukashii 気難しい
demented hakkyō shita 発狂した
demise shikyo 死去; *fig* shōmetsu 消滅
demitasse demitasu デミタス
demo (*protest*) demo デモ; (*tape*) demo-tēpu デモテープ
democracy (*system*) minshu-shugi 民主主義; (*country*) minshu-shugi-kokka 民主主義国家
democrat minshu-shugi-sha 民主主義者; ***Democrat*** POL minshutō-in 民主党員
democratic minshuteki (na) 民主的(な)
demo disk demo-disuku デモディスク
demolish *building* torikowasu 取り壊す; *argument* kutsugaesu 覆す
demolition (*of building*) torikowashi 取り壊し; (*of argument*) ronpa 論破
demon akuma 悪魔
demonstrate 1 *v/t* (*prove*) risshō suru 立証する; *machine* miseru 見せる **2** *v/i* (*politically*) demo o suru デモをする
demonstration (*show*) risshō 立証; (*protest*) demo デモ; (*of machine*) demonsutorēshon デモンストレーション
demonstrative: ***be*** ~ kanjō o soto ni dasu 感情を外に出す
demonstrator (*protester*) demo-sankasha デモ参加者
demoralized yaru ki o nakusaseru やる気をなくさせる
demoralizing yaru ki o nakusu やる気をなくす
den (*study*) shosai 書斎
denial (*of rumor, accusation*) hitei 否定; (*of request*) kyohi 拒否
denim denimu (no) デニム(の)
denims (*jeans*) jīnzu ジーンズ
Denmark Denmāku デンマーク
denomination (*of money*) gakumen 額面; (*religious*) shūha 宗派
dense (*thick*) koi 濃い; *foliage* missei shita 密生した; *crowd* misshū shita 密集した; (*stupid*) atama no warui 頭の悪い
densely: ~ ***populated*** jinkō no misshū shita 人口の密集した
density (*of population*) mitsudo 密度
dent 1 *n* hekomi へこみ **2** *v/t* hekomaseru へこませる
dental *treatment* ha (no) 歯(の); *hospital* shika (no) 歯科(の)
dentist haisha 歯医者
dentures ireba 入れ歯
deny *charge, rumor* hitei suru 否定する; *right, request* kyohi suru 拒否する
deodorant deodoranto デオドラント, bōshūzai 防臭剤
depart shuppatsu suru 出発する; ~ ***from*** (*deviate from*) … kara soreru …からそれる
department (*of company*) bu 部; ka 課; (*of university*) gakubu 学部, gakka 学科; (*of government*) shō 省; (*of store*) uriba 売り場
Department of Defense Kokubō-sōshō 国防総省; **Department of the Interior** Naimushō 内務省; **Department of State** Kokumushō 国務省; **department store** depāto

デパート

departure (*leaving*) shuppatsu 出発; (*of train, bus*) hassha 発車; (*of person from job*) taishoku 退職; (*deviation*) itsudatsu 逸脱; ***a new ~*** (*for goverment, organization*) shin-hōshin 新方針; (*for company*) shin-tenkai 新展開; (*for actor, writer*) shin-kyōchi 新境地

departure lounge shuppatsu-raunji 出発ラウンジ

departure time shuppatsu-jikoku 出発時刻

depend: ***that ~s*** bāi ni yoru 場合による; ***it ~s on the weather*** tenki ni yoru 天気による; ***I ~ on you*** anata o tayori ni shite imasu あなたを頼りにしています

dependable tayori ni naru 頼りになる

dependence, dependency izon 依存

dependent 1 *n* fuyō-kazoku 扶養家族 **2** *adj* tayotte iru 頼っている

depict (*in painting, writing*) egaku 描く

deplorable nagekawashii 嘆かわしい

deplore nageku 嘆く

deport kyōsei-sōkan suru 強制送還する

deportation kyōsei-sōkan 強制送還

deportation order kokugaitaikyo-meirei 国外退去命令

deposit 1 *n* (*in bank*) yokin 預金; (*of mineral*) kōmyaku 鉱脈; (*on purchase*) tetsukekin 手付け金 **2** *v/t money* yokin suru 預金する; (*put down*) oku 置く; *silt, mud* taiseki suru 堆積する

deposition LAW sensei-kyōjutsusho 宣誓供述書

depot (*train station*) eki 駅; (*bus station*) teiryū-jo 停留所; (*for storage*) chozō-jo 貯蔵所

depreciate *v/i* FIN kachi ga sagaru 価値が下がる

depreciation FIN kachi no teika 価値の低下

depress *person* yūutsu ni saseru 憂うつにさせる

depressed *person* yūutsu (na) 憂うつ(な)

depressing yūutsu (na) 憂うつ(な)

depression MED utsubyō うつ病; (*economic*) fukyō 不況; (*meteorological*) teikiatsu 低気圧

deprive: ***~ X of Y*** X kara Y o ubau XからYを奪う

deprived mazushii 貧しい

depth fuka-sa 深さ; (*of shelf*) okuyuki 奥行き; (*of voice*) hiku-sa 低さ; (*of color*) ko-sa 濃さ; (*of thought*) fuka-sa 深さ; ***in ~*** (*thoroughly*) tettei shite 徹底して; ***in the ~s of winter*** fuyu no massaichū 冬の真最中; ***be out of one's ~*** (*in water*) se no tatanai 背の立たない; (*in discussion etc*) tsuite ikenai ついていけない

deputation daihyō-dan 代表団

♦**deputize for** … no kawari o suru …の代わりをする

deputy dairi-nin 代理人

deputy leader fuku-rīdā 副リーダー

derail: ***be ~ed*** (*of train*) dassen suru 脱線する

deranged hakkyō shita 発狂した

derelict *adj* hōki sareta 放棄された

deride baka ni suru ばかにする

derision azakeri あざけり

derisive *remarks, laughter* azakeruyō (na) あざけるよう(な)

derisory *sum* kushō shite shimauyō (na) 苦笑してしまうよう(な)

derivative (*not original*) hasei (no) 派生(の)

derive *v/t* eru 得る; ***be ~d from*** (*of word*) … ni yurai suru …に由来する

derogatory keibetsuteki (na) 軽べつ的(な)

descend 1 *v/t* oriru 下りる; ***be ~ed from*** … no shison de aru …の子孫である **2** *v/i* (*of airplane*) oriru 降りる; (*of climber*) gezan suru 下山する; (*of road*) kudari ni naru 下りになる; (*of darkness*) oriru 下りる

descendant shison 子孫

descent (*from mountain*) gezan 下山; (*of airplane*) kōka 降下; (*ancestry*) kakei 家系; ***of Chinese ~***

chūgokukei no 中国系の
describe iiarawasu 言い表す; ***~ X as Y*** X o Y da to iu XをYだと言う
description byōsha 描写; (*of criminal*) ninsō 人相
desegregate jinshu, seibetsu ni yoru sabetsu o nakusu 人種、性別による差別をなくす
desert[1] *n* sabaku 砂漠; *fig* fumō no chi 不毛の地
desert[2] **1** *v/t* (*abandon*) misuteru 見捨てる **2** *v/i* (*of soldier*) dassō suru 脱走する
deserted sabireta さびれた
deserter MIL dassōhei 脱走兵
desertion iki 遺棄; MIL dassō 脱走
deserve … ni atai suru …に値する
design 1 *n* dezain デザイン; (*for building*) sekkei 設計; (*pattern*) moyō, 模様, dezain デザイン **2** *v/t* sekkei suru 設計する; *clothes* dezain suru デザインする; ***not ~ed for heavy use*** tashiyō ni taeru yō ni dezain sarete inai 多使用に耐える様にデザインされていない
designate *v/t person* shimei suru 指名する; *area* shitei suru 指定する
designer dezainā デザイナー; (*of building, car, ship*) sekkei-sha 設計者
designer clothes burando-mono ブランド物
design fault sekkei-misu 設計ミス
design school dezain-sukūru デザインスクール
desirable nozomashii 望ましい
desire *n* (*wish*) negai 願い; (*sexual*) yokubō 欲望
desk tsukue 机; (*in hotel*) furonto フロント
desk clerk furonto-gakari フロント係
desktop publishing desukutoppu-paburisshingu デスクトップパブリッシング
desolate *adj place* kōryō to shita 荒涼とした
despair 1 *n* zetsubō 絶望; ***in ~*** zetsubō shite 絶望して **2** *v/i* zetsubō suru 絶望する; ***~ of*** … ni zetsubō suru …に絶望する, *doing sth* … o akirameru …をあきらめる
desperate *person, action* hisshi (no) 必死(の); *situation* zetsubōteki (na) 絶望的(な); ***be ~ for a drink/cigarette*** nomitakute/tabako o suitakute tamaranai 飲みたくて/タバコを吸いたくてたまらない
desperation shinimonogurui 死に物狂い; ***an act of ~*** hisshi no kōdō 必死の行動
despise keibetsu suru 軽べつする
despite … nimo kakawarazu …にもかかわらず
despondent rakutan shita 落胆した
despot bōkun 暴君
dessert dezāto デザート
destination mokutekichi 目的地
destiny unmei 運命
destitute konkyū (no) 困窮(の)
destroy hakai suru 破壊する
destroyer NAUT kuchikukan 駆逐艦
destruction hakai 破壊
destructive *power* hakaiteki (na) 破壊的(な); *criticism* hikensetsuteki (na) 非建設的(な); *child* ranbō (na) 乱暴(な)
detach torihazusu 取りはずす
detachable torihazuseru 取りはずせる
detached (*objective*) reisei (na) 冷静(な)
detachment (*objectivity*) reisei-sa 冷静さ
detail *n* (*small point*) komakai ten 細かい点; (*piece of information*) shōsai 詳細; (*irrelevancy*) sasai na koto ささいなこと; ***in ~*** saibu ni watatte 細部にわたって
detailed komakai 細かい
detain (*hold back*) hikitomeru 引き止める; (*as prisoner*) kōryū suru 拘留する
detainee POL seijihan 政治犯
detect … ni kizuku …に気づく; (*of device*) tanchi suru 探知する
detection (*of crime*) hakken 発見; (*of smoke etc*) tanchi 探知
detective keiji 刑事; (*private*) shiritsu-tantei 私立探偵

detective novel suiri-shōsetsu 推理小説
detector (*for metal*) tanchi-ki 探知器; (*for drugs*) kenshutsu-ki 検出器
détente POL kinchō-kanwa 緊張緩和, detanto デタント
detention (*imprisonment*) kōkin 拘禁
deter soshi suru 阻止する; **~ *X from doing Y*** X ni Y suru no o omoi todomaseru XにYするのを思いとどませる
detergent senzai 洗剤
deteriorate waruku naru 悪くなる
determination (*resolution*) ketsui 決意
determine (*establish*) kakutei suru 確定する
determined kataku kesshin shite 堅く決心して; *effort* danko to shita 断固とした
deterrent *n* yokushiryoku 抑止力
detest hidoku kirau ひどく嫌う
detonate 1 *v/t* bakuhatsu saseru 爆発させる **2** *v/i* bakuhatsu suru 爆発する
detour *n* mawarimichi 回り道; (*diversion*) ukairo う回路
detract: **~ *from*** ... o sokonau ...を損なう
detriment: ***to the ~ of*** ... ni songai o ataete ...に損害を与えて
detrimental yūgai (na) 有害(な)
deuce (*in tennis*) jūsu ジュース
devaluation (*of currency*) heika-kirisage 平価切り下げ
devalue *currency* ... no heika o kirisageru ...の平価を切り下げる
devastate *crops, countryside, city* ... ni ōki na higai o motarasu ...に大きな被害をもたらす; *fig*: *person* uchinomesu うちのめす
devastating shōgekiteki (na) 衝撃的(な)
develop 1 *v/t film* genzō suru 現像する; *land, site* kaihatsu suru 開発する; *activity, business* hatten saseru 発展させる; (*design*) kaihatsu suru 開発する; (*improve on*) shinten saseru 進展させる; *illness, cold* hatsubyō saseru 発病させる **2** *v/i* (*grow*) sodatsu 育つ; (*of country, business*) hatten suru 発展する
developer (*of property*) kaihatsu-gyōsha 開発業者
developing country hatten-tojōkoku 発展途上国
development (*of film*) genzō 現像; (*of land, new drug*) kaihatsu 開発; (*of business, country*) hatten 発展; (*event*) shinten 進展; (*improving*) shinten 進展
device (*tool*) dōgu 道具; (*gadget*) sōchi 装置
devil akuma 悪魔
devious (*sly*) warugashikoi 悪賢い
devise kōan suru 考案する
devoid: **~ *of*** ... ni kakete iru ...に欠けている
devote *time, effort, money* ateru 充てる; *life* sasageru 捧げる
devoted *son etc* kenshinteki (na) 献身的(な); ***be ~ to a person*** hito ni kenshinteki de aru 人に献身的である
devotion (*to person*) kenshin 献身; (*to job*) chūsei 忠誠
devour *food* musaborikuu むさぼり食う; *book* musaboruyō ni yomu むさぼるように読む
devout keiken (na) 敬けん(な)
dew tsuyu 露
dexterity kiyō-sa 器用さ
diabetes tōnyōbyō 糖尿病
diabetic 1 *n* tōnyōbyō-kanja 糖尿病患者 **2** *adj* tōnyōbyō (no) 糖尿病(の)
diagonal *adj* naname (no) 斜め(の)
diagram zu 図
dial 1 *n* (*of clock*) moji-ban 文字盤; (*of meter*) keiki-ban 計器盤 **2** *v/i* TELEC denwa o kakeru 電話をかける **3** *v/t number* daiyaru suru ダイヤルする
dialect hōgen 方言
dialog taiwa 対話
dial tone hasshin'on 発信音
diameter chokkei 直径
diametrically: **~ *opposed*** seihantai (no) 正反対(の)

diamond (*jewel, in cards*) daiyamondo ダイヤモンド; (*shape*) daiyamondo-gata ダイヤモンド形, hishi-gata ひし形
diaper oshime おしめ
diaphragm ANAT ōkakumaku 横隔膜; (*contraceptive*) pessarī ペッサリー
diarrhea geri 下痢
diary (*for thoughts*) nikki 日記; (*for appointments*) techō 手帳
dice 1 *n* saikoro さいころ **2** *v/t* (*cut*) sai no me ni kiru さいの目に切る
dichotomy nibun 二分
dictate *v/t letter* kōjutsu suru 口述する
dictation kakitori 書き取り
dictator dokusai-sha 独裁者
dictatorial *tone of voice* sondai (na) 尊大(な); *person* wanman (na) ワンマン(な); *powers* dokusaiteki (na) 独裁的(な)
dictatorship dokusai-seiji 独裁政治
dictionary jisho 辞書
die shinu 死ぬ; *~ of cancer/AIDS* gan / eizu de shinu がん/エイズで死ぬ; ***I'm dying to know/leave*** shiritakute / tachisaritakute tamaranai 知りたくて/立ち去りたくてたまらない
♦ **die away** (*of noise*) dandan to kikoenaku naru だんだんと聞こえなくなる
♦ **die down** (*of noise*) chiisaku naru 小さくなる; (*of storm*) shizumaru 静まる; (*of fire*) kiete iku 消えていく; (*of excitement*) sameru 冷める
♦ **die out** (*of custom*) sutareru すたれる; (*of species*) zetsumetsu suru 絶滅する
diesel (*fuel*) dīzeru ディーゼル
diet 1 *n* (*regular food*) shokuseikatsu 食生活; (*for losing weight*) daietto ダイエット; (*for health reasons*) shokuji-ryōhō 食事療法 **2** *v/i* daietto suru ダイエットする
differ (*be different*) kotonaru 異なる; (*disagree*) iken ga awanai 意見が合わない
difference chigai 違い; (*argument*) iken no sōi 意見の相違; ***it doesn't make any ~*** (*doesn't change anything*) nani mo kawaranai 何も変わらない; (*doesn't matter*) dōdemo yoi どうでもよい
different (*dissimilar*) chigau 違う; (*distinct*) betsu (no) 別(の)
differentiate: ***~ between*** *things* … no kubetsu o suru …の区別をする; *people* sabetsu suru 差別する
differently chigau fū ni 違う風に; ***he expressed it ~*** kare wa chigau hyōgen o shita 彼は違う表現をした; ***they do things ~*** karera wa betsubetsu no yarikata o suru 彼等は別々のやり方をする
difficult muzukashii 難しい
difficulty muzukashi-sa 難しさ; ***have ~ doing …*** … suru no wa muzukashii …するのは難しい; ***with ~*** kurō shite 苦労して
dig 1 *v/t* horu 掘る **2** *v/i*: ***it was ~ging into me*** … ni kuikomu …に食い込む
♦ **dig out** (*find*) … o sagashidasu …を捜し出す
♦ **dig up** … o horiokosu …を掘り起こす; *information* … o saguridasu …を探り出す
digest *v/t* shōka suru 消化する; *information* yoku rikai suru よく理解する
digestible *food* shōka-shiyasui 消化しやすい
digestion shōka 消化
digit (*number*) sūji 数字; ***a 4 ~ number*** yonketa no sūji 4けたの数字
digital dejitaru-shiki (no) デジタル式(の)
dignified dōdō to shita 堂々とした
dignitary kōkan 高官
dignity kihin 気品
digress wakimichi e soreru わき道へそれる
digression dassen 脱線
dike (*wall*) teibō 堤防
dilapidated arehateta 荒れ果てた
dilate (*of pupils*) hirogaru 広がる
dilemma jirenma ジレンマ; ***be in a ~*** itabasami ni naru 板ばさみになる

diligent nesshin (na) 熱心(な)
dilute *v/t* usumeru 薄める
dim 1 *adj room, light* usugurai 薄暗い; *outline* bon'yari shita ぼんやりした; (*stupid*) atama no nibui 頭の鈍い; *prospects* kasuka (na) かすか(な) **2** *v/t*: **~ *the headlights*** heddoraito o shita ni mukeru ヘッドライトを下に向ける **3** *v/i* (*of lights*) kuraku naru 暗くなる
dime jussento-kōka 十セント硬貨
dimension (*measurement*) sunpō 寸法
diminish 1 *v/t* herasu 減らす **2** *v/i* genshō suru 減少する
diminutive 1 *n* aishō 愛称 **2** *adj* chiisai 小さい
dimple ekubo えくぼ
din *n* sōon 騒音
dine shokuji o suru 食事をする
diner (*person*) kyaku 客; (*restaurant*) shokudō 食堂
dinghy (*sailboat*) kogata yotto 小型ヨット; (*row boat*) gomu-bōto ゴムボート; (*inflatable*) kyūmei-bōto 救命ボート
dingy (*gloomy*) inki (na) 陰気(な); (*dirty*) usugitanai 薄汚ない
dining car shokudō-sha 食堂車; **dining room** shokudō 食堂; **dining table** shokutaku 食卓
dinner (*in the evening*) yūshoku 夕食; (*midday*) chūshoku 昼食; (*gathering*) dinā ディナー, enkai 宴会
dinner guest dinā no kyaku ディナーの客; **dinner jacket** takishīdo タキシード; **dinner party** dinā-pātī ディナーパーティー, enkai 宴会
dinosaur kyōryū 恐竜
dip 1 *n* (*swim*) hito-oyogi ひと泳ぎ; (*for food*) dippu ディップ; (*in road*) kubomi くぼみ **2** *v/t* … ni hitasu …に浸す; **~ *the headlights*** heddoraito o shita ni mukeru ヘッドライトを下に向ける **3** *v/i* (*of road*) kudarizaka ni naru 下り坂になる
diploma sotsugyō-shōsho 卒業証書
diplomacy gaikō 外交; (*tact*) josainasa 如才なさ
diplomat gaikōkan 外交官
diplomatic *corps* gaikōkan (no) 外交官(の); *solution* gaikō (no) 外交(の); (*tactful*) sotsu no nai そつのない
dire sashisematta 差し迫った
direct 1 *adj* chokusetsu (no) 直接(の); *flight* chokkō (no) 直行(の); *train* chokutsū (no) 直通(の); *person* sotchoku (na) 率直(な) **2** *v/t* (*to a place*) … ni michi o oshieru …に道を教える; *play* enshutsu suru 演出する; *movie* kantoku suru 監督する; *attention* mukeru 向ける
direct current ELEC chokuryū 直流
direction hōkō 方向; (*of play*) enshutsu 演出; (*of movie*) kantoku 監督; **~s** (*instructions*) shiji 指示; (*to a place*) michi 道; (*for use*) shiyō-hō 使用法; (*for medicine*) fukuyō-hō 服用法
direction indicator MOT winkā ウィンカー
directly 1 *adv* (*straight*) massugu ni 真っ直ぐに; (*soon*) mō sugu もうすぐ; (*immediately*) sugu ni すぐに **2** *conj* … suru to sugu ni …するとすぐに
director (*of company*) torishimariyaku 取締役; (*of movie*) kantoku 監督; (*of play*) enshutsu-ka 演出家
directory meibo 名簿; TELEC denwachō 電話帳
dirt yogore 汚れ
dirt cheap baka-yasui ばか安い
dirty 1 *adj* kitanai 汚い; (*pornographic*) waisetsu (na) わいせつ(な) **2** *v/t* yogosu 汚す
dirty trick hikyō na te 卑怯な手
disability shintai-shōgai 身体障害
disabled 1 *n*: ***the*** **~** shintai-shōgai-sha 身体障害者 **2** *adj* shintai-shōgai no aru 身体障害のある
disadvantage (*drawback*) furi na koto 不利なこと; ***be at a*** **~** furi na tachiba ni iru 不利な立場にいる
disadvantaged konkyū shite iru 困窮している
disadvantageous furi (na) 不利(な)

disagree iken ga awanai 意見が合わない
♦**disagree with** (*of person*) … to iken ga awanai …と意見が合わない; (*of food*) … no karada ni awanai …の体に合わない
disagreeable iya (na) いや(な)
disagreement iken no sōi 意見の相違; (*argument*) kenka けんか
disappear kieru 消える; (*run away*) shissō suru 失そうする
disappearance shissō 失そう
disappoint gakkari saseru がっかりさせる
disappointed gakkari shita がっかりした
disappointing kitaihazure (na) 期待はずれ(な)
disappointment shitsubō 失望
disapproval fusansei 不賛成
disapprove sansei shinai 賛成しない; ~ ***of X*** X ni hantai de aru Xに反対である
disarm 1 *v/t robber* … no buki o toriageru …の武器を取り上げる; *militia* busō-kaijo suru 武装解除する **2** *v/i* gunbi-shukushō suru 軍備縮小する
disarmament (*of militia*) busō-kaijo 武装解除; (*of country*) gunbi-shukushō 軍備縮小
disarming kokoro o nagomaseru 心をなごませる
disaster saigai 災害
disaster area hisaichi 被災地; *fig* (*person*) shippai-sha 失敗者
disastrous hisan (na) 悲惨(な)
disbelief: ***in*** ~ shinjirarenai to iu fū ni 信じられないという風に
discard suteru 捨てる
discern mitomeru 認める
discernible mitomerareru 認められる
discerning chigai no wakaru 違いのわかる
discharge 1 *n* (*from hospital*) taiin 退院; (*from army*) jotai 除隊 **2** *v/t* (*from hospital*) taiin saseru 退院させる; (*from army*) jotai saseru 除隊させる; (*from job*) kaiko suru 解雇する
disciple (*religious*) deshi 弟子
disciplinary chōkai (no) 懲戒(の)
discipline 1 *n* kiritsu 規律 **2** *v/t child, dog* shitsukeru しつける; *employee* bassuru 罰する
disc jockey disuku-jokkī ディスクジョッキー, dī-jē D J
disclaim hinin suru 否認する
disclose akiraka ni suru 明らかにする
disclosure (*of information, name*) kōhyō 公表; (*about scandal etc*) hakkaku 発覚
disco disuko ディスコ
discolor henshoku saseru 変色させる
discomfort (*pain*) karui itami 軽い痛み; (*embarrassment*) tōwaku 当惑
disconcert dogimagi saseru どぎまぎさせる
disconcerted dogimagi shita どぎまぎした; ***be*** ~ dogimagi suru どぎまぎする
disconnect *hose, appliance* torihazusu 取りはずす; *supply, service* tomeru 止める
disconsolate kanashii 悲しい
discontent fuman 不満
discontented fuman no aru 不満のある
discontinue *product* seizō-chūshi ni suru 製造中止にする; *train service* haishi suru 廃止する; *magazine* haikan ni suru 廃刊にする
discord MUS fukyō-waon 不協和音; (*in relations*) fuwa 不和
discotheque → ***disco***
discount 1 *n* waribiki 割引 **2** *v/t goods* waribiite baibai suru 割り引いて売買する; *theory* mushi suru 無視する
discourage (*dissuade*) … ni omoitodomaru yō ni iu …に思いとどまるようにいう; (*dishearten*) jishin o ushinawaseru 自信を失わせる
discover hakken suru 発見する; *talent* mitsukedasu 見つけ出す
discoverer hakken-sha 発見者
discovery hakken 発見

discredit *v/t person* … no shin'yō o kizutsukeru …の信用を傷つける; *theory* … ni gimon o nagekakeru …に疑問を投げかける
discreet *person* shinchō (na) 慎重(な); *restaurant* medatanai 目立たない
discrepancy mujun 矛盾
discretion shinchō-sa 慎重さ; ***at your ~*** anata no handan de あなたの判断で
discriminate: ***~ against*** … o sabetsu suru …を差別する; ***~ between*** … o kubetsu suru …を区別する
discriminating chigai no wakaru 違いのわかる
discrimination (*sexual*, *racial etc*) sabetsu 差別
discus SP enban 円盤
discuss hanashiau 話し合う; (*of article*) ronjiru 論じる
discussion (*talk*) hanashiai 話し合い; (*debate*) tōron 討論; (*in the press*) giron 議論
disease byōki 病気
disembark *v/i* (*from plane*) oriru 降りる; (*from ship*) gesen suru 下船する
disenchanted: ***~ with*** … ni genmetsu suru …に幻滅する
disengage hanasu 離す
disentangle hodoku ほどく
disfigure minikuku suru 醜くする
disgrace 1 *n* haji 恥; ***a ~*** (*person*) hajisarashi 恥さらし; ***it's a ~*** hidoi ひどい; ***in ~*** menboku o ushinatte 面目を失って **2** *v/t* hazukashimeru 辱める
disgraceful hazubeki 恥ずべき
disgruntled fuman (no) 不満(の)
disguise 1 *n* hensō 変装; (*costume, make-up*) hensō-dōgu 変装道具 **2** *v/t* kaeru 変える; *fear, anxiety* kakusu 隠す; ***~ oneself as*** … ni hensō suru …に変装する; ***he was ~d as*** kare wa … ni hensō shite ita 彼は…に変装していた
disgust 1 *n* ken'o 嫌悪 **2** *v/t* mukatsukaseru むかつかせる
disgusting *habit* iya (na) いや(な); *smell, food* kimochi no warui 気持ちの悪い; ***it is ~ that …*** … da to wa hidosugiru …だとはひどすぎる
dish (*part of meal*) ryōri 料理; (*container*) sara 皿
dishcloth shokkiaraiyō kurosu 食器洗い用クロス
disheartened gakkari shita がっかりした
disheartening gakkari saseru がっかりさせる
disheveled *hair*, *clothes* midareta 乱れた; *person* darashi no nai だらしのない
dishonest fushōjiki (na) 不正直(な)
dishonesty fushōjiki 不正直
dishonor *n* fumeiyo 不名誉; ***bring ~ on*** … ni doro o nuru …に泥を塗る
dishonorable fumeiyo (na) 不名誉(な)
dishwasher saraarai-ki 皿洗い機
dishwashing liquid senzai 洗剤
dishwater saraarai o shita mizu 皿洗いをした水
disillusion genmetsu saseru 幻滅させる
disillusionment genmetsu 幻滅
disinclined ki ga susumanai 気が進まない
disinfect shōdoku suru 消毒する
disinfectant shōdokuzai 消毒剤
disinherit … kara sōzokuken o ubau …から相続権を奪う
disintegrate barabara ni naru ばらばらになる; (*of marriage, building*) hōkai suru 崩壊する
disinterested (*unbiased*) kōhei (na) 公平(な)
disjointed matomari no nai まとまりのない
disk (*shape*) enban 円盤; COMPUT disuku ディスク; ***on ~*** furoppī ni hozon shite フロッピーに保存して
disk drive COMPUT disuku-doraibu ディスクドライブ
diskette furoppī-disuku フロッピーディスク
dislike 1 *n* hankan 反感 **2** *v/t* kirau 嫌う
dislocate *shoulder* dakkyū saseru 脱きゅうさせる
dislodge torihazusu 取り外す

disloyal uragirimono (no) 裏切り者(の)
disloyalty uragiri 裏切り
dismal *weather* iya (na) いや(な); *news, prospect* kurai 暗い; *person* (*sad*) inki (na) 陰気(な); *person* (*negative*) yūutsu (na) 憂うつ(な); *failure* mijime (na) みじめ(な)
dismantle *machine* bunkai suru 分解する; *organization* haishi suru 廃止する
dismay 1 *n* (*alarm*) tōwaku 当惑; (*disappointment*) shitsubō 失望 **2** *v/t* tōwaku saseru 当惑させる
dismiss *employee* kaiko suru 解雇する; *suggestion* shirizokeru 退ける; *idea, thought* suteru 捨てる; *possibility* mushi suru 無視する
dismissal (*of employee*) kaiko 解雇
disobedience fufukujū 不服従
disobedient hankōteki (na) 反抗的(な)
disobey … ni sakarau …に逆らう
disorder (*untidiness*) ranzatsu 乱雑; (*unrest*) bōdō 暴動; MED shōgai 障害
disorderly *room, desk* ranzatsu (na) 乱雑(な); *crowd* te ni oenai 手に負えない
disorganized mechakucha (na) めちゃくちゃ(な); *person* keikakusei no nai 計画性のない
disoriented konran shita 混乱した
disown kandō suru 勘当する
disparaging kenashita けなした
disparity sōi 相違
dispassionate (*objective*) reisei (na) 冷静(な)
dispatch *v/t* (*send*) hassō suru 発送する
dispensary (*in pharmacy*) chōzaishitsu 調剤室
dispense: ***~ with*** … nashi de sumaseru …なしで済ませる
disperse 1 *v/t* chirasu 散らす **2** *v/i* (*of crowd*) chitte iku 散っていく; (*of mist*) kieru 消える
displace (*supplant*) … ni totte kawaru …にとって代わる
display 1 *n* tenji 展示; (*in store window*) disupurē ディスプレー; COMPUT monitā モニター; ***be on ~*** (*at exhibition*) tenji shite aru 展示してある; (*be for sale*) chinretsu shite iru 陳列している **2** *v/t emotion* miseru 見せる; (*at exhibition*) tenji suru 展示する; (*for sale*) chinretsu suru 陳列する; COMPUT sukurīn ni hyōji suru スクリーンに表示する
display cabinet (*in museum, shop*) chinretsudana 陳列棚
displease okoraseru 怒らせる
displeasure ikari 怒り
disposable tsukaisute (no) 使い捨て(の); ***~ income*** tedori 手取り
disposal shobun 処分; (*of pollutants, nuclear waste*) haiki 廃棄; ***I am at your ~*** itsudemo kyōryoku shimasu いつでも協力します; ***put X at Y's ~*** X o Y no jiyū ni tsukaeru yōni suru XをYの自由に使えるようにする
dispose: ***~ of*** … o shimatsu suru …を始末する
disposed: ***be ~ to …*** (*willing*) … ki ga aru …気がある; ***be well ~ toward*** … ni kōiteki de aru …に好意的である
disposition (*nature*) kishitsu 気質
disproportionate futsuriai (na) 不つり合い(な)
disprove hanshō suru 反証する
dispute 1 *n* ronsō 論争; (*between countries*) funsō 紛争; (*industrial*) sōgi 争議 **2** *v/t* hanron suru 反論する; (*fight over*) arasou 争う
disqualify shikkaku to suru 失格とする
disregard 1 *n* mushi 無視 **2** *v/t* mushi suru 無視する
disrepair: ***in a state of ~*** hidoku itanda jōtai de ひどく傷んだ状態で
disreputable mittomonai みっともない; *area* ikagawashii いかがわしい
disrespect shitsurei 失礼
disrespectful shitsurei (na) 失礼(な)
disrupt *train service* midasu 乱す; *meeting, class* jama suru 邪魔する; (*intentionally*) bōgai suru 妨害する
disruption (*of train service*) konran

混乱; (*minor*) jama 邪魔; (*major*) bōgai 妨害

disruptive meiwaku (na) 迷惑(な)

dissatisfaction fuman 不満

dissatisfied fuman (na) 不満(な)

dissension iken no sōi 意見の相違

dissent 1 *n* hantai 反対 **2** *v/i*: ***~ from*** … ni hantai suru …に反対する

dissident *n* iken no chigau hito 意見の違う人

dissimilar kotonaru 異なる

dissociate: ***~ oneself from*** … to no kankei o hitei suru …との関係を否定する

dissolute fushidara (na) ふしだら(な)

dissolve 1 *v/t substance* tokasu 溶かす **2** *v/i* (*of substance*) tokeru 溶ける

dissuade omoi-todomaraseru 思いとどまらせる; ***~ X from Y*** X ni Y o omoi-todomaraseru XにYを思いとどまらせる

distance 1 *n* kyori 距離; ***in the ~*** tōku ni 遠くに **2** *v/t*: ***~ oneself from*** … kara kyori o oku …から距離をおく

distant tōi 遠い; (*aloof*) yosoyososhii よそよそしい

distaste ken'o 嫌悪

distasteful fuyukai (na) 不愉快(な)

distinct (*clear*) hakkiri shita はっきりした; (*different*) betsu (no) 別(の); ***as ~ from*** … to wa chigatte …とは違って

distinction (*differentiation*) kubetsu 区別; ***hotel of ~*** kōkyū-hoteru 高級ホテル; ***product of ~*** kōkyū-hin 高級品

distinctive dokutoku (na) 独特(な)

distinctly hakkiri to はっきりと; (*decidedly*) utagai naku 疑いなく

distinguish (*see*) hakkiri to mieru はっきりと見える; (*hear*) hakkiri to kikoeru はっきりと聞こえる; ***~ between X and Y*** X to Y no kubetsu o suru XとYの区別をする

distinguished (*famous*) yūmei (na) 有名(な); (*dignified*) jōhin (na) 上品(な)

distort yugameru ゆがめる

distract *person* jama suru 邪魔する; *attention* sorasu そらす

distracted (*worried*) uwa no sora (no) 上の空(の)

distraction (*of attention*) ki o chirasu mono 気を散らすもの; (*amusement*) kibarashi 気晴らし; ***drive … to ~*** … o gyakujō saseru …を逆上させる

distraught torimidashita 取り乱した

distress 1 *n* (*mental suffering*) kunō 苦悩; (*physical pain*) kutsū 苦痛; ***in ~*** *ship, aircraft* sōnan shite 遭難して **2** *v/t* (*upset*) kurushimeru 苦しめる

distress signal sōnan-shingō 遭難信号

distribute kubaru 配る; *wealth* bunpai suru 分配する; COM hanbai suru 販売する

distribution haifu 配布; (*of wealth*) bunpai 分配; COM ryūtsū 流通

distribution arrangement COM ryūtsu no tehai 流通の手配

distributor COM ryūtsū-gyōsha 流通業者

district chiku 地区

district attorney chihō-kenji 地方検事

distrust 1 *n* fushinkan 不信感 **2** *v/t* shinyō shinai 信用しない

disturb (*interrupt*) … no jama o suru …の邪魔をする; (*upset*) fuan ni saseru 不安にさせる; ***do not ~*** nyūshitsu goenryo kudasai 入室ご遠慮下さい

disturbance (*interruption*) jama 邪魔; ***~s*** bōdō 暴動

disturbed (*concerned, worried*) shinpai (na) 心配(な); (*mentally*) jōcho-fuantei (no) 情緒不安定(の)

disturbing dōyō saseru 動揺させる

disused heisa sareta 閉鎖された

ditch 1 *n* mizo 溝 **2** *v/t* F (*get rid of*) suteru 捨てる

dive 1 *n* tobikomi 飛び込み; (*underwater*) daibingu ダイビング; (*of plane*) kyūkōka 急降下; F (*bar etc*) ikagawashii bā いかがわしいバー; ***take a ~*** (*of dollar etc*) kyūkōka suru 急降下する **2** *v/i*

tobikomu 飛び込む; (*underwater*) daibingu o suru ダイビングをする; (*of plane*) kyūkōka suru 急降下する
diver (*off board*) tobikomi no senshu 飛び込みの選手; (*underwater*) daibā ダイバー
diverge bunki suru 分岐する
diverse samazama (na) 様々(な)
diversification COM takaku-keiei 多角経営
diversify *v/i* COM takaku-keiei suru 多角経営する
diversion (*for traffic*) ukairo う回路; ***create a ~*** ki o sorasu 気をそらす
diversity tayōsei 多様性
divert *traffic* ukai saseru う回させる; *attention* sorasu そらす
divest ***~ X of Y*** X kara Y o ubau XからYを奪う
divide wakeru 分ける; MATH waru 割る; *family* bunretsu saseru 分裂させる; *country* bunkatsu suru 分割する
dividend FIN haitōkin 配当金; ***pay ~s*** *fig* yaku ni tatsu 役に立つ
divine REL kami (no) 神(の); F subarashii すばらしい
diving (*from board*) tobikomi 飛び込み; (*scuba ~*) sukyūba-daibingu スキューバダイビング
diving board tobikomi-dai 飛び込み台
divisible warikireru 割り切れる
division MATH warizan 割り算; (*in party etc*) bunretsu 分裂; (*splitting into parts*) bunkatsu 分割; (*of company*) bu 部
divorce 1 *n* rikon 離婚; ***get a ~*** rikon suru 離婚する **2** *v/t* … to rikon suru …と離婚する **3** *v/i* rikon suru 離婚する
divorced rikon shita 離婚した; ***get ~d*** rikon suru 離婚する
divorcee (*man*) rikon shita dansei 離婚した男性; (*woman*) rikon shita josei 離婚した女性
divulge morasu 漏らす
DIY (= ***do-it-yourself***) nichiyō-daiku 日曜大工
DIY store doito ドイト
dizzy: ***feel ~*** memai ga suru めまいがする
DNA (= ***deoxyribonucleic acid***) deokishiribo-kakusan デオキシリボ核酸, dī-enu-ē DNA
do 1 *v/t* suru する; *one's hair* setto suru セットする; *Spanish, chemistry* benkyō suru 勉強する; *100mph etc* … no sokudo de susumu …の速度で進む; ***what are you ~ing tonight?*** kyō no yoru wa nani o suru no desu ka 今日の夜は何をするのですか; ***I don't know what to ~*** dō shitara ii ka wakarimasen どうしたらいいか分かりません; ***no, I'll ~ it*** iie, watashi ga shimasu いいえ、私がします; ***~ it right now!*** ima sugu shinasai 今すぐしなさい; ***have you done this before?*** kore o mae ni shita koto ga arimasu ka これを前にした事がありますか; ***have one's hair done*** kami o setto shite morau 髪をセットしてもらう **2** *v/i* (*be suitable, enough*) ma ni au 間に合う; ***that will ~!*** sore de jūbun da それで十分だ; ***~ well*** (*of person*) umaku yaru うまくやる; (*of business*) umaku iku うまくいく; ***well done!*** (*congratulations!*) omedetō おめでとう; ***how ~ you ~*** hajimemashite はじめまして **3** (*auxiliary*): ***~ you know him?*** kare o shitte imasu ka 彼を知っていますか; ***I don't know*** wakarimasen わかりません; ***~ be quick*** isoide yo 急いでよ; ***~ you like San Francisco? – yes I ~*** San Furanshisuko wa suki desu ka – hai, suki desu サンフランシスコは好きですか – はい、好きです; ***he works hard, doesn't he?*** kare wa nesshin ni hatarakimasu ne 彼は熱心に働きますね; ***don't you believe me?*** shinjiraremasen ka 信じられませんか; ***you ~ believe me, don't you?*** shinjite kuremasu ne 信じてくれますね; ***you don't know the answer, ~ you? – no I don't*** kotae o shirimasen ne – hai, shirimasen 答えを知りませんね – はい、知りません
♦**do away with** (*abolish*) … o

nakusu …をなくす
♦**do in** F: ***I'm done in*** hetoheto desu へとへとです
♦**do out of**: ***do X out of Y*** X o damashite Y o toriageru Xをだまして Yを取り上げる
♦**do over** (*do again*) … o yarinaosu …をやり直す
♦**do up** (*renovate*) … o kaishū suru …を改修する; (*fasten*) … o shimeru …を閉める; *buttons* … o tomeru …を留める; *laces* … o musubu …を結ぶ
♦**do with**: ***I could ~ …*** … ga hoshii …が欲しい; ***he won't have anything to ~ it*** kare wa sore to mattaku kakawaritakunai 彼はそれとまったくかかわりたくない
♦**do without 1** *v/i* nashi de sumaseru なしで済ませる **2** *v/t* … nashi de sumaseru …なしで済ませる
docile *person* sunao (na) 素直(な); *animal* jūjun (na) 従順(な)
dock[1] **1** *n* NAUT dokku ドック **2** *v/i* (*of ship*) dokku ni hairu ドックに入る; (*of spaceship*) dokkingu suru ドッキングする
dock[2] LAW hikoku-seki 被告席
dockyard zōsen-jo 造船所
doctor *n* MED isha 医者; (*form of address*) sensei 先生
doctorate hakase-gō 博士号
doctrine shugi 主義
docudrama dokyumentarī-dorama ドキュメンタリードラマ
document *n* bunsho 文書
documentary *n* dokyumentarī ドキュメンタリー
documentation shorui 書類
dodge *v/t blow* yokeru よける; *person*, *issue* sakeru 避ける; *question* hagurakasu はぐらかす
doe (*deer*) mejika 雌鹿
dog 1 *n* inu 犬 **2** *v/t* (*of bad luck*) … ni tsuite mawaru …について回る
dog catcher yaken-hokaku-nin 野犬捕獲人
dog-eared *book* tsukaifurushita 使い古した
dogged nebarizuyoi 粘り強い
doggie wanwan わんわん
doggy bag dogī-baggu ドギーバッグ
doghouse: ***be in the ~*** kirawarete iru 嫌われている
dogma kyōgi 教義
dogmatic kyōjō-shugiteki (na) 教条主義的(な)
do-gooder osekkai na jizen-ka おせっかいな慈善家
dog tag MIL ninshiki-hyō 認識票
dog-tired hetoheto ni tsukareta へとへとに疲れた
do-it-yourself nichiyō-daiku 日曜大工
doldrums: ***be in the ~*** (*of person*) yūutsu de aru 憂うつである; (*of economy*) keiki-chintai shite iru 景気沈滞している
♦**dole out** … o wakeru …を分ける
doll (*toy*) ningyō 人形; F (*attractive woman*) bijin 美人; F (*nice woman*) kawaii hito かわいい人
♦**doll up**: ***get dolled up*** kikazaru 着飾る
dollar doru ドル
dollop *n* hitosaji ひとさじ
dolphin iruka いるか
dome dōmu ドーム
domestic *adj chores* katei (no) 家庭(の); *news*, *policy* kokunai (no) 国内(の)
domestic animal petto ペット; (*for agriculture*) kachiku 家畜
domesticate *animal* kainarasu 飼い慣らす; ***be ~d*** (*of person*) kaji ni narete iru 家事に慣れている
domestic flight kokunai-sen 国内線
dominant omo (na) 主(な); *member* yūsei (na) 優勢(な); *opinion* shihaiteki (na) 支配的(な); BIO yūsei (no) 優性(の)
dominate shihai suru 支配する; *landscape* … ni sobieru …にそびえる
domination shihai 支配
domineering ōbō (na) 横暴(な)
donate *money* kifu suru 寄付する; *time* sasageru 捧げる; *toys*, *books* kizō suru 寄贈する; MED teikyō suru 提供する
donation (*of money*) kifu 寄付; (*of time*) kiyo 寄与; (*of toys*, *books*)

kizō 寄贈; MED teikyō 提供

donkey roba ろば

donor (*of money*) kizō-sha 寄贈者; MED teikyō-sha 提供者

donut dōnattsu ドーナッツ

doom *n* (*fate*) hiun 悲運; (*ruin*) hametsu 破滅

doomed *project* kanarazu shippai suru unmei (no) 必ず失敗する運命(の); ***we are ~*** (*bound to fail*) watashitachi wa shippai suru unmei ni aru 私達は失敗する運命にある; ***the ~ ship*** shizumu unmei no fune 沈む運命の船; ***the ~ plane*** tsuiraku suru unmei no hikōki 墜落する運命の飛行機

door to 戸, doa ドア; (*double ~s*) tobira 扉; (*entrance*) deiriguchi 出入口; ***there's someone at the ~*** dare ka kita mitai desu 誰か来たみたいです

doorbell buzā ブザー; **doorknob** doanobu ドアノブ, doa no totte ドアの取っ手; **doorman** doaman ドアマン; **doormat** matto マット; **doorstep** toguchi 戸口; **doorway** deiriguchi 出入口; (*in home*) genkan 玄関

dope 1 *n* (*drugs*) mayaku 麻薬; (*idiot*) manuke まぬけ; (*information*) jōhō 情報 **2** *v/t* kōfunzai o ataeru 興奮剤を与える

dormant *plant* kyūminchū (no) 休眠中(の); ~ ***volcano*** kyūkazan 休火山

dormitory ryō 寮

dosage tōyaku-ryō 投薬量

dose *n* ikkaibun 一回分

dot *n* ten 点; (*in e-mail address*) dotto ドット; ***on the ~*** (*exactly*) kikkari ni きっかりに

♦**dote on** … o yatara ni kawaigaru …をやたらにかわいがる

dotted line tensen 点線

double 1 *n* (*amount*) nibai (二)倍; (*referring to money*) baigaku 倍額; (*person*) sokkuri na hito そっくりな人; (*of movie star*) kaedama 替え玉; (*room*) daburu ダブル **2** *adj* (*twice as much*) (ni)bai (no) (二)倍(の); *whiskey* daburu (no) ダブル(の); *sink, oven* futatsu aru 二つある; *layer* nijū (no) 二重(の); *digit* futaketa no 二けた(の); ***in ~ figures*** futaketa no sūji de 二けたの数字で **3** *adv* bai (no) 倍(の); **4** *v/t* (ni)bai ni suru (二)倍にする; (*fold*) nijū ni suru 二重にする **5** *v/i* (ni)bai ni naru (二)倍になる

♦**double back** *v/i* (*go back*) hikikaesu 引き返す

♦**double up** (*in pain*) karada o futatsu ni oru 体を二つに折る; (*share*) dōshitsu suru 同室する

double-bass kontorabasu コントラバス; **double bed** daburubeddo ダブルベッド; **double-breasted** daburu (no) ダブル(の); **doublecheck** *v/t & v/i* saitenken suru 再点検する; **double chin** nijū-ago 二重あご; **doublecross** *v/t* … ni nimaijita o tsukau …に二枚舌を使う; **double door** tobira 扉; **double glazing** nijū-garasu 二重ガラス; **doublepark** *v/i* nijū-chūsha suru 二重駐車する; **double-quick**: ***in ~ time*** ōisogi de 大急ぎで; **double room** daburu-rūmu ダブルルーム

doubles (*in tennis*) daburusu ダブルス

doubt 1 *n* utagai 疑い; (*uncertainty*) gimon 疑問; ***be in ~*** gimon ga aru 疑問がある; ***no ~*** (*probably*) kitto きっと **2** *v/t* utagau 疑う

doubtful *remark, look* utagawashii 疑わしい; ***be ~*** (*of person*) utagai o motte iru 疑いをもっている; ***it is ~ whether…*** … to iu no wa utagawashii …というのは疑わしい

doubtfully utagawashige ni 疑わしげに

doubtless utagai nai 疑いない

dough kiji 生地; F (*money*) gennama 現なま

dove hato はと; *fig* hatoha はと派

dowdy dasai ださい

Dow Jones Average dau-heikin ダウ平均

down[1] *n* (*feathers*) umō 羽毛, daun ダウン

down[2] **1** *adv* (*downward*) shita no hō e 下の方へ; (*onto the ground*) shita ni 下に; ~ ***there*** (*near listener*) soko ni そこに; (*far from speaker / listener*) asoko ni あそこに; ***fall*** ~ ochiru 落ちる; ***$200*** ~ (*as deposit*) nihyaku doru sokkin de 200ドル即金で; ~ ***south*** (*direction*) minami e 南へ; (*location*) nanbu dewa 南部では; ***be*** ~ (*of price, rate*) sagatte iru 下がっている; (*of numbers amount*) hette iru 減っている; (*not working*) sadō shite inai 作動していない; F (*depressed*) yūutsu de aru 憂うつである **2** *prep*: ***run*** ~ ***the stairs*** kaidan o kakeoriru 階段を駆け降りる; ***the lava rolled slowly*** ~ ***the hill*** yōgan ga yukkuri oka o nagareochite itta 溶岩がゆっくり丘を流れ落ちて行った; ***the fish has distinctive markings*** ~ ***its back*** sakana no se ni wa me o hiku moyō ga aru 魚の背には目を引く模様がある; ***I looked*** ~ ***the list of names*** watashi wa namae no risuto o mita 私は名前のリストを見た; ***walk*** ~ ***the street*** (*along*) michi o aruku 道を歩く; ***third door on the left*** ~ ***this corridor*** kono rōka o zutto itta hidarite sanbanme no doa この廊下をずっと行った左手三番目のドア **3** *v/t drink* nomu 飲む; *food* nomikomu のみ込む; (*destroy*) uchiotosu 撃ち落とす

down-and-out *n* ochibureta hito 落ちぶれた人; **downcast** (*dejected*) gakkari shita がっかりした; **downfall** botsuraku 没落; (*of politician*) shikkyaku 失脚; **downgrade** *v/t* … no tōkyū o sageru …の等級を下げる; *employee* kōkaku suru 降格する; **downhearted** rakutan shita 落胆した; **downhill** *adv* kudarizaka (no) 下り坂(の); ***go*** ~ *fig* waruku naru 悪くなる; **downhill skiing** daunhiru-sukī ダウンヒルスキー; **download** COMPUT daunrōdo suru ダウンロードする; **downmarket 1** *adj* yasui 安い **2** *adv* taishūmuke ni 大衆向けに; **down payment** atamakin 頭金; **downplay** karuku atsukau 軽く扱う; **downpour** doshaburi どしゃ降り; **downright 1** *adj idiot* mattaku (no) まったく(の); ***a*** ~ ***lie*** makka na uso 真っ赤なうそ **2** *adv dangerous, stupid etc* tetteiteki ni 徹底的に; **downside** (*disadvantage*) warui men 悪い面; **downsize 1** *v/t car* kogataka suru 小型化する; *company* … no kibo o chiisaku suru …の規模を小さくする **2** *v/i* (*of company*) kibo o chiisaku suru 規模を小さくする; **downstairs 1** *adj* kaika (no) 階下(の) **2** *adv* kaika ni 階下に; **down-to-earth** *approach, person* genjitsuteki (na) 現実的(な); **down-town 1** *adj* hankagai (no) 繁華街(の) **2** *adv* hankagai ni 繁華街に; **downturn** (*in economy*) kakō 下降; **downward 1** *adj* shitamuki (no) 下向き(の) **2** *adv* shita no hō e 下の方へ

doze 1 *n* utatane うたたね **2** *v/i* utatane suru うたたねする

♦**doze off** utouto nemurikomu うとうと眠り込む

dozen dāsu ダース; ***~s of …*** nanjū mono … 何十もの…

drab saenai さえない

draft 1 *n* (*of air*) sukimakaze すきま風; (*of document*) shitagaki 下書き; MIL chōhei 徴兵; ~ ***(beer), beer on*** ~ nama-bīru 生ビール **2** *v/t document* … no shitagaki o suru … の下書きをする; MIL chōhei suru 徴兵する

draft dodger chōhei-kihisha 徴兵忌避者

draftee chōshūhei 徴集兵

draftsman seizukō 製図工; (*of plan*) ritsuan-sha 立案者

drafty sukimakaze no hairu すきま風の入る

drag 1 *n*: ***it's a*** ~ ***having to …*** … shinakute wa naranai no ga yakkai da … しなくてはならないのがやっかいだ; ***he's a*** ~ kare wa taikutsu na hito da 彼は退屈な人だ; ***the main*** ~ ōdōri 大通り; ***in*** ~ josō shite 女装して **2** *v/t* (*pull*) hikizuru 引きずる; *person* hikizuridasu 引きずり出す; (*search*) sarau さらう; ***I was***

feeling awful but I managed to ~ myself into work kibun ga hidoku warukatta ga nantoka shigoto ni dekaketa 気分がひどく悪かったが何とか仕事に出かけた; ***~ X into Y*** (*involve*) X o muriyari Y ni hikizurikomu Xをむりやり Yに引きずり込む; ***~ X out of Y*** (*get information from*) Y kara X o kikidasu YからXを聞きだす **3** *v/i* (*of time*) noronoro susumu のろのろ進む; (*of show, movie*) daradara nagabiku だらだら長引く

♦**drag away**: ***drag ... away from the TV*** ... o terebi kara hikihanasu ...をテレビから引き離す

♦**drag in** (*into conversation*) ... no koto o mochidasu ...のことを持ちだす

♦**drag on** daradara to nagabiku だらだらと長引く

♦**drag out** ... o nagabikaseru ...を長引かせる

♦**drag up** (*mention*) ... o mochidasu ...を持ちだす

dragon ryū 竜, doragon ドラゴン; *fig* onibaba 鬼ばば

dragonfly tonbo とんぼ

drain 1 *n* (*pipe*) haisuikan 排水管; (*under street*) mizo 溝; ***a ~ on resources*** kane no muda 金の無駄 **2** *v/t water* haisui suru 排水する; *oil* nuku 抜く; *vegetables* ... no mizu o kiru ...の水を切る; *land* ... ni haisui-setsubi o hodokosu ...に排水設備を施す; *glass, tank* kara ni suru 空にする; (*exhaust: person*) shōmō saseru 消耗させる **3** *v/i* (*of dishes*) kawaku 乾く

♦**drain away** (*of liquid*) ryūshutsu suru 流出する

♦**drain off** *water* ryūshutsu suru 流出する

drainage (*drains*) haisui-kan 排水管; (*of water from soil*) haisui 排水

drainpipe haisui-kan 排水管

drama dorama ドラマ; (*in theater, as study*) engeki 演劇

dramatic engeki (no) 演劇(の); (*exciting*) doramachikku (na) ドラマチック(な), gekiteki (na) 劇的(な); *gesture* ōgesa (na) 大げさ(な)

dramatist geki-sakka 劇作家

dramatization (*play*) kyakushoku 脚色

dramatize *story* kyakushoku suru 脚色する; *fig* ōgesa ni hyōgen suru 大げさに表現する

drape *v/t cloth, coat* kakeru 掛ける; ***~d in*** (*covered with*) ... de ōwareta ...でおおわれた

drapery hida no aru nunoji ひだのある布地

drapes kāten カーテン

drastic (*extreme*) kyokutan (na) 極端(な); *measures* bapponteki (na) 抜本的(な); *change* jūdai (na) 重大(な)

draw 1 *n* (*in match, competition*) hikiwake 引き分け; (*in lottery*) kujibiki くじ引き; (*attraction*) yobimono 呼び物 **2** *v/t picture, map* kaku かく; *cart, curtain* hiku 引く; *gun, knife* nuku 抜く; (*attract*) hikiyoseru 引き寄せる; (*lead*) hipparu 引っ張る; (*from bank account*) hikidasu 引き出す; ***he drew her closer*** kare wa kanojo o hikiyoseta 彼は彼女を引き寄せた **3** *v/i* e o kaku 絵をかく; (*in match, competition*) hikiwakeru 引き分ける; ***~ near*** chikazuku 近づく

♦**draw back 1** *v/i* (*recoil*) ushiro ni sagaru 後ろに下がる **2** *v/t* (*pull back*) ... o hikkomeru ...を引っ込める

♦**draw on 1** *v/i* (*approach*) chikazuku 近づく **2** *v/t* (*make use of*) ... o riyō suru ...を利用する

♦**draw out** *v/t billfold etc* ... o hikidasu ...を引き出す

♦**draw up 1** *v/t document* ... o sakusei suru ...を作成する; *chair* ... o hikiyoseru ...を引き寄せる **2** *v/i* (*of vehicle*) tomaru 止まる

drawback ketten 欠点

drawer[1] (*of desk etc*) hikidashi 引き出し

drawer[2]: ***be a good ~*** e o kaku no ga umai 絵を描くのがうまい

drawing suketchi スケッチ

drawing board gaban 画板; ***go back to the ~*** furidashi ni modoru 振り出しに戻る
drawl *n* yukkuri shita hanashi buri ゆっくりした話ぶり
dread *v/t* kowagaru 怖がる
dreadful hidoi ひどい
dreadfully (*very*) hidoku ひどく; *behave* tondemonaku とんでもなく
dream 1 *n* yume 夢 **2** *adj house etc* yume no yō (na) 夢のよう(な) **3** *v/t* … to iu yume o miru …という夢を見る; (*day~*) yumemiru 夢見る **4** *v/i* yume o miru 夢を見る; (*day~*) yumemiru 夢見る
♦**dream up** … o kangaedasu …を考え出す
dreamer (*day~*) musō-ka 夢想家
dreamy *voice, look* yumemiru yō (na) 夢見るよう(な)
dreary inki (na) 陰気(な)
dredge *canal* … no soko o sarau …の底をさらう
♦**dredge up** *fig* horiokosu 掘り起こす
dregs (*of coffee*) kasu かす; ***the ~ of society*** shakai no kuzu 社会のくず
drench *v/t* zubunure ni suru ずぶぬれにする; ***get ~ed*** zubunure ni naru ずぶぬれになる
dress 1 *n* (*for woman*) wanpīsu ワンピース; (*clothing*) fukusō 服装 **2** *v/t person* … ni fuku o kiseru …に服を着せる; *wound* … no teate o suru …の手当をする; ***get ~ed*** … ni fuku o kiseru …に服を着せる **3** *v/i* (*get ~ed*) fuku o kiru 服を着る; (*well, in black etc*) fukusō o shite iru 服装をしている
♦**dress up** *v/i* kichin to shita fukusō o suru きちんとした服装をする; (*in evening wear*) doresuappu suru ドレスアップする; (*wear a disguise*) kasō suru 仮装する; ***~ as X*** X ni kasō suru Xに仮装する
dress circle nikai-shōmenseki 二階正面席
dresser (*dressing table*) kyōdai 鏡台; (*in kitchen*) shokkidana 食器棚
dressing (*for salad*) doresshingu ドレッシング; (*for wound*) hōtai 包帯
dressing room THEA gakuya 楽屋
dressing table kyōdai 鏡台
dressmaker doresumēkā ドレスメーカー
dress rehearsal butai-geiko 舞台げいこ
dressy ereganto (na) エレガント(な)
dribble *v/i* (*of person*) yodare o tarasu よだれを垂らす; (*of water*) tareru 垂れる; SP doriburu suru ドリブルする
dried *fruit etc* kansō shita 乾燥した
drier → ***dryer***
drift 1 *n* (*of snow*) fukidamari 吹きだまり **2** *v/i* (*of snow*) fukidamaru 吹きだまる; (*of ship*) hyōryū suru 漂流する; (*go off course*) kōro o hazureru 航路をはずれる; (*of person*) samayou さまよう
♦**drift apart** (*of couple*) soen ni naru 疎遠になる
drifter nagaremono 流れ者
drill 1 *n* (*tool*) doriru ドリル; (*exercise*) bōsai-kunren 防災訓練; MIL gunji-kyōren 軍事教練 **2** *v/t hole* … ni ana o akeru …に穴をあける **3** *v/i* (*for oil*) horu 掘る; MIL kunren suru 訓練する
drilling rig (*platform*) kaijō-saiyu-kichi 海上採油基地
drily *remark* reitan ni 冷淡に
drink 1 *n* nomimono 飲物; (*alcoholic*) sake 酒; ***a ~ of …*** … ippai …一杯; ***go for a ~*** nomi ni iku 飲みに行く **2** *v/t* nomu 飲む **3** *v/i* nomu 飲む; (*consume alcohol*) sake o nomu 酒を飲む; ***I don't ~*** watashi wa osake o nomimasen 私はお酒を飲みません
♦**drink up 1** *v/i* (*finish drink*) nomihosu 飲み干す **2** *v/t* (*drink completely*) … o zenbu nomu …を全部飲む
drinkable inryōyō (no) 飲料用(の)
drinker sakenomi 酒飲み
drinking (*of alcohol*) inshu 飲酒
drinking water inryōsui 飲料水
drip 1 *n* (*liquid*) shizuku 滴; MED tenteki 点滴 **2** *v/i* shitataru し

たたる
dripping: ~ (***wet***) zubunure (no) ずぶぬれ(の)
drive 1 *n* (*journey*) michinori 道のり; (*outing*) doraibu ドライブ; (*energy*) yaruki やる気; COMPUT doraibu ドライブ; (*campaign*) undō 運動; ***it's a short ~ from the station*** eki kara kuruma de sugu desu 駅から車ですぐです; ***left-/ right-hand ~*** MOT hidari / migi-handoru no kuruma 左/右ハンドルの車 **2** *v/t vehicle* unten suru 運転する; (*own*) … ni notte iru …に乗っている; (*take in car*) nosete iku 乗せて行く; TECH ugokasu 動かす; ***that noise / he is driving me mad*** ano oto / kare no sei de ki ga kuruisō-da あの音/彼のせいで気が狂いそうだ **3** *v/i* unten suru 運転する
♦**drive at**: ***what are you driving at?*** nani o iitai no 何を言いたいの
♦**drive away 1** *v/t* … o kuruma de tsurete iku …を車で連れて行く; (*chase off*) … o oiharau …を追い払う **2** *v/i* hashirisaru 走り去る
♦**drive in** *v/t nail* … o uchikomu …を打ち込む
♦**drive off** → ***drive away***
drive-in *n* (*movie theater*) doraibuin-shiatā ドライブインシアター
driver untenshu 運転手, doraibā ドライバー
driver's license unten-menkyoshō 運転免許証
driveway kuruma-mawashi 車回し
driving 1 *n* unten 運転 **2** *adj rain* hageshii 激しい
driving force suishin-ryoku 推進力; **driving instructor** unten-kyōkan 運転教官; **driving lesson** jidōsha-kyōshū 自動車教習; **driving school** jidōsha-kyōshūjo 自動車教習所; **driving test** untenmenkyo-shiken 運転免許試験
drizzle 1 *n* kirisame 霧雨 **2** *v/i* kirisame ga furu 霧雨が降る
drone *n* (*noise*) būn to iu oto ぶーんという音
droop *v/i* tareru 垂れる; (*of plant*) shioreru しおれる; ***her shoulders ~ed*** kanojo wa kata o otoshita 彼女は肩を落とした
drop 1 *n* (*of rain*) shizuku 滴; (*small amount*) shōryō 少量; (*in price, temperature*) teika 低下; (*in number*) genshō 減少 **2** *v/t object* otosu 落とす; *person from car* orosu 降ろす; *person from team* jogai suru 除外する; (*stop seeing*) … to zekkō suru …と絶交する; (*give up*) yameru やめる; *charges, demand etc* torisageru 取り下げる; ***~ a line to*** … ni kantan na tegami o kaku …に簡単な手紙を書く **3** *v/i* ochiru 落ちる; (*decline*) sagaru 下がる; (*of wind*) shizumaru 静まる
♦**drop in** (*visit*) chotto tachiyoru ちょっと立ち寄る
♦**drop off 1** *v/t person* … o orosu …を降ろす; (*deliver*) … o oite iku …を置いて行く **2** *v/i* (*fall asleep*) nemurikomu 眠り込む; (*decline*) heru 減る
♦**drop out** (*withdraw*) datsuraku suru 脱落する; (*of school*) chūto-taigaku suru 中途退学する
dropout (*from school*) chūto-taigaku-sha 中途退学者; (*from society*) rakugo-sha 落後者
drops (*for eyes*) megusuri 目薬
drought kanbatsu 干ばつ
drown 1 *v/i* oboreshinu おぼれ死ぬ **2** *v/t person* dekishi saseru でき死させる; *sound* kesu 消す; ***be ~ed*** oboreshinu おぼれ死ぬ
drowsy nemui 眠い
drudgery tanchō na shigoto 単調な仕事
drug 1 *n* MED kusuri 薬; (*illegal*) mayaku 麻薬; ***be on ~s*** mayaku o yatte iru 麻薬をやっている **2** *v/t* kusuri o nomaseru 薬を飲ませる
drug addict mayaku-jōyō-sha 麻薬常用者; **drug dealer** mayaku-mitsubai-nin 麻薬密売人; **drug trafficking** mayaku-mitsubai 麻薬密売
druggist yakuzaishi 薬剤師
drugstore yakkyoku 薬局, doraggusutoa ドラッグストア

drum 1 *n* MUS doramu ドラム; (*Japanese-style*) taiko 太鼓; (*container*) doramu-kan ドラム缶
♦**drum into**: ***drum X into Y*** X o Y ni yakamashiku oshiekomu XをYにやかましく教え込む
♦**drum up**: ~ ***support*** kakki zukeru 活気づける
drummer doramā ドラマー; (*Japanese-style*) taiko-sōsha 太鼓奏者
drumstick MUS bachi ばち; (*of poultry*) tori no momoniku 鶏の腿肉
drunk 1 *n* nondakure 飲んだくれ **2** *adj* yopparatta 酔っ払った; ***get ~*** yopparau 酔っ払う
drunk driving inshu-unten 飲酒運転
drunken *voices*, *laughter* yopparatta 酔っ払った; *party* yopparai (no) 酔っ払い(の)
dry 1 *adj skin*, *clothes*, *mouth* kawaita 乾いた; *weather* ame no furanai 雨の降らない; *wine* karakuchi (no) 辛口(の); (*ironic*) hiniku (na) 皮肉(な); (*where alcohol is banned*) kinshu (no) 禁酒(の) **2** *v/t* kawakasu 乾かす; *dishes* fuite kawakasu 拭いて乾かす; ***~ one's eyes*** namida o fuku 涙を拭く **3** *v/i* kawaku 乾く
♦**dry out** (*of alcoholic*) sake o tatsu 酒を絶つ
♦**dry up** (*of river*) hiagaru 干上がる; (*of speaker*) kotoba ni tsumaru 言葉につまる; ***~!*** (*be quiet*) damarinasai 黙りなさい
dry-clean *v/t* doraikurīningu suru ドライクリーニングする; **dry-cleaner** doraikurīningu-ya ドライクリーニング屋; **dry-cleaning** (*clothes*) sentaku-mono 洗濯もの
dryer (*machine*) kansō-ki 乾燥機
DTP (= ***desktop publishing***) desukutoppu-paburisshingu デスクトップパブリッシング
dual nijū (no) 二重(の)
dub *movie* … no fukikae o suru …の吹替えをする
dubious ikagawashii いかがわしい; (*doubting*) utagawashii 疑わしい
duck 1 *n* (*wild*) kamo かも; (*domestic*) ahiru あひる **2** *v/i* hyoi to karada o kagameru ひょいと体をかがめる **3** *v/t one's head* hyoi to sageru ひょいと下げる; *question* kawasu かわす
due (*owed*) shiharawarerubeki 支払われるべき; (*proper*) tōzen (no) 当然(の); ***be ~*** (*of train, baby etc*) yotei de aru 予定である; (*of report, announcement*) kijitsu de aru 期日である; ***~ to*** (*because of*) … no tame …のため; ***be ~ to*** (*be caused by*) … no kekka de aru …の結果である; ***in ~ course*** sono uchi ni そのうちに; ***by the ~ date*** kijitsu made ni 期日までに
dull *weather* kumori (no) くもり(の); *sound* hakkiri shinai はっきりしない; *pain* nibui 鈍い; (*boring*) taikutsu (na) 退屈(な)
duly (*as expected*) todokōri naku 滞りなく; (*properly*) seitō ni 正当に
dumb (*mute*) kuchi no kikenai 口のきけない; (*stupid*) usunoro (no) うすのろ(の)
dummy (*for clothes*) manekin-ningyō マネキン人形
dump 1 *n* (*for garbage*) gomi-suteba ごみ捨て場; (*unpleasant place*) usugitanai basho 薄汚い場所 **2** *v/t* (*deposit*) oku 置く; (*dispose of*) suteru 捨てる; *nuclear waste* tōki suru 投棄する
dumpling dango だんご
dune sakyū 砂丘
dung fun ふん
dungarees ōbāōru オーバーオール
dunk *biscuit* tsukeru つける
duo (*singing*) nijūshō 二重唱; (*instrumental*) nijūsō 二重奏
duplex (apartment) mezonetto メゾネット
duplicate 1 *n* fukusei 複製; ***in ~*** seifuku nitsū ni shite 正副二通にして **2** *v/t* (*copy*) fukusei suru 複製する; (*repeat*) kurikaeshite iru 繰り返している
duplicate key aikagi 合い鍵
durable *material* taikyūsei no aru 耐久性のある; *relationship*

nagatsuzuki suru 長続きする
duration kikan 期間
duress: ***under*** ~ kyōhaku sarete 強迫されて
during … no aida ni …の間に; (*throughout*) … no aida zutto …の間ずっと
dusk tasogare たそがれ
dust 1 *n* hokori ほこり **2** *v/t* … no hokori o harau …のほこりを払う; ~ ***X with Y*** (*sprinkle*) Y o X ni furikakeru YをXにふりかける
dust cover (*for furniture*) hokoriyoke-kabā ほこりよけカバー; (*for book*) kabā カバー
duster (*cloth*) zōkin ぞうきん
dust jacket (*of book*) kabā カバー
dustpan chiritori ちりとり
dusty hokorippoi ほこりっぽい
Dutch 1 *adj* Oranda (no) オランダ(の); ***go*** ~ warikan ni suru 割り勘にする **2** *n* (*language*) Oranda-go オランダ語; ***the*** ~ Oranda-jin オランダ人
duty gimu 義務; (*task*) shokumu 職務; (*on goods*) zei 税; ***be on*** ~ kinmuchū de aru 勤務中である; ***be off*** ~ hiban de aru 非番である
duty-free 1 *adj* menzei (no) 免税(の) **2** *n* menzei-hin 免税品
duty-free shop mezei-ten 免税店
dwarf 1 *n* kobito 小人 **2** *v/t* chiisaku miseru 小さくみせる
♦**dwell on** … ni kodawaru …にこだわる
dwindle genshō suru 減少する
dye 1 *n* senryō 染料; (*for hair*) kezome 毛染め **2** *v/t* someru 染める
dying *person* shinikakatte iru 死にかかっている; *industry, tradition* kiekakatte iru 消えかかっている
dynamic *person* katsudōteki (na) 活動的(な)
dynamism katsuryoku 活力
dynamite *n* dainamaito ダイナマイト
dynamo TECH hatsudenki 発電機
dynasty ōchō 王朝; *fig* meimon 名門
dyslexia nandokushō 難読症
dyslexic 1 *adj* nandokushō (no) 難読症(の) **2** *n* nandokushō-kanja 難読症患者

E

each 1 *adj* sorezore (no) それぞれ(の) **2** *adv* sorezore それぞれ; ***they're $1.50*** ~ sorezore ichi doru gojū desu それぞれ1ドル50です; ***he gave us one*** ~ kare wa watashitachi ni hitstsuzutsu kureta 彼は私達にひとつずつくれた **3** *pron* sorezore それぞれ; ~ ***other*** otagai ni お互いに
eager nesshin (na) 熱心(な); ***he is ~ to buy a house*** kare wa shikiri ni ie o kaitagatte iru 彼はしきりに家を買いたがっている
eager beaver shigoto no mushi 仕事の虫
eagerly nesshin ni 熱心に
eagerness nesshin-sa 熱心さ
eagle washi わし
ear[1] (*of person, animal*) mimi 耳
ear[2] (*of corn*) mi 実
earache mimi no itami 耳の痛み
eardrum komaku 鼓膜
early 1 *adj* (*not late*) hayai 早い; (*ahead of time, in the near future*) hayame (no) 早め(の); (*farther back in time*) shoki (no) 初期(の); ~ ***October*** jūgatsu no hajime 十月の初め **2** *adv* (*not late, ahead of time*) hayaku 早く
early bird (*in morning*) hayaokidori 早起き鳥; (*who arrives before others*) hayaku kuru

hito 早く来る人

earmark: ***~ X for Y*** X o Y no tame ni totte oku XをYのために取っておく

earn kasegu 稼ぐ; *respect, holiday, drink etc* eru 得る

earnest majime (na) まじめ(な); ***in ~*** majime (na)(ni) まじめ(な)(に); ***I'm speaking in ~*** watashi wa majime ni hanashite imasu 私はまじめに話しています; ***I'm in ~ when I say that …*** watashi ga … to ittatoki majime datta 私が…と言ったときまじめだった

earnings shotoku 所得

earphones iyahon イヤホン

ear-piercing *adj* mimi o tsunzaku yō (na) 耳をつんざくよう(な)

earring iyaringu イヤリング

earshot: ***within ~*** koe no todoku han'i 声の届く範囲; ***out of ~*** yonde mo kikoenai tokoro ni 呼んでも聞こえないところに

earth (*soil*) tsuchi 土; (*world, planet*) chikyū 地球; ***where on ~ …?*** ittai doko (ni) (de)… 一体どこ(に) (で)…; ***where on ~ did you find it?*** ittai doko de mitsuketa no 一体どこで見つけたの; ***where on ~ have you been?*** ittai doko ni itte ita no 一体どこに行っていたの

earthenware *n* tōki 陶器

earthly konoyo (no) この世(の); ***it's no ~ use …*** …shite mo muda da … しても無駄だ

earthquake jishin 地震

earth-shattering sekai o yurugasu 世界を揺るがす

ease 1 *n* yōi-sa 容易さ; ***be or feel at ~*** ochitsuku 落ち着く; ***be or feel ill at ~*** ochitsukanai 落ち着かない; ***with ~*** yasuyasu to やすやすと **2** *v/t* (*relieve*) yawarageru 和らげる **3** *v/i* (*of pain*) karuku naru 軽くなる

♦**ease off 1** *v/t* (*remove*) … o yurumeru …をゆるめる **2** *v/i* (*of pain, rain*) yawaragu 和らぐ

easel īzeru イーゼル

easily (*with ease*) yōi ni 容易に; (*by far*) tashika ni 確かに

east 1 *n* higashi 東; (*of a country*) tōbu 東部; ***East*** (*Orient*) Tōyō 東洋 **2** *adj coast* higashi (no) 東(の); *wind* higashi kara (no) 東から(の) **3** *adv travel* higashi e 東へ

East China Sea Higashi-shinakai 東シナ海

Easter Fukkatsusai 復活祭

Easter egg Īsutā-eggu イースターエッグ

easterly *direction* higashi e (no) 東へ(の); *wind* higashi kara (no) 東から(の)

eastern tōbu (no) 東部(の); (*oriental*) tōyō (no) 東洋(の)

easterner tōbu-shusshin-sha 東部出身者

eastward higashi e 東へ

easy (*not difficult*) kantan (na) 簡単(な); (*relaxed*) yukkuri shita ゆっくりした; *life* kiraku (na) 気楽(な); ***take things ~*** (*slow down*) nonbiri yaru のんびりやる; ***take it ~!*** (*calm down*) ochitsuite 落ち着いて

easy chair anrakuisu 安楽いす

easy-going kodawaranai こだわらない

eat *v/t & v/i* taberu 食べる

♦**eat out** gaishoku suru 外食する

♦**eat up** *food* … o tabete shimau …を食べてしまう; *fig* … o tsukaitsukusu …を使い尽くす

eatable taberareru 食べられる

eaves hisashi ひさし

eavesdrop nusumigiki suru 盗み聞きする

ebb *v/i* (*of tide*) shio ga hiku 潮が引く

♦**ebb away** (*of courage, strength*) otoroeru 衰える

ebb tide hikishio 引き潮

eccentric 1 *adj* fūgawari (na) 風変わり(な) **2** *n* henjin 変人

echo 1 *n* kodama こだま **2** *v/i* hankyō suru 反響する **3** *v/t words* kurikaesu 繰り返す; *views* … ni dōchō suru …に同調する

eclipse 1 *n* (*of sun*) nisshoku 日食; (*of moon*) gesshoku 月食 **2** *v/t fig* shinogu しのぐ

ecological kankyō-hogo (no) 環境保護(の); ***~ balance*** seitaikei no baransu 生態系のバランス
ecologically friendly kankyō ni yasashii 環境にやさしい
ecologist kankyō-hozen-ron-sha 環境保全論者
ecology seitaigaku 生態学
e-commerce ī-komāsu e-コマース
economic keizaigaku (no) 経済学(の)
economical (*cheap*) keizaiteki (na) 経済的(な); (*thrifty*) tsumashii つましい
economically (*in terms of economics*) keizaiteki ni wa 経済的には; (*thriftily*) setsuyaku shite 節約して
economics (*science*) keizaigaku 経済学; (*financial aspects*) keizaiteki-sokumen 経済的側面
economist keizai-gakusha 経済学者
economize setsuyaku suru 節約する
♦**economize on** … o setsuyaku suru …を節約する
economy (*of a country*) keizai 経済; (*saving*) setsuyaku 節約
economy class ekonomī-kurasu エコノミークラス; **economy drive** ken'yaku-seishin 倹約精神; **economy size** otokuyō お徳用
ecosystem seitaikei 生態系
ecstasy uchōten 有頂天
ecstatic uchōten (no) 有頂天(の); *fan, welcome* nekkyōteki (na) 熱狂的(な)
eczema shisshin 湿疹
edge 1 *n* hashi 端; (*of knife*) hasaki 刃先; (*of cliff*) fuchi ふち; (*in voice*) surudo-sa 鋭さ; ***on ~*** iraira shite いらいらして **2** *v/t* fuchidoru 縁取る **3** *v/i* (*move slowly*) jirijiri to susumu じりじりと進む
edgewise: ***I couldn't get a word in ~*** kuchi o dasu yochi ga nai 口を出す余地がない
edgy iraira shite いらいらして
edible taberareru 食べられる
edit *text* kōetsu suru 校閲する; *book, newspaper, TV program, movie* henshū suru 編集する
edition han 版
editor (*of text*) kōetsu-sha 校閲者; (*of book*) henshū-sha 編集者; (*of magazine*) henshūchō 編集長; (*of newspaper*) henshū-kyokuchō 編集局長; (*of TV program, movie*) editā エディター; ***sports / political ~*** supōtsubu / seijibu-kisha スポーツ部/政治部記者
editorial 1 *adj* henshū (no) 編集(の) **2** *n* shasetsu 社説
EDP (= ***electronic data processing***) denshi-dēta-shori 電子データ処理
educate *child* kyōiku suru 教育する; *consumers* … ni oshieru …に教える
educated *person* kyōiku no aru 教育のある
education kyōiku 教育
educational kyōiku (no) 教育(の); *informative* kyōikuteki (na) 教育的(な)
eel (*fresh water*) unagi うなぎ; (*marine*) anago あなご
eerie kimi no warui 気味の悪い
effect *n* eikyō 影響; (*of overwork, detonation*) kekka 結果; ***take ~*** (*of medicine, drug*) kiku 効く; ***come into ~*** (*of law*) hakkō suru 発効する; ***have a positive ~*** kōka ga aru 効果がある
effective (*efficient*) kōkateki (na) 効果的(な); (*striking*) inshōteki (na) 印象的(な); (*valid*) yūkō (na) 有効(な); ***~ May 1*** gogatsu tsuitachi yori yūkō na 五月一日より有効な
effeminate nanjaku (na) 軟弱(な)
effervescent awadatsu 泡立つ; *personality* ikiiki shita 生き生きした
efficiency (*of person, machine*) nōryoku 能力
efficient *person* yūnō (na) 有能(な); *machine, method* kōritsuteki (na) 効率的(な)
efficiently kōkateki ni 効果的に, nōritsuteki ni 能率的に
effort (*struggle*) kurō 苦労; (*attempt*) doryoku 努力; ***make an ~ to do …*** … suru doryoku o suru …する努力

をする
effortless: ***he makes it look so ~*** kare wa zousa-naku yatte miseru 彼は造作なくやってみせる
effrontery atsukamashi-sa 厚かましさ
effusive netsuretsu (na) 熱烈(な)
e.g. tatoeba 例えば
egalitarian *adj* byōdō-shugi (no) 平等主義(の)
egg tamago 卵; (*of woman*) ranshi 卵子
♦**egg on** … o sosonokasu …をそそのかす
eggcup yudetamago-tate ゆで卵立て; **egghead** interi インテリ; **eggplant** nasu なす; **eggshell** tamago no kara 卵のから
ego PSYCH ego エゴ; (*self-esteem*) jisonshin 自尊心
egocentric jiko-chūshinteki (na) 自己中心的(な)
Egypt Ejiputo エジプト
Egyptian **1** *adj* Ejiputo (no) エジプト(の) **2** *n* Ejiputo-jin エジプト人
eiderdown (*quilt*) hanebuton 羽ぶとん
eight hachi 八; (*with countword 'tsu'*) yattsu 八つ
eighteen jūhachi 十八
eighteenth dai-jūhachi (no) 第十八(の)
eighth **1** *adj* dai-hachi (no) 第八(の) **2** *n* (*of month*) yōka 八日
eightieth *adj* dai-hachijū (no) 第八十(の)
eighty hachijū 八十
either **1** *adj* dochira ka (no) どちらか(の); (*both*) ryōhō (no) 両方(の); ***~ solution is OK*** ryōhō no kaiketsuhō tomo daijōbu desu 両方の解決法とも大丈夫です **2** *pron* dochira de mo どちらでも **3** *adv*: ***I won't go ~*** watashi mo ikanai 私も行かない **4** *conj*: ***~ … or …*** ka … ka …か…か; (*in negative sentence*) … mo … mo … も…も; ***you can have ~ rice or potatoes*** gohan ka jagaimo ka eraberu ごはんかじゃがいもか選べる; ***I haven't seen ~ Mike or Joanne*** Maiku ni mo Joannu ni mo atte imasen マイクにもジョアンヌにも会っていません
eject **1** *v/t cassette etc* toridasu 取り出す; *people* tsuihō suru 追放する **2** *v/i* (*from plane*) dasshutsu suru 脱出する
♦**eke out** motaseru もたせる
el → ***elevated railroad***
elaborate **1** *adj design* kotta 凝った; *scheme* shinchō ni keikaku shita 慎重に計画した **2** *v/i* kuwashiku noberu 詳しく述べる
elapse keika suru 経過する
elastic **1** *adj* danryokusei no aru 弾力性のある **2** *n* gomuhimo ゴムひも
elastic band wagomu 輪ゴム
elasticity danryokusei 弾力性
elasticized *waistband* gomu o tōshita ゴムを通した
elated ōyorokobi (no) 大喜び(の)
elation ōyorokobi 大喜び
elbow **1** *n* hiji ひじ **2** *v/t*: ***~ out of the way*** oshinokeru 押しのける
elder **1** *adj* toshiue (no) 年上(の); ***~ brother*** ani 兄; ***~ sister*** ane 姉 **2** *n* toshiue 年上
elderly nenpai (no) 年配(の)
eldest **1** *adj* ichiban toshiue (no) いちばん年上(の) **2** *n* sainenchō-sha 最年長者; ***you're the ~*** kimi ga ichiban toshiue da 君がいちばん年上だ
elect *v/t* senkyo suru 選挙する; ***~ to*** … suru koto o erabu …することを選ぶ
elected senkyo ni yotte erabareru 選挙によって選ばれる
election senkyo 選挙
election campaign senkyo-undō 選挙運動
election day sōsenkyobi 総選挙日
elective *subject* sentaku (no) 選択(の); *surgery* shinakutemo yoi しなくてもよい
elector yūken-sha 有権者; (*at Presidential election*) senkyo-nin 選挙人
electoral system senkyo-seido 選挙制度
electorate yūken-sha 有権者
electric denki (no) 電気(の); *fig*

shigekiteki (na) 刺激的(な)
electrical denki (no) 電気(の)
electric blanket denki-mōfu 電気毛布; **electric chair** denki-isu 電気いす; **electric fan** senpūki 扇風機
electrician denki-gishi 電気技師
electricity denki 電気
electrify *railway line, fence* denki o tōsu 電気を通す; *fig* shokku o ataeru ショックを与える
electrocute kandenshi saseru 感電死させる
electrode denkyoku 電極
electron erekutoron エレクトロン
electronic denshi-kōgaku (no) 電子工学(の)
electronic data processing denshi-dēta-shori 電子データ処理
electronic mail ī-mēru eメール
electronics denshi-kōgaku 電子工学
elegance yūga-sa 優雅さ
elegant yūga (na) 優雅(な)
element CHEM genso 元素
elementary (*rudimentary*) shoho (no) 初歩(の)
elementary school shōgakkō 小学校
elementary teacher shōgakkō-kyōshi 小学校教師
elephant zō 象
elevate mochiageru 持ち上げる
elevated railroad kōka-tetsudō 高架鉄道
elevation (*altitude*) kaibatsu 海抜
elevator erebētā エレベーター
eleven jūichi 十一
eleventh dai-jūichi (no) 第十一(の); ***at the ~ hour*** kiwadoi toki ni きわどいときに
eligible shikaku no aru 資格のある
eligible bachelor otto ni nozomashii dansei 夫に望ましい男性
eliminate *poverty etc* nakusu なくす; *village etc* keshisaru 消し去る; (*from inquiries*) jogai suru 除外する; (*kill*) massatsu suru 抹殺する; ***be ~ed*** (*from competition*) haitai suru 敗退する
elimination (*from competition*) haitai 敗退; (*of poverty etc*) bokumetsu 撲滅; (*murder*) massatsu 抹殺
elite 1 *n* erīto エリート **2** *adj* erīto (no) エリート(の); *troops* seiei (no) 精鋭(の)
elk herajika へらじか
ellipse daen だ円
elm nire no ki にれの木
elope kakeochi suru 駆け落ちする
eloquence yūben 雄弁
eloquent yūben (na) 雄弁(な)
eloquently yūben ni 雄弁に
else: ***anything ~?*** hoka ni nani ka 他に何か; ***if you've got nothing ~ to do*** moshi hoka ni nani mo nai nara もし他に何もないなら; ***no one ~*** hoka ni dare mo … nai 他にだれも…ない; ***everyone ~ is going*** hoka no hitotachi wa mina iku 他の人たちは皆行く; ***who ~ was there?*** hoka ni dare ga imashita ka 他にだれがいましたか; ***someone ~*** dare ka hoka no hito だれか他の人; ***something ~*** nani ka hoka no mono 何か他のもの; (*abstracts: suggestions, ideas*) nani ka hoka no koto 何か他のこと; ***let's go somewhere ~*** doko ka hoka no tokoro ni ikimashō どこか他のところに行きましょう; ***or ~*** samonai to さもないと
elsewhere hoka no basho de wa 他の場所では
elude *escape from* … kara nigeru …から逃げる; *avoid* nogareru 逃れる; ***her name ~s me*** kanojo no namae ga omoidasenai 彼女の名前が思い出せない
elusive *person* tsukamaenikui つかまえにくい
emaciated suijaku shita 衰弱した
e-mail 1 *n* ī-mēru eメール **2** *v/t person* … ni ī-mēru o okuru …にeメールを送る; *text* … o ī-mēru de okuru …をeメールで送る
e-mail address ī-mēru no adoresu eメールのアドレス
emancipated *woman* jiritsu shita 自立した
emancipation kaihō 解放

embalm … ni bōfu-shori o hodokosu …に防腐処理を施す
embankment teibō 堤防
embargo *n* yushutsu-kinshi 輸出禁止
embark (*on ship*) jōsen suru 乗船する; (*on plane*) tōjō suru 搭乗する
♦**embark on** (*begin*) … ni noridasu …に乗り出す
embarrass … ni kimazui omoi o saseru …に気まずい思いをさせる; (*put in awkward position*) komaraseru 困らせる; (*shame*) … ni haji o kakaseru …に恥をかかせる; (*cause to lose face*) … no menboku o tsubusu …の面目をつぶす; ***am I ~ing you?*** kimari ga warukatta desu ka きまりが悪かったですか
embarrassed *smile* kimari no warui きまりの悪い; ***I was ~*** hazukashikatta 恥ずかしかった
embarrassing hazukashii 恥ずかしい; (*awkward*) kimazui 気まずい; ***put … in an ~ position*** … ni kimari no warui omoi o saseru …にきまりの悪い思いをさせる
embarrassment kimazu-sa 気まずさ; (*shame*) haji 恥; ***I don't want to cause any ~*** kimazui omoi o sasetaku nai 気まずい思いをさせたくない
embassy taishikan 大使館
embellish sōshoku suru 装飾する; *story* junshoku suru 潤色する
embers moesashi 燃えさし
embezzle tsukaikomu 使い込む
embezzlement tsukaikomi 使い込み
embitter … ni nigai omoi o saseru …に苦い思いをさせる
emblem shinboru-māku シンボルマーク
embodiment keshin 化身
embody arawasu 表す; (*of person*) taigen suru 体現する
embolism sokusenshō そく栓症
emboss *metal* … ni enbosu-kakō o suru …にエンボス加工をする; *paper* … ni kataoshi-insatsu o suru …に型押し印刷をする; *fabric* … ni ukiori o hodokosu …に浮き織りを施す
embrace 1 *n* hōyō 抱擁 **2** *v/t* (*hug*) dakishimeru 抱き締める; (*take in*) fukumu 含む **3** *v/i* (*of two people*) dakiau 抱き合う
embroider … ni shishū o suru …に刺しゅうをする; *fig* … ni ohire o tsukeru …に尾ひれをつける
embroidery shishū 刺しゅう
embryo BIO hai 胚; (*fetus*) taiji 胎児
emerald (*precious stone*) emerarudo エメラルド; (*color*) emerarudo-iro エメラルド色
emerge (*appear*) arawareru 現れる; (*of truth*) akiraka ni naru 明らかになる; ***it has ~d that…*** … koto ga akiraka ni natta …ことが明らかになった
emergency kinkyū-jitai 緊急事態; ***in an ~*** kinkyū no bāi ni wa 緊急の場合には
emergency exit hijōguchi 非常口
emergency landing kinkyū-chakuriku 緊急着陸
emigrant *n* ijū-sha 移住者
emigrate ijū suru 移住する
emigration ijū 移住
eminent chomei (na) 著名(な)
eminently ichijirushiku 著しく
emission (*of gases*) haishutsu 排出
emotion kanjō 感情
emotional *problems, development* kanjōteki (na) 感情的(な); (*full of emotion*) kandōteki (na) 感動的(な)
empathize: ***~ with*** … ni kyōkan suru …に共感する
emperor kōtei 皇帝; (*of Japan*) Tennō 天皇; ***Emperor's Birthday*** Tennō-Tanjōbi 天皇誕生日
Emperor Hirohito Shōwa-Tennō 昭和天皇
emphasis (*stress*) kyōchō 強調; (*importance*) jūten 重点
emphasize kyōchō suru 強調する
emphatic hakkiri to shita はっきりとした
empire teikoku 帝国
employ yatou 雇う; *skills* katsuyō suru 活用する; *tool, method* riyō

suru 利用する; ***he's ~ed as a …*** kare wa … to shite yatowarete iru 彼は…として雇われている

employee jūgyōin 従業員

employer koyō-sha 雇用者

employment koyō 雇用; (*work*) shokugyō 職業; ***be seeking ~*** shoku o sagashite iru 職を探している

employment agency shokugyō-shōkaijo 職業紹介所

empress jotei 女帝; (*of Japan*) kōgō 皇后

emptiness (*of box, room*) karappo からっぽ; (*in heart*) munashi-sa むなしさ; (*of words, life*) kūkyo-sa 空虚さ

empty 1 *adj* karappo (no) からっぽ(の); *room, street, bus* dare mo inai だれもいない; *word* munashii むなしい; ***~ promises*** kara-yakusoku から約束 **2** *v/t drawer, pockets* … no nakami o akeru …の中身をあける; *glass, bottle* kara ni suru からにする **3** *v/i* (*of room, street*) kara ni naru からになる

emulate minarau 見習う

enable … dekiru yō ni suru …できるようにする; ***the money ~d him to go to university*** sono okane de kare wa daigaku ni iku koto ga dekita そのお金で彼は大学に行くことができた

enact *law* seitei suru 制定する; THEA jōen suru 上演する

enamel *n* hōrō ほうろう; (*on tooth*) enameru-shitsu エナメル質; (*paint*) enameru エナメル

encircle torikakomu 取り囲む

encl (= ***enclosure***(***s***)) dōfūbutsu 同封物

enclose (*in letter*) dōfū suru 同封する; *area* kakomu 囲む; ***please find ~d …*** … o dōfū itashimasu …を同封いたします

enclosure (*with letter*) dōfūbutsu 同封物

encore *n* ankōru アンコール

encounter 1 *n* deai 出会い **2** *v/t person* … ni deau …に出会う; *problem, resistance* … ni chokumen suru …に直面する

encourage *person* hagemasu 励ます; *participation* shōrei suru 奨励する; *violence* jochō suru 助長する; *growth* sokushin suru 促進する

encouragement hagemashi 励まし; (*from government etc*) shōrei 奨励

encouraging *news, report* hagemi ni naru 励みになる; *smile* hagemasu yō (na) 励ますよう(な)

♦**encroach on** *land* … ni shinnyū suru …に侵入する; *rights* shingai suru 侵害する; *time* tsubusu つぶす

encyclopedia hyakka-jiten 百科辞典

end 1 *n* (*extremity*) hashi 端; (*conclusion*) owari 終わり; (*purpose*) mokuteki 目的; ***in the ~*** tsui ni ついに; ***for hours on ~*** nanjikan demo 何時間でも; ***stand … on ~*** … o massugu ni tateru …をまっすぐに立てる; ***at the ~ of July*** shichigatsu no owari ni 七月の終わりに; ***put an ~ to*** … o owaraseru …を終わらせる **2** *v/t* oeru 終える **3** *v/i* owaru 終わる

♦**end up**: ***we ended up in Nagoya*** watashitachi wa Nagoya ni kite shimatta 私達は名古屋に来てしまった; ***we ended up buying …*** watashitachi wa … o kau koto ni natte shimatta 私達は…を買うことになってしまった

endanger kiken ni sarasu 危険にさらす

endangered species zetsumetsu-sunzen no shu 絶滅寸前の種

endearing kawairashii かわいらしい

endeavor 1 *n* doryoku 努力 **2** *v/t* doryoku suru 努力する

ending owari 終わ; GRAM gobi 語尾

endless *questioning etc* owari no nai 終わりのない; *desert* hateshi no nai 果てしのない

endorse *check* … ni uragaki o suru …に裏書きをする; *candidacy* suisen suru 推薦する; *product* senden suru 宣伝する

endorsement (*of check*) uragaki 裏書き; (*of candidacy*) suisen 推薦; (*of product*) senden 宣伝

end product saishū-seisanbutsu 最終生産物
end result saishū-kekka 最終結果
endurance (*physical*) jikyūryoku 持久力; (*mental*) nintai 忍耐
endure 1 *v/t* (*go through*) taeshinobu 耐え忍ぶ; (*tolerate*) gaman suru 我慢する **2** *v/i* (*last*) mochikotaeru 持ちこたえる
enduring eizoku suru 永続する
end-user mattan-shōhisha 末端消費者
enemy teki 敵; (*in war*) tekigun 敵軍
energetic *person* seiryokuteki (na) 精力的(な); *activity* seiryoku o tsukau 精力を使う; *fig: measures* seiryoku o katamuketa 精力を傾けた
energy seiryoku 精力; (*gas, electricity etc*) enerugī エネルギー
energy-saving *device* shō-ene (no) 省エネ(の)
enforce jisshi suru 実施する
engage 1 *v/t* (*hire*) yatou 雇う **2** *v/i* (*of clutch, gear*) ireru 入れる
♦**engage in** … ni kakawaru …にかかわる
engaged (*to be married*) kon'yaku shite iru 婚約している; ***get ~*** kon'yaku suru 婚約する
engagement (*appointment*) yakusoku 約束; (*to be married*) kon'yaku 婚約; MIL kōsen 交戦
engagement ring kon'yaku-yubiwa 婚約指輪
engaging *smile, person* hito o hikitsukeru 人を引き付ける
engine enjin エンジン
engineer 1 *n* gishi 技師; NAUT kikanshi 機関士; RAIL untenshi 運転士 **2** *v/t meeting etc* takuramu たくらむ
engineering kōgaku 工学
England Ingurando イングランド
English 1 *adj* Ingurando (no) イングランド(の) **2** *n* (*language*) Eigo 英語; ***the ~*** Ingurando-jin イングランド人
Englishman Ingurando-jin-dansei イングランド人男性
Englishwoman Ingurando-jin-josei イングランド人女性
engrave horu 彫る
engraving (*drawing*) hanga 版画; (*design*) chōban 彫版
engrossed: ***~ in*** … ni muchū de …に夢中で
engulf nomikomu 飲み込む
enhance *reputation, performance, effect* takameru 高める; *beauty, flavor* masu 増す
enigma nazo なぞ
enigmatic nazomeita なぞめいた
enjoy tanoshimu 楽しむ; ***I ~ skiing*** sukī ga suki de desu スキーが好きです; ***~ oneself*** tanoshii omoi o suru 楽しい思いをする; ***~!*** (*said to s.o. eating*) dōzo どうぞ
enjoyable tanoshii 楽しい
enjoyment tanoshimi 楽しみ
enlarge kakudai suru 拡大する; PHOT hikinobasu 引き伸ばす
enlargement kakudai 拡大; PHOT hikinobashi 引き伸ばし
enlighten (*educate*) keimō suru 啓もうする; (*inform*) … ni oshieru …に教える
enlightenment (*in Japanese philosophy*) satori 悟り
enlist 1 *v/i* MIL nyūtai suru 入隊する **2** *v/t*: ***~ X's help*** X no kyōryoku o eru Xの協力を得る
enliven … ni kakki o ataeru …に活気を与える
enormity (*of crime*) kyōaku-sa 凶悪さ; (*of task*) bōdai-sa 膨大さ
enormous kyodai (na) 巨大(な); *amount* bakudai (na) 莫大(な); *satisfaction, patience* taihen (na) 大変(な)
enormously hijō ni 非常に
enough 1 *adj* jūbun (na) 十分(な) **2** *pron* jūbun 十分; ***will $50 be ~?*** gojū doru de tarimasu ka 五十ドルで足りますか; ***I've had ~!*** mō takusan もうたくさん; ***that's ~, calm down!*** iikagen ni shinasai いいかげんにしなさい **3** *adv* jūbun ni 十分に; ***strangely ~*** fushigi ni mo 不思議にも
enquire, enquiry → ***inquire, inquiry***
enraged gekido shita 激怒した

enrich *vocabulary* hōfu ni suru 豊富にする; *s.o.'s life* yutaka ni suru 豊かにする
enroll *v/i* (*for a course*) tōroku suru 登録する
enrolment tōroku 登録
ensure kakujitsu ni suru 確実にする
entail tomonau 伴う; *cost, time* yō suru 要する
entangle: ***get ~d in*** (*in rope*) … ni karamaru …にからまる; (*in love affair*) … to kankei o motsu …と関係を持つ
enter 1 *v/t room, house* … ni hairu …に入る; *competition* … ni shutsujō suru …に出場する; *person, horse in race* shutsujō saseru 出場させる; *write down* kinyū suru 記入する; COMPUT nyūryoku suru 入力する **2** *v/i* hairu 入る; THEA tōjō suru 登場する; (*in competition*) shutsujō suru 出場する
enterprise (*initiative*) shinshu no kishō 進取の気性; (*venture*) jigyō 事業
enterprising shinshu no kishō ni tonda 進取の気性に富んだ
entertain 1 *v/t* (*amuse*) tanoshimaseru 楽しませる; (*as host*) motenasu もてなす; *idea* kōryo suru 考慮する **2** *v/i* (*have guests*) raikyaku o motenasu 来客をもてなす
entertainer (*as profession*) entāteinā エンターテイナー
entertaining *adj* omoshiroi おもしろい
entertainment tanoshimi 楽しみ
enthrall … no kokoro o ubau …の心を奪う
enthusiasm netsui 熱意
enthusiast fan ファン
enthusiastic netchū shite iru 熱中している
entice sasou 誘う
entire zentai (no) 全体(の); ***the ~ country*** zenkoku 全国; ***the ~ day*** maru ichinichi まる一日; ***the ~ family*** kazoku-zen'in 家族全員; ***the ~ world*** zensekai 全世界
entirely (*completely*) mattaku 全く; ***I'm not ~ satisfied*** watashi wa kanzen ni manzoku shite iru wake de wa nai 私は完全に満足しているわけではない
entitle … ni kenri o ataeru …に権利を与える; ***you're ~d to be angry*** okotte atarimae desu 怒って当たり前です
entitled *book* … ni taitoru o tsukeru …にタイトルをつける
entrance *n* (*doorway*) iriguchi 入り口; (*of house*) genkan 玄関; (*act of entering*) tōjō 登場; (*admission*) nyūjō 入場
entranced uchōten ni natta 有頂天になった
entrance fee nyūjōryō 入場料
entrant (*for exam*) juken-sha 受験者; (*in competition*) sanka-sha 参加者
entrenched *attitudes* korikatamatta 凝り固まった
entrepreneur kigyō-ka 企業家
entrepreneurial kigyō-ka (no) 企業家(の)
entrust: ***~ X with Y, ~ Y to X*** X o Y ni makaseru XをYに任せる
entry (*way in*) iriguchi 入り口; (*admission*) nyūjō 入場; (*to country*) nyūkoku 入国; (*for competition*) sanka-sha 参加者; (*item submitted*) shuppinbutsu 出品物; (*in diary, accounts*) kinyū 記入; ***no ~*** (*for cars*) shinnyū-kinshi 進入禁止; (*for people*) tachiiri-kinshi 立入禁止
entry form shutsujō-mōshikomi-yōshi 出場申し込み用紙
entry visa nyūkoku-biza 入国ビザ
envelop tsutsumu 包む; (*of mist etc*) ōu 覆う
envelope fūtō 封筒
enviable urayamashii うらやましい
envious urayamashige (na) うらやましげ(な); ***be ~ of*** … o netande iru …をねたんでいる
environment kankyō 環境
environmental *problem* kankyō (no) 環境(の); *consideration* kankyō ni tai suru 環境に対する

environmentalist kankyō-hogo-ronsha 環境保護論者
environmentally friendly kankyō ni yasashii 環境に優しい
environmental pollution kankyō-osen 環境汚染
environmental protection kankyō-hogo 環境保護
environs kinkō 近郊
envisage yosō suru 予想する
envoy kōshi 公使
envy 1 *n* netami ねたみ; ***be the ~ of*** senbō no mato de aru せん望の的である **2** *v/t* …ga urayamashii …がうらやましい; ***I ~ you your success*** anata no seikō ga urayamashii あなたの成功がうらやましい
epic 1 *n* taisaku 大作 **2** *adj journey* yūdai (na) 雄大(な)
epicenter shingenchi 震源地
epidemic ryūkō 流行
epilepsy tenkan てんかん
epileptic *n* tenkan-kanja てんかん患者
epileptic fit tenkan no hossa てんかんの発作
epilog epirōgu エピローグ
episode (*of story*) episōdo エピソード; (*of TV series*) ikkai 一回; (*event*) dekigoto 出来事
epitaph bohimei 墓碑銘
epoch jidai 時代
epoch-making kakkiteki (na) 画期的(な)
equal 1 *adj amount, number, value* hitoshii 等しい; *right, opportunity* byōdō (no) 平等(の); ***be ~ to*** *task* … ni taerareru …に耐えられる **2** *n* (*person*) dōtō no hito 同等の人; (*object*) hitteki suru mono 匹敵するもの **3** *v/t* (*in quantity*) … ni hitoshii …に等しい; (*be as good as*) … ni hitteki suru …に匹敵する; ***2 plus 2 ~s 4*** ni tasu ni wa 4 2たす2は4
equality byōdō 平等
equalize 1 *v/t* hitoshiku suru 等しくする **2** *v/i* SP dōten ni naru 同点になる
equalizer SP dōten-gōru 同点ゴール
equally *divide, apportion etc* byōdō ni 平等に; *intelligent, guilty etc* hitoshiku 等しく; ***~, …*** sore to dōji ni, … それと同時に、…
equate : ***~ X with Y*** X o Y to hitoshii to minasu XをYと等しいとみなす
equation MATH hōteishiki 方程式
equator sekidō 赤道
equilibrium kinkō 均衡
equinox (*spring*) shunbun 春分; (*autumnal*) shūbun 秋分
equip : ***be ~ped with*** … o sonaete iru …を備えている; ***he's not ~ped to handle it*** *fig* kare wa sore o atsukau kokoro no junbi ga dekite inai 彼はそれを扱う心の準備ができていない
equipment (*machinery*) setsubi 設備; (*tools*) yōgu 用具
equity FIN shisan 資産; ***equities*** (*shareholdings*) futsū-kabushiki 普通株式
equivalent 1 *adj* sōtō (no) 相当(の); ***be ~ to*** … ni sōtō suru …に相当する **2** *n* sōtō suru mono 相当するもの
era jidai 時代
eradicate konzetsu suru 根絶する
erase kesu 消す
eraser keshi-gomu 消しゴム; (*for blackboard*) kokuban-keshi 黒板消し
erect 1 *adj posture* chokuritsu shita 直立した **2** *v/t* tateru 建てる
erection (*of building etc*) kensetsu 建設; (*of penis*) bokki ぼっ起
erode (*of acid*) fushoku suru 腐食する; (*of rain, wind*) shinshoku suru 侵食する; *rights, power* okasu 侵す
erosion shinshoku 侵食; *fig* shingai 侵害
erotic erochikku (na) エロチック(な)
eroticism erochishizumu エロチシズム
errand tsukai 使い; ***run ~s*** … no tsukaibashiri o suru …の使い走りをする
erratic *behavior* toppi (na) とっぴ(な); *person* muraki (na) むら気(な); *performance, course* fuantei (na) 不安定(な); *heartbeat*

fukisoku (na) 不規則(な)
error machigai 間違い
error message COMPUT erā-messēji エラーメッセージ
erupt (*of volcano*) funka suru 噴火する; (*of violence*) hassei suru 発生する; (*be very angry*) okoridasu 怒り出す
eruption (*of volcano*) funka 噴火; (*of violence*) hassei 発生
escalate dandan kakudai suru だんだん拡大する
escalation gekika 激化
escalator esukarētā エスカレーター
escape 1 *n* (*of prisoner*) dassō 脱走; (*of gas*) more 漏れ; ***have a narrow ~*** karōjite manugareru かろうじて免れる **2** *v/i* (*of prisoner*) dassō suru 脱走する; (*of animal*) nigeru 逃げる; (*of gas*) moreru 漏れる **3** *v/t*: nogareru 逃れる; ***the name ~s me*** namae ga omoidasenai 名前が思い出せない
escape chute kinkyū-dasshutsu-sōchi 緊急脱出装置
escort 1 *n* dēto no aite デートの相手; (*guard*) goei 護衛 **2** *v/t* (*socially*) okutte iku 送っていく; (*as guard*) goei suru 護衛する
especial → ***special***
especially toku ni 特に
espionage supai-kōi スパイ行為
essay *n* essei エッセイ; (*academic*) shōronbun 小論文
essential *adj food, equipment* kaku koto no dekinai 欠くことのできない; (*crucial*) kanjin (no) 肝心(の)
essentially honshitsuteki ni 本質的に
establish *company* setsuritsu suru 設立する; (*create*) kakuritsu suru 確立する; (*determine*) kakutei suru 確定する; ***~ oneself as*** … to shite no chii o katameru …としての地位を固める
establishment (*firm, shop etc*) shisetsu 施設; ***the Establishment*** taisei 体制
estate (*area of land*) jisho 地所; (*of dead person*) zaisan 財産
esthetic *value, appeal* biteki (na) 美的(な); *building etc* shumi no yoi 趣味のよい
estimate 1 *n* mitsumori 見積り **2** *v/t* mitsumoru 見積もる
estimation: ***he has gone up / down in my ~*** kare ni taisuru watashi no hyōka wa agatta / sagatta 彼に対する私の評価は上がった/下がった; ***in my ~*** (*opinion*) watashi no miru tokoro de wa 私の見るところでは
estranged *wife, husband* bekkyochū (no) 別居中(の)
estuary irie 入り江
ETA (= ***estimated time of arrival***) tōchaku-yotei-jikoku 到着予定時刻
etching etchingu エッチング
eternal eien (no) 永遠(の)
eternity eien 永遠
ethical rinriteki (na) 倫理的(な); (*morally correct*) dōtokuteki (na) 道徳的(な)
ethics dōtoku 道徳; (*academic subject*) rinri-gaku 倫理学
ethnic minzoku (no) 民族(の)
ethnic group minzoku-shūdan 民族集団
ethnic minority shōsū-minzoku 少数民族
euphemism enkyoku-gohō えん曲語法
euphoria shifukukan 至福感
Europe Yōroppa ヨーロッパ
European 1 *adj* Yōroppa (no) ヨーロッパ(の) **2** *n* Yōroppa-jin ヨーロッパ人
euthanasia anrakushi 安楽死
evacuate (*clear people from*) … kara hinan saseru …から避難させる; (*leave*) … kara hinan suru …から避難する
evade *question* hagurakasu はぐらかす; *person* sakeru 避ける; *responsibility* kaihi suru 回避する
evaluate *performance* hyōka suru 評価する; *damage* satei suru 査定する
evaluation (*of performance*) hyōka 評価; (*of situation*) satei 査定
evangelist dendōshi 伝道師

evaporate (*of water*) jōhatsu suru 蒸発する; (*of confidence*) kiete nakunaru 消えてなくなる
evasion kaihi 回避; ***tax ~*** datsuzei 脱税
evasive kaihiteki (na) 回避的(な)
eve zen'ya 前夜
even 1 *adj* (*regular*) kisokuteki (na) 規則的(な); (*equal*) byōdō (na) 平等(な); (*level*) taira (na) 平ら(な); *number* gūsū (no) 偶数(の); ***get ~ with*** … ni shikaeshi o suru …に仕返しをする **2** *adv* … de sae mo …でさえも; ***~ he said it was good*** kare de sae mo sore wa yokatta to itta 彼でさえもそれはよかったと言った; ***the car ~ has a CD*** sono kuruma ni wa shīdī made aru その車にはＣＤまである; ***~ bigger / better*** sara ni ōkiku / yoku さらに大きく/よく; ***not ~*** … sae … nai …さえ…ない; ***he doesn't ~ try*** kare wa tamesu koto sae shinai 彼は試すことさえしない; ***~ so*** tatoe sō demo たとえそうでも; ***~ if*** tatoe … demo たとえ…でも **3** *v/t*: ***~ the score*** dōten ni suru 同点にする
evening ban 晩; ***in the ~*** yūgata ni 夕方に; ***this ~*** konban 今晩; ***good ~*** konban wa こんばんは
evening classes yakan-kōza 夜間講座; **evening dress** (*for woman*) ibuningu-doresu イブニングドレス; (*for man*) seisō 正装; **evening paper** yūkan 夕刊
evenly *distribute* kintō ni 均等に; *breathe* kisokuteki ni 規則的に; ***~ matched*** gokaku (no) 互角(の)
event dekigoto できごと; SP shumoku 種目; ***at all ~s*** tonikaku とにかく
eventful haran ni tonda 波乱に富んだ
eventual saishūteki (na) 最終的(な)
eventually (*finally*) tsui ni ついに; (*in time*) sono uchi ni そのうちに
ever *adv* ◊ (*in if clause*) itsuka いつか; ***if I ~ see you again*** moshi itsu ka mata aetara もしいつかまた会えたら; ◊ (*up to now / then*) ima made de 今までで; ***the worst movie ~ made*** ima made tsukurareta saiaku no eiga 今まで作られた最悪の映画; ***the best book I ~ read*** imamade yonda saikō no hon 今まで読んだ最高の本; ***have you ~ been to Japan?*** Nihon ni itta koto ga arimasu ka 日本に行ったことがありますか ◊: ***do you ~ see her now?*** kanojo ni ima mo atte iru no 彼女に今も会っているの; ***for ~*** itsu made mo いつまでも; ***~ since*** sore irai それ以来; ***~ since the accident*** sono jiko irai その事故以来
evergreen *n* jōryokuju 常緑樹
everlasting *love* eien (no) 永遠(の)
every subete (no) すべて(の); ***~ student has a computer*** subete no gakusei wa konpyūtā o motte iru すべての学生はコンピューターを持っている; ***~ week / month*** maishū / maitsuki 毎週/毎月; ***~ Sunday*** mainichiyōbi 毎日曜日; ***~ other day*** ichinichi oki ni 一日置きに; ***~ now and then*** tokidoki ときどき
everybody → ***everyone***
everyday *incident* arifureta ありふれた; *language* nichijō (no) 日常(の)
everyone minna 皆; ***I've spoken to ~ who knew her*** kanojo o shitte iru hito dare demo to hanashita 彼女を知っている人誰でもと話した
everything zenbu 全部
everywhere doko demo どこでも; (*wherever*) itaru tokoro ni いたるところに
evict tachinokaseru 立ち退かせる
evidence shōko 証拠; LAW shōko-bukken 証拠物件; ***give ~*** shōgen suru 証言する
evident akiraka (na) 明らか(な); ***it was ~ that*** … wa akiraka datta … は明らかだった
evidently (*clearly*) akiraka ni 明らかに; (*apparently*) dōyara どうやら
evil 1 *adj* ja-aku (na) 邪悪(な) **2** *n* ja-aku 邪悪
evoke *image* yobiokosu 呼び起こす
evolution (*of animal*) shinka 進化;

(*development*) hatten 発展
evolve *v/i* (*of animals*) shinka suru 進化する; (*develop*) hatten suru 発展する
ewe mehitsuji 雌羊
ex- moto ... 元...
ex *n* F (*wife*) zensai 前妻; (*husband*) zenpu 前夫
exact *adj time, word, amount* seikaku (na) 正確(な)
exactly (*precisely*) chōdo ちょうど; ***you look ~ like your mother*** anata wa okāsan ni sokkuri da あなたはお母さんにそっくりだ; ***that's ~ what I mean*** sore ga masa ni watashi no iō to shita koto da それがまさに私の言おうとしたことだ; ***~!*** sono tōri そのとおり; ***not ~*** chotto chigaimasu ne ちょっと違いますね
exaggerate 1 *v/t* kochō suru 誇張する **2** *v/i* ōgesa na iikata o suru 大げさな言い方をする
exaggeration ōgesa 大げさ
exam shiken 試験; ***sit an ~*** shiken o ukeru 試験を受ける; ***pass / fail an ~*** shiken ni ukaru / ochiru 試験に受かる/落ちる
examination (*of facts*) chōsa 調査; (*chemical analysis etc*) kensa 検査; (*of patient*) shinsatsu 診察; EDU shiken 試験; ***take an entrance ~*** juken suru 受験する
examine (*study*) chōsa suru 調査する; (*analyse*) kensa suru 検査する; *patient* shinsatsu suru 診察する; EDU shiken suru 試験する
examiner EDU shiken-kan 試験官
example rei 例; ***for ~*** tatoeba 例えば; ***set a good / bad ~*** yoi otehon / warui mihon to naru よいお手本/悪い見本となる
exasperated okotta 怒った
excavate *v/t* (*dig*) horu 掘る; (*of archeologist*) hakkutsu suru 発掘する
excavation hakkutsu 発掘
excavator pawāshaberu パワーシャベル
exceed (*be more than*) koeru 越える; (*go beyond*) kosu 越す
exceedingly kiwamete きわめて
excel 1 *v/i* sugurete iru 優れている; ***~ at*** ... ni hiidete iru ...に秀でている **2** *v/t*: ***~ oneself*** itsumo yori umaku yaru いつもよりうまくやる
excellence sugurete iru koto 優れていること
excellent sugureta 優れた
except ... igai wa ...以外は; ***~ for*** ... o nozoite wa ...を除いては; ***~ that*** ... to iu koto o nozokeba ...ということを除けば
exception reigai 例外; ***with the ~ of*** ... o nozoite wa ...を除いては; ***take ~ to*** ... ga ki ni iranai ...が気に入らない
exceptional (*very good*) tokubetsu ni sugureta 特別に優れた; (*special*) reigaiteki (na) 例外的(な)
exceptionally (*extremely*) toku ni 特に
excerpt bassui 抜粋
excess 1 *n*: ***eat / drink to ~*** tabe / nomi-sugiru 食べ/飲み過ぎる; ***in ~ of*** ... yori ōku ...より多く **2** *adj* kajō (no) 過剰(の)
excess baggage chōka-tenimotsu 超過手荷物
excess fare chōka-ryōkin 超過料金
excessive kajō (no) 過剰(の)
exchange 1 *n* (*of views, information*) kōkan 交換; (*between schools*) kōkan-ryūgaku 交換留学; ***in ~*** hikikae ni 引き換えに; ***in ~ for*** ... to hikikae ni ...と引き換えに **2** *v/t* (*in store*) torikaeru 取り替える; *addresses* torikawasu 取り交わす; *currency* ryōgae suru 両替する; ***~ X for Y*** X o Y to kōkan suru XをYと交換する
exchange rate kawase-sōba 為替相場
excitable kōfun shiyasui 興奮しやすい
excite (*make enthusiastic*) kōfun saseru 興奮させる
excited kōfun shita 興奮した; ***get ~*** kōfun suru 興奮する; ***get ~ about*** ... no koto de kōfun suru ...のことで興奮する

excitement kōfun 興奮
exciting wakuwaku suru わくわくする
exclaim sakebu 叫ぶ
exclamation sakebi 叫び
exclamation point kantanfu 感嘆符
exclude nozoku 除く, jogai suru 除外する; (*ban: from club etc*) shimedasu 締め出す
excluding … o nozoite …を除いて
exclusive *hotel, restaurant* kōkyū (na) 高級(な); *rights* yuiitsu (no) 唯一(の); *interview* dokusenteki (na) 独占的(な)
excruciating *pain* taegatai 耐えがたい
excursion ensoku 遠足
excuse 1 *n* iiwake 言い訳 **2** *v/t* (*forgive*) yurusu 許す; (*allow to leave*) … ga chūza suru no o yurusu …が中座するのを許す; **~ *X from Y*** X o Y kara menjo suru XをYから免除する; **~ *me*** (*to get attention*) sumimasen すみません; (*to get past*) chotto sumimasen ちょっとすみません; (*interrupting*) shitsurei desu ga 失礼ですが
execute *criminal* shokei suru 処刑する; *plan* jikkō suru 実行する
execution (*of criminal*) shokei 処刑; (*of plan*) jikkō 実行
executioner shikei-shikkō-nin 死刑執行人
executive *n* jūyaku 重役
executive briefcase kōkyū-burīfu-kēsu 高級ブリーフケース
executive washroom jūyakuyō-keshōshitsu 重役用化粧室
exemplary *conduct* mohanteki (na) 模範的(な)
exempt: ***be ~ from*** … o menjo sareru …を免除される
exercise 1 *n* (*physical*) undō 運動; EDU renshū-mondai 練習問題; MIL gunji-enshū 軍事演習; ***take ~*** undō suru 運動する **2** *v/t* *muscle* kitaeru 鍛える; *dog* undō saseru 運動させる; *caution, restraint* hatarakaseru 働かせる **3** *v/i* (*do exercise*) undō suru 運動する
exercise book EDU renshūchō 練習帳
exert *authority* kōshi suru 行使する; *influence* oyobosu 及ぼす; ***~ oneself*** doryoku suru 努力する
exertion doryoku 努力
exhale hakidasu 吐き出す
exhaust 1 *n* (*fumes*) haiki-gasu 排気ガス; (*pipe*) haikikan 排気管 **2** *v/t* (*tire*) tsukarehatesaseru 疲れ果てさせる; (*use up*) tsukaihatasu 使い果たす
exhaust fumes haiki-gasu 排気ガス
exhausted (*tired*) tsukarekitta 疲れ切った
exhausting hidoku tsukareru ひどく疲れる
exhaustion kyokudo no hirō 極度の疲労
exhaustive (*complete*) kanzen (na) 完全(な); (*thorough*) tetteiteki (na) 徹底的(な)
exhaust pipe haikikan 排気管
exhibit 1 *n* (*in exhibition*) tenjihin 展示品 **2** *v/t* (*of gallery*) tenji suru 展示する; (*of artist*) kōkai suru 公開する; (*give evidence of*) miseru 見せる
exhibition tenrankai 展覧会; (*of skill*) hakki 発揮; ***make an ~ of oneself*** hajisarashi na mane o suru 恥さらしなまねをする
exhibitionist medachitagariya 目立ちたがり屋
exhilarating ukiuki suru yō (na) うきうきするよう(な)
exile 1 *n* bōmei 亡命; (*person*) bōmei-sha 亡命者 **2** *v/t* tsuihō suru 追放する
exist sonzai suru 存在する; (*of animal*) seizon suru 生存する; ***~ on*** … de ikite iru …で生きている
existence sonzai 存在; (*life*) seikatsu 生活; ***in ~*** genzon (no) 現存(の); ***come into ~*** seiritsu suru 成立する
existing genzai (no) 現在(の)
exit *n* (*way out*) deguchi 出口; (*from highway*) intāchenji インターチェンジ; THEA taijō 退場
exonerate menjo suru 免除する; (*of*

serious offense) muzai ni suru 無罪にする
exorbitant hōgai (na) 法外(な)
exotic ekizochikku (na) エキゾチック(な)
expand 1 *v/t market, business* hirogeru 広げる **2** *v/i* (*of business*) kakuchō suru 拡張する; (*of city*) kakudai suru 拡大する; (*of population*) zōka suru 増加する; (*of metal*) bōchō suru 膨張する
♦**expand on** … ni tsuite kuwashiku noberu …について詳しく述べる
expanse hirogari 広がり
expansion (*of business*) kakuchō 拡張; (*of city*) kakudai 拡大; (*of population*) zōka 増加; (*of metal*) bōchō 膨張
expect 1 *v/t person, phonecall etc* machiukeru 待ち受ける; *rain etc* yosō suru 予想する; (*suppose*) … to omou …と思う; (*demand*) kitai suru 期待する **2** *v/i*: ***be ~ing*** (*be pregnant*) ninshin shite iru 妊娠している; ***I ~ so*** sō omoimasu そう思います
expectant matte iru 待っている
expectant mother ninpu 妊婦
expectation (*anticipation*) yosō 予想; (*hope*) kitai 期待; ***~s*** (*demands*) kitai 期待
expedient *n* shudan 手段
expedition tanken 探検; (*group*) tankentai 探検隊
expel *person* tsuihō suru 追放する
expend *energy* tsuiyasu 費やす
expendable *person* gisei ni shite yoi 犠牲にしてよい
expenditure shishutsu 支出
expense (*cost*) hiyō 費用; ***at the company's ~*** keihi de 経費で; ***a joke at my ~*** watashi o dashi ni shita jōdan 私をだしにした冗談; ***at the ~ of his health*** kenkō o gisei ni shite 健康を犠牲にして
expense account hitsuyō-keihi 必要経費
expenses keihi 経費
expensive *car, book, watch* kōka (na) 高価(な); *meal, hotel* nedan no takai 値段の高い; *lifestyle* kane no kakaru 金のかかる
experience 1 *n* keiken 経験 **2** *v/t* keiken suru 経験する
experienced jukuren shita 熟練した
experiment 1 *n* jikken 実験 **2** *v/i* jikken suru 実験する; ***~ on** animals* … de jikken suru …で実験する; ***~ with*** (*try out*) … o tameshite miru …を試してみる
experimental jikkenteki (na) 実験的(な)
expert 1 *adj* jukuren shita 熟練した; ***~ advice*** senmonka no iken 専門家の意見 **2** *n* senmonka 専門家, ekisupāto エキスパート
expertise gijutsu 技術, nōhau ノウハウ
expire yūkō-kigen ga kireru 有効期限が切れる; (*of contract*) shikkō to naru 失効となる
expiry kigengire 期限切れ
expiry date yūkō-kigen 有効期限
explain *v/t & v/i* setsumei suru 説明する
explanation setsumei 説明
explicit *instructions* meihaku 明白(な)
explicitly hakkiri to はっきりと
explode 1 *v/i* (*of bomb*) bakuhatsu suru 爆発する **2** *v/t bomb* bakuhatsu saseru 爆発させる
exploit[1] *n* igyō 偉業
exploit[2] *v/t person* sakushu suru 搾取する; *resources* riyō suru 利用する
exploitation (*of person*) sakushu 搾取
exploration tanken 探検; (*of idea*) kentō 検討
exploratory *surgery* shindan-mokuteki (no) 診断目的(の)
explore tanken suru 探検する; *possibility* kentō suru 検討する
explorer tankenka 探検家
explosion bakuhatsu 爆発; (*in population*) bakuhatsuteki na zōka 爆発的な増加
explosive *n* bakuyaku 爆薬
export 1 *n* (*action*) yushutsu 輸出; (*item*) yushutsuhin 輸出品 **2** *v/t goods* yushutsu suru 輸出する;

COMPUT waritsuke suru 割り付けする
export campaign yushutsu kyanpēn 輸出キャンペーン
exporter yushutsu-gyōsha 輸出業者
expose (*uncover*) mukidashi ni suru むき出しにする; *scandal* bakuro suru 暴露する; *person* … no shōtai o abaku …の正体をあばく; ***~ X to Y*** X o Y ni sarasu XをYにさらす
exposure sarasareru koto さらされること; MED teitaion-shō 低体温症; (*of dishonest behavior*) bakuro 暴露; ***36-~ film*** sanjūroku mai dori no firumu 36枚取りのフィルム
express 1 *adj* (*fast*) kyūkō (no) 急行(の); (*explicit*) meihaku (na) 明白(な) **2** *n* (*train*) kyūkō-ressha 急行列車; (*bus*) kyūkō-basu 急行バス **3** *v/t* (*speak of, voice*) iiarawasu 言い表す; *feelings* hyōgen suru 表現する; ***~ oneself well / clearly*** iitai koto o umaku / hakkiri noberu 言いたいことをうまく/はっきり述べる; ***~ oneself*** (*emotionally*) jiko o hyōgen suru 自己を表現する
express elevator kyūkō-erebētā 急行エレベーター
expression (*voiced*) hyōgen 表現; (*on face*) hyōjō 表情; (*phrase*) iimawashi 言い回し; (*expressiveness*) hyōgenryoku 表現力
expressive *face* hyōjō no yutaka (na) 表情の豊か(な); *gesture* hyōjō ni tomu 表情に富む
expressly (*explicitly*) meihaku ni 明白に; (*deliberately*) waza to わざと
expressway kōsoku-dōro 高速道路
expulsion (*from school*) taigaku-shobun 退学処分; (*of diplomat*) tsuihō 追放
exquisite (*beautiful*) yūbi (na) 優美(な)
extend 1 *v/t* (*make longer*) enchō suru 延長する; (*make larger*) kakuchō suru 拡張する; *thanks, congratulations* noberu 述べる **2** *v/i* (*of garden etc*) hirogaru 広がる
extension (*to house*) zōchiku 増築; (*of contract, visa*) enchō 延長; TELEC naisen 内線
extension cable enchō-kōdo 延長コード
extensive kōhan'i ni watatta 広範囲にわたった
extent (*degree*) teido 程度; ***to such an ~ that …*** … suru hodo …するほど; ***to a certain ~*** aru teido wa ある程度は
exterior 1 *adj* gaibu (no) 外部(の) **2** *n* (*of building*) gaibu 外部; (*of person*) gaiken 外見
exterminate *vermin* kujo suru 駆除する; *race* zetsumetsu suru 絶滅する
external gaibu (no) 外部(の)
extinct *species* zetsumetsu shita 絶滅した
extinction (*of species*) zetsumetsu 絶滅
extinguish *fire, cigarette* kesu 消す
extinguisher shōka-ki 消火器
extort: ***~ money from*** … kara kane o yusuritoru …から金をゆすり取る
extortion yusuri ゆすり
extortionate hōgai (na) 法外(な)
extra 1 *n* omake おまけ **2** *adj* yobun (no) 余分(の); ***be ~*** (*cost more*) warimashi-ryōkin ga iru 割増料金がいる **3** *adv* tokubetsu ni 特別に
extra charge warimashi-ryōkin 割増料金
extract[1] *n* bassui 抜粋
extract[2] *v/t nail etc* hikinuku 引き抜く; (*from pocket etc*) toridasu 取り出す; *coal, oil* saikutsu suru 採掘する; *tooth* nuku 抜く; *information* muriyari kikidasu 無理やり聞き出す
extraction (*of oil, coal*) saikutsu 採掘; (*of tooth*) basshi 抜歯
extradite hikiwatasu 引き渡す
extradition hikiwatashi 引き渡し
extradition treaty hikiwatashi-jōyaku 引き渡し条約
extramarital kongai (no) 婚外(の)
extraordinarily ijō ni 異常に
extraordinary namihazureta 並はずれた
extravagance zeitaku ぜいたく

extravagant (*with money*) zeitaku (na) ぜいたく(な)
extreme 1 *n* kyokutan 極端 **2** *adj* kyokutan (na) 極端(な); *views* kageki (na) 過激(な)
extremely kiwamete きわめて
extremist *n* kagekiha 過激派
extricate kyūshutsu suru 救出する
extrovert *n* gaikōteki na hito 外向的な人
exuberant *person* kakki no aru 活気のある
exult ōyorokobi suru 大喜びする
eye 1 *n* me 目; (*of needle*) hari no ana 針の穴; ***keep an ~ on*** … o mihatte iru …を見張っている **2** *v/t* jitto miru じっと見る
eyeball gankyū 眼球; **eyebrow** mayu まゆ; **eyeglasses** megane めがね; **eyelash** matsuge まつげ; **eyelid** mabuta まぶた; **eyeliner** airainā アイライナー; **eye shadow** aishadō アイシャドー; **eyesight** shiryoku 視力; **eyesore** mezawari 目ざわり; **eye strain** gansei-hirō 眼精疲労; **eyewitness** mokugeki-sha 目撃者

F

F (= ***Fahrenheit***) kashi 華氏
fabric kiji 生地
fabulous subarashii すばらしい
façade (*of building*) gaikan 外観; (*of person*) misekake 見せかけ
face 1 *n* kao 顔; ***~ to ~*** men to mukatte 面と向かって; ***lose ~*** menboku o ushinau 面目を失う **2** *v/t person* muku 向く; *the sea* menshite iru 面している
facelift kao no shiwatori seikei-shujutsu 顔のしわ取り整形手術
face value FIN gakumen 額面; ***take … at ~*** … o gakumen dōri ni uketoru …を額面通りに受け取る
facilitate sokushin suru 促進する
facilities setsubi 設備
fact jijitsu 事実; ***in ~, as a matter of ~*** jissai wa 実際は
factor yōin 要因
factory kōjō 工場
faculty (*hearing etc*) kinō 機能; (*at university*) gakubu 学部
fade *v/i* (*of color*) iro ga aseru 色があせる; (*of sound, light*) kiete iku 消えていく
faded *color, jeans* aseta あせた
fag F (*homosexual*) homo ホモ
Fahrenheit kashi 華氏
fail 1 *v/i* shippai suru 失敗する **2** *v/t exam* ochiru 落ちる
failure shippai 失敗
faint 1 *adj* kasuka (na) かすか(な) **2** *v/i* ki o ushinau 気を失う
fair[1] *n* (*fun~*) yūenchi 遊園地; COM mihon'ichi 見本市
fair[2] *adj hair* kinpatsu (no) 金髪(の); *complexion* shiroi 白い; (*just*) kōhei (na) 公平(な); (*not bad*) warukunai 悪くない; ***it's not ~*** sore wa fukōhei desu それは不公平です
fairly *treat* kōhei ni 公平に; (*quite*) kanari かなり
fairness (*of treatment*) kōhei-sa 公平さ
fairy yōsei 妖精
fairy tale *n* otogi-banashi おとぎ話
faith shinrai 信頼; REL shinkō 信仰
faithful seijitsu (na) 誠実(な); ***be ~ to one's partner*** pātonā ni seijitsu de aru パートナーに誠実である
fake 1 *n* nisemono 偽物 **2** *adj* nise (no) 偽(の)
fall[1] **1** *v/i* (*of person*) tentō suru 転倒する; (*from height*) tenraku suru 転落する; (*of government*) hōkai suru 崩壊する; (*of prices,*

temperature) teika suru 低下する; (*of exchange rate*) geraku suru 下落する; (*of night*) kuru 来る; ***it ~s on a Tuesday*** kayōbi ni ataru 火曜日にあたる; ***~ ill*** byōki ni naru 病気になる **2** *n* (*of person*) tentō 転倒; (*from height*) tenraku 転落; (*of government*) hōkai 崩壊; (*in price, temperature*) teika 低下; (*of exchange rate*) geraku 下落

♦**fall back on** … ni tayoru …に頼る

♦**fall down** taoreru 倒れる

♦**fall for** *person* … ni muchū ni naru …に夢中になる; (*be deceived by*) … ni damasareru …にだまされる

♦**fall out** (*of hair*) nukeru 抜ける; (*argue*) kenka suru けんかする

♦**fall over** (*of person*) korobu 転ぶ; (*of tree*) taoreru 倒れる

♦**fall through** (*of plans*) zasetsu suru ざ折する

fall[2] *n* (*autumn*) aki 秋

fallout hōshasei-rakkabutsu 放射性落下物, shi no hai 死の灰

false uso (no) うそ(の); (*mistaken*) machigatta 間違った

false alarm ayamari no keihō 誤りの警報

false teeth ireba 入れ歯

falsify henzō suru 変造する

fame meisei 名声

familiar *adj* (*intimate*) narenareshii なれなれしい; *name, form of address* shitashimi o kometa 親しみをこめた; ***be ~ with*** … o yoku shitte iru …をよく知っている; ***that sounds ~*** kiita koto ga aru 聞いたことがある

familiarity (*intimacy*) shitashi-sa 親しさ; (*with area etc*) chishiki 知識

familiarize narasu 慣らす; ***~ oneself with*** … ni najimu …になじむ

family kazoku 家族

family doctor kakaritsuke no isha かかりつけの医者; **family name** sei 姓; **family planning** kazoku-keikaku 家族計画

famine kikin ききん

famous yūmei (na) 有名(な); ***be ~ for …*** … de yūmei de aru …で有名である

fan[1] *n* (*supporter*) fan ファン

fan[2] **1** *n* (*for cooling*: *electric*) senpūki 扇風機; (*handheld*) sensu 扇子 **2** *v/t*: ***~ oneself*** aogu あおぐ

fanatic *n* mania マニア

fanatical nekkyōteki (na) 熱狂的(な)

fan belt MOT fanberuto ファンベルト

fancy dress kasō 仮装

fancy-dress party kasō-pātī 仮装パーティー

fang kiba きば

fanny pack uesuto pōchi ウエストポーチ

fantastic (*very good*) totemo subarashii とてもすばらしい; (*very big*) tohō mo nai 途方もない

fantasy kūsō 空想

far *adv* tōku ni 遠くに; (*much*) haruka ni はるかに; ***~ away*** haruka tōku ni はるか遠くに; ***~ off*** zutto tōku ni ずっと遠くに; ***how ~ is it to …*** …made dorekurai desu ka …までどれくらいですか; ***as ~ as the corner / hotel*** kado / hoteru made 角/ホテルまで; ***as ~ as I can see*** watashi no mita kagiri de wa 私の見た限りでは; ***as ~ as I know*** watashi no shiru kagiri de wa 私の知る限りでは; ***you've gone too ~*** (*in behavior*) anata wa chotto yarisugita あなたはちょっとやりすぎた; ***so ~ so good*** ima no tokoro umaku itte iru 今の所うまくいっている

farce chabangeki 茶番劇

fare (*for travel*) unchin 運賃

Far East Kyokutō 極東

farewell wakare 別れ

farewell party sōbetsukai 送別会

farfetched shinjigatai 信じがたい

farm *n* nōjō 農場

farmer nōjōshu 農場主

farmhouse nōka 農家

farmworker kosaku-nin 小作人

farsighted enshi (no) 遠視(の); *fig* senken no mei ga aru 先見の明がある

fart F **1** *n* he 屁 **2** *v/i* he o kogu 屁をこぐ

farther *adv* sara ni tōku ni さらに遠くに
farthest ichiban tōku ni 一番遠くに
fascinate *v/t* miryō suru 魅了する; ***be ~d by…*** … ni hikareru …にひかれる
fascinating miryokuteki (na) 魅力的(な)
fascination toriko ni naru koto とりこになること
fascism fashizumu ファシズム
fascist 1 *n* fashisuto ファシスト **2** *adj* kyokuu (no) 極右(の)
fashion *n* fasshon ファッション; (*manner*) ryūgi de 流儀で; ***in ~*** ryūkō shite 流行して; ***out of ~*** ryūkō okure de 流行おくれで
fashionable *clothes* ryūkō (no) 流行(の); *person, idea* imafū (no) 今風(の)
fashion-conscious ryūkō o ishiki shita 流行を意識した
fashion designer fasshon-dezainā ファッションデザイナー
fast[1] **1** *adj* hayai 速い; ***be ~*** (*of clock*) susunde iru 進んでいる **2** *adv* hayaku 速く; ***stuck ~*** kataku shimatte iru 固くしまっている; ***~ asleep*** gussuri nemutte ぐっすり眠って
fast[2] *n* (*not eating*) danjiki 断食
fasten 1 *v/t* shikkari shimeru しっかりしめる; ***~ X onto Y*** X o Y ni tomeru XをYに留める **2** *v/i* (*of dress etc*) tomaru 留まる
fastener (*for dress*) fasunā ファスナー; (*for lid*) tomegu 留め具
fast food fāsutofūdo ファーストフード; **fast-food restaurant** fāsutofūdo-restoran ファーストフードレストラン; **fast forward 1** *n* (*on video etc*) hayaokuri 早送り **2** *v/i* hayaokuri suru 早送りする; **fast lane** (*on road*) oikoshi-shasen 追い越し車線; **fast train** kaisoku 快速, kyūkō 急行
fat 1 *adj* futotta 太った **2** *n* (*on meat*) aburami 脂身
fatal chimeiteki (na) 致命的(な); *error* ketteiteki (na) 決定的(な)
fatality shibō-jiko 死亡事故
fatally: ***~ injured*** chimeishō o uketa 致命傷を受けた
fate unmei 運命
father *n* otōsan お父さん; (*talking to outsiders about one's own father*) chichi 父; ***become a ~*** chichioya ni naru 父親になる
fatherhood chichioya de aru koto 父親であること
father-in-law (*s.o. else's*) giri no otōsan 義理のお父さん; (*one's own*) giri no chichi 義理の父
fatherly chichioya no yō (na) 父親のよう(な)
fathom *n* NAUT hiro ひろ
fatigue *n* hirō 疲労
fatso *n* F debu でぶ
fatty 1 *adj* aburakkoi 脂っこい **2** *n* F (*person*) debu でぶ
faucet jaguchi 蛇口
fault *n* sekinin 責任; (*in machine etc*) kekkan 欠陥; (*in person*) ketten 欠点; ***it's your / my ~*** anata / watashi no sei desu あなた/私のせいです; ***find ~ with*** … no ara o sagasu …のあらを探す
faultless ketten no nai 欠点のない
faulty *goods* kekkan no aru 欠陥のある
favor (*service*) tasuke 助け; (*approval*) sansei 賛成; ***in ~ of*** … *vote, decide* no tame ni …のために; ***be in ~ of*** … ni sansei shite …に賛成して; ***do … a ~*** … no tanomi o kiku …の頼みを聞く; ***do me a ~!*** (*don't be stupid*) iikagen ni shite yo いいかげんにしてよ
favorable *reply etc* kōiteki (na) 好意的(な)
favorite 1 *n* okiniiri お気に入り; (*food*) kōbutsu 好物 **2** *adj* ichiban suki (na) 一番好き(な)
fax 1 *n* fakkusu ファックス; ***send … by ~*** … o fakkusu suru …をファックスする **2** *v/t* fakkusu de okuru ファックスで送る; ***~ X to Y*** Y ni X o fakkusu de okuru YにXをファックスで送る
FBI (= ***Federal Bureau of Investigation***) Ef-bī-ai エフ・ビー・アイ
fear 1 *n* osore 恐れ **2** *v/t* osoreru 恐れ

る
fearless daitanfuteki (na) 大胆不敵(な)
feasibility study jikkōsei-chōsa 実行性調査
feasible kanō (na) 可能(な)
feast *n* gochisō ごちそう
feat otegara お手柄
feather umō 羽毛
feature 1 *n* (*on face*) kaodachi 顔立ち; (*of city, building, plan, style*) tokuchō 特徴; (*article in paper*) tokushū-kiji 特集記事; (*movie*) chōhen-eiga 長編映画; ***make a ~ of*** … o ōkiku atsukau …を大きく扱う **2** *v/t* (*of movie*) shuen to suru 主演とする
February nigatsu 二月
federal renpō (no) 連邦(の)
federation renpō 連邦
fed up *adj* F unzari shite うんざりして; ***be ~ with*** … ni unzari shite iru …にうんざりしている
fee ryōkin 料金; (*of lawyer*) bengo-ryō 弁護料; (*of doctor*) shinsatsu-ryō 診察料; (*paid to professional*) sōdan-ryō 相談料; (*for entrance*) nyūjō-ryō 入場料; (*for membership*) kaihi 会費
feeble *person* yowayowashii 弱々しい; *attempt* muda (na) 無駄(な); *laugh* kasuka (na) かすか(な)
feed *v/t* … ni tabemono o ageru …に食べ物をあげる; *animal* … ni esa o yaru …にえさをやる
feedback kansō 感想
feel 1 *v/t* (*touch*) … ni sawaru …に触る; (*be aware of*) kanjiru 感じる; *pleasure, relief etc* oboeru 覚える; *pain* kanjiru 感じる; (*think*) … to omou …と思う **2** *v/i* kanjirareru 感じられる; ***it ~s like silk / cotton*** kinu / men no yō ni kanjirareru 絹/綿のように感じられる; ***your hand ~s hot / cold*** anata no te wa atsui / tsumetai あなたの手は熱い/冷たい; ***I ~ hungry / tired*** onaka ga suita / tsukareta mitai おなかがすいた/疲れたみたい; ***how are you ~ing today?*** kyō no kibun wa dō desu ka 今日の気分はどうですか; ***how does it ~ to be rich?*** okanemochi no kibun wa dō desu ka お金持ちの気分はどうですか; ***do you ~ like a drink / meal?*** nani ka nomitai / nani ka tabetai desu ka 何か飲みたい/何か食べたいですか; ***I ~ like going / staying*** ikitai / koko ni itai kibun desu 行きたい/ここにいたい気分です; ***I don't ~ like it*** watashi wa shitakunai 私はしたくない
♦ **feel up** (*sexually*) … ni chikan suru … にちかんする
♦ **feel up to…** … ga dekisō na ki ga suru …ができそうな気がする
feeler (*of insect*) shokkaku 触角
feelgood factor rakkan-yōin 楽観要因
feeling (*opinion*) kimochi 気持ち; (*emotion*) kanjō 感情; (*sensation*) kankaku 感覚; ***I have mixed ~s about him*** kare ni taishite fukuzatsu na kanjō o motte iru 彼に対して複雑な感情を持っている; ***what are your ~s about it?*** sore ni tsuite anata no kangaekata wa dō desu ka それについてあなたの考え方はどうですか
fellow *n* (*man*) yatsu やつ
fellow citizen (*of country*) kokumin 国民; (*of city*) shimin 市民; **fellow countryman** dōkokujin 同国人; **fellow man** ningen 人間
felony jūzai 重罪
felt *n* feruto フェルト
felt tip, felt-tip(ped) pen ferutopen フェルトペン
female 1 *adj animal, plant* mesu (no) 雌(の); (*relating to people*) josei (no) 女性(の) **2** *n* (*of animals, plants*) mesu 雌; (*person*) josei 女性; *pej* (*woman*) onna 女
feminine 1 *adj qualities* josei-rashii 女性らしい; GRAM josei (no) 女性(の); ***she's very ~*** kanojo wa totemo onnarashii 彼女はとても女らしい **2** *n* GRAM joseikei 女性形
feminism feminizumu フェミニズム
feminist 1 *n* feminisuto フェミニスト **2** *adj group* feminisuto (no) フェミニスト(の); *ideas* danjo-

dōkenshugi (no) 男女同権主義(の)
fence saku さく, fensu フェンス
♦**fence in** *land* … o kakoikomu …を囲い込む
fencing SP fenshingu フェンシング
fend: **~ *for oneself*** jikatsu suru 自活する
fender MOT fendā フェンダー
feng shui fūsui 風水
ferment[1] *v/i* (*of liquid*) hakkō suru 発酵する
ferment[2] *n* (*unrest*) konran 混乱
fermentation hakkō 発酵
fern shida シダ
ferocious *animal* dōmō (na) どう猛(な); *attack* hageshii 激しい
ferry *n* ferī フェリー
fertile *soil* hiyoku (na) 肥よく(な); *woman, animal* ninshinkanō (na) 妊娠可能(な)
fertility (*of soil*) hiyoku-sa 肥よくさ; (*of woman, animal*) seishokuryoku 生殖力
fertility drug hairan-yūhatsuzai 排卵誘発剤
fertilize *v/t ovum* jusei saseru 受精させる
fertilizer (*for soil*) hiryō 肥料
fervent *admirer* netsuretsu (na) 熱烈(な)
fester (*of sore*) kanō suru 化膿する
festival omatsuri お祭り
festive omatsurikibun (no) お祭り気分(の); ***the ~ season*** kurisumas no koro クリスマス(の)頃
festivities gyōji 行事
fetch *person* tsurete kaeru 連れてかえる; *thing* totte kuru 取ってくる; *price* … de ureru …で売れる
fetus taiji 胎児
feud *n* hanmoku 反目
fever netsu 熱
feverish netsuppoi 熱っぽい; *excitement* nekkyōteki (na) 熱狂的(な)
few 1 *adj* (*not many*) shōsū (no) 少数(の); ***we have ~ friends*** watashitachi wa tomodachi ga hotondo inai 私達は友達がほとんどいない; ***there are ~ of them left*** hotondo nokotte inai ほとんど残っていない; ***a ~*** ikutsuka (no) いくつか(の); (*people*) ikuninka (no) 幾人か(の); ***quite a ~, a good ~*** (*a lot*) kanari (no) かなり(の) **2** *pron* (*not many*) shōsū 少数; ***a ~*** ikutsuka 幾つか; ***a ~*** (*people*) ikuninka 幾人か; ***quite a ~, a good ~*** (*a lot*) kanari かなり; (*people*) kanari no hito かなりの人
fewer *adj* yori sukunai より少ない; ***~ than*** … yori sukunai …より少ない
fiancé kon'yaku-sha 婚約者
fiancée kon'yaku-sha 婚約者
fiasco daishippai 大失敗
fib *n* uso うそ
fiber sen'i 繊維
fiberglass *n* faibā-gurasu ファイバーグラス; **fiber optic cable** hikari faibā kēburu 光ファイバーケーブル; **fiber optics** (*subject*) sen'i-kōgaku 繊維光学
fickle kimagure (na) 気まぐれ(な)
fiction (*novels etc*) shōsetsu 小説; (*lie, exaggeration*) tsukuribanashi 作り話
fictitious kakū (no) 架空(の)
fiddle 1 *n* F (*violin*) baiorin バイオリン **2** *v/i*: **~ *with*** … o ijiru …をいじる; **~ (*around*) *with*** (*tamper with*) … o ijiru …をいじる **3** *v/t accounts, results* gomakasu ごまかす
fidelity seijitsu 誠実
fidget *v/i* sowasowa suru そわそわする
field *n* nohara 野原; (*with crops*) hatake 畑; SP kyōgi-jō 競技場; (*competitors in race*) kyōgi-sha 競技者; (*of research, knowledge etc*) bun'ya 分野; ***that's not my ~*** sore wa watashi no bun'ya de wa nai それは私の分野ではない
field events fīrudo-shumoku フィールド種目
fierce *adj animal* dōmō (na) どう猛(な); *wind, storm* mōretsu (na) 猛烈(な)
fiery *sunset* moetatsu 燃え立つ; *personality* hageshii 激しい
fifteen jūgo 十五
fifteenth dai-jūgo (no) 第十五(の)
fifth 1 *adj* dai-go (no) 第五(の) **2** *n*

(*of month*) itsuka 五日
fiftieth dai-gojū (no) 第五十(の)
fifty gojū 五十
fifty-fifty *adv* gobugobu ni 五分五分に
fig ichijiku いちじく
fight 1 *n* tatakai 戦い; (*argument*) kenka けんか; *fig* (*for survival, championship etc*) tatakai 闘い; (*in boxing*) bokushingu no shiai ボクシングの試合 **2** *v/t* … to tatakau …と戦う; *disease, injustice* … to tatakau …と闘う **3** *v/i* tatakau 戦う; (*argue*) kenka suru けんかする; (*for a cause, against injustice*) tatakau 闘う
♦**fight for** *rights, cause* … no tame ni tatakau …のために闘う
fighter tatakau hito 戦う人; (*airplane*) sentōki 戦闘機; (*boxer*) bokusā ボクサー; ***she's a ~*** kanojo wa tōshi da 彼女は闘士だ
figurative *usage* hiyuteki (na) 比ゆ的(な); *art* zōkei (no) 造形(の)
figure 1 *n* (*digit*) sūji 数字; (*of person*) sutairu スタイル; (*form, shape*) katachi 形 **2** *v/t* F (*think*) … to kangaeru …と考える
♦**figure on** F (*plan*) … o keikaku suru …を計画する
♦**figure out** (*understand*) … o rikai suru …を理解する; *calculation* keisan suru 計算する
figure skating figyua-sukēto フィギュアスケート
file[1] **1** *n also* COMPUT fairu ファイル **2** *v/t documents* fairu suru ファイルする
♦**file away** *documents* … o fairu ni irete seiri suru …をファイルにいれて整理する
file[2] *n* (*for wood, fingernails*) yasuri やすり
file cabinet seiriyō kyabinetto 整理用キャビネット
file manager COMPUT fairu-manejā ファイルマネジャー
Filipino 1 *adj* Firipin (no) フィリピン(の) **2** *n* (*person*) Firipin-jin フィリピン人
fill 1 *v/t* mitasu 満たす; *tooth* jūten suru 充てんする **2** *n*: ***eat one's ~*** onaka-ippai taberu おなかいっぱい食べる
♦**fill in** *form* … o kinyū suru …を記入する; *hole* … o umeru …を埋める
♦**fill in for** … no kawari o suru …の代わりをする
♦**fill out 1** *v/t form* … o kinyū suru …を記入する **2** *v/i* (*get fatter*) fukkura suru ふっくらする
♦**fill up 1** *v/t* … o ippai ni mitasu …をいっぱいに満たす **2** *v/i* (*of stadium, theater*) ippai ni naru いっぱいになる
fillet *n* hireniku ヒレ肉
fillet steak hire sutēki ヒレステーキ
filling 1 *n* (*in cake, sandwich etc*) nakami 中味; (*in tooth*) jūten 充てん **2** *adj food* onaka ga ippai ni naru おなかが一杯になる
filling station gasorin-sutando ガソリンスタンド
film 1 *n* (*for camera*) firumu フィルム; (*movie*) eiga 映画 **2** *v/t person, event* satsuei suru 撮影する
film-maker eiga-kantoku 映画監督
film star eiga-sutā 映画スター
filter 1 *n* firutā フィルター **2** *v/t coffee, liquid* kosu こす
♦**filter through** (*of news, reports*) jojo ni ikiwataru 徐々にいきわたる
filter tip firutā フィルター; (*cigarette*) firutā-tsuki no tabako フィルター付きのたばこ
filth yogore 汚れ
filthy fuketsu (na) 不潔(な); *language etc* gehin (na) 下品(な)
fin (*of fish*) hire ひれ
final 1 *adj* saigo (no) 最後(の); *decision* saishū (no) 最終(の) **2** *n* SP kesshōsen 決勝戦
finalist kesshōsen-shutsujōsenshu 決勝戦出場選手
finalize *plans, design* saishū-kettei suru 最終決定する
finally saigo ni 最後に; (*at last*) tsui ni ついに
finance 1 *n* zaisei 財政 **2** *v/t* yūshi suru 融資する
financial zaiseijō (no) 財政上(の)
financial year kaikei-nendo 会計年度

financier shusshi-sha 出資者
find *v/t* mitsukeru 見つける; ***if you ~ it too hot in here*** koko ga atsusugiru to omou nara ここが暑すぎると思うなら; ***~ X innocent / guilty*** LAW X ni yūzai / muzai hanketsu o kudasu Xに有罪/無罪判決を下す
♦**find out 1** *v/t* (*inquire*) … o shiraberu …を調べる; (*discover*) … ga wakaru …がわかる **2** *v/i* (*inquire*) shiraberu 調べる; (*discover*) wakaru わかる
fine[1] *adj day, weather* hare (no) 晴れ(の); *wine, performance, city* subarashii 素晴らしい; *distinction* komakai 細かい; *line* hosoi 細い; ***how's that? - that's ~*** dō datta - yokatta desu どうだった - よかったです; ***that's ~ by me*** watashi wa ōkē desu 私はOKです; ***how are you? - ~*** genki - genki desu 元気 - 元気です
fine[2] *n* (*penalty*) bakkin 罰金
finger *n* yubi 指
fingernail tsume つめ; **fingerprint** *n* shimon 指紋; **fingertip** yubisaki 指先; ***have … at one's ~s*** … ni seitsū shite iru …に精通している
finicky *person* urusai うるさい; *design, pattern* komakai 細かい
finish 1 *v/t* oeru 終える; ***~ doing …*** … suru no o oeru …するのを終える **2** *v/i* owaru 終わる **3** *n* (*of product*) shiagari 仕上がり; (*of race*) gōru ゴール
♦**finish off** *v/t wine* … o nonde shimau …を飲んでしまう; *job* … o oete shimau …を終えてしまう
♦**finish up** *v/t food* … o tabete shimau …を食べてしまう; ***he finished up living there*** kare wa kekkyoku soko ni sumu koto ni natta 彼は結局そこに住む事になった
♦**finish with** *v/t boyfriend etc* … to wakareru …と別れる
finishing line gōru ゴール
Finland Finrando フィンランド
Finn Finrando-jin フィンランド人
Finnish 1 *adj* Finrando (no) フィンランド(の) **2** *n* Finrando-go フィンランド語
fir momi no ki もみの木
fire 1 *n* hi 火; (*electric, gas*) hītā ヒーター; (*blaze*) kaji 火事; (*bonfire, campfire etc*) takibi たき火; ***be on ~*** moete iru 燃えている; ***catch ~*** hi ga tsuku 火がつく; ***set ~ to*** … ni hi o tsukeru …に火をつける **2** *v/i* (*shoot*) hassha suru 発射する **3** *v/t* F (*dismiss*) kaiko suru 解雇する
fire alarm kasai-hōchiki 火災報知機; **firearm** jūki 銃器; **fire department** shōbō-sho 消防署; **fire engine** shōbō-sha 消防車; **fire escape** hijō-kaidan 非常階段; *route* hijō-guchi 非常口; **fire extinguisher** shōka-ki 消火器; **firefighter** shōbō-shi 消防士; **firefly** hotaru ほたる; **fireman** shōbō-shi 消防士; **fireplace** danro 暖炉; **fireproof** *adj* taikasei (no) 耐火性(の); **fire truck** shōbō-sha 消防車; **firewood** maki まき; **fireworks** hanabi 花火; (*display*) hanabi no uchiage 花火の打ち上げ
firm[1] *adj grip, handshake* antei shita 安定した; *flesh, muscles* hikishimatta 引き締まった; *voice, decision* danko to shita 断固とした; ***a ~ deal*** kakujitsu na torihiki 確実な取り引き
firm[2] *n* COM kaisha 会社; (*of lawyers, accountants*) jimusho 事務所
first 1 *adj* dai-ichi (no) 第一(の) **2** *n* ichiban 一番; (*of month*) tsuitachi 一日 **3** *adv arrive, finish* ichiban ni 一番に; (*beforehand*) saisho ni 最初に; ***~ of all*** (*for one reason*) mazu saisho ni まず最初に; ***at ~*** hajime wa 初めは
first aid kyūkyū-shochi 救急処置; **first-aid box, first-aid kit** kyūkyū-bako 救急箱; **first-born** *adj* saisho ni umareta 最初に生まれた; **first-class 1** *adj* (*on boat, train*) ittō (no) 一等(の); (*on bullet train*) gurīn-sha (no) グリーン車(の); (*on airplane*) fāsuto kurasu (no) ファーストクラス(の); (*very*

good) ichiryū (no) 一流(の) **2** *adv* (*on boat, train*) ittō de 一等で; (*on bullet train*) gurīn de グリーンで; (*on airplane*) fāsuto kurasu de ファーストクラスで; **first floor** ikkai 一階; **firsthand** *adj* chokusetsu (no) 直接(の)

firstly mazu saisho ni まず最初に

first name namae 名前

first-rate ichiryū (no) 一流(の)

fiscal kaikei-jō (no) 会計上(の)

fish 1 *n* sakana 魚 **2** *v/i* tsuri o suru 釣りをする

fishbone sakana no hone 魚の骨

fisherman ryōshi 漁師

fishing tsuri 釣り

fishing boat gyosen 漁船; **fishing line** tsuri-ito 釣り糸; **fishing rod** tsuri-zao 釣りざお

fishmonger sakana-ya 魚屋

fish stick sakana no furai 魚のフライ

fishy F (*suspicious*) ayashii 怪しい

fist kobushi こぶし

fit[1] *n* MED hossa 発作; ***a ~ of rage / jealousy*** totsuzen no ikari / shitto 突然の怒り / しっと

fit[2] *adj* (*physically*) chōshi ga yoi 調子がよい; (*morally*) fusawashii ふさわしい; ***keep ~*** karada no chōshi o iji suru 体の調子を維持する

fit[3] **1** *v/t* (*of clothes*) … ni au …に合う; (*attach*) tsukeru 付ける **2** *v/i* (*of clothes*) au 合う; (*of piece of furniture etc*) hairu 入る **3** *n*: ***it is a good ~*** pittari da ぴったりだ; ***it's a tight ~*** kitchiri da きっちりだ

♦**fit in** (*of person in group*) tokekomu 溶け込む; ***it fits in with our plans*** watashitachi no keikaku ni umaku au 私達の計画にうまく合う

fitful *sleep* togiretogire (no) 途切れ途切れ(の)

fitness (*physical*) kenkō 健康

fitness center fittonesu kurabu フィットネスクラブ

fitted kitchen shisutemu kitchin システムキッチン

fitter *n* kumitatekō 組み立て工

fitting *adj* fusawashii ふさわしい

fittings setsubi 設備

five go 五; (*with count word 'tsu'*) itsutsu 五つ

fix 1 *n* F (*solution*) kaiketsu-hō 解決法; ***be in a ~*** F komatte iru 困っている **2** *v/t* (*attach*) toritsukeru 取り付ける; (*repair*) shūri suru 修理する; *meeting etc* tehai suru 手配する; *lunch* tsukuru 作る; *boxing match etc* yaochō o shikumu 八百長を仕組む; ***~ X onto Y*** X o Y ni toritsukeru XをYに取り付ける; ***I'll ~ you a drink*** watashi ga nomimono o tsukurimasu 私が飲み物を作ります

♦**fix up** *meeting* … o tehai suru …を手配する; ***it's all fixed up*** zenbu tehai sarete imasu 全部手配されています

fixed (*in one position*) kotei shita 固定した; *timescale, exchange rate* kimatta 決まった

fixture (*in room*) setsubi 設備; SP shiai 試合

flab (*on body*) tarumi たるみ

flabbergast: ***be ~ed*** F gyōten suru 仰天する

flabby *muscles, stomach* tarunda たるんだ

flag[1] *n* hata 旗

flag[2] *v/i* (*tire*) yowaru 弱る

flair (*talent*) sainō 才能; ***have a natural ~ for*** … no tenpu no sainō ga aru …の天賦の才能がある

flake *n* usui kakera 薄いかけら; (*of snow*) ippen 一片

♦**flake off** *v/i* hageochiru はげ落ちる

flaky *adj skin, paint* hageochi-yasui はげ落ちやすい

flaky pastry sō ni natta pesutorī 層になったペストリー

flamboyant *person* daitan (na) 大胆(な); *design* hade (na) 派手(な)

flame *n* honō ほのお

flammable kanensei (no) 可燃性(の)

flan pai パイ

flank 1 *n* (*of horse etc*) wakibara わき腹; MIL sokumen 側面 **2** *v/t*: ***be ~ed by*** … ni hasamarete iru …に挟まれている

flap 1 *n* (*of envelope, pocket*) futa ふた; (*of table*) tareita 垂れ板; ***be in a ~*** F kōfun shite iru 興奮している **2** *v/t wings* habataku 羽ばたく **3** *v/i* (*of flag etc*) hatameku はためく; F (*panic*) urotaeru うろたえる

flare *n* (*distress signal*) hatsuentō 発煙筒; (*in dress*) fureā フレアー

♦ **flare up** (*of violence*) boppatsu suru ぼっ発する; (*of illness, rash*) hassei suru 発生する; (*of fire*) moeagaru 燃え上がる; (*get very angry*) okoridasu 怒り出す

flash 1 *n* (*of light*) senkō せん光; PHOT furasshu フラッシュ; ***in a ~*** F atto iu ma ni あっという間に; ***have a ~ of inspiration*** hirameku ひらめく; ***~ of lightning*** inabikari いなびかり **2** *v/i* (*of light*) patto hikaru ぱっとひかる **3** *v/t headlights* tenmetsu saseru 点滅させる

flashback *n* (*in movie*) furasshubakku フラッシュバック

flashbulb furasshu no denkyū フラッシュの電球

flasher MOT jidō-tenmetsu-sōchi 自動点滅装置

flashlight kaichū-dentō 懐中電灯

flashy *pej* kebakebashii けばけばしい

flask mahōbin 魔法びん

flat 1 *adj surface, land* taira (na) 平ら(な); *beer* ki no nuketa 気の抜けた; *battery* kireta 切れた; *tire* panku shita パンクした; *shoes* hīru no nai ヒールのない; *sound, tone* tanchō (na) 単調(な); ***and that's ~!*** F zettai dakara ne 絶対だからね **2** *adv* MUS han'on sagete 半音さげて; ***~ out*** *work, run, drive* zensokuryoku de 全速力で

flat-chested mune no chiisai 胸の小さい

flat rate kin'itsu-ryōkin 均一料金

flatten *v/t land, road* taira ni suru 平らにする; (*by bombing, demolition*) hakai suru 破壊する

♦ **flatten out** *v/i* (*of land*) taira ni naru 平らになる

flatter *v/t* … ni oseji o iu …にお世辞を言う

flattering *comments* oseji (no) お世辞(の); *color, clothes* niau 似合う

flattery oseji お世辞

flavor 1 *n* fūmi 風味 **2** *v/t food* ajitsuke suru 味付けする

flavoring *n* chōmiryō 調味料

flaw *n* (*in glass, design*) kizu 傷; (*in system, plan etc*) ketten 欠点

flawless kanpeki (na) 完璧(な)

flea nomi のみ

flee *v/i* nigeru 逃げる

fleet *n* NAUT kansen 艦船; ***a ~ of …*** (*of taxis, trucks*) … no ichidan …の一団

fleeting *visit etc* tsuka no ma (no) つかのま(の); ***catch a ~ glimpse of*** chirari to miru ちらりと見る

flesh niku 肉; (*of fruit*) kaniku 果肉; ***meet / see a person in the ~*** jitsubutsu ni au 実物に会う

flex *v/t muscles* magenobashi suru 曲げ伸ばしする

flexible jūnan (na) 柔軟(な); ***I'm quite ~*** watashi wa yūzū ga kikimasu 私は融通が利きます

flick *v/t tail* hitofuri 一振り; ***he ~ed a fly off his hand*** kare wa hae o yubi de hajiita 彼ははえを指ではじいた; ***she ~ed her hair out of her eyes*** kanojo wa kami no ke ga me ni kakaranai yō ni haratta 彼女は髪の毛が目にかからない様にはらった

♦ **flick through** *book, magazine* parapara to pēji o mekuru ぱらぱらとページをめくる

flicker *v/i* (*of light, candle, screen*) chirachira suru ちらちらする

flies (*on pants*) zubon no chakku ズボンのチャック

flight (*in airplane*) bin 便; (*flying*) hikō 飛行; (*escape*) tōbō 逃亡; ***~ (of stairs)*** hitonobori no kaidan ひと上りの階段

flight crew jōmuin 乗務員; **flight deck** sōjū-shitsu 操縦室; **flight number** binmei 便名; **flight path** hikō-keiro 飛行経路; **flight recorder** furaito-rekōdā フライトレコーダー; **flight time** (*departure*) shuppatsu-jikoku 出発時刻; (*duration*) hikō-jikan 飛行時間

flighty karui 軽い
flimsy *structure, furniture* chachi (na) ちゃち(な); *dress, material* usui 薄い; *excuse* osomatsu (na) お粗末(な)
flinch shirigomi suru しりごみする
fling *v/t* hōridasu ほうり出す; ***she flung herself into his arms*** kanojo wa kare no ude no naka ni tobikonda 彼女は彼の腕のなかに飛び込んだ; ***~ oneself into a chair*** isu ni dosun to suwaru いすにどすんと座る
♦**flip through** *book, magazine* parapara to pēji o mekuru ぱらぱらとページをめくる
flipper (*for swimming*) ashihire 足ひれ
flirt 1 *v/i* kobiru こびる **2** *n* (*male*) purei-bōi プレイボーイ; (*female*) purei-gāru プレイガール
flirtatious ki o hiku yō (na) 気を引くよう(な)
float *v/i* uku 浮く; FIN (*of currency*) hendō suru 変動する
flock *n* (*of sheep*) mure 群れ
flog *v/t* (*whip*) muchiutsu むち打つ
flood 1 *n* kōzui 洪水 **2** *v/t* (*of river*) hanran saseru はんらんさせる; ***~ its banks*** (*of river*) kishi o hanran saseru 岸をはんらんさせる
flooding kōzui 洪水
floodlight *n* tōkō-shōmei 投光照明, furaddo-raito フラッドライト
floor *n* (*of room*) yuka 床, furoa フロア; (*story*) kai 階
floorboard yukaita 床板; **floor cloth** yukayō zōkin 床用雑巾; **floor lamp** furoarampu フロアランプ
flop 1 *v/i* dasatto taorekomu どさっと倒れ込む; F (*fail*) shippai suru 失敗する **2** *n* F (*failure*) shippai 失敗
floppy *adj* (*not stiff*) tarete iru 垂れている; (*weak*) darui だるい
floppy (disk) furoppī-disuku フロッピーディスク
florist hana-ya 花屋
flour komugiko 小麦粉
flourish *v/i* han'ei suru 繁栄する
flourishing *business, trade* sakan (na) 盛ん(な)
flow 1 *v/i* (*of river, current, traffic*) nagareru 流れる; (*of work*) susumu 進む **2** *n* (*of river, ideas*) nagare 流れ
flowchart furōchāto フローチャート
flower 1 *n* hana 花 **2** *v/i* hana ga saku 花が咲く
flower arrangement ikebana 生け花; **flowerbed** kadan 花壇; **flowerpot** uekibachi 植木鉢
flowery *pattern* hanamoyō (no) 花模様(の); *style of writing* ōgesa (na) 大げさ(な)
flu infuruenza インフルエンザ
fluctuate *v/i* hendō suru 変動する
fluctuation hendō 変動
fluency (*in a language*) ryūchō-sa 流ちょうさ
fluent *adj* ryūchō (na) 流ちょう(な); ***he speaks ~ Japanese*** kare wa Nihon-go o ryūchō ni hanasu 彼は日本語を流ちょうに話す
fluently ryūchō ni 流ちょうに
fluff: ***a bit of ~*** (*material*) chotto shita keba ちょっとした毛羽
fluffy *adj material, hair* fuwatto shita ふわっとした; *clouds* fuwafuwa shita ふわふわした; ***~ toy*** nuigurumi ぬいぐるみ
fluid *n* ryūdōtai 流動体
flunk *v/t* F *subject* shippai suru 失敗する
fluorescent keikō (no) 蛍光 (の)
flush 1 *v/t toilet* nagasu 流す; ***~ ... down the toilet*** ... o toire ni nagasu ...をトイレに流す **2** *v/i* (*of toilet*) nagareru 流れる; (*go red*) akaku naru 赤くなる **3** *adj* (*level*) ... to onaji takasa (no) ...と同じ高さ(の); ***be ~ with...*** ... to onaji takasa de aru ...と同じ高さである
♦**flush away** *v/i* (*down toilet*) nagasu 流す
♦**flush out** *rebels etc* ... o tatakidasu ...をたたき出す
fluster *v/t* menkurawaseru めんくらわせる; ***get ~ed*** urotaeru うろたえる
flute furūto フルート, yokobue 横笛
flutter *v/i* (*of bird, wings*) habataki suru 羽ばたきする; (*of flag*)

hatameku はためく; (*of heart*) dokidoki suru どきどきする
fly[1] *n* (*insect*) hae ハエ
fly[2] *n* (*on pants*) zubon no chakku ズボンのチャック
fly[3] **1** *v/i* (*of bird, airplane*) tobu 飛ぶ; (*in airplane*) hikōki de iku 飛行機で行く; (*of flag*) agaru 揚がる; (*rush*) tonde iku 飛んでいく; ***~ into a rage*** gekido suru 激怒する **2** *v/t airplane* sōjū suru 操縦する; *airline* … de ryokō suru …で旅行する; (*transport by air*) kūyu suru 空輸する
♦**fly away** (*of bird, airplane*) tonde iku 飛んで行く
♦**fly back** *v/i* (*travel back*) tonde kaeru 飛んで帰る
♦**fly in** **1** *v/i* (*of airplane, passengers*) tonde kuru 飛んで来る **2** *v/t supplies etc* … o hikōki de hakobu …を飛行機で運ぶ
♦**fly off** (*of hat etc*) tonde iku 飛んでいく
♦**fly out** **1** *v/i* hikōki de iku 飛行機で行く **2** *v/t* … o hikōki de hakobu …を飛行機で運ぶ
♦**fly past** (*in formation*) parēdo-hikō o suru パレード飛行をする; (*of time*) tobu yō ni sugiru 飛ぶように過ぎる
flying *n* hikōki de ryokō suru koto 飛行機で旅行する事
foam *n* (*on liquid*) awa 泡
foam rubber kihō-gomu 気泡ゴム
FOB (= ***free on board***) tsumikomi-watashi 積み込み渡し
focus *n* (*of attention*) chūshin 中心; PHOT pinto ピント; ***be the ~ of attention*** chūmoku no mato ni naru 注目の的になる; ***be in ~ / out of ~*** pinto ga atte iru / zurete iru ピントが合っている/ずれている
♦**focus on** *problem, issue* … no shōten o shiboru …の焦点を絞る; PHOT …ni pinto o awaseru …にピントを合わせる
fodder shiryō 飼料
fog kiri 霧
foggy *adj* kiri no tachikometa 霧の立ち込めた
foil[1] *n* (*silver ~ etc*) hoiru ホイル
foil[2] *v/t* (*thwart*) ura o kaku 裏をかく
fold **1** *v/t paper etc* oritatamu 折りたたむ; ***~ one's arms*** udegumi o suru 腕組みをする **2** *v/i* (*of business*) tsubureru つぶれる **3** *n* (*in cloth etc*) orime 折り目
♦**fold up** **1** *v/t* … o oritatamu …を折りたたむ **2** *v/i* (*of chair, table*) oritatameru 折りたためる
folder (*for documents*) fairu ファイル; COMPUT foruda フォルダ
folding oritatami-shiki (no) 折りたたみ式(の); ***~ chair*** oritatami-isu 折りたたみ椅子
foliage ha 葉
folk (*people*) hitobito 人々; ***my ~*** (*family*) watashi no shinseki 私の親せき; ***come in, ~s*** F minna みんな
folk dance fōku-dansu フォークダンス; **folk music** fōku-myūjikku フォークミュージック, minzoku-ongaku 民俗音楽; **folk singer** fōku-shingā フォークシンガー; (*Japanese-style*) min'yō-kashu 民謡歌手; **folk song** fōku-songu フォークソング; (*Japanese-style*) min'yō 民謡
follow **1** *v/t person* ato ni tsuite iku 後について行く; *road* … ni sotte iku …に沿って行く; *guidelines, instructions* … ni shitagau …に従う; *TV series, news* tsuzukete miru 続けて見る; (*understand*) rikai suru 理解する; ***~ me*** watashi ni tsuite kinasai 私についてきなさい **2** *v/i* tsuite iku ついていく; (*logically*) … to naru …となる; ***it ~s from this that …*** kono kekka kara …to iu koto ni naru この結果から…ということになる; ***as ~s*** tsugi no tōri 次のとおり
♦**follow up** *v/t letter, inquiry* … o forō suru …をフォローする
follower shinpō-sha 信奉者; (*of politician*) shiji-sha 支持者; (*of team, TV program*) fan ファン
following **1** *adj* tsugi (no) 次(の) **2** *n* (*people*) shiji-sha 支持者; ***the ~*** ika no koto 以下の事
follow-up meeting hikitsuzuki no

mītingu 引き続きのミーティング
follow-up visit (*to doctor etc*) saido no hōmon 再度の訪問
folly (*madness*) oroka-sa 愚かさ
fond (*loving*) yasashii 優しい; *memory* natsukashii 懐かしい; ***be ~ of…*** … ga suki de aru …が好きである
fondle kawaigaru かわいがる
fondness itsukushimi 慈しみ
font (*for printing*) fonto フォント
food tabemono 食べ物
food freak F gurume グルメ; **food mixer** dendō-awadateki 電動泡立て器; **food poisoning** shoku-chūdoku 食中毒
fool *n* baka 馬鹿; ***make a ~ of oneself*** waraimono ni naru 笑いものになる
♦**fool around** fuzakeru ふざける; (*sexually*) uwaki o suru 浮気をする
♦**fool around with** *knife, drill etc* … de fuzakeru …でふざける; (*sexually*) … to uwaki o suru …と浮気をする
foolish baka (na) 馬鹿(な)
foolproof machigaeyō no nai 間違えようのない
foot ashi 足; (*measurement*) fīto フィート; ***on ~*** aruite 歩いて; ***at the ~ of the page*** pēji no shita no bubun ni ページの下の部分に; ***at the ~ of the hill*** oka no fumoto ni 丘のふもとに; ***put one's ~ in it*** F shikujiru しくじる
football amerikan-futtobōru アメリカンフットボール; (*soccer*) sakkā サッカー; (*ball*) bōru ボール; **football player** amefuto-senshu アメフト選手; (*soccer*) sakkā-senshu サッカー選手; **footbridge** hodōkyō 歩道橋; **foothills** yamasuso やますそ
footing (*basis*) taisei 体勢; ***lose one's ~*** ashi o fumihazusu 足を踏み外す; ***be on the same / a different ~*** onaji / chigau tachiba ni aru 同じ/違う立場にある; ***be on a friendly ~ with …*** … to shitashii …と親しい
footlights futtoraito フットライト; **footnote** kyakuchū 脚注; **footpath** komichi 小道; (*in countryside*) shizen-hodō 自然歩道; **footprint** ashiato 足跡; **footstep** ashioto 足音; ***follow in X's ~s*** X no kokorozashi o tsugu Xの志を継ぐ; **footwear** hakimono はきもの
for ◊ (*purpose, destination etc*): ***a train ~ …*** …yuki no ressha …行きの列車; ***clothes ~ children*** kodomo yō no fuku 子供用の服; ***it's too big ~ you*** anata ni wa ōkisugiru あなたには大きすぎる; ***here's a letter ~ you*** anata ni tegami desu あなたに手紙です; ***this is ~ you*** kore wa anata ni desu これはあなたにです; ***what is there ~ lunch?*** ohiru wa nan desu ka お昼は何ですか; ***the steak is ~ me*** sutēki wa watashi desu ステーキは私です; ***what is this ~?*** kore wa nani ni tsukau no desu ka これは何に使うのですか; ***what ~?*** nan no tame ni 何のために ◊ (*time*): ***~ three days / ~ two hours*** mikkakan / nijikan 三日間/二時間; ***please get it done ~ Monday*** getsuyōbi made ni shiagete kudasai 月曜日までに仕上げて下さい ◊ (*distance*): ***I walked ~ a mile*** ichi-mairu arukimashita 1マイル歩きました; ***it stretches for a 100 miles*** hyaku-mairu ni watatte iru 100マイルに渡っている ◊ (*in favor of*): ***I am ~ the idea*** watashi wa sono kangae ni sansei desu 私はその考えに賛成です ◊ (*instead of, in behalf of*): ***let me do that ~ you*** watashi ni yarasete kudasai 私にやらせて下さい; ***we are agents ~ …*** watashitachi wa … no dairinin desu 私達は…の代理人です ◊ (*in exchange for*): ***I bought it ~ $25*** nijūgo-doru de kaimashita 二十五ドルで買いました; ***how much did you sell it ~?*** ikura de urimashita ka いくらで売りましたか
forbid kinjiru 禁じる; ***~ X to do Y*** X ni Y suru koto o kinjiru XにYすることを禁じる
forbidden *adj* kinjirareta 禁じられた; ***smoking ~*** kin'en 禁煙; ***parking ~*** chūsha-kinshi 駐車禁止

forbidding *rockface, prospect* kiken (na) 危険(な); *person* kowai 恐い
force 1 *n* (*violence*) bōryoku 暴力; (*of explosion, wind, punch*) chikara 力; ***come into ~*** jisshi sareru 実施される; ***the ~s*** MIL guntai 軍隊 **2** *v/t door, lock* kojiakeru こじ開ける; ***~ X to do Y*** X ni Y suru yō ni kyōsei suru XにYするように強制する; ***~ open*** kojiakeru こじ開ける
forced (*strained*) murijii (no) 無理強い(の); *confession* kyōseiteki (na) 強制的(な); ***~ smile*** tsukuri-warai 作り笑い
forced landing fujichaku 不時着
forceful *argument* tsuyoi 強い; *speaker* settokuryoku no aru 説得力のある; *character* kyōretsu (na) 強烈(な)
forceps pinsetto ピンセット
forcible *entry* chikarazuku (no) 力ずく(の); *argument* kōkateki (na) 効果的(な)
ford *n* asase 浅瀬
fore: ***come to the ~*** medatte kuru 目立ってくる
foreboding yokan 予感; **forecast 1** *n* yosō 予想; (*of weather*) yohō 予報 **2** *v/t* yosō suru 予想する; *weather* yohō suru 予報する; **forecourt** maeniwa 前庭; **forefathers** senzo 先祖; **forefinger** hitosashi-yubi 人差し指; **foregone**: ***it's a ~ conclusion*** sore wa me ni mieta kekka desu それは目に見えた結果です; **foreground** zenkei 前景; **forehand** (*in tennis*) foahando フォアハンド; **forehead** hitai 額
foreign gaikoku (no) 外国(の)
foreign affairs gaimu 外務
foreign currency gaikoku-tsūka 外国通貨
foreigner gaikoku-jin 外国人; *pej* gaijin 外人
foreign exchange gaikoku-kawase 外国為替; **foreign language** gaikoku-go 外国語; **Foreign Office** *Br* Gaimu-shō 外務省; **foreign policy** gaikō-seisaku 外交政策; **Foreign Secretary** *Br* Gaimu-daijin 外務大臣
foreman (*of jury*) baishinchō 陪審長; **foremost** ichiban (no) 一番(の); **forerunner** senku-sha 先駆者; **foresee** yosō suru 予想する; **foreseeable** yosoku dekiru 予測できる; ***in the ~ future*** chikai shōrai ni 近い将来に; **foresight** senken no mei 先見の明
forest mori 森
forestry ringyō 林業
foretaste maebure 前触れ
foretell yogen suru 予言する
forever eikyū ni 永久に
foreword maegaki 前書き
forfeit *v/t right etc* ushinau 失う
forge *v/t* (*counterfeit*) … o gizō suru …を偽造する
forger gizō-sha 偽造者
forgery (*bank bill*) gizō 偽造; (*document*) gizō-bunsho 偽造文書
forget wasureru 忘れる
forgetful wasureppoi 忘れっぽい
forget-me-not (*flower*) wasurenagusa わすれなぐさ
forgive *v/t & v/i* yurusu 許す
forgiveness yurushi 許し
fork *n* fōku フォーク; (*in road*) bunkiten 分岐点
♦**fork out** *v/i* F (*pay*) harau 払う
forklift (**truck**) fōkurifuto フォークリフト
form 1 *n* (*shape*) katachi 形; (*type*) shurui 種類; (*document*) yōshi 用紙; ***~ of address*** hanashikata 話し方 **2** *v/t* (*in clay etc*) katachizukuru 形作る; *friendship* musubu 結ぶ; *opinion* matomeru まとめる; *past tense etc* tsukuru 作る **3** *v/i* (*take shape, develop*) katachi ni naru 形になる
formal seishiki (no) 正式(の); *recognition etc* kōshiki (no) 公式(の); ***~ clothes*** seisō 正装
formality keishiki 形式; ***it's just a ~*** keishiki dake no koto desu 形式だけの事です
formally *adv speak* seishiki ni 正式に; *recognized* kōshiki ni 公式に; *behave* katakurushiku 堅苦しく
format 1 *v/t diskette* fōmatto suru

フォーマットする, shokika suru 初期化する; *document* keishiki o totonoeru 形式を整える **2** *n* (*size: of magazine, paper etc*) saizu サイズ; (*make-up: of program*) teisai 体裁
formation (*act of forming*) kōsei 構成; (*of airplanes*) fōmēshon フォーメーション
formative zōkei (no) 造形(の); ***in his ~ years*** kare no jinkaku keiseiki ni 彼の人格形成期に
former izen (no) 以前(の); ***the ~*** mae no mono 前のもの
formerly izen wa 以前は
formidable osoroshii 恐ろしい
formula MATH, CHEM kōshiki 公式; (*for success etc*) hiketsu 秘訣; (*for baby*) konamiruku 粉ミルク
formulate amidasu 編み出す
fort MIL toride とりで
forth: ***back and ~*** ittari kitari shite 行ったり来たりして; ***and so ~*** nado など
forthcoming (*future*) kondo (no) 今度(の); *personality* sotchoku (na) 率直(な)
fortieth dai-yonjū (no) 第四十(の)
fortnight *Br* nishūkan 二週間
fortress MIL yōsai 要さい
fortunate kōun (na) 幸運(な)
fortunately kōun ni mo 好運にも
fortune kōun 好運; (*lot of money*) zaisan 財産; ***it costs a ~ to live here*** koko ni sumu ni wa totemo okane ga kakarimasu ここに住むにはとてもお金がかかります
fortune-teller uranaishi 占い師
forty yonjū 四十
forward 1 *adv* mae ni 前に **2** *adj pej: person* zūzūshii ずうずうしい **3** *n* SP fowādo フォワード **4** *v/t letter* tensō suru 転送する
forwarding agent COM unsō-gyōsha 運送業者
forward planning keikaku 計画
fossil kaseki 化石
foster child satogo 里子
foster parents satooya 里親
foul 1 *n* SP fauru ファウル **2** *adj smell, taste* fuketsu (na) 不潔(な); *weather* warui 悪い **3** *v/t* SP hansoku suru 反則する
found *v/t school etc* sōritsu suru 創立する
foundation (*of theory etc*) kiso 基礎; (*organization*) zaidan 財団, kikin 基金; (*setting up*) setsuritsu 設立
foundations (*of house*) dodai 土台
founder *n* sōritsu-sha 創立者
foundry chūzō-kōjō 鋳造工場
fountain funsui 噴水
four yon 四, shi 四; (*with count word 'tsu'*) yottsu 四つ
four-star *adj hotel etc* yotsuboshi (no) 四つ星(の)
fourteen jūyon 十四
fourteenth dai-jūyon (no) 第十四(の)
fourth 1 *adj* dai-yon (no) 第四(の) **2** *n* (*of month*) yokka 四日
Fourth of May holiday Kokumin no kyūjitsu 国民の休日
fowl kakin 家禽
fox *n* kitsune きつね
fraction ichibu 一部; (*decimal*) bunsū 分数
fracture 1 *n* kossetsu 骨折 **2** *v/t* kossetsu suru 骨折する
fragile koware-yasui 壊れやすい
fragment hahen 破片
fragmentary danpenteki (na) 断片的(な)
fragrance ii kaori いい香り
fragrant kaori no ii 香りのいい
frail moroi もろい
frame 1 *n* (*of eyeglasses*) furēmu フレーム, fuchi 縁; (*of building, body*) honegumi 骨組み; (*of window*) waku 枠; (*of picture*) gaku 額; ***~ of mind*** kibun 気分 **2** *v/t picture* gakubuchi ni ireru 額縁に入れる; F *s.o.* wana ni kakeru わなにかける
framework honegumi 骨組, furēmu-wāku フレームワーク
France Furansu フランス
frank sotchoku (na) 率直(な)
frankly sotchoku ni 率直に; ***~, it's not worth it*** sotchoku ni itte sore wa suru kachi ga nai desu 率直に言ってそれはする価値がないです

frantic hankyōran (no) 半狂乱(の)
fraternal kyōdai (no) 兄弟(の)
fraud sagi 詐欺; (*person*) sagishi 詐欺師
fraudulent fusei (na) 不正(な)
frayed *cuffs* surikireru 擦り切れる
freak 1 *n* (*unusual event*) ijō 異常; (*two-headed person, animal etc*) kikei 奇形; F (*strange person*) henjin 変人; ***movie / jazz*** **~** F (*fanatic*) eiga / jazu mania 映画/ジャズマニア **2** *adj wind, storm etc* ijō (na) 異常(な)
freckle sobakasu そばかす
free 1 *adj* (*at liberty*) jiyū (na) 自由(な); (*no cost*) muryō (no) 無料(の); *room, table* aite iru 空いている; ***are you ~ this afternoon?*** kyō no gogo aite imasu ka 今日の午後空いていますか; ***~ and easy*** kutsuroida くつろいだ; ***for ~*** muryō de 無料で **2** *v/t prisoners* kaihō suru 解放する
freebie F keihin 景品
freedom jiyū 自由
freedom of the press hōdō no jiyū 報道の自由
free kick (*in soccer*) furī-kikku フリーキック; **freelance 1** *adj* furī (no) フリー(の) **2** *adv work* furī de フリーで; **freelancer** furī フリー; **free market economy** jiyū-keizai 自由経済; **free sample** muryō-sanpuru 無料サンプル; **free speech** genron no jiyū 言論の自由; **freeway** kōsoku-dōro 高速道路; **freewheel** *v/i* (*on bicycle*) dasei de hashiru 惰性で走る
freeze 1 *v/t food, river* kōraseru 凍らせる; *wages, bank account* tōketsu suru 凍結する; *video* seishi suru 静止する **2** *v/i* (*of water*) kōru 凍る; (*of weather*) hieru 冷える
♦**freeze over** kōru 凍る
freezer reitōko 冷凍庫
freezing 1 *adj* kōru yō (na) 凍るよう(な); ***it's ~ out here*** soto wa sugoku hiete imasu 外はすごく冷えています; ***it's ~*** (***cold***) (*of weather, water*) sugoku samui desu すごく寒いです; ***I'm ~*** (***cold***) karada ga sukkari hiete imasu 体がすっかり冷えています **2** *n* sesshi-reido 摂氏零度; ***10 degrees below ~*** hyōtenka-jūdo 氷点下十度
freezing compartment reitōko 冷凍庫
freezing point hyōten 氷点
freight *n* kamotsu 貨物; (*costs*) unsōryō 運送料
freight car (*on train*) kasha 貨車
freighter (*ship*) kamotsu-sen 貨物船; (*airplane*) kamotsu-ki 貨物機
freight train kamotsu-ressha 貨物列車
French 1 *adj* Furansu (no) フランス(の) **2** *n* (*language*) Furansu-go フランス語; ***the ~*** Furansu-jin フランス人
French doors furansu-mado フランス窓; **French fries** furenchi-furai フレンチフライ; **Frenchman** Furansu-jin dansei フランス人男性; **Frenchwoman** Fransu-jin josei フランス人女性
frequency hindo 頻度; RAD shūhasū 周波数
frequent[1] *adj* hinpan (na) 頻繁(な)
frequent[2] *v/t* yoku iku よく行く; *bar* kayō 通う
frequently shibashiba しばしば
fresh *fruit, meat etc* shinsen (na) 新鮮(な); (*cool*) sawayaka (na) さわやか(な); (*cold*) samui 寒い; (*new*) atarashii 新しい; (*impertinent*) namaiki (na) 生意気(な)
♦**freshen up 1** *v/i* sappari suru さっぱりする **2** *v/t room, paintwork* ... o moyōgae suru ...を模様替えする
freshman shinnyūsei 新入生
freshness (*of fruit, meat*) shinsen-sa 新鮮さ; (*of style, approach*) atarashi-sa 新しさ; (*of weather: coolness*) sawayaka-sa さわやかさ; (*coldness*) samu-sa 寒さ
freshwater *adj* mamizu 真水, tansui 淡水
fret *v/i* kuyokuyo nayamu くよくよ悩む
friction PHYS masatsu 摩擦; (*between people*) fuwa 不和

friction tape zetsuen-tēpu 絶縁テープ
Friday kin'yōbi 金曜日
fridge reizōko 冷蔵庫
friend tomodachi 友達; ***make ~s*** (*of one person*) tomodachi ga dekiru 友達ができる; (*of two people*) tomodachi ni naru 友達になる; ***make ~s with*** … to shitashiku naru …と親しくなる
friendly *adj atmosphere, meeting* yūkōteki (na) 友好的(な); *restaurant* igokochi no ii 居心地のいい; *person* hitonatsukoi 人なつこい; (*easy to use*) tsukai-yasui 使いやすい; ***be ~ with*** … to shitashii …と親しい
friendship yūjō 友情
fries furenchi-furai フレンチフライ
fright: ***give … a ~*** … o odorokasu …を驚かす
frighten *v/t* kowagaraseru 怖がらせる; ***be ~ed*** obieta おびえた; ***don't be ~ed*** kowagaranaide 怖がらないで; ***be ~ed of*** … o kowagaru …を怖がる
frightening osoroshii 恐ろしい
frigid (*sexually*) fukanshō (no) 不感症(の)
frill (*on dress etc*) furiru フリル; (*extra*) yokei na mono 余計な物
fringe (*on tablecloth, curtains etc*) heri へり; (*in hair*) maegami 前髪; (*edge*) hazure はずれ
frisk *v/t* … no bodīchekku o suru …のボディーチェックをする
frisky *puppy* genki (na) 元気 (な)
♦**fritter away** *time, fortune* … o rōhi suru …を浪費する
frivolous *person* karui 軽い; *pleasures* kudaranai 下らない
frizzy *hair* chijireta 縮れた
frog kaeru かえる
frogman daibā ダイバー
from ◊ (*in time*): ***~ 9 to 5 (o'clock)*** kuji kara goji made 九時から五時まで; ***~ the 18th century*** jūhasseiki kara 十八世紀から; ***~ today (on)*** kyō kara 今日から; ***~ next Tuesday*** tsugi no kayōbi kara 次の火曜日から ◊ (*in space*): ***~ here to there*** koko kara soko made ここからそこまで; ***we drove here ~ Tokyo*** watashitachi wa Tōkyō kara koko made kuruma de kita 私達は東京からここまで車で来た ◊ (*origin*): ***a letter ~ Jo*** jō kara no tegami ジョーからの手紙; ***a gift ~ the management*** keieijin kara no okurimono 経営陣からの贈り物; ***it doesn't say who it's ~*** dare kara kita no ka kaite inai 誰から来たのか書いていない; ***I am ~ New Jersey*** watashi wa Nyūjājī no shusshin desu 私はニュージャージーの出身です; ***made ~ bananas*** banana de tsukurarete iru バナナで作られている ◊ (*because of*): ***tired ~ the journey*** tabi de tsukarete iru 旅で疲れている; ***it's ~ overeating*** tabesugi kara kite iru 食べ過ぎから来ている
front 1 *n* (*of building, book*) shōmen 正面; (*of piece of paper*) omote 表; (*of car*) zenbu 前部; (*cover organization*) omotemuki 表向き; MIL senchi 戦地; (*of weather*) zensen 前線; ***in ~*** mae ni 前に; (*in a race*) rīdo shite リードして; ***in ~ of*** … no mae no …の前の; ***at the ~*** mae no hō ni 前の方に; ***at the ~ of*** … no zenbu ni …の前部に **2** *adj wheel, seat* mae (no) 前(の) **3** *v/t TV program* shikai o suru 司会をする
front cover hyōshi 表紙; **front door** genkan 玄関; **front entrance** shōmen-iriguchi 正面入り口
frontier kokkyō 国境; *fig* (*of science*) saisentan 最先端; (*of knowledge*) genkai 限界
front page (*of newspaper*) ichimen 一面; **front page news** ichimen no nyūsu 一面のニュース; **front row** saizenretsu 最前列; **front seat passenger** (*in car*) zenbu zaseki no jōkyaku 前部座席の乗客; **front-wheel drive** zenrin-kudō 前輪駆動
frost shimo 霜
frostbite tōshō 凍傷
frostbitten tōshō ni kakatta 凍傷にかかった

frosted glass suri-garasu すりガラス

frosting (*on cake*) aishingu アイシング

frosty *weather* shimo no orita 霜の降りた; *welcome* tsumetai 冷たい

froth awa 泡

frothy *cream etc* awa no yō (no) 泡のよう(な)

frown 1 *n* shikamettsura しかめっ面 **2** *v/i* kao o shikameru 顔をしかめる

frozen *feet etc* kogoeta 凍えた; *wastes of Siberia* kōtta 凍った; *food* reitō (no) 冷凍(の); ***I'm ~*** F sugoku hiete iru すごく冷えている

frozen food reitō-shokuhin 冷凍食品

fruit kudamono 果物, furūtsu フルーツ

fruitful *talks* minori aru 実りある

fruit juice furūtsu-jūsu フルーツジュース

fruit salad furūtsu-sarada フルーツサラダ

frustrate *v/t person* yokkyū-fuman ni saseru 欲求不満にさせる; *plans* zasetsu saseru ざ折させる

frustrated *look, sigh* yokkyū-fuman (no) 欲求不満(の)

frustrating iraira suru いらいらする

frustratingly *slow, hard* iraira saseru hodo いらいらさせるほど

frustration yokkyū-fuman 欲求不満; ***sexual ~*** seiteki-yokkyūfuman 性的欲求不満; ***the ~s of modern life*** kindaiteki na kurashi o naka no yokkyū-fuman 近代的な暮らしの中の欲求不満; ***a look of ~*** shitsubō no kao 失望の顔

fry *v/t* (*shallow-~*) yaku 焼く; (*stir-~*) itameru 炒める; (*deep-~*) ageru 揚げる

fried egg medamayaki 目玉焼き

fried potatoes poteto-furai ポテトフライ

frying pan furaipan フライパン

fuck *v/t* V yaru やる; ***~!*** kuso くそ; ***~ him / ~ that!*** kare nante dō demo ii / sore wa dō demo ii 彼なんてどうでもいい/それはどうでもいい

♦**fuck off** V useru うせる; ***~!*** jama shinaide じゃましないで

fucking V **1** *adj* kusoimaimashii くそいまいましい **2** *adv* kusoimaimashiku くそいまいましく; ***that's ~ stupid*** suggoku bakabakashii すっごくばかばかしい; ***that's ~ brilliant*** suggoku ii すっごくいい

fuel *n* nenryō 燃料

fugitive *n* tōbō-sha 逃亡者

fulfill *v/t* (*carry out*) hatasu 果たす; (*satisfy*) mitasu 満たす; ***feel ~ed*** (*in job, life*) mitasarete iru ki ga suru 満たされている気がする

fulfilling *job* jūjitsu shita 充実した

fulfillment (*of contract etc*) jitsugen 実現; (*moral, spiritual*) jūjitsu-kan 充実感

full *bottle, hotel, bus, diskette* ippai (no) いっぱい(の); *account* kanzen (na) 完全(な); *life* manzoku shita 満足した; *schedule, day* isogashii 忙しい; ***~ of*** … de ippai no …でいっぱいの; ***~ up*** *hotel etc* ippai no いっぱいの; (*with food*) onaka ga ippai no おなかがいっぱいの; ***pay in ~*** zenbu harau 全部払う

full coverage (*insurance*) zengaku-hoshō 全額補償; **full-grown** sukkari otona ni natta すっかり大人になった; **full-length** *dress* rongu (no) ロング(の); *mirror* zenshin (no) 全身(の); *movie* katto shite inai カットしていない

full moon mangetsu 満月; **full stop** piriodo ピリオド, shūshifu 終止符; **full-time 1** *adj job* seishain (no) 正社員(の); *teaching* jōkin (no) 常勤(の); *student* seiki (no) 正規(の) **2** *adv work* seishain de 正社員で; *teach* jōkin de 常勤で; *study* seiki ni 正規に

fully *booked* manpai ni 満杯に; *recovered* kanzen ni 完全に; *understand* jūbun ni 十分に

fumble *v/t catch, job* motatsuku もたつく

♦**fumble about** tesaguri suru 手探りする

fume: ***be fuming*** F (*angry*) kankan ni natte iru かんかんになっている

fumes (*from car*) haiki-gasu 排気ガス; (*from chemicals, machine*) gasu ガス
fun tanoshimi 楽しみ; ***it was great ~*** sore wa sugoku tanoshikatta それはすごく楽しかった; ***bye, have ~!*** jā tanoshinde ne じゃあ楽しんでね; ***for ~*** omoshirohanbun ni おもしろ半分に; ***make ~ of*** karakau からかう
function 1 *n* (*of machine part*) kinō 機能; (*of employee*) yakuwari 役割; (*reception etc*) gyōji 行事 **2** *v/i* hataraku 働く; ***~ as …*** … to shite kinō suru …として機能する
fund 1 *n* shikin 資金; (*governmental*) kikin 基金 **2** *v/t project* shikin o dasu 資金を出す
fundamental (*basic*) kisoteki (na) 基礎的(な); (*substantial*) kihonteki (na) 基本的(な); (*crucial*) jūyō (na) 重要(な)
fundamentally kihonteki ni 基本的に
funeral sōshiki 葬式
funeral home sōgijō 葬儀場
funfair yūenchi 遊園地
funicular (railway) kēburukā ケーブルカー
funnel *n* (*of ship*) jōgo じょうご
funnily (*oddly*) hen na fū ni へんな風に; (*comically*) omoshiroku おもしろく; ***~ enough*** okashi na koto ni おかしなことに
funny (*comical*) okashi (na) おかし(な); (*odd*) hen (na) へん(な)
fur kegawa 毛皮
furious (*angry*) gekido shite 激怒して; ***at a ~ pace*** mōretsu na hayasa de 猛烈な速さで
furnace (*in building*) boirā ボイラー; (*industrial*) ro 炉
furnish *room* sonaetsukeru 備え付ける; (*supply*) kyōkyū suru 供給する
furniture kagu 家具; ***a piece of ~*** kagu itten 家具一点
furry *animal* ke de ōwareta 毛で覆われた
further 1 *adj* (*additional*) sore ijō (no) それ以上(の); (*more distant*) sara ni susunda さらに進んだ; ***until ~ notice*** otte tsūchi suru 追って通知する; ***have you anything ~ to say?*** mada nani ka iu koto ga arimasu ka まだ何か言うことがありますか **2** *adv walk, drive* motto saki ni もっと先に; ***~, I want to say …*** kuwaete watashi wa … to iitai 加えて私は…と言いたい; ***2 miles ~ (on)*** sara ni ni-mairu さらに二マイル **3** *v/t cause etc* sokushin suru 促進する; *interests* tsukisusumeru 突き進める
furthest 1 *adj* ichiban tōku (no) 一番遠く(の) **2** *adv* ichiban tōku ni 一番遠くに
furtive *look* hisoka (na) ひそか(な)
fury (*anger*) gekido 激怒
fuse 1 *n* ELEC hyūzu ヒューズ **2** *v/i* ELEC hyūzu ga tobu ヒューズが飛ぶ **3** *v/t* ELEC … no hyūzu o tobasu …のヒューズを飛ばす
fusebox hyūzu-bokkusu ヒューズボックス
fuselage kitai 機体
fuse wire hyūzu-sen ヒューズ線
fusion yūgō 融合
fuss *n* hitosawagi 一騒ぎ; fuhei 不平; ***make a ~*** (*complain*) monku o iu 文句を言う; (*behave in exaggerated way*) ōsawagi o suru 大騒ぎをする; ***make a ~ of*** (*be very attentive to*) … o chiyahoya suru …をちやほやする
fussy *person* urusai うるさい; *design etc* korisugita 凝りすぎた; ***be a ~ eater*** tabemono ni urusai 食べ物にうるさい
futile muda (na) 無駄(な)
futon futon ふとん
future *n* (*of person, company*) shōrai 将来; (*of humanity, earth*) mirai 未来; GRAM miraikei 未来形; ***in ~*** korekarasaki これから先
futures FIN sakimono-torihiki 先物取引
futures market FIN sakimono-torihiki-shijō 先物取引市場
futuristic *design* zen'eiteki (na) 前衛的(な)
fuzzy *hair* kebadatta けばだった; (*out of focus*) boyaketa ぼやけた

G

gadget kigu 器具
gag 1 *n* sarugutsuwa 猿ぐつわ; (*joke*) gyagu ギャグ **2** *v/t person* sarugutsuwa o kamaseru 猿ぐつわをかませる; *the press* damaraseru 黙らせる
gain *v/t* (*acquire*) eru 得る; ***~ speed*** sokudo o masu 速度を増す; ***~ 10 pounds*** juppondo fueru 十ポンド増える
gale kyōfū 強風
gall bladder tannō 胆のう
gallery (*for art*) bijutsukan 美術館; (*art dealer's shop*) garō 画廊; (*in theater*) tenjō-sajiki 天井桟敷
galley (*on ship*) chōrishitsu 調理室
gallon garon ガロン; ***~s of tea*** tairyō no kōcha 大量の紅茶
gallop *v/i* gyaroppu ギャロップ
gallows kōshudai 絞首台
gallstone tanseki 胆石
gamble gyanburu ギャンブル, kakegoto 賭けごと
gambler bakuchiuchi ばくち打ち
gambling gyanburu ギャンブル, kakegoto 賭けごと
game *n* SP shiai 試合; (*child's*) asobi 遊び; (*in tennis*) gēmu ゲーム
gang ichimi 一味
gangster yakuza やくざ
♦ **gang up on** guru ni natte … o ijimeru ぐるになって…をいじめる
gangway tarappu タラップ
gap (*in teeth*, *clouds*) sukima すきま; (*between rich and poor etc*, *in time*) hedatari 隔たり; (*on the market*) zure ずれ
gape *v/i* (*of person*) pokan to kuchi o akete mitoreru ぽかんと口を開けて見とれる; (*of hole*) ōkiku hiraku 大きく開く
♦ **gape at** pokan to kuchi o akete … ni mitoreru ぽかんと口を開けて…に見とれる
gaping *hole* ōkiku hiraita 大きく開いた
garage (*for parking*) shako 車庫; garēji ガレージ; (*for repairs*) shūri-kōjō 修理工場; *Br* (*for gas*) gasorin-sutando ガソリンスタンド
garbage gomi ごみ; *fig* (*nonsense*) tawagoto たわごと; (*poor quality item*) dekisokonai 出来そこない
garbage can gomi-baketsu ごみバケツ
garden niwa 庭; ***Japanese ~*** Nihonteien 日本庭園
gardener engei-ka 園芸家; (*professional*) niwashi 庭師
gardening engei 園芸, gādeningu ガーデニング
gargle *v/i* ugai o suru うがいをする
garish kebakebashii けばけばしい
garland *n* hanawa 花輪
garlic ninniku にんにく
garment ifuku 衣服
garnish *v/t* kazaru 飾る
garrison *n* (*place*) chūtonchi 駐屯地; (*troops*) shubitai 守備隊
garter gātā ガーター
gas *n* kitai 気体; (*gasoline*) gasorin ガソリン
gash *n* fukai kizu 深い傷
gasket gasuketto ガスケット
gasoline gasorin ガソリン
gas pump kyūyu-ponpu 給油ポンプ
gasp *v/i* iki o nomu 息をのむ; ***~ for breath*** ikigire ga suru 息切れがする
gas pedal akuseru アクセル; **gas station** gasorin-sutando ガソリンスタンド; **gas works** gasu-kōjō ガス工場
gate mon 門; (*at airport*) gēto ゲート
gatecrash … ni oshikakeru …に押しかける
gateway iriguchi 入り口; *fig* michi 道
gather *v/t facts*, *information* atsumeru

集める; (*understand*) suisoku suru 推測する; ***I ~ that …*** … da to omou …だと思う; ***~ speed*** supīdo o masu スピードを増す

♦**gather up** *possessions* yoseatsumeru 寄せ集める

gathering (*group of people*) atsumari 集まり

gaudy kebakebashii けばけばしい

gauge 1 *n* keiki 計器 **2** *v/t* sokutei suru 測定する

gaunt yasekoketa やせこけた

gauze gāze ガーゼ

gay 1 *n* homo ホモ **2** *adj* homo (no) ホモ(の)

gaze 1 *n* shisen 視線 **2** *v/i* mitsumeru 見つめる

♦**gaze at** … o jitto mitsumeru …をじっと見つめる

GB (= ***Great Britain***) Eikoku 英国

GDP (= ***gross domestic product***) kokunai-sōseisan 国内総生産

gear *n* (*equipment*) sōbi 装備; (*in vehicles*) gia ギア

gear lever, **gear shift** hensoku-rebā 変速レバー

geisha geisha 芸者

gel (*for hair*) jeru ジェル; (*for shower*) bodīsōpu ボディーソープ

gem hōseki 宝石; *fig* (*book etc*) ippin 逸品; (*person*) kichō na hito 貴重な人

gender sei 性

gene idenshi 遺伝子; ***it's in his ~s*** kare no chi da 彼の血だ

general 1 *n* (*in army*) shōgun 将軍; ***in ~*** ippan ni 一般に **2** *adj* (*overall, miscellaneous*) ippanteki (na) 一般的(な); (*widespread*) zentaiteki (na) 全体的(な)

general election sōsenkyo 総選挙

generalization ippanka 一般化; ***that's a ~*** sore wa ippanron desu それは一般論です

generalize ippanka suru 一般化する

generally ippanteki ni 一般的に

generate (*create*) umidasu 生み出す; (*in linguistics*) seisei suru 生成する; *feeling* hikiokosu 引き起こす; ***~ electricity*** hatsuden suru 発電する

generation sedai 世代

generation gap sedai no danzetsu 世代の断絶

generator hatsudenki 発電機

generosity kimae no yosa 気前のよさ

generous (*with money*) kimae no yoi 気前のよい; (*not too critical*) kandai (na) 寛大(な); *portion etc* takusan (no) たくさん(の)

genetic idenshi (no) 遺伝子(の)

genetically idenshiteki ni 遺伝子的に

genetic engineering idenshi-kōgaku 遺伝子工学

genetic fingerprint idenshi-shimon 遺伝子指紋

geneticist idenshi-gakusha 遺伝子学者

genetics idenshi-gaku 遺伝子学

genial *person*, *company* shinsetsu (na) 親切(な)

genitals seiki 性器

genius tensai 天才

gentle yasashii 優しい

gentleman shinshi 紳士

gents (*toilet*) dansei-yō toire 男性用トイレ

genuine shōshin-shōmei (no) 正真正銘(の); seijitsu (na) 誠実(な)

geographical chiriteki (na) 地理的(な)

geography (*of area*) chiri 地理; (*subject*) chiri-gaku 地理学

geological chishitsugaku (no) 地質学(の)

geologist chishitsu-gakusha 地質学者

geology (*of area*) chishitsu 地質; (*subject*) chishitsu-gaku 地質学

geometric(al) kikagakuteki (na) 幾何学的(な)

geometry kikagaku 幾何学

geriatric 1 *adj* rōnen-igaku (no) 老年医学(の) **2** *n* rōnen-igaku 老年医学

germ baikin ばい菌; (*of idea etc*) me 芽

German 1 *adj* Doitsu (no) ドイツ(の) **2** *n* (*person*) Doitsu-jin ドイツ人; (*language*) Doitsu-go ドイツ語

Germany Doitsu ドイツ
germ warfare saikin-sensō 細菌戦争
gesticulate miburi de hanasu 身ぶりで話す
gesture *n* miburi 身ぶり; (*of friendship*) shirushi 印
get 1 *v/t* (*obtain*) te ni ireru 手に入れる; (*fetch*) totte kuru 取ってくる; (*receive*: *letter*) uketoru 受け取る; (*receive*: *knowledge*, *respect etc*) eru 得る; (*catch*: *bus*, *train etc*) … ni noru …に乗る; (*understand*) wakaru わかる ◊ (*become*) … ni naru …になる; ***~ worried / nervous*** shinpai / shinkeishitsu ni naru 心配/神経質になる ◊ (*causative*): ***~ X repaired*** X o shūri shite morau Xを修理してもらう; ***~ X to do Y*** X ni Y saseru XにYさせる; ***~ one's hair cut*** … no kami o kitte morau …の髪を切ってもらう; ***~ X ready*** X no junbi o suru Xの準備をする ◊ (*have opportunity*): ***I never got to meet her*** kanojo ni au kikai ga zenzen nakatta 彼女に会う機会が全然なかった; ***I didn't ~ to go there*** soko ni iku kikai ga nakatta そこに行く機会がなかった ◊ (*possess*): ***have got*** motte iru 持っている; ***she's got three of them*** kanojo wa mittsu motte iru 彼女は三つ持っている ◊ ***have got to*** (*must*): ***I have got to study / see him*** benkyōshinakereba / kare ni awanakereba naranai 勉強しなければ/彼に会わなければならない; ***I don't want to, but I' ve got to*** yaritaku nai kedo yaranakya やりたくないけどやらなきゃ **2** *v/i* (*arrive*) … ni tsuku …に着く
♦ **get about** (*travel*) achikochi ryokō suru あちこち旅行する; (*be mobile*) ugokimawaru 動き回る
♦ **get along** (*progress*) yatte iku やっていく; (*come to party etc*) iku 行く; (*with s.o.*) nakayoku yatte iku 仲よくやっていく
♦ **get at** (*criticize*) … o kenasu …をけなす; (*imply*, *mean*) iō to suru 言おうとする
♦ **get away 1** *v/i* (*leave*) tachisaru 立ち去る **2** *v/t*: ***get X away from Y*** Y kara X o toriageru YからXを取り上げる
♦ **get away with** … no batsu o ukenaide sumu …の罰を受けないですむ
♦ **get back 1** *v/i* (*return*) modoru 戻る; ***I'll ~ to you on that*** ato de henji o suru 後で返事をする **2** *v/t* (*obtain again*) … o torimodosu …を取り戻す
♦ **get by** (*pass*) tōrinukeru 通り抜ける; (*financially*) nantoka yatte iku なんとかやっていく
♦ **get down 1** *v/i* (*from ladder etc*) oriru 降りる; (*duck*) mi o kagameru 身をかがめる **2** *v/t* (*depress*) … o gakkuri saseru … をがっくりさせる
♦ **get down to** *work* … ni torikakaru …に取りかかる; *real facts* … ni tassuru …に達する
♦ **get in 1** *v/i* (*of train*, *plane*) tōchaku suru 到着する; (*come home*) uchi ni kaeru 家に着く; (*to car*) noru 乗る; ***how did they ~?*** (*of thieves*, *snakes etc*) dō yatte hairikonda no darō どうやって入り込んだのだろう **2** *v/t* (*to suitcase etc*) … o naka ni ireru …を中に入れる
♦ **get off 1** *v/i* (*from bus etc*) oriru 降りる; (*finish work*) owaru 終わる; (*not be punished*) manugareru 免れる **2** *v/t* (*remove*) … o toru …を取る; *clothes*, *footgear* … o nugu …を脱ぐ; ***~ the grass!*** shibafu kara denasai 芝生から出なさい
♦ **get off with** *Br* (*sexually*) … to ii naka ni naru …といい仲になる; ***~ a small fine*** shōgaku no bakkin de sumu 小額の罰金で済む
♦ **get on 1** *v/i* (*to bike*, *bus*, *train*) noru 乗る; (*be friendly*) umaku yatte iku うまくやっていく; (*of time*) tatsu たつ; (*become old*) toshi o toru 年をとる; (*make progress*) susumu 進む; ***it's getting on*** daibu jikan ga tatta だいぶ時間がたった; ***he's getting on*** kare wa

mō toshi da 彼はもう年だ; ***he's getting on for 50*** kare wa mō sugu go-jū ni naru 彼はもうすぐ五十になる **2** *v/t* … ni noru …に乗る; ***~ the bus / one's bike*** basu / jitensha ni noru バス/自転車に乗る; ***get one's hat on*** bōshi o kaburu 帽子をかぶる; ***I can't get these pants on*** kono zubon wa hakenai このズボンははけない
♦**get out 1** *v/i* (*from car etc*) deru 出る; (*from prison*) shussho suru 出所する; ***~!*** dete ike 出て行け; ***let's ~ of here*** koko o deyō ここを出よう; ***I don't ~ much these days*** watashi wa saikin amari gaishutsu shimasen 私は最近あまり外出しません **2** *v/t nail, sth jammed* … o torinozoku …を取り除く; *stain* … o toru …を取る; *gun, pen* … o nuku …を抜く
♦**get over** *fence, disappointment etc* … o norikoeru …を乗り越える; *lover etc* … o wasureru …を忘れる
♦**get over with**: ***let's get it over with*** sore o katazukete shimaō それを片付けてしまおう
♦**get through** TELEC denwa ga tsūjiru 電話が通じる; (*make self understood*) wakaraseru わからせる
♦**get to** (*reach*) … ni tsuku …に着く
♦**get up 1** *v/i* (*in morning*) okiru 起きる; (*from chair etc*) tachiagaru 立ち上がる; (*of wind*) okoru 起こる **2** *v/t hill* … o noboru …を登る
getaway (*from robbery*) tōsō 逃走
getaway car tōsō-sha 逃走車
get-together shinbokukai 親睦会
ghastly (*horrible*) hidoi ひどい
gherkin kyūri no pikurusu きゅうりのピクルス
ghetto hinmingai 貧民街
ghost yūrei 幽霊
ghostly bukimi (na) 無気味(な)
giant 1 *n* kyojin 巨人 **2** *adj* kyodai (na) 巨大(な)
gibberish tawagoto たわごと
giblets tori no zōmotsu 鳥の臓物
giddiness memai めまい
giddy memai ga suru めまいがする
gift okurimono 贈り物, gifuto ギフト
gifted sainō no aru 才能のある
giftwrap okurimono yō no hōsō o suru 贈り物用の包装をする
gigabyte COMPUT gigabaito ギガバイト
gigantic kyodai (na) 巨大(な)
giggle 1 *v/i* kusukusu warau くすくす笑う **2** *n* kusukusuwarai くすくす笑い
gill (*of fish*) era えら
gilt *n* kinmekki 金めっき; **~s** FIN yūryō kabu 優良株
gimmick kozaiku 小細工
gin jin ジン; ***~ and tonic*** jintonikku ジントニック
ginger (*spice*) shōga しょうが; akage 赤毛
gingerbread shōga-iri bisuketto しょうが入りビスケット
gingerly shinchō ni 慎重に
gipsy jipushī ジプシー
giraffe kirin きりん
girder *n* tessei no hari 鉄製の梁
girl onna no ko 女の子
girlfriend (*of boy*) kanojo 彼女; (*of girl*) onnatomodachi 女友達
girl guide gārugaido ガールガイド
girlie magazine nūdo-zasshi ヌード雑誌
girl scout gārusukauto ガールスカウト
gist yōten 要点
give ataeru 与える; (*from viewpoint of the giver*) ageru あげる; (*from viewpoint of the receiver*) kureru くれる; *present* okuru 贈る; (*supply: electricity etc*) kyōkyū suru 供給する; ***I can ~ you $5*** go doru ageru koto ga dekiru 五ドルあげることができる; ***can you ~ me $5?*** go doru kureru 五ドルくれる; ***~ her my love*** kanojo ni yoroshiku 彼女によろしく ◊: ***~ a groan*** umeku うめく; ***~ a talk*** hanashi o suru 話をする; ***~ a lecture*** kōgi o okonau 講義を行なう; ***~ a cry*** nakigoe o ageru 泣き声をあげる
♦**give away** (*as present*) … o hito ni ageru …を人にあげる; (*betray*) … o barasu …をばらす; ***give oneself***

away shōtai o arawasu 正体を現わす
♦**give back** … o kaesu …を返す
♦**give in 1** *v/i* (*surrender*) kōsan suru 降参する **2** *v/t* (*hand in*) … o watasu …を渡す
♦**give off** *smell, fumes* … o hassuru …を発する
♦**give onto** (*open onto*) … ni tsūjiru …に通じる
♦**give out 1** *v/t leaflets etc* … o kubaru …を配る **2** *v/i* (*of supplies, strength*) nakunaru なくなる
♦**give up 1** *v/t smoking etc* … o yameru …をやめる; ***give oneself up to the police*** keisatsu e jishu suru 警察へ自首する **2** *v/i* (*cease habit*) yameru やめる; (*stop trying*) akirameru あきらめる
♦**give way** (*of bridge etc*) kuzureru 崩れる
given name namae 名前
glacier hyōga 氷河
glad ureshii うれしい
gladly yorokonde 喜んで
glamor miryoku 魅力
glamorous miryokuteki (na) 魅力的(な)
glance *v/i* chiratto miru ちらっと見る; ~ ***at …*** … o chiratto miru …をちらっと見る
gland sen 腺
glandular fever sennetsu 腺熱
glare 1 *n* (*of sun, headlights*) giragira suru hikari ぎらぎらする光 **2** *v/i* (*of sun, headlights*) giragira hikaru ぎらぎら光る
♦**glare at** … o niramu …をにらむ
glaring *adj mistake* meihaku (na) 明白(な)
glass (*material*) garasu ガラス; (*for drink*) koppu コップ
glasses megane 眼鏡
glaze *n* uwagusuri 上薬
♦**glaze over** (*of eyes*) kasumu かすむ
glazed *expression* don'yori shita どんよりした
glazier garasu-ya ガラス屋
glazing mado-garasu 窓ガラス
gleam 1 *n* honoka na hikari ほのかな光 **2** *v/i* hikaru 光る
glee ōyorokobi 大喜び
gleeful ōyorokobi (no) 大喜び(の)
glib uwabe dake (no) うわべだけ(の)
glide *v/i* suberu 滑る
glider guraidā グライダー
gliding *n* (*sport*) guraidā-hikō グライダー飛行
glimmer 1 *n* (*of light*) kasuka na hikari かすかな光; ~ ***of hope*** kasuka na kibō no hikari かすかな希望の光 **2** *v/i* kasuka ni hikaru かすかに光る
glimpse 1 *n* hitome ひと目 **2** *v/t* chirari to hitome miru ちらりとひと目見る
glint 1 *n* kirameki きらめき **2** *v/i* (*of light*) kirameku きらめく; (*of eyes*) hikaru 光る
glisten kirakira hikaru きらきら光る
glitter pikapika hikaru ぴかぴか光る
glitterati yūmei-jin 有名人
gloat ninmari suru にんまりする; ~ ***over …*** … o ninmari to nagameru …をにんまりと眺める
global (*worldwide*) zensekaiteki (na) 全世界的(な); (*without exceptions*) zentaiteki (na) 全体的(な)
global economy sekai-keizai 世界経済; **global market** sekai-shijō 世界市場; **global warming** chikyū no ondanka 地球の温暖化
globe (*the earth*) chikyū 地球; (*model of earth*) chikyūgi 地球儀
gloom kuragari 暗がり; (*mood*) yūutsu 憂うつ
gloomy *room* kurai 暗い; *mood, person* yūutsu (na) 憂うつ(な)
glorious *weather* subarashii すばらしい; *victory* eikō aru 栄光ある
glory *n* eikō 栄光
gloss *n* (*shine*) tsuya つや; (*general explanation*) gaiyō 概要
glossary yōgoshū 用語集
gloss paint tsuyadashi-penki つや出しペンキ
glossy 1 *adj paper* tsuyadashi-jōshitsushi つや出し上質紙 **2** *n* (*magazine*) gurabia-zasshi グラビ

H

habit kuse 癖; (*routine*) shūkan 習慣
habitable sumeru 住める
habitat seisokuchi 生息地
habitual itsumo (no) いつも(の); *smoker*, *drinker* jōshūteki (na) 常習的(な)
hack *n* (*poor writer*) sanmon-bunshi 三文文士
hacker COMPUT hakkā ハッカー
hackneyed arifureta ありふれた
haddock tara たら
haggard yatsureta やつれた
haggle (*bargain*) negiru 値切る; (*argue*) yariau やり合う
haiku haiku 俳句
hail *n* (*big stones*) hyō ひょう; (*small stones*) arare あられ
hailstorm hyō / arare no arashi ひょう/あられの嵐
hair kami no ke 髪の毛; (*single*) ke 毛
hairbrush heaburashi ヘアブラシ; **haircut** heakatto ヘアカット; **hairdo** kamigata 髪型, heasutairu ヘアスタイル; **hairdresser** biyōshi 美容師; ***at the ~*** biyōin de 美容院で; **hairdrier, hairdryer** headoraiyā ヘアドライヤー; **hairless** ke no nai 毛のない; **hairpin** heapin ヘアピン; **hairpin curve** heapin-kābu ヘアピンカーブ; **hair-raising** mi no ke no yodatsu yō (na) 身の毛のよだつよう(な); **hair remover** datsumōzai 脱毛剤; **hair-splitting** *n* shōji ni kodawaru koto 詳事にこだわること; **hairstyle** heasutairu ヘアスタイル
hairy *arm*, *animal* kebukai 毛深い; F (*frightening*) mi no ke no yodatsu 身の毛のよだつ
half 1 *n* hanbun 半分; ***~ past ten*** jūji han 十時半; ***~ after ten*** jūji han 十時半; ***~ an hour*** sanjuppun 三十分; ***~ a pound*** hanpondo 半ポンド; ***~ the ...*** hanbun no ... 半分の... **2** *adj size* hanbun (no) 半分(の); *price* hangaku (no) 半額(の) **3** *adv eaten* hanbun dake 半分だけ; *asleep*, *hope* nakaba 半ば
half-hearted kinori no shinai 気乗りのしない; **half time** *n* SP hāfu-taimu ハーフタイム; **halfway 1** *adj stage*, *point* chūkan (no) 中間(の) **2** *adv*: ***~ between the two cities*** futatsu no toshi no chūkan de 二つの都市の中間で; ***it's ~ finished*** hanbun owatta 半分終わった
hall (*large room*) ōhiroma 大広間, hōru ホール; (*hallway*) genkan 玄関
halo gokō 後光
halt 1 *v/i* tomaru 止まる **2** *v/t* tomeru 止める **3** *n* teishi 停止; ***come to a ~*** teishi suru 停止する
halve *v/t* hanbun ni suru 半分にする
ham hamu ハム
hamburger hanbāgā ハンバーガー
hammer 1 *n* kanazuchi 金づち **2** *v/i* tataku たたく; (*with hammer*) tonkachi de tataku とんかちでたたく; ***~ at the door*** doa o gangan tataku ドアをがんがんたたく
hammock hanmokku ハンモック
hamper[1] *n* (*picnic ~*) pikunikku-yō basuketto ピクニック用バスケット
hamper[2] *v/t* (*obstruct*) samatageru 妨げる
hamster hamusutā ハムスター
hand 1 *n* te 手; (*of clock*) hari 針; (*worker*) hitode 人手; ***at ~, to ~*** sugu chikaku ni すぐ近くに; ***at first ~*** chokusetsu ni 直接に; ***by ~*** *write* te de 手で; *deliver* tewatashi de 手渡しで; ***on the one ~ ..., on the other ~...*** ippō dewa ... de, mō ippō dewa ... da 一方では...で、もう一方では...だ; ***be in ~*** (*being done*) ima yatte iru tokoro de 今

やっているところで; ***the job in ~*** tōmen no shigoto 当面の仕事; ***on your right ~*** migigawa ni 右側に; ***~s off!*** (*do not touch*) sawaranaide 触らないで; ***~s up!*** te o agero 手をあげろ; ***change ~s*** mochinushi ga kawaru 持ち主が変わる; (*of company*) keiei-sha ga kawaru 経営者が変わる

♦**hand down** *fig* tsutaeru 伝える

♦**hand in** teishutsu suru 提出する

♦**hand on** tewatasu 手渡す; *fig* … o tsutaeru …を伝える

♦**hand out** … o watasu …を渡す

♦**hand over** *knife, baton* … o tewatasu …を手渡す; *hostage etc* … o hikiwatasu …を引き渡す

handbag *Br* handobaggu ハンドバッグ; **handbook** handobukku ハンドブック; **handbrake** *Br* saidoburēki サイドブレーキ; **handcuffs** tejō 手錠

handicap *n* (*disability*) shintai-shōgai 身体障害; *fig* furi na jōken 不利な条件, handi ハンディ

handicapped (*physically*) shōgai no aru 障害のある; *fig* furi de aru 不利である

handicraft shugei 手芸

handiwork teshigoto 手仕事

handkerchief hankachi ハンカチ

handle 1 *n* totte 取っ手; (*of brush, umbrella*) e 柄; (*on door*) nobu ノブ **2** *v/t goods* atsukau 扱う; *case, deal* shori suru 処理する; *difficult person* atsukau 扱う; ***let me ~ this*** watashi ni makasete kudasai 私に任せてください

handlebars handoru ハンドル

hand luggage tenimotsu 手荷物; **handmade** tesei (no) 手製(の); **handrail** tesuri 手すり; **handshake** akushu 握手

hands-off kanshō shinai 干渉しない

handsome hansamu (na) ハンサム(な)

hands-on jissenteki (na) 実践的(な)

handwriting hisseki 筆跡

handwritten tegaki (no) 手書き(の)

handy *tool, device* benri (na) 便利(な); ***it might come in ~*** sore wa yaku ni tatsu kamo shirenai それは役に立つかもしれない

hang 1 *v/t picture* kakeru 掛ける; *person* kōshukei ni suru 絞首刑にする **2** *v/i* (*of dress, hair*) kakaru 掛かる **3** *n*: ***get the ~ of*** … no kotsu o nomikomu …のこつをのみ込む

♦**hang around** … o urotsuku …をうろつく

♦**hang on** *v/i* (*wait*) chotto matsu ちょっと待つ

♦**hang on to** (*keep*) … o motte iru …を持っている

♦**hang up** *v/i* TELEC kiru 切る

hangar kakunōko 格納庫

hanger (*for clothes*) hangā ハンガー, yōfuku-kake 洋服掛け

hang glider (*device*) hanguraidā ハングライダー

hang gliding hanguraidingu ハングライディング

hangover futsukayoi 二日酔い

♦**hanker after** … ni akogareru …にあこがれる

hankie, hanky F hankachi ハンカチ

haphazard detarame (na) でたらめ(な)

happen okoru 起こる; ***if you ~ to see him*** moshi kare ni tamatama attara もし彼にたまたま会ったら; ***what has ~ed to you?*** nani ga atta no 何があったの

♦**happen across** … o gūzen mitsukeru …を偶然見つける

happening dekigoto 出来事

happily tanoshisō ni 楽しそうに; (*willingly*) yorokonde 喜んで; (*luckily*) saiwai ni mo 幸いにも

happiness shiawase 幸せ

happy shiawase (na) 幸せ(な); *coincidence* kōun (na) 幸運(な)

happy-go-lucky nonki (na) のんき(な)

happy hour sābisutaimu サービスタイム

harass … ni iyagarase o suru …にいやがらせをする

harassed tsukareta つかれた

harassment iyagarase いやがらせ; ***sexual ~*** seiteki iyagarase 性的いやがらせ, sekuhara セクハラ

harbor 1 *n* minato 港 **2** *v/t criminal* kakumau かくまう; *grudge* kokoro ni idaku 心に抱く

hard *material* katai 硬い; *punch* hageshii 激しい; *training* kibishii 厳しい; (*difficult*) muzukashii 難しい; *facts*, *evidence* kakujitsu (na) 確実(な); **~ *of hearing*** mimi ga tōi 耳が遠い

hardback hādo kabā ハードカバー; **hard-boiled** *egg* katayude (no) 固ゆで(の); **hard copy** purinto プリント; **hard core** *n* chūshin-seiryoku 中心勢力; **hard currency** kōkankanō-tsūka 交換可能通貨; **hard disk** hādo disuku ハードディスク

harden 1 *v/t* kataku suru 固くする **2** *v/i* (*of glue*) katamaru 固まる; (*of attitude*) kataku naru 固くなる

hardheaded genjitsuteki (na) 現実的(な)

hardliner kyōkōha 強硬派

hardly hotondo … nai ほとんど…ない; ***I ~ know him*** watashi wa kare o hotondo shiranai 私は彼をほとんど知らない

hardness kata-sa 硬さ; (*difficulty*) kibishi-sa 厳しさ

hardsell oshiuri 押し売り

hardship konnan 困難

hard shoulder rokata 路肩

hard up ichimon-nashi 一文なし

hardware kanamonorui 金物類; COMPUT hādowea ハードウェア

hardware store kanamonoten 金物店

hard-working hatarakimono (no) 働き者(の); (*eager to learn*) benkyōka (no) 勉強家(の)

hardy jōbu (na) 丈夫(な)

hare nousagi 野うさぎ

harm 1 *n* gai 害; ***it wouldn't do any ~ to …*** … shite warui koto wa nai … して悪いことはない **2** *v/t* sokonau 損なう; *person* … ni kigai o kuwaeru …に危害を加える

harmful yūgai (na) 有害(な)

harmless mugai (na) 無害(な)

harmonious *sound* chōwa shita 調和した; *relationship* naka no yoi 仲のよい

harmonize MUS waon o tsukeru 和音をつける; *ideas* chōwa saseru 調和させる

harmony MUS hāmonī ハーモニー; (*in relationship etc*) chōwa 調和

harp hāpu ハープ

♦**harp on about** F … o kudokudo hanashitsuzukeru …をくどくど話し続ける

harpoon mori もり

harsh kibishii 厳しい

harvest *n* shūkaku 収穫

hash: ***make a ~ of*** F … o dainashi ni suru …を台なしにする

hash browns hasshu-buraun ハッシュブラウン

hashish hasshishi ハッシシ

haste: ***do … in ~*** … o awatete suru …をあわててする

hasty keisotsu (na) 軽率(な)

hat bōshi 帽子

hatch *n* (*for serving food*) haizenmado 配ぜん窓, hatchi ハッチ; (*on ship*) hatchi ハッチ

♦**hatch out** *v/i* (*of eggs*) kaeru かえる

hatchet teono 手おの

hate 1 *n* ken'o 嫌悪; (*deep*: *of the enemy*, *a country*) nikushimi 憎しみ **2** *v/t* hidoku kirau ひどく嫌う; (*deeply*) nikumu 憎む

hatred ken'o 嫌悪; (*deep*: *of enemy*, *a country*) nikushimi 憎しみ

haughty kōman (na) 高慢(な)

haul 1 *n* (*from robbery*) shūkaku 収穫; **~ *of fish*** gyokaku 漁獲 **2** *v/t* (*pull*) hipparu 引っ張る

haulage unsō 運送

haulage company unsō-gaisha 運送会社

haulier unsō-gaisha 運送会社

haunch shiri 尻

haunt 1 *v/t* (*of memory*) … no kokoro ni tsukimatou …の心につきまとう; ***this place is ~ed*** kono basho wa yūrei ga deru この場所は幽霊が出る **2** *n* yoku iku basho よく行く場所

have ◊ (*possess*) motte iru 持っている; *brother*, *sister etc* … ga iru …

がいる; *pet* katte iru 飼っている; ***do you ~ your passport with you?*** pasupōto motte iru パスポート持っている; ***I ~ two brothers*** watashi ni wa ani ga futari imasu 私には兄が二人います; ***he has red hair*** kare wa akai kami o shite imasu 彼は赤い髪をしています; ***I ~ small hands*** watashi no te wa chīsai 私の手は小さい ◊ *breakfast, lunch* toru とる; ***we had steak / fish*** watashitachi wa sutēki / sakana o tabeta 私達はステーキ/さかなを食べた; ***I'll ~ the apple pie*** watashi wa appuru pai ni shimasu 私はアップルパイにします ◊ (*requests*): ***can I ~ a cup of coffee?*** kōhī o itadakemasu ka コーヒーをいただけますか; ***can I ~ more time?*** mō sukoshi jikan ii desu ka もうすこし時間いいですか; ***do you ~ milk?*** (*to shopkeeper*) gyūnyū arimasu ka 牛乳ありますか; ***do you ~ a pen?*** pen mottemasu ka ペン持ってますか ◊: **~ (got) to** (*must*) ... shinakereba naranai ... しなければならない; ***you ~ to sign it first*** hajime ni shomei shinakereba naranai 初めに署名しなければならない; ***you don't ~ to leave*** ikanakute mo ii desu 行かなくてもいいです; ***if he doesn't want to stay with us, he doesn't ~ to*** moshi kare ga watashi-tachi to issho ni itaku nainara sōshinakute mo ii desu もし彼が私達と一緒にいたくないならそうしなくてもいいです ◊ (*causative*): **~ X done** X shite morau Xしてもらう; ***I'll ~ it repaired*** shūri shite morau yō ni suru 修理してもらうようにする; ***I had my hair cut*** kami o kitte moratta 髪を切ってもらった ◊ (*past tense*): ***I ~ come*** kita 来た; ***~ you seen her?*** kanojo o mikakemashita ka 彼女を見かけましたか ◊ (*tags*) ne ね、; ***you ~n't finished already, ~ you?*** mō owattanja nai yo ne もう終わったんじゃないよね

♦ **have back** ... o kaeshite morau ... を返してもらう; ***when can I have it back?*** itsu kaeshite moraemasu ka いつ返してもらえますか

♦ **have on** (*wear*) ... o mi ni tsukete iru ... を身につけている; (*have planned*) yotei ga aru 予定がある; ***do you have anything on for tonight?*** konban wa nani ka yotei ga arimasu ka 今晩は何か予定がありますか

haven *fig* hinan-basho 避難場所

havoc daikonran 大混乱; ***play ~ with*** mechamecha ni midasu めちゃめちゃに乱す

hawk taka たか; *fig* takaha たか派

hay hoshikusa 干し草

hay fever kafunshō 花粉症

hazard *n* kiken 危険

hazard lights MOT kiken-keikoku-sōchi 危険警告装置

hazardous kiken (na) 危険(な)

haze *n* kasumi かすみ

hazel (*tree*) hashibami はしばみ

hazelnut hēzerunattsu ヘーゼルナッツ

hazy *view, image* bon'yari shita ぼんやりした; *memories* mōrō to shita もうろうとした; ***I'm a bit ~ about it*** hakkiri shinai はっきりしない

he kare 彼; ***~ is American*** kare wa Amerika-jin desu 彼はアメリカ人です ◊ (*omission of pronoun*): ***where is ~? – ~ has left*** kare wa doko desu ka - mō ikimashita 彼はどこですかーもう行きました

head 1 *n* (*of person, nail*) atama 頭; (*boss, leader*) chō 長; (*of department*) buchō 部長; (*of company*) shachō 社長; (*of delegation*) daihyō-danchō 代表団長; (*on beer*) awa 泡; (*of line*) sentō 先頭; ***$15 a ~*** hitoribun jūgo doru 一人分十五ドル; ***~s or tails?*** ura ka omote ka 裏か表か; ***at the ~ of the list*** risuto no saisho ni リストの最初に; ***~ over heels*** *fall* massakasama ni 真っ逆さまに; *fall in love* sukkari すっかり; ***lose one's ~*** (*go crazy*) ki ga kurutta yō ni naru 気が狂ったようになる

2 *v/t* (*lead*) hikiiru 率いる; *ball* hedingu suru ヘディングする
headache zutsū 頭痛
headband hachimaki はちまき
header (*in soccer*) hedingu ヘディング; (*in document*) midashi 見出し
headhunter COM jinzai-sukauto-gakari 人材スカウト係, heddohantā ヘッドハンター
heading (*in list*) hyōdai 表題
headlamp heddoraito ヘッドライト; **headlight** heddoraito ヘッドライト; **headline** (*in newspaper*) midashi 見出し; ***make the ~s*** ōkiku midashi ni toriagerareru 大きく見出しに取り上げられる; **headlong** *adv fall* massakasama ni 真っ逆さまに; **headmaster** kōchō 校長; **headmistress** kōchō 校長; **head office** honsha 本社; **head-on 1** *adv crash* shōmen kara 正面から **2** *adj crash* shōmen (no) 正面(の); **headphones** heddohon ヘッドホン; **headquarters** honbu 本部; **headrest** heddoresuto ヘッドレスト; **headroom** (*under bridge*) akidaka 空き高; (*in car*) tenjō made no yutori 天井までのゆとり; **headscarf** sukāfu スカーフ; **headstrong** ganko (na) 頑固(な); **head teacher** kōchō 校長; **head waiter** bōi-chō ボーイ長; **headwind** mukaikaze 向かい風
heady me ga mawaru 目が回る; *drink, wine etc* yoi ga sugu mawaru 酔いがすぐ回る
heal 1 *v/t* naosu 治す **2** *v/i* naoru 治る
health kenkō 健康; (*condition*) karada no guai 体の具合; ***your ~!*** kanpai 乾杯
health club supōtsu-kurabu スポーツクラブ; **health food** kenkō-shokuhin 健康食品; **health food store** kenkō-shokuhinten 健康食品店; **health insurance** kenkō-hoken 健康保険; **health resort** kenkō-rizōto 健康リゾート
healthy kenkō (na) 健康(な); *food, lifestyle* kenkōteki (na) 健康的(な); *economy* kenzen (na) 健全(な)
heap *n* tsumikasane 積み重ね
♦**heap up** *v/t* … o tsumiageru …を積み上げる
hear kikoeru 聞こえる
♦**hear about** … ni tsuite kiku …について聞く
♦**hear from** (*have news from*) … kara renraku ga aru …から連絡がある
hearing chōkaku 聴覚; LAW chōmonkai 聴聞会; ***within ~*** kikoeru tokoro de 聞こえるところで; ***out of ~*** kikoenai tokoro de 聞こえないところで
hearing aid hochōki 補聴器
hearsay: ***by ~*** uwasa de うわさで
hearse reikyūsha 霊きゅう車
heart shinzō 心臓; (*of problem*) kakushin 核心; (*of city, organization*) chūshin 中心; ***know … by ~*** … o anki shite iru …を暗記している
heart attack shinzō-hossa 心臓発作; **heartbeat** kodō 鼓動; **heartbreaking** hitsū (na) 悲痛(な); **heartburn** muneyake 胸やけ; **heart failure** shinfuzen 心不全; **heartfelt** *sympathy* kokoro kara (no) 心から(の)
hearth roshō 炉床
heartless hijō (na) 非情(な)
heartrending hitsū (na) 悲痛(な)
hearts (*in cards*) hāto ハート
heart throb F akogare no mato あこがれの的
heart transplant shinzo-ishoku 心臓移植
hearty *appetite* ōsei (na) おう盛(な); *meal* tappuri (no) たっぷり(の); *person* meirō (na) 明朗(な)
heat *n* netsu 熱
♦**heat up** *food* … o atatameru …を温める; *room* … o atatameru …を暖める
heated *pool* onsui (no) 温水(の); *discussion* kōfun shita 興奮した
heater hītā ヒーター
heathen *n* ikyōto 異教徒
heating danbō 暖房
heatstroke nesshabyō 熱射病
heatwave neppa 熱波

heave *v/t* (*lift*) mochiageru 持ち上げる
heaven tengoku 天国; ***good ~s!*** oya, mā おや、まあ
heavy omoi 重い; *overcoat* atsui 厚い; *cold* hidoi ひどい; *rain* hageshii 激しい; *traffic* noroi のろい; *accent* tsuyoi 強い; *food* shitsukoi しつこい; *financial loss* tagaku (no) 多額(の); *loss of life* tasū (no) 多数(の); *bleeding* taryō (no) 多量(の); ***~ smoker*** hebī-sumōkā ヘビースモーカー; ***~ drinker*** nonbē 飲んべえ
heavy-duty ganjō (na) 頑丈(な)
heavyweight SP hebī-kyū (no) ヘビー級(の)
heckle *v/t* yajiru やじる
hectic yatara isogashii やたら忙しい
hedge *n* ikegaki 生け垣
hedgehog harinezumi はりねずみ
heed chūi 注意; ***pay ~ to …*** … ni chūi o harau …に注意を払う
heel (*of foot*) kakato かかと; (*of shoe*) hīru ヒール
heel bar kutsunaoshi 靴直し
hefty *person* gasshiri shita がっしりした; *suitcase* omokute ōkii 重くて大きい; *fine, cut* kōgaku (no) 高額(の)
height takasa 高さ; (*of person*) shinchō 身長; (*of plane*) kōdo 高度; (*of season*) massakari 真っ盛り
heighten *effect, tension* tsuyomeru 強める
heir sōzoku-nin 相続人
heiress sōzoku-nin 相続人
helicopter herikoputā ヘリコプター
hell jigoku 地獄; ***what the ~ are you doing?*** F ittai nani shitenda いったい何してんだ; ***what the ~ do you want?*** F ittai nani ga hoshittenda いったい何が欲しいってんだ; ***go to ~!*** F kutabatchimae くたばっちまえ; ***a ~ of a lot*** F sugoku すごく; ***one ~ of a nice guy*** F sugoi ii yatsu すごいいいやつ
hello konnichiwa こんにちは; TELEC moshimoshi もしもし
helm NAUT darin だ輪
helmet herumetto ヘルメット
help 1 *n* tasuke 助け; ***thanks for your ~*** tasukete kurete arigatō 助けてくれてありがとう **2** *v/t* tasukeru 助ける; ***~ oneself*** (*to food*) jiyū ni toru 自由に取る; ***I can't ~ it*** shō ga nai しょうがない; ***I couldn't ~ laughing*** omowazu waratte shimau 思わず笑ってしまう
helper tetsudai 手伝い, herupā ヘルパー
helpful yaku ni tatsu 役に立つ
helping (*of food*) hitomori ひと盛り
helpless (*unable to cope*) muryoku (na) 無力(な); (*powerless*) mubōbi (na) 無防備(な)
help screen COMPUT herupu-gamen ヘルプ画面
hem *n* (*of dress etc*) heri へり
hemisphere hankyū 半球
hemorrhage 1 *n* shukketsu 出血 **2** *v/i* taryō ni shukketsu suru 多量に出血する
hemp asa 麻
hen mendori めんどり
henchman *pej* kobun 子分
henpecked shiri ni shikareta 尻に敷かれた; ***~ husband*** kyōsai-ka 恐妻家
hepatitis kan'en 肝炎
her 1 *adj* ◊ kanojo no 彼女の; ***~ ticket*** kanojo no kippu 彼女の切符 ◊ (*omission of possessive*): ***she broke ~ arm*** kanojo wa ude no hone o otta 彼女は腕の骨を折った; ***she forgot ~ key*** kanojo wa kagi o wasureta 彼女はかぎを忘れた **2** *pron* kanojo 彼女; ***who? – ~*** dare – kanojo desu 誰ー彼女です; ***this is for ~*** kore wa kanojo ni desu これは彼女にです ◊ (*direct object*) kanojo o 彼女を; ***I know ~*** kanojo o shitte iru 彼女を知っている ◊ (*indirect object*) kanojo ni 彼女に; ***can you mail it to ~?*** kanojo ni okutte kureru 彼女に送ってくれる
herb kōsō 香草, hābu ハーブ
herb(al) tea hābutī ハーブティー
herd *n* mure 群れ
here *live, stay, sit down* koko ni ここに; *sleep, eat* koko de ここで; *come*

koko e ここへ; ***~'s to you!*** kimi ni kanpai 君に乾杯; ***~ you are*** (*giving sth*) hai, dōzo はい、どうぞ; ***~ we are!*** (*finding sth*) hora, koko ni atta ほらここにあった

hereditary *disease* idensei (no) 遺伝性(の)
heritage isan 遺産
hermit yosutebito 世捨て人
hernia MED herunia ヘルニア
hero eiyū 英雄, hīrō ヒーロー
heroic eiyūteki (na) 英雄的(な)
heroin heroin ヘロイン
heroine hiroin ヒロイン
heron aosagi アオサギ
herpes MED herupesu ヘルペス
herring nishin にしん
hers kanojo no mono 彼女のもの; ***it's ~*** kanojo no mono desu 彼女のものです
herself: ***she hurt ~*** kanojo wa kega o shita 彼女はけがをした; ***she saw ~ in the mirror*** kanojo wa kagami de jibun o mita 彼女は鏡で自分を見た; ***what does she think ~?*** kanojo wa dō kangaete iru no 彼女はどう考えているの; ***by ~*** (*without help*) jibun de 自分で; (*alone*) hitori de ひとりで
hesitate tamerau ためらう
hesitation tamerai ためらい
heterosexual *adj* isei-aisha 異性愛者
heyday massakari 真っ盛り
hi konnichiwa こんにちは
hibernate tōmin suru 冬眠する
hiccup *n* shakkuri しゃっくり; (*minor problem*) chotto shita mondai ちょっとした問題; ***have the ~s*** shakkuri suru しゃっくりする
hick *pej* F inakamono いなか者
hick town *pej* F inakamachi いなか町
hidden *meaning* kakusareta 隠された; *treasure* himitsu (no) 秘密(の)
hide[1] **1** *v/t* kakusu 隠す **2** *v/i* kakureru 隠れる
hide[2] *n* (*of animal*) kawa 皮
hide-and-seek kakurenbo かくれんぼ
hideaway kakurebasho 隠れ場所
hideous iya (na) いや(な); *crime* osoroshii 恐ろしい; *face* minikui 醜い
hiding[1] (*beating*) muchiuchi むち打ち
hiding[2]: ***be in ~*** kakurete iru 隠れている; ***go into ~*** kakureru 隠れる
hiding place kakurebasho 隠れ場所
hierarchy kaikyū-soshiki 階級組織
hi-fi haifai-sutereo ハイファイステレオ
high 1 *adj building, temperature, price, note, salary, speed* takai 高い; *wind* tsuyoi 強い; *quality* kōkyū (na) 高級(な); (*on drugs*) hai (na) ハイ(な); ***have a ~ opinion of*** … o takaku hyōka suru …を高く評価する; ***it is ~ time …*** mō … suru koro da もう…する頃だ **2** *n* MOT kōsoku-giya 高速ギヤ; (*in statistics*) saikō-kiroku 最高記録; EDU kōkō 高校 **3** *adv* takaku 高く; ***~ in the sky*** soratakaku 空高く; ***that's as ~ as we can go*** sore ga seiippai da それが精一杯だ
highbrow *adj* interimuke (no) インテリ向け(の); **highchair** bebī-isu ベビーいす; **highclass** kōkyū (na) 高級(な); **high diving** taka-tobikomi 高飛び込み; **high-frequency** tanpa 短波; **high-grade** yūryō (na) 優良(な); **high-handed** ōbō (na) 横暴(な); **high-heeled** haihīru o haita ハイヒールをはいた; **high jump** haijanpu ハイジャンプ; **high-level** toppureberu (no) トップレベル(の); **high life** zeitaku na seikatsu ぜいたくな生活; **highlight 1** *n* hairaito ハイライト **2** *v/t* (*with pen*, COMPUT) keikō-pen de kyōchō suru 蛍光ペンで強調する; **highlighter** (*pen*) keikō-pen 蛍光ペン
highly *desirable, likely* hijō ni 非常に; ***be ~ paid*** kōkyū o moratte iru 高給をもらっている; ***think ~ of*** … o takaku hyōka shite iru …を高く評価している
high-performance *drill* kōseinō (no) 高性能(の); *battery* jizoku-jikan no nagai 持続時間の長い;
high-pitched kandakai かん高い;

high point (*of life, career*) chōten 頂点, pīku ピーク; (*of program*) kuraimakkusu クライマックス; **high-powered** *engine* kōseinō (no) 高性能(の); *intellectual* senren sareta 洗練された; *salesman* yūnō (na) 有能(な);**high pressure 1** *n* (*weather*) kōkiatsu 高気圧 **2** *adj* TECH atsuryoku (no) 圧力(の); *salesman* oshiuri (no) 押し売り(の); *job, lifestyle* jūatsu no ōkii 重圧の大きい;**high priest** kōsō 高僧; **high school** kōkō 高校; **high society** jōryū-shakai 上流社会; **high-speed train** kōsoku-ressha 高速列車;**high-strung** shinkeishitsu (na) 神経質(な);**high tech 1** *n* haiteku ハイテク **2** *adj* haiteku (no) ハイテク(の); **high technology** haiteku ハイテク; **high-tension** *cable* kōden'atsu (no) 高電圧(の); **high tide** manchō 満潮;**high water** manchō 満潮; **highway** kansen-dōro 幹線道路; **high wire** tsunawatari no tsuna 綱渡りの綱

hijack 1 *v/t plane* haijakku suru ハイジャックする; *bus* nottoru 乗っ取る **2** *n* (*of plane*) haijakku ハイジャック; (*of bus*) nottori 乗っ取り

hijacker (*of plane, bus*) nottorihannin 乗っ取り犯人

hike[1] **1** *n* haikingu ハイキング; (*longer distance*) toho-ryokō 徒歩旅行 **2** *v/i* haikingu ni iku ハイキングに行く; (*longer distance*) toho-ryokō o suru 徒歩旅行をする

hike[2] *n* (*in prices*) hikiage 引き上げ

hiker haikā ハイカー

hilarious omoshiroi おもしろい

hill oka 丘; (*slope*) saka 坂

hillbilly *pej* F inaka-mono いなか者

hillside oka no chūfuku 丘の中腹

hilltop oka no ue 丘の上

hilly oka no ōi 丘の多い

hilt ken no tsuka 剣の柄

him kare 彼; ***who? – ~*** dare – kare desu 誰ー彼です; ***this is for ~*** kore wa kare ni desu これは彼にです ◊ (*direct object*) kare o 彼を; ***do you know ~?*** kare o shitte imasu ka 彼を知っていますか ◊ (*indirect object*) kare ni 彼に; ***can you mail it to ~?*** kare ni okutte kureru 彼に送ってくれる

himself: ***he hurt ~*** kare wa kega o shimashita 彼はけがをしました; ***he saw ~ in the mirror*** kare wa kagami de jibun o mita 彼は鏡で自分を見た ***what does he think ~?*** kare wa dō kangaete iru no 彼はどう考えているの; ***by ~*** (*without help*) jibun de 自分で; (*alone*) hitori de ひとりで

hinder samatageru 妨げる

hindrance (*bags, person*) jama 邪魔; (*lack of knowledge etc*) shōgai 障害

hindsight atojie あと知恵; ***with ~*** ato ni shite omoeba あとにして思えば

hinge *n* chōtsugai ちょうつがい

hint (*clue*) hinto ヒント; (*piece of advice*) jogen 助言; (*implied suggestion*) honomekashi ほのめかし; (*of red, sadness etc*) wazuka na ryō わずかな量; (*of spring, recovery*) kizashi 兆し

hip koshi 腰

hip pocket shiri-poketto 尻ポケット

hippopotamus kaba かば

hiragana hiragana ひらがな

hire *workers* yatou 雇う

his 1 *adj* ◊ kare no 彼の; ***~ ticket*** kare no kippu 彼の切符 ◊ (*omission of possessive*): ***he broke ~ arm*** kare wa ude no hone o otta 彼は腕の骨を折った; ***he forgot ~ key*** kare wa kagi o wasureta 彼はかぎを忘れた **2** *pron* kare no mono 彼のもの; ***it's ~*** kare no desu 彼のです

Hispanic 1 *adj* Raten-Amerika (no) ラテンアメリカ(の) **2** *n* Raten-Amerika-jin ラテンアメリカ人

hiss *v/i* (*of snake*) shūshū to iu oto o tateru しゅうしゅうという音を立てる; (*of audience*) shītto yajiru しーっとやじる

historian rekishi-ka 歴史家

historic rekishiteki ni yūmei (na) 歴史的に有名(な)

historical rekishijō (no) 歴史上(の)

history rekishi 歴史

hit 1 *v/t* tataku たたく; *ball* utsu 打つ; (*collide with*) … ni butsukaru …にぶつかる; ***he was ~ by a bullet*** kare wa dangan ni atatta 彼は弾丸に当たった; ***it suddenly ~ me*** (*I realized*) totsuzen sore o omoitsuita 突然それを思いついた; ***~ town*** (*arrive*) machi ni ikiataru 町に行き当たる **2** *n* (*blow*) dageki 打撃; MUS hitto ヒット; (*success*) daiseikō 大成功

♦**hit back** yarikaesu やり返す

♦**hit on** *idea* … o futo omoitsuku …をふと思いつく

♦**hit out at** (*criticize*) … o kokuhyō suru …を酷評する

hit-and-run *adj*: ***~ accident*** hikinige-jiko 引き逃げ事故; ***~ driver*** hikinige-untenshu 引き逃げ運転手

hitch 1 *n* (*problem*) mondai 問題; ***without a ~*** todokōrinaku 滞りなく **2** *v/t* hikkakeru 引っかける; ***~ X to Y*** X to Y o tsunagu XとYをつなぐ; ***~ a ride*** kuruma o hitchi-haiku suru 車をヒッチハイクする **3** *v/i* (*hitchhike*) hitchi-haiku suru ヒッチハイクする

♦**hitch up** *wagon*, *trailer* … o tsunagu …をつなぐ

hitchhike hitchi-haiku suru ヒッチハイクする; **hitchhiker** hitchi-haikā ヒッチハイカー; **hitchhiking** hitchi-haikingu ヒッチハイキング

hi-tech 1 *n* haiteku ハイテク **2** *adj* haiteku (no) ハイテク(の)

hitlist (*terrorist's*) satsugai-yoteisha-risuto 殺害予定者リスト; (*management's*) kubikiri-taishōsha-risuto 首切り対象者リスト; **hitman** koroshi-ya 殺し屋; **hit-or-miss** ikiataribattari 行き当たりばったり; **hit squad** sogekihan 狙撃班

HIV hito-men'eki-fuzen-uirusu ヒト免疫不全ウィルス

hive (*for bees*) subako 巣箱

hive off *v/t* COM bunri-dokuritsu saseru 分離独立させる

HIV-positive eichi-ai-bui-yōsei (no) ＨＩＶ陽性(の)

hoard 1 *n* takuwae 蓄え **2** *v/t* takuwaeru 蓄える

hoarse shagaregoe (no) しゃがれ声(の)

hoax *n* itazura いたずら

hobble *v/i* ashi o hikizutte aruku 足を引きずって歩く

hobby shumi 趣味

hobo furō-sha 浮浪者

hockey (*ice ~*) hokkē ホッケー

hog *n* (*pig*) buta 豚

hoist 1 *n* makiageki 巻き上げ機 **2** *v/t* (*lift*) mochiageru 持ち上げる; *flag* ageru 揚げる

Hokkaido Hokkaidō 北海道

hokum (*nonsense*) kodomodamashi 子供だまし; (*sentimental stuff*) tawagoto たわごと

hold 1 *v/t* (*in hands*) te ni motsu 手に持つ; (*in arms*) kakaeru 抱える; *s.o.'s hand* te o tsunagu 手をつなぐ; (*support, keep in place*) sasaeru 支える; *passport*, *license* motte iru 持っている; *prisoner*, *suspect* kōryū suru 拘留する; (*contain*) ireru koto ga dekiru 入れることができる; *job*, *post* … ni tsuite iru …についている; *course* iji suru 維持する; ***the crate ~s 6 bottles*** kono kēsu ni wa roppon ireru koto ga dekiru このケースには六本入れることができる; ***~ one's breath*** iki o korasu 息を凝らす; ***he can ~ his drink*** kare wa chotto ya sotto ja yowanai 彼はちょっとやそっとじゃ酔わない; ***~ … responsible*** … ni sekinin ga aru to omou …に責任があると思う; ***~ that …*** (*believe, maintain*) … da to shinjite iru …だと信じている; ***~ the line*** TELEC kirazu ni sono mama matsu 切らずにそのまま待つ **2** *n* (*in ship, plane*) kamotsu-shitsu 貨物室; ***catch ~ of*** … o tsukamu …をつかむ; ***lose one's ~ on*** (*on rope*) … no te o hanasu …の手を離す; ***lose one's ~ on reality*** genjitsu o miushinau 現実を見失う

♦**hold against**: ***hold X against Y*** X o ne ni motte Y o uramu Xを根に持ってYを恨む

♦**hold back 1** *v/t crowds* … o

oshitodomeru …を押しとどめる; *facts, information* … o kakusu …を隠す **2** *v/i* (*not tell all*) tamerau ためらう

♦**hold on** *v/i* (*wait*) matsu 待つ; TELEC kiranaide matsu 切らないで待つ; ***now ~ a minute!*** chotto matte ちょっと待って

♦**hold on to** (*keep*) … o motte iru …を持っている; *belief* … o mamoritsuzukeru …を守り続ける

♦**hold out 1** *v/t hand* … o sashidasu …を差し出す; *prospect* … o motaseru …を持たせる **2** *v/i* (*of supplies*) motsu もつ; (*of trapped miners etc*) mochikotaeru 持ちこたえる

♦**hold up** *v/t hand* … o ageru …をあげる; *bank etc* … o osotte kinpin o toru …を襲って金品を取る; (*make late*) … o okuraseru …を遅らせる; ***hold … up as an example*** … o rei to shite shimesu …を例として示す

♦**hold with** (*approve of*) … ni sansei suru …に賛成する

holder (*container*) iremono 入れ物, kēsu ケース; (*of passport, ticket etc*) shoyū-sha 所有者; (*of record*) hoji-sha 保持者

holding company oyagaisha 親会社

holdup (*robbery*) gōtō 強盗; (*delay*) okure 遅れ

hole ana 穴

holiday (*single day*) shukujitsu 祝日; (*period*) kyūka 休暇; ***take a ~*** yasumi o toru 休みを取る

holidaymaker kōrakukyaku 行楽客

Holland Oranda オランダ

hollow *object* karappo (no) 空っぽ(の); *cheeks* kubonda くぼんだ; *promise* uwabe dake (no) うわべだけ(の)

holly seiyō-hiiragi 西洋ひいらぎ

holocaust daigyakusatsu 大虐殺

hologram rittaieizō 立体影像, horoguramu ホログラム

holster horusutā ホルスター

holy shinsei (na) 神聖(な)

Holy Spirit Seirei 聖霊

Holy Week Seishūkan 聖週間

home 1 *n* katei 家庭; (*native country*) kokoku 故国; (*area, part of country*) kokyō 故郷; (*for animals*) seisokuchi 生息地; (*for old people*) rōjin-hōmu 老人ホーム; ***at ~*** (*in my house*) ie de 家で; (*in my country*) jibun no kuni de 自分の国で; SP honkyochi de 本拠地で; ***make oneself at ~*** kutsurogu くつろぐ; ***at ~ and abroad*** kuni no naigai de 国の内外で; ***work from ~*** zaitaku-kinmu suru 在宅勤務する **2** *adv* jitaku e 自宅へ; (*country*) kokoku e 故国へ; (*area, part of country*) kokyō e 故郷へ; ***go ~*** jitaku e kaeru 自宅へ帰る; (*to own country*) kokoku e kaeru 故国へ帰る; (*to area, part of country*) kokyō e kaeru 故郷へ帰る

home address jitaku no jūsho 自宅の住所; **homecoming** satogaeri 里帰り; **home computer** pasokon パソコン

homeless *adj* hōmuresu (no) ホームレス(の); (*temporarily*) ie no nai 家のない

homeloving kateiteki (na) 家庭的(な)

homely kateiteki (na) 家庭的(な); (*not good-looking*) kiryō no yoku nai 器量の良くない

homemade jikasei (no) 自家製(の); **home game** honkyochi de no shiai 本拠地での試合; **home movie** hōmu-mūbī ホームムービー

homeopathy homeopashī ホメオパシー, dōdoku-ryōhō 同毒療法

homesick: ***be ~*** homushikku ni naru ホームシックになる; **home town** kokyō 故郷; **homeward** *adv* ie ni mukatte 家に向かって; (*to one's country*) kokoku ni mukau 故国に向かう; **homework** EDU shukudai 宿題; **homeworking** COM zaitaku-kinmu (no) 在宅勤務(の)

homicide (*crime*) satsujin 殺人; (*police department*) satsujin-sōsa-ka 殺人捜査課

homograph dōkei-igigo 同形異義語

homophobia homo-girai ホモ嫌い

homosexual 1 *adj* dōseiai (no) 同性愛(の), homo (no) ホモ(の) **2** *n*

dōseiai-sha 同性愛者, homo ホモ
honest shōjiki (na) 正直(な)
honestly (*truthfully*) shōjiki ni 正直に; (*frankly*) sotchoku ni 率直に; **~!** mattaku まったく
honesty shōjiki 正直
honey hachimitsu はちみつ; F (*darling*) kawaii hito かわいい人; (*to husband*) anata あなた; (*to wife*) omae おまえ
honeycomb hachi no su はちの巣
honeymoon *n* hanemūn ハネムーン
Hong Kong Honkon 香港
honk *v/t horn* narasu 鳴らす
honor 1 *n* meiyo 名誉 **2** *v/t* uyamau 敬う
honorable rippa (na) 立派(な)
honorific language keigo 敬語
Honshu Honshū 本州
hood (*over head*) fūdo フード; (*over cooker*) ōi 覆い; MOT bonnetto ボンネット; F (*gangster*) chinpira チンピラ
hoodlum chinpira チンピラ
hoof hizume ひづめ
hook (*on wall, door*) yōfuku-kake 洋服掛け; (*on dress*) hokku ホック; (*for fishing*) tsuribari 釣り針; (*in golf, boxing*) fukku フック; ***off the ~*** TELEC juwaki o hazushite 受話器をはずして
hooked: ***be ~ on*** … ni muchū de … に夢中で; (*on drugs*) … chūdoku de … 中毒で
hooker F baishunfu 売春婦
hooky: ***play ~*** gakkō o saboru 学校をさぼる
hooligan fūrigan フーリガン
hooliganism ranbō 乱暴
hoop wa 輪
hoot 1 *v/t horn* būbū narasu ぶーぶー鳴らす **2** *v/i* (*of car*) kurakushon ga naru クラクションが鳴る; (*of owl*) hōhō to naku ほーほーと鳴く
hop[1] (*plant*) hoppu ホップ
hop[2] *v/i* (*of frog*) pyon to tobu ぴょんと飛ぶ; (*of person*) kataashi de tobu 片足で跳ぶ
hope 1 *n* nozomi 望み; ***there's no ~ of that*** sono mikomi wa amari nai その見込みはあまりない **2** *v/i* kibō o motsu 希望を持つ; ***~ for*** … o nozomu …を望む **3** *v/t*: ***I ~ you like it*** tsumaranai mono desu ga つまらないものですが; ***I ~ so*** sō da to yoi to omou そうだとよいと思う; ***I ~ not*** sō de nai to yoi to omou そうでないとよいと思う
hopeful kibō o motta 希望を持った; (*promising*) yūbō (na) 有望(な)
hopefully kitai shite 期待して; (*I / we hope*) dekireba できれば
hopeless *position, propect* zetsubōteki (na) 絶望的(な); (*useless: person*) dō shiyō mo nai どうしようもない
horizon chiheisen 地平線; (*at sea*) suiheisen 水平線
horizontal suihei (no) 水平(の)
hormone horumon ホルモン
horn (*of animal*) tsuno つの; MOT kurakushon クラクション
hornet suzumebachi すずめばち
horn-rimmed bekkōbuchi (no) べっ甲縁(の)
horny F (*sexually*) kōfun shita 興奮した
horoscope hoshiuranai 星占い
horrible osoroshii 恐ろしい
horrify: ***I was horrified*** zotto shimashita ぞっとしました
horrifying *experience* osoroshii 恐ろしい; *idea, prices* akireta あきれた
horror kyōfu 恐怖; ***the ~s of war*** sensō no sanka 戦争の惨禍
horror movie horā-eiga ホラー映画
hors d'oeuvre ōdoburu オードブル
horse uma 馬
horseback: ***on ~*** uma ni notte 馬に乗って; **horse chestnut** seiyō-tochinoki no mi 西洋とちのきの実; **horsepower** bariki 馬力; **horse race** keiba 競馬; **horse radish** seiyō-wasabi 西洋わさび; ***Japanese ~*** wasabi わさび; **horseshoe** teitetsu てい鉄
horticulture engei 園芸
hose *n* hōsu ホース
hospice hosupisu ホスピス
hospitable motenashi no yoi もてなしのよい

hospital byōin 病院; ***go into the ~*** nyūin suru 入院する
hospitality (o) motenashi (お)もてなし
host *n (at party, reception)* shujin'yaku 主人役; *(of TV program)* shikai-sha 司会者
hostage hitojichi 人質; ***be taken ~*** hitojichi ni torareru 人質にとられる
hostel *(for students)* gakuseiryō 学生寮; *(youth ~)* yūsu-hosuteru ユースホステル
hostess *(at party, reception)* shujin'yaku 主人役; *(on airplane)* suchuwādesu スチュワーデス; *(in bar)* hosutesu ホステス
hostile tekii no aru 敵意のある
hostility *(of attitude)* tekii 敵意; ***hostilities*** tekitai-kōi 敵対行為
hot *weather, day* atsui 暑い; *object, food, water* atsui 熱い; *(spicy)* karai 辛い; F *(good)* jōzu (na) 上手(な)
hot dog hottodoggu ホットドッグ
hotel *(Western-style)* hoteru ホテル; *(Japanese-style)* ryokan 旅館
hotplate dennetsuki 電熱器; **hot spot** *(military, political)* funsō-chitai 紛争地帯; **hot spring** onsen 温泉
hour jikan 時間
hourly *adj* ichijikan goto (no) 1時間ごと(の)
house *n* ie 家; ***at your ~*** anata no ie de あなたの家で
houseboat hausubōto ハウスボート; **housebreaking** oshikomi-gōtō 押し込み強盗; **household** kazoku 家族; **household name** dare demo shitte iru namae だれでも知っている名前; **house husband** shufu 主夫; **housekeeper** kaseifu 家政婦; **housekeeping** *(activity)* kaji 家事; *(money)* seikatsuhi 生活費; **House of Councilors** Sangiin 参議院; **House of Representatives** *(Japanese)* Shūgiin 衆議院; *(in USA)* Kain 下院; **housewarming (party)** hikkoshi-iwai no pātī 引越し祝いのパーティー; **housewife** shufu 主婦; **housework** kaji 家事
housing jūtaku 住宅; TECH kēsu ケース
housing conditions jūkankyō 住環境
hovel abaraya あばら屋
hover kūchū de teishi suru 空中で停止する
hovercraft hobākurafuto ホバークラフト
how dō yatte どうやって; ***~ do you open it?*** dō yatte akeru no どうやって開けるの; ***~ are you?*** konnichi wa こんにちは; *(long time since you met)* (o) genki desu ka (お)元気ですか; ***~ about ...?*** ... wa dō desu ka ...はどうですか; **~ much?** dono kurai どのくらい; **~ much is it?** *(cost)* sore wa ikura desu ka それはいくらですか; **~ many?** ikutsu いくつ; **~ funny/ sad!** nante okashiin darō / kanashiin darō なんておかしいんだろう/悲しいんだろう
however keredomo けれども; ***~ big / small they are*** dore hodo ōkikute mo / chiisakute mo どれほど大きくて/小さくても
howl *v/i (of dog)* tōboe suru 遠ぼえする; *(of person in pain)* wameku わめく; *(with laughter)* ōwarai suru 大笑いする
hub *(of wheel)* habu ハブ
hubcap hoīru-kyappu ホイールキャップ
♦**huddle together** mi o yoseau 身を寄せ合う
huff: ***be in a ~*** mutto shite iru むっとしている
hug *v/t* dakishimeru 抱き締める
huge *building, tree* kyodai (na) 巨大(な); *debt, difference* bakudai (na) ばく大(な)
hull *n* sentai 船体
hullabaloo sawagi 騒ぎ
hum 1 *v/t song, tune* hamingu suru ハミングする **2** *v/i (of person)* hanauta o utau 鼻歌を歌う; *(of machine)* būn to iu oto o tateru ぶーんという音を立てる
human 1 *n* ningen 人間 **2** *adj* ningen (no) 人間(の), hito (no) 人(の);

attitude, weakness ningen-rashii 人間らしい; *error* jin'iteki (na) 人為的(な)
human being ningen 人間
humane *society* ningenmi no aru 人間味のある; *treatment* ningenteki (na) 人間的(な)
humanitarian jindōteki (na) 人道的(な)
humanity (*human beings*) jinrui 人類; (*of attitude*) ningensei 人間性
human race jinrui 人類
human resources (*department*) jinjibu 人事部; (*personnel*) jinzai 人材
humble *person* tsutsumashii つつましい; *origins* iyashii 卑しい; *meal, house* shisso (na) 質素(な)
humdrum heibon (na) 平凡(な)
humid mushiatsui 蒸し暑い
humidifier kashitsuki 加湿器
humidity shikke 湿気; ***70% ~*** shitsudo nanajuppāsento 湿度70%
humiliate … ni haji o kakaseru …に恥をかかせる
humiliating kutsujokuteki (na) 屈辱的(な)
humiliation (*embarrassment*) haji 恥; (*indignity*) kutsujoku 屈辱; (*of enemy*) bujoku 侮辱
humility kenson 謙そん
humor (*comical*) yūmoa ユーモア; (*mood*) kigen 機嫌; ***sense of ~*** yūmoa no sensu ユーモアのセンス; ***he has a sense of ~*** kare wa yūmoa ga aru 彼はユーモアがある
humorous *movie, story* okashii おかしい; *person* yūmorasu (na) ユーモラス(な)
hump 1 *n* (*of camel, person*) kobu こぶ; (*on road*) moriagari 盛り上がり **2** *v/t* F (*carry*) katsuide hakobu 担いで運ぶ
hunch F (*idea*) yokan 予感
hundred hyaku 百
hundredth *adj* dai-hyaku (no) 第百(の)
hundredweight handoreddo-wēto ハンドレッドウェート
Hungarian 1 *adj* Hangarī (no) ハンガリー(の) **2** *n* (*person*) Hangarī-jin ハンガリー人; (*language*) Hangarī-go ハンガリー語
Hungary Hangarī ハンガリー
hunger kūfuku 空腹; (*starvation*) ue 飢え
hung-over futsukayoi (no) ふつか酔い(の)
hungry onaka o sukaseta お腹をすかせた; ***I'm ~*** onaka ga suita お腹がすいた
hunk: (***gorgeous***) ~ F takumashikute kakko ii otoko たくましくてかっこいい男
hunky-dory F daijōbu (na) 大丈夫(な)
hunt 1 *n* (*for animals*) kari 狩り; (*for criminal, missing child*) sōsaku 捜索; (*for new leader etc*) sukauto スカウト **2** *v/t animal* karu 狩る
♦ **hunt for** … o sagasu …を探す
hunter (*for sport*) kari o suru hito 狩をする人, hantā ハンター; (*for living*) ryōshi 猟師
hunting shuryō 狩猟
hurdle SP hādoru ハードル; *fig* (*obstacle*) shōgai 障害
hurdler SP hādoru-senshu ハードル選手
hurdles SP hādoru ハードル
hurl nagetsukeru 投げつける
hurray banzai 万歳
hurricane bōfūu 暴風雨; harikēn ハリケーン
hurried awatadashii あわただしい
hurry 1 *n* ōisogi 大急ぎ; ***be in a ~*** awatete iru あわてている **2** *v/i* isogu 急ぐ
♦ **hurry up 1** *v/i* isogu 急ぐ; ***~!*** isoide 急いで **2** *v/t* … o sekitateru …をせきたてる
hurt 1 *v/i* itamu 痛む; ***does it ~?*** itai desu ka 痛いですか **2** *v/t* itameru 痛める; (*emotionally*) kizutsukeru 傷つける; ***was anybody ~?*** keganin wa imashita ka 怪我人はいましたか
husband otto 夫
hush *n* chinmoku 沈黙; ***~!*** shizuka ni 静かに
♦ **hush up** *scandal etc* … o

momikesu …をもみ消す
husk (*of grain*) kara 殻
husky *adj* shagaregoe (no) しゃがれ声(の); *woman's voice* hasukī (na) ハスキー(な)
hustle 1 *n* hassuru ハッスル; ***~ and bustle*** zattō 雑踏 **2** *v/t person* isogasu 急がす; ***~ X into doing Y*** X ni muri ni Y saseru Xに無理にYさせる
hut koya 小屋
hyacinth hiyashinsu ヒヤシンス
hybrid *n* (*plant*, *animal*) zasshu 雑種, haiburiddo ハイブリッド
hydrangea ajisai あじさい
hydrant shōkasen 消火栓
hydraulic suiryoku (no) 水力(の); *brake* yuatsushiki (no) 油圧式(の)
hydroelectric suiryoku-hatsuden (no) 水力発電(の)
hydrofoil (*boat*) suichū-yokusen 水中翼船
hydrogen suiso 水素
hydrogen bomb suiso-bakudan 水素爆弾
hygiene eisei 衛生
hygienic eiseiteki (na) 衛生的(な)
hymn sanbika 賛美歌
hype *n* hade na puromōshon はでなプロモーション; *pej* kodai-senden 誇大宣伝
hyperactive hidoku ochitsuki no nai ひどく落ち着きのない; **hypermarket** ōgata-sūpāmāketto 大型スーパーマーケット; **hypersensitive** kabin (na) 過敏(な); **hypertension** kōketsuatsu 高血圧; **hypertext** COMPUT haipā tekisuto ハイパーテキスト
hyphen haifun ハイフン
hypnosis saimin-jōtai 催眠状態
hypnotherapy saimin-ryōhō 催眠療法
hypnotize (*by hypnotist*) … ni saiminjutsu o kakeru …に催眠術をかける; *fig* miwaku suru 魅惑する
hypochondriac *n* shinkishō-kanja 心気症患者
hypocrisy gizen 偽善
hypocrite gizen-sha 偽善者
hypocritical gizenteki (na) 偽善的(な)
hypothesis kasetsu 仮説
hypothermia teitaion-shō 低体温症
hypothetical kasetsujō (no) 仮説上(の)
hysterectomy shikyū-tekishutsu-shujutsu 子宮摘出手術
hysteria hisuterī ヒステリー
hysterical *person*, *laugh* hisuterikku (na) ヒステリック(な); (*very funny*) hidoku omoshiroi ひどくおもしろい; ***become ~*** hisuterī-jōtai ni naru ヒステリー状態になる
hysterics hisuterī no hossa ヒステリーの発作; (*laughter*) ōwarai 大笑い

I

I watashi 私; (*informal use by men*) boku ぼく; (*informal use by women*) atashi あたし; ***~ am American / a student*** watashi wa Amerika-jin / gakusei desu 私はアメリカ人/学生です ◊ (*omission of pronoun*): ***~ don't know*** shirimasen 知りません
ice kōri 氷; ***break the ~*** *fig* kinchō o hogusu 緊張をほぐす
♦**ice up** (*of engine*, *wings*) kōri ni ōwareru 氷に覆われる
iceberg hyōzan 氷山; **icebox** reitō shitsu 冷凍室; **icebreaker** (*ship*) saihyōsen 砕氷船; **ice cream** aisukurīmu アイスクリーム;

ice-cream parlor dezāto kafe デザートカフェ; **ice cube** kōri 氷
iced *drink* kōri-iri (no) 氷入り(の)
iced tea aisutī アイスティー; **iced coffee** aisukōhī アイスコーヒー; **iced water** ohiya お冷や
ice hockey aisuhokkē アイスホッケー
ice rink (aisu)sukēto-rinku (アイス)スケートリンク
icicle tsurara つらら
icon (*cultural*) gūzō 偶像; COMPUT aikon アイコン
icy *road*, *surface* kōri de ōwareta 氷で覆われた; *welcome* reitan (na) 冷淡(な)
idea kangae 考え; ***good ~!*** ii kangae da いい考えだ; ***I have no ~*** wakarimasen わかりません; ***it's not a good ~ to …*** … suru no wa ii kangae de wa nai …するのはいい考えではない
ideal (*perfect*) risōteki (na) 理想的(な)
idealistic risō no takai 理想の高い
identical mattaku onaji 全く同じ; ***~ twins*** ichiransei-sōseiji 一卵性双生児
identification mimoto-kakunin 身元確認; (*papers etc*) mibun-shōmei ni naru mono 身分証明になるもの
identify *person* miwakeru 見分ける; *cause*, *problem* akiraka ni suru 明らかにする; (*with a label*, *by analysis*) shikibetsu suru 識別する
identity mimoto 身元
identity card mibun-shōmeisho 身分証明書
ideology ideorogī イデオロギー
ideological ideorogī (no) イデオロギー(の)
idiom (*saying*) kan'yōku 慣用句
idiomatic kan'yōteki (na) 慣用的(な)
idiosyncrasy (*of style*) tokuisei 特異性; (*of person*, *behavior*) fūgawari na ten 風変わりな点
idiot baka ばか
idiotic baka (na) ばか(な)
idle 1 *adj* (*lazy*) namakemono (no) 怠け者(の); (*not busy*) hima (na) 暇(な); (*unemployed*) shitsugyōchū (no) 失業中(の); *threat* karui 軽い; *machinery* ugoite inai 動いていない; ***in an ~ moment*** hima na toki ni 暇なときに **2** *v/i* (*of engine*) aidoringu suru アイドリングする
♦ **idle away** *time etc* namakeru 怠ける
idol aidoru アイドル
idolize sūhai suru 崇拝する
idyllic bokkateki (na) 牧歌的(な)
if moshimo … naraba もしも…ならば; (*whether or not*) … kadōka …かどうか; ***~ you need any more information …*** moshimo hoka ni jōhō ga hitsuyō naraba もしも他に情報が必要ならば; ***I don't know ~ he will agree*** … kare ga sansei suru kadōka wakaranai 彼が賛成するかどうかわからない
igloo igurū イグルー
ignite *v/t* tenka suru 点火する
ignition (*in car*) tenka-sōchi 点火装置; ***~ key*** igunisshon-kī イグニッションキー
ignorance muchi 無知
ignorant muchi (na) 無知(な); (*rude*) reigishirazu (no) 礼儀知らず(の)
ignore mushi suru 無視する
ill guai no warui 具合の悪い; (*with specific illness*) byōki (no) 病気(の); ***fall ~***, ***be taken ~*** byōki ni naru 病気になる
illegal *strike*, *trade* higōhō (no) 非合法(の); *immigrant* fuhō (no) 不法(の); *parking* ihan (no) 違反(の); ***it's ~ to …*** … suru no wa hōritsu ihan da …するのは法律違反だ
illegible yomenai 読めない
illegitimate: ***be ~*** chakushutsu de nai 嫡出でない; ***~ child*** shiseiji 私生児
ill-fated fuun (na) 不運(な)
illicit fuhō (na) 不法(な)
illiterate monmō (no) 文盲(の)
ill-mannered busahō (na) 不作法(な)
ill-natured seikaku no warui 性格の悪い
illness byōki 病気

illogical fugōri (na) 不合理(な)
ill-tempered okorippoi 怒りっぽい
illtreat gyakutai suru 虐待する
illuminate *building etc* iruminēshon de kazaru イルミネーションで飾る
illuminating *remarks etc* wakariyasui わかりやすい
illusion gensō 幻想; (*false belief*) sakkaku 錯覚
illustrate *book* … ni sashie o ireru … に挿絵を入れる; (*with examples*) setsumei suru 説明する
illustration (*picture*) sashie 挿絵, irasuto イラスト; (*with examples*) setsumei 説明
illustrator irasutorētā イラストレーター
ill will tekii 敵意
image kōkei 光景; (*exact likeness*) ikiutsushi 生き写し; (*of politician, company*) imēji イメージ; (*of pop star etc*) sugata 姿
image-conscious imēji o ishiki shita イメージを意識した
imaginable sōzō dekiru 想像できる; ***the biggest / smallest size ~*** kangaerareru kagiri ichiban ōkii / chiisai saizu 考えられる限り一番大きい/小さいサイズ
imaginary sōzōjō (no) 想像上(の)
imagination (*ability to imagine*) sōzōryoku 想像力; ***it's all in your ~*** omoisugoshi desu 思い過ごしです
imaginative *child* sōzōryoku no yutaka (na) 想像力の豊か(な); *piece of work* sōzōsei ni tomu 想像性に富む
imagine sōzō suru 想像する; ***I can just ~ it*** sōzō ga tsuku 想像がつく; ***you're imagining things*** kangaesugi desu 考えすぎです
imbecile baka ばか
IMF (= ***International Monetary Fund***) Kokusai-tsūka-kikin 国際通貨基金
imitate maneru まねる
imitation (*copying*) mane まね; (*sth copied*) mozōhin 模造品; (*jewelry*) imitēshon イミテーション
immaculate yogore no nai 汚れのない; (*flawless*) ketten no nai 欠点のない
immaterial toru ni taranai 取るに足らない
immature mijuku (na) 未熟(な)
immediate (*in time*) sugu (no) すぐ(の); ***the ~ family*** kinshin-sha 近親者; ***in the ~ neighborhood*** sugu kinjo ni すぐ近所に
immediately sugusama すぐさま; ***~ after the bank / church*** ginkō / kyōkai no sugu saki 銀行/教会のすぐ先
immense kyodai (na) 巨大(な); *relief, longing* taihen (na) 大変(な)
immerse tsukeru つける; ***~ oneself in*** … ni fukeru …にふける
immersion heater yuwakashiki 湯沸かし器
immigrant *n* imin 移民
immigrate ijū suru 移住する
immigration (*act*) ijū 移住; ***Immigration*** (*government office*) nyūkoku-kanrikyoku 入国管理局
imminent sashisematta 差し迫った
immobilize *person* ugokenaku suru 動けなくする; *factory* sutoppu saseru ストップさせる; *car* sadō shinai yō ni suru 作動しないようにする
immoderate sessei no nai 節制のない
immoral fudōtoku (na) 不道徳(な)
immorality fudōtoku 不道徳
immortal fushi (no) 不死(の)
immortality fushi 不死
immune (*to illness, infection*) men'eki no aru 免疫のある; (*from ruling, requirement*) menjo sareta 免除された
immune system MED men'eki-shisutemu 免疫システム
immunity (*to infection*) men'eki 免疫; (*from ruling*) menjo 免除; ***diplomatic ~*** gaikōkan-tokken 外交官特権
impact *n* (*of meteorite, vehicle*) shōtotsu 衝突; (*effect*) eikyō 影響; (*of new manager etc*) shōgeki 衝撃
impair sokonau 損なう
impaired *hearing, sight* yowatta

弱った
impartial kōhei (na) 公平(な)
impassable *road* tōrenai 通れない
impasse (*in negotiations etc*) fukurokōji 袋小路
impassioned netsuretsu (na) 熱烈(な)
impassive *face* muhyōjō (na) 無表情(な)
impatience tanki 短気
impatient ki no mijikai 気の短い
impatiently iraira shite いらいらして
impeccable *turnout* mōshibun no nai 申し分のない; *English, Japanese* kanpeki (na) 完ぺき(な)
impeccably *dressed* mōshibun nai hodo 申し分ないほど; *pronounce, speak* kanpeki ni 完ぺきに
impede samatageru 妨げる
impediment ***speech ~*** gengo-shōgai 言語障害
impending sashisematta 差し迫った
impenetrable *mind* fukakai (na) 不可解(な)
imperative 1 *adj* dō shite mo hitsuyō (na) どうしても必要(な) **2** *n* GRAM meireikei 命令形
imperceptible chikakufunō (na) 知覚不能(な)
imperfect 1 *adj* fukanzen (na) 不完全(な) **2** *n* GRAM mikanryō-kei 未完了形
imperial teikoku (no) 帝国(の); *palaces* kōtei (no) 皇帝(の); ***Imperial Palace*** Kōkyo 皇居
impersonal ningenmi no nai 人間味のない
impersonate (*as a joke*) … no monomane o suru …の物まねをする; (*illegally*) … ni narisumasu …になりすます
impertinence namaiki 生意気
impertinent namaiki (na) 生意気(な)
imperturbable ochitsuita 落ち着いた
impervious: ***~ to*** … ni eikyō sarenai …に影響されない
impetuous mōretsu (na) 猛烈(な)
impetus (*of campaign etc*) hazumi はずみ
implement 1 *n* dōgu 道具 **2** *v/t measures etc* jikkō suru 実行する
implicate: ***~ X in Y*** X o Y ni kanrenzukeru XをYに関連付ける
implication (*inference*) imi 意味
implicit anmoku (no) 暗黙(の); *trust* zettaiteki (na) 絶対的(な)
implore … ni tangan suru …に嘆願する
imply (*mean*) imi suru 意味する; (*hint*) honomekasu ほのめかす
impolite reigishirazu (no) 礼儀知らず(の)
import 1 *n* yunyū 輸入 **2** *v/t* yunyū suru 輸入する
importance jūyōsei 重要性
important jūyō (na) 重要(な); *person* yūryoku (na) 有力(な)
importer yunyū-gyōsha 輸入業者
impose *tax* kasu 課す; ***~ oneself on*** … ni meiwaku o kakeru …に迷惑をかける
imposing medatsu 目立つ
impossibility fukanō 不可能
impossible fukanō (na) 不可能(な)
impostor peten-shi ぺてん師
impotence inpo インポ
impotent inpo (no) インポ(の)
impoverished mazushiku natta 貧しくなった
impractical *person* jōshiki ni kakete iru 常識に欠けている; *suggestion* higenjitsuteki (na) 非現実的(な)
impress (*give an impression to*) … ni yoi inshō o ataeru …によい印象を与える; (*of scenery*) … ni kandō o ataeru …に感動を与える; ***be ~ed by*** (*by s.o.*) … ni yoi inshō o ukeru …によい印象を受ける; (*by sth*) … ni kandō suru …に感動する; ***I'm not ~ed*** sore wa kanshin dekimasen ne それは感心できませんね
impression inshō 印象; (*impersonation*) monomane 物まね; ***make a good/bad ~ on*** … ni yoi/warui inshō o ataeru …によい/悪い印象を与える; ***I get the ~ that*** … to iu kanji ga suru …という感じがする

impressionable kanjiyasui 感じやすい
impressive inshōteki (na) 印象的(な)
imprint *n* (*of credit card*) kokuin 刻印
imprison keimusho ni ireru 刑務所に入れる
imprisonment (*act*) tōgoku 投獄; ***10 years'~*** jūnen no kinkokei 十年の禁固刑
improbable mikomi no nai 見込みのない
improper *behavior* futekisetsu (na) 不適切(な)
improve 1 *v/t* kaizen suru 改善する; *skills* jōtatsu saseru 上達させる **2** *v/i* yoku naru よくなる; (*of skills*) jōtatsu suru 上達する
improvement kaizen 改善; (*in skills*) jōtatsu 上達
improvise *v/i* THEA sokkyō de enjiru 即興で演じる; MUS sokkyō de ensō suru 即興で演奏する; ***we just had to ~*** sono ba o maniawasse de yarisugosu その場を間に合わせでやりすごす
impudent atsukamashii 厚かましい
impulse shōdō 衝動; ***do … on ~*** shōdōteki ni … o suru 衝動的に…をする; ***~ buy*** shōdōgai 衝動買い
impulsive shōdōteki (na) 衝動的(な)
impunity: ***with ~*** basserarezu ni 罰せられずに
impure fujun (na) 不純(な)
in 1 *prep* (*with verbs of being*) … ni …に; (*with verbs of activity*) … de …で; ***~ Washington / Japan*** (*live, stay*) Washinton / Nihon ni ワシントン/日本に; (*meet, work*) Washinton / Nihon de ワシントン/日本で; ***~ the box*** (*inside*) hako no naka ni 箱の中に; ***he put it ~ his pocket*** kare wa poketto no naka ni shimatta 彼はポケットの中にしまった; ***wounded ~ the leg / arm*** ashi / ude ni kega o shita 足/腕に怪我をした ◊ (*time*) … ni …に; ***~ 1999*** sen kyūhyaku kyūjū kyū nen ni 1999年に; ***~ two hours*** (*from now*) nijikan go ni 二時間後に; (*over period of*) nijikan de 二時間で; ***~ the morning*** asa ni 朝に; ***~ the summer*** natsu ni 夏に; ***~ August*** hachigatsu ni 八月に ◊ (*manner*) … de …で; ***~ English / Japanese*** Eigo / Nihongo de 英語/中国語で; ***~ a loud voice*** ōkina koe de 大きな声で; ***~ his style*** kare no yarikata de 彼のやり方で; ***dressed ~ yellow*** kiiroi fuku o kite iru 黄色い服を着ている ◊ (*while*): ***~ crossing the road*** michi o watatte iru toki ni 道をわたっているときに; ***~ agreeing to this*** (*by virtue of*) sansei shita tame ni 賛成したために ◊: ***the characters ~ his novel*** kare no shōsetsu no naka no tōjōjinbutsu 彼の小説の中の登場人物; ***~ Faulkner*** Fōkunā de wa フォークナーでは ◊: ***three ~ all*** zenbu de san 全部で三; ***one ~ ten*** (*of objects*) jū no uchi hitotsu 十のうち一つ; (*of people*) jūnin no uchi hitori 十人のうち一人 **2** *adv* (*at home*) ie ni 家に; (*in the building etc*) uchi ni 内に; (*arrived: train*) tōchaku shite 到着して; (*in its position*) naka ni 中に; ***~ here*** koko ni ここに **3** *adj* (*fashionable, popular*) hayari (no) はやり(の)
inability munō 無能
inaccessible ikizurai 行きづらい
inaccurate fuseikaku (na) 不正確(な)
inactive fukappatsu (na) 不活発(な)
inadequate *supply, space* fujūbun (na) 不十分(な); *person* muryoku (na) 無力(な)
inadvisable susumerarenai 勧められない
inanimate museibutsu (no) 無生物(の)
inapplicable tekiyō dekinai 適用できない
inappropriate futekitō (na) 不適当(な)
inarticulate *person* hakkiri shinai はっきりしない
inattentive fuchūi (na) 不注意(な)

inaudible kikoenai 聞こえない
inaugural *speech* shūninshiki (no) 就任式(の)
inaugurate *new building* rakusei suru 落成する; *service* kaigyō suru 開業する; *system* kaishi suru 開始する
inauguration (*of president*) shūninshiki 就任式
inborn umaretsuki (no) 生まれつき(の)
inbreeding kinshin-kōhai 近親交配
inc. (= ***incorporated***) kabushiki-gaisha 株式会社
incalculable *damage* hakari-shirenai はかりしれない
incapable muryoku (na) 無力(な); ***he's ~ of understanding*** kare wa rikai suru koto ga dekinai 彼は理解することができない
incendiary device shōidan 焼い弾
incense[1] *n* kō 香; REL senkō 線香
incense[2] *v/t* gekido saseru 激怒させる
incentive shigeki 刺激
incessant taema no nai 絶え間のない
incessantly taema naku 絶え間なく
incest kinshin-sōkan 近親相かん
inch *n* inchi インチ
incident dekigoto できごと; (*more serious*) jiken 事件
incidental fuzuiteki (na) 付随的(な); ***~ expenses*** zappi 雑費
incidentally tokoro de ところで
incinerator shōkyakuro 焼却炉
incision MED sekkai 切開
incisive *analysis* surudoi 鋭い
incite (*to riot*) sendō suru 扇動する; *violence* aoritateru あおりたてる; ***~ X to do Y*** X o sosonokashite Y saseru XをそそのかしてYさせる
inclement *weather* kibishii 厳しい
inclination (*tendency*) keikō 傾向; (*liking: for music*) konomi 好み; (*for travel*) ganbō 願望
incline : ***be ~d to do …*** (*tend to*) … suru keikō ni aru …する傾向にある; (*be willing to*) … shitai ki ga suru … したい気がする
inclose ,inclosure → ***enclose, enclosure***
include ireru 入れる; (*of price*) fukumu 含む
including *prep* … o fukumete …を含めて
inclusive **1** *adj price* issaikomi (no) 一切込み(の) **2** *prep* … o fukumete …を含めて; ***~ of*** … o fukumete … を含めて **3** *adv*: ***from Monday to Thursday ~*** getsuyōbi kara mokuyōbi made 月曜日から木曜日まで
incoherent tsujitsuma no awanai つじつまの合わない
income shūnyū 収入
income tax shotokuzei 所得税
incoming *flight* tōchaku suru 到着する; *phonecall* soto kara kakatte kuru 外からかかってくる; *mail* haitatsu sarete kuru 配達されてくる; *president* kōnin (no) 後任(の); ***~ tide*** ageshio 上げ潮
incomparable murui (no) 無類(の)
incompatibility (*of personalities*) seikaku no fuitchi 性格の不一致; (*of disk formats, systems*) gokansei no nasa 互換性のなさ
incompatible *personalities* aiirenai 相いれない; *formats, systems* gokansei no nai 互換性のない
incompetence munō 無能
incompetent *person, organization* munō (na) 無能(な); *piece of work* heta (na) 下手(な); ***be ~ to teach*** oshieru no ni muite inai 教えるのに向いていない
incomplete mikansei (no) 未完成(の); *account, statement* fukanzen (na) 不完全(な)
incomprehensible rikai dekinai 理解できない
inconceivable kangaerarenai 考えられない
inconclusive *argument* ketsuron ni tasshinai 結論に達しない; *evidence* fujūbun (na) 不十分(な)
incongruous chōwa shinai 調和しない
inconsiderate omoiyari no nai 思いやりのない
inconsistent *argument* mujun shita

矛盾した; *person* kimagure (na) 気まぐれ(な); *behavior*, *work* mura no aru むらのある

inconsolable nagusameyō no nai 慰めようのない

inconspicuous medatanai 目立たない

inconvenience *n* (*caused by s.o. / sth*) meiwaku 迷惑; (*of not having a car etc*) fuben-sa 不便さ

inconvenient *time*, *arrangement* tsugō no warui 都合の悪い; *place*, *not having a car etc* fuben (na) 不便(な)

incorporate (*include*) toriireru 取り入れる

incorporated COM kabushiki-gaisha 株式会社

incorrect fuseikaku (na) 不正確(な)

incorrectly fuseikaku ni 不正確に

incorrigible sukuigatai 救いがたい

increase 1 *v/t* ageru 上げる; *number*, *amount* fuyasu 増やす **2** *v/i* agaru 上がる; (*of number*, *amount*) fueru 増える; (*of confidence*) tsuku つく **3** *n* (*in number*) zōka 増加; (*in amount*) zōryō 増量; (*in value*) zōdai 増大

increasing zōka suru 増加する

increasingly masumasu ますます

incredible (*amazing*) shinjirarenai 信じられない; (*very good*) subarashii すばらしい

incriminate yūzai ni suru 有罪にする; **~ *oneself*** tsumi o mitomeru 罪を認める

incubator (*for chicks*) fukaki ふ化器; (*for babies*) jinkō-hoikuki 人工保育器

incur maneku 招く; *anger* kōmuru こうむる

incurable chiryō-fukanō (na) 治療不可能(な)

indebted *be ~ to* … ni taihen kansha shite iru …に大変感謝している

indecent waisetsu (na) わいせつ(な)

indecisive yūjū-fudan (no) 優柔不断(の)

indecisiveness yūjū-fudan 優柔不断

indeed (*in fact*) hontō ni 本当に, tashika ni 確かに; (*yes, agreeing*) sono tōri そのとおり; ***very much ~*** hontō ni 本当に

indefinable bakuzen to shita 漠然とした

indefinite *period*, *time* futei (no) 不定(の); **~ *article*** GRAM futei-kanshi 不定冠詞

indefinitely mukigen ni 無期限に

indelicate gehin (na) 下品(な)

indent 1 *n* (*in text*) atamasage 頭下げ **2** *v/t line* gyōtō o sageru 行頭を下げる

independence dokuritsu 独立

Independence Day Dokuritsu-kinenbi 独立記念日

independent *business*, *country* dokuritsu (no) 独立(の); (*financially*) jikatsu shite iru 自活している; *type of person* jiritsu shita 自立した; (*not state-owned*) minkan (no) 民間(の)

independently *treat* betsubetsu ni 別々に; **~ *of*** betsubetsu ni 別々に

indescribable ii yō no nai 言いようのない

indescribably *bad*, *beautiful* iiarawasenai hodo 言い表せないほど

indestructible hakai dekinai 破壊できない; *faith* kowarenai こわれない

indeterminate *length of time* bakuzen to shita ばく然とした

index (*for book*) sakuin 索引, indekkusu インデックス

index card sakuin-kādo 索引カード

index finger hitosashiyubi 人さし指

India Indo インド

Indian 1 *adj* Indo (no) インド(の) **2** *n* Indo-jin インド人; (*American*) Indian インディアン

Indian summer koharu-biyori 小春日和

indicate 1 *v/t* (*show*) shimesu 示す **2** *v/i* MOT winkā o dasu ウィンカーを出す

indication chōkō 徴候

indicator MOT winkā ウィンカー

indict kiso suru 起訴する
indifference mukanshin 無関心
indifferent mukanshin (na) 無関心(な); (*mediocre*) heibon (na) 平凡(な)
indigestible shōka dekinai 消化できない
indigestion shōka-furyō 消化不良
indignant fungaishita 憤慨した
indignation ikidōri 憤り
indirect *link* kansetsuteki (na) 間接的(な); *criticism* tōmawashi (na) 遠回し(な); ~ ***route*** mawarimichi 回り道
indirectly kansetsuteki ni 間接的に
indiscreet keisotsu (na) 軽率(な)
indiscretion (*act*) keisotsu (na) kōdō 軽率な行動
indiscriminate musabetsu (na) 無差別(な)
indispensable kakegae no nai 掛け替えのない
indisposed (*not well*) kibun ga warui 気分が悪い
indisputable meihaku (na) 明白(な)
indisputably meihaku ni 明白に
indistinct fumeiryō (na) 不明りょう(な)
indistinguishable miwake no tsukanai 見分けのつかない
individual **1** *n* kojin 個人 **2** *adj* (*separate*) koko (no) 個々(の); (*personal*) kojin (no) 個人(の)
individualist kojin-shugisha 個人主義者
individually koko ni 個々に
indivisible bunkatsu dekinai 分割できない
indoctrinate … ni fukikomu …に吹き込む
indolence taida 怠惰
indolent taida (na) 怠惰(な)
Indochina Indoshina インドシナ
Indochinese *adj* Indoshina-jin インドシナ人
Indonesia Indoneshia インドネシア
Indonesian **1** *adj* Indoneshia (no) インドネシア(の) **2** *n* (*person*) Indoneshia-jin インドネシア人
indoor okunai (no) 屋内(の), indoa (no) インドア(の)
indoors *go* okunai e 屋内へ; *stay* okunai ni 屋内に; *play* okunai de 屋内で
indulge **1** *v/t oneself* manzoku saseru 満足させる **2** *v/i*: ~ ***in*** … ni fukeru …にふける
indulgence (*of tastes, appetite etc*) tanoshimi 楽しみ; (*laxity*) amayakashi 甘やかし
indulgent (*not strict enough*) amai 甘い
industrial kōgyō (no) 工業(の)
industrial action sutoraiki ストライキ
industrial dispute rōdō-sōgi 労働争議
industrialist jitsugyōka 実業家
industrialize *v/t & v/i* kōgyōka suru 工業化する
industrial waste sangyō-haikibutsu 産業廃棄物
industrious kinben (na) 勤勉(な)
industry sangyō 産業, kōgyō 工業
ineffective kōka no nai 効果のない
ineffectual *person* munō (na) 無能(な)
inefficient *system* hinōritsuteki (na) 非能率的(な); *person* munō (na) 無能(な)
ineligible shikaku no nai 資格のない
inept *person* munō (na) 無能(な)
inequality fubyōdō 不平等
inescapable sakerarenai 避けられない
inestimable hakari-shirenai はかりしれない
inevitable sakerarenai 避けられない
inevitably hitsuzenteki ni 必然的に
inexcusable yurusarenai 許されない
inexhaustible *person* tsukare o shiranai 疲れを知らない; *supply* mujinzō (no) 無尽蔵(の)
inexpensive yasui 安い
inexperienced keiken no nai 経験のない
inexplicable setsumei no tsukanai 説明のつかない
inexpressible *joy* iiarawasenai 言い表せない

infallible zettai ni machigai no nai 絶対に間違いのない
infamous akumei no takai 悪名の高い
infancy (*of person*) yōnen-jidai 幼年時代; (*of state, institution*) shoki 初期
infant yōji 幼児
infantile *pej* kodomoppoi 子供っぽい
infantry hoheitai 歩兵隊
infantry soldier hohei 歩兵
infatuated: ***be ~ with*** … ni muchū ni naru …に夢中になる
infect … ni kansen suru …に感染する; (*of person*) byōki o utsusu 病気を移す; *food, water* osen suru 汚染する; ***become ~ed*** (*of person*) kansen suru 感染する; (*of wound*) baikin ga hairu ばい菌が入る
infection kansen 感染
infectious *disease* kansen suru 感染する; *laughter* hito ni utsuru 人に移る
infer: ***~ X from Y*** Y kara X o suiron suru YからXを推論する
inferior *quality, workmanship* ototta 劣った; ***be ~ to*** MIL … yori kai de aru …より下位である
inferiority (*in quality*) soaku-sa 粗悪さ
inferiority complex rettōkan 劣等感
infertile *soil* fumō (no) 不毛(の); *woman* funin (no) 不妊(の)
infertility (*of soil*) fumō 不毛; (*of woman*) funin 不妊
infidelity futei 不貞
infiltrate *v/t* shinnyū saseru 侵入させる
infinite mugen (no) 無限(の); *fig* bakudai (na) 莫大(な)
infinitive futeishi 不定詞
infinity mugen 無限
infirm yowatta 弱った
infirmary byōin 病院
infirmity byōki 病気
inflame *passions* aoritateru あおりたてる
inflammable kanensei (no) 可燃性(の)
inflammation MED enshō 炎症
inflatable *dinghy* fukuramasu koto ga dekiru ふくらますことができる
inflate *v/t tire, dinghy* fukuramasu ふくらます; *economy* infure ni suru インフレにする
inflation infure インフレ
inflationary (*of inflation*) infure (no) インフレ(の); (*causing inflation*) infure o hikiokosu インフレを引き起こす
inflection (*of voice*) yokuyō 抑揚
inflexible *attitude, person* yūzū no kikanai 融通のきかない
inflict: ***~ X on Y*** Y ni X o ataeru YにXを与える
in-flight kinai (no) 機内(の); ***~ entertainment*** kinai-entā teinmento 機内エンターテインメント
influence 1 *n* eikyō 影響; (*power to ~*) eikyōryoku 影響力; ***be a good / bad ~ on*** yoi / warui eikyō o … ni ataeru よい/悪い影響を…に与える **2** *v/t s.o.'s thinking* … ni eikyō o oyobosu …に影響を及ぼす; *decision* sayū suru 左右する
influential eikyōryoku no aru 影響力のある
influenza infuruenza インフルエンザ
inform tsūchi suru 通知する; ***~ X of Y*** X ni Y no koto o tsūchi suru XにYのことを通知する; ***keep me ~ed*** shirasenasai 知らせなさい
♦**inform on** … o mikkoku suru …を密告する
informal *conversation* kudaketa くだけた; *dress* fudan (no) 普段(の); *meeting* hikōshiki (no) 非公式(の)
informality kudaketa fun'iki くだけた雰囲気; ***the ~ of their dress*** karera no fudangi 彼らの普段着; ***given the ~ of the agreement …*** gōi ga hikōshiki nano de … 合意が非公式なので…
informant jōhō-teikyō-sha 情報提供者
information jōhō 情報, infomēshon インフォメーション
information science jōhō-kagaku 情報科学; **information scientist** jōhō-kagaku-sha 情報科学者;

information technology jōhō-kōgaku 情報工学
informative yūeki (na) 有益(な)
informer mikkoku-sha 密告者
infra-red *adj* sekigaisen (no) 赤外線(の)
infrastructure (*of economy, society, industry*) kiban 基盤; (*of organization*) kabu-soshiki 下部組織
infrequent tama (no) たま(の)
infuriate gekido saseru 激怒させる
infuriating hidoku haradatashii ひどく腹立たしい
infuse *v/i* (*of tea*) deru 出る
infusion (*of herb tea*) hābutī ハーブティー
ingenious kōmyō (na) 巧妙(な); *person* kiyō (na) 器用(な)
ingenuity kōmyō-sa 巧妙さ; (*of person*) kiyō-sa 器用さ
ingot jigane 地金
ingratiate: **~ *oneself with*** … ni toriiru …に取り入る
ingratitude onshirazu 恩知らず
ingredient (*in cooking*) zairyō 材料; *fig* (*for success*) yōso 要素
inhabit … ni sumu …に住む
inhabitable kyojū-kanō (na) 居住可能(な)
inhabitant jūmin 住民
inhale *v/t & v/i* suikomu 吸い込む
inhaler kyūnyūki 吸入器
inherit sōzoku suru 相続する
inheritance isan 遺産; (*characteristics*) iden 遺伝
inhibit *growth, conversation etc* yokusei suru 抑制する
inhibited yokusei sarete iru 抑制されている
inhibition yokusei 抑制
inhospitable *person* buaisō (na) 無愛想(な); *city* suminikui 住みにくい; *climate* kibishii 厳しい
in-house 1 *adj* shanai (no) 社内(の) **2** *adv work* shukkin shite 出勤して
inhuman zankoku (na) 残酷(な)
initial 1 *adj* hajime (no) 始め(の); *stage* shoki (no) 初期(の) **2** *n* kashira-moji 頭文字, inisharu イニシャル **3** *v/t document* … ni kashira-moji de shomei suru …に頭文字で署名する
initially hajime wa 始めは
initiate *v/t* (*start*) kaishi suru 開始する
initiation (*of new project*) kaishi 開始
initiative shudōken 主導権, inishiachibu イニシアチブ; ***do … on one's own ~*** mizukara susunde … suru 自ら進んで…する
inject *medicine, drug* chūsha suru 注射する; *fuel* chūnyū suru 注入する; *capital* tōnyū suru 投入する
injection MED chūsha 注射; (*of fuel*) chūnyū 注入; (*of cash*) tōnyū 投入
injure *person* kega o saseru 怪我をさせる; *oneself* kega suru 怪我する; *arm, leg* itameru 傷める
injured 1 *adj* kega o shita 怪我をした; *feelings* kizutsuita 傷ついた **2** *n*: ***the ~*** fushō-sha 負傷者
injury kega 怪我
injustice fukōsei 不公正
ink inku インク; (*Chinese ~*) sumi 墨; ***~ painting*** sumie 墨絵
inkjet (printer) inkujetto purintā インクジェットプリンター
inland nairiku (no) 内陸(の)
in-laws inseki 姻せき
inlay *n* zōgan-zaiku 象眼細工
inlet (*of sea*) irie 入り江; (*in machine*) chūnyūkō 注入口
inmate (*in prison*) jukei-sha 受刑者; (*in mental hospital*) nyūin-kanja 入院患者
inn ryokan 旅館
innate seirai (no) 生来(の)
inner *courtyard* uchigawa (no) 内側(の); *thoughts* naimen (no) 内面(の); ***~ ear*** naiji 内耳
inner city toshinbu 都心部
innermost mottomo oku (no) 最も奥(の); *feelings* kokoro no oku (no) 心の奥(の)
inner tube chūbu チューブ
innocence mujaki 無邪気; LAW muzai 無罪
innocent mujaki (na) 無邪気(な); LAW muzai (no) 無罪(の)
innovation kakushin 革新
innovative kakushinteki (na) 革新的

(な)
innovator kakushin-sha 革新者
innumerable kazoekirenai 数え切れない
inoculate yobō-sesshu suru 予防接種する
inoculation yobō-sesshu 予防接種
inoffensive gai ni naranai 害にならない
inorganic muki (no) 無機(の)
in-patient nyūin-kanja 入院患者
input 1 *n* (*into project etc*) enjo 援助; COMPUT nyūryoku 入力, inputto インプット **2** *v/t* (*into project*) enjo suru 援助する; COMPUT nyūryoku suru 入力する
input port COMPUT inputto-pōto インプットポート
inquest chōsa 調査
inquire toiawaseru 問い合わせる; **~ *into*** ... o chōsa suru ...を調査する
inquiry toiawase 問い合わせ
inquisitive shiritagari (no) 知りたがり(の)
insane kichigaijimita 気違いじみた; MED kyōki (no) 狂気(の)
insanitary hieiseiteki (na) 非衛生的(な)
insanity kyōki 狂気
insatiable aku koto no nai 飽くことのない
inscription mei 銘
inscrutable fukakai (na) 不可解(な)
insect konchū 昆虫
insecticide satchūzai 殺虫剤
insect repellent mushiyoke 虫よけ
insecure (*anxious*) fuan ni omotte iru 不安に思っている; (*not confident*) jishin ga nai 自信がない
insecurity (*anxiety*) fuan 不安 (*lack of confidence*) jishin no nasa 自信のなさ
insensitive *person* donkan (na) 鈍感(な); *remark* mushinkei (na) 無神経(な)
insensitivity donkan 鈍感; (*of remark*) mushinkei-sa 無神経さ
inseparable *issues* bunri dekinai 分離できない; *people* hanarerarenai 離れられない
insert 1 *n* (*in magazine etc*) orikomi kōkoku 折り込み広告 **2** *v/t* sashikomu 差し込む, ireru 入れる; **~ *X into Y*** X o Y ni sashikomu XをYに差し込む
insertion (*act*) sōnyū 挿入
inside 1 *n* (*of house, box*) naka 中, naibu 内部, uchigawa 内側; (*of road*) uchigawa-shasen 内側車線; ***somebody on the ~*** dare ka naijō ni tsūjite iru hito だれか内情に通じている人; **~ *out*** uragaeshi ni 裏返しに; ***turn X ~ out*** X o uragaeshi ni suru Xを裏返しにする; ***know X ~ out*** X o yoku shitte iru Xをよく知っている **2** *prep* ... no naka ni / e ...の中に/へ; **~ *the house*** ie no naka ni 家の中に; **~ *of 2 hours*** nijikan miman de 二時間未満で **3** *adv stay* naka ni 中に; *go, carry* naka e 中へ; *play, eat* naka de 中で; ***we looked ~*** watashitachi wa naka o mita 私達は中を見た **4** *adj* naka (no) 中(の), uchigawa (no) 内側(の); **~ *information*** naibu-jōhō 内部情報; **~ *lane*** SP inkōsu インコース; (*on road*) uchigawa-shasen 内側車線; **~ *pocket*** uchi-poketto 内ポケット
insider shōsokutsū 消息通
insider trading FIN insaidā-torihiki インサイダー取り引き
insides onaka おなか, hara 腹
insidious *disease* shiranai aida ni shinkō suru 知らない間に進行する; *means, trick* inken (na) 陰険(な); *effect* senzaiteki (na) 潜在的(な)
insight (*understanding*) dōsatsu 洞察; (*perception*) dōsatsuryoku 洞察力
insignificant toru ni taranai 取るに足らない; *person* jūyō de nai 重要でない
insincere seii no nai 誠意のない
insincerity fuseijitsu 不誠実
insinuate (*imply*) honomekasu ほのめかす
insist iiharu 言い張る; ***please keep it, I ~*** dōka, totte oite kudasai どうか、取っておいてください
♦**insist on** ... o yōkyū suru ...を要求する

insistent shitsukoi しつこい
insolent ōhei (na) 横柄(な)
insoluble *problem* kaiketsu dekinai 解決できない; *substance* tokenai 溶けない
insolvent hasan shita 破産した
insomnia fumin 不眠
inspect *work, tickets, baggage* kensa suru 検査する; *factory, school* shisatsu suru 視察する
inspection (*of work, tickets, baggage*) kensa 検査; (*of factory, school*) shisatsu 視察
inspector (*in factory*) kensa-gakari 検査係; (*on buses*) kensatsu-gakari 検札係
inspiration reikan 霊感, insupirēshon インスピレーション; (*very good idea*) myōan 妙案
inspire *respect etc* yobiokosu 呼び起こす; ***be ~d by*** … kara reikan o eru …から霊感を得る; (*be encouraged by*) … ni shokuhatsu sareru …に触発される
instability fuantei 不安定
instal(l) *computer, phone* toritsukeru 取り付ける; *software* insutōru suru インストールする
installation (*of new equipment*) toritsuke 取り付け; (*of software*) insutōru インストール; ***military ~*** gunji-shisetsu 軍事施設
installment (*of story, TV drama etc*) ichiwa 一話; (*payment*) ikkaibun no shiharai 一回分の支払い
installment plan bunkatsubarai 分割払い
instance (*example*) rei 例; ***for ~*** tatoeba 例えば
instant 1 *adj* sokuji (no) 即時(の) **2** *n* shunkan 瞬間; ***in an ~*** sugu ni すぐに
instantaneous sokuji (no) 即時(の)
instant coffee insutanto-kōhī インスタントコーヒー
instantly sokuza ni 即座に
instead sono kawari ni その代わりに; ***~ of*** … no kawari ni …の代わりに
instep ashi no kō 足の甲
instinct honnō 本能
instinctive honnōteki (na) 本能的(な)
institute 1 *n* (*association*) kyōkai 協会; (*academic*) gakkai 学会; (*educational*) kyōiku kikan 教育機関; (*research*) kenkyū-kikan 研究機関; (*special home*) shisetsu 施設 **2** *v/t new law, inquiry* mōkeru 設ける
institution (*governmental*) kikan 機関; (*something traditional*) kanrei 慣例; (*setting up*) setsuritsu 設立
instruct (*teach*) oshieru 教える; ***~ X to do Y*** X ni Y suru yō ni shiji suru XにYするように指示する
instruction shiyō-setsumei 使用説明; ***~s for use*** toriatsukai-setsumei 取扱説明
instruction manual toriatsukai-setsumeisho 取扱説明書
instructive yūeki (na) 有益(な)
instructor insutorakutā インストラクター
instrument MUS gakki 楽器; (*gadget, tool*) kigu 器具
insubordinate hankōteki (na) 反抗的(な)
insufficient fujūbun (na) 不十分(な)
insulate ELEC zetsuen suru 絶縁する; (*against cold*) dannetsu suru 断熱する
insulation ELEC zetsuen 絶縁; (*material*) zetsuentai 絶縁体; (*against cold*) dannetsu 断熱; (*material*) dannetsuzai 断熱材
insulin inshurin インシュリン
insult 1 *n* bujoku 侮辱 **2** *v/t* bujoku suru 侮辱する
insurance hoken 保険
insurance company hoken-gaisha 保険会社
insurance policy hoken-shōsho 保険証書
insure … ni hoken o kakeru …に保険をかける; ***be ~d*** hoken ni haitte iru 保険に入っている
insurmountable kokufuku dekinai 克服できない
intact (*not damaged*) mukizu (no) 無傷(の)
intake (*of college etc*) boshū-jin'in 募集人員

integrate *v/t* tokekomaseru 溶け込ませる
integrated circuit shūseki-kairo 集積回路
integrity (*honesty*) kōketsu 高潔
intellect chisei 知性
intellectual **1** *adj* chiteki (na) 知的(な) **2** *n* chishikijin 知識人, interi インテリ
intelligence chinō 知能; MIL jōhō 情報
intelligence service jōhōbu 情報部
intelligent rikō (na) 利口(な)
intelligible rikai dekiru 理解できる
intend : **~ *to …*** … tsumori de aru … するつもりである; ***that's not what I ~ed*** sō iu tsumori wa nakatta そういうつもりはなかった
intense mōretsu (na) 猛烈(な); *personality* jōnetsuteki (na) 情熱的(な)
intensify **1** *v/t effect, pressure* tsuyomeru 強める **2** *v/i* (*of pain*) tsuyoku naru 強くなる; (*of battle*) hageshiku naru 激しくなる
intensity hageshi-sa 激しさ
intensive *study, treatment* shūchūteki (na) 集中的(な)
intensive care (unit) shūchū-chiryōshitsu 集中治療室, ai-shī-yū ＩＣＵ
intensive course (*of language study*) shūchū-kōza 集中講座
intent : ***be ~ on doing …*** (*determined to do*) … shiyō to yonen ga nai … しようと余念がない; (*concentrating on*) … suru no ni muchū ni natte iru … するのに夢中になっている
intention ito 意図; ***I have no ~ of …*** (*refuse*) … no tsumori wa mattaku nai … のつもりはまったくない
intentional itoteki (na) 意図的(な); (*referring to negative things*) koi (no) 故意(の)
intentionally waza to わざと
interaction (*between departments etc*) kyōryoku 協力; (*between people*) fureai ふれあい; (*between chemicals*) sōgo-sayō 相互作用
interactive *software* taiwashiki (no) 対話式(の); *teaching* fureai no aru ふれあいのある
intercede chūsai suru 仲裁する
intercept *ball* intāseputo suru インターセプトする; *message* bōju suru 傍受する; *missile* tochū de geigeki suru 途中で迎撃する
interchange *n* MOT intāchenji インターチェンジ, rittai-kōsa 立体交差
interchangeable kōkan dekiru 交換できる
intercom intāhon インターホン
intercourse (*sexual*) seikō 性交
interdependent sōgo-izon shita 相互依存した
interest **1** *n* kyōmi 興味; (*financial*) rishi 利子; ***take an ~ in*** … ni kyōmi ga aru … に興味がある **2** *v/t* kyōmi o motaseru 興味を持たせる; ***does that offer ~ you?*** sono teian ni wa kyōmi ga arimasu ka その提案には興味がありますか
interested kyōmi o motta 興味を持った; ***be ~ in*** … ni kyōmi ga aru … に興味がある; ***thanks but I'm not ~*** sumimasen ga, kyōmi ga arimasen すみませんが、興味がありません
interesting omoshiroi おもしろい
interest rate riritsu 利率
interface **1** *n* intāfeisu インターフェイス **2** *v/i* intāfeisu de rendō suru インターフェイスで連動する
interfere kanshō suru 干渉する
♦**interfere with** *controls* … o ijiru … をいじる; *plans* … o jama suru … を邪魔する
interference kanshō 干渉; (*on radio*) jushin-shōgai 受信障害
interior **1** *adj* naibu (no) 内部(の) **2** *n* (*of house*) interia インテリア; (*of country*) nairiku 内陸
interior decorator interia-dezainā インテリアデザイナー; **interior design** shitsunai-sōshoku 室内装飾, interia-dezain インテリアデザイン; **interior designer** interia-dezainā インテリアデザイナー
interlude (*at theater, concert*) makuai 幕あい; (*period*) aima 合間

intermediary *n* chūkai-sha 仲介者
intermediate *adj* chūkyū (no) 中級(の)
intermission THEA kyūkei-jikan 休憩時間
intern *v/t* kōkin suru 拘禁する
internal naibu (no) 内部(の); *trade* kokunai (no) 国内(の)
internal combustion engine nainen-kikan 内燃機関
internally (*in body*) tainai ni 体内に; (*in organizaton*) naibu ni 内部に
Internal Revenue (Service) Kokuzeichō 国税庁
international *adj* kokusaiteki (na) 国際的(な)
international call kokusai-denwa 国際電話
International Court of Justice Kokusai-shihō-saibansho 国際司法裁判所
internationally kokusaiteki ni 国際的に
International Monetary Fund Kokusai-tsūka-kikin 国際通貨基金
Internet intānetto インターネット; ***on the ~*** intānetto ni インターネットに
internist naikai 内科医
interpret 1 *v/t* (*linguistically*) tsūyaku suru 通訳する; *comment* kaishaku suru 解釈する; *piece of music* ensō suru 演奏する; *role of Hamlet* enjiru 演じる **2** *v/i* tsūyaku suru 通訳する
interpretation (*linguistic*) tsūyaku 通訳; (*of piece of music, meaning*) kaishaku 解釈
interpreter tsūyaku 通訳
interrelated *facts* sōgo ni kankei shita 相互に関係した
interrogate jinmon suru 尋問する
interrogation jinmon 尋問
interrogative *n* GRAM gimonshi 疑問詞
interrogator jinmon-sha 尋問者
interrupt 1 *v/t speaker* … no hanashi ni warikomu …の話に割り込む **2** *v/i* jama o suru 邪魔をする
interruption jama 邪魔
intersect 1 *v/t* … to kōsa suru …と交差する **2** *v/i* kōsa suru 交差する
intersection MOT kōsaten 交差点
interstate *adj* kakushūkan (no) 各州間(の)
interval kankaku 間隔; (*at theater, concert*) kyūkei-jikan 休憩時間
intervene kanshō suru 干渉する; (*of police, military*) kainyū suru 介入する
intervention kanshō 干渉; (*of police, military*) kainyū 介入
interview 1 *n* (*on TV, in paper*) intabyū インタビュー; (*for job*) mensetsu 面接 **2** *v/t* (*on TV, for paper*) … ni intabyū suru …にインタビューする; (*for job*) mensetsu suru 面接する
interviewee (*on TV*) intabyū o ukeru hito インタビューを受ける人; (*for job*) mensetsu-juken-sha 面接受験者
interviewer (*on TV, for paper*) intabyūa インタビューア; (*for job*) mensetsu-sha 面接者
intestine chō 腸
intimacy (*of friendship*) shitashi-sa 親しさ; (*sexual*) nikutai-kankei 肉体関係
intimate *friend* shitashii 親しい; (*sexually*) fukai kankei no aru 深い関係のある; *thoughts* kojinteki (na) 個人的(な)
intimidate odosu 脅す
intimidation odoshi 脅し
into … no naka ni …の中に; ***he put it ~ his suitcase*** kare wa sūtsukēsu no naka ni shimatta 彼はスーツケースの中にしまった; ***translate ~ English*** Eigo ni hon'yaku suru 英語に翻訳する; ***be ~*** F (*like*) … ga suki de aru …が好きである; (*be involved with*) … ni nomerikomu …にのめり込む; ***when you're ~ the job*** shigoto ga wakatte kitara 仕事がわかってきたら
intolerable taerarenai 耐えられない
intolerant henkyō (na) 偏狭(な)
intoxicated yotta 酔った
intransitive verb jidōshi 自動詞

intravenous jōmyakunai (no) 静脈内(の)
intrepid yūkan (na) 勇敢(な)
intricate fukuzatsu (na) 複雑(な)
intrigue 1 *n* inbō 陰謀 **2** *v/t*: ***I would be ~d to know ...*** ... ga wakattara omoshiroi darō ...がわかったらおもしろいだろう
intriguing omoshiroi おもしろい
introduce *person* shōkai suru 紹介する; (*to chess etc*) oshieru 教える; *new technique etc* toriireru 取り入れる; ***~ X to Y*** X o Y ni shōkai suru XをYに紹介する; ***may I ~ ...?*** ... o goshōkai shimasu ...をご紹介します
introduction (*to person*) shōkai 紹介; (*to a new food, sport etc*) hajimete no keiken 初めての経験; (*in book*) jobun 序文; (*of new techniques etc*) dōnyū 導入
introvert *n* naikōteki na hito 内向的な人
intrude jama o suru 邪魔をする
intruder shinnyū-sha 侵入者
intrusion jama 邪魔
intuition chokkan 直感
invade shinryaku suru 侵略する
invalid[1] *adj argument* datō de nai 妥当でない; (*legally*) mukō (na) 無効(な)
invalid[2] *n* MED byōnin 病人
invalidate *claim, theory* mukō ni suru 無効にする
invaluable *help, contributor* kakegae no nai かけがえのない
invariably (*always*) itsumo いつも
invasion shinryaku 侵略
invent hatsumei suru 発明する
invention hatsumei 発明; (*product*) hatsumeihin 発明品
inventive hatsumei no sai no aru 発明の才のある
inventor hatsumei-sha 発明者
inventory mokuroku 目録
inverse *adj order* seihantai (no) 正反対(の)
invert gyaku ni suru 逆にする
inverted commas in'yōfu 引用符
invertebrate *n* musekitsui-dōbutsu 無せきつい動物
invest 1 *v/t* tōshi suru 投資する; *time, energy* tsugikomu つぎ込む **2** *v/i* tōshi suru 投資する
investigate chōsa suru 調査する; *crime* sōsa suru 捜査する
investigation chōsa 調査; (*of crime*) sōsa 捜査
investigative journalism chōsa-hōdō 調査報道
investment (*act*) tōshi 投資; (*amount*) tōshigaku 投資額
investor tōshi-sha 投資者
invigorating *climate* sawayaka (na) さわやか(な)
invincible *army, team* muteki (no) 無敵(の)
invisible me ni mienai 目に見えない
invitation shōtai 招待; (*card*) shōtaijō 招待状
invite shōtai suru 招待する; ***can I ~ you for a meal?*** issho ni shokuji shimasen ka 一緒に食事しませんか
invoice 1 *n* seikyūsho 請求書 **2** *v/t customer* ... no seikyūsho o okuru ...の請求書を送る
involuntary hanshateki (na) 反射的(な)
involve *hard work, expense* hitsuyō to suru 必要とする; (*concern*) ... ni kankei suru ...に関係する; ***what does it ~?*** sore ni wa nani ga hitsuyō desu ka それには何が必要ですか; ***get ~d with*** (*with sth*) ... ni kakawaru ...にかかわる; (*with s.o., emotionally*) ... to shitashiku naru ...と親しくなる
involved (*complex*) komiitta 込み入った
involvement (*in a project etc*) kakawariai かかわり合い; (*in crime, accident*) kankei 関係 (*as victim*) makizoe 巻き添え
invulnerable fujimi (no) 不死身(の)
inward 1 *adj thoughts* naishin (no) 内心(の); *direction* naka ni mukau 中に向かう **2** *adv* naka ni mukatte 中に向かって; (*into oneself*) naishin e 内心へ
inwardly (*in one's heart*) kokoro no naka de 心の中で
iodine yōso ヨウ素; (*as disinfectant*)

yōdochinki ヨードチンキ
IOU (= ***I owe you***) shakuyō-shōsho 借用証書
IQ (= ***intelligence quotient***) chinō-shisū 知能指数, ai-kyū ＩＱ
Iran Iran イラン
Iranian 1 *adj* Iran (no)イラン(の) **2** *n* (*person*) Iran-jin イラン人; (*language*) Iran-goha イラン語派
Iraq Iraku イラク
Iraqi 1 *adj* Iraku (no) イラク (の) **2** *n* (*person*) Iraku-jin イラク人
Ireland Airurando アイルランド
iris (*of eye*) kōsai こう彩; (*flower*) ayame あやめ
Irish 1 *adj* Airurando (no) アイルランド(の) **2** *n*: ***the ~*** Airurando-jin アイルランド人
Irishman Airurando-jin dansei アイルランド人男性
Irishwoman Airurando-jin josei アイルランド人女性
iron 1 *n* tetsu 鉄; (*for clothes*) airon アイロン **2** *v/t shirts etc* airon o kakeru アイロンをかける
ironic(al) hiniku (na) 皮肉(な)
ironing airon-gake アイロンがけ; ***do the ~*** airon-gake o suru アイロンがけをする
ironing board airon-dai アイロン台
ironworks seitetsujo 製鉄所
irony hiniku 皮肉
irrational fugōri (na) 不合理(な)
irreconcilable *positions* ryōritsu shinai 両立しない; *people* wakai dekinai 和解できない
irrecoverable torikaeshi no tsukanai 取り返しのつかない
irregular *intervals* fukisoku (na) 不規則(な); *sizes* fuzoroi (no) ふぞろい(の); *surface* dekoboko (no) 凸凹(の); (*against the rules*) kisoku ihan no 規則違反の
irrelevant mukankei (na) 無関係(な)
irreparable shūfuku dekinai 修復できない
irreplaceable *object*, *person* kakegae no nai かけがえのない
irrepressible *sense of humor* osaekirenai 抑えきれない; *person* kaikatsu (na) 快活(な)
irreproachable mōshibun no nai 申し分のない
irresistible *offer*, *smell* kotowarenai 断れない; *pleasures* osaekirenai 抑えきれない
irrespective: ***~ of*** … ni kakawarazu …にかかわらず
irresponsible musekinin (na) 無責任(な)
irretrievable torikaeshi no tsukanai 取り返しのつかない
irreverent fukei (na) 不敬(な)
irrevocable henkō dekinai 変更できない
irrigate kangai suru かんがいする
irrigation kangai かんがい
irrigation canal yōsuiro 用水路
irritable okorippoi 怒りっぽい
irritate (*annoy*) iraira saseru いらいらさせる; MED shigeki suru 刺激する
irritating *person*, *itch* iraira suru yō (na) いらいらするよう(な)
irritation iradachi いらだち; MED shigeki 刺激
Islam Isuramu-kyō イスラム教
Islamic Isuramu-kyō (no) イスラム教(の)
island shima 島; (***traffic***) ~ anzen-chitai 安全地帯
islander shima no hito 島の人
isolate (*separate*) kiri hanasu 切り離す; (*cut off*) koritsu saseru 孤立させる; (*identify*) tsukitomeru つきとめる; *gene*, *bacteria* bunri suru 分離する
isolated *house* koritsu shita 孤立した; *occurrence* tandoku (no) 単独(の)
isolation (*of a region*) koritsu 孤立; ***in ~*** hoka to kirihanashite 他と切り離して
isolation ward kakuri-byōtō 隔離病棟
Israel Isuraeru イスラエル
Israeli 1 *adj* Isuraeru (no) イスラエル(の) **2** *n* (*person*) Isuraeru-jin イスラエル人
issue 1 *n* (*matter*) mondai 問題; (*result*) kekka 結果; ***March ~*** (*of*

magazine) sangatsu-gō 三月号; ***the point at ~*** mondai to natte iru ten 問題となっている点; ***take ~ with*** … ni igi o tonaeru …に異議を唱える **2** *v/t coins, passports, visa* hakkō suru 発行する; *supplies* shikyū suru 支給する; *warning* dasu 出す

IT (= ***information technology***) jōhō-kōgaku 情報工学

it ◊ (*as subject*) sore wa / ga それは/が; (*as object*) sore o それを ◊ (*not translated*): ***~'s raining*** ame ga futte imasu 雨が降っています; ***~'s me / him*** watashi / kare desu 私/彼です; ***~'s Charlie here*** TELEC Chārī desu チャーリーです; ***I don't like ~*** watashi wa kirai desu 私は嫌いです; ***that's ~!*** (*that's right*) sono tōri そのとおり; (*finished*) kore de oshimai これでおしまい

Italian 1 *adj* Itaria (no) イタリア(の) **2** *n* (*person*) Itaria-jin イタリア人; (*language*) Itaria-go イタリア語

italic shatai 斜体

italics: shatai de 斜体で

Italy Itaria イタリア

itch 1 *n* kayumi かゆみ **2** *v/i* kayui かゆい

item (*on agenda*) kōmoku 項目; (*of news*) kiji 記事; (*on shopping list*) hinmoku 品目; (*thing, article*) shinamono 品物

itemize *invoice* kajōgaki ni suru 箇条書にする

itinerary ryokō-keikaku 旅行計画

its sore (no) それ(の); ***the dog has hurt ~ leg*** sono inu wa ashi o kega shite iru その犬は足を怪我している

itself: ***the dog hurt ~*** inu ga kega o shita 犬がけがをした; ***by ~*** (*alone*) jishin de 自身で; (*automatically*) sorejishin de それ自身で

ivory (*substance*) zōge 象牙

ivy tsuta つた

J

jab *v/t* tsuku 突く

jack MOT jakki ジャッキ; (*in cards*) jakku ジャック

♦**jack up** MOT … o jakki de mochiageru …をジャッキで持ち上げる

jacket (*coat*) jaketto ジャケット, uwagi 上着; (*of book*) kabā カバー

jacket potato *kawa goto yaita jagaimo* 皮ごと焼いたじゃがいも

jack-knife *v/i* oremagatte tachiōjō suru 折れ曲がって立ち往生する

jackpot ittōshōkin 一等賞金; ***hit the ~*** taikin o ateru 大金を当てる

jade *n* hisui ひすい

jagged gizagiza (no) ぎざぎざ(の)

jail keimu-sho 刑務所

jam[1] jamu ジャム

jam[2] **1** *n* MOT kōtsū-jūtai 交通渋滞; F (*difficulty*) pinchi ピンチ; ***be in a ~*** pinchi de aru ピンチである **2** *v/t* (*ram*) oshikomu 押し込む; (*cause to stick*) tsukkaesaseru つっかえさせる; *broadcast* bōgai suru 妨害する; ***be ~med*** (*very busy*) gyūgyūzume de aru ぎゅうぎゅう詰めである; (*of road*) jūtai shite iru 渋滞している; (*of door, window*) ugokanaku natte iru 動かなくなっている **3** *v/i* (*stick*) ugokanaku naru 動かなくなる; (*squeeze*) oshiiru 押し入る

jam-packed gyūgyūzume (no) ぎゅうぎゅう詰め(の)

janitor kanrinin 管理人

January ichigatsu 一月

Japan Nihon 日本, Nippon 日本

Japanese 1 *adj* Nihon (no) 日本

(の), Nippon (no) 日本(の) **2** *n* Nihon-jin 日本人, Nippon-jin 日本人; (*language*) Nihon-go 日本語, Nippon-go 日本語
Japanese-Chinese War (*1937-45*) Nitchū-sensō 日中戦争
Japanese tea ocha お茶
Japan Railways Jei-āru ジェイアール
Japan Self-Defense Forces Jieitai 自衛隊
jar[1] *n* (*container*) bin びん
jar[2] *v/i* (*of noise*) shinkei ni sawaru 神経にさわる; ***~ on*** … ni sawaru …にさわる
jargon senmon-yōgo 専門用語
jaundice ōdan 黄だん
jaw *n* ago あご
jaywalker shingō-mushi o suru hito 信号無視をする人
jaywalking shingō-mushi 信号無視
jazz jazu ジャズ
♦**jazz up** *tune* … o nigiyaka ni suru …をにぎやかにする; *room etc* … o hade ni suru …を派手にする
jealous shittobukai しっと深い; ***be ~ of …*** … o urayamashiku omou …をうらやましく思う
jealousy shitto しっと
jeans jīnzu ジーンズ, jīpan ジーパン
jeep jīpu ジープ
jeer **1** *n* yaji やじ **2** *v/i* yajiru やじる; ***~ at*** … o yajiru …をやじる
Jello zerī ゼリー
jelly jamu ジャム
jelly bean zerī-bīn ゼリービーン
jellyfish kurage くらげ
jeopardize kiken ni sarasu 危険にさらす
jeopardy: ***be in ~*** kiki ni sarasarete iru 危機にさらされている
jerk[1] **1** *n* guitto ugoku koto ぐいっと動く事 **2** *v/t* guitto hiku ぐいっと引く
jerk[2] F baka ばか
jerky *movement* pikupiku ugoku ぴくぴく動く; *train* gatagata ugoku ががたがた動く
jest **1** *n* jōdan 冗談; ***in ~*** jōdan de 冗談で **2** *v/i* jōdan o iu 冗談を言う
Jesus Iesu イエス
jet **1** *n* (*of water*) funshutsu 噴出; (*nozzle*) funshutsu-kō 噴出口; (*airplane*) jetto-ki ジェット機 **2** *v/i* (*travel*) jetto-ki de iku ジェット機で行く
jet-black makkuro (na) 真っ黒(な); **jet engine** jetto-enjin ジェットエンジン; **jetlag** jisa-boke 時差ぼけ
jettison suteru 捨てる; *fig* misuteru 見捨てる
jetty tottei 突堤
Jew Yudaya-jin ユダヤ人
jewel hōseki 宝石; *fig* (*person*) kichō na hito 貴重な人
jeweler hōseki-shō 宝石商
jewelry hōseki-rui 宝石類
Jewish Yudaya (no) ユダヤ(の); *father, girlfriend etc* Yudaya-jin (no) ユダヤ人(の)
jiffy: ***in a ~*** F sugu ni すぐに
jigsaw (puzzle) jigusō(pazuru) ジグソー（パズル）
jilt furu ふる
jingle **1** *n* (*song*) komāsharu-songu コマーシャルソング **2** *v/i* (*of coins*) charin to naru oto ちゃりんと鳴る音
jinx (*person*) engi no warui hito 縁起の悪い人; (*bad luck*) jinkusu ジンクス; ***there's a ~ on this project*** kono purojekuto ni wa jinkusu ga aru このプロジェクトにはジンクスがある
jitters: ***get the ~*** F agaru あがる
jittery F piripiri shita ぴりぴりした
job (*employment*) shoku 職; (*task*) shigoto 仕事; ***out of a ~*** shitsugyō shite 失業して; ***it's a good ~ that…*** … shite yokatta …して良かった; ***you'll have a ~*** (*it'll be difficult*) kurō suru 苦労する
job description shokumu-naiyō 職務内容; **job hunt**: ***be job hunting*** shūshoku-katsudō shite iru 就職活動している
jobless shitsugyō (no) 失業(の)
job satisfaction shigoto no jūjitsukan 仕事の充実感
jockey *n* kishu 騎手, jokkī ジョッキー
jog **1** *n* jogingu ジョギング; ***go for a***

~ jogingu shi ni iku ジョギングしに行く **2** *v/i* (*as exercise*) jogingu suru ジョギングする **3** *v/t elbow etc* kozuku 小突く; **~ *one's memory*** … no kioku o yobisamasu …の記憶を呼びさます

jogger (*person*) jogingu suru hito ジョギングする人

jogging jogingu ジョギング; ***go ~*** jogingu shi ni iku ジョギングしに行く

jogging suit suetto-sūtsu スエットスーツ

john F (*toilet*) toire トイレ

join 1 *n* tsugime 継ぎ目 **2** *v/i* (*of roads, rivers*) gōryū suru 合流する; (*become a member*) kanyū suru 加入する **3** *v/t* (*connect*) tsunagu つなぐ; *person* … to issho ni naru …と一緒になる; *club* … ni sanka suru …に参加する; (*go to work for*) … ni nyūsha suru …に入社する; (*of road*) gōryū suru 合流する

♦**join in** … ni sanka suru …に参加する

joiner tategu-ya 建具屋

joint 1 *n* ANAT kansetsu 関節; (*in woodwork*) tsugime 継ぎ目; (*of meat*) katamariniku かたまり肉; F (*place*) tamariba たまり場; (*of cannabis*) marifana マリファナ **2** *adj* (*shared*) kyōdō (no) 共同(の)

joint account kyōdō-yokin-kōza 共同預金口座; **joint-stock company** gōshi-gaisha 合資会社; **joint venture** gōben-jigyō 合弁事業, jointo-benchā ジョイントベンチャー

joke 1 *n* (*story*) jōdan 冗談; (*practical ~*) itazura いたずら; ***play a ~ on*** … o karakau …をからかう; ***it's no ~*** waraigoto ja nai 笑い事じゃない **2** *v/i* (*pretend*) karakau からかう; (*having a ~*) jōdan o iu 冗談を言う

joker (*person*) jōdan-zuki 冗談好き; *pej* yatsu やつ; (*in cards*) jōkā ジョーカー

joking: ***~ apart*** jōdan wa sateoki 冗談はさておき

jokingly fuzakete ふざけて

jolly *adj* yōki (na) 陽気(な)

jolt 1 *n* (*jerk*) yure 揺れ **2** *v/t* (*push*) … ni butsukaru …にぶつかる

jostle *v/t* osu 押す

♦**jot down** … o memo suru …をメモする

journal (*magazine*) zasshi 雑誌; (*diary*) nikki 日記

journalism hōdō 報道, jānarizumu ジャーナリズム

journalist kisha 記者, jānarisuto ジーナリスト

journey *n* ryokō 旅行; ***it's a five-hour ~*** gojikan no kōtei de aru 五時間の行程である

joy yorokobi 喜び

jubilant ōyorokobi (no) 大喜び(の)

jubilation kanki 歓喜

judge 1 *n* LAW saibankan 裁判官; (*in competition*) shinpan 審判, jajji ジャッジ **2** *v/t* handan suru 判断する; *person* hyōka suru 評価する; *competition* shinpan suru 審判する

judgment LAW hanketsu 判決; (*opinion*) iken 意見; (*good sense*) handan 判断

judicial shihō (no) 司法(の)

judicious kenmei (na) 賢明(な)

judo jūdō 柔道

juggle kyokugei o suru 曲芸をする; *fig* … no yarikuri o tsukeru …のやりくりをつける

juggler kyokugei-shi 曲芸師

juice jūsu ジュース

juicy mizumizushii みずみずしい; *news, gossip* omoshiroi おもしろい

July shichigatsu 七月

jumble *n* yoseatsume 寄せ集め

♦**jumble up** yoseatsumeru 寄せ集める

jump 1 *n* jampu ジャンプ; (*increase*) kyūjōshō 急上昇; ***give a ~*** (*of surprise*) bikkuri saseru びっくりさせる **2** *v/i* tobu 跳ぶ; (*in surprise*) dokitto suru どきっとする; (*increase*) kyūjōshō suru 急上昇する; ***~ to one's feet*** satto tachiagaru さっと立ち上がる; ***~ to conclusions*** karugarushiku ketsuron o dasu 軽々しく結論を出

す **3** *v/t fence etc* tobikoeru 跳び越える; F *(attack)* tobikakaru 飛びかかる

♦**jump at** *opportunity* … ni tobitsuku …に飛びつく

jumper SP jampā ジャンパー; *(horse)* shōgai-rēsu-yō kyōsōba 障害レース用競争馬

jumpy bikubiku shite iru びくびくしている

junction *(of roads)* kōsaten 交差点

June rokugatsu 六月

jungle janguru ジャングル, mitsurin-chitai 密林地帯

junior 1 *adj (subordinate)* shita (no) 下(の); *(younger)* toshishita (no) 年下(の) **2** *n (in rank)* kōhai 後輩; ***she is ten years my ~*** kanojo wa watashi yori jussai toshishita da 彼女は私より十歳年下だ

junk *(trash)* garakuta がらくた

junk food janku-fūdo ジャンクフード

junkie mayaku-jōshūsha 麻薬常習者

junk mail dairekuto-mēru ダイレクトメール

junkyard haihin-okiba 廃品置場

jurisdiction LAW shihōken 司法権

juror baishin-in 陪審員

jury baishin 陪審

just 1 *adj law* kōsei (na) 公正(な); *war, cause* seitō (na) 正当(な) **2** *adv (exactly)* chōdo ちょうど; *(only)* tada ただ; ***I've ~ got here*** watashi wa koko ni tsuita bakari desu 私はここに着いたばかりです; ***I've ~ seen her*** chōdo kanojo ni atta tokoro da ちょうど彼女に会ったところだ; ***~ about*** *(almost)* mō sukoshi de もうすこしで; ***I was ~ about to leave when …*** … shita toki watashi wa chōdo deru tokoro datta …したとき私はちょうど出るところだった; ***~ like that*** *(abruptly)* fui ni 不意に; *(exactly like that)* chōdo konna fū ni ちょうどこんな風に; ***~ now*** *(a few moments ago)* tsui sakki ついさっき; *(at the moment)* chōdo ima ちょうど今; ***~ you wait!*** chotto machinasai ちょっと待ちなさい; ***~ be quiet!*** chotto shizuka ni shinasai ちょっと静かにしなさい

justice shihō 司法; *(of cause)* seigi 正義

justifiable mottomo (na) もっとも(な)

justifiably tōzen ni 当然に; ***she ~ refused to agree*** kanojo ga sansei shinakatta no wa tōzen da 彼女が賛成しなかったのは当然だ

justification seitō na iiwake 正当な言い訳

justify seitōka suru 正当化する; *text* chōsei suru 調整する

justly *(fairly)* kōsei ni 公正に; *(rightly)* tōzen 当然

♦**jut out** *v/i* haridasu 張り出す

juvenile 1 *adj* shōnen (no) 少年(の); *pej* kodomoppoi 子供っぽい **2** *n fml* miseinen-sha 未成年者

juvenile delinquency shōnen-hikō 少年非行

juvenile delinquent *(male)* hikō-shōnen 非行少年; *(female)* hikō-shōjo 非行少女

K

k (= ***kilobyte***) kirobaito キロバイト; (= ***thousand***) sen 千

Kabuki Kabuki 歌舞伎

kamikaze kamikaze 神風

karaoke karaoke カラオケ

karate karate 空手

karate chop karate choppu 空手チョップ

katakanakatakana かたかな
keel*n* NAUT ryūkotsu 竜骨
keen(*intense*) hageshii 激しい
keep1 *n* (*maintenance*) kuibuchi 食いぶち, seikatsu-hi 生活費; ***for ~s*** F eikyū ni 永久に **2** *v/t* totte oku 取っておく; (*not give back*) motte iru 持っている; (*not lose*) tamotsu 保つ; (*detain*) hikitomeru 引き止める; (*in specific place*) shimatte oku しまっておく; *family* yashinau 養う; *animals* kau 飼う; ***~ a promise*** yakusoku o mamoru 約束を守る; ***~ ... company*** ... ni tsukiau ...に付き合う; ***~ ... waiting*** ... o mataseta mama ni suru ...を待たせたままにする; ***sorry to have kept you waiting*** o-matase shimashita お待たせしました; ***~ ... to oneself*** (*not tell*) ... o damatte iru ...を黙っている; ***~ X from Y*** (*not tell*) X o Y ni shirasenaide oku XをYに知らせないでおく; ***~ trying*** tsuzukete miru 続けてみる; ***~ interrupting*** jama shitsuzukeru 邪魔し続ける **3** *v/i* (*remain*) ... no mama de iru ...のままでいる; (*of food, milk*) motsu もつ
♦**keep away1** *v/i* chikazukanai 近付かない; ***~ from ...*** ... ni chikayoranai ...に近寄らない **2** *v/t* chikazukenai 近付けない
♦**keep back***v/t* (*hold in check*) ... o osaeru ...を抑える; *information* ... o kakushite oku ...を隠しておく
♦**keep down***v/t voice, costs etc* ... o osaeru ...を抑える; ***he can't keep anything down*** kare wa zenbu haite shimau 彼は全部吐いてしまう
♦**keep in**(*in hospital*) ... o nyūin saseru ...を入院させる; (*in school*) ... o hōkago ni nokosu ...を放課後に残す
♦**keep off1** *v/t* (*avoid*) ... o sakeru ...を避ける; ***~ the grass!*** shibafu ni hairanaide 芝生にはいらないで **2** *v/i* (*of rain*) furanaide iru 降らないでいる
♦**keep out***v/i* naka ni hairanai 中に入らない; (*of argument*) kuwawaranai 加わらない; ***~!*** (*as sign*) tachiiri-kinshi 立入禁止
♦**keep to***path* ... kara hanarenai ...から離れない; *rules* mamoru 守る
♦**keep up1** *v/i* (*when walking, running etc*) tsuite kuru ついてくる **2** *v/t pace, payments* tsuzukeru 続ける; *bridge* sasaeru 支える; *pants* osaeru 押さえる
♦**keep up with**... ni okurenaide tsuite iku ...に遅れないでついていく; (*stay in touch with*) ... to tsukiai o tsuzukeru ...とつき合いを続ける
keeping ***in ~ with*** ... to chōwa shite ...と調和して; (*with promises*) ... to itchi shite ...と一致して
kegchiisai taru 小さい樽
kelpkonbu こんぶ
kendokendō 剣道
kennelinugoya 犬小屋
kennelspetto-hoteru ペットホテル
kerneltane 種
kerosenetōyu 灯油
ketchupkechappu ケチャップ
kettleyakan やかん
key1 *n* (*to door, drawer*) kagi 鍵; COMPUT, MUS kī キー **2** *adj* (*vital*) jūyō (na) 重要(な) **3** *v/t* COMPUT nyūryoku suru 入力する
♦**key in***data* ... o nyūryoku suru ...を入力する
keyboardCOMPUT, MUS kī-bōdo キーボード; **keyboarder**COMPUT nyūryoku-operētā 入力オペレーター; **keycard**kādo-shiki no kagi カード式の鍵
keyed-upkinchō shite 緊張して
keyholekagiana 鍵穴; **keynote speech**kichō-enzetsu 基調演説; **keyring**kī-horudā キーホルダー
kick1 *n* kikku キック; F (*thrill*) kaikan 快感; (***just***) ***for ~s*** F omoshirohanbun de おもしろ半分で **2** *v/t* keru ける; F *habit* yameru やめる **3** *v/i* keru ける
♦**kick around***v/t ball* keru ける; (*treat harshly*) kozukimawasu 小突きまわす; F (*discuss*) kentō suru 検討する
♦**kick in1** *v/t* F *money* ... o dashiau ...を出し合う **2** *v/i* (*of boiler etc*)

sadō suru 作動する
♦**kick off** *v/i* kikku-ofu o suru キックオフをする, shiai-kaishi o suru 試合開始をする; F (*start*) hajimeru 始める
♦**kick out** *v/t* … o oidasu …を追い出す; ***be kicked out of the company / army*** kaisha / rikugun o oidasareru 会社/陸軍を追い出される
kickback F (*bribe*) ribēto リベート, wairo わいろ
kickoff kikku-ofu キックオフ, shiai-kaishi 試合開始
kid 1 *n* F (*child*) kodomo 子供; *pej* gaki がき; ***~ brother*** otōto 弟; ***~ sister*** imōto 妹 **2** *v/t* F karakau からかう **3** *v/i* F jōdan o iu 冗談を言う; ***only ~ding*** chotto karakatta dake desu ちょっとからかっただけです
kidder F itazurazuki いたずら好き
kidnap yūkai suru 誘拐する
kidnap(p)er yūkai-han 誘拐犯
kidnap(p)ing yūkai 誘拐
kidney ANAT jinzō じん臓; (*food*) kidonī キドニー
kill *v/t* korosu 殺す; *plant* karasu 枯らす; *time* tsubusu つぶす; ***be ~ed in an accident*** jiko de shinu 事故で死ぬ; ***~ oneself*** jisatsu suru 自殺する
killer (*murderer*) satsujin-han 殺人犯; (*cause of death*) inochitori 命取り
killing satsujin 殺人; ***make a ~*** (*lots of money*) ōmōke suru 大もうけする
kiln kama 窯
kilo → ***kilogram***
kilobyte kirobaito キロバイト
kilogram kiroguramu キログラム
kilometer kiromētā キロメーター
kimono kimono 着物; ***summer ~*** yukata 浴衣
kind[1] *adj* shinsetsu (na) 親切(な)
kind[2] *n* shurui 種類; (*make, brand*) kata 型; ***what ~ of …?*** donna shurui no … desu ka どんな種類の…ですか; ***all ~s of people*** arayuru hitobito あらゆる人々; ***nothing of the ~*** zenzen betsumono 全然別物; ***~ of sad / strange*** F nandaka sabishii / hen na 何だか寂しい/変な; ***it's ~ of green*** midoriiro no isshu da 緑色の一種だ
kindergarten yōchien 幼稚園
kind-hearted shinsetsu (na) 親切(な)
kindly 1 *adj* yasashii 優しい **2** *adv* shinsetsu ni mo 親切にも; (*please*) dōzo どうぞ
kindness shinsetsu 親切
king kokuō 国王; (*in cards*) kingu キング
kingdom ōkoku 王国
king-size(d) F kingu-saizu (no) キングサイズ(の), tokudai (no) 特大(の)
kink (*in hose etc*) yojire よじれ
kinky F kimyō (na) 奇妙(な); *sex* hentai (no) 変態(の)
kiosk kiosuku キオスク
kiss 1 *n* kisu キス **2** *v/t* … ni kisu suru …にキスする **3** *v/i* kisu o suru キスをする
kit (*equipment*) dōgubako 道具箱; (*for assembly*) kumitateyō buhin-setto 組み立て用部品セット
kitchen daidokoro 台所, kitchin キッチン
kitchenette daidokoro 台所, kitchin キッチン
kitchen sink *everything but the ~* F ari to arayuru mono ありとあらゆるもの
kite tako たこ
kitten koneko 子猫
kitty (*money*) kyōdō-tsumitatekin 共同積立金
klutz F (*clumsy person*) bukitcho ぶきっちょ
knack kotsu こつ
knead *dough* koneru こねる
knee *n* hiza ひざ
kneecap *n* hizakozō ひざ小僧, hiza no sara ひざの皿
kneel hizamazuku ひざまずく
knick-knacks komagoma shita mono こまごました物
knife 1 *n* naifu ナイフ **2** *v/t* naifu de sasu ナイフで刺す
knit 1 *v/t* amu 編む **2** *v/i* amimono o

suru 編み物をする
♦**knit together** (*of broken bone*) kuttsukeru くっつける
knitting amimono 編み物
knitwear nitto-wea ニットウェア
knob totte 取っ手
knock 1 *n* (*at door*) nokku ノック; (*blow*) shōgeki 衝撃 **2** *v/t* (*hit*) butsukeru ぶつける; (*to the floor*) taosu 倒す; F (*criticize*) kenasu けなす **3** *v/i* (*on the door*) nokku suru ノックする
♦**knock around 1** *v/t* (*beat*) … o naguru …を殴る **2** *v/i* F (*travel*) hōrō suru 放浪する
♦**knock down** (*of car*) haneru はねる; *wall, building* torikowasu 取り壊す; F (*in price*) nesage shita 値下げした
♦**knock out** nokku-auto suru ノックアウトする; (*of medicine*) gussuri nemuraseru ぐっすり眠らせる; *power lines etc* hakai suru 破壊する
♦**knock over** hikkurikaesu ひっくり返す; (*of car*) haneru はねる
knockdown: ***a ~ price*** hakaku no nedan 破格の値段
knockout *n* (*in boxing*) nokku-auto ノックアウト
knot 1 *n* musubime 結び目 **2** *v/t* musubu 結ぶ
knotty *problem* komiitta 込み入った
know *fact, city, subject*, (*have heard of: person*) shitte iru 知っている; (*be acquainted with: person*) shiriai de aru 知り合いである; (*understand*) wakatte iru わかっている; *language* dekiru できる; (*recognize*) ki ga tsuku 気がつく; ***get to ~*** *person* … to shiriai ni naru …と知り合いになる; *city* … ni nareru …に慣れる; ***I ~ what you mean*** anata no itteru koto ga wakaru あなたの言ってることがわかる; ***I ~ you!*** (*what you're like*) anatano koto wakatteiru あなたのことわかっている; ***don't I ~ you?*** watashi anata no koto shitte masu ka 私あなたのこと知ってますか **2** *v/i* shitte iru 知っている; ***I don't ~*** shirimasen 知りません; (*in despair, frustration*) wakarimasen わかりません; ***yes, I ~*** ē, shitte imasu ええ、知っています; (*I understand*) ē, wakatte imasu ええ、わかっています **3** *n*: ***be in the ~*** jijō ni tsūjite iru 事情に通じている
knowhow nōhau ノウハウ
knowing monoshiri-gao (no) ものしり顔(の)
knowingly (*wittingly*) koi ni 故意に; *smile etc* tokuigao de 得意顔で
know-it-all F shittakaburi suru hito 知ったかぶりする人
knowledge chishiki 知識; ***to the best of my ~*** watashi no shiru kagiri de wa 私の知る限りでは; ***have a good ~ of …*** … ni tsuite yoku shitte iru …についてよく知っている
knowledgeable chishiki no aru 知識のある; ***be ~ about music*** ongaku ni tsuite yoku shitte iru 音楽について良く知っている
knuckle yubi no tsukene no kansetsu 指の付け根の関節
♦**knuckle down** honki ni naru 本気になる
♦**knuckle under** kōsan suru 降参する
KO → ***knockout***
koi (*carp*) koi こい
Korea (*South*) Kankoku 韓国, *fml* Daikan-minkoku 大韓民国; (*North*) Kita-chōsen 北朝鮮, *fml* Chōsen-minshu-shugi-jinmin-kyōwakoku 朝鮮民主主義人民共和国; (*South & North*) Chōsen 朝鮮
Korean 1 *adj* (*South*) Kankoku (no) 韓国(の); (*North*) Kita-chōsen (no) 北朝鮮(の); (*South and North*) Chōsen (no) 朝鮮(の) **2** *n* (*South*) Kankoku-jin 韓国人; (*North*) Kita-chōsen-jin 北朝鮮人; (*South and North*) Chōsen-jin 朝鮮人; (*language*) Kankoku-go 韓国語, Chōsen-go 朝鮮語
kosher REL Yudaya no oshie ni kanatta ユダヤの教えにかなった; F tekitō (na) 適当(な)
kudos shōsan 称賛
Kyoto Kyōto 京都
Kyushu Kyūshū 九州

L

lab (*room*) jikken-shitsu 実験室; (*building*) kenkyū-jo 研究所
label 1 *n* raberu ラベル **2** *v/t bags* raberu o haru ラベルをはる
labor *n* (*work*) rōdō 労働; (*in pregnancy*) bunben 分べん; ***be in ~*** bunbenchū de aru 分べん中である
laboratory → ***lab***
laboratory technician kenkyū-gishi 研究技師
labored *style*, *speech* kushin shita 苦心した
laborer nikutai-rōdō-sha 肉体労働者
laborious mendō (na) 面倒(な)
Labor Thanksgiving Day Kinrō-kansha no hi 勤労感謝の日; **labor union** rōdō-kumiai 労働組合; **labor ward** bunben-shitsu 分べん室
lace *n* (*material*) rēsu レース; (*for shoe*) kutsuhimo 靴ひも
♦ **lace up** *shoes* … no himo o shimeru …のひもを締める
lack 1 *n* ketsubō 欠乏 **2** *v/t* … ni kakeru …に欠ける **3** *v/i*: ***be ~ing*** kakete iru 欠けている
lacquer *n* (*for hair*) heasupurē ヘアスプレー; (*paint*) urushi 漆
lacquerware shikki 漆器
lad wakamono 若者
ladder hashigo はしご
laden: ***~ with hay / parcels*** hoshikusa / nimotsu o tsunde 干し草/荷物を積んで
ladies' room joseiyō toire 女性用トイレ
ladle *n* shakushi しゃくし
lady shukujo 淑女
ladybug tentōmushi てんとうむし
lag *v/t pipes* dannetsuzai de ōu 断熱材で覆う
♦ **lag behind** okureru 遅れる
lager ragābīru ラガービール
lagoon kata 潟
laid-back nonbiri shita のんびりした
lake mizūmi 湖
lamb kohitsuji 子羊; (*meat*) kohitsuji no niku 子羊の肉, ramu ラム
lame *person* bikko (no) びっこ(の); *excuse* heta (na) 下手(な)
lament 1 *n* hitan 悲嘆 **2** *v/t* nageku 嘆く
lamentable *ignorance* nagekawashii 嘆かわしい; *supplies* hinjaku (na) 貧弱(な)
laminated raminēto sareta ラミネートされた
lamp ranpu ランプ
lamppost gaitō 街灯
lampshade sutando no kasa スタンドのかさ
land 1 *n* tochi 土地; (*property*) shoyūchi 所有地; (*shore*) riku 陸; (*country*) kuni 国; ***by ~*** rikuro de 陸路で; ***on ~*** rikujō de 陸上で; ***work on the ~*** (*as farmer*) nōfu to shite hataraku 農夫として働く **2** *v/t airplane* chakuriku saseru 着陸させる; *job* kakutoku suru 獲得する **3** *v/i* (*of airplane*) chakuriku suru 着陸する; (*of ball, sth thrown*) ochiru 落ちる
landing (*of airplane*) chakuriku 着陸; (*top of staircase*) ichiban ue no odoriba 一番上の踊り場
landing field kei-hikōjō 軽飛行場; **landing gear** chakuriku-sōchi 着陸装置; **landing strip** chakurikujō 着陸場
landlady (*of hostel*) onna-shujin 女主人; **landlord** (*of hostel*) shujin 主人; **landmark** mokuhyō 目標; *fig* kakkiteki-jiken 画期的事件; **land owner** jinushi 地主; **landscape 1** *n* keshiki 景色; (*painting*) fūkeiga 風景画 **2** *adv print* yokomuki de

横向きで; **landslide** jisuberi 地滑り; **landslide victory** attōteki na shōri 圧倒的な勝利
lane (*in country*) komichi 小道; (*alley*) roji 路地; MOT shasen 車線
language kotoba 言葉; (*of one's own country*) kokugo 国語; (*technical terms*) yōgo 用語; (*style, type of ~*) kotobazukai 言葉遣い; (*college subject*) gogaku 語学; ***foreign ~*** gaikokugo 外国語
lank *hair* nobite aburappoi 伸びて脂っぽい
lanky *person* yaseta やせた
lantern tesage-ranpu 手さげランプ
Lao (*language*)Rao-go ラオ語
Laos Raosu ラオス
Laotian 1 *adj* Raosu (no) ラオス(の) **2** *n* (*person*) Raosu-jin ラオス人
lap[1] *n* (*of track*) isshū 一周; (*in athletics*) rappu ラップ
lap[2] *n* (*of water*) nami no oto 波の音
lap[3] *n* (*of person*) hiza ひざ
♦**lap up** *drink, milk* … o nametsukusu …をなめ尽くす; *flattery* … o unomi ni suru …をうのみにする
lapel orieri 折り襟
laptop COMPUT rapputoppu ラップトップ
larceny (*charge*) settōzai 窃盗罪; (*act*) settō 窃盗
larder shokuryō-chozōshitsu 食料貯蔵室
large ōki (na) 大き(な); *sum of money* tagaku (no) 多額(の); *family, number of people* ōninzū (no) 大人数(の); *amount* taryō (no) 多量(の); ***the criminal is still at ~*** hannin wa mada tōsōchū de aru 犯人はまだ逃走中である
largely shu to shite 主として
lark (*bird*) hibari ひばり
larva yōchū 幼虫
laryngitis kōtōen こう頭炎
larynx kōtō こう頭
laser rēzā レーザー
laser beam rēzā-kōsen レーザー光線
laser printer rēzā-purintā レーザープリンター
lash[1] *v/t* (*with whip*) muchi de utsu むちで打つ
lash[2] *n* (*eyelash*) matsuge まつげ
♦**lash down** (*with rope*) shikkari shibaritsukeru しっかり縛りつける
last[1] *adj* (*in series*) saigo (no) 最後(の); *bus, train* saishū (no) 最終(の); (*preceding*) kono mae (no) この前(の); ***~ but one*** saigo kara nibanme 最後から二番目; ***~ night*** yūbe ゆうべ; ***~ but not least*** (*in speech*) saigo ni daiji na koto o nobemasu ga 最後に大事なことを述べますが; ***at ~*** tsui ni ついに; ***the week before ~*** ni shūkan mae 二週間前
last[2] *v/i* (*of weather, relationship*) tsuzuku 続く; (*of food, money*) nagamochi suru 長持ちする
lastly saigo ni 最後に
latch kakegane 掛け金
late (*behind time*) okureta 遅れた; (*for school, meeting*) chikoku shita 遅刻した; (*in day*) osoi 遅い; ***it's getting ~*** osoku natte kita 遅くなってきた; ***of ~*** saikin 最近; ***the ~ 19th / 20th century*** jūkyūseiki / nijusseiki-kōki 19世紀/20世紀後期; ***sorry I'm ~*** okurete sumimasen 遅れてすみません; ***sleep ~*** asane o suru 朝寝をする
lately saikin 最近
late night fare shin'ya-ryōkin 深夜料金
later *adv* ato de あとで; ***see you ~!*** jā, mata じゃあ、また; ***~ on*** ato de あとで
latest *news, girlfriend* saishin (no) 最新(の)
lathe *n* senban 旋盤
lather (*from soap*) awa 泡
lather (*sweat*) ase 汗
Latin America Raten-Amerika ラテンアメリカ
Latin American 1 *adj* Raten-Amerika (no) ラテンアメリカ(の) **2** *n* (*person*) Raten-Amerika-jin ラテンアメリカ人
latitude ido 緯度; (*freedom to act*) jiyū 自由

latter: ***the ~*** kōsha 後者
laugh 1 *n* warai 笑い; ***it was a ~*** omoshirokatta おもしろかった **2** *v/i* warau 笑う
♦**laugh at** *person* … o azawarau …をあざ笑う; *joke* omoshirogaru おもしろがる
laughing stock: ***make oneself a ~*** monowarai no tane ni naru もの笑いの種になる
laughter waraigoe 笑い声
launch 1 *n* (*boat*) ranchi ランチ; (*of rocket, missile*) hassha 発射; (*of ship*) shinsui 進水; (*of product*) hatsubai 発売 **2** *v/t rocket, missile* hassha suru 発射する; *ship* shinsui suru 進水する; *new product* hatsubai suru 発売する
launch(**ing**) **ceremony** hatsubai-kinenkai 発売記念会
launch(**ing**) **pad** hasshadai 発射台
launder sentaku suru 洗濯する; *money* senjō suru 洗浄する
laundromat koinrandorī コインランドリー
laundry (*in apartment building*) sentaku-shitsu 洗濯室; (*shop*) kurīningu-ten クリーニング店, randorī ランドリー; (*clothes*) sentakumono 洗濯もの; ***do one's ~*** sentaku o suru 洗濯をする
laurel (*tree*) gekkeiju 月桂樹
lavatory (*place*) toire トイレ; (*equipment*) benki 便器
lavender rabendā ラベンダー
lavish *adj meal* tappuri (no) たっぷり(の); *lifestyle* yutaka (na) 豊か(な); *reception* mono-oshimi shinai 物惜しみしない
law hōritsu 法律; (*subject*) hōgaku 法学; ***against the ~*** ihō de 違法で; ***forbidden by ~*** hō de kinjirareta 法で禁じられた
law court hōtei 法廷
lawful seitō (na) 正当(な)
lawless muhō (no) 無法(の)
lawn shibafu 芝生
lawn mower shibakariki 芝刈り機
lawsuit soshō 訴訟
lawyer bengoshi 弁護士
lax tenurui 手ぬるい
laxative *n* gezai 下剤
lay *v/t* (*put*) oku 置く; *cable, carpet* shiku 敷く; (*put down flat*) nekaseru 寝かせる; *eggs* umu 産む; V (*sexually*) yaru やる; ***get laid*** V yaru やる
♦**lay into** (*attack*) … o kōgeki suru …を攻撃する
♦**lay off** *workers* … o kaiko suru …を解雇する
♦**lay on** *food, entertainment* … o junbi suru …を準備する
♦**lay out** *objects* … o chinretsu suru …を陳列する; *page* … o reiauto suru …をレイアウトする
layer *n* sō 層; (*of society*) kaisō 階層
layman shirōto 素人
layout reiauto レイアウト
♦**laze around** namakeru 怠ける
lazy *person* namakete iru 怠けている; *day* nonbiri shita のんびりした
lb (= ***pound***(***s***)) pondo ポンド
LCD (= ***liquid crystal display***) ekishō-hyōji 液晶表示
lead[1] **1** *v/t procession* … no sentō ni tatsu …の先頭に立つ; *race* rīdo suru リードする; *company, team* hikiiru 率いる; (*guide, take*) annai suru 案内する **2** *v/i* (*in race, competition*) rīdo suru リードする; (*provide leadership*) rīdā ni naru リーダーになる; ***a street ~ing off the square*** hiroba kara dete iru michi 広場から出ている道; ***where is this ~ing?*** (*of argument, policy*) kore wa donna kekka o motarasu no ka これはどんな結果をもたらすのか **3** *n* (*in race*) rīdo リード; ***be in the ~*** rīdo shite iru リードしている; ***take the ~*** sentō ni tatsu 先頭に立つ; ***lose the ~*** rīdo o ushinau リードを失う
♦**lead on** (*go in front*) … o rīdo suru …をリードする
♦**lead up to** (*precede*) … ni dandan to mukau …にだんだんと向かう; ***what are you leading up to?*** anata wa ittai nani ga iitai no desu ka あなたはいったい何が言いたいのですか

lead² *n* (*for dog*) kusari 鎖
lead³ *n* (*substance*) namari 鉛
leader (*of group*, *team*) rīdā リーダー; (*in tournament etc*) toppu トップ; (*of league*) shui 首位; (*in race*) sentō 先頭
leadership (*ability to lead*) rīdā shippu リーダーシップ; (*leaders of country*, *organization*) shidōken 指導権; (*leaders of party*) tōshu 党首; ***under his ~*** kare no shidō de 彼の指導で; ***~ skills*** rīdāshippu o toru nōryoku リーダーシップをとる能力
leadership contest shidōken-arasoi 指導権争い; POL tōshu-senkyō 党首選挙
lead-free *gas* muen (no) 無鉛(の)
leading *runner* sentō (no) 先頭(の); *company*, *product* yūryoku (na) 有力(な)
leading-edge *adj technology* saisentan (no) 最先端(の)
leaf happa 葉っぱ; (*of book*) pēji ページ
♦**leaf through** … no pēji o parapara to mekuru …のページをぱらぱらとめくる
leaflet chirashi ちらし
league renmei 連盟; SP rīgu リーグ
leak 1 *n* (*of water*, *air*, *gas*) more 漏れ; (*hole*) ana 穴; (*of information*) rōei 漏えい **2** *v/i* moru 漏る
♦**leak out** (*of air*, *gas*, *news*) moreru 漏れる
leaky *pipe*, *boat* ana no aru 穴のある
lean¹ 1 *v/i* (*be at an angle*) katamuku 傾く; ***~ against*** (*of person*) … ni yorikakaru …に寄りかかる; (*of object*) … ni tatekakaru …に立てかかる **2** *v/t*: ***~ X against Y*** X o Y ni tatekakeru XをYに立てかける
lean² *adj meat* akami (no) 赤身(の); *style*, *prose* hikishimatta 引き締まった
leap 1 *n* (*jump*) chōyaku 跳躍; ***a great ~ forward*** ōkina shinpo 大きな進歩 **2** *v/i* tobu 跳ぶ; ***~ over*** … o tobikoeru …を跳び越える
leap year urūdoshi うるう年
learn narau 習う; ***~ how to*** … no shikata o narau …の仕方を習う
learner gakushū-sha 学習者
learning *n* (*knowledge*) gakushiki 学識; (*act*) gakushū 学習
learning curve gakushū-kyokusen 学習曲線; ***be on the ~*** manabi-tsuzukete iru 学び続けている
lease 1 *n* (*to lend*) chintai-keiyaku 賃貸契約; (*to borrow*) chinshaku-keiyaku 賃借契約 **2** *v/t* (*of owner*) chintai suru 賃貸する; (*of taker*) chinshaku suru 賃借する
♦**lease out** … o chintai suru …を賃貸する
lease purchase kaitori-opushon tsuki chintai 買い取りオプションつき賃貸
leash *n* (*for dog*) kusari 鎖
least 1 *adj* (*slightest*) goku wazuka (no) ごくわずか(の) **2** *adv* ichiban … de nai いちばん…でない; ***he had changed ~ ~*** kare ga ichiban kawaranakatta 彼がいちばん変わらなかった; ***the ~ expensive car*** ichiban yasui kuruma 一番安い車 **3** *n*: ***he drank the ~*** kare ga ichiban nomanakatta 彼がいちばん飲まなかった; ***not in the ~ surprised / disappointed*** sukoshi mo manzoku / gakkari shite inai 少しも満足/がっかりしていない; ***at ~*** sukunaku tomo 少なくとも
leather 1 *n* kawa 皮 **2** *adj* kawa (no) 皮(の)
leave 1 *n* (*vacation*) kyūka 休暇; ***on ~*** kyūka de 休暇で **2** *v/t town*, *city* hanareru 離れる; *park*, *museum* deru 出る; (*for another town*, *city*, *country*) tatsu 発つ; *company* saru 去る; (*graduate from*) sotsugyō suru 卒業する; (*desert*) misuteru 見捨てる; *husband*, *wife* … to wakareru …と別れる; (*not finish*: *food*, *drink*) nokosu 残す; *scar*, *memory* nokosu 残す; (*forget*, *leave behind*) okiwasureru 置き忘れる; ***let's ~ things as they are*** kono mama ni shite okō このままにしておこう; ***how did you ~ things with him?*** kare wa dō suru to itte

imashita ka 彼はどうすると言っていましたか; ***~ X alone*** (*not interfere with*) X o hotte oku Xをほっておく; ***~ it to me*** watashi ni makasete kudasai 私に任せてください; ***be left*** nokoru 残る; ***there is nothing left*** nani mo nokotte inai 何も残っていない **3** *v/i* (*of person*) tachisaru 立ち去る; (*of plane, train, bus*) … ga shuppatsu suru …が出発する; ***we left for New York*** Nyū Yōku ni shuppatsu shita ニューヨークに出発した

♦**leave behind** *v/t* (*intentionally*) … o oite iku …を置いていく; (*forget*) okiwasureru 置き忘れる

♦**leave on** *v/t hat* … o kabutta mama ni suru …をかぶったままにする; *coat* … o kita mama ni suru …を着たままにする; *TV, computer* … o tsukeppanashi ni suru …をつけっぱなしにする

♦**leave out** *v/t word, figure* … o habuku …を省く; (*not put away*) dashippanashi ni suru 出しっぱなしにする; ***leave me out of this*** watashi o makikomanaide kudasai 私を巻き込まないでください

leaving party sōbetsukai 送別会

lecture 1 *n* kōgi 講義; (*criticism*) sekkyō 説教 **2** *v/i* kōgi o suru 講義をする

lecturer kōshi 講師

LED (= ***light-emitting diode***) hakkō-daiōdo 発光ダイオード

ledge tana たな

ledger COM daichō 台帳

leek rīki リーキ

leer *n* (*sexual*) iyarashii metsuki いやらしい目つき; (*evil*) ijiwarui metsuki 意地悪い目つき

left 1 *adj* hidari (no) 左(の); POL saha (no) 左派(の) **2** *n* hidari 左, hidarigawa 左側; POL saha 左派; ***on the ~*** hidarigawa ni 左側に; ***on the ~ of*** … no hidarigawa ni …の左側に; ***to the ~*** *turn* hidari e 左へ **3** *adv turn* hidari ni 左に; *look* hidari o 左を

left-hand hidarite (no) 左手(の); *bend* hidarigawa (no) 左側(の);

left-hand drive hidari-handoru no kuruma 左ハンドルの車; **left-handed** hidarikiki (no) 左利き(の); **left-overs** (*food*) nokorimono 残り物; **left-wing** POL sayoku (no) 左翼(の); **left wing** SP refuto-uingu レフトウイング

leg ashi 足; ***he's pulling your ~*** kare wa kimi o karakatteiru 彼は君をからかっている

legacy isan 遺産

legal (*allowed*) gōhōteki (na) 合法的(な); (*relating to the law*) hōritsu (no) 法律(の)

legal adviser hōritsu-komon 法律顧問

legality gōhōsei 合法性

legalize gōhōka suru 合法化する

legend densetsu 伝説

legendary yūmei (na) 有名(な)

legible yomeru 読める

legislate hōritsu o seitei suru 法律を制定する

legislation (*laws*) hōritsu 法律; (*passing of laws*) hōritsu-seitei 法律制定

legislative *powers* rippōken no aru 立法権のある; *assembly* rippō (no) 立法(の)

legislature POL rippōfu 立法府

legitimate gōhōteki (na) 合法的(な)

leg room ashimoto no supēsu 足もとのスペース

leisure hima 暇; ***at your ~*** hima na toki ni 暇なときに

leisurely *pace* yuttari shita ゆったりした

leisure time yoka 余暇

lemon remon レモン

lemonade remonēdo レモネード

lemon juice remon-jūsu レモンジュース

lemon tea remon-tī レモンティー

lend: ***~ Y to X*** X ni Y o kasu XにYを貸す

length naga-sa 長さ; (*piece: of cloth, wood*) ippon 一本; ***at ~*** *describe, explain* kuwashiku 詳しく; (*eventually*) tsui ni ついに

lengthen nobasu 伸ばす

lengthy *speech, stay* nagai 長い
lenient kandai (na) 寛大(な)
lens renzu レンズ
lens cover renzu-kabā レンズカバー
Lent Shijunsetsu 四旬節
lentil hiramame ひら豆
leopard hyō ひょう
leotard reotādo レオタード
lesbian 1 *n* rezu レズ **2** *adj* rezu (no) レズ(の)
less ~ ***interesting / serious than …*** … hodo omoshiroku nai / shinkoku de nai …ほどおもしろくない/深刻でない; ***it cost ~ than …*** hiyō ga … hodo kakaranakatta 費用が…ほどかからなかった; ***~ than $200*** nihyaku doru 200ドル以下; ***eat / talk ~*** (*than one used to*) mae yori tabenai / shaberanai 前より食べない/しゃべらない
lesson (*in school*) jugyō 授業; (*for piano, swimming*) ressun レッスン
let *v/t* (*allow*): ***~ X do Y*** X ni Y saseru XにYさせる; ***~ me go!*** hanashite 放して; ***~ him come in*** kare o irete agete 彼をいれてあげて; ***~'s go*** ikō 行こう; ***~'s eat*** tabeyō 食べよう; ***~'s not argue*** iiarasō no wa yameyō 言い争うのはやめよう; ***she can hardly walk ~ alone run*** kanojo wa hashiru no wa iu made mo naku aruku koto mo dekinai 彼女は走るのは言うまでもなく歩くこともできない; ***~ go of*** (*of rope, handle*) … o hanasu …を放す
♦ **let down** *shades, hair* … o orosu …をおろす; (*disappoint*) … no kitai o uragiru …の期待を裏切る; (*make longer*) … no take o nobasu …の丈を伸ばす
♦ **let in** (*to house*) … o naka ni ireru …を中に入れる
♦ **let off** (*not punish*) … o hanasu …を放す; (*from car*) … o orosu …を降ろす
♦ **let out** (*of room, building*) soto ni dasu 外に出す; *jacket etc* haba o hirogeru 幅を広げる; *groan, yell* ageru あげる
♦ **let up** *v/i* (*stop*) yamu やむ
lethal chishi (no) 致死(の)
lethargic mukiryoku (na) 無気力(な)
letter (*of alphabet*) moji 文字; (*in mail*) tegami 手紙
letterhead (*heading*) retāheddo レターヘッド; (*headed paper*) retā heddo-iri no binsen レターヘッド入りの便せん
letter of credit COM shin'yō-shōkaijō 信用照会状
lettuce retasu レタス
letup: ***without a ~*** yasumazu 休まず
leukemia hakketsubyō 白血病
level 1 *adj field, surface* taira (na) 平ら(な); (*in competition, scores*) dōten (no) 同点(の); ***draw ~ with*** … to hikiwakeru …と引き分ける **2** *n* (*standard*) suijun 水準; (*in hierarchy*) chii 地位; (*amount, quantity*) reberu レベル; ***on the ~*** taira na men de 平らな面で; (*honest*) shōjiki (na) 正直(な)
level-headed reisei (na) 冷静(な)
lever 1 *n* (*on machine*) rebā レバー; (*bar*) teko てこ **2** *v/t* teko de ugokasu てこで動かす; ***~ open*** … o kojiakeru …をこじあける
leverage teko no sayō てこの作用; (*influence*) eikyōryoku 影響力
levy *v/t taxes* chōshū suru 徴収する
lewd waisetsu (na) わいせつ(な)
liability (*responsibility*) sekinin 責任; (*of taxpayer*) futan 負担
liability insurance songaibaishō-hoken 損害賠償保険
liable (*answerable*) sekinin no aru 責任のある; ***be ~ to*** (*likely*) … shigachi de aru …しがちである
♦ **liaise with** … to no renrakuyaku o tsutomeru …との連絡役を務める
liaison (*contacts*) renraku 連絡
liar usotsuki うそつき
libel 1 *n* hibō-bunsho ひぼう文書; LAW meiyo-kison 名誉棄損 **2** *v/t* chūshō suru 中傷する
liberal *adj* (*broad-minded*) kokoro no hiroi 心の広い; *portion etc* kimae no yoi 気前のよい; POL jiyū-shugi (no) 自由主義(の)

liberate jiyū ni suru 自由にする
liberated *woman* jiyū (na) 自由(な)
liberty jiyū 自由; ***at ~*** (*prisoner etc*) jiyū de 自由で; ***be at ~ to ...*** jiyū ni ... dekiru 自由に...できる
librarian shisho 司書
library toshokan 図書館
Libya Ribia リビア
Libyan **1** *adj* Ribia (no) リビア(の) **2** *n* Ribia-jin リビア人
license **1** *n* menkyo 免許; (*for car*) unten-menkyoshō 運転免許証 **2** *v/t* ninka suru 認可する; ***be ~d*** ninka o ukeru 認可を受ける
license number menkyo-bangō 免許番号; MOT nanbā ナンバー
license plate nanbāpurēto ナンバープレート
lick **1** *n* hitoname ひとなめ **2** *v/t* nameru なめる; ***~ one's lips*** shitanamezuri o suru 舌なめずりをする
licking : ***get a ~*** F (*defeat*) boromake suru ぼろ負けする
lid futa ふた
lie[1] **1** *n* (*untruth*) uso うそ **2** *v/i* uso o tsuku うそをつく
lie[2] *v/i* (*of person*) yoko ni naru 横になる; (*of animal*) nesoberu ねそべる; (*of place, building, object*) aru ある
♦**lie down** yoko ni naru 横になる
lieutenant (*in navy*) taii 大尉; (*in army*) chūi 中尉; (*in police*) keibuho 警部補
life (*being alive*) inochi 命; (*way of living*) seikatsu 生活; (*period of being alive*) isshō 一生; (*of machine*) jumyō 寿命; ***he had a happy / sad ~*** kare wa shiawase na / kanashii isshō o okutta 彼は幸せな/悲しい一生を送った; ***all her ~*** isshōgai 一生涯; ***that's ~!*** jinsei to wa sonna mono da 人生とはそんなものだ
life belt kyūmei-beruto 救命ベルト;
lifeboat kyūmei-bōto 救命ボート;
life expectancy heikin-jumyō 平均寿命;**lifeguard** kyūjoin 救助員;
life history seikatsushi 生活史;**life insurance** seimei-hoken 生命保険;
life jacket kyūmei-dōi 救命胴衣
lifeless *body* shinda 死んだ; *personality* seiki no nai 生気のない
lifelike ikiutsushi (no) 生き写し(の);**lifelong** isshō (no) 一生(の);
life preserver (*for swimmer*) kyūmeigu 救命具;**life-saving** *adj equipment, drug* jinmei-kyūjoyō (no) 人命救助用(の);**lifesized** jitsubutsudai (no) 実物大(の);**life-threatening** inochi ni kakawaru 命にかかわる;**lifetime** (*of person*) shōgai 生涯; ***in my ~*** watashi no ikite iru aida ni 私の生きている間に
lift **1** *v/t* mochiageru 持ち上げる **2** *v/i* (*of fog*) hareru 晴れる **3** *n Br* (*elevator*) erebētā エレベーター; ***give ... a ~*** (*in car*) ... o kuruma de okuru ...を車で送る
♦**lift off** *v/i* (*of rocket*) uchiagerareru 打ち上げられる
lift-off (*of rocket*) uchiage 打ち上げ
ligament jintai じん帯
light[1] **1** *n* hikari 光; (*lamp*) akari 明り; ***in the ~ of*** *fig* ... ni terashite ...に照らして; ***do you have a ~?*** hi o motte imasu ka 火を持っていますか **2** *v/t fire, cigarette* ... ni hi o tsukeru ...に火をつける; (*illuminate*) raitoappu suru ライトアップする **3** *adj* (*not dark*) akarui 明るい; *color* usui 薄い
light[2] **1** *adj* (*not heavy*) karui 軽い; *traffic* sukunai 少ない; *rain, wind* yowai 弱い **2** *adv*: ***travel ~*** migaru ni ryokō suru 身軽に旅行する
♦**light up** **1** *v/t* (*illuminate*) ... o raitoappu suru ...をライトアップする **2** *v/i* (*start to smoke*) hi o tsukeru 火をつける
light bulb denkyū 電球
lighten[1] *v/t color* akaruku suru 明るくする
lighten[2] *v/t load* karuku suru 軽くする
♦**lighten up** (*cheer up*) genki o dashite 元気を出して
lighter (*for cigarettes*) raitā ライター
light-headed (*dizzy*) atama ga

furafura suru 頭がふらふらする; **light-hearted** kiraku (na) 気楽(な); **lighthouse** tōdai 灯台
lighting shōmei 照明
lightly *touch* karuku 軽く; ***get off ~*** assari nogareru あっさり逃れる
lightness[1] (*of room, color*) keikai-sa 軽快さ
lightness[2] (*in weight*) karu-sa 軽さ
lightning inabikari 稲光
lightning conductor hiraishin 避雷針
light pen raitopen ライトペン; **lightweight** (*in boxing*) raito-kyū ライト級; **light year** kōnen 光年
like[1] **1** *prep* … no yō (na) …のよう(な); ***be ~*** (*resemble*) … no yō de aru …のようである; ***what is she ~?*** (*in looks, character*) kanojo wa donna hito desu ka 彼女はどんな人ですか; ***it' s not ~ him*** (*not his character*) karerashiku nai 彼らしくない **2** *conj* F (*as*) …yō ni … ように; ***~ I said*** watashi ga itta yō ni 私が言ったように
like[2] *v/t* … ga suki da …が好きだ; ***I ~ this one*** sore ga suki da それが好きだ; ***I ~ her*** kanojo ga suki da 彼女が好きだ; ***I would ~ …*** … ga hoshii … が欲しい; ***I would ~ to …*** … shitai …したい; ***would you ~ …*** … ga hoshii desu ka …が欲しいですか; ***would you ~ to …?*** … shitai desu ka …したいですか; ***~ to*** … no ga suki de aru …のが好きである; ***if you ~*** yokereba よければ
likeable sukareru 好かれる
likelihood mikomi 見込み; ***in all ~*** tabun 多分
likely (*probable*) arisō (na) ありそう(な); ***not ~!*** tondemonai とんでもない
likeness (*resemblance*) ruijiten 類似点
liking ***is it to your ~?*** anata no konomi ni attemasu ka あなたの好みに合ってますか; ***take a ~ to*** … ga ki ni iru …が気に入る
lilac (*flower*) rairakku ライラック; (*color*) fujiiro ふじ色
lily yuri ゆり
lily of the valley suzuran すずらん
limb teashi 手足
lime[1] (*fruit, tree*) raimu ライム
lime[2] (*substance*) sekkai 石灰
limegreen usumidoriiro うすみどり色
limelight ***be in the ~*** chūmoku no mato ni naru 注目の的になる
limit 1 *n* (*of endurance, patience*) genkai 限界; (*of age, weight, speed*) seigen 制限; (*of land, area*) kyōkai 境界; ***within ~s*** tekido ni 適度に; ***off ~s*** tachiiri-kinshi-chiku de 立ち入り禁止地区で; ***that's the ~!*** mō genkai da もう限界だ; ***5 glasses is my ~*** gurasu gohai ga watashi no genkai desu グラス五杯が私の限界です **2** *v/t* seigen suru 制限する
limitation genkai 限界
limited company *Br* kabushiki-gaisha 株式会社
limo, limousine rimujin リムジン
limp[1] *adj arm etc* darari to shita だらりとした; (*lacking energy*) genki no nai 元気のない
limp[2] *n*: ***he has a ~*** kare wa ashi o hikizutte aruite iru 彼は足を引きずって歩いている
line[1] *n* (*on paper, road*) sen 線; (*on tennis court*) rain ライン; TELEC denwasen 電話線; (*of people, trees*) retsu 列; (*of text*) gyō 行; (*of business*) hōmen 方面; ***the ~ is busy*** hanashichū desu 話中です; ***hold the ~ please*** sono mama omachi kudasai そのままお待ちください; ***draw the ~ at*** … ni gendo o oku …に限度を置く; ***~ of inquiry*** (*in police investigation*) sōsa-hōshin 捜査方針; ***~ of reasoning*** suiri no hōkō 推理の方向; ***stand in ~*** retsu ni narabu 列に並ぶ; ***in ~ with …*** (*conforming with*) … to itchi shite …と一致して; ***he's out of ~ there*** kare wa kisoku yaburi da 彼は規則破りだ
line[2] *v/t clothes* … ni ura o tsukeru … に裏をつける
♦**line up** *v/i* seiretsu suru 整列する
linen (*material*) asa 麻, rinen リネン;

(*for bed*) beddo-rinen ベッドリネン

liner (*ship*) teikisen 定期船

linesman SP senshin 線審, rainzuman ラインズマン

linger (*of person*) nakanaka tachisaranai なかなか立ち去らない; (*of pain*) nakanaka kienai なかなか消えない

lingerie ranjerī ランジェリー

linguist (*professional*) gengo-gakusha 言語学者; ***she's a good ~*** kanojo wa gaikokugo ga jōzu da 彼女は外国語が上手だ

linguistic gengo (no) 言語(の)

lining (*of clothes*) uraji 裏地

link 1 *n* (*between incidents, facts*) kanren 関連; (*between people, countries*) tsunagari つながり; (*in chain*) wa 輪 **2** *v/t* kanren saseru 関連させる

♦**link up** *v/i* tsunagaru つながる; (*with person*) gōryū suru 合流する

lion raion ライオン

lip kuchibiru 唇

lipread *v/i* dokushin suru 読唇する

lipstick kuchibeni 口紅

liqueur rikyūru リキュール

liquid 1 *n* ekitai 液体 **2** *adj* ekitai (no) 液体(の)

liquidation seisan 清算; ***go into ~*** seisan suru 清算する

liquidity kankinsei 換金性

liquor sake 酒

liquor store sakaya 酒屋

lisp 1 *n* shitatarazu no hatsuon 舌足らずの発音 **2** *v/i* shitatarazu ni hatsuon suru 舌足らずに発音する

list 1 *n* risuto リスト; (*of people*) meibo 名簿; (*of things*) mokuroku 目録 **2** *v/t* hyō ni suru 表にする

listen kiku 聞く

♦**listen in** nusumigiki suru 盗み聞きする; (*with listening device*) tōchō suru 盗聴する

♦**listen to** *radio* … o kiku …を聞く; *person* … no iu koto o kiku …の言うことを聞く

listener (*to radio*) chōshu-sha 聴取者; ***he's a good ~*** kare wa hito no hanashi o yoku kiku 彼は人の話をよく聞く

listings magazine terebi-zasshi テレビ雑誌

listless genki no nai 元気のない

liter rittoru リットル

literal mojidōri (no) 文字どおり(の)

literary bungaku (no) 文学(の)

literate: ***be ~*** yomikaki ga dekiru 読み書きができる

literature bungaku 文学; (*advertising*) insatsubutsu 印刷物; (*about a product*) katarogu カタログ

litter gomi ごみ; (*of animals*) hitohara no ko ひと腹の子

little 1 *adj* sukoshi (no) 少し(の); *town, house, hands* chīsai 小さい; *problem, mistake* sasai (na) ささい(な); *child* osanai 幼い; ***~ sister*** imōto 妹; ***~ brother*** otōto 弟; ***the ~ ones*** kodomotachi 子供たち; ***when I was ~*** watashi ga kodomo no koro 私が子供の頃; ***it's of ~ use*** yaku ni tatanai 役に立たない **2** *n*: ***the ~ I know*** nakenashi no chishiki なけなしの知識; ***a ~*** sukoshi 少し; ***a ~ bread / wine*** sukoshi no pan / wain 少しのパン/ワイン; ***a ~ is better than nothing*** sukoshi de mo nai yori mashi da 少しでもないよりましだ **3** *adv*: ***~ by ~*** sukoshi zutsu 少しずつ; ***a ~ better / bigger*** sukoshi yoi / ōkii 少しよい/大きい; ***a ~ before 6*** rokuji sukoshi mae 六時少し前

live[1] *v/i* (*reside*) sumu 住む; (*be alive*) ikiru 生きる

♦**live on 1** *v/t rice, bread* … o tabete ikiru …を食べて生きる **2** *v/i* (*continue living*) seizon suru 生存する

♦**live up**: ***live it up*** tanoshiku sugosu 楽しく過ごす

♦**live up to** … ni kotaeru …にこたえる

♦**live with** *person* … to issho ni kurasu …と一緒に暮らす

live[2] *adj broadcast* nama (no) 生(の); jikkyō (no) 実況(の); *ammunition* shiyō-kanō (na) 使用可能(な)

livelihood seikei 生計
lively *party* nigiyaka (na) にぎやか(な); *city, place* kakki no aru 活気のある; *music* yōki (na) 陽気(な); *person* ikiiki shita 生き生きした
liver MED kanzō 肝臓; (*food*) rebā レバー
livestock kachikurui 家畜類
livid (*angry*) gekido shita 激怒した
living 1 *adj* ikite iru 生きている; *language* genzai tsukawarete iru 現在使われている **2** *n* kurashi 暮し; ***earn one's ~*** seikei o tateru 生計を立てる; ***standard of ~*** seikatsu-suijun 生活水準
living room ima 居間, ribingu-rūmu リビングルーム
lizard tokage とかげ
load 1 *n* tsumini 積荷; ELEC fuka 負荷; ***~s of*** takusan no … たくさんの… **2** *v/t car* … ni noseru …にのせる; *camera* … ni firumu o ireru …にフィルムを入れる; *gun* … ni tama o komeru …に弾を込める; *software* rōdo suru ロードする; ***~ X onto Y*** X o Y ni tsumu XをYに積む
loaded F (*very rich*) okanemochi (no) お金持ち(の); (*drunk*) yopparatta 酔っぱらった
loaf ikkin 一斤; ***a ~ of bread*** ikkin no pan 一斤のパン
♦**loaf around** norakura suru のらくらする
loafer (*shoe*) rōfā ローファー
loan 1 *n* kashitsukekin 貸付金; ***on ~*** karite iru 借りている **2** *v/t* kasu 貸す; ***~ Y to X*** X ni Y o kasu XにYを貸す
loathe hidoku kirau ひどく嫌う
lobby robī ロビー; POL atsuryoku-dantai 圧力団体
lobster robusutā ロブスター
local 1 *adj* jimoto (no) 地元(の) **2** *n* (*person*) tochi no hito 土地の人; TELEC naisen 内線
local anesthetic kyokusho-masui 局所麻酔; **local call** TELEC shinai-tsūwa 市内通話; **local government** chihō-jichitai 地方自治体
locality basho 場所
locally *live, work* jimoto de 地元で
local produce jimoto no seisanbutsu 地元の生産物
local time genchi-jikan 現地時間
locate *new factory etc* oku 置く; (*identify position of*) basho o shimesu 場所を示す; ***be ~d*** aru ある
location (*siting*) basho 場所; (*identifying position of*) shozai no kakunin 所在の確認; ***on ~*** *movie* roke-chū de ロケ中で
lock[1] (*of hair*) fusa 房
lock[2] **1** *n* (*on door*) kagi 鍵 **2** *v/t door* … ni kagi o kakeru …に鍵をかける; ***~ X in position*** X o teiichi ni kotei suru Xを定位置に固定する
♦**lock away** … o genjū ni shimaikomu …を厳重にしまい込む
♦**lock in** *person* … o tojikomeru …を閉じ込める
♦**lock out** (*of house*) … o shimedasu …を締め出す; ***I locked myself out*** kagi o naka ni oita mama doa o shimete shimatta 鍵を中に置いたままドアを閉めてしまった
♦**lock up** (*in prison*) keimusho ni ireru 刑務所に入れる
locker rokkā ロッカー
locket roketto ロケット
locksmith jōmae-ya 錠前屋
locust inago いなご
lodge 1 *v/t complaint* teishutsu suru 提出する **2** *v/i* (*of bullet etc*) atatte tomaru 当たって止まる
lodger geshukunin 下宿人
loft yaneura 屋根裏; (*as apartment*) rofuto ロフト
lofty *heights* sobietatsu そびえ立つ; *ideals* sūkō (na) 崇高(な)
log (*wood*) maruta 丸太; (*record*) kiroku 記録; (*captain's, driver's*) nisshi 日誌
♦**log off** shūryō suru 終了する
♦**log on** kidō suru 起動する
♦**log on to** … o kidō suru …を起動する
logbook nisshi 日誌
log cabin maruta-goya 丸太小屋
logic ronri 論理

logical ronriteki (na) 論理的(な)
logistics keikaku no jisshi 計画の実施
logo rogo ロゴ
loiter urotsuku うろつく
lollipop bōtsuki kyandī 棒付きキャンディー
London Rondon ロンドン
loneliness (*of person*) kodoku 孤独; (*of place*) sabishi-sa 寂しさ
lonely *person* kodoku (na) 孤独(な); *place* sabishii 寂しい
loner ippiki-ōkami 一匹おおかみ
long[1] **1** *adj* nagai 長い; ***it's a ~ way*** tōi 遠い **2** *adv* nagaku 長く; ***don't be ~*** (*be back soon*) hayaku modotte kite 早く戻って来て; (*be quick*) isoide 急いで; ***5 weeks is too ~*** goshūkan wa nagasugiru 五週間は長過ぎる; ***will it take ~?*** nagaku kakarimasu ka 長くかかりますか; ***that was ~ ago*** sore wa daibu mae no koto da それはだいぶ前のことだ; ***~ before then*** sore yori daibu mae ni それよりだいぶ前に; ***before ~*** mamonaku まもなく; ***we can't wait any ~er*** watashitachi wa kore ijō matemasen 私たちはこれ以上待てません; ***he no ~er works here*** kare wa mō koko de wa hataraite imasen 彼はもうここでは働いていません; ***so ~ as*** (*provided*) … de aru kagiri wa …である限りは; ***so ~!*** sayōnara さようなら
long[2] *v/i*: ***~ for*** … o machinozomu …を待ち望む; ***I'm ~ing to see her again*** watashi wa kanojo ni aitakute tamaranai 私は彼女に会いたくてたまらない
long-distance *adj* chōkyori (no) 長距離(の)
longing *n* setsubō 切望
longingly setsubō shite 切望して
longitude keido 経度
long jump habatobi 幅跳び; **long-range** *missile* chōkyori (no) 長距離(の); *forecast* chōki (no) 長期(の); **long-sighted** enshi (no) 遠視(の); **long-sleeved** nagasode (no) 長袖(の); **long-standing** naganen ni wataru 長年にわたる; **long-term** *adj* chōki (no) 長期(の); **long wave** chōha 長波
look 1 *n* (*appearance*) mikake 見かけ; (*glance*) ikken 一見; ***give … a ~*** … o chiratto miru …をちらっと見る; ***have a ~ at*** (*examine*) … o chotto miru …をちょっと見る; ***can I have a ~?*** chotto mite mo ii desu ka ちょっと見てもいいですか; ***can I have a ~ around?*** (*in store etc*) gurutto mite mawatte mo ii desu ka ぐるっと見て回ってもいいですか; ***~s*** (*beauty*) yōbō 容ぼう **2** *v/i* miru 見る; (*seem*) … ni mieru …に見える; ***you ~ tired / different*** tsukarete / itsumo to chigatte mieru 疲れて/いつもと違って見える
♦**look after** *children* … no sewa o suru …の世話をする; *property* … no kanri o suru …の管理をする; *own interests* … o mamoru …を守る
♦**look around** *museum, city* … o gurutto mite mawaru …をぐるっと見て回る
♦**look at** … o miru …を見る; (*examine*) … o shiraberu …を調べる; (*consider*) … o kangaeru …を考える
♦**look back** … o furikaette miru …を振り返って見る
♦**look down on** … o mikudasu …を見下す
♦**look for** … o sagasu …を探す
♦**look forward to** … o tanoshimi ni shite matsu …を楽しみにして待つ
♦**look in on** (*visit*) … no tokoro ni tachiyoru …のところに立ち寄る
♦**look into** (*investigate*) … no naiyō o shiraberu …の内容を調べる
♦**look on 1** *v/i* (*watch*) bōkan suru 傍観する **2** *v/t*: ***~ X as Y*** (*consider*) X o Y da to minasu XをYだとみなす
♦**look onto** *garden, street* … ni menshite iru …に面している
♦**look out** *v/i* (*of window etc*) soto o miru 外を見る; (*pay attention*) ki o tsukeru 気をつける; ***~!*** abunai 危ない

♦**look out for** *mailman etc* … o sagashite miru …を捜してみる; (*be on guard against*) … ni chūi suru …に注意する
♦**look out of** *window* … kara soto o miru …から外を見る
♦**look over** *house* … o tenken suru …を点検する; *translation* … o shiraberu …を調べる
♦**look through** *magazine*, *notes* … o yoku shiraberu …をよく調べる
♦**look to** (*rely on*) … ni tayoru …に頼る
♦**look up 1** *v/i* (*from paper etc*) miageru 見上げる; (*improve*) jōshō suru 上昇する; (*of weather*) yoku naru よくなる; ***things are looking up*** yoku natte kite iru よくなって来ている **2** *v/t word*, *phone number* … o shiraberu …を調べる; (*visit*) … o hōmon suru …を訪問する
♦**look up to** (*respect*) … o sonkei suru …を尊敬する
lookout (*person*) mihari 見張り; ***be on the ~ for*** … no mihari o shite iru …の見張りをしている
♦**loom up** bon'yari arawareru ぼんやり現れる
loony F **1** *n* kichigai 気違い **2** *adj* ki no kurutta 気の狂った
loop *n* wa 輪
loophole (*in law etc*) nukeana 抜け穴
loose *connection* yurui ゆるい; *rope* tarunda たるんだ; *button* torekakatta 取れかかった; *clothes* yuttari shita ゆったりした; *morals* fushidara (na) ふしだら(な); *wording* aimai (na) あいまい(な); ***~ change*** bara no kozeni ばらの小銭; ***~ ends*** mikaiketsu-bubun 未解決部分
loosely *tied* yuruku ゆるく
loosely *worded* aimai ni あいまいに
loosen yurumeru ゆるめる
loot 1 *n* senrihin 戦利品 **2** *v/i* ryakudatsu suru 略奪する
looter ryakudatsu-sha 略奪者
♦**lop off** … o kiriotosu …を切り落とす
lop-sided katayotta 片寄った
Lord (*God*) Kamisama 神様; ***Lord's Prayer*** Shu no inori 主の祈り
lorry *Br* torakku トラック
lose 1 *v/t object* nakusu なくす; *match* … ni makeru …に負ける **2** *v/i* SP makeru 負ける; (*of clock*) okureru 遅れる; ***I'm lost*** michi ni mayotta 道に迷った; ***get lost!*** F (*go away*) usero うせろ; (*don't be stupid*) yamete やめて
♦**lose out** son o suru 損をする
loser SP haisha 敗者; (*in life*) rakugo-sha 落後者
loss (*of object*) funshitsu 紛失; (*through death*) sōshitsu 喪失; (*in business*) sonshitsu 損失; ***make a ~*** sonshitsu o dasu 損失を出す; ***be at a ~*** tohō ni kureru 途方に暮れる
lost ushinawareta 失われた
lost-and-found (office) ishitsubutsu-toriatsukaijo 遺失物取扱所
lot: ***a ~, ~s*** takusan たくさん; (*very, much*) totemo とても; ***a ~ of, ~s of*** takusan no たくさんの; ***a ~ better*** / ***easier*** totemo yoi / kantan とても良い/簡単
lotion rōshon ローション
lotus hasu はす
loud *voice*, *noise* ōkii 大きい; *music* urusai うるさい; *color* hade (na) はで(な)
loudspeaker supīkā スピーカー
lounge ima 居間; (*in hotel*, *airport*) robī ロビー
♦**lounge around** burabura suru ぶらぶらする
louse shirami しらみ
lousy saitei (no) 最低(の); (*ill*) kimochi no warui 気持ちの悪い
lout busahō na otoko 不作法な男
lovable aisubeki 愛すべき
love 1 *n* ai 愛; (*for child*, *pet*) aijō 愛情; (*romantic*) ren'ai 恋愛; (*for object*) aichaku 愛着; (*in tennis*) rabu ラブ; ***be in ~*** … ni koi shite iru …に恋している; ***fall in ~*** horeru ほれる; ***make ~*** sekkusu o suru セックスをする; ***what is it, my ~?*** (*man to woman*) nāni, anata なあに、あなた; (*woman to

man, mother to child) nāni なあに **2** *v/t* aisuru 愛する; ***~ to …*** … no ga daisuki de aru …のが大好きである

love affair ren'ai-kankei 恋愛関係; **love life** sekkusu-raifu セックスライフ; **love letter** raburetā ラブレター

lovely *face, hair* utsukushii 美しい; *color, tune* kirei (na) きれい(な); *person, character, holiday, weather, meal* subarashii すばらしい; ***we had a ~ time*** totemo tanoshikatta とっても楽しかった

lover aijin 愛人

loving *adj person* aijō no fukai 愛情の深い; *care* kokoro no komotta 心のこもった

low 1 *adj* hikui 低い; *salary, price etc* yasui 安い; *quality* somatsu (na) 粗末(な); ***be feeling ~*** genki ga nai 元気がない; ***be ~ on gas / tea*** gasorin / kōcha ga tarinai ガソリン/紅茶が足りない **2** *n* (*in weather*) teikiatsu 低気圧; (*in sales, statistics*) saitei-kiroku 最低記録

lowbrow *adj* kyōyō no hikui 教養の低い; **low-calorie** tei-karorī (no) 低カロリー(の); **low-cut** *dress* eriguri no fukai 襟ぐりの深い

lower *boat, sth to the ground* orosu 降ろす; *flag, hemline, pressure, price* sageru 下げる; *voice* hikuku suru 低くする

low-fat teishibō (no) 低脂肪(の); **lowkey** hikaeme (no) 控え目(の); **lowlands** teichi-chihō 低地地方; **low-pressure area** teikiatsu-iki 低気圧域; **low season** ofushīzun オフシーズン; **low tide** kanchō 干潮

loyal chūjitsu (na) 忠実(な)

lozenge (*shape*) hishigata ひし形; (*tablet*) torōchi トローチ

Ltd (= ***limited***) kabushiki-gaisha 株式会社

lubricant junkatsuyu 潤滑油

lubricate … ni abura o sasu …に油をさす

lubrication chūyu 注油

lucid (*clear*) wakariyasui わかりやすい; (*sane*) shōki (no) 正気(の)

luck un 運; ***bad ~*** fuun 不運; ***hard ~!*** zannen 残念; ***good ~*** kōun 幸運; ***good ~!*** ganbatte がんばって

♦ **luck out** F tsuite iru ついている

luckily un' yoku 運よく

lucky *person, coincidence, day* un no ii 運のいい; *number, charm* kōun (no) 幸運(の); *guess* magure (no) まぐれ(の); ***you were ~*** kimi wa un ga yokatta 君は運がよかった; ***he's ~ to be alive*** ikite iru nante kare wa un ga yokatta 生きているなんて彼は運がよかった; ***that's ~!*** sore wa tsuite iru それはついている

ludicrous bakageta ばかげた

luggage tenimotsu 手荷物

lukewarm nurui ぬるい; *reception* kinori no shinai 気乗りのしない

lull 1 *n* (*in storm, fighting*) koyami 小やみ; (*in conversation*) ma 間 **2** *v/t*: ***~ … into a false sense of security*** … o damashite anshin da to omowaseru …をだまして安心だと思わせる

lullaby komoriuta 子守歌

lumbago yōtsū 腰痛

lumber *n* (*timber*) zaimoku 材木

luminous hakkō suru 発光する

lump (*of sugar*) kakuzatō ikko 角砂糖一個; (*swelling*) shikori しこり, kobu こぶ

♦ **lump together** isshokuta ni suru 一緒くたにする

lump sum ikkatsubarai 一括払い

lumpy *sauce* dama ni natta だまになった; *mattress* dekoboko (no) 凸凹(の)

lunacy kyōki 狂気

lunar tsuki (no) 月(の)

lunatic *n* F ōbaka 大ばか

lunch chūshoku 昼食, hirugohan 昼ごはん; ***have ~*** chūshoku o toru 昼食をとる

lunch box (*packed lunch*) obentō お弁当; (*at station*) ekiben 駅弁; **lunch break** hiruyasumi 昼休み; **lunch hour** chūshokudoki 昼食時; **lunchtime** chūshokudoki 昼食時

lung hai 肺

lung cancer haigan 肺がん
♦**lunge at** … o tsuku …を突く
lurch *v/i* (*of person*) yoromeku よろめく; (*of ship, car*) yureru 揺れる
lure 1 *n* yūwaku 誘惑 **2** *v/t* (*into a trap*) obikiyoseru おびき寄せる
lurid *color* kebakebashii けばけばしい; *details* osoroshii 恐ろしい
lurk (*of person*) machibuse suru 待ち伏せする; (*of doubt*) tsukimatou つきまとう
luscious *fruit, dessert* amai 甘い; *woman, man* miryokuteki (na) 魅力的(な)
lust *n* yokubō 欲望
luxurious gōka (na) 豪華(な)
luxury 1 *n* zeitaku ぜいたく **2** *adj* gōka (na) 豪華(な)
lymph gland rinpasen リンパ腺
lynch … ni shikei o kuwaeru …に私刑を加える
lynx ōyamaneko おおやまねこ
lyricist sakushika 作詞家
lyrics kashi 歌詞

M

MA (= ***Master of Arts***) bungaku-shūshigō 文学修士号
ma'am okusan 奥さん; (*to younger woman*) ojōsan お嬢さん; (*to teacher*) sensei 先生
machine 1 *n* kikai 機械 **2** *v/t* (*on sewing machine*) mishin o kakeru ミシンをかける; TECH kikai de tsukuru 機械で作る
machine gun *n* kikanjū 機関銃
machine-readable konpyūtā de yomitori-kanō (no) コンピューターで読み取り可能(の)
machinery (*machines*) kikairui 機械類
machismo otokoppo-sa 男っぽさ
macho otokoppoi 男っぽい
mackerel saba さば
mackintosh reinkōto レインコート
macro COMPUT makuro マクロ
mad ki no kurutta 気の狂った; *idea* bakageta ばかげた; (*angry*) kankan ni hara o tateta かんかんに腹を立てた; ***be ~ about*** (*enthusiastic*) … ni netchū shite iru …に熱中している; ***this is driving me ~*** kono sei de ki ga kurui-sō da このせいで気が狂いそうだ; ***go ~*** ki ga kuruu 気が狂う; (*with enthusiasm*) ki ga kurutta yō ni kōfun suru 気が狂ったように興奮する; ***like ~*** *run, work* hisshi de 必死で
madden hidoku iradataseru ひどくいらだたせる
maddening hidoku haradatashii ひどく腹立たしい
made-to-measure ōdāmeido (no) オーダーメイド(の)
madhouse *fig* sōzōshii basho 騒々しい場所
madly hisshi ni 必死に; ***~ in love*** muchū ni natte iru 夢中になっている
madman kichigai 気違い
madness kyōki 狂気
Mafia : ***the ~*** Mafia マフィア
magazine (*printed*) zasshi 雑誌
maggot uji うじ
magic 1 *n* (*supernatural force*) mahō 魔法; (*charm*) maryoku 魔力; (*tricks*) tejina 手品; ***like ~*** tachidokoro ni たちどころに **2** *adj* mahō no yō (na) 魔法のよう(な)
magical *powers* mahō (no) 魔法(の); *moment* subarashii すばらしい
magician tejina-shi 手品師, majishan マジシャン
magic spell mahō 魔法
magic trick tejina 手品

magnanimous kandai (na) 寛大(な)
magnet jishaku 磁石
magnetic jishaku (no) 磁石(の); *personality* hito o hikitsukeru 人を引きつける
magnetism (*of person*) hito o hikitsukeru miryoku 人を引きつける魅力
magnificence sōdai-sa 壮大さ
magnificent *view, building* sōdai (na) 壮大(な); *decoration, work* migoto (na) みごと(な)
magnify kakudai suru 拡大する; *difficulties* kochō suru 誇張する
magnifying glass mushi-megane 虫眼鏡
magnitude ōki-sa 大きさ
mah-jong mājan 麻雀
maid otetsudai お手伝い; (*in hotel*) kyakushitsu-gakari 客室係
maiden name kyūsei 旧姓
maiden voyage shojo-kōkai 処女航海
mail 1 *n* yūbin 郵便; ***put X in the ~*** X o tōkan suru Xを投かんする **2** *v/t letter* yūsō suru 郵送する
mailbox (*in street*) posuto ポスト; (*of house*) yūbin'uke 郵便受け; COMPUT mērubokkusu メールボックス
mailing list yūsōsaki-meibo 郵送先名簿
mailman yūbin'ya-san 郵便屋さん; **mail-order catalog** tsūshin-hanbai-katarogu 通信販売カタログ; **mail-order firm** tsūshin-hanbai no kaisha 通信販売の会社
maim jūshō o owaseru 重傷を負わせる (*fugu ni naru* 不具になる)
main *adj* omo (na) 主(な)
mainframe ōgata-konpyūtā 大型コンピューター; **mainland** hondo 本土; ***on the ~*** hondo ni 本土に; **mainland China** Chūgoku hondo 中国本土
mainly omo ni 主に
main road kansen-dōro 幹線道路
main street ōdōri 大通り
maintain iji suru 維持する; *pace, speed* jizoku suru 持続する; *family* fuyō suru 扶養する; *innocence, guilt* shuchō suru 主張する; ***~ that*** … o ronjiru …を論じる
maintenance (*of machine, house*) mentenansu メンテナンス; (*money*) fuyōryō 扶養料; (*of law and order*) iji 維持
majestic dōdō to shita 堂々とした
major 1 *adj* shuyō (na) 主要(な); ***C ~*** MUS hachōchō ハ長調 **2** *n* MIL shōsa 少佐
♦**major in** … o senkō suru …を専攻する
majority daitasū 大多数; POL tokuhyō sa 得票差; ***be in the ~*** kahansū o shimeru 過半数を占める
make 1 *n* (*brand*) shurui 種類; ***a Japanese ~ of car*** Nihonsei no kuruma 日本製の車 **2** *v/t meal, dress, cake* tsukuru 作る; *coffee, tea* ireru 入れる; *movie, TV program* seisaku suru 製作する; *speech, statement etc* suru する; *bed* totonoeru 整える; *hole* akeru 開ける; (*manufacture*) seizō suru 製造する; (*earn*) kasegu 稼ぐ; MATH … ni naru …になる; ***~ X do Y*** (*compel, cause*) X ni Y saseru XにYさせる; ***you can't ~ me do it!*** muri ni yaraseyō tatte dame desu 無理にやらせようったってだめです; ***~ X happy*** X o shiawase ni suru Xを幸せにする; ***~ X angry*** X o okoraseru Xを怒らせる; ***~ a noise*** mono-oto o tateru 物音を立てる; ***made in Japan*** Nihonsei 日本製; ***~ it*** (*come to party, meeting*) deru 出る; (*arrive on time*) ma ni au 間に合う; (*succeed*) seikō suru 成功する; (*survive*) mochikotaeru 持ちこたえる; ***what time do you ~ it?*** ima nanji desu ka 今何時ですか; ***~ believe*** (*pretend*) … de aru furi o suru …であるふりをする; ***~ do with*** ma ni awaseru 間に合わせる; ***what do you ~ of it?*** sore o dō omoimasu ka それをどう思いますか
♦**make for** (*go toward*) … ni mukau …に向かう
♦**make off** isoide tachisaru 急いで立ち去る
♦**make off with** (*steal*) … o

mochinige suru …を持ち逃げする
♦ **make out** *v/t list* … o tsukuriageru …を作り上げる; (*see*) … o miwakeru …を見分ける; (*imply*) … to honomekasu …とほのめかす
♦ **make over**: ***make X over to Y*** X o Y ni yuzuru XをYに譲る
♦ **make up 1** *v/i* (*of woman*) keshō o suru 化粧をする; (*of actor*) mēkuappu o suru メークアップをする; (*after quarrel*) nakanaori suru 仲直りする **2** *v/t story, excuse* … o tsukuridasu …を作り出す; *face* … ni keshō o suru …に化粧をする; (*constitute*) kōsei suru 構成する; ***be made up of*** … de tsukurarete iru …で作られている; (*of class, group*) … de kōsei sarete iru …で構成されている; **~ *one's mind*** kesshin suru 決心する; ***make it up*** (*after quarrel*) nakanaori suru 仲直りする
♦ **make up for** … no umeawase o suru …の埋め合せをする
make-believe *n* misekake 見せかけ
maker (*of product*) seizō-gaisha 製造会社
makeshift ma ni awase (no) 間に合わせ(の)
make-up (*cosmetics*) keshōhin 化粧品
maladjusted kankyō-futekiō (no) 環境不適応(の)
Malay (*language*) Marē-go マレー語; (*person*) Marēshia-jin マレーシア人
Malaysia Marēshia マレーシア
Malaysian Marēshia (no) マレーシア(の)
male 1 *adj* dansei (no) 男性(の); *animal, bird, fish* osu (no) 雄(の) **2** *n* dansei 男性; (*animal, bird, fish*) osu 雄
male chauvinist (pig) danson-johi no (butayarō) 男尊女卑の(ブタ野郎)
male nurse kangoshi 看護士
malevolent akui o motta 悪意をもった
malfunction 1 *n* fuchō 不調 **2** *v/i* seijō ni ugokanai 正常に動かない
malice akui 悪意
malicious akui no aru 悪意のある
malignant *tumor* akusei (no) 悪性(の)
mall (*shopping ~*) shoppingu-sentā ショッピングセンター
malnutrition eiyō-shitchō 栄養失調
malpractice (*of doctor*) iryō-kago 医療過誤
maltreat gyakutai suru 虐待する
maltreatment gyakutai 虐待
mammal honyū-dōbutsu ほ乳動物
mammoth *adj* yama no yō (na) 山のよう(な)
man *n* otoko 男; (*human*) hito 人; (*humanity*) ningen 人間; (*in checkers*) koma こま
manage 1 *v/t business* keiei suru 経営する; *money* kanri suru 管理する; **~ *to*** nan to ka … suru 何とか…する **2** *v/i* (*cope*) dō ni ka kurashite iku どうにか暮していく; (*financially*) yarikuri suru やりくりする; ***can you ~?*** daijōbu desu ka 大丈夫ですか
manageable *hair* atsukai-yasui 扱いやすい; *work* dō ni ka shori suru どうにか処理できる
management keiei 経営; (*managers*) keieisha-gawa 経営者側, kanrishoku 管理職
management buyout keieijin no jishakabu kaishime 経営陣の自社株買い占め; **management consultant** keiei-konsarutanto 経営コンサルタント; **management studies** keiei-gaku 経営学; **management team** keiei-jin 経営陣
manager (*of restaurant, hotel*) shihai-nin 支配人, kanrishoku 管理職; (*of shop*) tenchō 店長
managerial keiei (no) 経営(の)
managing director senmu-torishimariyaku 専務取締役
Manchuria Manshū 満州
Mandarin Pekin-go 北京語
mandarin orange mikan みかん
mandate (*authority*) kengen 権限; (*task*) ninmu 任務

mandatory hissu (no) 必須(の)
mane (*of horse*) tategami たてがみ
maneuver 1 *n* sakusen 作戦; *fig* sakuryaku 策略 **2** *v/t* takumi ni ugokasu 巧みに動かす; *fig* takumi ni ayatsuru 巧みに操る
mangle *v/t* (*crush*) mechamecha ni suru 目茶目茶にする
manhandle *person* teara ni atsukau 手荒に扱う; *object* jinriki de ugokasu 人力で動かす
manhood (*maturity*) seinenki 成年期; (*virility*) otoko to shite no seiteki-nōryoku 男としての性的能力
man-hour jinji 人時
manhunt hannin-tsuiseki 犯人追跡
mania (*craze*) nekkyō 熱狂
maniac kyōjin 狂人
manicure *n* manikyua マニキュア
manifest 1 *adj* meihaku (na) 明白(な) **2** *v/t* akiraka ni suru 明らかにする; **~ *itself*** arawareru 表れる
manipulate *person* ayatsuru 操る; *bones* seitai-chiryō suru 整体治療する
manipulation (*of bones*) seitai 整体
manipulative hito o kōmyō ni ayatsuru yō (na) 人を巧妙に操るよう(な)
mankind jinrui 人類
manly otoko-rashii 男らしい
man-made jinkō (no) 人工(の)
manner (*of doing something*) hōhō 方法; (*attitude*) taido 態度
manners: ***good / bad ~*** yoi / warui gyōgi よい/悪い行儀; ***have no ~*** gyōgi ga warui 行儀が悪い
manpower jin'in 人員
mansion daiteitaku 大邸宅
mantelpiece, **mantelshelf** mantorupīsu マントルピース
manual 1 *adj* tesagyō (no) 手作業(の); *labor* nikutai (no) 肉体(の); *dexterity* tesaki (no) 手先(の) **2** *n* manyuaru マニュアル
manufacture 1 *n* seizō 製造 **2** *v/t* seizō suru 製造する
manufacturer seizō-gyōsha 製造業者
manufacturing (*industry*) seizōgyō 製造業
manure koyashi 肥やし
manuscript genkō 原稿
many 1 *adj* takusan (no) たくさん(の); **~ *times*** nando mo 何度も **2** *pron* tasū 多数; ***how ~ do you need?*** ikutsu hitsuyō desu ka いくつ必要ですか; ***a great ~*** totemo takusan no とてもたくさんの; ***a good ~*** kanari takusan no かなりたくさんの
map *n* chizu 地図
♦ **map out** … no keikaku o shikkari tateru …の計画をしっかり立てる
maple kaede かえで; ***Japanese ~*** momiji もみじ
mar sokonau 損なう; *event* dainashi ni suru 台無しにする
marathon (*race*) marason マラソン
marble (*material*) dairiseki 大理石
March sangatsu 三月
march 1 *n* kōshin 行進; (*protest*) demo-kōshin デモ行進 **2** *v/i* kōshin suru 行進する; (*in protest*) demo-kōshin suru デモ行進する
Mardi Gras Shanikusai no kayōbi 謝肉祭の火曜日
mare (*horse*) mesu-uma 雌馬
margarine māgarin マーガリン
margin (*of page*) yohaku 余白; (*profit ~*) rizaya 利ざや; ***by a narrow ~*** kiwadoi sa de きわどい差で
marginal (*slight*) wazuka (na) わずか(な)
marginally wazuka ni わずかに
marijuana, **marihuana** marifana マリファナ
marina marīna マリーナ
marinade *n* marine マリネ
marinate marine ni suru マリネにする
marine 1 *adj* umi (no) 海(の) **2** *n* (*soldier*) kaihei-taiin 海兵隊員
marital *problems* fūfu (no) 夫婦(の); **~ *status*** kon'in-kankei no umu 婚姻関係の有無
maritime umi (no) 海(の)
mark 1 *n* (*stain*) shimi 染み; (*sign, token*) shirushi 印; (*trace*) ato 跡; EDU tensū 点数; ***leave one's ~*** … ni

eikyō o ataeru …に影響を与える **2** *v/t* (*stain*) ato o tsukeru 跡をつける; EDU saiten suru 採点する; (*indicate*) shimesu 示す; (*commemorate*) kinen suru 記念する; **~ *time*** *fig* ashibumi-jōtai de aru 足踏み状態である **3** *v/i* (*of fabric*) shimi ga tsuku 染みがつく

♦**mark down** *goods* … o nebiki suru …を値引きする

♦**mark out** … ni sen o hiku …に線を引く; *fig* … o kubetsu suru …を区別する

♦**mark up** *price* … o neage suru …を値上げする

marked ichijirushii 著しい

marker (*highlighter*) keikō-pen 蛍光ペン

market 1 *n* ichiba 市場; (*for particular commodity*) shijō 市場; (*outlet*) hanro 販路; (*stock ~*) kabushiki-shijō 株式市場; ***on the ~*** shijō de 市場で **2** *v/t* shijō ni uri ni dasu 市場に売りに出す

market economy shijō-keizai 市場経済

market forces shijō-jissei 市場実勢

marketing māketingu マーケティング

market leader māketto līdā マーケットリーダー; **marketplace** (*in town*) ichiba 市場; (*for commodities*) shijō 市場; **market research** shijō-chōsa 市場調査; **market share** shijō-shea 市場シェア

mark-up rihaba 利幅

marmalade māmarēdo マーマレード

marquee tento テント

marriage (*institution*) kekkon 結婚; (*state of being married*) kekkon-seikatsu 結婚生活; (*wedding*) kekkonshiki 結婚式

marriage certificate kekkon-shōmeisho 結婚証明書

marriage counselor maridji-kaunserā マリッジカウンセラー

married kekkon shita 結婚した; ***be ~ to …*** … to kekkon shite iru …と結婚している

marry … to kekkon suru …と結婚する; (*of priest*) … no kekkonshiki o toriokonau …の結婚式をとり行う; ***get married*** kekkon suru 結婚する

marsh numachi 沼地

marshal *n* (*police officer*) keisatsu-shochō 警察署長

marshmallow mashumaro マシュマロ

marshy numachi (no) 沼地(の)

martial arts bujutsu 武術

martial law kaigenrei 戒厳令

martyr *n* REL junkyō-sha 殉教者; *fig* gisei-sha 犠牲者

martyred kunō shita 苦悩した

marvel 1 *n* (*person*) odorokubeki hito 驚くべき人 **2** *v/i*: **~ *at*** … ni odoroku …に驚く

marvelous subarashii すばらしい

Marxism Marukusu-shugi マルクス主義

Marxist 1 *adj* Marukusu-shugi (no) マルクス主義(の) **2** *n* Marukusu-shugi-sha マルクス主義者

mascara masukara マスカラ

mascot masukotto マスコット

masculine *pride* dansei (no) 男性(の); *appearance* danseiteki (na) 男性的(な)

masculinity otoko-rashisa 男らしさ; (*virility*) otoko to shite no seiteki-nōryoku 男としての性的能力

mash *v/t* tsubusu つぶす

mashed potatoes masshupoteto マッシュポテト

mask 1 *n* masuku マスク **2** *v/t* *feelings* kakusu 隠す

masochism mazohizumu マゾヒズム

masochist mazohisuto マゾヒスト

masquerade 1 *n fig* misekake みせかけ **2** *v/i*: **~ *as*** … no furi o suru …のふりをする

mass[1] **1** *n* (*great amount*) tairyō 大量; (*body*) katamari かたまり; ***a ~ of*** tairyō no … 大量の…; ***be a ~ of*** (*be covered in*) … de ippai de aru …でいっぱいである; ***~es of*** tasū no … 多数の… **2** *v/i* hitokatamari ni naru ひとかたまりになる

mass[2] REL misa ミサ
massacre 1 *n* daigyakusatsu 大虐殺; F boromake ボロ負け **2** *v/t* gyakusatsu suru 虐殺する; F (*in sport*) kotenpan ni yattsukeru こてんぱんにやっつける
massage 1 *n* massāji マッサージ **2** *v/t* massāji suru マッサージする; *statistics* sōsa suru 操作する
masseur massāji-shi マッサージ師
masseuse massāji-shi マッサージ師
massive *effort, increase* taihen (na) 大変(な); *building* dosshiri shita どっしりした
mass media masumedia マスメディア; **mass-produce** tairyō-seisan suru 大量生産する; **mass production** tairyō-seisan 大量生産
mast masuto マスト; RAD tettō 鉄塔
master 1 *n* (*of dog*) shujin 主人; (*of ship*) senchō 船長; ***be a ~ of*** ... no tatsujin de aru ...の達人である **2** *v/t skill, language* shūtoku suru 習得する; *situation* kokufuku suru 克服する
master bedroom mein-beddorūmu メインベッドルーム
master key masutā-kī マスターキー
masterly migoto (na) みごと(な)
mastermind 1 *n* kuromaku 黒幕 **2** *v/t* menmitsu ni keikaku o tateru 綿密に計画をたてる; *crime* kage de ito o hiku 陰で糸を引く; **Master of Arts** bungaku-shūshigō 文学修士号; **master of ceremonies** shikai-sha 司会者; **masterpiece** kessaku 傑作; **master's** (**degree**) shūshigō 修士号
mastery jukutatsu 熟達
masturbate masutābēshon o suru マスターベーションをする
mat *n* matto マット
match[1] (*for cigarette*) matchi マッチ
match[2] **1** *n* (*competition*) shiai 試合; (*marriage*) kekkon 結婚; ***be no ~ for*** totemo ... ni wa oyobanai とても...にはおよばない; ***meet one's ~*** kyōteki ni deau 強敵に出会う **2** *v/t* (*be the same as*) ... to chōwa suru ...と調和する; (*equal*) ... to dōtō de aru ...と同等である **3** *v/i* (*of colors, patterns*) chōwa suru 調和する
matchbox matchibako マッチ箱
matching osoroi (no) おそろい(の)
mate 1 *n* (*of animal*) tsugai no aite つがいの相手; NAUT kōkaishi 航海士 **2** *v/i* tsugai ni naru つがいになる
material 1 *n* (*fabric*) kiji 生地; (*substance*) busshitsu 物質 **2** *adj* busshitsuteki (na) 物質的(な)
materialism busshitsu-shugi 物質主義
materialist busshitsu-shugisha 物質主義者
materialistic busshitsu-shugiteki (na) 物質主義的(な)
materialize shutsugen suru 出現する
materials (*for specific activity*) yōgu 用具
maternal boseiteki (na) 母性的(な); *grandmother* hahakata (no) 母方(の)
maternity bosei 母性
maternity dress matanitī-wea マタニティーウェア; **maternity leave** sankyū 産休; **maternity ward** sanka-byōtō 産科病棟
math sūgaku 数学
mathematical *calculations* sūgaku (no) 数学(の); *mind* sūgakuteki (na) 数学的(な)
mathematician sūgaku-sha 数学者
mathematics sūgaku 数学
matinée machine マチネ
matriarch onnakachō 女家長
matrimony kekkon 結婚
matt tsuyakeshi (no) つや消し(の)
matter (*affair*) mondai 問題; PHYS busshitsu 物質; ***as a ~ of course*** tōzen no koto to shite 当然のこととして; ***as a ~ of fact*** jitsu o iu to 実を言うと; ***it's just a ~ of time*** tan ni jikan no mondai da 単に時間の問題だ; ***what's the ~*** (***with you***)***?*** dō shita no どうしたの; ***you're making ~s worse*** anata wa jijō o akka sasete iru あなたは事情を悪化させている; ***no ~ what***

she says kanojo ga nan to iō tomo 彼女が何と言おうとも **2** *v/i* jūyō de aru 重要である; ***it doesn't ~*** taishita koto de wa nai たいしたことではない

matter-of-fact jimuteki (na) 事務的(な)

mattress mattoresu マットレス

mature **1** *adj* (*grown-up*) seijuku shita 成熟した **2** *v/i* (*of person*) seijuku suru 成熟する; FIN manki ni naru 満期になる

maturity (*adulthood*) seijuku-ki 成熟期; (*in behavior*) seijuku 成熟; FIN manki 満期

maximize saidai ni suru 最大にする

maximum **1** *adj size, effort* saidai (no) 最大(の); *speed, salary* saikō (no) 最高(の) **2** *n* saidaigen 最大限; ***a ~ of …*** saidai … no 最大…の

May gogatsu 五月

may ◊ (*possibility*) … ka mo shirenai …かもしれない; ***he ~ have decided*** kare wa kesshin shita ka mo shirenai 彼は決心したかもしれない ◊ (*permission*) … shite mo ii …してもいい; ***~ I …?*** …shite mo ii desu ka …してもいいですか; ***you ~ as well*** …shite mo ii …してもいい

maybe tabun たぶん; ***you could ~ try…*** … o moshikashitara tameseru kamo …をもしかしたら試せるかも

May Day Mēdē メーデー

mayo, **mayonnaise** mayonēzu マヨネーズ

mayor shichō 市長

maze meiro 迷路

MB (= ***megabyte***) megabaito メガバイト

MBA (= ***Master in Business Administration***) keieigaku-shūshigō 経営学修士号

MBO (= ***management buyout***) keieijin no jishakabu kaishime 経営陣の自社株買い占め

MD (= ***Doctor of Medicine***) igaku-hakushigō 医学博士号

me watashi 私; ***with ~*** watashi to 私と; ***who?, ~?*** dare – watashi desu 誰ー私です ◊ (*direct object*) watashi o 私を; ***he doesn't know ~*** kare wa watashi o shiranai 彼は私を知らない ◊ (*indirect object*) watashi ni 私に; ***can you mail it to ~?*** watashi ni okutte moraemasu ka 私に送ってもらえますか

meadow bokusōchi 牧草地

meager wazuka (na) わずか(な)

meal shokuji 食事

meal ticket F kanezuru 金づる

mealtime shokuji-jikan 食事時間

mean[1] (*with money*) kechi (na) けち(な); (*nasty*) iji no warui 意地の悪い

mean[2] **1** *v/t* (*intend*) tsumori de aru つもりである; (*signify*) imi suru 意味する; ***~ to do X*** X suru tsumori de aru Xするつもりである; ***I really ~ it*** hontō ni sono tsumori de itte iru 本当にそのつもりで言っている; ***be ~t for*** (*be intended for*) … muke de aru …向けである; (*of remark*) … ni muketa mono de aru …に向けたものである; ***he ~s nothing to me*** kare nante watashi ni wa dōdemo yoi 彼なんて私にはどうでもよい **2** *v/i*: ***~ well*** yokare to omotte suru よかれと思ってする

meaning (*of word*) imi 意味

meaningful (*comprehensible*) imi o nasu 意味を成す; (*constructive*) igi no aru 意義のある; *glance* imiarige (na) 意味ありげ(な)

meaningless muimi (na) 無意味(な)

means (*financial*) zaisan 財産; (*way*) hōhō 方法; ***~ of transportation*** kōtsū-kikan 交通機関; ***by all ~*** (*certainly*) zehi dōzo ぜひどうぞ; ***by no ~*** kesshite … de nai 決して…でない; ***by ~ of*** … ni yotte …によって

meanwhile sono aida ni その間に

measles hashika はしか

measure **1** *n* (*step*) taisaku 対策; (*amount*) teido 程度 **2** *v/t* hakaru 測る **3** *v/i* aru ある

♦ **measure out** … o hakaritoru …を測りとる

♦ **measure up to** … ni kanau …にかなう

measurement sunpō 寸法; (*action*) sokutei 測定
meat niku 肉
meatball mītobōru ミートボール
meatloaf mītorōfu ミートローフ
mechanic (*for cars*) jidōsha-shūrikō 自動車修理工
mechanical *device* kikai (no) 機械(の); *gesture* kikaiteki (na) 機械的(な)
mechanically *fig* kikaiteki ni 機械的に
mechanism (*device*) kikai 機械; (*workings*) kōzō 構造
mechanize kikaika suru 機械化する
medal medaru メダル
medallion (*medal*) ōgata-medaru 大型メダル
medalist medarisuto メダリスト
meddle (*interfere*) kanshō suru 干渉する; (*tinker*) ijikuru いじくる
media ***the ~*** masukomi マスコミ
median strip chūō-bunritai 中央分離帯
mediate chōtei suru 調停する
mediation chōtei 調停
mediator chōtei-sha 調停者
medical 1 *adj college, student* igaku (no) 医学(の); *insurance* iryō (no) 医療(の); ***~ history*** byōreki 病歴; ***~ treatment*** iryō 医療 **2** *n* kenkō-shindan 健康診断
medical certificate kenkō-shindansho 健康診断書
Medicare *rōreisha-shinshōsha tō no iryō-hoken-seido* 老齢者身障者等の医療保険制度
medicated yakuyō (no) 薬用(の)
medication kusuri 薬
medicinal yakuyō (no) 薬用(の)
medicine kusuri 薬; (*science*) igaku 医学
medieval chūsei (no) 中世(の)
mediocre heibon (na) 平凡(な)
mediocrity (*of work etc*) heibon 平凡; (*person*) bonjin 凡人
meditate jukkō suru 熟考する; (*in yoga*) meisō suru めい想する
meditation (*thought*) jukkō 熟考; (*relaxation*) meisō めい想; ***seated ~*** zazen 坐禅
medium 1 *adj* chūgurai (no) 中位(の); *steak* midiamu (no) ミディアム(の) **2** *n* (*in size*) emu-saizu エムサイズ; (*means*) baitai 媒体; (*spiritualist*) reibai 霊媒; ***through the ~ of*** … o tōshite …を通して
medium-sized chūgurai no ōki-sa (no) 中位の大きさ(の)
medium wave chūha 中波
medley yoseatsume 寄せ集め; (*race, of songs*) medorē メドレー
meek otonashii おとなしい
meekly otonashiku おとなしく
meet 1 *v/t* … ni au …に会う; (*encounter*) … ni deau …に出会う; (*at airport etc*) demukaeru 出迎える; (*in competition*) … to taisen suru …と対戦する; (*of eyes*) … to au …と合う; (*satisfy*: *need*) mitasu 満たす; *deadline* mamoru 守る; *payment* shiharau 支払う; *standard* … ni tassuru …に達する **2** *v/i* au 会う; (*get to know each other*) shiriau 知り合う; (*in competition*) taisen suru 対戦する; (*of eyes*) au 合う; (*of committee*) kaigō suru 会合する **3** *n* kyōgikai 競技会
♦ **meet with** *person* … to kaiken suru …と会見する; *opposition, approval etc* … ni au …にあう
meeting (*unplanned*) deai 出会い; (*in business*) kaigi 会議; (*of committee*) kaigō 会合
megabyte megabaito メガバイト
Meiji Restoration Meijiishin 明治維新
melancholy yūutsu 憂うつ
mellow 1 *adj* yawaraka (na) 柔らか(な) **2** *v/i* (*of person*) maruku naru 円くなる
melodious ongakuteki (na) 音楽的(な)
melodramatic ōgesa (na) おおげさ(な)
melody merodī メロディー
melon meron メロン
melt 1 *v/i* tokeru 溶ける **2** *v/t* tokasu 溶かす
♦ **melt away** *fig* kiete nakunaru 消えてなくなる

♦**melt down** … o tokasu …を溶かす
melting pot rutsubo るつぼ
member ichiin 一員; (*of organization*) menbā メンバー; ***Member of Congress*** Kokkai-giin 国会議員
membership kaiin-shikaku 会員資格; (*of UN etc*) kaiin no chii 会員の地位; (*members*) kaiinsū 会員数
membrane maku 膜
memento kinenhin 記念品
memo memo メモ
memoirs kaikoroku 回顧録
memorable wasurerarenai 忘れられない
memorial 1 *adj concert* kinen (no) 記念(の); *service* tsuitō (no) 追悼(の) **2** *n* kinenhi 記念碑
Memorial Day Senbotusha-tsuitō-kinenbi 戦没者追悼記念日
memorize anki suru 暗記する
memory kioku 記憶; (*of vacation, childhood*) omoide 思い出; (*power of recollection*) kiokuryoku 記憶力; COMPUT memorī メモリー; ***have a good / bad ~*** kiokuryoku ga yoi / warui 記憶力がよい/悪い; ***in ~ of*** … o kinen shite …を記念して; (*on gravestone*) … o shinonde …をしのんで
menace 1 *n* (*threat*) kyōi 脅威; (*pest*) yakkai mono やっかい者 **2** *v/t* (*of person*) odosu 脅す; (*of flood etc*) obiyakasu 脅かす
menacing odosu yō (na) 脅すよう(な)
mend 1 *v/t* shūri suru 修理する **2** *n*: ***be on the ~*** kaifuku ni mukatte iru 回復に向かっている
menial *adj* tanjun (na) 単純(な)
meningitis nōmakuen 脳膜炎
menopause kōnenki 更年期
men's room danseiyō toire 男性用トイレ
menstruate seiri ga aru 生理がある
menstruation seiri 生理
mental *health, suffering* seishin (no) 精神(の); *ability* chinō (no) 知能(の); F (*crazy*) ki no kurutte iru 気の狂っている
mental arithmetic anzan 暗算; **mental cruelty** seishinteki-gyakutai 精神的虐待; **mental hospital** seishin-byōin 精神病院; **mental illness** seishinbyō 精神病
mentality (*intellect*) chisei 知性; (*mindset*) kangaekata 考え方
mentally kokoro no naka de 心の中で; *calculate etc* atama no naka de 頭の中で
mentally handicapped chiteki-shōgai no aru 知的障害のある
mentally ill seishinbyō (no) 精神病(の)
mention 1 *n*: ***he made no ~ of it*** kare wa sono koto wa nani mo iwanakatta 彼はそのことは何も言わなかった **2** *v/t* … no koto o hanasu …のことを話す; ***don't ~ it*** dō itashimashite どういたしまして
mentor *n* shidō-sha 指導者
menu *also* COMPUT menyū メニュー
mercenary 1 *adj* yokutokuzuku (no) 欲得ずく(の) **2** *n* MIL yōhei よう兵
merchandise shōhin 商品
merchandising shōhinka 商品化
merchant shōten-shu 商店主
merciful jihibukai 慈悲深い
mercifully kōun na koto ni 幸運なことに
merciless mujihi (na) 無慈悲(な)
mercury suigin 水銀
mercy jihi 慈悲; ***be at X's ~*** X no nasu ga mama de aru Xのなすがままである
mere hon no ほんの
merely tan ni … dake たんに…だけ
merge *v/i* (*of companies*) gappei suru 合併する
merger gappei 合併
merit 1 *n* (*worth*) kachi 価値; (*advantage*) chōsho 長所 **2** *v/t* … ni atai suru …に値する
merriment yōki na sawagi 陽気な騒ぎ
merry yōki (na) 陽気(な); ***Merry Christmas!*** Merī-Kurisumasu メリークリスマス
merry-go-round merīgōraundo メリーゴーラウンド

mesh *n* amime 網目
mesmerize … no me o ubau …の目を奪う
mess: ***who made this ~?*** konna ni chirakashita no wa dare desu ka こんなに散らかしたのはだれですか; ***I'm in a bit of a ~*** (*trouble*) komatta koto ni natta 困ったことになった; ***be a ~*** (*of room, desk*) chirakatte iru 散らかっている; (*of situation*) hidoku yakkai na koto ni natte iru ひどくやっかいなことになっている
♦**mess around** burabura suru ぶらぶらする
♦**mess around with** … o ijikurimawasu …をいじくり回す
♦**mess up** *room, papers* … o torichirakasu …を取り散らかす; *plans* … o dainashi ni suru …を台なしにする
♦**mess with** (*use*) … ni te o dasu …に手を出す; (*get involved with*) … ni kakawaru …にかかわる; (*upset, offend*) … ni chokkai o dasu …にちょっかいを出す
message messēji メッセージ, dengon 伝言; (*of movie, book*) nerai ねらい
messenger (*courier*) kyūsōbin 急送便; (*biker*) baiku-bin バイク便
messy *room* torichirakashita 取り散らかした; *person* darashi no nai だらしのない; *eater* tabechirakasu 食べ散らかす; *job* te no yogoreru 手の汚れる; *divorce etc* yakkai (na) やっかい(な)
metabolism shinchin-taisha 新陳代謝
metal 1 *n* kinzoku 金属 **2** *adj* kinzoku (no) 金属(の)
metallic *paint* kinzoku (no) 金属(の); *sound, taste* kinzokuteki (na) 金属的(な)
meteor ryūsei 流星
meteoric *fig* ryūsei no yō (na) 流星のよう(な)
meteorite inseki いん石
meteorological kishō (no) 気象(の)
meteorologist kishō-gakusha 気象学者
meteorology kishō-gaku 気象学
meter[1] (*for measuring*) mētā メーター; (*parking ~*) pākingu-mētā パーキングメーター
meter[2] (*length*) mētoru メートル
method hōhō 方法
methodical *search* soshikiteki (na) 組織的(な); *person* kichōmen (na) きちょうめん(な)
methodically soshikiteki ni 組織的に
meticulous *person* kichōmen (na) きちょうめん(な); *work, planning* genmitsu (na) 厳密(な)
meticulously kichōmen ni きちょうめんに
metric mētoruhō (no) メートル法(の)
metropolis daitoshi 大都市
metropolitan *adj* daitoshi (no) 大都市(の)
mew → ***miaow***
Mexican 1 *adj* Mekishiko (no) メキシコ(の) **2** *n* Mekishiko-jin メキシコ人
Mexico Mekishiko メキシコ
mezzanine (floor) chūnikai 中二階
miaow 1 *n* nyā にゃあ **2** *v/i* nyā to naku にゃあと鳴く
mickey mouse *adj pej* F *course, qualification* kudaranai くだらない
microchip maikurochippu マイクロチップ; **microcomputer** maikon マイコン; **microcosm** shōuchū 小宇宙; **microfilm** maikurofirumu マイクロフィルム; **microphone** maiku マイク; **microprocessor** maikuropurosessā マイクロプロセッサー; **microscope** kenbikyō 顕微鏡; **microscopic** bishō (no) 微小(の); **microwave** denshi-renji 電子レンジ
midair: ***in ~*** kūchū de 空中で
midday shōgo 正午
middle 1 *adj* mannaka (no) 真ん中(の) **2** *n* (*of room, garden*) mannaka 真ん中; (*of week, month*) nakaba 半ば; (*of meeting*) saichū 最中; ***in the ~ of*** (*of floor, room*) … no mannaka ni …の真ん中に; (*period of time*) … no nakagoro ni

…の中ごろに; ***be in the ~ of doing X*** X o shite iru saichū de aru Xをしている最中である
middle-aged chūnen (no) 中年(の); **the Middle Ages** Chūsei 中世; **middle-class** chūryū-kaikyū (no) 中流階級(の); **middle class(es)** chūryū-kaikyū 中流階級; **Middle East** Chūtō 中東; **middle man** nakagainin 仲買人; **middle name** midoru-nēmu ミドルネーム; **middle weight** *n* (*boxer*) midoru-kyū-senshu ミドル級選手
middling chūgurai (no) 中位(の)
midget *adj* gokushōgata (no) 極小型(の)
midnight gozen reiji 午前零時, mayonaka 真夜中; ***at ~*** mayonaka ni 真夜中に; **midsummer** manatsu 真夏; **midway** chūto ni 中途に; **midweek** *adv* shū no nakaba ni 週の半ばに; **Midwest** Chūseibu 中西部; **midwife** josanpu 助産婦; **midwinter** mafuyu 真冬
might[1] … ka mo shirenai …かもしれない; ***I ~ be late*** okureru ka mo shirenai 遅れるかもしれない; ***you ~ have told me!*** itte kuretara yokatta no ni 言ってくれたらよかったのに; ***you ~ as well spend the night*** hitoban tomaru hō ga ii darō 一晩泊まるほうがいいだろう
might[2] *n* chikara 力
mighty 1 *adj* kyōryoku (na) 強力(な) **2** *adv* F (*very*) sugoku すごく
migraine henzutsū 偏頭痛
migrant worker kisetsu-rōdōsha 季節労働者
migrate (*of people*) ijū suru 移住する; (*of bird*) idō suru 移動する
migration idō 移動
mike maiku マイク
mild *weather* odayaka (na) 穏やか(な); *person, voice* otonashii おとなしい; (*not spicy*) amakuchi (no) 甘口(の)
mildly (*slightly*) shōshō 少々; *say* odayaka ni 穏やかに
mildew shirokabi しろかび
mildness (*of weather, person, voice*) odayaka-sa 穏やかさ
mile mairu マイル
mileage sōkō-kyori 走行距離
milestone *fig* kakkiteki-jiken 画期的事件
militant 1 *adj* tōsōteki (na) 闘争的(な) **2** *n* tōshi 闘士
military 1 *adj* guntai (no) 軍隊(の); *spending, intervention* gunji (no) 軍事(の) **2** *n*: ***the ~*** guntai 軍隊
military academy rikugun-shikan-gakkō 陸軍士官学校
militia giyūgun 義勇軍
milk 1 *n* (*of cow*) gyūnyū 牛乳; (*of woman*) bonyū 母乳; (*of other animal*) chichi 乳 **2** *v/t* … no chichi o shiboru …の乳をしぼる
milk chocolate miruku-chokorēto ミルクチョコレート
milk shake sheiku シェイク
mill *n* (*for grain*) seifun-kōjō 製粉工場; (*for textiles*) bōseki-kōjō 紡績工場
♦**mill around** urouro suru うろうろする
millennium sennenkan 千年間
milligram miriguramu ミリグラム
millimeter mirimētā ミリメーター
million hyakuman 百万; ***hundred ~*** oku 億
millionaire hyakuman-chōja 百万長者
millstone *fig* omoni 重荷
mime *v/t* miburi de maneru 身ぶりでまねる
mimic 1 *n* monomane no umai hito 物まねのうまい人 **2** *v/t* … no monomane o suru …の物まねをする
mince *v/t* komakaku kizamu 細かく刻む
mincemeat minsumīto ミンスミート
mince pie minsupai ミンスパイ
mind 1 *n* (*intellect*) chisei 知性; (*sanity*) risei 理性; ***be out of one's ~*** ki ga kuruu 気が狂う; ***keep in ~*** … o oboete oku …を覚えておく; ***I've a good ~ to …*** … suru ki ga aru …する気がある; ***change one's ~*** kangae o kaeru 考えを変える; ***do you have something in ~?*** nani ka kangae ga aru no 何か考えがある

の; ***it didn't enter my ~*** sore wa omoitsukanakatta それは思いつかなかった; ***body and ~*** kokoro to karada 心と体; ***give … a piece of one's ~*** … ni hakkiri iu …にはっきり言う; ***make up one's ~*** kesshin suru 決心する; ***have something on one's ~*** nani ka o ki ni shite iru 何かを気にしている; ***keep one's ~ on*** … ni sennen suru …に専念する **2** *v/t* (*care*) ki ni suru 気にする; (*object to*) kamau かまう; (*look after*) … no sewa o suru …の世話をする; (*heed*) … no iu koto o kiku …の言うことを聞く; ***do you ~ if I smoke?*** tabako o sutte mo kamaimasen ka たばこを吸ってもかまいませんか; ***would you ~ opening the window?*** mado o akete itadakemasen ka 窓を開けていただけませんか; ***~ the step!*** ashimoto ni ki o tsukete 足元に気をつけて; ***~ your own business!*** ōki na osewa da 大きなお世話だ; ***~ you, …*** demo ne, … でもね、… **3** *v/i*: ***~!*** ki o tsukete 気をつけて; ***never ~!*** ki ni shinai 気にしない; ***I don't ~*** dotchi demo ii desu どっちでもいいです

mindful : ***be ~ of*** … o ki ni suru …を気にする

mindless *violence* oroka (na) 愚か(な)

mine[1] *pron* watashi no mono 私のもの; ***a friend of ~*** watashi no tomodachi 私の友達

mine[2] **1** *n* (*coal ~ etc*) kōzan 鉱山 **2** *v/i*: ***~ for*** … o saikutsu suru …を採掘する

mine[3] **1** *n* (*explosive*) jirai 地雷 **2** *v/t* … ni jirai o shikakeru …に地雷をしかける

minefield *also fig* jiraigen 地雷原

miner kōfu 坑夫

mineral kōbutsu 鉱物

mineral water mineraru-wōtā ミネラルウォーター

mingle *v/i* (*of sounds*) mazaru 混ざる; (*at party*) mazaru 交ざる

mini → ***miniskirt***

minibus maikurobasu マイクロバス

miniature *adj* kogata (no) 小型(の)

minimal saishōgen (no) 最小限(の); *cost* saiteigen (no) 最低限(の)

minimize saishō ni suru 最小にする; *cost* saitei ni suru 最低にする; (*downplay*) chiisaku miseru 小さく見せる

minimum **1** *adj* saitei (no) 最低(の) **2** *n*: ***a ~ of 10 people*** saitei jū nin 最低十人

minimum wage saitei-chingin 最低賃金

mining kōgyō 鉱業

miniskirt minisukāto ミニスカート

minister POL daijin 大臣; REL bokushi 牧師

ministerial POL daijin (no) 大臣(の)

ministry POL shō 省

mink (*fur*) minku ミンク; (*coat*) minku no kōto ミンクのコート

minor **1** *adj* chiisa (na) 小さ(な); *pain, operation* karui 軽い; ***D ~*** ni tanchō ニ短調 **2** *n* miseinen-sha 未成年者

minority shōsū 少数; ***be in the ~*** shōsūha de aru 少数派である

mint *n* (*herb*) minto ミント; (*chocolate*) minto-chokorēto ミントチョコレート; (*hard candy*) minto-kyandī ミントキャンディー

minus **1** *n* mainasu マイナス **2** *prep* (*without*) … nashi ni …なしに; ***42 ~ 18 is 24*** yonjūni hiku jūhachi wa nijūyon 42引く18は24; ***~ 10*** (*temperature*) reika jūdo 零下10度

minuscule hijō ni chiisai 非常に小さい

minute[1] *n* (*of time*) fun 分; ***in a ~*** sugu すぐ; ***just a ~*** chotto matte ちょっと待って; ***do you have a ~?*** chotto ii desu ka ちょっといいですか

minute[2] *adj* (*tiny*) kiwamete chiisai きわめて小さい; (*detailed*) shōsai (na) 詳細(な); ***in ~ detail*** shōsai ni 詳細に

minutes (*of meeting*) gijiroku 議事録

miracle kiseki 奇跡

miraculous kisekiteki (na) 奇跡的(な)

miraculously kisekiteki ni 奇跡的に
mirage shinkirō しん気楼
mirror 1 *n* kagami 鏡; MOT bakkumirā バックミラー **2** *v/t* utsusu 映す
misanthropist tsukiai no warui hito つき合いの悪い人
misapprehension: ***be under a ~*** gokai o shite iru 誤解をしている
misappropriate ōryō suru 横領する
misappropriation ōryō 横領
misbehave busahō ni furumau 不作法にふるまう
misbehavior busahō 不作法
miscalculate 1 *v/t* … no handan o ayamaru …の判断を誤る **2** *v/i* keisanchigai o suru 計算違いをする
miscalculation (*misjudgment*) gosan 誤算; (*in sums*) keisanmachigai 計算まちがい
miscarriage MED ryūzan 流産; ***~ of justice*** goshin 誤審
miscarry (*of plan*) zasetsu suru ざ折する
miscellaneous zatta (na) 雑多(な)
mischief (*naughtiness*) itazura いたずら
mischievous itazura (na) いたずら(な); (*malicious*) akui no aru 悪意のある
misconceived fubi (na) 不備(な)
misconception gokai 誤解
misconduct shokken-ran'yō 職権乱用
misconstrue gokai suru 誤解する
misdemeanor bizai 微罪
miser kechi けち
miserable (*unhappy*) mijime (na) みじめ(な); *life* aware (na) 哀れ(な); *weather* iya (na) いや(な); *news* itamashii 痛ましい
miserly wazuka (na) わずか(な); *person* kechi (na) けち(な)
misery (*wretchedness*) hisan-sa 悲惨さ; (*unhappiness*) mijime-sa みじめさ
misfire (*of scheme*) shippai suru 失敗する
misfit (*in society*) tekiō shinai hito 適応しない人
misfortune fuun 不運
misgiving fuan 不安
mishandle … no toriatsukai o ayamaru …の取り扱いを誤る
mishap jiko 事故
misinterpret gokai suru 誤解する
misinterpretation gokai 誤解
misjudge … no handan o ayamaru …の判断を誤る
mislay okiwasureru 置き忘れる
mislead … no gokai o maneku …の誤解を招く
misleading magirawashii 紛らわしい
mismanage *situation* … no shochi o shisokonau …の処置をしそこなう; *economy* … no kanri o shisokonau …の管理をしそこなう; *company* … no keiei ni shippai suru …の経営に失敗する
mismanagement (*of situation*) ayamatta shochi 誤った処置; (*of economy*) ayamatta kanri 誤った管理; (*of company*) ayamatta keiei 誤った経営
miso soup misoshiru 味噌汁
misplaced kentōhazure (na) 見当はずれ(な)
misprint *n* goshoku 誤植
mispronounce hatsuon o machigaeru 発音を間違える
misread *word, figures* yomichigaeru 読み違える; *situation* gokai suru 誤解する
misrepresent ayamatte tsutaeru 誤って伝える
miss[1]: ***Miss Smith*** Sumisu-san スミスさん
miss[2] **1** *n*: ***give X a ~*** X o yamete oku Xをやめておく **2** *v/t* (*not hit*) hazusu はずす; (*not meet*) … to ikichigau …と行き違う; (*emotionally: person*) … ga inaku natte sabishiku omou …がいなくなって寂しく思う; (*emotionally: place*) … ga natsukashii …がなつかしい; *bus, train, plane* … ni norisokonau …に乗りそこなう; (*not notice*) miotosu 見落とす; (*not be present at*) kesseki suru 欠席する **3** *v/i* hazusu はずす

♦**miss out on** *opportunity* … o nogasu …を逃す
misshapen bukakkō (na) 不格好(な)
missile misairu ミサイル; (*sth thrown*) tobidōgu 飛び道具
missing yukue-fumei (no) 行方不明(の); ***be*** ~ yukue-fumei de aru 行方不明である
mission (*task*) ninmu 任務; (*people*) shisetsudan 使節団
misspell … no tsuzuri o machigaeru …のつづりを間違える
mist kiri 霧
♦**mist over** (*of eyes*) kasumu かすむ
♦**mist up** (*of mirror*) kumoru 曇る
mistake 1 *n* machigai 間違い; ***make a*** ~ machigau 間違う; ***by*** ~ machigaete 間違えて **2** *v/t*: ~ ***X for Y*** X o Y to machigaeru XをYと間違える
mistaken: ***be*** ~ gokai shite iru 誤解している
mistress (*lover*) aijin 愛人; (*of servant*) onnashujin 女主人; (*of dog*) kainushi 飼い主
mistrust 1 *n* fushinkan 不信感 **2** *v/t* shin'yō shinai 信用しない
misty *weather* kiri no kakatta 霧のかかった; *eyes* kasunda かすんだ; *color* bon'yari shita ぼんやりした
misunderstand gokai suru 誤解する
misunderstanding (*mistake*) gokai 誤解; (*argument*) izakoza いざこざ
misuse 1 *n* goyō 誤用; (*dishonest*) akuyō 悪用 **2** *v/t* goyō suru 誤用する; (*dishonestly*) akuyō suru 悪用する
mitigating circumstances jōjō-shakuryō 情状酌量
mitt (*in baseball*) mitto ミット
mitten miton ミトン
mix 1 *n* kongō 混合; (*in cooking*) mazeawaseta mono 混ぜ合わせたもの; ***a*** ~ ***of people*** iroiro na hitotachi no mazatta gurūpu いろいろな人たちの混ざったグループ; ***pancake*** ~ (*ready to use*) pankēki-mikkusu パンケーキミックス **2** *v/t* mazeru 混ぜる **3** *v/i* (*socially*) tsukiau 付き合う
♦**mix up** … o gochamaze ni suru …をごちゃ混ぜにする; ***mix X up with Y*** X o Y to torichigaeru XをYと取り違える; ***be mixed up*** (*of person*) konran shite iru 混乱している; ***be mixed up in*** … to kankei ga aru …と関係がある; ***get mixed up with*** … to kakawariai ni naru …とかかわり合いになる
♦**mix with** (*associate with*) … to tsukiau …と付き合う
mixed *feelings* fukuzatsu (na) 複雑(な); *reviews* sanpi-ryōron (no) 賛否両論(の); *nuts* mikkusu shita ミックスした; (*racially*) kotonaru jinshu no mazatta 異なる人種の混ざった; (*religiously*) kotonaru shūkyō no mazatta 異なる宗教の混ざった
mixer (*for food*) mikisā ミキサー; (*drink*) *sōda nado kakuteru o tsukuru no ni hitsuyō na mono* ソーダなどカクテルをつくるのに必要なもの; ***she's a good*** ~ kanojo wa hitozukiai ga yoi 彼女は人付き合いがよい
mixture (*in cooking*) mazeawaseta mono 混ぜ合わせたもの; (*medicine*) kongōyaku 混合薬; ***a*** ~ ***of relief and anger*** ando to ikari no mazatta kimochi 安どと怒りの混ざった気持ち
mix-up techigai 手違い
moan 1 *n* (*of pain*) umeki うめき; (*complaint*) monku 文句 **2** *v/i* (*in pain*) umeku うめく; (*complain*) butsukusa iu ぶつくさ言う
mob 1 *n* gunshū 群衆; (*violent*) bōto 暴徒 **2** *v/t* muragaru 群がる
mobile 1 *adj person* ugoku koto no dekiru 動くことのできる **2** *n* (*for decoration*) mobīru モビール
mobile home torērāhausu トレーラーハウス
mobile phone *Br* keitai-denwa 携帯電話
mobility kadōsei 可動性
mobster gyangu ギャング; (*Japanese*) bōryokudan'in 暴力団員

mock 1 *adj surprise* misekake (no) みせかけ(の); *exams, election* mogi (no) 模擬(の) **2** *v/t* baka ni suru ばかにする; (*by mimicking*) … no mane o suru …のまねをする
mockery azakeri あざけり; (*travesty*) warai mono 笑いもの
mock-up mokei 模型
mode (*form*) yōshiki 様式; COMPUT mōdo モード
model 1 *adj employee, husband* risōteki (na) 理想的(な); *boat, plane* mokei (no) 模型(の) **2** *n* (*miniature*) mokei 模型; (*fashion* ~) fasshon-moderu ファッションモデル; ***male ~*** dansei-moderu 男性モデル **3** *v/t* … no moderu ni naru …のモデルになる **4** *v/i* (*for artist, photographer*) moderu ni naru モデルになる
modem modemu モデム
moderate 1 *adj heat, cold* hodoyoi ほどよい; *wealth, success, salary* mā mā (no) まあまあ(の); *exercise* tekido (no) 適度(の); *price* tegoro (na) 手ごろ(な); POL onken (na) 穏健(な) **2** *n* POL onkenha 穏健派 **3** *v/t* yawarageru やわらげる **4** *v/i* yawaragu やわらぐ
moderately tekido ni 適度に
moderation (*restraint*) setsudo 節度; ***in ~*** hodohodo ni ほどほどに
modern *history, medicine* gendai (no) 現代(の); *way of thinking* gendaiteki (na) 現代的(な), kindaiteki (na) 近代的(な)
modernization kindaika 近代化
modernize kindaika suru 近代化する
modest *house* sasayaka (na) ささやか(な); *amount, rate, improvement* tekido (na) 適度(な); *request* hikaeme (na) 控えめ(な); *clothes, role* jimi (na) 地味(な); (*not conceited*) kenkyo (na) 謙虚(な)
modesty (*of house*) shisso-sa 質素さ; (*of wage, improvement*) osomatsu-sa お粗末さ; (*lack of conceit*) kenkyo 謙虚
modification (*to machine*) kaizō 改造; (*to proposal*) shūsei 修正; (*to system*) kaisei 改正
modify *machine* kaizō suru 改造する; *proposal* shūsei suru 修正する; *system* kaisei suru 改正する
modular *furniture* yunitto-shiki (no) ユニット式(の)
module yunitto ユニット; ***space ~*** uchū-sen 宇宙船
moist shimetta 湿った
moisten shimeraseru 湿らせる
moisture shimerike 湿り気; (*in air*) shikke 湿気
moisturizer moisucharaizā モイスチャライザー
molar okuba 奥歯
molasses tōmitsu 糖蜜
mold[1] *n* (*on food*) kabi かび
mold[2] 1 *n* igata 鋳型 **2** *v/t clay etc* katadoru かたどる; *character* keisei suru 形成する
moldy *food* kabi no haeta かびのはえた
mole (*on skin*) hokuro ほくろ
molecular bunshi (no) 分子(の)
molecule bunshi 分子
molest *child, woman* … ni itazura o suru …にいたずらをする
mollycoddle amayakasu 甘やかす
molten yōkai shita 溶解した
mom F *n* mama ママ; (*talking to outsiders about one's own ~*) haha 母
moment shunkan 瞬間; ***at the ~*** ima no tokoro 今のところ; ***for the ~*** sashiatari 差し当たり; ***it'll only take a ~*** sore niwa isshun shika kakara nai それには一瞬しかかからない
momentarily (*for a moment*) ichijiteki ni 一時的に; (*in a moment*) sugu ni すぐに
momentary ichijiteki (na) 一時的(な)
momentous jūdai (na) 重大(な)
momentum ikioi 勢い
monarch kunshu 君主
monastery shūdōin 修道院; (*Buddhist*) sōbō 僧坊
monastic shūdōshi (no) 修道士(の); (*Buddhist*) sō (no) 僧(の); ***~ life***

shūdo-seikatsu 修道生活
Monday getsuyōbi 月曜日
monetary *policy* kin'yū (no) 金融(の); *system* tsūka (no) 通貨(の)
money okane お金; (*currency*) tsūka 通貨
money-lender kanekashi 金貸し; **money market** kin'yū-shijō 金融市場;**money order** yūbin-kawase 郵便為替
Mongolia Mongoruモンゴル
Mongolian 1 *adj* Mongoru (no) モンゴル (の) **2** *n* (*person*) Mongoru-jinモンゴル人
mongrel zasshu 雑種
monitor 1 *n* COMPUT sukurīn スクリーン **2** *v/t* kanshi suru 監視する
monk shūdōshi 修道士; (*Buddhist*) sō 僧
monkey saru さる; F (*child*) itazurakko いたずらっ子
♦**monkey around with** F ijikurimawasu いじくり回す
monkey wrench monkīrenchi モンキーレンチ
monkfish ankō あんこう
monogram *n* monoguramu モノグラム
monogrammed monoguramu iri (no) モノグラム入り(の)
monolog monorōgu モノローグ
monopolize dokusen suru 独占する
monopoly senbai 専売
monotonous *voice, song* tanchō (na) 単調(な); *job, movie* taikutsu (na) 退屈(な)
monotony tanchō-sa 単調さ
monsoon (*rain*) gōu 豪雨; (*wind*) kisetsufū 季節風; (*season*) uki 雨期
monsoon season uki 雨期
monster *n* kaibutsu 怪物; *fig* (*person*) hitodenashi ひとでなし
monstrosity bakadekkai bakari no shiromono ばかでっかいばかりの代物
monstrous (*shocking*) tondemonai とんでもない
month tsuki 月
monthly 1 *adj payment* maitsuki (no) 毎月(の); *magazine* gekkan (no) 月刊(の); *figures* ikkagetsu (no) 一ヶ月(の) **2** *adv* maitsuki 毎月 **3** *n* (*magazine*) gekkanshi 月刊誌
monument kinenhi 記念碑
mood (*frame of mind*) kigen 機嫌; (*bad ~*) fukigen 不機嫌; (*of meeting, country*) fun'iki 雰囲気; ***be in a good / bad ~*** kigen ga yoi / warui 機嫌がよい/悪い; ***be in the ~ for doing X*** X ga shitai kimochi de aru Xがしたい気持ちである
moody (*changing moods*) kibunya (no) 気分屋(の); (*bad-tempered*) fukigen (na) 不機嫌(な)
moon *n* tsuki 月
moonlight 1 *n* tsuki no hikari 月の光 **2** *v/i* F arubaito o suru アルバイトをする
moonlit night tsukiyo 月夜
moor *v/t boat* tsunagu つなぐ
moorings keiryūjo 係留所
moose herajika へらじか
mop 1 *n* (*for floor*) moppu モップ **2** *v/t floor* moppu de fuku モップでふく; *eyes, face* nuguu ぬぐう
♦**mop up** *spillage* … o fuku …をふく; *gravy* … ni tsukeru …につける; MIL … o sōtō suru …を掃討する
mope fusagikomu ふさぎ込む
moral 1 *adj dilemma, standards* dōtokuteki (na) 道徳的(な); *support, victory* seishinteki (na) 精神的(な); *person* seigikan no tsuyoi 正義感の強い; *behavior* tadashii 正しい **2** *n* (*of story*) kyōkun 教訓; **~s** dōtoku 道徳
morale shiki 士気
morality dōtoku 道徳
morbid byōteki (na) 病的(な)
more 1 *adj* motto ōku (no) もっと多く(の); ***some ~ tea?*** kōcha no okawari wa 紅茶のおかわりは; ***are there any ~ questions?*** shitsumon wa mada arimasu ka? 質問はまだありますか; ***there is no ~ money / coffee*** okane / kōhī wa mō arimasen お金/コーヒーはもうありません; ***a few ~ days / weeks*** ato sūjitsu / sūshūkan あと

数日/数週間; ***~ and ~ students/ companies*** masumasu ōku no gakusei/kigyō ますます多くの学生/企業; ***~ and ~ time*** masumasu nagai jikan ますます長い時間 **2** *adv* motto もっと; ***~ important*** motto daiji (na) もっと大事(な); ***~ and ~*** masumasu ますます; ***~ or less*** daitai だいたい; ***once ~*** mō ichido もう一度; ***~ than*** …以上; ***I don't live there any ~*** mō soko ni wa sunde imasen もうそこには住んでいません **3** *pron*: ***do you want some ~?*** mō sukoshi ikaga desu ka もう少しいかがですか; ***a little ~*** mō sukoshi もう少し

moreover sara ni さらに

morgue shitai-hokanjo 死体保管所

morning asa 朝; ***in the ~*** asa ni 朝に; (*tomorrow*) ashita no asa ni あしたの朝に; ***this ~*** kesa けさ; ***tomorrow ~*** ashita no asa あしたの朝; ***good ~*** ohayō gozaimasu おはようございます

moron manuke まぬけ

morose kimuzukashii 気難しい

morphine moruhine モルヒネ

morsel: ***a ~ of*** hitokuchi no… ひと口の…

mortal 1 *adj* itsuka shinu koto ni natte iru いつか死ぬことになっている; *blow* chimeiteki (na) 致命的(な); ***~ enemy*** fugutaiten no teki 不倶戴天の敵 **2** *n* ningen 人間

mortality shinu unmei 死ぬ運命; (*death rate*) shibōritsu 死亡率

mortar[1] MIL hakugekihō 迫撃砲

mortar[2] (*cement*) morutaru モルタル

mortgage 1 *n* jūtaku-rōn 住宅ローン **2** *v/t* teitō ni irete shakkin o suru 抵当に入れて借金をする

mortician sōgi-ya 葬儀屋

mortuary reianshitsu 霊安室

mosaic mozaiku モザイク

Moscow Mosukuwa モスクワ

mosquito ka 蚊

mosquito coil katorisenkō 蚊取り線香

mosquito net kaya 蚊帳

moss koke こけ

mossy koke de ōwareta こけでおおわれた

most 1 *adj* taitei (no) たいてい(の); ***he won the ~ votes*** kare ga mottomo ōku no tōhyō o eta 彼がもっとも多くの投票を得た **2** *adv* (*very*) taihen たいへん; ***the ~ beautiful/interesting*** mottomo utsukushii/omoshiroi 最も美しい/おもしろい; ***that's the one I like ~*** watashi ga ichiban suki na no wa sore desu 私が一番好きなのはそれです; ***~ of all*** nani yori mo 何よりも **3** *pron* hotondo ほとんど; ***at (the) ~*** seizei せいぜい; ***make the ~ of*** … o dekiru dake katsuyō suru …をできるだけ活用する; ***~ of her novels*** kanojo no shōsetsu no hotondo 彼女の小説のほとんど; ***~ of the time*** taitei たいてい

mostly (*mainly*) omo ni おもに; (*generally*) futsū wa 普通は

motel mōteru モーテル

moth ga 蛾

mother 1 *n* okāsan お母さん; (*talking to outsiders about one's own ~*) haha 母; ***become a ~*** hahaoya ni naru 母親になる **2** *v/t* (*look after like a mother*) … no sewa o yaku …の世話をやく; (*pamper*) amayakasu 甘やかす

motherboard COMPUT mazābōdo マザーボード; **motherhood** hahaoya de aru koto 母親であること; **mother-in-law** giri no okāsan 義理のお母さん; (*talking to outsiders about one's own ~*) giri no haha, 義理の母, shūtome しゅうとめ

motherly boseiteki na 母性的(な)

mother-of-pearl shinjubo 真珠母; **Mother's Day** Haha no hi 母の日; **mother tongue** bokokugo 母国語

motif (*design*) moyō 模様

motion 1 *n* ugoki 動き; (*of car, ship*) yure 揺れ; (*proposal*) dōgi 動議; ***set things in ~*** jikkō suru 実行する **2** *v/t*: ***he ~ed me forward*** kare wa watashi ni mae e deru yōni aizu shita 彼は私に前へ出るように合図した

motionless ugokanai 動かない
motivate yaruki ni saseru やる気にさせる
motivation dōki 動機
motive dōki 動機
motor mōtā モーター; (*of car*) enjin エンジン
motorbike ōtobai オートバイ; **motorboat** mōtābōto モーターボート; **motorcade** jidōsha no gyōretsu 自動車の行列; **motorcycle** ōtobai オートバイ; **motorcyclist** raidā ライダー; **motor home** kyanpingu-kā キャンピングカー
motorist doraibā ドライバー
motorscooter sukūtā スクーター
motor vehicle jidōsharyō 自動車両
motto mottō モットー, zayū no mei 座右の銘
mound (*hillock*) oka 丘; (*in baseball*) maundo マウンド; (*pile*) yama 山
mount 1 *n* (*mountain*) … san …山; (*horse*) jōyōba 乗用馬 **2** *v/t steps* noboru 上る; *horse, bicycle* … ni noru …に乗る; *campaign* hajimeru 始める; *photo* suetsukeru 据え付ける **3** *v/i* (*increase*) masu 増す
♦**mount up** tamaru たまる
mountain yama 山
mountain bike mauntenbaiku マウンテンバイク
mountaineer tozan-ka 登山家
mountaineering tozan 登山
mountainous yama no ōi 山の多い
mourn 1 *v/t death* nageki-kanashimu 嘆き悲しむ **2** *v/i*: **~ *for*** … no shi o nageki-kanashimu …の死を嘆き悲しむ
mourner chōmonkyaku 弔問客
mournful *person* kanashimi ni shizunda 悲しみに沈んだ; *song* kanashige (na) 悲しげ(な)
mourning mo 喪; ***be in ~*** mochū de aru 喪中である; ***wear ~*** mofuku o kiru 喪服を着る
mouse nezumi ねずみ; COMPUT mausu マウス
mouse mat COMPUT mausupaddo マウスパッド
mouth *n* kuchi 口; (*of river*) kakō 河口
mouthful (*of food*) hitokuchibun 一口ぶん
mouthorgan hāmonika ハーモニカ; **mouthpiece** (*of instrument*) mausupīsu マウスピース; (*spokesperson*) supōkusuman スポークスマン; **mouthwash** mausuwosshu マウスウォッシュ; **mouthwatering** yodare no desō (na) よだれの出そう(な)
move 1 *n* (*in chess, checkers*: *of piece*) te 手; (*turn to play*) ban 番; (*step, action*) ugoki 動き; (*change of house*) hikkoshi 引っ越し; ***get a ~ on!*** isoide 急いで; ***don't make a ~!*** ugokuna 動くな **2** *v/t object* ugokasu 動かす; *obstacle* dokasu どかす; (*transfer*) idō saseru 移動させる; (*emotionally*) kandō saseru 感動させる **3** *v/i* ugoku 動く; (*of traffic*) nagareru 流れる; (*transfer*) idō suru 移動する; ***~ to another school*** tenkō suru 転校する; ***~ house*** hikkoshi suru 引っ越しする
♦**move around** (*in room*) ugokimawaru 動き回る; (*from place to place*) hinpan ni hikkosu 頻繁に引っ越す
♦**move away** tachisaru 立ち去る; (*move house*) hikkoshite iku 引っ越して行く
♦**move in** hikkoshite kuru 引っ越して来る
♦**move on** (*to another town*) tachisaru 立ち去る; (*to another job / subject*) utsuru 移る
♦**move out** (*of house*) hikkosu 引っ越す; (*of area*) dete iku 出て行く
♦**move up** (*in league*) shōkaku suru 昇格する; (*in company*) shōshin suru 昇進する; (*in school*) shinkyū suru 進級する; (*make room*) tsumeru 詰める
movement ugoki 動き; (*organization*) undō 運動; (*of planet, moon*) unkō 運行; MUS gakushō 楽章
movers unsō-ya 運送屋

movie eiga 映画; ***go to a ~ / the ~s*** eiga ni iku 映画に行く; ***Japanese ~*** hōga 邦画; ***Western ~*** yōga 洋画
moviegoer eiga-fan 映画ファン
movie theater eigakan 映画館
moving (*which can move*) ugoku 動く; (*emotionally*) kandōteki (na) 感動的(な)
mow *grass* karu 刈る
♦**mow down** (*kill*) nagitaoshite korosu なぎ倒して殺す
mower shibakariki 芝刈機
MP (= ***Military Policeman***) kenpei 憲兵
mph (= ***miles per hour***) jisoku … mairu 時速…マイル
Mr … san …さん
Mrs … san …さん
Ms … san …さん
Mt Fuji Fuji-san 富士山
much 1 *adj* ōku (no) 多く(の); ***he has as ~ chance as you*** kare wa anata to onaji dake no chansu ga aru 彼はあなたと同じだけのチャンスがある; ***she does not have ~ money*** kanojo wa amari kane o motte inai 彼女はあまり金を持っていない **2** *adv* hijō ni 非常に, totemo とても; *better, higher, smaller* haruka ni はるかに; ***very ~*** hontō ni 本当に; ***as ~ as*** … … to onaji dake …と同じだけ; ***I thought as ~*** sonna koto da to omotte ita そんなことだと思っていた; ***you talk too ~*** anata wa shaberisugiru あなたはしゃべりすぎる; ***you did too ~*** yarisugi da やりすぎだ; ***I don't like it / him (very) ~*** sore / kare wa amari suki de wa arimasen それ/彼はあまり好きではありません **3** *pron* takusan たくさん; ***nothing ~*** taishita koto ja nai たいしたことじゃない
muck doro 泥
mucus nen'eki 粘液
mud doro 泥
muddle 1 *n* (*mess*) gochagocha ごちゃごちゃ; (*confusion*) konran 混乱 **2** *v/t person* konran saseru 混乱させる; *facts* kondō suru 混同する
♦**muddle up** *person* … o konran saseru …を混乱させる; *dates, papers etc* … o gochagocha ni suru …をごちゃごちゃにする
muddy doro darake (no) 泥だらけ(の)
muffin mafin マフィン
muffle hikuku suru 低くする
♦**muffle up** *v/i* kikomu 着込む
muffler MOT mafurā マフラー
mug[1] *n* (*for tea, coffee*) magukappu マグカップ; F (*face*) tsura 面
mug[2] *v/t* (*attack*) osotte kane o ubau 襲って金を奪う
mugger gōtō 強盗
mugging gōtō 強盗
muggy mushiatsui 蒸し暑い
mulberry kuwa 桑
mule (*animal*) raba らば; (*slipper*) surippa スリッパ
♦**mull over** … ni tsuite jikkuri kangaeru …についてじっくり考える
multi-journey ticket kaisūken 回数券
multilingual *person* sūkakokugo o hanaseru 数か国語を話せる; *country* sūkakokugo-heiyō (no) 数か国語併用(の)
multimedia *n* maruchi-media マルチメディア
multinational 1 *adj* takokuseki (no) 多国籍(の) **2** *n* COM takokuseki-kigyō 多国籍企業
multiple *adj* fukusū (no) 複数(の); *injuries* fukugō (no) 複合(の)
multiplication kakezan 掛け算
multiply 1 *v/t*: ***~ 3 by 4*** san ni yon o kakeru 3に4を掛ける; ***3 multiplied by 4 is 12*** san kakeru yon wa jūni 3掛ける4は12 **2** *v/i* fueru 増える; (*of animal, plant*) hanshoku suru 繁殖する
mumble 1 *n* butsubutsu iu koe ぶつぶつ言う声 **2** *v/t & v/i* butsubutsu iu ぶつぶつ言う
mumps otafukukaze おたふくかぜ
munch *v/t & v/i* kamishimete taberu かみしめて食べる
municipal (*of city*) shi (no) 市(の);

(*of town*) machi (no) 町(の); (*of local government*) chihō-jichitai (no) 地方自治体(の)

mural *n* hekiga 壁画

murder **1** *n* satsujin 殺人 **2** *v/t* satsugai suru 殺害する; *song* dainashi ni suru 台なしにする

murderer satsujin-hannin 殺人犯人

murderous *rage, look* hidoi ひどい

murmur **1** *n* tsubuyaki つぶやき **2** *v/t* tsubuyaku つぶやく

muscle kinniku 筋肉

muscular *pain, strain* kinniku (no) 筋肉(の); *person* kinniku-ryūryū (no) 筋肉隆々(の)

muse *v/i* monoomoi ni fukeru もの思いにふける

museum hakubutsukan 博物館; (*of art*) bijutsukan 美術館

mushroom **1** *n* kinoko きのこ; (*small white*) masshurūmu マッシュルーム **2** *v/i* kyūsoku ni seichō suru 急速に成長する

music ongaku 音楽; (*score*) gakufu 楽譜

musical **1** *adj* ongaku (no) 音楽(の); (*interested in music*) ongakuzuki (na) 音楽好き(な); (*talented*) onkan no yoi 音感のよい; *voice* mimi ni kokochi yoi 耳に心地よい **2** *n* myūjikaru ミュージカル

musical instrument gakki 楽器

musician (*classical*) ongakuka 音楽家; (*pop, jazz*) myūjishan ミュージシャン

mussel mūru-gai ムール貝

must ◊ (*necessity*) …nakereba naranai …なければならない; ***I ~ be on time*** watashi wa jikan o mamoranakereba naranai 私は時間を守らなければならない ◊ (*with negatives*) …te wa naranai …てはならない; ***I ~ n't be late*** chikoku shite wa naranai 遅刻してはならない ◊ (*probability*): ***it ~ be about 6 o'clock*** rokujigoro ni chigainai 6時ごろに違いない; ***they ~ have arrived by now*** karera wa mō tsuita ni chigainai 彼らはもう着いたに違いない

mustache kuchihige 口ひげ

mustard masutādo マスタード; (*Japanese*) karashi からし

musty kabikusai かび臭い

mute *adj* (*dumb*) kuchi no kikenai 口のきけない

muted *color* yawarakai 柔らかい; *criticism* yokusei shita 抑制した

mutilate setsudan suru 切断する

mutiny **1** *n* hanran 反乱 **2** *v/i* hanran o okosu 反乱を起こす

mutter *v/t & v/i* tsubuyaku つぶやく

mutton hitsuji no niku 羊の肉

mutual sōgo (no) 相互(の); (*shared*) kyōtsū (no) 共通(の)

muzzle **1** *n* (*of animal*) hanazura 鼻づら; (*for dog*) kuchiwa 口輪 **2** *v/t dog* … ni kuchiwa o tsukeru …に口輪をつける; ***~ the press*** atsuryoku o kakete hōdō o fūjiru 圧力をかけて報道を封じる

my ◊ watashi no 私の; ***~ ticket*** watashi no kippu 私の切符 ◊ (*omission of possessive*): ***I cut ~ finger*** watashi wa yubi o kega shimashita 私は指をけがしました; ***I forgot ~ key*** watashi wa kagi o wasuremashita 私はかぎを忘れました

myself : ***I hurt ~*** watashi wa kega o shimashita 私はけがをしました; ***I saw ~ in the mirror*** watashi wa kagami de jibun o mimashita 私は鏡で自分を見ました; ***by ~*** (*without help*) jibun de 自分で; (*alone*) hitori de ひとりで

mysterious (*unexplained*) fushigi (na) 不思議(な); (*enigmatic*) nazomeita なぞめいた

mysteriously fushigi na koto ni 不思議なことに

mystery nazo なぞ; (*story*) misuterī ミステリー

mystify kemuri ni maku 煙に巻く

myth shinwa 神話; *fig* henken 偏見

mythical shinwa (no) 神話(の); (*imaginary*) kakū (no) 架空(の)

mythology shinwa 神話

N

nab (*take for oneself*) tsukamu つかむ

nag 1 *v/i* (*of person*) kogoto o iu 小言を言う **2** *v/t* (*tell off*) … ni kogoto o iu …に小言を言う; ***~ X to do Y*** X ni Y suru yō ni urusaku segamu XにYするようにうるさくせがむ

nagging *person* kuchiurusai 口うるさい; *doubt* taezu tsukimatou 絶えずつきまとう; *pain* shitsukoi しつこい

nail (*for wood*) kugi くぎ; (*on finger*) tsume つめ

nail clippers tsume-kiri つめ切り; **nail file** tsume-yasuri つめやすり; **nail polish** manikyua マニキュア; **nail polish remover** jokōeki 除光液; **nail scissors** tsume-kiri-basami つめ切りばさみ; **nail varnish** manikyua マニキュア

naive sekenshirazu (na) 世間知らず(な)

naked hadaka no 裸(の); ***invisible to the ~ eye*** nikugan de wa mienai 肉眼では見えない

name 1 *n* namae 名前; (*family ~*) myōji 名字, sei 姓; (*of movie*) taitoru タイトル; ***what's your ~?*** onamae o onegaishimasu お名前をお願いします; ***call X ~s*** X ni akutai o tsuku Xに悪態をつく; ***make a ~ for oneself*** yūmei ni naru 有名になる **2** *v/t* nazukeru 名づける

♦ **name for**: ***name X for Y*** Y no na o totte X to nazukeru Yの名をとってXと名づける

namely sunawachi すなわち

namesake dōmei no hito 同名の人

nametag nafuda 名札

nanny *n* uba 乳母

nap *n* utatane うたた寝; ***have a ~*** utatane o suru うたた寝をする

nape: ***~ of the neck*** unaji うなじ

napkin (*table ~*) napukin ナプキン; (*sanitary ~*) seiriyō napukin 生理用ナプキン

narcotic *n* mayaku 麻薬

narcotics agent mayaku-sōsakan 麻薬捜査官

narrate narēshon o ireru ナレーションを入れる

narration narēshon ナレーション

narrative 1 *n* monogatari 物語 **2** *adj poem, style* monogatari-keishiki (no) 物語形式(の)

narrator narētā ナレーター

narrow *street, bed, mind* semai 狭い; *person, views* kyōryō (na) 狭量(な); *victory* kiwadoi きわどい

narrowly *win* karōjite かろうじて; ***~ escape*** … o karōjite nogareru …をかろうじて逃れる

narrow-minded kokoro no semai 心の狭い

nasal *voice* hana ni kakatta 鼻にかかった

nasty *person, thing to say* iji no warui 意地の悪い; *smell, weather* iya (na) いや(な); *cut, wound, disease* hidoi ひどい

nation kokka 国家

national 1 *adj identity, security* kokka (no) 国家(の); *airline* kokuyū (no) 国有(の); ***~ boundaries*** kokkyō 国境 **2** *n*: ***a Japanese ~*** Nihon-jin 日本人

national anthem kokka 国歌; **national debt** kokusai 国債; **National Foundation Day** Kenkoku-kinenbi 建国記念日

nationalism minzoku-shugi 民族主義

nationality kokuseki 国籍

nationalize kokuyūka suru 国有化する

national park kokuritsu-kōen 国立公園

native 1 *adj land, city* umarekokyō (no) 生まれ故郷(の); *people* dochaku (no) 土着(の); *plant* gensan (no) 原産(の); ***~ language*** bokokugo 母国語 **2** *n* (*local*) jimoto no hito 地元の人; (*tribesman*) genjūmin 原住民; ***a ~ of New York*** Nyū-Yōku umare no hito ニューヨーク生まれの人; ***she speaks Japanese like a ~*** kanojo wa neitibu-supīkā no yō ni Nihonogo o hanasu 彼女はネイティブスピーカーのように日本語を話す
native country bokoku 母国
native speaker neitibu-supīkā ネイティブスピーカー
NATO (= ***North Atlantic Treaty Organization***) Natō ナトー
natural shizen (no) 自然(の); (*obvious*) tōzen (no) 当然(の); ***a ~ blonde*** umaretsuki no burondo 生まれつきのブロンド
natural gas tennen-gasu 天然ガス
naturalist hakubutsu-gakusha 博物学者
naturalize: ***become ~d*** kika suru 帰化する
naturally (*of course*) tōzen 当然; *behave, speak* shizen ni 自然に; (*by nature*) motomoto もともと
natural science shizen-kagaku 自然科学
natural scientist shizen-kagaku-sha 自然科学者
nature shizen 自然; (*of person*) seishitsu 性質; (*of problem*) honshitsu 本質
nature reserve shizen-hogo-kuiki 自然保護区域
naughty gyōgi no warui 行儀の悪い; *photograph, word etc* etchi (na) エッチ(な)
nausea hakike 吐き気
nauseate mukamuka saseru むかむかさせる
nauseating *smell, taste* mukatsuku yō (na) むかつくよう(な); *person* zotto suru hodo iya (na) ぞっとするほどいや(な)
nauseous: ***feel ~*** hakike ga suru 吐き気がする
nautical umi (no) 海(の)
nautical mile kairi 海里
naval kaigun (no) 海軍(の)
naval base kaigun-kichi 海軍基地
navel heso へそ
navigable kōkō-kanō (na) 航行可能(な)
navigate *v/i* (*in ship, airplane*) kōkō suru 航行する; (*in car*) michiannai suru 道案内する; COMPUT … ni iku …に行く
navigation (*of ship, plane*) kōkō 航行; (*in car*) yūdō 誘導
navigator (*on ship*) kōkaishī 航海士; (*in airplane*) kōkūshi 航空士; (*in car*) nabigētā ナビゲーター
navy kaigun 海軍
navy blue 1 *n* kon'iro 紺色 **2** *adj* kon'iro (no) 紺色(の)
near 1 *adv* chikaku ni 近くに **2** *prep* … no chikaku ni …の近くに; ***~ the bank*** ginkō no chikaku ni 銀行の近くに **3** *adj* chikai 近い; ***the ~est bus stop*** ichiban chikai basu-tei いちばん近いバス停; ***in the ~ future*** chikai shōrai 近い将来
nearby *adv* chikaku ni 近くに
nearly hotondo ほとんどの場合 ◊ (*negative consequences*): ***he ~ got arrested*** kare wa ayauku taiho sareru tokoro datta 彼はあやうく逮捕されるところだった
near-sighted kinshi (no) 近視(の)
neat *room, desk* seiton sareta 整とんされた; *person* kichin to shita きちんとした; *whiskey* sutorēto (no) ストレート(の); *solution* tekisetsu (na) 適切(な); F (*terrific*) suteki (na) すてき(な)
necessarily hitsuzenteki ni 必然的に; ***that doesn't ~ mean that …*** kanarazushimo… to iu wake de wa nai 必ずしも…という訳ではない
necessary hitsuyō (na) 必要(な); ***it is ~ to …*** … suru koto ga hitsuyō da …することが必要だ
necessitate … o hitsuyō to suru …を必要とする
necessity hitsuyō 必要; (*thing*) hitsujuhin 必需品
neck kubi 首

necklace nekkkuresu ネックレス; **neckline** nekkurain ネックライン; **necktie** nekutai ネクタイ
née kyūsei 旧姓
need 1 *n* hitsuyō 必要; ***if ~ be*** moshi hitsuyō nara もし必要なら; ***in ~*** komatte 困って; ***be in ~ of*** ... o hitsuyō to shite iru ...を必要としている; ***there's no ~ to be rude / upset*** shitsurei ni suru / torimidasu hitsuyō wa nai 失礼にする/取り乱す必要はない **2** *v/t* hitsuyō to suru 必要とする; ***you ~ to buy one*** sore o kau hitsuyō ga arimasu それを買う必要があります; ***you don't ~ to wait*** anata wa matanakute mo ii desu あなたは待たなくてもいいです; ***I ~ to talk to you*** anata ni hanashi ga arimasu あなたに話があります; ***~ I say more?*** kore ijō iu hitsuyō ga arimasu ka これ以上言う必要がありますか
needle (*for sewing, on scale*) hari 針; MED chūshabari 注射針
needlework nuimono 縫い物
needy mazushii 貧しい
negative 1 *adj verb, sentence* hitei (no) 否定(の); *attitude, person* shōkyokuteki (na) 消極的(な); ELEC mainasu (no) マイナス(の) **2** *n*: ***answer in the ~*** nō to kotaeru ノーと答える
neglect 1 *n* hōchi 放置; (*of duty*) taiman 怠慢 **2** *v/t garden* hottarakashi ni suru ほったらかしにする; *one's health* mushi suru 無視する; ***~ to do*** ... shiwasureru ...し忘れる
neglected *garden* hottarakashi ni sareta ほったらかしにされた; *author* wasurerareta 忘れられた; ***feel ~*** wasurerarete iru to kanjiru 忘れられていると感じる
negligence taiman 怠慢
negligent fuchūi (na) 不注意(な)
negligible *quantity* toru ni taranai 取るに足らない
negotiable *salary, contract* kōshō no yochi no aru 交渉の余地のある
negotiate 1 *v/i* kōshō suru 交渉する **2** *v/t deal* torikimeru 取り決める; *obstacles* kirinukeru 切り抜ける; *curve* tōrinukeru 通り抜ける
negotiation kōshō 交渉
negotiator kōshō-sha 交渉者
Negro *n* Kokujin 黒人
neigh *v/i* inanaku いななく
neighbor kinjo no hito 近所の人
neighborhood chiiki 地域; ***in the ~ of ...*** *fig* oyoso ... およそ...
neighboring rinsetsu shita 隣接した; ***~ countries*** kinrin-shokoku 近隣諸国
neighborly shinsetsu (na) 親切(な)
neither 1 *adj* dochira no ... mo ... de nai どちらの...も...でない; ***~ applicant is any good*** dochira no shigan-sha mo tekisetsu de nai どちらの志願者も適切でない **2** *pron*: ***which do you want? – ~, thanks*** dochira ga hoshii – warui ga dochira mo hoshiku nai どちらが欲しい – 悪いがどちらも欲しくない **3** *conj*: ***~ my mother nor my father knew*** haha mo chichi mo shiranakatta 母も父も知らなかった; ***I told ~ my mother nor my father*** haha ni mo chichi ni mo iwanakatta 母にも父にも言わなかった **4** *adv*: ***~ do I*** watashi mo desu 私もです
neon light neon-tō ネオン灯
Nepal Nepāru ネパール
Nepalese 1 *adj* Nepāru (no) ネパール(の) **2** *n* (*person*) Nepāru-jin ネパール人
nephew oi おい
nerd F otaku オタク
nerve shinkei 神経; (*courage*) yūki 勇気; (*impudence*) zūzūshi-sa ずうずうしさ; ***it's bad for my ~s*** sore wa watashi no shinkei ni kotaeru それは私の神経にこたえる; ***get on X's ~s*** X no shinkei ni sawaru Xの神経にさわる
nerve-racking iraira suru いらいらする
nervous (*tense*) shinkeishitsu (na) 神経質(な); (*timid*) ki no chiisai 気の小さい; *twitch* shinkei (no) 神経(の); ***be ~ about doing X*** X suru no o shinpai shite iru Xするのを心配

している

nervous breakdown noirōze ノイローゼ

nervousness shinkei-kabin 神経過敏

nervous wreck: ***be a ~*** hidoku piripiri shite iru ひどくぴりぴりしている

nervy (*fresh*) zūzūshii ずうずうしい

nest *n* su 巣

nestle yorisou 寄り添う

net[1] *n* (*for fishing*) ami 網; (*for tennis*) netto ネット

net[2] *adj weight, amount* shōmi (no) 正味(の); ***~ price*** seika 正価

net curtain rēsu no kāten レースのカーテン

net profit junrieki 純利益

netsuke netsuke 根付け

nettle *n* irakusa いらくさ

network (*of contacts, cells*), COMPUT nettowāku ネットワーク

neurologist shinkeika-i 神経科医

neurosis shinkeishō 神経症

neurotic *adj* shinkei-kabin (no) 神経過敏(の)

neuter *v/t animal* kyosei suru 去勢する

neutral 1 *adj country* chūritsu (no) 中立(の); *color* chūkan (no) 中間(の) **2** *n* (*gear*) nyūtoraru ニュートラル; ***in ~*** nyūtoraru ni ニュートラルに

neutrality chūritsu 中立

neutralize chūwa suru 中和する

never ◊ (*future tense*) kesshite… nai 決して…ない; ***I'll ~ say that again*** sore o mō kesshite iwanai それをもう決して言わない ◊ (*past tense*) … koto ga nai … ことがない; ***I've ~ been there*** soko ni wa itta koto ga nai そこには行ったことがない ◊ (*in disbelief*) masaka まさか; ***you' re ~ going to believe this*** kore wa masaka shinjirarenai darō これはまさか信じられないだろう; ***you ~ promised, did you?*** masaka yakusoku shinakatta darō ne まさか約束しなかっただろうね

never-ending hateshinai 果てしない

nevertheless sore ni mo kakawarazu それにもかかわらず

new atarashii 新しい; ***this system is still ~ to me*** kono shisutemu ni wa mada narete inai このシステムにはまだ慣れていない; ***I'm ~ to the job*** watashi wa shigoto ni narete inai 私は仕事に慣れていない; ***that's nothing ~*** nani mo ima ni hajimatta koto ja nai 何も今に始まったことじゃない

newborn *adj* umaretate (no) 生まれたて(の)

newcomer (*to place*) shinzanmono 新参者; (*to company*) shinnyū-shain 新入社員

newly (*recently*) saikin 最近

newly-weds shinkon-kappuru 新婚カップル

new moon shingetsu 新月

news nyūsu ニュース; (*from friend, family*) tayori 便り; ***that's ~ to me*** sore wa watashi ni wa mattaku hatsumimi desu それは私にはまったく初耳です

news agency tsūshinsha 通信社; **newscast** TV nyūsu-hōsō ニュース放送; **newscaster** TV kyasutā キャスター; **news dealer** shinbun-zasshi-hanbaiten 新聞雑誌販売店; **news flash** nyūsu-sokuhō ニュース速報; **newspaper** shinbun 新聞; **newsreader** TV *etc* kyasutā キャスター; **news report** hōdō-kiji 報道記事; **newsstand** shinbun-uriba 新聞売り場; **newsvendor** shinbun'uri 新聞売り

New Year Shinnen 新年, Shōgatsu 正月; ***Happy ~!*** Akemashite omedetō gozaimasu 明けましておめでとうございます

New Year's Day Gantan 元旦, Ganjitsu 元日; **New Year's card** nengajō 年賀状; **New Year's Eve** Ōmisoka 大みそか

New York Nyū-Yōku ニューヨーク

New Zealand Nyū-Jīrando ニュージーランド

New Zealander Nyū-Jīrando-jin ニュージーランド人

next 1 *adj* (*in time, order*) tsugi (no) 次(の); (*in space*) tonari (no)

隣(の); ~ ***week*** raishū 来週; ***the ~ week / month he came back again*** sono yokushū / yokugetsu kare wa mata kaette kita その翌週/翌月彼はまた帰ってきた; ***who's ~?*** tsugi no kata dōzo 次の方どうぞ **2** *adv* tsugi ni 次に; ~ ***to*** (*beside*) … no tonari ni …の隣に; (*in comparison with*) hotondo … to onaji ほとんど…と同じ

next-door 1 *adj neighbor* tonari (no) 隣(の) **2** *adv live* tonari ni 隣に

next of kin mottomo chikai shinzoku もっとも近い親族

nibble *v/t* kajiru かじる

nice *person* shinsetsu (na) 親切(な); *weather, smile* ii いい; *party, trip, vacation* tanoshii 楽しい; *hair, color* kirei (na) きれい(な); *meal, food* oishii おいしい; ***be ~ to your little sister*** imōto ni yasashiku shite agenasai 妹にやさしくしてあげなさい; ***that's very ~ of you*** shinsetsu ni shite kudasatte arigatō gozaimasu 親切にしてくださってありがとうございます

nicely *written, presented* umaku うまく; (*pleasantly*) kimochi yoku 気持ちよく

niceties: ***social ~*** reigi 礼儀

niche (*in market*) nitchi ニッチ; (*suitable position*) tekisho 適所

nick *n* (*cut*) kireme 切れ目; ***in the ~ of time*** chōdo ii toki ni ちょうどいい時に

nickel nikkeru ニッケル; (*coin*) go-sento-kōka 五セント硬貨

nickname *n* nikkunēmu ニックネーム

niece mei めい

niggardly kechikechi shita けちけちした

night yoru 夜; (*in hotel*) ippaku 一泊; ***11 o'clock at ~*** yoru jūichiji 夜十一時; ***travel by ~*** yoru ni idō suru 夜に移動する; ***during the ~*** yoru ni 夜に; ***stay the ~*** tomaru 泊まる; ***a room for two ~s*** nihaku no yotei de hitoheya 二泊の予定で一部屋; ***work ~s*** yakin suru 夜勤する; ***good ~*** oyasumi nasai おやすみなさい; ***in the middle of the ~*** mayonaka ni 真夜中に

nightcap (*drink*) nezake 寝酒; **nightclub** naitokurabu ナイトクラブ; **nightdress** naitodoresu ナイトドレス; **nightfall**: ***at ~*** yūgure ni 夕暮れに; **night flight** yakan-furaito 夜間フライト; **nightgown** naitodoresu ナイトドレス

nightingale naichingēru ナイチンゲール

nightlife yoasobi 夜遊び

nightly 1 *adj* yogoto (no) 夜ごと(の) **2** *adv* yogoto ni 夜ごとに

nightmare akumu 悪夢

night porter yakan-furonto-gakari 夜間フロント係; **night school** yakan-gakkō 夜間学校; **night shift** yakan-kinmu 夜間勤務; **nightshirt** nemaki 寝巻き; **nightspot** naitosupotto ナイトスポット; **nighttime**: ***at ~*** yakan ni 夜間に

nimble subayai すばやい

nine kyū 九; (*with count word*) kokonotsu 九つ

nineteen jūkyū 十九

nineteenth dai-jūkyū (no) 第十九(の)

ninetieth dai-kyūjū (no) 第九十(の)

ninety kyūjū 九十

ninth 1 *adj* dai-kyū (no) 第九(の) **2** *n* (*of month*) kokonoka 九日

nip *n*: ***give X a ~*** (*pinch*) X o tsuneru Xをつねる; (*bite*) X ni kamitsuku Xにかみつく

nipple chikubi 乳首

nitrogen chisso 窒素

No[1] (~ *play*) Nō 能; ~ ***comedy*** kyōgen 狂言

no[2] **1** *adv* iie いいえ ◊ (*using 'yes', ie yes, that is right*): ***you don't know the answer, do you? – ~, I don't*** kotae ga wakaranai n deshō – hai wakarimasen 答えがわからないんでしょう－はい、わかりません **2** *adj* ***there's ~ coffee / tea left*** kōhī / kōcha wa sukoshi mo nokotte inai コーヒー/紅茶は少しも残っていない; ***I have ~ family*** watashi ni wa kazoku ga inai 私には

家族がいない; ***I'm ~ expert*** watashi wa ekisupāto de wa nai 私はエキスパートではない; ***~ smoking*** kin'en 禁煙; ***~ parking*** chūsha-kinshi 駐車禁止

nobility kōki-sa 高貴さ

noble *person* kōki (na) 高貴(な); *gesture* rippa (na) 立派(な)

nobody dare mo … (+ *neg verb*) だれも…; ***~ knows*** dare mo shiranai だれも知らない; ***there was ~ at home*** dare mo ie ni inakatta だれも家にいなかった

nod 1 *n* unazuki うなずき; ***give a ~*** (*agreeing*) unazuku うなずく; ***she greeted me with a ~*** kanojo wa watashi ni atama o sageta 彼女は私に頭を下げた **2** *v/i* (*agreeing*) unazuku うなずく; (*in greeting*) atama o sageru 頭を下げる

♦ **nod off** inemuri suru 居眠りする

no-hoper mikominashi 見込みなし

noise oto 音; (*unpleasant*) zatsuon 雑音

noisy yakamashii やかましい

nominal *amount* wazuka (na) わずか(な)

nominate (*appoint*) ninmei suru 任命する; ***~ X for a post*** X o shoku ni suisen suru Xを職に推薦する

nomination (*appointing*) ninmei 任命; (*proposal*) suisen 推薦

nominee kōho-sha 候補者

nonalcoholic arukōru o fukumanai アルコールを含まない

nonaligned chūritsu (no) 中立(の)

nonchalant heizen to shita 平然とした

noncommissioned officer kashikan 下士官

noncommittal aimai (na) あいまい(な)

nondescript arifureta ありふれた

none (*people*) … no dare mo …nai …のだれも…ない; (*things*) … no dore mo …nai …のどれも…ない; ***~ of the students has left yet*** gakusei wa dare mo satte inai 学生はだれも去っていない; ***~ of the apartments is vacant*** apāto wa dore mo aite inai アパートはどれも空いていない; ***there are ~ left*** hitotsu mo nokotte inai ひとつも残っていない; ***there is ~ left*** sukoshi mo nokotte inai 少しも残っていない

nonentity toru ni taranai hito 取るに足らない人

nonetheless sore demo nao それでもなお

nonexistent sonzai shinai 存在しない; **nonfiction** non-fikushon ノンフィクション; **non(in)flammable** funensei (no) 不燃性(の); **nonintervention** naisei-fukanshō 内政不干渉; **non-iron** *shirt* airon no iranai アイロンのいらない

no-no: ***that's a ~*** F sore wa dame desu それはだめです

no-nonsense *approach* genjitsu-rosen (no) 現実路線(の)

nonpayment fubarai 不払い; **nonpolluting** kankyō o osen shinai 環境を汚染しない; **nonresident** *n* (*in country*) hi-kyojūsha 非居住者; (*in hotel*) shukuhaku shite inai hito 宿泊していない人; **nonreturnable** kaette konai 返ってこない

nonsense tawagoto たわごと; ***don't talk ~*** baka na koto o iu na ばかなことを言うな; ***~, it's easy!*** tondemonai, kantan da とんでもない、簡単だ

nonskid *tires* suberidome o shita 滑り止めをした; **nonslip** *surface* suberanai 滑らない; **nonsmoker** (*person*) tabako o suwanai hito たばこを吸わない人; **nonstandard** hyōjungai (no) 標準外(の); **nonstick** *pans* tefuron-kakō (no) テフロン加工(の); **nonstop 1** *adj flight, train* chokkō (no) 直行(の); *chatter* taema nai 絶え間ない **2** *adv travel* chokkō de 直行で; *chatter, argue* taema naku 絶え間なく; **nonswimmer** kanazuchi かなづち; **nonunion** rōdō-kumiai ni zokusanai 労働組合に属さない; **nonviolence** hi-bōryoku 非暴力; **nonviolent** hi-bōryoku (no) 非暴力(の)

noodles menrui めん類; (*thick,*

white) udon うどん; (*brown*) soba そば; ***Chinese ~*** rāmen らーめん
nook sumi 隅
noon shōgo 正午; ***at ~*** shōgo ni 正午に
noose wanawa 輪縄
nor: ***~ do I*** watashi mo desu 私もです
norm (*of society etc*) kihan 規範
normal futsū (no) 普通(の); ***~ temperature*** (*of body*) heinetsu 平熱
normality seijō 正常
normalize *relationships* seijōka suru 正常化する
normally futsū wa 普通は; (*in a normal way*) seijō ni 正常に
north 1 *n* kita 北; ***to the ~ of*** … no kita ni …の北に **2** *adj* kita (no) 北(の) **3** *adv travel etc* kita no hō ni 北の方に; ***~ of*** … no kita ni …の北に
North America Kita-Amerika 北アメリカ; **North American 1** *adj* Kita-Amerika (no) 北アメリカ(の) **2** *n* Kita-Amerika-jin 北アメリカ人; **northeast** *n* hokutō 北東
northerly *adj* kita (no) 北(の)
northern kita (no) 北(の)
northerner hokubu-shusshin-sha 北部出身者
North Korea Kita-chōsen 北朝鮮, *fml* Chōsen-minshu-shugi-jinmin-kyōwakoku 朝鮮民主主義人民共和国; **North Korean 1** *adj* Kita-chōsen (no) 北朝鮮(の) **2** *n* Kita-chōsen-jin 北朝鮮人; **North Pole** Hokkyoku 北極; **North Vietnam** Kita-Betonamu 北ベトナム; **North Vietnamese 1** *adj* Kita-Betonamu (no) 北ベトナム(の) **2** *n* Kita-Betonamu-jin 北ベトナム人; **northward** kita no hō e 北の方へ; **northwest** *n* hokusei 北西
Norway Noruwē ノルウェー
Norwegian 1 *adj* Noruwē (no) ノルウェー(の) **2** *n* (*person*) Noruwē-jin ノルウェー人; (*language*) Noruwē-go ノルウェー語
nose hana 鼻; ***it was right under my ~!*** watashi no me no mae de 私の目の前で
♦**nose around** kagimawaru かぎ回る
nosebleed hanaji 鼻血; ***have a ~*** hanaji ga deru 鼻血が出る
nostalgia kyōshū 郷愁
nostalgic natsukashii 懐かしい
nostril hana no ana 鼻の穴
nosy sensakuzuki (na) せんさく好き(な); ***don't be ~*** sensaku shinaide せんさくしないで
not ◊ (*with verbs*) …nai …ない; (*past tense*) …nakatta …なかった; ***I am ~ finished*** watashi wa owatte inai 私は終わっていない; ***he didn't help*** kare wa tetsudawanakatta 彼は手伝わなかった ◊ (*when using masu*) …masen …ません; ***I don't know*** wakarimasen わかりません; ***I am ~ American*** watashi wa Amerika-jin de wa arimasen 私はアメリカ人ではありません ◊: ***~ this one, that one*** kore de wa nakute, sore desu これではなくて、それです; ***~ now*** ima wa dame desu 今はだめです; ***~ there*** soko wa dame desu そこはだめです; ***~ like that*** sō de wa naku そうではなく; ***~ before Tuesday / next week*** kayōbi / raishū ikō ni 火曜日/来週以降に; ***~ for me, thanks*** dōmo, demo watashi wa kekkō desu どうも、でも私は結構です; ***~ a lot*** (*degree*) anmari あんまり; (*quantity*) sukoshi dake 少しだけ
notable chūmoku ni atai suru 注目に値する
notary kōshōnin 公証人
notch *n* kizamime 刻み目
note *n* (*short letter*) mijikai tegami 短い手紙; MUS onpu 音符; (*memo to self*) memo メモ; (*comment on text*) chū 注; ***take ~s*** nōto o toru ノートをとる; ***take ~ of*** … ni chūi suru …に注意する
♦**note down** … o kakitomeru …を書き留める
notebook nōto ノート; COMPUT nōto-pasokon ノートパソコン
noted yūmei (na) 有名(な)
notepad memochō メモ帳
notepaper binsen 便せん

nothingnani mo … (+ *neg verb*) 何も…; ***there is ~ left*** nani mo nokotte inai 何も残っていない; ***I've had ~ to eat all day*** ichinichi-jū nani mo tabenakatta 一日中何も食べなかった; ***~ but*** tada … dake ただ…だけ; ***~ much*** taishite nani mo 大して何も; ***for ~*** (*free*) tada de ただで; (*for no reason*) riyū mo naku 理由もなく; ***I'd like ~ better*** (*accepting invitation*) yorokonde 喜んで; ***~ for me thanks*** kekkō desu, dōmo結構です、どうも

notice1 *n* (*on bulletin board*) keiji 掲示; (*in street*) harigami はり紙; (*advance warning*) keikoku 警告; (*in newspaper*) kōkoku 公告; (*to leave job / house*) tsūkoku 通告; ***at short ~*** girigiri no tsūtatsu de ぎりぎりの通達で; ***until further ~*** otte tsūchi ga aru made 追って通知があるまで; ***give X his / her ~*** (*to quit job*) X ni kaiko-tsūkoku suru Xに解雇通告する; ***hand in one's ~*** (*to employer*) jishoku-todoke o dasu 辞職届を出す; ***four weeks'~*** (*to employee*) yonshūkan no kaiko-tsūkoku 四週間の解雇通告; (*to employer*) yonshūkan no jishoku-todoke 四週間の辞職届; ***take ~ of*** … ni chūi o harau …に注意を払う; ***take no ~ of*** … o mushi suru …を無視する **2** *v/t* … ni ki ga tsuku …に気がつく

noticeablemedatta 目立った

notify… ni tsūchi suru …に通知する

notionkangae 考え

notionskomamono 小間物

notoriousakumei no takai 悪名の高い

nougatnugā ヌガー

nounmeishi 名詞

nourishingeiyō no aru 栄養のある

nourishmenteiyō 栄養

novel*n* shōsetsu 小説

novelistshōsetsu-ka 小説家

novelty(*being novel*) meatarashi-sa 目新しさ; (*sth novel*) meatarashii mono 目新しいもの

Novemberjūichigatsu 十一月

noviceshoshin-sha 初心者

nowima 今; ***~ and again, ~ and then*** tokidoki 時々; ***by ~*** ima made ni 今までに; ***from ~ on*** ima kara 今から; ***right ~*** genzai 現在; ***just ~*** (*at this moment*) ima wa 今は; (*a little while ago*) tsui sakki ついさっき; ***~, ~!*** (*warning*) korakora こらこら; ***~, where did I put it?*** sate, doko ni oitakke さて、どこに置いたっけ

nowadayskonogoro wa このごろは

nowheredoko ni mo … (+*neg verb*) どこにも…; ***there is ~ to stay*** doko ni mo tomaru tokoro ga nai どこにも泊まるところがない; ***it's ~ near finished*** sore wa mattaku owatte inai それはまったく終わっていない

nozzlenozuru ノズル

nuclearkaku (no) 核(の)

nuclear energygenshiryoku 原子力; **nuclear fission**kakubunretsu 核分裂; **nuclear-free zone** hikakuchitai 非核地帯; **nuclear physics**genshi-butsurigaku 原子物理学; **nuclear power** genshiryoku 原子力; **nuclear power station**genshiryoku-hatsudensho 原子力発電所; **nuclear reactor**genshiro 原子炉; **nuclear waste**kaku-haikibutsu 核廃棄物; **nuclear weapons**kaku-heiki 核兵器

nude1 *adj* hadaka (no) 裸(の) **2** *n* (*painting*) nūdo ヌード; ***in the ~*** hadaka de 裸で

nudge*v/t* sotto tsuku そっと突く

nudist*n* nūdisuto ヌーディスト

nuisance(*person*) meiwaku na hito 迷惑な人; (*thing*) yakkai na mono やっかいな物; (*having to do something*) mendō 面倒; ***make a ~ of oneself*** hito ni meiwaku o kakeru 人に迷惑をかける; ***what a ~!*** komatta mono da 困ったものだ

nuke*v/t* kakuheiki o tsukatte kōgeki suru 核兵器を使って攻撃する

null and voidmukō de 無効で

numb*arm, leg* shibireta しびれた; (*with cold*) kajikanda かじかんだ;

(*emotionally*) kankaku no nai 感覚のない
number 1 *n* (*figure*) sūji 数字; (*quantity*) kazu 数; (*of hotel room, house, phone ~ etc*) bangō 番号; ***a ~ of*** (*some*) ikuraka no… いくらかの…; (*quite a few*) kanari … no かなりの… **2** *v/t* (*put a number on*) bangō o tsukeru 番号をつける
numeral sūji 数字
numerate sūji ni tsuyoi 数字に強い
numerous tasū (no) 多数(の)
nun shūdōjo 修道女, ama 尼
nurse kangofu 看護婦; (*male*) kangoshi 看護士
nursery (*school*) hoikuen 保育園; (*for plants*) naedoko 苗床
nursery rhyme dōyō 童謡; **nursery school** hoikuen 保育園; **nursery school teacher** hobo 保母
nursing kango 看護
nursing home (*for old people*) rōjin-hōmu 老人ホーム
nut konomi 木の実; (*for bolt*) natto ナット; **~s** F (*testicles*) kintama きんたま
nutcrackers kurumiwari くるみ割り
nutrient yōbun 養分
nutrition eiyō 栄養
nutritious eiyō no aru 栄養のある
nuts *adj* F (*crazy*) ki ga kurutte 気が狂って; ***be ~ about*** … ni muchū de aru …に夢中である
nutshell: ***in a ~*** yō suru ni 要するに
nutty *taste* nattsu no fūmi no suru ナッツの風味のする; F (*crazy*) ki no kurutta 気の狂った
nylon 1 *n* nairon ナイロン **2** *adj* nairon (no) ナイロン(の)

O

oak (*tree*) kashi かし; (*wood*) ōku-zai オーク材; ***Japanese ~*** nara なら
oar ōru オール
oasis oashisu オアシス; *fig* ikoi no basho 憩いの場所
oath LAW sensei 宣誓; (*swearword*) nonoshiri-kotoba ののしり言葉; ***on ~*** sensei shite 宣誓して
oatmeal ōtomīru オートミール
oats ōto-mugi オート麦
obedience fukujū 服従
obedient iu koto o kiku 言うことを聞く
obey *the law* … ni shitagau …に従う; *parents* … no iu koto o kiku …の言うことを聞く
obituary *n* shibō-kiji 死亡記事
object[1] *n* (*thing*) mono 物; (*aim*) mokuteki 目的; GRAM mokutekigo 目的語
object[2] *v/i* hantai suru 反対する
♦ **object to** … ni hantai suru …に反対する
objection igi 異議
objectionable (*unpleasant*) iya (na) いや(な)
objective 1 *adj* kyakkanteki (na) 客観的(な) **2** *n* mokuteki 目的
obligation gimu 義務; ***be under an ~ to*** … ni giri ga aru …に義理がある
obligatory gimu (no) 義務(の); *qualifications* hitsuyō (na) 必要(な)
oblige: ***much ~d!*** dōmo arigatō どうもありがとう
obliging shinsetsu (na) 親切(な)
oblique 1 *adj reference* tōmawashi (no) 遠回し(の) **2** *n* (*in punctuation*) shasen 斜線
obliterate *city* kanzen ni hakai suru 完全に破壊する; *memory* kanzen ni wasureru 完全に忘れる
oblivion bōkyaku 忘却; ***fall into ~*** sukkari wasurerareru すっかり忘れ

られる
oblivious: ***be ~ of*** … ni zenzen ki ga tsukanai …に全然気がつかない
oblong *adj* chōhōkei (no) 長方形(の)
obnoxious ki ni sawaru 気にさわる
obscene waisetsu (na) わいせつ(な); *salary, poverty* monosugoi ものすごい
obscure (*hard to see*) usugurai 薄暗い; (*hard to understand*) wakarinikui わかりにくい; (*little known*) mumei (no) 無名(の)
observant chūibukai 注意深い
observation (*of stars etc*) kansatsu 観察; (*comment*) iken 意見
observatory kansokujo 観測所
observe *birds, wildlife* kansatsu suru 観察する; (*notice*) … ni ki ga tsuku …に気がつく
observer (*of human nature etc*) kansatsu-sha 観察者; (*at elections etc*) obuzābā オブザーバー
obsess: ***be ~ed by / with*** … ni toritsukarete iru …に取りつかれている
obsession (*with idea*) kyōhaku-kannen 強迫観念; (*with thing, person*) shūchaku 執着
obsessive *person* kodawaru こだわる; *behavior* toritsukareta yō (na) 取りつかれたよう(な)
obsolete sutareta すたれた
obstacle shōgaibutsu 障害物; (*to progress etc*) shōgai 障害
obstetrician sankai 産科医
obstinacy ganko 頑固
obstinate ganko (na) 頑固(な)
obstruct fusagu ふさぐ; *police* samatageru 妨げる
obstruction (*on road*) shōgaibutsu 障害物
obstructive *behavior, tactics* jama ni naru yō (na) じゃまになるような
obtain eru 得る
obtainable *products* te ni irerareru 手に入れられる
obvious akiraka (na) 明らか(な); (*not subtle*) akarasama (na) 明らさま(な)
obviously akiraka ni 明らかに; ***~!*** mochiron もちろん
occasion bāi 場合; (*event, ceremony*) gyōji 行事; (*opportunity*) kikai 機会
occasional tama (no) たま(の); ***I like the ~ whiskey*** watashi wa tama ni uisukī o nomu no ga suki desu 私はたまにウイスキーを飲むのが好きです
occasionally tama ni たまに
occult 1 *adj* okaruto (no) オカルト(の) **2** *n*: ***the ~*** okarutizumu オカルティズム
occupant (*of vehicle*) jōkyaku 乗客
occupation (*job*) shokugyō 職業; (*of country*) senryō 占領
occupy *one's time, mind* toru 取る; *position in company* shimeru 占める; *country* senryō suru 占領する
occur okoru 起こる; ***it ~red to me that*** … to iu kangae ga futo ukanda …という考えがふと浮かんだ
occurrence dekigoto できごと
ocean umi 海
Oceania Oseania オセアニア
o'clock: ***at five / six ~*** go / roku-ji ni 五/六時に
October jūgatsu 十月
octopus tako たこ
odd (*strange*) hen (na) 変(な); (*not even*) kisū (no) 奇数(の); ***the ~ one out*** (*thing*) hoka to wa chigau mono 他とは違う物; (*person*) hoka to wa chigau hito 他とは違う人; ***50 ~*** gojū chotto 五十ちょっと
odds: ***be at ~ with*** (*with people*) … to arasotte iru …と争っている; (*with proposal*) … to mujun suru …と矛盾する
odds and ends garakuta がらくた; (*things to do*) komakai ten 細かい点
odometer sōkō-kyorikei 走行距離計
odor nioi におい
of (*possession*) … no …の; ***the name ~ the hotel*** hoteru no namae ホテルの名前; ***the works ~ Dickens*** Dikenzu no sakuhin ディケンズの作品; ***five / ten minutes ~ twelve*** jūniji gofun / juppun mae

十二時五分/十分前; ***die ~ cancer / a stroke*** gan / shinzō-hossa de shinu がん/心臓発作で死ぬ; ***~ the three this is ...*** mittsu no uchi de kore ga … desu 三つのうちでこれが…です

off1 *prep* … kara …から; ***~ the main road*** (*away from*) ōdōri kara hanarete 大通りから離れて; (*leading off*) ōdōri kara haitta tokoro ni 大通りから入ったところに; ***$20 ~ the price*** nijū doru nedan kara waribiite 二十ドル値段から割り引いて; ***he's ~ his food*** kare wa shokuyoku ga nai 彼は食欲がない **2** *adv*: **be ~** (*of light,* TV) keshite aru 消してある; (*of machine*) tomatte iru 止まっている; (*of brake*) kakatte inai かかっていない; (*of lid, top*) shimete inai 閉めていない; (*not at work*) yasumi de aru 休みである; (*canceled*) chūshi ni naru 中止になる; ***we're ~ tomorrow*** (*leaving*) watashitachi wa ashita shuppatsu shimasu 私たちは明日出発します; ***I'm ~ to New York*** watashi wa Nyū-Yōku e ikimasu 私はニューヨークへ行きます; ***with his pants / hat ~*** zubon / bōshi o nuide ズボン/帽子を脱いで; ***take a day ~*** ichinichi yasumu 一日休む; ***it's 3 miles ~*** sore wa san mairu hanarete imasu それは三マイル離れています; ***it's a long way ~*** (*in distance*) sore wa tōi desu それは遠いです; (*in future*) sore wa saki no koto desu それは先のことです; ***drive ~*** kuruma de hashirisaru 車で走り去る; ***walk ~*** tachisaru 立ち去る **3** *adj*: ***the ~ switch*** suitchi スイッチ

offend *v/t* (*insult*) okoraseru 怒らせる

offender LAW hanzai-sha 犯罪者

offense LAW hanzai 犯罪

offensive 1 *adj behavior, remark* shitsurei (na) 失礼(な); *smell* iya (na) いや(な) **2** *n* MIL kōgeki 攻撃; ***go onto the ~*** kōgeki shihajimeru 攻撃し始める

offer 1 *n* teikyō 提供 **2** *v/t* teikyō suru 提供する; ***~ X Y*** *drink etc* X ni Y o susumeru XにYを勧める; *job* X ni Y o teikyō suru XにYを提供する

offhand *adj attitude* muzōsa (na) 無造作(な)

office (*building*) jimusho 事務所; (*room*) jimushitsu 事務室, ofisu オフィス; (*position*) shoku 職

office block ofisubiru オフィスビル

office hours kinmu-jikan 勤務時間; (*of doctor*) shinsatsu-jikan 診察時間

officer MIL shikan 士官; (*in police*) keisatsukan 警察官

official 1 *adj statement, visit* kōshiki (no) 公式(の); *organization* kōteki (na) 公的(な) **2** *n* kōmuin 公務員

officially (*strictly speaking*) omotemuki wa 表向きは

off-line *adj working, input* ofurainshiki (no) オフライン式(の); ***go ~*** rain o kiru ラインを切る

off-peak *rates, season* kansanki (no) 閑散期(の)

off-season 1 *adj rates* shīzun'ofu (no) シーズンオフ(の) **2** *n* shīzun'ofu シーズンオフ

offset *v/t losses* umeawaseru 埋め合わせる

offside 1 *adj* dōro no chūōgawa (no) 道路の中央側(の) **2** *adv* SP ofusaido (no) オフサイド(の)

offspring kodomo 子供

off-white *adj* ofuhowaito (no) オフホワイト(の)

often yoku よく

oil 1 *n* (*for machine*) sekiyu 石油; (*for food*) oiru オイル, abura 油; (*for skin*) oiru オイル **2** *v/t bearings* abura o sasu 油をさす

oil company sekiyu-gaisha 石油会社; **oil painting** aburae 油絵; **oil rig** kaijō-saiyu-kichi 海上採油基地; **oil tanker** sekiyu-tankā 石油タンカー; **oil well** yusei 油井

oily aburappoi 脂っぽい

ointment nankō 軟こう

ok *adv* (*as reply*) ōkē オーケー; ***can I? – ~*** ii desu ka – ii desu yo いい

ですか－いいですよ; ***is it ~ with you if I go home?*** ie ni kaette mo ii desu ka 家に帰ってもいいですか; ***that's ~ by me*** watashi wa kamaimasen 私はかまいません; ***are you ~?*** (*well, not hurt*) daijōbu desu ka 大丈夫ですか; ***are you ~ for Friday?*** kin'yōbi wa daijōbu desu ka 金曜日は大丈夫ですか; ***he's ~*** (*is a good guy*) kare wa ii hito desu 彼はいい人です; ***is this bus ~ for ...?*** kono basu wa ... e ikimasu ka このバスは...へ行きますか

Okinawa Okinawa 沖縄

old *person* toshi o totta 年をとった; *vehicle, building, joke* furui 古い; *custom* mukashi kara (no) 昔から(の); (*previous*) mae (no) 前(の); ***~ man / woman / people*** otoshiyori お年寄り; ***how ~ is he?*** kare wa ikutsu desu ka 彼はいくつですか; ***he's getting ~*** kare wa mō toshi desu 彼はもう年です

old age rōnen 老年

old-fashioned furui 古い; *pej* furukusai 古くさい

olive orību オリーブ

olive oil orību-oiru オリーブオイル

Olympic Games Orinpikku オリンピック

omelet omuretsu オムレツ

ominous fukitsu (na) 不吉(な)

omission (*in text, process*) shōryaku 省略; (*of person, name*) jogai 除外

omit *word, check* shōryaku suru 省略する; *person, name* jogai suru 除外する; ***~ to do X*** Xshiwasureru Xし忘れる

on 1 *prep* (*with verbs of being*) ... ni ...に; (*with verbs of activity*) ... de ...で; ***it's ~ the table*** tēburu ni aru テーブルにある; ***he wasn't ~ the bus*** kare wa basu ni notte inakatta 彼はバスに乗っていなかった; ***I traveled ~ the bus*** watashi wa basu de itta 私はバスで行った; ***I met him ~ the plane*** watashi wa hikōki de kare ni atta 私は飛行機で彼に会った; ***~ TV / the radio*** terebi / rajio de テレビ/ラジオで; ***~ Sunday*** nichiyōbi ni 日曜日に; ***~ the 1st of ...*** ... (no) tsuitachi ni ...(の)一日に; ***this is ~ me*** (*I'm paying*) kore wa watashimochi desu これは私持ちです; ***~ his arrival*** kare wa tōchaku suru to 彼は到着すると **2** *adv*: ***be ~*** (*of light, TV, computer*) tsuite iru ついている; (*of brake*) kakatte iru かかっている; (*of lid, top*) shimatte iru 閉まっている; (*of TV program: being broadcast*) hōei sarete iru 放映されている; (*of meeting etc: be scheduled to happen*) yotei sarete iru 予定されている; ***what's ~ tonight?*** (*on TV etc*) konban wa nani o yatte imasu ka 今晩は何をやっていますか; (*what's planned?*) konban no yotei wa nan desu ka 今晩の予定は何ですか; ***with his jacket ~*** uwagi o kite 上着を着て; ***with his hat ~*** bōshi o kabutte 帽子をかぶって; ***you're ~*** (*I accept your offer etc*) ii desu yo いいですよ; ***that's not ~*** (*not allowed, not fair*) sonna baka na koto wa nai そんなばかなことはない; ***~ you go*** (*go ahead*) dōzo どうぞ; ***walk / talk ~*** aruki / hanashi-tsuzukeru 歩き/話し続ける; ***and so ~*** nado など; ***~ and ~*** *talk etc* en'en to えんえんと **3** *adj*: ***the ~ switch*** suitchi スイッチ

once 1 *adv* (*one time*) ichido 一度; (*formerly*) katsute かつて; ***~ again, ~ more*** mō ichido もう一度; ***at ~*** (*immediately*) sugu ni すぐに; ***all at ~*** (*suddenly*) totsuzen 突然; (*together*) mattaku dōji ni まったく同時に; ***~ upon a time there was...*** (*person*) mukashi mukashi ... ga imashita 昔々...がいました; (*thing*) mukashimukashi ... ga arimashita 昔々...がありました **2** *conj* ittan ... sureba いったん...すれば; ***~ he has finished, he can leave*** (kare wa) ittan owatte shimaeba kaereru (彼は)いったん終わってしまえば帰れる

one 1 *n* (*number*) ichi 一 **2** *adj* (*with things*) hitotsu (no) 一つ(の); (*with people*) hitori (no) 一人(の)

3 *pron*: ***would you like ~?*** anata mo hoshii desu ka あなたも欲しいですか; ***I have a larger ~*** watashi wa ōki no o motte imasu 私は大きいのを持っています; ***~ is bigger than the other*** sore no hō ga mō ippō yori ōkii それの方がもう一方より大きい; ***which ~?*** (*thing*) dotchi どっち; (*person*) dare だれ; ***~ by ~*** (*things*) hitotsu zutsu 一つずつ; (*people*) hitori zutsu 一人ずつ; ***~ another*** otagai ni お互いに **4** *personal pron*: ***what can ~ say?*** nani ka iiyō ga arimasu ka 何か言いようがありますか; ***~ should take care of oneself*** hito wa jibun o taisetsu ni surubeki da 人は自分を大切にするべきだ

one-off *n* (*event*) ikkai kagiri no koto 一回限りのこと; (*person*) hoka ni rui no nai hito 他に類のない人; (*exception*) reigai 例外

one-parent family kataoya no katei 片親の家庭

oneself: ***by ~*** (*without help*) jibun-jishin de 自分自身で; (*alone*) hitori de ひとりで

one-sided ippōteki (na) 一方的(な); **one-way street** ippō-tsūkō 一方通行; **one-way ticket** katamichi-kippu 片道切符

onion tamanegi たまねぎ

on-line *adj* onrain (no) オンライン(の); ***go ~ to*** … ni setsuzoku suru …に接続する

on-line service COMPUT onrain-sābisu オンラインサービス

onlooker kenbutsunin 見物人

only 1 *adv* … dake …だけ; ***he's ~ 6*** kare wa hon no rokusai desu 彼はほんの六歳です; ***it's ~ one o'clock*** mada ichiji desu まだ一時です; ***not ~ X but also Y*** tada X dake de naku Y mo mata ただXだけでなくYもまた; ***~ just*** *manage* karōjite かろうじて **2** *adj* yuiitsu (no) 唯一(の); ***~ son / daughter*** hitori-musuko / musume 一人息子/娘

onset (*of illness*) hatsubyō 発病; (*of winter*) hajimari 始まり

onside *adv* SP onsaido オンサイド

onto: ***put X ~ Y*** (*on top of*) X o Y no ue ni oku XをYの上におく

onward (*in space*) zenpō e 前方へ; (*in time*) saki e 先へ; ***from … ~*** … ikō …以降

ooze 1 *v/i* (*of liquid, mud*) nijimideru にじみ出る **2** *v/t*: ***he ~s charm*** kare wa miryoku ni afurete iru 彼は魅力にあふれている

opaque futōmei (na) 不透明(な); ***~ glass*** kumori-garasu くもりガラス

OPEC (= ***Organization of Petroleum Exporting Countries***) OPEC

open 1 *adj door, window,* aita 開いた; *computer file* hiraita 開いた; *shop* eigyōchū (no) 営業中(の); *flower* saita 咲いた; (*honest, frank*) sōtchoku (na) 率直(な); *relationship* jiyū (na) 自由(な); *countryside* hirobiro to shita 広々とした; ***in the ~ air*** kogai de 戸外で; ***~ 24 hours*** nijūyojikan-eigyō ２４時間営業; ***~ all year round*** nenjū-mukyū 年中無休 **2** *v/t* hiraku 開く; *door, shop, window, bottle* akeru 開ける; *meeting* kaishi suru 開始する **3** *v/i* (*of door, shop*) hiraku 開く; (*of flower*) saku 咲く

♦ **open up** *v/i* (*of person*) uchitokeru 打ち解ける

open-air *adj meeting, concert* kogai (no) 戸外(の); *pool* okugai (no) 屋外(の)

open-ended *contract etc* mukigen (no) 無期限(の)

opening (*in wall etc*) sukima すき間; (*of movie, novel etc*) bōtō 冒頭; (*job*) aki 空き

openly (*frankly*) sotchoku ni 率直に

open-minded kokoro no hiroi 心の広い; **open plan office** ōpun-puran-ofisu オープンプランオフィス; **open ticket** ōpun-chiketto オープンチケット

opera opera オペラ

opera glasses opera-gurasu オペラグラス; **opera house** opera-hausu オペラハウス; **opera singer** opera-kashu オペラ歌手

operate 1 *v/i* (*of company*) eigyō

suru 営業する; (*of airline*) unkō suru 運航する; (*of bus service*) unkō suru 運行する; (*of machine*) ugoku 動く; MED shujutsu suru 手術する **2** *v/t machine* sōsa suru 操作する

♦ **operate on** MED … ni shujutsu o suru …に手術をする

operating instructions shiyō-setsumei 使用説明; **operating room** MED shujutsu-shitsu 手術室; **operating system** COMPUT operētingu-shisutemu オペレーティングシステム

operation MED shujutsu 手術; (*of machine*) sōsa 操作; ***~s*** (*of company*) jigyō-katsudō 事業活動; ***have an ~*** MED shujutsu o ukeru 手術を受ける

operator TELEC operētā オペレーター; (*of machine*) unten-sha 運転者; (*tour ~*) ryokō-dairiten 旅行代理店

ophthalmologist gankai 眼科医

opinion iken 意見; ***in my ~*** watashi no iken de wa 私の意見では

opponent aite 相手

opportunity kikai 機会

oppose … ni hantai suru …に反対する; ***be ~d to*** … ni hantai de aru …に反対である; ***as ~d to …*** … to taishōteki ni …と対照的に

opposite 1 *adj side of road,* mukōgawa (no) 向こう側(の); *end of town, direction* hantai (no) 反対(の); *views, characters* seihantai (no) 正反対(の); *meaning* gyaku (no) 逆(の); ***the ~ sex*** isei 異性 **2** *n* gyaku 逆

opposition (*to plan*) hantai 反対; POL yatō 野党

oppress *the people* yokuatsu suru 抑圧する

oppressive *rule* asseiteki (na) 圧制的(な); *weather* uttōshii うっとうしい

optical illusion me no sakkaku 目の錯覚

optician megane-ya 眼鏡屋

optimism rakkanron 楽観論

optimist rakkanron-sha 楽観論者

optimistic rakkanteki (na) 楽観的(な)

optimum 1 *adj* saiteki (na) 最適(な) **2** *n* saiteki-jōken 最適条件

option sentaku 選択

optional *subject* jiyū-sentaku (no) 自由選択(の); ***it's ~*** sore wa sentaku dekiru それは選択できる

optional extras opushon オプション

or … ka soretomo … ka …かそれとも…か; (*otherwise*) samonaito さもないと; ***he can't hear ~ see*** kare wa miru koto mo kiku koto mo dekinai 彼は見ることも聞くこともできない; ***~ else!*** samonaito taihen da yo さもないと大変だよ

oral *exam* kōtō (no) 口頭(の); *hygiene* kuchi (no) 口(の); ***~ sex*** ōraru-sekkusu オーラルセックス

orange 1 *adj* (*color*) orenji-iro (no) オレンジ色(の) **2** *n* (*fruit*) orenji オレンジ; (*color*) orenji-iro オレンジ色

orange juice orenji-jūsu オレンジジュース

orator enzetsu-sha 演説者

orbit 1 *n* kidō 軌道; ***send … into ~*** … o kidō ni noseru …を軌道に乗せる **2** *v/t the earth* kidō o egaite … o mawaru 軌道を描いて…を回る

orchard kajuen 果樹園

orchestra ōkesutora オーケストラ

orchid ran らん

ordeal shiren 試練

order 1 *n* (*command*) meirei 命令; (*sequence*) jun 順; (*orderliness: in society*) chitsujo 秩序; (*in one's life*) kiritsu 規律; (*for goods, in restaurant*) chūmon 注文; ***in ~ to*** … suru tame ni …するために; ***out of ~*** (*not functioning*) koshōchū de 故障中で; (*not in sequence*) junjo ga kurutte 順序が狂って **2** *v/t* (*put in sequence, proper layout*) seiri suru 整理する; *goods, meal* chūmon suru 注文する; ***~ X to do Y*** X ni Y suru yō ni meijiru XにYするように命じる **3** *v/i* (*in restaurant*) chūmon suru 注文する

orderly 1 *adj lifestyle* kiritsu-tadashii 規律正しい; *person*

kichōmen (na) きちょうめん(な) **2** *n* (*in hospital*) tsukisoi 付き添い
ordinary futsū (no) 普通(の)
ore kōseki 鉱石
organ ANAT kikan 器官 MUS orugan オルガン
organic *food, farming* munōyaku (no) 無農薬(の); ***~ fertilizer*** yūki-hiryō 有機肥料
organism seibutsu 生物
organization soshikitai 組織体; (*organizing*) kōsei 構成; (*of conference*) junbi 準備
organize *people, team* soshiki suru 組織する; *conference* junbi suru 準備する; *data* keitōdateru 系統立てる; *one's life* totonoeru 整える
organizer (*person*) shusai-sha 主催者
orgasm ōgazumu オーガズム
Orient Tōyō 東洋
orient *v/t* hōkō ni mukeru 方向に向ける; ***~ oneself*** hōkōzuke suru 方向付けする
Oriental 1 *adj* Tōyō (no) 東洋(の) **2** *n* Tōyō-jin 東洋人
origami origami 折り紙
origin kigen 起源; ***person of Japanese ~*** Nikkei no hito 日系の人
original 1 *adj* (*genuine*) honmono (no) 本物(の); (*not copied*) dokuji (no) 独自(の); (*first*) moto (no) もと(の) **2** *n* (*painting etc*) orijinaru オリジナル
originality dokusōsei 独創性
originally motomoto もともと; (*at first*) hajime wa 始めは
originate 1 *v/t scheme, idea* hajimeru 始める **2** *v/i*: ***~ in*** (*of idea, belief*) umareru 生まれる; (*of family*) shusshin de aru 出身である
originator (*of scheme etc*) kōan-sha 考案者; ***he's not an ~*** kare wa aideaman de wa nai 彼はアイデアマンではない
ornament *n* kazari 飾り
ornamental kazari (no) 飾り(の)
ornate *style etc* kotta 凝った
orphan *n* koji 孤児
orphanage yōgo-shisetsu 養護施設
orthopedic seikei-geka (no) 整形外科(の)
Osaka Ōsaka 大阪
ostentatious hade (na) 派手(な)
other 1 *adj* hoka (no) ほか(の); ***the ~ day*** (*recently*) senjitsu 先日; ***every ~ day / person*** ichinichi / hitori oki ni 一日/一人おきに **2** *n*: ***the ~*** (*thing*) hoka no mono ほかの物; (*person*) hoka no hito ほかの人; ***the ~s*** (*things*) mō ippō no mono もう一方の物; (*people*) mō ippō no hito もう一方の人
otherwise samonaito さもないと; (*differently*) chigau fū ni 違うふうに
otter kawauso かわうそ
ought *I ~ to know* watashi wa shiru hitsuyō ga aru 私は知る必要がある; ***you ~ to have done it*** sore o yatte okubeki datta それをやっておくべきだった
ounce onsu オンス
our ◊ watashitachi no 私たちの; ***~ mother*** watashitachi no haha 私たちの母 ◊ (*omission of possessive*): ***we forgot ~ keys*** watashitachi wa kagi o wasureta 私たちはかぎを忘れた
ours watashitachi no mono 私たちのもの
ourselves *by ~* (*without help*) jibuntachi de 私たち自身で; (*alone*) watashitachi dake de 私たちだけで
oust (*from office*) tsuihō suru 追放する
out *be ~* (*of light*) kirete iru 切れている; (*of fire*) kiete iru 消えている; (*of flower*) saite iru 咲いている; (*of sun*) dete iru 出ている; (*not at home*) rusu de aru 留守である; (*not in office*) gaishutsuchū de aru 外出中である; (*of calculations*) machigatte iru 間違っている; (*be published*) shuppan sarete iru 出版されている; (*of secret*) bareru ばれる; (*of scandal*) hakkaku suru 発覚する; (*no longer in competition*) haitai suru 敗退する; (*in baseball*) auto de aru アウトである; (*no longer in fashion*) ryūkōokure de

aru 流行遅れである; *~ here in Dallas* koko Darasu de wa ここダラスでは; ***he's ~ in the garden*** kare wa niwa ni dete imasu 彼は庭に出ています; **(*get*) *~!*** dete ike 出ていけ; **(*get*) *~ of my room!*** watashi no heya kara dete ike 私の部屋から出ていけ; ***that's ~!*** (*out of the question*) sore wa rongai da それは論外だ; ***he's ~ to win*** (*fully intending to*) kare wa katsu tsumori da 彼は勝つつもりだ

outboard motor sengai-enjin 船外エンジン

outbreak (*of violence, war*) boppatsu ぼっ発

outburst (*emotional*) bakuhatsu 爆発

outcast tsuihō sareta 追放された

outcome kekka 結果

outcry kōgi 抗議

outdated jidai-okure (no) 時代後れ(の)

outdo shinogu しのぐ

outdoor *toilet, facilities* okugai (no) 屋外(の); *activities, life* yagai (no) 野外(の)

outdoors *adv* soto ni 外に

outer *wall etc* sotogawa (no) 外側(の)

outer space uchū-kūkan 宇宙空間

outfit (*clothes*) hitosoroi no fuku ひとそろいの服; (*company*) kaisha 会社; (*organization*) soshiki 組織

outgoing *personality* gaikōteki (na) 外向的(な); ***~ flight*** shuppatsubin 出発便

outgrow *old ideas* … kara nukedasu …から抜け出す

outing (*trip*) ensoku 遠足

outlet (*of pipe*) hakeguchi はけ口; (*for sales*) hanbaiten 販売店; ELEC soketto ソケット

outline 1 *n* (*of person, building etc*) rinkaku 輪郭; (*of plan, novel*) aramashi あらまし **2** *v/t plans etc* aramashi o setsumei suru あらましを説明する

outlive … yori nagaiki o suru …より長生きをする

outlook (*prospects*) mitōshi 見通し

outlying *areas* chūshin o hanareta 中心を離れた

outnumber … yori kazu de masaru …より数で勝る

out of ◊ (*motion*): ***run ~ the house*** ie kara hashiridasu 家から走り出す; ***look ~ the window*** mado kara soto o miru 窓から外を見る ◊ (*position*): ***20 miles ~ Detroit*** Detoroito kara nijūmairu no tokoro de デトロイトから二十マイルの所で ◊ (*cause*): ***~ jealousy / curiosity*** netami / kōkishin kara ねたみ/好奇心から ◊ (*without*): ***we are ~ gas / beer*** gasorin / bīru ga kireta ガソリン/ビールが切れた ◊ (*from a group*): ***5 ~ 10*** jūnin chū gonin 十人中五人 ◊ (*not within range*): ***~ sight*** mienai tokoro de 見えない所で ◊ (*sheltered from*): ***keep ~ the sun*** chokusha-nikkō o sakete 直射日光を避けて

out-of-date jidai-okure (no) 時代遅れ(の)

out-of-the-way (*remote*) henpi (na) へんぴ(な)

outperform … yori sugurete iru … より優れている

output 1 *n* (*of factory*) seisandaka 生産高; COMPUT autoputto アウトプット **2** *v/t* (*produce*) seisan suru 生産する; COMPUT: *signal* … o shutsuryoku suru …を出力する

outrage 1 *n* (*feeling*) ikidōri いきどおり; (*act*) bōryoku-kōi 暴力行為 **2** *v/t person* … o gekido saseru …を激怒させる; ***I was ~d to hear …*** … to kiite hara ga tatta …と聞いて腹が立った

outrageous *acts* yurushigatai 許しがたい; *prices* akireta あきれた

outright 1 *adj winner* kanzen (na) 完全(な) **2** *adv win* kanzen ni 完全に; *kill* tetteiteki ni 徹底的に

outrun (*run faster than*) … yori hayaku hashiru …より速く走る; (*run for longer than*) … yori tōku e hashiru …より遠くへ走る

outset hajime 初め; ***from the ~*** hajime kara 初めから

outside 1 *adj surface, wall, lane*

sotogawa (no) 外側(の) **2** *adv sit* soto ni 外に; *go* soto e 外へ **3** *prep* … no soto de / ni …の外で/に; (*apart from*) … igai de wa …以外では; ***~ the USA*** Amerika igai de wa アメリカ以外では **4** *n* (*of building, case etc*) sotogawa 外側; ***at the ~*** saikō de 最高で

outside broadcast chūkei-hōsō 中継放送

outsider bugai-sha 部外者, tanin 他人; (*in race, election*) kachime no nai hito 勝ち目のない人

outsize *adj clothing* tokudai (no) 特大(の)

outskirts kōgai 郊外

outspoken sotchoku (na) 率直(な)

outstanding kesshutsu shita 傑出した; FIN miharai (no) 未払い(の)

outward *adj appearance* hyōmenteki (na) 表面的(な); ***~ journey*** ōro 往路

outwardly gaikenjō wa 外見上は

outweigh … yori masaru …より勝る

outwit dashinuku 出し抜く

oval *adj* daenkei (no) だ円形(の)

ovary ransō 卵巣

oven ōbun オーブン

over 1 *prep* (*above*) … no ue ni …の上に; (*across*) … no mukōgawa ni …の向こう側に; (*more than*) … yori ōku …より多く; (*during*) … no aida ni …の間に; ***travel all ~ Japan*** Nihonjū o tabi suru 日本中を旅する; ***you find them all ~ Japan*** sore wa Nihonjū doko ni demo aru それは日本中どこにでもある; ***let's talk ~ a meal / drink*** shokuji shinagara / nominagara hanasō 食事しながら/飲みながら話そう; ***we're ~ the worst*** saiaku wa sugita 最悪は過ぎた; ***she's ~ 40*** kanojo wa yonjussai o koete iru 彼女は四十歳を越えている **2** *adv*: ***be ~*** (*finished*) owari de aru 終わりである; (*left*) amatte iru 余っている; ***~ to you*** (*your turn*) anata no ban desu あなたの番です; ***~ in Europe*** (*with verbs of being*) Yōroppa ni ヨーロッパに; (*with verbs of activity*) Yōroppa de ヨーロッパに; ***~ here*** (*with verbs of being*) kochira ni こちらに; (*with verbs of activity*) kochira de こちらで; ***it hurts all ~*** karadajū itai desu 体中痛いです; ***painted white all ~*** ichimen shiro ni nurarete iru 一面白に塗られている; ***it's all ~*** kore de oshimai da これでおしまいだ; ***~ and ~ again*** nando mo nando mo 何度も何度も; ***do X ~ (again)*** X kurikaesu Xを繰り返す

overall *adj length* zentai (no) 全体(の); *cost* zenbu (no) 全部(の)

overawe: ***be ~d by*** … ni attō sareru …に圧倒される

overboard: ***man ~!*** dare ka ochitazo だれか落ちたぞ; ***go ~ for*** … ni do ga sugiru …に度が過ぎる

overcast *day, sky* kumotta くもった

overcharge *v/t* jissai yori takaku seikyū suru 実際より高く請求する

overcoat ōbā オーバー

overcome *difficulties* … ni uchikatsu …に打ち勝つ; ***be ~ by emotion*** kanjōteki ni mairu 感情的に参る

overcrowded chōman'in (no) 超満員(の)

overdo (*exaggerate*) yari-sugiru やりすぎる; (*in frying, grilling*) yaki-sugiru 焼きすぎる; *vegetables* ni-sugiru 煮すぎる; ***you're ~ing things*** kimi wa nan demo yari-sugiru 君は何でもやりすぎる

overdone *meat* yakisugita 焼きすぎた; *vegetables* nisugita 煮すぎた;

overdose *n* (*of sleeping pills etc*) chishiryō 致死量; (*of illegal substance*) yarisugi やりすぎ; (*given by doctor*) kajō-tōyo 過剰投与;

overdraft tōza-karikoshi 当座借越; ***have an ~*** (*authorized*) tōza-karikoshi ga mitomerarete iru 当座借越が認められている; ***have an ~*** (*unauthorized*) kōza ga karikoshi ni natte iru 口座が借り越しになっている; **overdraw** *account* karikosu 借り越す; ***be $800 ~n*** happyaku doru karikoshite iru 800ドル借り越している; **overdrive**

MOT ōbādoraibu オーバードライブ; **overdue** *apology, alteration* okureta 遅れた; **overestimate** kadai ni hyōka suru 過大に評価する; **overexpose** *photograph* roshutsu-kado ni suru 露出過度にする

overflow *v/i* (*of water*) afureru あふれる; (*of river*) hanran suru はんらんする

overgrown *garden* kusabōbō (no) 草ぼうぼう(の); ***he's an ~ baby*** kare wa sodachisugi no akanbō da 彼は育ちすぎの赤ん坊だ

overhaul *v/t engine* ōbāhōru suru オーバーホールする; *plans* minaosu 見直す

overhead 1 *adj railway* kōka (no) 高架(の); ***~light*** tenjō no denki 天井の電気 **2** *n* FIN kansetsu-keihi 間接経費

overhear futo mimi ni suru ふと耳にする

overjoyed ōyorokobi (no) 大喜び(の)

overland 1 *adj route* rikuro (no) 陸路(の) **2** *adv travel* rikuro de 陸路で

overlap *v/i* (*of tiles, periods of time*) kasanaru 重なる; (*of theories*) kyōtsū suru bubun ga aru 共通する部分がある

overload *v/t vehicle* … ni ni o tsumisugiru …に荷を積みすぎる; ELEC … ni fuka o kakesugiru …に負荷をかけすぎる

overlook (*of building etc*) miorosu 見下ろす; (*not see: accidentally*) miotosu 見落とす; (*deliberately*) minogasu 見逃す

overly kado ni 過度に; ***not ~ …*** amari … de nai あまり…でない

overnight *adv* ippaku 一泊

overnight bag shōryokōyō no kaban 小旅行用のかばん

overpaid kyūryō ga shiharawaresugi (no) 給料が支払われすぎ(の)

overpass kōka-dōro 高架道路

overpower *v/t* (*physically*) oshitaosu 押し倒す

overpowering *smell* kyōretsu (na) 強烈(な); *sense of guilt* attōteki (na) 圧倒的(な)

overpriced … ni takane o tsukesugiru …に高値をつけすぎる

overrated kadai-hyōka sareta 過大評価された

overrule *decision* mukō ni suru 無効にする

overrun *country* shinryaku suru 侵略する; *time* chōka suru 超過する; ***be ~ with*** … de ippai de aru …でいっぱいである

overseas 1 *adv live* kaigai ni 海外に; *work* kaigai de 海外で; *travel* kaigai o 海外を **2** *adj travel* kaigai (no) 海外(の); *visitor* kaigai kara (no) 海外から(の)

oversee kantoku suru 監督する

oversight miotoshi 見落とし

oversleep nesugosu 寝過ごす

overtake (*in work, development*) … o shinogu …をしのぐ; *Br* MOT … ni oitsuku …に追いつく

overthrow *government* taosu 倒す

overtime 1 *n* (*in the evening*) zangyō 残業; (*on Sunday, holiday*) kyūjitsu-shukkin 休日出勤; SP enchōsen 延長戦 **2** *adv* (*in the evening*) zangyō de 残業で; (*on Sunday, holiday*) kyūjitsu-shukkin de 休日出勤で

overture MUS jokyoku 序曲; ***make ~s to*** … ni mōshiire o suru …に申し入れをする

overturn 1 *v/t* hikkurikaesu ひっくり返す; *government* datō suru 打倒する **2** *v/i* (*of vehicle*) hikkurikaeru ひっくり返る

overweight futori-sugi (no) 太りすぎ(の)

overwhelm attō suru 圧倒する; ***be ~ed by*** (*very pleased: by response*) … no tame ni mune ga ippai ni naru …のために胸が一杯になる

overwork 1 *n* karō 過労; ***death from ~*** karōshi 過労死 **2** *v/i* hataraki-sugiru 働きすぎる **3** *v/t employee* hatarakase-sugiru 働かせすぎる; *machine* tsukai-sugiru 使いすぎる

owe *v/t* … ni shakkin o shite iru …に借金をしている; ***~ … $500*** … ni gohyaku doru karite iru …に500ドル借りている; ***~ … an apology*** … ni ayamaranakereba naranai …に謝らなければならない; ***how much do I ~ you?*** ikura haraeba ii desu ka いくら払えばいいですか
owing to … no tame ni …のために
owl fukurō ふくろう
own[1] *v/t* shoyū suru 所有する
own[2] **1** *adj* jibun-jishin (no) 自分自身(の) **2** *pron*: ***a car / an apartment of my ~*** jibun no kuruma / apāto 自分の車/アパート; ***on my / his ~*** hitori de ひとりで
♦ **own up** hakujō suru 白状する
owner shoyū-sha 所有者
ownership shoyū-ken 所有権
oxide sankabutsu 酸化物
oxygen sanso 酸素
oyster kaki かき
ozone ozon オゾン
ozone layer ozon-sō オゾン層

P

pace 1 *n* (*step*) ipo 一歩; (*speed*) pēsu ペース **2** *v/i*: aruku 歩く; ***~ up and down*** urouro to arukimawaru うろうろと歩き回る
pacemaker MED, SP pēsumēkā ペースメーカー
Pacific: ***the ~*** (***Ocean***) Taiheiyō 太平洋
Pacific Rim: ***the ~*** kan-Taiheiyō 環太平洋; ***~ countries*** kan-Taiheiyō-shokoku 環太平洋諸国
Pacific War (*1941-45*) Taiheiyō-sensō 太平洋戦争
pacifier oshaburi おしゃぶり
pacifism heiwa-shugi 平和主義
pacifist *n* heiwa-shugi-sha 平和主義者
pacify nadameru なだめる
pack 1 *n* (*back~*) bakku-pakku バックパック; (*of sausages etc*) pakku パック; (*of cereal, cigarettes*) hako 箱; (*of candy*) fukuro 袋; (*of cards*) hitokumi 一組 **2** *v/t* tsumeru 詰める; *bag* … ni nimotsu o tsumeru …に荷物を詰める **3** *v/i* nizukuri o suru 荷造りをする
package 1 *n* (*parcel*) kozutsumi 小包; (*of offers etc*) ikkatsu-keiyaku 一括契約 **2** *v/t* (*in packs*) hōsō suru 包装する; (*for promotion*) pakkēji suru パッケージする
package deal (*for vacation*) setto-hanbai セット販売
package tour pakku-ryokō パック旅行
packaging (*of product*) hōsō 包装; (*of rock star etc*) imēji イメージ
packed (*crowded*) komiatta 込み合った
packet kobukuro 小袋, pakku パック
pact kyōtei 協定
pad[1] **1** *n* (*piece of cloth etc*) paddo パッド; (*for writing*) binsen 便せん **2** *v/t* (*with material*) … ni tsumemono o suru …に詰めものをする; *speech, report* hikinobasu 引き延ばす
pad[2] *v/i* (*move quietly*) sotto aruku そっと歩く
padded *jacket, shoulders* kata-paddo no haitta 肩パッドの入った
padding (*material*) tsumemono 詰めもの; (*in speech etc*) yodan 余談
paddle[1] **1** *n* (*for canoe*) padoru パドル, kai かい **2** *v/i* (*in canoe*) kogu こぐ
paddle[2] *v/i* (*in water*) bachabacha oyogu ばちゃばちゃ泳ぐ
paddock (*on farm*) shōbokujō 小牧場; (*at racetrack*) padokku パドック
padlock 1 *n* nankinjō 南京錠 **2** *v/t*

gate … ni nankinjō o kakeru …に南京錠をかける; **~ X to Y** X ni kagi o kakete Y ni tomeru Xに鍵をかけてYに止める
page[1] *n* pēji ページ; **~ number** pēji ページ
page[2] *v/t* (*call*) yobidasu 呼び出す
pager pokettoberu ポケットベル
pagoda tō 塔
paid employment ***be in ~*** shigoto o motte iru 仕事を持っている
pail baketsu バケツ
pain itami 痛み; ***be in ~*** itami ga aru 痛みがある; ***take ~s to …*** … suru no ni hone o oru …するのに骨を折る; ***a ~ in the neck*** F (*person*) iya na yatsu いやなやつ
painful *arm, leg etc* itai 痛い; (*distressing*) tsurai つらい; (*laborious*) konnan (na) 困難(な)
painfully (*extremely*) hijō ni 非常に
painkiller itamidome 痛み止め
painless mutsū (no) 無痛(の); (*not problematic*) tayasui たやすい
painstaking *work* hone no oreru 骨の折れる; *worker* kinben (na) 勤勉(な)
paint 1 *n* (*for wall*) penki ペンキ; (*for artist*) enogu 絵の具 **2** *v/t wall etc* … ni penki o nuru …にペンキを塗る; *picture* kaku 描く **3** *v/i* (*as art form*) e o kaku 絵を描く
paintbrush hake はけ; (*of artist*) efude 絵筆
painter (*decorator*) penki-ya ペンキ屋; (*artist*) ekaki 絵かき, gaka 画家
painting (*picture*) e 絵; (*decorating*) penkinuri ペンキ塗り
paintwork tosō 塗装
pair (*of animals, birds*) tsugai つがい; (*of people*) futarigumi 二人組; SP pea ペア; (*of objects*) tsui 対; ***a ~ of shoes / sandals*** kutsu / sandaru issoku 靴/サンダル一足; ***a ~ of scissors*** hasami itchō はさみ一丁; ***a ~ of pants*** zubon itchaku ズボン一着
pajama jacket pajama no uwagi パジャマの上着
pajama pants pajama no zubon パジャマのズボン
pajamas pajama パジャマ
Pakistan Pakisutan パキスタン
Pakistani 1 *adj* Pakisutan (no) パキスタン(の) **2** *n* Pakisutan-jin パキスタン人
pal F tomodachi 友達; ***hey ~, got a light?*** nē, matchi motte nai ねー、マッチ持ってない
palace kyūden 宮殿
palate kōgai 口がい; *fig* mikaku 味覚
palatial gōka (na) 豪華(な)
pale *person* aojiroi 青白い; ***look ~*** kaoiro ga warui 顔色が悪い; ***go ~*** aozameru 青ざめる; ***~ pink / blue*** usui pinku-iro / burū うすいピンク色/ブルー
pallet (*for goods*) nidai 荷台
pallor irojiro-sa 色白さ
palm[1] (*of hand*) tenohira 手のひら
palm[2] (*tree*) yashi やし
palpitations MED dōki 動き
paltry *sum* wazuka (na) わずか(な)
pamper amayakasu 甘やかす
pamphlet panfuretto パンフレット
pan 1 *n* furaipan フライパン **2** *v/t* F (*criticize*) kokiorosu こきおろす
♦ **pan out** ***let's wait and see how things ~*** chotto matte dō naru ka mite miyo ちょっと待ってどうなるか見てみよう
pancake hottokēki ホットケーキ
panda panda パンダ
pandemonium daikonran 大混乱
pane (*of glass*) madogarasu 窓ガラス
panel (*section*) paneru パネル; ***a ~ of experts*** senmonka no ichidan 専門家の一団
paneling panerubari パネル張り
panhandle *v/i* F monogoi o suru 物乞いをする
panic 1 *n* panikku パニック **2** *v/i* (*of person*) awateru あわてる; (*of crowd*) panikku-jōtai ni naru パニック状態になる; ***don't ~*** awateruna あわてるな
panic selling FIN rōbai uri ろうばい売り
panic-stricken panikku-jōtai ni natta パニック状態になった

panorama panorama パノラマ
panoramic panorama (no) パノラマ(の)
pansy (*flower*) panjī パンジー
pant *v/i* ikigire suru 息切れする
panties pantī パンティー
pants zubon ズボン; ***a pair of ~*** zubon itchaku ズボン一着
pantyhose pantīsutokkingu パンティーストッキング
paper 1 *n* (*material*) kami 紙; (*news~*) shinbun 新聞; (*wall~*) kabegami 壁紙; (*academic*) ronbun 論文; (*examination ~*) shiken 試験; ***~s*** (*documents*) shorui 書類; (*identity ~s*) mibun-shōmeisho 身分証明書; ***a piece of ~*** kamikire ichimai 紙切れ一枚; ***Japanese ~*** washi 和紙 **2** *adj* kami (no) 紙(の) **3** *v/t walls* … ni kabegami o haru …に壁紙をはる
paperback pēpābakku ペーパーバック; **paper bag** kamibukuro 紙袋; **paper clip** kurippu クリップ; **paper cup** kamikoppu 紙コップ; **paperwork** shorui-jimu 書類事務
par (*in golf*) pā パー; ***be on a ~ with*** … to dōtō de aru …と同等である; ***feel below ~*** itsumo no chōshi de nai いつもの調子でない
parachute 1 *n* parashūto パラシュート **2** *v/i* parashūto de oriru パラシュートで降りる **3** *v/t supplies* parashūto de otosu パラシュートで落とす
parade 1 *n* (*procession*) parēdo パレード **2** *v/i* (*to celebrate*) parēdo suru パレードする; (*to be noticed*) koremiyogashi ni aruku これみよがしに歩く; (*of soldiers*) kōshin suru 行進する **3** *v/t knowledge, new car* misebirakasu 見せびらかす
paradise tengoku 天国; (*biblical*) Eden no sono エデンの園
paradox gyakusetsu 逆説, paradokkusu パラドックス
paradoxical gyakusetsuteki (na) 逆説的(な)
paradoxically gyakusetsuteki ni 逆説的に
paragraph danraku 段落
parallel 1 *n* (*line*) heikō 平行; (*of latitude*) isen 緯線; *fig* ruijiten 類似点; ***do two things in ~*** futatsu no koto o heiretsu shite okonau 二つのことを並列して行う **2** *adj line* heikō (no) 平行(の) **3** *v/t* (*match*) … ni hitteki suru …に匹敵する
paralysis mahi 麻ひ
paralyze mahi saseru 麻ひさせる; *fig* … no kinō o mahi saseru …の機能を麻ひさせる
paramedic iryō-hojoin 医療補助員
parameter seigen-han'i 制限範囲
paramilitary 1 *adj* jungunjiteki (na) 準軍事的(な) **2** *n* jungunji-soshiki no kōseiin 準軍事組織の構成員
paramount saikō (no) 最高(の); ***be ~*** mottomo jūyō de aru もっとも重要である
paranoia saigishin さいぎ心
paranoid *adj* kangurisugi (no) かんぐりすぎ(の)
paraphernalia mochimono 持ち物
paraphrase *v / t* iikaeru 言いかえる
paraplegic *n* kahanshin-mahi no hito 下半身麻ひの人
parasite kiseichū 寄生虫
parasol parasoru パラソル
paratrooper rakkasanhei 落下傘兵
parcel kozutsumi 小包
♦**parcel up** kozutsumi ni suru 小包にする
parch *v/t*: ***be ~ed*** (*of person*) nodo ga karakara de aru のどがからからである
pardon 1 *n* LAW onsha 恩赦; ***I beg your ~?*** (*what did you say?*) nan to osshaimashita ka 何とおっしゃいましたか; ***I beg your ~*** (*I'm sorry*) gomen nasai ごめんなさい **2** *v/t* yurusu 許す; LAW shamen suru 赦免する; ***~ me?*** nan to osshaimashita ka 何とおっしゃいましたか
pare (*peel*) … no kawa o muku …の皮をむく
parent oya 親; ***~s*** ryōshin 両親
parental oya (no) 親(の)
parent company oyagaisha 親会社
parent-teacher association pītīē

PTA

park[1] (*area*) kōen 公園

park[2] *v/t&v/i* MOT chūsha suru 駐車する

parka anorakku アノラック

parking MOT chūsha 駐車; ***no ~*** chūsha-kinshi 駐車禁止

parking brake saidoburēki サイドブレーキ; **parking garage** chūshajō 駐車場; **parking lot** chūshajō 駐車場; **parking meter** pākingu-mētā パーキングメーター; **parking place** chūsha-supēsu 駐車スペース; **parking ticket** chūsha-ihan no yobidashijō 駐車違反の呼び出し状

parliament gikai 議会

parliamentary gikai (no) 議会(の)

parole 1 *n* karishussho 仮出所; ***be on ~*** karishussho shite iru 仮出所している **2** *v/t* karishussho saseru 仮出所させる

parrot ōmu おうむ

parsley paseri パセリ

part 1 *n* (*portion*) ichibu 一部; (*section*) bu 部; (*area*) bubun 部分; (*of country*) chihō 地方; (*of machine*) buhin 部品; (*in play, movie*) yaku 役; MUS pāto パート; (*in hair*) wakeme 分け目; ***take ~ in*** … ni sanka suru …に参加する; ***mix two ~s vinegar with three ~s oil*** su ni, abura san no wariai de mazeru 酢2、油3の割合で混ぜる **2** *adv* (*partly*) ichibubun wa 一部分は **3** *v/i* wakareru 別れる **4** *v/t* wakeru 分ける

♦**part with** tebanasu 手放す

part exchange shitadori 下取り; ***take … in ~*** … o shitadori suru …を下取りする

partial (*incomplete*) bubunteki (na) 部分的(な); ***be ~ to*** … ga suki de aru …が好きである

partially bubunteki ni 部分的に

participant sanka-sha 参加者

participate sanka suru 参加する; ***~ in*** … ni sanka suru …に参加する

participation sanka 参加

particle PHYS ryūshi 粒子; (*small amount*) kakera かけら

particular (*specific*) tokutei (no) 特定(の); (*special*) tokubetsu (no) 特別(の); (*fussy*) yakamashii やかましい; ***in ~*** toku ni 特に; ***this ~ morning / case*** sono asa / kono bāi ni kagitte その朝/この場合に限って; ***for a ~ reason*** toku ni riyū ga atte 特に理由があって

particularly toku ni 特に

parting (*of people*) wakare 別れ

partition 1 *n* (*screen*) majikiri 間仕切り; (*of country*) bunkatsu 分割 **2** *v/t country* bunkatsu suru 分割する

♦**partition off** … o shikiru …を仕切る

partly bubunteki ni 部分的に; ***that's ~ the reason*** sore mo riyū no hitotsu da それも理由の1つだ

partner COM kyōdō-keiei-sha 共同経営者; (*at work*) kumu aite 組む相手; (*husband, wife*) haigū-sha 配偶者; (*in long-term relationship*) koibito 恋人; (*in particular activity*) pātonā パートナー

partnership (*business*) kyōdō-keiei-jigyō 共同経営事業; (*relationship*: *in business*) kyōdō-keiei-sha 共同経営者; (*in dance, sport*) kyōryoku-kankei 協力関係; POL kyōryoku 協力

part of speech hinshi 品詞; **part owner** kyōdō-shoyū-sha 共同所有者; **part-time 1** *adj* pātotaimu (no) パートタイム(の), baito (no) バイト(の); *teacher* hijōkin (no) 非常勤(の) **2** *adv work* pātotaimu de パートタイムで

party 1 *n* (*celebration*) pātī パーティー; POL seitō 政党; (*group of people*) ichidan 一団; ***be a ~ to*** … ni kuwawaru …に加わる **2** *v/i* F omoikiri asobu 思い切り遊ぶ

pass 1 *n* (*for entry*) nyūjōken 入場券; (*permit*) tsūkōshō 通行証; (*membership card*) kaiinshō 会員証; (*for public transportation*) teikiken 定期券; SP pasu パス; (*in mountains*) tōge 峠; ***make a ~ at*** … ni mōshon o kakeru …にモーションをかける **2** *v/t* (*hand*) watasu 渡す; *salt* mawasu 回す; (*go past*) tōrisugiru 通り過ぎる; MOT oikosu 追い越す; (*go beyond*) koeru 越える; (*approve*) kaketsu suru 可決する; *new drug* ninka suru 認可する; SP pasu suru パスする; **~ *an exam*** shiken ni gōkaku suru 試験に合格する; **~ *sentence*** LAW hanketsu o kudasu 判決を下す; **~ *the time*** jikan o sugosu 時間を過ごす **3** *v/i* (*of time*) tatsu たつ; (*in exam*) ukaru 受かる; SP pasu suru パスする; (*go away*) kieru 消える

♦**pass around** … o mawasu …を回す

♦**pass away** (*die*) nakunaru 亡くなる

♦**pass by 1** *v/t* (*go past*) … o tōrisugiru …を通り過ぎる **2** *v/i* (*go past*) tōrisugiru 通り過ぎる

♦**pass on 1** *v/t information,* … o tsutaeru …を伝える; *book* … o mawasu …を回す; *costs, savings* … o mawasu …を回す **2** *v/i* (*die*) shinu 死ぬ

♦**pass out** (*faint*) ki o ushinau 気を失う

♦**pass through** *town* … o tōrinukeru …を通り抜ける

♦**pass up** *opportunity* … o miokuru …を見送る

passable *road* tsūkō-kanō (na) 通行可能(な); (*acceptable*) māmā (no) まあまあ(の)

passage (*corridor*) tsūro 通路; (*from poem, book*) issetsu 一節; (*of time*) keika 経過

passageway tsūro 通路

passenger jōkyaku 乗客

passenger seat joshuseki 助手席

passer-by tsūkōnin 通行人

passion jōnetsu 情熱; (*sexual desire*) jōyoku 情欲

passionate jōnetsuteki (na) 情熱的(な)

passive 1 *adj* ukemi (no) 受身(の) **2** *n* GRAM ukemi 受身; ***in the ~*** ukemi de 受身で

pass mark gōkakuten 合格点;

passport pasupōto パスポート;

passport control (*arrivals*) nyūkoku-shinsa 入国審査; (*departures*) shukkoku-shinsa 出国審査; **password** pasuwādo パスワード

past 1 *adj* (*former*) izen (no) 以前(の); ***the ~ few days*** kono sūjitsu この数日; ***that's all ~ now*** sore wa mō owatta koto da それはもう終わったことだ **2** *n* kako 過去; ***in the ~*** kako ni 過去に **3** *prep* (*in time*) … o sugite …を過ぎて; (*in position*) … o tōrisugite …を通り過ぎて; ***it's half ~ two*** niji han desu 二時半です **4** *adv*: ***run / walk ~*** hashitte / aruite tōrisugiru 走って/歩いて通り過ぎる

paste 1 *n* (*adhesive*) nori のり **2** *v/t* (*stick*) nori de haru のりではる

pastel 1 *n* (*color*) pasuteru パステル **2** *adj* pasuteru-chō (no) パステル調(の)

pastime shumi 趣味

pastor bokushi 牧師

past participle kako-bunshi 過去分詞

pastrami pasutorami パストラミ

pastry (*for pie*) pai-kiji パイ生地; (*small cake*) pēsutorī ペーストリー

past tense kakokei 過去形

pasty *adj face* aojiroi 青白い

pat 1 *n*: ***with a ~ of her hand*** te o karuku tatakinagara 手を軽くたたきながら; ***give … a ~ on the back*** *fig* … o homeru …を褒める **2** *v/t* karuku tataku 軽くたたく

patch 1 *n* (*on clothing*) tsugi つぎ; (*area*) ichibu 一部; ***be not a ~ on*** … to wa kurabemono ni naranai …とは比べものにならない; ***go through a bad ~*** junchō ni ikanai jiki ni naru 順調にいかない時期になる **2** *v/t clothing* … ni tsugi o ateru …につぎを当てる

♦**patch up** (*repair*) … ni ōkyū no shochi o suru …に応急の処置をする; *quarrel* nakanaori suru 仲直りする

patchwork 1 *n* (*needlework*) patchiwāku パッチワーク **2** *adj*

quilt patchiwāku de dekita パッチワークでできた
patchy *fog* mura no aru むらのある; *work, performance* fukanzen (na) 不完全(な)
patent 1 *adj* meihaku (na) 明白(な) **2** *n* (*for invention*) tokkyo 特許 **3** *v/t invention* … no tokkyo o toru …の特許を取る
patent leather enameru-gawa エナメル革
patently akiraka ni 明らかに
paternal *relative* chichikata (no) 父方(の); *pride, love* chichioya (no) 父親(の)
paternalism kanshō 干渉
paternalistic kanshōgamashii 干渉がましい
paternity chichioya de aru koto 父親であること
path komichi 小道; (*to the front door, also fig*) michi 道
pathetic aware (na) 哀れ(な); F (*very bad*) nasakenai hodo heta (na) 情けないほど下手(な)
pathological byōteki (na) 病的(な)
pathologist byōrigaku-sha 病理学者
pathology byōrigaku 病理学
patience nintai 忍耐
patient 1 *n* kanja 患者 **2** *adj* gamanzuyoi 我慢強い; ***just be ~!*** gaman shinasai 我慢しなさい
patiently gamanzuyoku 我慢強く
patio terasu テラス
patriot aikoku-sha 愛国者
patriotic aikokuteki (na) 愛国的(な)
patriotism aikoku-shin 愛国心
patrol 1 *n* junkai 巡回, patorōru パトロール; ***be on ~*** junkaichū de aru 巡回中である **2** *v/t streets, border* junkai suru 巡回する
patrol car patokā パトカー; **patrolman** junsa 巡査;**patrol wagon** shūjin-gosō-sha 囚人護送車
patron (*of store, movie house*) kokyaku 顧客; (*of artist, charity etc*) kōen-sha 後援者
patronize (*be condescending to*) … ni meuebutta taido o toru …に目上ぶった態度を取る
patronizing meuebutta 目上ぶった
patter 1 *n* (*of rain etc*) parapara to iu oto ぱらぱらという音; F (*of salesman*) urikomi 売り込み **2** *v/i* parapara to oto o tatete ochiru ぱらぱらと音を立てて落ちる
pattern *n* (*on fabric*) moyō 模様; (*for knitting, sewing*) katagami 型紙; (*model*) mihon 見本; (*in behavior, events*) patān パターン
patterned moyōiri (no) 模様入り(の)
paunch taikobara 太鼓腹
pause 1 *n* ma 間 **2** *v/i* (*in speaking*) ma o akeru 間をあける; (*in doing sth*) chūdan suru 中断する **3** *v/t tape* ichiji-teishi suru 一時停止する
pave hosō suru 舗装する; ***~ the way for*** … e no michi o hiraku …への道を開く
pavement (*roadway*) hosō 舗装; *Br* (*sidewalk*) hodō 歩道
paving stone shikiishi 敷石
paw 1 *n* (*of animal*) ashi 足; F (*hand*) te 手 **2** *v/t* F sawaru 触る
pawn[1] *n* (*in chess*) pōn ポーン; *fig* tesaki 手先
pawn[2] *v/t* shichi ni ireru 質に入れる
pawnbroker shichi-ya 質屋
pawnshop shichi-ya 質屋
pay 1 *n* kyūryō 給料; ***in the ~ of*** … ni yatowarete …に雇われて **2** *v/t employee* … ni shiharau …に支払う; *sum, bill* harau 払う; ***~ attention*** chūi o harau 注意を払う; ***~ X a compliment*** X o homeru Xを褒める **3** *v/i* shiharai o suru 支払いをする; (*be profitable*) mōkaru もうかる; ***it doesn't ~ to …*** … suru no wa wari ni awanai …するのは割に合わない; ***~ for*** *purchase* … no daikin o shiharau …の代金を支払う; ***you'll ~ for this!*** kitto kono mukui o ukeruzo きっとこの報いを受けるぞ
♦ **pay back** *person* … ni kane o kaesu …に金を返す; *loan* … o kaesu …を返す; (*get revenge on*) … ni shikaeshi o suru …に仕返しをする
♦ **pay in** (*to bank*) … o haraikomu … を払い込む

♦**pay off 1** *v/t debt* … o sukkari hensai suru …をすっかり返済する; *corrupt official* … o baishū suru …を買収する **2** *v/i* (*be profitable*) hikiau 引き合う
♦**pay up** sukkari harau すっかり払う
payable shiharaubeki 支払うべき
pay check kyūryō 給料
payday kyūryōbi 給料日
payee uketori-nin 受取人
pay envelope kyūryōbukuro 給料袋
payer shiharai-nin 支払い人
payment (*of bill*) shiharai 支払い; (*money*) shiharai-kingaku 支払い金額
pay phone kōshū-denwa 公衆電話
payroll (*money*) kyūryō-sōgaku 給料総額; (*employees*) jūgyōin-meibo 従業員名簿; ***be on the ~*** yatowarete iru 雇われている
PC (= ***personal computer***) pasokon パソコン; (= ***politically correct***) shakaiteki ni tadashii 社会的に正しい
pea endōmame えんどう豆
peace heiwa 平和; (*quietness*) shizuke-sa 静けさ; ***~ of mind*** kokoro no yasuragi 心の安らぎ
peaceable *person* odayaka (na) 穏やか(な)
Peace Corps Heiwa-butai 平和部隊
peaceful (*quiet*) shizuka (na) 静か(な); (*not violent*) heiwa (na) 平和(な)
peacefully heiwa ni 平和に; ***sleep ~*** anmin suru 安眠する
peach momo 桃
peacock kujaku くじゃく
peak 1 *n* (*of mountain*) chōjō 頂上; (*mountain*) mine 峰; *fig* pīku ピーク **2** *v/i* pīku ni tassuru ピークに達する
peak hours pīku-ji ピーク時
peanut pīnattsu ピーナッツ; ***get paid ~s*** F wazuka na kyūryō o uketoru わずかな給料を受け取る; ***that's ~s to him*** F hashitagane はした金
peanut butter pīnattsu-batā ピーナッツバター
pear (*oriental*) nashi なし; (*western*) seiyōnashi 西洋なし
pearl shinju 真珠
Pearl Harbor Shinjuwan 真珠湾
peasant nōmin 農民
pebble koishi 小石
pecan pekan ペカン
peck 1 *n* (*kiss*) karui kisu 軽いキス **2** *v/t* (*bite*) tsutsuku つつく; (*kiss*) … ni karuku kisu o suru …に軽くキスをする
peculiar (*strange*) myō (na) 妙(な); ***~ to*** … ni dokutoku (na) …に独特(な)
peculiarity (*strangeness*) kuse 癖; (*special feature*) tokuchō 特徴
pedal 1 *n* (*of bike*) pedaru ペダル **2** *v/i* (*turn ~s*) pedaru o fumu ペダルを踏む; (*cycle*) jitensha o kogu 自転車をこぐ
pedantic shakushi-jōgi (na) しゃくし定規(な)
pedestal (*for statue*) dai 台
pedestrian *n* hokō-sha 歩行者
pedestrian precinct sharyō-tachiiri-kinshi-kuiki 車両立ち入り禁止区域
pediatrician shōnikai 小児科医
pediatrics shōnika 小児科
pedicab rintaku 輪タク
pedigree 1 *n* (*of dog*) kettō 血統 **2** *adj* junketsu (no) 純血(の)
pee *v/i* F oshikko o suru おしっこをする
peek *v/i* nozokimi suru のぞき見する
peel 1 *n* kawa 皮 **2** *v/t fruit, vegetables* … no kawa o muku …の皮をむく **3** *v/i* (*of nose, shoulders*) mukeru むける; (*of paint*) hageochiru はげ落ちる
peep → ***peek***
peephole nozokiana のぞき穴
peer[1] *n* (*equal*) dōhai 同輩; (*in school*) dōkyūsei 同級生
peer[2] *v/i* jitto miru じっと見る; ***~ through the mist*** kiri o tōshite jitto miru 霧を通してじっと見る; ***~ at*** jitto miru じっと見る
peeved F okotta 怒った
peg *n* (*for hat, coat*) fukku フック; (*for tent*) pegu ペグ; ***off the ~*** kisei

(no) 既製(の)
pejorative keibetsuteki (na) 軽べつ的(な)
pellet chiisana tama 小さな玉; (*bullet*) sandan 散弾
pelt 1 *v/t*: **~ *X with Y*** X ni Y o nagetsukeru XにYを投げつける **2** *v/i*: ***they ~ed along the road*** zenryoku de hashiru 全力で走る; ***it's ~ing down*** ame ga hidoku futte iru 雨がひどく降っている
pelvis kotsuban 骨盤
pen[1] *n* (*ballpoint ~*) bōrupen ボールペン; (*fountain ~*) mannenhitsu 万年筆
pen[2] (*enclosure*) ori おり
pen[3] → ***penitentiary***
penalize (*punish*) shobatsu suru 処罰する; SP … ni penarutī o kasuru …にペナルティーを科する; (*disadvantage*) furi ni suru 不利にする
penalty (*punishment*) batsu 罰; (*fine*) bakkin 罰金; SP penarutī ペナルティー
penalty area SP penarutī-eria ペナルティーエリア
penalty clause iyaku-jōkō 違約条項
pencil enpitsu 鉛筆
pencil sharpener enpitsu-kezuri 鉛筆削り
pendant (*necklace*) pendanto ペンダント
pending 1 *prep* … (suru) made … (する)まで **2** *adj*: ***be ~*** (*awaiting a decision*) mikettei de aru 未決定である; LAW shinrichū de aru 審理中である; (*about to happen*) sashisematte iru 差し迫っている
penetrate (*of knife*) kantsū suru 貫通する; (*of water, smell*) … ni shimikomu …にしみ込む; (*of sun, light*) tōru 通る; *market* … ni sannyū suru …に参入する
penetrating *stare, sound* tsukisasu yō (na) 突き刺すよう(な); *analysis* surudoi 鋭い
penetration (*by enemy*) shinnyū 侵入; (*of market*) sannyū 参入
pen friend penfurendo ペンフレンド
penicillin penishirin ペニシリン
peninsula hantō 半島
penis penisu ペニス
penitence kōkai 後悔
penitent *adj* kōkai shite iru 後悔している
penitentiary keimusho 刑務所
pen name pennēmu ペンネーム
pennant penanto ペナント
penniless muichimon (no) 無一文(の)
pen pal penfurendo ペンフレンド
pension nenkin 年金
♦ **pension off** … o oharaibako ni suru …をお払い箱にする
pension fund nenkin-kikin 年金基金
pensive mono-omoi ni shizunda もの思いに沈んだ
Pentagon: ***the ~*** Amerika-kokubō-sōshō アメリカ国防総省
penthouse saijōkai no apāto 最上階のアパート
pent-up usseki shita うっ積した
penultimate saigo kara nibanme (no) 最後から二番目(の)
peony botan ぼたん
people hitobito 人々; (*inhabitants*) jūmin 住民; (*race, tribe*) minzoku 民族; ***two ~*** futari ふたり; ***ten ~*** jūnin 十人; ***the ~*** (*citizens*) shimin 市民; ***the American ~*** Amerika-kokumin アメリカ国民; ***other ~*** hoka no hito tachi 他の人たち; ***~ say …*** … to iu uwasa de aru …といううわさである
pepper (*spice*) koshō こしょう; (*vegetable*) pīman ピーマン
peppermint (*candy*) minto-kyandī ミントキャンディー; (*flavoring*) pepāminto ペパーミント
pep talk: ***give a ~*** happa o kakeru 発破をかける
per … ni tsuki …につき
per annum ichinen ni tsuki 一年につき
perceive (*with senses*) chikaku suru 知覚する; (*view, interpret*) uketoru 受け取る
percent pāsento パーセント; ***10 ~*** juppāsento 十パーセント

percentage wariai 割合
perceptible ninshiki dekiru 認識できる
perceptibly ninshiki dekiru hodo ni 認識できるほどに
perception (*with senses*) chikaku 知覚; (*of situation*) ninshiki 認識; (*insight*) dōsatsuryoku 洞察力
perceptive *person, remark* surudoi 鋭い
perch 1 *n* (*for bird*) tomarigi 止り木 **2** *v/i* (*of bird*) tomaru 止まる; (*of person*) koshikakeru 腰掛ける
percolate *v/i* (*of coffee*) hairu はいる
percussion dagakki 打楽器
percussion instrument dagakki 打楽器
perfect 1 *n* GRAM kanryōkei 完了形 **2** *adj* (*flawless*) kanpeki (na) 完ぺき(な); (*ideal*) uttetsuke (no) うってつけ(の) **3** *v/t* kansei suru 完成する
perfection kanpeki 完ぺき; ***to ~*** kanpeki ni 完ぺきに
perfectionist *n* kanpeki-shugi-sha 完ぺき主義者
perfectly kanpeki ni 完ぺきに; (*totally*) mattaku 全く
perforated *line* mishinme (no) ミシン目(の)
perforations mishinme ミシン目
perform 1 *v/t* (*carry out*) okonau 行う; *play* jōen suru 上演する; *piece of music* ensō suru 演奏する **2** *v/i* (*of actor*) enzuru 演ずる; (*of theater group*) kōen suru 公演する; (*of musician*) ensō suru 演奏する; ***~ well*** (*of machine*) seinō ga yoi 性能がよい; ***~ badly*** (*of machine*) seinō ga warui 性能が悪い
performance (*by actor*) engi 演技; (*by theater company*) kōen 公演; (*by musician*) ensō 演奏; (*of employee, company etc*) seiseki 成績; (*by machine*) seinō 性能
performance car kōseinō-sha 高性能車
performer (*actor, dancer*) engi-sha 演技者; (*musician*) ensō-sha 演奏者
perfume kōsui 香水; (*of flower*) kaori 香り
perfunctory ii kagen (na) いい加減(な)
perhaps tabun たぶん; ***you could ~ try…*** … o moshikashitara tameseru kamo …をもしかしたら試せるかも
peril kiken 危険
perilous kiken (na) 危険(な)
perimeter shūi 周囲
perimeter fence bōgyo-fensu 防御フェンス
period (*time*) kikan 期間; (*menstruation*) seiri 生理; (*punctuation mark*) piriodo ピリオド; ***I don't want to, ~!*** sore wa iya nan desu, ijō それはいやなんです、以上
periodic shūkiteki (na) 周期的(な)
periodical *n* zasshi 雑誌
periodically teikiteki ni 定期的に
peripheral 1 *adj* (*not crucial*) samatsu (na) さ末(な) **2** *n* COMPUT shūhen-kiki 周辺機器
periphery shūhen 周辺
perish (*of rubber*) boroboro ni naru ぼろぼろになる; (*die*) shinu 死ぬ
perishable *food* kusariyasui 腐りやすい
perjure: ***~ oneself*** gishō suru 偽証する
perjury gishō 偽証
perk *n* (*of job*) yakutoku 役得
♦**perk up 1** *v/t* … o genki-zukeru …を元気づける **2** *v/i* genki ni naru 元気になる
perky (*cheerful*) akarui 明るい
perm 1 *n* pāma パーマ **2** *v/t* pāma o kakeru パーマをかける
permanent *adj* eikyūteki (na) 永久的(な); ***~ employee*** seishain 正社員; ***~ job*** teishoku 定職; ***~ address*** teijūsho 定住所
permanently eikyū ni 永久に
permissible yurusareru 許される
permission kyoka 許可
permissive amai 甘い
permit 1 *n* kyokashō 許可証 **2** *v/t* kyoka suru 許可する; ***~ X to do Y*** X ga Y suru no o kyoka suru XがYするのを許可する

perpendicular *adj* suichoku (no) 垂直(の)
perpetual (*permanent*) eikyūteki (na) 永久的(な); (*continual*) taema nai 絶え間ない
perpetually (*continually*) hikkirinashi ni ひっきりなしに
perpetuate eizoku saseru 永続させる
perplex nayamaseru 悩ませる
perplexed tomadotta とまどった
perplexity tomadoi とまどい
persecute (*oppress*) hakugai suru 迫害する; (*hound*) urusaku nayamasu うるさく悩ます
persecution hakugai 迫害
perseverance konki 根気
persevere ganbaru がんばる
persimmon kaki 柿
persist (*last*) tsuzuku 続く; (*keep on*) koshitsu suru 固執する; **~ *in doing X*** Xshitsuzukeru Xし続ける
persistence (*perseverance*) konkizuyo-sa 根気強さ; (*continuation*) jizoku 持続
persistent nebarizuyoi 粘り強い; (*negative sense*) shitsukoi しつこい; *rain* itsu made mo tsuzuku いつまでも続く
persistently (*continually*) itsu mademo いつまでも
person hito 人; ***in* ~** jibun de 自分で
personal *opinion, life* kojinteki (na) 個人的(な); *belongings, secretary* kojin (no) 個人(の); (*private*) shiteki (na) 私的(な); ***don't make* ~ *remarks*** hito o kizutsukeru koto wa iuna 人を傷つけることは言うな
personal assistant kojin-hisho 個人秘書; **personal computer** pāsonaru-konpyūtā パーソナルコンピューター; **personal hygiene** karada no eisei 体の衛生
personality jinkaku 人格; (*celebrity*) yūmeijin 有名人; ***he has no* ~** kare wa kosei ga nai 彼は個性がない
personally (*for my part*) watashi to shite wa 私としては; (*in person*) jibun de 自分で; ***don't take it* ~** ki o waruku shinaide kudasai 気を悪くしないでください
personal pronoun ninshō-daimeishi 人称代名詞
personal stereo wōkuman ウォークマン®
personnel shokuin 職員; (*department*) jinjibu 人事部
personnel manager jinji-buchō 人事部長
perspiration hakkan 発汗
perspire ase o kaku 汗をかく
persuade settoku suru 説得する; **~ *X to do Y*** X o settoku shite Y saseru Xを説得してYさせる
persuasion settoku 説得
persuasive settokuryoku no aru 説得力のある
pertinent tekisetsu (na) 適切(な)
perturb fuan ni saseru 不安にさせる
perturbing fuan (na) 不安(な)
pervasive *influence, ideas* hirogaru 広がる
perverse (*awkward*) tsumujimagari (no) つむじ曲り(の)
perversion (*sexual*) seiteki-tōsaku 性的倒錯
pervert *n* (*sexual*) hentai 変態
pessimism hikanron 悲観論
pessimist hikanron-sha 悲観論者
pessimistic hikanteki (na) 悲観的(な)
pest (*insect*) gaichū 害虫; (*animal*) gaijū 害獣; F (*person*) yakkaimono やっかいもの
pest control gaichū-kujo 害虫駆除
pester urusaku itte komaraseru うるさく言って困らせる; **~ *X to do Y*** X ni Y suru yō ni segande komaraseru XにYするようにせがんで困らせる
pesticide satchūzai 殺虫剤
pet 1 *n* (*animal*) petto ペット; (*favorite*) okiniiri お気に入り **2** *adj* otokui (no) お得意(の) **3** *v/t animal* naderu なでる **4** *v/i* (*of couple*) pettingu suru ペッティングする
petal hanabira 花びら
♦ **peter out** (*of path*) dandan nakunaru だんだんなくなる; (*of*

rain) shidai ni yamu しだいにやむ
petite kyasha (na) きゃしゃ(な)
petition *n* seigansho 請願書
petrified kyōfu ni karitaterareta 恐怖に駆り立てられた
petrify kyōfu ni karitateru 恐怖に駆り立てる
petrochemical *adj* sekiyu-kagaku (no) 石油化学(の)
petroleum sekiyu 石油
petty *person, behavior* kokoro no semai 心の狭い; *details, problem* toru ni taranai 取るに足らない
petty cash tōzayō genkin 当座用現金
petulant *person* okorippoi 怒りっぽい; *remark* okotta yō (na) 怒ったよう(な)
pew kyōkai no zaseki 教会の座席
pewter shirome しろめ
pharmaceutical seiyaku (no) 製薬(の)
pharmaceuticals kusuri 薬
pharmacist (*in store*) yakuzaishi 薬剤師
pharmacy (*store*) yakkyoku 薬局
phase (*stage*) dankai 段階
♦**phase in** … o dankaiteki ni dōnyū suru …を段階的に導入する
♦**phase out** … o dankaiteki ni haishi suru …を段階的に廃止する
PhD (= ***Doctor of Philosophy***) hakase-gō 博士号
pheasant kiji きじ
phenomenal odoroku hodo (no) 驚くほど(の)
phenomenally sugoku すごく
phenomenon genshō 現象
philanthropic nasakebukai 情け深い
philanthropist jizen-ka 慈善家
philanthropy jizen-jigyō 慈善事業
Philippines: ***the ~*** Firipin-shotō フィリピン諸島
philistine *n* kyōyō no nai hito 教養のない人
philosopher tetsugaku-sha 哲学者
philosophical tetsugakuteki (na) 哲学的(な); *fig* reisei (na) 冷静(な)
philosophy tetsugaku 哲学; (*of life*) jinseikan 人生観
phobia kyōfushō 恐怖症
phone 1 *n* denwa 電話 **2** *v/t* … ni denwa o kakeru …に電話をかける **3** *v/i* denwa o suru 電話をする
phone book denwachō 電話帳; **phone booth** kōshū-denwa-bokkusu 公衆電話ボックス; **phone call** denwa 電話; **phone number** denwa-bangō 電話番号
phon(e)y *adj name, address* uso (no) うそ(の); *bill, accent* nise (no) 偽(の); *person* shin'yō dekinai 信用できない
photo *n* shashin 写真
photo album arubamu アルバム; **photocopier** kopī-ki コピー機; **photocopy 1** *n* kopī コピー **2** *v/t* kopī suru コピーする
photogenic shashin'utsuri no yoi 写真うつりのよい
photograph 1 *n* shashin 写真 **2** *v/t* … no shashin o toru …の写真をとる
photographer kameraman カメラマン
photography shashin-satsuei 写真撮影
phrase 1 *n* GRAM ku 句; (*what s.o. said*) kotoba 言葉; (*expression*) iikata 言い方 **2** *v/t* hyōgen suru 表現する
phrasebook kaiwa-hyōgenshū 会話表現集
physical 1 *adj* (*bodily*) shintaiteki (na) 身体的(な); *attraction, labor* nikutaiteki (na) 肉体的(な); ***the ~ world*** busshitsukai 物質界 **2** *n* MED kenkō-shindan 健康診断
physical handicap shintai-shōgai 身体障害
physically shintaiteki ni 身体的に, nikutaiteki ni 肉体的に
physician naikai 内科医
physicist butsuri-gakusha 物理学者
physics butsurigaku 物理学
physiotherapist butsuri-ryōhōshi 物理療法士
physiotherapy butsuri-ryōhō 物理療法
physique taikaku 体格
pianist pianisuto ピアニスト

piano piano ピアノ
pick 1 *n*: ***take your ~*** suki na no o erande kudasai 好きなのを選んでください **2** *v/t* (*choose*) erabu 選ぶ; *flowers* tsumu 摘む; *fruit* mogu もぐ; ***~ one's nose*** hanakuso o hojiru 鼻くそをほじる **3** *v/i*: ***~ and choose*** yorigonomi suru より好みする
♦**pick at**: ***~ one's food*** honno sukoshi shika tabenai ほんの少ししか食べない
♦**pick on** (*treat unfairly*) … o ijimeru …をいじめる; (*select*) … o erabidasu …を選び出す
♦**pick out** (*identify*) … o miwakeru …を見分ける
♦**pick up 1** *v/t* … o toriageru …を取り上げる; (*from ground*) … o hiroiageru …を拾い上げる; (*collect: person*) … o mukae ni iku …を迎えに行く; *dry cleaning etc* … o tori ni iku …を取りに行く; *information* … o atsumeru …を集める; (*in car*) … o noseru …を乗せる; (*in sexual sense*) … o hikkakeru …をひっかける; *language, skill* … o oboeru …を覚える; *habit* … o mi ni tsukeru …を身につける; *illness* … ni kakaru …にかかる; (*buy*) … o te ni ireru …を手に入れる; *criminal* … o taiho suru …を逮捕する **2** *v/i* (*improve*) yoku naru よくなる
picket 1 *n* (*of strikers*) pike ピケ **2** *v/t* kanshi suru 監視する
picket fence kuisaku くい柵
picket line pikerain ピケライン
pickle *v/t* suzuke ni suru 酢漬けにする
pickled plum umeboshi 梅干し
pickled vegetables (*Japanese-style*) tsukemono 漬物
pickles pikurusu ピクルス
pickpocket suri すり
pick-up (truck) kogata-torakku 小型トラック
picky F konomi no urusai 好みのうるさい
picnic 1 *n* pikunikku ピクニック **2** *v/i* pikunikku o suru ピクニックをする
picture 1 *n* e 絵; (*photo*) shashin 写真; ***keep … in the ~*** … ni jijō o shirasete oku …に事情を知らせておく **2** *v/t* sōzō suru 想像する
picture book ehon 絵本
picturesque e no yō ni utsukushii 絵のように美しい
pie pai パイ
piece (*fragment*) kakera かけら; (*component*) bubun 部分; (*in board game*) koma こま; ***a ~ of pie / bread*** hitokire no pai / pan 一切れのパイ/パン; ***a ~ of string / ribbon*** ippon no himo / ribon 一本のひも/リボン; ***a ~ of advice / information*** chotto shita adobaisu / jōhō ちょっとしたアドバイス/情報; ***a ~ of music*** ikkyoku no ongaku 一曲の音楽; ***go to ~s*** uchinomesareru 打ちのめされる; ***take to ~s*** barabara ni suru ばらばらにする
♦**piece together** *broken plate* … o tsunagiawaseru …をつなぎ合わせる; *facts, evidence* … o matomeageru …をまとめ上げる
piecemeal *adv* sukoshi zutsu 少しずつ
piecework *n* dekidakabarai no shigoto 出来高払いの仕事
pierce (*penetrate*) tsuranuku 貫く; (*of bullet*) kantsū suru 貫通する; *ears* … ni piasu o suru …にピアスをする
piercing *noise* mimi o tsunzaku 耳をつんざく; *eyes* sasu yō (na) 刺すよう(な); *wind* mi ni shimiru 身にしみる
pig (*animal*) buta 豚; (*unpleasant person*) butayarō 豚野郎
pigeon hato はと
pigheaded gōjō (na) 強情(な)
pigpen (*also fig*) buta-goya 豚小屋; **pigskin** buta-gawa 豚皮; **pigtail** osagegami おさげ髪
pile yama 山; ***a ~ of work*** yama hodo no shigoto 山ほどの仕事
♦**pile up 1** *v/i* (*of work, bills*) tamaru たまる **2** *v/t* … o tsumiageru …を積み上げる

piles MED ji ぢ
pile-up MOT tamatsuki-shōtotsu 玉突き衝突
pilfering kosodoro こそ泥
pilgrim junrei-sha 巡礼者
pilgrimage junrei 巡礼
pill kusuri 薬; ***the ~*** (*contraceptive ~*) piru ピル; ***be on the ~*** piru o nonde iru ピルを飲んでいる
pillar hashira 柱
pillion (*of motor bike*) kōbu-zaseki 後部座席
pillow *n* makura まくら
pillowcase makura-kabā まくらカバー
pilot 1 *n* (*of airplane*) pairotto パイロット **2** *v/t airplane* … no pairotto o tsutomeru …のパイロットを務める
pilot plant shiken-kōjō 試験工場
pilot scheme shikenteki na keikaku 試験的な計画
pimp *n* ponbiki ポン引き
pimple nikibi にきび
PIN (= ***personal identification number***) anshō-bangō 暗証番号
pin 1 *n* (*also in bowling*) pin ピン; (*for sewing*) machibari 待ち針; (*badge*) burōchi ブローチ **2** *v/t* (*hold down*) osaetsukeru 押さえつける; (*attach*) pin de tomeru ピンで留める
♦**pin down**: ***pin … down to a date*** … ni nichiji o yakusoku saseru …に日時を約束させる
♦**pin up** *notice* gabyō de tomeru 画びょうで留める
pinball (*upright*) pachinko パチンコ
pincers yattoko やっとこ
pinch 1 *n*: ***a ~ of salt*** shio hitotsumami 塩一つまみ; ***at a ~*** masaka no toki ni wa まさかの時には **2** *v/t* tsuneru つねる **3** *v/i* (*of shoes*) shimetsukeru 締めつける
pine[1] *n* (*tree*) matsu 松
pine[2] *v/i*: ***~ for*** koishigaru 恋しがる
pineapple painappuru パイナップル
ping 1 *n* chin to iu oto ちんという音 **2** *v/i* chin to iu oto ga suru ちんという音がする
ping-pong pinpon ピンポン
pink *adj* pinku-iro (no) ピンク色(の)
pinnacle *fig* zetchō 絶頂
pinpoint (*identify*) tsukitomeru つきとめる; (*accurately describe*) seikaku ni shimesu 正確に示す
pins and needles: ***have ~*** shibireru しびれる
pinstripe *adj* pinsutoraipu ピンストライプ
pint painto パイント
pin-up (girl) pinnappu no moderu ピンナップのモデル
pioneer 1 *n fig* senku-sha 先駆者 **2** *v/t* … no michi o hiraku …の道をひらく
pioneering *adj work* senkuteki (na) 先駆的(な)
pious shinjinbukai 信心深い
pip *n* (*of fruit*) tane 種
pipe 1 *n* (*for smoking, gas etc*) paipu パイプ; ***water ~*** suidōkan 水道管 **2** *v/t* paipu de hakobu パイプで運ぶ
♦**pipe down** damaru 黙る
piped music yūsen-ongaku-hōsō 有線音楽放送
pipeline yusōkan 輸送管; ***in the ~*** shinkōchū de 進行中で
piping hot atsuatsu (no) 熱々(の)
pirate *v/t software* … no kaizokuban o tsukuru …の海賊版を作る
piss V **1** *v/i* (*urinate*) shōben o suru 小便をする **2** *n* shōben 小便
pissed V (*annoyed*) mutto shita むっとした; *Br* (*drunk*) yopparatta 酔っ払った
pistol pisutoru ピストル
piston pisuton ピストン
pit *n* (*hole*) ana 穴; (*coal mine*) tankō 炭坑; (*in fruit*) tane 種
pitch[1] *n* MUS chōshi 調子
pitch[2] **1** *v/i* (*in baseball*) tōkyū suru 投球する **2** *v/t tent* haru 張る; *ball* nageru 投げる
pitch black makkura (na) 真っ暗(な)
pitcher[1] (*baseball*) pitchā ピッチャー
pitcher[2] (*container*) mizusashi 水差し

piteous aware (na) 哀れ(な)
pitfall otoshiana 落し穴
pith (*of fruit*) nakakahi 中果皮
pitiful *sight* aware (na) 哀れ(な); *excuse etc* nasakenai 情けない
pitiless reikoku (na) 冷酷(な)
pittance suzume no namida すずめの涙
pity 1 *n* awaremi 哀れみ; ***it's a ~ that*** … to wa zannen desu …とは残念です; ***what a ~!*** zannen 残念; ***take ~ on*** kinodoku ni omou 気の毒に思う **2** *v/t person* kinodoku ni omou 気の毒に思う
pivot *v/i* kaiten suru 回転する
pizza piza ピザ
placard purakādo プラカード
place 1 *n* basho 場所; (*bar, restaurant*) mise 店; (*apartment, house*) uchi うち; (*in book*) yomikake no tokoro 読みかけの所; (*in race, competition*) jun'i 順位; (*seat*) seki 席; ***at my / his ~*** watashi / kare no uchi de 私/彼のうちで; ***in ~ of*** … no kawari ni …のかわりに; ***feel out of ~*** bachigai ni kanjiru 場違いに感じる; ***take ~*** okoru 起こる; (*of ceremony*) okonawareru 行われる; ***in the first ~*** (*firstly*) mazu daiichi ni まず第一に; (*in the beginning*) somosomo そもそも **2** *v/t* (*put*) oku 置く; (*identify*) … ga dare ka omoidasu …がだれか思い出す; ***~ an order*** chūmon suru 注文をする
place mat ranchonmatto ランチョンマット
placid ochitsuita 落ち着いた
plague 1 *n* ekibyō 疫病 **2** *v/t* (*bother*) nayamasu 悩ます
plaice karei かれい
plain¹ *n* heichi 平地
plain² 1 *adj* (*clear, obvious*) meihaku (na) 明白(な); (*not elaborate*) kanso (na) 簡素(な); (*not flavored*) fūmi no tsuite inai 風味のついていない; (*not pretty*) saenai さえない; (*not patterned*) muji (no) 無地(の); (*blunt*) sotchoku (na) 率直(な); ***~ chocolate*** burakku-chokorēto ブラックチョコレート **2** *adv* akiraka ni 明らかに; ***it's ~ crazy*** mattaku dōka shite iru まったくどうかしている
plain clothes: ***in ~*** shifuku de 私服で
plainly (*clearly*) akiraka ni 明らかに; (*bluntly*) sotchoku ni 率直に; (*simply*) kanso ni 簡素に
plain-spoken sotchoku (na) 率直(な)
plaintiff genkoku 原告
plaintive kanashisō (na) 悲しそう(な)
plait 1 *n* (*in hair*) osagegami おさげ髪 **2** *v/t hair* amu 編む
plan 1 *n* (*project*) keikaku 計画; (*intention*) kangae 考え; (*drawing*) zumen 図面 **2** *v/t* (*prepare*) keikaku suru 計画する; (*design*) sekkei suru 設計する; ***~ to do, ~ on doing*** … suru tsumori de aru …するつもりである **3** *v/i* keikaku suru 計画する
plane¹ *n* (*airplane*) hikōki 飛行機
plane² (*tool*) kanna かんな
planet wakusei 惑星
plank (*of wood*) ita 板; *fig* (*of policy*) seitō-kōryō no shuyō-kōmoku 政党綱領の主要項目
planning keikaku 計画; ***at the ~ stage*** keikakuchū de 計画中で
plant¹ 1 *n* shokubutsu 植物 **2** *v/t* ueru 植える
plant² *n* (*factory*) kōjō 工場; (*equipment*) kikai-setsubi 機械設備
plantation purantēshon プランテーション
plaque (*on wall*) meiban 銘板; (*on teeth*) shikō 歯こう
plaster 1 *n* (*on wall, ceiling*) shikkui しっくい **2** *v/t wall, ceiling* … ni shikkui o nuru …にしっくいを塗る; ***be ~ed with*** (*with posters, notices*) … ga betabeta hatte aru …がべたべた張ってある; (*with make-up etc*) … ga betabeta nutte aru …がべたべた塗ってある
plaster cast gipusu ギプス
plastic 1 *n* purasuchikku プラスチック **2** *adj* purasuchikku-sei (no) プラスチック製(の)

plastic bag binīru-bukuro ビニール袋; **plastic money** kurejitto-kādo クレジットカード; **plastic surgeon** keisei-gekai 形成外科医; **plastic surgery** keisei-geka 形成外科; (*cosmetic*) seikei-shujutsu 整形手術
plate *n* sara 皿; (*of metal*) kinzokuban 金属板; (*license ~*) nanbā-purēto ナンバープレート
plateau kōgen 高原
platform (*stage*) endan 演壇; *fig* (*political*) kōryō 綱領; RAIL purattohōmu プラットホーム; **~ 6** roku-bansen 六番線
platform ticket nyūjōken 入場券
platinum 1 *n* purachina プラチナ **2** *adj* purachina-sei (no) プラチナ製(の)
platitude kimarimonku 決まり文句
platonic *relationship* puratonikku (na) プラトニック(な)
platoon (*of soldiers*) shōtai 小隊
platter (*for food*) ōzara 大皿
plausible *excuse* mottomorashii もっともらしい
play 1 *n* THEA geki 劇; (*on TV*) dorama ドラマ; (*of children*) asobi 遊び; TECH asobi あそび; SP purē プレー **2** *v/i* (*of children*) asobu 遊ぶ; (*of musician*) ensō suru 演奏する; (SP: *perform*) suru する; (SP: *take part*) shutsujō suru 出場する **3** *v/t musical instrument, music* hiku 弾く; *wind instrument* fuku 吹く; *game* suru する; *opponent* … to shiai o suru …と試合をする; (*perform: Macbeth etc*) jōen suru 上演する; *particular role* enjiru 演じる; *pirates, house* … gokko o shite asobu …ごっこをして遊ぶ; **~ *a joke on*** karakau からかう
♦ **play around** (*be unfaithful*) asobimawaru 遊びまわる; **~ *with*** … to asobimawatte iru …と遊びまわっている
♦ **play down** … o karuku atsukau …を軽く扱う
♦ **play up** (*of machine, tooth*) chōshi ga waruku naru 調子が悪くなる; (*of child*) atsukainikuku naru 扱いにくくなる
playact (*pretend*) furi o suru ふりをする
playback saisei 再生
playboy purēbōi プレーボーイ
player SP senshu 選手; (*musician*) ensō-sha 演奏者; (*actor*) haiyū 俳優
playful *punch* honki de nai 本気でない; *person, dog* yōki (na) 陽気(な)
playground asobiba 遊び場
playing card toranpu トランプ
playing field undōjō 運動場
playwright geki-sakka 劇作家
plaza (*for shopping*) shoppingu-sentā ショッピングセンター
plea *n* tangan 嘆願
plead *v/i*: **~ *for*** tangan suru 嘆願する; **~ *guilty*** tsumi o mitomeru 罪を認める; **~ *not guilty*** muzai o shuchō suru 無罪を主張する; **~ *with*** … ni kongan suru …に懇願する
pleasant *weather* kimochi no yoi 気持ちのよい; *room, hotel* kaiteki (na) 快適(な); *person* kanji no ii 感じのいい; *meal* tanoshii 楽しい
please 1 *adv* dōzo どうぞ; ***will you pass the salt ~*** sumimasen ga, shio o totte itadakemasu ka すみませんが、塩をとっていただけますか; ***close the door ~*** doa o shimete kudasai ドアを閉めてください; ***more tea? - yes, ~*** ocha no okawari wa - hai, arigatō お茶のおかわりは-はい、ありがとう; **~ *do*** ē, dōzo ええ、どうぞ **2** *v/t* yorokobasu 喜ばす; **~ *yourself*** katte ni shinasai 勝手にしなさい
pleased yorokonda 喜んだ; **~ *to meet you*** hajimemashite はじめまして
pleasing *design, person* kanji no ii 感じのいい; *weather, sound* kokochiyoi 心地よい
pleasure (*happiness, satisfaction*) yorokobi 喜び; (*enjoyment*) tanoshimi 楽しみ; (*not business*) asobi 遊び; ***it's a ~*** (*you're welcome*) dō itashimashite どういたしまして; ***with ~*** yorokonde 喜

んで

pleat *n* (*in skirt*) purītsu プリーツ

pledge 1 *n* (*promise*) yakusoku 約束; (*security*) teitō 抵当 **2** *v/t* (*promise*) chikau 誓う

Pledge of Allegiance Chūsei no Chikai 忠誠の誓い

plentiful jūbun (na) 十分(な)

plenty: **~ *of*** (*a lot of*) takusan (no) たくさん(の); (*enough*) jūbun (na) 十分(な); ***that's* ~** jūbun desu 十分です; ***there's ~ for everyone*** minna no bun jūbun ni arimasu みんなの分十分にあります

pliable jūnan (na) 柔軟(な)

pliers penchi ペンチ; ***a pair of ~*** penchi itchō ペンチ一丁

plight kukyō 苦境

plod *v/i* (*walk*) tobotobo aruku とぼとぼ歩く

♦**plod along** (*with a job*) kotsukotsu hataraku こつこつ働く

plodder (*at work*) jimichi na hito 地道な人; (*at school*) gariben がり勉

plot[1] *n* (*land*) jisho 地所

plot[2] **1** *n* (*conspiracy*) inbō 陰謀; (*of novel*) suji 筋 **2** *v/t&v/i* takuramu たくらむ

plotter inbō-sha 陰謀者; COMPUT purottā プロッター

plow 1 *n* suki すき **2** *v/t & v/i* tagayasu 耕す

♦**plow back** *profits* … o saitōshi suru …を再投資する

pluck *v/t eyebrows* nuku 抜く; *chicken* … no hane o mushiru …の羽をむしる

♦**pluck up**: **~ *courage*** yūki o dasu 勇気を出す

plug 1 *n* (*for sink, bath*) sen 栓; (*electrical*) puragu プラグ; (*spark ~*) tenka-puragu 点火プラグ; (*for new book etc*) senden 宣伝 **2** *v/t hole* … ni sen o suru …に栓をする; *new book etc* senden suru 宣伝する

♦**plug away** F kotsukotsu yaru こつこつやる

♦**plug in** *v/t* puragu o sashikomu プラグを差し込む

plum 1 *n* puramu プラム; (*Japanese*) ume 梅 **2** *adj* F oishii おいしい

plumage tori no hane 鳥の羽

plumb *adj* suichoku (no) 垂直(の)

plumber haikankō 配管工

plumbing (*pipes*) haikan 配管

plummet (*of airplane*) suichoku ni rakka suru 垂直に落下する; (*of prices*) kyūraku suru 急落する

plump *adj person, hand* potchari shita ぽっちゃりした; *baby, chicken* marumaru to futotta まるまると太った

♦**plump for** … o erabu …を選ぶ

plunge 1 *n* tobikomi 飛び込み; (*in prices*) kyūraku 急落; ***take the ~*** omoikitte yatte miru 思い切ってやってみる **2** *v/i* tobikomu 飛び込む; (*of prices*) kyūraku suru 急落する **3** *v/t hand* tsukkomu 突っ込む; *knife* tsukisasu 突き刺す; ***the city was ~d into darkness*** totsuzen machijū ga makkura ni natta 突然街中が真っ暗になった; ***the news ~d him into despair*** sono nyūsu o kiite kare wa zetsubō ni ochiitta そのニュースを聞いて彼は絶望に陥った

plunging *neckline* munamoto no aita 胸元の開いた

plural 1 *adj* fukusū (no) 複数(の) **2** *n* fukusūkei 複数形

plus 1 *prep*: ***2 ~ 2 is 4*** ni tasu ni wa yon da ２足す２は４だ; ***~ tax*** zeikin o kuwaete 税金を加えて; ***children ~ teachers*** kodomotachi no hoka ni sensei 子供たちの他に先生 **2** *adj* ijō 以上; ***$500 ~*** gohyaku doru ijō 500ドル以上 **3** *n* (*symbol*) purasu プラス; (*advantage*) riten 利点 **4** *conj* (*moreover, in addition*) sore ni kuwaete それに加えて

plush gōka (na) 豪華(な)

plywood beniya-ita ベニヤ板

p.m. gogo (no) 午後(の)

pneumatic kūki no haitta 空気の入った

pneumatic drill kūki-doriru 空気ドリル

pneumonia haien 肺炎

poach[1] *v/t* (*cook*) yuderu ゆでる

poach[2] **1** *v/i* (*for fish*) mitsuryō

suru 密漁する; (*for bird, animal*) mitsuryō suru 密猟する **2** *v/t fish* mitsuryō suru 密漁する; *bird, animal* mitsuryō suru 密猟する

poached egg otoshitamago 落し卵

P.O. Box shishobako 私書箱

pocket 1 *n* poketto ポケット; ***line one's own ~s*** shifuku o koyasu 私腹をこやす; ***be out of ~*** son o suru 損をする **2** *adj* (*miniature*) kogata (no) 小型(の) **3** *v/t* (*steal*) chakufuku suru 着服する; (*put in ~*) poketto ni shimau ポケットにしまう

pocketbook (*purse*) handobaggu ハンドバッグ; (*billfold*) saifu 財布; (*book*) bunkobon 文庫本;**pocket calculator** dentaku 電卓; **pocketknife** pokettonaifu ポケットナイフ

podium endai 演台; MUS shikidai 指揮台

poem shi 詩

poet shijin 詩人

poetic shiteki (na) 詩的(な)

poetic justice inga-ōhō 因果応報

poetry shi 詩

poignant itamashii 痛ましい

point 1 *n* (*of pencil, knife*) saki 先; (*in competition, exam*) tensū 点数; (*purpose*) imi 意味; (*moment*) jiten 時点; (*in argument, discussion*) yōten 要点; (*in decimals*) ten 点; (*decimal ~*) shōsūten 少数点; ***beside the ~*** kentōchigai de 見当違いで; ***be on the ~ of doing X*** X suru tokoro de aru Xするところである; ***get to the ~*** hondai ni hairu 本題に入る; ***there's no ~ in waiting / trying*** matte ite mo / tsuzukete mo muimi da 待っていても/続けても無意味だ **2** *v/i* sasu 指す **3** *v/t gun* mukeru 向ける

♦**point at** (*with finger*) … o yubisasu …を指さす

♦**point out** *sights* … o sashishimesu …を指し示す; *advantages etc* … o shiteki suru …を指摘する

♦**point to** (*with finger*) … o sasu …を指す; *fig* (*indicate*) … o shimesu …を示す

point-blank 1 *adj refusal* tantō-chokunyū (na) 単刀直入(な); ***at ~ range*** shikin-kyori de 至近距離で **2** *adv refuse, deny* kippari to きっぱりと

pointed *remark* shinratsu (na) しんらつ(な)

pointer (*for teacher*) sashibō 指し棒; (*hint*) jogen 助言; (*sign, indication*) shishin 指針

pointless muimi (na) 無意味(な); ***it's ~ trying to persuade him*** kare o settoku-shiyō to suru no wa muimi da 彼を説得しようとするのは無意味だ

point-of-sale hanbaiten 販売店; (*promotional material*) hanbaisokushin zairyō 販売促進材料

point of view kanten 観点

poise ochitsuki 落ち着き

poised *person* ochitsuita 落ち着いた

poison 1 *n* doku 毒 **2** *v/t person, animal* … ni doku o moru …に毒を盛る; *water, land* osen suru 汚染する; *relationship* dame ni suru だめにする

poisonous yūdoku (na) 有毒(な)

poke *v/t* (*prod*) tsutsuku つつく; (*stick*) tsukkomu 突っ込む; ***~ fun at*** … o karakau …をからかう; ***~ one's nose into*** … o sensaku suru …をせん索する; ***~ one's head out of the window*** mado no soto ni atama o tsukidasu 窓の外に頭を突き出す

♦**poke around** sagashimawaru 探し回る

poker (*card game*) pōkā ポーカー

poky (*cramped*) semakurushii 狭苦しい

Poland Pōrando ポーランド

polar (*Arctic*) hokkyoku (no) 北極(の); (*Antarctic*) nankyoku (no) 南極(の)

polar bear shirokuma 白くま

polarize *v/t* ryōkyokuka suru 両極化する

Pole Pōrando-jin ポーランド人

pole[1] (*of wood, metal*) bō 棒

pole[2] (*of earth*) kyoku 極

polevault *n* bōtakatobi 棒高跳び
police *n* keisatsu 警察
police box kōban 交番; **policeman** keikan 警官; **police state** keisatsu-kokka 警察国家; **police station** keisatsu-sho 警察署; **policewoman** fujin-keikan 婦人警官
policy[1] (*of government*) seisaku 政策; (*of company, individual*) hōshin 方針
policy[2] (*insurance ~*) hoken-shōken 保険証券
polio shōni-mahi 小児まひ
Polish 1 *adj* Pōrando (no) ポーランド(の) **2** *n* Pōrando-go ポーランド語
polish 1 *n* (*product*) tsuyadashi つや出し; (*nail ~*) manikyua マニキュア; ***shoe ~*** kutsuzumi 靴墨 **2** *v/t* migaku 磨く; *speech* … ni migaki o kakeru …に磨きをかける
♦**polish off** *food* … o tairageru …を平らげる
♦**polish up** *skill* … o fukushū suru …を復習する; *work* … no shiage o suru …の仕上げをする
polished *performance* senren sareta 洗練された
polite reigi-tadashii 礼儀正しい
politely teinei ni ていねいに
politeness reigitadashi-sa 礼儀正しさ
political *career* seiji (no) 政治(の); *consideration, problem* seijiteki (na) 政治的(な); ***~ party*** seitō 政党; ***~ correspondent*** seijibu-kisha 政治部記者
politically correct shakaiteki ni tadashii 社会的に正しい
politician seijika 政治家
politics seiji 政治; ***what are his ~?*** kare no seiji ni kan suru kangaekata wa dō nan desu ka 彼の政治に関する考え方はどうなんですか
poll 1 *n* (*survey*) seron-chōsa 世論調査; ***the ~s*** (*election*) tōhyō 投票; ***go to the ~s*** tōhyō suru 投票する **2** *v/t* *people* … no seron-chōsa o suru …の世論調査をする; *votes* kakutoku suru 獲得する
pollen kafun 花粉
pollen count kafunsū 花粉数
polling booth tōhyō-yōshi-kinyūjo 投票用紙記入所
pollster seron-chōsain 世論調査員
pollutant osen-busshitsu 汚染物質
pollute osen suru 汚染する
pollution osen 汚染
polo neck tātorunekku タートルネック
polo shirt poroshatsu ポロシャツ
polyester poriesuteru ポリエステル
polyethylene poriechiren ポリエチレン
polystyrene porisuchiren ポリスチレン
polyunsaturated tafuhōwa (no) 多不飽和(の)
pompous mottaibutta もったいぶった
pond ike 池
ponder *v/i* jukkō suru 熟考する
pony ponī ポニー
ponytail ponītēru ポニーテール
poodle pūdoru プードル
pool[1] (*swimming ~*) pūru プール; (*of water, blood*) tamari たまり
pool[2] (*game*) pūru プール
pool[3] *v/t resources* mochiyoru 持ちよる
pool hall tamatsukijō 玉突き場
pool table pūru-dai プール台
pooped F hetoheto ni tsukareta へとへとに疲れた
poor 1 *adj* (*not wealthy*) mazushii 貧しい; (*not good*) heta (na) 下手(な); (*unfortunate*) aware (na) 哀れ(な); ***be in ~ health*** kenkō ga sugurenai 健康がすぐれない; ***~ old Tony!*** Tonī mo kinodoku ni トニーも気の毒に **2** *n*: ***the ~*** mazushii hitobito 貧しい人々
poorly 1 *adv* heta ni 下手に **2** *adj* (*unwell*) kibun ga sugurenai 気分がすぐれない
pop[1] **1** *n* (*noise*) pon to iu oto ぽんという音 **2** *v/i* (*of balloon etc*) pon to iu oto o tateru ぽんという音を立てる **3** *v/t cork* pon to nuku ぽんと抜く; *balloon* pān to haretsu saseru

ぱーんと破裂させる

pop[2] **1** *n* MUS poppusu ポップス **2** *adj* poppusu (no) ポップス(の)

pop[3] (*father*) tōchan 父ちゃん

pop[4] F (*put*) hyoi to ireru ひょいと入れる

♦**pop up** *v/i* (*appear*) hyokkori arawareru ひょっこり現われる

popcorn poppukōn ポップコーン

pope Rōma-hōō ローマ法王

poppy popī ポピー

Popsicle® aisukyandī アイスキャンディー

pop song poppusu ポップス

popular ninki no aru 人気のある; *belief, support* ippan (no) 一般(の)

popularity ninki 人気

populate shokumin suru 植民する

population jinkō 人口

porcelain 1 *n* jiki 磁器 **2** *adj* jiki (no) 磁器(の)

porch beranda ベランダ

porcupine yama-arashi やまあらし

pore (*of skin*) keana 毛穴

♦**pore over** *designs, map* … o jukkō suru …を熟考する; *document* … o jukudoku suru …を熟読する

pork butaniku 豚肉

porn *n* poruno ポルノ

porn(o) *adj* poruno (no) ポルノ(の)

pornographic poruno (no) ポルノ(の)

pornography poruno ポルノ

porous kyūsui shiyasui 吸水しやすい

port[1] *n* (*town*) minatomachi 港町; (*area*) minato 港

port[2] *adj* (*left-hand*) sagen (no) 左げん(の)

portable 1 *adj* keitaiyō (no) 携帯用(の) **2** *n* COMPUT rapputoppu ラップトップ; (*TV set*) keitaiyō terebi 携帯用テレビ

porthole NAUT gensō げん窓

portion *n* bubun 部分; (*of food*) ichininmae 1人前

portrait 1 *n* (*painting, photograph*) shōzōga 肖像画; (*depiction*) byōsha 描写 **2** *adv print* tatemuki 縦向き

portray (*of artist*) … no shōzō o egaku …の肖像を描く; (*of actor*) … no yaku o enjiru …の役を演じる; (*of author*) egaku 描く

portrayal (*by actor*) engi 演技; (*by author*) byōsha 描写

Portugal Porutogaru ポルトガル

Portuguese 1 *adj* Porutogaru (no) ポルトガル(の) **2** *n* (*person*) Porutogaru-jin ポルトガル人; (*language*) Porutogaru-go ポルトガル語

pose 1 *n* (*pretense*) misekake 見せかけ **2** *v/i* (*for artist, photographer*) pōzu o toru ポーズをとる; **~ as** … no furi o suru …のふりをする **3** *v/t*: **~ a problem** mondai o umu 問題を生む

position 1 *n* (*location*) ichi 位置; (*stance*) shisei 姿勢; (*in race, competition*) jun'i 順位; (*occupied by soldiers*) jinchi 陣地; (*point of view*) iken 意見; (*situation*) tachiba 立場; (*job*) shoku 職; (*status*) chii 地位; ***fourth ~*** (*in race*) daiyon'i 第四位 **2** *v/t* haichi suru 配置する

positive *attitude* sekkyokuteki (na) 積極的(な); *response* maemuki (na) 前向き(な); *medical test* yōsei (no) 陽性(の); GRAM genkyū (no) 原級(の); ELEC purasu (no) プラス(の); ***be ~*** (*sure*) jishin ga aru 自信がある; ***are you sure? - I'm ~*** tashika desu ka - machigai arimasen 確かですか - 間違いありません

positively (*decidedly*) mattaku まったく; (*definitely*) tashika ni 確かに

possess *car, house* shoyū suru 所有する; *sth that can be carried* shoji suru 所持する; *skills* … ga aru …がある

possession (*of car, house*) shoyū 所有; (*of sth that can be carried*) shoji 所持; (*thing owned*) shoyūbutsu 所有物; ***~s*** shoyūbutsu 所有物

possessive *person* dokusen'yoku no tsuyoi 独占欲の強い; GRAM shoyūkaku (no) 所有格(の)

possibility kanōsei 可能性

possible kanō (na) 可能(な); ***the quickest ~ route*** saitan no michi 最短の道; ***the highest ~ speed*** saidaigen no supīdo 最大限のスピード; ***the best ~ …*** dekirudake yoi … できるだけよい…
possibly dekirudake できるだけ; (*perhaps*) osoraku おそらく; ***that can't ~ be right*** sore wa totemo tadashii to wa omoenai それはとても正しいとは思えない; ***could you ~ tell me the time?*** jikan o oshiete itadakemasen ka 時間を教えていただけませんか
post[1] **1** *n* (*of wood, metal*) hashira 柱 **2** *v/t notice* haru はる; *profits* kōhyō suru 公表する; ***keep ~ed*** (*informed*) … ni shiraseru …に知らせる
post[2] **1** *n* (*place of duty*) shoku 職; (*of soldier*) mochiba 持ち場 **2** *v/t soldier, employee* haizoku suru 配属する; *guards* haichi suru 配置する
postage yūsōryō 郵送料
postal yūbin (no) 郵便(の)
postcard hagaki はがき
postdate sakihizuke ni suru 先日付にする
poster posutā ポスター
posterior *n* F oshiri おしり
posterity kōsei 後世
postgraduate 1 *n* daigakuinsei 大学院生 **2** *adj* daigakuin (no) 大学院(の)
posthumous shigo (no) 死後(の)
posthumously shigo ni 死後に
posting (*assignment*) haizoku 配属
postmark keshiin 消印
postmortem kenshi 検死
post office yūbinkyoku 郵便局
postpone enki suru 延期する
postponement enki 延期
posture shisei 姿勢
postwar sengo (no) 戦後(の)
pot[1] (*for cooking in*) nabe なべ; (*for coffee, tea*) potto ポット; (*for plant*) uekibachi 植木鉢
pot[2] F (*marijuana*) marifana マリファナ
potato jagaimo じゃがいも
potato chips poteto-chippusu ポテトチップス
potent *medicine* kikime no aru 効き目のある
potential 1 *adj* kanō (na) 可能(な); *customer, problem* senzaiteki (na) 潜在的(な); *failure* okoriuru 起こりうる **2** *n* kanōsei 可能性
potentially senzaiteki ni 潜在的に
pothole (*in road*) ana 穴
potter *n* tōkō 陶工
pottery (*activity*) tōgei 陶芸; (*items*) tōki 陶器; (*place*) tōki-seizōjo 陶器製造所
potty *n* (*for baby*) omaru おまる
pouch (*bag*) pōchi ポーチ
poultry (*birds*) kakin 家きん; (*meat*) toriniku 鳥肉
pounce *v/i* (*of animal*) tobikakaru とびかかる; *fig* kyūshū suru 急襲する
pound[1] *n* (*weight*) pondo ポンド
pound[2] (*for strays*) ori おり; (*for cars*) kuruma-okiba 車置き場
pound[3] *v/i* (*of heart*) dokidoki suru どきどきする; ***~ on*** *door, desk* … o dondon tataku …をどんどんたたく; ***~ on the roof*** (*of rain*) yane ni tatakitsukeru 屋根にたたきつける
pound sterling Igirisu-pondo イギリスポンド
pour 1 *v/t drink* tsugu つぐ; *oil, water* ireru 入れる **2** *v/i*: ***it's ~ing (with rain)*** doshaburi da どしゃ降りだ
♦**pour out** *drink* … o tsugu …をつぐ; *troubles* … o buchimakeru …をぶちまける
pout *v/i* fukureru 膨れる
poverty hinkon 貧困
poverty-stricken hijō ni binbō (na) 非常に貧乏(な)
powder 1 *n* kona 粉; (*for face*) oshiroi おしろい **2** *v/t face* … ni oshiroi o nuru …におしろいを塗る
powder room keshōshitsu 化粧室
power 1 *n* (*strength*) chikara 力; (*of engine*) shutsuryoku 出力; (*authority*) kenryoku 権力; (*of parliament*) kengen 権限; (*energy*) dōryoku 動力; (*electricity*) denryoku 電力; ***atomic ~***

genshiryoku 原子力; ***in ~*** POL seiken o nigitta 政権を握った; ***fall from ~*** POL shikkyaku suru 失脚する **2** *v/t*: ***be ~ed by*** … de ugoku … で動く
power cut teiden 停電
powerful *blow, drug* kyōryoku (na) 強力(な); *car, engine* bariki no aru 馬力のある; *man, union* yūryoku (na) 有力(な)
powerless muryoku (na) 無力(な); ***be ~ to …*** … suru chikara ga nai … する力がない
power line densen 電線; **power outage** teiden 停電; **power station** hatsudensho 発電所; **power steering** pawā-sutearingu パワーステアリング; **power unit** pawā-yunitto パワーユニット
PR (= ***public relations***) pīāru ピーアール
practical *experience* jissaiteki (na) 実際的(な); *studies, work* jitchi (no) 実地(の); *person* genjitsuteki (na) 現実的(な); *color, knowledge* jitsuyōteki (na) 実用的(な)
practical joke warufuzake 悪ふざけ
practically *behave, think* genjitsuteki ni 現実的に; (*almost*) jisshitsuteki ni 実質的に
practice 1 *n* (*not theory*) jissen 実践; (*training*) renshū 練習; (*rehearsal*) keiko けいこ; (*custom*) shūkan 習慣; ***in ~*** (*in reality*) jissai ni wa 実際には; ***be out of ~*** renshū-busoku de aru 練習不足である **2** *v/i* renshū suru 練習する **3** *v/t* renshū suru 練習する; ***~ law*** bengoshi o shite iru 弁護士をしている; ***~ medicine*** isha o shite iru 医者をしている
pragmatic jitsuyōteki (na) 実用的(な)
pragmatism jitsuyō-shugi 実用主義
prairie sōgen 草原
praise 1 *n* shōsan 称賛 **2** *v/t* shōsan suru 称賛する
praiseworthy shōsan ni atai suru 称賛に値する
prank itazura いたずら
prattle *v/i* mudabanashi o suru むだ話をする
pray inoru 祈る
prayer inori no kotoba 祈りの言葉; (*praying*) inori 祈り
preach 1 *v/i* (*in church*) sekkyō o suru 説教をする; (*moralize*) osekkyō o suru お説教をする **2** *v/t sermon* … ni tsuite sekkyō o suru …について説教をする
preacher sekkyōshi 説教師
precarious fuantei (na) 不安定(な)
precariously fuantei ni 不安定に
precaution yōjin 用心; ***take ~s*** (*use contraceptive*) hinin suru 避妊する
precautionary *measure* yōjin no tame (no) 用心のため(の)
precede *v/t* (*in time*) … yori saki ni kuru …より先に来る; (*go ahead of*) … yori saki ni iku …より先に行く
precedence: ***take ~*** yūsen sareru 優先される; ***take ~ over …*** … yori yūsen suru …より優先する
precedent senrei 先例
preceding mae (no) 前(の)
precinct (*district*) chiku 地区
precious kichō (na) 貴重(な)
precipitate *v/t crisis* hayameru 早める
précis *n* yōyaku 要約
precise seikaku (na) 正確(な)
precisely seikaku ni 正確に; ***~!*** sono tōri そのとおり
precision seikaku-sa 正確さ
precocious *child* sōjuku (na) 早熟(な)
preconceived: ***~ idea*** sennyūkan 先入観
precondition zentei-jōken 前提条件
predator (*animal*) hoshoku-dōbutsu 捕食動物
predecessor (*in job*) zennin-sha 前任者; (*machine*) mae no mono 前のもの
predestination unmei no yoteisetsu 運命の予定説
predicament kukyō 苦境
predict yogen suru 予言する
predictable yosō no tsuku 予想のつく
prediction yogen 予言

predominant *question, color* medatsu 目立つ; *mood* attōteki (na) 圧倒的(な)
predominantly attōteki ni 圧倒的に
predominate … ga yūsei de aru … が優勢である
prefabricated purehabu (no) プレハブ(の)
preface *n* jobun 序文
prefecture ken 県
prefer … no hō o konomu …のほうを好む; **~ X to Y** Y yori X no hō ga suki de aru YよりXのほうが好きである; **~ to do** … suru hō ga suki de aru …するほうが好きである
preferable nozomashii 望ましい; **be ~ to** … yori nozomashii …より望ましい
preferably dekireba できれば
preference konomi 好み
preferential yūsen (no) 優先(の)
prefix sēttōji 接頭辞
pregnancy ninshin 妊娠
pregnant ninshin shite iru 妊娠している
prehistoric senshi-jidai (no) 先史時代(の)
prejudice 1 *n* henken 偏見 **2** *v/t person* … ni henken o idakaseru …に偏見を抱かせる; *chances* sokonau 損なう
prejudiced henken no aru 偏見のある
preliminary *adj* yobiteki (na) 予備的(な)
premarital konzen (no) 婚前(の)
premature *action, decision* hayamatta 早まった; *death, arrival* hayasugita 早過ぎた; **~ baby** mijukuji 未熟児
premeditated keikakuteki (na) 計画的(な)
premier *n* POL shushō 首相
première *n* (*of movie*) fūkiri 封切り; (*of play*) shonichi 初日
premises (*of business*) shikichi 敷地; (*of store*) mise 店
premium *n* (*in insurance*) hokenryō 保険料
premonition yokan 予感
prenatal shussan mae (no) 出産前(の)
preoccupied uwa no sora (no) うわの空(の)
preparation (*act*) junbi 準備; **in ~ for** … no junbi de …の準備で; **~s** junbi 準備
prepare 1 *v/t* … no junbi o suru …の準備をする; **be ~d to do X** (*willing*) yorokonde X suru 喜んでXする **2** *v/i* junbi suru 準備する
preposition zenchishi 前置詞
preposterous tohō mo nai 途方もない
prerequisite hissu-jōken 必須条件
prescribe (*of doctor*) shohō suru 処方する
prescription MED shohōsen 処方せん
presence iru koto 居ること; **in the ~ of** … no mae de …の前で
presence of mind kiten 機転
present[1] **1** *adj* (*current*) genzai (no) 現在(の); **be ~** iru いる; (*at conference, meeting, in class*) shusseki shite iru 出席している **2** *n*: **the ~** genzai 現在; GRAM genzaikei 現在形; **at ~** ima no tokoro 今のところ
present[2] **1** *n* (*gift*) purezento プレゼント **2** *v/t award, bouquet* okuru 贈る; *program* teikyō suru 提供する; **~ X with Y, ~ Y to X** X ni Y o okuru XにYを贈る
presentation (*of new product*) shōkai 紹介, purezen プレゼン; (*of plan*) teiji 提示; (*of meal etc*) misekata 見せ方
present-day gendai (no) 現代(の)
presently (*at the moment*) ima no tokoro 今のところ; (*soon*) mamonaku まもなく
preservation hozon 保存
preservative *n* hozonzai 保存剤
preserve 1 *n* (*domain*) ryōiki 領域 **2** *v/t standards, peace etc* iji suru 維持する; *wood, building, food* hozon suru 保存する
preside *v/i* (*at meeting*) gichō o tsutomeru 議長を務める; **~ over** *meeting* … no gichō o tsutomeru …の議長を務める

presidency (*office of president*) daitōryō no chii 大統領の地位; (*term as president*) daitōryō no ninki 大統領の任期
president POL daitōryō 大統領; (*of company*) shachō 社長
presidential daitōryō (no) 大統領(の)
press 1 *n*: ***the ~*** shinbun-zasshi 新聞雑誌; (*journalists*) hōdōjin 報道陣 **2** *v/t button* osu 押す; (*urge*) sekasu せかす; *hand* nigirishimeru 握りしめる; *grapes* shiboru しぼる; *clothes* … ni airon o kakeru …にアイロンをかける **3** *v/i*: ***~ for*** segamu せがむ
press conference kisha-kaiken 記者会見
pressing *adj* kinkyū (no) 緊急(の)
pressure 1 *n* atsuryoku 圧力; (*of work, demands*) jūatsu 重圧; ***be under ~*** puresshā o kanjiru プレッシャーを感じる; ***be under ~ to do*** … suru yō ni atsuryoku o kakerareru …するように圧力をかけられる **2** *v/t* … ni atsuryoku o kakeru …に圧力をかける
prestige meisei 名声
prestigious *award* nadakai 名高い; *school* meimon (no) 名門(の)
presumably tabun 多分
presume … to suitei suru …と推定する; ***~ to do …*** atsukamashiku mo … suru 厚かましくも…する
presumption (*of innocence, guilt*) suitei 推定
presumptuous okogamashii おこがましい
pre-tax zeikomi (no) 税込み(の)
pretend 1 *v/t* … no furi o suru …のふりをする **2** *v/i* furi o suru ふりをする
pretense misekake 見せかけ
pretentious kidotta 気取った
pretext kōjitsu 口実
pretty 1 *adj woman, house* kirei (na) きれい(な); *child, doll* kawairashii かわいらしい **2** *adv* (*quite*) kanari かなり
prevail katsu 勝つ
prevailing *opinion* ippanteki (na) 一般的(な); *wind* yoku fuku よく吹く
prevent fusegu 防ぐ; ***~ X (from) doing Y*** X ga Y suru no o samatageru XがYするのを妨げる
prevention bōshi 防止
preventive yobō (no) 予防(の)
preview *n* (*of movie*) shishakai 試写会; (*trailer*) yokokuhen 予告編; (*of exhibition*) nairan 内覧
previous mae (no) 前(の)
previously mae ni 前に
prewar senzen (no) 戦前(の)
prey *n* emono 獲物
♦**prey on** … o totte kuu …を取って食う; *fig* (*of conman etc*) … o kuimono ni suru …を食い物にする
price 1 *n* nedan 値段 **2** *v/t* COM … ni nedan o tsukeru …に値段をつける
priceless hijō ni kichō (na) 非常に貴重(な)
price war nebiki-kyōsō 値引き競争
prick[1] **1** *n* (*pain*) chikutto suru itami チクッとする痛み **2** *v/t* (*jab*) sasu 刺す
prick[2] *n* V (*penis*) chinpoko ちんぽこ; (*person*) iya na yatsu いやなやつ
♦**prick up**: ***~ one's ears*** (*of dog*) mimi o tateru 耳を立てる; (*of person*) mimi o sobadateru 耳をそば立てる
prickle (*on plant*) toge とげ
prickly *fabric, beard* chikuchiku suru ちくちくする; *plant* togedarake (no) とげだらけ(の)
pride 1 *n* (*in person, achievement*) jiman 自慢; (*self-respect*) jisonshin 自尊心, puraido プライド; (*arrogance*) unubore うぬぼれ **2** *v/t*: ***~ oneself on*** … o hokori ni suru …を誇りにする
priest (*Christian*) shisai 司祭; (*Buddhist*) sōryo 僧侶; (*Shinto*) kannushi 神主
primarily omo ni 主に
primary 1 *adj* shuyō (na) 主要(な) **2** *n* POL yobi-senkyo 予備選挙
prime 1 *n*: ***be in one's ~*** jinsei no sakari ni aru 人生の盛りにある **2** *adj example, reason* mottomo jūyō (na) もっとも重要(な); ***of ~***

importance saijūyō (no) 最重要(の)

prime minister sōri-daijin 総理大臣, shushō 首相

prime time TV gōruden-awā ゴールデンアワー

primitive *man, culture* genshi (no) 原始(の); *tool, conditions* genshiteki (na) 原始的(な)

prince ōji 王子

princess ōjo 王女

principal 1 *adj* shuyō (na) 主要(な) **2** *n* (*of school*) kōchō 校長

principally omo ni 主に

principle (*in moral sense*) shugi 主義; (*rule*) genri 原理; ***on ~*** shugi to shite 主義として; ***in ~*** gensokuteki ni wa 原則的には

print 1 *n* (*in book, newspaper etc*) insatsu sareta moji 印刷された文字; (*photograph*) purinto プリント; ***out of ~*** zeppan de 絶版で; ***wood block ~*** ukiyoe 浮世絵 **2** *v/t* insatsu suru 印刷する; (*using block capitals*) katsujitai de kaku 活字体で書く

♦ **print out** *text, file* purinto-auto suru プリントアウトする

printed matter insatsubutsu 印刷物

printer (*person*) insatsu-gyōsha 印刷業者; (*machine*) purintā プリンター

printing press insatsuki 印刷機

printout purinto-auto プリントアウト

prior 1 *adj engagement* saki (no) 先(の); *knowledge* jizen (no) 事前(の) **2** *prep*: ***~ to*** … yori mae ni …より前に

prioritize (*put in order of priority*) … no yūsen-jun'i o kimeru …の優先順位を決める; (*give priority to*) yūsen saseru 優先させる

priority (*sth urgent*) yūsen-jikō 優先事項; (*most important thing*) saijūyō-jikō 最重要事項; ***have ~*** yūsen suru 優先する

prison keimusho 刑務所

prisoner shūjin 囚人; ***take ~*** … o horyo ni suru …を捕虜にする

prisoner of war horyo 捕虜

privacy puraibashī プライバシー

private 1 *adj life, conversation* shiteki (na) 私的(な); *office* kojinyō (no) 個人用(の); *property* shiyū (no) 私有(の); *industry* minkan (no) 民間(の); *school* shiritsu (no) 私立(の); *place* hitome ni tsukanai 人目につかない; *thought* hisoka (na) 秘か(な); *person* uchiki (na) 内気(な); (*on letter*) shinten 親展; (*on door*) kankeisha-igai-tachiiri-kinshi 関係者以外立ち入り禁止; ***~ room*** koshitsu 個室; ***~ patient*** shihi-chiryō no kanja 私費治療の患者 **2** *n* MIL heisotsu 兵卒; ***in ~*** hito no inai tokoro de 人のいないところで

privately (*in private*) hito no inai tokoro de 人のいないところで; *funded, owned* shiteki ni 私的に; (*inwardly*) kojinteki ni 個人的に

private sector minkan-kigyō 民間企業

privilege (*special treatment*) tokken 特権; (*honor*) meiyo 名誉

privileged tokken no aru 特権のある; (*honored*) kōei (na) 光栄(な)

prize 1 *n* shō 賞 **2** *v/t* taisetsu ni suru 大切にする

prizewinner jushō-sha 受賞者

prizewinning jushō shita 受賞した

pro[1] *n*: ***the ~s and cons*** sanpi-ryōron 賛否両論

pro[2] (*professional*) puro プロ

pro[3]: ***be ~ …*** (*in favor of*) … sanseiha de aru …賛成派である

probability mikomi 見込み

probable arisō (na) ありそう(な)

probably tabun たぶん

probation LAW shikkō-yūyo 執行猶予; ***on ~*** (*in job*) shiyōkikanchū de 試用期間中で

probation officer hogo-kansatsukan 保護観察官

probation period (*in job*) shiken-saiyō-kikan 試験採用期間

probe 1 *n* (*investigation*) chōsa 調査; MED saguribari 探り針; ***space ~*** uchū-tansaki 宇宙探査機 **2** *v/t* saguribari de saguru 探り針で探る; (*investigate*) chōsa suru 調査する

problem mondai 問題; (*trouble*) toraburu トラブル; ***I don't want to be a ~*** toraburu ni wa naritaku nai トラブルにはなりたくない; ***no ~*** ii desu yo いいですよ
procedure tetsuzuki 手続き
proceed 1 *v/i* (*go*: *of people*) susumu 進む; (*of work etc*) shinkōsuru 進行する **2** *v/t*: ***~ to do X*** X shihajimeru Xし始める
proceedings ichibu-shijū 一部始終
proceeds shūeki 収益
process 1 *n* katei 過程; ***in the ~*** (*while doing it*) sono katei de その過程で **2** *v/t food, raw materials* kakō suru 加工する; *data* shori suru 処理する; *application etc* shinsa suru 審査する
procession gyōretsu 行列
processor COMPUT enzanshori-sōchi 演算処理装置
proclaim sengen suru 宣言する
prod 1 *n* hitotsuki ひと突き **2** *v/t* tsuku 突く
prodigy: (***child***) ~ tensai 天才
produce 1 *n* (*fruit and vegetables*) seisanbutsu 生産物 **2** *v/t commodity* seisan suru 生産する; (*bring about*) motarasu もたらす; (*bring out*) toridasu 取り出す; *play, movie, TV program* seisaku suru 製作する
producer (*of commodity*) seisan-sha 生産者, seizō-gaisha 製造会社; (*country*) seisankoku 生産国; (*of play, movie, TV program*) purodyūsā プロデューサー
product seihin 製品; (*result*) kekka 結果
production seisan 生産; (*of machinery, automobiles*) seisaku 製作; (*of play, movie, TV program*) seisaku 制作
production capacity seisan-nōryoku 生産能力
production costs seisakuhi 製作費
productive seisanryoku no takai 生産力の高い; *meeting* seisanteki (na) 生産的(な)
productivity seisansei 生産性
profane *language* gehin (na) 下品(な)
profess (*claim*) kōgen suru 公言する
profession shokugyō 職業
professional 1 *adj* (*not amateur*) puro (no) プロ(の); *advice, help* senmonka (no) 専門家(の); *piece of work* puro-nami (no) プロ並み(の); ***turn ~*** puro ni tenkō suru プロに転向する **2** *n* (*doctor, lawyer etc*) senmonshoku no hito 専門職の人; (*not an amateur*) puro プロ
professionally *play sport* puro to shite プロとして; (*well, skillfully*) takumi ni 巧みに
professor kyōju 教授
proficiency jukuren 熟練
proficient jukuren shita 熟練した
profile (*of face*) yokogao 横顔; (*description*) gaiyō 概要
profit 1 *n* rieki 利益 **2** *v/i*: ***~ by, ~ from*** … kara rieki o eru …から利益を得る
profitability shūekisei 収益性
profitable mōke ni naru もうけになる
profit margin rizaya 利ざや
profound *thought* shin'en (na) 深遠(な); *hatred* fukai 深い; *shock, effect* tsuyoi 強い
profoundly fukaku 深く; *shock* tsuyoku 強く
prognosis yochi 予知
program 1 *n* keikaku 計画; (*on radio, TV*) bangumi 番組; (*in theater,* COMPUT) puroguramu プログラム **2** *v/t* COMPUT … ni puroguramu o ireru …にプログラムを入れる
programmer COMPUT puroguramā プログラマー
progress 1 *n* shinpo 進歩; ***make ~*** shinpo suru 進歩する; ***in ~*** shinkōchū de 進行中で **2** *v/i* (*advance in time*) shinkō suru 進行する; (*move on*) susumu 進む; (*make progress*; *in lesson*) jōtatsu suru 上達する; ***how is the work ~ing?*** shigoto wa donna guai ni hakadotte imasu ka 仕事はどんな具合にはかどっていますか

progressive *adj* dankaiteki (na) 段階的(な); (*enlightened*) shinpoteki (na) 進歩的(な)
progressively dandan to だんだんと
prohibit kinshi suru 禁止する
prohibition kinshi 禁止; ***Prohibition*** Kinshuhō-jidai 禁酒法時代
prohibitive *prices* hōgai (na) 法外(な)
project[1] *n* (*plan*) keikaku 計画; EDU kenkyū-kadai 研究課題; (*housing area*) jūtaku-danchi 住宅団地
project[2] **1** *v/t figures, sales* yosō suru 予想する; *movie* eisha suru 映写する **2** *v/i* (*stick out*) tsukideru 突き出る
projection (*forecast*) mitsumori 見積もり
projector (*for slides*) eishaki 映写機
prolific *writer, artist* tasaku (na) 多作(な)
prolong enchō suru 延長する
prom (*school dance*) dansu-pātī ダンスパーティー
prominent *nose* takai 高い; *chin* tsukideta 突き出た; (*significant*) jūyō (na) 重要(な)
promiscuity dare to demo neru koto 誰とでも寝ること
promiscuous aite o erabanai 相手を選ばない
promise 1 *n* yakusoku 約束 **2** *v/t person* … ni yakusoku suru …に約束する; **~ *to* …** … to yakusoku suru …と約束する; **~ *X to Y*** Y ni X o yakusoku suru YにXを約束する **3** *v/i* yakusoku suru 約束する
promising zento-yūbō (na) 前途有望(な)
promote *employee* shōshin saseru 昇進させる; (*encourage, foster*) sokushin suru 促進する; COM senden suru 宣伝する
promoter (*of sports event*) shusaisha 主催者
promotion (*of employee*) shōshin 昇進; (*of scheme, idea*) sokushin 促進; COM hanbai-sokushin 販売促進
prompt 1 *adj person* jikan o mamoru 時間を守る; *train* teikoku kikkari (no) 定刻きっかり(の); (*speedy*) jinsoku (na) 迅速(な) **2** *adv*: ***at two o'clock ~*** niji kikkari ni 二時きっかりに **3** *v/t* (*cause*) … no kikkake to naru … のきっかけとなる; *actor* … ni serifu o tsukeru …にせりふをつける; **~ *X to do Y*** X ni Y saseru XにYさせる **4** *n* COMPUT puronputo プロンプト
promptly (*on time*) kikkari ni きっかりに; (*immediately*) sokuza ni 即座に
prone: ***be ~ to*** … shigachi de aru … しがちである
pronoun daimeishi 代名詞
pronounce *word* hatsuon suru 発音する; (*declare*) … to sengen suru … と宣言する
pronounced *accent* meihaku (na) 明白(な); *views* kakko to shita 確固とした
pronunciation hatsuon 発音
proof *n* shōko 証拠; (*of book*) kōseizuri 校正刷り
prop 1 *v/t* tatekakeru 立てかける **2** *n* (*in theater*) kodōgu 小道具
♦ **prop up** … o sasaeru …を支える
propaganda puropaganda プロパガンダ
propel suishin suru 推進する
propellant (*in aerosol*) kōatsu-gasu 高圧ガス
propeller sukuryū スクリュー
proper (*real*) chanto shita ちゃんとした; (*correct*) tadashii 正しい; (*fitting*) tekitō (na) 適当(な)
properly chanto ちゃんと
property shoyūbutsu 所有物; (*land*) tochi 土地
property developer tochi-kaihatsu-gyōsha 土地開発業者
prophecy yogen 予言
prophesy … to yogen suru …と予言する
proportion wariai 割合; (*part, percentage*) bubun 部分; **~*s*** (*dimensions*) tsuriai つり合い
proportional hirei shita 比例した
proposal (*suggestion*) teian 提案; (*of*

marriage) puropōzu プロポーズ
propose 1 *v/t* (*suggest*) teian suru 提案する; (*plan*) keikaku suru 計画する **2** *v/i* (*to marry*) puropōzu suru プロポーズする
proposition 1 *n* teian 提案 **2** *v/t woman* … ni iiyoru …に言い寄る
proprietor ōnā オーナー
proprietress josei-ōnā 女性オーナー
prose sanbun 散文
prosecute *v/t* LAW kiso suru 起訴する
prosecution LAW kiso 起訴; (*lawyers*) kensatsugawa 検察側
prosecutor → ***public prosecutor***
prospect 1 *n* (*chance, likelihood*) nozomi 望み; (*thought of sth in the future*) mikomi 見込み; **~s** mitōshi 見通し **2** *v/i*: **~ for** *gold* … o shikutsu suru …を試堀する
prospective mikomi no aru 見込みのある
prosper han'ei suru 繁栄する
prosperity han'ei 繁栄
prosperous *person, business* seikō shita 成功した; *city, country* han'ei shita 繁栄した
prostitute *n* baishunfu 売春婦; ***male* ~** danshō 男娼
prostitution baishun 売春
prostrate: ***be ~ with grief*** hitan ni kurete iru 悲嘆にくれている
protect hogo suru 保護する, mamoru 守る
protection hogo 保護
protection money mikajimeryō みかじめ料
protective *clothing, equipment* hogoyō (no) 保護用(の); *mother* sewazuki (no) 世話好き(の)
protein tanpakushitsu たんぱく質
protest 1 *n* kōgi 抗議; (*demonstration*) kōgi-shūkai 抗議集会 **2** *v/t* … to shuchō suru …と主張する; (*object to*) … ni hantai suru …に反対する **3** *v/i* kōgi suru 抗議する
Protestant 1 *n* Purotesutanto プロテスタント **2** *adj* Purotesutanto (no) プロテスタント(の)
protester kōgi-sha 抗議者
protocol gaikō-girei 外交儀礼
prototype genkei 原型
protracted nagabiita 長引いた
protrude *v/i* tsukideru 突き出る
proud *owner, father* hokorashige (na) 誇らしげ(な); (*independent*) jisonshin no tsuyoi 自尊心の強い; (*arrogant*) unubore ga tsuyoi うぬぼれが強い; ***be ~ of*** … o hokori ni omou …を誇りに思う
proudly hokorashige ni 誇らしげに
prove shōmei suru 証明する
proverb kotowaza ことわざ
provide (*for society, school*) kyōkyū suru 供給する; (*for person*) ataeru 与える; ***~ Y to X, ~ X with Y*** X ni Y o ataeru XにYを与える; **~d** (***that***)… to iu jōken de …という条件で
♦**provide for** *family* … o yashinau …を養う; (*of law etc*) … ni sonaeru …に備える
province shū 州
provincial *city* chihō (no) 地方(の); *pej* shiya no semai 視野の狭い
provision (*supply*) kyōkyū 供給; (*of law, contract*) jōkō 条項
provisional jōkentsuki (no) 条件つき(の)
proviso jōken 条件
provocation chōhatsu 挑発
provocative chōhatsuteki (na) 挑発的(な)
provoke (*cause*) hikiokosu 引き起こす; (*annoy*) okoraseru 怒らせる
prow NAUT senshu 船首
prowess shuwan 手腕
prowl *v/i* urotsuku うろつく
prowler urotsuku hito うろつく人
proximity chika-sa 近さ
proxy (*authority*) inin 委任; (*person*) dairinin 代理人
prude kamatoto かまとと
prudence shinchō-sa 慎重さ
prudent shinchō (na) 慎重(な)
prudish kamatotobutta かまととぶった
prune[1] *n* purūn プルーン
prune[2] *v/t plant* sentei suru せん定する; *fig* kiritsumeru 切り詰める

pry sensaku suru せん索する
♦**pry into** … no koto o sensaku suru …のことをせん索する
PS (= ***postscript***) tsuishin 追伸
pseudonym pen-nēmu ペンネーム
psychiatric seishinka (no) 精神科(の)
psychiatrist seishinkai 精神科医
psychiatry seishin-igaku 精神医学
psychic 1 *adj* chōnōryoku (no) 超能力(の) **2** *n* chōnōryoku-sha 超能力者
psychoanalysis seishin-bunseki 精神分析
psychoanalyst seishin-bunsekii 精神分析医
psychoanalyze … no seishin-bunseki o suru …の精神分析をする
psychological shinriteki (na) 心理的(な); *research, study* shinrigakuteki (na) 心理学的(な)
psychologically shinriteki ni 心理的に
psychologist shinri-gakusha 心理学者
psychology shinrigaku 心理学
psychopath seishin-ijōsha 精神異常者
pub pabu パブ; (*Japanese-style*) izakaya 居酒屋
puberty shishunki 思春期
pubic hair inmō 陰毛
public 1 *adj* (*in ~*) kōzen (no) 公然(の); (*of the ~*) kokumin (no) 国民(の); (*not private*) ōyake (no) 公(の); (*for the ~*) kōkyō (no) 公共(の); (*open to the ~*) kōkai (no) 公開(の); *school, library* kōritsu (no) 公立(の); ***~ bath*** sentō 銭湯 **2** *n*: ***the ~*** ippan no hitobito 一般の人々; (*citizens*) kokumin 国民; ***open to the ~*** ippankōkai sarete iru 一般公開されている; ***in ~*** hitomae de 人前で
publication (*of book, report*) shuppan 出版; (*by newspaper: of photographs*) kōhyō 公表; (*of story*) hōdō 報道; (*book, newspaper*) shuppanbutsu 出版物
publicity (*advertisements*) senden 宣伝; (*media attention*) chūmoku 注目; ***it got a lot of ~*** chūmoku o atsumeta 注目を集めた
publicize (*make known*) kōhyō suru 公表する; COM senden suru 宣伝する
publicly kōzen to 公然と
public prosecutor kensatsukan 検察官; **public relations** kōhō-katsudō 広報活動; **public school** kōritsu-gakkō 公立学校; **public sector** kōei-bumon 公営部門
publish shuppan suru 出版する
publisher (*company*) shuppan-sha 出版社; (*person*) hakkō-sha 発行者
publishing shuppan 出版
publishing company shuppan-sha 出版社
puddle *n* mizutamari 水たまり
puff 1 *n*: ***a ~ of smoke*** ippuku 一服; ***a ~ of wind*** ichijin no kaze 一陣の風 **2** *v/i* (*pant*) aegu あえぐ
puffy *eyes* harebottai はれぼったい; *face* mukunda むくんだ
pull 1 *n* (*on rope*) hippari 引っ張り; F (*appeal*) miryoku 魅力; F (*influence*) eikyōryoku 影響力 **2** *v/t* hipparu 引っ張る; *tooth* hikinuku 引き抜く; *muscle* itameru 痛める **3** *v/i* hipparu 引っ張る
♦**pull apart** … o hikihanasu …を引き離す
♦**pull away** *v/t* … o hikihanasu …を引き離す
♦**pull down** (*lower*) … o hikiorosu …を引き下ろす; (*demolish*) … o torikowasu …を取り壊す
♦**pull in** (*of bus, train*) tōchaku suru 到着する
♦**pull off** *leaves* … o mogitoru …をもぎ取る; *clothes* … o nugu …を脱ぐ; F (*succeed in*) … o yaritogeru …をやり遂げる
♦**pull out 1** *v/t* … o nuku …を抜く; *troops* … o tettai saseru …を撤退させる **2** *v/i* (*of an agreement, a competition*) te o hiku 手を引く; (*of troops*) tettai suru 撤退する; (*of ship*) shuppatsu suru 出発する
♦**pull through** (*from an illness*) kaifuku suru 回復する
♦**pull together 1** *v/i* (*cooperate*)

kyōryoku suru 協力する **2** *v/t*: ***pull oneself together*** ki o shizumeru 気を静める

♦**pull up1** *v/t* (*raise*) … o hippariageru …を引っ張り上げる; *plant, weeds* … o hikinuku …を引き抜く **2** *v/i* (*of car etc*) tomaru 止まる

pulley kassha 滑車

pulp (*of fruit*) kaniku 果肉; (*for paper-making*) parupu パルプ

pulpit sekkyōdan 説教壇

pulsate (*of blood*) myaku-utsu 脈打つ; (*of rhythm*) kodō suru 鼓動する

pulse myakuhaku 脈拍

pulverize funsai suru 粉砕する

pump1 *n* (*machine*) ponpu ポンプ; (*gas ~*) kyūyu-ponpu 給油ポンプ **2** *v/t water* ponpu de okuru ポンプで送る; *air* ponpu de ireru ポンプで入れる

♦**pump up** ponpu de kūki o ireru ポンプで空気を入れる

pumpkin kabocha かぼちゃ

pun dajare だじゃれ

punch1 *n* (*blow*) panchi パンチ; (*tool*) ana-akeki 穴あけ機 **2** *v/t* (*with fist*) kobushi de naguru こぶしで殴る; *hole, ticket* akeru 開ける

punch line ochi 落ち

punctual jikan ni seikaku (na) 時間に正確(な)

punctuality jikan o mamoru koto 時間を守ること

punctually jikan dōri ni 時間どおりに

punctuate kutōten o utsu 句読点を打つ

punctuation kutōten no uchikata 句読点の打ち方

punctuation mark kutōten 句読点

puncture1 *n* ana 穴 **2** *v/t* … ni ana o akeru …に穴を開ける

pungent shigekiteki (na) 刺激的(な)

punish *person* bassuru 罰する

punishing *schedule* kitsui きつい

punishment batsu 罰; LAW keibatsu 刑罰

puny *person* yaseppochi (no) やせっぽち(の)

pup (*young dog*) koinu 子犬

pupil[1] (*of eye*) dōkō どう孔

pupil[2] (*student*) seito 生徒; (*disciple*) deshi 弟子

puppet (*on strings*) ayatsuri-ningyō 操り人形; (*finger ~*) yubiningyō 指人形; *fig* kairai かいらい

puppet government kairai-seifu かいらい政府

puppy koinu 子犬

purchase[1]1 *n* (*action*) kōnyū 購入; (*object*) kōnyūhin 購入品 **2** *v/t* kōnyū suru 購入する

purchase[2] (*grip*) tegakari 手がかり

purchaser kaite 買い手

pure *silk, gold* junsui (na) 純粋(な); *air, water, sound* sunda 澄んだ; (*morally*) junketsu (na) 純潔(な)

purely tan ni 単に

purge1 *n* (*of political party*) shukusei 粛清 **2** *v/t* shukusei suru 粛清する

purify *water* jōka suru 浄化する

Puritan REL Seikyōto 清教徒

puritanical genkaku (na) 厳格(な)

purity junsui-sa 純粋さ; (*moral*) junketsu 純潔

purple *adj* murasaki (no) 紫(の)

Purple Heart MIL meiyo-senshō-kunshō 名誉戦傷勲章

purpose mokuteki 目的; ***on ~*** waza to わざと

purposeful danko to shita 断固とした

purposely waza to わざと

purr *v/i* (*of cat*) gorogoro to nodo o narasu ごろごろとのどを鳴らす

purse *n* (*pocketbook*) handobaggu ハンドバッグ

pursue *v/t person* tsuiseki suru 追跡する; *career, aim* tsuikyū suru 追求する; *course of action* tsuzukeru 続ける

pursuer tsuiseki-sha 追跡者

pursuit (*chase*) tsuiseki 追跡; (*of happiness etc*) tsuikyū 追求; (*pastime*) shumi 趣味; ***those in ~*** otte 追っ手

pus umi うみ

push1 *n* (*shove*) hitooshi ひと押し **2** *v/t* (*shove*) osu 押す; (*pressure*)

sekitateru せきたてる; *drugs* mitsubai suru 密売する; **be ~ed for** … ga nakute komatte iru …がなくて困っている; **be ~ing 40** yonjū ni chikazuku 四十に近づく
3 *v/i* osu 押す
♦**push along** *cart etc* oshisusumu 押し進む
♦**push away** … o oshiyaru …を押しやる
♦**push off 1** *v/t lid* … o oshiageru …を押し上げる **2** *v/i* F (*leave*) saru 去る; **~!** itte shimae 行ってしまえ
♦**push on** *v/i* (*continue*) saki e susumu 先へ進む
♦**push up** *prices* … o oshiageru …を押し上げる
push-button oshi-botan 押しボタン
pusher (*of drugs*) mayaku-mitsubai-nin 麻薬密売人
push-up udetatefuse 腕立て伏せ
pushy gōin (na) 強引(な)
puss, pussy (cat) neko-chan 猫ちゃん
put (*place*) oku 置く; *question* dasu 出す; **~ the cost at …** … to hiyō o mitsumoru …と費用を見積もる
♦**put aside** *money* … o totte oku …を取っておく; *work* … o chūdan suru …を中断する
♦**put away** (*in closet etc*) … o shimau …をしまう; (*in prison*) … o keimusho ni ireru …を刑務所に入れる; (*in mental home*) … o seishin-byōin ni ireru …を精神病院に入れる; (*consume*) … o tairageru …を平らげる; *money* … o chokin suru …を貯金する; *animal* … o shimatsu suru …を始末する
♦**put back** (*replace*) … o kaesu …を返す
♦**put by** *money* … o tameru …をためる
♦**put down** … o oku …を置く; *deposit* … o atamakin to shite harau …を頭金として払う; *rebellion* … o chin'atsu suru …を鎮圧する; (*belittle*) … o kenasu …をけなす; (*in writing*) … o kaku …を書く; **put one's foot down** (*in car*) supīdo o dasu スピードを出す; (*be firm*) danko to shita taido o toru 断固とした態度を取る; **put X down to Y** (*attribute*) X o Y no sei to minasu XをYのせいとみなす
♦**put forward** *idea etc* teian suru 提案する
♦**put in** … o ireru …を入れる; *time* … o tsugikomu …をつぎ込む; *claim* … o teishutsu suru …を提出する
♦**put in for** … o shinsei suru …を申請する
♦**put off** *light, radio, TV* kesu 消す; (*postpone*) enki suru 延期する; (*deter*) omoi-todomaraseru 思いとどまらせる; (*repel*) fukai ni saseru 不快にさせる; **the experience put me off shellfish** sono keiken no sei de watashi wa kai ga iya ni natta その経験のせいで私は貝がいやになった
♦**put on** *light, radio, TV* … o tsukeru …をつける; *tape, music, glasses, brake* … o kakeru …をかける; *jacket, shirt* … o kiru …を着る; *shoes, pants* … o haku …をはく; *gloves* … o hameru …をはめる; *hat* … o kaburu …をかぶる; *make-up* … o suru …をする; (*perform*) … o jōen suru …を上演する; (*assume*) … no furi o suru …のふりをする; **~ weight** futoru 太る; **she's just putting it on** kanojo wa tan ni furi o shite iru dake desu 彼女は単にふりをしているだけです
♦**put out** *hand* … o sashidasu …を差し出す; *fire, light* … o kesu …を消す
♦**put through** (*on phone*) … o tsunagu …をつなぐ
♦**put together** (*assemble*) … o kumitateru …を組み立てる; (*organize*) … o soshiki suru …を組織する
♦**put up** *v/t hand, hair, prices* … o ageru …を上げる; *person* … o tomeru …を泊める; (*erect*) … o tateru …を建てる; *poster, notice* … o kakageru …を掲げる; *money* … o

teikyō suru ... を提供する; ***~ up for sale*** uri ni dasu 売りに出す
♦ **put up with** (*tolerate*) ... o gaman suru ...を我慢する
putty pate パテ
puzzle 1 *n* (*mystery*) nazo なぞ; (*game*) pazuru パズル; (*jigsaw ~*) jigusō-pazuru ジグソーパズル; (*crossword ~*) kurosuwādo-pazuru クロスワードパズル **2** *v/t* komaraseru 困らせる
puzzling wake no wakaranai わけのわからない
PVC pori-enka-binīru ポリ塩化ビニール
pylon tettō 鉄塔

Q

quack¹ 1 *n* (*of duck*) gāgā naku koe がーがー鳴く声 **2** *v/i* gāgā naku がーがー鳴く
quack² F (*bad doctor*) yabuisha やぶ医者
quadrangle (*figure*) shikakkei 四角形; (*courtyard*) nakaniwa 中庭
quadruped yotsuashi (no) 四つ足(の)
quadruple *v/i* yonbai ni naru 四倍になる
quadruplets yotsugo 四つ子
quaint *cottage* kofū (na) 古風(な); *ideas etc* kimyō (na) 奇妙(な)
quake 1 *n* (*earthquake*) jishin 地震 **2** *v/i* (*of earth*) yureru 揺れる; (*with fear*) furueru 震える
qualification (*from university etc*) shikaku 資格; (*of remark etc*) jōken 条件; ***have the right ~s for a job*** shigoto ni tekishita shikaku o motte iru 仕事に適した資格を持っている
qualified *doctor, engineer etc* nintei sareta 認定された; (*restricted*) gentei sareta 限定された; ***I am not ~ to judge*** watashi ni handan suru shikaku wa nai 私に判断する資格はない
qualify 1 *v/t* (*of degree, course etc*) ... ni shikaku o ataeru ...に資格を与える; *remark etc* gentei suru 限定する **2** *v/i* (*get degree etc*) shikaku o toru 資格を取る; ***our team has qualified for the semi-final*** watashitachi no chīmu wa junkesshō ni susunda 私達のチームは準決勝に進んだ; ***that doesn't ~ as ...*** sore wa ... to mitomerarenai それは...と認められない
quality shitsu 質; (*characteristic*) tokuchō 特徴
quality control (*activity*) hinshitsu-kanri 品質管理; (*department*) hinshitsu-kanribu 品質管理部
qualm gimon 疑問; ***have no ~s about ...*** ... ni taishite nani mo gimon o kanjinai ...に対して何も疑問を感じない
quantify ... o ryō de arawasu ...を量で表す
quantity ryō 量
quarantine *n* kakuri 隔離
quarrel 1 *n* kenka けんか **2** *v/i* kenka suru けんかする
quarrelsome kenkappayai けんかっぱやい
quarry (*for mining*) ishikiriba 石切り場
quart kuwōto クウォート
quarter 1 *n* yonbun no ichi 四分の一; (*25 cents*) nijūgo sento dama 25セント玉; (*part of town*) chiku 地区; ***a ~ of an hour*** jūgo fun 十五分; ***a ~ of 5*** go ji jūgo fun mae 五時十五分前; ***~ after 5*** go ji jūgo fun 五時十五分 **2** *v/t* yontōbun

suru 四等分する

quarterback SP kuwōtābakku クウォーターバック; **quarterfinal** junjun-kesshō 準々決勝; **quarterfinalist** junjun-kesshō-shutsujō-senshu 準々決勝出場選手

quarterly 1 *adj* shihanki (no) 四半期(の) **2** *adv publish* kikan de 季刊で; *pay* shihanki goto ni 四半期毎に

quarternote MUS shibu-onpu 四分音符

quarters MIL heisha 兵舎

quartet MUS karutetto カルテット

quartz suishō 水晶

quaver 1 *n* (*in voice*) furuegoe 震え声 **2** *v/i* (*of voice*) furueru 震える

queen joō 女王

queen bee joō-bachi 女王ばち

queer (*peculiar*) hen (na) 変(な)

quench *flames* kesu 消す; ***~ one's thirst*** nodo no kawaki o iyasu のどの渇きをいやす

query 1 *n* shitsumon 質問 **2** *v/t* (*express doubt about*) … ni toitadasu …に問いただす; (*check*) kiku 聞く; ***~ X with Y*** Y ni X o kiku YにXを聞く

question 1 *n* shitsumon 質問; (*matter*) mondai 問題; ***in ~*** (*being talked about*) wadai (no) 話題(の); (*in doubt*) mondai (no) 問題(の); ***it's a ~ of money / time*** okane no / jikan no mondai da お金の/時間の問題だ; ***that's out of the ~*** sore wa mondai-gai da それは問題外だ **2** *v/t person* … ni shitsumon suru …に質問する; LAW jinmon suru 尋問する; (*doubt*) utagau 疑う

questionable *honesty* utagawashii 疑わしい; *figures, statement* fushin (na) 不審(な)

questioning *look, tone* utagawashige (na) 疑わしげ(な)

question mark gimonfu 疑問符

questionnaire ankēto アンケート

quick hayai 速い; ***be ~!*** hayaku 早く; ***let's have a ~ drink*** chotto nomi ni ikō ちょっと飲みに行こう; ***can I have a ~ look?*** chotto mite mo ii desu ka ちょっと見てもいいですか; ***that was ~!*** hayakatta ne 早かったね

quicksand ryūsa 流砂; **quicksilver** suigin 水銀; **quickwitted** kiten no kiku 機転のきく

quiet *voice, music engine* shizuka (na) 静か(な); *life* heion (na) 平穏(な); *town, street* kansan to shita 閑散とした; *person* mono-shizuka (na) 物静か(な); ***keep ~ about*** … o damatte iru …を黙っている; ***~!*** shizuka ni 静かに

♦**quieten down 1** *v/t children* shizuka ni saseru 静かにさせる **2** *v/i* (*of children*) shizuka ni naru 静かになる; (*of situation*) osamaru 収まる

quilt (*on bed*) kakebuton 掛け布団

quinine kinīne キニーネ

quip 1 *n* jōdan 冗談 **2** *v/i* jōdan o iu 冗談を言う

quirky kimagure (na) 気まぐれ(な)

quit 1 *v/t job* yameru 辞める; ***~ doing X*** X suru no o yameru Xするのを止める **2** *v/i* (*leave job*) yameru 辞める; COMPUT owari ni suru 終わりにする

quite (*fairly*) kanari かなり; (*completely*) mattaku まったく; ***not ~ ready*** mada junbi ga dekite inai まだ準備ができていない; ***I didn't ~ understand*** watashi wa amari yoku wakaranakatta 私はあまりよく分からなかった; ***is that right? - not ~*** sore de ii – chotto chigau それでいい-ちょっと違う; ***~!*** sono tōri そのとおり; ***~ a lot*** kanari かなり; ***it was ~ a surprise*** sore wa kanari odoroki datta それはかなり驚きだった

quits: ***be ~ with*** … to aiko da …とあいこだ

quiver *v/i* (*of voice, hand*) furueru 震える; (*of leaf*) yureru 揺れる

quiz 1 *n* kuizu クイズ **2** *v/t* shitsumon suru 質問する

quiz program kuizu-bangumi クイズ番組

quota wariate 割り当て
quotation (*from author*) in'yō 引用; (*price*) mitsumori 見積もり; ***give X a ~ for Y*** X ni Y no mitsumori o dasu XにYの見積もりを出す
quotation marks in'yōfu 引用符
quote 1 *n* (*from author*) in'yō 引用; (*price*) mitsumori 見積もり; (*quotation mark*) in'yōfu 引用符 **2** *v/t text* inyō suru 引用する; *price* … no mitsumori o dasu …の見積もりを出す **3** *v/i*: ***~ from an author*** aru chosha kara in'yō suru ある著者から引用する

R

rabbit usagi うさぎ
rabies kyōkenbyō 狂犬病
raccoon araiguma あらいぐま; ***~ dog*** tanuki たぬき
race[1] *n* (*of people*) jinshu 人種
race[2] **1** *n* SP kyōsō 競走, rēsu レース; *fig* kyōsō 競争, rēsu レース; ***the ~s*** (*horse ~s*) keiba 競馬 **2** *v/i* (*run fast*) isoide iku 急いで行く; SP kyōgi ni deru 競技に出る; ***he ~d through his meal / work*** kare wa ōisogi de shokuji o shita / shigoto o shita 彼は大急ぎで食事をした/仕事をした **3** *v/t*: ***I'll ~ you*** anata to kyōsō suru あなたと競争する
racecourse keiba-jō 競馬場; **racehorse** kyōsō-ba 競走馬; **racetrack** (*for athletes*) torakku トラック; (*for cars*) sākitto サーキット
racial jinshu (no) 人種(の); ***~ equality*** jinshu-byōdō 人種平等
racing kyōsō 競争
racing car rēshingu-kā レーシングカー
racing driver rēsā レーサー
racism jinshu-sabetsu 人種差別
racist 1 *n* jinshu-sabetsu-shugi-sha 人種差別主義者 **2** *adj* jinshu-sabetsuteki (na) 人種差別的(な)
rack 1 *n* (*for parking bikes*) rakku ラック; (*for bags on train,*) tana 棚; (*for CDs*) tate 立て **2** *v/t*: ***~ one's brains*** chie o shiboru 知恵を絞る
racket[1] SP raketto ラケット
racket[2] (*noise*) sōon 騒音; (*criminal activity*) sagi 詐欺
radar rēdā レーダー
radiant *smile, appearance* kagayaku yō (na) 輝くよう(な)
radiate *v/i* (*of heat, light*) hōsha suru 放射する
radiation PHYS hōshanō 放射能
radiator rajiētā ラジエーター
radical 1 *adj* konponteki (na) 根本的(な); POL *views* kyūshinteki (na) 急進的(な); *person* kageki (na) 過激(な) **2** *n* POL kyūshin-ha 急進派
radicalism POL kyūshin-shugi 急進主義
radically konponteki ni 根本的に
radio rajio ラジオ; ***on the ~*** rajio de ラジオで; ***by ~*** musen de 無線で
radioactive hōshasei (no) 放射性(の); **radioactivity** hōshanō 放射能; **radio alarm** mezamashi-rajio 目覚ましラジオ; **radio station** rajio-hōsōkyoku ラジオ放送局; **radiotherapy** hōshasen-ryōhō 放射線療法
radish hatsuka-daikon はつかだいこん
radius hankei 半径
raffle *n* kuji くじ
raft ikada いかだ
rafter hari はり
rag (*for cleaning etc*) zōkin ぞうきん; ***~s*** (*clothes*) boro ぼろ
rage 1 *n* gekido 激怒; ***be in a ~*** ikarikurutte iru 怒り狂っている; ***all***

the ~ būmu (no) ブーム(の) **2** *v/i* (*of person*) ikarikuruu 怒り狂う; (*of storm*) arekuruu 荒れ狂う
ragged *clothes etc* boroboro (no) ぼろぼろ(の)
raid 1 *n* (*by troops, police*) shūgeki 襲撃; (*by robbers*) gōtō 強盗; FIN urikuzushi 売り崩し **2** *v/t* (*of troops, police*) shūgeki suru 襲撃する; (*of robbers*) gōtō ni hairu 強盗に入る
raider (*on bank etc*) gōtō 強盗
rail (*on track*) rēru レール; (*hand* ~) tesuri 手すり; (*for towel*) kake 掛け; ***by*** ~ ressha de 列車で
railings (*around park etc*) saku さく
railroad tetsudō 鉄道
railroad station eki 駅
rain 1 *n* ame 雨; ***in the*** ~ ame no naka de 雨の中で; ***the ~s*** uki 雨季 **2** *v/i* ame ga furu 雨が降る; ***it's ~ing*** ame ga futte iru 雨が降っている
rainbow niji にじ; **raincheck** ***can I take a ~ on that?*** tsugi no kikai de ii kashira 次の機会でいいかしら; **raincoat** reinkōto レインコート; **raindrop** amadare 雨垂れ; **rainfall** kōsuiryō 降水量; **rain forest** urin 雨林; **rainstorm** bōfūu 暴風雨
rainy amemoyō 雨模様; ***it's*** ~ amemoyō de aru 雨模様である
rainy season uki 雨季; (*in Japan*) tsuyu 梅雨
raise 1 *n* (*in salary*) shōkyū 昇給 **2** *v/t shelf etc* mochiageru 持ち上げる; *offer* ageru 上げる; *children* sodateru 育てる; *question* teiki suru 提起する; *money* atsumeru 集める
raisin hoshibudō 干しぶどう
rake *n* (*for garden*) kumade くま手
rally *n* (*meeting, reunion*) shūkai 集会; (*for cars, in tennis*) rarī ラリー
♦**rally around 1** *v/i* tasuke ni kuru 助けに来る **2** *v/t*: ~ ***X*** X no tokoro ni tasuke ni kuru Xの所に助けに来る
RAM (= ***random access memory***) ramu ラム
ram 1 *n* ohitsuji 雄ひつじ **2** *v/t ship, car* … ni shōtotsu suru …に衝突する
ramble 1 *n* (*walk*) haikingu ハイキング **2** *v/i* (*walk*) haikingu suru ハイキングする; (*when speaking*) toritomenaku naru とりとめなくなる; (*talk incoherently*) toritome no nai hanashi o suru とりとめのない話をする
rambler (*walker*) haikā ハイカー
rambling 1 *n* (*walking*) haikingu ハイキング; (*in speech*) kanwa 閑話 **2** *adj speech* toritome no nai とりとめのない
ramp surōpu スロープ; (*for raising vehicle*) ranpu ランプ
rampage 1 *v/i* abaremawaru 暴れまわる **2** *n*: ***go on the*** ~ abaremawatte iru 暴れまわっている
rampart jōheki 城壁
ramshackle gatagata (no) がたがた(の)
ranch daibokujō 大牧場
rancher bokujō-keiei-sha 牧場経営者
rancid kusatta 腐った
rancor urami うらみ
R & D (= ***research and development***) kenkyū-kaihatsu 研究開発
random 1 *adj* teatari-shidai (no) 手当たり次第(の); (*in statistics*), COMPUT musakui (no) 無作為(の); ~ ***sample*** musakui-chūshutsu 無作為抽出 **2** *n*: ***at*** ~ teatari-shidai ni 手当たり次第に
range 1 *n* (*of products*) haba 幅; (*of voice*) seiiki 声域; (*of gun*) shatei-kyori 射程距離; (*of airplane*) kōzoku-kyori 航続距離; (*of mountains*) sanmyaku 山脈 **2** *v/i*: ~ ***from X to Y*** X kara Y no han'i XからYの範囲
ranger (*forest* ~) shinrin-keibi-taiin 森林警備隊員
rank 1 *n* MIL kaikyū 階級; (*in society*) chii 地位; ***the ~s*** MIL heishi 兵士 **2** *v/t* … ni kakuzuke suru …に格付けする
♦**rank among** … no uchi ni kazoerareru …のうちに数えられる
ransack kumanaku sagasu くまなく

探す
ransom minoshirokin 身の代金; ***hold … to ~*** … o hitojichi ni shite minoshirokin o yōkyū suru …を人質にして身の代金を要求する
rant: ***~ and rave*** ōgoe de wamekichirasu 大声でわめきちらす
rap 1 *n* (*at door etc*) tonton tataku oto とんとんたたく音; MUS rappu ラップ **2** *v/t table etc* tonton tataku とんとんたたく
♦**rap at** *window etc* … o tonton tataku …をとんとんたたく
rape 1 *n* gōkan 強かん **2** *v/t* gōkan suru 強かんする
rape victim gōkan no higai-sha 強かんの被害者
rapid hayai 速い
rapidity haya-sa 速さ
rapids kyūryū 急流
rapist gōkan-sha 強かん者
rapture uchōten 有頂天
rapturous nekkyōteki (na) 熱狂的(な)
rare (*infrequent*) mare (na) まれ(な); (*unusual*) mezurashii めずらしい; *steak* rea レア
rarely metta ni…nai めったに…ない
rarity chinpin 珍品
rascal itazurakko いたずらっ子
rash[1] MED hasshin 発しん
rash[2] *action, behavior* keisotsu (na) 軽率(な)
raspberry kiichigo 木いちご, razuberī ラズベリー
rat *n* nezumi ねずみ
rate 1 *n* rēto レート; (*price*) ryōkin 料金; (*speed*) sokudo 速度; ***~ of interest*** FIN rishi 利子; ***at an hourly ~ of*** (*be paid at*) jikankyū… de 時間給…で; ***at this ~*** (*at this speed*) kono sokudo de この速度で; (*carrying on like this*) kono chōshi de wa この調子では **2** *v/t* (*consider, rank*) hyōka suru 評価する
rather kanari かなり; (*polite understatement*) sukoshi 少し; ***I would ~ stay here*** watashi wa dochiraka to iu to koko ni itai desu 私はどちらかと言うとここにいたいです; ***or would you ~ …?*** sō de nakereba mushiro …shitai desu ka そうでなければむしろ…したいですか
ration 1 *n* haikyū-bun 配給分 **2** *v/t supplies* haikyū suru 配給する
rational *person* riseiteki (na) 理性的(な); *method etc* gōrīteki (na) 合理的(な)
rationality gōrisei 合理性
rationalization (*of production etc*) gōrika 合理化
rationalize 1 *v/t production* gōrika suru 合理化する; *emotions, one's actions etc* seitōka suru 正当化する **2** *v/i* seitōka suru 正当化する
rat race kyōsō-shakai 競争社会
rattle 1 *n* (*noise*) garagara to iu oto がらがらという音; (*toy*) garagara がらがら **2** *v/t chains etc* … ni garagara oto o tatesaseru …にがらがら音を立てさせる **3** *v/i* (*of chains etc*) garagara oto ga suru がらがら音がする; (*of crates*) gatagata oto ga suru がたがた音がする
♦**rattle off** *poem, list* … o surasura iu …をすらすら言う
rattlesnake garagarahebi がらがらへび
ravage: ***~d by war*** sensō de hakai sareta 戦争で破壊された
rave *v/i* (*talk deliriously*) uwagoto o iu うわ言を言う; (*talk wildly*) wameku わめく; ***~ about*** (*enthuse*) … o homesoyasu …をほめそやす
raven watarigarasu わたりがらす
ravenous *appetite* harapeko (no) 腹ペコ(の)
rave review kōhyō 好評
ravine keikoku 渓谷
raving: ***~ mad*** kyōran shita 狂乱した
ravishing miwakuteki (na) 魅惑的(な)
raw *meat, vegetable* nama (no) 生(の); *sugar, iron* kakō shite inai 加工していない
raw materials genryō 原料
ray kōsen 光線; ***a ~ of hope***

hitosuji no kibō 一筋の希望
razor kamisori かみそり
razor blade kamisori no ha かみそりの刃
re COM … ni kanshite …に関して
reach 1 *n*: ***within ~*** te no todoku tokoro 手の届くところ; ***out of ~*** te no todokanai tokoro 手の届かないところ; ***the bus station is within easy ~ of the house*** basutei wa uchi no sugu chikaku ni arimasu バス停はうちのすぐ近くにあります **2** *v/t city etc* … ni tsuku …に着く; (*go as far as*) … ni todoku …に届く; *decision, agreement* … ni tassuru …に達する; (*contact*) … ni renraku suru …に連絡する
♦**reach out** *v/i* ude o nobasu 腕を伸ばす
react hannō suru 反応する
reaction hannō 反応
reactionary 1 *n* POL handō-shugi-sha 反動主義者 **2** *adj* POL handōteki (na) 反動的(な)
reactor (*nuclear*) genshiro 原子炉
read 1 *v/t* yomu 読む; *diskette* yomitoru 読み取る **2** *v/i* yomu 読む; ***~ to*** … ni yomikikaseru …に読み聞かせる
♦**read out** *v/t* (*aloud*) …o rōdoku suru …を朗読する
♦**read up on** … o tetteiteki ni kenkyū suru …を徹底的に研究する
readable *handwriting* yomeru 読める; *book* yomaseru 読ませる
reader (*person*) dokusha 読者
readily *admit, agree* susunde 進んで
readiness: **be *in a state of ~*** junbi ga totonotte iru 準備が整っている; ***surprised at their ~ to agree*** karera no susunde sansei suru taido ni odoroita 彼らの進んで賛成する態度に驚いた
reading (*activity*) dokusho 読書; (*from meter etc*) kiroku 記録
reading matter yomimono 読み物
readjust 1 *v/t equipment, controls* chōsetsu suru 調節する **2** *v/i* (*to situation*) … ni nareru …に慣れる
read-only file COMPUT yomidashi-sen'yō-fairu 読み出し専用ファイル
read-only memory COMPUT yomidashi-sen'yō-memorī 読み出し専用メモリー
ready (*prepared*) junbi ga dekita 準備ができた; (*willing*) susunde… suru 進んで…する; ***get*** (***oneself***) ***~*** junbi suru 準備する; ***get X ~*** X no junbi o suru Xの準備をする
ready-made *stew etc* dekiai (no) 出来合い(の); *solution* kisei (no) 既製(の)
ready-to-wear kiseifuku (no) 既製服(の)
real hontō (no) 本当(の); *gold, leather* honmono (no) 本物(の)
real estate fudōsan 不動産
real estate agent fudōsan-ya 不動産屋
realism genjitsu-shugi 現実主義
realist genjitsu-shugi-sha 現実主義者
realistic genjitsuteki (na) 現実的(な)
reality jijitsu 事実
realization jikkan 実感; (*of hopes, plan*) jitsugen 実現
realize *v/t* kizuku 気付く; *hopes, plan* jitsugen suru 実現する; FIN rieki o ageru 利益を上げる; ***I ~ now that …*** watashi wa ima … ni ki ga tsuita 私は今…に気が付いた
really hontō ni 本当に; ***~?*** hontō 本当; ***not ~*** (*not much*) anmari あんまり
real time COMPUT riarutaimu リアルタイム
real-time COMPUT riarutaimu (no) リアルタイム(の)
realtor fudōsan-ya 不動産屋
reap shūkaku suru 収穫する
reappear futatabi arawareru 再び現れる
rear 1 *n* kōbu 後部 **2** *adj legs* ushiro (no) 後ろ(の); *seats, wheels, lights* kōbu (no) 後部(の)
rearm *v/t & v/i* saigunbi suru 再軍備する
rearmost saikōbi (no) 最後尾(の)
rearrange *flowers, furniture* narabenaosu 並べ直す; *schedule*

saichōsei suru 再調整する
rear-view mirror bakku-mirā バックミラー
reason 1 *n* (*faculty*) risei 理性; (*cause*) riyū 理由 **2** *v/i*: **~ *with*** … o settoku suru …を説得する
reasonable *person, behavior* funbetsu no aru 分別のある; *price* datō (na) 妥当(な); ***a ~ number of people*** māmā no ninzū まあまあの人数
reasonably *act, behave* jōshikiteki ni 常識的に; (*quite*) kanari かなり
reassure anshin saseru 安心させる
reassuring anshin saseru 安心させる
rebate (*money back*) haraimodoshi 払い戻し
rebel 1 *n* POL hangyaku-sha 反逆者; (*against parents*) hankō-bunshi 反抗分子; **~ *troops*** hanran-gun 反乱軍 **2** *v/i* POL hanran o okosu 反乱を起こす; (*against parents*) hankō suru 反抗する
rebellion POL hanran 反乱; (*against parents*) hankō 反抗
rebellious hankōteki (na) 反抗的(な)
rebound *v/i* (*of ball etc*) hanekaeru はね返る
rebuff *n* kyozetsu 拒絶
rebuild *wall* tatenaosu 建て直す; *relationship* tatenaosu 立て直す
rebuke *v/t* hinan suru 非難する
recall *v/t ambassador* yobimodosu 呼び戻す; (*remember*) omoidasu 思い出す
recapture MIL dakkan suru 奪還する; *criminal* saitaiho suru 再逮捕する; *emotion* torimodosu 取り戻す
receding *hair* hagete kite iru はげてきている
receipt (*for money*) ryōshū-sho 領収書, reshīto レシート; (*for goods*) juryō-sho 受領書; ***acknowledge ~ of*** … o tashika ni uketorimashita koto o oshirase shimasu …を確かに受け取りましたことをお知らせします; **~*s*** FIN shūnyū 収入
receive uketoru 受け取る
receiver (*of letter*) uketorinin 受取人; TELEC juwaki 受話器; RAD jushinki 受信機
receivership: ***be in ~*** kanzainin no kanrika ni aru 管財人の管理下にある
recent saikin (no) 最近(の)
recently saikin 最近
reception (*in company*) uketsuke 受付; (*in hotel*) furonto フロント; (*formal party*) resepushon レセプション; (*welcome*) kangei 歓迎; (*for radio, phone*) jushin 受信
reception desk (*in company*) uketsuke 受付; (*in hotel*) furonto フロント
receptionist (*in company*) uketsuke-gakari 受付係; (*in hotel*) furonto-gakari フロント係
receptive: ***be ~ to*** … ni maemuki de aru …に前向きである
recess (*in wall etc*) kubomi くぼみ; EDU yasumi-jikan 休み時間; (*of Congress*) kyūkai 休会
recession keiki-kōtai 景気後退
recharge *battery* jūden suru 充電する
recipe reshipi レシピ
recipient uketorinin 受取人
reciprocal sōgo (no) 相互(の)
recital MUS risaitaru リサイタル
recite *poem* anshō suru 暗唱する; *details, facts* rekkyo suru 列挙する
reckless mucha (na) 無茶(な)
reckon (*think, consider*) omou 思う
♦**reckon with**: ***have X to ~*** X o kōryo ni ireru Xを考慮に入れる
reclaim *land from sea* umetateru 埋め立てる; *lost items* torimodosu 取り戻す
recline *v/i* motareru もたれる
recluse inton-sha 隠とん者
recognition (*of state, s.o.'s achievements*) shōnin 承認; (*of person*) ninshiki 認識; ***changed beyond ~*** miwake ga tsukanai hodo kawatta 見分けがつかないほど変わった
recognizable miwake ga tsuku 見分けがつく
recognize *person, voice, tune* … ni oboe ga aru …に覚えがある;

symptoms kakunin suru 確認する; POL: *state* shōnin suru 承認する; ***it can be ~d by …*** … de kakunin dekiru …で確認できる
recollect omoidasu 思い出す
recollection omoide 思い出
recommend susumeru 勧める
recommendation suisen 推薦
reconcile *people* nakanaori saseru 仲直りさせる; *facts, differences* chōwa saseru 調和させる; ***~ oneself to …*** … o shikata ga nai to ukeireru …をしかたがないと受け入れる; ***be ~d*** (*of two people*) nakanaori suru 仲直りする
reconciliation (*of people*) wakai 和解; (*of facts, differences*) chōwa 調和
recondition shūri suru 修理する
reconnaissance MIL teisatsu 偵察
reconsider *v/t & v/i* kangaenaosu 考え直す
reconstruct *city* saiken suru 再建する; *one's life* tatenaosu 立て直す; *crime* saigen suru 再現する
record 1 *n* MUS rekōdo レコード; SP *etc* saikō-kiroku 最高記録; (*written document, in database etc*) kiroku 記録; ***~s*** kiroku 記録; ***say off the ~*** … o hikōshiki ni iu …を非公式に言う; ***have a criminal ~*** zenka ga aru 前科がある; ***have a good ~ for*** … ni yoi jisseki o agete iru …に良い実績を上げている **2** *v/t* (*on tape etc*) rokuon suru 録音する; (*in writing*) kiroku suru 記録する
record-breaking kiroku-yaburi (no) 記録破り(の)
recorder MUS rikōdā リコーダー
record holder kiroku-hojisha 記録保持者
recording rokuon 録音
recording studio rokuon-sutajio 録音スタジオ
record player rekōdo-pureiyā レコードプレイヤー
recoup *losses* torimodosu 取り戻す
recover 1 *v/t sth lost, stolen* torimodosu 取り戻す; *composure* kaifuku suru 回復する **2** *v/i* (*from illness*) genki ni naru 元気になる
recovery (*of sth lost, stolen*) kaishū 回収; (*from illness*) kaifuku 回復; ***he has made a good ~*** kare wa sukkari kaifuku shita 彼はすっかり回復した
recreation goraku 娯楽
recruit 1 *n* MIL shinpei 新兵; (*to company*) shinnyū-shain 新入社員 **2** *v/t new staff* boshū suru 募集する
recruitment boshū 募集
recruitment drive boshū-katsudō 募集活動
rectangle chōhōkei 長方形
rectangular chōhōkei (no) 長方形(の)
recuperate kaifuku suru 回復する
recur kurikae sareru 繰り返される; (*of illness*) saihatsu suru 再発する
recurrent tabitabi okoru 度々起こる
recycle sairiyō suru 再利用する
recycling risaikuru リサイクル
red 1 *adj* akai 赤い **2** *n* aka 赤; ***be in the ~*** (*of person*) shakkin shite iru 借金している; ~ (*of account*) akaji de aru 赤字である
Red Cross Sekijūji 赤十字
redden *v/i* (*blush*) akaku naru 赤くなる
redecorate *v/t* kaisō suru 改装する
redeem *debt* shōkan suru 償還する; *sinners* sukuu 救う
redeeming: ***~ feature*** torie 取り柄
redevelop *part of town* saikaihatsu suru 再開発する
red-handed: ***catch X ~*** X o genkōhan de tsukamaeru Xを現行犯で捕まえる;**redhead** akage no hito 赤毛の人;**red-hot** sugoku atsui すごく熱い;**red light** (*at traffic light*) akashingō 赤信号;**red light district** akasen-chiku 赤線地区;**red meat** akami no niku 赤身の肉;**redneck** *hoshu-ha rōdō-sha kaikyū no hakujin* 保守派労働者階級の白人;**red pepper** tōgarashi とうがらし;**red tape** kanryō-shugi 官僚主義
reduce herasu 減らす; *speed, price* sageru 下げる; *size* chiisaku suru 小さくする
reduction genshō 減少; (*of price*)

nesage 値下げ
redundant (*unnecessary*) yobun (na) 余分(な)
reed BOT ashi あし
reef (*in sea*) anshō 暗礁
reef knot komamusubi こま結び
reek *v/i* niou 臭う; **~ of …** … no nioi ga punpun suru …の臭いがぷんぷんする
reel *n* (*of film*) rīru リール; (*of thread*) maki 巻
refer *v/t*: **~ a decision / problem to …** … ni kettei / mondai o itaku suru …に決定/問題を委託する
♦ **refer to** (*allude to*) … o honomekasu …をほのめかす; *dictionary etc* … o sanshō suru …を参照する
referee SP shinpan 審判; (*for job*) mimoto-hoshōnin 身元保証人
reference (*allusion*) genkyū 言及; (*for job*) suisenjō 推薦状; **with ~ to** … ni kanshite …に関して
reference book sankōtosho 参考図書
reference number shōkai-bangō 照会番号
referendum jūmin-tōhyō 住民投票
refill *v/t tank* … ni hojū suru …に補充する; *glass* … ni mō ippai tsugu …にもう一杯つぐ
refine *oil, sugar* seisei suru 精製する; *technique* senren suru 洗練する
refined *manners* senren sareta 洗練された
refinery seisei-jo 精製所
reflation rifureishon リフレーション
reflect 1 *v/t light* hansha suru 反射する; **be ~ed in …** … ni utsutte iru …に映っている **2** *v/i* (*think*) yukkuri kangaeru ゆっくり考える
reflection hansha 反射; (*consideration*) jukkō 熟考
reflex (*in body*) hansha-nōryoku 反射能力
reflex reaction hansha-undō 反射運動
reform 1 *n* kaikaku 改革 **2** *v/t* kaikaku suru 改革する
refrain[1] *v/i* tsutsushimu 慎む; **please ~ from smoking** kitsuen wa goenryo kudasai 喫煙はご遠慮下さい
refrain[2] *n* (*in song etc*) kurikaeshi 繰り返し
refresh *person* genki-zukeru 元気づける; **feel ~ed** kibun ga sawayaka ni naru 気分がさわやかになる
refresher course kenshū-kai 研修会
refreshing *drink* sawayaka (na) さわやか(な); *experience* sugasugashii すがすがしい
refreshments keishoku 軽食
refrigerate reizō suru 冷蔵する
refrigerator reizōko 冷蔵庫
refuel 1 *v/t airplane* … ni nenryō o hokyū suru …に燃料を補給する **2** *v/i* (*of airplane*) nenryō no hokyū o ukeru 燃料の補給を受ける
refuge hinan-basho 避難場所; **take ~** (*from storm etc*) hinan suru 避難する
refugee nanmin 難民
refund 1 *n* haraimodoshi 払い戻し **2** *v/t* haraimodosu 払い戻す
refusal kyozetsu 拒絶
refuse *gift* kotowaru 断る; *permission* kyohi suru 拒否する; *invitation* jitai suru 辞退する; **~ to do X** X suru no o kotowaru …Xするのを断る
regain *control, the lead* torimodosu 取り戻す
regard 1 *n*: **have great ~ for** … o sonkei suru …を尊敬する; **in this ~** kore ni kanshite これに関して; **with ~ to** … ni kanshite …に関して; (**kind**) **~s** keigu 敬具; **give my ~s to Yoko** Yōko san ni yoroshiku otsutae kudasai ようこさんによろしくお伝え下さい; **with no ~ for …** … ni okamainaku …にお構いなく **2** *v/t*: **~ X as Y** X o Y to omou XをYと思う; **as ~s …** … ni kanshite wa …に関しては
regarding … ni kanshite wa …に関しては
regardless kamawazu ni 構わずに; **~ of** … ni mo kakawarazu …にもかかわらず

regime (*government*) seiji-taisei 政治体制
regiment *n* rentai 連隊
region chiiki 地域; ***in the ~ of*** yaku … 約…
regional chihō (no) 地方(の)
register 1 *n* tōrokubo 登録簿 **2** *v/t birth, death* todokederu 届け出る; *vehicle* tōroku suru 登録する; *letter* kakitome ni suru 書留めにする; *emotion* arawasu 表す; ***send a letter ~ed*** kakitome de okuru 書留で送る **3** *v/i* (*at university*) nyūgaku-tetsuzuki o suru 入学手続きをする; (*for a course*) jukōtetsuzuki o suru 受講手続きをする; (*with police*) tōroku suru 登録する
registered letter kakitome-shokan 書留書簡
registration (*vehicle number*) tōroku 登録; (*of birth, death*) todokede 届出; (*at university*) nyūgaku-tetsuzuki 入学手続; (*for course*) jukō-tetsuzuki 受講手続
regret 1 *v/t* kōkai suru 後悔する; *loss* kuyamu 悔やむ; *inconvenience* sumanai to omou すまないと思う **2** *n* kōkai 後悔
regrettable zannen (na) 残念(な)
regrettably zannen nagara 残念ながら
regular 1 *adj* teikiteki (na) 定期的(な); *breathing* kisokuteki (na) 規則的(な); *pattern, shape* taishōteki (na) 対称的(な); (*normal, ordinary*) tsūjō (no) 通常(の) **2** *n* (*at bar etc*) jōren 常連
regulate *costs* kisei suru 規制する; *machine* chōsetsu suru 調節する
regulation (*rule*) kisoku 規則; (*of expenditure*) kisei 規制; (*of machine*) chōsetsu 調節
rehabilitate shakaifukki saseru 社会復帰させる
rehearsal rihāsaru リハーサル
rehearse 1 *v/t* … no rihāsaru o suru …のリハーサルをする **2** *v/i* rihāsaru o suru リハーサルをする
reign 1 *n* chisei 治世; *fig* shihai 支配 **2** *v/i* kunrin suru 君臨する; *fig* shihai suru 支配する
reimburse haraimodosu 払い戻す; (*for damage*) benshō suru 弁償する
rein tazuna 手綱
reincarnation rinne 輪ね
reinforce *structure* hokyō suru 補強する; *army* kyōka suru 強化する; *beliefs* urazukeru 裏付ける
reinforced concrete tekkin-konkurīto 鉄筋コンクリート
reinforcements MIL engun 援軍
reinstate *person in office* fukki saseru 復帰させる; *paragraph etc* moto ni modosu 元に戻す
reject *v/t* kyozetsu suru 拒絶する; *applicant* fusaiyō ni suru 不採用にする; *goods* uketsukenai 受け付けない
rejection kyozetsu 拒絶; (*of applicant*) fusaiyō 不採用
relapse MED saihatsu 再発; ***have a ~*** saihatsu suru 再発する
relate 1 *v/t story* hanasu 話す; ***~ X to Y*** X to Y o musubitsukeru XとYを結び付ける **2** *v/i*: ***~ to …*** (*be connected with*) … ni kankei ga aru …に関係がある; ***he doesn't ~ to people*** kare wa hito to shitashiku shinai 彼は人と親しくしない
related (*by family*) ketsuen-kankei (no) 血縁関係(の); *events, ideas etc* kankei ga aru 関係がある
relation (*in family*) shinseki 親せき; (*connection*) kankei 関係; ***business / diplomatic ~s*** shigoto / gaikō kankei 仕事/外交関係
relationship kankei 関係; (*sexual*) nikutai kankei 肉体関係
relative 1 *n* shinseki 親せき **2** *adj* sōtaiteki (na) 相対的(な); ***X is ~ to Y*** X wa Y ni yoru XはYによる
relatively hikakuteki 比較的
relax 1 *v/i* kutsurogu くつろぐ; ***~!, don't get angry*** ochitsuite okoranaide 落ち着いて怒らないで **2** *v/t muscle* hogusu ほぐす; *pace of work* yurumeru 緩める
relaxation kibarashi 気晴らし
relay 1 *v/t message* tsutaeru 伝える;

radio, TV signals chūkei suru 中継する **2** *n*: **~ (*race*)** rirē リレー
release 1 *n* (*from prison*) shakuhō 釈放; (*of CD etc*) hatsubai 発売 **2** *v/t prisoner* shakuhō suru 釈放する; *parking brake* hanasu 放す; *CD etc* hatsubai suru 発売する; *information* kōhyō suru 公表する; *movie* kōkai suru 公開する
relent taido ga nanka suru 態度が軟化する
relentless (*determined*) shūnen-bukai 執念深い; *rain etc* taema no nai 絶え間のない
relevance kanren 関連
relevant kanren suru 関連する; ***is this ~ to our discussion?*** kore wa watashitachi no giron ni tekisetsu na mono desu ka これは私達の議論に適切なものですか
reliability (*of person, machine*) shinraisei 信頼性; (*of information*) shinpyōsei 信ぴょう性
reliable *person, machine* shinrai dekiru 信頼できる; *information* shin'yō dekiru 信用できる
reliably kakujitsu ni 確実に; ***I am ~ informed that …*** … o tashika na suji kara kiita tokoro ni yoru to … を確かな筋から聞いたところによると
reliance izon 依存; **~ *on*** … o shin'yō suru …を信用する
relic ibutsu 遺物
relief ando 安ど; (*in art*) ukibori 浮き彫り; ***that's a ~*** hotto shita ほっとした
relieve *pressure, pain* yawarageru 和らげる; (*take over from*) … to kōtai suru …と交替する; ***be ~d*** (*at news etc*) anshin suru 安心する
religion shūkyō 宗教
religious shūkyō (no) 宗教(の); *person* shinjinbukai 信心深い
religiously (*conscientiously*) kichin to きちんと
relish 1 *n* (*sauce*) tsukeawase 付け合わせ; (*pleasure*) tanoshimi 楽しみ **2** *v/t prospect* tanoshimu 楽しむ
relive *the past* tsuitaiken suru 追体験する
relocate *v/i* idō suru 移動する
reluctance ki ga susumanai koto 気が進まないこと
reluctant ki ga susumanai 気が進まない; ***be ~ to do X*** X suru koto ni ki ga susumanai Xすることに気が進まない
reluctantly iyaiya-nagara いやいやながら
♦**rely on** (*depend on*) … ni tayoru … に頼る; (*count on*) shin'yō suru 信用する; **~ *X to do Y*** Y suru koto o X ni tayoru YすることをXに頼る
remain (*be left*) nokoru 残る; (*stay*) todomaru とどまる; ***they ~ unconvinced*** karera wa kakushin dekinai mama de iru 彼らは確信できないままでいる
remainder nokori 残り; MATH sa 差
remains (*of body*) itai 遺体
remand 1 *v/t*: **~ *in custody*** … o kōchi suru …を拘置する **2** *n*: ***be on ~*** kōchi-chū de aru 拘置中である
remark 1 *n* hatsugen 発言 **2** *v/t* … to iu …と言う
remarkable subarashii すばらしい
remarkably ijō ni 異常に
remarry *v/i* saikon suru 再婚する
remedy *n* MED, *fig* chiryōhō 治療法
remember 1 *v/t s.o., sth* omoidasu 思い出す; ***I must ~ to do …*** … suru no o oboete okanakereba naranai …するのを覚えておかなければならない; **~ *to lock the door*** doa no kagi o kakeru no o wasurenai de ドアのかぎをかけるのを忘れないで; **~ *me to her*** kanojo ni yoroshiku otsutae kudasai 彼女によろしくお伝え下さい **2** *v/i*: ***I don't ~*** oboete inai 覚えていない
remind: **~ *X to do Y*** X ni Y o wasurenai yō ni chūi suru XにYを忘れないように注意する; ***Tokyo ~s me of …*** Tōkyō wa watashi ni … o omoidasaseru 東京は私に…を思い出させる; ***you ~ me of your sister*** anata o miru to onēsan o omoidasu あなたを見るとお姉さんを思い出す
reminder omoidasaseru mono 思い

出させる物; *letter* oboegaki 覚え書き; COM saisokujō 催促状
reminisce omoidebanashi o suru 思い出話をする
reminiscent: ***be ~ of*** … o omoidasaseru …を思い出させる
remnant nokori 残り
remorse hageshii kōkai 激しい後悔
remorseless *person* reikoku (na) 冷酷(な); *pace, demands* yōsha nai 容赦ない
remote *village* henpi (na) へんぴ(な); *possibility, connection* kasuka (na) かすか(な); (*aloof*) hanareta 離れた; *ancestor* tōi 遠い
remote access COMPUT rimōto-akusesu リモートアクセス
remote control rimōto-kontorōru リモートコントロール
remotely *related, connected* wazuka ni わずかに; ***just ~ possible*** wazuka ni kanōsei ga aru わずかに可能性がある
removal jokyo 除去; MED setsujo 切除
remove torinozoku 取り除く; MED setsujo suru 切除する; *feet* dokeru どける; *demonstrators* oiharau 追い払う; *top, lid* toru 取る; *coat etc* nugu 脱ぐ; *doubt, suspicion* toriharau 取り払う
remuneration hōshū 報酬
remunerative wari no au 割の合う
rename atarashii namae o tsukeru 新しい名前をつける
render *service* suru する; ***~ X helpless / unconscious*** X o muryoku ni / kizetsu saseru Xを無力に/気絶させる
rendering (*of music*) ensō 演奏
rendez-vous (*romantic*) machiawase 待ち合わせ; MIL shūketsu-chiten 集結地点
renew *contract, license* kōshin suru 更新する; *discussions* saikai suru 再開する
renewal (*of contract etc*) kōshin 更新; (*of discussions*) saikai 再開
renounce *title, rights* hōki suru 放棄する
renovate kaizō suru 改造する
renovation kaizō 改造
renown meisei 名声
renowned yūmei (na) 有名(な)
rent 1 *n* yachin 家賃; ***for ~*** kashiie ari 貸し家あり **2** *v/t apartment, car* kariru 借りる; (*~ out*) kasu 貸す
rental (*for apartment*) yachin 家賃; (*for TV etc*) chintai-ryō 賃貸料
rental agreement chintai-keiyakusho 賃貸契約書
rental car renta-kā レンタカー
rent-free *adv* chintairyō nashi de 賃貸料なしで
reopen 1 *v/t* saikai suru 再開する **2** *v/i* (*of theater etc*) saikai suru 再開する
reorganization (*of business, schedule*) saihensei 再編成; (*of room*) moyōgae 模様替え
reorganize *business, schedule* saihensei suru 再編成する; *room* moyōgae suru 模様替えする
rep COM sērusuman セールスマン
repaint nurinaosu 塗り直す
repair 1 *v/t* shūri suru 修理する **2** *n*: ***be in a good / bad state of ~*** teire ga ikitodoite iru / inai 手入れが行き届いている/いない
repairman shūri-ya 修理屋
repatriate sōkan suru 送還する
repay *money* haraimodosu 払い戻す; *person* ongaeshi o suru 恩返しをする
repayment hensai 返済
repeal *v/t law* haishi suru 廃止する
repeat 1 *v/t sth said* kurikaeshite iu 繰り返して言う; *performance, experience* kurikaesu 繰り返す; ***am I ~ing myself?*** mata onaji koto itte imasu ka また同じことを言っていますか **2** *v/i* kurikaeshite iu 繰り返して言う; ***I ~, do not touch it*** kurikaeshimasu, sore ni sawaranaide 繰り返します、それに触らないで **3** *n* TV *etc* saihōsō 再放送
repeat business COM tsuika no torihiki 追加の取り引き
repeated saisan (no) 再三(の)
repeat order COM saichūmon 再注文

repel *v/t invaders, attack* gekitai suru 撃退する; *insects* oiharau 追い払う; (*disgust*) mukatsukaseru むかつかせる
repellent 1 *n* (*insect* ~) mushiyoke 虫よけ **2** *adj* totemo iya (na) とてもいや(な)
repent kōkai suru 後悔する
repercussions eikyō 影響
repetition (*of word, event etc*) kurikaeshi 繰り返し; (*repeating things*) chōfuku 重複
repetitive *style* kudoi くどい; *work* kurikaeshi (no) 繰り返し(の)
replace (*put back*) moto ni modosu 元に戻す; (*take the place of*) … ni kawaru …に代わる
replacement (*person: permanent*) kōkei-sha 後継者; (*person: temporary*) kōtai-yōin 交代要員; (*thing*) daiyōhin 代用品
replacement part torikae-buhin 取替部品
replay 1 *n* (*recording*) saisei 再生; (*game*) saishiai 再試合 **2** *v/t game* … no saishiai o suru …の再試合をする
replica fukusei 複製, repurika レプリカ
reply 1 *n* henji 返事 **2** *v/t* … to henji suru …と返事する **3** *v/i* henji suru 返事する
report 1 *n* (*account*) hōkoku-sho 報告書; (*by journalist*) hōdō 報道 **2** *v/t facts* hōdō suru 報道する; (*to authorities*) hōkoku suru 報告する; ***~ one's findings to X*** X ni ketsuron o hōkoku suru Xに結論を報告する; ***~ X to the police*** keisatsu ni X no koto o tsūhō suru 警察にXのことを通報する; ***he is ~ed to be in Hong Kong*** kare wa Honkon ni iru to hōkoku sarete iru 彼は香港にいると報告されている **3** *v/i* (*of journalist*) hōkoku suru 報告する; (*present oneself*) shuttō suru 出頭する
♦**report to** (*be accountable to*) …ga jōshi de aru …が上司である
report card EDU tsūchi-hyō 通知票
reporter kisha 記者
repossess COM kaishū suru 回収する
reprehensible hinansubeki 非難すべき
represent (*act for*) … no dairi o suru …の代理をする; (*stand for*) … no tenkei de aru …の典型である; *one's country etc* daihyō suru 代表する; (*of images in painting etc*) hyōgen suru 表現する
representative 1 *n* dairi 代理; (*of nation*) daihyō 代表; COM sērusuman セールスマン; POL kain-giin 下院議員 **2** *adj* (*typical*) tenkeiteki (na) 典型的(な)
repress *revolt* yokuatsu suru 抑圧する; *feelings, urges* osaeru 抑える; *laugh* koraeru こらえる
repression POL dan'atsu 弾圧
repressive POL dan'atsuteki (na) 弾圧的(な)
reprieve 1 *n* LAW shikeishikkō-yūyo 死刑執行猶予; *fig* enki 延期 **2** *v/t prisoner* shikei-shikkō o yūyo suru 死刑執行を猶予する
reprimand *v/t* shisseki suru 叱責する
reprint 1 *n* zōsatsu 増刷 **2** *v/t* zōsatsu suru 増刷する
reprisal hōfuku 報復; ***take ~s*** hōfuku suru 報復する
reproach 1 *n* hinan 非難; ***be beyond ~*** mōshibun no nai 申し分のない **2** *v/t* hinan suru 非難する
reproachful togameru yō (na) とがめるよう(な)
reproduce 1 *v/t atmosphere, mood* saigen suru 再現する; *painting, document* fukusei suru 複製する **2** *v/i* BIO hanshoku suru 繁殖する
reproduction BIO hanshoku 繁殖; (*of sound, images*) saisei 再生; (*piece of furniture*) fukusei 複製
reproductive BIO hanshoku (no) 繁殖(の)
reptile hachūrui は虫類
republic kyōwakoku 共和国
Republican 1 *n* Kyōwatōin 共和党員 **2** *adj* Kyōwatō (no) 共和党(の)
Republic of Korea Daikan-minkoku 大韓民国

repudiate (*deny*) hitei suru 否定する
repulsive ken'o subeki 嫌悪すべき
reputable hyōban no yoi 評判の良い
reputation hyōban 評判; ***have a good / bad ~*** hyōban no yoi / warui 評判の良い/悪い
request 1 *n* yōsei 要請; (*on radio program*) rikuesuto リクエスト; ***on ~*** irai shidai de 依頼次第で **2** *v/t* onegai suru お願いする
require (*need*) …ga hitsuyō de aru が必要である; ***it ~s great care*** sore wa taihen na chūi ga hitsuyō desu それは大変な注意が必要です; ***as ~d by law*** hōritsu ni yotte yōkyū sarete iru 法律によって要求されている
required hitsuyō (na) 必要(な)
requirement (*need*) yōkyū 要求; (*condition*) jōken 条件
reroute *airplane etc* ukai saseru う回させる
rerun *tape* saisei suru 再生する
rescue 1 *n* kyūjo 救助; ***come to X's ~*** X o tasuke ni kuru Xを助けに来る **2** *v/t* kyūjo suru 救助する
rescue party kyūjo-tai 救助隊
research *n* kenkyū 研究
♦**research into** … ni tsuite kenkyū suru …について研究する
research and development kenkyū-kaihatsu 研究開発
research assistant kenkyū-joshu 研究助手
researcher kenkyū-sha 研究者
research project kenkyū-purojekuto 研究プロジェクト
resemblance ruijiten 類似点
resemble … ni nite iru …に似ている
resent … ni hara o tateru …に腹を立てる
resentful okotte iru 怒っている
resentment urami 恨み
reservation (*of room, table*) yoyaku 予約; (*mental*) utagai 疑い; (*special area*) tokubetsu-horyūchi 特別保留地; ***I have a ~*** yoyaku shite arimasu 予約してあります
reserve 1 *n* (*store*) bichiku 備蓄; (*aloofness*) enryo 遠慮; SP hoketsu 補欠; ***~s*** FIN junbikin 準備金; ***keep X in ~*** X o totte oku Xを取っておく **2** *v/t seat, table* yoyaku suru 予約する; *judgment* horyū suru 保留する
reserved *person, manner* hikaeme (na) 控えめ(な); *table, seat* yoyaku (no) 予約(の)
reservoir chosuichi 貯水池
reside kyojū suru 居住する
residence (*house etc*) jūtaku 住宅; (*stay*) zaijū 在住
residence permit zairyū-kyoka 在留許可
resident 1 *n* kyojū-sha 居住者; (*in hotel*) shukuhaku-kyaku 宿泊客 **2** *adj manager etc* rejidento (no) レジデント(の)
residential district jūtakuchi 住宅地
residue zanryūbutsu 残留物
resign 1 *v/t position* jinin suru 辞任する; ***~ oneself to*** akiramete … o mitomeru あきらめて…を認める **2** *v/i* (*from job*) jinin suru 辞任する
resignation (*from job*) jinin 辞任; (*mental*) akirame あきらめ
resigned akirameta あきらめた; ***we have become ~ to the fact that …*** watashitachi wa … to iu jijitsu o akiramete mitometa 私達は…という事実をあきらめて認めた
resilient *personality* tachinaori no hayai 立ち直りの早い; *material* nagamochi suru 長持ちする
resin jushi 樹脂
resist 1 *v/t enemy, advances, new measures* teikō suru 抵抗する; *temptation* gaman suru 我慢する **2** *v/i* teikō suru 抵抗する
resistance teikō 抵抗; (*to disease, heat etc*) teikō-ryoku 抵抗力
resistant: ***~ to heat*** tainetsu (no) 耐熱(の); ***~ to rust*** taishoku (no) 耐食(の)
resolute danko to shita 断固とした
resolution (*decision*) ketsugi 決議; (*New Year ~*) kesshin 決心; (*determination*) kyōko na ishi 強固な意志; (*of problem*) kaiketsu 解決;

(*of image*) kaizō-ryoku 解像力
resolve *problem, mystery* kaiketsu suru 解決する; **~ *to do X*** Xshiyō to kesshin suru Xしようと決心する
resort 1 *n* (*place*) kōrakuchi 行楽地, rizōto リゾート; ***as a last ~*** saigo no shudan to shite 最後の手段として
resounding *success, victory* kanzen (na) 完全(な)
resource shigen 資源
resourceful rinki-ōhen (no) 臨機応変(の)
respect 1 *n* sonkei 尊敬; (*consideration*) sonchō 尊重; ***show ~ to*** … ni keii o harau …に敬意を払う; ***with ~ to*** … ni kanshite wa … に関しては; ***in this / that ~*** kore ni kanshite wa これに関しては; ***in many ~s*** iroiro na ten de 色々な点で; ***pay one's last ~s to*** … no meifuku o inoru …のめい福を祈る **2** *v/t person* sonkei suru 尊敬する; *opinion, privacy* sonchō suru 尊重する; *law* mamoru 守る
respectable rippa (na) 立派(な)
Respect-for-the-Aged Day Keirō no hi 敬老の日
respectful reigi-tadashii 礼儀正しい
respectfully teinei ni 丁寧に
respective sorezore (no) それぞれ(の)
respectively sorezore それぞれ
respiration kokyū 呼吸
respirator MED jinkōkokyū-sōchi 人工呼吸装置
respite kyūsoku 休息; ***without ~*** yasuminaku 休みなく
respond (*answer*) kotaeru 答える; (*react*) ōjiru 応じる; (*to treatment*) kōka o arawasu 効果を表す
response (*answer*) kotae 答え; (*reaction*) hannō 反応
responsibility sekinin 責任; (*duty*) gimu 義務; (*in job*) shokumu 職務; ***a job with ~*** sekinin no aru shigoto 責任のある仕事; ***accept ~ for*** sekinin o toru 責任を取る
responsible (*liable, for children, production etc*) sekinin ga aru 責任がある; (*trustworthy*) shinrai dekiru 信頼できる; (*involving responsibility: job*) sekinin no omoi 責任の重い
responsive *audience, brakes* yoku hannō suru よく反応する
rest[1] **1** *n* yasumi 休み **2** *v/i* yasumu 休む; **~ *on*** (*be based on*) … ni motozuku …に基づく; (*lean against*) … ni tatekakeru …にたてかける; ***it all ~s with him*** kare no handan ni kakatte iru 彼の判断にかかっている **3** *v/t* (*lean, balance etc*) yorikakeru 寄り掛ける
rest[2]: ***the ~*** nokori 残り
restaurant resutoran レストラン
restaurant car shokudōsha 食堂車
rest cure ansei 安静
rest home yōrōin 養老院
restless ochitsukanai 落ち着かない; ***have a ~ night*** nemurenai 眠れない
restoration (*of building*) shūfuku 修復; (*of health*) kaifuku 回復
restore *building etc* shūfuku suru 修復する; *health* kaifuku suru 回復する
restrain *dog, troops* seishi suru 制止する; *emotions* osaeru 抑える; **~ *oneself*** jibun o osaerarenai 自分を抑えられない
restraint (*moderation*) setsudo 節度
restrict seigen suru 制限する; ***I'll ~ myself to …*** … ni seigen suru …に制限する
restricted *view* kagirareta 限られた
restricted area MIL tachiiri-kinshi no basho 立ち入り禁止の場所
restriction seigen 制限
rest room otearai お手洗
result *n* kekka 結果; (*of exam*) seiseki 成績; ***as a ~ of this*** kono kekka この結果
♦**result from** … no kekka …の結果
♦**result in** … ni owaru …に終わる
resume *v/t* … ni modoru …に戻る
résumé rirekisho 履歴書
resurface 1 *v/t roads* hosō shinaosu 舗装し直す **2** *v/i* (*of problems*)

saifujō suru 再浮上する; (*of person*) saitōjō suru 再登場する
resurrection REL Kirisuto no fukkatsu キリストの復活
resuscitate ikikaeraseru 生き返らせる
retail 1 *adv* kourine de 小売値で **2** *v/i*: kouri sareru 小売りされる; **~ at …** … de kouri suru …で小売りする
retailer kouri-gyōsha 小売業者
retail price kouri-kakaku 小売価格
retain tamotsu 保つ
retainer FIN komon-ryō 顧問料
retaliate hōfuku suru 報復する
retaliation hōfuku 報復
retarded chie-okure (no) 知恵後れ(の)
retire *v/i* (*from work*) taishoku suru 退職する
retired taishoku shita 退職した
retirement taishoku 退職
retirement age teinen 定年
retiring hikkomijian (no) 引込み思案(の)
retort 1 *n* shippegaeshi しっぺ返し **2** *v/i* iikaesu 言い返す
retrace *footsteps* hikikaesu 引き返す
retract *v/t claws, undercarriage* hikkomeru 引っ込める; *statement* tekkai suru 撤回する
retreat 1 *v/i* MIL taikyaku suru 退却する; (*in discussion etc*) hikisagaru 引き下がる **2** *n* MIL taikyaku 退却; (*place*) kakurega 隠れ家
retrieve *sth lost* torimodosu 取り戻す; *larger object* kaishū suru 回収する; COMPUT kensaku suru 検索する
retriever (*dog*) retorībā レトリーバー
retroactive *law etc* sakanoboru さかのぼる
retrograde *move, decision* atomodori (no) 後戻り(の)
retrospect: ***in ~*** furikaette miru to 振り返ってみると
retrospective *n* kaiko 回顧
return 1 *n* (*coming back, going back*) kikan 帰還; (*giving back*) henkyaku 返却; COMPUT, (*in tennis*) ritān リターン; ***by ~ (of post)*** orikaeshi de 折り返しで; ***~s*** (*profit*) rieki 利益; ***many happy ~s (of the day)*** otanjōbi omedetō gozaimasu お誕生日おめでとうございます **2** *v/t* (*give back*) henkyaku suru 返却する; (*put back*) modosu 戻す; *favor, invitation* kaesu 返す **3** *v/i* (*go back, come back*) kaeru 帰る; (*of good times, doubt etc*) modoru 戻る
return flight kaeri no bin 帰りの便
return journey kaeri 帰り
reunification saitōitsu 再統一
reunion atsumari 集まり; EDU dōsōkai 同窓会
reunite *v/t old friends* saikai saseru 再会させる; *country* saitōgō suru 再統合する
reusable sairiyō dekiru 再利用できる
reuse sairiyō suru 再利用する
rev *n* kaiten 回転; ***~s per minute*** maifun-kaitensū 毎分回転数
♦ **rev up** *v/t engine* … o fukasu …をふかす
revaluation kiriage 切り上げ
reveal (*make visible*) miseru 見せる; (*make known*) akiraka ni suru 明らかにする; *feelings* shimesu 示す
revealing *remark* akiraka ni suru 明らかにする; *dress* hada o arawa ni suru 肌をあらわにする
revelation igai na hakken 意外な発見; (*scandalous*) bakuro 暴露
revenge *n* fukushū 復しゅう; ***take one's ~ on*** … ni fukushū suru …に復しゅうする
revenue shūnyū 収入; (*of government*) sainyū 歳入
reverberate (*of sound*) hibiku 響く
Reverend: ***the ~ John Smith*** Jon Sumisu shi ジョンスミス師
reverent uyauyashii うやうやしい
reverse 1 *adj sequence* gyaku (no) 逆(の) **2** *n* (*opposite*) gyaku 逆; (*back*) ura 裏; MOT bakku バック **3** *v/t sequence* gyaku ni suru 逆にする; *vehicle* bakku saseru バックさ

せる; *decision* hikkurikaesu ひっくり返す **4** *v/i* MOT bakku suru バックする
review 1 *n* (*of book, movie*) hihyō 批評; (*of troops*) eppei 閲兵; (*of situation etc*) saikentō 再検討 **2** *v/t book, movie* hihyō suru 批評する; *troops* eppei suru 閲兵する; *situation etc* saikentō suru 再検討する; EDU fukushū suru 復習する
reviewer (*of book, movie*) hyōron-ka 評論家
revise *v/t text, figures* shūsei suru 修正する; *opinion* kaeru 変える
revision (*of text, figures*) shūsei 修正; (*of opinion*) henkō 変更
revival (*of custom etc*) fukkatsu 復活; (*of patient*) kaifuku 回復; THEA ribaibaru リバイバル
revive 1 *v/t custom, old style etc* fukkatsu saseru 復活させる; *patient* ishiki o kaifuku saseru 意識を回復させる; *economy* kaifuku saseru 回復させる; THEA saijōen suru 再上演する **2** *v/i* (*of business, exchange rate etc*) kaifuku suru 回復する; (*of patient*) ishiki o torimodosu 意識をとりもどす
revoke *law, license* mukō ni suru 無効にする
revolt 1 *n* hangyaku 反逆 **2** *v/i* hangyaku suru 反逆する
revolting (*disgusting*) mukatsukaseru むかつかせる
revolution POL *etc* kakumei 革命; (*turn*) kaiten 回転
revolutionary 1 *n* POL kakumei-ka 革命家 **2** *adj spirit, forces* kakumei (no) 革命(の); *ideas* kakumeiteki (na) 革命的(な)
revolutionize kakumei o okosu 革命を起こす
revolve *v/i* kaiten suru 回転する
revolver riborubā リボルバー
revolving door kaiten-doa 回転ドア
revue THEA rebyū レビュー
revulsion ken'o 嫌悪
reward 1 *n* (*financial*) shōkin 賞金; (*benefit derived*) hōbi ほうび **2** *v/t* (*financially*) shōkin o ataeru 賞金を与える
rewarding tame ni naru ためになる
rewind *v/t film, tape* makimodosu 巻き戻す
rewrite *v/t* kakinaosu 書き直す
rhetoric retorikku レトリック
rheumatism ryūmachi リューマチ
rhinoceros sai さい
rhubarb rubābu ルバーブ
rhyme 1 *n* in 韻 **2** *v/i* in o fumu 韻を踏む; ***~ with ...*** ... to in o fumu ...と韻を踏む
rhythm rizumu リズム
rib *n* rokkotsu ろっ骨
ribbon ribon リボン
rice kome 米; (*cooked*) gohan ご飯
rice ball onigiri おにぎり; **rice bowl** gohan-jawan ご飯茶碗; **rice cooker** suihanki 炊飯器; **rice cracker** senbei せんべい; **ricefield** suiden 水田; **rice wine** sake 酒
rich 1 *adj* kanemochi (no) 金持ち(の); *country* yutaka (na) 豊か(な); *soil* hiyoku (na) 肥よく(な); *food* kotteri shita こってりした **2** *n*: ***the ~*** kanemochi 金持
rid: ***get ~ of*** ... o torinozoku ...を取り除く; *feeling, state of affairs* ... kara nukedasu ...から抜け出す
ride 1 *n* (*on horse*) jōba 乗馬; (*in vehicle*) doraibu ドライブ; (*journey*) ryokō 旅行; ***do you want a ~ into town?*** machi made notte ikimasen ka 町まで乗って行きませんか **2** *v/t horse, bike* ... ni noru ...に乗る **3** *v/i* (*on horse*) jōba o suru 乗馬をする; (*on bike*) jitensha ni noru 自転車に乗る; (*in vehicle*) kuruma ni noru 車に乗る
rider (*on horse*) kishu 騎手; (*on bike*) norite 乗り手
ridge (*on earth*) une 畝; (*of mountain*) one 尾根; (*of roof*) teppen 天辺
ridicule 1 *n* azakeri あざけり **2** *v/t* azakeru あざける
ridiculous bakageta ばかげた
ridiculously bakabakashii hodo ばかばかしいほど
riding (*on horseback*) jōba 乗馬
rifle *n* raifuru ライフル
rift (*in earth*) kiretsu 亀裂; (*in party*

etc) tairitsu 対立

rig 1 *n* (*oil ~*) yusei-kussakusōchi 油井掘削装置; (*truck*) torakku トラック **2** *v/t elections* fuseisōsa suru 不正操作する

right 1 *adj* (*correct*) tadashii 正しい; (*morally*) seitō (na) 正当(な); (*fair, just*) tekisetsu (na) 適切(な); (*proper, appropriate*) tekitō (na) 適当(な); (*not left*) migi (no) 右(の); ***be ~*** (*be correct*) tadashii 正しい; (*of clock*) seikaku de aru 正確である; ***that's ~!*** sono tōri そのとおり; ***put things ~*** naosu 直す → ***alright*** **2** *adv* (*directly*) sugu すぐ; (*correctly*) tadashiku 正しく; (*completely*) sukkari すっかり; (*not left*) migi ni 右に; ***~ now*** (*immediately*) ima sugu ni 今すぐに; (*at the moment*) ima 今; ***~ on time*** chōdo no jikan ちょうどの時間 **3** *n* (*civil, legal etc*) kenri 権利; (*not left*) migi 右; POL uha 右派; ***on the ~*** migi ni 右に; POL uha (no) 右派(の); ***turn to the ~, take a ~*** migi ni magaru 右に曲がる; ***be in the ~*** tadashii 正しい; ***know ~ from wrong*** shinjitsu o shiru 真実を知る

right-angle chokkaku 直角; ***at ~s to …*** … to chokkaku ni …と直角に

rightful *heir, owner etc* seitō (na) 正当(な)

right-hand *adj* migi (no) 右(の); ***on the ~ side*** migigawa (no) 右側(の); **right-hand drive** MOT migi-handoru (no) 右ハンドル(の); **right-handed** migikiki (no) 右利き(の); **right-hand man** migiude 右腕; **right of way** (*in traffic*) yūsen-ken 優先権; (*across land*) tsūkō-ken 通行権; **right wing 1** *n* POL uyoku 右翼; (*within party*) uha 右派; SP raito-uingu ライトウイング **2** *adj* POL uyoku (no) 右翼(の); (*within party*) uha (no) 右派(の); **right-wing extremism** POL kyokuu 極右; **right-winger** POL uyoku 右翼

rigid *material* katai 固い; *principles* kibishii 厳しい; *attitude* yūzū no kikanai 融通の利かない

rigor (*of discipline*) genkaku-sa 厳格さ; ***the ~s of the winter*** fuyu no kibishi-sa 冬の厳しさ

rigorous *discipline* kibishii 厳しい; *tests, analysis* genmitsu (na) 厳密(な)

rim (*of wheel*) rimu リム; (*of cup*) fuchi 縁; (*of eyeglasses*) furēmu フレーム

ring[1] (*circle*) wa 輪; (*on finger*) yubiwa 指輪; (*in boxing, at circus*) ringu リング

ring[2] 1 *n* (*of bell*) beru no naru oto ベルの鳴る音; (*of voice*) hibiki 響き **2** *v/t bell* narasu 鳴らす **3** *v/i* (*of bell*) naru 鳴る; ***please ~ for attention*** goyō no sai wa beru o narashite kudasai ご用の際はベルを鳴らして下さい

ringleader shubō-sha 首謀者

ring-pull puru-tabu プルタブ

rink rinku リンク

rinse 1 *n* (*for hair color*) hea-dai ヘアダイ **2** *v/t clothes, dishes* susugu すすぐ; *hair* rinsu suru リンスする

riot 1 *n* bōdō 暴動 **2** *v/i* bōdō o okosu 暴動を起こす

rioter bōto 暴徒

riot police kidōtai 機動隊

rip 1 *n* (*in cloth etc*) sakeme 裂け目 **2** *v/t cloth etc* saku 裂く; ***~ open …*** o yabutte akeru …を破って空ける

♦ **rip off** F (*cheat*) damasu だます; *customers* fukkakekeru 吹っかける

ripe *fruit* ureta 熟れた

ripen *v/i* (*of fruit*) juku suru 熟する

ripeness (*of fruit*) seijuku 成熟

rip-off *n* F sagi 詐欺

ripple (*on water*) sazanami さざ波

rise 1 *v/i* (*from chair etc*) tachiagaru 立ち上がる; (*of sun*) noboru 昇る; (*of rocket*) ririku suru 離陸する; (*of price, temperature, water level*) agaru 上がる **2** *n* (*in price, temperature, water level*) jōshō 上昇; (*in salary*) shōkyū 昇給

rising sun: ***the land of the ~*** hi izuru tokoro no kuni 日出ずる処の国

risk 1 *n* kiken 危険; ***take a ~*** kiken o okasu 危険を冒す **2** *v/t* kiken ni sarasu 危険にさらす; *reputation* kiken o okasu 危険を冒す; ***let's ~ it*** yatte miyō やってみよう
risky kiken (na) 危険(な)
ritual 1 *n* gishiki 儀式 **2** *adj* gishikiteki (na) 儀式的(な)
rival 1 *n* raibaru ライバル **2** *v/t* … ni hitteki suru …に匹敵する; ***I can't ~ that*** kore ni wa katenai これには勝てない
rivalry kyōsō 競争
river kawa 川
riverbed kawadoko 川床
riverside kawagishi 川岸
rivet 1 *n* ribetto リベット **2** *v/t* ribetto de tomeru リベットで留める; ***~ X to Y*** Y ni X o ribetto de tomeru YにXをリベットで留める
road dōro 道路; ***it's just down the ~*** sugu soko desu すぐそこです
roadblock kenmon-sho 検問所; **road hog** ranbō na doraibā 乱暴なドライバー; **road holding** (*of vehicle*) sōkōanteisei 走行安定性; **road map** dōro-chizu 道路地図; **roadside**: ***at the ~*** dōrowaki ni 道路脇に; **roadsign** dōro-hyōshiki 道路標識; **roadway** shadō 車道; **road works** dōro-kōji 道路工事; **roadworthy** seibi sareta 整備された
roam samayou さまよう
roar 1 *n* (*of traffic, engine*) gōon ごう音; (*of lion*) hoegoe ほえ声; (*of person*: *in anger*) wamekigoe わめき声 **2** *v/i* (*of engine*) gōon o tateru ごう音を立てる; (*of lion*) hoeru ほえる; (*of person*: *in anger*) wameku わめく; ***~ with laughter*** ōwarai suru 大笑いする
roast 1 *n* (*beef etc*) rōsuto ロースト **2** *v/t* yaku 焼く; *nuts, coffee* iru いる **3** *v/i* (*of food*) yakeru 焼ける; ***we're ~ing*** F sugoku atsui すごく暑い
roast beef rōsuto-bīfu ローストビーフ
roast pork rōsuto-pōku ローストポーク
rob *person, bank* …kara ubau …から奪う; ***I've been ~bed*** watashi wa gōtō ni osowareta 私は強盗に襲われた
robber gōtō 強盗
robbery gōtō 強盗
robe (*of judge, priest*) shikifuku 式服; (*bath~*) basu-rōbu バスローブ
robin komadori こまどり
robot robotto ロボット
robust *person* takumashii たくましい; *economy* kenzen (na) 健全(な); *structure* ganjō (na) 頑丈(な)
rock 1 *n* ganseki 岩石; (*small*) ishi 石; MUS rokku ロック; ***on the ~s*** *drink* on za rokku オンザロック; *of marriage* hatan sunzen de 破たん寸前で **2** *v/t cradle* yuri ugokasu 揺り動かす; *baby* ayasu あやす; (*surprise*) dōyō saseru 動揺させる **3** *v/i* (*on chair*) yure ugoku 揺れ動く; (*of boat*) yureru 揺れる
rock bottom: ***reach ~*** donzoko ni ochiru どん底に落ちる
rock-bottom *prices* sokone (no) 底値(の)
rocket 1 *n* roketto ロケット **2** *v/i* (*of prices etc*) kyūjōshō suru 急上昇する
rocking chair yuriisu 揺りいす
rock 'n' roll rokkun-rōru ロックンロール
rock star rokku-stā ロックスター
rocky *beach, path* iwadarake (no) 岩だらけ(の)
rod bō 棒; (*for fishing*) tsuri-zao 釣ざお
rodent gesshirui げっ歯類
rogue akutō 悪党
role yakuwari 役割
role model risō no sugata 理想の姿
roll 1 *n* (*bread*) rōru-pan ロールパン; (*of film*) maki 巻き; (*of thunder*) todoroki とどろき; (*list, register*) meibo 名簿 **2** *v/i* (*of ball etc*) korogaru 転がる; (*of boat*) yureru 揺れる **3** *v/t*: ***~ X into a ball*** X o maite tama ni suru Xを巻いて玉にする
♦**roll over 1** *v/i* negaeri o utsu 寝返りを打つ **2** *v/t person, object* … o korogasu …を転がす; (*renew*)

kōshin suru 更新する
♦**roll up 1** *v/t sleeves* … o makuru … をまくる **2** *v/i* F (*arrive*) arawareru 現れる
roll call tenko 点呼
roller (*for hair*) kārā カーラー
roller blade *n* rōrā-burēdo ローラーブレード;**roller coaster** jetto-kōsutā ジェットコースター;**roller skate** *n* rōrā-sukēto ローラースケート
rolling pin menbō めん棒
ROM (= ***read only memory***) romu ロム
Roman Catholic 1 *n* Katorikku-shinja カトリック信者 **2** *adj* Katorikku (no) カトリック(の)
Roman script Rōmaji ローマ字
romance (*affair*) ren'ai 恋愛; (*novel*) ren'ai-shōsetsu 恋愛小説; (*movie*) ren'ai-eiga 恋愛映画
romantic romanchikku (na) ロマンチック(な)
roof yane 屋根
roof rack MOT rūfu-rēru ルーフレール
room heya 部屋; (*space*) basho 場所; (*scope*) yochi 余地; ***there's no ~ for …*** … no basho ga nai …の場所がない; ***Japanese-style ~*** washitsu 和室
room clerk furonto フロント; **roommate** rūmu-mēto ルームメート;**room service** rūmu-sābisu ルームサービス
roomy *house etc* hirobiro to shita 広々とした; *clothes* yuttari shita ゆったりした
root ne 根; (*of word*) gokan 語幹; (*of problem*) kongen 根源; **~s** (*of person*) rūtsu ルーツ
♦**root out** (*get rid of*) … o nekosogi ni suru …を根こそぎにする; (*find*) … o sagashidasu …を捜し出す
rope rōpu ロープ
♦**rope off** … o rōpu de shikiru …をロープで仕切る
rose BOT bara ばら
rostrum endan 演壇
rosy *cheeks* akai 赤い; *future* akarui 明るい; *color* barairo (no) ばら色(の)
rot 1 *n* (*in wood*) fuhai 腐敗; (*in teeth*) mushiba 虫歯 **2** *v/i* (*of food, wood*) kusaru 腐る; (*of teeth*) mushiba ni naru 虫歯になる
rotate *v/i* kaiten suru 回転する
rotation kaiten 回転; ***do X in ~*** X o kōtai de suru Xを交替でする
rotten *food, wood etc* kusatta 腐った; *trick, thing to do* hiretsu (na) 卑劣(な); *weather, luck* hidoi ひどい
rough 1 *adj surface* zarazara shita ざらざらした; *hands, skin, crossing, seas* areta 荒れた; *voice* shagareta しゃがれた; (*violent*) ranbō (na) 乱暴(な); (*approximate*) daitai だいたい; *town, area* chian no warui 治安の悪い; ***~ draft*** shitagaki 下書き **2** *adv*: ***sleep ~*** nojuku suru 野宿する **3** *n* (*in golf*) rafu ラフ **4** *v/t*: ***~ it*** genshiteki na seikatsu o suru 原始的な生活をする
roughage (*in food*) sen'i 繊維
roughly (*approximately*) daitai だいたい
roulette rūretto ルーレット
round 1 *adj* marui 丸い; ***in ~ figures*** daitai だいたい **2** *n* (*of mailman etc*) junkai 巡回; (*of toast*) hitokire 一切れ; (*of drinks*) kai 回; (*of competition*) kaisen 回戦; (*in boxing match*) raundo ラウンド **3** *v/t the corner* magaru 曲がる **4** *adv & prep* → ***around***
♦**round off** *edges* … o maruku suru …を丸くする; *meeting, evening* … o oeru …を終える
♦**round up** *figure* … o kiriageru …を切り上げる; *suspects, criminals* … o kenkyo suru …を検挙する
roundabout *adj way of saying sth* tōmawashi (no) 遠回し(の); *route* tōmawari (no) 遠回り(の);**round trip** ōfuku 往復;**round trip ticket** ōfuku-kippu 往復切符
round-up (*of cattle*) kakiatsumeru koto かき集めること; (*of suspects, criminals*) kenkyo 検挙; (*of news*) matome まとめ

rouse (*from sleep*) okosu 起こす; *interest, emotions* hikiokosu 引き起こす

rousing *speech etc* nekkyōteki (na) 熱狂的(な)

route rūto ルート; (*walking*) tōrimichi 通り道

routine 1 *adj* (*customary*) nichijō (no) 日常(の); (*predictable*) okimari (no) お決まり(の) **2** *n* (*habitual behavior*) shūkan 習慣; (*set sequence of events*) itsumo no tejun いつもの手順; ***as a matter of ~*** okimari no shigoto お決まりの仕事

row[1] (*line*) retsu 列; ***5 days in a ~*** itsuka renzoku de 五日連続で

row[2] **1** *v/t boat* kogu こぐ **2** *v/i* bōto o kogu ボートをこぐ

rowboat bōto ボート

rowdy ranbō (na) 乱暴(な); *party* sozō shii 騒々しい

row house terasu-hausu テラスハウス

royalty ōzoku 王族; (*on book etc*) inzei 印税

rub *v/t* kosuru こする

♦**rub down** (*to clean*) kosutte migaku こすって磨く

♦**rub off 1** *v/t dirt* … o kosuritoru …をこすり取る; *paint etc* hagasu はがす **2** *v/i*: ***it rubs off on you*** anata ni utsuru あなたにうつる

rubber 1 *n* (*material*) gomu ゴム **2** *adj* gomu (no) ゴム(の)

rubble gareki がれき

ruby (*jewel*) rubī ルビー

rucksack ryukku sakku リュックサック

rudder kaji かじ

ruddy *complexion* kesshoku no yoi 血色の良い

rude *person* burei (na) 無礼(な); *behavior, language* gehin (na) 下品(な); ***it is ~ to …*** … suru no wa burei de aru …するのは無礼である; ***I didn't mean to be ~*** burei na mane o suru tsumori de wa nakatta 無礼なまねをするつもりではなかった

rudeness burei 無礼

rudimentary *skills* shohoteki (na) 初歩的(な); *knowledge* kisoteki (na) 基礎的(な)

rudiments kiso 基礎

ruffian gorotsuki ごろつき

ruffle 1 *n* (*on dress*) hidakazari ひだ飾り **2** *v/t hair, clothes* midasu 乱す; *person* dōyō saseru 動揺させる; ***get ~d*** dōyō suru 動揺する

rug shikimono 敷き物; (*blanket*) hizakake ひざ掛け

rugged *scenery, cliffs* kewashii 険しい; *face* hori no fukai 彫りの深い; *resistance* ganken (na) 頑健(な)

ruin 1 *n* hakai 破壊; **~s** iseki 遺跡; ***in ~s*** *city, building*) kōhai shite 荒廃して; *plans, marriage* dame ni natte だめになって **2** *v/t party, birthday, vacation* dame ni suru だめにする; *plans* kowasu 壊す; *reputation* kegasu 汚す; ***be ~ed*** (*financially*) hasan suru 破産する

rule 1 *n* (*of club, game*) kisoku 規則, rūru ルール; (*of monarch*) tōchi 統治; (*for measuring*) monosashi 物差し; ***as a ~*** gaishite 概して **2** *v/t country* shihai suru 支配する; ***the judge ~d that …*** saibankan ga … to saitei suru 裁判官が…と裁定する **3** *v/i* (*of monarch*) tōchi suru 統治する

♦**rule out** … o jogai suru …を除外する

ruler (*for measuring*) monosashi 物差し; (*of state*) shihai-sha 支配者

ruling 1 *n* kettei 決定 **2** *adj*: ***~ party*** yotō 与党

rum (*drink*) ramu-shu ラム酒

rumble *v/i* (*of stomach*) gorogoro naru ゴロゴロ鳴る; (*of train in tunnel*) gōon o hibikasete hashiru ごう音を響かせて走る

♦**rummage around** hikkurikaeshite sagasu ひっくり返して探す

rummage sale garakuta-ichi がらくた市

rumor 1 *n* uwasa うわさ **2** *v/t*: ***it is ~ed that …*** … to iu uwasa da …と言ううわさだ

rump (*of animal*) shiri しり

rumple *clothes, paper* kushakusha ni suru くしゃくしゃにする
rumpsteak ranpusutēki ランプステーキ
run 1 *n* (*on foot*) kakeashi 駆け足; (*in pantyhose*) densen 伝線; (THEA: *of play*) renzoku-kōen 連続公演; ***go for a ~*** jogingu suru ジョギングする; ***make a ~ for it*** (*run away*) nigeru 逃げる; ***a criminal on the ~*** tōsōchū no hannin 逃走中の犯人; ***in the short ~*** mesaki no koto to shite kangaeru to 目先の事として考えると; ***in the long ~*** nagai me de miru to 長い目で見ると; ***a ~ on the dollar*** doru no kaininki shūchū ドルの買い人気集中 **2** *v/i* (*of person, animal*) hashiru 走る; (*of river, paint, make-up*) nagareru 流れる; (*of trains etc*) unkō suru 運行する; (*of nose*) hanamizu ga tareru 鼻水が垂れる; (*of faucet*) deru 出る; (*of play*) renzoku-kōen suru 連続公演する; (*of engine, machine*) sadō suru 作動する; (*of software*) tsukaeru 使える; (*in election*) shutsuba suru 出馬する; ***~ for President*** daitōryō-sen ni shutsuba suru 大統領選に出馬する **3** *v/t race* kyōgikai ni deru 競技会に出る; *3 miles etc* hashiru 走る; *business, hotel, project etc* keiei suru 経営する; *software* sadō suru 作動する; *car* tsukau 使う; ***would you like me to ~ you to the station?*** eki made okurimashō ka 駅まで送りましょうか; ***he ran his eye down the page*** kare wa pēji ni me o hashiraseta 彼はページに目を走らせた
♦**run across** (*meet*) … ni dekuwasu …に出くわす; (*find*) … o gūzen mitsukeru …を偶然見つける
♦**run away** nigeru 逃げる
♦**run down 1** *v/t* (*by car*) … o hiku …をひく; (*criticize*) … o kenasu …をけなす; *stocks* … o herasu …を減らす **2** *v/i* (*of battery*) kireru 切れる
♦**run into** (*meet*) … ni dekuwasu …に出くわす; *difficulties* … ni butsukaru …にぶつかる
♦**run off 1** *v/i* nigedasu 逃げ出す **2** *v/t* (*print*) … o insatsu suru …を印刷する
♦**run out** (*of contract*) kireru 切れる; (*of supplies*) nakunaru なくなる; ***time is running out*** jikangire ni natte kita 時間切れになってきた
♦**run out of** *time, patience* … ga nakunaru …がなくなる; *supplies* …ga kireru …が切れる; ***I ran out of gas*** gasuketsu ni narimashita ガス欠になりました
♦**run over 1** *v/t* (*in car*) … o hiku …をひく; ***can we ~ the details again?*** mō ichido shōsai ni me o tōshite ii desu ka もう一度詳細に目を通していいですか **2** *v/i* (*of water etc*) … ga afureru …があふれる
♦**run through** (*rehearse, go over*) rihāsaru o suru リハーサルをする; *details* tōsu 通す
♦**run up** *v/t debts, bill* … ga kasamu …がかさむ; *clothes* … o isoide tsukuru …を急いで作る
run-down *person* hetoheto (no) へとへと(の); *area, building* sabirete iru さびれている
rung (*of ladder*) dan 段
runner (*athlete*) sōsha 走者
runner-up ni chaku no hito 二着の人
running 1 *n* SP kyōsō 競走; (*jogging*) jogingu ジョギング; (*of business*) keiei 経営 **2** *adj*: ***for two days ~*** futsuka-kan renzoku 二日間連続
running water (*supply*) suidōsui 水道水
runny *liquid* mizuppoi 水っぽい; *egg* yurui 緩い; *nose* tareru 垂れる
run-up SP josō 助走; ***in the ~ to*** … e no junbi-kikan de …への準備期間で
runway kassōro 滑走路
rupture 1 *n* (*in pipe*) haretsu 破裂; (*in relations*) ketsuretsu 決裂; MED herunia ヘルニア **2** *v/i* (*of pipe etc*) haretsu suru 破裂する
rural inaka (no) 田舎(の); *economy* chihō (no) 地方(の)
rush 1 *n* ōisogi 大急ぎ; ***do X in a ~*** X

o ōisogi de suru Xを大急ぎでする; ***be in a*** ~ isoide iru 急いでいる; ***what's the big ~?*** dōshite sonna ni isoide iru no desu ka どうしてそんなに急いでいるのですか **2** *v/t person* isogaseru 急がせる; *meal* isoide tabesaseru 急いで食べさせる; ***~ X to the hospital*** X o ōisogi de byōin ni tsurete itta Xを大急ぎで病院に連れていった **3** *v/i* isogu 急ぐ

rush hour rasshu-awā ラッシュアワー

Russia Roshia ロシア

Russian 1 *adj* Roshia (no) ロシア(の) **2** *n* Roshia-jin ロシア人; (*language*) Roshia-go ロシア語

Russo-Japanese War (*1904-05*) Nichiro-sensō 日露戦争

rust 1 *n* sabi さび **2** *v/i* sabiru さびる

rustle *v/i* (*of silk*) sarasara to naru さらさらと鳴る; (*of leaves*) kasakasa to naru かさかさと鳴る

♦ **rustle up** F *meal* … o tebayaku ryōri suru …を手早く料理する

rust-proof *adj* sabinai さびない

rust remover sabitorizai さび取り剤

rusty sabita さびた; *French, math etc* …ga dame ni natta …がだめになった; ***I'm a little ~*** sukoshi dame ni natte imasu すこしだめになっています

rut (*in road*) wadachi わだち; ***be in a ~*** kata ni hamaru 型にはまる

ruthless reikoku (na) 冷酷(な)

ruthlessness reikoku 冷酷

rye raimugi ライ麦

rye bread raimugi-pan ライ麦パン

S

sabbatical *n* (*of academic*) kenkyū-kyūka 研究休暇

sabotage 1 *n* hakai-kōsaku 破壊工作 **2** *v/t* hakai suru 破壊する

saccharin *n* sakkarin サッカリン

sachet (*of shampoo, cream etc*) ko-bukuro 小袋

sack *n* ō-bukuro 大袋

sacred shinsei (na) 神聖(な)

sacrifice 1 *n* (*act*) gisei 犠牲; (*person, animal sacrificed*) ikenie いけにえ; ***make ~s*** *fig* gisei o harau 犠牲をはらう **2** *v/t* ikenie to shite sasageru いけにえとして捧げる; *freedom etc* gisei ni suru 犠牲にする

sad kanashii 悲しい; *face* kanashisō (na) 悲しそう(な)

saddle *n* kura くら

sadism sadizumu サディズム

sadist sadisuto サディスト

sadistic kagyakuteki (na) 加虐的(な)

sadly *look, sing etc* kanashi-sō ni 悲しそうに; (*regrettably*) zannen na koto ni 残念なことに

sadness kanashimi 悲しみ

safe 1 *adj* (*not dangerous*) anzen (na) 安全(な); (*not in danger*) buji (na) 無事(な); *investment, prediction* kakujitsu (na) 確実(な) **2** *n* kinko 金庫

safeguard 1 *n* anzen-taisaku 安全対策; ***as a ~ against*** … ni taisuru anzen-taisaku to shite …に対する安全対策として **2** *v/t* hogo suru 保護する

safekeeping ***give X to Y for ~*** Y ni X o hokan shite morau yō ni azukeru YにXを保管してもらうように預ける

safely *arrive* buji ni 無事に; *drive* anzen ni 安全に; *assume* machigainaku 間違いなく; ***they will be ~ looked after*** karera wa machigainaku sewa o shite moraemasu 彼らは間違いなく世話をしてもらえます

safety anzen 安全; (*of investment*) anzensei 安全性; ***be in ~*** buji de aru 無事である; ***reach ~*** anzen na tokoro ni tadori-tsuku 安全なところにたどりつく

safety-conscious anzen-ishiki no takai 安全意識の高い; **safety first** anzen-daiichi (no) 安全第一(の); **safety pin** anzen-pin 安全ピン

sag 1 *n* (*in ceiling etc*) tawami たわみ **2** *v/i* (*of ceiling, rope*) tarumu たるむ; (*of output, tempo*) naka-darumi suru 中だるみする

sage (*herb*) sēji セージ

sail 1 *n* ho 帆; (*trip*) kōkai 航海; ***go for a ~*** sēringu ni iku セーリングに行く **2** *v/t yacht* sēringu suru セーリングする **3** *v/i* sēringu suru セーリングする; (*depart*) shukkō suru 出港する

sailboard 1 *n* sāfu-bōdo サーフボード **2** *v/i* windo-sāfin o suru ウィンドサーフィンをする

sailboarding windosāfin ウィンドサーフィン

sailboat yotto ヨット

sailing SP sēringu セーリング

sailing ship hansen 帆船

sailor (*in the navy*) suihei 水兵; SP yottoman ヨットマン; ***be a good / bad ~*** funayoi shinai / suru hito 船酔いしない/する人

saint seijin 聖人

sake: ***for my / your ~*** watashi / anata no tame ni 私/あなた のために; ***for the ~ of*** … no tame ni …のために

sake sake 酒; ***sweet ~*** amazake 甘酒; ***cold ~*** hiya 冷や; ***hot ~*** atsukan 熱かん

sake cup choko ちょこ

sake flask tokkuri とっくり

salad sarada サラダ

salad dressing doresshingu ドレッシング

salary kyūryō 給料

salary scale kyūryō-taikei 給料体系

sale hanbai 販売; (*reduced prices*) tokubai 特売, sēru セール; ***for ~*** (*sign*) urimono 売り物; ***be on ~*** hanbai sarete iru 販売されている; (*at reduced prices*) yasuuri sarete iru 安売りされている

sales (*department*) eigyō-bu 営業部

sales clerk ten'in 店員; **sales figures** uriagedaka 売上高; **salesman** sērusuman セールスマン; **sales manager** eigyō-kachō 営業課長; **sales meeting** hanbai-kaigi 販売会議

saliva daeki だ液

salmon sake さけ

saloon (*bar*) bā バー

salt shio 塩

saltcellar shioire 塩入れ

salty shiokarai 塩辛い

salutary *experience* yūeki (na) 有益(な)

salute 1 *n* MIL keirei 敬礼; ***take the ~*** keirei o ukeru 敬礼を受ける **2** *v/t* … ni aisatsu suru …にあいさつする **3** *v/i* aisatsu suru あいさつする

salvage *v/t* sukuidasu 救い出す

salvation tamashii no kyūsai 魂の救済

Salvation Army Kyūseigun 救世軍

same 1 *adj* onaji 同じ **2** *pron*: ***the ~*** (*things*) onaji mono 同じ物; (*abstracts*) onaji koto 同じこと; ***Happy New Year – the ~ to you*** Akemashite omedetō gozaimasu – kochira koso Akemashite omedetō gozaimasu 明けましておめでとうございますーこちらこそ、明けましておめでとうございます; ***he's not the ~ any more*** kare wa mō moto no kare de wa nai 彼はもう元の彼ではない; ***but all the ~, it does seem strange*** tonikaku hen da とにかく変だ; ***but I still love her all the ~*** yappari kanjo o aishite iru やっぱり彼女を愛している; ***men are all the ~*** otoko wa mina nitari yottari de aru 男は皆似たり寄ったりである; ***it's all the ~ to me*** watashi wa nan demo kamaimasen 私は何でもかまいません **3** *adv*: ***look / sound the ~*** onaji ni mieru / kikoeru 同じに見える/聞こえる

sample *n* mihon 見本, sanpuru サンプル
Samurai Samurai 侍; *~ sword* katana 刀
sanction 1 *n* (*approval*) ninka 認可; (*penalty*) seisai 制裁 **2** *v/t* (*approve*) ninka suru 認可する
sanctity shinsei-sa 神聖さ
sanctuary REL seiiki 聖域; (*for animals*) hogo-kuiki 保護区域
sand 1 *n* suna 砂 **2** *v/t* (*with sandpaper*) … ni yasuri o kakeru …にやすりをかける
sandal sandaru サンダル; ***Japanese ~*** zōri ぞうり
sandbag suna-bukuro 砂袋
sand dune sakyū 砂丘
sander (*tool*) kenmaki 研磨機
sandpaper 1 *n* kami-yasuri 紙やすり **2** *v/t* kami-yasuri de migaku 紙やすりで磨く; **sandpit** sunaba 砂場; **sandstone** sagan 砂岩
sandwich 1 *n* sandoitchi サンドイッチ **2** *v/t*: ***be ~ed between two …*** … no aida ni hasamarete iru …の間に挟まれている
sandy *beach, soil* suna (no) 砂(の); *hair* sunairo (no) 砂色(の)
sane shōki (no) 正気(の)
sanitarium ryōyō-sho 療養所
sanitary *conditions, installations* eiseiteki (na) 衛生的(な)
sanitary napkin seiriyō napukin 生理用ナプキン
sanitation (*sanitary installations*) eisei-setsubi 衛生設備; (*removal of waste*) gesui-setsubi 下水設備
sanitation department eiseikyoku 衛生局
sanity shōki 正気
Santa Claus Santa-kurōsu サンタクロース
sap 1 *n* (*in tree*) jueki 樹液 **2** *v/t s.o.'s energy* yowaraseru 弱らせる
sapphire *n* (*jewel*) safaia サファイア
sarcasm hiniku 皮肉
sarcastic iyami (na) 嫌み(な)
sardine iwashi いわし
sash (*on dress, uniform*) kazariobi 飾り帯; (*in window*) sasshi サッシ
sashimi sashimi さしみ
Satan Maō 魔王
satellite (*natural*) eisei 衛星; (*man-made*) jinkō-eisei 人工衛星
satellite dish parabora-antena パラボラアンテナ
satellite TV eisei-terebi 衛星テレビ
satin saten サテン
satire fūshi 風刺
satirical fūshiteki (na) 風刺的(な)
satirist fūshi-sakka 風刺作家
satisfaction manzoku 満足; ***get ~ out of*** … ni manzoku o miidasu …に満足を見出す; ***a feeling of ~*** manzoku-kan 満足感; ***is that to your ~?*** oki ni meshimashita deshō ka お気に召しましたでしょうか
satisfactory manzoku no iku 満足のいく; (*just good enough*) nami (no) 並み(の); ***this is not ~*** kore de wa manzoku dekinai これでは満足できない
satisfy *customers* manzoku saseru 満足させる; *needs* … ni ōjiru …に応じる; *conditions, hunger, desires* mitasu 満たす; ***I am satisfied*** (*had enough to eat*) manpuku desu 満腹です; ***I am satisfied that*** (*convinced*) watashi wa … to kakushin shite iru 私は…と確信している; ***I hope you're satisfied!*** kore de manzoku shita deshō これで満足したでしょう
Saturday doyōbi 土曜日
sauce sōsu ソース
saucepan katate-nabe 片手なべ
saucer ukezara 受け皿
saucy *person* namaiki (na) 生意気(な); *dress* shareta しゃれた
Saudi Arabia Sauji-Arabia サウジアラビア
Saudi (Arabian) 1 *adj* Sauji-Arabia (no) サウジアラビア(の) **2** *n* (*person*) Sauji-Arabia-jin サウジアラビア人
sauna sauna サウナ
saunter nonbiri to aruku のんびりと歩く
sausage sōsēji ソーセージ
savage 1 *adj animal* dōmō (na) どう猛(な); *attack* zannin (na) 残忍

(な); *criticism* zankoku (na) 残酷(な) **2** *n* yaban-jin 野蛮人

save 1 *v/t* (*rescue*) sukuu 救う; *money* tameru ためる; *time* setsuyaku suru 節約する; (*collect*) totte oku 取っておく; COMPUT hozon suru 保存する; *goal* fusegu 防ぐ; ***you could ~ yourself a lot of effort*** anata no tema ga unto habukeru あなたの手間がうんと省ける **2** *v/i* (*put money aside*) chokin suru 貯金する; (*in soccer*) tokuten o fusegu 得点を防ぐ; (*in baseball*) sēbu suru セーブする **3** *n* SP sēbu セーブ

♦**save up for** … no tame ni chokin suru …のために貯金する

saving (*amount saved*) setsuyaku 節約; (*activity*) chochiku 貯蓄

savings chokin 貯金

savings account futsū-yokin-kōza 普通預金口座

savings bank futsū-ginkō 普通銀行

savior REL kyūseishu 救世主; (*Christian*) Kirisuto キリスト

savor *v/t* ajiwau 味わう

savory *adj* (*salty*) shioaji (no) 塩味(の); (*spicy*) piritto shita ぴりっとした

saw *n* (*tool*) nokogiri のこぎり

♦**saw off** nokogiri de kiriotosu のこぎりで切り落とす

sawdust ogakuzu おがくず

saxophone sakusofōn サクソフォーン

say 1 *v/t* iu 言う; ***can I ~ something?*** hitokoto iwasete moraemasu ka 一言言わせてもらえますか; ***that is to ~*** tsumari つまり; ***what do you ~ to that?*** anata wa dō omoimasu ka あなたはどう思いますか **2** *n*: ***have one's ~*** iibun ga aru 言い分がある

saying kotowaza ことわざ

scab (*on cut*) kasabuta かさぶた

scaffolding ashiba 足場

scald *v/t* yakedo saseru やけどさせる

scale[1] (*on fish*) uroko うろこ

scale[2] **1** *n* (*size*) kibo 規模; (*on thermometer etc*) memori 目盛り; (*of map*) shukushaku 縮尺; MUS onkai 音階; ***on a larger / smaller ~*** dai kibo / shō kibo ni 大規模/小規模に **2** *v/t cliffs etc* noboru 登る

scale drawing shukuzu 縮図

scales hakari はかり; (*for person*) taijūkei 体重計

scalp *n* atamo no kawa 頭の皮

scalpel mesu メス

scalper shitsukoku kan'yū suru hito しつこく勧誘する人

scam F sagi 詐欺

scan 1 *v/t horizon* miwatasu 見渡す; *page* … ni zatto me o tōsu …にざっと目を通す; MED sukyan o kakeru スキャンをかける; COMPUT sukyanā o kakete sagasu スキャナーをかけて探す **2** *n* MED sukyan スキャン

♦**scan in** COMPUT sukyanā de yomikomu スキャナーで読み込む

scandal sukyandaru スキャンダル

scandalous tondemonai とんでもない

scanner MED sukyan スキャン; COMPUT sukyanā スキャナー

scantily: ***~ clad*** hotondo nani mo kite inai ほとんど何も着ていない

scanty *clothes* hada o roshutsu shita 肌を露出した

scapegoat migawari 身代わり

scar 1 *n* kizuato 傷跡 **2** *v/t* … ni kizuato o nokosu …に傷跡を残す

scarce (*in short supply*) fujūbun (na) 不十分(な); ***make oneself ~*** (*go away*) tachisaru 立ち去る; (*stay away*) hikkonde iru 引っ込んでいる

scarcely hotondo…nai ほとんど…ない; ***I ~ know her*** watashi wa hotondo kanojo o shiranai 私はほとんど彼女を知らない

scarcity fusoku 不足

scare 1 *v/t* kowagaraseru 怖がらせる; ***be ~d of*** … o kowagaru …を怖がる **2** *n* (*alarm*) kyōfu 恐怖; (*panic*) panikku パニック; ***give … a ~*** … o bikkuri saseru …をびっくりさせる

♦**scare away** … o odoshite oiharau …を脅して追い払う

scarecrow kakashi かかし
scaremonger dema o tobasu hito デマを飛ばす人
scarf (*around neck*) mafurā マフラー; (*over head*) sukāfu スカーフ
scarlet *adj* hiro (no) ひ色(の)
scarlet fever shōkōnetsu しょう紅熱
scary *music, movie* kowai 怖い
scathing tsūretsu (na) 痛烈(な)
scatter 1 *v/t leaflets,* baramaku ばらまく; *seeds* maku まく; ***be ~ed all over the room*** heyajū ni chirakatte iru 部屋中にちらかっている **2** *v/i* (*of crowd etc*) chirijiri ni naru ちりぢりになる
scatterbrained chūi-sanman (na) 注意散漫(な)
scattered *family, villages* tenzai shite iru 点在している; ***~ showers*** niwaka-ame にわか雨
scenario sujigaki 筋書き; (*of movie*) shinario シナリオ
scene THEA ba 場; (*view, sight*) jōkyō 情況; (*of accident, crime etc*) genba 現場; (*of novel, movie*) butai 舞台; (*argument*) ōsawagi 大騒ぎ; ***make a ~*** sōdō o okosu 騒動を起こす; ***~s*** THEA haikei 背景; ***jazz / rock ~*** jazu / rokku no bun'ya ジャズ/ロックの分野; ***behind the ~s*** butaiura de 舞台裏で; *fig* kage de 陰で
scenery keshiki 景色; THEA butai-sōchi 舞台装置
scent *n* (*smell*) kaori 香り; (*perfume*) kōsui 香水; (*of animal*) shūseki 臭跡
schedule 1 *n* (*of events, work*) sukejūru スケジュール; (*for trains etc*) jikoku-hyō 時刻表; (*of lessons*) jikan-wari 時間割; ***be on ~*** (*of work, workers, etc*) yotei dōri de aru 予定どおりである; (*of train etc*) teikoku dōri de aru 定刻どおりである; ***be behind ~*** (*of work, workers, train etc*) yotei yori okureru 予定より遅れる **2** *v/t* (*put on schedule*) yotei suru 予定する; ***it's ~d for completion next month*** raigetsu ni kansei ga yotei sarete imasu 来月に完成が予定されています
scheduled flight teikibin 定期便
scheme 1 *n* keikaku 計画; (*plot*) takurami たくらみ **2** *v/i* (*plot*) takuramu たくらむ
scheming *adj* haraguroi 腹黒い
schizophrenia seishin-bunretsushō 精神分裂症
schizophrenic 1 *n* seishinbunretsushō-kanja 精神分裂症患者 **2** *adj* seishin-bunretsushō (no) 精神分裂症(の)
scholar gakusha 学者
scholarship (*scholarly work*) gakumon 学問; (*financial award*) shōgakukin 奨学金
school gakkō 学校; (*university*) daigaku 大学
schoolbag gakusei-kaban 学生かばん; **schoolboy** danshi-seito 男子生徒; **schoolchildren** seito 生徒; **school days** gakusei-jidai 学生時代; **schoolgirl** joshi-seito 女子生徒; **schoolteacher** sensei 先生
sciatica zakotsu-shinkeitsū 座骨神経痛
science kagaku 科学
science fiction SF
scientific kagakuteki (na) 科学的(な)
scientist kagaku-sha 科学者
scissors hasami はさみ
scoff[1] *v/t* (*eat fast*) gatsugatsu taberu がつがつ食べる; (*eat all of*) tairageru 平らげる
scoff[2] *v/i* azawarau あざ笑う
♦ **scoff at** … o azawarau …をあざ笑う
scold *v/t* shikaru しかる
scoop 1 *n* (*for ice cream*) sābā サーバー; (*for mud*) sukoppu スコップ; (*story*) sukūpu スクープ **2** *v/t* (*pick up*) sukui ageru すくい上げる
♦ **scoop up** … o hiroi ageru …を拾い上げる
scooter sukūtā スクーター
scope han'i 範囲; (*opportunity*) yochi 余地; (*freedom*) jiyū 自由
scorch *v/t* kogasu 焦がす
scorching hot yaketsuku yō ni atsui 焼けつくように暑い

score1 *n* SP tokuten 得点; (*written music*) gakufu 楽譜; (*of movie etc*) sukoa スコア; ***what's the ~?*** tokuten wa dō natte imasu ka 得点はどうなっていますか; ***have a ~ to settle with*** … ni urami o harasu …に恨みを晴らす **2** *v/t goal, point* tokuten suru 得点する; (*cut: line*) kirime o tsukeru 切り目をつける **3** *v/i* tokuten suru 得点する; (*keep the ~*) kiroku suru 記録する; ***that's where he ~s*** soko ga kare no tsuyomi da そこが彼の強みだ

scorer(*of goal, point*) tokuten-sha 得点者; (*scorekeeper*) kiroku-gakari 記録係

scorn1 *n* keibetsu 軽べつ; ***pour ~ on*** … o keibetsu suru …を軽べつする **2** *v/t idea, suggestion* hanetsukeru はねつける

scornfulkeibetsu shita 軽べつした

ScotSukottorando-jin スコットランド人

Scotch(*whiskey*) Sukotchi uisukī スコッチウイスキー

ScotlandSukottorando スコットランド

ScottishSukottorando (no) スコットランド(の)

scot-free ***get off ~*** buji ni nigeru 無事に逃げる

scoundrelakutō 悪党

scour[1](*search*) sagashimawaru 捜しまわる

scour[2]*pans* goshigoshi arau ごしごし洗う

scout*n* (*boy ~*) bōi sukauto ボーイスカウト

scowl1 *n* shikamettsura しかめっ面 **2** *v/i* kao o shikameru 顔をしかめる

scram[F] sassa to useru さっさと失せる; ***~!*** sassa to usero さっさと失せろ

scramble1 *n* (*rush*) awatadashi-sa 慌ただしさ **2** *v/t message* hachō o kaeru 波長を変える **3** *v/i* (*climb*) saki o arasotte yojinoboru 先を争ってよじ登る; ***he ~d to his feet*** kare wa kyū ni tachiagatta 彼は急に立ち上がった

scrambled eggssukuranburu eggu スクランブルエッグ

scrap1 *n* (*metal*) kuzu くず; (*fight*) kenka けんか; (*little bit*) sukoshi 少し **2** *v/t plan, paragraph etc* yameru やめる

scrapbooksukurappu bukku スクラップブック

scrape1 *n* (*on paint etc*) kosuru koto こすること **2** *v/t paint, one's arm etc* kosuru こする; *vegetables* muku むく; ***~ a living*** nantoka seikatsu suru 何とか生活する

♦**scrape through**(*in exam*) nantoka pasu suru 何とかパスする

scrap heapgomi no yama ごみの山; ***good for the ~*** suteru shikanai 捨てるしかない

scrap metalkuzutetsu くず鉄

scrappy*work* zatsu (na) 雑(な)

scratch1 *n* (*mark*) hikkakikizu 引っかき傷; ***have a ~*** (*to stop itching*) kaku かく; ***start from ~*** zero kara hajimeru ゼロから始める; ***not up to ~*** jūbun de nai 充分でない **2** *v/t* (*mark: skin, paint*) hikkaku 引っかく; (*because of itch*) kaku かく **3** *v/i* (*of cat, nails*) hikkaku 引っかく

scrawl1 *n* nagurigaki なぐり書き **2** *v/t* nagurigaki suru なぐり書きする

scream1 *n* himei 悲鳴 **2** *v/i* himei o ageru 悲鳴をあげる

screech1 *n* (*of tires*) kī to naru oto キーとなる音; (*scream*) kanakirigoe 金切り声 **2** *v/i* (*of tires*) kī to oto o tateru キーと音を立てる; (*scream*) kanakirigoe o ageru 金切り声をあげる

screen1 *n* (*in room, hospital*) tsuitate ついたて; (*decorative*) byōbu 屏風; (*protective*) maku 幕; (*in movie theater*) sukurīn スクリーン; COMPUT gamen 画面; ***on the ~*** (*in movies*) eiga ni deru 映画に出る; ***on (the) ~*** COMPUT gamen ni deru 画面に出る **2** *v/t* (*protect, hide*) ōikakusu 覆い隠す; *movie* eisha suru 映写する; (*for security reasons*) shinsa suru 審査する

screenplayeiga no shinario 映画の

シナリオ; **screen saver** COMPUT sukurīn sēbā スクリーンセーバー; **screen test** ōdishon オーディション

screw 1 *n* neji ねじ; V (*sex*) sekkusu セックス **2** *v/t* neji de tomeru ねじで留める; V sekkusu suru セックスする; F (*cheat*) damasu だます; ***~ X to Y*** X o Y ni neji de tomeru XをYにねじで留める

♦**screw up 1** *v/t eyes* … o shikameru …をしかめる; *piece of paper* … o marumeru …を丸める; F (*make a mess of*) … o dainashi ni suru …を台無しにする **2** *v/i* F (*make a bad mistake*) dame ni suru だめにする

screwdriver doraibā ドライバー

screwed up F (*psychologically*) dame ni naru だめになる

screw top neji buta ねじぶた

scribble 1 *n* hashirigaki 走り書き **2** *v/t* (*write quickly*) hashirigaki suru 走り書きする **3** *v/i* rakugaki suru 落書きする

script (*for play etc*) kyakuhon 脚本; (*form of writing*) moji 文字

Scripture: ***the (Holy) ~s*** Seisho 聖書

scriptwriter kyakuhon-ka 脚本家

scroll *n* (*manuscript*) makimono 巻き物; ***hanging ~*** kakejiku 掛け軸

♦**scroll down** *v/i* COMPUT sukurōru suru スクロールする

♦**scroll up** *v/i* COMPUT sukurōru suru スクロールする

scrounger takari たかり

scrub *v/t floor, hands* goshigoshi arau ごしごし洗う

scrubbing brush (*for floor*) burashi ブラシ

scruffy misuborashii みすぼらしい

♦**scrunch up** *plastic cup etc* … o baritto tsubusu …をばりっとつぶす

scruples ryōshin no togame 良心のとがめ; ***have no ~ about doing X*** nan no tamerai mo naku X suru 何のためらいもなくXする

scrupulous (*with moral principles*) seijitsu (na) 誠実(な); (*thorough*) kichōmen (na) きちょうめん(な); *attention to detail* menmitsu (na) 綿密(な)

scrutinize (*examine*) menmitsu ni shiraberu 綿密に調べる

scrutiny menmitsu na chōsa 綿密な調査; ***come under ~*** kanshi sarete iru 監視されている

scuba diving sukyūba daibingu スキューバダイビング

scuffle *n* rantō 乱闘

sculptor chōkoku-ka 彫刻家

sculpture *n* chōkoku 彫刻

scum ukikasu 浮きかす; *pej* (*people*) kasu かす

scythe *n* kusakarigama 草刈りがま

sea umi 海; ***by the ~*** kaigan 海岸

sea bass suzuki すずき; **sea bream** tai たい; **Sea Day** Umi no hi 海の日; **seafaring** *nation* kaiyō (no) 海洋(の); **seafood** gyokairui 魚介類, shīfūdo シーフード; **seafront** kaigandōri 海岸通り; **seagoing** *vessel* en'yō-kōkaiyō (no) 遠洋航海用(の); **seagull** kamome かもめ

seal[1] *n* (*animal*) azarashi あざらし

seal[2] **1** *n* (*on document*) inshō 印章; TECH fū 封 **2** *v/t container* mippei suru 密閉する

♦**seal off** *area* … o fūsa suru …を封鎖する

sea level: ***above ~*** kaibatsu 海抜 ; ***below ~*** kaimenka 海面下

seam *n* (*on garment*) nuime 縫い目; (*of ore*) hakusō 薄層

seaman sen'in 船員

Sea of Japan nihonkai 日本海; **Sea of Okhotsk** Ohōtsuku-kai オホーツク海; **seaport** minatomachi 港町; **sea power** (*nation*) kaigun no chikara 海軍の力

search 1 *n* chōsa 調査; (*for happiness*) tsuikyū 追求; COMPUT kensaku 検索 **2** *v/t city, files* sagasu 捜す

♦**search for** … o sagasu …を捜す

searching *adj look, question* surudoi 鋭い

searchlight sāchiraito サーチライト; **search party** sōsaku-tai 捜索隊; **search warrant** katakusōsaku-

reijō 家宅捜索令状
seasick funayoi (no) 船酔い(の); ***get ~*** funayoi suru 船酔いする; **seaside** umibe 海辺; ***at the ~*** umibe de 海辺で; ***go to the ~*** umibe ni iku 海辺に行く; **seaside resort** umibe no kōrakuchi 海辺の行楽地
season *n* (*winter etc*) kisetsu 季節; (*for tourism etc*) shīzun シーズン
seasoned *wood* kansō shita 乾燥した; *traveler etc* keiken yutaka (na) 経験豊か(な)
seasoning chōmiryō 調味料
season ticket (*for bus etc*) teikiken 定期券; (*for football, opera*) shīzun chiketto シーズンチケット
seat 1 *n* zaseki 座席; (*of pants*) shiri しり; ***please take a ~*** osuwari kudasai お座りください **2** *v/t* (*have seating for*) seki ga aru 席がある; ***please remain ~ed*** seki ni tsuita mama de ite kudasai 席に着いたままでいてください
seat belt shīto-beruto シートベルト
sea urchin uni うに
seaweed kaisō 海草; (*dried to eat*) nori のり
secluded hitozato hanareta 人里離れた
seclusion kakuri 隔離
second 1 *n* (*of time*) byō 秒; (*of month*) futsuka; ***just a ~*** chotto matte kudasai ちょっと待って下さい **2** *adj* dai-ni (no) 第二(の); ***~ biggest*** nibanme ni ōkii 二番目に大きい **3** *adv* nibanme ni 二番目に; *come in* nii de 二位で **4** *v/t motion* shiji suru 支持する
secondary nijiteki (na) 二次的(な); ***of ~ importance*** amari jūyō de nai あまり重要でない
secondary education chūtō-kyōiku 中等教育
second best *adj* nibanme ni yoi 二番目によい; **second class** *adj ticket* nitō 二等; **second gear** MOT sekando セカンド; **second hand** (*on clock*) byōshin 秒針;
secondhand 1 *adj* chūko (no) 中古(の) **2** *adv buy* chūko de 中古で
secondly daini ni 第二に
second-rate niryū (no) 二流(の)
second thoughts: ***I've had ~*** ki ga kawatta 気が変わった
secrecy himitsu ni suru koto 秘密にすること; ***the X51 was developed in great ~*** ekkusu gojūichi wa himitsuri no uchi ni kaihatsu sareta X51は秘密裏のうちに開発された
secret 1 *n* himitsu 秘密; ***do X in ~*** hisoka ni X suru ひそかにXする **2** *adj passage* himitsu (no) 秘密(の); *work* kimitsu 機密
secret agent supai スパイ
secretarial *job* hisho (no) 秘書(の)
secretary hisho 秘書; POL daijin 大臣
Secretary of State Kokumu-chōkan 国務長官
secrete (*give off*) bunpitsu suru 分泌する; (*hide away*) kossori kakusu こっそり隠す
secretion (*of liquid*) bunpitsu 分泌; (*liquid secreted*) bunpitsu-butsu 分泌物; (*hiding*) intoku 隠匿
secretive himitsushugi (no) 秘密主義(の)
secretly naimitsu de 内密で
secret police himitsu keisatsu 秘密警察
secret service himitsu-chōhōkikan 秘密諜報機関
sect shūha 宗派
section bubun 部分; (*of book, text*) shō 章; (*of company, department*) …bu …部
sector (*of city*) kuiki 区域; (*of society*) bumon 部門; (*of diskette, lung*) bubun 部分
secular sezoku (no) 世俗(の)
secure 1 *adj shelf etc* kotei sareta 固定された; *job, feeling* antei shita 安定した **2** *v/t shelf* kotei suru 固定する; *help* kakuho suru 確保する
security (*in job*) hoshō 保証; (*guarantee*) tanpo 担保; (*at airport etc*) keibi 警備; (*department*) keibi-bumon 警備部門; (*of beliefs etc*) kakushin 確信; ***securities*** FIN yūka-shōken 有価証券; ***securities***

market FIN shōken-shijō 証券市場
security alert (*state*) keikai-taisei 警戒態勢; (*warning*) keikai-keihō 警戒警報; **security check** sekyuritī-chekku セキュリティーチェック; **security-conscious** keibi-ishiki no takai 警備意識の高い; **security forces** bōeigun 防衛軍; **security guard** keibiin 警備員; **security risk** (*person*) kiken-jinbutsu 危険人物
sedan MOT sedan セダン
sedative *n* chinseizai 鎮静剤
sediment chindenbutsu 沈殿物
seduce yūwaku suru 誘惑する
seduction (*sexual*) yūwaku 誘惑
seductive *dress* miwakuteki (na) 魅惑的(な); *offer* miryokuteki (na) 魅力的(な)
see miru 見る; (*understand*) wakaru わかる; ***I ~*** wakarimashita わかりました; ***can I ~ the manager?*** manējā ni aemasu ka マネージャーに会えますか; ***you should ~ a doctor*** isha ni itta hō ga ii desu 医者に行ったほうがいいです; ***~ home*** … o ie made okuru …を家まで送る; ***I'll ~ you to the door*** genkan made okurimasu 玄関まで送ります; ***~ you!*** mata ne またね
♦ **see about** (*attend to*) … o torihakarau …を取り計らう
♦ **see off** (*at airport etc*) … o okuru …を送る; (*chase away*) … o oiharau …を追い払う
♦ **see to**: ***~ it that X gets done*** X ga okonawareru yō ni ki o tsukeru X が行われるように気をつける
seed tane 種; (*in tennis*) shīdo シード; ***go to ~*** (*of person, district*) sakari o sugiru 盛りを過ぎる
seedling nae 苗
seedy *bar, district* misuborashii みすぼらしい
seeing (that) … de aru kara …であるから
seeing eye dog mōdōken 盲導犬
seek 1 *v/t employment* sagasu 捜す; *truth* motomeru もとめる **2** *v/i* sagasu 捜す
seem … no yō ni mieru …のように見える; ***it ~s that …*** … no yō ni omowareru …のように思われる
seemingly mita tokoro de wa 見たところでは
seep (*of liquid*) shimideru 染み出る
♦ **seep out** (*of liquid*) sukoshi zutsu deru 少しずつでる
seesaw shīsō シーソー
see-through *dress, material* shīsurū (no) シースルー(の)
segment ichibu 一部; (*of orange*) fukuro 袋
segmented bundan sareta 分断された
segregate bunri suru 分離する
segregation sabetsu 差別
seismology jishin-gaku 地震学
seize tsukamu つかむ; *opportunity* toraeru とらえる; (*of customs, police etc*) ōshū suru 押収する
♦ **seize up** (*of engine*) ugokanaku naru 動かなくなる
seizure MED hossa 発作; (*of drugs etc*) ōshū 押収
seldom metta ni nai めったにない
select 1 *v/t* erabidasu 選び出す **2** *adj* (*exclusive*) erabareta 選ばれた
selection (*choosing*) sentaku 選択; (*that / those chosen*) senbatsu 選抜; (*assortment*) korekushon コレクション
selection process senbatsu-hōhō 選抜方法
selective sentaku suru chikara no aru 選択する力のある
self jiko 自己
self-addressed envelope jibun ate no fūtō 自分あての封筒; **self-assured** jishin no aru 自信のある; **self-catering apartment** jisuiyō no apāto 自炊用のアパート; **self-centered** jiko-chūshin (no) 自己中心(の); **self-confessed** jinin suru 自認する; **self-confidence** jishin 自信; **self-confident** jishin no aru 自信のある; **self-conscious** uchiki (na) 内気(な); **self-contained** *apartment* setsubi-kanbi (no) 設備完備(の); **self-control** jisei 自制; **self-defense** jiko-bōei 自己防衛; **self-discipline**

jiko-kisei 自己規制; **self-doubt** jiko-fushin 自己不信; **self-employed** jieigyō (no) 自営業(の); **self-evident** jimei (no) 自明(の); **self-interest** riko-shugi 利己主義

selfish wagamama (na) わがまま(な)

selfless muyoku (no) 無欲(の)

self-made man tatakiage no hito たたき上げの人; **self-possessed** ochitsuita 落ち着いた; **self-reliant** jiritsu shita 自立した; **self-respect** jisonshin 自尊心; **self-righteous** *pej* hitoriyogari (no) 独りよがり(の); **self-satisfied** *pej* jiko-manzoku (no) 自己満足(の); **self-service** *adj* serufu-sābisu (no) セルフサービス(の)

sell 1 *v/t* uru 売る; ***you have to ~ yourself*** jibun o urikomanakute wa narimasen 自分を売り込まなくてはなりません **2** *v/i* (*of products*) uru 売る

seller urite 売り手

selling *n* COM eigyō 営業

selling point COM sērusu pointo セールスポイント

semen seieki 精液

semester gakki 学期

semi (*truck*) torērā トレーラー

semicircle han'en 半円; **semicircular** han'en (no) 半円(の); **semiconductor** ELEC handōtai 半導体; **semifinal** junkesshō 準決勝

seminar seminā セミナー

semiskilled *adj* hanjukuren (no) 半熟練(の)

senate jōin 上院

senator jōin-giin 上院議員

send *v/t* okuru 送る; ***~ X to Y*** *thing* X oY ni okuru XをYに送る; *person* X oY no tokoro e ikaseru XをYのところへ行かせる; ***~ her my best wishes*** kanojo ni yoroshiku itte oite kudasai 彼女によろしく言ってください

♦**send back** … o hensō suru …を返送する; *food in restaurant* … o kaesu …を返す

♦**send for** *doctor, help* … o yobu yō ni tanomu …を呼ぶように頼む

♦**send in** *troops* … o haken suru …を派遣する; *next interviewee* … o tōsu …を通す; *application form* … o teishutsu suru …を提出する

♦**send off** *letter etc* … o hassō suru …を発送する

♦**send up** (*mock*) … o karakau …をからかう

sender (*of letter*) sashidashi-nin 差出人

senile mōroku shita もうろくした

senility mōroku もうろく

senior (*older*) nenchō (no) 年長(の); (*in rank*) jōi (no) 上位(の); ***be ~ to*** (*in rank*) … yori jōi (no) …より上位(の)

senior citizen kōrei-sha 高齢者

sensation (*feeling*) kankaku 感覚; (*surprise event*) sensēshon センセーション; (*s.o. / sth very good*) daininki 大人気

sensational *news, discovery* sensēshonaru (na) センセーショナル(な); (*very good*) subarashii 素晴らしい

sense 1 *n* (*meaning*) imi 意味; (*purpose, point*) ito 意図; (*common ~*) jōshiki 常識; (*of sight, smell etc*) kankaku 感覚; (*feeling*) kanji 感じ; ***in a ~*** aru imi de wa ある意味では; ***talk ~, man!*** majime ni shite yo まじめにしてよ; ***it doesn't make ~*** imi ga wakarimasen 意味がわかりません; ***there's no ~ in trying / waiting*** shite mo / matte mo muda desu しても/待っても無駄です **2** *v/t s.o.'s presence* kanjiru 感じる

senseless (*pointless*) muimi (na) 無意味(な)

sensible *person, decision* jōshiki no aru 常識のある; *advice* kenmei (na) 賢明(な)

sensitive *skin* binkan (na) 敏感(な); *person* shinkeishitsu (na) 神経質(な)

sensitivity (*of skin, person*) binkan-sa 敏感さ

sensual kannōteki (na) 官能的(な)

sensuality kōshoku 好色

sensuous kansei ni uttaeru 感性に訴える

sentence 1 *n* GRAM bun 文; LAW senkoku 宣告 **2** *v/t* LAW hanketsu o senkoku suru 判決を宣告する
sentiment (*sentimentality*) kanshō 感傷; (*opinion*) iken 意見
sentimental kanshōteki (na) 感傷的(な)
sentimentality kanshō 感傷
sentry mihari 見張り
separate 1 *adj* wakeru 分ける; ***keep X ~ from Y*** X to Y o wakeru XとYを分ける **2** *v/t* wakeru 分ける; *people* hikihanasu 引き離す; ***~ X from Y*** X o Y to kubetsu suru XをYと区別する **3** *v/i* (*of couple*) bekkyo suru 別居する
separated *couple* bekkyo shita 別居した
separately betsubetsu ni 別々に
separation bunri 分離; (*of couple*) bekkyo 別居
September kugatsu 九月
septic kansen shita 感染した; ***go ~*** (*of wound*) kansen suru 感染する
sequel tsuzuki 続き
sequence *n* renzoku 連続; ***in ~*** junban ni 順番に; ***out of ~*** barabara ni ばらばらに; ***the ~ of events*** ichiren no dekigoto 一連の出来事
serene odayaka (na) 穏やか(な)
sergeant (*army*) gunsō 軍曹; (*police*) junsa-buchō 巡査部長
serial *n* rensai 連載
serialize (*on TV, radio*) tsuzukimono toshite hōsō suru 続き物として放送する; (*in magazine, newspaper*) rensai suru 連載する
serial killer renzoku-satsujinhan 連続殺人犯; **serial number** seizō bangō 製造番号; **serial port** COMPUT shiriaru pōto シリアルポート
series (*of numbers, events*) renzoku 連続
serious *situation, damage* jūdai (na) 重大(な); *illness* omoi 重い; (*person: earnest*) majime (na) まじめ(な); *company* katai 堅い; ***I'm ~*** watashi wa honki desu 私は本気です; ***listen, this is ~*** nē, kore wa jūdai desu ねー、これは重大です; ***we'd better take a ~ look at it*** shinken ni mita hō ga ii desu 真剣に見たほうがいいです
seriously *injured* hidoku ひどく; *understaffed* shinkoku ni 深刻に; ***~ intend to ...*** honki de…shiyō to 本気で…しようと; ***~?*** hontō 本当; ***take X ~*** X o majime ni uketomeru Xをまじめに受けとめる
sermon sekkyō 説教
servant shiyōnin 使用人
serve 1 *n* (*in tennis*) sābu サーブ **2** *v/t food, meal* dasu 出す; *customer* ... no yō o ukagau . . . の用をうかがう; *one's country, the people* ... ni tsukaeru . . . に仕える; ***it ~s you / him right*** jigō-jitoku da 自業自得だ **3** *v/i* (*give out food*) shokuji o dasu 食事を出す; (*as politician etc*) tsutomeru 勤める; (*in tennis*) sābu suru サーブする
♦ **serve up** *meal* … o dasu …を出す
server SP, COMPUT sābā サーバー
service 1 *n* (*to customers*) sābisu サービス; (*for vehicle, machine*) tenken-shūri 点検修理; (*in tennis*) sābisu サービス; ***the ~s*** heieki 兵役 **2** *v/t vehicle, machine* tenken-shūri suru 点検修理する
service area sābisu-eria サービスエリア; **service charge** (*in restaurant, club*) sābisu-ryō サービス料; **service industry** sābisu-sangyō サービス産業; **serviceman** MIL gunjin 軍人; **service provider** COMPUT purobaidā プロバイダー; **service sector** sābisu-sangyō サービス産業; **service station** gasorin sutando ガソリンスタンド
session kaigi 会議; (*with analyst, consultant etc*) sōdan 相談; (*of aerobics etc*) sesshon セッション
set 1 *n* (*of tools, books etc*) isshiki 一式; (*group of people*) nakama 仲間; MATH shūgō 集合; THEA: *scenery* setto セット; (*where a movie is made*) satsuei-genba 撮影現場; (*in tennis*) setto セット; ***television ~*** terebi-juzōki テレビ受像機 **2** *v/t* (*place*) oku 置く; *movie, novel etc*

settei suru 設定する; *date, time, limit* sadameru 定める; *mechanism* chōsei suru 調整する; *alarm clock, broken limb* awaseru 合わせる; *jewel* hamekomarete iru はめこまれている; (*for exam*) *text, book* totonoeru 整える; **~ *the table*** shokutaku no yōi o suru 食卓の用意をする; **~ *a task for*** shigoto o… ni ataeru 仕事を…に与える **3** *v/i* (*of sun*) shizumu 沈む; (*of glue*) katamaru 固まる **4** *adj views, ideas* kata ni hamatta 型にはまった; ***be dead ~ on*** … ni kataku kesshin suru …に堅く決心する; ***be very ~ in one's ways*** kata ni hamatte iru 型にはまっている; **~ *book* / *reading*** (*in course*) shitei-tosho 指定図書; **~ *meal*** teishoku 定食

♦**set apart**: ***set X apart from Y*** X o Y to kubetsu suru XとYを区別する

♦**set aside** (*for future use*) … o totte oku …を取っておく

♦**set back** (*in plans etc*) … o okuraseru …を遅らせる; ***it set me back $400*** yonhyaku doru kakaru 四百ドルかかる

♦**set off 1** *v/i* (*on journey*) shuppatsu suru 出発する **2** *v/t explosion, chain reaction* … o hikiokosu …を引き起こす

♦**set out 1** *v/i* (*on journey*) shuppatsu suru 出発する; **~ *to do X*** (*intend*) X shiyō to kokoromiru Xしようと試みる **2** *v/t proposal* … o setsumei suru …を説明する; *goods* … o naraberu …を並べる

♦**set to** (*start*) torikakaru 取りかかる

♦**set up 1** *v/t company* … o setsuritsu suru …を設立する; *system* … o tachiageru …を立ち上げる; *equipment, machine* … o junbi suru …を準備する; *market stall* … o setchi suru …を設置する; F (*frame*) … o wana ni kakeru …をわなにかける **2** *v/i* (*in business*) kaigyō suru 開業する

setback kōtai 後退

setting (*of novel etc*) settei 設定; (*of house*) kankyō 環境

settle 1 *v/i* (*of bird*) tomaru とまる; (*of liquid*) sumaseru すませる; (*of dust*) shizumeru 静める; (*to live*) ochitsuku 落ち着く **2** *v/t dispute, argument* ketchaku o tsukeru 決着をつける; *issue, uncertainty* kaiketsu suru 解決する; *s.o.'s debts* harau 払う; *check* seisan suru 清算する; ***that ~s it!*** sore de kimari それで決まり

♦**settle down** *v/i* (*stop being noisy*) shizumaru 静まる; (*stop wild living*) teijū suru 定住する; (*in an area*) ochitsuku 落ち着く

♦**settle for** (*take, accept*) … de te o utsu …で手を打つ

settlement (*of claim, debt*) kessai 決済; (*of dispute*) ketchaku 決着; (*payment*) shiharai 支払; (*of building*) chinka 沈下

settler kaitaku-imin 開拓移民

set-up (*structure*) soshiki 組織; (*relationship*) kankei 関係; F (*frame-up*) wana わな

seven nana 七

seventeen jūnana 十七

seventeenth dai jūnana (no) 第十七(の)

seventh 1 *adj* dai nana (no) 第七(の) **2** *n* (*of month*) nanoka 七日

seventieth dai-nanajū (no) 第七十(の)

seventy nanajū 七十

sever *arm, cable etc* setsudan suru 切断する; *relations* tatsu 絶つ

several 1 *adj* ikutsu ka (no) 幾つか(の); *people* ikunin ka (no) 幾人か(の) **2** *pron* ikutsu ka 幾つか

severe *penalty, winter* kibishii 厳しい; *teacher* genkaku (na) 厳格(な); **~ *illness*** taibyō 大病

severely *punish* kibishiku 厳しく; *speak, stare* hageshiku 激しく; *injured, disrupted* hidoku ひどく

severity (*of illness, penalty*) shinkoku-sa 深刻さ; (*of look, winter etc*) kibishi-sa 厳しさ

sew 1 *v/t* nuu 縫う **2** *v/i* nuimono o suru 縫い物をする

♦**sew on** … o nuitsukeru …を縫いつける

sewage gesui 下水
sewage plant gesuishorijō 下水処理場
sewer gesuidō 下水道
sewing (*skill*) saihō 裁縫; (*that being sewn*) nuimono 縫い物
sewing machine mishin ミシン
sex (*act*) sekkusu セックス; (*gender*) seibetsu 性別; ***have ~ with*** sekkusu o suru セックスをする
sexual seiteki (na) 性的(な)
sexual harrassment sekuhara セクハラ; **sexual intercourse** seikō 性交
sexually transmitted disease seikō-kansen byō 性交感染病
sexy sekushī (na) セクシー(な)
shabby *coat etc* yoreyore (no) よれよれ(の); *treatment* hiretsu (na) 卑劣(な)
shack hottate goya 掘っ建て小屋
shade 1 *n* hikage 日陰; (*for lamp*) kasa かさ; (*of color*) iroai 色合い; (*on window*) buraindo ブラインド; ***in the ~*** hikage ni 日陰に **2** *v/t* (*from sun, light*) kage ni suru 陰にする
shadow *n* kage 陰
shady *spot* hikage (no) 日陰(の); *character, dealings* ikagawashii いかがわしい
shaft (*of axle*) kaitenjiku 回転軸; (*of mine*) tatekō 縦抗
shaggy *hair, dog* mojamoja (no) もじゃもじゃ(の)
shake 1 *n* furu koto 振ること; ***give X a good ~*** X o hageshiku yusaburu Xを激しく揺さぶる **2** *v/t* furu 振る; ***~ hands*** akushu suru 握手する; ***~ hands with*** … to akushu suru …と握手する; ***~ one's head*** kubi o furu 首を振る **3** *v/i* (*of hands, voice*) furueru 震える; (*of building*) yureru 揺れる
shaken (*emotionally*) dōyō suru 動揺する
shake-up saihensei 再編成
shaky *table etc* gatagata (no) がたがた(の); (*after illness, shock*) furafura (no) ふらふら(の); *grasp of sth, grammar etc* ayashii 怪しい
shall: ***I ~ do my best*** besuto o tsukushimasu ベストをつくします; ***~ we go now?*** ikimashō ka 行きましょうか
shallow *water* asai 浅い; *person* asahaka (na) 浅はか(な)
shame 1 *n* haji 恥; ***bring ~ on*** … no kao ni doro o nuru …の顔に泥を塗る; ***what a ~!*** zannen da 残念だ; ***~ on you!*** haji o shire 恥を知れ **2** *v/t* hazukashimeru 辱める; ***~ X into doing Y*** X o hajiirasete Y saseru Xを恥じ入らせてYさせる
shameful hazubeki 恥ずべき
shameless hajishirazu (no) 恥知らず(の)
shampoo 1 *n* shanpū シャンプー; ***a ~ and set*** shanpū to setto シャンプーとセット **2** *v/t* shanpū suru シャンプーする
shape 1 *n* katachi 形 **2** *v/t clay* katachizukuru 形づくる; *s.o.'s life* hōkōzukeru 方向づける; *the future* kettei suru 決定する
shapeless *dress etc* kakkō warui 格好悪い
shapely *figure* sutairu no ii スタイルのいい
share 1 *n* wakemae 分け前; FIN kabu 株; ***do one's ~ of the work*** jibun no buntan no shigoto o suru 自分の分担の仕事をする **2** *v/t* wakeru 分ける; *room, bed* kyōyō suru 共用する; *s.o.'s feelings, opinions* wakachiau 分かち合う **3** *v/i* buntan suru 分担する; ***do you mind sharing with Patrick?*** (*bed, room, table*) Patorikku to issho demo kamaimasen ka パトリックと一緒でもかまいませんか
♦**share out** bunpai 分配
shareholder kabunushi 株主
shark same さめ
sharp 1 *adj knife* surudoi 鋭い; *mind* rikō (na) 利口(な); *pain* hageshii 激しい; *taste* piritto shita ピリッとした **2** *adv* MUS han'on takaku 半音高く; ***at 3 o'clock ~*** chōdo ちょうど
sharpen *knife* togu 研ぐ; *skills* surudoku suru 鋭くする

shatter 1 *v/t glass* konagona ni waru 粉々に割る; *illusions* dainashi ni suru 台無しにする **2** *v/i* (*of glass*) konagona ni wareru 粉々に割れる

shattered F (*exhausted*) totemo tsukareta とても疲れた; (*very upset*) gakkuri kita がっくりきた

shattering *news, experience* shokkingu (na) ショッキング(な); *effect* bikkuri saseru びっくりさせる

shave 1 *v/t & v/i* soru そる **2** *n* higesori ひげそり; ***have a ~*** hige o soru ひげをそる; ***that was a close ~*** kan'ippatsu no tokoro deshita 間一髪のところでした

♦ **shave off** *beard* soriotosu そりおとす; *bit of wood* kiriotosu 切り落とす

shaven *head* sotta そった

shaver (*electric*) denki-kamisori 電気かみそり

shaving brush higesoriyō burashi ひげそり用ぶらし

shaving soap higesoriyō kurīmu ひげそり用クリーム

shawl shōru ショール

she ◊ kanojo 彼女; ***she's a doctor*** kanojo wa isha desu 彼女は医者です ◊ (*omission of pronoun*): ***who is ~? ~ is my daughter*** are wa dare desu ka – musume desu あれは誰ですか–娘です

shears hasami はさみ

sheath *n* (*for knife*) saya さや; (*contraceptive*) kondōmu コンドーム

shed[1] *v/t blood, tears* nagasu 流す; *leaves* otosu 落とす; ***~ light on*** *fig* hikari o sosogu 光を注ぐ

shed[2] *n* koya 小屋

sheep hitsuji 羊

sheepdog bokuyōken 牧羊犬

sheepish hazukashisō (na) 恥ずかしそう(な)

sheepskin *adj* hitsuji no kegawa 羊の毛皮

sheer *adj madness, luxury* mattaku (no) 全く(の); *drop, cliffs* kiritatta 切り立った

sheet (*for bed*) shītsu シーツ; ***a ~ of paper / glass*** ichimai no kami / garasu 一枚の紙/ガラス

shelf tana 棚; ***shelves*** tana 棚

shell 1 *n* (*of mussel etc*) kaigara 貝殻; (*of egg*) kara 殻; (*of tortoise*) kōra 甲羅; MIL bakuhatsubutsu 爆発物; ***come out of one's ~*** *fig* jibun no kara o yaburu 自分の殻を破る **2** *v/t peas* muku むく; MIL hōgeki suru 砲撃する

shellfire hōgeki 砲撃; ***come under ~*** hōgeki sareru 砲撃される

shellfish kōkakurui 甲殻類

shelter 1 *n* (*refuge*) hinan-sho 避難所; (*construction*) amayadori no basho 雨宿りの場所 **2** *v/i* (*from rain, bombing etc*) hinan suru 避難する **3** *v/t* (*protect*) mamoru 守る

sheltered *place* mamorarete iru 守られている; ***lead a ~ life*** seken no aranami kara mamorareta seikatsu o okuru 世間の荒波から守られた生活を送る

sherry sherī-shu シェリー酒

shiatsu shiatsu 指圧

shield 1 *n* tate 盾; (*sports trophy*) tategata-torofī 盾型トロフィー; TECH shīrudo シールド **2** *v/t* (*protect*) hogo suru 保護する

shift 1 *n* (*in attitude, thinking*) henka 変化; (*switchover*) tenkan 転換; (*in direction of wind etc*) henka 変化; (*period of work*) kōtai 交替 **2** *v/t* (*move*) ugokasu 動かす; *stains etc* torinozoku 取り除く; ***~ the emphasis onto*** kyōchō suru tokoro o … ni kaeru 強調するところを…に変える **3** *v/i* (*move*) ugoku 動く; (*in attitude, opinion*) kawaru 変わる; (*of wind*) hōkō ga kawaru 方向が変わる; ***that's ~ing!*** F sore wa hayai それは速い

shift key COMPUT shifuto kī シフトキー

shift work kōtaisei no shigoto 交替制の仕事

shifty *pej* zurui ずるい

shifty-looking *pej* ayashige na kaotsuki (no) 怪しげな顔つき(の)

Shikoku Shikoku 四国

shimmer *v/i* chirachira hikaru ちらちら光る
shin *n* mukōzune 向うずね
shine 1 *v/i* (*of sun, moon*) kagayaku 輝く; (*of shoes etc*) hikaru 光る; *fig* (*of student etc*) sugureru 優れる **2** *v/t flashlight etc* terasu 照らす
shingle (*on beach*) jari 砂利
shingles MED obijō-hōshin 帯状疱疹
Shinto Shintō 神道
Shinto altar kamidana 神棚
Shinto priest kannushi 神主
ship 1 *n* fune 船 **2** *v/t* (*send*) okuru 送る; (*send by sea*) funabin de okuru 船便で送る
shipment (*consignment*) kamotsu-yusō 貨物輸送
shipowner senshu 船主
shipping (*sea traffic*) senpaku 船舶; (*sending*) hassō 発送; (*sending by sea*) funabin 船便
shipping company unsōgyō 運送業
shipshape *adj* seizen to shita 整然とした; **shipwreck 1** *n* nanpa 難破 **2** *v/t* nanpa suru 難破する; ***be ~ed*** nanpa shita 難破した; **shipyard** zōsen-sho 造船所
shirk kaihi suru 回避する
shirt shatsu シャツ; ***in his ~ sleeves*** uwagi nashi de 上着なしで
shit F **1** *n* kuso くそ; (*bad quality goods, work*) garakuta がらくた; ***I need a ~*** unko shitai うんこしたい **2** *v/i* daiben o suru 大便をする **3** *interj* kuso' くそっ
shitty F hidoi ひどい
shiver *v/i* furueru 震える
shock 1 *n* shokku ショック; ELEC dengeki 電撃; ***be in ~*** MED shokku jōtai ni aru ショック状態にある **2** *v/t* shokku o ataeru ショックを与える; ***be ~ed by*** bikkuri saserareru びっくりさせられる
shock absorber MOT kanshōki 緩衝器
shocking *behavior, poverty* shōgekiteki (na) 衝撃的(な); F (*very bad*) hidoi ひどい
shoddy *goods* mikake daoshi (no) 見かけ倒し(の); *behavior* keibetsu subeki 軽べつすべき
shoe kutsu 靴
shoelace kutsu-himo 靴ひも; **shoestore** kutsu-ya 靴屋; **shoestring**: ***do X on a ~*** shōgaku-shikin de X suru 小額資金でXする
Shogun Shōgun 将軍
Shogunate Bakufu 幕府
♦**shoo away** shitto itte oiharau しっと言って追い払う
shoot 1 *n* BOT shinme 新芽 **2** *v/t* utsu 撃つ; (*and kill*) uchikorosu 撃ち殺す; *movie* satsuei suru 撮影する; ***~ X in the leg*** X no ashi o utsu Xの足を撃つ
♦**shoot down** *airplane* uchiotosu 撃ち落とす; *suggestion* hanetsukeru はねつける
♦**shoot off** (*rush off*) tobidasu 飛び出す
♦**shoot up** (*of prices*) kyūjōshō suru 急上昇する; (*of children*) kyū ni seichō suru 急に成長する; (*of new suburbs etc*) kyū ni hatten suru 急に発展する
shooting star nagare-boshi 流れ星
shop 1 *n* mise 店; ***talk ~*** shigoto no hanashi o suru 仕事の話をする **2** *v/i* kaimono o suru 買い物をする; ***go ~ping*** kaimono ni iku 買い物に行く
shopkeeper tenshu 店主
shoplifter manbiki 万引き
shopper kaimono-kyaku 買い物客
shopping (*activity*) kaimono 買い物; (*items*) katta shinamono 買った品物; ***do one's ~*** … ga kaimono o suru …が買い物をする
shopping mall shoppingu-sentā ショッピングセンター
shop steward rōdōkumiai-daihyōiin 労働組合代表委員
shore kishi 岸; ***on ~*** riku de 陸で
short 1 *adj* (*in height*) se no hikui 背の低い; *road, distance, time* mijikai 短い; ***be ~ of*** … ga tarinai …が足りない **2** *adv*: ***cut a vacation / meeting ~*** kyūka / mītingu o mijikaku kiriageru 休暇/ミーティングを短く切り上げる; ***stop a person ~*** kyū ni tachidomaru 急に立ち止まる; ***go ~***

of …nashi de sumasu …なしですます; ***in ~*** yō suru ni 要するに
shortage fusoku 不足
short circuit *n* shōto ショート; **shortcoming** ketten 欠点; **shortcut** chikamichi 近道
shorten *v/t* mijikaku suru 短くする
shortfall fusoku 不足; **shorthand** *n* sokki 速記; **shortlist** *n* (*of candidates*) saishū-kōho-sha 最終候補者; **short-lived** tsukanoma (no) つかの間(の)
shortly (*soon*) sugu ni すぐに; ***~ before ten o'clock*** jūji sukoshi mae ni 十時少し前に
shorts han-zubon 半ズボン; (*underwear*) pantsu パンツ
shortsighted kingan (no) 近眼(の); *fig* kinshiganteki (na) 近視眼的(な); **short-sleeved** hansode (no) 半そで(の); **short-staffed** hitode-busoku (no) 人手不足(の); **short story** tanpen-shōsetsu 短編小説; **short-tempered** tanki (na) 短気(な); **short-term** tankikan (no) 短期間(の); **short time**: ***be on ~*** sōgyō-tanshuku suru 操業短縮する; **short wave** tanpa 短波
shot (*from gun*) hassha 発射; (*photograph*) shotto ショット; (*injection*) chūsha 注射; ***be a good / poor ~*** shageki no umai / heta na hito 射撃のうまい/下手な人; ***like a ~*** *accept, run off* teppōdama no yō ni 鉄砲弾のように
shotgun sandanjū 散弾銃
should …subeki de aru …すべきである; ***what ~ I do?*** dō shitara ii desu ka どうしたらいいですか; ***you ~n't do that*** sore o subeki de nai それをすべきでない; ***that ~ be long enough*** jūbun nagai to omoimasu 充分長いと思います; ***you ~ have heard him!*** kare no iu koto o kiite itara 彼の言うことを聞いていたら
shoulder *n* kata 肩
shoulder blade kenkōkotsu 肩甲骨
shout 1 *n* ōgoe 大声 **2** *v/i* donaru 怒鳴る **3** *v/t order* ōgoe de iu 大声で言う
♦**shout at** … o donaru …を怒鳴る
shouting *n* sakebigoe 叫び声
shove 1 *n* hitooshi ひと押し **2** *v/t & v/i* osu 押す
♦**shove in** *v/i* (*in line-up*) tsukkomu 突っ込む
♦**shove off** *v/i* F (*go away*) dete iku 出て行く
shovel *n* shaberu シャベル
show 1 *n* THEA, TV shō ショー; (*display*) hyōgen 表現; ***on ~*** (*at exhibition*) tenjichū 展示中; ***it's all done for ~*** *pej* zenbu misekake dake de aru 全部見せかけだけである **2** *v/t passport, ticket* miseru 見せる; *interest, emotion* arawasu 表す; (*at exhibition*) tenji suru 展示する; *movie* jōei suru 上映する; ***~ X to Y*** Y ni X o miseru YにXを見せる **3** *v/i* (*be visible*) mieru 見える; (*of movie*) jōei sareru 上映される; ***does it ~?*** wakaru わかる
♦**show off 1** *v/t skills* … o miseru …を見せる **2** *v/i pej* misebirakasu 見せびらかす
♦**show up 1** *v/t faults etc* … o abaku …を暴く; ***don't show me up in public*** mina no mae de haji o kakasenaide 皆の前で恥をかかせないで **2** *v/i* (*arrive*) arawareru 現れる; (*be visible*) mieru 見える
show business geinōkai 芸能界
showdown taiketsu 対決
shower 1 *n* (*of rain*) niwaka-ame にわか雨; (*to wash*) shawā シャワー; ***take a ~*** shawā o abiru シャワーを浴びる **2** *v/i* shawā o abiru シャワーを浴びる **3** *v/t*: ***~ X with compliments / praise*** X o homechigiru Xをほめちぎる
shower cap shawā-kyappu シャワーキャップ; **shower curtain** shawā-kāten シャワーカーテン; **showerproof** *adj* bōsui (no) 防水(の)
show jumping shōgaihietsu 障害飛越
show-off unubore-ya うぬぼれや
showroom shōrūmu ショールーム; ***in ~ condition*** hotondo shinpin no jōtai de ほとんど新品の状態で

showy *jacket, behavior* hade (na) 派手(な)
shred 1 *n* (*of paper etc*) danpen 断片; (*of evidence etc*) kirehashi 切れ端 **2** *v/t paper* shureddā ni kakeru シュレッダーにかける; (*in cooking*) mijingiri ni suru みじん切りにする
shredder shureddā シュレッダー
shrewd nukeme no nai 抜け目のない
shriek 1 *n* himei 悲鳴 **2** *v/i* himei o ageru 悲鳴をあげる
shrimp ebi えび
shrine jinja 神社
shrink *v/i* (*of material*) chijimu 縮む; (*of support etc*) heru 減る
shrink-wrap rappu de tsutsumu ラップで包む
shrink-wrapping (*process*) rappu-hōsō ラップ包装; (*material*) rappu ラップ
shrivel (*of skin*) shiwa ga yoru しわがよる; (*of material*) chijimu 縮む
shrub kanboku かん木
shrubbery uekomi 植え込み
shrug 1 *n* kata o sukumeru koto 肩をすくめること **2** *v/t & v/i*: **~ (*one's shoulders*)** kata o sukumeru 肩をすくめる
shudder 1 *n* (*of fear, disgust*) miburui 身震い; (*of earth etc*) yure 揺れ **2** *v/i* (*with fear, disgust*) furueru 震える; (*of earth, building*) yureru 揺れる
shuffle 1 *v/t cards* kiru 切る **2** *v/i* (*in walking*) ashi o hikizutte aruku 足を引きずって歩く
shun sakeru さける
shut 1 *v/t* shimeru 閉める **2** *v/i* shimaru 閉まる; ***they were ~*** shimatte iru 閉まっている
♦ **shut down 1** *v/t business* … o heisa suru …を閉鎖する; *computer* … o shūryō suru …を終了する **2** *v/i* (*of business*) heisa ni naru 閉鎖になる; (*of computer*) shūryō suru 終了する
♦ **shut up** *v/i* (*be quiet*) damaru 黙る; ***~!*** damare 黙れ
shutter (*on window,* PHOT) shattā シャッター
shuttle *v/i* ōfuku suru 往復する
shuttlebus shatoru-basu シャトルバス; **shuttlecock** SP shatoru シャトル; **shuttle service** orikaeshi-unten 折返し運転
shy hazukashigari (no) 恥ずかしがり(の)
shyness uchiki 内気
Siamese twins shamu-sōseiji シャム双生児
sick byōki (no) 病気(の); *sense of humor* burakku yūmoa ブラックユーモア; *society* kusatta 腐った; ***I'm going to be ~*** (*vomit*) hakisō desu 吐きそうです; ***be ~ of*** (*fed up with*) … ni unzari suru …にうんざりする
sicken 1 *v/t* (*disgust*) mukatsukaseru むかつかせる **2** *v/i* byōki ni naru 病気になる; ***be ~ing for*** … no shōjō o shimesu …の症状を示す
sickening fukai (na) 不快(な)
sickle kama かま
sick leave byōketsu 病欠; ***be on ~*** byōketsuchū (no) 病欠中(の)
sickly *person* byōjaku (na) 病弱(な); *color* aojiroi 青白い
sickness byōki 病気
side *n* (*of box, house*) sokumen 側面; (*of room, field*) gawa 側; (*of mountain*) sanpuku 山腹; (*of person*) waki わき; SP chīmu チーム; ***take ~s*** (*favor one side*) mikata o suru 味方をする; ***take ~s with*** … o shiji suru …を支持する; ***I'm on your ~*** watashi wa anata no mikata desu 私はあなたの味方です; ***~ by ~*** narande 並んで; ***at the ~ of the road*** rokata ni 路肩に; ***on the big / small ~*** sukoshi ōkii / chiisai 少し大きい/小さい
♦ **side with** … no mikata o suru …の味方をする
sideboard shokkidana 食器棚; **side dish** tsukeawase 付け合わせ; **side effect** fukusayō 副作用; **sidelight** MOT saidoraito サイドライト; **sideline 1** *n* fukugyō 副業 **2** *v/t*: ***feel ~d*** hazusareta ki ga suru はずされた気がする; **side street** wakimichi わき道; **sidetrack**: ***get***

~ed yokomichi ni soreru 横道にそれる; **sidewalk** hodō 歩道; **sidewalk café** kafeterasu カフェテラス; **sideways** *adv* yokomuki ni 横向きに

siege hōi 包囲; ***lay ~ to*** … o hōi-kōgeki suru …を包囲攻撃する

sieve *n* furui ふるい

sift *v/t corn, ore* furui ni kakeru ふるいにかける; *data* genmitsu ni shiraberu 厳密に調べる

♦**sift through** *data* … o genmitsu ni shiraberu …を厳密に調べる

sigh 1 *n* tameiki ため息; ***heave a ~ of relief*** hotto tameiki o tsuku ほっとため息をつく **2** *v/i* tameiki o tsuku ため息をつく

sight *n* kōkei 光景; (*power of seeing*) shiryoku 視力; ***~s*** (*of city*) keshiki 景色; ***catch ~ of*** … o mitsukeru …を見つける; ***know by ~*** mishitte iru 見知っている; ***within ~ of*** mieru tokoro ni 見えるところに; ***out of ~*** mienai tokoro ni 見えないところに; ***what a ~ you are!*** kimi wa mirareta mono de wa nai yo きみは見られた物ではないよ; ***lose ~ of*** *objective etc* … o miushinau …を見失う

sightseeing kankō 観光; ***go ~*** kankō ni dekakeru 観光に出かける

sightseeing tour kankō-ryokō 観光旅行

sightseer kankō-kyaku 観光客

sign 1 *n* (*indication*) chōkō 兆候; (*road ~*) hyōshiki 標識; (*on shop, building*) hyōji 表示; ***it's a ~ of the times*** jidai no nagare desu 時代の流れです **2** *v/t document* … ni shomei suru …に署名する **3** *v/i* shomei suru 署名する

♦**sign up** *v/i* (*for course*) jukō-tetsuzuki o suru 受講手続きをする

signal 1 *n* aizu 合図; RAIL shingō 信号; ***be sending out all the right / wrong ~s*** tadashii / machigatta shingō o okuru 正しい/間違った信号を送る **2** *v/i* (*of driver*) aizu suru 合図する

signatory shomei-sha 署名者; (*to treaty*) chōin-sha 調印者

signature shomei 署名

signature tune tēma-ongaku テーマ音楽

signature seal inkan 印鑑

significance igi 意義

significant *event etc* jūyō (na) 重要(な); (*large*) kanari (no) かなり(の)

signify imi suru 意味する

sign language shuwa 手話

signpost annai-hyōshiki 案内標識

silence 1 *n* (*of place*) seijaku 静寂; (*of person*) chinmoku 沈黙; ***in ~*** *work, march* mugon de 無言で; ***~!*** shizuka ni 静かに **2** *v/t* damaraseru 黙らせる

silencer (*on gun*) shōon sōchi 消音装置

silent shizuka (na) 静か(な); *movie* musei (no) 無声(の); ***stay ~*** (*not comment*) genkyū shinai 言及しない

silent partner tōshi suru dake no shain 投資するだけの社員

silhouette *n* shiruetto シルエット

silicon shirikon シリコン

silicon chip shirikon chippu シリコンチップ

silicone shirikon シリコン

silk 1 *n* kinu 絹 **2** *adj shirt etc* kinu (no) 絹(の)

silly baka (na) ばか(な)

silver 1 *n* gin 銀 **2** *adj ring* gin (no) 銀(の); *hair* ginpatsu (no) 銀髪(の)

silver medal gin medaru 銀メダル

silver-plated gin mekki (no) 銀めっき(の)

similar ruiji shita 類似した

similarity ruiji 類似

simmer *v/i* (*in cooking*) torobi de torotoro niru とろ火でとろとろ煮る; (*with rage*) bakuhatsu sunzen de aru 爆発寸前である

♦**simmer down** shizumaru 静まる

simple (*easy*) kantan (na) 簡単(な); (*not very bright*) tanjun (na) 単純(な)

simplicity kantan-sa 簡単さ

simplify kantan ni suru 簡単にする

simplistic kantan ni shita 簡単にした

simply (*absolutely*) mattaku 全く; (*in a simple way*) tan ni 単に; ***it's ~ the best*** sore wa mattaku saikō desu それは全く最高です
simulate shimyurēto suru シミュレートする
simultaneous dōji (no) 同時(の)
simultaneously dōji ni 同時に
sin 1 *n* tsumi 罪 **2** *v/i* tsumi o okasu 罪を犯す
since 1 *prep* irai 以来; ***~ last week*** senshū irai 先週以来 **2** *adv* sore irai それ以来; ***I haven't seen him ~*** sore irai kare ni atte imasen それ以来彼に会っていません **3** *conj* (*expressions of time*) …shite irai …して以来; (*seeing that*) …dakara …だから; ***~ you left*** anata ga satte irai あなたが去って以来; ***~ you don't like it*** anata wa sore ga kirai dakara あなたはそれが嫌いだから
sincere seijitsu (na) 誠実(な)
sincerely seijitsu ni 誠実に; *hope* kokoro kara 心から
sincerity seijitsu-sa 誠実さ
sinful tsumibukai 罪深い
sing *v/t & v/i* utau 歌う
Singapore Shingapōru シンガポール
Singaporean 1 *adj* Shingapōru (no) シンガポール (の) **2** *n* (*person*) Shingapōru-jin シンガポール人
singe *v/t* kogasu 焦がす
singer kashu 歌手
single 1 *n* (*sole*) hitotsu dake (no) 一つだけ(の); (*not double*) hitoe no 一重(の); (*not married*) dokushin (no) 独身(の); ***there wasn't a ~ person there*** soko ni wa dare mo inakatta そこには誰も居なかった; ***in ~ file*** ichiretsu-jūtai de 一列縦隊で **2** *n* MUS shinguru-ban シングル盤; ***~s*** (*in tennis*) shingurusu シングルス
♦ **single out** (*choose*) … o erabu …を選ぶ; (*distinguish*) kubetsu suru 区別する
single-breasted shinguru (no) シングル(の); **single-handed 1** *adj* dokuryoku (no) 独力(の) **2** *adv* dokuryoku de 独力で; **single-minded** hitamuki (na) ひたむき(な); **single mother** shinguru-mazā シングルマザー; **single parent** kataoya (no) 片親(の); **single parent family** (*father only*) fushi katei 父子家庭; (*mother only*) boshi katei 母子家庭
singular GRAM **1** *adj* tansū (no) 単数(の) **2** *n* tansūkei 単数形; ***in the ~*** tansūkei (no) 単数形(の)
sinister ayashige (na) 怪しげ(な)
sink 1 *n* nagashi 流し **2** *v/i* (*of ship, object, sun*) shizumu 沈む; (*of interest rates, pressure etc*) ochikomu 落ち込む; ***he sank onto the bed*** kare wa beddo ni taorekonda 彼はベッドに倒れ込んだ **3** *v/t ship* shizumeru 沈める; *funds* tsugikomu つぎ込む
♦ **sink in** *v/i* (*of liquid*) shimikomu 染み込む; ***it still hasn't really sunk in*** mada jūbun ni rikai shite inai まだ充分に理解していない
sinner zainin 罪人
Sino-Japanese War (*1894-95*) Nisshin-sensō 日清戦争
sinusitis MED jōmyaku-dōen 静脈洞炎
sip 1 *n* hitokuchi 一口 **2** *v/t* sukoshi zutsu nomu 少しずつ飲む
sir (*to teacher*) sensei 先生; (*to customer*) okyaku-san お客さん; ***excuse me, ~*** chotto sumimasen ちょっとすみません
siren sairen サイレン
sirloin sāroin サーロイン
sister (*own, elder*) ane 姉; (*s.o. else's, elder*) onēsan お姉さん; (*own, younger*) imōto 妹; (*s.o. else's, younger*) imōtosan 妹さん; ***~s*** shimai 姉妹
sister-in-law (*older*) giri no onēsan 義理のお姉さん; (*younger*) giri no imōto 義理の妹; (*s.o. else's*) giri no imōtosan 義理の妹さん; (*talking to outsiders about one's own ~*) giri no ane 義理の姉
sit 1 *v/i* suwaru 座る **2** *v/t exam* ukeru 受ける
♦ **sit down** suwaru 座る
♦ **sit up** (*in bed*) okinaoru 起き直る;

(*straighten back*) kichin to suwaru きちんと座る; (*wait up*) okite iru 起きている
sitcom renzoku hōmu komedī 連続ホームコメディー
site 1 *n* basho 場所 **2** *v/t new offices etc* … no yōchi o sadameru …の用地を定める
sitting (*of committee, court*) kaikichū 会期中; (*for artist*) sesshon セッション; (*for meals*) shokuji-jikan 食事時間
sitting room ribingu-rūmu リビングルーム
situated: ***be*** ~ ichi shite iru 位置している
situation jōsei 情勢; (*of building etc*) ritchi-jōken 立地条件
six roku 六
sixteen jūroku 十六
sixteenth dai-jūroku (no) 第十六(の)
sixth 1 *adj* dai-roku (no) 第六(の) **2** *n* (*of month*) muika 六日
sixtieth dai-rokujū (no) 第六十(の)
sixty rokujū 六十
size ōki-sa 大きさ; (*of jacket, shoes*) saizu サイズ
♦ **size up** … o hyōka suru …を評価する
sizeable kanari ōki (na) かなり大き(な)
sizzle shūshū oto o tateru シュウシュウ音をたてる
skate 1 *n* sukēto スケート **2** *v/i* sukēto o suru スケートをする
skateboard *n* sukēto-bōdo スケートボード
skater sukētā スケーター
skating sukēto スケート
skeleton gaikotsu がい骨
skeleton key masutā-kī マスターキー
skeptic utagaibukai hito 疑い深い人
skeptical kaigiteki na 懐疑的(な)
skepticism gimon 疑問
sketch 1 *n* suketchi スケッチ; THEA shōhin 小品 **2** *v/t* shasei suru 写生する
sketchbook suketchi bukku スケッチブック
sketchy ōzappa (na) 大雑把(な)
ski 1 *n* sukī スキー **2** *v/i* sukī o suru スキーをする
skid 1 *n* surippu スリップ **2** *v/i* surippu suru スリップする
skier sukīyā スキーヤー
skiing sukī スキー
ski lift sukī-rifuto スキーリフト
skill gijutsu 技術
skilled jukuren (no) 熟練(の)
skilled worker jukuren-kō 熟練工
skillful jōzu (na) 上手(な)
skim *surface* hyōmen o kasumete tobu 表面をかすめて飛ぶ
♦ **skim off** *the best* … o erabitoru …を選び取る
♦ **skim through** *text* zatto me o tōsu ざっと目を通す
skimmed milk sukimu miruku スキムミルク
skimpy *account etc* fujūbun (na) 不十分(な); *little dress* mijikasugiru 短すぎる
skin 1 *n* hifu 皮膚 **2** *v/t* kawa o hagu 皮をはぐ
skin diving sukin daibingu スキンダイビング
skinny yaseta やせた
skin-tight karada ni pittari (no) 体にぴったり(の)
skip 1 *n* (*little jump*) sukippu スキップ **2** *v/i* sukippu suru スキップする **3** *v/t* (*omit*) tobasu 飛ばす
ski pole sukī stokku スキーストック
skipper NAUT senchō 船長; (*of team*) kyaputen キャプテン
skirt *n* sukāto スカート
ski run gerende ゲレンデ
ski tow sukītō スキートー
skull zugaikotsu 頭がい骨
sky sora 空
skylark hibari ひばり; **skylight** tenmado 天窓; **skyline** sukairain スカイライン; **skyscraper** chōkōsō-biru 超高層ビル
slab (*of stone*) sekiban 石版; (*of cake etc*) atsugiri 厚切り
slack *rope* yurui ゆるい; *discipline* tarunda たるんだ; *person* iikagen (na) いい加減(な); *work* fuchūi (na) 不注意(な); *period* kakki no

nai 活気のない

slacken *v/t rope* yurumeru 緩める; *pace* otosu 落とす

♦**slacken off** *v/i* (*of trading*) heru 減る; (*of pace*) ochiru 落ちる

slacks surakkusu スラックス

slam 1 *v/t door* batan to shimeru バタンと閉める **2** *v/i* (*of door etc*) batan to shimaru バタンと閉まる

♦**slam down** … o gachan to oku …をガチャンと置く

slander 1 *n* waruguchi 悪口 **2** *v/t* chūshō suru 中傷する

slang surangu スラング; (*of a specific group*) ingo 隠語

slant 1 *v/i* katamuku 傾く **2** *n* keisha 傾斜; (*given to a story*) mikata 見方

slanting naname (no) 斜め(の); *eyes* tsuriagatta つり上がった

slap 1 *n* (*blow*) hirateuchi 平手打ち **2** *v/t* pishatto utsu ピシャッと打つ

slash 1 *n* (*cut*) kirikizu 切り傷; (*in punctuation*) surasshu スラッシュ **2** *v/t skin etc* satto kiru さっと切る; *prices, costs* kirisageru 切り下げる; **~ *one's wrists*** tekubi o kiru 手首を切る

slate *n* surēto スレート

slaughter 1 *n* (*of animals*) tosatsu と殺; (*of people*) gyakusatsu 虐殺 **2** *v/t animal* tosatsu suru と殺する; *people* gyakusatsu suru 虐殺する

slave *n* dorei 奴隷

slay korosu 殺す

slaying (*murder*) satsujin 殺人

sleazy *bar, character* misuborashii みすぼらしい

sled(ge) *n* sori そり

sledge hammer hanmā ハンマー

sleep 1 *n* nemuru 眠る; ***go to ~*** neru 寝る; ***I need a good ~*** watashi ni wa tappuri no suimin ga hitsuyō desu 私にはたっぷりの睡眠が必要です; ***I couldn't get to ~*** nemurenakatta 眠れなかった **2** *v/i* nemuru 眠る

♦**sleep on** *v/t decision* … o yukkuri kangaeru …をゆっくり考える

♦**sleep with** (*have sex with*) … to sekkusu o suru …とセックスをする

sleeping bag nebukuro 寝袋; **sleeping car** shindai-sha 寝台車; **sleeping pill** suimin'yaku 睡眠薬

sleepless *night* nemurenai 眠れない

sleepwalker muyūbyō-sha 夢遊病者

sleepy *yawn* nemui 眠い; *town* kakki no nai 活気のない; ***I'm ~*** watashi wa nemui 私は眠い

sleet *n* mizore みぞれ

sleeve (*of jacket etc*) sode そで

sleeveless sodenashi (no) そでなし(の)

sleight of hand kōmyō na hayawaza 巧妙なはやわざ

slender *figure, arms* hossori shita ほっそりした; *chance, income, margin* wazuka (na) わずか(な)

slice 1 *n* hitokire ひときれ; *fig* (*of profits etc*) wakemae 分け前 **2** *v/t loaf etc* usuku kiru 薄く切る

sliced bread usugiri no pan 薄切りのパン

slick 1 *adj performance* subarashii 素晴らしい; *pej* (*cunning*) kuchi no umai 口のうまい **2** *n* (*of oil*) yumaku 油膜

slide 1 *n* (*for kids*) suberidai 滑り台; PHOT suraido スライド **2** *v/i* suberu 滑る; (*of exchange rate etc*) genshō suru 減少する **3** *v/t* suberaseru 滑らせる

sliding door hikido 引き戸; (*room partition in Japan*) fusuma ふすま; (*made of paper*) shōji しょうじ

slight 1 *adj* wazuka (na) わずか(な); *person, figure* kyasha (na) きゃしゃ(な); ***have a ~ headache*** sukoshi zutsū ga suru 少し頭痛がする; ***no, not in the ~est*** sukoshi mo…nai 少しも…ない **2** *n* (*insult*) bujoku 侮辱

slightly sukoshi 少し

slim 1 *adj* hossori shita ほっそりした; *chance* wazuka (na) わずか(な) **2** *v/i* daietto suru ダイエットする

slime nurunuru shita mono ぬるぬるした物

slimy *liquid* nebaneba shita ねばねばした; *person* pekopeko shita ペ

こぺこした
sling 1 *n* (*for arm*) sankaku-kin 三角巾 **2** *v/t* (*throw*) hōru ほうる
slip 1 *n* (*on ice etc*) surippu スリップ; (*mistake*) machigai 間違い; ***a ~ of paper*** ichimai no kamikire 一枚の紙切れ; ***a ~ of the tongue*** ukkari iu うっかり言う; ***give … the ~*** … o maku …をまく **2** *v/i* (*on ice etc*) suberu 滑る; (*decline*: *of quality etc*) teika suru 低下する; ***he ~ped out of the room*** kare wa kossori heya kara dete itta 彼はこっそり部屋から出ていった **3** *v/t* (*put*) suberikomaseru 滑り込ませる; ***he ~ped it into his briefcase*** (kare wa sore o) burīfukēsu ni suberikomaseta (彼はそれを)ブリーフケースに滑り込ませた
♦**slip away** (*of time*) sugiru 過ぎる; (*of opportunity*) kiesaru 消え去る; (*die*) shizuka ni iki o hikitoru 静かに息を引き取る
♦**slip off** *v/t coat* … o nugu …を脱ぐ
♦**slip out** *v/i* (*go out*) nukedasu 抜け出す
♦**slip up** *v/i* (*make mistake*) machigau 間違う
slipped disc tsuikanban herunia つい間板ヘルニア
slipper heyabaki 部屋ばき
slippery suberiyasui 滑りやすい
slipshod zonzai (na) ぞんざい(な)
slit 1 *n* (*tear*) sakeme 裂け目; (*hole*) sukima すき間; (*in skirt*) suritto スリット **2** *v/t* kirihiraku 切り開く
slither *v/i* zuruzuru suberu ずるずる滑る
slobber *v/i* yodare o tarasu よだれを垂らす
slogan surōgan スローガン
slop *v/t* kobosu こぼす
slope 1 *n* katamuki 傾き; (*of mountain*) sanpuku 山腹; ***be built on a ~*** shamen ni taterarete iru 斜面に建てられている **2** *v/i* naname ni naru 斜めになる; ***the road ~s down to the sea*** dōro wa umi no hō e kudarizaka ni natte iru 道路は海の方へ下り坂になっている
sloppy *work, editing* zusan (na) ずさん(な); (*in dressing*) darashinai だらしない; (*too sentimental*) kanshōteki (na) 感傷的(な)
sloshed F (*drunk*) yopparatta 酔っ払った
slot *n* tōnyūguchi 投入口; (*in schedule*) jikantai 時間帯
♦**slot in 1** *v/t* … o hamekomu …をはめ込む **2** *v/i* hairu 入る
slot machine (*for vending*) jidōhanbai-ki 自動販売機; (*for gambling*) surotto mashin スロットマシン
slouch *v/i* maekagami ni naru 前かがみになる
slovenly darashinai だらしない
slow osoi 遅い; ***be ~*** (*of clock*) okurete iru 遅れている
♦**slow down 1** *v/t* … o okuraseru …を遅らせる; *traffic* supīdo o otosaseru スピードを落とさせる **2** *v/i* osoku naru 遅くなる; ***the doctor told her to ~*** oisha-san wa kanojo ni yukkuri suru yō ni itta お医者さんは彼女にゆっくりするように言った
slowdown (*in production*) gensan 減産
slow motion: ***in ~*** surō mōshon de スローモーションで
slug *n* (*animal*) namekuji なめくじ
sluggish kanman (na) 緩慢(な)
slum *n* suramugai スラム街
slump 1 *n* (*in trade*) fukeiki 不景気 **2** *v/i* (*economically*) bōraku suru 暴落する; (*collapse*: *of person*) dosun to taoreru ドスンと倒れる
slur 1 *n* (*on s.o.'s character*) chūshō 中傷 **2** *v/t words* mogomogo iu もごもご言う
slurred *speech* fumeiryō (na) 不明りょう(な)
slush *n* handoke no yuki 半解けの雪; *pej* (*sentiment*) kanshōteki na hanashi 感傷的な話
slush fund fusei-shikin 不正資金
slut darashinai onna だらしない女
sly zurui ずるい; ***on the ~*** kossori to こっそりと

smack 1 *n* hirateuchi 平手打ち **2** *v/t child* pishatto utsu ピシャッと打つ; *bottom* butsu ぶつ

small 1 *adj* chiisai 小さい **2** *n*: ***the ~ of the back*** koshi no kubireta bubun 腰のくびれた部分

small change kozeni 小銭; **small hours** yonaka 夜中; **smallpox** tennentō 天然痘; **small print** saiji-bubun 細字部分; **small talk** sekenbanashi 世間話

smart 1 *adj* (*elegant*) iki (na) いき(な); (*intelligent*) atama ga ii 頭がいい; *pace* hayai 速い; ***get ~ with*** … ni taishite namaiki ni naru …に対して生意気になる **2** *v/i* (*hurt*) uzuku うずく

smart card sumāto kādo スマートカード

♦**smarten up** *v/t* … o kogirei ni suru …をこぎれいにする

smash 1 *n* (*noise*) gachan to iu oto ガチャンという音; (*car crash*) shōtotsu 衝突; (*in tennis*) sumasshu スマッシュ **2** *v/t* (*break*) mechamecha ni kowasu めちゃめちゃに壊す; (*hit*) kyōda suru 強打する; ***~ to pieces*** … o konagona ni suru …を粉々にする **3** *v/i* (*break*) konagona ni naru 粉々になる; ***the driver ~ed into …*** untenshu wa … ni tsukkon de itta 運転手は…に突っ込んでいった

smash hit F dai hitto 大ヒット

smashing F subarashii 素晴らしい

smattering: ***I have a ~ of Chinese*** watashi wa Chūgoku-go o sukoshi kajitta 私は中国語を少しかじった

smear 1 *n* (*of ink etc*) shimi 染み; MED tofu-kensa 塗布検査; (*on character*) chūshō 中傷 **2** *v/t paint etc* … ni nuritsukeru …に塗り付ける; *character* chūshō suru 中傷する

smear campaign chūshō gassen 中傷合戦

smell 1 *n* nioi におい; ***it has no ~*** nioi ga shinai においがしない; ***sense of ~*** shūkaku 臭覚 **2** *v/t* nioi ga suru においがする **3** *v/i* (*unpleasantly*) niou におう; (*sniff*) nioi o kagu においをかぐ; ***what does it ~ of?*** nan no nioi ga shimasu ka 何のにおいがしますか; ***you ~ of beer*** bīru no nioi ga suru ビールのにおいがする

smelly kusai くさい

smile 1 *n* hohoemi ほほ笑み **2** *v/i* hohoemu ほほ笑む

♦**smile at** … ni hohoemu …にほほ笑む

smirk 1 *n* niyaniya-warai にやにや笑い **2** *v/i* niyaniya-warau にやにや笑う

smog sumoggu スモッグ

smoke 1 *n* kemuri 煙; ***have a ~*** tabako o suu たばこを吸う **2** *v/t cigarettes* suu 吸う; *bacon* ibusu いぶす **3** *v/i* tabako o suu たばこを吸う; ***I don't ~*** watashi wa tabako o suwanai 私はたばこを吸わない

smoker (*person*) kitsuen-ka 喫煙家

smoking kitsuen 喫煙; ***no ~*** kin'en 禁煙

smoking compartment RAIL kitsuen-sha 喫煙車

smoky *room, air* kemui 煙い

smolder (*also fig*) kusuburu くすぶる

smooth 1 *adj surface, skin, sea* nameraka (na) なめらか(な); *ride* shizuka (na) 静か(な); *transition* junchō (na) 順調(な); *pej*: *person* oseji no umai お世辞のうまい **2** *v/t hair* nadetsukeru なでつける

♦**smooth down** (*with sandpaper etc*) nameraka ni suru なめらかにする

♦**smooth out** *paper, cloth* … o nobasu …をのばす

♦**smooth over**: ***smooth things over*** kaiketsu suru 解決する

smother *flames* … ni …o kabusete kesu …に…をかぶせて消す; *person* chissoku saseru 窒息させる; ***~ with kisses*** … ni kisu o abiseru …にキスを浴びせる

smudge 1 *n* shimi 染み **2** *v/t* yogosu 汚す

smug hitoriyogari (no) 独りよがり(の)

smuggle *v/t* mitsuyu suru 密輸する

smuggler mitsuyu-gyōsha 密輸業者

smuggling mitsuyu 密輸
smutty *joke, sense of humor* waisetsu (na) わいせつ(な)
snack *n* keishoku 軽食
snack bar keishokudō 軽食堂
snag (*problem*) shōgai 障害
snail katatsumuri かたつむり
snake *n* hebi 蛇
snap 1 *n* patan to iu oto パタンという音; PHOT sunappu shashin スナップ写真 **2** *v/t* (*break*) pokin to oru ぽきんと折る; (*say sharply*) kamitsuku かみつく **3** *v/i* (*break*) pokin to oreru ぽきんと折れる **4** *adj decision* kyū (na) 急(な)
♦ **snap up** *bargain* … o tobitsuite kau …を飛びついて買う
snappy *person, mood* kamitsukisō (na) かみつきそう(な); *decision, response* hayai 速い; (*elegant*) shareta しゃれた
snapshot snappu shashin スナップ写真
snarl 1 *n* (*of dog*) unari うなり **2** *v/i* ha o mukidashite unaru 歯をむき出してうなる
snatch 1 *v/t* (*steal*) hittakuru ひったくる; (*kidnap*) yūkai suru 誘拐する **2** *v/i* hittakuru ひったくる
snazzy iki (na) 粋(な)
sneak 1 *v/t* (*remove, steal*) kossori toru こっそりとる; **~ *a glance at*** … o nusumimi ru …を盗み見る **2** *v/i*: **~ *into the room / out of the room*** kossori heya ni hairu / heya o deru こっそり部屋に入る/部屋を出る
sneakers sunīkā スニーカー
sneaking: ***have a ~ suspicion that …*** … o hisoka ni utagatte iru …をひそかに疑っている
sneaky F (*crafty*) inken (na) 陰険(な)
sneer 1 *n* reishō 冷笑 **2** *v/i* azawarau あざ笑う
sneeze 1 *n* kushami くしゃみ **2** *v/i* kushami o suru くしゃみをする
sniff 1 *v/i* (*to clear nose*) hana o susuru はなをすする; (*of dog*) kunkun kagu くんくんかぐ **2** *v/t* (*smell*) nioi o kagu においをかぐ
sniper sogekihei 狙撃兵
snitch F **1** *n* (*telltale*) tsugeguchi-ya 告げ口屋 **2** *v/i* tsugeguchi suru 告げ口する
snob kidori-ya 気取り屋
snobbish kidotta 気取った
snooker biriyādo ビリヤード
♦ **snoop around** hisoka ni nozokimawaru ひそかにのぞき回る
snooty gōman (na) ごう慢(な)
snooze 1 *n* inemuri 居眠り; ***have a ~*** inemuri suru 居眠りする **2** *v/i* inemuri suru 居眠りする
snore *v/i* ibiki o kaku いびきをかく
snoring *n* ibiki いびき
snorkel shunōkeru シュノーケル
snort *v/i* (*of bull, horse*) hana o narasu 鼻を鳴らす; (*of person: disdainfully*) fun to hana o narasu ふんと鼻を鳴らす
snout (*of pig, dog*) hana 鼻
snow 1 *n* yuki 雪 **2** *v/i* yuki ga furu 雪が降る
♦ **snow under**: ***be snowed under with …*** … de totemo isogashii …でとても忙しい
snowball yukidama 雪玉; **snowbound** yuki ni tojikomerareta 雪に閉じ込められた; **snow chains** MOT chēn チェーン; **snowdrift** yuki no fukidamari 雪の吹きだまり; **snowdrop** matsuyukisō まつゆきそう; **snowflake** yuki no hitohira 雪のひとひら; **snowman** yukidaruma 雪だるま; **snowplow** josetsuki 除雪機; **snowstorm** fubuki 吹雪
snowy *weather* yuki no ōi 雪の多い; *roads, hills* yuki no tsumotta 雪の積もった
snub 1 *n* bujoku 侮辱 **2** *v/t* bujoku suru 侮辱する
snub-nosed shishibana (no) しし鼻(の)
snug atatakaku kokochi yoi 暖かく心地よい; (*tight-fitting*) pittari atta ぴったり合った
♦ **snuggle down** kokochi yoku yokotawaru 心地よく横たわる
♦ **snuggle up to** … ni yorisou …に

寄り添う

so 1 *adv*: **~ *hot* / *cold*** totemo atsui / samui ここはとても暑い/寒い; ***not ~ much*** amari あまり; **~ *much better* / *easier*** zutto yoi / kantan na ずっと良い/簡単な; ***eat* / *drink* ~ *much*** takusan tabeta / nonda たくさん食べた/飲んだ; **~ *many …*** takusan … たくさん…; **~ *am* / *do I*** watashi mo sō desu わたしもそうです; **~ *is she* / *does she*** kanojo mo sō desu 彼女もそうです; ***and ~ on*** … nado …など **2** *pron*: ***I hope ~*** sō kibō shimasu そう希望します; ***I think ~*** sō omoimasu そう思います; ***you didn't tell me – I did ~*** watashi ni iwanakatta deshō - watashi wa sō iimashita 私に言わなかったでしょう 私はそういいました; ***50 or ~*** daitai gojussai 大体五十歳 **3** *conj* (*for that reason*) sono kekka その結果; (*in order that*) node ので; ***and ~ I missed the train*** sō iu wake de densha ni noriokuremashita そういう訳で電車に乗り遅れました; **~ (*that*) *I can come too*** …nanode watashi mo koraremasu …なので私も来られます; **~ *what?*** sore de それで

soak *v/t* (*steep*) tsukeru つける; (*of water, rain*) nurasu ぬらす

♦**soak up** *liquid* … o kyūshū suru …を吸収する

soaked bishonure ni natta びしょぬれになった

so-and-so F (*unknown person*) daresore 誰それ; (*annoying person*) aitsu あいつ

soap *n* (*for washing*) sekken 石けん

soap (opera) renzoku merodorama 連続メロドラマ

soapy *water* sekken darake (no) 石けんだらけ(の)

soar (*of rocket etc*) maiagaru 舞い上がる; (*of prices*) kyūjōshō suru 急上昇する

sob 1 *n* susurinaki すすり泣き **2** *v/i* nakijakuru 泣きじゃくる

sober (*not drunk*) shirafu (no) しらふ(の); (*serious*) majime (na) まじめ(な)

♦**sober up** yoi ga sameru 酔いが覚める

so-called (*referred to as*) iwayuru いわゆる; (*incorrectly referred to as*) nabakari (no) 名ばかり(の)

soccer sakkā サッカー

sociable shakōteki (na) 社交的(な)

social *adj* shakai (no) 社会(の); (*recreational*) shakō (no) 社交(の)

socialism shakai-shugi 社会主義

socialist 1 *adj* shakai-shugi (no) 社会主義(の) **2** *n* shakai-shugisha 社会主義者

socialize tsukiau 付き合う

social work shakaifukushi-jigyō 社会福祉事業

social worker sōsharu-wākā ソーシャルワーカー

society shakai 社会; (*organization*) kyōkai 協会; (*informal club*) kurabu クラブ

sociology shakai-gaku 社会学

sock[1] kutsushita 靴下

sock[2] **1** *n* (*punch*) kyōda 強打 **2** *v/t* (*punch*) kyōda suru 強打する

socket ELEC soketto ソケット; (*of arm*) kataguchi 肩口; (*of eye*) ganka 眼か

soda (*~ water*) sōda ソーダ; (*ice-cream ~*) kurīmu sōda クリームソーダ; (*soft drink*) saidā サイダー

sofa sofa ソファ

sofa-bed sofabeddo ソファベッド

soft yawarakai 柔らかい; (*lenient*) yasashii 優しい; ***have a ~ spot for*** …ga daisuki da …が大好きだ

soft drink seiryō-inryōsui 清涼飲料水

soften 1 *v/t position* nanka suru 軟化する; *impact, blow* yawarageru 和らげる **2** *v/i* (*of butter, ice cream*) yawarakaku naru 柔らかくなる

softly shizuka ni 静かに

software sofuto ソフト

soggy mizubitashi (no) 水浸し(の); *pastry* betobeto shita べとべとした

soil 1 *n* (*earth*) tsuchi 土 **2** *v/t* yogosu 汚す

solar energy taiyō-enerugī 太陽エネルギー

solar panel taiyō-denchiban 太陽電池板
soldier gunjin 軍人
sole[1] *n* (*of foot*) ashi no ura 足の裏; (*of shoe*) kutsu no soko 靴の底
sole[2] *adj* yuiitsu (no) 唯一(の)
solely …dake …だけ
solemn (*serious*) genshuku (na) 厳粛(な); *promise* shinken (na) 真剣(な)
solid *adj* (*hard*) katai 固い; (*without holes*) sukima no nai すき間のない; *gold, silver* junsui (no) 純粋(の); (*sturdy*) ganjō (na) 頑丈(な); *evidence* kakko taru 確固たる; *support* shikkari shita しっかりした
solidarity kessoku 結束
solidify *v/i* katamaru 固まる
solitaire (*game*) hitori toranpu 一人トランプ
solitary *life* kodoku (na) 孤独(な); *walk* hitoridake (no) 一人だけ(の); (*single*) tatta hitori dake (no) たった一人だけ(の)
solitude kodoku 孤独
solo 1 *n* MUS dokusō 独奏 **2** *adj* tandoku (no) 単独(の)
soloist sorisuto ソリスト
soluble *substance* tokeru 溶ける; *problem* kaiketsu dekiru 解決できる
solution kaitō 解答; (*mixture*) yōeki 溶液
solve toku 解く
solvent *adj* (*financially*) shiharai-nōryoku no aru 支払能力のある
somber *dark* kurai 暗い; (*serious*) shinkoku (na) 深刻(な)
some 1 *adj* (*with countable nouns*) ikutsuka (no) 幾つか(の), sukoshi 少し; (*with uncountable nouns*) ikuraka (no) 幾らか(の), sukoshi 少し; ***~ people say that …*** …to itteru hito mo imasu …と言ってる人も居ます; ***would you like ~ water / cookies?*** (sukoshi) mizu / kukkī wa ikaga desu ka (少し)水は/クッキーはいかがですか; ***~ woman I met on the train*** densha de atta aru onna 電車で会ったある女 **2** *pron* (*for countable nouns*) ikutsuka (no) 幾つか(の), sukoshi 少し; (*for uncountable nouns*) ikuraka (no) 幾らか(の), sukoshi 少し; ***~ of my relatives think …*** … to omotte iru shinseki mo imasu …と思っている親戚もいます; ***~ of the group*** gurūpu no nanninka グループの何人か; ***would you like ~?*** sukoshi ikaga 少しいかが; ***give me ~*** sukoshi kudasai 少し下さい **3** *adv* (*a bit*) sukoshi 少し; ***we'll have to wait ~*** sukoshi matanakereba narimasen 少し待たなければなりません
somebody dareka 誰か
someday itsu no hi ka いつの日か
somehow (*by one means or another*) nantoka shite 何とかして; (*for some unknown reason*) nazeka なぜか
someone → ***somebody***
someplace → ***somewhere***
somersault 1 *n* tonbogaeri とんぼ返り **2** *v/i* tonbogaeri suru とんぼ返りする
something nanika 何か; ***would you like ~ to drink / eat?*** nanika nomimasen ka / tabemasen ka 何か飲みませんか/食べませんか; ***is ~ wrong?*** nanika okashii desu ka 何かおかしいですか
sometime sono uchi そのうち; ***~ last year*** kyonen no itsuka 去年のいつか
sometimes tokidoki 時々
somewhere 1 *adv* (*with verbs of being*) dokoka de どこかで; (*with verbs of activity*) dokoka ni どこかに **2** *pron* dokoka どこか
son musuko 息子
song uta 歌
songwriter sakushi-ka 作詞家
son-in-law giri no musuko 義理の息子
son of a bitch V kono yarō この野郎
soon (*in a short time*) mō sugu もうすぐ; (*a short time after*) sugu ni すぐに; ***how ~ can you be ready to leave?*** dono kurai de deru junbi ga dekimasu ka どのくらい

で出る準備ができますか; ***it's too ~ to say...*** ... o handan suru ni wa hayasugiru ...を判断するには早すぎる; ***as ~ as*** ... suru to sugu ni ... するとすぐに; ***as ~ as possible*** dekiru dake hayaku できるだけ早く; ***~er or later*** itsuka wa いつかは; ***the ~er the better*** hayakereba hayai hodo ii 早ければ早いほどいい

soot susu すす

soothe *person* nagusameru なぐさめる; *pain* yawarageru やわらげる

sophisticated *person, tastes* senren sareta 洗練された; *machine* kōdo (na) 高度(な)

sophomore ninensei 二年生

soprano *n* sopurano ソプラノ

sordid *affair, business* kitanai 汚い

sore 1 *adj* (*painful*) itai 痛い; F (*angry*) kizutsuku 傷つく; ***is it ~?*** itai desu ka 痛いですか **2** *n* kizuguchi 傷口

sorrow *n* kanashimi 悲しみ

sorry *sight* sabishisō (na) さびしそう(な); *day* kanashii 悲しい; ***(I'm) ~!*** (*apologizing*)sumimasen すみません; ***I'm ~*** (*regretting*) sumimasen ga すみませんが; ***I'm ~ but I can't help*** mōshiwake arimasen ga tetsudaemasen 申し訳ありませんが手伝えません ***I won't be ~ to leave here*** koko o saru no wa zannen dewa nai ここを去るのは残念ではない ***I feel ~ for her*** kanojo ni dōjō suru 彼女に同情する

sort 1 *n* shurui 種類; ***~ of ...*** F chotto... ちょっと...; ***is it finished? – ~ of*** F owarimashita ka – daitai 終わりましたか – だいたい **2** *v/t* bunrui suru 分類する; COMPUT sōto suru ソートする

♦ **sort out** *papers* ... o seiri suru ...を整理する; *problem* kaiketsu suru 解決する

so-so *adv* māmā まあまあ

soul REL tamashii 魂; *fig* (*of nation etc*) seishin 精神; (*character*) kyarakutā キャラクター; (*person*) hito 人

sound[1] **1** *adj* (*sensible*) kenjitsu (na) 堅実(な); (*healthy*) kenzen (na) 健全(な) **2** *adv*: ***~ asleep*** gussuri nemutte ぐっすり眠って

sound[2] **1** *n* oto 音; (*noise*) sawagi 騒ぎ **2** *v/t* (*pronounce*) hatsuon suru 発音する; MED chōshin suru 聴診する; ***~ one's horn*** kurakushon o narasu クラクションを鳴らす **3** *v/i*: ***that ~s interesting*** sore wa omoshiro-sō da それはおもしろそうだ; ***that ~s like a good idea*** ii aidea no yō da いいアイデアのようだ; ***she ~ed happy*** kanojo wa shiawase-sō datta 彼女は幸せそうだった

soundly *sleep* gussuri ぐっすり; *beaten* koppidoku こっぴどく

soundproof *adj* bōon (no) 防音(の)

soundtrack saundotrakku サウンドトラック

soup sūpu スープ; ***clear ~*** sumashijiru すまし汁

soup bowl sūpu-zara スープ皿

sour *adj apple, orange* suppai 酸っぱい; *milk* suppaku natta 酸っぱくなった; *expression, comment* ijiwaru (na) 意地悪(な)

source *n* minamoto 源; (*of river*) suigenchi 水源地; (*person*) jōhōgen 情報源

south 1 *adj* minami (no) 南(の) **2** *n* minami 南; (*of country*) nanbu 南部; ***to the ~ of ...*** ... no minami ni ...の南に **3** *adv* minami ni 南に

South Africa Minami-Afurika 南アフリカ; **South African 1** *adj* Minami-Afurika (no) 南アフリカ(の) **2** *n* Minami-Afurika-jin 南アフリカ人; **South America** Nanbei 南米; **South American 1** *adj* Nanbei (no) 南米(の) **2** *n* Nanbei-jin 南米人; **southeast 1** *n* nantō 南東 **2** *adj* nantō (no) 南東(の) **3** *adv* nantō ni 南東に; ***it's ~ of ...*** ... no nantō desu ...の南東です; **Southeast Asia** Tōnan Ajia 東南アジア; **Southeast Asian** *adj* Tōnan Ajia (no) 東南アジア(の); **southeastern** nantōbu (no) 南東部(の)

southerly *adj* minami kara (no) 南から(の)
southern nanbu (no) 南部(の)
South Korea Kankoku 韓国; **South Korean 1** *adj* Kankoku (no) 韓国(の) **2** *n* Kankoku-jin 韓国人
southward *adv* nanpō e 南方へ
southwest 1 *n* nansei 南西 **2** *adj* nansei (no) 南西(の) **3** *adv* nansei ni 南西に; ***it's ~ of …*** … no nansei desu …の南西です
southwestern nanseibu (no) 南西部(の)
souvenir o-miyage おみやげ
sovereign *adj state* dokuritsu shita 独立した
sovereignty (*of state*) shuken 主権
Soviet Union Sobieto-renpō ソビエト連邦
sow¹ *n* (*pig*) mesubuta 雌豚
sow² *v/t seeds* maku まく
soy bean daizu 大豆
soy sauce shōyu しょうゆ
space *n* (*outer ~*) uchū-kūkan 宇宙空間; (*area*) yohaku 余白; (*room*) basho 場所
♦**space out** kankaku o oku 間隔を置く
spacebar COMPUT supēsu-bā スペースバー; **spaceship** uchū-sen 宇宙船; **space shuttle** supēsu-shatoru スペースシャトル; **space station** uchū-sutēshon 宇宙ステーション; **spacesuit** uchū-fuku 宇宙服
spacious hirobiro to shita 広々とした
spade sukoppu スコップ; **~s** (*in cards*) supēdo スペード
Spain Supein スペイン
span *v/t* … ni oyobu …に及ぶ; (*of bridge*) … ni kakatte iru …かかっている
Spaniard Supein-jin スペイン人
Spanish 1 *adj* Supein (no) スペイン(の) **2** *n* (*language*) Supein-go スペイン語
spank … no shiri o tataku …のしりをたたく
spare 1 *v/t time, money* ataeru 与える; (*do without*) …nashi de sumasu …なしで済ます; ***can you ~ me 5 minutes*** watashi ni gofun kurenai 私に五分くれない; ***can you ~ me $50?*** gojū doru kashite kurenai 五十ドル貸してくれない; ***can you ~ the time?*** jikan o tsukureru 時間をつくれる; ***there are 5 to ~*** yobun ni goko arimasu 余分に五個あります **2** *adj* yobi (no) 予備(の) **3** *n* (*part*) kōkan-buhin 交換部品
spare ribs supearibu スペアリブ; **spare room** yobi no heya 予備の部屋; **spare time** yoka 余暇; **spare tire, spare wheel** supea taiya スペアタイヤ
spark *n* hibana 火花
sparkle *v/i* kagayaku 輝く
sparkling wine happō-wain 発泡ワイン
spark plug tenka-puragu 点火プラグ
sparrow suzume すずめ
sparse *vegetation* tenzai suru 点在する
sparsely: ***~ populated*** jinkō-mitsudo no hikui 人口密度の低い
spatter *v/t mud, paint* … ni hanekakeru …にはねかける
speak 1 *v/i* hanasu 話す; (*make a speech*) enzetsu suru 演説する; ***we're not ~ing (to each other)*** watashitachi wa (otagai ni) kuchi o kiiteinai 私達は(お互いに)口をきいていない; ***can I ~ to Charles – ~ing*** Chārusu-san wa irasshaimasu ka – watashi desu チャールスさんはいらっしゃいますかー 私です **2** *v/t foreign language* hanasu 話す; ***~ one's mind*** jibun no kangae o hakkiri iu 自分の考えをはっきり言う
♦**speak for** … o daiben suru …を代弁する
♦**speak out** sotchoku ni iken o noberu 率直に意見を述べる
♦**speak up** (*speak louder*) ōki na koe de hanasu 大きな声で話す
speaker (*at conference*) enzetsu-sha 演説者; (*orator*) yūben-ka 雄弁家; (*of sound system*) supīkā ス

ピーカー

spearmint supeamintо スペアミント

special tokubetsu (na) 特別(な)

specialist senmon-ka 専門家; MED senmon-i 専門医

♦**specialize in** … o senmon ni suru …を専門にする; *subject* … o senkō suru …を専攻する

specially → ***especially***

specialty tokushoku 特色; (*food*) jiman-ryōri 自慢料理

species shu 種

specific tokutei (no) 特定(の)

specifically toku ni 特に

specifications (*of machine etc*) shiyō 仕様

specify shitei suru 指定する; *details* meisai ni shirusu 明細に記す

specimen (*sample*) mihon 見本; MED hyōhon 標本

speck (*of dust, soot*) tsubu 粒

spectacle (*impressive sight*) supekutakuru スペクタクル

spectacular *adj profit, success* gekiteki (na) 劇的(な); *view, building* gōka (na) 豪華(な)

spectator kankyaku 観客

spectator sport miru supōtsu 見るスポーツ

spectrum *fig* han'i 範囲

speculate *v/i* okusoku suru 憶測する; FIN tōki suru 投機する

speculation okusoku 憶測; FIN tōki 投機

speculator FIN tōki-ka 投機家

speech (*address*) supīchi スピーチ; (*in play*) serifu せりふ; (*ability to speak*) hanasu nōryoku 話す能力; (*way of speaking*) hanashikata 話し方

speechless koe mo denai 声も出ない

speech defect gengo-shōgai 言語障害; **speech therapist** gengo-ryōhōshi 言語療法士; **speech writer** supīchi-raitā スピーチライター

speed 1 *n* haya-sa 速さ; (*of car, plane etc*) supīdo スピード; ***at a ~ of 150 mph*** maiji hyakugojū mairu no hayasa de 毎時百五十マイルの速さで **2** *v/i* isogu 急ぐ; (*drive too quickly*) ihan-sokudo de hashiru 違反速度で走る

♦**speed by** sugisaru 過ぎ去る

♦**speed up 1** *v/i* supīdo ga agaru スピードが上がる **2** *v/t* … no supīdo o ageru …のスピードを上げる

speedboat mōtābōto モーターボート

speedily subayaku 素早く

speeding *n* supīdo-ihan スピード違反

speeding fine supīdo-ihan no bakkin スピード違反の罰金

speed limit seigen-sokudo 制限速度

speedometer sokudo-kei 速度計

speedy hayai 速い

spell[1] *v/t & v/i* tsuzuru つづる

spell[2] *n* (*period of time*) sukoshi no aida 少しの間; ***I'll take a ~ at the wheel*** kōtai shite watashi ga unten shimasu 交替して私が運転します

spellbound miserareta 魅せられた; **spellcheck** COMPUT superu-chekku スペルチェック; ***do a ~ on …*** … ni superu-chekku o kakeru …にスペルチェックをかける; **spellchecker** COMPUT superu-chekkā スペルチェッカー

spelling tsuzuri つづり, superingu スペリング

spend *money* tsukau 使う; *time* sugosu 過ごす; ***don't ~ too much time on it*** sore ni jikan o kakesuginai de それに時間をかけ過ぎないで

spendthrift *n pej* rōhi-ka 浪費家

sperm seishi 精子; (*semen*) seieki 精液

sperm bank seishi-ginkō 精子銀行

sphere kyū 球; *fig* (*field*) bun'ya 分野; ***~ of influence*** eikyō no oyobu han'i 影響の及ぶ範囲

spice *n* (*seasoning*) kōshinryō 香辛料

spicy *food* kōshinryō no kiita 香辛料の利いた

spider kumo くも

spiderweb kumo no su くもの巣
spike *n* (*of railings*) kugi くぎ; (*of plant*) toge とげ; (*on shoe*) supaiku スパイク; (*of animal*) hari 針
spill 1 *v/t* kobosu こぼす **2** *v/i* koboreru こぼれる
spin[1] **1** *n* (*turn*) kaiten 回転 **2** *v/t* kaiten saseru 回転させる **3** *v/i* (*of wheel*) kaiten suru 回転する; ***my head is ~ning*** kurakura suru くらくらする
spin[2] *v/t wool, cotton* tsumugu 紡ぐ; *web* su o tsukuru 巣をつくる
♦ **spin around** (*of person, car*) kaiten suru 回転する
♦ **spin out** … o hikinobasu …を引き延ばす
spinach hōrensō ほうれん草
spinal sebone (no) 背骨(の)
spinal column sebone 背骨
spin doctor supōkusuman スポークスマン; **spin-dry** *v/t* dassui suru 脱水する; **spin-dryer** dassui-ki 脱水機
spine (*of person, animal*) sebone 背骨; (*of book*) se 背; (*on plant*) toge とげ; (*on hedgehog*) hari 針
spineless *fig* ikuji no nai 意気地のない
spin-off fukusanbutsu 副産物
spiral 1 *n* rasenkei ら旋形 **2** *v/i* (*rise quickly*) kyūjōshō suru 急上昇する
spiral staircase rasen kaidan ら旋階段
spire sentō せん塔
spirit *n* (*as opposed to body*) seishin 精神; (*of dead person*) rei 霊; (*energy*) katsuryoku 活力; (*courage*) kiryoku 気力; (*attitude*) keikō 傾向; ***we did it in a ~ of cooperation*** watashitachi wa kyōryoku no seishin de sore o shimashita 私達は協力の精神でそれをしました
spirited (*energetic*) seiryokuteki (na) 精力的(な)
spirit level suijunki 水準器
spirits[1] (*alcohol*) jōryūshu 蒸留酒
spirits[2] (*morale*) shiki 士気; ***be in good / poor ~*** kibun wa jōjō de aru / saiaku de aru 気分は上々である/最悪である
spiritual *adj* reiteki (na) 霊的(な)
spiritualism kōreisetsu 降霊説
spiritualist *n* kōreijutsu-sha 降霊術者
spit *v/i* (*of person*) tsuba o haku つばを吐く; ***it's ~ting with rain*** ame ga shitoshito futte iru 雨がしとしと降っている
♦ **spit out** *food etc* … o hakidasu …を吐き出す
spite *n* akui 悪意; ***in ~ of*** … ni mo kakawarazu …にもかかわらず
spiteful ijiwaru (na) 意地悪(な)
spitting image: ***be the ~ of*** … ni sokkuri de aru …にそっくりである
splash 1 *n* (*noise*) zabun to iu oto ザブンという音; (*small amount: of liquid, of color*) sukoshi (no) 少し(の) **2** *v/t person* mizu o tobichirasu 水を飛び散らす; *water, mud* hanekakeru 跳ねかける **3** *v/i* mizu o haneru 水を跳ねる; (*of water*) tobichiru 飛び散る
♦ **splash down** (*of spacecraft*) chakusui suru 着水する
♦ **splash out** taikin o tsukau 大金を使う
splendid gōka (na) 豪華(な)
splendor gōka-sa 豪華さ
splint *n* MED fukuboku 副木
splinter 1 *n* (*of wood, bone*) hahen 破片, toge とげ **2** *v/i* kudakeru 砕ける
splinter group bunretsu gurūpu 分裂グループ
split 1 *n* (*in material*) sakeme 裂け目; (*in wood*) wareme 割れ目; (*disagreement*) bunretsu 分裂; (*division, share*) bunpai 分配 **2** *v/t* (*damage*) saku 裂く; *logs* waru 割る; (*cause disagreement in*) bunretsu saseru 分裂させる; (*divide*) wakeru 分ける **3** *v/i* (*tear*) sakeru 裂ける; (*of wood etc*) wareru 割れる; (*disagree*) bunretsu suru 分裂する
♦ **split up** *v/i* (*of couple*) wakareru 別れる
split personality PSYCH nijū-

jinkaku 二重人格
splitting *adj*: **~ *headache*** atama ga waresō na zutsū 頭が割れそうな頭痛
spoil *v/t* dame ni suru だめにする; *child* amayakasu 甘やかす
spoilsport F za o shirakesaseru hito 座を白けさせる人
spoilt *adj child* amayaka sareta 甘やかされた; ***be ~ for choice*** erabu no ni komaru 選ぶのに困る
spoke (*of wheel*) supōku スポーク
spokesman supōkusu-man スポークスマン
spokesperson supōkusu-pāson スポークスパーソン
spokeswoman josei-supōkusuman 女性スポークスマン
sponge *n* suponji スポンジ
♦**sponge off** F ... ni takaru ...にたかる
sponger F takari たかり
sponsor 1 *n* (*for immigration, membership*) hoshōnin 保証人; (*of radio, TV program, event*) suponsā スポンサー **2** *v/t* (*for immigration, membership*) hoshōnin to naru 保証人となる; *program, event* suponsā ni naru スポンサーになる
sponsorship kōen 後援
spontaneous jihatsuteki (na) 自発的(な)
spooky F obake no desō (na) お化けの出そう(な)
spool *n* (*for thread*) itomaki 糸巻き; (*for film*) rīru リール
spoon *n* supūn スプーン
spoonfeed *fig* amayakasu 甘やかす
spoonful supūn-ippai スプーン一杯
sporadic barabara (no) バラバラ(の)
sport *n* supōtsu スポーツ
sporting *event* supōtsu (no) スポーツ(の); (*fair*) kōhei (na) 公平(な); (*generous*) kimae ga ii 気前がいい; ***a ~ gesture*** kōhei na kōi 公平な行為
sportscar supōtsu-kā スポーツカー; **sportscoat** supōtsu-jaketto スポーツジャケット; **Sports Day** Taiiku no hi 体育の日; **sports journalist** supōtsu-kisha スポーツ記者; **sportsman** supōtsu-man スポーツマン; **sports news** supōtsu-nyūsu スポーツニュース; **sports page** supōtsu-ran スポーツ欄; **sportswoman** supōtsu-ūman スポーツウーマン
sporty *person* supōtsu-zuki (na) スポーツ好き(な); *clothes* supōtī (na) スポーティー(な)
spot[1] (*pimple*) nikibi にきび; (*caused by measles etc*) dekimono できもの; (*part of pattern*) mizutama 水玉
spot[2] (*place*) basho 場所; ***on the ~*** (*in the place in question*) genba de 現場で; (*immediately*) sono ba de その場で; ***put X on the ~*** X o komaraseru Xを困らせる
spot[3] *v/t* (*notice, identify*) mitsukeru 見つける
spot check nukitori-kensa 抜き取り検査; ***carry out spot checks*** (*of customs, police*) nukiuchi-kensa o suru 抜き打ち検査をする
spotless seiketsu (na) 清潔(な)
spotlight *n* supottoraito スポットライト
spotted *fabric* mizutama moyō (no) 水玉模様(の)
spotty (*with pimples*) nikibidarake (no) にきびだらけ(の)
spouse *fml* haigū-sha 配偶者
spout 1 *n* sosogiguchi 注ぎ口 **2** *v/i* (*of liquid*) hotobashiru ほとばしる
sprain 1 *n* nenza ねんざ **2** *v/t* nenza suru ねんざする
sprawl *v/i* (*lying*) nesoberu ねそべる; (*sittin*) darashinaku suwaru だらしなく座る; (*of city*) zatsuzen to shita basho 雑然とした場所; ***send ~ing*** ... o jimen ni tatakinomesu ...を地面に叩きのめす
sprawling *city* mukeikaku ni hirogatta 無計画に広がった
spray 1 *n* (*of water*) shibuki しぶき; (*paint, for hair*) supurē スプレー **2** *v/t* furikakeru ふりかける; ***~ X with Y*** X ni Y o furikakeru XにYをふりかける
spraygun fukitsuke-ki 吹き付け機

spread 1 *n* (*of disease, religion etc*) hirogari 広がり; F (*big meal*) gochisō ごちそう **2** *v/t* (*lay*) hirogeru 広げる; *butter, jam* nuru 塗る; *news, rumor, disease* hiromeru 広める; *arms, legs* nobasu 伸ばす **3** *v/i* hiromaru 広まる; (*of butter*) nuru 塗る

spreadsheet COMPUT supureddoshīto スプレッドシート

spree: ***go*** (***out***) ***on a ~*** F bakasawagi suru ばか騒ぎする; ***go on a shopping ~*** shōdōgai o suru 衝動買いをする

sprightly kakushaku to shita かくしゃくとした

spring[1] *n* (*season*) haru 春

spring[2] *n* (*device*) bane ばね

spring[3] **1** *n* (*jump*) chōyaku 跳躍; (*stream*) izumi 泉 **2** *v/i* tobiagaru 飛び上がる; ***~ from*** …kara kite iru …からきている

springboard tobiita 飛び板; **spring chicken**: ***she's no ~*** F kanojo wa mō wakaku wa nai 彼女はもう若くはない; **spring-cleaning** ōsōji 大掃除; **springtime** shunki 春期; **Spring Equinox Day** Shunbun no hi 春分の日

springy *mattress, ground* danryokusei no aru 弾力性のある; *walk* keikai (na) 軽快(な)

sprinkle *v/t* furikakeru ふりかける; ***~ X with Y*** X ni Y o furikakeru XにYをふりかける

sprinkler supurinkurā スプリンクラー

sprint 1 *n* zenryoku-shissō 全力疾走; SP tankyori-kyōsō 短距離競走 **2** *v/i* zensokuryoku de hashiru 全速力で走る

sprinter SP tankyori-senshu 短距離選手

sprout 1 *v/i* (*of seed*) hatsuga suru 発芽する **2** *n*: me 芽; (***Brussels***) ***~s*** mekyabetsu 芽キャベツ

spruce *adj* kogirei (na) こぎれい(な)

spur *n fig* shigeki 刺激; ***on the ~ of the moment*** shōdōteki ni 衝動的に

♦**spur on** (*encourage*) … e to karitateru …へとかりたてる

spurt 1 *n* (*in race*) supāto スパート; ***put on a ~*** rasuto-supāto o kakeru ラストスパートをかける **2** *v/i* (*of liquid*) fukidasu 噴き出す

spy 1 *n* supai スパイ **2** *v/i* supai o suru スパイをする **3** *v/t* me ni suru 目にする

♦**spy on** … o saguru …をさぐる

squabble 1 *n* kenka けんか **2** *v/i* kenka suru けんかする

squalid fuketsu (na) 不潔(な)

squalor fuketsu-sa 不潔さ

squander *money* rōhi suru 浪費する

square 1 *adj* (*in shape*) seihōkei (no) 正方形(の); ***~ mile / yard*** heihō mairu / yādo 平方マイル/ヤード **2** *n* (*shape*) seihōkei 正方形; (*in town*) hiroba 広場; (*in board game*) masu ます; MATH nijō 二乗; ***we're back to ~ one*** furidashi ni modoru 振り出しに戻る

square root heihōkon 平方根

squash[1] *n* (*vegetable*) uririui うり類

squash[2] *n* (*game*) sukasshu スカッシュ

squash[3] *v/t* (*crush*) tsubureru つぶれる

squat 1 *adj* (*in shape*) zunguri shita ずんぐりした **2** *v/i* (*sit*) shagamu しゃがむ; (*illegally*) fuhō-kyojū suru 不法居住する

squatter fuhōkyojū-sha 不法居住者

squeak 1 *n* (*of mouse*) chūchū naku koe チューチュー鳴く声; (*of hinge*) kīkī kishimu oto キーキーきしむ音 **2** *v/i* (*of mouse*) chūchū naku チューチュー鳴く; (*of hinge, shoes*) kīkī naru キーキー鳴る

squeal 1 *n* kanakirigoe 金切り声; (*of brakes*) kī to kishimu oto キーときしむ音 **2** *v/i* kanakirigoe o ageru 金切り声をあげる; (*of brakes*) kishimu きしむ

squeamish sugu ni kimochi ga waruku naru すぐに気持ちが悪くなる

squeeze 1 *n*: ***he gave her hand a ~*** kare wa kanojo no te o gyutto nigirishimeta 彼は彼女の手をぎゅっと握り締めた **2** *v/t* (*press*) gyutto nigirishimeru ぎゅっと握り締める; (*remove juice from*) gyutto shiboru ぎゅっと絞る

♦ **squeeze in 1** *v/i* (*to a car etc*) tsumekomareru 詰め込まれる **2** *v/t* ... o oshikomu ...を押し込む

♦ **squeeze up** *v/i* (*to make space*) tsumeru 詰める

squid ika いか

squint *n* shashi 斜視

squirm (*wriggle*) karada o kuneraseru 体をくねらせる; (*in embarrassment*) mojimoji suru もじもじする

squirrel *n* risu りす

squirt 1 *v/t* fukikakeru 噴きかける **2** *n* F (*pej*) namaiki na yatsu 生意気なやつ

stab 1 *n*: ***have a ~ at*** F ... o chotto yatte miru ...をちょっとやってみる **2** *v/t person* sasu 刺す

stability antei 安定

stabilize 1 *v/t prices, currency, boat etc* antei saseru 安定させる **2** *v/i* (*of prices etc*) antei suru 安定する

stable[1] *n* (*for horses*) umagoya 馬小屋

stable[2] *adj* antei shita 安定した

stack 1 *n* (*pile*) yama 山; (*smoke~*) entotsu 煙突 **2** *v/t* tsumikasaneru 積み重ねる

stadium kyōgijō 競技場, sutajiamu スタジアム

staff *n* (*employees*) shain 社員; (*teachers, in government office*) shokuin 職員

staffer shain 社員; (*in government office*) shokuin 職員

staffroom (*in school*) shokuin-shitsu 職員室

stage[1] (*in life, project etc*) dankai 段階; (*of journey*) kōtei 行程

stage[2] **1** *n* THEA butai 舞台; ***go on the ~*** yakusha ni naru 役者になる **2** *v/t play* jōen suru 上演する; *demonstration, strike* okonau 行う

stage door gakuya-guchi 楽屋口

stagger 1 *v/i* yoromeku よろめく **2** *v/t* (*amaze*) bikkuri suru びっくりする; *coffee breaks etc* zurasu ずらす

staggering shinjirarenai 信じられない

stagnant *water* yodonda よどんだ; *economy* teitai shita 停滞した

stagnate (*of person, mind*) dareru だれる

stag party sutaggu-pātī スタッグパーティー

stain 1 *n* (*dirty mark*) shimi 染み; (*for wood*) chakushokuzai 着色剤 **2** *v/t* (*dirty*) yogosu 汚す; *wood* chakushoku suru 着色する **3** *v/i* (*of wine etc*) shimi ni naru 染みになる; (*of fabric*) yogoreru 汚れる

stained-glass window sutendo-gurasu no mado ステンドグラスの窓

stainless steel 1 *n* sutenresu ステンレス **2** *adj* sutenresu (no) ステンレス(の)

stain remover shiminuki 染み抜き

stair dan 段; ***the ~s*** kaidan 階段

staircase kaidan 階段

stake 1 *n* (*of wood*) kui くい; (*when gambling*) kakekin 賭け金; (*investment*) tōshi 投資; ***be at ~*** kiken ni sarasarete iru 危険にさらされている **2** *v/t tree* kui de sasaeru くいで支える; *money* kakeru 賭ける; *person* enjo suru 援助する

stale *bread* furuku natta 古くなった; *air* yodonda よどんだ; *news* furukusai 古くさい

stalemate (*in chess*) tezumari 手詰まり; *fig* kōchaku-jōtai こう着状態

stalk[1] *n* (*of plant*) kuki 茎; (*of fruit*) e 柄

stalk[2] *v/t* (*follow*) ou 追う; *person* tsukimatou つきまとう

stalker (*of person*) sutōkā ストーカー

stall[1] *n* (*at market*) yatai 屋台; (*for cow, horse*) kachikugoya no heya 家畜小屋の部屋

stall[2] **1** *v/i* (*of plane, engine*) enjin ga tomaru エンジンが止まる; (*of vehicle*) ensuto suru エンストする; (*play for time*) jikankasegi suru 時間稼ぎする **2** *v/t engine* tomeru 止める; *s.o.* hikitomeru 引き止める

stallion taneuma 種馬
stalwart *adj* shikkari shita しっかりした
stamina sutamina スタミナ
stammer 1 *n* domori どもり **2** *v/i* domoru どもる
stamp[1] **1** *n* (*for letter*) kitte 切手; (*device*) kokuin 刻印; (*mark made with device*) sutanpu スタンプ **2** *v/t document, passport* sutanpu o osu スタンプを押す
stamp[2] *v/t*: ***~ one's feet*** ashi o fumitsukeru 足を踏みつける
♦**stamp out** (*eradicate*) … o konzetsu suru …を根絶する
stampede *n* (*of cattle*) shūdan-bōsō 集団暴走; (*of people*) sattō 殺到
stance (*position*) shisei 姿勢
stand 1 *n* (*at exhibition*) sutando スタンド; (*witness ~*) shōnin-seki 証人席; (*support, base*) dai 台; ***take the ~*** LAW shōgen suru 証言する **2** *v/i* (*be situated*: *of person*) tatte iru 立っている; (*of object*) oite aru 置いてある; (*of building*) tatte iru 建っている; (*as opposed to sit*) tatsu 立つ; (*rise*) tachiagaru 立ち上がる; ***~ still*** jitto shite iru じっとしている; ***where do I ~ with you?*** watashi wa anata ni totte nani na no desu ka 私はあなたにとって何なのですか **3** *v/t* (*tolerate*) gaman suru 我慢する; (*put*) oku 置く; ***you don't ~ a chance*** anata ni wa chansu ga arimasen あなたにはチャンスがありません; ***~ one's ground*** ato e hikanai 後へ引かない
♦**stand back** sagaru 下がる
♦**stand by 1** *v/i* (*not take action*) bōkan suru 傍観する; (*be ready*) taiki suru 待機する **2** *v/t person* shiji suru 支持する; *decision* koshu suru 固守する
♦**stand down** (*withdraw*) mi o hiku 身を引く
♦**stand for** (*tolerate*) … o gaman suru …を我慢する; (*represent*) … no ryaku de aru …の略である
♦**stand in for** … no dairi o suru …の代理をする
♦**stand out** medatsu 目立つ
♦**stand up 1** *v/i* tachiagaru 立ち上がる **2** *v/t* F … ni machibōke o kuwasu …に待ちぼうけを食わす
♦**stand up for** … o mamoru …を守る
♦**stand up to** … ni tachimukau …に立ち向かう
standard 1 *adj* (*usual*) tsūrei no 通例(の) **2** *n* (*level of excellence*) suijun 水準; (*expectation*) kijun 基準; TECH kikaku 規格; ***be up to ~*** kijun ni tassuru 基準に達する; ***not be up to ~*** hyōjun ika de aru 標準以下である
standardize *v/t* kikakuka suru 規格化する
standard of living seikatsu-suijun 生活水準
standby: ***on ~*** (*for flight*) kyanseru machi (no) キャンセル待ち(の)
standby passenger kyanseru machi no kyaku キャンセル待ちの客
standing *n* (*in society etc*) chii 地位; (*repute*) hyōban 評判; ***a musician / politician of some ~*** chii no aru ongakuka / seijika 地位のある音楽家/政治家
standing order *Br* jidō-furikae 自動振替
standing room (*in theater*) tachimiseki 立ち見席; (*in bus*) tachiseki 立ち席
standoffish yosoyososhii よそよそしい; **standpoint** kanten 観点; **standstill**: ***be at a ~*** teishi shite iru 停止している; ***bring to a ~*** tomaru 止まる
staple[1] *n* (*foodstuff*) shuyō-shokuryōhin 主要食料品
staple[2] **1** *n* (*fastener*) hotchikisu no hari ホッチキスの針 **2** *v/t* tomeru とめる
staple diet shushoku 主食
staple gun sutēpuru-gan ステープルガン
stapler hotchikisu ホッチキス®
star 1 *n* hoshi 星; *fig* sutā スター **2** *v/t* (*of movie*) shuen saseru 主演させる **3** *v/i* (*in movie*) shuen suru 主演する

starboard *adj* ugen (no) 右げん(の)
stare 1 *n* gyōshi 凝視 **2** *v/i* jitto mitsumeru じっと見つめる; ***~ at*** … o niramu …をにらむ
starfish hitode ひとで
stark 1 *adj landscape* kōryō to shita 荒涼とした; *reminder, contrast etc* akarasama (na) 明らさま(な) **2** *adv*: ***~ naked*** maruhadaka de 丸裸で
starling mukudori むくどり
Stars and Stripes Seijōki 星条旗
start 1 *n* hajimari 始まり; ***get off to a good / bad ~*** (*in race, marriage, career*) kōchō na / fuchō na sutāto o kiru 好調な/不調なスタートをきる; ***from the ~*** hajime kara はじめから; ***well, it's a ~!*** sā, kore ga shuppatsuten desu さあ、これが出発点です **2** *v/i* hajimaru 始まる; (*of engine, car*) shidō suru 始動する; ***~ing from tomorrow*** ashita kara hajimaru 明日から始まる **3** *v/t* hajimeru 始める; *engine, car* shidō suru 始動する; *business* sōritsu suru 創立する; ***~ to do X*** X o hajimeru Xを始める
starter (*part of meal*) zensai 前菜; (*of car etc*) sutātā スターター
starting point (*for walk etc*) shuppatsu-chiten 出発地点; (*for discussion, thesis*) kiten 起点
starting salary hajime no kyūryō 初めの給料
startle odorokasu 驚かす
startling odoroku yō (na) 驚くよう(な)
starvation kiga 飢餓
starve *v/i* ueru 飢える; ***~ to death*** uejini suru 飢え死にする; ***I'm starving*** F onaka ga pekopeko desu おなかがペコペコです
state[1] **1** *n* (*of car, house etc*) jōtai 状態; (*part of country*) shū 州; (*country*) kokka 国家; ***the States*** Beikoku 米国 **2** *adj capital etc* shū (no) 州(の); *banquet etc* kōshiki (no) 公式(の)
state[2] *v/t* noberu 述べる
State Department Kokumushō 国務省
statement (*to police*) chinjutsu 陳述; (*announcement*) seimei 声明; (*bank ~*) kōzashūshi-hōkokusho 口座収支報告書; ***make a ~*** chinjutsu o suru 陳述をする; (*of government*) seimei o happyō suru 声明を発表する
state of emergency kinkyū-jitai 緊急事態
state-of-the-art *adj* saishin-gijutsu (no) 最新技術(の)
statesman ōmono seijika 大物政治家
state trooper shū-keisatsukan 州警察官
state visit kōshiki-hōmon 公式訪問
static (electricity) seidenki 静電気
station 1 *n* RAIL eki 駅; RAD, TV channeru チャンネル **2** *v/t guard etc* haichi suru 配置する; ***be ~ed at*** (*of soldier*) … ni chūton shite iru …に駐屯している
stationary tomatte iru 止まっている
stationery bunbōgu 文房具
stationery store bunbōgu-ten 文房具店
station wagon wagon-sha ワゴン車
statistical tōkeijō (no) 統計上(の)
statistically tōkeijō 統計上
statistics (*science*) tōkei-gaku 統計学; (*figures*) tōkei 統計
statue zō 像
Statue of Liberty Jiyū no Megamizō 自由の女神像
status (*position*) chii 地位; (*class*) mibun 身分
status symbol suteitasu-shinboru ステイタスシンボル
statute hōritsu 法律
staunch *adj* chūjitsu (na) 忠実(な)
stay 1 *n* taizai 滞在 **2** *v/i* (*in a place*) taizai suru 滞在する; (*in a condition*) … no mama de iru …のままでいる; ***I don't want to ~ at home all day*** ichinichijū ie ni itaku nai 一日中家にいたくない; ***~ in a hotel*** hoteru ni tomaru ホテルに泊まる; ***~ right there!*** soko o ugokanaide そこを動かないで; ***~ put*** todomaru とどまる
♦**stay away** chikazukanai 近づか

ない

♦**stay away from** … o sakeru …を避ける

♦**stay behind** inokoru 居残る

♦**stay up** (*not go to bed*) okite iru 起きている

steadily *improve etc* chakuchaku to 着々と

steady 1 *adj* (*not shaking*) shikkari shita しっかりした; (*regular*) antei shita 安定した; (*continuous*) chakujitsu (na) 着実(な) **2** *adv*: ***be going ~*** majime ni tsukiau まじめに付き合う; ***~ on!*** ochitsuite 落ち着いて **3** *v/t* antei saseru 安定させる

steak sutēki ステーキ

steal 1 *v/t money etc* nusumu 盗む **2** *v/i* (*be a thief*) nusumi o suru 盗みをする; (*move quietly*) kossori iku こっそり行く

stealthy hisoka (na) ひそか(な)

steam 1 *n* suijōki 水蒸気 **2** *v/t food* musu 蒸す

♦**steam up 1** *v/i* (*of window*) jōki de kumoru 蒸気で曇る **2** *v/t*: ***be steamed up*** F punpun okoru プンプン怒る

steamer (*for cooking*) mushiki 蒸し器

steam iron suchīmu-airon スチームアイロン

steel 1 *n* kōtetsu 鋼鉄 **2** *adj* kōtetsusei (no) 鋼鉄製(の)

steep[1] *adj hill etc* kewashii 険しい; F *prices* mechakucha takai めちゃくちゃ高い

steep[2] *v/t* (*soak*) hitasu 浸す

steeplechase (*in athletics*) shōgaibutsu-sō 障害物走

steer[1] *n* (*animal*) kyosei sareta koushi 去勢された子牛

steer[2] *v/t car, boat* unten suru 運転する; *person* … ni michibiku …に導く; *conversation* … ni mukeru …に向ける

steering MOT sutearingu ステアリング

steering wheel handoru ハンドル

stem[1] *n* (*of plant*) miki 幹; (*of pipe*) jiku 軸; (*of word*) gokan 語幹

♦**stem from** … ni kiin suru …に起因する

stem[2] *v/t* (*block*) tomeru 止める

stemware ashitsuki-gurasu 足付きグラス

stench akushū 悪臭

step 1 *n* (*pace*) ippo 一歩; (*stair*) dan 段; (*measure*) kōdō 行動; ***~ by ~*** sukoshi zutsu 少しずつ **2** *v/i* fumiireru 踏み入れる

♦**step down** (*from post etc*) jinin suru 辞任する

♦**step out** *v/i* (*go out for a short time*) chotto deru ちょっと出る

♦**step up** *v/t* (*increase*) … o suteppu-appu suru …をステップアップする

stepbrother (*son of stepfather*) ifu kyōdai 異父兄弟; (*son of stepmother*) ibo kyōdai 異母兄弟; **stepdaughter** mama-musume まま娘; **stepfather** mama-chichi まま父; **stepladder** kyatatsu 脚立; **stepmother** mama-haha まま母

stepping stone tobiishi 飛び石; *fig* fumidai 踏み台

stepsister (*daughter of stepfather*) ifu-shimai 異父姉妹; (*daughter of stepmother*) ibo-shimai 異母姉妹

stepson mama-musuko まま息子

stereo *n* sutereo ステレオ

stereotype *n* koteigainen 固定概念, sutereotaipu ステレオタイプ

sterile *woman, man* funin (no) 不妊(の); MED sakkin shita 殺菌した

sterilize *woman* hinin-shujutsu o suru 避妊手術をする; *equipment* sakkin suru 殺菌する

sterling *n* FIN Eikoku-tsūka 英国通貨

stern *adj* kibishii 厳しい

steroids suteroido ステロイド

stethoscope chōshinki 聴診器

Stetson® sutettoson ステットソン

stevedore kōwan-rōdōsha 港湾労働者

stew *n* shichū シチュー

steward (*on plane, ship*) suchuwādo スチュワード

stewardess (*on plane, ship*) suchuwādesu スチュワーデス

stick[1] *n* (*wood*) bōkire 棒切れ; (*of*

policeman) konbō こん棒; (*walking ~*) sutekki ステッキ; ***the ~s*** F inaka 田舎

stick² **1** *v/t* (*with adhesive*) haritsukeru はり付ける; F (*put*) tsukkomu 突っ込む **2** *v/i* (*jam*) ugokanaku naru 動かなくなる; (*adhere*) hittsuku 引っ付く

♦**stick around** F kono hen de urouro suru この辺でうろうろする

♦**stick by** F ... o misutenai ...を見捨てない

♦**stick out** *v/i* (*protrude*) tsukideru 突き出る; (*be noticeable*) medatsu 目立つ

♦**stick to** (*of sth sticky*) ... ni hittsuku ...に引っ付く; F *path, advice* ... kara hanarenai ...から離れない; F (*when following s.o.*) ... ni haritsuku ...に張り付く

♦**stick together** F kuttsuite iru くっ付いている

♦**stick up** *poster* ... o haritsukeru ...をはり付ける

♦**stick up for** F ... o aku made mamoru ...をあくまで守る

sticker sutekkā ステッカー

sticking plaster bansōkō ばんそうこう

stick-in-the-mud: ***he's such a ~!*** kare wa hontō ni hoshuteki da na 彼は本当に保守的だな

sticky *hands, surface* betobeto shita べとべとした; *label* nori no tsuita のりの付いた

stiff **1** *adj brush, leather* katai 堅い; *muscle, body* kowabatta こわばった; *mixture, paste* katai 固い; (*in manner*) katakurushii 堅苦しい; *drink* tsuyoi 強い; *competition, fine* kibishii 厳しい **2** *adv*: ***be scared ~*** F totemo bikkuri suru とてもびっくりする; ***be bored ~*** F totemo taikutsu suru とても退屈する

stiffen *v/i* kowabaru こわばる

♦**stiffen up** (*of muscle*) kataku naru 堅くなる

stifle *v/t yawn, laugh* osaeru 抑える; *criticism, debate* yokuatsu suru 抑圧する

stifling ikigurushii 息苦しい

stigma omei 汚名

stilettos (*shoes*) haihīru ハイヒール

still¹ **1** *adj* shizuka (na) 静か(な) **2** *adv* ugokanai de 動かないで; ***keep ~!*** ugokanai de 動かないで; ***stand ~!*** sono mama tatte ite そのまま立っていて

still² *adv* (*yet*) mada まだ; (*nevertheless*) sore demo それでも; ***do you ~ want it?*** mada sore ga hoshii desu ka まだそれが欲しいですか; ***she ~ hasn't finished*** kanojo wa mada owatte imasen 彼女はまだ終わっていません; ***she might ~ come*** kanojo wa mada kuru kamo shiremasen 彼女はまだ来るかもしれません; ***they are ~ my parents*** karera wa sore demo watashi no oya desu 彼らはそれでも私の親です; ***~ more*** sara ni さらに

stillborn: ***be ~*** shizan shita 死産した

stilted katakurushii 堅苦しい

stimulant kakuseizai 覚せい剤

stimulate *person* kōfun saseru 興奮させる; *growth, demand* shigeki suru 刺激する

stimulating shigekiteki (na) 刺激的(な)

stimulation shigeki 刺激

stimulus (*incentive*) shigeki 刺激

sting **1** *n* (*from bee, jellyfish*) mushisasare 虫刺され; ***I felt a ~ on my elbow*** watashi wa hiji ga mushi ni sasareta no o kanjimashita 私はひじが虫に刺されたのを感じました **2** *v/t* (*of bee, jellyfish*) sasu 刺す **3** *v/i* (*of eyes*) hirihiri suru ひりひりする; (*of scratch*) shimiru しみる

stinging *remark, criticism* gusatto kuru ぐさっとくる

stingy F kechi (na) けち(な)

stink **1** *n* akushū 悪臭; F (*fuss*) monchaku もん着; ***make a ~*** F monchaku o okosu もん着を起こす **2** *v/i* niou 臭う; F (*be very bad*) hidoi ひどい

stint *n* ninki 任期; ***do one's ~ in the army*** rikugun de ninki o tsutomeru 陸軍で任期を勤める

♦**stint on** … o kechiru …をけちる
stipulate jōken to suru 条件とする
stipulation jōken 条件
stir 1 *n*: ***cause a ~*** sawagi o okosu 騒ぎを起こす **2** *v/t soup etc* kakimazeru かき混ぜる **3** *v/i* (*of sleeping person*) miugoki suru 身動きする
♦**stir up** *crowd* hikiokosu 引き起こす; *bad memories* kokoro o kakimidasu 心をかき乱す
stir-crazy: ***be ~*** F ikarete ita いかれていた
stir-fry *v/t* tsuyobi de itameru 強火でいためる
stirring *music, speech* kandōteki (na) 感動的(な)
stitch 1 *n* (*in sewing*) hitohari 一針; (*in knitting*) hitoami 一編み; ***~es*** MED hōgō 縫合; ***she needed six ~es*** kanojo wa rokuhari mo nuwanakereba narimasen deshita 彼女は六針も縫わなければなりませんでした; ***take the ~es out*** basshi suru 抜糸する; ***have a ~*** wakibara ga itamu わき腹が痛む **2** *v/t* (*sew*) nuu 縫う
♦**stitch up** *wound* … o hōgō suru …を縫合する
stitching (*stitches*) nuime 縫い目
stock 1 *n* (*reserves*) shigen 資源; (COM: *in store*) shōhin 商品; (*animals*) kachikurui 家畜類; FIN kabushiki 株式; (*of food*) chozōhin 貯蔵品; ***be in / out of ~*** zaiko ga aru / nai 在庫がある/ない; ***take ~*** kentō suru 検討する **2** *v/t* COM mise ni oku 店に置く
♦**stock up on** … o kaidame suru …を買いだめする
stockbroker kabushiki-nakagai-nin 株式仲買人; **stock exchange** shōken-torihiki-sho 証券取引所; **stockholder** kabunushi 株主
stocking sutokkingu ストッキング
stock market kabushiki-shijō 株式市場; **stockmarket crash** kabushiki-shijō no bōraku 株式市場の暴落; **stockpile 1** *n* (*of food, weapons*) bichiku 備蓄 **2** *v/t* bichiku suru 備蓄する; **stockroom** chozōshitsu 貯蔵室; **stocktaking** tanaoroshi 棚卸し
stocky gasshiri shita がっしりした
stock-still: ***stand ~*** jitto shite じっとして
stodgy *food* kotteri shita こってりした
stomach 1 *n* (*insides*) i 胃; (*abdomen*) onaka おなか **2** *v/t* (*tolerate*) gaman suru 我慢する
stomach-ache fukutsū 腹痛
stone *n* (*material*) ishi 石; (*pebble*) koishi 小石; (*precious ~*) hōseki 宝石
stoned F (*on drugs*) itte shimatte iru いってしまっている
stone-deaf mattaku mimi no kikoenai まったく耳の聞こえない
stonewall *v/i* F iinogare suru 言い逃れする
stony *ground, path* ishi darake (no) 石だらけ(の)
stool (*seat*) sutsūru スツール
stoop[1] **1** *n*: ***have a ~*** nekoze de aru 猫背である; ***walk with a ~*** maekagami ni natte aruku 前かがみになって歩く **2** *v/i* (*bend down*) kagamu かがむ; (*have bent back*) koshi ga magaru 腰が曲がる
stoop[2] *n* (*porch*) pōchi ポーチ
stop 1 *n* (*for train*) eki 駅; (*for bus*) teiryūjo 停留所; ***come to a ~*** tomaru 止まる; ***put a ~ to*** … o yamesaseru …をやめさせる **2** *v/t* (*put an end to, prevent*) yamesaseru やめさせる; (*cease*) yameru やめる; *person on street, car, bus, train* tomeru 止める; ***~ talking immediately!*** ima sugu oshaberi o yamenasai! 今すぐおしゃべりをやめなさい; ***I ~ped her from leaving*** watashi wa kanojo ga saru no o yamesasemashita 私は彼女が去るのをやめさせました; ***it has ~ped raining*** ame ga yande imasu 雨がやんでいます; ***~ a check*** kogitte no shiharai o teishi suru 小切手の支払いを停止する **3** *v/i* (*come to a halt*) tomaru 止まる; (*of rain, snow*) yamu やむ
♦**stop by** (*visit*) yoru 寄る

♦**stop off** yoru 寄る
♦**stop over** tachiyoru 立ち寄る
♦**stop up** *sink* tsumaru 詰まる
stopgap sonobashinogi その場しのぎ; **stoplight** (*traffic light*) teishi-shingō 停止信号; (*brake light*) burēki-ranpu ブレーキランプ; **stopover** (*in air travel*) tochū-kōki 途中降機
stopper (*for bath, bottle*) sen 栓
stopping: ***no ~*** teisha-kinshi 停車禁止
stop sign ichijiteishi-hyōshiki 一時停止標識
stopwatch sutoppu-wotchi ストップウォッチ
storage hokan 保管; ***put in ~*** … o hokan shite morau …を保管してもらう; ***be in ~*** hokan sarete iru 保管されている
storage capacity COMPUT kioku-yōryō 記憶容量
storage space oshiire 押し入れ
store 1 *n* mise 店; (*stock*) takuwae 蓄え; (*storehouse*) sōko 倉庫 **2** *v/t* shimau しまう; COMPUT hozon suru 保存する
storefront tentō 店頭; **storehouse** sōko 倉庫; **storekeeper** shōten-shu 商店主; **storeroom** sōko 倉庫; **store window** shō-windō ショーウィンドウ
storm *n* arashi あらし
storm drain haisuikō 排水溝; **storm window** bōfūyō-mado 防風用窓; **storm warning** bōfū-keihō 暴風警報
stormy *weather* aremoyō (no) 荒れ模様(の); *relationship* hageshii 激しい
story[1] (*tale*) monogatari 物語; (*account*) hanashi 話; (*newspaper article*) kiji 記事; F (*lie*) tsukuri-banashi 作り話
story[2] (*of building*) kai 階
stout *adj person* futotta 太った; *boots* ganjō (na) 頑丈(な)
stove (*for cooking*) renji レンジ; (*for heating*) sutōbu ストーブ
stow shimau しまう
♦**stow away** *v/i* mikkō suru 密航する
stowaway mikkō-sha 密航者
straight 1 *adj line, hair, back* massugu (na) まっすぐ(な); (*honest, direct*) shōjiki (na) 正直(な); (*not criminal*) matomo (na) まとも(な); *whiskey etc* sutorēto (no) ストレート(の); (*tidy*) kichin to shita きちんとした; (*conservative*) majime (na) まじめ(な); (*not homosexual*) dōseiai de nai 同性愛でない; ***be a ~ A student*** yūshū na gakusei de aru 優秀な学生である **2** *adv* (*in a straight line*) massugu ni まっすぐに; (*directly, immediately*) sugu ni すぐに; (*clearly*) chanto ちゃんと; ***stand up ~!*** massugu tatte まっすぐ立って; ***look X ~ in the eye*** X no me o massugu mitsumeru Xの目をまっすぐ見つめる; ***go ~*** F (*of criminal*) katagi ni naru 堅気になる; ***give it to me ~*** F hakkiri itte kure はっきりいってくれ; ***be ~ ahead*** massugu mae ni aru まっすぐ前にある; ***drive ~ on*** massugu iku まっすぐ行く; ***~ ahead*** *look* massugu miru まっすぐ見る; ***carry ~ on*** (*of driver etc*) sonomama massugu iku そのまままっすぐ行く; ***~away, ~ off*** sugu ni すぐに; ***~ out*** sotchoku ni 率直に; ***~ up*** (*without ice*) kōri nashi de 氷なしで
straighten *v/t* massugu ni suru まっすぐにする
♦**straighten out 1** *v/t situation* … o kaiketsu suru …を解決する **2** *v/i* (*of road*) massugu ni naru まっすぐになる
♦**straighten up** *v/i* nobi o suru 伸びをする
straightforward (*honest, direct*) shōjiki (na) 正直(な); (*simple*) tanjun (na) 単純(な)
strain[1] **1** *n* (*on rope*) hari 張り; (*on engine, heart, person*) futan 負担 **2** *v/t* (*injure*) itameru 痛める; *finances, budget* futan o kakeru 負担をかける
strain[2] *v/t vegetables* mizuke o kiru 水気を切る; *oil, fat etc* kosu こす

strainer (*for vegetables*) koshiki こし器; ***tea ~*** chakoshi 茶こし
strait kaikyō 海峡
straitlaced genkaku (na) 厳格(な)
strand[1] *n* (*of hair, wool*) ippon 一本
strand[2] *v/t* zashō saseru 座礁させる; ***be ~ed*** ashidome sareru 足留めされる
strange (*odd*) hen (na) 変(な); (*unknown, foreign*) shiranai 知らない
strangely (*oddly*) hen ni 変に; ***~ enough*** kimyō na koto ni 奇妙なことに
stranger (*person you don't know*) mishiranu hito 見知らぬ人; ***I'm a ~ here myself*** watashi wa koko de wa yosomono desu 私はここではよそ者です
strangle shimekorosu 絞め殺す
strap *n* (*of purse, dress*) katahimo 肩ひも; (*of watch*) bando バンド; (*of shoe*) sutorappu ストラップ
♦**strap in** … no shītoberuto o shimeru …のシートベルトを締める
strapless katahimo nashi (no) 肩ひも無し(の)
strategic senryakuteki (na) 戦略的(な)
strategy senryaku 戦略
straw[1] mugiwara 麦わら; ***that's the last ~!*** mō gaman dekinai もう我慢できない
straw[2] (*for drink*) sutorō ストロー
strawberry ichigo いちご
stray 1 *adj animal* hagureta はぐれた; *bullet* nagareta 流れた **2** *n* (*dog*) nora-inu 野良犬; (*cat*) nora-neko 野良猫 **3** *v/i* (*of animal*) hagureru はぐれる; (*of child*) mayou 迷う; *fig* (*of eyes, thoughts*) soreru それる
streak (*of dirt, paint*) suji 筋; ***he's got a mean ~*** kare ni wa sukoshi ijiwaru na tokoro ga arimasu 彼には少し意地悪なところがあります **2** *v/i* (*move quickly*) subayaku hashiru 素早く走る **3** *v/t*: ***be ~ed with*** … de shima ni natte iru …でしまになっている
stream 1 *n* ogawa 小川; ***a ~ of*** (*of people, complaints*) ichiren no … 一連の…; ***come on ~*** kadōshihajimeru 稼動し始める **2** *v/i* (*of people*) zokuzoku to dete kuru 続々と出てくる; ***sunlight ~ed into the room*** hizashi ga heya ni sashikondekita 日差しが部屋に差し込んできた
streamer kami-tēpu 紙テープ
streamline *v/t fig* gōrika suru 合理化する
streamlined *car, plane* ryūsenkei (no) 流線形(の); *fig*: *organization* gōrika sareta 合理化された
street tōri 通り
streetcar romen-densha 路面電車; **streetlight** gaitō 街灯; **streetpeople** hōmuresu ホームレス; **streetwalker** baishunfu 売春婦; **streetwise** *adj* jijōtsū (no) 事情通(の)
strength tsuyo-sa 強さ; (*of emotion, friendship, currency, physical ~*) chikara 力; (*strong point*) tsuyomi 強み; (*of organization*) seiryoku 勢力
strengthen 1 *v/t* tsuyoku suru 強くする **2** *v/i* tsuyoku naru 強くなる
strenuous hageshii 激しい; *effort* nesshin (na) 熱心(な)
stress 1 *n* (*emphasis*) jūten 重点; (*on syllable*) kyōsei 強勢; (*tension*) sutoresu ストレス; ***be under ~*** sutoresu no aru ストレスのある **2** *v/t syllable* kyōsei o oku 強勢を置く; *importance etc* kyōchō suru 強調する; ***I must ~ that …*** watashi wa … o kyōchō shinakute wa narimasen 私は…を強調しなくてはなりません
stressed out F sutoresu ga tamatte iru ストレスがたまっている
stressful sutoresu no ōi ストレスの多い
stretch 1 *n* (*of land, water*) hirogari 広がり; ***at a ~*** (*nonstop*) ikki ni 一気に **2** *adj fabric* shinshukusei no aru 伸縮性のある **3** *v/t material* nobasu 伸ばす; *income* yarikuri suru やりくりす

る; F *rules* mageru 曲げる; ***he ~ed out his hand*** kare wa te o nobashita 彼は手を伸ばした; ***a job that ~es me*** watashi o nobashite kureru shigoto 私を伸ばしてくれる仕事 **4** *v/i* (*to relax muscles*) nobi o suru 伸びをする; (*to reach sth*) karada o nobasu 体を伸ばす; (*extend*) hirogaru 広がる; (*of fabric*) nobiru 伸びる; ***~ from X to Y*** (*extend*) X kara Y e nobite iru XからYへ伸びている

stretcher tanka 担架

strict *person* kibishii 厳しい; *instructions, rules* genmitsu (na) 厳密(な)

strictly kibishiku 厳しく; ***it is ~ forbidden*** sore wa kibishiku kinjirarete imasu それは厳しく禁じられています

stride **1** *n* ōmata 大また; ***take X in one's ~*** X o nannaku ukeireru Xを難なく受け入れる **2** *v/i* ōmata de aruku 大またで歩く

strident kandakai 甲高い; *fig: demands* shitsukoi しつこい

strike **1** *n* (*of workers*) sutoraiki ストライキ; (*in baseball, bowling*) sutoraiku ストライク; (*of oil*) hakken 発見; ***be on ~*** sutoraikichū de aru ストライキ中である; ***go on ~*** sutoraiki ni hairu ストライキに入る **2** *v/i* (*of workers*) sutoraiki o suru ストライキをする; (*of disaster*) osou 襲う; (*of clock*) utsu 打つ **3** *v/t* (*hit*) utsu 打つ; (*of disaster, illness*) osou 襲う; *match* tsukeru つける; (*of idea, thought*) kokoro ni ukabu 心に浮かぶ; *oil* hakken suru 発見する; ***she struck me as being ...*** kanojo wa … de aru to iu kanji o ataeta 彼女は…であるという感じを与えた

♦**strike out** *v/t* (*delete*) … ni sen o hiite kesu …に線を引いて消す

strikebreaker sutoyaburi スト破り

striker (*person on strike*) sutoraiki-sankasha ストライキ参加者

striking (*marked*) medatsu 目立って; (*eye-catching*) kiwadatte 際立って

string *n* (*cord*) himo ひも; (*of violin, cello etc*) gen 弦; (*of tennis racket*) gatto ガット; ***~s*** (*musicians*) gengakki-sōsha 弦楽器奏者; ***pull ~s*** ito o hiku 糸を引く; ***a ~ of*** (*series*) ichiren no … 一連の…

♦**string along** **1** *v/i* tsuite iku ついて行く **2** *v/t*: ***string X along*** X o damasu Xをだます

♦**string up** F … o shibarikubi ni suru …を縛り首にする

stringed instrument gengakki 弦楽器

stringent kibishii 厳しい

string player gengakki-sōsha 弦楽器奏者

strip **1** *n* (*comic ~*) koma-manga コマ漫画; ***a ~ of land*** hosonagai tochi 細長い土地; ***a ~ of cloth*** hosonagai ippen no nunokire 細長い一片の布切れ **2** *v/t* (*remove*) hagasu はがす; (*undress*) hadaka ni suru 裸にする; ***~ X of Y*** X kara Y o toriageru XからYを取り上げる **3** *v/i* (*undress*) hadaka ni naru 裸になる

strip club sutorippu-goya ストリップ小屋

stripe shima しま; (*indicating rank*) sodeshō そで章

striped shimamoyō (no) しま模様(の)

stripper sutorippā ストリッパー

strip show sutorippu-shō ストリップショー

striptease sutorippu-shō ストリップショー

strive **1** *v/t*: ***~ to do X*** Xshiyō to doryoku suru Xしようと努力する **2** *v/i*: ***~ for*** … no tame ni doryoku suru …のために努力する

stroke **1** *n* MED nōshukketsu 脳出血; (*in writing*) kaku 画; (*in Chinese characters*) kakusū 画数; (*style of swimming*) eihō 泳法; ***~ of luck*** omoigakenai kōun 思いがけない幸運; ***she never does a ~ (of work)*** kanojo wa zenzen (shigoto) o shinai 彼女は全然(仕

事)をしない **2** *v/t* naderu なでる
stroll 1 *n* sanpo 散歩 **2** *v/i* yukkuri aruku ゆっくり歩く
stroller (*for baby*) isugata-bebīkā いす型ベビーカー
strong *currency, smell, person, wind, alcohol* tsuyoi 強い; *structure* ganjō (na) 頑丈(な); *candidate* yūryoku (na) 有力(な); *support* kyōryoku (na) 強力(な); *tea, coffee, taste* koi 濃い; *views, objections* kyōko (na) 強固(な)
stronghold *fig* kyoten 拠点
strongly tsuyoku 強く
strong-minded danko to shita 断固とした
strong-willed ishi no tsuyoi 意志の強い
structural kōzōteki (na) 構造的(な); **~ *engineering*** kōzō-kōgaku 構造工学
structure 1 *n* (*sth built*) kōzō 構造; (*mode of construction*) kōsei 構成 **2** *v/t* kōsei suru 構成する
struggle 1 *n* (*fight*) arasoi 争い; (*hard time*) kutō 苦闘 **2** *v/i* (*with person*) arasou 争う; (*have a hard time*) kurō suru 苦労する **3** *v/t*: **~ *to do X*** X ni kutō suru Xに苦闘する
strum kakinarasu かき鳴らす
strut *v/i* kidotte aruku 気取って歩く
stub 1 *n* (*of cigarette*) suigara 吸い殻; (*of check, ticket*) hanken 半券 **2** *v/t*: **~ *one's toe*** tsumasaki o butsukeru つま先をぶつける
♦**stub out** tabako o momikesu たばこをもみ消す
stubble (*of beard*) bushōhige 無精ひげ
stubborn ganko (na) 頑固(な); *defense* kyōko (na) 強固(な)
stubby mijikakute futoi 短くて太い
stuck: ***be ~ on*** F … ni noboseru …にのぼせる
stuck-up F kōmanchiki (na) 高慢ちき(な)
student (*at high school*) seito 生徒; (*at university*) gakusei 学生
student nurse minarai-kangofu 見習い看護婦
student teacher kyōiku-jisshūsei 教育実習生
studio (*of artist, sculptor*) atorie アトリエ; (*recording ~, TV ~*) sutajio スタジオ; (*film ~*) satsuei-sho 撮影所; (*apartment*) wanrūmu-manshon ワンルームマンション
studious benkyōzuki (na) 勉強好き(な)
study 1 *n* (*room*) shosai 書斎; (*learning*) benkyō 勉強; (*investigation*) kenkyū 研究 **2** *v/t* (*at school, university*) benkyō suru 勉強する; (*observe*) kansatsu suru 観察する; (*examine*) shiraberu 調べる **3** *v/i* benkyō suru 勉強する
stuff 1 *n* (*things, belongings*) mono 物 **2** *v/t turkey* tsumemono o suru 詰め物をする; **~ *X into Y*** X o Y ni oshikomu XをYに押し込む
stuffed toy nuigurumi ぬいぐるみ
stuffing (*for turkey, in chair, toy*) tsumemono 詰め物
stuffy *room* mutto shita むっとした; *person* furukusai 古くさい
stumble *v/i* tsumazuku つまずく
stumble across … o gūzen mitsukeru …を偶然見つける
stumble over tsumazuite kokeru つまずいてこける; *words* tsumaru つまる
stumbling block shōgai 障害
stump 1 *n* (*of tree*) kirikabu 切り株 **2** *v/t* (*of question*) heikō saseru 閉口させる
♦**stump up** F kane o dasu 金を出す
stun (*of blow*) kizetsu saseru 気絶させる; (*of news*) shokku o ataeru ショックを与える
stunning (*amazing*) bikkuri saseru びっくりさせる; (*very beautiful*) utsukushii 美しい
stunt *n* (*for publicity*) senden-kōi 宣伝行為; (*in movie*) sutanto スタント
stuntman sutantoman スタントマン
stupefy bōtto saseru ぼーっとさせる
stupendous namihazureta 並外れた
stupid baka (na) ばか(な)
stupidity oroka-sa 愚かさ

stupor ishikimōrō 意識もうろう
sturdy jōbu (na) 丈夫(な)
stutter *v/i* domoru どもる
style *n* (*method, manner*) yōshiki 様式; (*fashion*) ryūkō 流行; (*elegance*) yūga-sa 優雅さ, sutairu スタイル; **~ of writing** buntai 文体; **go out of ~** ryūkōokure ni naru 流行遅れになる
stylish jōhin (na) 上品(な)
stylist sutairisuto スタイリスト
subcommittee shō-iinkai 小委員会
subcompact (**car**) junkogata-jidōsha 準小型自動車
subconscious: **the ~** (**mind**) senzai-ishiki 潜在意識
subcontract *v/t* shitauke saseru 下請けさせる
subcontractor shitauke-gaisha 下請け会社
subdivide *v/t* saibunkatsu suru 再分割する
subdued shizuka (na) 静か(な); *light, colo* yawarakai 柔らかい
subheading komidashi 小見出し
subject 1 *n* (*of country*) kokumin 国民; (*topic*) shudai 主題; (*branch of learning*) kamoku 科目; GRAM shugo 主語; **change the ~** wadai o kaeru 話題を変える **2** *adj*: **be ~ to** … suru keikō ga aru …する傾向がある; **~ to availability** *ticket* kūseki-jōkyō ni yorimasu 空席状況によります; *product* kazu ni kagiri ga arimasu 数に限りがあります **3** *v/t* … ni sarasu …にさらす; **~ X to torture** X o gōmon ni kakeru Xを拷問にかける
subjective shukanteki (na) 主観的(な)
sublet *v/t* matagashi suru 又貸しする
submachine gun kei-kikanjū 軽機関銃
submarine sensuikan 潜水艦
submerge 1 *v/t* … o shizumeru …を沈める **2** *v/i* (*of submarine*) sensui suru 潜水する
submission (*surrender*) kōfuku 降伏; (*to committee etc*) hōkoku 報告
submissive jūjun (na) 従順(な)
submit *v/t plan, proposal* teishutsu suru 提出する
subordinate 1 *adj* hojoteki (na) 補助的(な) **2** *n* buka 部下
subpoena 1 *n* shōkan-jō 召喚状 **2** *v/t person* shōkan suru 召喚する
♦**subscribe to** *magazine etc* … o teiki-kōdoku suru …を定期購読する; *theory* … ni dōi suru …に同意する
subscriber (*to magazine*) teiki-kōdoku-sha 定期購読者
subscription kōbai-keiyaku 購買契約
subsequent sono ato (no) その後(の)
subsequently sono ato その後
subside (*of flood waters*) hiku ひく; (*of winds*) yamu やむ; (*of building*) chinka suru 沈下する; (*of panic*) osamaru 収まる
subsidiary *n* kogaisha 子会社
subsidize joseikin o ataeru 助成金を与える
subsidy joseikin 助成金
♦**subsist on** … de ikinagaraeru … で生きながらえる
subsistence farmer jikyū-jisoku no nōka 自給自足の農家
subsistence level saitei-seikatsusuijun 最低生活水準
substance (*matter*) busshitsu 物質
substandard hyōjun-ika (no) 標準以下(の)
substantial sōtō (na) 相当(な); *meal* tappuri shita たっぷりした
substantially (*considerably*) kanari (no) かなり(の); (*in essence*) jisshitsuteki ni 実質的に
substantiate shōmei suru 証明する
substantive jisshitsuteki (na) 実質的(な)
substitute 1 *n* (*for person*) dairi 代理; (*for commodity*) daiyōhin 代用品; SP hoketsu 補欠 **2** *v/t*: **~ X for Y** Y no kawari ni X o tsukau Yの代わりにXを使う **3** *v/i*: **~ for** … no kawari o suru …の代わりをする
substitution (*act*) okikae 置き換え; **make a ~** SP senshu-kōtai o suru 選手交代をする
subtitle 1 *n* jimaku 字幕 **2** *v/t movie*

jimaku o tsukeru 字幕をつける
subtle bimyō (na) 微妙(な); *person* kōmyō (na) 巧妙(な)
subtract *v/t number* hiku 引く; ***~ X from Y*** Y kara X o hiku YからXを引く
suburb kōgai 郊外; ***the ~s*** kōgai 郊外
suburban kōgai (no) 郊外(の); *attitudes, lifestyle* inaka kusai 田舎くさい
subversive 1 *adj* hakaiteki (na) 破壊的(な) **2** *n* hakai-bunshi 破壊分子
subway chikatetsu 地下鉄
subzero *adj* reika (no) 零下(の)
succeed 1 *v/i* seikō suru 成功する; (*of emperor, in office*) keishō suru継承する; ***~ in doing X*** X suru koto ni seikō suru Xすることに成功する **2** *v/t* (*come after*) … no ato o tsugu …の後を継ぐ; (*in office*) kōnin suru 後任する
succeeding sono ato (no) その後(の)
success seikō 成功; ***be a ~*** seikō suru 成功する
successful seikō shita 成功した
successfully umaku うまく
succession (*sequence*) renzoku 連続; (*in office*) ōi-keishō 王位継承; ***in ~*** renzoku shite 連続して
successive renzoku shite 連続して; ***~ managers have tried to …*** manējātachi wa aitsuide … o tameshitemita マネージャー達は相次いで…を試してみた
successor kōnin-sha 後任者
succinct kanketsu (na) 簡潔(な)
succulent *meat, fruit* shiru ga ōkute oishii 汁が多くておいしい
succumb (*give in*) taerarenai 耐えられない; ***~ to temptation*** yūwaku ni makeru 誘惑に負ける
such 1 *adj*: ***~ a*** (*so much of a*) sonna そんな; ***it was ~ a surprise!*** sore wa hontō ni odoroki datta それは本当に驚きだった; ***he gave me ~ a fright*** kare wa watashi o hontō ni bikkuri saseta 彼はわたしを本当にびっくりさせた; ***~ as*** … no yō na …のような; ***there is no ~ word as …*** … no yō na kotoba wa sonzai shinai …のような言葉は存在しない **2** *adv* totemo とても; ***~ a nice day*** totemo otenki no ii hi とてもお天気のいい日; ***and, as ~, she deserves…*** sorenari ni kanojo wa … ni atai suru それなりに彼女は…に値する; ***the job as ~ is not interesting*** shigoto jitai wa omoshiroku nai 仕事自体はおもしろくない
suck *candy* nameru なめる; ***~ one's thumb*** oyayubi o suu 親指を吸う; ***~ X from Y*** Y kara X o suitoru YからXを吸い取る
♦**suck up 1** *v/t* … o kyūshū suru …を吸収する **2** *v/i*: ***~ to*** goma o suru ごまをする
sucker F (*person*) kamo かも; F (*lollipop*) bōtsuki-kyandē 棒付きキャンデー
suction kyūin 吸引
sudden totsuzen (no) 突然(の); ***all of a ~*** totsuzen 突然
suddenly totsuzen 突然
suds (*soap ~*) sekken no awa 石けんの泡
sue *v/t* … o kiso suru … を起訴する
suede *n* suēdo スエード
suffer 1 *v/i* (*be in pain*) kurushimu 苦しむ; (*deteriorate*) akka suru 悪化する; ***be ~ing from*** … de kurushinde iru …で苦しんでいる **2** *v/t loss* kōmuru 被る; *setback* kurushimu 苦しむ
suffering *n* kurushimi 苦しみ
sufficient jūbun (na) 十分(な)
sufficiently jūbun ni 十分に
suffocate 1 *v/i* chissoku suru 窒息する **2** *v/t* chissoku saseru 窒息させる
suffocation chissoku 窒息
sugar 1 *n* satō 砂糖 **2** *v/t* … ni satō o ireru …に砂糖を入れる
sugar bowl satō ire 砂糖入れ
sugar cane satō kibi 砂糖きび
suggest *v/t* (*propose*) teian suru 提案する; (*imply*) shisa suru 示唆する; ***I ~ that we stop now*** ima yame masen ka 今止めませんか

suggestion (*proposal*) teian 提案; (*implication*) shisa 示唆
suicide jisatsu 自殺; ***commit ~*** jisatsu suru 自殺する
suit 1 *n* (*for men*) sebiro 背広, sūtsu スーツ; (*for women*) sūtsu スーツ; (*in cards*) kumifuda 組札 **2** *v/t* (*of clothes, color*) … ni niau …に似合う; ***~ yourself!*** katte ni shiro 勝手にしろ; ***be ~ed for*** … ni teki shite iru …に適している
suitable tekitō (na) 適当(な); *time* tsugō no ii 都合のいい
suitcase sūtsukēsu スーツケース
suite (*of rooms*) suīto-rūmu スイートルーム; (*furniture*) kagu-isshiki 家具一式; MUS kumikyoku 組曲
sukiyaki sukiyaki すきやき
sulfur iō 硫黄
sulk *v/i* suneru すねる
sulky suneta すねた
sullen suneta すねた
sultry *climate* mushiatsui 蒸し暑い; (*sexually*) kannōteki (na) 官能的(な)
sum (*total*) gōkei 合計; (*amount*) kingaku 金額; (*in arithmetic*) keisan-mondai 計算問題; ***a large ~ of money*** tagaku no kane 多額の金; ***~ insured*** hoshō sareta kingaku 保証された金額; ***the ~ total of his efforts*** kare no doryoku no subete 彼の努力のすべて
♦ **sum up 1** *v/t* (*summarize*) … o yōyaku suru …を要約する; (*assess*) … o hyōka suru …を評価する **2** *v/i* LAW *baishin ni saiban no yōten o setsumei suru* 陪審に裁判の要点を説明する
summarize *v/t* yōyaku suru 要約する
summary *n* yōyaku 要約
summer natsu 夏
summit (*of mountain*) chōjō 頂上; *fig* chōten 頂点; POL shunō-kaigi 首脳会議, samitto サミット
summon *staff, ministers* yobu 呼ぶ; *meeting* shōshū suru 招集する
♦ **summon up** *strength* … o furuitataseru …を奮い立たせる
summons LAW shuttō-meirei 出頭命令
sumo sumō 相撲
sumo wrestler sumō tori 相撲取り
sump (*for oil*) aburadame 油だめ
sun taiyō 太陽; ***in the ~*** hinata 日なた; ***out of the ~*** hikage 日陰; ***he has had too much ~*** kare wa nikkō ni atarisugita 彼は日光に当たりすぎた
sunbathe nikkōyoku suru 日光浴する; **sunblock** hiyake-dome 日焼け止め; **sunburn** hiyake 日焼け; **sunburnt** hidoku hi ni yaketa ひどく日に焼けた
Sunday nichiyōbi 日曜日
sundial hidokei 日時計
sundries zakka 雑貨; (*expenses*) zappi 雑費
sunglasses sangurasu サングラス
sunken *cheeks* yasekoketa やせこけた
sunny *day* hareta 晴れた; *disposition* kaikatsu (na) 快活(な); ***it's ~*** yoku harete imasu よく晴れています
sunrise hinode 日の出; **sunset** nichibotsu 日没; **sunshade** hiyoke 日よけ; (*parasol*) higasa 日傘; **sunshine** nikkō 日光; **sunstroke** nisshabyō 日射病; **suntan** hiyake 日焼け; ***get a ~*** hiyake suru 日焼けする
super 1 *adj* F sugoi すごい **2** *n* (*janitor*) kanrinin 管理人
superb subarashii 素晴らしい
superficial *comments, analysis* hyōmenteki (na) 表面的(な); *person* usupperai 薄っぺらい; *wounds* asai 浅い
superfluous yokei (na) 余計(な)
superhuman *efforts* chōjinteki (na) 超人的(な)
superintendent (*of apartment block*) kanrinin 管理人
superior 1 *adj* (*better*) yori sugureta よりすぐれた; *pej*: *attitude* gōman (na) ごう慢(な) **2** *n* (*in organization*) jōshi 上司; (*in society*) meue no hito 目上の人
supermarket sūpāmāketto スー

パーマーケット; **supernatural** **1** *adj powers* chōshizen (no) 超自然(の) **2** *n*: ***the ~*** chōshizen-genshō 超自然現象; **superpower** POL chōtaikoku 超大国;
supersonic chōonsoku (no) 超音速(の)
superstition meishin 迷信
superstitious *person* meishin-bukai 迷信深い
supervise kantoku suru 監督する
supervisor (*at work*) kantoku 監督
supper yūshoku 夕食
supple jūnan (na) 柔軟(な)
supplement (*payment*) hosoku-ryōkin 補足料金
supplier COM nōnyū-gyōsha 納入業者
supply 1 *n* kyōkyū 供給; ***~ and demand*** juyō to kyōkyū 需要と供給; ***supplies*** (*food*) chozōhin 貯蔵品; (*materials*) zaikohin 在庫品 **2** *v/t goods* kyōkyū suru 供給する; ***~ X with Y*** X ni Yo kyōkyū suru X にYを供給する; ***be supplied with*** …ga sōbi sarete iru …が装備されている
support 1 *n* (*for structure*) shichū 支柱; (*backing*) shien 支援 **2** *v/t building, structure* sasaeru 支える; (*financially*) yashinau 養う; (*back*) shiji suru 支持する
supporter shiji-sha 支持者; (*fan*) fan ファン
supportive kyōryokuteki (na) 協力的(な)
suppose (*imagine*) …da to omou …だと思う; ***I ~ so*** sō deshō ne そうでしょうね; ***be ~d to …*** (*be meant to*) … suru hazu ni natte iru …するはずになっている; (*be said to be*) … to iwarete iru …と言われている; ***you are not ~d to …*** (*not allowed to*) …shite wa ikenai koto ni natte iru … してはいけない事になっている
suppository MED zayaku 座薬
suppress *rebellion* chin'atsu suru 鎮圧する; *feelings* osaeru 抑える
suppression (*of rebellion*) chin'atsu 鎮圧; (*of feelings*) yokusei 抑制
supremacy yūsei 優勢
supreme *effort, courage* saikō (no) 最高(の); ***~ commander*** saikō-shireikan 最高司令官
Supreme Court Saikō-saibansho 最高裁判所
surcharge *n* tsuika-ryōkin 追加料金
sure 1 *adj* kakujitsu (na) 確実(な); ***I'm ~*** hontō desu 本当です; ***I'm not ~*** yoku wakarimasen よくわかりません; ***be ~ about*** … wa tashika de aru …は確かである; ***make ~ that …*** … o ki o tsukeru …を気をつける **2** *adv* tashika ni 確かに; ***~ enough*** an no jō 案の定; ***it ~ is hot today*** F kyō wa hontō ni atsui desu 今日はほんとうに暑いです; ***~!*** mochiron もちろん
surely (*in negative sentence*) masaka まさか; (*in affirmative sentence*) kitto きっと; (*gladly*) mochiron もちろん
surf 1 *n* (*on sea*) uchiyoseru nami 打ち寄せる波 **2** *v/t*: ***~ the Net*** netto sāfin o suru ネットサーフィンをする
surface 1 *n* (*of table, object*) hyōmen 表面; (*of water*) suimen 水面; ***on the ~*** *fig* hyōmenjō wa 表面上は **2** *v/i* (*of swimmer, submarine*) suimen ni fujō suru 水面に浮上する; (*appear*) sugata o arawasu 姿を表す
surface mail futsū-yūbin 普通郵便
surfboard sāfu-bōdo サーフボード
surfer (*on sea*) sāfā サーファー
surfing sāfin サーフィン
surge *n* (*in current, demand, growth*) kyūzō 急増; (*of interest etc*) takamari 高まり
♦ **surge forward** (*of crowd*) tosshin suru 突進する
surgeon gekai 外科医
surgery geka 外科; ***undergo ~*** geka-shujutsu o ukeru 外科手術を受ける
surgical gekateki (na) 外科的(な)
surly buaisō (na) 無愛想(な)
surmount *v/t difficulties* norikoeru 乗り越える

surname myōji 名字
surpass koeru 越える
surplus 1 *n* yojō 余剰 **2** *adj* yojō (no) 余剰(の)
surprise 1 *n* odoroki 驚き; ***it'll come as no ~ to hear that…*** … o kiite mo odorokanai …を聞いても驚かない **2** *v/t* odorokasu 驚かす; ***be ~d*** odoroita yō da 驚いたようだ
surprising odoroku beki 驚くべき; ***it is not ~ that he left the firm*** kare ga kaisha o yameta no wa igai de wa nakatta 彼が会社を辞めたのは意外ではなかった
suprisingly odoroku hodo 驚く程
surrender 1 *v/i* (*of army*) kōfuku suru 降伏する **2** *v/t weapons etc* hikiwatasu 引き渡す **3** *n* kōfuku 降伏; (*of weapons etc*) hikiwatashi 引き渡し
surrogate mother dairibo 代理母
surround 1 *v/t* kakomu 囲む; ***be ~ed by …*** … ni kakomarete iru …に囲まれている **2** *n* (*of picture etc*) fuchi 縁
surrounding *adj* shūi (no) 周囲(の)
surroundings kankyō 環境
survey 1 *n* (*of literature etc*) gaisetsu 概説; (*of consumer habits etc*) chōsa 調査; (*of building*) sokuryō 測量 **2** *v/t* (*look at*) miwatasu 見渡す; *building* sokuryō suru 測量する
surveyor sokuryō-gishi 測量技師
survival seizon 生存
survive 1 *v/i* (*of species*) ikinokoru 生き残る; (*of patient*) tasukaru 助かる; ***how are you? - surviving*** dō - nantoka yatte iru yo どう -何とかやっているよ; ***his two surviving daughters*** kare no ikinokotta futari no musumetachi 彼の生き残った二人の娘達 **2** *v/t accident, operation* ikinobiru 生き延びる; (*outlive*) …yori nagaiki suru …より長生きする
survivor seizon-sha 生存者; ***he's a ~*** *fig* kare wa fujimi da 彼は不死身だ
susceptible (*emotionally*) eikyō o ukeyasui 影響を受けやすい; ***be ~ to the cold / heat*** samusa / atsusa ni binkan de aru 寒さ/暑さに敏感である
sushi sushi すし
suspect 1 *n* yōgi-sha 容疑者 **2** *v/t person* utagau 疑う; (*suppose*) … to omou …と思う
suspected *murderer* utagai o kakerarete iru 疑いをかけられている; *cause, heart attack etc* utagai no aru 疑いのある
suspend (*hang*) tsurusu つるす; (*from office, duties*) teishoku-shobun ni suru 停職処分にする
suspenders (*for pants*) sasupendā サスペンダー
suspense sasupensu サスペンス
suspension (*in vehicle*) sasupenshon サスペンション; (*from duty*) teishoku 停職
suspension bridge tsuribashi つり橋
suspicion utagai 疑い
suspicious (*causing suspicion*) ayashii 怪しい; (*feeling suspicion*) utagai-bukai 疑い深い; ***be ~ of …*** … o utagatte iru …を疑っている
sustain iji suru 維持する
swab *n* shōdokumen 消毒綿
swagger: ***walk with a ~*** ibatte aruku 威張って歩く
swallow[1] *v/t & v/i* nomikomu 飲み込む
swallow[2] *n* (*bird*) tsubame つばめ
swamp 1 *n* numachi 沼地 **2** *v/t*: ***be ~ed with*** … de ippai ni naru …で一杯になる
swampy jimejime shita じめじめした
swan hakuchō 白鳥
swap 1 *v/t*: ***~ X for Y*** X to Y o kōkan suru XとYを交換する **2** *v/i* kōkan suru 交換する
swarm 1 *n* (*of bees*) mure 群れ **2** *v/i* (*of ants, tourists etc*) muragaru 群がる; ***the town was ~ing with*** machi wa… de ippai de aru 町は…で一杯である
swarthy asaguroi 浅黒い
swat *v/t insect, fly* tataku たたく
sway 1 *n* (*influence, power*) shihai 支配 **2** *v/i* yureru 揺れる

swear *v/i* (*use swearword*) akutai o tsuku 悪態をつく; (*promise*) chikau 誓う; LAW sensei suru 宣誓する; **~ *at*** ... o nonoshiru ...をののしる

♦**swear in** *witnesses etc* sensei-shūnin suru 宣誓就任する

swearword akutai 悪態

sweat 1 *n* ase 汗; ***covered in ~*** asebisshori ni naru 汗びっしょりになる **2** *v/i* ase o kaku 汗をかく

sweater sētā セーター

sweatshirt torēnā トレーナー

sweaty *hands, smell* asebanda 汗ばんだ

Swede Suwēden-jin スウェーデン人

Sweden Suwēden スウェーデン

Swedish 1 *adj* Suwēden (no) スウェーデン(の) **2** *n* Suwēden-go スウェーデン語

sweep 1 *v/t floor, leaves* haku 掃く **2** *n* (*long curve*) ōki na kābu 大きなカーブ

♦**sweep up** *v/t mess* ... o hakiyoseru ...を掃き寄せる

sweeping *adj generalization, statement* jippahitokarage (no) 十把一からげ(の); *changes* zenmenteki (na) 全面的(な)

sweet *adj taste, tea* amai 甘い; F (*kind*) shinsetsu (na) 親切(な); F (*cute*) kawaii かわいい

sweet and sour *adj* amazuppai 甘酸っぱい

sweetcorn tōmorokoshi とうもろこし

sweeten *v/t drink, food* amaku suru 甘くする

sweetener (*for drink*) kanmiryō 甘味料

sweetheart koibito 恋人

sweet potato satsuma-imo さつま芋

swell 1 *v/i* (*of limb*) hareru 腫れる **2** *adj* F (*good*) suteki (na) 素敵(な) **3** *n* (*of sea*) uneri うねり

swelling *n* MED hare 腫れ

sweltering udaru yō (na) うだるよう(な)

swerve *v/i* (*of driver, car*) soreru それる

swift *adj* hayai 速い

swim 1 *v/i* oyogu 泳ぐ; ***go ~ming*** oyogi ni iku 泳ぎに行く; ***my head is ~ming*** atama ga mawatte iru 頭が回っている **2** *n* suiei 水泳; ***go for a ~*** oyogi ni iku 泳ぎに行く

swimmer oyogu hito 泳ぐ人; ***she's a good ~*** kanojo wa oyogu no ga umai 彼女は泳ぐのがうまい

swimming suiei 水泳

swimming pool pūru プール

swimsuit mizugi 水着

swindle 1 *n* sagi 詐欺 **2** *v/t* damashitoru だまし取る; ***~ X out of Y*** Y kara X o damashitoru YからXをだまし取る

swine F (*person*) iya na yatsu いやなやつ

swing 1 *n* yure 揺れ; (*for child*) buranko ブランコ; ***~ to the Democrats*** Minshutō ni katamuku 民主党に傾く **2** *v/t* furu 振る **3** *v/i* yureru 揺れる; (*turn*) muki ga kawaru 向きが変わる; (*of public opinion etc*) kawaru 変わる

swing-door jizai-doa 自在ドア

Swiss 1 *adj* Suisu (no) スイス(の) **2** *n* (*person*) Suisu-jin スイス人

switch 1 *n* (*for light*) suitchi スイッチ; (*change*) tenkan 転換 **2** *v/t* (*change*) kirikaeru 切り替える; (*swap*) torikaeru 取り替える **3** *v/i* (*change*) kirikaeru 切り替える

♦**switch off** *v/t lights, TV* ... o kesu ...を消す; *engine, PC* ... o kiru ...を切る

♦**switch on** *v/t lights, TV* ... o tsukeru ...をつける; *PC* ... no suitchi o ireru ...のスイッチを入れる; *engine* ... o kakeru ...をかける

switchboard kōkandai 交換台

switchover (*to new system*) kirikaeru 切り替える

Switzerland Suisu スイス

swivel *v/i* mawaru 回る

swollen hareta 腫れた; *stomach* fukureta 膨れた

swoop *v/i* (*of bird*) maioriru 舞い下りる

♦**swoop down on** *prey* ... ni tobikakaru ...に飛びかかる

♦**swoop on** (*of police etc*) ... o teire

suru ...を手入れする
sword katana 刀
swordfish kajiki かじき
sycamore kaede かえで
syllable onsetsu 音節
syllabus kōgi-gaiyō 講義概要
symbol (*character*) kigō 記号; (*in poetry etc*) shōchō 象徴
symbolic shōchōteki (na) 象徴的(な)
symbolism shōchōteki-imi 象徴的意味
symbolize shōchō suru 象徴する
symmetric(al) taishōteki (na) 対称的(な)
symmetry taishō 対称
sympathetic (*showing pity*) dōjōteki (na) 同情的(な); (*understanding*) kōiteki (na) 好意的(な); ***be ~ toward a person / an idea*** hito ni / kangae ni kōiteki de aru 人に/考えに好意的である
♦**sympathize with** *person* ... ni dōjō suru ...に同情する; *views* ... ni kyōkan suru ...に共感する
sympathizer POL shien-sha 支援者
sympathy (*pity*) dōjō 同情; (*understanding*) kyōkan 共感
symphony kōkyōkyoku 交響曲
symptom MED shōjō 症状; *fig* kizashi 兆し
symptomatic: ***be ~ of*** MED ... no shōjō ga aru ...の症状がある; *fig* ... no kizashi ga aru ...の兆しがある
synchronize *watches* jikan o awaseru 時間を合わせる; *operations* dōji ni ugokasu 同時に動かす
synonym dōigo 同意語
syntax tōgoron 統語論
synthetic gōsei (no) 合成(の)
syphilis baidoku 梅毒
syringe chūshaki 注射器
syrup shiroppu シロップ
system soshiki 組織; (*method*) hōhō 方法; (*of grammar, categorization etc*) taikei 体系; (*computer*) shisutemu システム; ***the braking / digestive ~*** burēki / shōkaki keitō ブレーキ/消化器系統
systematic *approach* soshikiteki (na) 組織的(な)
systematically *analyze, study* keitōteki ni 系統的に; *destroy* tetteiteki ni 徹底的に
systems analyst COMPUT shisutemu-anarisuto システムアナリスト

T

tab *n* (*for pulling*) tsumami つまみ; (*in text*) tabu タブ; ***~ up the tab*** kanjō o harau 勘定を払う
table *n* shokutaku 食卓, tēburu テーブル; (*of figures*) hyō 表
tablecloth fukin ふきん
tablespoon tēburu-supūn テーブルスプーン; (*measure*) ōsaji 大さじ
tablet MED jōzai 錠剤
table tennis takkyū 卓球
tabloid *n* (*newspaper*) taburoido タブロイド
taboo *adj* tabū (no) タブー(の)
tacit anmoku (no) 暗黙(の)
tack 1 *n* (*nail*) byō びょう **2** *v/t* (*sew*) byō de tomeru びょうで留める **3** *v/i* (*of yacht*) magiru 間切る
tackle 1 *n* (*equipment*) yōgu 用具; (*for fishing*) tsuri-dōgu 釣り道具; SP takkuru タックル **2** *v/t* SP takkuru suru タックルする; *problem* torikumu 取り組む; *intruder* tobikakaru 飛びかかる
tacky *paint, glue* betobeto shita べとべとした; (*cheap, poor quality*) yasuppoi 安っぽい; *behavior*

kokoro no semai 心の狭い
tact kiten 気転
tactful josainai 如才ない
tactical sakuryaku ni tomu 策略に富む
tactics sakusen 作戦
tactless kiten no kikanai 気転の利かない
tadpole otamajakushi おたまじゃくし
tag (*label*) fuda 札
tail *n* shippo 尻尾
tail light bitō 尾灯
tailor yōfuku-ya 洋服屋
tailor-made *suit* shitate (no) 仕立て(の); *solution* mokuteki ni au yō ni tsukutta 目的に合うようにつくった
tail wind oikaze 追い風
Taiwan Taiwan 台湾
Taiwanese **1** *adj* Taiwan (no) 台湾(の) **2** *n* Taiwan-jin 台湾人; (*dialect*) Taiwan-go 台湾語
take *v/t* (*remove*) toru 取る; (*steal*) nusumu 盗む; (*transport, accompany*) tsurete iku 連れて行く; (*accept: money, gift*) uketoru 受け取る; *credit cards* tsukau 使う; (*study: math, French*) toru 取る; *photograph, photocopy* toru 撮る; *exam, degree* ukeru 受ける; *shower* abiru 浴びる; *stroll* sanpo suru 散歩する; *s.o.'s temperature* hakaru 計る; (*endure*) gaman suru 我慢する; (*require*) hitsuyō to suru 必要とする; (*time*) kakaru かかる; ***how long does it ~?*** dorekurai kakarimasu ka どれくらいかかりますか; ***I'll ~ it*** (*when shopping*) kaimasu 買います
♦**take after** … ni nite iru …に似ている
♦**take away** *pain* … o torinozoku …を取り除く; *object* … o katazukeru …を片づける; MATH … o hiku …を引く; ***take X away from Y*** X kara Y o toriageru XからYを取り上げる
♦**take back** (*return: object*) … o kaesu …を返す; *person* … o okuru …を送る; *husband etc* … o ukeireru …を受け入れる; ***that takes me back*** sore ga omoidasaseru それが思い出させる
♦**take down** (*from shelf*) … o motte kuru …を持ってくる; *scaffolding* … o hazusu …をはずす; *pants* … o nugu …を脱ぐ; (*write down*) … o kakitomeru …を書き留める
♦**take in** (*indoors*) … o toriireru …を取り入れる; (*give accommodation*) … o tomeru …を泊める; (*make narrower*) … o tsumeru …をつめる; (*deceive*) … o damasu …をだます; (*include*) … o fukumu …を含む
♦**take off** **1** *v/t clothes, hat* … o nugu …を脱ぐ; *10% etc* … o toru …を取る; (*mimic*) … no mane suru …の真似する; ***can you take a bit off here?*** (*to barber*) konohen o chotto katto shite moraemasen ka この辺をちょっとカットしてもらえませんか; ***take a day/week off*** ichinichi/isshūkan yasumi o toru 一日/一週間休みをとる **2** *v/i* (*of airplane*) ririku suru 離陸する; (*become popular*) ninki ga deru 人気が出る
♦**take on** *job* … o toru …を取る; *staff* … o yatou …を雇う
♦**take out** (*from bag, pocket*) … o toridasu …を取り出す; *stain* … o torinozoku …を取り除く; *appendix, tonsils, word from text* … o toru …を取る; *tooth* … o nuku …を抜く; *money from bank* … o hikidasu …を引き出す; (*to dinner etc*) … o shokuji ni tsurete iku …を食事に連れて行く; (*romantically*) … o dēto ni tsurete iku …をデートに連れて行く; *dog* … o sanpo ni tsurete iku …を散歩に連れて行く; *insurance policy* … ni kanyū suru …に加入する; ***take it out on*** … ni ataru …にあたる
♦**take over** **1** *v/t company etc* … o nottoru …を乗っ取る; ***tourists ~ the town*** … o kankōkyaku ga machi o senryō suru …を観光客が

町を占領する **2** *v/i* (*of new management etc*) hikitsugu 引き継ぐ; (*do sth in s.o.'s place*) kōtai suru 交代する

♦**take to** (*like*) suki ni naru 好きになる; (*form habit of*) suru yō ni naru するようになる

♦**take up** *carpet etc* … o hagasu …をはがす; (*carry up*) … o motte iku …を持って行く; *dress etc* … o mijikaku suru …を短くする; *judo, Spanish* … o narai hajimeru …を習い始める; *offer* … o ukeru …を受ける; *new job, hobby* … o hajimeru …を始める; *space, time* … o shimeru …を占める; ***I'll take you up on your offer*** anata no mōshide o ukeireru あなたの申し出を受け入れる

take-home pay tedori-kyūryō 手取り給料; **takeoff** (*of airplane*) ririku 離陸; (*impersonation*) mane 真似; **takeover** COM baishū suru 買収する; **takeover bid** kabushiki-kōkai-kaitsuke 株式公開買い付け

takings uriage 売り上げ

talcum powder tarukamu-paudā タルカムパウダー

tale monogatari 物語

talent sainō 才能

talented sainō ga aru 才能がある

talk 1 *v/i* hanasu 話す; ***can I ~ to …?*** …san to hanasemasu ka …さんと話せますか; ***I'll ~ to him about it*** watashi ga kare ni hanashite okimasu 私が彼に話しておきます **2** *v/t English etc* hanasu 話す; *business, politics* hanashiau 話し合う; ***~ X into Y*** X ni Y o settoku suru XにYを説得する **3** *n* (*conversation*) kaiwa 会話; (*lecture*) kōgi 講義; ***he's all ~*** *pej* kare wa kuchisaki dake no hito desu 彼は口先だけの人です

♦**talk over** … o hanashiau …を話し合う

talkative oshaberi (na) おしゃべり(な)

talk show tōku-shō トークショー

tall takai 高い; *person* se ga takai 背が高い

tall order muzukashii yōkyū 難しい要求

tall story mayutsuba-mono まゆつばもの

tame *animal* kainarasareta 飼い慣らされた; *joke etc* tsumaranai つまらない

♦**tamper with** ijiru いじる

tampon tanpon タンポン

tan 1 *n* (*from sun*) hiyake 日焼け; (*color*) shakudōiro 赤銅色 **2** *v/i* (*in sun*) hi ni yakeru 日に焼ける **3** *v/t leather* kawa o namesu 皮をなめす

tandem (*bike*) futarinori no jitensha 二人乗りの自転車

tangerine mikan みかん

tangle *n* motsure もつれ

♦**tangle up**: ***get tangled up*** (*of string etc*) motsureru もつれる

tango *n* tango タンゴ

tank tanku タンク; MOT tankusha タンク車; MIL sensha 戦車; (*for skin diver*) sanso-bonbe 酸素ボンベ

tanker (*ship*) tankā タンカー; (*truck*) tanku rōrī タンクローリー

tanned hi ni yaketa 日に焼けた

tantalizing jirashita じらした

tantamount ***be ~ to*** … to onaji de aru …と同じである

tantrum kanshaku かんしゃく

tap 1 *n* jaguchi 蛇口 **2** *v/t* (*knock*) karuku utsu 軽く打つ; *phone* tōchō suru 盗聴する

♦**tap into** *resources* … o riyō suru …を利用する

tap dance *n* tappu-dansu タップダンス

tape 1 *n* (*for recording*) kasetto-tēpu カセットテープ; (*sticky*) setchaku-tēpu 接着テープ **2** *v/t conversation etc* rokuon suru 録音する; (*with sticky ~*) hittsukeru 引っつける

tape deck tēpu-dekki テープデッキ; **tape drive** COMPUT tēpu-doraibu テープドライブ; **tape measure** makijaku 巻尺

taper *v/i* shidai ni hosoku naru 次第に細くなる

♦**taper off** (*of production, figures*)

shidai ni heru 次第に減る
tape recorder tēpu-rekōdā テープレコーダー
tape recording tēpu-rokuon テープ録音
tapestry tapesutorī タペストリー
tar *n* tāru タール
tardy osoi 遅い
target 1 *n* (*in shooting*) mato 的; (*for sales, production*) mokuhyō 目標 **2** *v/t market* mato ni suru 的にする
target date mokuhyō-kijitsu 目標期日; **target group** COM taishō-gurūpu 対象グループ; **target market** taishō-shijō 対象市場
tariff (*price*) ryōkinhyō 料金表; (*tax*) kanzei 関税
tarmac (*at airport*) kūkō-epuron 空港エプロン
tarnish *v/t metal* … no kōtaku o kumoraseru …の光沢を曇らせる; *reputation* … o kegasu …を汚す
tarpaulin bōsui-shīto 防水シート
tart *n* taruto タルト
task shigoto 仕事
task force tokubetsu-taisakuhonbu 特別対策本部; MIL kidō-butai 機動部隊
tassel fusa 房
taste 1 *n* (*sense*) mikaku 味覚; (*of food etc*) aji 味; (*in clothes, art etc*) konomi 好み; ***he has no ~*** kare wa sensu ga nai 彼はセンスがない **2** *v/t food* ajimi suru 味見する; *freedom etc* ajiwau 味わう
tasteful shumi no yoi 趣味のよい
tasteless *food* mazui まずい; *remark* taikutsu (na) 退屈(な)
tasty oishii おいしい
tatami mat tatami たたみ
tattered boroboro ni natta ぼろぼろになった
tatters: ***in ~*** *clothes* boroboro ni natte ぼろぼろになって; *reputation, career* zutazuta ni natte ずたずたになって
tattoo *n* irezumi いれずみ
taunt 1 *n* azakeri あざけり **2** *v/t* azakeru あざける
taut pin to hatta ぴんと張った
tax 1 *n* zeikin 税金; ***before ~*** zeikomi 税込み; ***after ~*** zeibikigo 税引き後 **2** *v/t people, product* kazei suru 課税する
taxation (*act*) kazei 課税; (*taxes*) zeikin 税金
tax code takkusu-kōdo タックスコード; **tax-deductible** shotoku kara kōjo sareru 所得から控除される; **tax-free** menzei (no) 免税(の)
taxi takushī タクシー
taxidriver takushī-untenshu タクシー運転手
taxi rank takushī-noriba タクシー乗り場
tax payer nōzei-sha 納税者
tax return (*form*) kakutei-shinkokusho 確定申告書
tea (*drink*) cha 茶; (*meal*) gogo no ocha 午後のお茶; ***Japanese ~*** ocha お茶; ***green ~*** ryokucha 緑茶
teabag tībaggu ティーバッグ
tea ceremony sadō 茶道
teach 1 *v/t person, subject* oshieru 教える;***~ X to do Y*** X ni Y o oshieru XにYを教える **2** *v/i* kyōshi o suru 教師をする
teacher kyōshi 教師, sensei 先生
teacher training kyōin-kenshū 教員研修
teaching (*profession*) kyōshoku 教職
teaching aid hojo-kyōzai 補助教材
teaching assistant joshu 助手
tea cloth fukin ふきん; **teacup** kōcha-jawan 紅茶茶碗; (*for green tea*) yunomi ゆのみ; **tea drinker** kōcha o konomu hito 紅茶を好む人
teak chīku チーク
tea leaves cha no ha 茶の葉
team chīmu チーム
team spirit danketsushin 団結心
teamster trakku no untenshu トラックの運転手
teamwork chīmuwāku チームワーク
teapot tīpotto ティーポット
tear[1] **1** *n* (*in cloth etc*) sakeme 裂け目 **2** *v/t paper, cloth* hikisaku 引き裂く; ***be torn between two alternatives*** itabasami ni naru 板ばさみになる **3** *v/i* (*run fast*)

mōretsu na ikioi de hashiru 猛烈な勢いで走る; (*drive fast*) mōretsu na ikioi de unten suru 猛烈な勢いで運転する
♦ **tear up** *paper* … o yaburu …を破る; *agreement* … o haki suru …を破棄する
tear[2] (*in eye*) namida 涙; ***be in ~s*** namida ni kureru 涙にくれる
teardrop namida no hitoshizuku 涙のひとしずく
tearful namida de ippai (no) 涙でいっぱい(の)
tear gas sairui-gasu 催涙ガス
tearoom tīrūmu ティールーム
tease *v/t* ijimeru いじめる
tea service, tea set tīsetto ティーセット
teaspoon tīspūn ティースプーン
teat chikubi 乳首
tea towel fukin ふきん
technical senmonteki (na) 専門的(な)
technicality (*technical nature*) senmonteki-jikō 専門的事項; LAW hōritsujō no tetsuzuki 法律上の手続き; ***that's just a ~*** komakai koto 細かい事
technically (*strictly speaking*) genmitsu ni wa 厳密には; *written* kami no ue de wa 紙の上では
technician gishi 技師
technique gijutsu 技術
technological kagaku-gijutsu (no) 科学技術(の)
technology kagaku-gijutsu 科学技術
technophobia kagaku-gijutsu-kyōfushō 科学技術恐怖症
tedious taikutsu (na) 退屈(な)
tee *n* (*in golf*) tī ティー
teem: ***be ~ing with rain*** doshaburi de aru 土砂降りである; ***be ~ing with tourists / ants*** ryokō-sha / ari de ippai de aru 旅行者/ありで一杯である
teenage *fashions* tīn'eijā (no) ティーンエイジャー(の); ***~ boy / girl*** jūdai no shōnen / shōjo 十代の少年/少女
teenager tīn'eijā ティーンエイジャー
teens: ***be in one's ~*** jūdai de aru 十代である; ***reach one's ~*** jūdai ni naru 十代になる
telecommunications denki-tsūshin 電気通信
telegram denpō 電報
telegraph pole denshinbashira 電信柱
telepathic terepashī (no) テレパシー(の); ***you must be ~!*** anata wa terepashī ga aru ni chigainai あなたはテレパシーがあるに違いない
telepathy terepashī テレパシー
telephone 1 *n* denwa 電話; ***be on the ~*** (*be speaking*) hanashichū de aru 話中である; (*have a phone*) denwa o hiite iru 電話をひいている **2** *v/t person* … ni denwa o kakeru …に電話をかける **3** *v/i* denwa suru 電話する
telephone booth kōshū-denwa bokkusu 公衆電話ボックス; **telephone call** denwa 電話; **telephone directory** denwachō 電話帳; **telephone exchange** denwa-kōkanshitsu 電話交換室; **telephone number** denwa-bangō 電話番号
telephoto lens bōen-renzu 望遠レンズ
telesales denwa-sērusu 電話セールス
telescope bōenkyō 望遠鏡
televise terebi-hōsō suru テレビ放送する
television terebi-hōsō テレビ放送; (*set*) terebi テレビ; ***what's on ~ tonight?*** konban terebi de nani o yatte imasu ka 今晩テレビで何をやっていますか; ***watch ~*** terebi o miru テレビを見る
television program terebi-bangumi テレビ番組; **television set** terebi テレビ; **television studio** sutajio スタジオ
tell 1 *v/t story* hanasu 話す; *lie* tsuku つく; *the difference* wakaru わかる; ***~ X Y*** X ni Y o iu XにYを言う; ***don't ~ Mom*** okāsan ni wa iu na お母さん

には言うな; ***could you ~ me the way to …?*** … e no michi o oshiete itadakemasu ka …への道を教えていただけますか; ***~ X to do Y*** X ni Y suru yō ni iu XにYするように言う; ***you're ~ing me!*** sono tōri da その通りだ **2** *v/i* (*have effect*) kikime ga aru 効き目がある; ***the heat is ~ing on him*** atsusa ga kare no mi ni kotaeru 暑さが彼の身にこたえる; ***time will ~*** jikan ga oshiete kureru 時間が教えてくれる

♦**tell off** (*reprimand*) … o shikaru …をしかる

teller (*in bank*) madoguchi 窓口

telltale 1 *adj signs* kakushikirenai 隠しきれない **2** *n* tsugeguchi suru hito 告げ口する人

temp 1 *n* (*employee*) rinji-shokuin 臨時職員, haken 派遣 **2** *v/i* rinji-yatoi de hataraku 臨時雇いで働く

temper (*bad ~*) kigen 機嫌; ***be in a ~*** fukigen de aru 不機嫌である; ***keep one's ~*** heisei o tamotsu 平静を保つ; ***lose one's ~*** hara o tateru 腹を立てる

temperament kishitsu 気質

temperamental (*moody*) kimagure (na) 気まぐれ(な)

temperature ondo 温度; (*fever*) netsu 熱; ***have a ~*** netsu ga aru 熱がある

temple[1] REL shinden 神殿; (*Japanese*) tera 寺

temple[2] ANAT komekami こめかみ

tempo tenpo テンポ

temporarily ichijiteki ni 一時的に

temporary ichiji (no) 一時(の)

tempt yūwaku suru 誘惑する

temptation yūwaku 誘惑

tempting *offer, invitation* miwakuteki (na) 魅惑的(な); *food* oishisō (na) おいしそう(な)

tempura tenpura てんぷら

ten jū 十

tenacious tsuyoi 強い

tenant shakuchi-nin 借地人

tend[1] *v/t* (*look after*) … no sewa o suru …の世話をする

tend[2]: ***~ to do X*** X suru keikō ga aru Xする傾向がある; ***~ toward*** … ni narigachi de aru …になりがちである

tendency keikō 傾向

tender[1] *adj* (*sore*) itai 痛い; (*affectionate*) yasashii 優しい; *steak* yawarakai 柔らかい

tender[2] *n* COM nyūsatsu 入札

tenderness (*soreness*) itami 痛み; (*of kiss etc*) yasashi-sa 優しさ; (*of steak*) yawaraka-sa 柔らかさ

tendon ken 腱

tennis tenisu テニス

tennis ball tenisu-bōru テニスボール; **tennis court** tenisu-kōto テニスコート; **tennis player** tenisu-pureiyā テニスプレイヤー; **tennis racket** tenisu-raketto テニスラケット

tenor *n* MUS tenōru テノール

tense[1] *n* GRAM jisei 時制

tense[2] *adj muscle* pin to hatta ピンと張った; *voice, person* kinchō shita 緊張した; *moment* haritsumeta 張り詰めた

♦**tense up** *v/i* (*of muscles*) haru 張る; (*of person*) kinchō suru 緊張する

tension (*of rope*) hariguai 張りぐあい; (*in atmosphere, voice*) kinchō 緊張; (*in movie, novel*) kinpaku 緊迫

tent tento テント

tentacle shokushu 触手

tentative shikenteki (na) 試験的(な); *smile* tameraigachi (na) ためらいがち(な)

tenterhooks: ***be on ~*** yakimoki shite iru やきもきしている

tenth 1 *adj* dai-jū (no) 第十(の) **2** *n* (*of month*) tōka 十日

tepid *water* namanurui なまぬるい; *reaction* netsui no nai 熱意のない

term (*period of time*) kikan 期間; (*condition*) jōken 条件; (*word*) yōgo 用語; ***be on good / bad ~s with*** … to ii / warui kankei de aru …といい/悪い関係である; ***in the long ~*** nagai me de mireba 長い目で見れば; ***in the short ~*** mesaki wa 目先は; ***come to ~s with*** … o ukeireru …を受け入れる

terminal 1 *n* (*at airport*) tāminaru ターミナル; (*for buses*) basu-tā minaru バスターミナル; (*for containers*) kontena コンテナ; ELEC tanshi 端子; COMPUT tanmatsu 端末 **2** *adj illness* makki (no) 末期(の)

terminally: **~ *ill*** makki no byōki 末期の病気

terminate 1 *v/t contract* owaraseru 終わらせる; *pregnancy* chūzetsu suru 中絶する **2** *v/i* owaru 終わる

termination (*of contract*) shūryō 終了; (*of pregnancy*) chūzetsu 中絶

terminology senmon-yōgo 専門用語

terminus (*for buses, trains*) tāminaru ターミナル

terrace (*on hillside*) dandan-batake 段々畑; (*patio*) terasu テラス

terra cotta terakotta テラコッタ

terrain chikei 地形

terrestrial 1 *n* chikyūjō no seibutsu 地球上の生物 **2** *adj*: **~ *television*** chijōha-terebi 地上波テレビ

terrible hidoi ひどい

terribly (*very*) totemo とても

terrific sugoi すごい

terrifically (*very*) sugoku すごく

terrify totemo kowagaraseru とても怖がらせる; ***be terrified*** kyōfu ni karareta 恐怖にかられた

terrifying osoroshii 恐ろしい

territorial ryōdo (no) 領土(の)

territorial waters ryōkai 領海

territory ryōdo 領土; *fig* ryōiki 領域

terror kyōfu 恐怖

terrorism tero テロ

terrorist terorisuto テロリスト

terrorist organization tero-soshiki テロ組織

terrorize obiesaseru おびえさせる

test 1 *n* shiken 試験, tesuto テスト **2** *v/t* tamesu 試す

testament (*to s.o.*) shōko 証拠; ***Old / New Testament*** REL Kyū / Shin'yaku Seisho 旧/新約聖書

testicle kōgan こう丸

testify *v/i* LAW shōgen suru 証言する

testimonial *n* suisenjō 推薦状

test tube shikenkan 試験管

test-tube baby shikenkan-bebī 試験管ベビー

testy tanki (na) 短気(な)

tetanus hashōfū 破傷風

tether 1 *v/t horse* tsunagu つなぐ **2** *n* tsunagi-zuna つなぎ綱; ***be at the end of one's ~*** genkai ni tasshite iru 限界に達している

text honbun 本文

textbook kyōkasho 教科書

textile orimono 織物

texture tezawari 手触り; (*of food*) shitazawari 舌触り

Thai 1 *adj* Tai (no) タイ(の) **2** *n* (*person*) Tai-jin タイ人; (*language*) Tai-go タイ語

Thailand Tai タイ

than …yori …より; ***bigger / faster ~ me*** watashi yori ōkii / hayai 私より大きい/速い; ***more ~ 50*** gojū yori takusan 五十よりたくさん

thank *v/t* … ni kansha suru …に感謝する; **~ *you*** arigatō gozaimasu ありがとうございます; ***no ~ you*** kekkō desu 結構です

thanks kansha 感謝; **~!** arigatō ありがとう; **~ *to*** … no okage de …のおかげで

thankful kansha shite iru 感謝している

thankfully kansha shite 感謝して; (*luckily*) arigatai koto ni ありがたいことに

thankless *task* wari ni awanai 割に合わない

Thanksgiving (Day) Kanshasai 感謝祭

that 1 *adj* (*further away from both speaker and listener*) ano あの; (*nearer to listener, previously known to listener*) sono その; **~ *one*** are あれ; sore それ **2** *pron* ◊ (*further away from both speaker and listener*) are あれ; (*nearer to listener, previously known to listener*) sore それ; ***what's ~?*** (*pointing at sth*) are / sore wa nan desu ka あれ/それは何ですか; ***who's ~?*** (*pointing at photo*) ano hito / sono hito wa dare desu ka あの人/その人はだれですか; (*when there's a noise outside*) dochirasama desu ka どちら様ですか; **~*'s mine*** are / sore wa watashi no desu あれ/それは私のです; ***~'s very kind*** sore wa shinsetsu desu ne それは親切ですね ◊ (*relative*): ***the person / car ~ you saw*** anata ga mita hito / kuruma あなたが見た人/車 **3** *conj*: ***I think ~ …*** watashi wa … to omou 私は…と思う **4** *adv* (*so*) sore hodo それ程; ***~ big*** sore hodo ōkii それ程大きい

thaw *v/i* (*of snow*) tokeru 溶ける; (*of frozen food*) kaitō suru 解凍する

the ◊ (*no equivalent in Japanese*): ***~ border*** kokkyō 国境 ◊ (*identifying or with previous reference*) sono その; ***~ doctor who treated me*** watashi o chiryō shita sono isha 私を治療したその医者; ***is that ~ ring he gave you?*** sono yubiwa ga kare kara moratta mono nano その指輪が彼からもらったものなの; ***~ blue bag is mine*** sono aoi kaban wa watashi no desu その青いかばんは私のです ◊: ***~ sooner ~ better*** hayakereba hayai hodo ii 速ければ速いほどいい

theater gekijō 劇場

theatrical engeki (no) 演劇(の); (*overdone*) wazatorashii わざとらしい

theft nusumi 盗み

their ◊ karera no 彼らの; (*of female subjects also*) kanojora no 彼女らの; (*of inanimate objects*) sorera no それらの ◊ (*omission of possessive*): ***they forgot ~ keys*** karera wa kagi o wasureta 彼らはかぎを忘れた ◊ (*his or her*): ***somebody has left ~ bag here*** dare ka ga kaban o koko ni wasurete iru 誰かがここにかばんを忘れている

theirs karera no mono 彼らのもの; (*of female subjects also*) kanojora no mono 彼女らのもの; ***a friend of ~*** karera no tomodachi no hitori 彼らの友達の一人

them ◊ ***who do you mean? - ~*** dare no koto o itteru no - karera 誰のことを言ってるの一彼ら; ***without ~*** (*people*) karera nashi de 彼らなしで; (*things*) sorera nashi de それらなしで ◊ (*direct object*) karera o 彼らを; (*female also*) kanojora o 彼女らを; (*things*) sorera o それらを; ***do you know ~?*** karera o shitte imasu ka 彼らを知っていますか ◊ (*indirect object*) karera ni 彼らに; (*female also*) kanojora ni 彼女らに; (*things*) sorera ni それらに; ***I sent it to ~*** karera ni sore o okutta 彼らにそれを送った ◊ (*him or her*): ***if a person asks for help, you should help ~*** moshi dare ka ga tasuke o motomete itara, tasukete ageru beki da もし誰かが助けを求めていたら、助けてあげるべきだ

theme tēma テーマ

theme park tēma-yūenchi テーマ遊園地

theme song tēma-songu テーマソング

themselves: ***they hurt ~*** (*male*) karera wa kega o shita 彼らはけがをした; (*female also*) kanojora wa kega o shita 彼女らはけがをした; ***they saw ~ in the mirror*** karera wa jibuntachi o kagami de mita 彼らは自分達を鏡でみた; ***what do they think ~?*** karera wa dō kangaete iru no 彼らはどう考えているの; ***but the boxes ~ have no value*** sono hako wa sore dake dewa kachi ga nai その箱はそれだけでは価値がない; ***by ~*** (*alone*) jibuntachi dake de 自分達だけで; (*without help*) jibuntachi de 自分達で

then (*at that time*) sono tōji その当時; (*after that*) sorekara それから; (*deducing*) sorenara それなら; ***by ~*** soremade ni それまでに

theology shingaku 神学

theoretical rironteki (na) 理論的(な)

theory riron 理論; ***in ~*** rironteki ni wa 理論的には

therapeutic chiryōhō (no) 治療法(の)

therapist serapisuto セラピスト

therapy serapī セラピー

there (*with verbs of being*) asoko ni あそこに; (*with verbs of activity*) asoko de あそこで; ***I used to live ~*** watashi wa izen asoko ni sunde ita 私は以前あそこに住んでいた; ***I used to work ~*** watashi wa izen asoko de hataraite ita 私は以前あそこで働いていた; ***over ~ / down ~*** asoko あそこ; ***~ is / are*** (*of person, animal*) … ga iru …がいる; (*polite*) … ga imasu …がいます; (*of things*) … ga aru …がある; (*polite*) … ga arimasu …があります; ***is / are ~ …?*** (*of person, animal*) … ga imasu ka …がいますか; (*of things*) …ga arimasu ka …がありますか; ***~ is / are not*** (*of person, animal*) …ga inai …がいない; (*polite*) …ga imasen …がいません; ~ (*of things*) …ga nai …がない; (*polite*) … ga arimasen … がありません; ***~ you are*** (*giving sth*) hai dōzo はい どうぞ; (*finding sth*) hora ほら; (*completing sth*) hai dekimashita はい できました; ***~ and back*** ōfuku 往復; ***~ he is!*** imashita いました; ***~, ~*** nēnē ねーねー

thereabouts sono kurai そのくらい

therefore shitagatte 従って

thermometer (*for room*) ondokei 温度計; MED taionkei 体温計

thermos flask mahōbin 魔法瓶

thermostat sāmosutatto サーモスタット

these 1 *adj* kono この **2** *pron* kore これ

thesis ronbun 論文

they karera 彼ら; (*female also*) kanojora 彼女ら; (*things*) sorera それら; ***~ are American*** karera wa Amerika-jin desu 彼らはアメリカ人です ◊ (*omission of pronoun*): ***where are ~? – ~ have left*** karera wa doko desu ka – mō ikimashita 彼らはどこですか－もう行きました ◊ (*he or she*): ***if anyone looks at this, ~ will see that …*** moshi dareka ga kore o mitara … to wakaru darō もし誰かがこれをみたら…とわかるだろう; ***if somebody thinks ~ know the answer*** moshi dareka ga seikai o shitte iru to omottara もし誰かが正解を知っていると思ったら ◊ (*impersonal*): ***~ say that …*** … to iwarete iru …と言われている; ***~ are going to change the law*** tōkyoku wa hōritsu o kaeru tsumori desu 当局は 法律を変えるつもりです

thick *hair* ōi 多い; *soup, fog* koi 濃い; *wall, book* atsui 厚い; (*stupid*) nibui 鈍い

thicken *sauce* koku suru 濃くする

thickset zunguri shita ずんぐりした

thickskinned donkan (na) 鈍感(な)

thief dorobō 泥棒

thigh momo もも

thimble yubinuki 指貫

thin *hair, soup, coat* usui 薄い; *person, line* hosoi 細い

thing mono 物; (*abstract*) koto 事; ***~s*** (*belongings*) mochimono 持ち物; ***how are ~s?*** chōshi wa dō desu ka 調子はどうですか; ***good ~ you told me*** itte kurete tasukarimashita 言ってくれて助かりました; ***what a ~ to do / say!*** nante koto o shita no / itta no なんてことをしたの/言ったの

thingumajig F nantoka iu mono 何とかいうもの

think kangaeru 考える, omou 思う; ***I ~ so*** sō omoimasu そう思います; ***I don't ~ so*** sōda to wa omoimasen そうだとは思いません; ***I ~ so too*** watashi mo sō omoimasu 私もそう思います; ***what do you ~?*** dō omoimasu ka どう思いますか; ***what do you ~ of it?*** sore o dō omoimasu ka それをどう思いますか; ***I can't ~ of anything more*** kore ijō kangaeraremasen これ以上考えられません; ***~ hard!*** yoku kangaenasai よく考えなさい; ***I'm ~ing about emigrating*** ijū shiyō ka to omotte imasu 移住しようかと思っています

♦ **think over** … o yoku kangaeru …をよく考える

♦ **think through** … o shinchō ni kangaeru …を慎重に考える

♦ **think up** *plan* … o kangaedasu …

を考え出す

third 1 *adj* dai san (no) 第三(の) **2** *n* dai san banme 第三番目; (*of month*) mikka 三日; (*in race*) san'i 三位; (*fraction*) sanbun no ichi 三分の一

thirdly dai san ni 第三に

third-party insurance songaibaishō-hoken 損害賠償保険; **third-rate** sanryū (no) 三流(の); **Third World** Daisan-sekai 第三世界

thirst nodo no kawaki 喉の渇き

thirsty: ***I'm ~*** nodo ga kawaite iru 喉が渇いている; ***it's ~ work*** nodo no kawaku shigoto da のどの渇く仕事だ

thirteen jūsan 十三

thirteenth dai-jūsan (no) 第十三(の)

thirtieth dai-san jū (no) 第三十(の)

thirty sanjū 三十

this 1 *adj* kono この; ***~ one*** kore これ **2** *pron* kore これ; ***~ is good*** kore wa ii これはいい; ***~ is...*** (*introducing*) kochira wa ... san desu こちらは...さんです; TELEC ... to mōshimasu ga ...と申しますが **3** *adv* koregrai これぐらい; ***~ big*** koregurai ōkii これぐらい大きい

thorn toge とげ

thorough *search* tetteiteki (na) 徹底的(な); *knowledge* kanzen (na) 完全(な); *person* tettei shite iru 徹底している

thoroughbred (*horse*) sarabureddo サラブレッド

those 1 *adj* (*further away from both speaker and listener*) ano あの; (*nearer to listener, previously known to listener*) sono その **2** *pron* (*further away from both speaker and listener*) are あれ; (*nearer to listener, previously known to listener*) sore それ

though 1 *conj* (*although*) keredomo けれども; ***~ it might fail*** shippai suru kamo shirenai ga 失敗するかもしれないが; ***as ~*** ... no yō ni ...のように **2** *adv* demo でも; ***it's not finished ~*** owatte inai keredo 終わっていないけれど

thought (*single*) kangae 考え; (*collective*) shisō 思想

thoughtful kangaekonda 考え込んだ; (*considerate*) omoiyari no aru 思いやりのある

thoughtless keisotsu (na) 軽率(な)

thousand sen 千; ***ten ~*** man 万; ***~s of*** tasū no... 多数の...

thousandth dai-issen (no) 第一千(の)

thrash *v/t* utsu 打つ; SP uchimakasu 打ち負かす

♦ **thrash around** (*with arms etc*) furimawasu 振り回す

♦ **thrash out** *solution* ... o dakai suru ...を打開する

thrashing ōda 殴打

thread 1 *n* ito 糸; (*of screw*) nejiyama ネジ山 **2** *v/t needle* ... ni ito o tōsu ...に糸を通す; *beads* tōsu 通す

threadbare surikireta すりきれた

threat kyōhaku 脅迫; (*to national security, environment*) kyōi 脅威

threaten kyōhaku suru 脅迫する; *national security, environment* obiyakasu 脅かす

threatening *gesture, tone* osoroshii 恐ろしい; ***~ sky*** aresō na sora 荒れそうな空

three san 三; (*with countword*) mittsu 三つ

three-quarters *n* yonbun no san 四分の三

thresh *corn* dakkoku suru 脱穀する

threshold (*of house*) shikii 敷居; (*limit*) genkai 限界; (*of new age*) sakaime 境目; ***on the ~ of*** ... no iriguchi ni ...の入り口に; ***I have a low pain ~*** watashi no itami ni tai suru genkai wa hikui 私の痛みに対する限界は低い

thrift ken'yaku 倹約

thrifty shisso (na) 質素(な)

thrill 1 *n* suriru スリル **2** *v/t*: ***be ~ed*** wakuwaku suru わくわくする

thriller surirā-mono スリラー物

thrilling wakuwaku saseru わくわくさせる

thrive (*of plant*) sodatsu 育つ; (*of

firm, economy) sakaeru 栄える
throat nodo のど
throat lozenges nodo-ame のどあめ
throb 1 *n* (*of heart*) kodō 鼓動; (*of music*) rizumu リズム **2** *v/i* (*of heart*) kodō suru 鼓動する; (*of music*) rizumu o utsu リズムを打つ
thrombosis kessenshō 血栓症
throne ōza 王座
throttle 1 *n* (*on motorbike, boat*) surottoru スロットル **2** *v/t* (*strangle*) … no nodo o shimeru … ののどを絞める
♦**throttle back** *v/i* gensoku suru 減速する
through 1 *prep* ◊ (*across*) yokogitte 横切って; ***go ~ the city*** machi o tōri nukeru 町を通り抜ける ◊ (*with time*): ***~ the winter / summer*** fuyu / natsu jū 冬/夏中; ***Monday ~ Friday*** getsuyōbi kara kin'yōbi made 月曜日から金曜日まで ◊ (*by means of*) … o tōshite …を通して; ***arranged ~ him*** kare o tōshite tehai shita 彼を通して手配した **2** *adv*: ***wet ~*** bishonure de びしょぬれで; ***watch a movie ~*** eiga o saigo made miru 映画を最後まで見る; ***read a book ~*** hon o yomitōsu 本を読み通す **3** *adj*: ***be ~*** (*of couple*) owaru 終わる; (*have arrived*: *of news etc*) todoku 届く; ***you're ~*** TELEC tsunagarimashita つながりました; ***I'm ~ with him*** kare to wa owatta 彼とは終わった; ***give me the paper back when you're ~ with it*** yomiowattara shinbun o kaeshite kudasai 読み終わったら新聞を返してください
through flight chokkō-bin 直行便
throughout 1 *prep*: ***~ the day*** shūjitsu 終日; ***~ the night*** shūya 終夜; ***~ one's life*** shōgai o tsūjite 生涯を通じて; ***~ the war*** sensō no aidajū 戦争の間中; ***~ the book*** hon no hajime kara owari made 本の初めから終わりまで **2** *adv* (*in all parts*) zenbu 全部
through train chokkō-ressha 直行列車
throw 1 *v/t* nageru 投げる; (*of horse*) furiotosu 振り落とす; (*disconcert*) konran saseru 混乱させる; *party* hiraku 開く **2** *n* nage 投げ
♦**throw away** … o suteru …を捨てる
♦**throw out** *old things* … o suteru … を捨てる; *drunk, husband* … o oidasu …を追い出す; *plan* … o kyakka suru …を却下する
♦**throw up 1** *v/t ball* … o nageru … を投げる; ***~ one's hands*** odoroku 驚く **2** *v/i* (*vomit*) haku 吐く
throw-away *remark* sarigenai さりげない; (*disposable*) tsukaisute (no) 使い捨て(の)
throw-in SP surō in スローイン
thru → ***through***
thrush (*bird*) tsugumi つぐみ
thrust *v/t* (*push hard*) tsuyoku osu 強く押す; ***~ X into Y's hands*** X o Y no te ni oshitsukeru XをYの手に押しつける; ***~ one's way through the crowd*** hitogomi o oshiwakete susumu 人込みを押し分けて進む
thud *n* dosun to ochiru oto ドスンと落ちる音
thug yakuza やくざ
thumb 1 *n* oyayubi 親指 **2** *v/t*: ***~ a ride*** hitchi-haiku suru ヒッチハイクする
thumbtack gabyō 画びょう
thump 1 *n* (*blow*) naguru koto 殴ること; (*noise*) gotsun to iu oto ゴツンという音 **2** *v/t person* naguru 殴る; ***~ one's fist on the table*** kobushi de tēburu tataku こぶしでテーブルをたたく **3** *v/i* (*of heart*) shinzō gadokidoki suru 心臓がドキドキする; ***~ on the door*** doa o dondon tataku ドアをドンドンたたく
thunder *n* kaminari 雷
thunderstorm raiu 雷雨
thundery *weather* kaminari no kisō (na) 雷のきそう(な)
Thursday mokuyōbi 木曜日
thus (*in this way*) kōshite こうして; (*as a consequence*) shitagatte 従って

thwart dame ni suru だめにする
thyroid (**gland**) kōjōsen 甲状腺
Tibet Chibetto チベット
Tibetan 1 *adj* Chibetto (no) チベット(の) **2** *n* (*person*) Chibetto-jin チベット人; (*language*) Chibetto-go チベット語
tick 1 *n* (*of clock*) kachikachi naru oto カチカチなる音; (*checkmark*) chekku no shirushi チェックの印 **2** *v/i* (*of clock*) kachikachi naru カチカチなる
♦ **tick off** … o shikaru …をしかる
ticket kippu 切符
ticket barrier kaisatsu-guchi 改札口; **ticket collector** kaisatsu-gakari 改札係; **ticket inspector** shashō 車掌; **ticket machine** kippu-hanbaiki 切符販売機; **ticket office** (*at station*, THEA) kippu-uriba 切符売場
tickle 1 *v/t person* kusuguru くすぐる **2** *v/i* (*of material*) chikuchiku suru チクチクする; (*of person*) kusuguttai くすぐったい
ticklish *person* kusuguttagari (no) くすぐったがり(の)
tidal wave tsunami 津波
tide shio 潮の干満; ***high ~*** manchō 満潮; ***low ~*** kanchō 干潮; ***the ~ is in / out*** manchō / kanchō da 満潮/干潮だ
tidy *person, habits* kichin to shita きちんとした; *room, house* kogirei (na) こぎれい(な)
♦ **tidy up 1** *v/t room, shelves* … o katazukeru …を片づける; ***tidy oneself up*** kichin to suru きちんとする **2** *v/i* katazukeru 片づける
tie 1 *n* (*necktie*) nekutai ネクタイ; (SP: *even result*) hikiwake 引き分け; ***he doesn't have any ~s*** kare ni wa nani mo sokubaku suru mono ga nai 彼には何も束縛するものがない **2** *v/t knot* musubu 結ぶ; *hands* tsunagu つなぐ **3** *v/i* SP dōten ni naru 同点になる
♦ **tie down** (*with rope*) … o shibaritsukeru …を縛り付ける; (*restrict*) … o kōsoku suru …を拘束する
♦ **tie up** *person* … o shibaru …を縛る; *laces, hair* … o musubu …を結ぶ; *boat* … o tsunagu …をつなぐ; ***I'm tied up tomorrow*** ashita wa isogashii 明日は忙しい
tier (*of hierarchy*) sō 層; (*in stadium*) dan 段
tiger tora トラ
tight 1 *adj clothes* kitsui きつい; *security* kibishii 厳しい; (*hard to move*) katai 堅い; (*properly shut*) kichin to shimatte iru きちんと閉まっている; (*not leaving much time*) kitsui きつい; F (*drunk*) dekiagatte iru 出来上がっている **2** *adv hold* shikkari しっかり; *shut* kichin to きちんと
tighten *screw* kataku shimeru 堅く絞める; *control, security* kibishiku suru 厳しくする; ***~ one's grip on*** … o shikkari nigiru …をしっかり握る
♦ **tighten up** *v/i* (*in discipline, security*) kibishiku naru 厳しくなる
tight-fisted kechi (na) けち(な)
tightrope tsuna-watari no tsuna 綱渡りの綱
tile tairu タイル
till[1] → ***until***
till[2] (*cash register*) reji レジ
till[3] *v/t soil* tagayasu 耕す
tilt 1 *v/t* katamukeru 傾ける **2** *v/i* katamuku 傾く
timber zaimoku 材木
time jikan 時間; (*occasion*) kai 回; ***~ is up*** jikangire de aru 時間切れである; ***for the ~ being*** ima no tokoro 今のところ; ***have a good ~*** tanoshimu 楽しむ; ***have a good ~!*** tanoshinde ne 楽しんでね; ***what's the ~?***, ***what ~ is it?*** ima nanji desu ka 今何時ですか; ***the first ~*** hajimete 初めて; ***four ~s*** yon kai 四回; ***~ and again*** nankai mo 何回も; ***all the ~*** zutto ずっと; ***they came in two / three at a ~*** karera wa futari / sannin zutsu haitte kita 彼らは二人/三人ずつ入って来た; ***at the same ~*** *speak, reply etc* dōji ni 同時に; (*however*) shikashi しかし; ***be in ~*** ma ni au 間に合う;

on **~** jikan dōri 時間どおり; ***in no ~*** sugu ni すぐに
time bomb jigen bakudan 時限爆弾; **time clock** (*in factory*) taimu-rekōdā タイムレコーダー;**time-consuming** jikan no kakaru 時間のかかる;**timelag** jikan no zure 時間のずれ;**time limit** shimekiri 締め切り
timely taimingu ga ii タイミングがいい
time out SP taimu-auto タイムアウト
timer taimā タイマー
timesaving *n* jikan no setsuyaku 時間の節約;**timescale** (*of project*) nagare 流れ;**time switch** taimā タイマー;**timetable** (*for trains*) jikokuhyō 時刻表; (*at school*) jikanwari 時間割;**timewarp** wāpu ワープ;**time zone** jikantai 時間帯
timid okubyō(na) 憶病(な)
timing (*choosing a time*) taimingu タイミング; (*of actor, dancer*) ma no torikata 間の取り方
tin (*metal*) suzu すず
tinfoil hoiru ホイル
tinge: ***a ~ of red*** akamigakatta iro 赤みがかった色; ***a ~ of sadness*** monoganashi-sa もの悲しさ
tingle *v/i* hirihiri itamu ひりひり痛む
♦**tinker with** … o ijiru …をいじる
tinkle *n* (*of bell*) rinrin to naru oto リンリンと鳴る音
tinsel mōru モール
tint 1 *n* (*of color*) iroai 色合い; (*in hair*) kezome 毛染め **2** *v/t hair* kami o someru 髪を染める
tinted *glasses* iro no tsuita 色のついた; *paper* irotsuki (no) 色つき(の)
tiny totemo chiisai とても小さい
tip[1] *n* (*of stick, finger*) saki 先; (*of mountain*) chōjō 頂上; (*of cigarette*) sentan 先端
tip[2] **1** *n* (*piece of advice*) mimiyori no jōhō 耳寄りの情報; (*money*) chippu チップ **2** *v/t waiter etc* chippu o watasu チップを渡す
♦**tip off** … o naihō suru …を内報する
♦**tip over** *glass, liquid* … o hikkurikaesu …をひっくりかえす; ***he tipped water all over me*** kare wa watashi ni mizu o kakemashita 彼はわたしに水をかけました
tipped *cigarettes* firutā no tsuita フィルターのついた
tippy-toe: ***on ~*** tsumasakidachi de つま先立ちで
tipsy chotto yopparatta ちょっと酔っ払った
tire[1] *n* taiya タイヤ
tire[2] **1** *v/t* tsukare saseru 疲れさせる **2** *v/i* tsukareru 疲れる; ***he never ~s of it*** kare wa zenzen sore ni akinai 彼は全然それにあきない
tired tsukareta 疲れた; ***be ~ of***… ni unzari shita …にうんざりした
tireless *efforts* fudan (no) 不断(の)
tiresome taikutsu (na) 退屈(な)
tiring tsukareru 疲れる
tissue ANAT soshiki 組織; (*handkerchief*) orimono 織物
tissue paper tisshu pēpā ティッシュペーパー
tit[1] (*bird*) shijūkara しじゅうから
tit[2]: ***~ for tat*** shippegaeshi しっぺ返し
tit[3] V (*breast*) chibusa 乳房
title dai 題; (*of person*) katagaki 肩書き; LAW kenri 権利
titter *v/i* kusukusu warau くすくす笑う
to 1 *prep*: ***~ Japan*** Nihon e 日本へ; ***~ Chicago*** Shikago e シカゴへ; ***go ~ my place*** watashi no uchi ni iku 私の家に行く; ***walk ~ the station*** eki made aruku 駅まで歩く; ***~ the north / south of*** … no kita / minami e …の北/南へ; ***give X ~ Y*** X o Y ni ageru XをYにあげる; ***from Monday ~ Wednesday*** getsuyōbi kara suiyōbi made 月曜日から水曜日まで; ***from 10 ~ 15 people*** jūnin kara jūgonin made 十人から十五人まで **2** (*with verbs*) … suru koto …すること; ***~ speak*** hanasu koto 話すこと; ***~ shout*** sakebu koto 叫ぶこと; ***learn ~ drive*** unten o narau 運転を習う; ***it's nice ~ eat*** oishii desu おいしいです; ***too heavy ~ carry*** omosugite motenai 重過ぎて持てない; ***~ honest with you …*** shōjiki ni iu to

正直に言うと **3** *adv*: ***~ and fro*** ittari kitari 行ったり来たり
toad hikigaeru ひきがえる
toadstool doku kinoko 毒きのこ
toast 1 *n* tōsuto トースト; (*when drinking*) kanpai 乾杯; ***propose a ~ to*** … ni kanpai …に乾杯 **2** *v/t* (*when drinking*) kanpai suru 乾杯する
tobacco tabako タバコ
toboggan *n* sori そり
today kyō 今日
toddle (*of child*) yochiyochi aruku よちよち歩く
toddler yochiyochi aruki no yōji よちよち歩きの幼児
toe 1 *n* ashi no yubi 足の指; (*of shoe*) tsumasaki つま先 **2** *v/t*: ***~ the line*** kitaidōri ni furumau 期待どうりに振る舞う
toffee kyandī キャンディ
tofu tōfu とうふ
together issho ni 一緒に; (*at the same time*) dōji ni 同時に
toil *n* kurō 苦労
toilet toire トイレ; ***go to the ~*** toire ni iku トイレに行く
toilet paper toiretto pēpā トイレットペーパー
toiletries senmen yōgu 洗面用具
token (*sign*) shirushi しるし; (*gift ~*) shōhinken 商品券
Tokyo Tōkyō 東京
tolerable *pain etc* gaman dekiru 我慢できる; (*quite good*) kanari yoi かなりよい
tolerance kan'yō 寛容
tolerant kan'yō (na) 寛容(な)
tolerate *noise, person* kyoyō suru 許容する; ***I won't ~ it!*** gaman dekinai 我慢できない
toll[1] *v/i* (*of bell*) naru 鳴る
toll[2] (*deaths*) gisei-sha no kazu 犠牲者の数
toll[3] (*for bridge, road*) tsūkō-ryō 通行料; TELEC chōkyori-tsūwaryō 長距離通話料
toll booth ryōkin-sho 料金所; **toll-free** TELEC furī-daiaru フリーダイアル; **toll road** yūryō-dōro 有料道路
tomato tomato トマト
tomato ketchup tomato-kechappu トマトケチャップ
tomb haka 墓
tomboy otenba おてんば
tombstone hakaishi 墓石
tomcat osuneko おす猫
tomorrow ashita 明日; ***the day after ~*** asatte あさって; ***~ morning*** ashita no asa 明日の朝; ***tomorrow ~*** ashita no yoru 明日の夜
ton ton トン
tone (*of color*) nōtan 濃淡; (*of musical instrument*) neiro 音色; (*of conversation etc*) chōshi 調子; (*of neighborhood*) fun'iki 雰囲気; ***~ of voice*** kuchō 口調
♦ **tone down** *demands, criticism* yawarageru 和らげる
toner tonā トナー
tongs (*for sugar*) satō-basami 砂糖ばさみ; (*for ice*) kōri-basami 氷ばさみ; (*for fire*) hi-basami 火ばさみ; (*for hair*) kote こて
tongue *n* shita 舌
tonic MED kyōsōzai 強壮剤
tonic (water) tonikku wōtā トニックウォーター
tonight konban 今晩
tonsillitis hentōsen-en 扁桃腺炎
tonsils hentōsen 扁桃腺
too (*also*) …mo mata … もまた; (*excessively*) …sugiru …すぎる; ***me ~*** watashi mo 私も; ***~ big / hot*** ōki-sugiru / atsu-sugiru 大きすぎる/熱すぎる; ***~ much rice*** gohan ga ō-sugiru ごはんが多すぎる; ***eat ~ much*** tabe-sugiru 食べ過ぎる
tool dōgu 道具
tooth ha 歯
toothache haita 歯痛
toothbrush ha-burashi 歯ブラシ
toothless hanashi (no) 歯なし(の)
toothpaste ha-migaki 歯磨き
toothpick tsumayōji つまようじ
top 1 *n* (*of mountain, tree*) sentan 先端; (*upper part*) ue 上; (*lid: of bottle etc, pen*) futa ふた; (*of the class, league*) ichiban 一番; (*clothing*) uwagi 上着; (MOT: *gear*) toppu gia トップギア; ***on ~ of*** …

no ue ni …の上に; ***at the ~ of*** … no ichiban ni …の一番に; ***at the ~ of the tree*** kozue ni こずえに; ***at the ~ of the mountain*** chōjō ni 頂上に; ***get to the ~*** (*of company etc*) toppu ni noboritsumeru トップにのぼりつめる; ***be over the ~*** (*exaggerated*) yari-sugiru やりすぎる **2** *adj branches* saikō (no) 最高(の); *floor* saijōkai 最上階; *management, official* saikō-kanbu 最高幹部; *player* sugureta senshu 優れた選手; *speed, note* saikō 最高 **3** *v/t* … no ue o ōu の上をおおう; ***~ped with cream*** ue o kurīmu de kazatta 上をクリームで飾った

♦**top up** *glass, tank* … o ue ni tsugitasu …を上につぎたす

top hat shiruku hatto シルクハット; **topheavy** atamadekkachi (no) 頭でっかち(の); **top knot** chonnmage ちょんまげ

topic wadai 話題

topical wadai (no) 話題(の)

topless *adj* toppuresu (no) トップレス(の)

topmost *branches, floor* ichiban ue (no) 一番上(の)

topping (*on pizza*) toppingu トッピング

topple 1 *v/i* kuzureochiru 崩れ落ちる **2** *v/t government* taosu 倒す

top secret *adj* saikō-kimitsu (no) 最高機密(の)

topsy-turvy *adj* (*in disorder*) sakasama (no) 逆さま(の); *world* konran-jōtai (no) 混乱状態(の)

torch (*with flame*) taimatsu たいまつ

torment 1 *n* kurushimi 苦しみ **2** *v/t person, animal* itametsukeru 痛めつける; ***~ed by doubt*** utagai ni nayamasareta 疑いに悩まされた

tornado tatsumaki 竜巻

torrent gekiryū 激流; (*of abuse, words*) renpatsu 連発; ***~ of lava*** yōganryū 溶岩流

torrential dohaburi (no) 土砂降り(の)

tortoise kame かめ

torture 1 *n* gōmon 拷問 **2** *v/t* gōmon ni kakeru 拷問にかける

toss 1 *v/t ball* nageru 投げる; *rider* furiotosu 振り落とす; *salad* kakimazeru かき混ぜる; ***~ a coin*** koin o nagete kimeru コインを投げて決める **2** *v/i*: ***~ and turn*** negaeri o utsu 寝返りをうつ

total 1 *n* gōkei 合計 **2** *adj sum, amount* gōkei (no) 合計(の); *disaster, idiot* hidoi ひどい; *stranger* mattaku (no) まったく(の) **3** *v/t* F *car* mechamecha (no) めちゃめちゃ(の)

totalitarian zentai-shugi (no) 全体主義(の)

totally mattaku まったく

tote bag ōgata no tesage baggu 大型の手提げバッグ

totter (*of person*) yoromeku よろめく

touch 1 *n* (*act of touching*) tezawari 手ざわり; (*sense*) kanshoku 感触; (*little bit*) sukoshi 少し; SP tatchi タッチ; ***lose ~ with*** … to renraku ga todaeru …と連絡が途絶える; ***keep in ~ with*** … to renraku shite iru …と連絡している; ***we kept in ~*** yaritori o tsuzukeru やりとりを続ける; ***be out of ~*** … to sesshoku o ushinau …の感触を失う **2** *v/t* sawaru 触る; (*emotionally*) kandō saseru 感動させる **3** *v/i* sawaru 触る; (*of two lines etc*) sesshoku suru 接触する

♦**touch down** *v/i* (*of airplane*) chakuriku suru 着陸する; SP tatchidaun suru タッチダウンする

♦**touch on** (*mention*) … ni chotto furete oku …にちょっと触れておく

♦**touch up** *photo* … o shūsei suru …を修正する

touchdown (*of airplane*) chakuriku 着陸; SP tatchidaun タッチダウン

touching *adj* mune o utsu 胸をうつ

touchline SP saidorain サイドライン

touchy *person* shinkeishitsu (na) 神経質(な)

tough *person* ki no tsuyoi 気の強い; *meat* katai 固い; *question, exam* muzukashii 難しい; *material* tsuyoi 強い; *punishment* omoi 重い

tough guy tafu gai タフガイ

tour 1 *n* ryokō 旅行 **2** *v/t area* ryokō suru 旅行する
tourism kankō jigyō 観光事業
tourist kankōkyaku 観光客
tourist (information) office kankō annaisho 観光案内所
tournament tōnamento トーナメント
tour operator ryokō-gaisha 旅行会社
tousled *hair* midareta 乱れた
tow 1 *v/t car, boat* hipparu 引っ張る **2** *n*: ***give X a ~*** X o ken'in suru Xをけん引する
♦**tow away** *car* ken'in sarete motte ikareru けん引されて持っていかれる
toward *prep* … no hō e …の方へ
towel taoru タオル
tower *n* tō 塔
town machi 町
town council chōgikai 町議会; **town councilor** chōgikai-giin 町議会議員; **town hall** shiyakusho 市役所
towrope ken'in-rōpu けん引ロープ
toxic yūdoku (na) 有毒(な)
toy omocha おもちゃ
♦**toy with** *object* … o ijikuru …をいじくる; *idea* … o chotto kangaete iru …をちょっと考えている
trace 1 *n* (*of substance*) ato 跡 **2** *v/t* (*find*) sagashidasu 捜し出す; *footsteps* shiraberu 調べる; (*draw*) utsusu 写す
track *n* (*path*) komichi 小道; (*for racing*) kōsu コース; RAIL tetsudō senro 鉄道線路; ***~ 10*** RAIL jūbansen 十番線; ***keep ~ of*** … o kiroku suru …を記録する
♦**track down** … o mitsukedasu …を見つけ出す
tracksuit suwetto sūtsu スウェットスーツ
tractor torakutā トラクター
trade 1 *n* (*commerce*) bōeki 貿易; (*profession, craft*) shokugyō 職業 **2** *v/i* (*do business*) torihiki suru 取り引きする; ***~ in*** … o atsukau …を扱う **3** *v/t* (*exchange*) kōkan suru 交換する; ***~ X for Y*** X o Y to kōkan suru XをYと交換する
♦**trade in** *v/t* (*when buying*) … o shitadori suru …を下取りする
trade fair mihon'ichi 見本市; **trademark** tōroku-shōhyō 登録商標; **trade mission** bōeki-shisetsudan 貿易使節団
trader FIN torēdā トレーダー
trade secret kigyō-himitsu 企業秘密
tradesman (*plumber etc*) shokunin 職人
trade(s) union rōdō-kumiai 労働組合
tradition dentō 伝統, iitsutae 言い伝え
traditional dentōteki (na) 伝統的(な)
traditionally dentōteki ni 伝統的に
traffic *n* (*on roads*) kōtsū 交通; (*at airport*) ōrai 往来; (*in drugs*) mitsubaibai 密売買
♦**traffic in** *drugs* … o mitsubaibai suru …を密売買する
traffic circle rōtarī ロータリー; **traffic cop** F kōtsū-keisatsukan 交通警察官; **traffic island** anzen-chitai 安全地帯; **traffic jam** kōtsū-jūtai 交通渋滞; **traffic light** shingō 信号; **traffic police** kōtsū-keisatsu 交通警察; **traffic sign** kōtsū-hyōshiki 交通標識; **traffic warden** kōtsū-kanshiin 交通監視員
tragedy higeki 悲劇
tragic higeki (no) 悲劇(の)
trail 1 *n* (*path*) michi 道; (*of blood*) ato 跡 **2** *v/t* (*follow*) ato o tsukeru 跡をつける; (*tow*) hipparu 引っぱる **3** *v/i* (*lag behind*) okure o toru 後れを取る
trailer (*pulled by vehicle*) torērā トレーラー; (*mobile home*) torērā hausu トレーラーハウス; (*of movie*) yokokuhen 予告編
train[1] *n* ressha 列車; ***go by ~*** ressha de iku 列車で行く
train[2] **1** *v/t team, athlete* kitaeru 鍛える; *employee* kyōiku suru 教育する; *dog* chōkyō suru 調教する **2** *v/i* (*of team, athlete*) kitaeru 鍛える; (*of teacher etc*) kenshū suru 研修する
trainee kenshūsei 研修生

trainer SP torēnā トレーナー; (*of dog*) chōkyō-shi 調教師
trainers *Br* (*shoes*) sunīkā スニーカー
training (*of staff*) kenshū 研修; SP renshū 練習; ***be in ~*** SP renshū o tsunde iru 練習を積んでいる; ***be out of ~*** SP renshū-busoku de aru 練習不足である
training course kenshū kōsu 研修コース
training scheme renshū-keikaku 練習計画
train station eki 駅
trait tokushoku 特色
traitor hangyaku-sha 反逆者
tramp *v/i* omoi ashidori de aruku 重い足取りで歩く
trample *v/t* fumitsukeru 踏みつける; ***be ~d to death*** fumikorosareru 踏み殺される; ***be ~d underfoot*** fumikorosare-sōni naru 踏み殺されそうになる
♦ **trample on** *person, object* … o fumitsukeru …を踏みつける
trampoline toranporin トランポリン
trance yume-utsutsu 夢うつつ; ***go into a ~*** kōkotsu-jōtai ni naru こうこつ状態になる
tranquil shizuka (na) 静か(な)
tranquility seijaku 静寂
tranquilizer seishin-anteizai 精神安定剤
transact *deal, business* okonau 行う
transaction torihiki 取引
transatlantic Taiseiyō ōdan (no) 大西洋横断(の)
transcendental chōshizenteki (na) 超自然的(な)
transcript (*of meeting, trial*) kiroku-bunsho 記録文書
transfer 1 *v/t* idō saseru 移動させる **2** *v/i* (*switch*) kirikaeru 切り替える; (*in travel*) idō suru 移動する **3** *n* idō 移動; (*in travel*) norikae 乗り換え; (*of money*) sōkin 送金
transferable *ticket* jōto dekiru 譲渡できる
transform *v/t* henkei saseru 変形させる
transformation henkei 変形
transformer ELEC hen'atsuki 変圧器
transfusion yuketsu 輸血
transistor toranjisutā トランジスター; (*radio*) rajio ラジオ
transit ***in ~*** *goods, passengers* idōchū (no) 移動中(の)
transition utsurikawari 移り変わり
transitional katoki (no) 過渡期(の)
transit lounge norikae-kyakuyō-raunji 乗り換え客用ラウンジ
translate hon'yaku suru 翻訳する
translation hon'yaku 翻訳
translator hon'yaku-sha 翻訳者
transliterate on'yaku suru 音訳する
transmission (*of program*) dentatsu 伝達; (*of disease*) densen 伝染; MOT hensokuki 変速機
transmit *program* okuru 送る; *disease* utsusu うつす
transmitter RAD, TV sōshinki 送信機
transpacific Taiheiyō-ōdan (no) 太平洋横断(の)
transparent tōmei (no) 透明(の); (*obvious*) miesuita 見え透いた
transplant MED **1** *v/t* ishoku suru 移植する **2** *n* ishoku 移植
transport 1 *v/t* yusō suru 輸送する **2** *n* yusō 輸送
transportation yusō-kikan 輸送機関; ***means of ~*** kōtsū-kikan 交通機関; ***public ~*** kōkyō-kōtsūkikan 公共交通機関; ***Department of Transportation*** Un'yushō 運輸省
transvestite fukusōtōsaku-sha 服装倒錯者
trap 1 *n* (*for animal*) wana わな; (*question, set-up etc*) sakuryaku 策略; ***set a ~ for*** … o wana ni kakeru …をわなにかける **2** *v/t animal* … ni wana o shikakeru …にわなをしかける; *person* wana ni kakeru わなにかける; ***be ~ped*** (*by enemy, etc*) hamatta はまった; ***be ~ped by the flames*** honō ni torikakomareta 炎にとりかこまれた
trapdoor otoshido 落とし戸
trapeze kūchū-buranko 空中ブランコ
trappings (*of power*) tokuten 特典

trash (*garbage*) kuzu くず; (*poor product*) garakuta がらくた; (*book, movie*) dasaku 駄作; ***he's ~*** kare wa kudaranai hito da 彼はくだらない人だ
trashcan kuzuire くず入れ
trashy *goods* kudaranai くだらない
traumatic shōgekiteki (na) 衝撃的(な)
travel 1 *n* ryokō 旅行; ***~s*** ryokō-chū 旅行中 **2** *v/i* ryokō suru 旅行する; (*to work*) tsūkin suru 通勤する; ***~ by boat / train*** fune / densha de iku 船/電車で行く **3** *v/t*: ***I ~ 15 miles by car every day*** mainichi jūgo mairu kuruma de hashiru 毎日15マイル車で走る
travel agency ryokō-sha 旅行社
travel bag ryokō-kaban 旅行かばん
traveler ryokō-sha 旅行者
traveler's check toraberāzu-chekku トラベラーズチェック
travel expenses shutchō-ryohi 出張旅費; **travel insurance** ryokō-hoken 旅行保険; **travelsick** norimonoyoi shita 乗り物酔いした
trawler torōru-sen トロール船
tray (*for food etc*) bon 盆; (*to go in oven*) ōbun-zara オーブン皿; (*in printer, copier*) torei トレイ
treacherous *person* fuseijitsu (na) 不誠実(な); *current, road* kiken (na) 危険(な)
treachery uragiri 裏切り
tread 1 *n* ashioto 足音; (*of tire*) toreddo トレッド **2** *v/i* aruku 歩く
♦ **tread on** *s.o.'s foot* … o fumu …を踏む
treason hangyakuzai 反逆罪
treasure 1 *n* takara 宝; ***he is a ~*** kare wa subarashii hito da 彼はすばらしい人だ **2** *v/t gift etc* taisetsu ni suru 大切にする
treasurer kaikei-gakari 会計係
Treasury Department Ōkura-shō 大蔵省
treat 1 *n* tanoshimi 楽しみ; ***it was a real ~*** totemo tanoshikatta desu とても楽しかったです; ***I have a ~ for you*** anata o yorokobasu mono ga arimasu あなたを喜ばすものがあります; ***it's my ~*** (*I'm paying*) watashi no ogori desu 私のおごりです **2** *v/t materials* shori suru 処理する; *illness* chiryō suru 治療する; (*behave toward*) atsukau 扱う; ***~ X to Y*** X ni Y o ogoru XにYをおごる
treatment (*of materials*) toriatsukai 取り扱い; (*of illness*) chiryō 治療; (*of people*) taigū 待遇
treaty jōyaku 条約; ***the Japan-US Security Treaty*** Nichibeianzen-hoshōjōyaku 日米安全保障条約
treble[1] (*singer*) bōi-sopurano ボーイソプラノ
treble[2] **1** *adv*: ***~ the price*** nedan ga sanbai ni naru 値段が三倍になる **2** *v/i* sanbai ni naru 三倍になる
tree ki 木
tremble furueru 震える; (*of building*) yureru 揺れる
tremendous (*very good*) subarashii すばらしい; (*enormous*) monosugoi ものすごい
tremendously hijō ni 非常に
tremor (*of earth*) shindō 震動
trench zangō ざんごう
trend keikō 傾向; (*fashion*) ryūkō 流行
trendy hayari (no) はやり(の)
trespass … ni fuhō-shinnyū suru …に不法侵入する; ***no ~ing*** tachiiri-kinshi 立ち入り禁止
♦ **trespass on** *land* … ni fuhō-shinnyū suru …に不法侵入する; *privacy* … o shingai suru …を侵害する
trespasser fuhō-shinnyū-sha 不法侵入者
trial LAW saiban 裁判; (*of equipment*) tesuto テスト; ***on ~*** LAW saiban ni kakerarete 裁判にかけられて; ***have on ~*** *equipment* … o tameshite miru …を試してみる
trial period (*for employee*) shiyō-kikan 試用期間; (*for equipment*) tesuto-kikan テスト期間
triangle sankakkei 三角形
triangular sankaku (no) 三角(の)
tribe shuzoku 種族
tribunal shingi-iinkai 審議委員会
tributary shiryū 支流

trick 1 *n* (*to deceive*) keiryaku 計略; (*knack*) kotsu こつ; ***play a ~ on*** … o damasu …をだます **2** *v/t* damasu だます; ***~ X into doing Y*** X o damashite Y saseru XをだましてYさせる

trickery keiryaku 計略

trickle *v / i* sukoshi zutsu nagareru 少しずつ流れる

trickster sagishi 詐欺師

tricky (*difficult*) yayakoshii ややこしい

tricycle sanrinsha 三輪車

trifle (*triviality*) sasai na koto ささいなこと

trifling kudaranai くだらない

trigger *n* hikigane 引き金

♦**trigger off** … no hikigane ni naru …の引き金になる

trim 1 *adj* (*neat*) teire sareta 手入れされた; *figure* hikishimatta 引き締まった **2** *v/t hair, hedge* kirisoroeru 切りそろえる; *budget, costs* kiritsumeru 切り詰める; (*decorate: dress*) kazaru 飾る **3** *n* (*light cut*) karikomi 刈り込み; ***just a ~, please*** (*to hairdresser*) soroete kudasai そろえてください; ***in good ~*** chōshi no ii 調子のいい

trimming (*on clothes*) kazari 飾り; ***with all the ~s*** *dish* tsukeawase zenbu to 付け合わせ全部と; *fig* fuzokuhin zenbu to 付属品全部と

trinket sōshingu 装身具

trio MUS sanjūsō 三重奏

trip 1 *n* (*journey*) ryokō 旅行 **2** *v/i* (*stumble*) tsumazuku つまずく **3** *v/t* (*make fall*) ... no ashi o sukuu . . . の足をすくう

♦**trip up 1** *v/t* (*make fall*) … no ashi o sukuu …の足をすくう; (*cause to go wrong*) … o konran saseru …を混乱させる **2** *v/i* (*stumble*) ashi o sukuwareru 足をすくわれる; (*make a mistake*) hema o suru へまをする

tripe ushi no i 牛の胃

triple → ***treble***[2]

triplets mitsugo 三つ子

tripod PHOT sankyaku 三脚

trite arifureta ありふれた

triumph *n* shōri 勝利

trivial sasai (na) ささい(な)

triviality heibon 平凡

trombone toronbōn トロンボーン

troops guntai 軍隊

trophy torofī トロフィー

tropic kaikisen 回帰線

tropical nettai (no) 熱帯(の)

tropics nettaichihō 熱帯地方

trot *v/i* hayaashi de kakeru 速足でかける

trouble 1 *n* (*difficulties*) kurō 苦労; (*disease*) byōki 病気; (*inconvenience*) mendō 面倒; (*quarrel*) sawagi 騒ぎ; (*armed conflict*) funsō 紛争; ***go to a lot of ~ to do X*** X suru no ni hone o oru Xするのに骨を折る; ***no ~!*** daijōbu 大丈夫; ***get into ~*** mendō na koto ni naru 面倒なことになる **2** *v/t* (*worry*) nayamaseru 悩ませる; (*bother, disturb*) meiwaku o kakeru 迷惑をかける; (*of back, liver etc*) chōshi o waruku suru 調子を悪くする

trouble-free koshō no nai 故障のない; **troublemaker** toraburu-mēkā トラブルメーカー; **troubleshooter** (*mediator*) chōteinin 調停人; **troubleshooting** mondai-kaiketsu 問題解決

troublesome mendō (na) 面倒(な)

trousers *Br* zubon ズボン

trout masu ます

truce kyūsen 休戦

truck torakku トラック

truck driver torakku no untenshu トラックの運転手; **truck farm** shijōmuke-yasaien 市場向け野菜園; **truck farmer** shijōmuke-yasai saibai-gyōsha 市場向け野菜栽培業者; **truck stop** keishokudō 軽食堂

trudge 1 *v/i* tobotobo aruku とぼとぼ歩く **2** *n* omoi ashidori 重い足取り

true *story, friend* hontō (no) 本当(の); ***come ~*** (*of hopes, dream*) genjitsu ni naru 現実になる

truly hontō ni 本当に; ***Yours ~*** keigu 敬具

trumpet *n* toranpetto トランペット

trunk (*of tree*) miki 幹; (*of body*) dō 胴; (*of elephant*) hana 鼻; (*container, of car*) toranku トランク

trust 1 *n* shinrai 信用; FIN shintaku 信託 **2** *v/t* shin'yō suru 信用する; ***I ~ you*** anata o shin'yō suru あなたを信用する

trusted shin'yō sareta 信用された

trustee jutaku-sha 受託者

trustful, trusting shin'yō shiyasui 信用しやすい

trustworthy ate ni naru 当てになる

truth shinjitsu 真実; ***the eternal ~s of …*** … no eien no shinri …の永遠の真理

truthful seijitsu (na) 誠実(な)

try 1 *v/t* tamesu 試す; LAW saiban suru 裁判する; ***~ to do X*** Xshiyō to suru Xしようとする **2** *v/i* tamesu 試す; ***you must ~ harder*** motto ganbaranakereba narimasen もっとがんばらなければなりません **3** *n* kokoromi 試み; ***can I have a ~?*** (*of food*) tabete mite mo ii desu ka 食べてみてもいいですか; (*at doing sth*) tameshitemite mo ii desu ka 試してみてもいいですか

♦**try on** *clothes* … o shichaku suru …を試着する

♦**try out** *machine, method* … o tameshitemiru …を試してみる

trying (*annoying*) tsurai つらい

T-shirt tī-shatsu ティーシャツ

tsunami tsunami 津波

tub (*bath*) furo-oke 風呂おけ; (*of liquid*) kame かめ; (*for yoghurt, ice cream*) iremono 入れ物

tubby *adj* zunguri shita ずんぐりした

tube (*pipe*) kuda 管, chikatetsu 地下鉄; (*of toothpaste, ointment*) chūbu チューブ

tubeless *tire* chūburesu taiya チューブレスタイヤ

tuberculosis kekkaku 結核

tuck 1 *n* (*in dress*) hida ひだ **2** *v/t* (*put*) shimaikomu しまい込む

♦**tuck away** (*put away*) … o shimaikomu …をしまい込む; (*eat*) … o kakikomu …をかき込む

♦**tuck in 1** *v/t children* … o kurumu …をくるむ; *sheets* … o hasami komu …を挟み込む **2** *v/i*: ***~!*** tappuri tabenasai たっぷり食べなさい

♦**tuck up** *sleeves etc* … o makuru …をまくる; ***tuck X up in bed*** X o nekasu Xを寝かす

Tuesday kayōbi 火曜日

tuft taba 束

tug 1 *n* NAUT tagubōto タグボート; ***I felt a ~ at my sleeve*** sode o hippararerū no o kanjita そでを引っ張られるのを感じた **2** *v/t* (*pull*) hipparu 引っ張る

tuition: ***private ~*** katei-kyōshi 家庭教師

tulip chūrippu チューリップ

tumble *v/i* taoreru 倒れる

tumbledown tsuburesō (na) つぶれそう(な)

tumbler (*for drink*) gurasu グラス; (*in circus*) karuwaza-shi 軽業師

tummy onaka おなか

tummy ache onakaita おなか痛

tumor shuyō しゅよう

tumult sōdō 騒動

tumultuous sōzōshii 騒々しい

tuna maguro まぐろ; (*canned*) tsuna ツナ

tune 1 *n* merodī メロディー; ***in ~*** chōshi ga atte iru 調子が合っている; ***out of ~*** chōshi ga hazurete iru 調子がはずれている **2** *v/t instrument* chōritsu suru 調律する

♦**tune in** *v/i* RAD, TV channeru o awaseru チャンネルをあわせる

♦**tune in to** *v/t* RAD, TV … ni channeru o awaseru …にチャンネルをあわせる

♦**tune up 1** *v/i* (*of orchestra*) chōshi o awaseru 調子を合わせる **2** *v/t engine* … o chōsei suru …を調整する

tuneful merodī no utsukushii メロディーの美しい

tuner (*hi-fi*) chūnā チューナー

tunic EDU chunikku チュニック

tunnel *n* tonneru トンネル

turbine tābin タービン

turbot ōhirame 大ひらめ

turbulence (*in air travel*) rankiryū

乱気流
turbulent areru 荒れる
turf shiba 芝
Turk Toruko-jin トルコ人
Turkey Toruko トルコ
turkey shichimenchō 七面鳥
Turkish 1 *adj* Toruko (no) トルコ(の) **2** *n* (*language*) Toruko-go トルコ語
turmoil konran 混乱
turn 1 *n* (*rotation*) kaiten 回転; (*in road*) kābu カーブ; (*in vaudeville*) dashimono 出し物; ***take ~s doing X*** kōtai de X o suru 交替でXをする; ***it's my ~*** watashi no junban desu 私の順番です; ***it's not your ~ yet*** mada anata no junban ja nai まだあなたの順番じゃない; ***take a ~ at the wheel*** sukoshi unten suru 少し運転する; ***do X a good ~*** X no tame ni naru koto o suru Xのためになることをする **2** *v/t wheel* kaiten saseru 回転させる; *corner* magaru 曲がる; ***~ one's back on*** … ni se o mukeru …に背を向ける **3** *v/i* (*of driver, car*) magaru 曲がる; (*of wheel*) kaiten suru 回転する; ***~ right / left here*** koko de migi / hidari ni magatte ここで右/左に曲がって; ***it has ~ed sour / cold*** suppaku / samuku naru すっぱく/寒くなる; ***he has ~ed 40*** kare wa yonjūdai ni natte iru 彼は四十代になっている
♦ **turn around 1** *v/t object* … o hōkō-tenkan suru …を方向転換する; *company* kōten saseru 好転させる; (COM: *deal with*) taisho suru 対処する **2** *v/i* (*of person*) furikaeru 振り返る; (*of car*) muki o kaeru 向きを変える
♦ **turn away 1** *v/t* (*send away*) … o oiharau …を追い払う **2** *v/i* (*walk away*) muki o kaete tachisaru 向きを変えて立ち去る; (*look away*) kao o somukeru 顔を背ける
♦ **turn back 1** *v/t edges, sheets* … o orikaesu …を折り返す **2** *v/i* (*in walking, procedure*) hikikaesu 引き返す
♦ **turn down** *v/t offer, invitation* … o kotowaru …を断る; *volume, TV* o chiisaku suru …を小さくする; *heating* … o yowaku suru …を弱くする; *edge, collar* … o orikaesu …を折り返す
♦ **turn in 1** *v/i* (*go to bed*) neru 寝る **2** *v/t* (*to police*) mikkoku suru 密告する
♦ **turn off 1** *v/t radio, TV etc* … o kesu …を消す; *faucet, heater, engine* … o tomeru …を止める; F (*sexually*) … o unzarisaseru …をうんざりさせる **2** *v/i* (*of car, driver*) waki e hairu わきへ入る; (*of machine*) kieru 消える
♦ **turn on 1** *v/t radio, TV, engine etc* … o tsukeru …をつける; *faucet, heater* … o ireru …をいれる; F (*sexually*) … o kōfun saseru …を興奮させる **2** *v/i* (*of machine*) tsuku つく
♦ **turn out 1** *v/t lights* … o kesu …を消す **2** *v/i*: ***as it turned out*** kekkyoku no tokoro 結局のところ
♦ **turn over 1** *v/i* (*in bed*) negaeri o utsu 寝返りをうつ; (*of vehicle*) hikkuri kaeru ひっくり返る **2** *v/t* (*put upside down*) tenpuku saseru 転覆させる; *page* mekuru めくる; FIN shōbai o suru 商売をする
♦ **turn up 1** *v/t collar* … o orikaesu …を折り返す; *volume* … o ageru …をあげる; *heating* … o tsuyoku suru …を強くする **2** *v/i* (*arrive*) arawareru 現れる
turning magarikado 曲がり角
turning point fushime 節目
turnip kabu かぶ
turnout (*of people*) shussekiritsu 出席率; **turnover** FIN uriage 売り上げ; **turnpike** yūryō-kōsokudōro 有料高速道路; **turnstile** kaitenshiki kido 回転式木戸; **turntable** (*of record player*) kaitenban 回転盤
turquoise *adj* aomidoriiro (no) 青緑色(の)
turret (*of castle*) shōtō 小塔; (*of tank*) jūza 銃座
turtle kame かめ
turtleneck (sweater) tātorunekku タートルネック
tusk kiba きば
tutor 1 *v/t* oshieru 教える **2** *n* (***private***) ~ katei-kyōshi 家庭教師

tuxedo takishīdo タキシード
TV terebi テレビ; ***be on ~*** terebi de yatte iru テレビでやっている; ***~ program*** terebi bangumi テレビ番組
twang 1 *n*: ***the ~ of his accent*** hana ni kakatta akusento 鼻にかかたアクセント **2** *v/t guitar string* būn to narasu ブーンと鳴らす
tweezers pinsetto ピンセット
twelfth dai-jūni (no) 第十二(の)
twelve jūni 十二
twentieth 1 *adj* dai-nijū (no) 第二十(の) **2** *n* (*of month*) hatsuka 二十日
twenty nijū 二十
twice nikai 二回; ***~ as much*** nibai 二倍
twiddle ijiru いじる; ***~ one's thumbs*** yubi o moteasobu 指をもてあそぶ
twig *n* koeda 小枝
twilight tasogare たそがれ
twin futago 双子
twin beds tsuin-beddo ツインベッド
twinge (*of pain*) uzuki うずき
twinkle *v/i* (*of stars*) kirakira hikaru キラキラ光る; (*of eyes*) kagayaku 輝く
twin town shimai-toshi 姉妹都市
twirl 1 *v/t* kurukuru mawasu くるくる回す **2** *n* (*of cream etc*) uzumaki kazari うずまき飾り
twist 1 *v/t* nejiru ねじる; ***~ one's ankle*** nenza suru ねんざする **2** *v/i* (*of road, river*) magarikuneru 曲がりくねる **3** *n* (*in rope*) nejire ねじれ; (*in road*) kābu カーブ; (*in plot, story*) hineri ひねり
twisty *road* magarikunetta 曲がりくねった
twit F bakamitai ばかみたい
twitch 1 *n* (*nervous*) keiren けいれん **2** *v/i* (*jerk*) keiren suru けいれんする
twitter *v/i* (*of birds*) saezuru さえずる
two ni 二; (*with count word*) futatsu 二つ; ***the ~ of them*** sono futatsu その二つ
two-faced uraomote no aru 裏表のある
two-way traffic taimen-kōtsū (no) 対面交通(の)
tycoon ōmono 大物
type 1 *n* (*sort*) taipu タイプ; ***what ~ of …?*** donna taipu no… どんなタイプの… **2** *v/i* (*use a keyboard*) taipu o utsu タイプを打つ **3** *v/t* (*with a typewriter*) taipu suru タイプする
typewriter taipu-raitā タイプライター
typhoid (fever) chō-chifusu 腸チフス
typhoon taifū 台風
typhus chifusu チフス
typical tenkeiteki (na) 典型的(な); ***that's ~ of you / him!*** anatarashii / karerashii あなたらしい / 彼らしい
typically gaishite 概して; ***~ American*** tenkeiteki na Amerika-jin 典型的なアメリカ人
typist taipisuto タイピスト
tyrannical bōkun (no) 暴君(の)
tyrannize shiitageru 虐げる
tyranny assei 圧制
tyrant bōkun 暴君

U

ugly minikui 醜い
UK (= ***United Kingdom***) Eikoku 英国
ulcer kaiyō かいよう
ultimate (*best, definitive*) kyūkyoku (no) 究極(の); (*final*) saishū (no)

最終(の); (*fundamental*) konponteki (na) 根本的(な)
ultimately (*in the end*) kekkyoku 結局
ultimatum saigotsūchō 最後通ちょう
ultrasound MED chōonpa 超音波
ultraviolet *adj* shigaisen (no) 紫外線(の)
umbilical cord heso no o へその緒
umbrella kasa 傘
umpire *n* shinpan 審判
umpteen: ***I have told you ~ times*** F nankai mo itta deshō 何回も言ったでしょう
UN (= ***United Nations***) Kokuren 国連
unable: ***be ~ to do X*** X suru koto ga dekinai …することができない
unacceptable mitomerarenai 認められない; ***it is ~ that*** … wa mitomerarenai …は認められない
unaccountable setsumei dekinai 説明できない
unaccustomed: ***be ~ to*** … ni narete inai …に慣れていない
unadulterated (*absolute*) mattaku (no) 全く(の)
un-American Amerika-jin rashikunai アメリカ人らしくない
unanimous *verdict* manjō-itchi (no) 満場一致(の); ***be ~ on*** … ni zenkai itchi de aru …に全会一致である
unanimously manjō-itchi de 満場一致で
unapproachable *person* chikazukinikui 近づきにくい
unarmed *person* busō shite inai 武装していない; ***~ combat*** buki o tsukawanai bujutsu 武器を使わない武術
unassuming kidoranai 気取らない
unattached (*without a partner*) tsukiatte iru hito no inai 付き合っている人のいない
unattended hottarakashi (no) ほったらかし(の); ***leave ~*** … o hottarakashi ni suru …をほったらかしにする
unauthorized mukyoka (no) 無許可(の); (*lacking official approval*) muninka (no) 無認可(の)
unavoidable sakerarenai 避けられない
unavoidably: ***be ~ detained*** hikitomerareru no o sakerarenakatta 引き止められるのを避けられなかった
unaware: ***be ~ of*** … ni ki ga tsukanai …に気が付かない
unawares: ***catch X ~*** X ni fuiuchi o kuwaseru Xに不意打ちを食わせる
unbalanced katayotta 偏った; *design* baransu no warui バランスの悪い; PSYCH kurutta 狂った
unbearable taerarenai 耐えられない; *person* gaman dekinai 我慢できない
unbeatable *team, quality* subarashii 素晴らしい
unbeaten *team* muteki (no) 無敵(の)
unbeknownst: ***~ to*** … ni kizukarezu ni …に気付かれずに
unbelievable shinjirarenai 信じられない; F *heat, value* sugoi すごい; ***he's ~*** F (*very good / bad*) kare wa tondemonai 彼はとんでもない
unbias(s)ed kōsei (na) 公正(な)
unblock *pipe* tsumari o torinozoku 詰まりを取り除く
unborn onaka no naka (no) お腹の中(の)
unbreakable *plates* kowarenai 壊れない; *world record* yaburu koto no dekinai 破ることのできない
unbutton botan o hazusu ボタンをはずす
uncalled-for yokei (na) 余計(な)
uncanny bukimi (na) 不気味(な); *knack* hitonami-hazureta 人並みはずれた
unceasing taemanai 絶え間ない
uncertain *future, origins* hakkiri shinai はっきりしない; *weather* fuantei (na) 不安定(な); ***be ~ about*** … ni tsuite hakkiri wakaranai …についてはっきりわからない
uncertainty (*of the future*) fukakujitsu 不確実; ***there is still ~ about*** … ni wa mada fukakujitsu

na tokoro ga aru …にはまだ不確実なところがある

unchecked: ***let X go ~*** X o chekku shinaide sumasu Xをチェックしないですます

uncle oji おじ; (*s.o. else's*) ojisan おじさん

uncomfortable *chair* kokochi-warui 心地悪い; *sitting position* ochitsukanai 落ち着かない; ***feel ~ about*** … o fuan ni kanjiru …を不安に感じる; ***I feel ~ with him*** kare to iru to kizumari de aru 彼といると気詰まりである

uncommon mezurashii 珍しい; ***it's not ~*** mezurashiku nai 珍しくない

uncompromising dakyō shinai 妥協しない

unconcerned kanshin no nai 関心のない; ***be ~ about*** … o ki ni shiteinai …を気にしていない

unconditional mujōken (no) 無条件(の)

unconscious MED ishikifumei (no) 意識不明(の); PSYCH muishiki (no) 無意識(の); ***knock ~*** shisshin saseru 失神させる; ***be ~ of*** (*not aware*) … ni ki ga tsukanai …に気が付かない

uncontrollable *anger, desire* osaerarenai 抑えられない; *children* te ni oenai 手に負えない

unconventional kata ni hamaranai 型にはまらない

uncooperative hikyōryokuteki (na) 非協力的(な)

uncork *bottle* … no koruku-sen o nuku …のコルク栓を抜く

uncover (*remove cover from*) … no ōi o toru …の覆いを取る; *plot* bakuro suru 暴露する; *ancient remains* hakkutsu suru 発掘する

undamaged higai o ukete inai 被害を受けていない

undaunted: ***carry on ~*** kujikenaide tsuzukeru くじけないで続ける

undecided kimatte inai 決まっていない; ***be ~ about*** … ni tsuite mada kimete inai …についてまだ決めていない

undeniable hitei dekinai 否定できない

undeniably tashika ni 確かに

under 1 *prep* … no shita ni …の下に; (*less than*) …miman de …未満で; ***it is ~ review / investigation*** sore wa minaoshi-chū / chōsa-chū de aru それは見直し中/調査中である **2** *adv* (*anesthetized*) muishiki-jōtai ni 無意識状態に

underage *drinking etc* miseinen (no) 未成年(の); ***be ~*** miseinen de aru 未成年である

underarm *adv throw* shitate nage (no) 下手投げ(の)

undercarriage chakuriku-sōchi 着陸装置

undercover *adj agent* naimitsu (no) 内密(の)

undercut *v/t* COM …yori yasui ne de uru …より安い値で売る

underdog jakusha 弱者

underdone *meat* namayake (no) 生焼け(の)

underestimate *v/t person, skills, task* mikubiru 見くびる

underexposed PHOT roshutsu-busoku (no) 露出不足(の)

underfed eiyōbusoku (no) 栄養不足(の)

undergo *surgery, treatment* ukeru 受ける; *experience* keiken suru 経験する

underground 1 *adj passage etc* chika (no) 地下(の); POL: *resistance, newpaper etc* chikasoshiki (no) 地下組織(の) **2** *adv work* chika de 地下で; ***go ~*** POL chika ni moguru 地下にもぐる

undergrowth shitabae 下生え

underhand *adj* (*devious*) fusei (na) 不正(な)

underlie *v/t* (*form basis of*) … no kiso ni natte iru …の基礎になっている

underline *v/t text* kasen o hiku 下線を引く

underlying *causes, problems* kihonteki (na) 基本的(な)

undermine *s.o.'s position* yowameru 弱める; *theory* yurugasu 揺るがす

underneath 1 *prep* … no shita ni … の下に **2** *adv* shita ni 下に
underpants pantsu パンツ
underpass (*for pedestrians*) chikadō 地下道
underprivileged megumarenai 恵まれない
underrate *v/t* mikubiru 見くびる
undershirt hadagi 肌着
undersized *person* kogara (no) 小柄(の)
underskirt pechikōto ペチコート
understaffed hitodebusoku (no) 人手不足(の)
understand 1 *v/t* rikai suru 理解する; ***I ~ that you*** anata wa … da to kiite imasu あなたは…だと聞いています; ***they are understood to be in Canada*** karera wa Kanada ni iru to omowarete iru 彼らはカナダにいると思われている **2** *v/i* wakaranai わからない
understandable rikai dekiru 理解できる
understandably: ***they were ~ annoyed*** karera ga mutto shita no wa tōzen da 彼らがむっとしたのは当然だ
understanding 1 *adj person* omoiyari no aru 思いやりのある **2** *n* (*of problem, situtation*) rikai 理解; (*agreement*) gōi 合意; ***on the ~ that*** … no jōken de …の条件で
understatement hikaeme na hyōgen 控えめな表現
undertake *task* hikiukeru 引き受ける; ***~ to do X*** (*agree to*) X o suru koto o hikiukeru Xをすることを引き受ける
undertaking (*enterprise*) jigyō 事業; (*promise*) yakusoku 約束
undervalue *v/t* kashō-hyōka suru 過小評価する
underwear shitagi 下着
underweight *adj* taijū-fusoku (no) 体重不足(の)
underworld (*criminal*) ankokugai 暗黒街; (*in mythology*) ano yo あの世
underwrite *v/t* FIN … no hoken o hikiukeru …の保険を引き受ける
undeserved *praise* fusōō (na) 不相応(な); *blame* futō (na) 不当(な)
undesirable konomashiku nai 好ましくない; ***~ elements*** konomashiku nai renchū 好ましくない連中
undisputed *champion, leader* monku nashi (no) 文句無し(の)
undo *parcel, envelop* akeru 開ける; *wrapping, shoelaces* hodoku ほどく; *buttons* hazusu はずす; *shirt* nugu 脱ぐ; *s.o. else's work* muda ni suru 無駄にする
undoubtedly utagau yochi naku 疑う余地なく
undreamt-of *riches* yume ni mo omowanai 夢にも思わない
undress 1 *v/t* ifuku o nugaseru 衣服を脱がせる; ***get ~ed*** ifuku o nugu 衣服を脱ぐ **2** *v/i* ifuku o nugu 衣服を脱ぐ
undue (*excessive*) yokei (na) 余計(な)
unduly futō ni 不当に
unearth *ancient remains* hakkutsu suru 発掘する; *fig* (*find*) hakken suru 発見する; *secret* abaku 暴く
unearthly: ***at this ~ hour*** tondemonai jikan ni とんでもない時間に
uneasy *relationship, peace* fuantei (na) 不安定(な); ***feel ~ about*** … o fuan ni kanjiru …を不安に感じる
uneatable taberarenai 食べられない
uneconomic fukeizai (na) 不経済(な)
uneducated mugaku (no) 無学(の)
unemployed shitsugyō shita 失業した; ***the ~*** shitsugyō-sha 失業者
unemployment shitsugyō 失業
unending hateshinai 果てしない
unequal fubyōdō (na) 不平等(な); ***be ~ to the task*** sono shigoto ni wa taerarenai その仕事には耐えられない
unerring *judgment, instinct* kakujitsu (na) 確実(な)
uneven *quality* fuzoroi (no) 不ぞろい(の); *surface, ground* dekoboko (no) でこぼこ(の)

unevenly *distributed, applied* fukisoku ni 不規則に; *~ matched* tsuriatte inai 釣り合っていない
uneventful tanchō (na) 単調(な)
unexpected omoigakenai 思いがけない
unexpectedly fui ni 不意に
unfair futō (na) 不当(な)
unfaithful *husband, wife* uwaki (na) 浮気(な); ***be ~ to*** … ni taishite fuseijitsu de aru …に対して不誠実である
unfamiliar shiranai 知らない; ***be ~ with*** … o yoku shiranai …を良く知らない
unfasten *belt* hazusu はずす
unfavorable *report, conditions* yoku nai 良くない; *review* hihanteki (na) 批判的(な)
unfeeling *person* reikoku (na) 冷酷(な)
unfinished mikansei (no) 未完成(の); ***leave ~*** … o tochū de hotte oku …を途中でほっておく
unfit (*physically*) undōbusoku (no) 運動不足(の); (*morally*) … ni fumuki (na) …に不向き(な); ***be ~ to eat / drink*** nomu / taberu no ni tekishite inai 飲む/食べるのに適していない
unfix *part* torihazusu 取り外す
unflappable heizen to shita 平然とした
unfold 1 *v/t sheets* hirogeru 広げる; *letter* hiraku 開く; *one's arms* hodoku ほどく **2** *v/i* (*of story etc*) tenkai suru 展開する; (*of view*) hirogaru 広がる
unforeseen omoigakenai 思いがけない
unforgettable wasurerarenai 忘れられない
unforgivable yurusenai 許せない; ***that was ~ of you*** sore wa yurusenai それは許せない
unfortunate (*wretched*) aware (na) 哀れ(な); (*unlucky*) fukō (na) 不幸(な); *choice of words* mazui まずい; ***that's ~ for you*** sore wa zannen da それは残念だ
unfortunately zannen nagara 残念ながら
unfounded konkyo no nai 根拠のない
unfriendly fushinsetsu (na) 不親切(な); *software* tsukai nikui 使いにくい
unfurnished kagutsuki de nai 家具付きでない
ungodly: ***at this ~ hour*** tondemonai jikan ni とんでもない時間に
ungrateful onshirazu (no) 恩知らず(の)
unhappiness fukō 不幸
unhappy fukō (na) 不幸(な); *customers etc* fuman (na) 不満(な); ***be ~ with an explanation*** setsumei ni fuman ga aru 説明に不満がある
unharmed buji (na) 無事(な)
unhealthy *person* fukenkō (na) 不健康(な); *food, conditions* kenkō ni warui 健康に悪い; *atmosphere, economy* fukenzen (na) 不健全(な)
unheard-of (*shocking*) zendaimimon (no) 前代未聞(の); (*unknown*) shirarete inai 知られていない
unhurt buji (na) 無事(な)
unhygienic hieiseiteki (na) 非衛生的(な)
unification tōitsu 統一
uniform 1 *n* seifuku 制服; (SP) yunifōmu ユニフォーム **2** *adj* ittei (no) 一定(の)
unify tōitsu suru 統一する
unilateral ippōteki (na) 一方的(な)
unimaginable sōzō dekinai 想像できない
unimaginative sōzōteki de nai 創造的でない; (*boring*) taikutsu (na) 退屈(な)
unimportant jūyō de nai 重要でない
uninhabitable hito ga sumenai 人が住めない
uninhabited mujin (no) 無人(の)
uninjured kizutsuite inai 傷ついていない
unintelligible rikai dekinai 理解できない
unintentional koi de nai 故意でない
unintentionally muishiki ni 無意識に

uninteresting tsumaranai つまらない
uninterrupted *sleep, two hours' work* togirenai 途切れない
union POL rengō 連合; (*labor ~*) rōdō-kumiai 労働組合
unique dokutoku (no) 独特(の); F (*very good*) yunīku (na) ユニーク(な); ***with his own ~ humor*** kare dokutoku no yūmoa 彼独特のユーモア
unit (*of measurement*) tan'i 単位; (*section: of machine, structure*) yunitto ユニット; (*part with separate function*) buhin 部品; (*department*) bu 部; MIL butai 部隊
unit cost COM tanka 単価
unite 1 *v/t* hitotsu ni suru 一つにする; *country* ketsugō suru 結合する **2** *v/i* danketsu suru 団結する
united hitotsu ni natta 一つになった; *effort* danketsu shita 団結した
United Kingdom Rengō-ōkoku 連合王国
United Nations 1 *n* Kokusai-rengō 国際連合 **2** *adj* Kokuren (no) 国連の
United States (**of America**) (Amerika) Gasshūkoku (アメリカ)合衆国
unity kessoku 結束; (*harmony*) chōwa 調和
universal fuhenteki (na) 普遍的(な)
universally fuhenteki ni 普遍的に
universe uchū 宇宙
university daigaku 大学; ***he is at ~*** kare wa daigakusei desu 彼は大学生です
unjust futō (na) 不当(な)
unkempt *appearance* darashi no nai だらしのない; *hair* mojamoja (no) もじゃもじゃ(の)
unkind fushinsetsu (na) 不親切(な)
unknown 1 *adj* shirarete inai 知られていない **2** *n*: ***a journey into the ~*** michi no sekai e no tabi 未知の世界への旅
unleaded *adj* muen (no) 無鉛の
unless: ***don't say anything ~ you're sure*** moshi tashika de nakereba nanimo iu na もし確かでなければ何も言うな; ***~ he pays us tomorrow…*** moshi kare ga ashita harawanai nara… もし彼が明日払わないなら…
unlike *prep* … to chigatte …と違って; ***it's ~ him to drink so much*** sonna ni takusan nomu nante kare rashikunai そんなにたくさん飲むなんて彼らしくない; ***the photograph was completely ~ her*** shashin wa kanojo to zenzen nite inai 写真は彼女と全然似ていない
unlikely arisō mo nai ありそうもない; ***he is ~ to win*** kare wa kachisō de nai 彼は勝ちそうでない; ***it is ~ that*** … to iu koto wa arisō mo nai …ということはありそうもない
unlimited museigen (no) 無制限(の)
unlisted: ***be ~*** denwachō ni dete inai 電話帳に出ていない
unload *truck* ni o orosu 荷を下ろす; *goods* …kara ni o orosu …から荷を下ろす
unlock kagi o akeru 鍵を開ける
unluckily un no warui koto ni 運の悪い事に
unlucky *day, choice* fuun (na) 不運(な); *number* engi no warui 縁起の悪い; *person* fukō (na) 不幸(な); ***that was so ~ for you!*** sore wa un ga warukatta ne それは運が悪かったね
unmade-up *face* suppin (no) 素っぴん(の)
unmanned *spacecraft* mujin (no) 無人(の)
unmarried mikon (no) 未婚(の)
unmistakable machigaeyō no nai 間違えようのない
unmoved (*emotionally*) kokoro o ugokasarenai 心を動かされない
unmusical *person* ongakuteki de nai 音楽的でない; *sounds* mimizawari (na) 耳障り(な)
unnatural fushizen (na) 不自然(な); ***it's not ~ to be annoyed*** mutto shite tōzen de aru むっとして当然である
unnecessary fuhitsuyō (na) 不必要(な)

unnerving ki o sogu-yō (na) 気をそぐよう(な)
unnoticed: ***it went ~*** miotosarete ita 見落とされていた
unobtainable *goods* te ni ireru koto no dekinai 手に入れる事のできない; ***the number is ~*** TELEC kono bangō wa genzai tsukawarete orimasen この番号は現在使われておりません
unobtrusive *person* hikaeme (na) 控えめ(な); *thing* medatanai 目立たない
unoccupied *building, house* hito no sunde inai 人の住んでいない; *person* burabura shite iru ぶらぶらしている; **~ *post*** ketsuin 欠員; **~ *room*** akibeya 空き部屋
unofficial kōhyō sarete inai 公表されていない; *strike, action* kōnin sarete inai 公認されていない
unofficially hikōshiki ni wa 非公式には
unpack 1 *v/t* … no nakami o dashite katazukeru …の中身を出して片づける **2** *v/i* nimotsu o dashite katazukeru 荷物を出して片づける
unpaid *work* mukyū (no) 無給(の); *invoice* miharai (no) 未払い(の)
unpleasant fuyukai (na) 不愉快(な); ***he was very ~ to her*** kare wa kanojo ni totemo burei datta 彼は彼女にとても無礼だった
unplug *v/t TV, computer* konsento o nuku コンセントを抜く
unpopular *person* ninki no nai 人気のない; *decision* fuhyō (no) 不評(の)
unprecedented zenrei no nai 前例のない; ***it was ~ for a woman to …*** josei ga … suru no wa zendai-mimon datta 女性が…するのは前代未聞だった
unpredictable yosō dekinai 予想できない
unprincipled sessō no nai 節操のない
unpretentious *person, style,* hikaeme (na) 控えめ(な); *hotel* hade de nai 派手でない
unproductive *meeting, discussion* hiseisanteki (na) 非生産的(な); *soil* minori no nai 実りのない
unprofessional *person, behavior* shokugyōrinri ni hansuru 職業倫理に反する; *workmanship* shirōto (no) 素人(の)
unprofitable rieki no nai 利益のない
unpronounceable hatsuon shinikui 発音しにくい
unprotected *borders* bōbi nashi (no) 防備なし(の); *machine* kabā nashi (no) カバーなし(の); **~ *sex*** kondōmu nashi no sekkusu コンドームなしのセックス
unprovoked *attack* seitō na riyū no nai 正当な理由のない
unqualified *worker, doctor etc* shikaku no nai 資格のない
unquestionably (*without doubt*) utagai mo naku 疑いもなく
unquestioning *attitude, loyalty* utagawanai 疑わない
unravel *v/t string, knitting* hogusu ほぐす; *mystery, complexities* kaimei suru 解明する
unreadable *book* yominikui 読みにくい
unreal (*not matching reality*) higenjitsuteki (na) 非現実的(な); (*that doesn't actually exist*) kakū (no) 架空(の); ***this is ~!*** F shinjirarenai 信じられない
unrealistic higenjitsuteki (na) 非現実的(な)
unreasonable *person* riseiteki de nai 理性的でない; *demand, expectation* futō (na) 不当(な)
unrelated *issues* kankei no nai 関係のない; *people* shinzoku de nai 親族でない
unrelenting yōsha nai 容赦ない
unreliable *person* shinrai dekinai 信頼できない; *car, machine* ate ni naranai 当てにならない
unrest fuan 不安
unrestrained *emotions* yokusei sarenai 抑制されない
unroadworthy rojō-shiyō ni tekishite inai 路上使用に適していない

unroll *v/t carpet, scroll* hirogeru 広げる
unruly te ni oenai 手に負えない
unsafe kiken (na) 危険(な); ***~ to drink / eat*** nomu / taberu no ni tekishite inai 飲む/食べるのに適していない
unsanitary *conditions, drains* hieiseiteki (na) 非衛生的(な)
unsatisfactory fumanzoku (na) 不満足(な)
unsavory *person, reputation* konomashikunai 好ましくない; *district* ikagawashii いかがわしい
unscathed *person* mukizu (no) 無傷(の); *thing* songai o ukete inai 損害を受けていない
unscrew … no neji o nuku …のネジを抜く; *top* nejitte akeru ねじって開ける
unscrupulous akutoku 悪徳
unselfish omoiyari no aru 思いやりのある
unsettled *issue* mikettei (no) 未決定(の); *weather, stock market* kawariyasui 変わりやすい; *lifestyle* ochitsukanai 落ち着かない; *bills* miharai (no) 未払い(の)
unshaven bushōhige (no) 無精ひげ(の)
unsightly minikui 醜い
unskilled mijuku (na) 未熟(な)
unsociable buaisō (na) 無愛想(な)
unsophisticated *person, beliefs* senren sarete inai 洗練されていない; *equipment* tanjun (na) 単純(な)
unstable *person* jōcho-fuantei (na) 情緒不安定(な); *structure, region, economy* fuantei (na) 不安定(な)
unsteady (*on one's feet*) furafura shita ふらふらした; *ladder* guragura shita ぐらぐらした
unstinting ***she was ~ in her efforts*** kanojo wa oshiminai doryoku o shita 彼女は惜しみない努力をした; ***she was ~ in her generosity*** kanojo wa oshiminai yasashi-sa o ataeta 彼女は惜しみない優しさを与えた
unstuck ***come ~*** (*of notice etc*) hagareru はがれる; F (*of plan etc*) dame ni naru だめになる
unsuccessful *writer etc* urete inai 売れていない; *candidate* rakusen shita 落選した; *party* tsumaranai つまらない; *attempt* shippai shita 失敗した; ***he tried but was ~*** kare wa yatte mita ga shippai datta 彼はやってみたが失敗だった
unsuccessfully *try, apply* shippai shite 失敗して
unsuitable futekitō (na) 不適当(な); *clothes* bachigai (no) 場違い(の)
unsuspecting kizuite inai 気付いていない
unswerving *loyalty, devotion* kakko to shita 確固とした
unthinkable kangaerarenai 考えられない
untidy *room, desk,* chirakatta 散らかった; *hair, appearance* darashinai だらしない
untie *knot, laces* hodoku ほどく; *prisoner* nawa o toku 縄を解く
until 1 *prep* …made …まで; ***from Monday ~ Friday*** getsuyōbi kara kin'yōbi made 月曜日から金曜日まで; ***I can wait ~ tomorrow*** ashita made matemasu 明日まで待てます; ***not ~ Friday*** kin'yōbi made wa dame da 金曜日まではだめだ; ***it won't be finished ~ July*** shichigatsu made wa owaranai deshō 七月までは終わらないでしょう **2** *conj* … suru made …するまで; ***can you wait ~ I'm ready?*** watashi no junbi ga dekiru made matte kureru 私の準備ができるまで待ってくれる; ***they won't do anything ~ you say so*** karera wa anata ga sō iu made nani mo shinai de shō 彼らはあなたがそう言うまで何もしないでしょう
untimely ori no warui 折りの悪い; ***~ death*** hayajini 早死に
untiring *efforts* tayumanu たゆまぬ
untold *riches, suffering* hakarishirenai はかりしれない; *story* akiraka ni sarete inai 明らかにされていない
untranslatable hon'yaku dekinai 翻

訳できない

untrue uso (no) うそ(の)

unused[1] *goods* mishiyō (no) 未使用(の)

unused[2]: ***be ~ to…*** … ni narete inai …に慣れていない; ***be ~ to doing X*** X suru koto ni narete inai Xすることに慣れていない

unusual (*rare*) mezurashii 珍しい; (*strange*) kawatta 変わった

unusually mezurashiku 珍しく; ***it is ~ cold for the time of year*** kono jiki ni shite wa hijō ni samui この時期にしては非常に寒い

unveil *memorial etc* … no jomakushiki o okonau …の除幕式を行う; *secret* akasu 明かす

unwell kibun ga warui 気分が悪い

unwilling: ***be ~ to do X*** X suru no o iyagatte iru Xするのを嫌がっている

unwind 1 *v/t tape* hodoku ほどく **2** *v/i* (*of tape*) hodokeru ほどける; (*of story*) hakkiri suru はっきりする; (*relax*) kutsurogu くつろぐ

unwise asahaka (na) 浅はか(な)

unwrap *v/t gift* akeru 開ける

unwritten: ***~ rule*** fubunritsu 不文律

unzip *v/t dress etc* fasunā o sageru ファスナーを下げる; COMPUT asshuku fairu o kaitō suru 圧縮ファイルを解凍する

up 1 *adv* ue e 上へ; ***~ in the sky*** sora no ue ni空の上に ***~ on the roof*** yane no ue ni 屋根の上に; ***~ here / there*** kono / ano ue この/あの上; ***be ~*** (*out of bed*) okite iru; (*of sun*) nobotte iru 昇っている; (*be built*) tatte iru ; (*of shelves*) sonaetsukerarete iru 備え付けられている; (*of prices, temperature*) agatte iru ; (*have expired*) kigen ga kirete iru 期限が切れている; ***your time is ~*** jikan-gire desu 時間切れです; ***what's ~?*** nani ka atta 何かあった; ***~ to the year 1989*** sen kyūhyaku hachijūkyū nen made 千九百八十九年まで; ***he came ~ to me*** kare ga watashi no tokoro ni yatte kita 彼が私のところにやって来た; ***what are you ~ to these days?*** saikin dō shite iru 最近どうしている; ***what are those kids ~ to?*** ano kodomotachi wa nani yatte irun darō あの子供たちは何やっているんだろう; ***be ~ to something*** (***bad***) nani ka takurande iru 何かたくらんでいる; ***I don't feel ~ to it*** watashi wa sore ni tsuite ikenai to omoimasu 私はそれについていけないと思います; ***it's ~ to you*** anata shidai desu あなた次第です; ***it is ~ to them to solve it*** karera no sekinin de kaiketsu suru koto desu 彼らの責任で解決することです; ***be ~ and about*** (*after illness*) okireru yō ni naru 起きれるようになる **2** *prep* ue ni 上に; ***further ~ the mountain*** yama no ue no hō ni 山の上の方に; ***he climbed ~ a tree*** kare wa ki ni nobotta 彼は木に登った; ***they ran ~ the street*** tōrizoi ni hashitta 通り沿いに走った; ***the water goes ~ this pipe*** mizu wa kono paipu o agatte iku 水はこのパイプを上がっていく; ***we traveled ~ to Sendai*** watashitachi wa Sendai e ryokō shita 私達は仙台へ旅行した **3** *n*: ***~s and downs*** ukishizumi 浮き沈み

upbringing shitsuke しつけ

upcoming *adj* (*forthcoming*) mamonaku yatte kuru まもなくやって来る

update 1 *v/t file, records* kōshin suru 更新する; ***~ X on Y*** Y no saishinjōhō o X ni shiraseru Yの最新情報をXに知らせる **2** *n* (*of files, records*) kōshin 更新; (*software version*) saishinban 最新版; ***can you give me an ~ on the situation?*** saishin no jōkyō o oshiete kuremasu ka 最新の状況を教えてくれますか

upgrade 1 *v/t computer, product etc* hinshitsu o takameru 品質を高める; (*replace with new versions*) gurēdo appu suru グレードアップする; *ticket* kakuage suru 格上げする

upheaval (*emotional*) dōyō 動揺; (*physical*) hendō 変動; (*political,

social) dōran 動乱
uphill 1 *adv walk* ue no hō e 上のほうへ **2** *adj struggle* taihen (na) 大変(な)
uphold *traditions, rights* mamoru 守る; (*vindicate*) mitomeru 認める
upholstery (*covering*) *isu ni hatta kiji* いすに張った生地; (*padding*) *isu ni tsukau tsumemono* いすに使う詰め物
upkeep *n* (*of buildings, parks etc*) iji-kanri 維持管理
upload *v/t* COMPUT sābā ni dēta o okuru サーバーにデータを送る
upmarket *adj restaurant, hotel* kōshotoku-sō (no) 高所得層(の)
upon → ***on***
upper *part of sth* jōbu (no) 上部(の); *stretches of a river* jōryū (no) 上流(の)
upper atmosphere taikiken no saijōsō 大気圏の最上層; **upper-class** jōryū-kaikyū (no) 上流階級(の); **upper classes** jōryū-kaikyū 上流階級; **upper deck** uekanban 上甲板
upright 1 *adj citizen* shōjiki (na) 正直(な) **2** *adv sit* massugu ni 真っすぐに
upright (piano) tate piano たてピアノ
uprising bōdō 暴動
uproar (*loud noise*) ōsawagi 大騒ぎ; (*protest*) kōgi 抗議
upset 1 *v/t drink, glass* hikkurikaesu ひっくり返す; (*emotionally*) kanashimaseru 悲しませる **2** *adj* (*emotionally*) kanashimu 悲しむ; ***get ~ about*** … de kanashimu …で悲しむ; ***have an ~ stomach*** onaka o kowashite iru おなかをこわしている
upsetting tsurai つらい
upshot (*result*) kekka 結果
upside down *adv* sakasama ni 逆さまに; ***turn ~*** *box etc* … o sakasama ni suru …を逆さまにする
upstairs 1 *adv* ue no kai ni 上の階に; ***he went ~*** kare wa nikai ni itta 彼は二階に行った **2** *adj room* ue no kai (no) 上の階(の)
upstart *n* nariagari 成り上がり
upstream *adv* jōryū ni 上流に
uptight F (*nervous*) piripiri shita ぴりぴりした; (*inhibited*) katakurushii 堅苦しい
up-to-date *information* saishin (no) 最新(の); *fashions* saishin-ryūkō (no) 最新流行(の)
upturn (*in economy*) kōten 好転
upward *adv fly, move* uemuki ni 上向きに; ***~ of 10,000*** ichiman o koeta 一万を超えた
uranium uraniumu ウラニウム
urban toshi (no) 都市(の)
urbanization toshika 都市化
urchin gaki がき; ***street ~*** furōji 浮浪児
urge 1 *n* shōdō 衝動 **2** *v/t*: ***~ X to do Y*** X ni Y suru yō ni susumeru XにYするように勧める
♦ **urge on** … o hagemasu …を励ます
urgency kinkyūsei 緊急性
urgent *job, letter* kinkyū (na) 緊急(な); ***be in ~ need of*** … no hitsuyō ni semararete iru …の必要に迫られている; ***is it ~?*** kinkyū no yō desu ka 緊急の用ですか
urinate hainyō suru 排尿する
urine nyō 尿
urn tsubo つぼ
US (= ***United States***) Gasshūkoku 合衆国
us ◊ ***who's that? – it's ~*** dare desu ka - watashitachi desu 誰ですか – 私達です; ***that's for ~*** sore wa watashitachi no tame desu それは私達のためです ◊ (*direct object*) watashitachi o 私達を; ***they helped ~*** karera wa watashitachi o tasuketa 彼らは私達を助けた ◊ (*indirect object*) watashitachi ni 私達に; ***can you fax it to ~?*** watashitachi ni fakkusu shite moraemasu ka 私達にファックスしてもらえますか
USA (= ***United States of America***) Amerika-gasshūkoku アメリカ合衆国
usable shiyō dekiru 使用できる
usage (*linguistic*) kan'yō 慣用
use 1 *v/t tool, word* tsukau 使う;

skills, knowledge katsuyō suru 活用する; *s.o.'s car* kariru 借りる; *a lot of gas* shōhi suru 消費する; *pej person* riyō suru 利用する; ***I could ~ a drink*** F nomitai 飲みたい **2** *n* shiyō 使用; ***be of great ~ to*** … no totemo yaku ni tatsu …のとても役に立つ; ***be of no ~ to*** … no zenzen yaku ni tatanai …の全然役に立たない; ***is that of any ~?*** nanika no yaku ni tatsu 何かの役に立つ; ***it's no ~*** muda desu 無駄です; ***it's no ~ trying / waiting*** yatte mo muda desu / matte mo muda desu やっても無駄です/待っても無駄です

♦**use up** … o tsukaihatasu …を使い果たす

used[1] *car etc* chūko (no) 中古(の)

used[2]: ***be ~ to*** … ni narete iru …に慣れている; ***get ~ to*** … ni narete kuru …に慣れてくる; ***be ~ to doing X*** X suru no ni narete iru … するのに慣れている; ***get ~ to doing X*** X suru no ni narete kuru X するのに慣れてくる

used[3]: ***I ~ to like / know him*** izen kare o suki datta / shitte ita 以前彼を好きだった/知っていた; ***I don't work there now, but I ~ to*** ima soko de wa hataraite inai, shikashi izen wa hataraite ita 今そこでは働いていない しかし、以前は働いていた

useful yaku ni tatsu 役に立つ

usefulness jitsuyōsei 実用性

useless *information* yaku ni tatanai 役に立たない; F *person* yakutatazu (no) 役立たず(の); *machine, computer* tsukaenai 使えない; ***it's ~ trying*** yattemo muda de aru やっても無駄である

user (*of product*) shiyō-sha 使用者

user-friendly tsukaiyasui 使いやすい

usher *n* annaigakari 案内係

♦**usher in** *new era* … no sakigake to naru …の先駆けとなる

usual itsumo (no) いつも(の); (*customary*) futsū (no) 普通(の); ***as ~*** itsumo no yō ni いつもの様に; ***the ~, please*** itsumo no kudasai いつもの下さい

usually futsū wa 普通は

utensil yōgu 用具; ***kitchen ~*** daidokoro-yōhin 台所用品

uterus shikyū 子宮

utility (*usefulness*) jitsuyōsei 実用性; ***public utilities*** kōkyō-jigyō 公共事業

utilize riyō suru 利用する

utmost 1 *adj caution, difficulty* saidai (no) 最大(の); *tact, skill* saikō (no) 最高(の) **2** *n*: ***do one's ~*** saizen o tsukusu 最善を尽くす

utter 1 *adj* kanzen (na) 完全(な) **2** *v/t sound* hassuru 発する

utterly mattaku 全く

U-turn yū-tān Uターン; (*in policy*) hyakuhachijūdo no hōkō-tenkan 百八十度の方向転換

V

vacant *building* aite iru 空いている; *position* ketsuin ni natte iru 欠員になっている; *look, expression* utsuro (na) うつろ(な)

vacate *room* akeru 空ける

vacation *n* kyūka 休暇; ***be on ~*** kyūkachū de aru 休暇中である; ***go to … on ~*** … de kyūka o sugosu … で休暇を過ごす

vacationer kōrakukyaku 行楽客

vaccinate … ni yobō-sesshu o suru …に予防接種をする; ***be ~d against …*** … ni tai suru yobō-sesshu o ukete iru …に対する予防

接種を受けている
vaccination wakuchin-sesshu ワクチン接種
vaccine wakuchin ワクチン
vacuum 1 *n* PHYS shinkū 真空; *fig* (*in one's life*) kūhaku 空白 **2** *v/t floors* sōjiki o kakeru 掃除機をかける
vacuum cleaner denki-sōjiki 電気掃除機; **vacuum flask** mahōbin 魔法瓶; **vacuum-packed** shinkū-pakku (no) 真空パック(の)
vagina chitsu 膣
vaginal chitsu (no) 膣(の)
vague *answer, wording* aimai (na) あいまい(な); *feeling, resemblance* hakkiri shinai はっきりしない; *taste of sth* honoka (na) ほのか(な); ***he was very ~ about it*** kare wa sore ni tsuite zenzen hakkiri shite inai 彼はそれについて全然はっきりしていない
vaguely *answer* bakuzen to 漠然と; (*slightly*) nantonaku 何となく; *possible* tabun たぶん
vain 1 *adj person* unuborete iru うぬぼれている; *hope* muda (na) 無駄(な) **2** *n*: ***in ~*** munashiku むなしく; ***their efforts were in ~*** karera no doryoku wa muda datta 彼等の努力は無駄だった
valet (*person*) meshitsukai 召し使い
valet service (*for clothes*) kurīningu sābisu クリーニングサービス; (*for cars*) kuruma no sensha sābisu 車の洗車サービス
valiant yūkan (na) 勇敢(な)
valid *passport, document* yūkō (na) 有効(な); *reason, argument* datō (na) 妥当(な)
validate (*with official stamp*) yūkō ni suru 有効にする; (*back up*) shōmei suru 証明する
validity (*of reason, argument*) datōsei 妥当性; (*of ticket, document*) yūkōsei 有効性
valley tani 谷
valuable 1 *adj help, advice* kichō (na) 貴重(な); *jewel* kōka (na) 高価(な) **2** *n*: **~s** kichōhin 貴重品
valuation (*estimate*) kachi 価値; (*value as calculated by expert*) hyōka 評価; ***at his ~*** kare no hyōka de wa 彼の評価では
value 1 *n* kachi 価値; (*expressed in monetary terms*) kakaku 価格; ***be good ~*** kachi ga aru 価値がある; ***get ~ for money*** kane ni miau mono o eru 金に見合うものを得る; ***rise / fall in ~*** kachi ga agaru / sagaru 価値が上がる/下がる **2** *v/t s.o.'s friendship, one's freedom* sonchō suru 尊重する; ***I ~ your advice*** anata no jogen o sonchō shimasu あなたの助言を尊重します; ***have an object ~d*** kachi no mitsumori o suru 価値の見積もりをする
valve barubu バルブ; (*in heart*) ben 弁
van ban バン
vandal kokoronai hakai-sha 心無い破壊者
vandalism hakai-kōdō 破壊行動
vandalize hakai suru 破壊する
vanilla 1 *n* banira バニラ **2** *adj* banira (no) バニラ(の)
vanish kieru 消える
vanity (*of person*) kyoeishin 虚栄心; (*of hopes*) munashi-sa むなしさ
vanity case keshō-pōchi 化粧ポーチ
vantage point (*on hill etc*) kansatsuten 観察点
vapor jōki 蒸気
vaporize *v/t* (*of bomb*) jōhatsu saseru 蒸発させる
vapor trail hikōki-gumo 飛行機雲
variable 1 *adj amount* sadamaranai 定まらない; *moods, weather* kawariyasui 変わりやすい **2** *n* MATH, COMPUT hensū 変数
variation henka 変化
varicose vein jōmyakuryū 静脈瘤
varied *quality* samazama (na) 様々(な); *range* iroiro (na) 色々(な); *diet* katayoranai 偏らない
variety henka 変化; (*type*) shurui 種類; ***a ~ of things to do*** suru koto ga iroiro aru する事が色々ある
various (*several*) samazama (na) 様々(な); (*different*) iroiro (na) 色々

(な)
varnish 1 *n* (*for wood*) nisu ニス; (*for nails*) manikyua マニキュア **2** *v/t wood* … ni nisu o nuru …にニスを塗る; *nails* … ni manikyua suru …にマニキュアする
vary 1 *v/i* henka suru 変化する; ***it varies*** sono toki ni yotte chigau その時によって違う **2** *v/t* henka o tsukeru 変化をつける
vase kabin 花瓶
vast *desert, city* kōdai (na) 広大(な); *collection* bōdai (na) 膨大(な); *knowledge, sum of money* bakudai (na) ばく大(な)
vaudeville baraetī-shō バラエティーショー
vault[1] *n* (*in roof*) marutenjō 丸天井; **~s** (*for wine*) chika-chozōshitsu 地下貯蔵室; (*of bank*) kinkoshitsu 金庫室
vault[2] **1** *n* SP chōba 跳馬 **2** *v/t fence etc* tobikoeru 飛び越える
VCR (= ***video cassette recorder***) bideo ビデオ
veal koushiniku 子牛肉
vegan 1 *n* kanzen-saishokushugi-sha 完全菜食主義者 **2** *adj* kanzen-saishokushugi (no) 完全菜食主義(の)
vegetable yasai 野菜
vegetarian 1 *n* saishoku-shugisha 菜食主義者 **2** *adj* saishoku-shugi (no) 菜食主義(の)
vehicle kuruma 車; (*for information etc*) shudan 手段
veil 1 *n* bēru ベール **2** *v/t* bēru de ōu ベールで覆う
vein ANAT jōmyaku 静脈
Velcro® *n* berukuro ベルクロ
velocity sokudo 速度
velvet *n* berubetto ベルベット
vending machine jidō-hanbaiki 自動販売機
vendor LAW urite 売り手
veneer (*on wood*) keshōbari 化粧張り; (*of politeness etc*) misekake 見せかけ
venereal disease seibyō 性病
venetian blind itasudare 板すだれ
vengeance fukushū 復しゅう; ***with a ~*** mōretsu ni 猛烈に
venison shikaniku しか肉
venom (*of snake*) doku 毒
vent *n* (*for air*) tsūkikō 通気孔; ***give ~ to*** *feelings, emotions* … o hakidasu …を吐き出す
ventilate *room, building* … no kanki o suru …の換気をする
ventilation kanki 換気
ventilation shaft kankikō 換気孔
ventilator kanki-sōchi 換気装置
ventriloquist fukuwajutsu-shi 腹話術師
venture 1 *n* (*undertaking*) benchā-jigyō ベンチャー事業; COM tōki 投機 **2** *v/i* omoikitte… suru 思い切って…する
venue kaisaichi 開催地
veranda pōchi ポーチ; (*in Japanese houses*) engawa 縁側
verb dōshi 動詞
verdict LAW hyōketsu 評決; (*opinion, judgment*) iken 意見
verge *n* (*of road*) rokata 路肩; ***be on the ~ of*** *ruin, collapse* … no sunzen de aru …の寸前である; *of tears* ima ni mo…shisō de aru 今にも…しそうである
♦**verge on** …dōzen de aru …同然である
verification shōmei 証明; (*confirmation*) kakunin 確認
verify (*check out*) shōmei suru 証明する; (*confirm*) kakunin suru 確認する
vermin (*animals*) gaijū 害獣; (*fleas, lice*) gaichū 害虫
vermouth berumotto ベルモット
vernacular *n* hanashi-kotoba 話し言葉
versatile *person* tasai (no) 多才(の); *machine, tool* tsukaimichi no ōi 使い道の多い
versatility (*of person*) tasai 多才; (*of machine, tool*) bannō 万能
verse (*poetry*) shi 詩; (*part of poem, song*) setsu 節
versed: ***be well ~ in*** … ni kuwashii …に詳しい
version kata 型; (*of book, report*) ban 版; (*of events*) setsumei 説明

versus SP, LAW tai 対
vertebra sekitsuikotsu せきつい骨
vertebrate *n* sekitsui-dōbutsu せきつい動物
vertical suichoku (no) 垂直(の)
vertigo memai めまい
very 1 *adv* totemo とても; ***was it cold? – not ~*** samukatta – anmari 寒かった – あんまり; ***the ~ best*** saikō (no) 最高(の) **2** *adj* chōdo ちょうど; ***in the ~ act*** genkōhan de 現行犯で; ***that's the ~ thing I need*** kore ga masa ni watashi ga hitsuyō to shite iru mono desu これがまさに私が必要としている物です; ***the ~ thought of*** … o kangaeta dake de …を考えただけで; ***right at the ~ top / bottom*** sono ichiban ue / shita その一番上/下
vessel NAUT fune 船
vest besuto ベスト
vestige (*of previous civilization etc*) keiseki 形跡; (*of truth*) kakera かけら
vet[1] (*for animals*) jūi 獣医
vet[2] *v/t applicants etc* shinsa suru 審査する
veteran 1 *n* (*of war*) taieki-gunjin 退役軍人; (*old hand*) beteran ベテラン **2** *adj* (*old*) beteran (no) ベテラン(の); (*experienced*) rōren (na) 老練(な)
veterinarian jūi 獣医
veto 1 *n* kyohiken 拒否権 **2** *v/t* … ni kyohiken o kōshi suru …に拒否権を行使する
vexed (*worried*) komatta 困った; ***the ~ question of …*** … no yakkai na mondai …のやっかいな問題
via keiyu de 経由で
viable *life form* seichō dekiru 成長できる; *company* ikinokoresō (na) 生き残れそう(な); *alternative, plan* jikkō kanō (na) 実行可能(な)
vibrate *v/i* shindō suru 振動する
vibration shindō 振動
vice akutoku 悪徳; ***the problem of ~*** akugyō 悪行
vice president (*of company*) fuku-shachō 副社長; (*senior executive*) baisu-purejidento バイスプレジデント; POL fuku-daitōryō 副大統領
vice squad fūzokuhanzai-torishimarihan 風俗犯罪取り締まり班
vice versa gyaku no bāi mo onaji 逆の場合も同じ
vicinity kinjo 近所; ***in the ~ of*** *the church etc* … no kinjo ni …の近所に; *$500 etc* oyoso … およそ…
vicious *dog* dōmō (na) どう猛(な); *attack, temper, criticism* zankoku (na) 残酷(な)
victim gisei-sha 犠牲者
victimize gisei ni suru 犠牲にする
victor shōri-sha 勝利者
victorious shōri o eta 勝利を得た
victory shōri 勝利; ***win a ~ over …*** … ni katsu …に勝つ
video 1 *n* bideo ビデオ; ***have X on ~*** X o bideo ni totte aru Xをビデオにとってある **2** *v/t* bideo ni rokuga suru ビデオに録画する
video camera bideo-kamera ビデオカメラ; **video cassette** bideo-tēpu ビデオテープ; **video conference** TELEC terebi-kaigi テレビ会議; **video game** terebi-gēmu テレビゲーム; **videophone** terebi-denwa テレビ電話; **video recorder** bideo-tēpu-rekōdā ビデオテープレコーダー; **video recording** bideo-rokuga ビデオ録画; **videotape** bideo-tēpu ビデオテープ
Vietnam Betonamu ベトナム
Vietnamese 1 *adj* Betonamu (no) ベトナム(の) **2** *n* Betonamu-jin ベトナム人; (*language*) Betonamu-go ベトナム語
view 1 *n* keshiki 景色; (*of situation*) iken 意見; ***in ~ of*** … o kangaeru to …を考えると; ***be on ~*** (*of paintings*) tenjichū de aru 展示中である; ***with a ~ to*** … suru tsumori de …するつもりで **2** *v/t & v/i* miru 見る
viewer TV shichō-sha 視聴者
viewfinder PHOT faindā ファインダー
viewpoint mikata 見方; (*place*) kansatsu-chiten 観察地点
vigor (*energy*) genki 元気

vigorous *person,* kappatsu (na) 活発(な); *shake* ikioi no aru 勢いのある; *denial* tsuyoi 強い
vile *smell* hidoi ひどい; *thing to do* geretsu (na) 下劣(な)
village mura 村
villager murabito 村人
villain akunin 悪人
vindicate (*show to be correct*) … no tadashi-sa o shōmei suru …の正しさを証明する; (*show to be innocent*) … no keppaku o shōmei suru …の潔白を証明する; ***I feel ~d*** watashi wa seitōsei o mitomerareta to kanjita 私は正当性を認められたと感じた
vindictive fukushūshin ni moeta 復しゅう心に燃えた
vine budō no ki ぶどうの木
vinegar su 酢
vineyard budōen ぶどう園
vintage 1 *n* (*of wine*) budō-shūkakunen ぶどう収穫年 **2** *adj* (*classic*) tenkeiteki (na) 典型的(な)
violate *rules, treaty* ihan suru 違反する; *sanctity* kegasu 汚す
violation (*of rules, treaty*) ihan 違反; (*of sanctity*) bōtoku 冒とく; ***traffic ~*** kōtsū-ihan 交通違反
violence (*of person, movie*) bōryoku 暴力; (*of emotion, reaction*) hageshi-sa 激しさ; (*of gale*) mōi 猛威; ***outbreak of ~*** hanran no boppatsu 反乱のぼっ発
violent *person, movie* bōryokuteki (na) 暴力的(な); *emotion, reaction, storm* hageshii 激しい; ***have a ~ temper*** hageshii kishō de aru 激しい気性である
violently *react* hageshiku 激しく; *object* hidoku ひどく; ***fall ~ in love with*** hageshiku … ni koi o suru 激しく…に恋をする
violet (*color*) murasakiiro 紫色; (*plant*) sumire すみれ
violin baiorin バイオリン
violinist baiorin-sōsha バイオリン奏者
VIP (= ***very important person***) yōjin 要人, VIP ブイアイピー
viral uirusu (no) ウイルス(の)
virgin (*male*) dōtei 童貞; (*female*) shojo 処女
virginity (*male*) dōtei 童貞; (*female*) shojo 処女; ***lose his ~*** dōtei o ushinau 童貞を失う; ***lose her ~*** shojo o ushinau 処女を失う
virile *man* otokorashii 男らしい; *prose* chikarazuyoi 力強い
virility otokorashi-sa 男らしさ; (*sexually*) seiteki-nōryoku 性的能力
virtual jijitsujō (no) 事実上(の)
virtually jisshitsuteki ni wa 実質的には
virtual reality kasō-genjitsu 仮想現実
virtue bitoku 美徳; ***in ~ of*** … de aru koto de …であることで
virtuoso MUS meijin 名人
virtuous kōketsu (na) 高潔(な)
virulent *disease* akusei (no) 悪性(の)
virus MED, COMPUT uirusu ウイルス
visa sashō 査証, biza ビザ
visibility shikai 視界
visible *object, anger* me ni mieru 目に見える; *difference* akiraka (na) 明らか(な); ***not ~ to the naked eye*** nikugan de wa mienai 肉眼では見えない
visibly *different* me ni miete 目にみえて; ***he was ~ moved*** kare wa akiraka ni kandō shite ita 彼は明らかに感動していた
vision (*eyesight*) shiryoku 視力; (*foresight, of a new world*) bijon ビジョン; REL *etc* maboroshi 幻
visit 1 *n* (*to person*) hōmon 訪問; (*to place, country, city*) kenbutsu 見物; ***pay a ~ to the doctor / dentist*** isha / haisha ni iku 医者/歯医者に行く; ***pay X a ~*** X o tazuneru Xを訪ねる **2** *v/t person* hōmon suru 訪問する; *place, country, city* tazuneru 訪ねる; *doctor, dentist* … ni iku …に行く
visiting card meishi 名刺
visiting hours (*at hospital*) menkai-jikan 面会時間
visitor (*guest*) kyaku 客; (*to museum etc*) nyūkan-sha 入館者;

(*tourist*) kankōkyaku 観光客
visor (*of helmet*) men 面; (*of cap*) tsuba つば
visual shikakuteki (na) 視覚的(な)
visual aid shikaku-kyōzai 視覚教材
visual display unit monitā モニター
visualize sōzō suru 想像する
visually shikakuteki ni 視覚的に
visually impaired me no fujiyū (na) 目の不自由(な)
vital (*essential*) jūyō (na) 重要(な); ***it is ~ that …*** … suru koto wa jūyō da …することは重要だ
vitality (*of person*) genki 元気; (*of city*) kakki 活気
vitally: ***~ important*** kiwamete jūyō (na) 極めて重要(な)
vital organs *seimei-iji ni hitsuyō na kikan* 生命維持に必要な器官
vital statistics (*of woman*) surī-saizu スリーサイズ
vitamin bitamin ビタミン
vitamin pill bitamin-zai ビタミン剤
vivacious kappatsu (na) 活発(な)
vivacity kaikatsu 快活
vivid *color* azayaka (na) 鮮やか(な); *memory* hakkiri shita はっきりした; *imagination* kappatsu (na) 活発(な)
V-neck bui-nekku ブイネック
vocabulary goi 語い; (*list of words*) yōgoshū 用語集
vocal koe (no) 声(の); (*expressing opinions*) hakkiri mono o iu はっきり物を言う
vocal cords seitai 声帯
vocal group MUS bando バンド
vocalist MUS bōkaru ボーカル
vocation (*calling*) tenshoku 天職; (*profession*) shokugyo 職業; ***have a ~ for*** … ni shimeikan o motsu …に使命感を持つ
vocational *guidance* shokugyō (no) 職業(の)
vodka wokka ウォッカ
vogue ryūkō 流行; ***be in ~*** ninki ga aru 人気がある
voice 1 *n* koe 声 **2** *v/t opinions* hyōmei suru 表明する
voicemail rusuban-denwa sābisu 留守番電話サービス
void 1 *n* (*space*) uchū-kūkan 宇宙空間; *fig* (*emptiness*) kūkyo 空虚 **2** *adj*: ***~ of*** …ga nai …がない
volatile *personality* kimagure (na) 気まぐれ(な)
volcano kazan 火山
volley *n* (*in tennis*) borē ボレー; ***a ~ of gunfire*** issei-shageki 一斉射撃
volleyball barēbōru バレーボール
volt boruto ボルト
voltage den'atsu 電圧
volume (*of container*) yōseki 容積; (*of liquid*) yōryō 容量; (*of work, business, etc*) ryō 量; (*of book*) satsu 冊, kan 巻; (*of radio etc*) boryūmu ボリューム
volume control boryūmu-chōsetsu ボリューム調節
voluntary *adj helper* jihatsuteki (na) 自発的(な); *work* borantia (no) ボランティア(の)
volunteer 1 *n* borantia ボランティア; MIL shigan-sha 志願者 **2** *v/i* jihatsuteki ni… suru 自発的に…する
voluptuous kannōteki (na) 官能的(な)
vomit 1 *n* hedo へど **2** *v/i* haku 吐く
♦**vomit up** … o haku …を吐く
voracious *appetite* ōsei (no) 旺盛(の)
vote 1 *n* tōhyō 投票; (*process*) hyōketsu 票決; (*votes cast*) tōhyōsū 投票数; ***have the ~*** tōhyōken o motsu 投票権を持つ **2** *v/i* POL tōhyō suru 投票する; ***~ for / against …*** … ni sansei / hantai no tōhyō o suru …に賛成/反対の投票をする **3** *v/t*: ***they ~d him President*** karera wa tōhyō de kare o daitōryō ni kimeta 彼等は投票で彼を大統領に決めた; ***they ~d to stay behind*** karera wa nokoru koto ni tōhyō de kimeta 彼らは残ることに投票で決めた
♦**vote in** *member* … ni senshutsu sareru …に選出される
♦**vote on** *issue* … ni tsuite tōhyō suru …について投票する
♦**vote out** (*of office*) tōhyō de tsuihō

suru 投票で追放する
voter (*entitled to vote*) yūken-sha 有権者; (*who votes*) tōhyō-sha 投票者
voting POL tōhyō 投票
voting booth tohyōyōshi-kinyūsho 投票用紙記入所
♦**vouch for** … o hoshō suru …を保証する
voucher (*for gas*) kūpon クーポン; (*for food*) shokken 食券; (*gift* ~) shōhinken 商品券
vow 1 *n* chikai 誓い **2** *v/t*: **~ *to do X*** X suru to chikau Xすると誓う
vowel boin 母音
voyage (*by sea*) funatabi 船旅; (*in space*) uchū-ryokō 宇宙旅行
vulgar *person, language* gehin (na) 下品(な)
vulnerable (*to attack*) kōgeki sareyasui 攻撃されやすい; (*to criticism etc*) kizutsukiyasui 傷つきやすい
vulture hagetaka はげたか

W

wad *n* (*of paper*) taba 束; (*of absorbent cotton*) katamari 固まり; ***a ~ of $100 bills*** hyaku doru satsu no taba 百ドル札の束
waddle *v/i* (*of baby, duck*) yochiyochi aruku よちよち歩く; (*of person*) yotayota aruku よたよた歩く
♦**wade across** mizu no naka o aruite wataru 水の中を歩いて渡る
♦**wade through** *book*… o kurō shite yomu …を苦労して読む
wafer (*cookie*) uehāsu ウエハース
waffle[1] *n* (*to eat*) waffuru ワッフル
waffle[2] *v/i* tsumaranai hanashi o suru つまらない話をする
wag 1 *v/t tail, finger* furu 振る **2** *v/i* (*of tail*) yureru 揺れる
wage[1] *v/t war* okonau 行う
wage[2] *n* kyūryō 給料
wage earner chingin-rōdō-sha 賃金労働者
waggle *v/t hips, tail* furu 振る; *ears, eyebrows* ugokasu 動かす; *loose screw, tooth etc* guragura ugokasu ぐらぐら動かす
wagon: ***be on the ~*** F sake o tatte iru 酒を断っている
wail 1 *n* (*of person, baby*) nakigoe 泣き声; (*of siren*) unari うなり **2** *v/i* (*of person, baby*) nakisakebu 泣き叫ぶ; (*of siren*) unaru うなる
waist koshi 腰, uesuto ウエスト
waistcoat *Br* besuto ベスト
waistline dōmawari 胴回り; (*of clothes*) uesuto ウエスト
wait 1 *n*: ***have a long ~*** nagaku matasareru 長く待たされる **2** *v/i* matsu 待つ; ***we'll ~ until he's ready*** kare no junbi ga dekiru made machimasu 彼の準備ができるまで待ちます **2** *v/t meal* matsu 待つ; **~ *table*** ueitā / ueitoresu o suru ウエイター/ウエイトレスをする
♦**wait for** … o matsu …を待つ; **~ *me!*** matte 待って
♦**wait on** *person* … ni kyūji suru …に給仕する
♦**wait up** nenaide matsu 寝ないで待つ
waiter ueitā ウエイター; **~*!*** sumimasen すみません
waiting *n* matsu koto 待つこと; ***no ~ sign*** teisha-kinshi no hyōji 停車禁止の表示
waiting list junban-machi no meibo 順番待ちの名簿
waiting room machiaishitsu 待合室
waitress ueitoresu ウエイトレス
wake[1]: **~ (*up*) 1** *v/i* me ga sameru 目

が覚める **2** *v/t* okosu 起こす
wake² (*of ship*) kōseki 航跡; ***in the ~ of*** … ni hikitsuzuite …に引き続いて; ***follow in the ~ of*** … ni hikitsuzuite kuru …に引き続いて来る
wake-up call mōningu-kōru モーニングコール
walk 1 *n* toho 徒歩; (*path*) hodō 歩道; ***it's a long / short ~ to the office*** kaisha made chotto aruku / aruite sugu da 会社までちょっと歩く/歩いてすぐだ; ***go for a ~*** sanpo ni iku 散歩に行く **2** *v/i* aruku 歩く; (*as opposed to taking the car / bus etc*) aruite iku 歩いていく; (*hike*) haikingu suru ハイキングする **3** *v/t dog* sanpo ni tsurete iku 散歩に連れて行く; ***~ the streets*** (*walk around*) arukimawaru 歩き回る
♦**walk out** (*of spouse, from room etc*) dete iku 出て行く; (*go on strike*) sutoraiki suru ストライキする
♦**walk out on** *spouse* … o misuteru …を見捨てる
walker (*hiker*) yamaaruki no hito 山歩きの人; (*for baby, old person*) hokōki 歩行器; ***be a slow / fast ~*** aruku no ga osoi / hayai 歩くのが遅い/速い
walkie-talkie toranshībā トランシーバー
walk-in closet ōkii kurōzetto 大きいクローゼット
walking (*as opposed to driving*) aruki 歩き; (*hiking*) haikingu ハイキング; ***be within ~ distance*** aruite ikeru kyori ni aru 歩いて行ける距離にある
walking stick sutekki ステッキ
walking tour toho-ryokō 徒歩旅行
Walkman® wōkuman ウォークマン; **walkout** (*strike*) sutoraiki ストライキ; **walkover** (*easy win*) rakushō 楽勝; **walk-up** *n* erebētā no nai apāto エレベーターのないアパート
wall (*also fig*) kabe 壁; ***go to the ~*** (*of company*) tōsan suru 倒産する
wallet satsuire 札入れ
wallop F **1** *n* (*blow*) panchi パンチ **2** *v/t* butsu ぶつ; *opponent* uchinomesu 打ちのめす
wallpaper 1 *n* kabegami 壁紙 **2** *v/t* … ni kabegami o haru …に壁紙をはる
Wall Street Wōru-gai ウォール街
wall-to-wall carpet shikikomi kāpetto 敷込みカーペット
walnut kurumi クルミ
waltz *n* warutsu ワルツ
wan *face* aozameta 青ざめた
wand mahō no tsue 魔法のつえ
wander *v/i* (*roam*) buratsuku ぶらつく; (*stray*) mayou 迷う; (*of attention*) yokomichi ni soreru 横道にそれる
♦**wander around** burabura suru ぶらぶらする
wane *v/i* (*of interest*) usureru 薄れる; (*of moon*) kakeru 欠ける
wangle *v/t* F umai guai ni te ni ireru うまい具合に手に入れる
want 1 *n*: ***for ~ of*** …ga nai node …がないので **2** *v/t* …ga hoshii …が欲しい; (*need*) …ga hitsuyō de aru …が必要である; ***~ to do X*** X ga shitai Xがしたい; ***I ~ to stay here*** watashi wa koko ni itai desu 私はここにいたいです; ***do you ~ to come too? – no, I don't ~ to*** anata mo kitai – iie, watashi wa ikitaku nai あなたも来たい – いいえ、私は行きたくない; ***you can have whatever you ~*** anata no suki na mono nandemo totte kudasai あなたの好きなもの何でも取ってください; ***it's not what I ~ed*** sore wa watashi no hoshikatta mono de wa nai それは私の欲しかった物ではない; ***she ~s you to go back*** kanojo wa anata ni modotte hoshii 彼女はあなたに戻って欲しい; ***he ~s a haircut*** kare wa katto ni iku beki desu 彼はカットに行くべきです **3** *v/i*: ***~ for nothing*** nani mo fujiyū shite inai 何も不自由していない
want ad kyūjin-kōkoku 求人広告
wanted (*by police*) shimei-tehai chū (no) 指名手配中(の)
wanting: ***be ~ in*** … ni kakete iru …

に欠けている
wanton *adj* akui no aru 悪意のある
war *n* sensō 戦争; ***be at ~*** sensōchū de aru 戦争中である; ***~ criminal*** senpan 戦犯
warble *v/i* (*of bird*) saezuru さえずる
ward *n* (*in hospital*) byōtō 病棟; (*child*) hikōken-nin 被後見人
♦ **ward off** … o kawasu …をかわす
warden (*of prison*) shochō 所長
wardrobe (*for clothes*) yōfuku-dansu 洋服ダンス; (*clothes*) yōfuku-isshiki 洋服一式
warehouse sōko 倉庫
warfare sensō 戦争
warhead dantō 弾頭
warily yōjin bukaku 用心深く
warm *adj* atatakai 暖かい; *welcome, smile* kokoro kara (no) 心から(の)
♦ **warm up 1** *v/t* … o atatameru …を暖める **2** *v/i* atatamaru 暖まる; (*of athlete etc*) wōmuappu suru ウォームアップする
warmhearted kokoro no atatakai 心の温かい
warmly *dressed* atatakaku 暖かく; *welcome, smile* kokoro kara 心から
warmth atataka-sa 暖かさ; (*of welcome, smile*) atatakami 温かみ
warn keikoku suru 警告する
warning *n* keikoku 警告; ***without ~*** yokoku nashi ni 予告なしに
warp 1 *v/t wood* hizumaseru ひずませる; *character* yugameru ゆがめる **2** *v/i* (*of wood*) yugamu ゆがむ
warped *fig* hinekureta ひねくれた
warplane gun'yōki 軍用機
warrant 1 *n* reijō 令状 **2** *v/t* (*deserve, call for*) … ni atai suru …に値する
warranty hoshō 保証; ***be under ~*** hoshō-kikanchū de aru 保証期間中である
warrior senshi 戦士
warship gunkan 軍艦
wart ibo いぼ
wartime senji 戦時
wary yōjin-bukai 用心深い; ***be ~ of*** … ni yōjin suru …に用心する
wash 1 *n*: ***have a ~*** arau 洗う; ***that jacket / shirt needs a ~*** sono jaketto wa / sono shatsu wa arau beki da そのジャケットは/そのシャツは洗うべきだ **2** *v/t* arau 洗う; *clothes* sentaku suru 洗濯する **3** *v/i* senmen suru 洗面する
♦ **wash up** *v/i* (*wash one's hands and face*) senmen suru 洗面する
washable sentaku dekiru 洗濯できる
washbasin, washbowl senmenki 洗面器
washcloth hando-taoru ハンドタオル
washed out tsukarekitta 疲れ切った
washer (*for faucet etc*) zagane 座金; → ***washing machine***
washing sentakumono 洗濯物; ***do the ~*** sentaku o suru 洗濯をする
washing machine sentakuki 洗濯機
Washington (*city*) Washinton ワシントン
washroom otearai お手洗い
wasp (*insect*) hachi はち
waste 1 *n* rōhi 浪費; (*from industrial process*) haikibutsu 廃棄物; ***it's a ~ of time / money*** jikan / okane no mudazukai da 時間/お金の無駄使いだ **2** *adj* fuyō (no) 不用(の) **3** *v/t* mudazukai suru 無駄使いする
♦ **waste away** yaseotoroeru やせ衰える
wasteful fukeizai (na) 不経済(な)
wasteland arechi 荒れ地; **wastepaper** kamikuzu 紙くず; **wastepaper basket** kuzukago くずかご; **waste product** haikibutsu 廃棄物
watch 1 *n* (*timepiece*) udedokei 腕時計; ***keep ~*** mihari o suru 見張りをする **2** *v/t movie, TV* miru 見る; (*look after*) … ni ki o tsukeru …に気をつける **3** *v/i* miru 見る
♦ **watch for** … o matte iru …を待っている
♦ **watch out** ki o tsukeru 気を付ける; ***~!*** ki o tsukete 気を付けて
♦ **watch out for** … ni ki o tsukeru …に気を付ける
watchdog kanshi-iinkai 監視委員会

watchful chūi-bukai 注意深い
watchmaker tokei-ya 時計屋
water 1 *n* mizu 水; **~s** NAUT ryōkai 領海 **2** *v/t plant* mizu o yaru 水をやる **3** *v/i* (*of eyes*) namida ga deru 涙が出る; ***my mouth is ~ing*** yodare ga dete iru よだれが出ている
♦ **water down** *drink* mizu de usumeru 水で薄める
watercolor (*painting*) suisaiga 水彩画; (*paint*) suisai-enogu 水彩絵の具; **watercress** kureson クレソン; **waterfall** taki 滝
watering can jōro じょうろ
water level suii 水位; **water lily** suiren スイレン; **waterline** (*on ship*) kissuisen 喫水線; **waterlogged** shinsui shita 浸水した; **watermark** sukashi 透かし; **watermelon** suika スイカ; **water polo** suikyū 水球; **waterproof** *adj* bōsui (no) 防水(の); **waterside** *n* mizube (no) 水辺(の); ***at the ~*** mizube ni / de 水辺に/で; **waterskiing** suijō-sukī 水上スキー; **watertight** *compartment* mizu o tōsanai 水を通さない; **waterway** suiro 水路; **waterwings** ukiwa 浮き輪
watery mizuppoi 水っぽい
watt watto ワット
wave[1] *n* (*in sea*) nami 波
wave[2] **1** *n* (*of hand*): ***with a ~ of his hand*** kare wa te o futte 彼は手を振って **2** *v/i* (*with hand*) te o furu 手を振る; **~ *to*** … ni te o furu …に手を振る **3** *v/t flag etc* furu 振る
wavelength RAD shūhasū 周波数; ***be on the same ~*** *fig* hachō ga au 波長が合う
waver yuragu 揺らぐ
wavy *line* kunekune shita くねくねした; *hair* uēbu no kakatta ウエーブのかかった
wax *n* (*for floor, furniture*) wakkusu ワックス; (*in ear*) mimiaka 耳あか
way 1 *n* (*method, manner*) hōhō 方法; (*route*) iku michi 行く道; ***this ~*** (*like this*) kono yarikata このやり方; (*in this direction*) kono hōkō この方向; ***please come this ~*** kochira e dōzo こちらへどうぞ; ***by the ~*** (*incidentally*) tokoro de ところで; ***by ~ of*** (*via*) …keiyu de …経由で; (*in the form of*) … to shite …として; ***in a ~*** (*in certain respects*) aru imi de wa ある意味では; ***be under ~*** shinkōchū de aru 進行中である; ***give ~*** MOT shinro yuzure 進路譲れ; (*collapse*) kuzureru 崩れる; ***give ~ to*** (*be replaced by*) … ni totte kawaru …に取って代わる; ***have one's (own) ~*** omoidōri ni suru 思い通りにする; ***OK, we'll do it your ~*** wakatta anata no omoidōri ni shimashō 分かったあなたの思い通りにしましょう; ***lead the ~*** sentō ni tatte iku 先頭に立っていく; ***lose one's ~*** mayou 迷う; ***be in the ~*** jama ni naru 邪魔になる; ***it's on the ~ to the station*** sore wa eki ni iku tochū ni aru それは駅に行く途中にある; ***I was on my ~ to the station*** eki ni iku tochū deshita 駅に行く途中でした; ***no ~!*** jōdan ja nai 冗談じゃない; ***there's no ~ he can do it*** kare ni wa zettai dekinai 彼には絶対できない **2** *adv* F (*much*) suggoku すっごく; ***it's ~ too soon to decide*** kimeru no ni wa hayasugiru 決めるのには早過ぎる; ***they are ~ behind with their work*** karera no shigoto wa suggoku okurete iru 彼等の仕事はすっごく遅れている
way in iriguchi 入り口; **way of life** seikatsu-yōshiki 生活様式; **way out** deguchi 出口; *fig* kaiketsuhō 解決法
we watashitachi 私達, wareware 我々; ***~ are Americans / students*** watashitachi wa Amerika-jin / gakusei desu 私達はアメリカ人/学生です ◊ (*omission of pronoun*): ***~ don't know*** shirimasen 知りません
weak yowai 弱い; *tea, coffee* usui 薄い; *currency* yasui 安い; (*morally*) ishi ga yowai 意志が弱い
weaken 1 *v/t* yowaku suru 弱くする

2 *v/i* yowaku naru 弱くなる; (*of health*) otoroeru 衰える; (*morally*) yowaki ni naru 弱気になる
weakling kyojaku 虚弱; (*morally*) yowamushi 弱虫
weakness jakuten 弱点; ***have a ~ for*** (*liking*) … ni me ga nai …に目がない
wealth zaisan 財産, tomi 富; ***a ~ of*** hōfu na … 豊富な…
wealthy yūfuku (na) 裕福(な)
weapon buki 武器
wear 1 *n*: ***the engine has had a lot of ~ and tear*** enjin ga sukkari itande iru エンジンがすっかり痛んでいる; ***clothes for everyday ~*** heifuku 平服 **2** *v/t shirt, dress, suit raincoat, special clothing* kiru 着る; *hat* kaburu かぶる; *shoes, socks, skirt, pants, pantyhose* haku はく; *necktie* shimeru 締める; *brassiere* tsukeru つける; *gloves, ring* hameru はめる; *make-up* suru する; *glasses* kakeru かける; (*damage*) tsukai-furusu 使い古す; ***what was he ~ing?*** kare wa nani o kite ita no 彼は何を着ていたの **3** *v/i* (*of carpet, fabric*: *wear out*) surikireru 擦り切れる; (*last*) motsu もつ
♦**wear away 1** *v/i* suriheru 擦り減る **2** *v/t* … o suriherasu …を擦り減らす
♦**wear off** (*of effect, feeling*) kieru 消える
♦**wear out 1** *v/t* (*tire*) … o tsukare saseru …を疲れさせる; *shoes* … o suriherasu …を擦り減らす **2** *v/i* (*of shoes, carpet*) suriheru 擦り減る
wearing (*tiring*) tsukareru 疲れる
weary tsukarehateta 疲れ果てた
weather 1 *n* tenki 天気; ***be feeling under the ~*** kibun ga warui 気分が悪い **2** *v/t crisis* norikiru 乗り切る
weather-beaten fūu ni sarasareta 風雨にさらされた; **weather chart** tenkizu 天気図; **weather forecast** tenki-yohō 天気予報; **weatherman** tenki-yohō-gakari 天気予報係
weave 1 *v/t cloth* oru 織る; *basket* amu 編む **2** *v/i* (*move*) nū yō ni susumu 縫うように進む
Web[1]: **the ~** webu ウェブ
web[2] (*of spider*) kumo no su くもの巣
webbed feet mizukakino aru ashi 水かきのある足
web page webu-pēji ウエブページ
web site webu-saito ウエブサイト
wedding kekkonshiki 結婚式
wedding anniversary kekkon-kinenbi 結婚記念日; **wedding cake** uedingu-kēki ウエディングケーキ; **wedding day** kekkon no hi 結婚の日; **wedding dress** uedingu-doresu ウエディングドレス; **wedding ring** kekkon-yubiwa 結婚指輪
wedge *n* (*to hold sth in place*) kusabi くさび; (*of cheese etc*) hitokire 一切れ
Wednesday suiyōbi 水曜日
weed 1 *n* zassō 雑草 **2** *v/t* kusatori o suru 草取りをする
♦**weed out** … o torinozoku …を取り除く
weed-killer josōzai 除草剤
week shū 週; (*duration*) shūkan 週間; ***a ~ tomorrow*** raishū no ashita 来週の明日
weekday heijitsu 平日, uīkudē ウイークデー
weekend shūmatsu 週末, uīkuendo ウイークエンド; ***on the ~*** shūmatsu ni 週末に
weekly 1 *adj* maishū (no) 毎週(の) **2** *n* (*magazine*) shūkan 週刊 **3** *adv* maishū 毎週
weep shikushiku naku しくしく泣く
weigh[1] **1** *v/t* omo-sa o hakaru 重さを量る **2** *v/i* omo-sa ga … de aru 重さが…である; ***how much does the bag ~?*** kaban no omo-sa wa ikura desu ka かばんの重さはいくらですか; ***how much do you ~?*** taijū wa dono kurai arimasu ka 体重はどのくらいありますか
weigh[2]: ***~ anchor*** ikari o ageru いかりを上げる
♦**weigh down**: ***be weighed down***

with … no omomi de shizumu …の重みで沈む; *with worries* … de ki o omoku saseru …で気を重くさせる
♦ **weigh up** (*assess*) … o hyōka suru …を評価する
weight (*of person*) taijū 体重; (*of object*) omo-sa 重さ
weightlessness mujūryoku 無重力
weightlifter jūryōage-senshu 重量挙げ選手
weightlifting jūryōage 重量挙げ
weir seki せき
weird hen (na) 変(な)
weirdo *n* F hen na hito 変な人
welcome 1 *adj* kangei subeki 歓迎すべき; ***you're ~!*** dō itashimashite どういたしまして; ***you're ~ to try some*** dōzo tameshite mite kudasai どうぞ試してみてください **2** *n also fig* kangei 歓迎 **3** *v/t guests* kangei suru 歓迎する; *decision etc* ureshiku omou うれしく思う
weld *v/t* yōsetsu suru 溶接する
welder yōsetsu-kō 溶接工
welfare shiawase 幸せ; (*financial assistance*) fukushi 福祉; ***be on ~*** seikatsu-hogo o ukete iru 生活保護を受けている
welfare check seikatsu-hogo no kogitte 生活保護の小切手; **welfare state** fukushi-kokka 福祉国家; **welfare work** fukushi-jigyō 福祉事業; **welfare worker** sōsharu-wākā ソーシャルワーカー
well[1] *n* (*for water*) ido 井戸; ***oil ~*** yusei 油井
well[2] **1** *adv* yoku よく; ***as ~*** (*too*) … mo …も; ***as ~ as*** (*in addition to*) … no hoka ni …のほかに; (*do sth*) … to onaji gurai …と同じぐらい; ***it's just as ~ you told me*** anata ga itte kurete yokatta あなたが言ってくれてよかった; ***very ~*** (*acknowledging an order*) hai wakarimashita はいわかりました; (*reluctant acceptance*) yoku wakarimashita よくわかりました; ***~, ~!*** (*surprise*) ē' エーッ; ***~ …*** (*uncertainty, thinking*) ētto … えーっと… **2** *adj*: ***be ~*** genki de aru 元気である; ***feel ~*** kibun ga ii 気分がいい; ***get ~ soon!*** hayaku yoku natte 早く良くなって
well-balanced *person* jōshiki no aru 常識のある; *meal, diet* baransu no toreta バランスの取れた; **well-behaved** gyōgi no ii 行儀のいい; **well-being** kōfuku 幸福; **well-done** *meat* shikkari yaketa しっかり焼けた; **well-dressed** minari no yoi 身なりの良い; **well-earned** jibun de hataraite eta 自分で働いて得た; **well-known** yūmei (na) 有名(な); **well-made** yoku dekita 良く出来た; **well-mannered** reigi tadashii 礼儀正しい; **well-off** yūfuku (na) 裕福(な); **well-read** hakushiki (no) 博識(の); **well-timed** taimingu no ii タイミングのいい; **well-to-do** yūfuku (na) 裕福(な); **well-worn** tsukai furushita 使い古した
west 1 *n* nishi 西; ***the West*** (*nations*) Nishigawa-shokoku 西側諸国; (*part of a country*) seibu 西部 **2** *adj* nishi (no) 西(の) **3** *adv* nishi e 西へ; ***~ of*** … no nishi no hō ni …の西の方に
West Coast (*of USA*) Nishikaigan 西海岸
westerly nishitori (no) 西寄り(の)
western 1 *adj* nishi (no) 西(の); ***Western*** Nishigawa (no) 西側(の) **2** *n* (*movie*) seibugeki 西部劇
Westerner Seiyōjin 西洋人
westernized seiyōka 西洋化
westward nishi e 西へ
wet *adj* nureta ぬれた; (*rainy*) ame no ōi 雨の多い; ***"~ paint"*** penki-nuritate ペンキ塗りたて; ***be ~ through*** bishonure ni naru びしょぬれになる
whack F **1** *n* (*blow*) kyōda 強打 **2** *v/t* hippataku 引っぱたく
whale kujira 鯨
whaling hogei 捕鯨
wharf *n* hatoba 波止場
what 1 *pron* ◊ (*interrogative*) nani 何; ***~ is that?*** sore wa nan desu ka それは何ですか; ***~ is it?*** (*~ do you want?*) nannano 何なの; ***~!*** (*astonishment*) nani' 何; ***~ about***

some dinner? yūshoku ni shimasen ka 夕食にしませんか; ***~ about heading home?*** ie ni kaerimasen ka 家に帰りませんか; ***~ for?*** (*why?*) dōshite どうして; ***so ~?*** sore de それで ◊ (*relative*): ***I don't know ~ you're talking about*** anata ga nani o itte iru no ka wakarimasen あなたが何を言っているのか分かりません; ***take ~ you need*** hitsuyō na mono o totte kudasai 必要なものを取って下さい; ***this is ~ I wanted*** kore ga watashi no hoshikatta mono desu これが私の欲しかったものです **2** *adj* dono どの; ***~ university are you at?*** dono daigaku ni itte iru no どの大学に行っているの; ***~ experience have you had?*** don na keiken ga arimasu ka どんな経験がありますか; ***~ color is the car?*** kuruma wa nani iro desu ka 車は何色ですか ; ***~ a beautiful girl!*** nante kirei na onna no ko darō 何てきれいな女の子だろう

whatever 1 *pron* nan demo 何でも; (*regardless of what*) … ni kakawarazu …にかかわらず; ***~ people say*** hito no iukoto ni kakawarazu 人の言うことにかかわらず **2** *adj* donna… demo どんな…でも; ***you have no reason ~ to worry*** anata wa mattaku shinpai suru hitsuyō wa arimasen あなたはまったく心配する必要はありません

wheat komugi 小麦

wheedle: ***~ X out of Y*** kuchiguruma ni nosete Y kara X o damashitoru 口車に乗せてYからXをだましとる

wheel 1 *n* sharin 車輪; (*steering ~*) handoru ハンドル **2** *v/t bicycle* osu 押す **3** *v/i* (*of birds*) senkai suru 旋回する

♦ **wheel around** kyū ni mukinaoru 急に向き直る

wheelbarrow teoshi-guruma 手押し車; **wheelchair** kurumaisu 車いす; **wheel clamp** ihan-chūsha no sharindome 違反駐車の車輪止め

wheeze *v/i* zeizei iu ゼイゼイ言う

when 1 *adv* itsu いつ; ***~ is breakfast?*** asagohan wa itsu desu ka 朝ご飯はいつですか **2** *conj* toki 時; ***~ I was a child*** watashi ga kodomo datta toki 私が子供だった時; ***~ I've finished*** watashi ga owattara 私が終わったら; ***it was the year ~*** … no toshi datta …の年だった; ***on the day ~ he was born*** kare ga umareta hi ni 彼が生まれた日に

whenever (*any time*) … suru toki wa itsu demo …する時はいつでも; (*each time*) … suru tabi ni …する度に; ***call me ~ you like*** itsu demo denwa shite いつでも電話して

where 1 *adv* doko ni どこに; ***~ do you come from?*** anata wa doko no shusshin desu ka あなたはどこの出身ですか **2** *conj*: ***the hotel ~ the Beatles stayed*** Bītoruzu ga tomatta hoteru ビートルズが泊まったホテル; ***this is ~ I used to live*** koko wa watashi ga izen sunde ita tokoro desu ここは私が以前住んでいた所です

whereabouts 1 *n* ibasho 居場所 **2** *adv* dono atari ni どの辺りに; ***~ did you lose it?*** dono atari de nakushita no desu ka どの辺りでなくしたのですか

whereas … ga が; ***~ he thought …, the others …*** kare wa … to kangaeta ga, hoka no hitotachi wa 彼は…と考えたが、他の人達は

wherever 1 *conj* doko ni …shite mo どこに…しても; ***sit ~ you like*** doko de mo suki na tokoro ni suwatte kudasai どこでも好きな所に座って下さい **2** *adv* ittai doko ni 一体どこに; ***~ can he be?*** kare wa ittai doko ni iru no 彼は一体どこにいるの

whet *appetite* sosoru そそる

whether …ka dō ka …かどうか; ***~ you approve or not*** anata ga mitomete mo mitomenakute mo あなたが認めても認めなくても

which 1 *adj* dono どの, dochira (no) どちら(の); (*referring to people*) dono hito どの人; ***~ one is yours?***

dochira ga anata no desu ka どちらがあなたのですか; **~ student would you select?** dono gakusei o erabimasu ka どの学生を選びますか **2** *pron* ◊ (*interrogative*) dore どれ; (*referring to people*) dono hito どの人; **~ do you like best?** dore ga ichiban suki desu ka どれが一番好きですか; **take one, it doesn't matter ~** dore de mo ii kara totte kudasai どれでもいいから取って下さい ◊ (*relative*): **the house, ~ was designed by XYZ** XYZ no dezain shita ie XYZのデザインした家; **the chair on ~ I'm sitting** watashi ga suwatte iru isu 私が座っているいす

whichever 1 *adj*: **~ style you choose** anata ga dono sutairu o erabu ni shite mo あなたがどのスタイルを選ぶにしても; **choose ~ color you like** suki na iro o dore demo erande 好きな色をどれでも選んで **2** *pron* dore demo どれでも

whiff (*smell*) kasuka na kaori かすかな香り

while 1 *conj* … suru aida …する間; (*although*) … suru ni mo kakawarazu …するにもかかわらず; (*whereas*) … de aru no ni …であるのに **2** *n*: **a long ~** nagai aida 長い間; **for a ~** shibaraku no aida しばらくの間; **I haven't seen you for a ~** hisashiburi desu 久しぶりです; **I'll wait a ~ longer** mō sukoshi machimashō もう少し待ちましょう

♦**while away** burabura sugosu ぶらぶら過ごす

whim kimagure 気まぐれ

whimper 1 *n* kawaisō na nakigoe かわいそうな泣き声 **2** *v/i* kawaisō na nakigoe o dasu かわいそうな泣き声をだす

whine *v/i* (*of dog*) kunkun naku くんくん泣く; F (*complain*) nakigoto o iu 泣き言を言う

whip 1 *n* muchi むち **2** *v/t* (*beat*) muchiutsu むち打つ; *cream* awadateru 泡立てる; F (*defeat*) uchimakasu 打ち負かす

♦**whip out** F (*take out*) … o satto toridasu …をさっと取り出す

♦**whip up** (*arouse*) … o aoru …をあおる

whipping (*beating*) muchiuchi むち打ち; F (*defeat*) haiboku 敗北

whirl 1 *n*: **my mind is in a ~** kōfun shite atama ga mawatte iru 興奮して頭が回っている **2** *v/i* kurukuru mawaru くるくる回る; (*of leaves*) uzumaku 渦巻く

whirlpool (*in river*) uzumaki 渦巻; (*for relaxation*) jakūji ジャクージ

whirlwind tsumujikaze つむじ風

whirr *v/i* unaru うなる

whisk 1 *n* (*kitchen utensil*) awadateki 泡立て器 **2** *v/t eggs* awadateru 泡立てる

♦**whisk away** … o subayaku katazukeru …を素早く片付ける

whiskers (*of man, animal*) hige ひげ

whiskey uisukī ウイスキー; **~ and soda** haibōru ハイボール; **~ and water** mizuwari 水割り

whisper 1 *n* sasayaki ささやき **2** *v/t & v/i* sasayaku ささやく

whistle 1 *n* (*sound*) kuchibue 口笛; (*device*) fue 笛 **2** *v/i* kuchibue o fuku 口笛をふく; (*of wind*) pyūtto naru ぴゅうーっと鳴る **3** *v/t* kuchibue de fuku 口笛で吹く

white 1 *n* (*color*) shiro 白; (*of egg*) shiromi 白身; (*person*) hakujin 白人 **2** *adj* shiroi 白い; (*pale*) aojiroi 青白い; *person* hakujin (no) 白人(の)

white-collar worker howaito-karā no sararīman ホワイトカラーのサラリーマン;**White House** Howaito-hausu ホワイトハウス; **white lie** tsumi no nai uso 罪のないうそ;**white meat** shiromi no niku 白身の肉;**white-out** (*for text*) shūseieki 修正液;**whitewash** *n* suisei-hakushoku-toryō 水性白色塗料; *fig* gomakashi ごまかし;**white wine** shiro wain 白ワイン

whittle *wood* kezuru 削る

♦**whittle down** … o herasu …を減らす

whizz: **be a ~ at** F … no tensai de

aru …の天才である
♦ **whizz past** (*of time, car*) byūn to tōrisugiru ビューンと通り過ぎる
whizzkid F tensai 天才
who ◊ (*interrogative*) dare 誰; ***~'s that guy?*** ano hito wa dare desu ka あの人は誰ですか ◊(*relative*): ***the woman ~ saved the boy*** otoko no ko o tasuketa fujin 男の子を助けた婦人; ***I don't know ~ to believe*** dare o shinjireba ii ka wakaranai 誰を信じればいいか分からない
whoever dare demo 誰でも; ***~ can that be?*** ittai dare darō 一体誰だろう
whole 1 *adj* zentai (no) 全体(の); ***the ~ town / country*** machi-zentai / kuni-zentai 町全体/国全体; ***the ~ night*** yorujū 夜中; ***it's a ~ lot easier / better*** zutto kantan da / zutto ii ずっと簡単だ/ずっといい **2** *n* zentai 全体; ***the ~ of the United States*** Amerika zentai アメリカ全体; ***on the ~*** zentai to shite 全体として
whole-hearted kokoro kara (no) 心から(の); **wholesale 1** *adj* oroshi (no) 卸(の); *fig* musabetsu (no) 無差別(の) **2** *adv* oroshi de 卸で; **wholesaler** ton'ya 問屋; **wholesome** kenkō ni yoi 健康に良い; *fig* kenzen (na) 健全(な)
wholly kanzen ni 完全に
whom *fml* dare o / ni 誰を/に
whooping cough hyakunichizeki 百日ぜき
whore *n* baita 売女
whose 1 *pron* ◊ (*interrogative*) dare no mono 誰の物; ***~ is this?*** kore wa dare no mono desu ka これは誰の物ですか ◊ (*relative*): ***a man ~ wife has left him*** tsuma ni suterareta otoko 妻に捨てられた男; ***a country ~ economy is booming*** keizai ga kakkizuite iru kuni 経済が活気付いている国 **2** *adj* dare (no) 誰(の); ***~ bike is that?*** kore wa dare no jitensha desu ka これは誰の自転車ですか
why dōshite どうして, naze なぜ; ***~ do you ask?*** naze kikun desu ka なぜ聞くんですか; ***~ not?*** dōshite iya na no どうしていやなの; (*agreeing to suggestion*) ii kangae da いい考えだ; ***~ don't you come?*** (*suggesting*) kimasen ka 来ませんか; ***I don't know ~ I said that*** dōshite sonna koto o itta no ka wakarimasen どうしてそんな事を言ったのかわかりません; ***that's ~*** dakara だから
wick shin しん
wicked (*evil*) jaaku (na) 邪悪(な); (*mischievous*) ijiwaru (na) 意地悪(な)
wicker tōami とう編み
wicker chair tō no isu とうのいす
wicket (*in station, bank etc*) madoguchi 窓口
wide *adj* hiroi 広い; *experience* hōfu (na) 豊富(な); ***be 12 foot ~*** haba jūni fīto de aru 幅十二フィートである
wide-awake sukkari me ga sameta すっかり目が覚めた
wide-angle lens kōkaku-renzu 広角レンズ
widely *used, known* hiroku 広く
widen 1 *v/t* hiroku suru 広くする **2** *v/i* hiroku naru 広くなる
wide-open hiroku hiraita 広く開いた
widespread hirogatta 広がった
widow mibōjin 未亡人
widower otokoyamome 男やもめ
width hiro-sa 広さ
wield *weapon, power* furimawasu 振りまわす
wife tsuma 妻; (*talking to outsiders about one's own ~ also*) kanai 家内; (*s.o. else's*) okusan 奥さん
wig katsura かつら
wiggle *v/t hips* kunerasu くねらす; *loose screw etc* guragura ugokasu ぐらぐら動かす
wild 1 *adj animal, flowers* yasei (no) 野生(の); *land, sea* areta 荒れた; *teenager* ranbō (na) 乱暴(な); *party* ōsawagi (no) 大騒ぎ(の); *scheme* toppi (na) 突飛(な); *applause* kōfun shita 興奮した; ***be***

~ ***about …*** (*enthusiastic*) … ni muchū de aru …に夢中である; ***go ~*** kyōki suru 狂喜する; (*become angry*) gekido suru 激怒する; ***run ~*** (*of children*) katte kimama o suru 勝手気ままをする; (*of plants*) nobihōdai ni suru 伸び放題にする **2** *n*: ***the ~s*** kōya 荒野

wilderness mikaichi 未開地

wildfire: ***spread like ~*** matataku ma ni hirogaru 瞬く間に広がる; **wildgoose chase** mudaashi 無駄足; **wildlife** yasei-dōbutsu 野生動物

will[1] *n* LAW yuigon 遺言

will[2] *n* (*~power*) ishi 意志

will[3]: ***I ~ let you know tomorrow*** ashita shirasemasu 明日知らせます; ***~ you be there too?*** anata mo iku no あなたも行くの; ***I won't be back until late*** osoku narimasu 遅くなります; ***you ~ call me, won't you?*** denwa shite kureru yo ne 電話をしてくれますよね; ***I'll pay for this – no, I ~*** watashi ga koko wa haraimasu ― iie watashi ga harai masu 私がここは払います – いいえ私が払います; ***the car won't start*** kuruma ga ugokanai 車が動かない; ***~ you tell her that …?*** kanojo ni … to itte kureru 彼女に…と言ってくれる; ***~ you have some more tea?*** mō sukoshi ocha wa ikaga desu ka もう少しお茶はいかがですか; ***~ you stop that!*** yamenasai 止めなさい

willful *person* wagamama (na) わがまま(な); *action* koi (no) 故意(の)

willing *worker, attitude* iyoku no aru 意欲のある; ***be ~ to do X*** kokoroyoku X suru 快くXする

willingly (*with pleasure*) yorokonde 喜んで; (*readily*) susunde 進んで

willingness (*of worker*) iyoku 意欲; ***his ~ to help*** kare no susunde tetsudaō to iu kimochi 彼の進んで手伝おうという気持ち

willow yanagi 柳

willpower ishi no chikara 意志の力

willy-nilly (*at random*) nariyuki-makase ni 成り行きまかせに

wilt *v/i* (*of plant*) shioreru しおれる

wily zurugashikoi ずる賢い

wimp F yowamushi 弱虫

win 1 *n* shōri 勝利 **2** *v/t* … ni katsu … に勝つ; *lottery, money, prize* ateru 当てる; ***~ an election*** tōsen suru 当選する **3** *v/i* katsu 勝つ

wince *v/i* kao ga kowabaru 顔がこわばる

winch *n* uinchi ウインチ

wind[1] **1** *n* kaze 風; (*flatulence*) gasu ガス; ***get ~ of*** … o kagitsukeru … をかぎつける **2** *v/t*: ***be ~ed*** iki ga kireru 息が切れる

wind[2] **1** *v/i* (*of path, river*) magaru 曲がる; (*of ivy*) karamitsuku 絡み付く **2** *v/t* karamaseru 絡ませる; *scarf* makitsukeru 巻き付ける

♦ **wind down 1** *v/i* (*of party etc*) ochitsuku 落ち着く **2** *v/t car window* … o akeru …を空ける; *business* … o shukushō suru …を縮小する

♦ **wind up 1** *v/t clock* … o neji o maku …をネジを巻く; *car window* … o shimeru …を閉める; *speech, presentation* … o shimekukuru …を締めくくる; *affairs* … o oeru …を終える; *company* … o tatamu …を畳む **2** *v/i* (*finish*) owaru 終わる; ***~ in the hospital*** byōin ni iku koto ni naru 病院に行くことになる

windfall tanabota 棚ぼた

winding magarikunetta 曲がりくねった

wind instrument kangakki 管楽器

windmill fūsha 風車

window mado 窓; ***in the ~*** (*of store*) shōuindō ni ショーウインドーに

windowpane madogarasu 窓ガラス; **window-shop**: ***go ~ping*** uindō-shoppingu suru ウインドーショッピングする; **windowsill** mado no shitawaku 窓の下枠

windshield furontogarasu フロントガラス; **windshield wiper** waipā ワイパー; **windsurfer** sāfā サーファー; (*board*) sāfu-bōdo サーフボード; **windsurfing** uindosāfin ウインドサーフィン

windy *weather, day* kaze no tsuyoi 風の強い; ***it's getting ~*** kaze ga

tsuyoku natte kita 風が強くなってきた
wine wain ワイン
wine list wainrisuto ワインリスト
wing *n* hane 羽; (*of plane*) tsubasa 翼; SP uingu ウイング
wink 1 *n* uinku ウインク **2** *v/i* (*of person*) uinku suru ウインクする; **~ *at*** … ni uinku suru …にウインクする
winner (*of race*) shō-sha 勝者; (*of prize*) jushō-sha 受賞者; (*of election, lottery*) tōsen-sha 当選者
winning *adj* katta 勝った; *number* atatta 当たった
winning post kesshōten 決勝点
winnings shōkin 賞金
winter *n* fuyu 冬
winter sports uintā-supōtsu ウインタースポーツ
wintry fuyurashii 冬らしい
wipe *v/t* fuku ふく; *eyes, feet* nuguu ぬぐう; *tape* kesu 消す
♦ **wipe out** (*kill, destroy*) … o zenmetsu saseru …を全滅させる; *debt* … o hensai suru …を返済する
wire harigane 針金; ELEC densen 電線
wireless *n* rajio ラジオ
wire netting kanaami 金網
wiring ELEC denki-haisen 電気配線
wiry *person* sujibatta 筋張った
wisdom (*of person*) chie 知恵; (*of action*) kenmei-sa 賢明さ
wisdom tooth oyashirazu 親知らず
wise kashikoi 賢い
wisecrack *n* iyami 嫌み
wise guy *pej* shittakaburi-ya 知ったかぶり屋
wisely *act* kenmei ni 賢明に
wish 1 *n* nozomi 望み; ***best ~es*** omedetō おめでとう **2** *v/t* nozomu 望む; ***I ~ that …*** …sureba ii no ni to omou …すればいいのにと思う; ***~ X well*** X no kōun o inoru Xの幸運を祈る; ***I ~ed him good luck*** kare no kōun o inoru to iimashita 彼の幸運を祈ると言いました
♦ **wish for** … o nozomu …を望む
wishful thinking kibōteki-kansoku 希望的観測
wishy-washy *person* yūjū-fudan (no) 優柔不断(の); *color* usui 薄い
wisteria fuji 藤
wistful zannen sō (na) 残念そう(な)
wit (*humor*) yūmoa ユーモア; (*person*) yūmoa no aru hito ユーモアのある人; ***be at one's ~s' end*** dō sureba ii ka wakaranakunaru どうすればいいかわからなくなる
witch majo 魔女
with ◊ (*accompanied by*) … to …と; ***she came ~ her little sister*** kanojo wa imōto to kita 彼女は妹と来た; ***a treaty ~ Japan*** Nihon to no jōyaku 日本との条約; ***are you ~ me?*** (*do you understand?*) wakarimasu ka 分かりますか; ***~ no money*** kane nashi de 金なしで ◊ (*proximity*) … to issho ni …と一緒に; ***I live ~ my aunt*** watashi wa oba to issho ni sunde iru 私はおばと一緒に住んでいる ◊ (*agency*) … de …で; ***stabbed ~ a knife*** naifu de sashita ナイフで刺した; ***decorated ~ flowers*** hana de kazatta 花で飾った ◊ (*cause*) kyōfu de furueta 恐怖で震えた; ***shivering ~ fear*** ◊ (*possession*) … no …の; ***the house ~ the red door*** akai doa no uchi 赤いドアの家; ***a girl ~ brown eyes*** chairo no me no onna no ko 茶色の目の女の子; ***we need someone ~ experience*** watashitachi wa dareka keiken no aru hito ga hitsuyō desu 私達は誰か経験のある人が必要です ◊: ***~ a smile / ~ a wave*** hohoende / te o futte ほほ笑んで/手を振って ◊: ***be angry ~ X*** X ni hara o tatete iru Xに腹をたてている
withdraw 1 *v/t complaint, application* torikesu 取り消す; *money from bank* hikidasu 引き出す; *troops* tettai saseru 撤退させる **2** *v/i* (*of competitor*) mi o hiku 身を引く; (*of troops*) tettai suru 撤退する
withdrawal (*of complaint, application*) torikeshi 取り消し; (*of money*) hikidashi 引き出し; (*of troops*) tettai 撤退; (*from drugs*)

shiyō-chūshi 使用中止
withdrawal symptoms kindan-shōjō 禁断症状
withdrawn *adj person* hikkomigachi (na) 引っ込みがち(な)
wither kareru 枯れる
withhold *consent, payment* horyū suru 保留する; *information, name* kakusu 隠す
within *prep* (*inside*) … no naka de …の中で; (*in expressions of time*) …inai de …以内で; (*in expressions of distance*) … no han'inai de …の範囲内で; ***we kept ~ the budget*** watashitachi wa yosan nai ni osamemashita 私達は予算内に収めました; ***~ my power*** watashi no chikara no oyobu han'i de 私の力の及ぶ範囲で; ***~ reach*** te no todoku tokoro ni 手の届くところに
without …nashi de …なしで; ***~ looking / ~ asking*** nani mo minaide / nani mo shitsumon shinaide 何も見ないで/何も質問しないで
withstand … ni taeru …に耐える
witness 1 *n* (*at trial*) shōnin 証人; (*of accident, crime*) mokugeki-sha 目撃者; (*to signature*) hoshō-nin 保証人 **2** *v/t accident, crime* mokugeki suru 目撃する; *signature* hoshō-nin toshite sain suru 保証人としてサインする
witness stand shōninseki 証人席
witticism jōdan 冗談
witty yūmoa no aru ユーモアのある
wobble (*of bike, table*) guragura suru ぐらぐらする; (*of legs*) yoromeku よろめく
wobbly *table* fuantei (na) 不安定(な); *voice* furueru 震える
wolf 1 *n* (*animal*) ōkami おおかみ; *fig* (*womanizer*) onnatarashi 女たらし **2** *v/t*: ~ **(*down*)** gatsugatsu taberu がつがつ食べる
wolf whistle *n josei ni mukete dansei ga narasu kuchibue* 女性に向けて男性がならす口笛
woman josei 女性
woman doctor joi 女医
womanizer onnatarashi 女たらし
womanly onna-rashii 女らしい
woman priest josei-shisai 女性司祭
womb shikyū 子宮
women's lib ūman ribu ウーマンリブ
women's libber ūman ribu no katsudōka ウーマンリブの活動家
wonder 1 *n* (*amazement*) odoroki 驚き; ***no ~!*** tōzen da 当然だ; ***it's a ~ that …*** … wa odoroki da …は驚きだ **2** *v/i* … no koto o kangaeru …の事を考える **3** *v/t*: ***I ~ why she said that*** naze kanojo ga sō itta no ka na to omou なぜ彼女がそういったのかなと思う; ***I ~ what he's like*** kare wa donna hito kashira 彼はどんな人かしら; ***I ~ if you could help*** tetsudatte kudasaimasen ka 手伝って下さいませんか
wonderful subarashii 素晴らしい
wood mokuzai 木材; (*forest*) hayashi 林
wooded ki de ōwareta 木で覆われた
wooden (*made of wood*) mokusei (no) 木製(の)
woodpecker kitsutsuki きつつき;
woodwind MUS mokkan-gakki pāto 木管楽器パート; **woodwork** (*wooden parts*) mokuzōbu 木造部; (*activity*) mokkō-zaiku 木工細工
wool keito 毛糸
woolen 1 *adj* ūru (no) ウール(の) **2** *n* ūru ウール
word 1 *n* ◊ (*unit of language*) tango 単語; ***this is a new ~*** kore wa atarashii tango desu これは新しい単語です ◊ (*with a number, in linguistics*) go 語; ***500 ~s*** gohyaku-go 500語 ◊ (*way of expressing sth*) kotoba 言葉; ***there is no ~ for it in …*** … go niwa sono kotoba wa nai …語にはその言葉はない; ***a polite ~ for …*** … no teinei na kotoba …のていねいな言葉 ◊ (*news*) shirase 知らせ; ***is there any ~ from …?*** …kara nani ka shirase ga atta …から何か知らせがあった; ◊ (*promise*) yakusoku 約束; ***you have my ~***

yakusoku shimasu 約束します ◊ (*of song*): **~s** kashi 歌詞 ◊ (*expressions*): ***have ~s*** (*argue*) kuchigenka suru 口げんかする; ***have a ~ with*** … to hanasu …と話す **2** *v/t article, letter* kotoba o erabu 言葉を選ぶ

wording iimawashi 言い回し

word processing wāpuro de no bunsho-sakusei ワープロでの文書作成

word processor (*software*) wāpuro ワープロ

work 1 *n* shigoto 仕事; (*of art, literature*) sakuhin 作品; ***be out of ~*** shitsugyō shite iru 失業している; ***be at ~*** shigotochū de aru 仕事中である; ***I go to ~ by bus*** basu de tsūkin suru バスで通勤する **2** *v/i* (*of person*) hataraku 働く; (*study*) benkyō suru 勉強する; (*of machine*) ugoku 動く; (*succeed*) kiku 効く; ***what are you ~ing on?*** ima nani ni torikunde imasu ka 今何に取り組んでいますか; ***I used to ~ with him*** watashi wa izen kare to hataraite imashita 私は以前彼と働いていました; ***how does it ~?*** (*of device*) dō iu fū ni ugoku no desu ka どういう風に動くのですか **3** *v/t employee* hatarakaseru 働かせる; *student* benkyō saseru 勉強させる; *machine* ugokasu 動かす

♦ **work off** *bad mood, anger* … no uppun o harasu …のうっぷんを晴らす; *flab* … o herasu …を減らす

♦ **work out 1** *v/t problem* … o kaiketsu suru …を解決する; *solution* … o mitsukeru …を見つける **2** *v/i* (*at gym*) torēningu suru トレーニングする; (*of relationship etc*) umaku iku うまく行く

♦ **work out to** (*add up to*) … ni naru …になる

♦ **work up** *enthusiasm* … o hikiokosu …を引き起こす; *appetite* … o okosaseru …を起こさせる; ***get worked up*** (*angry*) ki ga tatsu 気が立つ; (*nervous*) iraira suru いらいらする

workable *solution* jikkō dekiru 実行できる

workaholic *n* shigoto-chūdoku 仕事中毒

worker rōdō-sha 労働者; (*in office*) sararīman サラリーマン; ***she's a good ~*** (*of student*) kanojo wa yoku benkyō suru 彼女はよく勉強する

work day (*hours of work*) shūgyō-jikan 就業時間; (*not a holiday*) kinmubi 勤務日; **workforce** rōdōryoku 労働力; **work hours** kinmu-jikan 勤務時間

working class rōdōsha-kaikyū 労働者階級; **working-class** rōdōsha-kaikyū (no) 労働者階級(の); **working knowledge** kiso-chishiki 基礎知識

workload shigotoryō 仕事量; **workman** shokunin 職人; **workmanlike** takumi (na) 巧み(な); **workmanship** dekibae 出来栄え; **work of art** geijutsu-sakuhin 芸術作品; **workout** torēningu トレーニング; **work permit** rōdō-biza 労働ビザ; **workshop** sagyōba 作業場; (*seminar*) wāku-shoppu ワークショップ; **work station** wāku-sutēshon ワークステーション

world sekai 世界; ***the ~ of computers / the theater*** konpyūtā / engeki no sekai コンピューター/演劇の世界; ***out of this ~*** F tobikiri (no) とびきり(の)

worldly sezokuteki (na) 世俗的(な); *person* sesai ni taketa 世才にたけた; ***~ goods*** zaisan 財産

world power sekaiteki-kyōkoku 世界的強国

world war sekaitaisen 世界大戦

worldwide 1 *adj* sekaiteki (na) 世界的(な) **2** *adv* sekaijū ni 世界中に

worm *n* mimizu みみず

worn-out *shoes, carpet, part* tsukaifurushita 使い古した; *person* hetoheto ni naru へとへとになる

worried shinpaisō (na) 心配そう(な)

worry 1 *n* shinpai 心配 **2** *v/t* shinpai saseru 心配させる; (*upset*) ... ga ki ni naru . . . が気になる **3** *v/i* shinpai suru 心配する; ***it will be***

alright, don't ~! daijōbu dakara shinpai shinaide 大丈夫だから心配しないで
worrying shinpai (na) 心配(な)
worse 1 *adj* sara ni warui 更に悪い **2** *adv* sara ni waruku 更に悪く
worsen *v/i* akka suru 悪化する
worship 1 *n* sūhai 崇拝 **2** *v/t* sūhai suru 崇拝する; *fig* netsuai suru 熱愛する
worst 1 *adj* saiaku (no) 最悪(の) **2** *adv* mottomo hidoku 最もひどく **3** *n*: ***the ~*** saiaku no jitai 最悪の事態; ***the ~ of the bad weather*** akutenkō no saiaku no bubun 悪天候の最悪の部分; ***if the ~ comes to ~*** saiaku no bāi ni wa 最悪の場合には
worth *adj*: ***$20 ~ of gas*** nijū doru bun no gasorin 二十ドル分のガソリン; ***be ~*** (*in monetary terms*) … no kachi ga aru …の価値がある; ***be ~ reading / seeing*** yomu / miru kachi ga aru 読む / 見る価値がある; ***be ~ it*** yaru kachi ga aru やる価値がある
worthless *object* kachi ga nai 価値がない; *person* yakutatazu (no) 役立たず(の)
worthwhile *cause* tame ni naru ためになる; ***be ~*** (*beneficial, useful*) yaku ni tatsu 役に立つ; (*worth the effort, worth doing*) … suru kachi ga aru …する価値がある
worthy … ni fusawashii …にふさわしい; *cause* … ni atai suru …に値する; ***be ~ of*** (*deserve*) … ni atai suru …に値する
would: ***I ~ help if I could*** dekireba tetsudaimasu できれば手伝います; ***I said that I ~ go*** watashi wa iku to iimashita 私は行くと言いました; ***I told him I ~ not leave unless ….*** kare ni… de nakereba dete ikanai to iimashita 彼に…でなければ出て行かないと言いました; ***~ you like to go to the movies?*** eiga ni ikimasen ka 映画に行きませんか; ***~ you mind if I smoked?*** tabako o sutte mo ii desu ka タバコをすってもいいですか; ***~ you tell her that …?*** … to kanojo ni tsutaete moraemasu ka …と彼女に伝えてもらえますか; ***~ you close the door?*** doa o shimete moraemasu ka ドアを締めてもらえますか; ***I ~ not have been so angry if …*** moshi … nara watashi wa sonna ni okoranakatta deshō もし…なら私はそんなに怒らなかったでしょう
wound 1 *n* kizu 傷 **2** *v/t* (*with weapon,*) … ni kizu o owaseru …に傷を負わせる; (*with remark*) kizutsukeru 傷つける
wow *interj* wā' わーっ
wrap *v/t parcel, gift* tsutsumu 包む; (*wind, cover*) maku 巻く
♦**wrap up** *v/i* (*against the cold*) atatakai fukusō o suru 暖かい服装をする
wrapper (*on candy etc*) tsutsumi 包み; (*of book*) kabā カバー
wrapping hōsō-zairyō 包装材料
wrapping paper hōsōshi 包装紙
wreath hanawa 花輪
wreck 1 *n* zangai 残がい; (*of ship*) nanpasen 難破船; ***be a nervous ~*** shinkei ga maitte iru 神経が参っている **2** *v/t ship* nanpa saseru 難破させる; *car, plans, career, marriage* dainashi ni suru 台無しにする
wreckage (*of car, plane*) zangai 残がい
wrecker rekkā-sha レッカー車
wrecking company jikosha-toriatsukai-gyōsha 事故車取扱業者
wrench 1 *n* (*tool*) supana スパナ; (*injury*) nenza ねんざ **2** *v/t* (*injure*) nenza suru ねんざする; (*pull*) mogitoru もぎ取る
wrestle … to kakutō suru …と格闘する
♦**wrestle with** *problems* … ni torikumu …に取り組む
wrestler resurā レスラー
wrestling resuringu レスリング
wrestling contest resuringu no shiai レスリングの試合
wriggle *v/i* (*squirm*) kunekune suru

くねくねする; (*along the ground*) hau はう
♦**wriggle out of** … o kirinukeru … を切り抜ける
♦**wring out** *v/t cloth* … o shiboru … を絞る
wrinkle 1 *n* shiwa しわ **2** *v/t clothes* shiwa o yoseru しわを寄せる **3** *v/i* (*of clothes*) shiwa ga yoru しわが寄る
wrist tekubi 手首
wristwatch udedokei 腕時計
write 1 *v/t* kaku 書く; *check* kiru 切る **2** *v/i* ji o kaku 字を書く; (*of author*) hon o kaku 本を書く; (*send a letter*) tegami o kaku 手紙を書く
♦**write down** … o kakitomeru …を書き留める
♦**write off** *debt* … o chōkeshi ni suru …を帳消しにする; *car* … o shūri-fukanō ni suru …を修理不可能にする
writer sakka 作家; (*of a document etc*) kakite 書き手
write-up hihyō 批評
writhe *v/i* mimodae suru 身もだえする
writing (*as career*) chojutsugyō 著述業; (*hand-~*) hisseki 筆跡; (*words*) bunshō 文章; (*script*) moji 文字; ***in ~*** shomen de 書面で
writing paper binsen 便せん
wrong 1 *adj* machigatta 間違った; (*morally*) yokunai 良くない; ***be ~*** (*of person, answer, clock*) machigatte iru 間違っている; (*morally*) yoku nai koto da 良くないことだ; ***what's ~?*** dōshita no どうしたの; ***there is something ~ with the car*** kono kuruma wa dokoka okashii この車はどこかおかしい **2** *adv* machigatte 間違って; ***go ~*** (*of person*) machigau 間違う; (*of marriage, plan etc*) umaku ikanai うまくいかない **3** *n* fusei 不正; ***be in the ~*** machigatte iru 間違っている
wrongful futō (na) 不当(な)
wrongly machigatte 間違って
wrong number bangō-machigai 番号間違い
wry hinikuppoi 皮肉っぽい

X

xenophobia gaikokujin-girai 外国人嫌い
X-ray 1 *n* ekkusu-sen X線; (*picture*) rentogen-shashin レントゲン **2** *v/t* … no rentogen-shashin o toru …のレントゲン写真を撮る

Y

yacht yotto ヨット
yachting yotto-asobi ヨット遊び
yachtsman yottonori ヨット乗り
Yank *n* F yankī ヤンキー
yank *v/t* hipparu 引っ張る
yap *v/i* (*of dog*) kyankyan hoeru きゃんきゃんほえる; F (*talk a lot*) pechakucha shaberu ぺちゃくちゃ

しゃべる
yard[1] (*of prison, institution etc*) kōnai 構内; (*behind house*) uraniwa 裏庭; (*for storage*) okiba 置き場
yard[2] (*measurement*) yādo ヤード
yardstick handan no shakudo 判断の尺度
yarn *n* (*thread*) ito 糸; F (*story*) horabanashi ほら話
yawn 1 *n* akubi あくび **2** *v/i* akubi suru あくびする
year toshi 年; (*with count word*) nen 年; ***two / three ~s*** ni / san nen 二/三年; ***for ~s*** nannen mo 何年も; ***this ~*** kotoshi 今年; ***next ~*** rainen 来年; ***last ~*** kyonen 去年; ***12 ~s old*** jūni-sai 十二才
yearly 1 *adj salary* ichinenkan (no) 1年間(の); *event, result* maitoshi (no) 毎年(の) **2** *adv* maitoshi 毎年
yearn *v/i* setsubō suru 切望する
♦**yearn for** … ni akogareru …にあこがれる
yearning *n* akogare あこがれ
yeast īsuto イースト
yell 1 *n* sakebigoe 叫び声 **2** *v/i* sakebu 叫ぶ **3** *v/t* … to sakebu …と叫ぶ
yellow 1 *n* kiiro 黄色 **2** *adj* kiiro (no) 黄色(の)
yellow pages ierōpēji イエローページ
yelp 1 *n* himei 悲鳴 **2** *v/i* himei o ageru 悲鳴をあげる
yen FIN en 円
yes hai はい; ***John! – ~?*** Jon – nani ジョン – なに ◊ (*using 'no', ie no, that is not right*): ***you don't know the answer, do you? – oh ~, I do*** kotae ga wakaranain deshō-iie wakarimasu 答えがわからないんでしょう–いいえ、わかります
yesman *pej* iesuman イエスマン
yesterday kinō 昨日; ***the day before ~*** ototoi おととい
yet 1 *adv* kore made de これまでで; ***as ~*** mada まだ; ***have you finished ~?*** mō owarimashita ka もう終わりましたか; ***he hasn't arrived ~*** mada kare wa kite imasen まだ彼は来ていません; ***is he here ~? – not ~*** mō kare wa kimashita ka – mada desu もう彼はきましたか – まだです; ***~ bigger / longer*** sara ni ōkiku / nagaku さらに大きく/長く **2** *conj* soredemo それでも; ***~ I'm not sure*** soredemo yoku wakarimasen それでもよくわかりません
yield 1 *n* (*from fields*) shūkaku 収穫; (*from investment*) rieki 利益 **2** *v/t fruit, interest* motarasu もたらす **3** *v/i* (*give way*) yuzuru 譲る
yoghurt yōguruto ヨーグルト
Yokohama Yokohama 横浜
yolk kimi 黄身
you ◊ (*singular: polite*) anata あなた; (*familiar*) kimi きみ; (*plural: polite*) anatatachi あなたたち; (*familiar*) kimitachi きみたち; ***~ are very kind*** anata wa totemo shinsetsu da あなたはとても親切だ; ***he knows ~*** kare wa anata o shitte imasu 彼はあなたを知っています; ***I told ~ you before*** anata ni mae ni hanashimashita あなたに前に話しました ◊ (*omission of pronoun*): ***are ~ sure?*** honto ほんと ◊ (*impersonal*): ***~ never know*** dō naru ka wakarimasen ne どうなるかわかりませんね; ***it's good for ~*** tame ni naru ためになる
young wakai 若い
youngster wakamono 若者
your ◊ (*singular: polite*) anata no あなたの; (*familiar*) kimi no きみの; (*plural: polite*) anatatachi no あなたたちの; (*familiar*) kimitachi no きみたちの ◊ (*omission of possessive*): ***did you bring ~ passport?*** pasupōto motte kimashita ka パスポート持ってきましたか
yours (*singular: polite*) anata no mono あなたのもの; (*familiar*) kimi no mono きみのもの; (*plural: polite*) anatatachi no mono あなたたちのもの; (*familiar*) kimitachi no mono きみたちのもの; ***a friend of***

~ anata no tomodachi no hitori あなたの友達の一人; ***Yours ...*** (*at end of letter*) keigu 敬具
yourself: ***did you hurt ~?*** (*polite*) anata wa kega o shimashita ka あなたはけがをしましたか; (*familiar*) kimi wa kega o shita no きみはけがをしたの; ***did you see ~ in the mirror?*** anata wa jibun de kagami o mimashita ka あなたは自分で鏡を見ましたか; ***by ~*** (*alone*) hitori de ひとりで; (*without help*) jibun de 自分で
yourselves: ***did you hurt ~?*** (*polite*) anatatachi wa kega o shimashita ka あなた達はけがをしましたか; (*familiar*) kimitachi wa kega o shita no きみ達はけがをしたの; ***did you see ~ in the mirror?*** anatatachi wa jibun de kagami o mimashita ka あなた達は自分で鏡を見ましたか; ***by ~*** (*alone*) anatatachi dake de あなた達だけで; (*without help*) jibuntachi de 自分達で
youth (*young man*) seinen 青年; (*young people*) seishōnen 青少年
youthful wakawakashii 若々しい
youth hostel yūsu-hosuteru ユースホステル

Z

zap *v/t* COMPUT (*delete*) sakujo suru 削除する; F (*kill*) korosu 殺す; F (*hit*) naguru なぐる
♦**zap along** F (*move fast*) subayaku ugokimawaru すばやく動き回る
zapped F (*exhausted*) kutakuta (no) くたくた(の)
zappy F *car, pace* kibikibi shita きびきびした; (*lively*) ikiiki shita いきいきした; (*energetic*) seiryokuteki (na) 精力的(な)
zeal netsujō 熱情
zebra shimauma しまうま
Zen Zen 禅
Zen Buddhism Zenshū 禅宗
zero zero ゼロ; ***10 below ~*** reika jūdo 零下10度
zero growth zero-seichō ゼロ成長
♦**zero in on** (*identify*) ... ni shūchū suru ...に集中する
zest (*zeal*) netsui 熱意
zigzag 1 *n* jiguzagu ジグザグ **2** *v/i* jiguzagu ni susumu ジグザグに進む
zilch F nani mo 何も
zinc aen 亜鉛
♦**zip up** *v/t dress, jacket* ... no fasunā o shimeru ...のファスナーを締める; COMPUT asshuku suru 圧縮する
zip code yūbin-bangō 郵便番号
zipper fasunā ファスナー
zodiac kōdōtai 黄道帯; ***signs of the ~*** seiza 星座
zombie F (*barely human person*) zonbi ゾンビ; ***feel like a ~*** (*exhausted*) hetoheto ni tsukarete iru へとへとに疲れている
zone chitai 地帯
zoo dōbutsuen 動物園
zoological dōbutsugaku (no) 動物学(の)
zoology dōbutsugaku 動物学
zoom F (*move fast*) mōsupīdo de susumu 猛スピードで進む
♦**zoom in on** PHOT ... o kurōzu-appu suru ...をクローズアップする
zoom lens zūmu-renzu ズームレンズ

Numbers and Dates

0	**zero, rei**	ゼロ, 零
1	**ichi**	一
2	**ni**	二
3	**san**	三
4	**yon, shi**	四
5	**go**	五
6	**roku**	六
7	**nana, shichi**	七
8	**hachi**	八
9	**kyū**	九
10	**jū**	十
11	**jū-ichi**	十一
12	**jū-ni**	十二
13	**jū-san**	十三
20	**ni-jū**	二十
21	**ni-jū-ichi**	二十一
30	**san-jū**	三十
35	**san-jū-go**	三十五
40	**yon-jū**	四十
50	**go-jū**	五十
60	**roku-jū**	六十
70	**nana-jū**	七十
80	**hachi-jū**	八十
90	**kyū-jū**	九十
100	**hyaku**	百
101	**hyaku-ichi**	百一
200	**ni-hyaku**	二百
300	**san-byaku**	三百
400	**yon-hyaku**	四百
500	**go-hyaku**	五百
600	**rop-pyaku**	六百
700	**nana-hyaku**	七百
800	**hap-pyaku**	八百
900	**kyū-hyaku**	九百
1,000	**sen**	千
2,000	**ni-sen**	二千
3,000	**san-zen**	三千
4,000	**yon-sen**	四千
5,000	**go-sen**	五千
6,000	**roku-sen**	六千
7,000	**nana-sen**	七千
8,000	**hass-sen**	八千
9,000	**kyū-sen**	九千
10,000	**ichi-man**	一万
20,000	**ni-man**	二万
100,000	**jū-man**	十万
1,000,000	**hyaku-man**	百万
2,000,000	**ni-hyaku-man**	二百万
10,000,000	**sen-man**	千万
100,000,000	**ichi-oku**	一億

Ordinal numbers

Ordinal numbers are formed by putting **dai** in front of the cardinal numbers:

1st	**dai-ichi**	第一
2nd	**dai-ni**	第二
3rd	**dai-san**	第三

Dates

1st	**tsuitachi**	一日
2nd	**futsuka**	二日
3rd	**mikka**	三日
4th	**yokka**	四日
5th	**itsuka**	五日
6th	**muika**	六日
7th	**nanoka**	七日
8th	**yōka**	八日
9th	**kokonoka**	九日
10th	**tōka**	十日
11th	**jū-ichi-nichi**	十一日
12th	**jū-ni-nichi**	十二日
13th	**jū-san-nichi**	十三日
14th	**jū-yokka**	十四日
15th	**jū-go-nichi**	十五日
16th	**jū-roku-nichi**	十六日
17th	**jū-nana-nichi**	十七日
18th	**jū-hachi-nichi**	十八日
19th	**jū-ku-nichi**	十九日
20th	**hatsuka**	二十日
21st	**ni-jū-ichi-nichi**	二十一日
22nd	**ni-jū-ni-nichi**	二十二日
23rd	**ni-jū-san-nichi**	二十三日
24th	**ni-jū-yokka**	二十四日
25th	**ni-jū-go-nichi**	二十五日
26th	**ni-jū-roku-nichi**	二十六日
27th	**ni-jū-nana-nichi**	二十七日
28th	**ni-jū-hachi-nichi**	二十八日
29th	**ni-jū-ku-nichi**	二十九日
30th	**san-jū-nichi**	三十日
31st	**san-jū-ichi-nichi**	三十一日